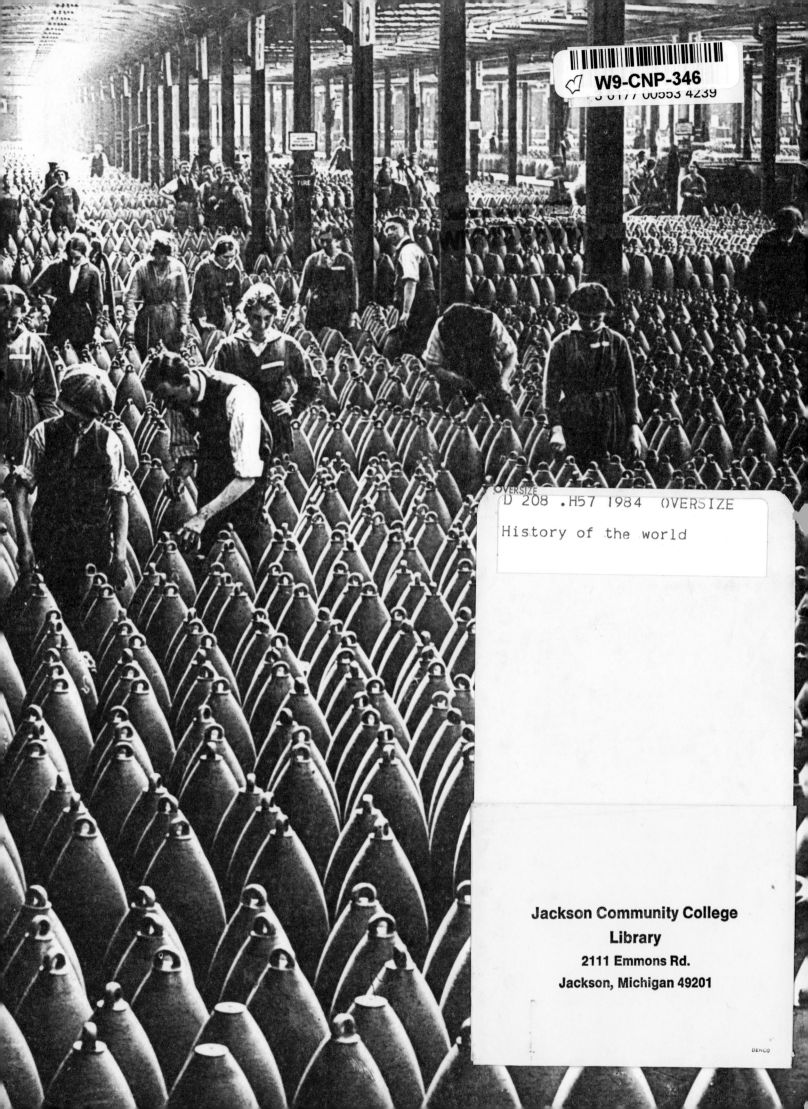

HISTORY OF THE WORLD

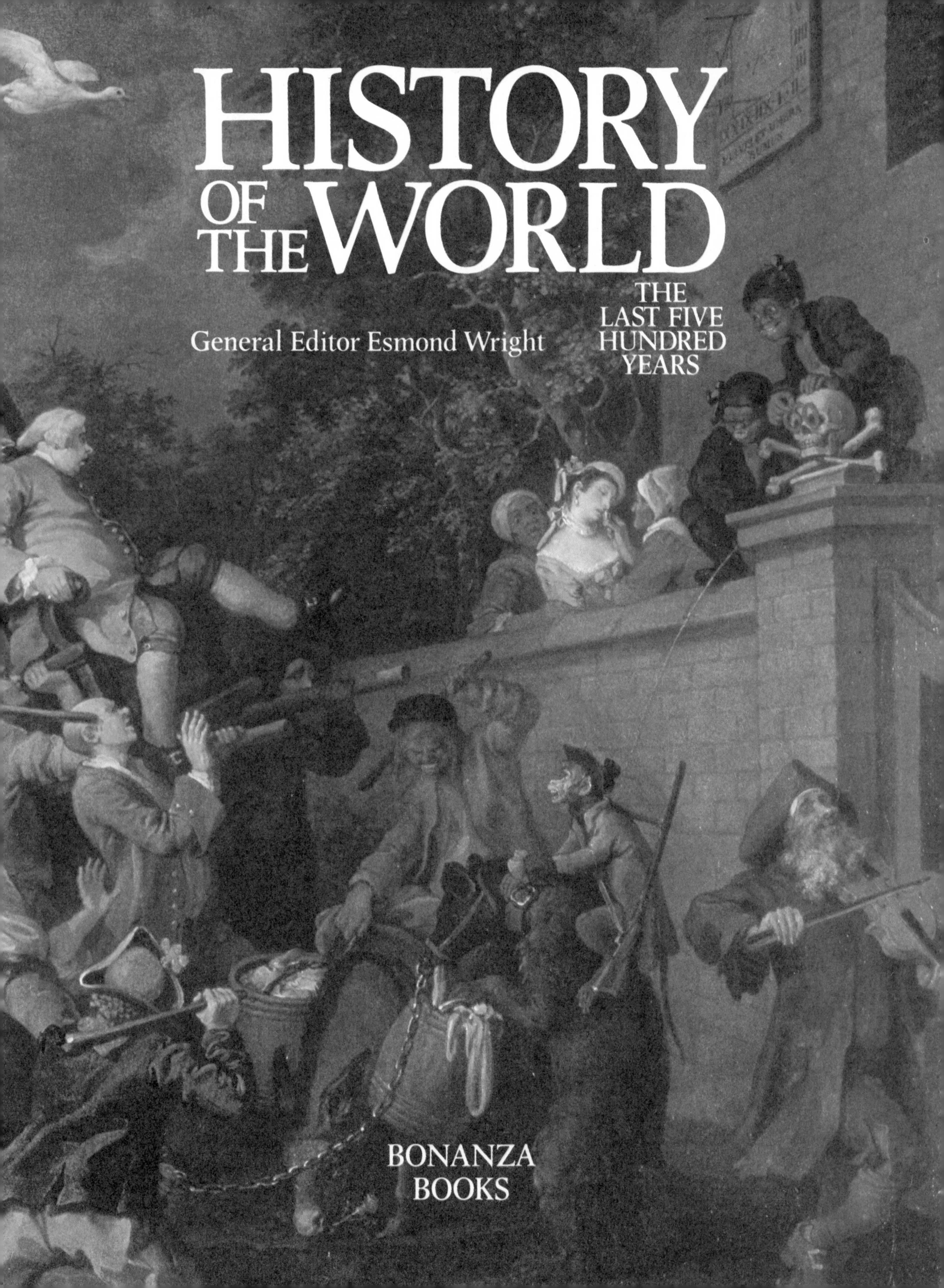

HISTORY
OF THE WORLD

General Editor Esmond Wright

THE
LAST FIVE
HUNDRED
YEARS

BONANZA
BOOKS

General Editor
Esmond Wright
Professor of American History
University of London

Contributors
Christopher Andrew
Geoffrey Barraclough
Asa Briggs
David Buisseret
John Burnett
G. R. Elton
Peter Furtado
David Gillard
Gerald S. Graham
Neil Grant
Nathaniel Harris
J. A. Hawgood
James Henderson
R. Horsman
F. C. Jones
Robert Knecht
William H. McNeill
George Metcalf
R. R. Palmer
C. Duncan Rice
George Shepperson
Alan Smith
Frank Thistlethwaite
David Thomson
J. J. Tumelty

This 1984 edition is published by Bonanza Books,
distributed by Crown Publishers Inc.
and prepared for them by
Newnes Books
a division of The Hamlyn Publishing Group Limited,
84–88 The Centre, Feltham, Middlesex, England
TW13 4BH

Original text
© 1969 The Hamlyn Publishing Group Limited
Revised and updated 1979, 1984
This edition
© 1984 Newnes Books, a division of The Hamlyn
Publishing Group Limited

Library of Congress Cataloging in Publication Data:
Main entry under title:

The History of the world.

    Originally published: London: Hamlyn Pub. Group,
1969.
    Includes index.
    1. History, Modern.   I. Wright, Esmond.
D208.H57 1984   909.08   84–6472

ISBN 0–517–436442

h g f e d c b a

Printed in Yugoslavia

Part I
THE WARS OF RELIGION

Page 10

Introduction

Chapter 1
Economic and Social Change

Page 13

Chapter 2
The Reformation

Page 21

Chapter 3
Habsburg-Valois Rivalry

Page 28

Chapter 4
The Tudors

page 42

Chapter 5
Sixteenth-century Spain

Page 52

Chapter 6
The Counter-Reformation

Page 61

Chapter 7
France from 1500 to 1640

Page 66

Chapter 8
Spain under Philip III and Philip IV

Page 75

Chapter 9
The Thirty Years' War

Page 82

Manière de brûler ceux qui ont été condannez par l'INQUISITION.

Part I

THE WARS OF RELIGION

Introduction

Among the deplorable ages in the sad history of Europe, the near-century which followed upon the Religious Peace of Augsburg in 1555 stands high for horror and unpleasantness. War dominated it: war against the Turks, wars among the powers, civil wars in France, the Netherlands and England, war over principle, ideology and profit. And war got ever more frightful, ending in the destruction of Central Europe, as the brutalized armies of the Thirty Years' War swept across once prosperous realms. In the wake of war came plague, typhus and dysentery, killing far more than even the improved firearms of the day could kill—both weapons and disease being assisted by the incompetent medicine of the time. Assassination grew common, intolerance and inhumanity (encouraged by the fanaticisms of faiths that claimed a monopoly of the Christian message of redemption) ever more dominant. The men and women who ruled that world rarely evoke feelings of admiration; some of the best of them fell to the axe, the bullet or the knife. Small-minded intriguers and incompetent meddlers for the most part sat on the thrones of Spain, France, the Holy Roman Empire and Rome; the men of political vision were few. It is little wonder that not only the English came to look with admiration to the relatively prosperous reign of Elizabeth I, whose greatest achievement, in retrospect, turned out to be her survival on the throne for forty-five years, in spite of all that enemies, plotters and doctors could do.

The age was not unaware of its horrors, and some men set about the tasks of reconciliation and peace. There were those who wished to put an end to the quarrels among Christians: philosophers like Richard Hooker who thought to preserve the peaceful traditions of a moderate Christianity among the assertive arrogances of the sects, mystics like St John of the Cross who wished to bring peace to this world by turning its thoughts exclusively to the next, sceptics like Montaigne who pointed out that the causes for which men wished to kill and die did not exist. Hugo Grotius laid the foundations of international law and order among the ruins created by the collapse of common causes. Both James I of England and Henry IV of France devised and promoted idealistic schemes of universal peace on the basis of solemn treaties and settlements among the nations. But of practical effects there were none; indeed, each year seemed to make the situation worse.

What was wrong with Europe? In the first place, it does appear that at this time its political structure was exceptionally unstable, exceptionally devoid of balance and control. The prolonged decline of France in her civil wars left Spain supremely powerful, but there was always something unreal about the Spanish dominance. The redistribution of Charles V's empire had left that ancient trouble centre, the Rhineland and Burgundy, under the distant control of an alien power in Madrid: the result was the Dutch rebellion which effectively destroyed Philip II's chance of bringing peace by force. In the feeble hands of Maximilian II and Rudolph II, the eastern Habsburg power, in any case confronted with a continuous threat from the Ottoman Turks, allowed the splintering of Germany to become permanent. The jockeying for position among those princelings kept the pot on the boil, embroiled every European country from Sweden to Hungary and led directly to the disasters of the seventeenth century. Such chance as Spain might have had to impose herself on this ceaseless turmoil was lost by the miserable government of Philip III in the days of Lerma and in consequence of the restlessly aggressive revival of France. As everyone battled for himself, the devil came in the end to take the foremost, too.

The conflicts of interests were to some extent polarized and altogether intensified by the religious split. It is customary today to deny that this was an age when religion determined policy; and it is perfectly true that most princes were ready, under pressure, to adapt their faith to their interest. The loyalties of religion grew ever less urgent, till in the end a cardinal of the Church of Rome, in alliance with the Swedish and German defenders of Protestantism, resolved the situation by demolishing the champions of the Counter-Reformation. Nevertheless, the battle between the Catholics and Protestants was real, and the wars would have been both less continuous and less violent if the combatants had not been led by men whose banners carried the conflicting messages of a conquering God. In particular, the seemingly remorseless and irresistible reconquest of so much territory by the Papacy drove the Protestants to put their fate in the hands of extremists. The Calvinists and the Catholic Church after the Council of Trent (1545–63) did not command everyone's allegiance; much happened that conflicted with the claims of the militant faiths; but militancy and the bitter will to fight nonetheless grew out of those faiths.

Besides, the Europe engaged in these murderous activities suffered the strains and uncertainties which go with economic crisis and social transformation. Perhaps it would be best to see the age as one in which a new (or partly new) aristocracy, borne up by landed possession and dependent on the king's favour, built up its hold on society and politics. It is true that bourgeois societies throwing off aristocratic dependence did come into being in the Netherlands and Switzerland and that manifestations of the old anti-monarchial policies of the European nobility continued to occur and in the east continued to be effective. But what happened in the main was not so much a social upheaval or the replacement of one class by another, as rather the transformation of a ruling class pulling in fresh elements, absorbing the cultural achievements of the Renaissance, and accommodating itself to the service of princes with absolute power.

The great inflation and population increase of the sixteenth century swelled the coffers of the landowners upon whom in the end the mass production and distribution of food depended; the new technology of war gave overwhelming power to centralized control; resistance was generally less possible, and the frequent outbursts of social discontent were ever less able to win success. It was an age in which the possessors tightened their hold till fears of the people and limitations on the exercise of power that had existed time out of mind could at long last be safely ignored. Even in England and the Netherlands, the ruling classes maintained their command in the midst of rebellions which they prevented from expanding into social revolution.

Of course, this was also the age of Shakespeare, Montaigne and Cervantes; of Veronese, Tintoretto, Velasquez and Rubens; of Kepler and Galileo. There were many who faced their dreadful time with steadfast sense and good humour. Yet, when all is done, one looks upon that century and sees the three horrible Philips who ruled and ruined Spain; the silly Stuarts who drove an obedient realm into civil war; the cynical Henry IV and the savage Richelieu, both men of vast ability who sought power for power's sake and little else; the asinine Rudolph II, in his castle at Prague, neglecting the problems of empire for the fascinations of alchemy. One sees Drake, confusing enterprise with piracy, and Wallenstein, squeezing great wealth from war and then committing his fortunes to the planets. And on all sides there stand embattled ranks convinced that their faith entitles—nay, compels—them to kill.

Chapter 1

Economic and Social Change

Europeans had travelled beyond the limits of their continent before the Renaissance, but in the fifteenth century a number of countries which had so far played no part in exploration began to send expeditions into uncharted seas. As a result of their efforts new lands were discovered, old superstitions shattered, hitherto respectable theories disproved and new sources of wealth tapped. The great overseas discoveries of the fifteenth and sixteenth centuries, in addition to being remarkable achievements in themselves, had far-reaching effects on the economic and social life of Europe. The opening up of the Cape route to the Spice Islands by the Portuguese threatened the monopoly hitherto enjoyed by Italian, particularly Venetian, merchants, while the discovery by the Spaniards of gold and silver Central and South America led to an increase of the amount of money circulating in Europe.

Among the goods which reached Europe from the Far East in the Middle Ages spices were particularly important. By the fifteenth century most of this trade came to Europe by sea. The goods were carried by Arab merchants from places like Malacca or Calicut across the Indian Ocean to ports along the Persian Gulf or Red Sea, whence they were carried by boat or overland to markets in Egypt or the Levant. Here they were bought by Venetian merchants who carried them the rest of the way to Europe. In short, the goods were bought and sold several times over, each time becoming more expensive. Moreover, the various governments straddling the route imposed heavy tolls and duties, so that the ultimate cost of the goods far exceeded their original price.

The Portuguese doubtless hoped that by discovering an alternative route to the Far East they would be able to obtain cheaper spices at least for themselves, but they were less successful than was once assumed. Although the Cape route to the East was free from tolls and duties and could be controlled from one extremity to the other by a single trading interest, it was almost twice as long as the old route. The risk of shipwreck and of cargoes deteriorating was consequently greater. The Portuguese were also less experienced than their rivals in handling and shipping goods, while Lisbon was less conveniently situated than Venice for the distribution of spices to the rest of Europe. Furthermore, the Portuguese were obliged to take military action in the Indian Ocean to protect their trade and, in an attempt to destroy that of their competitors, they had to spend a large amount of money on forts, ships, armaments and men. Thus it appears unlikely that they made large profits out of the spice business.

Had the Portuguese succeeded in destroying the trade of the Venetians and Arabs they would have been completely successful, but this did not happen. After a temporary setback early in the sixteenth century the old trade through the Levant revived. By 1560 it was so brisk that a Portuguese diplomat in Rome even suggested that his master should seriously think of importing spices that way himself if only he could come to terms with the Turks!

The recovery of the old trade was largely a result of the corruption and inefficiency of Portuguese officials in the East, who were ready to ignore it in return for a share of the profits. Thus the Portuguese spice trade was only a qualified success. The once popular notion that it caused the decline of Venice is no longer tenable. Piracy in the Mediterranean undermined the Venetian commercial structure to a much greater extent.

While the Portuguese were founding an empire in the Far East, the Spaniards created an empire of their own in Central and South America. Though the settlers were interested mainly in cattle, horses and sheep, they established sugar and tobacco plantations on coastal areas and discovered gold and silver.

During the first forty years of the sixteenth century the chief metal export from America was gold, either taken from the natives as barter or booty or mined in a primitive way by the conquistadores. However, in the 1540s, large deposits of silver were found at Potosi and Guanajuato. Mining was left to private enterprise but the Spanish government reserved to itself a proportion of the metal, known as the *quint,* approximately a fifth. Government agents were posted in America to prevent concealment and smuggling. All the bullion had to pass through the House of Trade in Seville, which was under the jurisdiction of the Council of the Indies. The government also controlled the supply of mercury which was used for extracting the silver from the ore.

Originally the bullion was carried to Spain by individual merchant ships which were armed and expected to defend themselves if attacked. Piracy, though, developed to such an extent that, in 1564, the Spanish government set up a system of convoys which sailed twice a year, in April and August. This proved quite efficient. The convoys reached their destination safely, except in 1628 when one was captured by the Dutch and in 1656 when another was intercepted by the English. On arrival the ships were carefully inspected by representatives of the

Above, merchants of the city of Hamburg in the 1490s. Ports throughout the northern and western coasts of Europe flourished at this time, as trade shifted from the Mediterranean to the Atlantic.

Below, a fifteenth-century Venetian galley, armed with both cannon and infantry; its power at sea formed the basis of Venice's expansion during the Italian Wars of the early sixteenth century. National Maritime Museum, London.

On page 10, a French engraving of the burning of heretics by the Inquisition. The Roman Inquisition was less notorious than the Spanish for its pursuit of heresy, but the activities of the Jesuits in opposing Protestantism made it feared to a similar extent.

House of Trade before anyone was allowed ashore. The treasure was then transported to Seville where it was weighed and stored pending its disposal. Officially some eighteen thousand tons of silver and two hundred tons of gold reached Spain between 1521 and 1660.

The price revolution

A most important phenomenon of the sixteenth century was a rise in prices which affected the whole of Europe. This had serious social repercussions: people who depended on fixed incomes suffered, while others who lived by trade or speculation could grow rich quickly. Political life reflected these social changes.

The extent of the so-called price revolution is not easily assessed, for the documentary evidence available to the historian is difficult to interpret and often incomplete. Evidence exists only for certain areas and particular commodities. Little is known about the price of ordinary commodities like butter or cheese in England, but a fair amount about that of woollen cloth and other textiles. Variations in the size and quality of cloth, however, are not always indicated, so that it is often impossible to compare the prices of goods. The evidence for cereals is good but the price varied from year to year according to the harvests and even from district to district. Thus, it is impossible to compile a really accurate price index for the sixteenth century.

Despite these technical difficulties it would appear that the prices of basic consumable goods in England tripled by 1580 and quadrupled by 1600, a process which was reflected in other countries as well. In Flanders the price of wheat was 93 percent higher in 1521–22 than in the previous year, and in Hainaut 115 percent. In Antwerp there was a sharp rise in the price of fuel and the value of rents. In Spain there was a 2·8 percent average annual increase in prices from 1501 to 1562 and a 1·3 percent increase from 1562 to 1600. By comparison with more modern times the inflation of the sixteenth century was not particularly severe. It has been calculated that prices went up 400 percent in ninety years, whereas in the twentieth century they may have risen by as much in only forty years. But the price revolution came at the end of a long period of stable prices and sixteenth century society was less able to adapt itself to changing conditions than its modern counterpart.

Inflation occurs when 'too much money chases too few goods'. In the sixteenth century the scarcity of food and other commodities was blamed on such human weaknesses as idleness or greed. Sir Thomas More in *Utopia* blamed 'the unreasonable covetousness of a fewe' for 'the great dearth of victualles'. He believed that food was running short because greedy landlords were turning their land over to sheep on account of the profits to be made out of the sale of

wool. In 1533 Thomas Starkey asserted that 'a great part of these people which we have here in our country is either idle or ill-occupied.

In 1556, however, another explanation of the price revolution was advanced by Martín de Azpilcueta of the University of Salamanca. He showed that 'money is worth more when and where it is scarce than where it is abundant. We see by experience', he wrote,

that in France, where money is scarcer than in Spain, bread, cloth and labour are worth much less. And even in Spain, in times when money was scarcer, saleable goods and labour were given for very much less than after the discovery of the Indies, which flooded the country with gold and silver.

This theory was further expounded in 1568 by the French lawyer, Jean Bodin, in a published reply to M. de Malestroit, who had blamed successive debasements of the coinage for the inflation.

Recently, however, the theory that the importation of precious metals from America was the principal cause of the price revolution has been largely discredited. American treasures did not begin to reach Europe in sizeable quantities until the middle of the sixteenth century, yet prices had begun to rise in the preceding fifty years. Moreover, much of the silver that reached Spain was immediately re-exported to pay for its imports, to maintain its armies abroad and to repay loans made by foreign bankers. As a result Spain suffered from a dearth rather than a surplus of gold and silver. This meant that in the seventeenth century it was obliged to adopt a billon currency, that is, base metal mixed with gold and silver. It would seem, therefore, that the price rise in Spain was a credit, not a monetary, inflation.

Population growth

In recent years the view has been adopted that a major cause of the price revolution was a rise in the population of Europe. This created a growing demand for food, fuel and clothing. As productivity failed to keep pace with this demand, goods became scarce and prices rose.

Again the sources available to the historian are unsatisfactory: no censuses or reliable estimates exist for any whole country in the sixteenth century. Information has to be pieced together from materials like parish registers, tax returns or muster rolls, which are frequently inaccurate or misleading. All the available evidence, however, points to a general rise in the population of Europe during the century. Some towns even doubled in size. In 1500 there were only five European cities with 100,000 inhabitants or more; by 1600 the number had grown to twelve or thirteen. The population of London may have gone up from fifty thousand to two hundred thousand. Certainly the city was making very heavy demands on the hinterland for food supplies, as were other towns like Bristol and Norwich.

In 1500 Seville had about sixty thousand

inhabitants. During the next two or three decades the number dropped as a result of epidemics and emigration, but it had risen to one hundred and fifty thousand by 1588. Smaller towns expanded to such an extent that they often had to build outside their walls and in the large cities there was much overcrowding. The growth in population was also felt in the countryside where there was fierce competition for limited amounts of farm land. Yet by modern standards sixteenth century Europe was thinly populated: the population of England rose from three and a half million in 1500 to five million in 1600 and that of the Holy Roman Empire from twelve to twenty million.

It is not difficult to see how the rise in population of the sixteenth century would affect prices. Wherever peasants farmed their land on temporary leases landlords could, and often did, raise their rents. Those tenants who could not afford the new rents left the land and either joined the armies of vagabonds who roamed about the countryside or flocked to the towns.

The rise in population meant an increased demand for food. To some extent this was met by improved methods of agriculture and the introduction of new crops such as rice in the Po valley. But most European farmers were illiterate and unable to read the new manuals of husbandry or, if they could, they lacked the capital necessary to carry out the improvements recommended. Consequently demand outstripped supply.

The price of other agricultural products was also affected by the rise in population. Until about 1550 wool prices in England and Spain (the only two countries which produced wool for an international market) rose even more rapidly than grain prices. This encouraged landlords to turn arable land into pasture. They enclosed common land and depopulated villages to make room for their flocks. This inevitably aggravated the problem of food supplies.

In Spain sheep-farming was practised on a huge scale in Castile where the soil and the climate were not favourable to other forms of cultivation. Each year enormous flocks of sheep were moved from the mountains of Old Castile to winter in the south. They were supposed to follow certain predetermined tracks but would often damage crops and cause soil erosion. Continual disputes arose between ordinary farmers and the guild of sheep farmers, called the Mesta, which enjoyed the full backing of the crown.

Above, sixteenth-century illustration from an edition of Marco Polo's voyages; Europeans were beginning to discover other races and societies and consequently found a new interest in earlier travellers.

Top, Harvesting, by Pieter Brueghel; the paintings of peasant life of the mid-sixteenth century by Brueghel, despite their emphasis on hard work, show the relative prosperity and stability of the Low Countries. Metropolitan Museum, New York.

Opposite top, Portuguese carracks of the mid-sixteenth century; at this date the Portuguese controlled much of the carrying trade of the Far East.

Opposite bottom, a sixteenth-century French port with ocean-going trading ships.

In 1501 the Mesta was given the right to use for ever and at fixed rents any land it had once used as pasture. The Spanish monarchy supported the Mesta in this way because it received a quick and sure revenue from taxes on sheep and the sale of wool. Arable farming was discouraged by this policy and Spain accordingly suffered from a serious shortage of grain. After 1506 it become more independent on foreign imports.

Spain was not the only country which failed to produce enough food for its growing population. After a severe famine in 1590–91 all the countries bordering on the western Mediterranean had to import grain from the Baltic. More Dutch and Hanseatic ships than ever before passed through the Sound between Denmark and Sweden laden with rye from Poland, Prussia and Pomerania. The newly constructed port of Leghorn (Livorno) became the main distributing centre in Italy for northern grain. The number of ships entering the port shot up from about 200 in 1592–93 to nearly 2,500 in 1609–10. The northerners had better crews and cheaper ships than the Italians, who began to lose the commercial dominance in this and in other aspects of the carrying trade which they had hitherto enjoyed.

If European agriculture failed to cope with the rising demand for food, the manufacturing industries proved more adaptable. Most of them did not require much fixed capital and they could use the increased labour force available. Only the guilds with their regulations limiting the number of apprentices and journeymen a master might employ stood in the way of greater productivity. But capitalist entrepreneurs could always go into the countryside or small country towns, where the people were only too glad to earn a little extra money by spinning and weaving at home. Alternatively the capitalists could take over the guilds and employ the master craftsmen on piece rates. Because the manufacturing industries were better able to keep abreast of the rising demand the price of their products did not go up as much as that of grain.

Although wages tended to go up in the sixteenth century they were seldom able to catch up with prices. In England and other countries, for example, the wages of building workers doubled during the century but food prices rose four or five times above their original level. It cannot be doubted, then, that wage earners were worse off in terms of real wages at the end of the century than at the beginning even allowing for the fact that retail prices did not go up as much as wholesale ones and that manufactured goods cost relatively less than food.

When the disparity between wages and prices became apparent in about 1530 a serious undercurrent of discontent developed among the labouring poor, occasionally flaring up into open revolt. If unemployment and low wages became combined with revolutionary religious propaganda the result could be devastating, as was shown by the Anabaptist take-over of Münster in 1534. Only those wage-earners who held land fixed at the old rate actually benefited from the price revolution, since, as their rent declined in value, they were able to get more for their produce on the local market.

Much has been written about the so-called 'rise of the gentry' in sixteenth-century England, but the picture is still far from clear. Some country gentlemen who held moderately large estates certainly did very well at this time, but it is difficult to say whether their success was a result of favourable market conditions or to royal favour. Other members of the gentry declined but no one has yet been able to work out exactly the ratio of 'declining' to 'rising' gentry. Nor was there anything new about merchants putting their capital in land with a view to becoming gentlemen or even members of the aristocracy. English society had always been fluid and the expanding economy of the sixteenth century simply offered wider opportunities for the movement of persons and capital.

A similar dearth of statistical evidence precludes a clear assessment of the effects of the price revolution on rural society in other parts of Europe. In Hainaut, and perhaps in the other Walloon provinces of the Netherlands, owners of reasonably large estates did better out of rising prices than smaller landowners. In France, on the other hand, it would seem that the lesser nobility were less successful in adjusting their rents to the economic situation. This would explain why so many were ready to join the armies engaged in the Wars of Religion. It is possible, however, that most of these were younger sons who had suffered as a result of the legal devices employed by their seniors to prevent the fragmentation of their estates.

On the whole the nobility in France, Spain and Italy managed to weather the storm of the price revolution quite well by raising rents or entry fines (premiums on transferring tenancies) at least as fast as prices and by exacting feudal dues and seigneurial monopolies. The upper nobility received gifts of pensions, lands and offices from the crown in return for their military and administrative services.

In Germany the social effects of the price revolution varied from one locality to another. In the west the nobility found it difficult to raise rents except in Bavaria and

Austria where the ruling princes supported their claims to raise entry fines. In southwest Germany the princes provoked a considerable amount of peasant unrest by substituting autocratic Roman law for local custom, by taking over village and seigneurial jurisdiction and by imposing new taxes.

In Holstein and Denmark the nobles profited from high prices by acting as middlemen between the peasants and foreign merchants seeking grain and dairy produce. In northeast Germany and Poland they made the most of the growing market for rye, timber and furs in western and southern Europe. They raised a cheap labour force to farm their huge demesnes by tying the peasants to their holdings and exacting heavy labour services from them. The local princes did nothing to protect the peasants from this 'new serfdom' as they depended on the landowners or *Junkers* for money grants.

The golden age of Antwerp

European expansion overseas widened the scope of international trade and stimulated far-reaching changes in its organization and methods.

In the course of the sixteenth century the main focus of international trade shifted from the Mediterranean to the North Sea and the Atlantic, and Antwerp rose to a preeminent position. Within fifty years this city attracted to itself a high proportion of Europe's trade, becoming at the same time one of the largest money markets and an industrial centre. Its population rose from about fifty thousand in 1500 to around one hundred thousand in 1550, and these figures do not include a large floating population of foreign merchants.

Experience had shown that Lisbon was not a convenient centre for the distribution of spices to the rest of Europe. The Portuguese needed to exchange them for grain, metals and cloth. For centuries the Netherlands had been an important trading centre accessible to traders from many countries. In 1499, therefore, the Portuguese decided to establish their spice staple at Antwerp.

Important as this event was, it was not the only reason for the city's golden age. The deepening of the river Scheldt linking Antwerp to the North Sea enabled ships which had been obliged previously to anchor in the estuary to go up river and unload directly at the port instead of having to trans-ship their cargoes. As a result the number of ships paying anchorage dues rose steeply during the century.

Antwerp was situated close to a network of rivers leading to the south. It was the terminus of a comparatively toll-free land route from Germany, so that even before the coming of the Portuguese it was thronged with German merchants who traded mainly in metals and fustians. Many English cloth merchants were there too. All these traders were attracted not only by the city's geographical situation but also by the favourable conditions attached to its two annual fairs. By the 1540s it was handling eighty percent of the Netherlands trade and exporting about three times as much as London.

In addition to being a clearing-house for goods, Antwerp imported a considerable quantity of food for its fast-growing population and this in turn gave rise to local industries like fish-curing and sugar-refining. Its main industry, however, was the finishing of English cloth, which necessitated the importation of dyes from southern Europe and America and of alum (used to fix the colours) from the papal states. Antwerp manufactured armaments and church bells and exported a wide range of goods such as furniture, tapestries, paintings, jewellery, glassware, books, paper, maps and musical instruments.

The growth of capitalism

Antwerp was also one of the foremost money markets in Europe. Originally merchants would transact business with each other directly but by the sixteenth century they had begun to work through bankers. These had often started their careers as merchants in various commodities and had then switched to trading in money, which

offered larger and quicker returns.

This was true of the great family business of Fugger, based at Augsburg in south Germany. Its fortunes were founded on the cloth trade but in the fifteenth century the scope of its activities was much enlarged by Jacob Fugger the Rich (1459–1525). He added silks and velvets, spices, metals and jewels to the linens and fustians which had been the firm's original commodities. To sell these goods he set up a chain of counting houses and merchandise depots in all the great cities of central and western Europe. At the same time he went into the metal trade, gaining control of the output of silver, copper and iron in central Europe and of silver and mercury in Spain. Jacob Fugger then bought or financed mines to extend his monopoly.

By the sixteenth century the firm of Fugger had become the leading banking house in Europe. Its wealth was so great that it was even able to come to the rescue of impecunious princes. In return for mining concessions it would do almost anything for the Habsburgs and it was largely owing to its financial assistance that Charles V was elected emperor in 1519. When he delayed over the repayment of his debt Jacob Fugger lost no time in bluntly reminding him: 'it is well known that your Majesty without me might not have acquired the imperial crown'.

The development of banking was closely bound up with the trade boom of the sixteenth century. Few merchants ever paid cash in Antwerp: they bought and sold their goods by means of bills of exchange provided by the bankers. They relied on advances and settled their accounts by instalments. The complex transactions that took place offered incomparable opportunities for speculation. At first, interest rates were high and erratic but they settled down by the 1540s to between twelve and fifteen percent. Henry VIII of England borrowed about a million pounds on the Antwerp market during the last four years of his reign.

The sixteenth century was an age of feverish speculation. The stock exchanges of Antwerp and Lyons were permanent establishments, unlike the old medieval fairs which had been held only from time to time. Merchants setting off on long voyages at sea began to insure their lives. State lotteries and loans made their appearance. An innovation deserving special notice was the creation of the *rentes sur l' Hôtel de Ville* in 1522. The French king, Francis I, obtained a loan from the general public against the security not of the state but of the municipal government of Paris. In return the lenders were promised an annual *rente* representing an interest of about eight percent. In 1555 Henry II launched the *Grand Parti* (Great Deal) of Lyons which started a great rush of investors.

The decline of Antwerp

The golden age of Antwerp was short-lived. In 1549 the Portuguese, finding that they could get silver more easily and cheaply from Spain and that the Germans were willing to trade directly with Lisbon, withdrew their spice staple. This blow was followed by the collapse of the English cloth trade. As a result of the English government's devaluation of silver in 1550, the Merchant Adventurers were able to export a record amount of cloth to Antwerp, causing a temporary glut. When sterling was revalued in the following year the price of cloth shot up and the trade suffered a setback from which it never fully recovered during the rest of the century.

All this coincided with a slump in the Spanish-American trade, a renewal of war between the King of France and the emperor, two successive harvest failures and a round of national bankruptcies. The Spanish government transformed all its debts into state bonds or *juros*. Its example was soon followed by the Netherlands, French and Portuguese governments. As a result the Antwerp bankers defaulted on their obligations and the small investors who had financed the government loans were severely hit. The final blows were struck after the outbreak of the Dutch revolt. In 1576 Antwerp was sacked by Spanish troops, and in 1585 the Scheldt was closed by the Dutch.

Above, a view of Antwerp; in the sixteenth century this city became the trading centre of northern Europe, for wool, cloth, wheat and banking, as well as being the centre of the trade in diamonds. National Scheepvaartmuseum, Antwerp.

Left, The Fight between Carnival and Lent by Pieter Brueghel; the pagan festival of Carnival still flourished, especially in the Mediterranean countries, and was greatly opposed by the Reformation.

Opposite top left, cartographers at work in the sixteenth century. The development of navigational skills led to many scientific advances, in astronomy, physics and geography, and special schools were founded to teach these new sciences to the seamen.

Opposite bottom left, an agricultural scene from a book of 1502. The population of western Europe rose in the next century, and a reorganization of agriculture was necessary, both to feed the towns and to provide for industries such as cloth.

Opposite right, this painting of a banker and his wife, by Quentin Massys, shows the spirit of early sixteenth-century capitalism of the Low Countries in action – frugality, devotion to work and relative equality between the sexes. Musée du Louvre, Paris.

ABRAHAM VON WERDT.

Protestantism and capitalism

How far was the rise of capitalism connected with the Reformation? In 1904 the German sociologist, Max Weber, argued that the Protestant concept of the 'calling'—the interpretation of worldly avocations as divinely appointed and capable of fulfilment in a spirit of worship—enabled the Protestant to pursue his daily life energetically and profitably. The Roman Church, he alleged, had condemned the world and opposed economic development, particularly the taking of interest. The Protestant ethic was thus seen as the essential prerequisite for the growth of modern capitalism. Finally, Weber argued, capitalism had developed to a greater extent in Protestant than in Catholic countries, while the Reformation had found its most enthusiastic followers among traders and industrialists.

Attractive as the Weber thesis may seem, it does not stand up well to investigation. Capitalism existed before the Reformation and the late medieval Church was not totally opposed to the taking of interest. In the late fifteenth century the Franciscans established benevolent funds for loans to the poor and charged interest on them to cover administrative costs. The Lateran Council of 1515 recognized the impossibility of interest-free loans. Thus Calvin was not being revolutionary when he grudgingly defended usury at five percent in certain carefully guarded circumstances. Protestant preaching consistently denounced acquisitiveness as sinful. The concept of the calling certainly implied that a man could serve God in the world, but it did not suggest that profit should be his main object in life.

It is also not true to say that capitalism reached its fullest expression in Protestant as distinct from Catholic countries. It was strong in the Netherlands long before Calvinism reached there and it hardly existed in Calvin's own stronghold of Geneva. Jacob Fugger, who once declared his intention to continue enlarging his fortune as long as he could, was not a Protestant. In short, no good reason exists for linking Protestantism and capitalism in any significant way.

Chapter 2

The Reformation

The Reformation was far more than a movement directed against abuses in the Roman Church; it was the culmination of a complex situation with roots deeply buried in the medieval past.

Serious abuses did exist, of course, in the Church on the eve of the Reformation. One of the most widespread was pluralism, the accumulation of more than one benefice in the hands of one man. Often this was economically justified. In an age of inflation it was not always possible for a clergyman to live on the income of a single benefice, so he obtained a papal dispensation to hold more than one. Pluralism was spiritually insidious, however, for it necessarily entailed absenteeism and the neglect of pastoral duties.

Another common abuse was clerical ignorance. Few educational opportunities existed even for the clergy outside the universities, and only a relatively small proportion of clergymen were graduates properly equipped to teach the faith. Among the regular clergy there was a fair amount of laxity about the observance of monastic rules: the choral office was neglected, the refectory abandoned, fasting neglected, silence at meals ignored and the teaching of novices was inadequate. At the highest level of the Church nepotism was a serious problem. One of the worst offenders in this respect was Pope Sixtus IV, who created his nephews cardinals or made them lords of cities. The Renaissance popes generally were much more concerned with their temporal interests in Italy than with their responsibilites as spiritual leaders.

Clerical abuses were a cause of anti-clericalism in the late Middle Ages, but they had always existed and churchmen realized the need to remedy them. Decline and renewal were normal processes in the evolution of the Church, which had been largely built up by successive generations of reformers. The Reformation was not primarily a movement of the laity against the clergy. It was largely a movement of the clergy against the growth of centralization in the Church.

The crisis in the Church was constitutional as well as moral. The papacy had become an absolute monarchy: it controlled ecclesiastical appointments through the system of 'reservations' and 'nominations'

and it taxed the clergy by means of annates (payments claimed by the pope from the first year's revenue of a new benefice) and tenths (ten percent on all clerical incomes). This caused much discontent among the clergy and the demand arose for a reform of the Church in its head as well as its members. But who was to carry out this reform? Could the papacy be trusted to reform itself?

In the fourteenth century the theory was advanced that the responsibility of reforming the Church lay with a general council of the Church, not with the pope. A disputed election to the papacy in 1378 enabled the conciliarists to put their ideas into practice. If the Council of Constance (1414–18) succeeded in healing the Great Schism, it failed to curb papal authority, and the Council of Basle (1431–49) was equally unsuccessful. By their radicalism the conciliarists had unconsciously harmed the cause of reform, for the popes were thereafter reluctant to call another council, fearing that their authority would be challenged. As a result reform was left to the initiative of individuals whose activities were necessarily limited to particular religious houses or dioceses.

Church versus state

The constitutional conflict within the Church was paralleled by another crisis caused by the emergence of powerful secular forces. The kings and princes of Europe wanted complete mastery of their own states. They aimed at controlling the lives, thoughts and pockets of their subjects. The Church, with its own legal and fiscal organization cutting across national boundaries, was an obstacle in the path of the royal efforts to achieve a centralized administration. Friction between Church and state had always existed, but it now reached a dangerous intensity. The Reformation often took the form of a movement by national lay rulers to achieve their independence from an international Church which had outlived its day.

Finally the Reformation was a reaction againsy the doctrinal teaching of the Church which had ceased to satisfy large sections of the clergy and laity. Throughout Europe the late fifteenth century was marked by a profound spiritual restlessness. People were no longer content to accept the truth, they wanted to understand it. As the Renaissance helped to sharpen their minds they began to re-examine the sources of Christianity, particularly the writings of St Paul.

It is undeniable that a connection existed between the Renaissance and the Reformation but, as the quarrel between Erasmus and Luther over the question of free will was to demonstrate, a deep ideological gulf divided the two movements. Whereas Renaissance scholars believed in man's ability to better himself by his own efforts, the leaders of the Reformation saw him as utterly incapable of achieving salvation without God's grace.

Above, a drawing of Erasmus by Albrecht Dürer; Erasmus' criticisms of the abuses of the Catholic church have led him to be called 'the foster-father of the Reformation', although he disagreed with Luther on many points. Musée du Louvre, Paris.

Opposite top, a printing press at Nuremburg in the fifteenth century. Printing with movable type had been invented in the 1450s and very quickly spread throughout Europe. Many printers were supporters of the New Learning and the Reformation.

Opposite bottom, Amsterdam in the sixteenth century. The city grew rapidly to become the main trading centre of northern Europe, especially as its rival Antwerp suffered during the Dutch War of Independence in the 1570s.

Luther

Martin Luther was born on 10 November 1483 at Eisleben, on the edge of the Thuringian Forest. Though a miner, his father, Hans, was not poor and soon after Martin's birth he moved to Mansfeld where he became part owner of six shafts and two foundries and a town councillor. He was thus able to give Martin a good education.

Luther's childhood appears to have been perfectly normal. His parents were serious, hard-working and devout but not unduly strict or cruel. As a schoolboy Luther mastered Latin and became a good musician. In 1501 he was sent to the University of Erfurt, where he gained the reputation of being cheerful, witty, hard-working and devout.

Religion already meant so much to Luther that he decided not to become a lawyer, as his father had intended, but to enter the Order of Augustinian Hermits in Erfurt. It is often said that he reached this decision after he had narrowly escaped death in a thunderstorm, but he really made up his mind after a long search for God.

From an early age Luther was deeply preoccupied with the question of his own salvation. As a monk and a priest he did all the customary acts of penance: he deliberately inflicted pain upon himself by beating his own body, and spent hours confessing his sins, but peace of mind continued to elude him. In 1510 he was sent to Rome but he returned disillusioned. 'Like a fool', he said later, 'I took onions to Rome and brought back garlic.'

In 1511 Luther was transferred to Wittenberg where he was persuaded to take his doctorate and become a preacher. But he was still groping for the truth. God appeared to him as a demanding and angry judge, not as a gracious and merciful father. His vision of God was at times so terrifying that he once compared it with seeing the Devil.

Then came the light. In 1513 as he was preparing his lectures on the Psalms he began to question the traditional meaning given to the biblical term 'righteousness'. He turned to the text in the first chapter of St Paul's *Epistle to the Romans*: 'For therein is the righteousness of God revealed from faith to faith: as it is written, The just shall live by faith'. Gradually Luther began to see righteousness in a new light: as a forgiving righteousness, not as a punitive one, whereby God reconciled sinful man to Himself. 'When I had realized this', he wrote, 'I felt myself absolutely born again. The gates of Paradise had been flung open and I had entered. There and then the whole of Scripture took on another look to me.'

From this time onwards Luther devoted himself to the task of revealing the truth to his fellow men by liberating Scripture from the false interpretation of the schoolmen. He did not become widely known, however, until November 1517, when he protested against the sale of indulgences by posting up his famous ninety-five theses on the door of the castle church at Wittenberg.

Indulgences were papal certificates releasing men from some of the penalties of sin, and a famous case of their misuse occurred when Albert of Hohenzollern declared that he wished to become Archbishop of Mainz. He already held the sees of Magdeburg and Halberstadt, although he was not old enough to be a bishop at all. The pope was prepared to overlook these impediments in return for the enormous fee of ten thousand ducats. As Albert did not have the money he borrowed it from the Fuggers. The pope assisted him to repay the loan by authorizing a sale of indulgences on condition that half the proceeds would go to the Fuggers and half to the rebuilding of St Peter's in Rome.

Although the certificates of indulgence were carefully worded to exclude the notion that divine forgiveness could be purchased and sold, John Tetzel, who hawked them around in Saxony, indulged in unscrupulous salesmanship. He pointed to the dead souls languishing in the torments of purgatory crying out for relief. 'As soon as the coin in the coffer rings', he explained, 'the soul from purgatory springs.'

When Luther was told about Tetzel's activities he remarked: 'I'll knock a hole into his drum', yet his indignation was not provoked by the sale of indulgences so much as the doctrine upon which it was based, which was incompatible with his own belief in justification by faith. He was deeply concerned about the way in which people assumed that an indulgence was a remission not merely of penalty but also of guilt.

The ninety-five theses were not extreme. They were simply intended to start an academic debate. Within a few weeks, however, they were printed and widely circulated in Switzerland and Germany. The Dominicans in Saxony espoused Tetzel's cause and pressed charges against Luther in Rome. But because of the political situation the papacy failed to act swiftly.

Although the Emperor Maximilian was still alive, it was clear that his days were numbered and that a successor would soon have to be elected. From the papacy's point of view the safest candidate was Frederick the Wise, Elector of Saxony, who happened to be Luther's lord. Frederick did not sympathize with his attack on indulgences but was determined that he should be given a fair hearing on German soil.

In 1518 Luther was ordered to appear before Cardinal Cajetan at Augsburg. The cardinal urged him to revoke his doctrines without preliminary discussion but Luther refused. In June 1519 he was drawn into a debate at Leipzig with the redoubtable Dominican, John Eck. It began as a harmless metaphysical exchange but soon shifted on to the much more dangerous question of papal authority. Eck was prompted to accuse Luther of Hussitism by his contention that Scripture, not the papacy, was the ultimate authority in religious matters.

After the Leipzig debate Luther published several works in which he elaborated his view of the sacraments. They did not in his view function automatically but through faith in the promises of Christ. He doubted if they numbered more than three: baptism, communion, penance. By 1520 he had rejected the Catholic doctrine of transubstantiation according to which, when the priest pronounces the words 'this is my body', the substance of the bread and wine on the altar is changed into the flesh and blood of Christ while continuing to look, taste and feel as before. Luther accepted that the bread and wine are the body of Christ but denied that their substance was changed. God, he argued, is everywhere and in everything, and in administering the sacrament the priest merely serves as an agent in the self-disclosure of God. To this extent Luther continued to believe that God was actually present in the sacrament, so that Catholics and Lutherans shared the doctrine of God's Real Presence.

Meanwhile many people rallied to Luther's side without always understanding the fundamental reasons of his protest. Ulrich von Hutten wished to draw him into a national revolt against Rome. Another humanist, Philip Melanchthon (1497–1560), became his right-hand man and did much to systematize his theology. The great painter, Albrecht Dürer, belonged to a circle of Lutheran intellectuals at Nuremberg. The Imperial Knights, whose unique constitutional position was being threatened by the territorial princes, also came out in support of Luther.

In June 1520 the pope at last condemned Luther in the Bull *Exsurge domine* while allowing him sixty days in which to retract.

Luther's retort was to throw into a bonfire the Bull along with the whole body of canon law before a gathering of university teachers and students. As a result of this incident he was excommunicated in January 1521.

In the meantime, Luther published three pamphlets of great significance. *The Address to the Christian Nobility of the German Nation,* which was written in German, called on the German rulers to reform the papacy and the entire ecclesiastical hierarchy. In *The Babylonian Captivity of the Church* Luther outlined his theology and condemned the papacy for depriving Christians of direct access to God through faith. Yet he had not given up hope of making his peace with the Church. In *The Freedom of a Christian Man* he expounded in a conciliatory tone, for the pope's attention, his idea of the evangelical life, albeit without retracting his views.

The newly elected emperor, Charles V, though not opposed to Church reform or even to a curbing of papal authority, intended to defend the old faith. He feared that rebellion against the Church would easily lead to rebellion against the state. Yet he could not ignore the wishes of the German people and those of the electors, so he agreed to summon Luther to explain himself at the Diet of Worms. Many of the reformer's friends warned him of the dangers of accepting the invitation, even with a safe-conduct in his pocket. But Luther, confident in the power of the Gospel, announced that he would go to Worms even if there were 'as many devils in it as there were tiles on the roofs of the houses'.

When he appeared before the emperor and the Estates he was asked to retract his views, but he refused. He boldly declared,

Unless I am convinced of error by the testimony of Scripture or by clear reason I cannot and will not recant anything, for it is neither safe not honest to act against one's conscience. God help me. Amen.

As no compromise seemed feasible Luther was given permission to return to Wittenberg. On his way through the Thuringian forest, however, he was spirited off by his friends to the Wartburg castle where he remained for almost a year. In May 1521 he was placed under the imperial ban, but Charles V could not enforce the edict, so that Luther continued his activities without interruption.

In addition to works condemning priestly confession and absolution, monastic vows and clerical celibacy, he produced in the incredibly short time of eleven weeks a translation into German of the New Testament, five thousand copies of which were sold in two months. Meanwhile, his followers, including many members of the regular clergy, preached his doctrine in the towns. They were joined by all kinds of agitators with views far more extreme than Luther's. At Wittenberg, Carlstadt and Zwilling set

out to destroy all that remained of the old religious order. The arrival of the Zwickau 'prophets' coincided with riots in which religious images were destroyed and Luther, who strongly disapproved of violence, had to come out of hiding to restore order. He and his friends then began to construct a Church in accordance with the teaching of the gospel.

With the assistance of printing the Reformation spread rapidly to many parts of the empire. By 1528 Brandenburg, Brunswick-Lüneburg, Schleswig-Holstein, Mansfeld and Silesia had become Lutheran. The most popular form of Reformation literature was the pamphlet illustrated by woodcuts. Some of these were designed by Lucas Cranach the Elder (1472–1553), to whom we are indebted for the best portraits of Luther. Hymns and religious plays also helped to popularize the Reformation. Luther himself composed hymns, the best known being *Ein' Feste Burg* (*God is our refuge*). The poet Heine called it 'the Marseillaise of the Reformation'.

The Peasants' War

Popular as it was, the Lutheran movement could not satisfy the social aspirations of the lower orders of German society. The peasants in particular were dissatisfied with their status, which was being depressed by the reception of Roman Law, and wanted to be relieved of many feudal obligations and fiscal burdens. For a time they translated Luther's doctrines into social terms and looked to him as a leader, but if he sympathized with their complaints he was

Above, a painting of the four evangelists stoning the pope for his worldliness and corruption; this work by Girolamo da Treviso illustrates that opposition to the abuses of the Church was not confined to north of the Alps. Royal Collection.

Below, Knight, Death and Devil (1513) by Albrecht Dürer; the idea of the resolute combating the real distractions of the devil was one that Luther felt personally. British Museum, London.

Opposite, Martin Luther (1483–1546) painted by Lucas Cranach; Luther had a curiously ambivalent attitude towards authority, demanding freedom from the rules of the Church but insisting on the absolute subjection of the individual to God.

consistently opposed to violent action on their part. However, his *Admonition to Peace* came too late. In June 1524 the Peasants' War had broken out in the Black Forest and it quickly spread to many parts of Germany.

In Saxony and Thuringia Thomas Münzer, a former disciple of Luther, exploited the upheaval to fulfil a mystical vision. Denouncing the princes as 'godless rascals', he issued bloodcurdling orders of the day, signed 'the Sword of Gideon'. Luther was appalled by the turn of events. In *Against the Murdering Hordes of Peasants* he encouraged the princes to 'strike, throttle, thrust, each man who can, secretly or openly and bear in mind that nothing is more poisonous, harmful or devilish than a rebellious man'. Luther feared that the revolt would compromise his own movement, but his attitude was consistent with his theology: civil government and the existing social order were divinely instituted; to rebel against them was an offence against God.

The Peasants' War ended bloodily. When the princes offered terms to the rebels assembled at Frankenhausen, Münzer told them that God had promised them victory and that he would catch the princes' cannon balls in the folds of his cloak. Without cavalry or guns, however, the peasants could do nothing. As the first cannon balls fell upon them they fled in panic and were cut down by the princes' cavalry. Münzer, who was found hiding in a cellar, was tortured and beheaded. As a result of Luther's role in the Peasants' War his movement lost much of its popular appeal. Many peasants and townsmen, feeling that he had let them down, turned to Anabaptism, a more radical form of Protestantism.

After 1525 the religious situation in Germany crystallized. The Catholic princes formed the League of Dessau while the Lutherans banded together at Torgau. Because of the Lutheran majority at the Diet of Speyer in 1526 a law was passed making each prince responsible for his own

Gallia non alio tantum se Flamine Jactat,
Nec se alio tollit Scotia Vate magis. O 2.

religious policy. This was revoked three years later by a Catholic majority in the Diet. The Lutherans protested against this decision—hence the term 'Protestant'. But the reformers lacked unity.

In 1529 a conference was called at Marburg to settle differences between the Lutherans and the Zwinglians of Switzerland and south Germany. It failed because Luther and Zwingli could not agree on the interpretation of the communion service or Eucharist. This disunity occurred at the worst possible time, for in 1530 Charles V was able to turn his attention to Germany. At the Diet of Augsburg the Protestants produced not one confession of faith but three, while the Catholics refused to make any doctrinal concessions.

Zwingli

Huldreych Zwingli (1484–1531) departed from Catholic doctrine in 1519 and more radically than Luther. Whereas the latter adhered to the doctrine of Christ's Real Presence in the Eucharist, Zwingli considered the communion service to be simply commemorative. The two reformers also disagreed about baptism, justification by faith and other doctrinal questions.

Fundamentally they differed in their view of human nature. Zwingli was closer to the humanist in his belief that man could acquire faith by studying the Word of God. He was als more of a fundamentalist in that he would accept only practices enjoined by Scripture. Thus, he rejected fasting, clerical celibacy, religious images and church music. His attachment to the Bible was shown by his activities as a preacher and church organizer in Zürich after the bishop's authority had been removed. The Bible was translated and published in Zürich in 1530, four years before the appearance of Luther's German Bible.

Perhaps Zwingli's most important contribution was the stress he placed on discipline. Under his influence matrimonial and moral questions were submitted to a special court made up of clergymen and city magistrates. This identified Church and state in a way that Luther had never envisaged. Zwingli was the most politically minded of the leading reformers. Having taken part in the Italian wars, he was strongly opposed to the mercenary system and persuaded Zürich to give it up. But the poorer Catholic cantons in the Swiss Confederation depended on it for their livelihood. A war developed between them and Zürich and Zwingli was killed at the Battle of Kappel (October 1531). Thereafter Swiss Protestantism lost it belligerency. Under Heinrich Bullinger (1504–75) it concentrated on its spiritual work.

Anabaptism

From the start of the Reformation various reformers showed more radical tendencies than Luther or Zwingli. Because they were generally opposed to infant baptism they became known as Anabaptists (from the Greek word for 'baptising again'). However, their views differed widely, ranging from a passive attitude towards life with devotional contemplation (quietism) to the active promotion of Christ's reign on earth (chiliasm). They sprang up in different places more or less simultaneously and lacked any cohesion.

The first known case of an adult baptism was administered in Zürich in 1525 by Conrad Grebel, who argued that a man was not born into a Church but accepted on profession of faith and the promise to lead a holy life. Because they believed that the professed believers were separate from the world, most Anabaptists refused to serve the state in any capacity. As a result they became regarded as a disruptive influence in society and were fiercely persecuted by the civil authorities and by Catholics and Protestants. After their expulsion from Zürich in 1525 they carried their ideas to southern Germany, Upper Austria, Moravia, Hungary, the Netherlands and elsewhere.

One of the Anabaptist leaders in the Netherlands, David Joris, saw himself as the prophet of the coming millennium, but the quietism of his *Book of Wonders* (1542) was not reflected in the careers of Jan Matthys of Haarlem and Jan Beuckelsz of Leyden. They sent out a call to arms against all unbelievers and in February 1534 led a revolution in the episcopal city of Münster in Westphalia. Common ownership of all things on the basis of the Bible was introduced.

When Matthys died in April, Beuckelsz assumed the title of king under the name of Jan van Leyden. His introduction of polygamy and his unbridled brutality caused considerable resentment, facilitating the city's recapture by Philip of Hesse and the local bishop in June 1535. The Anabaptist leaders were tortured to death and their bodies placed in iron cages and hung in the tower of the Lambert church. Vigorous action was taken at the same time against Anabaptists everywhere in Europe. Their movement became respectable only when it was purged of its radical elements under Menno Simons (1496–1561). From East Friesland his congregation spread to many parts of Europe and America.

John Calvin

Whereas Lutheranism remained largely confined to Germany and Scandinavia and soon lost much of its dynamic force, Calvinism spread from France and Geneva to many parts of Europe, seriously threatening the survival of Catholicism in the second half of the sixteenth century.

John Calvin was born at Noyon in Picardy on 10 July 1509. His father, Gérard Cauvin (Calvin being derived from the Latin form of the name), was a lawyer employed by the cathedral chapter. He obtained two benefices for his son and in 1523 sent him to Paris for his education. At the Collège de la Marche he was taught by Mathurin Cordier, an excellent Latin scholar. Then he was moved to the Collège de Montaigu where Erasmus and Rabelais had studied. The damp walls, disgusting food and harsh discipline nearly ruined his health.

In 1528 his father decided to change the direction of his eduction from theology to law. He was sent to Orléans and to Bourges. Here he also learned Greek and possibly some Hebrew from Melchior Wolmar, a Lutheran scholar. In 1531 Calvin was released by his father's death from the obligation to continue his legal studies. He returned to Paris and devoted his attention to humanism. In April 1532 he published his first work, a commentary on Seneca's *De Clementia*.

No one knows exactly when Calvin first embraced Protestant ideas, but it was probably in about 1533, when he became associated with Gérard Roussel and other evangelicals. His conversion soon brought him into trouble with the authorities. In November 1533 his friend, Nicholas Cop, rector of the University of Paris, delivered an inaugural address betraying Lutheran sympathies. This provoked a strong reaction and Calvin, who was suspected of having written the address, escaped to Saintonge, where he may have started work on his *Institutes* in a fine library placed at his disposal by Louis du Tillet. He called on Jacques Lefèvre d'Ètaples, the founder of French evangelicalism, who was living in retirement at Nérac.

After resigning his ecclesiastical benefices Calvin visited Poitiers and Orléans where he preached and administered the Lord's Supper in a Protestant form. In October 1534 a campaign of persecution was unleashed against Protestants after they had affixed posters attacking the Mass in a number of French towns. Calvin fled to Strasbourg and Basle, where the first edition of his *Institutes of the Christian Religion* was published in March 1536.

Although the *Institutes* was subsequently altered and enlarged, the first edition contained the basic elements of the Calvinistic doctrine. It emphasized the majesty and absolute sovereignty of God and the hopeless corruption of man as a consequence of the Fall. Though predestination was implied in this doctrine, Calvin did not lay stress upon it until later.

Another important aspect of his doctrine was the authority which he gave to scripture, but he made clear that it was not sufficient to read the Bible; it had to be understood, and this required the help of the Holy Spirit. He had no time for a purely mystical approach to religion. Finally, while Calvin believed that the true Church was invisible and made up of the elect of God, he also believed in the necessity of a visible Church, independent of, yet related to, the state.

In later years Calvin devoted much of his time to the elaboration, clarification and enlargement of the *Institutes*. The sixth and last edition on 1559 was five times bigger than the first and was arranged differently. The first French translation was published in 1541. This was an important event not only for the popularization of the Reformation but also for the development of French vernacular literature.

In 1536, after a journey to Italy, Calvin returned to France to deal with some family business. He then planned to go to Strasbourg but, as the direct road was blocked by an imperial army, he made a detour to Geneva, expecting to stop there only one night. The city, however, was in the midst of a religious revolution led by the fiery French Protestant exile, Guillaume Farel, who persuaded Calvin to remain and help him. Calvin described what happened as follows:

Farel strained every nerve to detain me. Having learned that my heart was set on

Below, illustration of 1607 ridiculing the beliefs of the Anabaptists.

Bottom, Adam and Eve (1504) by Albrecht Dürer; although this work was done before the rise of Protestantism, the themes of the fall of man and original sin figured highly in the preoccupations of the Reformers. Staatliche Museen zu Berlin.

Opposite, John Calvin (1509–64), who developed a form of Protestantism which gave the individual responsibility for his own spiritual welfare.

up of the twelve elders and five pastors. It gathered once a week to admonish, reprimand and correct citizens who had opposed the official doctrine, stayed away from church or behaved in an un-Christian way. The consistory, which could also excommunicate, undertook its work with more enthusiasm than tact. Citizens were summoned before it for the most trivial deviations from the straight and narrow path, while more serious offences were punished with great severity. Between 1542 and 1546 seventy-six persons were banished from Geneva and fifty-eight executed for heresy, adultery, blasphemy or witchcraft.

For the first five years after his return to Geneva Calvin got along relatively well with the city authorities. He helped to recodify the city's laws and to revise the constitution and his advice was sought on many matters ranging from defence to fire prevention. Yet his leadership was seriously challenged after 1545 when a number of prominent citizens strongly objected to the consistory's activities. In the end, however, he managed to assert his authority.

Calvin's hold on Geneva depended on the faithful exercise of his duties as preacher and teacher. He was therefore very zealous in maintaining 'the pure doctrine' and in rooting out heresy. Sebastian Castellio was banished for denying the inspiration of the Song of Solomon, while Jerome Bolsec suffered the same fate after he had argued that the doctrine of predestination implied that God was the cause of all sin.

In August 1553 Michael Servetus, who had published books repudiating the doctrine of the Holy Trinity, was foolhardy enough to visit Geneva. He was at once arrested, tried and burnt. Calvin justified the execution in *A Defense of the Orthodox Faith,* but Castellio protested against this use of force. In *Concerning Heretics, Whether they are to be Persecuted* he argued that to burn heretics was contrary to Christ's merciful teaching. Most Protestant leaders, however, sided with Calvin. After the Servetus affair his authority in Geneva was unchallenged and in 1559 he was made a citizen.

An event of prime significance for the development of Calvinism was the founding of the Genevan Academy in June 1559. Its first rector was the French humanist, Theodore Beza (1519–1605), who eventually succeeded Calvin as leader of his movement. The academy was divided into a primary or 'private' school, in which the young were taught French, Latin, Greek and the elements of logic, and a secondary or 'public' school, in which Greek, Hebrew, theology and philosophy were taught. Tuition in both was free and the student received a certificate of attendance, not a degree, at the end of his course. At Calvin's death in 1564 the 'private school' numbered 1200 students and the 'public school' 300. The latter were mostly foreigners who, after they had finished their studies, carried Calvin's

devoting myself to private studies he uttered an imprecation that God would curse my retirement and the tranquillity of my studies which I sought if I should withdraw and refuse to give assistance when the need was so pressing. I felt as if God from heaven had laid His mighty hand to arrest me. . . . I was so stricken with terror that I desisted from the journey I had undertaken.

Because of the strange circumstances which had combined to bring him to Geneva, Calvin believed that he had been commissioned by God to build there a truly Christian community. The task did not prove easy, for the leading citizens of Geneva were motivated by political rather than religious considerations. Having overthrown the authority of the bishop, they undertook 'to live in this holy evangelical law and word of God' and to abandon 'all masses and other papal ceremonies and abuses, images and idols'. When, however, Calvin and Farel tried to enforce discipline among them by means of excommunication they resisted and, following a number of incidents, asked the reformers to leave.

Calvin retired to Strasbourg where he became pastor to the congregation of French exiles and married Idelette of Buren. Although his basic ideas did not change, he developed his views on predestination and church organization under Bucer's influence.

In Calvin's absence the political and religious situation in Geneva became so chaotic that he was soon invited to return. At the insistence of his friends he decided to follow God's will and reappeared in the city in June 1541. The authorities gave him a beautiful house and garden near the lake and a salary. Helped by six council members he promptly drew up a new constitution for the Genevan Church called the Ecclesiastical Ordinances.

The Genevan Church was allowed more independence than those of Luther or Zwingli. The chief innovation of the ordinances was the recognition of the four offices of pastor, teacher, elder and deacon. The pastors, numbering five at first, constituted the venerable company. They were responsible for preaching the Gospel, administering the sacraments and admonishing members. New pastors were elected by the venerable company with the approval of the city council.

Frequent services were provided in Geneva's three parishes. The teachers who had the duty of instructing the young in 'sound doctrine' were examined by a two-man committee. The twelve elders were laymen responsible for the enforcement of discipline. Each supervised one of Geneva's twelve districts and was expected to visit each family at least once a year. The deacons assisted the pastors in supervising poor relief, visiting the sick and needy and administering the city hospital.

The central part of the constitution of the Genevan Church was the consistory made doctrine back to their own countries.

Calvin went further than Luther in encouraging the Christian to serve God through as well as in his calling. His followers participated actively in political, economic and social life. Success in business came to be regarded as evidence of self-denial and hard work to the glory of God. But if Calvin's example encouraged the bourgeois virtues, it is important to remember that he constantly stressed the traditional Christian virtues of self-sacrifice, humility and joy in God's salvation. Contrary to common belief, Calvin did not initiate a law permitting the taking of interest; he simply gave his approval to an existing law protecting the poor from exorbitant rates. The idea that Calvin was responsible for the rise of capitalism is absurd. His chief concern was moral and religious.

When the final edition of the *Institutes* appeared in 1559 Calvin's doctrine was complete and predestination had become central to it. This was not Calvin's invention; it was rooted in Augustinian and scholastic theology and was shared by the other reformers. Calvin simply made its implications clearer.

Predestination means that before the beginning of the world God chose some men (the elect) for eternal salvation, regardless of their merits in life, and left others to suffer eternal damnation, the fate which all men deserve. This doctrine did not lead to fatalism among Calvin's followers; on the contrary, they were confident that God had chosen them for salvation. The elect, according to Calvin, were those who publicly professed their faith and covenant with God, walked in the ways of God and participated in the sacraments. The clarity of these criteria goes far to explain Calvinistic activism. Certainty of election was accompanied by confidence in the future and hope of establishing a Christian commonwealth on earth.

The spread of Calvinism

The Calvinists were only able to carry out their aims on a large scale in Scotland and in New England; elsewhere they formed an active minority which tried to overcome all obstacles.

From the beginning Calvin was deeply concerned with the progress of the Reformation in his native land. The Huguenots, as the French Calvinists were called (the origin of the word is uncertain), formed themselves into small compact groups. They met in heavily curtained rooms or secluded spots in the countryside to worship or read the Bible. As they grew in size pastors trained in Geneva were sent out secretly to attend to their spiritual needs. Despite fierce persecution under Henry II (1547–59) Calvinism continued to gain strength. It was adopted by many nobles and even by some members of the royal family.

In 1555 the first French Calvinist church with a formal church service, regular preaching and administration of the sacraments and a consistory of elders was set up in Paris, and in the next few years similar congregations appeared all over France. They sent their pastors and elders to the first national synod in Paris in 1559, at which a confession of faith was adopted. A centralized organization was established, consisting of local consistories, regional colloquies, provincial synods and a national synod. By 1561 the national synod represented more than 2000 congregations.

Persecution soon obliged the Huguenots to take up arms against the state. Many were implicated in the Conspiracy of Amboise (March 1560), an unsuccessful attempt to seize the young king, Francis II, and to get rid of his Catholic advisers. Calvin, however, refused to condone rebellion. 'Better', he wrote in 1561, 'that we should all perish one hundred times than that the cause of the Gospel and Christianity should be exposed to such opprobrium'. He sent Beza to take part in a religious debate with the Catholics sponsored by the regent, Catherine de' Medici. Although the Colloquy of Poissy was a failure, a certain measure of toleration was granted to the Huguenots by the edict of January 1562. The result was a strong Catholic reaction led by the Duke of Guise and his supporters. In March 1562 some Huguenots were slaughtered in a barn at Vassy. This was followed by other bloody deeds which precipitated the outbreak of the religious wars.

Calvinism penetrated the Low Countries mainly after the peace of Cateau-Cambrésis (1559). It became a strong motive behind the resistance to Spanish rule which culminated in the outbreak of the Dutch revolt in 1566.

Englishmen first made serious contact with Calvinism when many of them went into exile on the continent under Mary Tudor (1553–58). They hoped that Elizabeth would accede to their wishes on their return and were bitterly disappointed by her religious settlement. Neither wholly Protestant nor unashamedly Catholic but uniting elements of both, it threw Protestant enthusiasts into confusion. As a London priest remarked it was 'halflie forward and more than halflie backward'.

John Knox, who had been to Geneva, carried Calvinism to Scotland. The Lords of the Congregation, who opposed Mary Stuart and the French alliance, formed the Scottish covenant in 1557. Following the Treaty of Edinburgh in 1560 the Scottish Parliament adopted a confession of faith drawn up by Knox.

Within the empire Calvinism took root mainly in the Palatinate, but it also made deep inroads in eastern Europe, notably in Poland and Bohemia.

Wherever it established itself it was characterized by a heroic certainty which the Wars of Religion were to bring into the open.

Above, Calvinist publication of 1584 attacking the Catholic belief in relics. The Reformation led to a large number of satirical pamphlets and woodcuts, as the religious debates took place as much on a popular level as among theologians and politicians.

Opposite, the Calvinist church in Lyon, France, in 1564; its decoration was minimal and the focus of attention was the pulpit rather than the altar. Bibliothèque Publique et Universitaire, Geneva.

Chapter 3

Habsburg-Valois Rivalry

The European political scene in the first half of the sixteenth century was dominated by three young monarchs, Francis I of France (1515–47), Henry VIII of England (1509–47) and the Holy Roman emperor, Charles V (1519–56).

The accession of Francis I to the French throne on I January 1515 was largely fortuitous. Although he was descended from King Charles V, he was only the cousin and son-in-law of his predecessor and would not have become king if Louis XII had been blessed with a son. At the age of twenty-one Francis seemed the very embodiment of ideal kingship. He was intelligent, lively and quite well educated, eloquent, affable and dignified, brave, proud and ambitious. According to an English chronicler, Edward Hall, he was 'a goodly Prince, stately of countenance, mery of chere, broune coloured, great iyes, high nosed, bigge lipped, Faire brested and shoulders, small legges, and long fete.'

On the debit side Francis was extravagant, impetuous and wilful. He made lavish gifts to his mother, Louise of Savoy, and to his friends and showed a strong inclination to authoritarianism, which brought him into collision more than once with the *parlement* of Paris, the supreme court of justice, whose duty it was to uphold the so-called 'fundamental laws' of the kingdom.

Policy, which was determined by the king and his councillors along, was consistently directed towards strengthening royal power at the expense of surviving feudal liberties. The territorial unification of France was taken a stage further by the formal annexation of Brittany in 1532 and by the confiscation of the Bourbonnais following the treason of its duke in 1523. Some attempt was also made to streamline the machinery of government, notably by the establishment of a central treasury.

Francis I was also an outstanding patron of scholarship and the arts. Leonardo da Vinci, Andrea del Sarto, Benvenuto Cellini, Il Rosso and Francesco Primaticcio were among the great Italian artists who visited his court. He built magnificent *châteaux* or palaces in the valley of the Loire in and around Paris, including the Louvre, Chambord and Fontainebleau. With the encouragement of the humanist, Budé, he established public lectureships in the classics which eventually developed into the Collège de France.

From the start of his reign Francis was determined to avenge the series of disasters that had befallen French arms in 1513. Like every other prince of his time he had been educated for war and had already gained some experience of fighting in Guienne and Gascony. As the descendant of Valentina Visconti, he too had a claim to the Duchy of Milan, constituting an honorable pretext for aggression. His accession, therefore, did not mark any new departure in French foreign policy; the Italian wars were to continue.

Emperor Charles V

France's most important neighbour was Charles, Duke of Burgundy, the future emperor Charles V, a shy and unprepossessing youth of fifteen. He was the son of Philip the Fair and Joanna of Castile and the grandson of Emperor Maximilian and of Ferdinand of Aragon. When his father died in 1506 he inherited all the Burgundian territories (Franche-Comté, Luxembourg, Brabant, Flanders, Holland, Zeeland, Hainaut and Artois) except the Duchy of Burgundy itself, which had been annexed by France in 1477.

Though Charles was cosmopolitan by blood, he was a Burgundian by birth and upbringing. His favourite author as a child had been Olivier de la Marche, the panegyrist of Charles the Bold, under whom Burgundy had become one of the most powerful states in Europe. As he grew up his heart and mind were bent on one purpose: to rebuild his mutilated inheritance.

In 1515, however, the effective head of his government was Guillaume de Croy, lord of Chièvres, who, as a Walloon, wanted peace with France. So Francis was able to neutralize Charles for the time being without difficulty.

Henry VIII of England

The young king of England was anything but shy and unprepossessing. Tall and well-built, he had auburn hair 'combed straight and short in the French fashion, and a round face so very beautiful that it would become a pretty woman'. An observer thought him 'much handsomer than any sovereign in Christendom, a great deal handsomer than the King of France'. Henry was one of the best sportsmen of his day, excelling in archery, wrestling, jousting and tennis. He was also a good linguist, an accomplished musician and a reasonably competent amateur theologian.

Vanity, jealousy and cruelty were Henry VIII's principal faults. In particular he was anxious that his physical attainments should not be surpassed by those of his young rival across the Channel. An Italian envoy wrote,

His Majesty came into our arbour and addressing me in French, said 'Talk with me awhile. The King of France, is he as tall as I am?' I told him there was but little difference. He continued, 'Is he as stout?' I said he was not; and he then enquired, 'What sort of legs has he?' I replied 'Spare'. Whereupon he opened the front of his doublet, and placing his hand on his thigh, said, 'Look here; and I have also a good calf to my leg'.

Yet, suspicious and envious as he was, Henry was not inclined to pick a quarrel with Francis at this stage. Having already had a taste of war he was content for the time being to enjoy himself and to leave policy making in the capable hands of his almoner, Wolsey, who wanted peace in Christendom.

Francis I lost no time completing the military preparations begun by his predecessor. By the summer of 1515 he had assembled an army about forty thousand strong at Lyons. The Swiss, on their part, were keeping a close watch on the main Alpine passes. The king, faced with the choice of either fighting his way through them or bypassing them, chose to do the latter. The French army threaded its way through the difficult Col d'Argentière and suddenly appeared in Piedmont, forcing the Swiss to fall back rapidly towards Milan. Some of the cantons began to negotiate peace terms, but the rest launched a surprise attack on the French camp at Marignano 13 September.

The battle which ensued was one of the fiercest of the Italian Wars. It lasted for the best part of two days and its outcome was decided only at the eleventh hour when the Venetians intervened on the French side. Losses were heavy; the gravediggers counted 16,500 bodies. Marshal Trivulzio, who had fought in eighteen battles, called Marignano 'a battle of giants'.

It certainly marked the end of an epoch. The Swiss ceased to be an independent factor in Italian politics. The myth of their invincibility had been exploded and, by the Eternal Peace of Fribourg (1516), they bound themselves to the service of France. Henceforth their role in European wars was simply that of mercenaries.

In Italy the effects of Marignano were important. Francis I became Duke of Milan and Massimiliano Sforza retired to France on a pension. Pope Leo X yielded Parma and Piacenza to the king in return for a guarantee that the Medici would remain in Florence. In December 1515 the pope and the king met in Bologna and put their signatures to a mutually advantageous concordat.

On 23 January 1516 the balance of power in Europe was badly shaken when Ferdinand of Aragon died. He was succeeded by his grandson, Charles of Burgundy, who had so far tried to keep on good terms with Francis I. His inheritance comprised not only Aragon and Castile but also Naples and Navarre. As Duke of Burgundy, Charles had implicitly recognized the Albret claim to Navarre, but he could hardly be expected to do so now. Equally ominous was the search instituted by Francis in the archives of Provence for evidence supporting his own claim to Naples. For a time the *status quo* was maintained by the Treaty of Noyon, but, if Erasmus hoped for a new era of peace, the elements of discord were only thinly veiled.

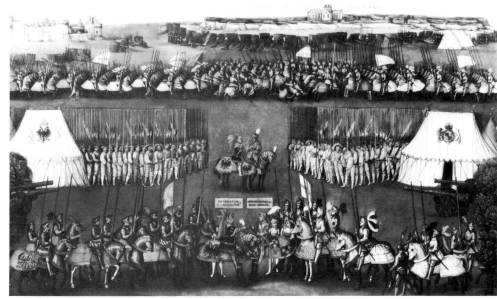

Above, meeting between Henry VIII and the Holy Roman Emperor Maximilian I (ruled 1493–1519). The emperor's patronizing attitude towards the foreign ambitions of the young English king led Henry into several expensive and abortive attempts to invade France. Royal Collection.

Left, Francis I of France (ruled 1515–47), painted by Jean Clouet. Like his life-long rival Henry VIII, Francis was a typically ostentatious Renaissance prince, concerned primarily with glory.

Below left, Charles V; King of Spain, Holy Roman Emperor, Duke of Burgundy, Duke of Austria, King of the Romans, were just a few of his many titles. Wallace Collection, London.

Opposite, Henry VIII (ruled 1509–47) sailing to meet Francis I in 1520. Henry put a lot of effort into rebuilding and modernizing the English navy, which was essential for his effective participation in European politics.

The imperial election

In 1517 the Emperor Maximilian fell gravely ill. The Holy Roman Empire was elective, not hereditary. Its ruler was chosen by seven electors: the archbishops of Mainz, Cologne and Trier, the King of Bohemia, the Count-palatine, the Duke of Saxony and the Margrave of Brandenburg. Nothing obliged them to choose a member of the house of Habsburg or even a German. Theoretically, they were supposed to put imperial interests first but in practice their own personal advantage had precedence. Though they solemnly promised to vote 'without the least intrigue, reward, salary or promise of any kind' the majority were willing to take bribes.

As early as 1516 four of the electors invited the French king, Francis I, to stand for the empire. He accepted if only to prevent Maximilian's grandson, Charles, from becoming preponderant in Europe by adding the German territories to his already extensive dominions. Charles was immediately advised to win the electors over by bribery. At the Diet of Augsburg in 1518 Maximilian persuaded five electors to vote for Charles. But when the emperor died in January 1519 they indicated their readiness to take new bids from the candidates.

Germany soon became a vast auction room. By scattering gold in all directions French agents tried to create the impression that their master had inexhaustible means. In fact, his credit was poor. To scrape enough money together for the electors Francis had to borrow from his subjects and to sell offices and parts of his demesne. Pope Leo X agreed to support the king as the lesser of two evils, for it was a principle of papal policy to prevent the empire and the kingdom of Naples from falling into the same hands. As for Henry VIII of England, he secretly offered himself as a third candidate.

Public opinion was very important in the election. Using sermons and broadsheets, Habsburg agents stirred up hatred of everything French. The King of France was also hampered by the fact that the German bankers denied him exchange facilities.

While his rival was able to use bills of exchange, Francis had to send ready cash, at his own risk. Once it had to be put into bags and dragged along the bottom of the Rhine by boats.

In June 1519 the electors assembled in Frankfurt and all foreigners were ordered to leave the city. The heat was intense, plague raged in the outskirts and the army of the Swabian League stood menacingly by. On 28 June, after several days of feverish lobbying, Charles was unanimously elected. As the Germans rejoiced wildly at the news, the French agents hastened back to France, narrowly escaping molestation.

War with the emperor

In 1521 war broke out between Francis I and Charles V. It was provoked by the King of France who wanted to prevent Charles from going to Italy to be crowned emperor by the pope. Not wishing to go to war himself at this stage, Francis made use of Robert de la Marck, lord of Sedan, and Henri d'Albret, King of Navarre. But he misjudged the emperor's ability to strike back. An imperial army under the count of Nassau overran de la Marck's territories and advanced to within a few miles of the French border. In June a French army that had invaded Spanish Navarre was decisively defeated at Esquiros. In Italy, Pope Leo X overthrew his alliance with France and bestowed the investiture of Naples on Charles V.

By the summer Francis was anxious to stop the war and accepted an offer of mediation from Henry VIII. A conference was held at Calais under the presidency of Cardinal Wolsey. In August the cardinal went to Bruges and signed a secret treaty with the emperor, promising him English help if the war did not end by November. The Calais conference soon became a farce.

Meanwhile the war continued. For three weeks Massau besieged Mézières which Bayard defended heroically. Eventually the imperialists retreated leaving a trail of destruction behind them. In the south, the French captured Fuenterrabia, the key to Spain, and in Italy they relieved Parma. In

November, the Calais conference ended unsuccessfully. Wolsey returned home complaining that he was 'sore tempestyd in mind by the outwardness of the chauncelers and oratours on every side'. The improvement in Francis's fortunes proved short lived. The expulsion of the French from Milan in November was quickly followed by the capitulation of Tournai in the north.

Following the death of Leo X in December 1521, Adrian of Utrecht, Charles V's old tutor and regent in Spain, was elected pope. This caused much resentment in France, but Adrian VI turned out to be a humble and devout man who approached his duties in a truly Christian spirit. He hoped to pacify Christendom so that its princes might unite against the Turks.

In April 1522 the French suffered a major setback in Italy when Marshal Lautrec was defeated at La Bicocca near Milan. England chose this moment to declare war on France and in September an expeditionary force under the Earl of Surrey invaded Picardy. Meanwhile the Turkish sultan, Süleyman the Magnificent, captured Rhodes which the knights of St John of Jerusalem had held since 1309. On learning of this the pope exclaimed 'Alas, for Christendom! I should have died happy if I had united the Christian princes to withstand our enemy.' As Francis I prepared to cross the Alps again, Adrian joined the emperor and his allies in a league for the defence of Italy.

The treason of Charles of Bourbon

In 1515 Charles of Bourbon was a handsome young man with a distinguished war record. As constable of France he was responsible for military administration in peacetime and was entitled by custom, if not by right, to command the vanguard under the king in wartime. The first clear sign of discord between him and the king occurred in October 1521 when he was not given command of the vanguard during the campaign in northern France.

Angered by the king's efforts to cheat him of his inheritance, Bourbon entered into secret negotiations with the emperor. In July he signed a treaty promising to lead a rebellion in return for the hand of one of Charles V's sisters. His plan was to wait until Francis had gone to Italy with his army before revealing himself. But the plot was soon discovered.

Meanwhile Francis's patience ran out. He ordered the arrest of the duke's chief accomplices and deferred his own journey to Italy. Finding himself almost trapped, Bourbon fled into the mountains of Auvergne and eventually made his way to imperial territory while the allies tried unsuccessfully to invade France from three directions. Although Bourbon's revolt had failed ignominiously, it had obliged the King of France to alter his plans.

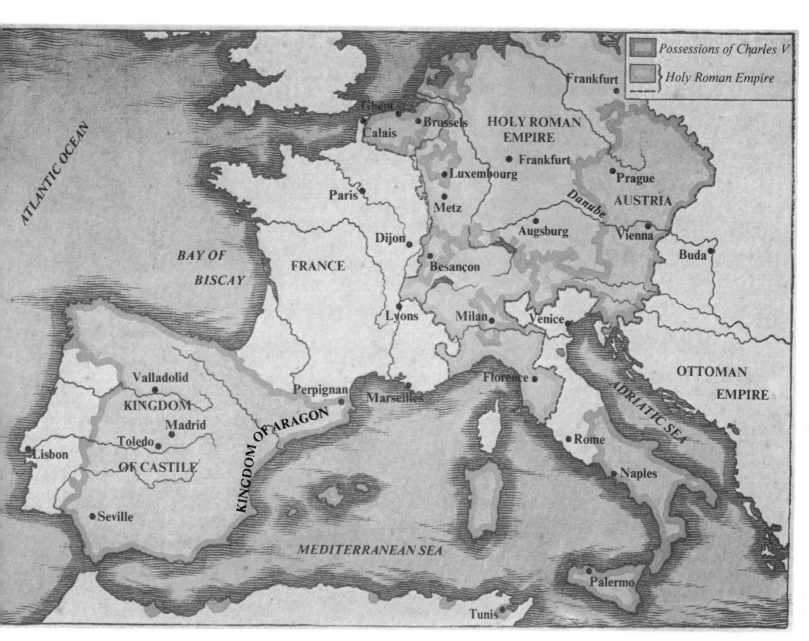

Above, Francis I and Henry VIII meeting near Calais in 1520 at a great diplomatic showpiece known as the Field of the Cloth of Gold. Despite days of feasting and jousting, no alliance was agreed, and Henry allied with Charles V shortly afterwards.

Top, the empire of Charles V at its height.

Left, the siege train of Maximilian I, the Holy Roman emperor (ruled 1493–1519); artillery played an increasingly important role in the wars of the sixteenth century and led to a new style of siege warfare and defensive planning. Nevertheless such a siege train was costly and ponderous. Graphische Sammlung Albertina, Vienna.

Opposite, Henry VIII arriving at the Field of the Cloth of Gold in 1520.

31

In July 1524 the imperial army, now commanded by Bourbon, followed up its victory in Italy by invading Provence. The duke hoped that his former vassals in central France would rally to his standard and help him on his way to Lyons and Paris, but they remained quiet. The duke was also let down by his allies and Marseilles proved an insuperable obstacle. While the garrison bravely endured heavy bombardments, Francis I rebuilt an army and marched to Avignon. Seeing that his communications were threatened, Bourbon had to beat a hasty retreat along the coast and the king reoccupied Provence.

Bourbon's retreat from Provence enabled Francis to put into effect his long-deferred plan of leading another invasion of Italy himself and besieged Pavia, the second largest city in the duchy of Milan.

In January 1525 an imperial army marched from Lodi to relieve Pavia. For three weeks the two armies faced each other without making a move. But an acute shortage of supplies obliged the imperialists to take the offensive.

On 23 February a team of sappers, using only rams and picks, breached the wall in three places and the imperial troops poured into the park, taking the French completely by surprise. Francis managed to rally his cavalry and charged through the enemy centre but his infantry lagged behind and suffered heavy losses, Meanwhile the Pavia garrison came into the open, obliging the French to fight on two fronts. Francis tried desperately to rally his men but, after his horse had been killed under him, he was surrounded and captured.

At the end of the battle some eight thousand Frenchmen lay dead on the field, including Admiral Bonnivet and other close friends of the king. Pavia was the biggest massacre of French nobles since Agincourt. The imperialists claimed the loss of only seven hundred men. Charles V received the

news of his victory in Madrid on 10 March. Characteristically, he forbade noisy rejoicings, arranged services of thanksgiving and retired to his private oratory. On his instructions the King of France, who spent the first three months of his captivity at Pizzighettone in Lombardy, was treated with all the consideration due to his rank.

For a long time the King of France expected to be released on generous terms, but the emperor was not prepared to be magnanimous at the expense of his own political interest. In March he was urged by his ally, Henry VIII, to join him in the conquest and dismemberment of France. The King of England argued that there had never been so good an opportunity 'utterly to extinct the regiment of the French king and his line,

or any other Frenchmen, from the crown of France'. Without waiting for Charles' reply, Henry asked his subjects for an 'Amicable Grant' and prepared to invade France.

But the emperor needed to think carefully before continuing the war. Despite his resounding victory, he was still faced by many problems: in Italy his army was unpaid and mutinous, in Germany the Peasants' War had broken out, and in the east the Turkish threat remained. His chandellor, Gattinara, who believed that a continuation of the war would only benefit England, advised him to show 'the magnanimity of the lion and the mercy of God the Father'. Charles consequently opened negotiations with Francis.

Although the emperor's sentiments were

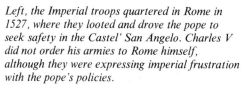

generous, his peace terms were harsh.
Francis was to cede Burgundy and all the
other territories that Charles the Bold had
held at his death; Bourbon was to be reinstated and given Provence as an independent kingdom; and Henry VIII's French
claims were to be satisfied. The King of
France rejected these terms at the end of
April. He was prepared to make substantial
concessions but refused to cede an inch of
French territory. Early in May the imperial
authorities decided to move him to Naples,
but he persuaded the viceroy, Lannoy, to
take him to Spain instead. Meanwhile, his
mother, Louise of Savoy, who ruled France
in his absence, sent an appeal for help to the
Turkish sultan, Süleyman the Magnificent,
and in August 1525 signed the Peace of

Moore with England.

When Margaret of Angoulême visited
Spain to offer a ransom for her brother,
Charles V insisted on the surrender of Burgundy. In the end Francis saw that he would
never regain his freedom unless he gave way.
By the Treaty of Madrid he abandoned the
duchy and all his Italian claims and agreed
to hand over his two sons as hostages.

As soon as he had been released, however,
Francis declared that he was not bound to
keep promises extorted from him under
duress. His repudiation of the Treaty of
Madrid was immediately followed by the
formation of a new coalition against the
emperor, called the Holy League of Cognac.
It comprised France, the papacy, Venice,
Florence and the Milan of Francesco

Sforza. The imperialists in Italy, who were commanded by Bourbon, were vulnerable, being penniless, numerically weak and hated by the population. Yet they were able to hold their own, for the Duke of Urbino, who commanded the league's army, was excessively cautious and Francis failed to send the military help expected of him. As a result Sforza, who had been besieged in Milan castle, had to capitulate and Bourbon's army left the Lombard plain.

The sack of Rome

As the imperial army, now reinforced by a powerful contingent of German mercenaries, marched on Rome, Pope Clement VII tried desperately to avert a disaster. He signed a truce with the emperor, but Bourbon's men refused to be deflected from their course. They were cold, hungry and short of money; only the expectation of booty kept them together. Clement offered to buy them off, but he could not meet their exorbitant demands. On the 6 May 1527 they launched an assault on the virtually defenceless city.

Among the first to fall was the Duke of

Bourbon, who was struck by a cannon ball or bullet as he scaled the city's ramparts. His death had the effect of inflaming his already wild and uncontrollable men. They broke into the city and swept across it like a mountian torrent in flood, killing, burning and looting. The pope, some cardinals and about three thousand people took refuge in the castle of Sant' Angelo. The sack continued for more than a week. Indescribable atrocities were committed. People were tortured for money without respect for age, sex or status. The Lutheran troops attacked anything ecclesiastical with special relish. 'From every side'. wrote an eye-witness, 'came cries, the clash of arms, the shrieks of women and children, the crackling of flames, the crash of falling roofs.'

It is impossible to be precise about the number of people who died in the sack of Rome. In two districts alone 2,000 bodies were cast into the Tiber and 9,800 buried. The booty of the soldiers was incalculable; Clement VII estimated the damage at ten million gold ducats. The Sistine Chapel was used as stables and the Vatican Library was saved only because Philibert, Prince of

Orange, who replaced Bourbon, had his headquarters in the palace.

A month after the sack a Spaniard described the Holy City as follows:

No bells ring, no churches are open, no masses are said, Sundays and feastdays have ceased. The rich shops of the merchants are turned into stables, the most splendid palaces are stripped bare; many houses are burnt to the ground; in others the doors and windows are broken and carried away; the streets are changed into dunghills. The stench of dead bodies is terrible; men and beasts have a common grave and in the churches I have seen corpses that dogs have gnawn. In the public places tables are set close together at which piles of ducats are gambled for. The air rings with blasphemies fit to make good men, if such there be, wish that they were deaf. I know nothing wherewith I can compare it, except it be the destruction of Jerusalem.

The sack of Rome shook Francis I out of his lethargy and precipitated another French invasion of Italy, this time under Marshal Lautrec. He recaptured Lombardy, except Milan, and early in 1528 laid siege to Naples. The city was saved by the defection to the imperial side of the Genoese admiral, Andrea Doria, and by an epidemic of typhus or cholera which carried off Lautrec and thousands of his men. In June 1529 another French army, under the Count of Saint Pol, was defeated at Landriano in north Italy.

These events convinced the pope that he had nothing to gain by remaining neutral. 'I have quite made up my mind', he declared, 'to become an imperialist, and to live and die as such.' Clement VII wanted Charles V to help to restore the Medici to power in Florence. On 29 June, therefore, his nuncio signed the Treaty of Barcelona with the emperor. In return for Charles' military assistance, the pope promised to crown him emperor and to absolve all who had taken part in the sack of Rome. The pope's nephew, Alessandro de' Medici, married the emperor's illegitimate daughter, Margaret.

By now Francis I also wished for a respite. A meeting was arranged at Cambrai between his mother, Louise of Savoy, and the emperor's aunt, Margaret of Austria, who ruled the Netherlands. Despite the many differences which existed between the two sides, a settlement was reached known as the Peace of Cambrai or Peace of the Ladies on the third of August.

The Turkish threat to Christendom

In July 1529 Charles V sailed from Barcelona to Genoa. His purpose was to pacify Italy in order to attend to more pressing problems elsewhere. In Germany, the Lutheran heresy was rapidly gaining ground and in central Europe the Ottoman Turks were once again on the move.

Since the fourteenth century the Ottomans had been expanding steadily westward. Under Mehmed II they had captured Constantinople, penetrated far into the Balkans and expelled the Venetians from Euboea; under Selim 'the Terrible' (1512–20) they had conquered Syria, Palestine and Egypt.

The West heaved a sigh of relief when Selim the Terrible died. His twenty-six-year-old son, Süleyman, was reputed to be 'a gentle lamb', but he soon showed himself no less bellicose than his predecessors. In 1521 he captured Belgrade and in 1522 attacked Rhodes. The Knights of St John, who held the island, had long harassed

Muslim trade and plundered ships taking pilgrims to Mecca. The siege lasted 145 days and the Turks lost heavily in men and material, but eventually the garrison capitulated.

For three years Süleyman was content to rest on his laurels, but in 1526 he again marched on Hungary at the head of an enormous army. The Hungarians were hopelessly divided between a 'court' party, led by the young king, Louis II, and a 'national' party, led by John Zápolyai, Prince of Transylvania. On 29 August they came up against the Turks on the plain of Mohacs. With insane overconfidence their cavalry charged into the jaws of the sultan's guns only to be shattered to pieces. King Louis and most of his nobles were left dead on the field. Ten days later the victors entered Buda.

Because of Mohacs the defence of Christendom devolved on the Habsburgs, more especially on Charles V's brother, Ferdinand, who now became king of Bohemia and of Hungary. His rival, Zápolyai, turned to the sultan, who recognized him as vassal and king. When Ferdinand called on Süleyman to withdraw from some of the fortresses he had conquered, the sultan declared that he would come to Vienna to satisfy him.

A major offensive on the Danube was a severe test of Ottoman military resourcefulness. Although the campaign season lasted from mid-April to the end of October, the sultan's army could not expect to cross the Sava before July. Rivers had to be spanned by pontoon bridges, roads had to be made over difficult ground, and bad weather frequently impeded progress. Some guns and munitions were carried by boats on the Danube, but most had to be loaded on waggons, carts or beasts of burden. Abundant food was necessary as the retreat might lie through devastated areas.

These difficulties and the premature onset of winter explain why Süleyman failed to capture Vienna in 1529. Incessant rain and flooded rivers prevented him reaching the city before September. Thus Ferdinand had enough time to give it a strong garrison. The Turks had to succeed quickly as their food was running low, but all their assaults were repulsed, so on 14 October Süleyman gave the order to retreat. In 1532 he again marched against the Habsburgs but was held up by the heroic resistance of the small town of Güns. Having lost three precious weeks, he gave up his plan, signed a truce with Ferdinand and became involved in a war with the Persians.

Because of the Turkish threat Charles V was unable to visit Rome in 1529. He asked Clement VII to meet him at Bologna instead. In the course of the four months which they spent together a mutually satisfactory settlement of the Italian situation was reached. Francesco Sforza was restored to power in Milan, Venice promised to give back Ravenna and Cervia to the pope, and an imperial army under the Prince of Orange was sent to besiege Florence in aid of the Medici. In February 1530 Charles V received the crowns of Lombardy and of the Holy Roman Empire amid all the traditional pomp and ceremony. He then moved on to Germany to preside over the doctrinal bickerings of the Diet of Augsburg.

Charles V and the German Lutherans

Although the emperor stood by the pope and his own Edict of Worms, he was anxious to achieve a religious settlement in Germany and treated the Lutherans with courtesy. At his invitation they drew up a confession of faith which was read in the Diet on 25 June. It was mainly Melanchthon's work and was so remarkably conciliatory that it was described by the Bishop of Augsburg as 'the pure truth'. Yet the Catholic theologians would have nothing to do with it. A committee of theologians from both sides failed to break the deadlock. In September, Charles issued a recess in which he promised a General Council within a year and forbade Lutheran innovations in the meantime. The Lutherans rejected the recess and in December formed a defensive alliance, called the Schmalkaldic League.

In 1532, however, a temporary political unity was achieved when the Turks again threatened Christendom. A truce was signed at Nuremberg which enabled Charles to raise a powerful army. After the Turkish retreat he returned to Bologna where he spent the winter trying in vain to persuade Clement VII to call a General Council. In April he returned to Spain.

In the emperor's absence the Lutheran princes again looked to France for support. Early in 1534 Philip of Hesse met Francis I secretly at Bar-le-Duc and obtained a subsidy which he used to restore Duke Ulrich of Württemberg, who had been dispossessed by the Habsburgs in 1520. Charles V was warned that Germany was full of French agents. In 1535 the Schmalkaldic League was renewed for another ten years. Yet the German princes were not yet prepared to ally with Francis against Charles, being still afraid of the Turkish menace and distrustful of the French king because of his persecution of Protestants in his own country.

The conquest of Tunis

The struggle between Christendom and the Infidel was fought not only in the Danube valley but also in the Mediterranean. Even before the fall of Rhodes pirates operating from North African ports had harassed shipping and terrorized the coastal villages of Spain and Italy. The most dreaded of them was Khayr ad-Dīn Barbarossa, who controlled Algiers as a vassal of the Turkish sultan. In 1532 he was appointed grand admiral of the Ottoman fleet and in 1534 he ravaged the coasts of south Italy with more than a hundred ships and expelled Muley Hasan, Charles V's ally, from Tunis.

The emperor could not allow the Turks to dominate the central Mediterranean and to threaten his kingdoms of Sicily and Naples. In 1535, therefore, he assembled a large fleet at Barcelona and an army at Cagliari in Sardinia. Then, on 10 June, the entire expedition sailed for Africa.

Its first objective was the fortress of La Goletta, guarding the narrow entrance to the Bay of Tunis. Although Charles was suffering acutely from gout, nothing would keep him from the front lines. The siege lasted nearly three weeks and the emperor's men suffered severely from the intense heat and shortage of water, but on 14 July they launched an assault from several directions and the defenders fled. Many French guns with the fleur-de-lys embossed on their barrels were among the rich booty found in the fortress and Barbarossa's fleet of eighty-two galleys was captured in the harbour. Charles then seized Tunis while Barbarossa made his escape to Algiers.

The conquest of Tunis was undoubtedly Charles V's greatest personal triumph. The whole world marvelled at his might. When Charles visited Sicily in the autumn of 1535 his triumph seemed complete. As he rode beneath magnificent arches, trophies and inscriptions, the crowds shouted 'Long live our victorious emperor, father of the fatherland, conqueror of Africa, peace-maker of Italy!'

The Castilian empire in the New World

By 1535 Charles V was also master of the New World. The *conquistadores* had gone to America at their own expense and looked forward to living on slave labour, but the Spanish government did not intend a new feudalism to take root overseas, while the Church was concerned that the natives should be treated fairly. An influential advocate of their rights was the Dominican friar, Bartolomé de Las Casas. By about 1550 an official policy had emerged. The Indies were treated as dependencies of the crown of Castile, administered through a distinct royal council. The Indians were free men and direct subjects of the crown.

The Castilians (the Aragonese were deliberately excluded) in the New World comprised soldiers, missionaries and administrators. The good behaviour of the soldiers had to be bought with grants of land (*encomiendas*) and minor salaried offices. They expressed themselves through town councils which were really oligarchies exercising wide administrative powers. Alongside the soldiers were friars from the

missionary orders, especially the Franciscans, who undertook the education and peaceful conversion of the natives. Finally, there were the lawyers who kept a close watch on the activities of the provincial governors and viceroys through the *audiencias* or courts of appeal. All important decisions, however, were taken in Spain, which did not make for efficiency.

Stock farming was the typical occupation of the New World Spaniard, arable farming being mainly in Indian hands. Horses, cattle and sheep were imported in large numbers and great estates grew up around ranch houses. In the tropical coast lands sugar was produced. African negroes, who

Above, a seventeenth-century allegorical painting of Charles V; as well as ruling one of the largest empires in history, he aimed to be the defender of Christendom itself, against its enemies within and without. Rijksmuseum, Amsterdam.

Top, Charles V hunting with John Frederick, Duke of Saxony and a leader of the Lutherans, at Torgau, according to a painting by Lucas Cranach. John Frederick was eventually defeated at Mühlberg in 1547.

Opposite left, Flemish engraving of Charles V. Rijksmuseum, Amsterdam.

Opposite right, the siege of Tunis of 1535, one of Charles V's greatest triumphs. His army included Muslim cavalry, even though Tunis was an Ottoman garrison. Kunstsammlungen, Coburg.

could be enslaved as they were not Castilian subjects, were imported to work the plantations.

Spain also imported gold and silver from the New World. To begin with mining was a relatively simple matter of prospecting and washing in streams, but very productive silver mines were discovered at Potosí in 1545 and Zacatecas in 1548. Extensive plant was set up to extract silver from the ore, usually by a mercury amalgamation process. The crown claimed a fifth of all the metal produced and employed a large number of agents to weigh, test and stamp the silver ingots as they issued from the mines and to prevent smuggling. In about the middle of the century a convoy system was devised to protect the bullion cargoes crossing the Atlantic.

Charles V's empire

Personal government and particularism (the desire of certain countries to govern themselves) were the essential characteristics of Charles V's vast empire.

The grand chancellor, Mercurino de Gattinara (1518–30), believed that the imperial title gave Charles authority over the whole world for it was 'ordained by God himself . . . and approved by the birth, life and death of our Redeemer Christ.' Like his compatriot Dante he saw the empire as a unified whole centred on Italy and the emperor as legislator for the whole world 'following the path of the good emperor Justinian'.

But this vision died with Gattinara. In practice the empire was unified only in the emperor's person: otherwise it had no common institutions. To deal with the vast amount of paper work Charles was assisted by two secretaries, one for Spain, Italy and the Mediterranean, the other for territories north of the Alps. The two secretaries, Francisco de los Cobos and Nicholas Perrenot, Lord of Granvelle, were men of considerable ability, but they were not as significant as Gattinara had been before 1530.

Charles V also employed members of his family as governors-general, regents or even kings in his dominions. The Netherlands, the empire itself and Spain were always entrusted to a Habsburg or his consort after 1529. Non-royal viceroys were appointed only in the Italian territories. The emperor was ably served by his relatives, notably by the two regents of the Netherlands, his aunt, Margaret of Austria (1518–30), and his sister, Mary of Hungary (1531–5).

Yet Charles reserved to himself ultimate control over policy and administration. Despite the enormous distances which messengers had to cover, he insisted on taking all important decisions himself in consultation with those advisers who accompanied him on his constant travels. This did not make for efficient administration especially as Charles was unable to take decisions

Boundary
of the empire
Habsburg lands
Hohenzollern lands
Wittelsbach lands
Ecclesiastical states

Wettin lands
Ernestine Saxony
Albertine Saxony

NORTH SEA
POMERANIA
Lübeck
Hamburg
ARCHBISHOPRIC
OF BREMEN
Bremen
HOLLAND
BRANDENBURG
Berlin
ZEELAND
Münster
Magdeburg
Antwerp
Halberstadt
Wittenberg
Brussels
HESSE
Eisleben
Muhlberg
Cologne
Eisenach
Erfurt
SAXONY
Dresden
Liège
Marburg
Gotha
Zwickau
LUXEMBOURG
Fulda
Annaberg
Cracow
Frankfurt
am Main
Bamberg
Prague
Mainz
RHENISH
Trier
Würzburg
BOHEMIA
MORAVIA
Worms
UPPER
Heidelberg
PALATINATE
PALATINATE
Nuremberg
Regensburg
Strasbourg
WÜRTTEMBERG
Ingolstadt
BAVARIA
HUNGARY
Augsburg
Passau
Munich
Vienna
Basle
Zürich
AUSTRIA
Salzburg
FRANCHE
COMTÉ
Kappel
TYROL
HABSBURG
TURKISH
Berne
HUNGARY
POLAND
SILESIA
FRANCE
NETHERLANDS

quickly. He also kept a firm control over public appointments and all forms of patronage. Hence the passionate longing of his subjects that he should reside with them.

The emperor's failure to develop a centralized organization for his empire outside his own person was not, however, solely because of the view he took of his office. It was a result of the intense particularism existing in the different countries making up the empire. The Sicilians, the Spaniards, the Germans and, above all, the Netherlanders were intensely devoted to their own laws, customs, privileges and institutions, and would not have tolerated any diminution of them in the interest of a more unified empire. In 1534, for example, the Estates-General rejected a proposal for a defensive union in the Netherlands because they felt it would undermine provincial liberties.

Charles preferred to comply with vested interests, local traditions and his own immediate financial needs rather than attempt to impose some kind of economic unity on the empire. It was for this reason that the Aragonese were not allowed to participate in the Spanish colonial trade, despite Castile's inability to supply the colonists with all the manufactured goods they needed.

Nowhere was this pervasive particularism more evident than in the Netherlands.

Charles wanted them to contribute their share of the imperial expenditure and he was successful up to a point, but the Estates insisted that the redress of grievances must precede any discussion of new taxes and that they should control the collection and expenditure of revenues.

As taxation became heavier after 1530 there was a growing volume of discontent which culminated in Ghent's refusal in 1539 to pay its share of taxes voted by the Estates-General. The rebellion had to be quelled by force and the punishment inflicted on the citizens was severe. Ghent forfeited all its rights and privileges, its public treasure was confiscated and its arms were taken away.

Religion was another source of serious trouble in the Netherlands. Lutheranism reached Antwerp in 1519 and made many converts. It was followed by Anabaptism with its apocalyptic vision of the Kingdom of God on earth and its revolutionary appeal to the socially oppressed. Charles V dealt with heresy much more vigorously in the Netherlands than in Germany where he was less powerful. About 1600 heretics, including the Englishman, William Tyndale, were put to death in the Netherlands during his reign.

Yet Charles never had to face a general revolt in the Netherlands. This was because the provinces did not always see eye to eye

Above, the Holy Roman Empire in the sixteenth century, made up of many semi-independent states ruled over by an emperor, who was elected by the seven chief princes but who was by this time traditionally an Austrian Habsburg.

Opposite, window from Brussels Cathedral made in 1537 showing the Emperor Charles V with his wife; Charles was always popular in the Netherlands but his decision to make the Low Countries part of the Spanish Empire in 1555 was widely resented.

and also because the emperor was sometimes prepared to compromise. Thus he allowed certain provinces to exclude the Inquisition and mitigated the harshness of his anti-heresy laws in their application to Antwerp. But the fact remains that the situation in the Netherlands was not calm under Charles V. The general revolt which broke out under Philip II in 1564 was the result of a financial, religious and political crisis that had been developing for some time. In fact, the Habsburg system in the Netherlands was on the verge of dissolution by 1555.

During the last decade of his reign Charles V was concerned mainly with three questions: his rivalry with France, the Turkish threat and heresy in Germany. They overlapped to some extent, since Francis I continued to intrigue with the Turks and the German Protestants.

In November 1535 the Milanese question was reopened by the death of Francesco Sforza without issue. Francis claimed his duchy for the Duke of Orléans and in February 1536 a French army overran Savoy and occupied Turin. Charles strongly denounced this action in a speech before the new pope, Paul III, and his court. He even challenged Francis to a duel. In order to relieve the pressure on Milan he invaded Provence but the scorched-earth tactics of Anne de Montmorency, constable of France, exhausted his men. Finding that Marseilles was impregnable, he retreated to Italy and signed the Truce of Nice (June 1538). Soon afterwards he met Francis at Aiguesmortes and in 1539 passed through France on his way to quell the Ghent revolt. No peace treaty was signed, however, and in 1542 the war flared up again. Charles made an alliance with Henry VIII and visited Germany to obtain aid. Then, in July 1544, he invaded France and even threatened Paris, while Henry VIII besieged Boulogne. But as

Charles wanted a respite to deal with the German situation he signed the Peace of Crépy in September.

The Turks meanwhile continued their aggression in the Mediterranean. Doria's defeat at Prevesa in 1538 destroyed the emperor's hopes of carrying the war into the eastern Mediterranean. Thereafter he had to be content with limited objectives.

In October 1541 he planned to strike hard at Algiers. An impressive armada sailed from the Balearics but it was so severely damaged by a storm off the African coast that the expedition was abandoned. In 1543 Khayr ad-Dīn captured Nice and his fleet was allowed to winter at Toulon. It was described as a second Constantinople with a lively slave market where Christians were offered for sale. When the old corsair died in 1546 his work was carried on by the equally formidable Dragut, who conquered Tripoli in 1551. The western Mediterranean was not freed from the Turkish menace until Don John of Austria's great victory at Lepanto in 1571.

The Peace of Crépy enabled Charles to attend the German question. Behind a smokescreen of doctrinal discussions he proceeded to detach Maurice of Saxony and others from the Schmalkaldic League. He was also reconciled with the Catholic Duke of Bavaria. The Diet of Regensburg (June 1546) showed that a conflict was inevitable. While the Catholics called on the reformers to attend the Council of Trent on the pope's terms, the Protestants demanded a reform of the Church by a diet. Charles meanwhile made an alliance with the pope against the Protestants.

The war between the emperor and the Protestant princes began with a long series of skirmishes. A decision, however, was reached at Mühlberg 24 April 1547 when Charles suddenly fell upon the flank of John Frederick's army. The fighting was soon over and the emperor claimed that he had lost less than ten men killed and wounded. When John Frederick was led into the emperor's presence he exclaimed: 'Most mighty and gracious emperor, I am your captive'. 'Ah!', rejoined Charles, 'you call me emperor now, do you? You lately gave me another style.' (The princes had distributed broadsheets calling him 'Charles of Ghent, who thinks he is emperor'.)

Charles hoped to use his victory to establish an imperial league on the lines of the Swabian League, a confederation of south German towns formed in 1487. The pope's decision to move the council from Trent to Bologna helped to bring him closer to the German Protestants. At the Diet of Augsburg (September 1547) he stated his determination to bring the council back to Trent. He expected the Lutherans to attend it there and in the meantime to live in peace with the Catholics.

On 30 June 1548 he issued the Augsburg *Interim* which aimed at keeping the possibilities of conciliation open. Its underlying

assumption was that a council would some day reach a settlement which both sides were held to have accepted in principle. In practice the *Interim* worked out as *cuius regio, eius religio,* i.e., subjects must follow the faith of their ruler.

In September 1551 King Henry II of France declared war on the emperor and soon afterwards entered into negotiations with Maurice of Saxony and other German Protestants. In exchange for a subsidy they recognized Henry as vicar in the empire and allowed him to occupy the 'three bishoprics' of Metz, Toul and Verdun, as well as Cambrai and other imperial cities whose language was not German. Charles V found himself trapped in Germany without any money to raise an army. He thought of making a dash to the Netherlands but was advised not to do so by his sister, Mary of Hungary. She claimed, moreover, that she had no money or means of raising any.

During May 1552 Maurice of Saxony tried to capture the emperor at Innsbruck, but Charles gave him the slip across the Brenner pass and down the Drave valley to Villach in Carinthia. Some years later he recalled how two Lutheran emissaries had met him on a mountain track and made him an offer: if he would only listen to the Protestant princes they would not pursue him but would go with him against the Turk and set him on the throne of Constantinople. But Charles had told them that he wanted no more realms, only Christ crucified, and had spurred on his horse and left them.

Having failed in his attempt to seize the emperor, Maurice of Saxony came to terms with his brother, Ferdinand, at Passau in August 1552 and joined him in a campaign against the Turks in the course of which he was killed. Meanwhile, Charles determined to oust the French from Metz in spite of his sister's advice that he should desist from so dangerous an enterprise. He could not allow Henry II to threaten the Netherlands and the route connecting them with Franche-Comté. The siege of Metz was begun in November 1552 but the city was well fortified and ably defended by the Duke of Guise. Bombardments, mining operations and assaults all failed. Early in January Charles decided to withdraw.

Ferdinand was now left in sole charge of German affairs and at the Diet of Augsburg in September 1555 constitutional form was given to the concessions made three years before to the late Maurice of Saxony. Lutheranism was given equal legal status with Catholicism within the empire, though explicit provision was made to continue the endeavours to restore unity.

Charles V's attempt to re-establish the medieval concept of a united Christendom under the joint leadership of emperor and pope had foundered. Having already relinquished the government of his German dominions, he now decided to hand over the rest of his responsibilities, though not the imperial title itself, to his son, Philip. In

October 1555 he laid down the sovereignty
of the Netherlands and in January 1556
divested himself of the Spanish crowns and
their dependencies. He then retired to a
country palace adjoining the monastery of
Yuste in Spain, where he held court and
continued, amid his devotions, to take a
keen interest in the fortunes of his empire
until his death in 1558.

Henceforth the nature of his empire
changed radically. Instead of being a universal, Christian empire with a Burgundian
soul, it became a Spanish, Catholic empire
with a Castilian soul. As the flow of American silver to Spain increased during the
second half of the century, the Netherlands
ceased to be economically the most advanced
and wealthiest part of the empire. The wars
in Italy and Germany demonstrated the
superiority of Spanish troops over all others.
The emperor's council shed its international
character and became dominated by Spaniards or Hispano-Italians. In Spain itself
Erastianism was superseded by an uncompromising orthodoxy reflected in the
activities of the Inquisition. Under its new
king, Philip II, Spain became the spearhead
of the Counter-Reformation.

Part of Philip's inheritance was the age-
old conflict with the Valois kings. His
accession was followed by a renewal of war
with France, but weariness on both sides led
to the Treaty of Cateau-Cambrésis (3 April
1559). France kept Metz, Toul and Verdun
as well as Calais which it had recently
taken from England, but it abandoned
claims in Italy and restored Savoy and Piedmont to Duke Emmanuel-Philibert. Despite
its gains France emerged from the Italian
wars in debilitated condition. Its financial
resources were exhausted and the peace
freed large numbers of soldiers for the civil
wars which were about to devastate the
country.

Chapter 4

The Tudors

The accession of Henry VII in 1485 was for long regarded as a watershed in English history. It was seen as the beginning of a 'new monarchy' able to impose its will on the turbulent nobles who had torn the country apart in the Wars of the Roses. The first Tudor, it was alleged, had infused new life into the dormant machinery of government and by careful management had built up the royal revenues to such an extent that he was able to bequeath more than a million pounds in gold and silver to his son. However, it has recently been shown that some of the administrative reforms attributed to Henry, notably his use of the Chamber as a department of national finance, were initiated by his predecessors. His financial achievement was generally less spectacular than was once supposed. It cannot be proved that he died a millionaire. Nor did 1485 mark the end of civil unrest, which flared up during Henry VII's reign in the revolts of Lambert Simnel and Perkin Warbeck.

Yet Henry VII's achievement was not negligible. Legally he had a very poor claim to the throne. On his father's side he had no claim at all. His mother belonged to the Beaufort family, which traced its illegitimate descent from John of Gaunt. Richard II had legitimized the family but Henry IV had debarred it from the throne. Many people had a better claim than Henry Tudor, notably the young Earl of Warwick, the son of Edward IV's brother, Clarence.

Henry's method of overcoming these disadvantages was forceful and direct. He proclaimed himself king by the grace of God, seeing that the Almighty had given him the victory at Bosworth and made Parliament register his accession and the right of his heirs to succeed to the throne. As for Warwick, he was beheaded. By marrying his children into some of the royal families of Europe Henry VII succeeded in establishing his dynasty on a firm and internationally respectable footing. This was his greatest achievement.

The Henrician Reformation

Another obstacle which the Tudors had to overcome was the survival of independent jurisdictions within the kingdom. The most important was the Church, which had its own law courts and owed allegiance to the pope. As long as it remained independent, the king could not call himself master in his own house. Henry VIII solved this problem by severing the traditional connection with Rome and setting himself up as Supreme Head of the English Church. By so doing he immeasurably enhanced the prestige of kingship; having fixed the crown firmly on his head, he added a halo.

The Henrician Reformation was not just 'an act of state', however, it was also a popular movement. Lollardy (the heretical movement founded by John Wycliffe in the fourteenth century) was far from extinct by the end of the fifteenth century. The act books of the ecclesiastical tribunals and the bishops' registers show a steady rise in the number of prosecutions, abjurations and punishments for heresy from the 1480s onwards.

Dissent was concentrated in Buckinghamshire, London, Essex and Kent, but there were Lollards also at Coventry and in the large diocese of York. Although Lollardy lacked a central administration its wandering missionaries kept scattered congregations in touch with each other. Most Lollards belonged to the common people, though skilled workers outnumbered labourers and husbandmen. They also included some lesser clergymen, London merchants and many women.

It has been claimed that Lollardy provided 'a spring-board of critical dissent from which the Protestant Reformation could overleap the walls of orthodoxy'. Lollards certainly helped to disseminate Lutheran literature, notably Tyndale's *New Testament*. It is arguable, though, that Lollardy was a hindrance to the spread of Lutheranism, for it provided an alternative form of dissent at the popular level and provoked a rigorous campaign of persecution which was well under way by the time Lutheranism first appeared in England.

Luther's name became known in London soon after he had posted up his ninety-five theses. Copies of his works were sent to England by John Froben, the Basle printer, as early as 1519 and they continued to circulate despite censorship measures taken by the government. They were smuggled in by merchants trading with Antwerp or Germany and distributed by the Society of Christian Brethren, which has been aptly described as a kind of 'forbidden book of the month club'. Yet Lutheranism made relatively few converts in England. It was avidly taken up by some young intellectuals at Cambridge, who used to gather at the White Horse Tavern, and it found support among German merchants of the London Steelyard. Otherwise its impact on the English public at large seems to have been small.

Henry VIII's government was opposed to Luther from the start. In May 1521 Wolsey presided over a solemn book-burning at St Paul's Cross, at which John Fisher, Bishop of Rochester, preached a sermon against the new doctrine. Sir Thomas More, who was equally hostile to it, conducted a visitation of the London Steelyard and was empowered by the bishop of London to read Lutheran books so as to reply to them in English. Henry VIII himself attacked Luther in a book called *Assertio Septem Sacramentorum,* for which he was given the title of 'Defender of the Faith' by the pope. Yet only a few years later Henry cast aside his allegiance to Rome.

The royal 'divorce' and the break with Rome

As an act of state the Henrician Reformation was anything but doctrinal. It stemmed directly from the king's determination to obtain an annulment of his first marriage to Catherine of Aragon so as to be free to marry Anne Boleyn. The 'king's great matter' was closely bound up with the succession problem. All Catherine's children had died, except Mary, and the absence of a male heir threatened the survival of the Tudor dynasty.

The prospect of a woman ruler, for which there was no satisfactory precedent in English history, was viewed with apprehension. If she were to marry a foreigner, England would become tied to the destinies of another country. This had to be avoided and Henry was confident that the pope would allow him to remarry, for Catherine had been the wife of his deceased brother, Arthur, and the Bible said: 'And if a man shall take his brother's wife, it is an unclean thing . . . they shall be childless.'

If Clement VII had been a different person Henry would probably have got what he wanted, but the pope was a timid and shifty character, mainly interested in the political situation in Italy. The moral issues raised by Henry's demand for an annulment did not worry him. He even suggested that the king might be allowed to have two wives at once. What really concerned him was that Catherine was the emperor's aunt and that if he gave way to Henry he would lose Charles V's military assistance on which depended the restoration of the Medici to power in Florence. He authorized Wolsey and Campeggio (the Italian papal legate) to try the king's divorce suit in England in 1529 but secretly instructed his legate to procrastinate. Eventually he revoked the case to Rome after he had given a verbal promise not to do so.

An immediate consequence of the pope's action was the fall of Cardinal Wolsey in October 1529. For three years thereafter Henry VIII ruled without a chief minister. It has been suggested that royal policy during these years was 'unimaginative, bombastic and sterile' and that it only became 'direct, simple and successful' after Thomas Cromwell's ascendancy in 1532. Henry VIII did not wish to break with Rome, however, until every approach had been

tried. What a triumph he would have scored if the pope had given way!

The aim of the king's policy was to put pressure on the pope by a campaign of intimidation against the Church of England. In 1531 he extorted a subsidy from the clergy after he had accused them of offending the law of the realm by exercising their independent jurisdiction. As the pope failed to react the campaign was intensified. In 1532 the English Church gave up its legislative independence in a document called the *Surrender of the Clergy*. The death of Archbishop Warham in the same year enabled Henry to appoint his own creature, Thomas Cranmer, as primate. In May 1533 he declared the king's marriage null and void at a special court held in Dunstable. The decree came none too soon for Henry was already secretly married to Anne Boleyn. She was crowned in June and in September Elizabeth was born.

In the meantime a frontal attack was mounted by Thomas Cromwell on papal authority in England. This was done by means of statute law. Never before had Parliament been called upon to participate so actively in policy-making. The Reformation Parliament lasted on and off from 1529 to 1536. It has been called the first modern Parliament because its members were at last given a chance to know each other and to form groups, though nothing comparable with the modern party system as yet existed. Henry did not need to bully its members; a fundamental harmony of interests existed between them.

The most important act passed in 1533 was the Act of Appeals. Its resounding preamble to the effect 'that this realm of England is an Empire' implied that England was a country independent of any external authority, temporal or spiritual. Under the Act of Supremacy Henry VIII became Supreme Head of the English Church.

Anti-clericalism was strong in England in the early sixteenth century, yet it could not be taken as certain that Henry's religious policy would not be resisted. A campaign of anti-papal propaganda was therefore mounted by the government and an example made of Sir Thomas More and John Fisher, Bishop of Rochester, after they had refused to take the Succession Oath imposed on all the king's subjects. This declared that the succession to the throne was vested in the children of Henry's second marriage. Fisher had supported Queen Catherine and More had shown his disapproval of royal policy by resigning the chancellorship in 1532. They were found guilty of high treason and beheaded on Tower Green in 1535.

In 1536 an act was passed dissolving the smaller monasteries, which were alleged to be centres of 'manifest sin, vicious, carnal and abominable living'. This charge was largely unfounded; the government's real motive was the confiscation of monastic wealth. Although the larger monasteries were described as 'great, honourable and solemn' in 1536, they were not spared three years later.

The dissolution of the monasteries was one of the most spectacular revolutions in English history. Within four years landed property worth nearly twenty million pounds passed from one set of owners to another. It was put on the market at a time when land was much in demand and a vested interest in the Reformation was thus established.

From the doctrinal standpoint no radical

Reformation came about as a result of the Henrician. The Ten Articles which Convocation adopted in 1536 made no concessions to the Lutherans despite a conciliatory phraseology. *The Bishops' Book* of 1537 was a conservative statement of belief. Two years later the Act of Six Articles laid down heavy penalties for those who denied the doctrine of transubstantiation and other fundamental Catholic beliefs. Even if Henry himself did incline towards a less orthodox position towards the end of his reign, England did not become a Protestant country till the reign of Edward VI.

Edward VI

The first major crisis which the Tudor monarchy had to face was the minority of Edward VI, who was only nine at his accession in January 1547. His father, Henry VIII, had provided for a council of regency of equal members but its first act was to appoint one of its members, Edward Seymour, Earl of Hertford, as Protector and Duke of Somerset.

Being a man of liberal views, Somerset began by sweeping away Henry VIII's stringent treason laws and the old laws

against heresy. People were suddenly able to debate freely and openly about religion, and the situation soon got out of hand. Preachers stormed in their pulpits; printing presses produced a flood of libels and satires; Protestant divines flocked to England from the continent.

Though sympathetic to the Protestant cause, Somerset did not wish to provoke the mass of the people, who continued to worship as they had always done. He therefore embarked on a policy of piecemeal religious change aimed at causing the least offence to anyone. Cranmer's Order of Communion of 1548 contained nothing flagrantly hostile to Catholic beliefs, and the first Prayer Book of 1549 was 'an ingenious essay in ambiguity'. It left much of the old order as it was, though religious services were henceforth to be held in English instead of Latin.

In general the Prayer Book was accepted without resistance, but in Devon and Cornwall it provoked a serious popular rising known as the Western Rebellion. This was ruthlessly crushed by John Russell, Earl of Bedford.

Somerset's social policy also ended in catastrophe and bloodshed. By 1547 the economic situation had become critical:

Above, Thomas Wolsey (c. 1473–1530), who administered England during the first twenty years of Henry VIII's reign. As well as being a fine organizer, Wolsey was a cardinal who hoped to use his position to bring peace to Europe and a supporter of the humanists.

Above left, an engraving of the island of Utopia, the frontispiece to Thomas More's book of the same name published in 1516. A friend of Erasmus, More became Lord Chancellor in 1529 but was executed in 1535 when he refused to accept the Henrician Reformation.

Opposite top, Hampton Court Palace, outside London, first built by Henry VIII's minister Thomas Wolsey but taken over and enlarged by the king as a palace for his second wife Anne Boleyn.

Opposite bottom, John Foxe, an English Protestant, published a Book of Martyrs in 1559; it contained a number of accounts of the suffering of English Protestants at the hands of the Catholics. This illustration shows the exhumation of Wycliffe's bones in 1425.

On page 43, the royal coat of arms adopted by the Tudor dynasty, incorporating both the red and the white rose, the symbols of the opposing factions in the Wars of the Roses; heraldic symbolism had genuine political importance at this time. Victoria and Albert Museum, London.

prices were rising steadily and landowners tried to keep abreast of inflation by resorting to expedients which caused social hardship and unrest. They enclosed arable land, turning it into pasture so as to take advantage of the cloth boom, encroached on common land and went in for rack-renting. At first the government merely made the situation worse by selling off the lands of the dissolved chantries to speculators and continuing the debasement of the coinage begun by Henry VIII.

In 1548, however, Somerset tried to put into effect some of the reforms advocated by a group of enlightened theorists called the Commonwealth Men. He introduced a Subsidy Act to restrict enclosure by taxing sheep and cloth and set up a special commission to enforce existing anti-enclosure statutes. The upshot of this well-intentioned policy was another revolt.

During the summer of 1549 the common people of Norfolk rose under Robert Ket's leadership. Unlike the western rebels, they were not concerned with religion. Their enemies were the gentry, who were refusing to comply with the government's economic measures. Since they regarded the Protector as their friend, they did not march on London but simply staged a kind of sit-down strike outside Norwich. Even so, their movement constituted a threat to the security of the state and was mercilessly put down by Somerset's rival in the council, John Dudley, Earl of Warwick.

Somerset's rule could not survive two major rebellions in one year. He was overthrown in October 1549 and subsequently beheaded, his place being taken by Dudley, who assumed the title of Duke of Northumberland. After siding with the Catholics, Northumberland now joined the extreme Protestants in order to despoil the Church. He ordered the destruction of service books, religious statues and paintings and went far towards depriving bishops of their secular power and property. The second Prayer Book of 1552 altered the communion service and simplified ceremonial so as to get away from the Catholic idea of the mass as a sacrifice. Henceforth the communion was to be celebrated on a table instead of an altar, ordinary bread was to be used and the celebrant was not to wear special vestments or make devotional gestures. The doctrine of the Real Presence was repudiated by Cranmer's Forty-two Articles in 1553.

If Northumberland's religious policy was radical, his economic and social policy was thoroughly reactionary. The Subsidy Act of 1548 was repealed and the Enclosure Commission allowed to lapse. To prevent social unrest the scope of treason was again enlarged, certain gentlemen were allowed to raise cavalry units at the public expense and the sheriff's military powers were transferred to a new official, the lord-lieutenant. Yet Northumberland did did try to reverse the debasement of the coinage and encouraged English overseas enterprise.

Northumberland's power depended on the survival of the young king, whose health was precarious. If Mary Tudor, who was the duke's enemy and a Catholic, came to the throne he and his policy were doomed. So Northumberland bullied the king and his council into altering the succession in favour of his own daughter-in-law, Lady Jane Grey. But when Edward died, on 6 July 1553, Mary managed to give Northumberland the slip and the whole nation, including the royal council, rallied to her side. In a desperate bid to save his skin the duke proclaimed her himself but his volte-face deceived no one. He was arrested and executed, while the unfortunate Lady Jane Grey, her husband and Cranmer were imprisoned in the Tower of London.

Mary Tudor

In 1553 Tudor England entered upon a second crisis. Having survived a minority it now had to overcome the predicament of being ruled by a thirty-seven-year-old Catholic spinster. The accession of Mary Tudor, Henry VIII's daughter by Catherine of Aragon, threatened the survival of both the Tudor dynasty and the English Reformation.

Mary was sincere, devout, kind and cultured but she lacked administrative and political skill. 'I know the queen', wrote the imperial ambassador, 'to be good, easily influenced, inexpert in worldly matters, and

PARVVLE PATRISSA, PATRIÆ VIRTVTIS ET HÆRES
ESTO, NIHIL MAIVS MAXIMVS ORBIS HABET,
GNATVM VIX POSSVNT COELVM ET NATVRA DEDISSE,
HVIVS QVEM PATRIS, VICTVS HONORET HONOS.
ÆQVATO TANTVM, TANTI TV FACTA PARENTIS,
VOTA HOMINVM, VIX QVO PROGREDIANTVR, HABENT
VINCITO, VICISTI. QVOT REGES PRISCVS ADORAT
ORBIS, NEC TE QVI VINCERE POSSIT, ERIT.

a novice all round. . . . To tell you between ourselves, I believe if God does not preserve her she will be lost.' In fact, Mary turned out to be a pathetic failure.

The queen aimed at restoring the old religion, but first she had to secure her succession, for if she remained single the throne would eventually pass to her Protestant half-sister, Elizabeth, who would surely undo her work. The choice of a husband, however, was not easy. The chancellor, Stephen Gardiner, would have liked Mary to marry an English nobleman, but she accepted instead the future Philip II of Spain, thereby bringing her kingdom into the Habsburg orbit.

Mary's decision caused the Kentish rebellion of Sir Thomas Wyatt in 1554. Though he pretended to champion the Prayer Book, he was really opposed to the Spanish marriage. His revolt failed because the Londoners would not join it, and its chief result was the unjust execution of Lady Jane Grey and her husband.

The royal marriage was celebrated at Winchester on 25 July 1554. Philip tactfully agreed to stand down should Mary predecease him without leaving an heir and promised not to appoint Spaniards to important posts in England. Yet the marriage was unpopular, for Englishmen were no longer economically dependent on trade with the Spanish Netherlands and feared that the Spanish Inquisition might be introduced into their country.

Originally Mary asked for nothing more than toleration for Catholics, but she soon began to revert to the religious position that had existed before the schism and Protestant extremists went into temporary exile on the continent. Edward VI's religious legislation was annulled by Parliament and the title of 'Supreme Head' in the royal style was replaced by a convenient 'etc.'.

In November 1554 Cardinal Reginald Pole returned to England as papal legate. He absolved the nation of the spiritual penalties it had incurred by its schism and heresy and wisely refrained from demanding the restoration of Church lands that had been secularized. But the reversion to Catholicism was marred by a campaign of persecution without parallel in English history. Altogether some 300 people were burnt for their beliefs, mainly in southeast England. Most of them were humble folk, though Cranmer was among the victims.

In 1557 Mary allowed herself to be dragged into a war with France which resulted in the loss of Calais, England's last continental foothold. Such was the price of the Spanish marriage which had in any case proved barren. Sterility was the keynote of Mary's reign. She died, execrated by her subjects, on 17 November 1558.

Elizabeth I

Little is known about Queen Elizabeth's religious convictions. She disapproved of

Above, the future King Edward VI of England (ruled 1547–53), painted by Hans Holbein. Edward died before he was able to impress his will on the policies of his advisers. National Maritime Museum, London.

Above left, Thomas Cromwell (c. 1485–1540), England's chief minister from 1531 to 1540. He masterminded the English Reformation, reorganized the administrative system and oversaw the dissolution of the monasteries. He was executed in 1540. Frick Collection New York.

Opposite left, Henry VIII of England (ruled 1509–47), painted by Hans Holbein. Henry became increasingly tyrannical in his later years, and his expensive foreign policies produced no tangible results.

Opposite right, Anne Boleyn (1507–36); Henry's love for her and his frustration with Catharine of Aragon's inability to bear him a son was sufficient to cause England's break with the Church of Rome. National Gallery of Art, Washington.

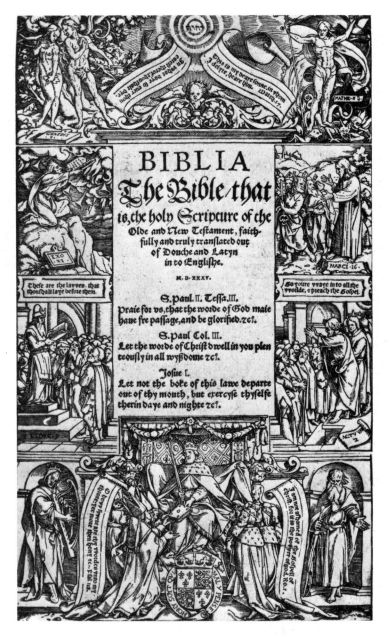

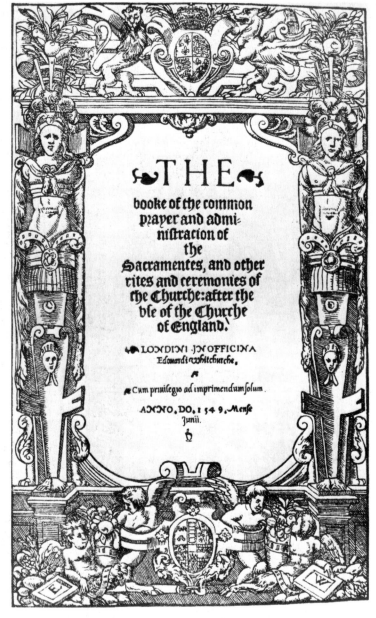

theological pedantry and clerical marriage; otherwise she kept her beliefs very much to herself. As the daughter of Henry VIII and Anne Boleyn she could hardly be expected to retain the papal supremacy, yet she had no wish to provoke her more conservative subjects by adopting extreme Protestantism. Her original intention was probably to win the Marian bishops over before proceeding to any change of doctrine, but this was not acceptable to certain Protestant hotheads in Parliament. They tried to force a complete Protestant programme on her and the result was a more extreme compromise than the queen had originally envisaged.

The Act of Supremacy of April 1559 restored the royal supremacy, while the Act of Uniformity, passed in the same month, imposed a new Prayer Book. The queen, because of her sex, was described as 'supreme governor' of the English Church, not as supreme head. The new doctrine stood roughly halfway between the Prayer Books of 1549 and 1552. All the Marian bishops except one refused to take the Oath of Supremacy and were accordingly de-

prived, but a majority of the lesser clergy submitted. The settlement was rounded off by the adoption of the Thirty-nine Articles by Convocation in 1563. Like all compromises it failed to satisfy the extremists on both sides. The Puritan, John Field, described it as, 'a certain kind of religion, framed out of man's own brain and fantasy, far worse than that of popery (if worse may be), patched and pieced out of theirs and ours together'.

Elizabeth was probably wise not to throw in her lot with either the Catholics or the Protestants. By steering a middle course she united all moderate-minded Englishmen and avoided becoming intimately associated with the big religious power blocks on the continent.

In the first decade of Elizabeth's reign the Catholics were not troublesome. Many conformed outwardly to the settlement while continuing to worship in their own way. Philip II persuaded the pope not to excommunicate the queen as he needed England's friendship against France, the traditional enemy of Spain. But the Rebellion of the

Northern Earls in 1569 created a false impression abroad that only a signal from Rome was needed to overthrow Elizabeth. Pius V therefore excommunicated her and all who continued to obey her. The Catholics were thus forced to choose between loyalty to the state and allegiance to their faith.

A number of young English Catholics went abroad where they were trained in special colleges at Douai, Valladolid, Rome and elsewhere as missionaries to rescue their homeland from heresy. They began to return in 1574 and operated secretly from country houses up and down the country. The first Jesuit mission led by Edmund Campion and Robert Persons arrived in 1580. The government reacted by means of penal legislation. The fine for recusancy was raised to twenty pounds a month and an intensive drive was launched against missionary priests. Campion was among those martyred. Yet Catholicism was able to make headway, for local officials were sometimes unwilling to enforce the penal laws. After 1588 Catholics were persecuted less, for they had remained quiet during the Armada

L. Receiue my spirit.

Left, Thomas Cranmer (1489–1556), the Archbishop of Canterbury under Henry VIII and Edward VI, being burned at the stake under Mary for his guiding role in the introduction of Protestantism to England.

Below, Mary I of England (ruled 1553–58), painted by the Spaniard Antonio Moro. Despite her nickname Bloody Mary, her persecution of the Protestants was not unduly severe for the times; many of the people she forced into exile went to Geneva where they learnt a far more radical form of Protestantism than England had previously known.

Opposite left, the title page of the Coverdale Bible of 1535, a new English translation by Miles Coverdale. Despite such efforts of the Protestants, Henry VIII was reluctant to accept a Lutheran liturgy in England, and it was not until Edward VI's accession that Protestantism was firmly established.

Opposite right, the title page to the Book of Common Prayer *of 1549, written by the Archbishop of Canterbury Thomas Cranmer. The book represented an attempt to impose a uniform religion on the whole of England; but it was amended in 1552 and again in 1559.*

The extreme Protestants or Puritans were also a serious problem to Elizabeth. The Presbyterians hoped to rebuild the Church on the Geneva model by getting rid of bishops and the royal supremacy, while the Separatists wanted freedom to worship outside the framework of a national Church.

Trouble began in 1559 when the Puritans objected to the survival of certain 'popish' practices, notably the use of vestments. Archbishop Parker campaigned vigorously against nonconformity among the clergy and emerged victorious from the Vestiarian controversy. Meanwhile Puritan members of Parliament put forward bills to reform the Church but were each time foiled by the queen.

About 1569 Puritanism assumed a more revolutionary aspect. By attacking the bishops Thomas Cartwright and John Field, to mention only two of the leaders, were indirectly threatening the queen's quasi-episcopal authority. In 1583 Archbishop Whitgift required all the clergy to subscribe to the royal supremacy, the Prayer Book and the Thirty-nine Articles under pain of deprivation. Largely as a result of his efforts, Puritanism declined and was driven underground where it remained until its revival under James I.

An important feature of Elizabeth's reign was the growing importance of the House of Commons where the country gentry were preponderantly represented. Even boroughs were represented by country gentlemen who usually owed their seats to the patronage of some great nobleman. Parliament enabled young gentlemen to go to London, which was fast becoming the social centre of the kingdom.

The Tudor period saw an extension of parliamentary privilege, but as late as 1558 freedom of speech was not well defined. Some members claimed the right to discuss religion, the succession and foreign affairs, but the queen believed such matters should be raised only with her prior consent. In 1566 Paul Wentworth put three questions to the House which suggested that the queen's ban on any discussion of the succession amounted to a breach of privilege. Ten years later his brother, Peter, resumed the attack. He declared,

In this house which is termed a place of free speech, there is nothing so necessary for the preservation of the prince and the state as free speech, and without, it is a scorn and mockery to call it a Parliament House, for in truth it is none, but a very school of flattery, and so a fit place to serve the devil and his angels in, and not to glorify God and the Commonwealth.

Parliamentary opposition to the crown, then, did not begin with the Stuarts, but under Elizabeth it was fundamentally loyal. What the members feared above all was that they would lose her and all that she stood for. The queen's feelings for her Commons were also tempered by affection. 'I think they speak out of zeal to their countries', she declared, 'and not out of spleen or malevolent affection.'

The age of Drake

To many people the reign of Elizabeth I is above all the age of Drake.

Until the 1550s England showed little interest in exploration. The reasons for this apathy were economic and political. It exported its cloth to Antwerp and did not need to look for markets elsewhere; Spain controlled Antwerp and was England's natural ally against France. In the second half of the century this situation changed

completely. The Antwerp market crashed and Englishmen had to find other outlets for their goods; France was crippled by its civil wars. Thus England was left free to encroach upon the Spanish colonial sphere which it had hitherto respected.

The primary motive of English overseas enterprise was commercial. Englishmen hoped to trade with Cathay (China), which was reputedly rich in gold and spices, but all the known routes to the Far East were closed to them. Their only course was to find a new route to the Far East in the northern hemisphere. The attempt made by Hugh Willoughby and Richard Chancellor to find a northeast passage in 1553 failed, but it did lead to the establishment of commercial relations with Russia. In 1576 Martin Frobisher claimed that he had found the northwest passage. He brought back an Eskimo and pieces of black ore said to contain gold. In fact he had only found a Canadian cul-de-sac and the ore turned out to be worthless. Yet the search for a northwest passage continued.

Privateering became important in the 1560s. With the deterioration of Anglo-Spanish relations, English captains began to see possibilities of gain by penetrating the Carribbean. John Hawkins at first hoped to trade legally with the Spanish colonies but the disaster that befell him at San Juan de Ulua, when his fleet was almost destroyed by the Spaniards as it was refitting in the harbour, convinced him otherwise. Francis Drake then set out to inflict as much damage as possible on the Spaniards and in the course of his circumnavigation of the world (1577–80) he seized a considerable quantity of treasure.

Until the late 1560s Englishmen gave little thought to colonization. It was suggested by Humphrey Gilbert in his *Discourse* (1556), and in 1585 the first English colony was founded at Roanoke, a low-lying island off the coast of modern North Carolina. Though it proved a failure, the experience gained paved the way for the foundation of Jamestown in the next century.

Above, Elizabeth I of England presiding over a meeting of parliament, Elizabeth was unable to prevent the House of Commons from discussing topics that she considered the royal prerogative, including religion, foreign politics and monopolies.

Above left, Francis Drake (c. 1540–96) in a miniature by Nicholas Hilliard. Explorer, pirate and harasser of the Spaniards, Drake was the archetypal Elizabethan seaman who created the legend of English sea power in a space of twenty or thirty years. National Portrait Gallery, London.

Opposite, the Ermine Portrait of Elizabeth I of England (ruled 1558–1603), one of many official portraits of the queen intended to link her image with suitable mythical or literary concepts. In this case, the ermine represents purity and chastity.

Chapter 5

Sixteenth-Century Spain

'If death came from Madrid', said the Spanish viceroy at Naples, 'we should all live a long time.' The chronic delays of the Madrid administration were notorious and at the centre of them was the lonely and conscientious Philip II. During his reign, Spain became the first European power to operate on a global scale. The country which launched the great Armada of invasion against England in 1588 was without exaggeration the most powerful nation in the whole world.

In Europe itself the King of Spain was also after 1580, the King of Portugal, King of Naples and Sicily, Duke of Milan and Lord of the Netherlands. Outside Europe he was ruler of territories stretching from Macao to Lima. As may be imagined so extensive and impressive a facade had many flaws and by the end of the century fissures were beginning to split the structure. But if it is true that neither the financial nor the administrative resources of any sixteenth-century European state were sufficient to meet the demands of such global possibilities, it is also true that the Spanish Empire was no figment of the imagination. To the men of the time it was quite simply the greatest power on earth.

The basis of this power was the formidable strength of the Spanish army, based in turn on its excellent infantry; the fleets of the two greatest maritime powers of the time; the immense physical wealth which flowed in from the American empires, and a sense of national purpose and justification in the eyes of God.

The king had an unshakable, indeed almost fanatical belief in his own divine mission as the champion of the Catholic Church in its struggle with the forces of the new Protestant states and wedded to this was the parallel conviction that it was the destiny of Spain to lead the forces of light. 'I do not propose to be the ruler of heretics', he said and he not only effectively crushed all signs of heresy in his own kingdoms but also kept the southern provinces of the Netherlands Catholic. Besides this he scored a notable victory over the Turk, arch-enemy of Christendom, and indirectly was responsible for preventing the accession of a Protestant monarch to the throne of France.

Philip II

For more than eighty years of the sixteenth century, Spain was ruled by two men, father and son. The father, Charles V, was brought up at the cosmopolitan court of Burgundy and was constantly about his business throughout the length and breadth of Europe. On the other hand, his solitary and introverted son, Philip II, apart from brief visits to France and England, where he married Mary Tudor and was for a while co-ruler of England, retired to Spain when he was only thirty-two and thereafter never left the Iberian peninsula.

Before he was forty, Philip had commissioned the architect for his huge new palace complex, El Escorial, some thirty miles outside Madrid and, as the years went by, he spent more and more time in the dark and labyrinthine interior of this austere building. At the centre stood the royal chapel and within the palace were also to be found not only the administrative offices of state but the state rooms of the court, the mausoleum of the royal family and a monastic community. Such was the environment in which Philip, by choice, conducted the business of the world's mightiest empire.

Philip's composure and reserve were legendary and undoubtedly remarkable, but to picture him as a neurotic recluse would be to exaggerate. He was certainly slow in coming to decisions but prudence was usually justified. Since Philip was the sole co-ordinator in his administration and took on himself an immense amount of paper work, literally directing an empire from a desk, business was delayed still further; and while he was thoroughly professional, he had a fatal inability to distinguish high policy from trivia.

When Charles V finally resigned the kingship in 1556 his son, Philip II, inherited as his most immediate problem the sixty-year-old conflict with France over the claims of the rival dynasties in Italy. There was also a dispute about the frontiers of the Burgundian Netherlands which had to be settled. Philip, involving his wife, Mary of England, in the struggle, and even waging war on the pope for his support of the French, fought the war to a satisfactory conclusion. He settled his differences with the French king

by the important treaty of Cateau-Cambrésis, returning numerous towns and villages on the northern and eastern frontiers of France in return for the French recognition of his position in Milan. The French also surrendered Corsica, a vital post on the Spanish sea route to Naples, but they recovered Calais from the English. The treaty was signed in 1559 and in the same year Philip went back to Spain.

Once he had returned to his country he established his new capital at Madrid. It had the advantage of being an administrative capital without history which was at the geographical centre of the peninsula. In addition, since it was neutral in the eyes of the various regional populations in the country, it did not invite the political jealousy which would have been focused on any of the old capitals which might have been chosen. From Madrid, and later from El Escorial, Philip administered the daily affairs of his kingdom, rarely leaving his capital city and using the councils at the capital and the viceroys in the non-Castilian parts of his empire. Philip's reliance on Castilian officials and his fixed residence in Castile created problems. The fact that of the many languages spoken throughout his dominions Castilian was the only one which he could speak at all fluently also contributed to the unrest in Flanders and Aragon. In both cases this was to flare up into open revolt.

The revolt in Flanders

The highly urbanized area of the Low Countries, whose livelihood was commerce and whose neighbour was Protestant Germany, was a fertile ground for the doctrines of the reformers. In the earlier decades of the century the dangerously liberal views of the great Dutch reformer Erasmus had won a considerable following in Spain itself. The trend had been stopped by the leaders of the Counter-Reformation in Spain and the rigours of the Holy Office of the Inquisition.

Philip, whose religious conviction verged on fanaticism, began to enforce the existing laws with rigour and appointed new bishops himself. This offended even Catholic opinion as unwarranted royal intervention in the affairs of the Church. The Protestant cause grew in natural opposition to the aggressive actions of the alien administration. It was also fostered by the immigration of Calvinists in the 1560s, the representatives of an organized anti-authoritarian and international movement. The situation progressively deteriorated and in 1566 the explosion occurred with wide-scale rioting. The efficiency of Calvinist agitation was a new threat to the regime which tightened up its measures.

The following year Philip sent in the Duke of Alba, one of his top ranking generals, with orders to restore 'law and order' and to suppress heresy. Alba's religious fervour was equal to that of his master and there ensued a reign of terror in which thousands lost their lives.

The Netherlands had been subjected to crippling levels of taxation from the time of the Habsburg accession to the crown of Spain, since they were the richest European provinces in the Spanish Empire. The position was exacerbated still further when Alba imposed new levies in 1572, which not only raised the rate but also denied the estates general the right to assess the distribution of the burden and thus infringed the privileges of its powerful members. But this year marked a new and serious setback for the Spaniards. Although they were impregnable from the land they were highly vulnerable to seaborne attack and for some years this attack had been pressed by privateers from the northern provinces who had their bases in England. In 1572 they were expelled from England and descended in force on the shores of the Low Countries; in the same year these 'Sea Beggars' took the ports of Brill and Flushing and most of Zeeland and Holland. Philip replaced Alba with a new governor, Requesens, but his attempts at a more moderate policy failed and he had to resort to force.

The Spanish army was an uncertain amalgam of various nationalities and its instability was increased by long arrears of pay. In 1576, the year of Requesens' death, the army got completely out of hand and in November, after a skirmish with rebel troops, ran amok in the streets of Antwerp and subjected the great city to a brutal and horrible sack. As a result the rebels, that is the predominantly Catholic movement in the south and the 'Sea Beggars' in the north, formed an alliance against the foreign invader, the Pacification of Ghent. Yet the unity was more apparent than real and the divisions between the Calvinist burghers and the southern Catholic nobles were still there waiting only to be exploited.

As his next governor Philip appointed his half brother Don John of Austria, the hero of the Battle of Lepanto, who seems to have hoped that the Netherlands could be used as a base for an attack on England. He was not the last Spanish general to think so, but he was never given the opportunity to explore the practicalities of the project. Before he was even admitted as governor by the

Above, the Spanish infantry regiments, known as tercios, *formed the finest army in sixteenth-century Europe. They were armed with pikes and muskets. Here they are seen relaxing after capturing Valenciennes in 1567.*

Left, Miguel de Cervantes (1547–1616), the greatest writer of the Spanish Renaissance, publishing his novel Don Quixote *in 1605–15. He spent five years in the 1570s as a slave of the Barbary pirates and the viceroy of Algiers.*

Opposite, the Spanish Armada of 1588, the first great European naval battle in which both sides relied on cannonades and broadsides rather than the medieval tactic of boarding the enemy vessel and fighting hand to hand.

estates general, he had to promise to observe the traditional liberties of the territories and to withdraw Spanish troops, and although he later recalled them before his death in 1578 he did not succeed in establishing his authority against the power of the rebels.

In the same year (1578) the rift widened between the Catholics and the Calvinist townsfolk who were led by William the Silent, the Prince of Orange. The problem was further exacerbated when Philip appointed as governor general Alexander Farnese, Duke of Parma, one of the greatest soldiers of the age and one of Spain's most brilliant statesmen. Farnese quickly came to terms with the Catholic nobility in the south. He promised to withdraw Spanish troops and guarantee the privileges of the aristocrats against the growing power of the bourgeoisie if they withdrew their provinces from the rebels. But the final issue was decided on the battlefield.

Parma had all the ideal qualities of a great commander, courage, vigour and the willingness and ability to share the full rigours of campaigning with his men. In addition he displayed a brilliant sense of timing and a previously unequalled feeling for the terrain of the Low Countries themselves. In him

SIXTEENTH-CENTURY SPAIN

1500	
	Charles V becomes emperor (1519)
1525	
	Birth of Philip II (1527)
1550	
	Abdication of Charles V and the accession of Philip II (1556)
	Building of El Escorial (1563–84)
	Alba sent to restore order in Netherlands (1567)
	Death of Don Carlos (1568)
	Battle of Lepanto (1571)
	'Sea Beggars' seize Brill, Flushing and most of Zealand and Holland (1572)
1575	
	Sack of Antwerp (1576)
	Alexander Farnese becomes Governor of the Netherlands (1578)
	Philip II elected King of Portugal (1580)
	William the Silent assassinated (1584)
	Defeat of the Spanish Armada (1588)
	Revolt in the Aragon (1590)
	Death of Philip II (1598)
1600	

even William the Silent found his equal, and thanks to the tenacity and effectiveness of his great general's conduct of the war Philip of Spain could claim to have saved at least the southern provinces of the Low Countries for Catholicism.

In an indirect sense Alexander Farnese was the founder of the modern state of Belgium. In a far more direct sense he was author of the continuing reputation of Spanish arms in the later sixteenth century, welding the diverse nationalities and military traditions of his troops into a precise and deadly instrument of military power.

The revolt of the Netherlands, which began in the 1560s, continued for a further twenty years after the formal declaration of independence of the northern provinces in 1581 by William the Silent, who was assassinated three years later. However Spain did not recognize the independence of the new state until the Treaty of Westphalia of 1648.

It is clear that a struggle of such intensity and duration must have had its origins in something deeper than the policy of one man, Some of the factors leading to the break have already been outlined, but it must also be realized that during the later years of the sixteenth century and the beginning of the seventeenth the Dutch had matured as a sea power. They were thus building the foundations of their maritime empire and were gaining an unquenchable sense of national identity and patriotic pride.

As has been noticed elsewhere, one of the busiest trade routes of early modern Europe was that between the Iberian peninsula and the Low Countries, since wool was transported from the north coast Spanish ports to Flanders so that it could be manufactured into cloth. Trading in luxuries also developed later as the Portuguese capital of Lisbon became the European entrepot for the spices, silks and other treasures brought back from the Indies. When therefore in 1594 Philip closed Lisbon to the Protestant merchants of the Low Countries because he was pursuing economic sanctions against them, the response was direct Dutch sailings to the Indies and, in 1602, the founding of the Dutch East India Company.

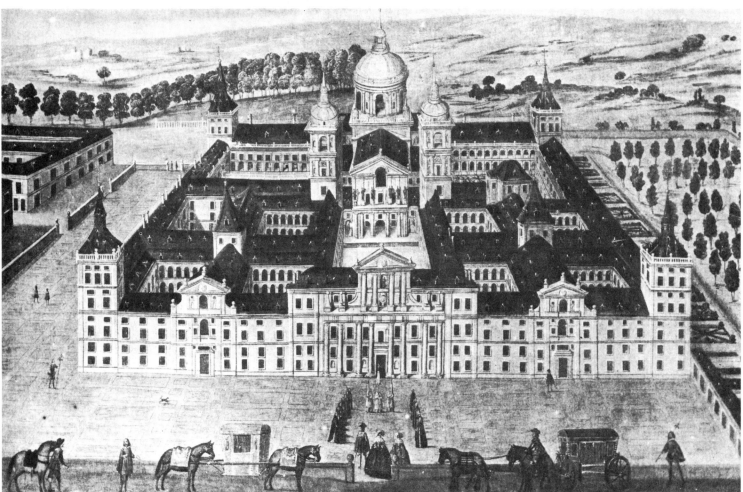

54

The annexation of Portugal

For the sixty years between 1580 and 1640, the dream of generations of Spanish kings seemed to have been realised: with the accession of Philip II of Spain to the throne of Portugal in 1580, the Iberian peninsula became a single political as well as a geographical unit. The name of 'Spain' had been used since the Middle Ages, but to describe the whole of the peninsula; indeed when Pope Alexander VI granted Ferdinand of Aragon the title of king of Spain, Manuel of Portugal lodged a complaint against the misuse of the term. But throughout the century the two states, which together controlled the only colonial empires of their century, had been growing closer together by a series of dynastic marriages. When therefore in 1578 the disastrous reign of Sebastian of Portugal came to an end on the fateful field of Alcazar-Kebir in Morocco Spain had not only virtually unanswerable arguments in terms of military power but

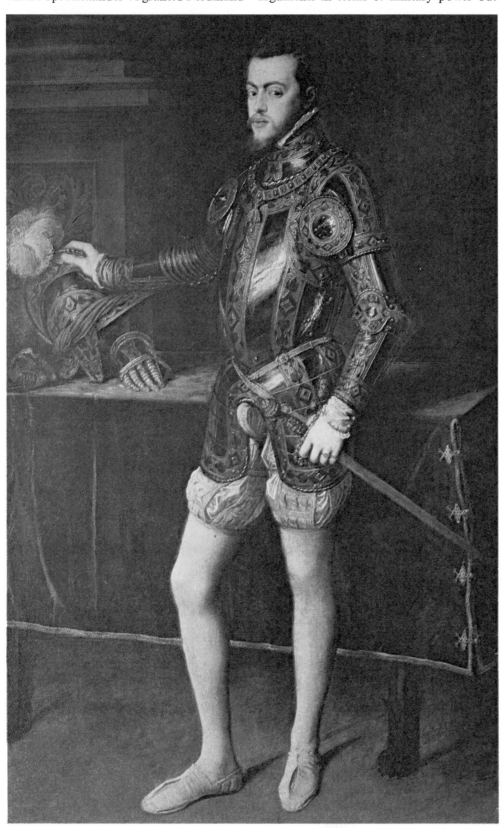

Below, Philip II of Spain (ruled 1556–98) in a portrait by Titian. Philip saw himself as the ever-vigilant guardian of the interests of the Catholic church as well as the defender of a vastly wealthy empire in the New World. Prado, Madrid.

Opposite top left, the siege of Haarlem in 1572–73 by the Spanish troops. This was a turning point in the revolt of the Netherlands against the Spaniards. The town defended heroically but eventually 2,000 of its citizens were killed. As a result, the Netherlands became far more united in the revolt.

Opposite top right, Lisbon in the late sixteenth century, after Portugal had been joined to the kingdom of Spain. Lisbon was no longer the great port of earlier in the century.

Opposite bottom, the Escorial, a combination of monastery and palace built by Philip II of Spain near Madrid in 1563–84. Its grid-iron layout was intended to symbolize the grill on which St Lawrence was martyred.

a condition of his wedding to a Spanish princess, Manuel had reluctantly agreed to the forcible expulsion of all unconverted Jews in 1496. The Portuguese officials did their utmost to arrange the conversion of these valuable citizens and any who did become *conversos* (that is converts) were assured that their beliefs would be free from investigation for the following twenty years.

A major problem for Portugal was the drain on her resources of manpower—the riches of the east which had given King Manuel his sobriquet were hard to win and the cost in both men and ships was terrible. The lure of quick riches from seafaring attracted not only the merchants as entrepreneurs but also the labourers as seamen and by the middle of the century Portugal was not only an importer of food stuffs but also had a huge black slave population. By the time of the Spanish conquest then, Portugal was too exhausted to offer any serious resistance.

The Spanish Inquisition

The most sinister of the institutions which were brought into Portugal under the pressure of her powerful neighbour was undoubtedly the Inquisition. It had been set up in Spain in the time of the Catholic Kings. From the beginning it was free from papal control, even being granted, in 1559, independent jurisdiction over bishops. In the reign of Charles V it became a department of state, developing in the fourth and fifth decade of the sixteenth century into the large and oppressive apparatus of thought control which became notorious.

The barbarities of torture and execution employed by the Inquisition were the commonplaces of interrogation and justice of the time; the particular objections to the Inquisition lay in its encouragement of public corruption and private betrayal. The condemned heretic lost not only his life and his honour but also stood to lose his lands. His trial might have been the result of denunciation by an unnamed informer, possibly a relation, and he might be held in prison for years before his case came to trial and then longer still while awaiting a verdict.

The apparatus of informers, denunciations, forced confessions and a public habit of watchfulness are unfortunately all too common in the twentieth century, but although the ritual of the show trial is still familiar the ceremony of the *auto-de-fé* (loosely to be translated as Act of Faith) is fortunately no longer practised. Even in an age of public executions it was outstanding. Crowds would assemble on specially constructed stands in the main squares of towns to watch the mass burning of the condemned heretics, while those who had recanted would process in penitence through the streets. King Philip's first public act in Spain was a personal attendance at an *auto-da-fé* in Valladolid.

also the best claims to the throne by the laws of succession.

A caretaker monarchy was set up under the aged Cardinal Henry who was crowned king and even announced his willingness to marry in the hope of a legitimate Portuguese heir. But no papal dispensation was forthcoming and this last sturdy representative of the great house of Avis died a few months later without having had the opportunity of performing this final service for his country.

His death left the field clear for Philip who, as both nephew and son-in-law of the late king's father, John, was convinced of the superiority of his claim to that of his only rival, Anthony Prior of Crato, who was the illegitimate nephew of King John. But despite his successful diplomacy and bribery among the Portuguese aristocracy, Philip found himself obliged to put on a show of force in view of the militant popular support which Anthony, as the only hope of an independent Portugal, attracted. The campaign swept Anthony and his supporters before it and in 1580 the Cortes was obliged to elect Philip II King of Portugal.

In the eighty years preceding Philip's takeover, Portugal had been consolidating the work of her explorers and merchants so as to produce one of the world's great maritime empires. At home the costs of such an empire to such a small metropolitan country did fatal damage to the economy. This was weakened still further by the huge dowries which John III (1521–57) bestowed on his daughters and, most crippling of all, by the expenses of Sebastian's absurd enterprise against the sultan of Morocco. Quite apart from the terrible loss in manpower and the costs of the expedition itself, the ransoms of the numerous noble prisoners came to well over a million *cruzados*.

The century had opened with the reign of Manuel I, the Fortunate (1495–1521), who continued John II's forceful disciplining of the nobility. Also, learning from the example of Ferdinand of Aragon, Manuel prepared the way for the crown's takeover of the mastership of the military Order of Christ. In other respects the kings of Portugal followed the example of their neighbour. Indeed in some cases they had no choice. As

The Place & manner of Execution of Persons condemn'd by the Inquisition.

In the view of Philip's commitment to the re-establishment of orthodox Catholicism throughout Europe the Inquisition was obviously fundamental to his policy. If it was sometimes the vehicle of corrupt practices it was an important factor in the destruction of Protestantism in the Peninsula. During his father's reign action against Jewish *conversos*, too, had become even more severe with the passing of laws to enforce *Limpieza*, that is, the exclusion from public office those not of pure Old Christian descent: no candidate would be admitted to public office who could not prove the purity of his gentile blood. Under Philip the activities of the Inquisition were extended to the field of censorship, while in 1559 students were forbidden to travel abroad.

War against the infidel

In the 1560s Philip saw that the laws against the Moriscos of Granada were more rigorously enforced, in the same way that he had striven to establish orthodoxy amongst his Christian subjects. After their forcible conversion to Christianity in 1502, the Moors of this ancient Muslim kingdom had been able to buy the tolerance of the Christian kings. They were thus able to continue their former customs, dress, language and even, in some cases, religious observances. However, in the sixteenth century social and religious non-conformity were often closely associated and the Moors of Granada were often suspected, with some justice, of conspiracy, supported by their fellow Muslims in North Africa.

In 1568, the year after Philip had introduced his new measures against Muslim practices, the Moriscos of Granada rose in a revolt. This threatened the security of Christians and Spain and had it been vigorously supported by the Islamic powers might seriously have subverted the state of the Catholic Monarch. But the sultan took the opportunity of Philip's diversion in Granada to attack Cyprus, and Algiers reconquered Tunis.

Philip called in his half-brother, Don John of Austria, who had to summon troops from Italy. The Moriscos, who had already suffered the full rigours of the police methods of the Inquisition and who had in their turn massacred hundreds of their Christian oppressors, were now cruelly put down. They fled for refuge to the mountains of Alpujarras, the campaign of terror taking Don John two years to complete. When

Above, an auto-da-fé, or the burning of heretics by the Spanish Inquisition; the Inquisition's surreptitious methods and its insistence on prosecuting every deviation from the orthodox Catholic line made it hated and feared throughout Europe.

Opposite, Alessandro Farnese, the Duke of Parma (1545–92), one of Philip II's greatest generals; as well as fighting at Lepanto in 1571, he won permanent control of the southern Netherlands for Spain and assisted the Catholic cause in the French Wars of Religion. Musées Royaux des Beaus Arts de Belgique, Brussels.

the revolt was finally broken the Moriscos were forcibly deported and scattered throughout the length and breadth of Spain and their place was taken by 12,000 peasant families from the Christian north.

No sooner had the internal threat been eliminated than Philip received a call for aid from the Christian powers of the eastern Mediterranean against the Turkish force besieging Cyprus. Mindful of his self-imposed task as defender of the faith, Philip answered the call and despatched a fleet of some 200 galleys to help Venice and the papacy. Again Don John had the command, but he arrived too late to relieve the siege of Cyprus so he sought out the enemy in the bay of Lepanto, on the north coast of the Peloponnese. In the epic fight which followed the Christian fleet utterly destroyed its infidel enemy and the fame of the victory spread thoughout Europe. However the fruits of victory were meagre.

When the news of the defeat reached Constantinople the sultan, although furious with his dead Admiral, Ali Pasha, was not dismayed. 'The beard is singed,' he observed, 'it will grow again.' The observation, famous in another context in which the exultant compatriots of Sir Francis Drake may have missed its full import, was very just. Despite the loss of 210 ships the Turks were not long in repairing their shattered navy. The King of Spain, distracted by the continuing rebellion of his Christian yet heretic subjects in the Netherlands, only gained the recapture of Tunis as the fruits of victory.

The Holy League of allies which had defeated the Turk broke up on the death of the pope in the following year and Venice had to resign herself to the loss of Cyprus. Meanwhile the victorious admiral who had urged that the victory should be followed up by an attack on Constantinople and the destruction of Ottoman power, was despatched to the more prosaic task of putting down rebellion in the Low Countries.

Revolt in Aragon

In the sheer extent of the territories which he controlled and the forces which he could command, Philip of Spain excelled all the world's rulers except possibly the emperor of China. Yet so grandoise were his aims that they exceeded even the huge revenues which flowed annually into the Spanish treasury. In the early years of his reign he himself reckoned that the crown was in debt to the tune of seven times its national income, and some years later he was paying more interest than his combined total revenues. It is estimated that the Armada alone cost the Spanish exchequer ten million ducats and the yearly drain of the revolt in the Netherlands was a seemingly interminable wastage. Yet to Philip it must have seemed that such expenditure was unavoidable if his aims of a reunited Christendom and a united Spain were to be achieved. He did not intend to be the ruler of heretics and he was determined to be the sole ruler of Spain.

In this second aim his policy was in direct conflict with the intentions and ambitions of the once great partner in the Spanish dual monarchy, the kingdom of Aragon. The Catholic monarchs, Ferdinand and Isabella had carefully defined and separated the interests and autonomies of their two kingdoms thereby faithfully reflecting the wishes of their peoples. At that time it was the Castilians who at first feared the domination of the King of Aragon, but by the end of the sixteenth century the roles had been reversed. The administration of the joint kingdom was dominated by Castilians, the merchants of Barcelona had been excluded from the new world of the Indies, and the oppressive scrutiny of the Holy Office was an ever present reminder of the authority of the Castilian-speaking king.

The main cause of Aragonese discontent was the *fueros*, the ancient liberties of the kingdom which were invoked by the nobility to protect archaic feudal privileges and jurisdiction over the peasantry. The real grudge of the nobles, above all, the lesser nobility who lacked the influence and oppotunity open to the magnates, was their effective exclusion from the high offices of state in favour of Castilians. By and large Philip respected the Aragonese constitution, but he was impatient with the second kingdom's insubordination, and so he decided, in 1588, to impose a non-Aragonese viceroy on the country. The justiciar's court refused to acknowledge the validity of the title and regionalist opposition mounted. It broke out into rebellion two years later around the

person of Antonio Perez, the king's once powerful and ambitious secretary.

Perez had been under arrest for some years for his initiation of the murder of Don John of Austria's secretary. Philip, who had at first been inclined to believe Perez's fabrications of treason against his half brother, was implicated but was now determined to eliminate his deceitful adviser. When, therefore, Perez escaped and fled to Aragon and the justiciar, urged on by members of the lesser nobility, refused to surrender him to the king, Philip fell back on the Inquisition, the only body whose powers overrode the *fueros*.

The arrest of Perez on a trumped up charge of heresy led to rioting in Saragossa, but most of the other towns of the kingdom as well as the leading magnates declared themselves for Philip against the 'knights of liberty' (minor nobility and gentry) who had released Perez. Philip's forces marched on the capital, put down the rebels and executed the justiciar. Two years later an invading force under Perez was easily defeated, with the aid of Aragonese contingents, and at the *cortes* of June 1592 the constitution of Aragon was modified though not suppressed.

The Invincible Armada

'You are engaging upon the most important undertaking by God's church for many hundreds of years, with every conceivable pretext for a just and holy war.' The words are taken from one of the many sermons preached in the pulpits of Lisbon during the spring of 1588 to encourage the soldiers and crews of the great Armada which was assembling there.

Philip had maintained a pacific if not exactly amicable policy towards Elizabeth of England since her accession, even at one stage offering to marry her as he had done her Catholic sister Mary; and from the point of view of Spanish supremacy in Europe there was good reason for his policy. The natural heir to Elizabeth, Mary Queen of Scots, was undoubtedly a good Catholic but, in view of her close ties with the powerful French family of Guise, Philip could hardly have regarded her as the ideal queen of England. To expand Spanish resources on setting a friend of France on the throne of England would be a quixotic way for Spain to further the victory of Catholicism. Not only was Philip not prepared to open the way to Mary, but he was also reluctant to undermine the authority of Elizabeth. This was even though the activities of her seadogs Hawkins and Drake in the Spanish Main had brought him to the brink of supporting the rising of 1569. Yet in the following year, after it had failed, he dramatically opposed the papal excommunication of Elizabeth, forbidding the publication of the Bull in Spain and even trying to prevent its reaching England.

The accession of Pope Sixtus V in 1585 introduced a new factor into Spanish papal relations. Just as Philip would not promote a solution to the English problem which favoured the power of France, so the pope

Above, the great crescent formation of the Spanish Armada of 1588, followed by the much smaller English fleet. The bulk of the Spanish fleet was made up of troop-carrying vessels; only fifty were fighting craft and even these were less manoeuvrable than the English ships. National Maritime Museum, London.

Opposite, the converted Moors, or Moriscos, of southern Spain were forcibly dispersed throughout the country in the 1570s; the episode exacerbated the economic stagnation caused by the lack of a strong urban middle class in Spain.

was fearful of seeing the massive power of Spain gain new influence in the north. In the words of a modern historian, 'The domination of the church by the crown was probably more complete in Spain than in any other part of Europe, including Protestant countries.' So real was the pope's fear of seeing this influence extended to the northern kingdom that Sixtus at first hoped by a diplomacy of concilation to win Elizabeth back to Rome. Philip II could have told him how wrong he was, and the execution of Mary in 1587 finally convinced the pope that there was no way out but alliance with Spain. Yet even now, when the king sought financial aid, it was only to be met with a promise from the wily pontiff that the papal treasury would pay out one million ducats in cash when the first Spanish soldier set foot on English soil. From the first Sixtus was sceptical:

The king and his armada are becoming ridiculous, while Queen Elizabeth knows how to manage her affairs. If that woman were only a Catholic she would be loved by us more than any other sovereign for she has great qualities. . . . That Spanish Armada gives us anxieties. We have strong presentiments that it will not succeed.

Yet, with the annexation of Portugal, Philip's finances had improved and the increase in English aid to the Low Countries reinforced the arguments of those of his advisers who urged that the revolt would only be put down when England had been conquered. In 1586, Elizabeth sent not only money but troops under the command of the Earl of Leicester himself. And then, in February the following year, came the execution of Mary Queen of Scots. Philip, who had shown increasing interest in investigating the enterprise against England, now perhaps saw the great danger of a queen friendly to France removed.

Preparations begin

In March 1587 he ordered the beginning of preparations under the directions of the ageing Santa Cruz, who some years previously had drawn up the first specifications for such an enterprise. Either his enthusiasm had waned or, more likely, the full complexity of mounting the expedition only became apparent when work was started in earnest. Whatever the reason, Santa Cruz was unable to press on with the preparations as quickly as the impatient king demanded.

Matters were not helped when, in May, Cadiz harbour was raided by Drake who destroyed not only several great ships but also the vital seasoned timbers 'from which the barrels for the fleet's provisions were to have been made. The King of Spain's beard had been well and truly singed and the daring exploit ended in tangible profit when Drake captured the treasure carrack *San Felipe*. This was only the most sensational of the innumerable delays which dogged the fitting out of the Armada so that, despite all the king's urgings, the fleet was still not in a fit condition to sail when in February 1588 Santa Cruz died. His successor, the Duke of Medina Sidonia, was appalled by what he found—rotting provisions, fevered crews, ships in need of repair and, above all, pitifully few large guns.

The Spaniards at the time, and many historians since, have made Medina Sidonia the scapegoat for the failure of the whole expedition. The appointment was indeed inapposite as the poor man himself was painfully aware; he confessed to being totally inexperienced in sea-going command and begged to be spared the responsibility. But King Philip insisted and the duke had no option. However, there was one thing in his favour—none of the proud and contentious officers of the fleet could object to taking orders from a man who outranked them all in social station. And Medina Sidonia used his authority to the best possible effect in procuring a further delay in the sailing date and, as far as was possible, made good the terrible deficiencies which his predecessor had left him. Thus when, on 9 May, the grand fleet finally set sail from Lisbon its equipment and provisions were in as good a state as was possible. Even so it was necessary to put in again at Corunna to take on fresh victuals and water and because of this and the terrible weather conditions it was not until late in July that the great Spanish invasion fleet finally arrived at the mouth of the English Channel.

The epic running fight which followed and the final scattering of the huge Armada by fire-ships in the roads of Calais traditionally belong more to the folk history of Britain, and the names of Drake, Hawkins, Frobisher and Admiral Howard are listed among the heroes. And yet it should be realized that up to the very last moment the English commanders treated the enemy with considerable respect. Indeed they had been unable to inflict any mortal damage on the Spaniards until the dangerous crescent formation was finally shattered and dispersed by the use of fire ships when it was anchored in the roads of Calais.

Despite his inexperience, Medina Sidonia showed immense and justified tenacity in taking his formidable but slow-moving force through the lines of the agile and more powerfully gunned ships which the enemy provided. Both his own presence of mind and the considerable seamanship of his crews ensured that the Spaniards were able to maintain their formation. The fleet itself was carrying troops, but the main invasion force was to be the army which Parma had assembled on the Dutch coast and which was to be ferried across in transport barges.

In so far as the English fleet was still intact Medina Sidonia had failed. Nevertheless, against all the odds, he had brought his escort to the rendezvous point. The fact that his ammunition was now practically exhausted was a result of the failure of the king and Santa Cruz to see that adequate preparation was made for the enterprise. Nor was it the fault of the admiral that his great ships could not get close enough inshore to protect the transports from the Dutch fleet which was patrolling the coast. The king had known the danger from the outset. He had received reports both from Medina Sidonia and Parma stating that since the deep sea ports Brill and Flushing were in rebel hands and there was an insufficient number of shallow draft vessels to combat the Dutch the whole strategy of the invasion was invalid.

Broken in spirit, out of ammunition and desperately short of supplies, the once proud Armada made its terrible way through the icy waters round the north of Scotland and down the murderous shores of Ireland; only half of its one hundred and thirty ships returned to Spain. However, one section of the fleet did complete its voyage, without breaking station or losing a single ship, and that was the guardship squadron of Carrera de Indias. It was by far the most efficient branch of the Spanish navy and had been taken off the trans-Atlantic run for this operation.

Philip did not regard the English enterprise as closed. He took the news of the disaster with his customary calm and is supposed to have commented: 'I sent my ships to fight against men, not the winds and the waves of God.' Indeed he seems to have actually begun roughing out the plans for a second expedition. But, to quote an American historian: 'If any one year marks the division between the triumphant Spain of the first two Habsburgs and the defeatist disillusioned Spain of their successors, that year is 1588.'

Despite the heroic endeavours and considerable achievements of Philip II of Spain, the century which followed his death witnessed the uninterrupted decline of Spanish power and the domination of Europe by his arch-enemy France. The story was complete when in 1702 a Bourbon dynasty was set upon the throne of Spain.

Chapter 6

The Counter-Reformation

In the face of the mounting Protestant menace, the Roman Catholic Church began setting her house in order. The most effective agents of this reform were the Council of Trent and the new Order of Jesus. thanks to their efforts much formerly Catholic territory was recovered, and many pagan peoples were Christianized.

Long before the great renewal of the years 1540 to 1570, there had been stirrings of reform within the Catholic church. In Spain, for instance, in the later fifteenth century, Cardinal Ximenes had entirely revitalized the old structure, correcting monastic abuses, appointing zealous bishops, founding schools and so on. In France too there were reforming prelates like bishop Briçonnet of Meaux. In Italy itself there was the Oratory of Divine Love, an association of pious laymen and clerics which met for the first time in 1517. However, all these movements were fated to remain local as long as the papacy remained unreformed. In the first part of the century the popes continued to be primarily interested in Italian politics and personal pleasure. They thus failed to see the force behind the movement and to make those moves which might early have contained it.

It was under Clement VII (1523–34) that the papacy suffered its worst humiliation, when Rome itself was taken and sacked by troops of the Holy Roman Empire in 1527. To much of Europe this seemed symbolic of the collapse of the ancient church, while the Protestant Lutheran movement was daily gaining fresh adherents in Germany and elsewhere.

Clement VII's successor was a man no less worldly than he but one who was able to appreciate the nature of the crisis. Paul III saw that the time was past for sterile Italian bickerings, and that the papacy's task was now to unite the Catholic world against the Turks and the Protestants. Not that he accepted the divisions within Christianity as final. In his early years, at any rate, he knew and appreciated the works of the Christian humanist Erasmus and hoped for a reconciliation with the Protestants.

Paul was responsible for organizing or approving the weapons used by the old church in its new offensive: the council, the Jesuits, the Capuchins, the Inquisition and the Index. He intervened actively in European politics, excommunicating the King of England, encouraging the Holy Roman emperor to unite with the King of France against the Turk, and censuring the King of France for his immoral conduct. He also set his own house straight. If there were still few saints at Rome, at any rate after his passing there were fewer incompetent and uninterested prelates than there had been.

Ignatius Loyola

This reform of the central organization was greatly assisted by the growth of the Jesuits. It all began in 1521 when a young Spanish soldier, Ignatius Loyola, was severely injured while attempting to hold Pamplona against the French forces. Deprived at the age of thirty of the possibility of pursuing his chosen career of arms, Loyola took up reading during his convalescence and soon began to experience the same kind of spiritual anguish as that suffered by Luther.

Like the great German reformer, Loyola started from a deeply-felt realization of the sinfulness of man and of his helplessness if deprived of God's grace. Going on from there, Loyola found great comfort in the redeeming message of Christ and in the conviction that salvation was possible through apostolic action. Hence the development of his determination to consecrate his life *ad majorem Dei gloriam*: to the greater glory of God, the future motto of the Jesuits.

Like a good soldier, he converted these personal reflections into a practical manual, which he called the *Spiritual Exercises*, much as one might speak of exercises with the sword, pike or musket. This little manual, which became the devotional guide of the Jesuits, is not a catechism, concerned with faith and doctrine, but is essentially what its title promises: a course of spiritual exercises designed to train the future soldier of Christ.

Loyola realized that he could accomplish nothing without further study, and so, his enthusiasm having become suspect in Spain, he came to France, to work on theology, philosophy, the natural sciences and languages at the Sorbonne. There his capacity for hard work and his unfailing geniality greatly impressed his young fellow-students, several of whom began to fall under his spell as a leader of men. Six of them became particularly attached to him: François de Jassu from Navarre (the future Saint Francis Xavier), the Spaniard Diego Lainez, Pierre Lefèvre from Savoy, the Spaniards Nicolas Bobadilla and Alonso Salmeron and Simon Rodriguez, member of a great Portuguese family.

On 15 August 1534 these seven went up to Montmartre, and there took together three vows, of poverty, chastity and of a pilgrimage to the Holy Land. Then they set out for Venice, whence they planned to set sail for the Middle East. Along the way they

Above, a Jesuit missionary, painted by Jusepe de Ribera. Such missionaries were highly educated and disciplined; their main policy in the sixteenth century was to gain positions of power within the royal households and to establish schools. The most successful Jesuit campaign was staged in Poland in the 1580s. Museo Poldi, Pezzoli, Milan.

gathered companions for the adventure and gave themselves the name of the 'Company of Jesus'.

However, when the time came to leave, Loyola had doubts. Not only was he short of funds, but friends suggested that things had changed so radically over the past few years that there was now as much to be done in Europe as in the Holy Land. Loyola thought for a while of entering the new Theatine order but in the end resolved to found his own, whose basis would be obedience to the pope. Perhaps it was rather a military concept, this idea of creating around the head of the church an impregnable citadel. Anyway, Paul III rapidly saw what great use the Order could be to the papacy, and on 27 September 1540 he granted it official recognition in the Bull 'on the government of the church militant'.

It took ten years or so for the Company to settle down and work out its organization. Loyola borrowed here and there such features of the other orders as seemed appropriate but never lost sight of the primary function of the Jesuits—support of, and obedience to, the pope. New members were chosen not only for their moral but also for their physical qualities: they had to be sturdy to work effectively.

Within the Company, fasting and contemplation were minimized so as to allow the maximum possible time 'in the world'. The Jesuit training lasted for fifteen years, beginning with the mastery of the *Spiritual Exercises* and going on to study the classics, philosophy and theology. After that the young aspirant might well teach in one of the

many colleges the Jesuits set up, before finally being ordained a priest. After that, he could still advance in rank within the Company, perhaps eventually to become its 'general'. The use of this title for the head of the Jesuits was very characteristic, as was the idea that within the Company advancement came through merit, efficiency and excellence. Of the virtues, humility seemed less important than strength of mind.

This organization was marvellously well calculated to serve the papacy's ends. 'Provinces' were set up all over the world, and in them missionary activity went on apace. Very soon the Jesuits won a name for their schools, which flourished not only in Europe—and especially in France and Germany—but also in all the regions penetrated by Catholic Europeans. Within Europe virtually the whole of the Catholic governing classes came to send their children to Jesuit schools, and in countries of mixed religion like France they often received Protestants as well. So they came to wield a remarkable influence over the ways of thought of the people who counted in every country. They also proved adept at penetrating the highest social circles, often as confessors to kings and noblemen.

But the activities of the Jesuits were not confined to elegant salons. All over the world they were to be found, from the snowy wastes of Canada to the jungles of India, preaching, instructing, converting. Some entered even too wholeheartedly into the customs of their regions and had to be repudiated by their provincial superiors. Many were martyred by the savage peoples among whom they lived. All were a testimony to the dynamism of Loyola's vision and the effectiveness of his organization.

The Council of Trent

Meanwhile, following great difficulties overcome largely by the insistence of Paul III, a general council of the church had been called at the little town of Trent, on the borders of what are now Italy and Austria. the opening sessions were bedevilled by the oroblem of what should be done about the Protestants and by the unwillingness of the French and Spanish sovereigns to let their 'national' prelates commit themselves to any greater degree of papal control.

However, as the sessions went on the council began to get to grips with the most pressing problems in organization and doctrine. The reform of abuses was perhaps the easiest and certainly the most effective aspect of the council's work. Henceforward the popes were men of irreproachable moral character. The cardinals were elected according to less worldly standards. The bishops were chosen for their evangelical zeal and for their learning. Above all, the council reformed the whole position of priests. Henceforward they had to undergo severe training in special seminaries, and their celibate status was confirmed.

The doctrinal aspect of the council's work was in some ways less satisfactory. But it had at any rate the great advantage of letting Catholics clearly know what they had to believe, rather as the *Institutes of the Christian Religion* gave clear instructions to Calvinists in what they must hold to be true.

The council reaffirmed the theological importance of tradition, which might be just as directly inspired as the Bible. A definitive edition of the scriptures was prepared and published in 1592. Against Luther, the fathers took care to redefine the place of faith in its traditional terms, in no sense to be isolated from works. Against Calvin, they were at pains to emphasize both the freewill of man and the infinite mercy of God, which made predestination unthinkable. Finally, they reaffirmed the validity of all seven sacraments, insisting particularly on the real presence of Christ in the sacrament of the Eucharist.

After the announcement of the council's decisions after 1563, Catholics knew how to think. The doctrinal messages of Trent were successfully spread throughout Catholic Europe not only in catechisms but also by paintings, sculpture and music. Architecture itself was pressed into the service of the renewed church with the adoption of the baroque, the so-called 'Jesuit style'.

Alongside these positive aspects of the ancient church's revival went two repressive measures, the Inquisition and the Index. First used against medieval heretics, the Inquisition had already been revived in Spain in 1478 and in 1542 was extended to all the Catholic countries under the name of the 'Holy Office'. There is no doubt that it succeeded in stamping out Protestantism in Spain and Italy, but at a cost to the freedom and spontaneity of society there that only late became evident.

Much the same reflections come to mind

in considering the work of the Index devised in 1557. Although it doubtless ensured the destruction of many worthless books, it also encouraged the kind of censorship fatal to the growth and development of social and cultural institutions.

Philip II

Given the political and religious divisions of Europe in the second half of the sixteenth century, it was inconceivable that the Counter-Reformation could remain a purely spiritual affair. So it was that the cause of Trent came to be taken up by Philip II of Spain, who in extremely uneasy alliance with Rome became the champion of the ancient church's revival.

Against the pagan Turks, Philip was remarkably successful. In 1571, with the aid of the Venetian fleet and papal diplomacy, he inflicted such a defeat on the sultan's fleet at Lepanto that the western Mediterranean was henceforward free from large forces of Turkish warships.

He was less successful in his campaigns against the heretical Europeans. Elizabeth of England long held him in suspense with her enigmatic religious policy, and when he finally decided to invade in 1588 the Invincible Armada came to grief.

In the Netherlands the revolt of 1566 eventually led to the establishment of the autonomous United Provinces in the north of the country, even though during four decades Philip II had tried to impose Spanish rule and Catholicism on the whole of the Low Countries. However, if the

Above, the Battle of Lepanto in 1571, at which an alliance of the Papacy, the Spaniards and the Venetians defeated the Ottoman fleet. The victory gave the Catholics a greater confidence in dealing with opposition inside Europe as well. National Maritime Museum, London.

Left, an interrogation by the Inquisition; faced with the spread of independent thinking through widespread education and the popularity of printing, the Inquisition fell back on a belief in authority and tradition to test an individual's adherence to Catholicism.

Opposite, the Council of Trent, painted by Titian in 1586. Despite its interruptions and delays (the Council was convened in 1545–47, 1551–52 and 1562–63), it managed to arrive at a firm restatement of Catholic doctrine, as the original intention of a reconciliation with the Protestants was abandoned. Musée du Louvre, Paris.

63

seven provinces of the north escaped him, the ten of the south did not, and in the so-called 'Spanish Netherlands' there developed a thriving culture epitomized early in the next century by the work of Rubens.

In France, too, the Spanish intervention was not altogether unsuccessful. The two expeditions led from the Low Countries by the Spanish general Parma retrieved the situation for the Catholic forces before Paris (1590) and Rouen (1592), and even if Henry of Navarre did eventually become King of France it was not without having to abjure Protestantism. Philip II played his part in this abjuration, which opened the way to a great flowering of Catholicism in early seventeenth-century France.

This spiritual revival owed a good deal to the work of the Jesuits, who from the mid-sixteenth century onwards had been establishing schools and colleges in the areas particularly affected by Protestantism. However, it owed much as well to other orders, some of which reflected very faithfully the new spiritual zeal of the period.

Typical of these orders was the Congregation of the Mission, founded in 1624 by St Vincent de Paul. Its members were to evangelize the French countryside in total obedience to the diocesan bishop. St Vincent de Paul, in collaboration with Louis de Marillac, also founded in 1633 the Company of Daughters of Charity, to work among the poor. He was a very dynamo of a man,

founding seminaries, reforming older orders and organizing charitable work for all the needy: foundlings, beggars, prisoners, galley-slaves, old soldiers and so on.

Another remarkable figure in French Catholicism of the early seventeenth century was Pierre de Bérulle. Founder of the Oratorian order in France (1611), he also encouraged Madame de Sainte-Beuve to found the order of Ursulines, which by the mid-seventeenth century had over 250 schools in France. The Ursuline schools did not aim to turn out well-educated women but young women of strong moral character, resolved to run their families, and to reform society, in accordance with Catholic principles. The educational principles of the Ursulines owed much to the advice of St François de Sales, whose combination of mysticism and dynamic charitable activity is very typical of this phase of the Catholic renewal.

Both the Oratorian and the Ursuline orders derived from Italy, where again the influence of the decisions taken at Trent was strongly felt. There the outstanding bishop was St Charles Borromeo (1538–84). Nephew of Pius IV, Borromeo had attended the closing sessions of the Council of Trent and then returned to Rome. There, in 1562, he went through the *Spiritual Exercises* and emerged a changed man.

Taking priest's orders, he reduced his life to one of ascetic simplicity and besought

the pope to let him return to his See of Milan. Permission was finally granted on the accession of the saintly Pius V (1566–72), and Borromeo at once set about reforming the archdiocese.

Provincial and diocesan councils were regularly held. Three seminaries were established, and when they could not easily be staffed by Jesuits Borromeo founded his own order, the oblates of St Ambrose, to fill the posts. He encouraged the order of Barnabites to preach their spectacular missions within his diocese. He founded a congregation of Ursulines. He encouraged and commissioned the work of ecclesiastical musicians, including Palestrina. He established a whole series of elementary schools within his See. In short, he was actively and energetically concerned with anything which could revive Christian life in the archdiocese of Milan. It is easy to comprehend the great effect of the Counter-Reformation when we reflect that Borromeo was only one of many prelates who were taking similar action all over Catholic Europe.

In Spain the Catholic reformation took a rather different form. The church had been largely reformed in the days of Cardinal Ximenes and had been 'purified' since then by the ferocious activity of the Inquisition. Consequently, the great Counter-Reformation figures of St Teresa of Avila and St John of the Cross, while not negligible from the point of view of reform, especially

MISERICORDIAS DOMINI · INETERNVM CANTABO

in the monasteries, are chiefly remarkable for their mystical writings. Some indeed have affirmed that, with the Inquisition raging as it was, mysticism was the final refuge for personal religion.

The political Counter-Reformation was not very successful in England or the United Provinces. It also failed to affect Scandinavia and the north German provinces. However, a combination of political and cultural penetration was very successful for the Catholic cause in southern and central Germany during the later sixteenth century. This advance was led by the Jesuits and Capuchins, who skilfully won the friendship of secular rulers and then, by establishing their remarkable colleges and universities, won back whole regions for the ancient church.

The great name associated with this movement is that of St Peter Canisius, provincial of the Jesuits in Germany, Austria and Bohemia after 1556. Not content with founding colleges, he produced a masterly catechism in 1556 and conducted successful preaching tours all over his province. Steadily Catholic influence and Jesuit colleges penetrated central and even northern Germany, until by 1600 the disunited Protestants were everywhere in retreat. Alas, this peaceful reconquest was destined to come to a violent end, for the Catholic revival was sowing the seeds for the 'thirty years' war'.

IVLIVS TERTIVS PONTIFEX MAX

Chapter 7

France from 1500 to 1640

On paper France in the early sixteenth century appeared to be an unusually unified state. The English, who in previous centuries had controlled much of the northern and western regions of France, were now confined to the town of Calais, and the important Duchy of Brittany was virtually absorbed into France in 1488 (formally becoming part of the kingdom in 1532). The kings Louis XII and Francis I were commanding figures who were engaged in a long struggle for primacy in Europe with the Habsburgs and the Tudors, fighting in the Low Countries and in Italy. Although in the long run these wars were to prove indecisive, France made one permanent gain after the victory of Marignano in 1515, which Francis followed up by the Concordat of Bologna made with the Pope the following year. According to its terms, the French monarch was given an unprecedented degree of autonomy in controlling the major ecclesiastical appointments within his realm. With this vast new field of royal patronage, with his strong standing army, and with his style of monarchy symbolized by the palace of Fontainebleau which he built in the Renaissance manner, Francis I seemed set fair to create a powerful new monarchy in control of the largest nation in Europe.

The reigns of his successors showed both the unity of the kingdom and the authority of its monarch to be precarious. Geographically, France was a disparate country, with many regional cultures and economies, and many of these regions, dukedoms, provinces, counties and cities retained their ancient rights and privileges. Throughout the sixteenth century the Crown would be faced with the problem of asserting itself over local loyalties and interests, often in areas that would prove intractable to permanent military conquest. Many approaches were tried: military control, alliance with the local aristocracy, a crude appeal to the prejudices of the people; but none satisfactorily created a genuine consensus of government.

One technique invented by Francis I and developed by the last Valois kings as well as their Bourbon successors was the sale

of offices, in the royal courts, the central administration and local government. This was an attempt at one stroke both to create a new group of officials loyal to the king, and to raise extra revenue for the Crown. It did not wholly succeed, however, in forging a new authority in the regions distinct from that of the old nobility. Indeed, many nobles themselves bought the right to dispose of these offices, and thereby acquired a new sphere in which to build up their own power blocs – a fact which contributed to a French version of the 'bastard feudalism' that had been seen in fifteenth-century England. The Valois kings failed to use the opportunity of these new offices to introduce a drastic reform of local administration; their interests lay more in the financial expedients and in buying the loyalty of the individual office-holders, rather than in establishing a new or centralized bureaucracy.

Meanwhile the old social order was gradually changing. Throughout the sixteenth century the population of France continued to rise, perhaps by as much as a third between 1470 and 1560. At the same time France was suffering, like the rest of Europe, from rising prices. In the countryside these two factors combined to depress the peasantry, for whom land was scarce, and to hold wages down; in many areas medium-sized farming units tended to become consolidated into much larger holdings controlled by the nobility, thus further reducing the likelihood of the emergence of a stabilizing group of wealthy peasants. Many were driven to the towns, but only Lyons and a few other large centres could offer substantial industrial employment. On the other hand the bourgeoisie, the merchants and the lawyers, and those who had been able to benefit from the military contracts, had done well out of the price rise. As the towns

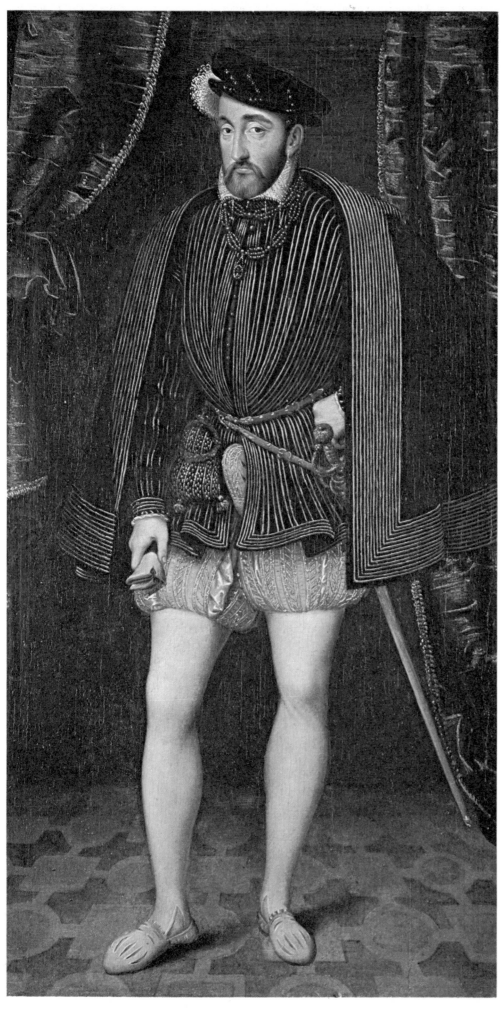

Opposite top, a dance at the court of Henry III (reigned 1574–89); throughout the civil wars the royal court flourished, although it never attained the spectacular qualities of the court of Elizabeth I of England. Musée du Louvre, Paris.

Opposite centre, Francis I of France (reigned 1515–47); he was a typical Renaissance prince, eager for glory in war and not above allying himself with the Turks against the Holy Roman emperor to win it. Galleria degli Uffizi, Florence.

Opposite below, Claude of France, the wife of Francis I and the daughter of Louis XIII, who was the cousin of Francis. Cathedral of Saint-Denis.

Left, Henry II of France (reigned 1547–59), the muscular king whose main contribution to the history of his country was to marry Catherine de' Medici. However, she did not win any great importance until the reigns of their sons. Musée du Louvre, Paris.

developed in size, wealth and social complexity, so they experienced their own social tensions. These were expressed both in the form of conflicts between various groups of inhabitants, and also in a strongly voiced sense of civic pride and independence, often heard in the *parlements* of the seven largest provincial cities.

Even so, many of the wealthy bourgeoisie tended to leave their home towns and buy estates in the country. As in England this gave rise to a widespread fear that these 'new men' would fail to fulfil the landlord's customary obligations to his tenants, a fear that contributed to the feeling that things in general were changing for the worse. Some bourgeois won admittance to the ranks of the aristocracy, and anxiety was felt that even that bastion of the traditional social order was being undermined, as yet other recruits to its ranks came from those who had bought titles to go with their royal offices, and from those who made entirely fraudulent claims to noble status.

The kingdom, then, was weakened by a variety of local and group interests, all anxious to advance, or at least protect, their position in a climate of social and economic change. Though not intrinsically hostile to royal authority, they would be prepared to obstruct any royal initiatives that threatened their position. This obstructiveness took many forms: local and courtly factionalism (especially among the nobility, whose readiness to rebel might lead so far as to treat with a foreign power); a reluctance to authorize (on the part of the *parlements* and Estates) or to pay royal taxes; and, among the lower orders who had few other forms of political expression, a frequent and alarming willingness to riot. The king's court itself was riven by long-standing hostilities into three camps: the Guises and their supporters,

the Bourbons and the Montmorencies, each of whom had a provincial power-base more solid than the king himself could command as well as their own systems of patronage. A monarch needed a strong character to assert his rule over this nation.

The challenge of Protestantism

The Concordat of Bologna may have satisfied those whose hostility to the Papacy was primarily nationalistic, but it did nothing to improve the spiritual or pastoral condition of the French church, for Francis used his new command over clerical appointments for political rather than religious ends. Ignorant, impoverished and hypocritical parish clergy were as notorious in France as elsewhere in Europe. Some regions of France, particularly in the south and south-west, had a legacy of heresy from the Middle Ages deeply rooted in the local culture; and the advent of humanist ideas among the educated and made available in print made French intellectuals ready to listen to new religious ideas. The realm of the Most Christian King was as fertile a ground as any for questioning the teachings of Rome.

Lutheranism entered the country in the 1520s, but spread only slowly. From 1534 Francis adopted a policy of rooting it out by force, even though the *parlements*, on whom fell the main task of carrying out the policy, were half-hearted in their support of it. From the 1540s the influence of Calvin, himself a Frenchman and based close to France in Geneva, became more prevalent and won support initially from the artisan and poorer urban classes. Energetic and well-educated Calvinist missionaries founded Reformed churches in towns all over France, and soon won over many noble families, old and new, to their

faith. In the 1550s these nobles tended to wrest control of their local churches from the ministers, and thereafter members of the nobility such as Condé and Coligny emerged as national leaders of the Reformed church. With other great families, notably the Guises, supporting repression of the Calvinists (or Huguenots as they came to be called), the religious issue became firmly entrenched as an element of the complex power struggles of mid sixteenth-century France. And though the Huguenot nobility introduced Calvinism into their estates and seigneurial lands, the spread of the new religion tended to highlight the divide between town and country, with churches flourishing in almost every major town in the 1550s, whereas the peasants adopted Calvinism with much less enthusiasm.

The coming of the civil wars

Francis I was succeeded in 1547 by his son Henry II, who vigorously continued his father's policy of pursuing the Protestants as heretics, though the main result was to strengthen their discipline and popularity. After the Treaty of Cateau-Cambresis of

April 1559 in which he at last made peace with the Habsburgs, he was about to launch a major offensive against the Protestants when, in July of the same year, he was killed in a joust and was succeeded by his fifteen-year-old son Francis II.

Francis' reign, which lasted only eighteen months, revealed the instability of the position of the France monarchy, as factionalism at court went out of control and the strongly anti-Huguenot Guise family dominated the royal council. Their supremacy led the Protestants to prepare to defend themselves by arms, and to strengthen their ties with the anti-Guise grouping at court. Calvinism was still spreading quickly throughout the nation, winning widespread support particularly in the towns of the south; and at this point its leaders entertained the hope that the royal council itself could be won over. In 1561 Catherine de' Medici, regent and mother of the new king nine-year-old Charles IX, usurped the power of the by-now highly unpopular Guises and called an assembly of the Protestant and Catholic church leaders to attempt to reconcile their differences. This 'Colloquy of Poissy', which was attended by Theodore Beza on the part of the Protestants, was concerned mainly with theological dispute but failed to bring any tangible results; but it was followed by a royal edict granting relative freedom of worship throughout the kingdom. These acts began Catherine's long fight to achieve a moderate solution to the religious tension and to win for the Crown

a modicum of independence from the aristocrat factions.

Even so fighting between Catholics and Huguenots broke out in the spring of 1562. Paris quickly became a Catholic power-base, but the early fighting left several cities, including Lyons, Rouen and Orleans, in the hands of their Huguenot inhabitants. It became apparent that Huguenot power was to be found in the peripheries of the kingdom, in Normandy, in much of the region from the Loire to the Dordogne, in Gascony, and in a broad stretch eastwards from there through Montauban to Avignon and up the Rhône as far as Lyons. However, the Huguenots were rarely in total control of any district – they would lose Lyons shortly afterwards – and with this limited geographical base and after a spate of iconoclasm with which many Huguenots greeted the outbreak of hostilities and which lost them much moderate support, their aspirations to become the new national church were effectively ended. On the other hand they would prove extremely hard to destroy as a military force. Henceforward, the wars of religion, consisting of campaigns waged by the nobility and the royal army in the name of the religious cause, would be paralleled on both sides by a high level of sectarian violence, the incidence of which was outside the control of the military or political leaders.

The progress of the wars

In 1563 the Duke of Guise was assassinated and Montmorency (the other Catholic leader at this time) a captive of the Huguenots, and Catherine de' Medici had a chance to assert the royal position as head of the Catholic cause. She attempted to end the warfare by offering (in the Edict

Above, the Massacre of St Bartholomew, on 24 August 1572, in which the Catholics murdered several thousand Huguenots in Paris and the provinces; the event led to the outbreak of the fourth civil war.

Above left, Henry IV (reigned 1589–1610): although he was able to bring the civil wars to a close by leading the growing party of politiques, who preferred peace to religious conviction, he could not secure his throne until he renounced Protestantism in 1593. Musée du Louvre, Paris.

Opposite above right, Gaspard de Coligny (1519–72): a successful admiral who was converted to Protestantism in 1559. He led the Protestant cause with the Duke of Condé in the 1560s, but his murder was eventually ordered by Catherine de' Medici who feared his policy of war with Spain. Bibliothèque Nationale, Paris.

Opposite below right, Charles IX (reigned 1560–74): his affection for Coligny was the main cause of Catherine's hatred for the admiral and her plot to murder him. The king was made to assent to the plot by his mother. Musée Condé, Chantilly.

Opposite left, the massacre of St Bartholomew and the murder of Coligny in his bed; Coligny was the prime target for the Catholics, and his idealism made him much loved among the Huguenots.

of Amboise) freedom of worship to the nobles, but otherwise allowed the Huguenots the right to hold services only in towns in specified areas. This was accepted only grudgingly on either side, and even though she attempted to boost personal loyalty for the king with a long progress of herself and Charles through southern France in 1564-5, Catherine could not prevent the emergence of a popular extremist Catholic party, especially strong in Paris and prepared if need be to ally with Spain against her in order to destroy the Huguenots. Henceforward the Catholics could pose a threat to the French monarchy at least as dangerous as that of the Protestants.

Warfare broke out again in 1567 as the Huguenots began to fear this alliance with Spain, and Catherine was driven to support the extreme Catholic position. The Huguenots, led now by Coligny and Condé, established their headquarters at La Rochelle on the west coast in 1568. A peace was made once more in 1570; the king's sister was married to the Bourbon Henry of Navarre, one of the Protestant leaders, and Coligny won a respected place at court. Plans were made – encouraged, it was thought, by Coligny – to unite the kingdom by launching an attack on the Spanish in the Netherlands, who were embarrassed by the outbreak of their own religious-provincial revolt. But on 22 August 1572 Coligny was wounded by an assassin hired by the Guises; and two days later, following reports that the Huguenots planned reprisals on the royal family, Catherine and Charles ordered the gates of Paris to be closed. The 'Massacre of St Bartholomew' began, in which 2,000 Huguenots were killed in Paris alone, and similar violence broke out in many cities, including Lyons and Orleans.

The massacre ended any Huguenot dreams of using influence at court to win their cause, and it identified Catherine and Charles permanently with the extreme Catholic position. La Rochelle was besieged for seven months from November 1572, but it did not fall. The hardening of the ideological divide, and the evident military stalemate gave rise to a new party, prepared openly to oppose the Crown but in favour of toleration and peace. This was led by Alençon (the king's youngest brother) and his party was known as the *politiques*. In certain regions, notably the Languedoc, the *politiques* prevented the implementation of the royal policy of suppressing Huguenot military power, and instead concluded a separate peace with the Protestants. This so frustrated the royal cause that after the death of Charles IX and accession of his brother Henry III in May 1574, a new peace was agreed.

Despite an attempt by the Guises to set up a 'Holy League' to force the king to impose religious uniformity on France, an attempt that was thwarted when the king declared himself head of the League, Henry contrived to maintain the peace virtually unbroken for eight years. But he failed to use the opportunity to develop the independence of the Crown or to rebuild the broken ties and trust with even those parts of the nobility who were anxious for a permanent end to the warring. The truce therefore came to an end when

Alençon, who had been Henry's heir, died in 1584, leaving Henry of Navarre, who was now the Huguenot leader, the heir to the throne. The prospect of a Protestant king of France brought the re-emergence of the Catholic League, this time motivated not by the nobility but by townsmen who throughout the wars had shown a consistent degree of extremism and violence. The League allied itself with Spain, produced its own rival claimant to the throne, took control of many towns of northern France, and forced the king to revoke the toleration on which the peace of 1576 had been based.

The war of the three Henries

Despite his uneasy alliance with the League, Henry III mistrusted its aims and its threat to traditional authority and legitimacy. He raised his armies against it, and there followed the 'war of the three Henries', in which he, Henry of Navarre and Henry, Duke of Guise who was at the head of the League, all jockeyed for power in a three-cornered contest. In May 1588 Guise entered Paris against royal orders; the Parisians resorted (for the first time in their history) to building barricades and drove the king out of the city. Henry III was constrained to make Guise commander-in-chief of the royal army and to summon a meeting of the Estates General which was expected to enforce the full programme of the League. By the time it met, however, the League's ally Spain had been humiliated in its attempt to send the Armada to invade England; the Estates proved unwilling to vote the funds needed to conduct the large campaigns that would be necessary to extirpate the many Huguenot strongholds; they voted instead for a reduction in taxation.

To overcome this new stalemate and to relieve the humiliations he had suffered, the king had Guise murdered in December 1588. The result was that many League towns, including Paris and a large swathe of northern France, declared outright opposition to the king, and began to develop ideas of republicanism. Many moderate

Above, a dance at the court of Henry IV of France; Henry won the support of most of the French nobility through his policies of compromise and planning for the future. Musée du Louvre, Paris.

Opposite, Henry IV of France (reigned 1589–1610), defeating the Catholic League at the Battle of Arques in 1589. Henry was unable to complete the victory over the League, which received assistance from Philip II of Spain, but he was able to conciliate the Catholics instead by renouncing his Protestantism. Château de Versailles.

71

Catholics declared for the king against the League; Henry allied himself with Henry of Navarre, and together they laid siege to Paris in 1589. They were about to assault the city's defences when a monk who supported the League assassinated Henry III.

The re-establishment of royal power

Henry of Navarre, now Henry IV, had a reputation as a great soldier with a strong army; but he was forced immediately to raise the siege. Although unwilling at this stage to alienate his core of Protestant supporters by undergoing a personal religious conversion, he was able to allay the initial Catholic fears of the accession of a Protestant king by undertaking to protect the Catholic religion throughout France. He won important victories against the League at Arques in 1589 and Ivry in 1590, and the League called on support from Spain against him; but Henry's successful defence against the renowned armies of Parma combined with the unpopularity of the League's overt use of foreign intervention won over to Henry increased support from the country at large, particularly among the northern nobility who had been reassured by his *politique* approach to the religious question.

Within the League the military frustrations and the desperate conditions caused by the long wars and a series of poor harvests brought their own tensions, particularly between the poorer townsmen and their bourgeois leaders. This culminated in the execution of two senior members of the *parlement* by the Paris mob in 1591, an act which lost the League much support from the wealthier classes.

Faced with ebbing confidence and finding that Spain's support proved both militarily ineffective and politically inept, the League began to negotiate with Henry in 1593. He responded in July of that year by taking the decisive step to securing his throne by renouncing his Protestant faith. He entered Paris in triumph in 1594, where he took good care to be generous to many of the Leaguers and buy their loyalty. By now it was evident that further opposition to his rule would be limited, and he won new support with campaigns against Spain in 1595-8. In 1598 he finally ended the wars of religion by issuing the Edict of Nantes (from a town which had itself been a League centre). This gave liberty of conscience to Protestants throughout the realm, and gave them the right to worship in certain areas. Special courts were to be set up to deal with sectarian questions, and the Huguenots were allowed to maintain a hundred strongholds as security.

This was hardly a new solution, nor was it especially popular with any party; the

parlements were reluctant to ratify it. But Henry had succeeded in creating a consensus in support of his rule, and in destroying the ambitions of his rivals. He was now able to begin to assert royal authority over the many local rights and privileges that had grown up and might have destroyed his settlement. The wars of religion, which had been followed with a great deal of interest by all of France's powerful neighbours, had not, after all, succeeded in destroying the nation's territorial integrity; but they did spell the end for the early sixteenth-century belief that the ruler should dictate the religion of his people. On both sides the wars had brought justifications for rebellion, and even for tyrannicide; but other thinkers, notably Jean Bodin, began to advocate toleration and to argue that the monarchy should be a sovereign power within the state and, though it should be restrained by concern for the welfare of the realm, local interests had no right to protect themselves against the state.

Henry IV

Despite the Edict of Nantes and his own Protestant background, Henry was forced by both the Catholic majority among the nobility and the dictates of France's diplomatic situation not to appear too tolerant to the Huguenots. He was anxious to protect France against a revival of the traditionally hostile strength of Habsburg Spain, and most of the policies of his reign after 1598 were developed with this in view, rather than in a search to resolve the country's domestic difficulties. He supported the Dutch Protestant rebels against

Spain, married Marie de' Medici, the daughter of the Duke of Tuscany, one of his greatest creditors, and sought to use French influence to disrupt Spanish authority over the welter of small states on France's eastern border which formed Spain's vital communications link with the Netherlands.

Although he adopted a policy of generosity to his old enemies, internally Henry did not court popularity from any single power-group in the country. He took care to prevent the nobility banding together against his rule, and sought to disrupt old systems of allegiance by forging new marriage links among the nobility. But, despite the occasional sharp move against a rebellious noble, he was not able to take decisive action to end the intrinsic independence of the leading aristocrats of France. He tended to rely for his government on a group of families who had traditionally been associated with the royal administration, and a central figure emerged in the form of the *surintendant de finances*, the Duke of Sully, who was a long-standing associate of the king, and came to be the most prominent representative of the Huguenot interest at court. Sully and Henry worked together on re-creating the economic substructure of France, building roads, bridges and canals; and in strengthening the royal military establishment, greatly expanding the fleet in the Mediterranean, the arsenals and the fortifications of the frontier provinces. Certain industries, notably silk and tapestries, emerged under royal patronage, and parts of Paris were ambitiously rebuilt; but little was done to increase prosperity in the older trades and industries. Sully also

introduced a new financial expedient in the form of the *paulette*, a controversial arrangement under which an official could buy over a number of years the right for his son to inherit his office; and in general, Sully's financial management combined with Henry's inexpensive foreign policy contrived in large part to restore the royal finances.

Henry IV has gone down in French history as a great monarch, re-uniting France after its recent turmoils and creating new prosperity. This view today seems exaggerated, as it is now clear that France as a whole saw very little economic growth in the first half of the seventeenth century; and the continued instability of the realm even under his rule can be seen in the reactions to the last crisis of his reign. In 1610 he seemed to be ready to intervene in the German state of Jülich-Cleves to support the Protestant candidate for the dukedom against that of the Spaniards. Although this policy accorded well with his anti-Habsburg policy, it caused distress to the Catholic advocates of a European-wide counter-offensive against Protestantism. On 14 May 1610, before his intentions in the crisis were clear, Henry was fatally stabbed in his coach in Paris, by a Catholic countryman who insisted under torture that he had acted alone but had felt impelled to kill Henry, according to the Jesuit doctrine of tyrannicide, for his betrayal of the Catholic cause. The prospect

of a minority under Henry's nine-year-old son Louis XIII seemed likely to re-open all France's old wounds.

The regent, Henry's widow Marie de' Medici, was not able to prevent a return to noble factionalism, despite abandoning Henry's military ambitions in the Empire and creating a new marriage alliance with Spain. The Huguenots feared a renewal of the repression and strengthened their defences, but the first challenge to Marie's rule came in 1614 from the Protestant Condé. Henry's work in preventing any nobles from maintaining solid power-blocs paid off, however, and Condé's revolt evaporated, resulting only in an unsatisfactory summoning of the Estates General, its last meeting before 1789.

In 1617 Louis decided to break free from his mother's control and, inspired by his falconer whom he made Duke of Luynes, he exiled Marie who rallied the opposition and conducted a war against the king in 1620. By this time, the emerging crisis of the Thirty Years' War should have demanded both a more positive French foreign policy, and a careful approach to the issue of the Huguenots; but by subduing the Huguenot lands of Béarn, Luynes drove many Protestants, led by the Duke of Rohan, back into revolt. By 1622 they had lost many important strongholds, and this revolt together with the news from the Empire hardened the anti-Protestant line of many Catholics.

Richelieu

Marie de' Medici had returned to the royal council in 1622, and two years later was joined by her protégé, the Cardinal Richelieu, whose political and administrative talents were already well known. Richelieu's initial moves were to undertake an anti-Habsburg and pro-Protestant foreign policy, marrying the king's sister to the future Charles I of England, agreeing to help the beleaguered Elector Palatine and cutting the Spanish communications link by taking the strategic Valtelline region. But with the threat of a Spanish riposte he allied once more with Spain, and took the opportunity to eradicate Huguenot military strength. In 1627 he laid siege to La Rochelle, the Huguenot capital, and despite the chaotic intervention of the English against him, he took the town in 1628 and razed its defences. There were sporadic Huguenot risings in the south in the ensuing years, but their military presence in France had effectively been destroyed. Richelieu, whose priorities in both internal affairs and foreign policy concerned protecting the interests of the state and cared little for religious enthusiasm, issued the Peace of Alais of 1629 to confirm the freedom of conscience that had been enshrined in the Edict of Nantes; he thereby ended religious strife in France for a generation.

The king's wars of the 1620s had created a huge financial strain, and gave rise to new protests at the means used to raise royal finances. The main expedient of these years was to exploit the *paulette* to raise as much as possible from royal officials, a policy that led to considerable opposition in the courts and *parlements* and a reluctance on the part of the officials to suppress local unrest as at Dijon and Aix.

This new tendency on the part of the localities to rebel against central government led Richelieu to introduce *intendants* as financial officers of the crown who could cut across old jurisdictional boundaries.

Discontent at this attack on traditional privileges, fear of the implications of his foreign policy and distrust of his toleration of the Huguenots brought opposition to a head in 1630 when Marie de' Medici, his old patron, sought Richelieu's downfall and replacement by Michel de Maraillac; but on the critical 'Day of Dupes' in November 1630 the King opted to retain the services of the Cardinal.

Thereafter Richelieu had unprecedented power. He was in control of all the major offices of state, and built up a vast network of patronage in many facets of the nation's life. He introduced *intendants* to most regions of France, and widened their powers; they now acted not merely as tax-collectors but as judicial officers and as direct agents of government authority in the regions. He patronized the development of French arts, and founded the *Academie Française* in 1634. He also sought to take charge of public opinion by a programme of governmental pamphleteering. He attempted to develop a commercial expansion, also under royal control, by means of trading companies to encourage merchants and colonization, especially in the Americas. Although these last measures had limited success, they and Richelieu's building of an Atlantic fleet to match that of the Mediterranean did serve to redirect France's commercial vigour. The combination of attacking ancient privilege and expanding governmental activity into new fields allowed Richelieu to lay the foundations for absolutism.

It was done at great cost. In 1630 Richelieu supported the intervention of the Protestant hero Gustavus Adolphus of Sweden in the Thirty Years' War, although he also attempted to compromise and keep France itself free from direct involvement in the war. In 1635 his arachnoid diplomacy collapsed, however, and he was forced to declare war on Spain; and thereafter the cost of the war proved enormous. In 1640 his army consisted of 160,000 men, far larger than ever before. His attempts to stimulate the French economy had brought nothing like the levels of growth that were necessary to sustain such a commitment, and more and more effort was devoted to raising taxes. Between 1630 and 1648, the burden of taxation in France increased by 300 per cent, the vast majority of which was wrung from the peasantry. The problem of feeding and billeting the armies imposed an even more arduous burden; and localized or regional revolts against taxation and billeting, or bread riots against high prices and shortages, broke out regularly from 1630 to 1660.

Despite the size of the armies, France was unable to win any decisive victories in the campaigns that were intended slowly to expand her eastern frontier towards what was seen as the 'natural frontier' of the Rhine. In 1636 a Spanish invasion threatened Paris, but the merchants voted Richelieu large enough sums to deal with the emergency. Nevertheless opposition at court, which had long been brewing around Gaston d'Orleans, the king's brother, and Anne of Austria, the Queen, led to a revival of aristocratic plotting which culminated in 1642 in the rising of the Marquis de Cinq-Mars against the Cardinal. However none of these plots posed a serious threat to his rule which continued until his death in 1642.

Chapter 8

Spain under Philip III and Philip IV

At the beginning of the seventeenth century, the power of the Spanish kings still seemed invincible. Philip III (1598–1621) ruled not only extensive and wealthy regions of Europe but also immense territories in the New World, from which he drew great supplies of silver. It would not have been easy to predict in 1600 that in fifty years' time this great empire would have been generally defeated in Europe. Yet so it was; the Dutch formally gained their independence in 1648, and the French ate into Spanish possessions all along the Rhine. In 1640 the Portuguese broke away, and only in Italy did the Spaniards remain in control of their territories for a little longer.

The latter years of Philip II's reign saw a series of poor harvests in Castile (by 'Castile' is meant the whole group of central provinces) and this time of famine was followed, as so often happened, by a great plague during the years 1599 and 1600. However, these spectacular catastrophes were in a sense not unexpected, for Castilian agriculture had been showing signs of weakness for at least fifty years previously. Whereas at the start of the century central Spain had been a great corn producing region, by 1570 it was heavily dependent on imports of grain from northern and eastern Europe. Many peasants fled from their holdings, driven to despair by the harshness of nature and the demands of the tax-gatherers.

If agriculture was in full decline, industry and commerce were also faltering. By the end of the century the Spanish colonies in the New World had become largely self-sufficient in those commodities which the Spaniards had formerly exported to them. Any attempt by the Spaniards to switch to new products was hampered by the fact that English and Dutch interlopers increasingly tended to encroach on the former Spanish preserve and to satisfy the colonists' fresh requirements with their own products. The Spaniards, like most imperial peoples, were loth to change the attitudes and methods which had won them such remarkable successes.

That is not to say that they were unwilling to think about their predicament. The later sixteenth century saw the publication of many works by the so-called *arbitristas* ('projectors', or formulators of policy), and their advice was always the same: reduce government expenditure, revise the tax-structure so that it was more equitably shared among classes and provinces, encourage immigration and offer new incentives to farmers and manufacturers.

Philip III and Lerma

1598 saw not only the death of Philip II but also the Treaty of Vervins, marking the end of the war with France. Philip's successor therefore had an interval of peace in which to put his house in order. Philip III, however, was not the man to take this chance. He soon allowed himself to fall into the hands of a favourite, the Duke of Lerma, and together they adopted a policy of masterly inertia, hoping in Micawberish fashion that something would turn up to remedy the monarchy's deep-rooted ills. Needless to say, nothing did turn up, and during the reign of Philip III (1598–1621) Spain's economic and social discontents went from bad to worse.

The royal bankruptcy of 1607 forced upon Lerma the one constructive act of his period of power: the conclusion of a truce with the United Provinces in 1609. That year also saw the expulsion of the Moriscos, an act which has for generations been seized on by historians eager to perpetuate the Black Legend of Spanish ignorance and bigotry. The Moriscos were in fact Moors who had been forcibly 'converted' to Christianity

Above, Philip III of Spain (reigned 1598–1621). Hampton Court Palace.

Top, The European possessions of Philip III.

Opposite left, the Luxembourg Palace, Paris, built between 1615 and 1620 for Marie de' Medici.

Opposite right, The Duc de Richelieu (1585–1642), known as the 'eminence grise'. Musée du Louvre, Paris.

after the reconquest of 1492. Needless to say, the loyalty of these 'New Christians' was suspect, and it is certain that in the early seventeenth century they were intriguing not only with the Muslim Turks in north Africa but also with the French Protestants in Béarn.

To these good political reasons for their expulsion were added less reputable economic ones. Many Valencian lords whose tenants were Old Christians were envious of the prosperity apparently brought to their neighbours by Morisco tenants, and many small men among the Old Christians were frankly hungry for the Moriscos' land. So in 1609 the expulsion was carried through, and of a total Morisco population of about 300,000 perhaps 275,000 were obliged to take ship for the inhospitable shores of north Africa.

In the Black Legend this act has been made to look like an economic catastrophe. But in fact its effects are very difficult to assess, for most of the Moriscos, although hard-working, were not great proprietors or businessmen, and it is possible that many of the jobs and plots of land which they vacated were filled quickly enough. All the same, what might have been a politically acceptable act in a prosperous country was one of grave imprudence in a kingdom whose economy was declining as rapidly as Spain's was; if the expulsion was not a political crime, it was certainly an economic blunder of the first order.

Philip IV and Olivares

Philip III died in 1621 and was succeeded by his son Philip IV. That year too the truce of 1609 with the Dutch expired, so that the young king was at once faced with the need

to confront his enemies. Philip IV was more intelligent than his father but had the same lack of drive. Therefore it was fortunate that he chose as his chief minister the dynamic Duke of Olivares, who had been a gentleman of his household.

Throughout his ministry Olivares was torn between two conflicting aims. He appreciated the arguments of the *arbitristas*, and realized that economic, fiscal and administrative reforms were essential if the Spanish monarchy were to retain its power.

At the same time, he inherited the Castilian ambitions for European and indeed worldwide leadership. In fact, it was impossible to pursue these two goals simultaneously, as time would show.

From the start Olivares was obliged to face up to the Dutch and to order a considerable increase in expenditure on the Atlantic fleet. Simultaneously, he authorized a great expansion in the army of Flanders, so that for 1622 projected expenditure was about double projected income. To meet this deficit, he cut royal pensions drastically and pushed through some of the minor reforms called for by the *arbitristas*.

What was needed, however, was to persuade the other provinces, and particularly

Catalonia and Portugal, to help Castile to shoulder the increasingly heavy military burden. Thus during 1624 Olivares worked out the details of the so-called 'Union of Arms', which was to be achieved by all the different components of the monarchy combining to support an army 140,000 strong. Early in 1626 he and the king attended meetings of the *cortes* or parliaments of Aragon, Valencia and Catalonia and succeeded in extracting from them, if not full assent to the Union of Arms, at least substantial contributions for the common military effort.

Meanwhile some of Olivares' other projects were going ahead well. In 1625 Spanish troops captured Breda from the Dutch, and that same year there was founded at Madrid the *colegia imperial*. This was a Jesuit academy for the sons of nobles, designed to provide not only a humanistic education but also a training in the military arts. Olivares hoped that this college would remedy what he sometimes called a 'lack of leadership' among the Spanish people. By 1627 he could boast of considerable reforms achieved at home and of significant victories won abroad.

The year 1628, however, proved to be the turning-point in his administration. In that year it looked as if he could at last concentrate seriously on domestic reform, for the English were disunited, the Habsburgs were victorious in Germany and Richelieu was fully occupied by the Huguenots in France.

This great and final chance for a drastic reorganization of domestic policy was however lost, because Olivares could not resist intervening in the war which broke out over the succession to Mantua (1628–31). Thereafter Spain became increasingly involved in the German aspects of the Thirty Years' War and was obliged to squander what remained of her resources in the struggle against the French and their allies.

At first this struggle did not go badly, and in 1636, as we have seen, a Spanish force seriously threatened Paris. However, by the late 1630s it was clear that Spain's enemies were getting the upper hand, as each year brought a fresh disaster. In 1637 came the loss of Breda, recaptured by the Dutch, 1638 the fall of Breisach, and with it the loss of Spanish control over the route between Italy and the Netherlands, 1639 the defeat of a great Spanish fleet in the Downs and the end of any hope of sending relief to Spanish troops in the Netherlands.

But it was 1640 which was the really disastrous year. Castilian troops had been sent into Catalonia to repel the French attack from the north. As no money was available, they had been billeted on the Catalans, and in the early spring of 1640 many clashes took place between these troops and their unwilling hosts. At first Olivares reacted with severity, but as this only aggravated the populace he eventually ordered the viceroy to attempt to appease

Above, the Spanish flagship in action in the Battle of the Downs in 1639, at which the Dutch demonstrated their control of the Channel and ended Spanish hopes of prolonging their resistance to Dutch independence. Nederlandsch Historisch Scheepvaart Museum, Amsterdam.

Opposite top left, the expulsion of the Moriscos, or converted Moors, from Spain in 1609; Philip was unwilling to be king of a country peopled by converts of dubious faith. For the most part the Moriscos had inhabited the southern regions of Spain, especially Granada. Museo del Prado, Madrid.

Opposite bottom left, the Duke of Olivares (1587–1645), painted by Velasquez. Olivares was chief minister of Spain from 1620 to 1641, and his need to promote Spain's interests in the Thirty Years' War resulted in widespread opposition to his rule, especially in the non-Castilian parts of Spain. Hispanic Society of America, New York.

Opposite bottom right, The Relief of Cadiz in 1625, painted by Francisco de Zurbaran in 1634. Museo del Prado, Madrid.

the Catalans by concessions. Too late; the viceroy was himself hunted down and killed, while the rebels proclaimed Louis XIII Count of Barcelona, which now formed part of the republic of Catalonia.

Richelieu had encouraged and organized the revolt of the Catalans; he seems also to have subsidized the Portuguese rebellion, which broke out in December 1640 and resulted in the establishment of John IV as an independent king. With his resources already strained to the limit. Olivares could do little about this secession; he struggled on for a couple of years but then resigned in 1643 and died half-mad in 1645. So ended his valiant attempt to bring order into the chaotic peninsula under a unified central government.

Rocroi and after

The year of his resignation saw the defeat of the hitherto invincible Spanish infantry at Rocroi; thereafter it was just a question of how soon Spain could make peace and how humiliating would be the price she would have to pay. The successor of Olivares was his nephew, Don Luis de Haro, and this discreet, self-effacing courtier was well-suited to retrieve what could be recovered from the general wreck.

In spite of another bankruptcy in 1647, in the following year he succeeded in persuading the Dutch, who by now were beginning to fear the rising power of France, to make a peace. It was at Münster in October 1648 that the seventy-year long struggle was formally ended, when Spain at last recognized the independence and sovereignty of the United Provinces.

Meanwhile there was for a time doubt whether Madrid could recover Catalonia, let alone Portugal. Throughout the mid-1640s the eastern provinces, Aragon and Valencia as well as Catalonia, seemed to be tottering off into independence. However, Olivares' very failure to establish a unified central government was now, paradoxically enough, the saving of the monarchy. In the eastern provinces the

nobility had retained a considerable degree of independence, and the aristocracy there now saw that a loose confederation with Madrid was preferable to a perilous autonomy, in which revolutionary elements might begin to have more influence.

So the Valencians and Aragonese came once more to acknowledge a loose dependence on the government of Haro. Meanwhile the Catalans had lost much of their French support when Mazarin's government became preoccupied with its own internal troubles, and after a slow and painful campaign the Castilian troops were able to recapture Barcelona late in 1652. Thus the possibility of the peninsula reverting to a political structure of three or more sovereign units was averted, the provinces not only fearing to encourage their own revolutionary element but also realizing that dependence on a powerful French monarchy would in the long run be more harmful to them than a loose attachment to the feeble crown at Madrid.

During the 1650s, indeed, the French government was so weakened by internal problems that the Castilian armies were even able to push Mazarin's forces back here and there. By 1659 it was possible for Haro to conclude a relatively favourable peace with France. This so-called 'Treaty of the Pyrenees' recognized that Spain had lost Artois as well as Roussillon and parts of Cerdagne, but this settlement seems moderate bearing in mind Spain's desperate position in 1640.

Her main loss was, of course, the kingdom of Portugal, which remained independent under the Duke of Braganza, John IV. Castile had only acquired Portugal in 1580, and sixty years had not been long enough to reconcile the traditional hostility between the peoples. Moreover, Portugal was independent in a way that Catalonia could never hope to be; she not only had a ready-made dynasty in the Braganza family but could also look to her Atlantic connections for a sound economic basis to her power. In fact, during the 1650s the Portuguese succeeded in reversing the trend of the previous decades when they expelled the Dutch from Brazil; after that they were well set on the way to real independence and a moderate prosperity.

The Spaniards did not recognize Portuguese independence until 1668. By then Philip IV had been dead for three years, having been succeeded by his son Charles II, an apparently sickly individual whose death would be daily awaited by European diplomats for the next thirty-five years. The infanta Maria Teresa had in 1660 married Louis XIV of France, thereby encouraging those French pretensions to the Spanish throne which would only be shattered by the long and costly war of the Spanish succession early in the next century.

All that, however, is another sad tale. No historian who has described the sequence of Spanish decline can resist trying to understand why it came about. For most eighteenth-century 'enlightened' writers, it was the inevitable result of superstitious religion, allied to 'Spanish sloth'. Clearly this explanation is inadequate to explain the transition from the triumphant Spain of the mid-sixteenth century to the wreck of the mid-seventeenth century. However, it does bring out two features of Spanish society which crucially influenced the development of the peninsula: its peoples were devoted to the old church, and they did prize the military virtues above commercial techniques.

Nor was this surprising, given their history: that of a small Christian kingdom, at first penned into the northwestern corner, gradually recovering land from the Moors until the triumphant reconquest of Granada in 1492. During this process, lasting for many centuries, Spanish Christianity acquired a zeal and a militancy which were not found in the more settled regions of western Europe like France or Italy. In a sense, it was this long formation in the struggle against the Moors which made the Spanish conquest of the New World so successful. The conquistadores and their followers were clearly the product of a Catholic and military society such as existed at that time.

However, what had been virtues in 1300 or 1500 were beginning to become vices by 1600. By then the need was for a society which could adapt itself to changing circumstances in order to strengthen its empire in Europe and overseas; more specifically, for a society which could strengthen its economic framework by adopting new techniques in agriculture and industry as well as commerce. It is not surprising that Spanish society, founded in response to quite different challenges, could not rapidly make this transition. Its failure is characteristic of the inability of imperial peoples to adjust to the new realities of power.

So while Dutch and English interlopers drove an ever more thriving trade with the Spanish colonies, industry and trade in the peninsula declined, and political problems

became more and more pressing. For the sake of convenience we have used the terms 'Spain' and 'Spaniard', but in fact the political structure of the peninsula was such that these terms do not mean much during the sixteenth and seventeenth centuries. The fifteenth-century union of Castile and Aragon was a dynastic marriage, never consummated on an economic and political level. For all intents and purposes, 'Spain' really meant 'Castile'; the Aragonese continued throughout the period to be excluded from both the burdens and the fruits of empire.

Eventually, of course, the burden of colonizing the New World and subjecting the Old became too much even for the Castilians, and they tried—most notably in the time of Olivares—to draw the rest of the peninsula more fully into their plans. By then though it was too late; defeat in war, economic decline and the inevitable tensions of a mixed society combined to bring on the collapse of the 1640s. It has been well said that 'Castile has made Spain, and Castile has destroyed it'.

The end of the golden age

The sixteenth century saw remarkable achievements in almost every aspect of human activity. There were great mystics like St John of the Cross and St Teresa of Avila, great political theorists like Francisco de Vitoria and Bartolomé de Las Casas, great architects like Juan de Herrera; the list seems endless and extends as well into the natural sciences. The reigns of Philip III and Philip IV witnessed a less varied cultural activity and were chiefly

Above, The Surrender of Breda *(1634), painted by Diego Velasquez (1599–1660). Museo del Prado, Madrid.*

Opposite left, Philip IV of Spain (reigned 1621–65), portrayed by Velasquez. During his reign Spain had to acknowledge the independence of both the United Provinces and Portugal, which had rebelled in 1640, but he was able to avoid permanent French control of Catalonia. Museo del Prado, Madrid.

Opposite right, The Burial of the Count of Orgaz *(1586) by El Greco (1545–1614). Portraits of the notables of Toledo are here juxtaposed with a grand vision of heaven. Santo Tomé, Toledo.*

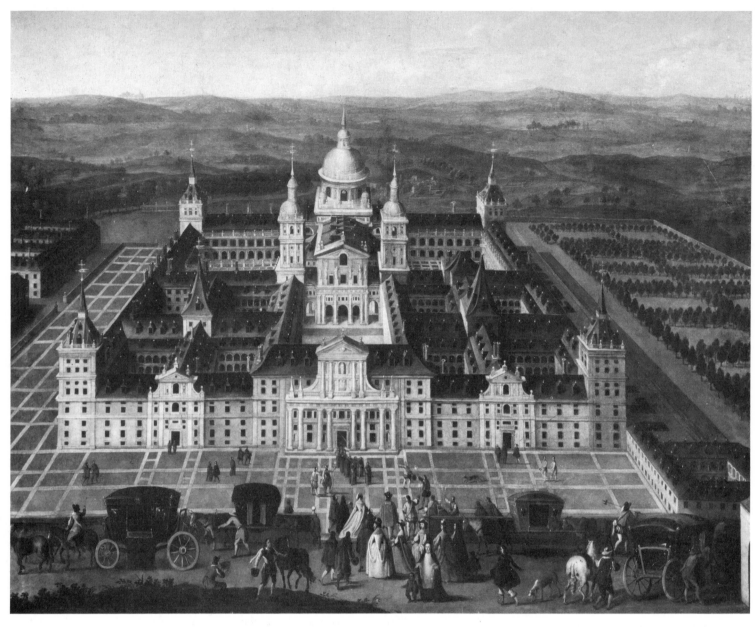

remarkable for their literature and their painting. No doubt this had something to do with the economic situation. The fact, for instance, that the Plaza Mayor of Madrid (1617–19) was the one major new enterprise undertaken at this time probably reflects Spain's increasing impoverishment.

Literature, however, does not demand investment on a large scale, and the wealth of writers in early seventeenth-century Spain is extraordinary. Miguel de Cervantes lived until 1616, producing his works not only during the heroic decades but also during those of disillusionment. *Don Quixote* he created an immortal figure, humanely mocking knightly ideals. This baroque sense of 'illusionism' pervades the work of Cervantes' successors, writers like Lope de Vega Carpio (1562–1635), Francisco Quevedo (1580–1645) and Pedro Calderon de la Barca (1600–81). All were obsessed by the contrast between fact and fancy, between the ideal and the real, between the world as it was and the world as it might have been. So Calderon could write his celebrated and symptomatic *Life Is a Dream*, and Quevedo

could typically exclaim that 'our life is but a comedy, and the whole world a comic theatre'.

It is, perhaps, not too farfetched to suggest that seventeenth-century Spanish writers took refuge in fantasy because the realities of the Spanish situation were too harsh to be faced. It is certainly true that they remained impregnated with the idea that all human activities are vain in comparison with the transcendent reality of God, and some of them carried this conviction over into their lives. Calderon, for instance, entered holy orders in middle age after serving in the royal armies. So one may assume that what was psychologically true for some of the leading writers was also true for the many Spaniards who shared with them these polarizing loyalties.

The concepts of honour and faith underlying much of the literature of the period also inspired seventeenth-century Spanish painters. El Greco (1545–1614), near-contemporary of Cervantes, showed the way in his mystically realistic canvasses, one of the most characteristic of which is the *Burial of*

the Count of Orgaz. Later in the century the works of Bartolome Murillo (1617–82) provided powerful propaganda for the Roman Church of the Counter-Reformation. Murillo is especially remarkable for the skill and feeling with which he painted the Virgin Mary. The subjects of Francisco de Zurburan (1598–1664), too, were usually religious; either tranquil, determined female saints, or monkish ascetics whose intense devotion is most realistically portrayed.

The greatest of them all, of course, was Diego Velasquez (1599–1660). Velasquez drew his inspiration from the Crown rather than from the church and showed an unparalleled virtuosity in his paintings of the Spanish royal family. One of his most famous canvasses shows *The Surrender of Breda* and is unforgettable for the way in which the lances of the victorious Spanish army dominate the right background. In much of his work, however, there is a strain of disillusionment—look, for instance, at many of his royal portraits—which seems to echo the same strain in the great dramatists. The Spaniards of the seventeenth century had lost the easy self-confidence of their fathers, but in literature and art they were technically supreme in expressing this mood of disenchantment.

The Spanish possessions in Europe

Curiously enough, one of the great master-painters of the age, Peter Paul Rubens (1577–1640), was produced by the small and battered Spanish Netherlands. Deprived by the Dutch of access to the sea, the southern Netherlands were about to enter a period of political effacement which would last until the re-opening of the Scheldt in the early nineteenth century restored to Antwerp access to the high seas.

In Italy the Spaniards still held much territory and were particularly concerned to retain their route to the Low Countries, which passed through Genoa and Milan before continuing through Switzerland, Franche-Comté and Luxembourg. Energetic Spanish proconsuls like the Count of Fuentes ensured that even in the days of Philip III Spanish rule was uncontested in Genoa and the Milanese.

To the northwest of this central bloc lay the duchy of Savoy, whose rulers would tread a delicate line for the next century between France and Spain—a policy of masterly vacillation rewarded at Utrecht in 1713, when the reigning duke received the crown of Sicily and so set his house on the way to becoming Italy's first royal line. To the northeast of the Spanish bloc were the possessions of Venice. During the seventeenth century the proud republic fell into an irreversible decline, as the economic foundations of her power were sapped. Yet she retained her political independence and a degree of agricultural prosperity right down to the nineteenth century.

In central Italy the chief princes were the dukes of Tuscany, Spanish clients, and the popes. After the triumphant years of the Counter-Reformation the papacy too declined, as was exemplified by its exclusion from the peace treaties of the middle of the seventeenth century. All the same, Rome continued to be the centre of a now world-wide network of bishops and religions, exercising a steady if unspectacular influence on all the regions colonized by Catholic Europeans. The great city was also at this period being architecturally transformed, most notably by the genius of Bernini (1598–1680).

In southern Italy the Spaniards controlled the kingdom of Naples and the island of Sicily, and, as in the north, they retained their power through the action of vigorous viceroys like the Duke of Osuna. Naples and Sicily were very heavily taxed during the first half of the seventeenth century, and in 1647 the Neopolitan populace, led by a young fishmonger called Masaniello, broke into spontaneous revolt.

At first the Spanish viceroy, the Duke of Arcos, was disconcerted and indeed narrowly escaped with his life. But then, as it became clear to the Neapolitan nobility that they would not profit by the establishment of the republic, the revolt lost momentum, and in 1648 the Spaniards were able to reassert their power. The repression was horribly thorough, and in Naples as in the rest of Italy the Spaniards experienced little more trouble until their Italian possessions passed to the house of Austria by the treaty of Rastadt (1714).

In the long run, this repressive rule had disastrous consequences for Italy. Her central political and economic position was already being challenged by the development of the Atlantic world, and the stifling influence of the Spanish rule meant that the peoples of the peninsula had no chance of adapting themselves to the new economic, political and cultural patterns. Italy, which in the sixteenth century and earlier had been the mistress of Europe in economic and cultural affairs, had by the end of the seventeenth century become one of Europe's stagnant backwaters.

Above, the piazza of St Peter's Cathedral, in Rome, designed by Bernini and one of the greatest expressions of the Baroque in town planning.

Opposite, the Escorial, a combination of palace, monastery and mausoleum, built by Philip II in 1563–84, shown here in a painting of the seventeenth century. Musée du Louvre, Paris.

Chapter 9

The Thirty Years' War

The title of this chapter, drawn from the conventions of historiography, is misleading. We are concerned here not merely with a 'German' conflict originating in 1618 and ending in 1648 but with a European convulsion which, first making itself felt in 1609, was not settled until 1659. This fifty years' war is incomprehensible without a knowledge of those non-German conflicts which helped to determine its development, chiefly of course the abiding rivalry between the Bourbons (of whom the first was Henry IV) and the Spanish, as well as the Austrian Habsburgs. By the time the dust had begun to settle, in 1660, the political shape of Europe for the next two centuries was beginning to emerge.

The conflict known as the Thirty Years' War arose directly out of the religious and administrative settlement of the mid-sixteenth century known as the Peace of Ausburg. For religious affairs, this treaty aimed at freezing the positions achieved by the Catholics and Lutherans—the Calvinists were excluded—in 1555. Evidently, it was severely strained in the decades which followed by the continuing progress of Lutheranism and even more by the development of Calvinism. Moreover, once the tide began to turn in Germany against the reformed churches, the champions of the ancient church could find many infringements of the treaty on which to base their claims to repossess formerly Catholic territories.

The Augsburg settlement was not merely a religious truce but also included provisions for keeping peace within the ten 'circles' of the Holy Roman Empire. In principle each of these was controlled by a presiding prince dependent on the emperor, but in practice the territorial princes—of whom the most outstanding were the seven imperial electors—enjoyed a large degree of freedom. One of the issues at stake in the struggle was precisely this: how close a control could the emperor exercise over his crumbling feudal pyramid?

Within Germany, then, the interests at stake were complex enough. What further complicated the long struggle was the fact that these internal conflicts were overlaid by other rivalries among the European powers. The Swedes and the Danes, for

instance, were crucially interested in the control of the shores of the Baltic. The Dutch could not look on unconcerned while territories in the Rhineland changed hands. The French saw in the German struggle an occasion to prosecute their ancient campaign against the Habsburgs. Even the King of England at one stage intervened in the struggle, singularly ineffectively it is true.

The international nature of the conflict was clear from the start. When in 1608 the Protestant princes and cities formed a defensive pact, the Union, it was to Henry IV of France that they looked for support. Similarly, the Catholic league founded a few months later relied from the start on subsidies from Philip III of Spain.

France and Spain also intervened quite openly in the first dispute to test the strength of these two hostile camps. This dispute broke out over the succession to the Rhineland duchy of Jülich-Cleves, whose duke died without heir in 1609. There were both Protestant and Catholic claimants. At first Jülich was occupied by the imperial emissary, but then he was expelled by Dutch troops, aided by a French contingent.

In the early months of 1610 Henry IV of France was mobilizing a large army, with a view to consolidating the Protestant position in the Rhineland and elsewhere. This projected campaign would no doubt have led to a general conflict, but the French king was assassinated before it could get under way. The imperial side was unable to take advantage of his disappearance, since these were the uncertain last months of the unstable emperor, Rudolf II (1576–1612). Moreover, the new rulers, Marie de Medici in Paris and Mathias at Vienna were moderates for the time being. The spectre of a general war thus disappeared.

The Bohemian War (1618–27)

The next major dispute arose over the throne of Bohemia. This predominantly Protestant kingdom, with proud memories both of independence and of the days of the fifteenth-century reformer John Hus, was governed from Prague by a group of Catholic nobles. The Habsburgs claimed that the crown of Bohemia fell by heredity to the Holy Roman emperor, and the Bohemians had in fact accepted both Rudolf II (1576–1612) and Mathias (1612–19) as their king.

Before the death of Mathias in 1619, they had also agreed that his successor should be Ferdinand of Styria, a prince noted for the ruthlessness with which he had crushed Protestantism out of his Austrian territories. Encouraged by the acceptance of Ferdinand, the Catholic group at Prague stepped up their attempts to reconvert the kingdom, and by 1618 their actions had so exasperated the Protestant majority that the latter resolved to break from the Habsburgs. The symbolic occasion of this break was the famous 'defenestration of Prague', when two of the Catholic governors and their secretary were thrown out of the window of the castle in which the Protestant nobles were assembled.

The consequences of this act of rebellion had been weighed by the Bohemian nobles, who in the inevitable struggle with the Habsburgs expected to get help from the Protestant powers of Europe—notably Holland, England and Sweden. Thus when Mathias died in 1619 they proceeded with the election of Frederick, the elector palatine of the Rhine, as his successor, declaring the claims of Ferdinand to be rejected. Almost as soon as Frederick had been elected King

of Bohemia, however, Ferdinand was elected emperor; clearly the latter's first act would be to move against his rebellious Bohemian subjects.

At this stage the behaviour of the Bohemian rebels was foolish and vague in the extreme. Having elected the ineffectual Frederick as their king, they did little to help him. Had they attempted to win over the middle and lower classes in Bohemia to his cause, they might have been able to present a united front to the imperial armies. As it was, rather like the noble rebels of Catalonia or Naples a little later, they refused to abandon their feudal privileges in favour of the common cause. Moreover, they failed to gain that help from abroad on which they were counting. The kings of England and of Sweden were unwilling to involve themselves, and the Dutch were at this period distracted by a constitutional crisis which ended in the execution of the Dutch statesman Oldenbarneveldt after a highly irregular trial for treason.

So in 1620 the imperial armies entered Bohemia virtually unopposed. They brushed Frederick's army aside before Prague at the battle of the White Hill and entered the capital in triumph. The royal family fled to the Netherlands, and the subjection of Bohemia was set in hand. By 1627 it had become a hereditary Habsburg possession, administered by royal officials, with towns and nobles curbed, German the official language and Catholicism the only permitted religion.

The Danish War (1625–29)

The subjection of Bohemia was in a sense a sideshow, since none of the major Protestant powers had cared to come to its help. In the early 1620s the true focus of the conflict was the Rhineland, where hostilities had broken out following the termination in 1621 of the Dutch-Spanish truce of 1609. The Spanish general Spinola undertook campaigns which enjoyed a steady success; he recovered Jülich in 1622 and in 1625 Breda itself fell to Spanish arms.

Meanwhile Olivares had planned a great shipping and trading alliance to break the power of the Dutch. The members of this alliance were to be Spain, the Spanish Netherlands, the Hansa towns and Poland; with this combination Olivares hoped to carry to war into the Dutch preserves in the Baltic and so to ease the pressure on the Spanish colonies in the New World. The Dutch were thoroughly alarmed by this plan, for which Spinola's successes seemed to be laying sound foundations, and so in 1625 by the treaty of The Hague they formed an offensive alliance with England and Denmark.

The chief captain of the anti-imperial forces was Ernest of Mansfeld, and their campaign opened in 1626. They were opposed, however, by the remarkable imperial General Wallenstein, whose colleague Tilly in August inflicted a severe defeat on the Danes at Lutter. Meanwhile the allies' other thrusts at the Habsburg perimeter were not very successful, largely because they could not manage to co-ordinate their efforts. The chief feature of the later 1620s was Wallenstein's steady extension and consolidation of his power in north Germany, in accordance with Olivares' plans for an economic and military offensive against the Dutch. Wismar fell to him in 1627 and Rostock in 1628; only Stralsund held out, thanks to the fleets of Denmark and Sweden. By 1629 the anti-imperial league was defeated; the English were willing enough to withdraw, and the Danes accepted the peace of Lübeck, agreeing to interfere no more in German affairs.

The Emperor Ferdinand now took advantage of his excellent position to issue an imperial decree known as the 'edict of restitution'. This document is often represented as primarily religious, enforcing the restoration to the old church of all property seized since 1552 and so re-establishing the power of Catholicism throughout northern and northwestern Germany. However, it also had great constitutional significance, for in recognizing Habsburg rule over that region it seemed to give to the emperor those absolute powers which the German princes had for centuries sought to deny him. Hence the edict stirred up great resentment among the princes, Catholic as well as Protestant, and at Regensburg in 1630 the electors succeeded in forcing Ferdinand to dismiss Wallenstein, whom they rightly saw as the chief instrument of the emperor's forward policy. In the long run, by making plain Ferdinand's religious and constitutional ambitions, the edict of restitution was a great blunder. Ferdinand did not know how to hasten slowly, and consequently lost his great general just when he needed him most.

The Swedish phase (1630–34)

After the withdrawal of the Danes, a new and more formidable antagonist appeared in the north: Gustavus Adolphus, after some months of deliberation, resolved to pit his armies against those of the Habsburgs. The Swedish king had since his accession in 1611 effected a remarkable reorganization of his kingdom. Whereas in countries like France the offices of the ancient nobility—constable, marshal and so on—were being crushed out by the emergence of new bureaucratic forms, in Sweden Gustavus Adolphus contrived to bring off a happy marriage between them and the councils which he set up for the army, for finances, for justice and so on.

This efficient administrative structure was backed by an economy which thrived on Dutch business enterprise and particularly on the lucrative export of Swedish copper. Many of the new industries were based on military products, and Gustavus Adolphus proved adept at reorganizing his army so as to profit by the ideas of Maurice of Nassau, the late Prince of Orange, who had virtually established Dutch independence; the artillery was made relatively light and mobile, the cavalry and infantry were trained to fight in smaller units, and the three arms were brought under more effective battlefield control.

The soldiers of Sweden also enjoyed exceptionally high morale. By his victories over the Poles and Russians the king had rapidly become a great hero-figure, and in their German campaigns the Swedes were

MAGDEBURG.

Left, Axel Oxenstierna (1583–1654), the Swedish chancellor who controlled the administration of his country from 1612 to his death. His financial and commercial efficiency provided the backing required for Gustavus Adolphus' spectacular campaigns. Vitterhetsakademien, Stockholm.

Below, Gustavus Adolphus in action in the Battle of Dirschau. Kungl. Husgeradskammaren, Stockholm.

Opposite, the capture of the Protestant town of Magdeburg by the imperial troops under Tilly in 1631; some 25,000 people were killed and the city was burned down. The Thirty Years' War caused destruction in central Europe unparalleled until the twentieth century.

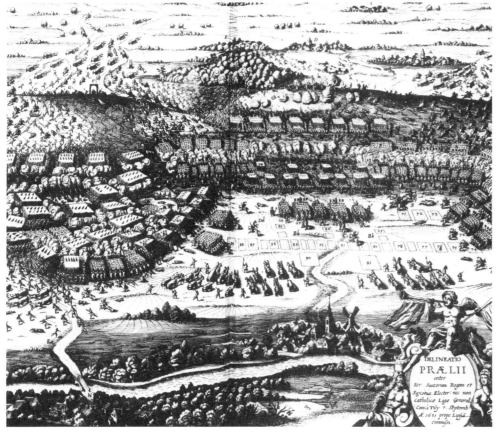

convinced that they came not only to save the provinces from Habsburg tyranny but also to snatch Protestantism from the grips of the Scarlet Woman: the Counter-Reformation. The king and his great minister Oxenstierna were also determined to exclude the Habsburgs from the Baltic and so to foil the grandiose economico-military plan of Olivares.

It was the constitutional and economic aspects of the campaign which were stressed in the preamble to the Treaty of Bärwalde, which was signed in 1631 with the envoys of Richelieu. This treaty was a great triumph for Swedish diplomacy as it secured a large annual subsidy from the French with virtually no strings attached to it. Gustavus Adolphus was therefore well placed for the campaign of 1631. In the spring of that year the imperial troops took and sacked Magdeburg, an event which provided excellent propaganda for the anti-Habsburg cause. In fact it was more of a blunder than a crime on the part of the imperial general Tilly, who had been counting on the city's supplies for his impending campaign and now saw them largely destroyed. Gustavus Adolphus caught up with Tilly just north of Leipzig in September 1631. In the ensuing Battle of Breitenfeld, the new Swedish

tactics proved greatly superior to the traditional Spanish order of battle. Having successfully resisted the first shock of the imperial cavalry, Gustavus smashed their infantry with his artillery and went on to complete their rout with his highly mobile groups of horse.

Then he advanced into the heart of Germany, taking up his winter-quarters at Mainz. Needless to say, there was despair in the camp of the imperialists, who had seemed on the verge of triumph only two years earlier. In April 1632 Wallenstein was recalled and began to reorganize his forces for the new campaigning season.

It is not clear what Gustavus Adolphus' intentions were, but it seems that he was progressing from his earlier notion of a Swedish protectorate over the German princes to the idea of a frank annexation of certain regions of Germany. In any case, his plans never came to fruition, for in the course of his victorious battle against Wallenstein at Lützen in November 1632 he was killed.

Perhaps it would have been better for Sweden if Oxenstierna had now decided to cut his losses and withdraw his forces. But the chancellor decided to fight on, and in September 1634 his army was decisively defeated at Nördlingen by an imperial army with a strong Spanish contingent.

Thus ended the phase of the war in which Sweden played the major role. After many complicated intrigues, the emperor had had Wallenstein legally but unjustly put to death the previous February, and so when the French declared war on Spain in May 1635 the struggle entered a new phase with new leaders.

The French phase (1635–48)

In this new phase religious and constitutional considerations plainly took second place to the Habsburg-Bourbon power struggle. This was shown not only by the fact that the chief opponent of Catholic Austria was Catholic France led by Cardinal Richelieu but also by the conclusion in May 1635 of the Peace of Prague, which in settling German affairs received the assent of the major princes. Thereafter, in short, the main issues were not the fate of the Counter-Reformation or of princely liberties but the question of whether or not Richelieu could break the power of Olivares.

In 1636 the Spaniards carried the war into France, and one of their armies penetrated almost to Paris, while others operated in Lorraine and Franche-Comté. However, with this lightning offensive the Spaniards had shot their bolt, and the ensuing campaigns saw the increasing predominance of the French and their Dutch and English allies. Throughout 1637 the French were successfully recovering their ancient province of Artois, while the Dutch besieged and took Breda. The following year Bernard of Saxe-Weimar took Breisach, thus cutting the 'Spanish road' between Italy and the Netherlands; it was at this siege that the young Turenne, later to become one of France's most successful commanders, first showed his skill. In 1639 the Spaniards lost the last armada of any size that they were able to equip, when the Dutch won a running battle in the English channel. Then the disastrous year of 1640 was followed in 1643 by the Battle of Rocroi and by the fall of Olivares.

By the early 1640s, in fact, most of the belligerents were ready to begin peace negotiations. Ferdinand II had died in 1637, and his successor Ferdinand III, of a more realistic temperament, was ready to renounce vast imperial ambitions in favour of a policy of consolidation of the inner kernel of Habsburg lands. In France Richelieu had been succeeded in 1642 by Mazarin, while the Battle of Rocroi convinced the Dutch that the threat in future might well lie not in Madrid or Vienna but in Paris. So it was that the negotiations at Münster and Osnabrück, whose outcome would be known as the Treaty of Westphalia (1648), slowly got under way.

The Treaty of Westphalia (1648)

After many complicated deliberations it was agreed that the maxim *cuius regio, eius religio* (literally 'of whom the region, of him the religion' meaning that regions should adopt the religion of their rulers) should be abandoned; henceforward dissident subjects were to be allowed freedom of worship, except in the hereditary Habsburg lands. The struggle between the princes and towns on one side, and the absolutist claims of the emperor on the other, was decided emphatically in favour of the former, as the German 'states' were allowed full sover-

eignty. This abdication of imperial claims was completed by the recognition of the independence not only of the Dutch Republic but also of the Swiss cantons.

Each of the main contestants also gained at the expense of the empire. France acquired Alsace and the imperial cities and bishoprics of Metz, Toul and Verdun, Sweden received a large part of Pomerania, and to Brandenburg fell not only the rest of Pomerania but also various smaller territories which almost linked the duchy of Brandenburg with its Rhineland possessions.

The significance of the settlement was clear: if the Swedes eventually failed to hold their acquisitions on the south shore of the Baltic, the French and the Prussians acquired territories which set them on the road to greater expansion in the ensuing decades. After Westphalia it began to be clear, for instance, that not Saxony but Brandenburg-Prussia would be the power of the future in northern Germany. Equally significant was the eclipsing of the empire and of the papacy. The Habsburg turned to that consolidation of their hereditary lands which was to be so successfully accomplished in the next half-century, and the papacy was forced to realize that it could no longer rely on ecclesiastical sanctions in order to make its voice heard in European politics. In diplomatic history the assemblies at Münster and Osnabrück were important as the

first of a long series of reunions at which, following major wars, European statesmen met to adjust their boundaries in accordance with the new realities of power.

The continuation of the Franco-Spanish struggle (1648–59)

There had been no agreement in the Westphalian negotiations between the representatives of France and of the Spanish Habsburgs, and so their struggle continued. Between 1648 and 1652 the French were crippled by their internal dissensions, but once Mazarin had put an end to the *fronde* he was able to turn French arms against the old enemy. At first the struggle was fairly equal, but then in 1656 Cromwell's England joined the French, and in the 1658 campaign the allies' superiority showed as fortress after fortress fell in the Spanish Netherlands.

So it was that in 1659 Spain was ready to come to terms with France and to put an end to a century and a half of broken warfare. The Treaty of the Pyrenees from the French point of view supplemented the territorial gains already made in 1648. This time it was Roussillon and Cerdagne in the Pyrenees and Artois on the northeastern frontier which passed to the French crown, along with certain fortresses in Lorraine

whose possession meant that sooner or later the whole duchy would also be absorbed. The long nightmare of Habsburg encirclement was over. Time would show that the French were as little capable of using their new power moderately as the Spaniards had been in the previous decades.

The effects of the war

For military historians the period between 1609 and 1659 is full of interest. During the preceding two or three decades most of the new military tactics had been worked out in the United Provinces, under the direction of Maurice of Nassau. After 1617, however, the initiative passed to the Swedes, who under Gustavus Adolphus took up and developed many of the Dutch ideas.

The chief of these was the division of the army into small self-contained units. Whereas the Spanish *tercio* consisted of a solid mass of 3,000 or so men, the basic unit in Gustavus' army numbered only about 500 and fought not in a solid mass, relying on weight, but often in an extended line, in which the power of small firearms could better be brought into action. Instead of the older method of slow 'rolling' fire, Gustavus introduced the 'salvo', delivered at close range and calculated to throw the leading ranks of the enemy into disarray.

This missile blow would be followed by the brute shock of a calvalry charge, for the Swedes gave up the device of the caracole, by which the horsemen wheeled up to deliver pistol-shots at the enemy, and reverted to the more effective device of crushing the enemy foot down by sheer weight. Of course, this cavalry attack could only be successful once the front ranks of the enemy pikemen had been severely mauled, and this was the task either of the musketeers or of the gunners, using their mobile field-pieces.

The Swedish factories, under the direction of the Dutchman Louis de Geer, were at this time turning out light, quick-firing artillery, which could quickly be brought up to take advantage of the tactical situation. Needless to say, this close collaboration between infantry, cavalry and artillery called for a high degree of skill on the part of all the soldiers and their commanders, and it was to develop this skill that the Swedish troops were endlessly drilled and put through mock manoeuvres.

This tactical revolution, which was to carry the military art to a level of technical perfection scarcely exceeded before the nineteenth century, was not accompanied by any corresponding change in military organization. Supplies continued to be raised in very haphazard fashion, either by taking them from the surrounding countryside or by uncertain private contractors. Moreover, the very chain of command remained ill-defined. Not only Wallenstein, but also French leaders like Condé were closer in their independence to the *condottieri* of Renaissance Italy than they were to the generals of the later seventeenth century.

The very imperfections of the logistical support meant that armies remained relatively small. A general who could muster 30,000 trained men would nearly always outnumber his adversary. Indeed the strongest French army employed in Germany at this period numbered only 14,000 men. When this figure is compared with the 400,000 soldiers whom Louis XIV is said to have had under arms towards the end of the seventeenth century, it is clear that the so-called 'military revolution', as far as scale of operations goes, did not get under way until the latter half of the century.

Moreover, such armies as were raised tended to be disbanded during the winter, and it was regarded as rather 'caddish' of Gustavus of Sweden that he launched many of his offensives almost out of season.

The relatively small size of armies, and their restricted season of operations, bear on another problem, that of the economic effects of the war. These have commonly been described as nothing less than catastrophic and as retarding for generations the regions affected. In fact, things seem to have been much less dramatic. Population, for instance, seems actually to have increased in the Germanic regions from about sixteen million in 1600 to about seventeen million in 1650. Obviously it is possible to cite instances of dramatic decline, particularly in the theatres of war, but very often such reductions in the number of inhabitants were temporary. Once the armies had gone, people returned home.

Sometimes too districts did lose many of their inhabitants, not because they died, but because they emigrated to regions offering a better livelihood. The number of citizens in Cologne, for instance, declined sharply after about 1610; but this was because many of the wealthiest men and their families were moving to Hamburg, whose commercial prospects now seemed brighter. Often these emigrations were rapidly compensated by a high birthrate; for example, Antwerp lost many of her inhabitants to Amsterdam in the late sixteenth century and yet continued to grow in numbers from about 45,000 in 1600 to about 67,000 in 1700. Clearly the temporary depletion of one town or region might be the making of others.

Even towns directly affected by military operations did not necessarily suffer. Danzig, for instance, was often blockaded in the late 1620s, and yet this does not seem to have prevented a steady increase in her trade. Often, indeed, military operations stimulated commercial activity, by temporarily disrupting the trade of rival centres. This was certainly the case with Danzig itself, which profited greatly by the distraction of the Dutch between 1621 and 1625 and also during the Anglo-Dutch war of 1652–3.

Even physical damage does not seem to have had the dire effects imagined by some historians. Leipzig, for instance, saw great battles fought before her gates (Lützen and Breitenfeld) during the 1630s, and both then and during the 1640s suffered several successful assaults both by the imperialists and by the Swedes. All the same, Leipzig throughout this period continued to grow, overtaking her former rivals Nuremberg, Cologne and Frankfurt, and emerging in 1650 as second only to Hamburg. Clearly the legend of catastrophic destruction has been much exaggerated. In fact towns and individuals which knew how to adapt to new circumstances were able not only to survive but also to flourish during this period, and the region in general made marked economic progress between 1600 and 1650.

The myth of the Thirty Years' War

The legend of the widespread devastation was largely the work of writers like Pufendorf, who were hired to improve the 'image' of the rulers of Brandenburg-Prussia. For historians like this the struggle was between Habsburg tyranny and the high-minded Protestant German princes, in the course of which such devastation was wreaked that it could only be repaired by rulers of the calibre of Frederick William of Brandenburg, known as 'the Great Elector'.

So much then for the myth of widespread destruction; what of the idea that the struggle was one for religious freedom? It would be impossible to assign such motives to the Elector of Brandenburg, who, as one historian has recently said, 'sold himself without any scruples successively or almost simultaneously to Sweden, Poland, Denmark, the Netherlands, the emperor and France'. In the case of the Swedes, there is no doubt that the idea of the Lion of the North come to rescue Protestants from the Habsburg menace had much to commend it as propaganda. But Gustavus and Oxenstierna were in fact at least as concerned with establishing themselves on the southern shores of the Baltic as with 'freeing' their co-religionists in Germany. The same is true of the King of Denmark, whose unhappy intervention seems to have been primarily motivated by a desire to seize the declining Hanseatic towns on the North Sea and Baltic.

The notion that the struggle was primarily one for 'German' constitutional liberties can be discarded also. The shifting alliances, which arrayed the princes now on the side of the emperor and now on that of his adversaries, were clearly the result not of a calculation of long-term constitutional interest but of the impulse to profit by short-term political possibilities or perhaps merely to survive. Any attempt to imprison the

EUROPE IN THE SIXTEENTH AND SEVENTEENTH CENTURIES

Date	Rulers	Political events	Culture and religion
1515	Henry VIII (1509–47)	Battle of Marignano (1515)	Death of Bramante (1444–1514)
	Francis I (1515–47)	Concordat between the pope and Francis I (1516)	Oratory of Divine Love (1517)
	Charles I of Spain (1516–56)	Charles I of Spain elected Holy Emperor (Charles V, 1519–56)	Death of Raphael (1483–1520)
			Luther at Worms (1521)
	Pope Clement VII (1523–34)	Sack of Rome (1527)	
	Pope Paul III (1534–49)	Act of Supremacy (1534)	Recognition of the Jesuits (1540)
			Opening sessions of the council of Trent (1545)
	Henry II of France (1547–59)		Death of Luther (1483–1546)
1550		Peace of Augsburg (1555)	Saint Peter Canisius provincial in Germany (1556)
		French capture Calais (1558)	
	Philip II of Spain (1556–98)	Treaty of Cateau-Cambrésis	
	Elizabeth of England (1558–1603)	Bankruptcies at Lyons and Antwerp (1559)	
	Francis II of France (1559–60)	Conspiracy of Amboise (1560)	
	Charles IX of France (1560–74)	Colloquy of Poissy (1561)	Closing sessions of the council of Trent (1563)
		Edict of Amboise (1563)	Death of Michelangelo (1475–1564) and of Jean Calvin (1509–64)
		Catherine de Medici's great tour (1564–5)	
	Pope Pius V (1566–72)	Meaux incident and battle of Saint-Denis (1567)	
		Treaty of Longjumeau (1568)	
		Treaty of Saint-Germain (1570)	
		Protestants to French court (1571)	
	William the Silent (1572–84)	Massacre of Saint Bartholomew (1572)	
		Siege of La Rochelle (1572–3)	
1575	Henry III of France (1574–89)	Edict of Beaulieu (1576)	Death of Titian (1477–1576)
	Emperor Rudolf II (1576–1612)	Treaty of Bergerac (1577)	Death of Andrea Palladio (1508–80)
	Maurice of Nassau (1584–1625)	Death of the duke of Anjou (1584)	Death of Saint Teresa of Avila (1515–82)
		Treaty of Nemours (1585)	Death of Pierre Ronsard (1524–85)
	Henry IV of France (1589–1610)	Battles of Coutras and of Auneau (1587)	
		Failure of the Armada (1588)	
		'Day of barricades' at Paris and murder of the Guises (1588)	Death of Michel de Montaigne (1533–92)
	Pope Clement VIII (1592–1605)	Battle of Arques (1589)	
		Battle of Ivry (1590)	
		States-General of the League at Paris and conversion of Henry IV (1593)	Death of Palestrina (1524–94)
		Henry IV enters Paris (1594)	
	Philip III of Spain (1598–1621)	Edict of Nantes and treaty of Vervins (1598)	
1600		Charter of the English East India Company (1600)	
		Founding of the Dutch East India Company (1602)	
	James I of England (1603–25)	Gunpowder plot (1605)	
		Philip III repudiates his debts (1607)	
	Pope Paul V (1605–21)	Formation in Germany of the Union and of the League (1608)	
		Expulsion of the Moriscos (1609)	
1600 (contd)		Truce between Spain and Holland, and founding of the Bank of Amsterdam (1609)	Death of El Greco (1545–1614)
	Louis XIII of France (1610–43)	War is averted by the death of Henry IV (1610)	Death of Cervantes (1547–1616) and of Shakespeare (1564–1616)
	Emperor Mathias (1612–19)	Death of the Concinis (1617)	
		Defenestration of Prague (1618)	
		Assassination of Oldenbarneveldt (1619)	
	Emperor Ferdinand II (1619–37)	Battle of the White Hill (1620)	
		Spaniards capture Jülich (1622)	
	Philip IV of Spain (1621–65)	Richelieu becomes chief minister (1624)	
1625	Charles I of England (1625–49)	Battle of Lutter (1626)	
	Frederick Henry (1625–47)	Siege and capture of La Rochelle (1627–8)	
		Wallenstein captures Wismar (1628)	
		Edict of restitution and peace of Lübeck (1629)	
		Treaty of Bärwalde, sack of Magdeburg and Battle of Breitenfeld (1631)	Death of John Donne (1573–1631)
		Battle of Lützen and execution of Montmorency (1632)	
		Battle of Nördlingen (1634)	
		Peace of Prague and declaration of war by France on Spain (1635)	Death of Lope de Vega (1562–1635) and of Jacques Callot (1592–1635)
		Spaniards invade France (1636)	Publication of René Descartes' *Discourse on Method* (1637)
	Emperor Ferdinand III (1637–57)	Dutch recapture Breda (1637)	
		French capture Breisach (1638)	
		Spanish fleet destroyed in the Downs (1639)	
		Revolt of Portugal and of Catalonia (1640)	Death of Rubens (1577–1640)
		Civil war in England (1642)	Death of Van Dyck (1599–1641)
	Louis XIV (1643–1715)	Battle of Rocroi and resignation of Olivares (1643)	
		Revolt in Naples (1647)	
		Treaties of Münster and of Osnabrück (1648)	Death of Monteverdi (1567–1643)
	Charles II of England (1649–85)	Execution of Charles I (1649)	Death of Grotius (1583–1645)
		Fronde parlementaire (1649)	
1650		*Fronde des princes* (1650–2)	Death of Descartes (1596–1650)
		Spaniards recapture Barcelona (1652)	
		Oliver Cromwell becomes 'Lord Protector' (1653)	
		English capture Jamaica (1655)	
		Death of Cromwell (1658)	
	Emperor Leopold I (1657–1705)	Treaty of the Pyrenees (1659)	
		Charles II enters London and Louis XIV marries the infanta (1660)	Death of Velasquez (1599–1660)
		Death of Mazarin (1661)	Death of Pascal (1598–1662)

struggle in some kind of all-explanatory definition is bound to fail, for it was at the same time a religious, political, constitutional and economic struggle, waged not only in Germany but all over Europe and lasting not thirty but something like fifty years.

The career of Wallenstein provides an excellent example of the mixed nature both of the motives and of the fortunes of the participants in the struggle. Wallenstein was born into the minor Bohemian nobility and received a thoroughly Protestant education at school and university. When he was twenty, he was converted by a Jesuit, who introduced him at the imperial court and secured for him an advantageous marriage. Thereafter Wallenstein's prodigious talents as a financier and military organizer carried him to a series of dazzling conquests; Duke of Friedland in 1625, by 1630 he owned enormous areas of north Germany and had arsenals from which he supplied all sides in the struggle. He was equally unselective in his choice of collaborators, who ranged from conventional Catholics to overt Protestants; Wallenstein himself was more interested in astrology than theology.

Wallenstein's fate was as extraordinary as his rise. Having become a sort of co-emperor, thanks rather to his genius than to his alliance with any constitutional or religious movement, he was, as we have seen, dismissed at the demand of the princes, reinstated in the emperor's hour of need and finally murdered when the emperor came to regard him as a dangerous rival. In his extraordinary talents Wallenstein resembles Napoleon, but unlike the great Corsican he lived at a time when the hereditary principle was still too strong for adventurers to clothe their bids for power with a cloak of legality. In its motives and progress his career defies logical analysis; like the so-called 'Thirty Years' War', it cannot be fitted into the neat categories of historiography.

Opposite left, a battle fought within sight of the city of Leipzig, which was then an important cultural centre. The effects of the war, economically and demographically, have been the subject of long dispute among historians.

Opposite top right, Wallenstein (1583–1634), the great imperial general who used his military power for political ends, trying to negotiate with the Swedes on his own account to bring the war to a close.

Opposite bottom right, the assassination of Wallenstein in 1634 in his castle in Bohemia by the agents of the emperor.

Part II

THE NEW EUROPE

Introduction

From the point of view of world history, the outstanding development of the whole period from 1500 to 1700 was the expansion of Europe. Until 1500 man had lived in regional isolation, and Europe had been hemmed in, isolated and vulnerable, by the civilization of Islam, the great Muslim empires and the conquerors from the steppes of Asia. After 1500 the process was reversed and Europe began to press out on the world with a new momentum, which continued unabated right down to 1947.

Traditionally we date the expansion of Europe from the voyages of Columbus in 1492 and Vasco da Gama in 1497, and it is true that the Spanish conquistadores laid the foundations of a great colonial empire in South and Central America between 1520 and 1550, though they destroyed Aztec civilization in the process. But it was in the seventeenth century that voyages of discovery and trading and sheer exploitation gave way to colonization in the true sense of the word and that the Dutch, French and British empires were established. The foundation of Virginia in 1607 (earlier attempts at colonization had failed) and of Massachusetts in 1620, of Acadia (or Nova Scotia) and Quebec in 1605 and 1608, and of New Amsterdam on Manhatten Island in 1612, marked the beginning of a new stage in European and world history.

Parallel with the colonization of the New World was the great movement of Russian expansion across Siberia. One band of Russians reached the Arctic coast in 1645; two years later another reached the shores of the Pacific; and the first stage of Russian expansion in Asia was formally completed by the Treaty of Nerchinsk between Russia and China in 1689. Taken together, these different waves of expansion, eastwards and westwards, were the most important developments of the seventeenth century in the longer perspective of world history. They are also important in a shorter and more narrowly European perspective. The new knowledge of the world which resulted—of the old world as well as the new—and the widening of horizons consequent upon contact with the ancient civilizations of China and the Indies profoundly affected the seventeenth-century European's view of the world and his attitude to himself and his past. In particular, the irreconcilability of the new knowledge with biblical tradition prepared the way for a new, secular view of world history. This was evident from about 1655, when the French Calvinist Isaac de la Peyrère found it impossible to reconcile Chinese history with the story of Adam and Eve, and the Dutch historian Hornius composed the first truly universal history, which included both China and pre-Columbian America.

This change in men's attitude to history, and the secularization of thought which it illustrates, is only one example of a more far-reaching transformation which is usually described as the 'scientific revolution' of the seventeenth century. This revolution, which extended far beyond the limits of natural science and affected the whole intellectual atmosphere of Europe after about 1680, marks a great turning point in the history of European thought and civilization. The age of Newton saw the emergence of most of the characteristic attitudes of the modern mind. Far more than the Renaissance it marked 'the dividing line between medieval and modern', and that is the reason, above all others, why historians today pick out the seventeenth century as the time of 'the foundation of modern Europe'

The great transformation of European life and attitudes came relatively late in the century. Thomas Hobbes' *Leviathan* is often acclaimed as the first enunciation of the modern theory of sovereignty, but two of its four books deal specifically with the Christian Commonwealth and with the Kingdom of Darkness. Hobbes, atheist though he is said to have been, was firmly anchored in the old world of religion and demonology. But with a writer like Locke, whose second *Treatise on Government* appeared in 1689, we are in another, firmly secular and pragmatic, environment. The years between 1651, when *Leviathan* was published, and 1689 are the great watershed. Historians have spilt a great deal of ink trying to probe the causes of the change. We shall probably never know exactly the answer. But one thing that is certain is that Europe underwent a great crisis and testing-time in the 1640s and 1650s, and when it emerged its character and temper, as well as its political structure, were different.

Political and military history is the necessary background for understanding the social and intellectual changes this crisis brought about. It is also of importance in its own right. Here also the seventeenth century saw a process of modernization. both in the internal structure of government and in the balance of political forces, which mark a major advance towards the Europe we know.

In part at least, this process of modernization was the consequence of a military revolution, associated with the name of Gustavus Adolphus of Sweden, the significance of which extended far beyond the purely military sphere. This was a period when the demands of finance, recruitment and equipment for ever growing armies forced governments to interfere increasingly in the lives of their subjects. 'Just as the modern state was needed to create the standing army,' one writer has said, 'so the army created the modern state.' The little principality of Brandenburg, for example, increased its military forces from 900 to 80,000 men within a hundred years, and though Brandenburg was in some respects exceptional a similar process was taking place through the length and breadth of continental Europe.

As a result of the exigencies of war, in other words, modern administrations began visibly to take shape. A second result of the wars of the seventeenth century was the re-drawing of the political map of Europe on lines familiar to us all. At the beginning of the seventeenth century that was not the case. Spain was still the dominant power in Europe, Holland its greatest financial and commercial centre, Poland a force to be reckoned with in the east; and in the north it looked as though Sweden was in the process of carving out a mighty empire on the Baltic. How different the map of Europe would have been, how strangely changed its destinies, if the possibilities inherent in this constellation of forces had been realized! By the end of the seventeenth century it was obvious that they would not be. Germany and Italy, it is true, were still 'geographical expressions,' though their future outlines were reasonably clear. But the circle of Great Powers was closing. Brandenburg under the Great Elector (1640–88) had taken the first steps which later—though no one could have foreseen it at the time—were to make it the nucleus of a new German empire. Austria, having driven back the Turks from the very gates of Vienna, assumed the position in southeast Europe which it was destined to retain until 1918. And Russia, emerging from its 'time of troubles', became an integral part of the Concert of Europe. By the time of the peace of Utrecht in 1713 the European balance of power, the framework of European politics and international relations for the next two centuries, was in existence. The foundations of modern Europe had been laid. It is surprising how firm they remained, withstanding the shocks of the French Revolution and of the Industrial Revolution, until that fateful day in 1914 when the old Europe went into the melting-pot. Today, after the shattering experience of two world wars, we have passed into a new age, a post-European age of global politics, when Europe is faced by a resurgent Asia and Africa and dwarfed by the two great superpowers on its flanks. The old Europe, whose beginnings in the seventeenth century we now trace is no more.

Chapter 10

Seventeenth-century England

In March 1603, on the death of Queen Elizabeth, King James VI of Scotland became James I of England as well. When he travelled southwards the following month he received a rapturous reception from his new subjects. Their enthusiasm was to some extent a commentary on the last years of Elizabeth's reign. As the seventeenth century progressed people looked back on the Elizabethan era as a golden age, but in 1603 there was considerable discontent in England. The last decade of the sixteenth century had brought difficulties for the country. These included the war with Spain—which had begun in 1585—financial problems, the Crown's relations with parliament, increasing corruption in the administration and the social distress which

accompanied a series of bad harvests in the mid-1590s. The queen and her chief minister, Lord Burghley, an ageing conservative whose policies had served the country well in the early years of the reign, had no new ideas to offer to meet changing conditions and, as a result, at the time of Elizabeth's death her popularity was perhaps at its lowest level of the entire reign.

James therefore ascended the throne amidst great goodwill. No section of the community had higher expectations of the new monarch than the Catholics, who had been subjected to intermittent persecution during Elizabeth's reign. James at first held out hopes of a relaxation of the severe Elizabethan penal laws, which threatened their property and even their lives, but as a result of the consequent rapid growth in the number of those who openly declared themselves Catholic he took alarm and the policy of persecution was resumed.

Some of the bolder spirits among the Catholics, led by Robert Catesby, a Warwickshire squire, and Guy Fawkes, an Englishman who had served in the Spanish armies, resorted in despair to the Gunpowder Plot, a scheme to blow up King, Lords and Commons at the opening of parliament on 5 November 1605.

The conspirators leased a cellar under the Parliament House and placed in it twenty barrels of gunpowder with a number of iron bars on top to make the blast even more

Below, James I of England (reigned 1603–25) and VI of Scotland (reigned 1567–1625), and his wife Anne of Denmark, both painted by Nicholas Hilliard. James was unable to comprehend many of the political problems facing him as King of England, and his political, religious and financial policies all left his parliaments infuriated with his rule.

On page 92. The Card Players (c. 1665) by Pieter de Hooch. Musée du Louvre, Paris.

Robert Winter Christopher Wright Iohn Wright Thomas Percy Guido Fawkes Robert Catesby Thomas Winter

Bates

destructive. The government got wind of the plot, the cellar was searched, and the ringleaders were killed or executed. In 1606, in the ensuing anti-Catholic hysteria, parliament passed two further penal statutes and Catholics continued to be persecuted throughout the early Stuart period.

James's initial reluctance to persecute his Catholic subjects reflected to a considerable extent, his genuine hatred of violence, an admirable personal quality which extended to an intense dislike of wars. He was determined to bring the conflict with Spain to a speedy end. This was done in August 1604. The terms of the treaty, which was concluded after negotiations in London, reflected the stalemate which prevailed in the war. James gave practically nothing away, standing his ground on all the points at issue between the two countries, in particular England's claims to trading rights in the New World.

The end of the war and the vast expenses which accompanied it, together with the better harvests of the first decade of the seventeenth century and James's initial popularity, augured well for a successful reign. Unfortunately, however, there was another, much less happy side of the picture. Though he did have good points, James had serious defects of character. He was lazy, he was extravagant, and he had exalted ideas of the divine right of kings—their right to rule unquestioned—which led to conflicts with parliament. James's laziness—he much preferred hunting to the hard work of routine government business—was to some

extent redressed in the early years of the reign by the diligence of his principal minister, Robert Cecil, who was created Earl of Salisbury in 1605. As secretary of state and later as lord treasurer as well, Salisbury toiled away endlessly over his papers while the king hunted and feasted.

James's extravagance had more immediately serious effects. Elizabeth had left a debt of perhaps £350,000. James who scattered money lavishly among the Scottish favourites who accompanied him to England and spent far more on the royal household than Elizabeth had ever done, soon increased this. By 1608, the year Salisbury became lord treasurer, it stood at perhaps £600,000. Salisbury managed to reduce this to under £300,000 by 1610, but there was still a large deficit on the annual budget—well over £100,000.

In these circumstances Salisbury supported the Great Contract, a scheme which was discussed in parliament in 1610; it proposed the abolition of certain antiquated royal prerogatives which were burdensome to the king's subjects in return for a fixed annual compensation of £200,000. The scheme was eventually abandoned because of mutual suspicion between Crown and Commons. It has been argued that, if it had gone through, it might have given the Crown virtual financial independence of parliament. This is speculation—we can only guess what James would have done with the money. One thing is certain. The failure of the Contract marked the end of Salisbury's political power. He remained in

office until his death in 1612, but the king had lost confidence in the man who had been the principal protagonist of the failed Contract.

King and Commons

In 1611 James dissolved his first parliament. His bitter words to Salisbury about it reflected his disillusionment both with the House of Commons and with his principal minister. 'Your greatest error', he wrote, 'has been that you ever expected to draw honey out of gall, being a little blinded with the self-love of your own counsel in holding together of this parliament, whereof all men were despaired, as I have often told you, but yourself alone.'

The clashes between Crown and Commons in the parliament of 1604–11—there were many other disputes besides that over the Contract—showed very clearly that already in the first decade of the seventeenth century there were important differences between the Crown and the House of Commons, which mainly comprised representatives of the gentry class. At that time the overwhelming majority of the peers were loyal supporters of the king and the government, but with James I's and Charles I's lavish additions to the peerage between 1615 and 1628, increasing the number of English peers from eighty-one to a hundred and twenty-six, a split developed within the ranks of the aristocracy. Many members of the older peerage despised the new 'upstarts', and in the parliaments of the 1620s there was a significant opposition group to the Crown in the Lords as well as in the Commons.

The peerage and gentry taken together formed the English political community, and the Crown depended on their general cooperation and goodwill for the successful running of the country. There were several reasons why that cooperation was very clearly breaking down in the second and third decades of the century.

One of the most important was the increasing gap between the 'Court', that is, the king and his entourage, and the 'Country', those members of the aristocracy and gentry who had no access to the profits of office or the largesse which James I distributed so freely to his chosen favourites, like the worthless Robert Carr, created Earl of Somerset, on whom the king showered gifts and honours between 1611 and 1615. Somerset was disgraced in 1616 following disclosures of his complicity in a sordid murder, but he was soon replaced by a new favourite, George Villiers, created Duke of Buckingham in 1623, who was the dominant influence in the kingdom from 1618 until 1628. Under the regimes of Carr and Buckingham corruption at court and in the administration became a scandal, offices and honours being openly sold in the interest of the favourites.

Those noblemen and gentlemen outside the charmed circle of the court, and some within it, looked on the situation with growing distaste. By 1628 the position of Buckingham, who was as secure in the friendship of Charles I (1625–49) as he had been in the affections of James I, had become one of the greatest grievances in the kingdom, a leading obstacle to the improvement of relations between the king and his subjects. He was not, however, by any means the only obstacle, as clashes between Crown and Commons in 1629, the year after Buckingham's assassination, were to show very plainly.

Another source of conflict was the continuing financial needs of the Crown, especially after the outbreak of war with Spain in 1624, a conflict which lasted until 1630. The parliaments of 1624 and 1625 voted some money—though not nearly enough—for the prosecution of the war, but in 1626 the Commons refused to consider any supply until their grievances had been redressed. They proceeded with a formal impeachment of the Duke of Buckingham, and Charles had to dissolve parliament to prevent the continuation of attacks on his favourite. As no money had been forthcoming for the war effort he then had recourse to a forced loan, which caused widespread resentment. Some gentlemen refused to pay and were imprisoned. Their appeal to the courts was turned down in 1627 when the King's Bench upheld Charles's view that he had the right to imprison men without showing specific cause. This decision,

together with unparliamentary taxation, was attacked in the Petition of Right, a statement of the liberties of the subject drawn up by the House of Commons in 1628.

Charles grudgingly agreed to the Petition, though he made it quite plain that he interpreted it as merely confirming existing liberties (as he understood them) and not creating new ones. By 1628, therefore, the war and the growing financial problems which attended it had led to serious disputes and great ill-feeling between Crown and Commons.

Charles's religious ideas also provoked trouble with many of his subjects, and that trouble too was reflected in the parliaments of the 1620s. He supported the Arminian party within the Church, a group led by William Laud, who was made Bishop of London in 1628 and Archbishop of Canterbury in 1633. Laud and his followers stressed the freedom of men's wills as opposed to the Anglican Church's traditional emphasis on predestination—the idea that God determined each soul's destiny in advance and that men were powerless to aid their salvation by their own efforts.

Many moderate Anglicans regarded Laud's theology with as much suspicion as the Puritan wing of the Church did, but it was the Puritans who took the lead in opposing not only Laud's theological ideas but also his change in Church services, changes designed to restore some of the dignity and beauty of pre-Reformation ritual. To the Puritans some of his innovations, such as railing off the altar and his insistence on kneeling at communion, suggested the doctrine of the real presence in the sacrament—one of the very foundations of Catholicism. This explains the bitterness of their opposition, both inside and outside parliament. James I had already made life

difficult enough for the Puritans, and in 1620 a large group of them had set sail in the *Mayflower* for America, where they hoped for freedom to practise their religion as they pleased. When in March 1629 parliament was adjourned amid excited scenes in the Commons, it was religious issues which raised the greatest passions in the hearts of members. They acclaimed a resolution asserting that anyone who proposed innovations in religion—a clear reference to Laud and his followers—should be considered 'a betrayer of the liberties of England and an enemy to the same'.

Charles rules alone

The crisis in the relationship between Crown and Commons in 1628–9 made Charles decide to rule without calling parliament, which he did for the next eleven years. The key to the whole situation during this period was the financial position of the Crown. Charles had to obtain sufficient money to administer the country without recourse to parliament. This meant keeping out of wars —peace was made with Spain in 1630—and exploiting the royal prerogative for financial ends. Ship money, the most important of the numerous fiscal devices of the personal rule, was imposed on the whole country from 1636 onwards. There were good precedents, going back to the sixteenth century, for raising this tax in coastal shires in times of national emergency. The money was used to equip fleets to defend these areas against possible attacks from abroad. Charles, however, argued that the whole country benefited, at least indirectly, from the protection this afforded and that all counties should contribute to the tax. He also contended that he alone had the right to decide when an emergency existed. The judges upheld the king's views in Hampden's case (1637), but only by a majority of seven to five. Still, it looked as if Charles had obtained the right to impose a non-parliamentary tax which could easily become a regular levy.

Ship money and all the other financial expedients which were employed improved the royal revenue, which rose from about £600,000 a year at the beginning of the 1630s to about £900,000 a year at the end of the decade. Even this increase was not enough, however, to wipe out the large Crown debts, and Charles had to borrow more money to pay off these previous liabilities. In other words, his continuing solvency depended on his ability to obtain loans, and it was clear that any sudden large demand upon his purse—a war, for example—would necessitate the calling of parliament. Crisis point came for the king in 1638 when his Scottish subjects openly defied his authority.

The trouble in Scotland arose from Charles's and Laud's efforts to impose their religious ideas there. The climax came in 1637 when they tried to introduce a new prayer book, based on that of the Church of England. The Scots refused to accept this and at the beginning of 1638 the National Covenant, a document asserting Scotland's rights to its traditional religious and civil

liberties, was drawn up and signed by large numbers of Scotsmen. The king decided to coerce the Scots. It was a fateful decision, as it set in motion the events which led directly to civil war. It soon became clear that Charles did not have sufficient financial resources to impose his will in Scotland. In 1640, therefore, he was forced to call parliament. The first parliament which met that year, the Short Parliament, was dissolved hastily without voting the king any money. Its successor, the famous Long Parliament, which opened in November 1640, was one of the most important in English history.

At the beginning of the Long Parliament the king had little support in the House of Commons, and in 1641 he had to agree to a series of measures which profoundly and, as it turned out, permanently modified the structure of the English state. The institutions of conciliar government created during the Tudor period, notably the courts of Star Chamber and High Commission and the other prerogative courts, upon which James I and Charles I had depended for the enforcement of their policies, were swept away and Parliament embarked on a radical course of restoring its old position vis-à-vis the Crown.

The death of Strafford

The Commons also succeeded in 1641 in disposing of Thomas Wentworth, Earl of Strafford, the king's ablest minister, who was condemned to death by act of attainder and executed in May. Charles never forgave himself for consenting to Strafford's death, and there is no doubt that the earl's abilities would have been of the greatest use to him in the years ahead. The Commons, however, were determined that he should die. They feared that otherwise he might succeed in enforcing the royal will in England with the same ruthlessness he had shown during his rule in Ireland, where he had represented the king as lord deputy during the 1630s.

Events in Ireland contributed to the breakdown of the virtual unanimity which was a striking feature in the House of Commons during the early months of 1641. So did religious differences among MPs. The Commons were united in their desire to do away with Arminian practices—Laud was imprisoned in 1641—but some members wanted to go much further and abolish espiscopacy altogether, 'root and branch', This Puritan policy was abhorrent to many middle of the road Anglicans and it played a large part in the reaction towards the king's side which was apparent by the autumn of 1641. That reaction can be seen very clearly in the voting on the Grand Remonstrance, a summary of parliament's previous grievances against the Crown and a statement of further measures necessary to satisfy their wishes. John Pym, the ablest of the parliamentarian leaders and a supporter of the 'root and branch' policy, obtained a majority of only eleven votes (159 to 148) for the document when it was passed in November. Broadly speaking, those who voted for the Remonstrance wished for further radical changes in church and state, while those who voted against it were convinced that previous measures had been sufficient.

While the Remonstrance was being discussed news of a great Irish Catholic revolt against English authority reached London. Coming at such a time, this rebellion was a very important link in the chain of events leading to the outbreak of civil war in England. It was obvious that an army would have to be raised to crush the revolt, but the Commons as a whole were not prepared to concede control of it to the king. They feared that it might be turned against themselves. The king, on the other hand, was not prepared to surrender his control of the armed forces, the very basis of the royal prerogative.

In January 1642 he tried personally to arrest five of his leading opponents in the House of Commons. They had been warned and had already fled and the king had to withdraw baffled. This attempted coup was very unwise. It lost Charles a good deal of the moderate support which he had gained and left a virtually unbridgeable gulf of fear and suspicion between him and his opponents. Soon afterwards he left London and during the early part of 1642 the country drifted towards civil war. General hostilities began in September.

The civil war

Few historical subjects have provoked more discussion or greater disagreement among historians than the causes of the English Civil War. Only one thing is certain: no one explanation or group of explanations is entirely satisfactory. The best interpretation of the origins of the war is probably one which takes the widest possible view of its causes, and the English revolution should be seen in a European as well as in a local context. Much attention has recently been devoted to the social and economic background of

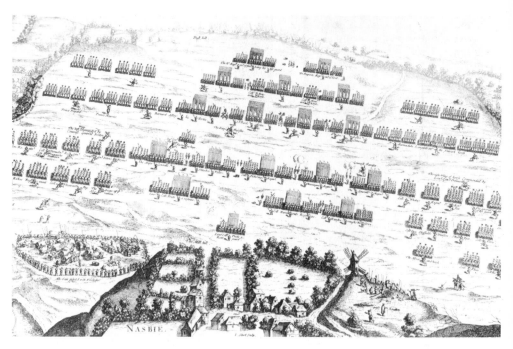

the political conflict. No generally accepted picture has emerged, but many historians see economic and social developments behind the obvious political fact that the leadership in the struggle against the Crown was taken by the gentry and their lawyer allies rather than by the aristocracy. This, it can be argued, reflected a relative increase in the wealth and political maturity of those middling groups in society—principally the landed gentry—which were increasingly resentful of the Crown's exactions. These were the people who looked to the common law to defend their interests and who were finally prepared to risk an open conflict with the king.

Any comprehensive interpretation must also take into account the increasing division between the Laudian and Puritan parties in the Church in the years before the Civil War, the constitutional conflicts of the reigns of James I and Charles I and the significance of the foreign policy of the first two Stuarts. Despite the wars of 1624–30, this was generally friendly towards Spain, still the arch-champion of militant Catholicism and as such anathema to most Englishmen.

The First Civil War lasted from 1642 until 1646. It ended with the defeat of the king, and during its course Oliver Cromwell, who dominated English history in the 1650s, emerged as a significant figure on the political stage. When the struggle began—and now we are speaking in the broadest possible terms—Charles controlled the north and west, the poorer part of the country, while the richer southern and eastern regions of the kingdom supported parliament. The king had an initial superiority in the quality of his troops, notably of his cavalry, but he failed to exploit this effectively, and the parliamentarians, who concluded an alliance with the Scots in 1643, took the initiative from that year onwards. The royal forces in the north were

defeated at Marston Moor in 1644 and in the following year the king's own army in the Midlands was beaten at Naseby. In 1646 Charles realized that further resistance was useless and surrendered to the Scots.

It was during the later stages of the war that Oliver Cromwell really made his mark. Cromwell, who came from East Anglian gentry stock, was an Independent in religion. As such he was one of a growing body of men who believed in the right of the congregation of each church to choose its own minister and worship in its own way. Cromwell's great contribution to parliament's victory in the war was as an organizer and trainer of cavalry. By its end he was second-in-command of the New Model Army, an efficient military force which had been organized in 1645 under the command of Sir Thomas Fairfax. Independency was very strong in the army, but it was much weaker in parliament, where both houses were dominated by Presbyterians who drew strength from their alliance with the Scots.

The king's execution

The two following years, 1646–8, were occupied by a series of tortuous intrigues in which the principal parties were Charles, the army, parliament and the Scots. The outcome was a Second Civil War, fought in 1648 between the Scots, who had allied with Charles, and the army. The Scots were soon defeated and the army leaders decided that they must get rid of Charles, the 'man of blood' whose intrigues had been responsible for the renewal of conflict. This provoked a direct clash with the Presbyterians in parliament, who had maintained an equivocal attitude during the Second Civil War but had eventually reopened negotiations with the king. The army took drastic action. In December 1648, the Presbyterian MPs were excluded from the Commons and only some seventy members, army supporters,

were allowed to remain. The purged parliament, in alliance with the army, set up a special court to try the king, who was executed in January 1649. Immediately afterwards the monarchy and the House of Lords were abolished.

It is easy to condemn Charles I's execution as a crime—there was, of course, no legal process by which a sovereign could be arraigned—but less easy to show what other solution was possible. Charles had many virtues both as a man and as a king. He was a faithful husband and a dutiful father. He was sincerely religious, and he worked hard at the routine business of kingship. Despite these admirable qualities, however, it can be argued that the most notable defect of his character—his total untrustworthiness—made his final execution necessary. Throughout the period between 1642 and 1648 he played his opponents off against one another with a total lack of scruple, which he himself would have justified by arguing that he was entitled to use virtually any means available to preserve the monarchy and the Church of England. In these circumstances he inevitably alienated any goodwill which remained among his enemies.

Although, therefore, the king in some ways brought about his own death, the very fact of his execution was a heavy burden for the regicides to bear. In England itself many people were horrified at his death. An eyewitness records that after the execution 'there was such a groan by the thousands then present, as I never heard before'.

Abroad the reaction was almost universally hostile, and in the United Provinces and Spain envoys of the new government were murdered by the hostile populace.

This new government took the form of a Commonwealth, with the remaining members of the House of Commons, the Rump as it came to be called, as the supreme authority in the state. Between 1649 and 1651 Cromwell reconquered Ireland and once again defeated the Scots who intervened on behalf of Charles I's son, the future Charles II. These victories made Cromwell, now the acknowledged leader of the army, the most powerful man in the state, though on many issues he did not see eye to eye with the Rump. There were clashes over foreign policy—Cromwell was unhappy about the war between England and the United Provinces which broke out in 1652—over the slowness of the Rump in reforming the country's archaic legal system, and, above all, over its determination to perpetuate its own existence. Cromwell and the army wanted a general election for a new parliament, but in April 1653 the Rump decided to have piecemeal by-elections with existing members keeping their seats. Cromwell then dissolved the Rump by force.

Between July and December 1653 he tried what was perhaps the most extraordinary constitutional experiment ever attempted in England, the Nominated Parliament, sometimes called the Barebones Parliament, after Praise-God Barbon, a London tradesman who was one of the MPs for the City. Its members were not elected in the normal

only one chamber. Under the Humble Petition and Advice his powers as protector were increased, and a second chamber, the so-called 'Other House', was instituted. Originally the Humble Petition and Advice proposed to restore the monarchy, with Cromwell as king. He hesitated but in the end, under pressure from the army, refused the Crown. It is clear that Cromwell, who throughout his career was involved in so many constitutional experiments, was not wedded to any particular form of government. Its structure was always a secondary consideration in his eyes. It was, he thought, 'but a mortal thing', merely 'dross and dung compared with Christ'. For Cromwell religious considerations came first.

Cromwell the radical

In his attitude towards religion Cromwell was far in advance of his time. He had a deep and abiding belief in men's right to freedom of conscience and throughout his protectorate, tried to secure as wide a measure of religious toleration as was compatible with the safety of the state. The Cromwellian Church, set up in 1654, covered a wide spectrum of religious beliefs. No agreement on ritual or doctrine was required from its members except for the acceptance of the main principles of Christianity. In the words of a distinguished historian, 'it was not so much a Church as a confederation of Christian sects working together for righteousness under the control of the state.'

Outside this tolerant Establishment dissenters were allowed freedom of worship as long as their conduct did not threaten the integrity of the state. Anglicanism, which did constitute such a threat, was in theory banned but in practice enjoyed a wide degree of toleration. Even Catholics, who were regarded by most Englishmen of the day as idolators, and, like Anglicans, were not officially tolerated, were treated with a good deal of leniency. Cromwell's belief in wide religious toleration was very different from the attitude of the two protectorate parliaments of 1654 and 1656, which were dominated by moderate Presbyterians and conservative Independents who sought a much clearer definition of the doctrine of the state Church and wanted to exclude large sections of English Protestantism from legal recognition and protection.

Cromwell, a radical in religious matters, was profoundly conservative in his social attitudes. He saw secular society as an ordered hierarchy based on private property and regarded democratic or crypto-democratic ideas with abhorrence. He showed this very clearly in his attitude towards the Levellers, a group of men both inside and outside the army who were a power of some importance in England between 1647 and 1649. They advocated, among other reforms, a wide extension of the franchise in parliamentary elections. Cromwell thought

way. They were 'godly' men chosen by the leading army officers. The Nominated Parliament therefore reveals very clearly Cromwell's belief in the efficacy of religion in solving the problems of human society; he thought that if he collected a body of devout men they would soon put the state in order. He was disillusioned. The new parliament soon split into moderate and radical wings, the radicals pressing for the abolition of tithes and for sweeping law reforms. The alarm of the moderates at these proposals led them, with the encouragement of some of the more conservative army officers, especially General

Lambert, to meet unusually early one morning in December and, in the absence of many of their radical colleagues, to surrender their authority to Cromwell.

In December 1653, therefore, Cromwell had to construct another constitutional settlement. The new government which was set up was based on a written constitution produced by Lambert. This 'Instrument of Government' as it was called was the foundation of Cromwell's rule until it was replaced in 1657 by the 'Humble Petition and Advice'. By the Instrument Cromwell, with the title of Lord Protector, shared power with a parliament which consisted of that this might lead in due course to social as well as political equality. His horror was reflected in his words to the Council of State early in 1649: 'You have no other way to deal with these men but to break them in pieces. . . . If you do not break them they will break you.' He then proceeded himself to suppress the London Levellers and Leveller-led mutinies in the army. The year 1649 brought the end of the Levellers as a serious political force and as a focus for potential social revolution. Throughout the 1650s the traditional social hierarchy remained undisturbed in Cromwell's England.

Cromwell pursued an active foreign policy. England had been a power of secondary importance in European affairs during the reigns of James I and Charles I, but he made the country feared and respected abroad. As at home, religious idealism played an important role in his policies. He hastened to make peace with the Protestant United Provinces in 1654 and in 1656 engaged in a war, waged in both the West Indies and Europe, against Spain, still regarded as the arch-enemy of Protestantism. In 1658 he won a bridgehead on the continent, when, following an Anglo-French victory over Spain at the Battle of the Dunes, the allies captured the town of Dunkirk, which was later handed over to England.

In September of the same year Cromwell died. The protectorate, which depended so much on his personality, did not long survive him. His ineffectual son and successor, Richard Cromwell, who did not have the support of the army leaders, was pushed into private life in 1659 when the Rump of the Long Parliament was restored. This now represented an alliance between the army leaders and anti-protectorate Republicans, but soon army and parliament fell out. The country seemed to be drifting towards anarchy. The situation was saved by George Monck, Cromwell's commander-in-chief in Scotland. He marched his well disciplined army south and restored those members of the House of Commons who had been purged in 1648. It soon voted to dissolve itself, and when elections for a new parliament were held monarchists won a large majority. The way was open for the restoration of Charles II, who arrived in London, amidst scenes of great rejoicing, in May 1660.

The period between 1642 and 1660 was a unique interlude in English history. During these years the Puritans took advantage of their victory over the established rulers of the country to impose a moral code which proved as distasteful to the populace at large as it was satisfactory to the whole range of Puritan opinion from the conservative Presbyterians of the Long Parliament to the radical sectaries of the Commonwealth and Protectorate.

Accepting the Scriptures as an absolute code of behaviour, they exacted Biblical penalties for moral offences: a law of 1650, for example, imposed the death sentence for adultery.

Other legislation tried to stamp out drunkenness, swearing and gambling and to preserve the sanctity of the Sabbath. Such attempts to interfere with everyday social habits met, however, with little success. They did turn the bulk of the population into active enemies of Puritan morality and paved the way for the hedonistic atmosphere of the reign of Charles II.

On the restoration of 1660, the House of Lords and the Established Church of England returned along with the monarchy. The events of 1640 to 1660 could not,

Above, Oliver Cromwell (1599–1658), who ruled England after 1649 as head of the army and from 1653 as lord protector. Like many of the parliamentary leaders, he was anxious to preserve the social system of the time, to allow religious toleration and to prevent any body such as an established church or the monarchy to have sovereignty over the people. National Portrait Gallery, London.

Opposite, England and Wales during the Civil War, in 1644. Charles' support came mainly from the west country, and his capital was at Oxford. With the resources of London at their disposal, the parliamentarians had overwhelming material superiority.

however, be obliterated. The monarchy of Charles II and the restoration Church of Juxon and Sheldon were very different institutions from the pre-civil war kingship and the Laudian Church of England.

As far as the monarchy is concerned Charles II had none of the apparatus for personal rule that all his predecessors in the sixteenth and seventeenth centuries had possessed. The prerogative courts which had been abolished by the Long Parliament in 1641 were not restored and the common law courts reigned supreme. The events of 1640 to 1660 had also reduced the power and prestige of the Crown in a more intangible way. A section of the English political community had waged a successful war against the king and had later executed him in public. The death of Charles I on the scaffold was a permanent reminder to later monarchs that they might be held to account by their people.

In the Church the idea of comprehension —the theory that every English man and woman should belong to the state Church as well as to the state itself—was for all practical purposes abandoned soon after the restoration. This was because the Puritans, who had dominated religious life during the Interregnum, and the restored hierarchy of the Established Church could not settle their differences. Efforts were made to do so at the Savoy Conference of 1661 but no agreement was reached, and when the bishops produced a revised version of the prayer book the Puritan leaders found it quite unacceptable. The book was, however, incorporated in an Act of Uniformity, passed in 1662, and all ministers were required both to use the book and to make public declarations of 'unfeigned assent and consent' to all its contents. By the end of 1662 nearly 2,000 ministers had lost their livings—a much more sweeping change in the personnel of the Church than had occurred at any one time during the 1640s and 1650s.

Many of these ministers set up independent congregations which were subject to persecution under the Clarendon Code, a series of repressive laws against dissenters passed between 1661 and 1665. The intensity of persecution, however, varied a good deal and many congregations survived. Their continuing existence symbolized the end of the Tudor and early Stuart ideal of a united Christian society in which Church and state were one.

The House of Lords, just like the Crown, lost prestige as a result of the Interregnum. Neither the peers nor the Commons ever forgot that between 1649 and 1657 the upper house had been abolished. In the last resort England could do without a house of peers.

The new king

Charles II certainly never forgot that the country had done without a king for eleven

years. He was resolved not to 'go on his travels' again, and that determination explains why he was never prepared to make heroic stands on matters of conscience, except when the exclusion movement attempted to debar his brother James from the throne and thus destroy the very principle to which he (Charles) owed his crown, that of hereditary right. Charles, in fact, wanted to enjoy life, and the country as a whole was sympathetic to a monarchy and court which so openly rejected the rigours of Puritan morality. The king, unassuming and friendly, surrounded by his dogs and his mistresses, was personally popular.

In 1660 Charles took as his chief minister Edward Hyde, Earl of Clarendon, who had been the mainstay of the Royalist party in exile. He fell from power after the Dutch War of 1665–67 had revealed appalling inefficiency in his administration and went into exile abroad, where he wrote his *History of the Rebellion and Civil Wars in England*, still one of the finest pieces of English historical writing.

It was during the Dutch War that two of the most dramatic episodes of Restoration history took place—the Great Plague and the Great Fire of London. The plague, which raged from the spring of 1665 to the end of 1666, was the last, and one of the worst, of a series of outbreaks which had occurred in England in the three centuries following the Black Death in 1348. At its height in London, in autumn 1665, thousands died each week, many of them covered with the huge sores which were the most appalling signs of the plague's visitation.

Then, just as the plague was waning, came the Great Fire, which swept through the City of London for five days in September 1666, destroying more than 13,000 houses and more than eighty churches, including London's historic cathedral, old St Paul's. The tragedy of the fire, though it was a traumatic experience for the citizens of the capital, did, however, provide the opportunity for rebuilding London. This produced not only a city of superior private houses but also Wren's magnificent series of London churches, over fifty in all, including his masterpiece, new St Paul's.

Between 1667 and the early 1670s, while his capital was beginning to recover from the plague and the fire, Charles relied for advice on a group of ministers—themselves holding very different views on many subjects—who came to be known as the Cabal. In 1673, however, Sir Thomas Osborne, who had shown considerable financial ability as Treasurer of the Navy, was appointed Lord Treasurer and soon achieved primacy in the kings counsels. He was created Earl of Danby in 1674 and remained in office until 1679. Danby tried to wean Charles away from a pro-French foreign policy out of tune with the growing fears of most of his subjects about Louis XIV's expansionist ambitions. Charles had signed the treaty of Dover with France in 1670. By this he agreed, in return for a subsidy, to join France in war against the Dutch. By secret clauses he also promised to declare openly, at a time of his own choosing, his loyalty to the Catholic religion.

As a result of this treaty England joined France in attacking the Dutch in 1672, but in the autumn of the following year the Commons, suspicious of the French alliance, refused to vote supplies for the continuance of the war. Charles was forced to make a separate peace with the Dutch in 1674. For most of the rest of the 1670s Danby tried to persuade Charles to adopt an openly Protestant stance in foreign affairs, but the king shrank away from a complete break with France. Then, at the end of 1678, everything else was overshadowed by the Popish Plot.

It was in 1678 that Titus Oates, a liar and a scoundrel of the first order, announced that he had secret information about a plot by the Pope and the Jesuits to kill the king

and place his brother James, Duke of York, an avowed Catholic, on the throne. Protestant Englishmen of the day were prepared to believe almost anything about Catholics and by the time parliament met in October London was in ferment. The plot was the only subject of discussion and when Oates obtained support from the Earl of Shaftesbury, a skilful and unscrupulous politician who believed in strictly limited monarchy, the situation became serious for the government. Shaftesbury took advantage of the anti-Catholic feeling produced by the plot to try to secure James's exclusion from the throne. He won the support of three successive Houses of Commons between 1679 and 1681, but Charles refused to consider depriving his brother of the succession. When he dissolved the parliament of 1681 the Whigs—as those who favoured exclusion had come to be called to distinguish them from the Tory supporters of hereditary right—talked of armed resistance. In the end, however, they dispersed quietly. Charles had won.

He took advantage of the royalist reaction which followed the defeat of the exclusionist movement to remodel the borough corporations, which elected most MPs. Many of these were Whig strongholds, but the new charters which Charles imposed upon them made it probable that in future elections they would select royalist MPs.

A Catholic monarch

James II felt the benefit of these changes immediately after his accession to the throne

in 1685. His first parliament was loyal to the point of subservience. Despite this, however, his reign lasted for only three years. The reason was basically James's desire to restore the Catholic faith to an official and respected place in English society at a time when the great majority of Englishmen still feared and detested it. In such a situation there was sure to be serious conflict.

James tried to further the cause of Catholicism by a variety of measures, each of which increased antagonism towards the Crown in the country at large. He appointed Catholics to high office in both the army and civil government, he set up an ecclesiastical commission reminiscent of the old Court of High Commission, he received a papal envoy at Whitehall, he issued declarations of indulgence suspending the penal laws against Catholics and dissenters. He wanted to persuade parliament to repeal the penal laws altogether, but in order to achieve this he had to set about a further remodelling of the municipal corporations. Charles II's reforms, it is true, had handed control of the boroughs over to fervent Tories, but these men were committed Anglicans as well and clearly would not have been prepared to approve of measures harmful to the position of the Church of England. James's reforms meant that in many boroughs the parliamentary franchise and the administration of justice were handed over to Catholics and dissenters. He also instituted a great purge of Anglican county notables.

In 1686 and 1687 most of the established JPs in England and Wales, the effective rulers of the country in the localities, were

Above, James, Duke of York, painted in 1661. James was the brother of Charles II, and as he became overtly Catholic, and as it became clear that Charles would have no legitimate heirs, attempts were made to exclude James from the throne. Nevertheless, he acceded as James II in 1685. Victoria and Albert Museum, London.

Top, the Great Fire of London in September 1666, which practically devastated the whole of the city, and enabled it to be rebuilt on more spacious lines. Half its population lost their homes.

Opposite, an English doctor during the Great Plague of 1665–66; more than 70,000 people died during this last great outbreak of bubonic plague.

replaced by men of inferior social rank. These changes caused the most profound resentment among the propertied classes who felt that the country was faced with two major threats, one to the whole established fabric of society, the other to the position of the Church of England. The crowning blow from their point of view was the birth of a son and heir to James in June of 1688. Until then the Crown's opponents could take comfort in the thought that he would be succeeded by one of his Protestant daughters.

In this situation seven prominent Englishmen signed an invitation to William of Orange, ruler of Holland, a grandson of Charles I and husband of James's elder daughter Mary, to come to England and save the country from James's policies. William landed in November and the following month James fled to France. The stage was set for the joint accession of William and Mary to the throne and the settlement of 1689.

Thus the political and constitutional history of seventeenth-century England was dominated by conflicts between the Crown and large numbers of its subjects. Domestic arguments did not, however, prevent the country from expanding abroad or inhibit literary and scientific developments. The century saw the foundation of an English colonial empire in America and a great expansion in both the volume and the content of English trade. These developments set the scene for further advances in the eighteenth century when the country emerged as a great colonial, commercial and financial power. In the field of culture and

science Englishmen made unique contributions to the age. The names of Shakespeare, Bacon, Milton, Hobbes, Locke, Dryden and Newton—a roll-call of genius—are sufficient explanation of the fact that, by the end of the century, England was challenging France for the intellectual leadership of Europe.

Chapter 11

The Golden Age of the United Provinces

In 1609 the Spanish government concluded a military truce with the Seven United Provinces of the Netherlands which had been in revolt against its authority since the 1570s. Philip III of Spain was not prepared at that time to recognize formally the complete sovereignty which his rebellious subjects had claimed since the 1580s, but his government had negotiated with them 'as if' they were an independent power. Although Spain was thus forced by military and financial exhaustion to concede what amounted to practical recognition of sovereign authority to the northern Netherlands, the king and his advisers had some consolation. Thanks to the military genius of the Duke of Parma the southern Netherlands, which in the 1570s had also seemed likely to break away, had been recovered for Spain in the early 1580s. The Netherlands were thus divided—permanently as it turned out. The factors which determined the line of division were not linguistic or religious—there were many Dutch speakers in the Spanish Netherlands and very many Catholics in the north—but geographic and military: the position of the Spanish and Dutch forces in the country at the time of the truce determined the frontier.

The seven provinces which had struggled against Spain for some forty years to win their freedom were to enjoy a glorious career in the seventeenth century as the world's greatest commercial power, but in 1609 powerful forces in the country feared that its independence might be short-lived. Those who took this view believed that the truce was a great mistake. The Spanish government, they argued, had concluded it from a position of weakness but with a view to renewing the struggle later, after a period of peace had enabled the still mighty Spanish Empire to mobilize new resources. The principal protagonist of this view was Prince Maurice of Orange, son of William the Silent. He held the position of *stadtholder* (governor) in five of the seven provinces, an office which gave him considerable influence in the internal affairs of each province and of the country as a whole. He had strong support among the more zealous Calvinists, men who regarded any agreement with the Spaniards, short of complete victory, as a sign of weakness.

On the other side stood the ruling 'regent' families, who dominated the states or governing assemblies of each of the provinces and through them the States-General of the United Provinces. The regents were an oligarchy of wealthy burghers, particularly strong in Holland, the dominant province in the Union, who thought, on the whole, that the advantage of the state would best be served by peace. They believed firmly in the need to subject the Church to the secular power. The Calvinist ministers and the enthusiasts among their flocks, on the other hand, stressed the independent rights of the Church; they criticized not only the eagerness of the regents to negotiate with the Spanish heretics but also their readiness to extend toleration at home to the large number of Catholic and Protestant dissenters. The leader of the regent party and the man who was principally responsible for the successful negotiation of the 1609 truce was Oldenbarnevelt, advocate (that is principal official) of the States of Holland. His disagreement with Prince Maurice over the conclusion of the truce was the beginning of a conflict between the two men which was to end in tragedy in 1619.

Religious divisions

The whole domestic history of the republic in the years before the renewal of war with Spain in 1621 was dominated by disputes in which religion and politics were inextricably intermingled. The religious side of the conflict turned on a theological dispute between two professors at the University of Leyden in Holland. One of these, Arminius, put forward views on free will which stressed man's ability to help to determine the fate of his soul by his own efforts. The other, Gomarus, stressed the traditional Calvinist concept of predestination, the idea that God has decided each soul's fate in advance and that man is powerless to aid his salvation by his own efforts.

These rival ideas became involved with politics in 1610, when the supporters of Arminius, a minority in the ministry, set out their views on the disputed questions in a Remonstrance, which they presented to the States of Holland, together with a request for protection from their opponents. The States, with their firm views on the responsibility of the secular power for ecclesiastical affairs, could hardly refuse an appeal couched in these terms. Under Oldenbarnevelt's leadership they granted the desired protection, an action which infuriated the majority among the ministry who followed Gomarus. In the heated atmosphere thus engendered the States' subsequent efforts at mediation between the two sides did little to help matters, and in 1611 the Gomarists presented a Counter-Remonstrance containing their own views on the points at issue. For the next few years the arguments of Remonstrants and

Above, Johan van Oldenbarnevelt (1547–1619), the Dutch statesman who championed the rule of the merchants, and of the state of Holland, within the United Provinces from the 1580s until his execution.

Opposite left, the arrival of William of Orange in England in November 1688; his invasion, which had probably been planned before he was invited to sail to England, was universally welcomed and the coup was achieved virtually without bloodshed.

Opposite top right, Francis Bacon (1561–1626), the English scientist who argued for the adoption of the scientific method – observation and hypothesis – and who served as lord chancellor after 1618, until he was convicted of accepting bribes in 1621. National Portrait Gallery, London.

Opposite bottom right, John Milton (1608–74), the poet of Paradise Lost, *who was a supporter of the parliamentary cause in the civil war, argued for freedom of speech in his pamphlet* Areopagitica *(1644) and discussed many of the ideas of the religious sects in his poetry. National Portrait Gallery, London.*

Opposite bottom left, an English plate of 1691 celebrating the accession of William and Mary. The Glorious Revolution was supported by almost all sectors of English society, Ashmolean Museum, Oxford.

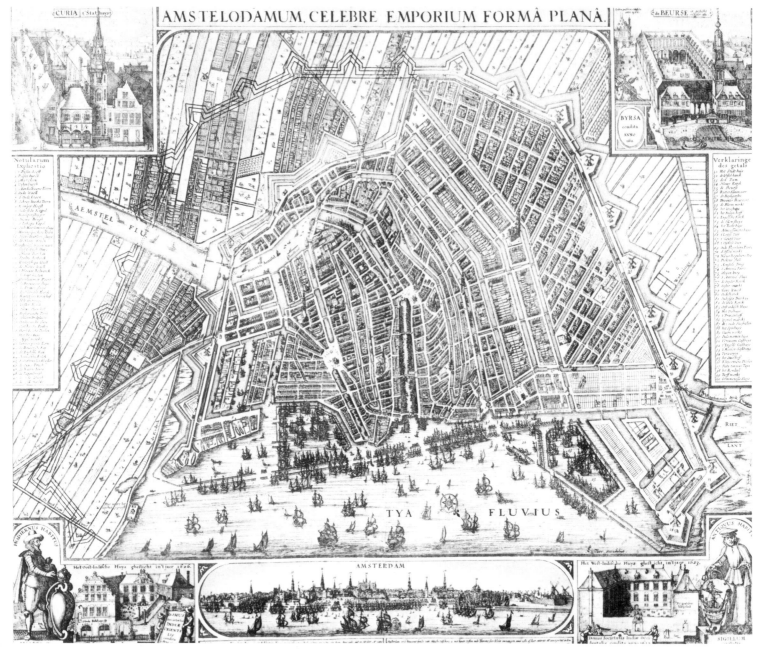

Counter-Remonstrants resounded throughout the province of Holland and indeed throughout the United Provinces as a whole. Prince Maurice, alienated from Oldenbarnevelt as a result of the truce of 1609 and at odds with him in subsequent years over other issues of foreign policy, openly joined the Counter-Remonstrant side in 1617. The political issue was thus very clearly joined: a struggle between Maurice and Oldenbarnevelt for the dominant position in the state, a conflict no less real because it was waged under the cloak of high religious principles.

Arminianism had comparatively little support outside Holland, and the other states tended to follow the lead of their Counter-Remonstrant ministers. Accordingly the majority in the States-General supported the Gomarists against the States of Holland which, though with loud and important dissenting voices, particularly from Amsterdam, were for the Arminian party. Matters came to a climax in August 1618 when Maurice, acting on a warrant from the states-general, ordered the arrest of Oldenbarnevelt. He followed this up by purging the advocate's supporters from the town councils of Holland and replacing them with Counter-Remonstrants. The States of Holland, thus transformed, authorized the trial of Oldenbarnevelt before an extraordinary court which, in May 1619 sentenced him to death for jeopardizing 'the position of the faith . . . and of the state'. He was executed the following day. It was a poor reward for a man who had probably done more than any other, with the exception of William the Silent himself, to establish the Dutch republic.

Prince Maurice

Even before Oldenbarnevelt's trial and execution a national synod of the Church, from which Remonstrants were excluded, had met at Dort and condemned Arminian doctrines. The leading Remonstrant ministers were banished from the country and their supporters excluded from public office and denied the right to freedom of worship, though freedom of conscience was still allowed: there was no suggestion of enforcing attendance at the State Church. The events of 1618–19 were, of course, a great triumph for Prince Maurice. From then until his death in 1625 he was virtually supreme in the state. In 1621, however, Maurice turned his attention away from the internal affairs of the Republic and focused it on the war with Spain, which broke out again that year on the expiry of the twelve-year truce.

This war, the second stage of the great struggle against Spain, lasted until the Treaty of Münster in 1648, when the Spanish government at last formally recognized the sovereignty of the United Provinces and also their territory in the southern Netherlands—parts of Flanders and Brabant—which had been conquered during the

war. Indeed, during the 1640s Maurice's successor, his brother Frederick Henry, became more and more committed to a personal foreign policy which took little heed of the real interests of the republic. That policy combined support for the royalists in England—his son William had married Princess Mary, daughter of Charles I, in 1641—with a continuing dependence on and even subservience to the growing power of France, which had been the republic's ally in the war but which might and indeed later did prove as great a threat to the Netherlands' liberties as Spain had ever been. His death, therefore, came at a most opportune time for the peace party, as his son and successor, William II, lacked the influence and experience necessary to prevent the conclusion of the agreements the war against Spain without Dutch aid.

William, however, was not prepared to accept the situation. He was determined to renew the war and also, if possible, to secure the restoration of his brother-in-law Charles Stuart in England. These ambitious plans, which necessitated the maintenance of a large army, led to bitter conflict with the States of Holland and at one time civil war seemed imminent. In November 1650, however, William died. Eight days later his only child, the future William III, was born. There could be no question of appointing the infant prince to his father's dignities and between 1650 and 1672 most of the republic's provinces were without a stadtholder.

This was the 'republican' period, a distinctive phase in Dutch history. It was ushered in by the Grand Assembly, which met at the Hague in 1651. The States of Holland hoped that this body which represented all the provincial estates, would produce a new form of government for the republic. Their hope was disappointed, but the Assembly did take important decisions which greatly strengthened the control of the individual provinces over the army. As a result the armed forces of the country were virtually split into seven. This was a considerable triumph for the centrifugal tendencies within the United Provinces; indeed, after 1651 the country seemed more like a union of independent states than a federal republic.

Power follows wealth

The years 1650–1 thus witnessed a 'revolution' in the United Provinces. William II's attempt to enforce his personal foreign policy, an attempt which would surely have had important constitutional results if it had succeeded, was followed by his early and unexpected death and a reaction in which the views of the ruling regent oligarchy of Holland won the day. Indeed, in the decentralized republic of 1651–72 Holland's position was stronger than ever. This was partly a result of its intrinsic economic strength—it was by far the wealthiest province, contributing some fifty-eight per cent of the total taxes of the union—and partly because of the emergence in 1652 of John de Witt, a statesman of note, as grand pensionary of Holland.

De Witt's policy was fundamentally conservative. Essentially, he wanted to preserve the status quo of 1651 both at home

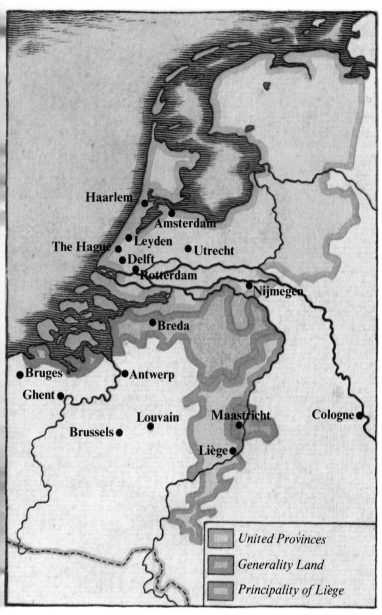

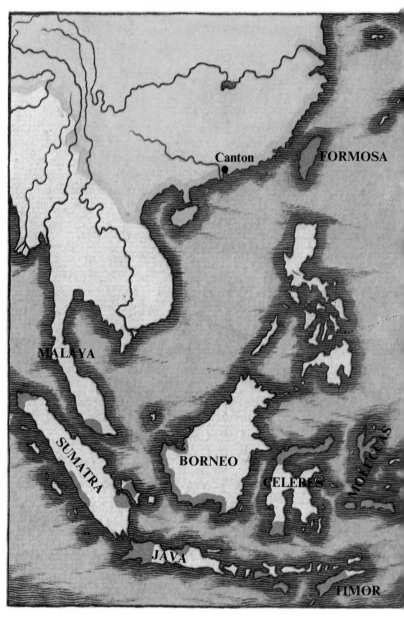

United Provinces

Generality Land

Principality of Liège

and abroad. The great threats to this ambition came from the House of Orange and its partisans at home and from England and France abroad. The Orange family was not resigned to the loss of its great position in the republic; England was jealous of the commercial dominance of the United Provinces; and after 1668 France, under Louis XIV, was determined to humble the country which had opposed her political ambitions in the Spanish Netherlands during the War of Devolution. De Witt's system thus collapsed in ruins in 1672 with the Anglo-French attack on the republic and the restoration of the office of stadtholder to the House of Orange in the person of William III. The people held de Witt responsible for the disasters of the French invasion, and in August 1672 he and his brother were lynched at the Hague. Like Oldenbarnevelt he deserved a better fate. He had served the republic to the best of his very considerable abilities and it is difficult to see what he could have done to prevent the French invasion.

From 1672 until his death thirty years later William III dominated the history of

the United Provinces. When he assumed office it seemed that, because of the successes of French arms the republic was on the brink of dissolution. By 1674, however, the French had withdrawn from Dutch soil. This was a result of at least as much of Louis XIV's errors as of William III's energy, but the events of 1672–4 gave the latter a prestige as saviour of his country which stood him in good stead in later years. After the end of the war in 1678 the United Provinces enjoyed a decade of peace, but William's régime in the republic, just like his rule in England after 1689, was dominated by his determination to oppose Louis XIV's ambitions and to reduce the power of France. He had the satisfaction of living to see the first major check to French power in the war of 1688–97 and died in 1702 at the beginning of the long and costly struggle over the Spanish succession. This war put an end to France's hopes of dominating Europe but at the same time imposed a strain on Dutch resources from which the republic never really recovered.

Even before William's death the effects of war in the 1690s had considerably reduced

his popularity. That had been at its height in the 1670s. In 1674 the States of Holland and Zeeland made his title a hereditary office and in 1675 the States-General did the same for his offices of captain-general and admiral-general of the union. By 1700, however, the lower middle classes in particular were suffering severely from the increased burdens of war taxation. The middle class as a whole resented William's failure to curtail the power of the ruling regent oligarchy. They also objected to the growing corruption in appointments to official posts which secured the nomination of his own followers and obtained much needed revenue to further the war effort.

The social system

An outline political and diplomatic history of the United Provinces in the seventeenth century with its ecclesiastical squabbles and recurrent conflicts between the House of Orange and the republican party does little to suggest a 'golden age': quite the

contrary. Yet there is no doubt that the seventeenth century was the greatest period in the history of the Netherlands. It witnessed a commercial and imperial expansion and cultural flowering which were among the wonders of the contemporary world and which should not be obscured by the often sordid details of domestic political rivalries.

The imperial expansion of the United Provinces took place against a social background entirely different from that of any other country in Europe. It is not easy to make generalizations about the social structure of the republic, which varied greatly from province to province. The nobility, for example, was much more important in Guelderland than in Holland, where it was numerically weak and economically insignificant. Holland, of course, dominated the union, and it is not altogether unrealistic to take the social situation there as representative of the ethos of life in the country as a whole during the period of its greatest glory.

Holland was dominated by its urban patriciate, the 'regent' class, which by the middle of the seventeenth century had established itself firmly as a burgher oligarchy in control of the administration and economic life of the province. It is not easy to estimate the number of regent families, but they certainly formed a very small minority of the population—perhaps only one in every thousand belonged to the regent class. Below them in the social hierarchy there was a large middle class with wide variations of income and status but all sharing to some extent in the prosperity which unparalleled economic expansion brought. Even the artisans and other members of the lower classes who thronged the province's cities and towns enjoyed on the whole a standard of life which would have been the envy of their fellows in other European countries. Moreover, the really poor were not neglected. Dutch workhouses, orphanages and other charitable institutions may have been primitive by modern standards, but they were far in advance of anything found in most other countries at the time.

This variegated population belonged to a number of religious groups. Perhaps a

Above, The Shipbuilder and his Wife, *painted by Rembrandt Van Rijn (1606–69), prosperous members of the Dutch middle classes. National Maritime, Museum, London.*

Above left, Michael de Ruyter (1607–91), the Dutch admiral who supported Denmark in 1658–59, and commanded the fleet during the Second Anglo-Dutch War.

Top, the Dutch burning the English fleet at anchor in the River Medway during the Second Anglo-Dutch War in 1667.

Top left, the Battle of the Sound, in 1658, in which the Dutch narrowly defeated a Swedish fleet and managed to end the Swedish domination of Denmark. Rijksmuseum, Amsterdam.

Opposite left, the United Provinces according to the Treaty of Münster, whereby Spain at last recognized their independence. The Generality Land was a part of the southern Netherlands conquered by the United Provinces and ceded to them by Spain; and the Principality of Liège was still technically part of the Holy Roman Empire.

Opposite right, the Dutch empire in the East Indies, won in the early seventeenth century by the Dutch East India Company.

third of the population—and now we are speaking of the union as a whole—belonged to the official Reformed Church as it emerged at the Synod of Dort. Nearly half may have been Catholics, and the remainder were Remonstrants, Lutherans, Baptists and adherents of numerous small sects. There was freedom of conscience; the state Church made no systematic effort to enforce Calvinism, but freedom of worship was restricted and dissenters often found it difficult to hold administrative posts. All in all, however, the religious policy of the Dutch states was liberal. Certainly, when compared with contemporary France, where the Huguenots were subjected to violent persecution, it was a model of enlightenment.

The population of the United Provinces thus enjoyed a combination of religious freedom and economic prosperity which was unique in Europe. The prosperity was based upon the success of Dutch trade. Although the foundations of Dutch commercial greatness had been laid in the Middle Ages it was only during the period of the revolt against Spain, probably sometime between the 1590s and the 1620s, that the northern Netherlands became unquestionably the leading seafaring and trading nation in the world. Dutch commercial preponderance in the seventeenth century was based upon a combination of factors: the geographical situation of the republic, ideally placed to act as an entrepôt for the trade of northern and central Europe; the long seafaring traditions of the country's maritime provinces; the absence of state interference in economic life; the fact that the States-General had neither the authority nor the desire to introduce economic planning; and the absence, at least for most of the century, of really efficient competitors.

It was a combination of these factors which enabled a group of Amsterdam merchants to tell the States of Holland 'during the truce, through our economic management and exertions we have sailed all nations off the seas, drawn almost all trade from other lands hither and served the whole of Europe with our ships.' This was not an exaggerated boast.

French, English and Mediterranean ports were filled with Dutch vessels carrying raw materials or manufactured goods which they sold or exchanged for other commodities. Grain and naval stores were obtained in the Baltic, cloth in England, linens in Germany, salt and wines in France. oil, fruit and silks in the Mediterranean. From America came sugar, from the East Indies spices and other luxuries.

This great Dutch carrying trade was centred in the ports of Holland, especially in the town of Amsterdam. By the mid-seventeenth century Amsterdam was one of the great cities of Europe, with a population of perhaps 150,000. It was the centre of the Baltic trade, the great source of its prosperity, and of the West and East Indian trades. During the seventeenth century, however, Amsterdam became much more than the world's greatest port. It also became the centre of the international money market, outstripping Venice and Genoa. The accumulation of capital in the United Provinces which made this development possible was based on the country's trading successes and was aided by the policy of the town government of Amsterdam which in 1609 set up a Bank designed to finance international trade. It had considerable success and by the mid-seventeenth century the republic was clearly the leading financial as well as the leading commercial power in the world. This was very plain at the time of Louis XIV's invasion in 1672. In that year, when the rate of interest on the Dutch national debt stood at only $3\frac{3}{4}$ percent there was a negligible response to a French public loan even when offered at $5\frac{1}{2}$ percent.

Most of the ships which constantly filled the port of Amsterdam were engaged in European trade, but an increasing number sailed to and from other continents, notably the Americas and Asia. In the seventeenth century the republic won two empires, one in America and the other in the East Indies. She soon lost most of her American acquisitions but her great East Indian possessions remained a valuable asset until the twentieth century.

Wealth from the Spice Islands

The republic's possessions in the East Indies were controlled by the Dutch East India Company which became, in the seventeenth century, the most powerful European institution in Asia and the greatest trading corporation in the world. The company had been founded in 1602 to regulate and protect the already considerable trade carried on by the Dutch in the eastern seas. This was necessary because that trade was challenged by the traditional dominance of Portugal in the area, and Portugal, then a possession of the Spanish crown, was inevitably involved in Spain's war against her rebellious Netherlands provinces.

The company was given full authority in the east, with the right to maintain military forces on sea and by land, to make war and peace, coin money and found colonies. Under two great proconsuls, Coen and Van Diemen, whose careers in the East Indies spanned the period between 1618 and 1645, it made spectacular progress, founding its capital at Batavia on the island of Java, obtaining and then consolidating a hold on the Moluccas, the fabulous 'spice islands', which were, in the eyes of the company's servants, the most valuable part of the whole eastern commercial system, and expelling the Portuguese from Malacca and from part of Sri Lanka. In 1652 the company established a colony at the Cape of Good Hope on the southern tip of Africa and after 1660 consolidated its hold on the East Indies as a whole.

The company's chief imports into Holland were spices and textiles. The latter, principally silks and cotton piece goods, became more and more important as the century advanced and by 1700 were the most valuable part of the eastern trade. Although it was first and foremost a commercial organization the company's conquests and the need to supervise and control the native principalities in the Indies involved it in heavy expenses. In 1669 it possessed forty ships of war and 10,000 soldiers in addition to its 150 trading vessels. Military expenditure as heavy as this soon reduced its profits and in addition it suffered from servants who tended to promote their own private trading interests at the expense of those of the company as a whole. By 1700 therefore the company had begun to decline. This decline was, of course, entirely relative. Although its profits were less than they had been in the great years of the seventeenth century it remained a very important body until nearly 1800.

The East India Company was founded principally as a trading body. The reasons for the inception of the West India Company in 1621 were different. It was formed essentially to fight against Portugal and

Spain in the Americas and was thus an instrument of war rather than a commercial company. It soon captured some islands in the West Indies but its principal efforts were made in Brazil and in New Netherland, a Dutch colony centred on Manhattan island, which it took over in 1623. New Netherland was ceded to England in 1667 after the second Dutch war, and substantial conquests made in northeastern Brazil after 1630 had to be abandoned to the Portuguese by the 1650s. The prospects of a Dutch American empire, which came to the fore only in the early years of the seventeenth century, ahd thus collapsed by the 1660s.

The arts

The Dutch expansion overseas, symbolized by the creation of the West and East India Companies, was paralleled by the expansion of Dutch cultural horizons at home. The seventeenth century was the great age of Dutch art and literature. The growing numbers and wealth of the middle class in the republic led to an increasing demand for aesthetic satisfaction, a demand which produced forms of artistic expression different from those found in the absolutist and Baroque culture which dominated most of the rest of western Europe.

Painting was by far the most important of the Dutch arts. There was little scope for notable architecture or sculpture. These, in the seventeenth century, depended largely on the existence of patrons dedicated to conspicuous consumption, great princes and cardinals, or nobles of the highest rank, the kind of men who were not to be found in the Netherlands. On the other hand, those who enjoyed even modest prosperity could aspire to the ownership of paintings. Thousands of Dutchmen did. The pictures which they bought were characterized by realism and by infinite variety: still-lifes, landscapes, seascapes, individual and group portraits, views of towns, studies of animals, pictures of the interiors of churches—to select just some of the subjects favoured by Dutch artists of the time. There were dozens of good Dutch painters in the seventeenth century, several great ones—like Frans Hals, who painted really splendid portrait groups, and Jan Vermeer of Delft, who produced magnificent scenes of his native towns—and one unquestioned genius, Rembrandt, a man whose work can never be adequately described but which, with its humanity and its inner simplicity, gives the impression that its creator had looked at some of the great secrets of the universe. To prove the point it is only necessary to look at his wonderful series of self-portraits, which depict the physical and spiritual development of a genius.

The greatness of Dutch literature in the seventeenth century has received less general recognition than the greatness of its painting, but in both prose and poetry it was a

time of the highest achievement. Cats, Huygens, Hooft and Vondel, to mention only four names, wrote verse and prose of the highest calibre. Vondel, regarded by his fellow countrymen as their greatest poet, on a par with Shakespeare, has never won equal recognition in other countries, but the perennial fascination which he has exercised over the minds of Netherlands through such plays as *Lucifer* (1654) and *Jephta* (1659) makes him the worthy leader of a golden age in literature.

When he died in 1679 that golden age was almost over, in other aspects of Dutch life as well as in literature. Dutch cultural inspiration, as well as the country's economic and political strength, declined in the eighteenth century. The political and economic deterioration must not be exaggerated or antedated. The United Provinces entered the war of the Spanish Succession as a great power, and her commercial and financial predominance in Europe lasted well into the eighteenth century. But already by 1700 there were signs that the rising power of England, with a larger population and superior natural resources, would in a generation or so outstrip her in both trade and finance. The cultural decline came earlier and was more dramatic. By 1680 the great age of Dutch painting and literature was over. The men of genius had died leaving no successors.

Above, A Group Portrait of the Officers of the St Hadrian Militia, *painted in 1633 by Franz Hals; Dutch portraits of civic officials and people carrying out their public duties were common in the seventeen century. Frans Halsmuseum, Haarlem.*

Left, Self-portrait at a Window, *by Rembrandt, done in 1640. Although more poetical than the work of any of his contemporaries, Rembrandt's paintings and etchings reflect the popular taste for self-portraits and subjects of human curiosity.*

Opposite, Interior with Soldiers, *painted by Pieter de Hooch (c. 1629–c. 1677). Such scenes of relaxation and conviviality are said to express the love of life and lack of pretentiousness of the Dutch bourgeoisie. National Gallery, London.*

Chapter 12

The Changing Pattern of Europe

When Louis XIV assumed personal charge of his kingdom in 1661, France was the greatest power in Europe. She had achieved that position as a result of a long struggle with the Austrian and Spanish branches of the Habsburg family, a conflict which, in its most recent phase, had lasted from 1635 to 1659. The Austrian Habsburgs, headed by the Holy Roman emperor, were humiliated at the Treaty of Westphalia in 1648, when France not only gained the three bishoprics of Metz, Toul and Verdun, comprising important territories on her eastern frontier, but the emperor's rights in Alsace as well. In 1659 the Treaty of the Pyrenees, which brought the Spanish phase of the war to an end, gave her the provinces of Roussillon and Cerdagne, Spanish territory lying to the north of the Pyrenees and most of Artois in the Spanish Netherlands as well.

The Treaty of the Pyrenees demonstrated clearly to the world at large that the great days of the Spanish Empire were over. In the sixteenth century Spain had been the dominant power. After her acquisition of Portugal in 1580 she controlled the greatest empire that the world had yet seen, with far flung possessions in Europe, Africa, Asia and the Americas. That empire had largely been created by the Castilian provinces which formed the heartland of the Iberian peninsula, and the strength and stability of Spain as a whole depended on the continuing power of Castile. The years between 1590 and 1620, however, saw a rapid erosion of the three fundamental foundations of Castile's greatness, rising population, productivity and the revenue which she obtained from her American colonies. The decline of Castile's ability to support the burdens of empire led the Count-Duke of Olivares, Philip IV's leading minister from 1621 to 1643, to turn to the kingdoms of Portugal and Aragon for greater contributions. This led to revolts there, and these, in turn, further weakened the empire as a whole. By 1661 Spain was very clearly in decline.

The greatness of France in 1661 was founded at least as much on the weaknesses of the other European states as on her own intrinsic strength. Wherever Louis looked conditions seemed favourable for extending French influence. The newly restored Charles II of England was preoccupied with the settlement of his kingdom after the upheavals of 1640 to 1660 and was in any case an admirer of Louis. The United Provinces, under John de Witt, were preoccupied with defending their commercial supremacy and preventing a return to power of the House of Orange. Moreover, they had fought with France against Spain in the 1630s and 1640s and, though very well aware of the potential threat of growing French power, continued their traditional anti-Spanish stance.

Louis, therefore, had nothing to fear from England or the Dutch. He had equally little cause to worry about the Emperor Leopold I. From the 1660s until the 1680s Leopold's main preoccupation was the defence of his own hereditary Austrian and Hungarian dominions against the Ottoman Turks. The Turkish Empire, which had declined sharply in power in the early seventeenth century under a series of incompetent sultans, revived dramatically after 1656 with campaigns against Austria and Hungary, which culminated in the siege of Vienna, the imperial capital, in 1683. Leopold, so strongly threatened in the east, was in a very weak position to resist French ambitions in the west.

Of the other states, the vast Russian Empire was hardly, in the mid-seventeenth century, part of Europe at all. It had a large population and great unexploited natural resources but its army was inefficient by west European standards and its administration primitive. Russian foreign policy centred around its immediate neighbours, the Ottoman Empire, Poland and Sweden. The vast Polish state was in decline, but Sweden, in 1661 the dominant country in the Baltic, was a great European power, a position which she had won under Gustavus Adolphus and in alliance with France during the Thirty Years War. In 1660, however, she lost a notable warrior-king, Charles X, and a regency became essential for the four-year-old Charles XI. The main aim of the regency in foreign policy was to preserve Swedish dominance in the north. This determination led to tactical switches in Sweden's alliances in the 1660s, though the tradition of friendship with France remained strong. She did not have the ability, even if she had had the will, to undertake sustained resistance to French ambitions in the west.

The weaknesses of most of the European states appeared doubly dramatic when contrasted with France's intrinsic strength. France's population was about eighteen million, perhaps three times as large as that of England or Spain and about eight times greater than that of the United Provinces or Sweden. Even the vast Russian Empire had fewer inhabitants. France had other impressive natural resources, notably fertile soil, and in the early years of Louis' personal rule, under Colbert's direction, financial reforms and industrial development added to the country's strength. The army steadily increased in size, from under 100,000 in the early 1660s to nearly 400,000 during the war of the Spanish Succession. In addition, under the direction of two administrators of genius, Michel le Tellier and his son, the Marquis de Louvois, its munitions and supply services were greatly improved and discipline in all ranks was tightened up. Moreover, Louis had at the beginning of his reign, the greatest generals in Europe, Turenne and Condé.

There was no naval tradition in France comparable with her great military reputation, dating back to the Middle Ages. Colbert, however, resolved to make France a great naval power. He built dockyards, ordered French ships to be constructed at home rather than abroad and developed an elaborate bureaucratic machine for the government of the navy. By the time of his death in 1683 France was almost ready to challenge England and Holland for control of the seas. Indeed, at the beginning of the War of the League of Augsburg in 1688 it looked as if France might become the dominant naval power. This possibility was ended in 1692 at the Battle of La Hogue, when the French under Admiral Tourville were decisively defeated by an Anglo-Dutch fleet. The French navy never recovered from this blow and by the end of Louis' reign England had clearly outdistanced France as the country with the most powerful war fleet in the world.

The army and navy were, of course, Louis' ultimate weapons in international affairs, but he had one more subtle instrument. Like his army, Louis' diplomatic service was unrivalled in Europe. When he assumed personal power the foreign office consisted of a few clerks. By the time of his death it had become a large bureau with elaborate archives and a whole host of officials who supplied much of the information upon which royal policy decisions were based. Abroad, Louis kept permanent ambassadors in all the leading European countries except Russia and in addition residents of subordinate rank in the lesser states, such as the German and Italian principalities. These representatives were on the whole capable and conscientious men. No other country equalled France in the number or quality of its agents abroad, and no other country was able to provide its diplomats with the lavish subsidies which Louis distributed freely in order to win friends.

The quest for glory

With these great sources of strength behind him Louis could confidently embark on an ambitious foreign policy. What was his real aim? It has been claimed that the issue of the Spanish succession was the pivot of Louis' whole foreign policy, but this question was all-important only in the later years of the reign. Other interpretations, that Louis' policies were determined by a desire to

extend France to her natural frontiers or by a wish to increase French influence in Germany, are open to even greater objection. It may be more realistic to argue that Louis was, above all, resolved to reduce still further the already waning power of the Habsburgs. Such a view, however, neglects the obsessive determination with which he set out to crush the United Provinces in the early 1670s. It is probable that the primary motive for Louis' actions was a desire for glory: glory for France but, above all, glory for himself.

Louis' quest for glory and the reactions of the other European states to it can be followed in four wars—the War of Devolution (1667–8), the Dutch War (1672–8), the War of the League of Augsburg (1688–97) and the War of the Spanish Succession (1701–13)—and also in the 'reunions' policy of the early 1680s.

In the War of Devolution Louis fought against Spain, in theory to safeguard the rights of his wife, the Spanish princess, Maria Theresa, to territory in the Spanish Netherlands but in practice to win territory for France and military reputation for his armies and himself. He achieved considerable triumphs, first of all by isolating Spain internationally—a fine achievement for his splendid diplomatic service—and then by winning notable victories in the field. These successes, however, alarmed England, Holland and Sweden, and in 1668 these three countries formed a Triple Alliance, designed to force France to make peace. Louis did agree to peace in 1668, though it is not certain how far the Triple Alliance influenced him. One thing is clear, however; he never forgave the Dutch for their intrigues against him. As a result of the War of Devolution he gained a number of important towns in the Spanish Netherlands for France, and after 1668 he planned to extend still further French influence in the north east, this time by an attack on the Dutch.

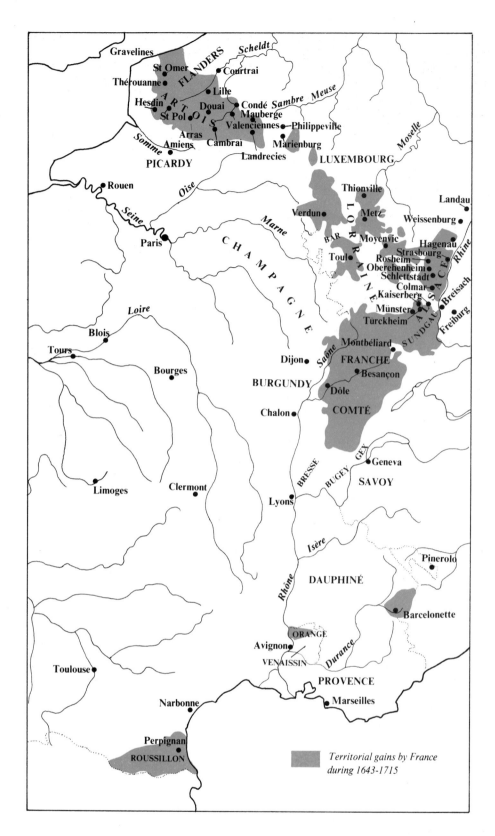

REDIIT CONCORDIA FRATRVM.

Amsterdam. This brought a temporary respite to the Dutch and during 1673 and 1674 they obtained much needed allies. There was a virtual diplomatic revolution in these years as the other European powers, terrified by the prospect of a complete French victory, hastened to support the United Provinces. By the end of 1674 Louis was at war with the emperor, Spain and most of the leading German princes. In addition he had lost the support of England, for in 1674 Charles II was forced by parliamentary pressure to make peace with the Dutch. As a result of these changes in the international scene Louis was forced to withdraw from Dutch territory, and after 1674 he waged war chiefly against the Habsburgs.

The war was brought to an end by a series of treaties signed at Nymegen in 1678 and 1679. Louis obtained very favourable terms from Spain. The great territory of Franche Comté was confirmed as a French possession and, although several of the towns in the Spanish Netherlands which France had gained at the Treaty of Aix-la-Chapelle were restored, she obtained in exchange a string of other strongholds including Saint-Omer and Ypres.

The treaty with the Dutch was much less to Louis' liking, as he made no territorial gains at all from the republic. Very clearly, his objective of crushing the Dutch had not been realized. Nevertheless, the Peace of Nymegen probably represents the summit of his power and success in Europe. In the later stages of the war, he had fought against a great coalition, yet his armies had never been beaten.

After Nymegen, Louis' confidence was high and he tried to achieve further triumphs by his 'reunions' policy. His idea was to exploit the vague wording of recent treaties, such as that of Westphalia, which, in ceding lands to France, often failed to make clear the precise limits of the territory granted.

Territorial gains by France during 1643-1715

He worked as hard in the years after 1668 to isolate the United Provinces as he had to isolate Spain in the period before 1667 and with almost equal success—Brandenburg was the republic's only ally in 1672. His and his diplomats' greatest triumph was the break-up of the Triple Alliance. In 1670 by the Secret Treaty of Dover, which reflected Charles II's personal views on foreign policy, England allied with France against the Dutch, and in April 1672 Sweden, in return for a subsidy, agreed to oppose any German prince who supported Holland.

Louis was thus able in 1672 to join England in an attack on the United Provinces in the knowledge that the diplomatic situation was decisively in his favour. With his huge army, some 120,000 strong and led by generals of genius, he won a series of great victories.

In the summer of 1672 the capture of Amsterdam seemed imminent: the very existence of the United Provinces was in the balance. At this point the republic saved itself by piercing the walls and dykes along the banks of some of its numerous canals and rivers and thus flooding a large area around

From 1679 onwards he set up a number of 'chambers of reunion', which assigned large stretches of territory in western Germany to France. By 1681 French sovereignty had been proclaimed over the whole of Alsace, including the city of Strasbourg. Louis also won important successes in the Spanish Netherlands, where he captured Luxembourg in 1684.

Spain, infuriated by French attacks on her possessions, had declared war in 1683, but she was much too weak to have any real hope of success. In 1684 she had to agree to a twenty-year truce, by which France was left in possession of Alsace, Strasbourg, Luxembourg and some territory in Spanish Flanders. Spain had been unable to find allies against France because the general diplomatic situation in Europe was still favourable to Louis, though this was the last period when that was true. In 1683,

the Austrian Habsburgs were fighting for their lives against the Turks and Charles II of England was a French pensioner. By the end of 1688, when the next great military conflict broke out in western Europe, the emperor was winning notable victories in the east against a retreating Ottoman army. Above all, William of Orange had become King of England.

France's enemies gather

Between 1684 and 1688 Louis took a series of steps which could almost have been designed to unite his enemies against him. In 1685 his revocation of the Edict of Nantes, which had safeguarded the rights of French Protestants, infuriated all the Protestant powers of Europe. In 1687 he quarrelled violently with the pope over the

conduct of the French ambassador in Rome, and in 1688 he tried to intrude his own candidate, Cardinal Furstenburg, into the important Electorate of Cologne against the wishes of both pope and emperor. Moreover, he also invaded and devastated the Palatinate in support of the flimsy claims of his sister-in-law, the Princess Elizabeth Charlotte, to that territory.

This final aggression led to the outbreak of war with the emperor. In 1689–90 a grand coalition was formed against Louis consisting of England, the Dutch, the emperor, Spain, Saxony, Savoy, Hanover, Bavaria and Brandenburg.

The war was fought in Flanders, Germany, Italy and Spain as well as at sea. France won some notable military successes, but the naval defeat at La Hogue in 1692 marked the beginning of a permanent decline in her strength at sea, while the bad harvest of 1693 brought famine and discontent at home. By 1695 it was clear that the strain of waging war against most of Europe was too much even for France and in 1697 peace was concluded at Ryswick. Louis made very great concessions, probably because the long expected death of the ailing Charles II of Spain seemed imminent and he was anxious to obtain part of the inheritance for his son, the Dauphin Louis.

He agreed to give up all his reunions' acquisitions gained since 1679, except for Strasbourg and the town of Landau, and to abandon his candidates for the electorates of Cologne and the Palatinate. He recognized William III as King of England, made considerable concessions to the Dutch, and agreed that they should be allowed to garrison, for their own protection, a series of border fortresses in the Spanish Netherlands.

The issue of the Spanish succession, uppermost in Louis' mind in 1697, dominated the remainder of his reign. Charles II of Spain had no children or brothers, but his two half-sisters—daughters of Philip IV by his first wife—had married into the reigning houses of France and Austria. The elder, Maria Theresa, had married Louis XIV, the younger, Margaret Theresa, the Emperor Leopold I. Louis and Leopold had further dynastic connections with the Spanish Habsburgs through their mothers, who were both daughters of Philip III. The French royal house and the Austrian imperial family thus had the best hereditary claims to the Spanish throne, and as early as 1668 Leopold and Louis had signed a partition treaty providing for the division of the Spanish dominions between them on Charles II's death.

In 1698, however, after much haggling, France, England and the United Provinces reached a settlement by which the greater part of the Spanish dominions was to go to the Electoral Prince of Bavaria. He was a grandson of Leopold I but had little chance of inheriting the Habsburg's hereditary possessions or the imperial crown. In this way it was made clear that Spain was not to be united either with France or with the Empire. Louis did, however, obtain Sicily, Sardinia and the Tuscan ports for the dauphin, a splendid inheritance which would pass in due course to the French crown and make France a dominant power in Italy. It was also agreed that the Archduke Charles, Leopold's second son, should get the Duchy of Milan. Such terms, it need hardly be said, were quite unacceptable to the emperor.

The fate of an empire

Any slight chance which the arrangement of 1698 may have had of success collapsed in February 1699 when the electoral prince died. A few months later France, England and the United Provinces agreed on a second treaty, by which the Archduke Charles was to get Spain, the Spanish

120

Netherlands and the Spanish Empire overseas and the dauphin was to obtain Milan (which he was then to exchange for the duchy of Lorraine) as well as the territory which he had been promised in 1698. The emperor, however, refused to accept these provisions—he feared the aggrandizement of France in Italy.

In Spain the treaty provoked an outburst of fury: Spaniards were indignant that foreigners should presume to settle the fate of their empire without even consulting them. Charles II himself was determined that the Spanish inheritance should be preserved intact. In October 1700, after much hesitation, he signed a will which made Philip, Duke of Anjou, second son of the dauphin, his sole heir. If Anjou refused, the inheritance was to pass to his younger brother, the Duke of Berry. If he too declined, it was to go to the Archduke Charles. Louis accepted the will on behalf of his grandson, but this decision did not immediately lead to a general war. The hostility of the emperor was certain, but the English and Dutch governments recognized Philip as King of Spain.

It was only a series of unwise actions by Louis—difficult to understand in the delicate diplomatic situation of the time—which led to the War of the Spanish Succession. He took measures to safeguard Philip's rights to the French throne, drove the Dutch from the barrier fortresses in the Spanish Netherlands which they had been allowed to garrison in 1697, obtained commercial advantages for France in Spain's American colonies and, in September 1701, on the death of James II, recognized the Old Pretender as James III, King of England. War was officially declared in May 1702, though the French and Austrians had

already been engaged in hostilities in Italy since the spring of the previous year.

The odds were heavily against Louis in the conflict. His three main opponents, England, the United Provinces and Austria, had support from Brandenburg, Hanover, Denmark and the Palatinate, while he had the support of only Spain, Savoy, Portugal, Bavaria and Cologne. Spain was a liability to be defended against allied attacks rather than an asset, and in 1703 Savoy and Portugal changed sides. The latter's desertion in particular was a bitter blow for Louis. It gave his enemies a convenient land base from which to assault Spain, already vulnerable to attack from the powerful Dutch and English navies, which commanded the seas.

The French army, with fewer troops than the allies, had to conduct operations in Spain and Italy and along the whole eastern boundary of France. With such considerable commitments Louis had to stand on the defensive, an unusual posture for France. Moreover, for the first time in his reign, his opponents' generals were much better than his own. Marlborough and Eugene, the principal allied commanders, demonstrated that they were soldiers of genius, whereas France, though she had distinguished service from Marshal Villars, no longer had officers of the calibre of Turenne and Condé. In 1704, at Blenheim in Germany, Eugene and Marlborough inflicted a crushing defeat on a large French and Bavarian army, the first really serious reverse suffered by France on the battlefield during the entire reign of Louis XIV. It was a portent of things to come. Further defeats in the Netherlands at Ramillies (1706), Oudenarde (1708) and Malplaquet (1709) reduced France to desperate military straits. To make matters worse the winter of 1708–9 was appallingly severe in France and many peasants were faced with the threat of starvation.

In this situation Louis was prepared to make almost any concession to obtain peace, but the allies' demand that he should provide military aid to help in the expulsion of his grandson from Spain was too humiliating for him to accept. The French nation rallied around him in this desperate time, and colossal efforts were made to raise new troops. The allies had overreached themselves: after 1709 prospects improved for France. Spain as a whole showed that it stood behind Philip V and was not prepared to accept an Austrian king. In 1710 a Tory government anxious for peace came to power in England. Above all, in 1711, on the death of the Emperor Joseph I, the Archduke Charles ascended the imperial throne. If he were to be established as king of Spain as well, the whole balance of power in Europe would be seriously affected.

These developments and an important French victory at Denain in the Netherlands in 1712 meant that Louis was able to obtain more favourable treatment in the peace

Left, an allegorical painting of William III presenting liberty to Europe, done by James Thornhill in the 1720s. As champion of the Protestant cause, William was able to pose as the opponent of authoritarianism and centralization generally. Painted Hall, Royal Naval College, Greenwich.

Opposite, the Battle of La Hogue in 1692, at which the Anglo-Dutch fleet defeated the French, commanded by Tourville. The French navy was no match for the strength of the two most powerful navies of Europe combined. National Maritime Museum, London.

settlement of 1713–14 than would have seemed possible in 1709. By the treaties of Utrecht (1713) and Rastadt (1714) Philip V was allowed to retain Spain and the Spanish Empire in the New World, although the Spanish possessions in Italy and the Netherlands passed to Austria. The Dutch right to a 'barrier' against France was confirmed. Louis recognized Anne as Queen of England and made considerable commercial and colonial concessions to England in the New World.

When Louis died in 1715, therefore, he had the satisfaction of seeing his grandson established on the throne of Spain and of leaving to his successor Louis XV a larger France that he had inherited in 1643—he did not lose in 1713 the territorial gains made as a result of his triumphs up to the 1680s. It is clear, however, that between about 1685 and 1715 the balance of power had swung strongly against France. In 1683–4, the years of the siege of Vienna and the truce of Ratisbon, France had been by far the most powerful state in Europe and there seemed a real possibility that she might establish complete dominance on the continent. In 1715, because of her large population and great natural resources, she was still the strongest single power, but the reverses of the years between 1688 and 1713 meant that she had ceased to threaten the very existence of her neighbours. Moreover, the treaties of 1713–14, together with the treaty of Nystadt, which brought the Great Northern War of 1700–21 to an end, marked the rise of England, Austria and Russia to the status of great powers, a position which none of them had really enjoyed in 1683.

The rise of England

In the early 1680s England, under Charles II, had been little more than a French tributary state. Between 1688 and 1713, however, under William III and Queen Anne, she had built up her strength at an astonishing rate and had been the paymaster of the coalitions which humbled Louis XIV. In 1715 she was certainly a power of the very first rank and by far the greatest naval power in the world.

In 1680 Austria, too, had been a comparatively weak state, controlling only a strip of Hungary to the east. By 1715 the position was very different. Following a series of brilliant victories against the Turks in the years after 1683, she gained control of the whole of Hungary. In the west, as a result of the settlements of 1713–14, she obtained the Spanish Netherlands. Milan, the Tuscan ports, Naples and Sardinia. This was a vast accession of territory and population. In 1715 Austria, like England, was unquestionably a great power.

Russia hardly counted in the European states system in 1680, but by 1715, as a result of Peter the Great's victories against Sweden, she controlled the southern coastline of the Baltic Sea, a position confirmed by the Treaty of Nystadt in 1721. In 1715 Russia was by far the greatest power in northern Europe, though it was not until well on in the eighteenth century that the full impact of her new strength was felt in western Europe.

Among the other notable European states in 1715 the United Provinces was entering a period of relative political and economic decline, while Sweden, a great power in the 1680s, was well on the way to third-rate status. Spain, under its new Bourbon dynasty, was to witness something of a revival in the early eighteenth century but in 1715 was both poor and weak.

None of these changes, except the decline of Holland and, perhaps, the revival of Spain, boded well for France. In the age of Louis XIV she was the greatest international power. In the eighteenth century other nations challenged her for that title.

Chapter 13

France under Louis XIV

Louis XIV was four when he succeeded his father in 1643. His regent and mother, Anne of Austria, confirmed the Sicilian Cardinal Mazarin in the position of first minister to which he had been appointed on Richelieu's death the previous year. Mazarin established close personal ties with Anne and followed Richelieu's policy of a centralized bureaucratic government, exploiting every conceivable avenue to raise money sufficient for the commitments of war with Spain. Important victories on the battlefields of Rocroi (1643) and Lens (1648) maintained the government's prestige, while Mazarin proved effective at defusing the opposition factions against his rule, although regional revolts continued to break out with regularity against the endless demands for taxes.

Nevertheless by 1648 the strain of war had virtually bankrupted the government, and the Paris *parlement* came out in open opposition to proposals for new taxes; in this they were supported by royal officials angered at the prospect of the renewal of the *paulette*. They proposed legislation to restore the princes of the blood to their old position in the royal administration in the place of the new bureaucrats; and the *parlements* of other towns similarly forced the revocation of the powers of the *intendants*. When Mazarin attempted to arrest the *parlementaire* leaders the people of Paris resorted to the barricades and drove the king and government from the city.

It was apparent that neither side wanted a full-scale civil war, and a compromise reached in 1649 ended this phase of the rebellion, known as the *fronde parlementaire*. However the damage done to authority of the provincial adminstration brought violence from many cities from Normandy to Provence, and devastation to the countryside which worsened the hardships of a series of disastrous harvests. The Duke of Condé, the hero of Rocroi and Lens, became the focus for noble discontent with Mazarin, and leader of the so-called *fronde des princes*. Civil war and intrigue resulted in two periods of exile for Mazarin and a march in 1652 by Condé from his power-base in Bordeaux to Paris where his impetus fizzled out. By February

1653 Mazarin was firmly in control once more. Although the *frondes* never had the impact of the wars of religion, or the scope of the English civil war, they left a lasting legacy in convincing the young king of the need to wield an absolute monarchical power.

The 1650s saw the continuation of the war with Spain, the re-establishment of the *intendancy* and the old systems of adminstration and fund-raising, while Mazarin slowly educated Louis in the business of government. The now-familiar revolts against taxation came to a head in 1659 with a major rebellion in Provence. Louis himself led an army into Aix and Marseilles the following year, and destroyed the region's military and administrative autonomy. This victory symbolized his arrival as a powerful monarch who would use all his will and power to counter provincial and aristocratic rebelliousness.

'L'état, c'est moi'

Mazarin died in 1661 and Louis saw no need to replace him. For the rest of his reign he would work hard at creating a state that could reflect his belief in the divinely given authority of the monarch over every other authority in the realm, whether noble, representative or ecclesiastical. Louis' reign therefore saw not only the establishment of a glorious monarchical vision at Versailles, where every great aristocrat felt impelled to attend as a planet orbiting around the Sun-King, even at the cost of losing touch with his old connections in the provinces on which aristocratic independence of the Crown had always been based; it also saw the curtailment of the *parlement's* powers in 1673, while the Estates General were never called at all. Regional privileges were ruthlessly overriden and the monarch

Above, the Galerie des Glaces *at Versailles, designed by Jules Hardouin Mansart. The walls are decorated with green marble and the ceiling with allegories of the apotheosis of Louis XIV.*

Opposite left, John Churchill, Duke of Marlborough (1650–1722), the English general who created an efficient English army, and won the independence to use it as he wished in the Blenheim campaign of 1704. National Portrait Gallery, London

Opposite right, William III of England (reigned 1689–1702) and Stadtholder of the United Provinces. National Portrait Gallery, London.

Below, Louis and Colbert visiting the Gobelins tapestry factory, according to a tapestry produced by that very factory. Colbert bought the factory for the government in 1662, and it was the centre of production of both furniture and tapestries for the court until the 1690s, when furniture production there was ended. Musée des Gobelins, Paris.

became as never before the origin of all power in the land.

The court of Versailles was the wonder of Europe, and epitomized to foreigners, whether sympathetic or critical to Louis, the King's absolutist ambitions. He began work on expanding his father's old palace in the 1660s, and moved his court there permanently in 1682. Its size and magnificence were unprecedented (as was appropriate for Europe's largest and, in terms of population and natural resources, wealthiest kingdom) and the subordination of the nobility to the *minutiae* of court etiquette perfectly expressed Louis' ideal of a hierarchical state in which the king was answerable only to God.

The grandeur of Versailles, and of the state that had its home there, was partly illusory. Louis had inherited great financial difficulties that bound his freedom of action; and if he brooked no challenges to his rule, treating offenders of all sorts with exemplary harshness, he rarely went out of his way to induce such challenges in the first place. Like his predecessors, he leant heavily on a small group of families committed to working in the royal administration. The first and greatest of these servants was Jean-Baptiste Colbert, the son of a draper, who came to prominence in 1661 and was appointed controller-general of finances in 1665. By 1670 his jurisdiction covered most areas of French life, except the army.

Colbert's success was in reducing the Crown's chronic indebtedness; this was achieved primarily by reforming the system of taxation. He restructured the *taille*, bringing it down to a realistic level and ensuring that it was regularly collected; to overcome the wide-ranging exemptions enjoyed by the nobility, he turned increasingly to indirect forms of taxation; and by changing the system of tax farming he was able to ensure that a larger proportion of taxes paid actually reached the Crown – rising from 37 per cent in 1661 to 65 per cent six years later. Such means gave Louis a peacetime revenue of a size that previous monarchs had known only in the emergencies of war.

Much of the extra revenue was spent on extending the scope of royal patronage and on military preparations, building elaborate fortifications on the eastern frontier, expanding the army and navy in size and equipment. Domestically, Colbert sought to follow the policies of Sully and Henry IV in encouraging trade by improving the transport network – joining the Atlantic and Mediterranean by canal – and by abolishing many local restrictions on the internal movement of goods. He encouraged industries by bringing in skilled workers from other countries, and attempted to build up overseas trade by organizing trading companies. He was able to do little for

agriculture, however, on which the bulk of the nation's prosperity rested, and Louis' commitment to military spending did not leave enough money over to stimulate industry to the extent that was required. French trade, for the most part based on the peripheries of the kingdom away from Paris, suffered badly from the extreme centralization of the state.

Colbert's name has been linked with the doctrine of mercantilism, according to which trade is treated as an arm of state policy, the main object being to accumulate bullion for use in financing wars: money was for power, not for prosperity. The king's subjects were expected to control all aspects of the nation's trade, since France could not be dependent on the goodwill of foreign merchants, and trade with foreign countries should not be allowed to diminish the nation's stock of natural or monetary resources. Thus Colbert encouraged luxury textile manufacture for export, but proposed high tariffs on all imports to keep out middlemen. Whether or not mercantilism was a coherent policy, it was bound to increase tension with neighbouring nations, notably the Dutch whose prosperity was founded on their position in the carrying trade, both in Europe and beyond. The restrictive tariffs that Colbert set in 1667 were a virtual declaration of economic warfare on the Dutch.

The relative health of France's fiscal and economic state achieved by Colbert was swiftly undermined by the outbreak of actual war with the Dutch in 1672. This initiated a new period of long, expensive and unsatisfactory wars in which Louis' slow march towards the 'natural frontier' of the Rhine was obstructed by the general fear among his neighbours that he intended to be master of the whole of Europe. After Colbert's death in 1683 no other minister

was equal to coping with the financial situation and, as Louis found it more and more hard to raise money through the sale of offices, he resorted increasingly to indirect taxes, most notoriously the *gabelle* or salt-tax. By Louis' death in 1715 France was again virtually bankrupt, and was no nearer building up a strong mercantile base to resolve the problem. Instead Louis' taxes merely served to depress the peasantry still further and his death was widely greeted with relief rather than mourning.

Religious conflicts

Louis' reign was marked by three religious crises, all expressions in the ecclesiastical sphere of his desire for absolute power within his realm. Personally Louis was a conventional Catholic; after 1684 under the influence of his secret wife Mme de Maintenon he adopted a sombre piety but in general he had little interest in theology.

At the start of his reign there were between one and two million Huguenots in France, found particularly in the financial, commercial and industrial sectors of the economy. Since 1629 they had posed no political threat, and France enjoyed a degree of religious peace.

At first Louis' attitude to them was moderate, and he attempted to encourage peaceful conversion. But in 1679 he began to withdraw their privileges: the churches were destroyed, schools closed down, Huguenots removed from public office, civil rights taken away, and soldiers billeted on Protestant families.

This policy resulted in a stream of conversions, and in 1685 Louis formally revoked the Edict of Nantes, outlawing all Huguenot worship, whether public or private, and ordering all Protestant ministers to leave the country. The Catholics at home and abroad reacted with delight, but to Protestants, especially in London and Amsterdam, the Revocation set the seal on their view of Louis as the arch-enemy of liberty and truth. Some 200,000 Huguenots, many of them skilled craftsmen, fled abroad, where they encouraged this view of Louis as a tyrant, while the loss of their talents did nothing to help France's economic lethargy. Both diplomatically and domestically the Revocation marked, if it did not cause, the start of a decline in Louis' fortunes; his enemies were confirmed in their resolve, and he was increasingly embroiled in the paralyzing difficulties of organizing his huge military campaigns.

Louis' religious problems were not only with Protestants. The Council of Bologna which had given the French Crown the right to control ecclesiastical appointments in 1516 had certain grey areas, notably the right of the Crown to enjoy the fruits of vacant sees. In 1673 Louis reasserted this right, and supported the Gallican theorists who disputed the Pope's sovereignty over the General Council and who claimed that papal bulls must be ratified by the *parlements* before their writ could run in France. In 1681 Louis summoned a General Council of the French church which declared that kings were not subject to the Pope in temporal affairs and that General Councils were superior to the Papacy.

By 1689 a third of French bishoprics were empty, but Louis was beginning to feel the diplomatic impact of the Pope's hostility to his position. Consequently a compromise position was reached in 1693, at which point he turned to attack the Jansenists, a Catholic group who supported the teachings of Cornelius Jansen, an early seventeenth-century bishop of Ypres. Jansen had argued, like Calvin, that man's sin is so great that he can be saved neither by faith nor good works, but only by the grace of God. This doctrine approached predestinarianism, and was at odds with the dominant Jesuit teaching. Jansenism, best known today in the writings of Blaise Pascal, inspired a moral rigour and unworldliness, and became the focus of religious critics of contemporary Catholicism.

In 1653 Jansenism was declared a heresy, and Louis took it upon himself to root it out in France, expelling the nuns of the well-known convent of Port-Royal in 1664. In 1668 a theological compromise was reached but in 1693 Louis' fear of a Jansenist conspiracy revived. In 1705 he persuaded the pope to condemn the movement again, and in 1709 he closed the Port-Royal convent once more. He failed, however, to destroy the Order, but spent many of his declining years worrying about what many people considered an anachronistic dispute.

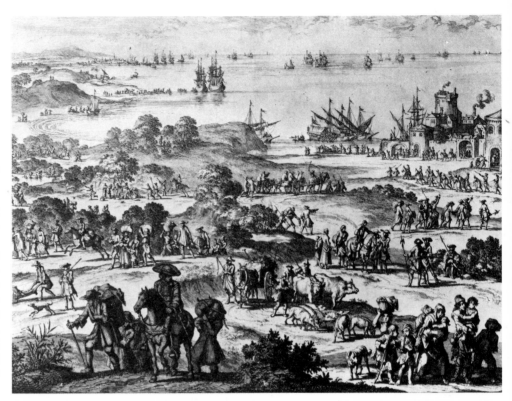

Chapter 14

Russia of the Romanovs

Throughout the seventeenth century observers from the West found it difficult to think of Russia as part of Europe. Accounts of the country by foreign travellers and diplomats were almost unanimous in emphasizing its 'Asiatic' aspects, such as the arbitrary and despotic form of government and the subjection of women and their virtual exclusion from society. The obverse of the almost unlimited power of the ruler, the complete subjection of the Russian people, reinforced this impression of an oriental despotism.

By 1600 the idea of the 'slave-born Muscovite' was firmly enshrined in English literature—the phrase occurs in Sir Philip Sidney's poem *Astrophel and Stella*. Such ideas symbolized the fact that the new Romanov dynasty, which came to power in the early seventeenth century, occupied the throne of a country which seemed barbarous to the more sophisticated nations of western Europe.

The election of Michael Romanov to the throne of Russia in 1613 marked the end of a period of dramatic upheavals in Russian history. The 'Time of Troubles', as the years 1598 to 1613 are called, had witnessed Polish invasions and occupation of the country, several changes of dynasty and, above all, a gigantic social ferment in which the peasantry protested violently against the oppressions of the government and their landlords in general and the growing burdens of serfdom in particular. The origins of that revolutionary social movement can be traced back to the developments of the fifteenth century and earlier, but, despite its long antecedents and the extent and savagery of the storm in which it culminated, it left few permanent marks on the political and social structure of the country. The fundamental fact of previous Russian political life—the absolutism of the tsars—emerged virtually unscathed from the upheavals. The great majority of the peasants who had played a prominent part in the movement were returned to the tender mercies of masters whose one real remedy for discontented serfs was continuous and brutal use of the knout.

The Orthodox Church, endowed with enormous estates and vast privileges in 1598, retained both throughout these years of turmoil. It is true that the storms of 1598 to 1613 completed the downfall of the great influence previously enjoyed by the ancient Russian princely and noble families, but this was merely the culmination of a trend which had been continuing throughout the sixteenth century, and the fact that the nobility of birth was replaced by a 'service' nobility, which owed its rise to the influence which it derived from holding court and state offices, meant that the change was essentially merely one of personnel—there was certainly no remodelling of the social structure.

Michael, the first Romanov tsar, the man who had the task of maintaining internal peace and stability after the Troubles, was not well equipped for his task. A sickly youth of sixteen when he came to the throne, he was dominated first of all by his forceful mother and then, from 1619 onwards, by his father Filaret, who had previously been a prisoner in Poland. Filaret became patriarch or head of the Russian Church, was recognized as co-ruler with his son and, in practice, governed the country until his death in 1633. Michael himself died in 1645 and was succeeded by his only son Alexis, then sixteen years old.

The new tsar, a man of conservative mind, pious to the point of bigotry, showed few signs of real ability in matters of state—his main preoccupations seem to have been with complicated church and court ceremonies—and the conduct of government business was left to favourites and officials. When he died in 1676 his eldest son, Fedor, a delicate, unassertive boy of fourteen, succeeded to the throne. Fedor's early death in 1682 precipitated a struggle for power between rival branches of the imperial family, a struggle which was the prelude to the reign of Peter the Great.

Reforming the government

The conservatism of Michael, Alexis and Fedor, helps to explain the continuity between Russian political and social developments in the sixteenth and seventeenth centuries. Before the upheavals of the Time of Troubles the tendency had been towards increasing centralization and regimentation, a tendency which was resumed under the Romanovs. The central administration of the country was carried on through *prikazy*, government departments inherited from the sixteenth century. There were a large number of these in Michael's reign, perhaps as many as fifty in all. The authority of the different *prikazy* often overlapped and the whole system was both unwieldy and inefficient. During the seventeenth century improvements were made. Some *prikazy* were merged, while others were grouped together under the control of a single official. These reforms, though their importance must not be overrated, did help

Opposite above, a Dutch engraving of Protestants leaving France in the 1660s.

Opposite below, a view of the Palace of Versailles, painted in the late seventeenth century by Jean-Baptiste Martin. Château de Versailles.

to prepare the way for the administrative reforms of Peter the Great.

The tendency towards centralization was more immediately obvious at local level, where administration in the seventeenth century was carried on by governors appointed by the central authorities and by elected officials. The elected local officials, who dated from the reign of Ivan the Terrible (1533–84), might seem at first sight to be exceptions to the rule of growing centralization. In fact, from the very start they were government agents rather than representatives of local interests, and this aspect of their role developed in the seventeenth century.

The main duty of such officials was the unpopular one of collecting taxes from their fellow-citizens, a task for which they received no pay from the government. Their good behaviour was guaranteed by heavy penalties for misdemeanours and by the fact that the local communities which elected them were collectively responsible for their actions. In these circumstances, 'local self-government' was a mockery. Local officials were simply unpaid agents of the central government. They functioned under the close supervision of the governors who were, for all practical purposes, the supreme masters of the territories under their control. Most governors exploited their position to the full, and a complaint of 1642 declared that they had 'reduced the people of all stations to beggary and . . . stripped them to the bone'.

Like the administrative history of seventeenth-century Russia, the social history can be viewed essentially as a continuation of sixteenth-century trends. The great themes of sixteenth-century social history were the development of serfdom and the increasing regimentation of the population as a whole in the interests of the state. Serfdom had originated in Russia long before 1500, but it developed rapidly during the course of the sixteenth century. There were two main reasons for this. First of all, the central government tried, for fiscal purposes, to keep peasants living on state land from moving away. Second, peasants living on private estates became increasingly indebted to their masters. In these circumstances, more and more peasants became tied to the land.

Serfdom

The great Code of Laws issued in 1649 confirmed the developments of the previous century and a half and restricted still further the rights of the peasants, reducing virtually the whole of the Russian peasantry to serfdom. Indeed, the framers of the Code embodied in it the idea of the complete subordination of all classes in the community to the interests of the state as they saw them. This applied just as much to the two other great classes, the burghers and the nobles, as it did to the peasants. Burghers

were forbidden to move from the towns where they were living when the Code was issued—a provision largely designed to prevent tax evasion—and the nobility, who were given the sole right to own estates farmed by servile labour, became a hereditary caste whose main duty was military service to the state.

The provisions of the Code were, of course, honoured as much in the breach as in the observance. Despite its failures, however, the main idea which it enshrined was to dominate almost the whole of later Russian history.

Alexis and Fedor, despite their conservatism, did, in one respect at least, show themselves to be less hidebound than many of their subjects. They accepted changes in church ritual and in the phrasing of certain religious texts which were anathema to large numbers of Russians and which produced an important and permanent schism in the Russian Church. The matters at issue seem incredibly trivial today, but minor points of ceremonial, such as the use of three instead of two fingers in making the sign of the cross, provoked the most ferocious cruelties from the authorities and the staunchest resistance and utmost heroism from the 'Old Believers', as those who resisted the changes came to be called.

The changes, which brought Russia into line with other Orthodox Churches, were approved by a great Church council which met in the autumn of 1666 and continued its work until 1667. This council, which was attended by the patriarchs of Alexandria and Antioch and by representatives of other important branches of the Eastern Church, anathematized all who refused to accept the revised texts and the new ritual. The extent of resistance to the decisions of 1667 bears witness to the attachment to traditional religious observances which characterized a large part of the population of Russia. For them, formal piety was the very essence of the faith and they saw in the changes the abandonment of Christianity itself. During the years up to about 1690, when the most

violent persecutions took place, thousands of Old Believers burned themselves to death to escape contamination by the new 'heresy.'

The schism of the later seventeenth century weakened the inner religious life of the official Church by depriving it of many of its more devout members. It also weakened its position in relation to the state. In its efforts to suppress the Old Believers it had to rely more and more on the power and goodwill of the tsar. This was the situation which, in the early eighteenth century, enabled Peter the Great to reduce the Church to the position of a department of state.

Russia begins to look west

The changes in the Church can hardly be regarded as 'progressive'—they were an attempt to return to the pure Orthodoxy of the past—but, despite the profoundly conservative ethos of Russian life at all levels, there were areas in which new ideas did break into the country. The so-called 'westernization' of Russia, itself a misleading term, started long before the reign of Peter the Great, who is traditionally regarded by historians as its most distinguished protagonist. In the sixteenth century Ivan the Terrible imported foreign artisans and craftsmen, and a special suburb of Moscow, the 'German' quarter as it was known, was set aside for them. This settlement was abolished during the Time of Troubles but was restored in 1652 as a result of the large influx of foreigners during the reign of Michael and the early years of Alexis. The government was afraid that native Russians might be contaminated by the habits and heresies of the foreigners, hence the attempted segregation, but it was impossible to keep foreign habits from influencing, at least to some extent, the upper classes in Moscow. Even the tsar himself was affected. He introduced foreign furniture into the palace, established an orchestra, instituted theatrical performances and developed a liking for the ballet.

The immigration of foreigners, which made possible the beginnings—at a very superficial level—of western cultural influence in Russia was, however, permitted and encouraged by the government for severely practical reasons. The Russian army was much inferior to those of its neighbours, especially to that of Sweden, both in the quality of its troops and in the weapons at its disposal. Many foreign soldiers of fortune were employed in the seventeenth century in an effort to improve the fighting standards of the army, and attempts were made to exploit Russia's natural resources in the service of the armed forces by encouraging the immigration of industrialists and craftsmen who were ordered to train native Russians in their skills. In this way it was hoped that Russia would eventually become independent of foreign technical aid. That, of course, was very much a long-term ambition; the country was not only sadly lacking in skilled manpower of every kind but also in the educational institutions which were the necessary prerequisite for technical advances.

The anxiety of seventeenth-century tsars to improve their armed forces reflected the fact that a very large part of their reigns was spent at war, almost half the total period between 1613 and 1682. These wars were fought against Sweden, Poland, the Tartars and the Turks, often on several fronts at the same time. The seventeenth century was the great age of Swedish power. That power was based on the genius of a series of warrior kings, Gustavus Adolphus, Charles X, Charles XII, on the efficiency and patriotism of her armies, on the exploitation of her natural resources of tin and copper and, above all, on the relative weakness of her neighbours, especially Poland and Russia. These temporary advantages were nullified by the growth of Russian power under Peter the Great, and when Sweden suffered a series of setbacks in the early eighteenth century she did not have reserves of population and natural resources (her copper industry was by that time in decline) to fall back on. In the seventeenth century, however, she was much too strong for Russia and kept her away from the shores of the Baltic, a traditional area for Russian expansionist ambitions.

Seventeenth-century Russia, which thus faced Sweden at the height of her power, fought against a Polish state which was already in decline.

The sixteenth century had been Poland's golden age. Then she was the predominant political power in east central Europe. In 1572, however, the great Jagellonian dynasty which had ruled the country since the four-teenth century died out and a process of progressive political disintegration began under a series of elected kings who were forced to concede more and more power to the land-owning gentry or *szlachta* who, by the middle of the seventeenth century, had gained a dominant voice in the country. That dominance received institutional form in 1652 with the introduction of the notori-ous *liberum veto*. By applying the veto any member of the Diet (the Polish parliament) —a body dominated by the *szlachta*—could not only defeat the legislation under con-sideration but also nullify all laws previously agreed in that session of the Diet and dis-solve the Diet itself.

In the hands of the selfish *szlachta* the *liberum veto*—which was merely the most striking provision of a constitution which by the mid-seventeenth century had deprived the Polish king of all real power—was an instrument of anarchy. Against a Poland faced with such formidable internal political weaknesses, Russia had some military suc-cesses. Between 1654 and 1689 a compli-cated and bloody struggle took place between the two countries for control of the

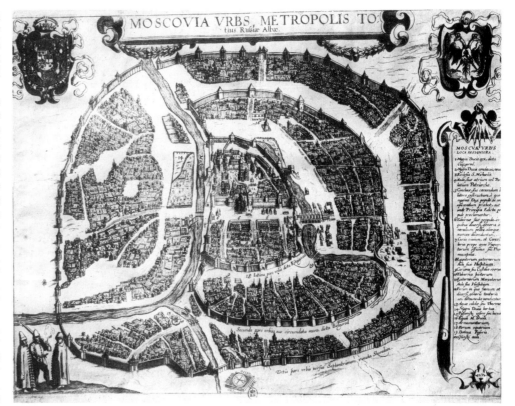

Ukraine. Russia emerged with substantial territorial gains, including the city of Kiev, but she had expended immense sums of men and money in the process and her victories did not render her southern frontier more secure; that still remained at the mercy of the nomadic Tartars, backed by the power of the Ottoman Empire.

Peter the Great

The history of Russia in the seventeenth century, then, is a story of conservatism in both Church and state. The tsars and their advisers were suspicious of all outside influ-ences which might contaminate the true Russian heritage. They were, it is true, prepared to accept changes in the Church which were anathema to large sections of the population, but these changes were merely

Above, Archangel in the seventeenth century; the town had been founded in 1584 and it was the main port of Russia until the early eighteenth century; the fact that it was on an inlet of the Arctic Ocean and was icebound for much of the year contributed much to the isolation of Russia. National Maritime Museum, London.

Top, Moscow in the seventeenth century, centred upon the Kremlin or citadel; an English trading mission, led by Richard Chancellor, had visited the city in 1553, but a hundred years later foreign visitors were still a rarity.

Opposite, Alexis Mihailovitch, Tsar of Russia (reigned 1645–76), whose reign saw the start of the creation of modern Russia, with the institution of serfdom and the union of the Ukraine with Russia.

a return to the stream of genuine Orthodox tradition from which Russia had departed through ignorance. The 'westernization' of the country—if the term must be used—was an attempt to introduce western technical and military expertise into Russia under strictly regulated conditions, an attempt to increase the power of the state, not to change the social milieu. The population as a whole was subjected to a regimentation which was never entirely effective but which aimed, as the Code of 1649 showed, at the subjection of the individual to the needs of the state.

In this situation general standards of personal behaviour were almost incredibly low. Tsar Alexis won the reputation of being a kindly man, but even he used his fists freely on the highest state dignitaries, and frequent and often sadistically violent beatings with the knout were not only commonplace but were the lot of high and low, young and old, women as well as men. Drunkenness was common, and incest and sexual perversion were rife, especially among the lower classes, where big families were often crowded into a single room.

Contemporary observers, both Russian and foreign, are unanimous about the brutality and general coarseness of conduct which were the rule rather than the exception in Russia. The country which Peter the Great was called upon to rule must have been a hell for those with sensitive natures, if any such were able to survive until maturity in the conditions just described.

Peter's formal accession to the throne came in 1682, on the death of Fedor. Fedor was survived by a brother Ivan, a half-blind, mentally defective youth of fifteen, by six sisters—all children of Alexis by his first wife Maria Miloslavsky and by a half brother, Peter, Alexis's son by a second wife, Nathalie Naryshkin. This situation was the signal for a series of intrigues between the

rival Naryshkin and Miloslavsky clans. At first the robust, ten-year-old Peter was proclaimed tsar, but the Miloslavsky fought back under the leadership of Sophie, one of Alexis's daughters, a very ambitious woman of twenty-five. She conducted a skilful propaganda campaign, directed against the Naryshkin, among the *streltsy*, a semi-military organization which was stationed in the capital and whose members engaged in trading activities in addition to their military duties. By promising them increased pay and privileges she won their support, and on three successive days in May 1682 the *streltsy* invaded the Kremlin and put some of Peter's Naryshkin relatives to death in full view of the young tsar.

As a result of this coup d'etat Ivan and Peter were proclaimed joint tsars. Power, however, passed to Sophie, who became regent. The events of May 1682 must have been a traumatic experience for Peter. Some historians have used the bloody events of these days to explain the cruelties and contradictions of his later career. One thing at least seems certain. When Peter had to

deal with a *streltsy* revolt in 1698, when he was in full control of the government, memories of the events of 1682 must have stirred in his mind. It is worth noting that the rebels of 1698 were treated with a cruelty which even Ivan the Terrible had never exceeded.

Sophie's rule lasted for seven years and was brought to an end largely by her own ambitions. She seems to have planned to get rid of her brothers and proclaim herself sole ruler. The *streltsy* refused to support her and she was deprived of power and locked up in a convent. After her downfall Ivan and Peter ruled jointly, although the former took no part in the actual business of government. He died in 1696.

When he became sole tsar, Peter's character was already fully formed. During Sophie's regency he had lived in a small village on the outskirts of Moscow. There he formed a miniature army and developed an interest in ships, an interest inspired by his discovery of an old English sailing boat in a barn.

This enthusiasm for maritime matters was

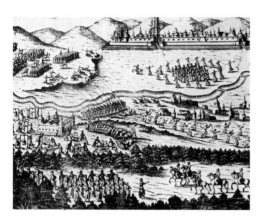

confirmed when he visited Archangel in 1693 and 1694. It was on the first visit that he first actually saw the sea. In the years immediately after Sophie's fall he seems to have taken little interest in affairs of state. He preferred to organize large-scale army manoeuvres and build boats. When he did visit the capital, he rarely went to the Kremlin, but spent most of his time in the company of friends in the German settlement. There, at the centre of a group of foreign and Russian companions headed by the Scotsman, Patrick Gordon, the Swiss, Francis Lefort, and the Russian, Alexander Menshikov, Peter was exposed to the influence of Western ideas as well as to the pleasures of drinking and hunting. By 1695, in fact, when he undertook his first campaign against Azov, a Turkish port on the Black Sea, Peter had already shown great interest in the three influences which were subsequently to dominate his reign: the army, the sea, and western Europe.

The 1695 campaign was a failure, but Peter returned to the fray the following year, when, with the aid of a hastily constructed fleet, he captured Azov. In 1697 he decided to visit western Europe in person, to find out what it was really like and to study navigation, shipbuilding and the military arts in general. The tsar travelled incognito throughout his trip, which included visits to Brandenburg, the United Provinces, England and Austria. The incognito, however, was loosely observed—it would have been difficult to maintain in any event in view of Peter's remarkable appearance; he was a giant of a man over six and a half feet tall. He returned to Moscow via Vienna, which he left earlier than expected in order to deal with a *streltsy* rebellion which had broken out in his capital. His bloody repression of the revolt was followed by the disbandment of the *streltsy* regiments stationed in the capital. The political power of what had been Russia's praetorian guard was thus broken once and for all.

As a result of his first visit to the west Peter brought to Moscow hundreds of western technicians and artisans. The journey had stimulated his curiosity about other countries and later in his reign he made further visits abroad, including a notable trip to France in 1717.

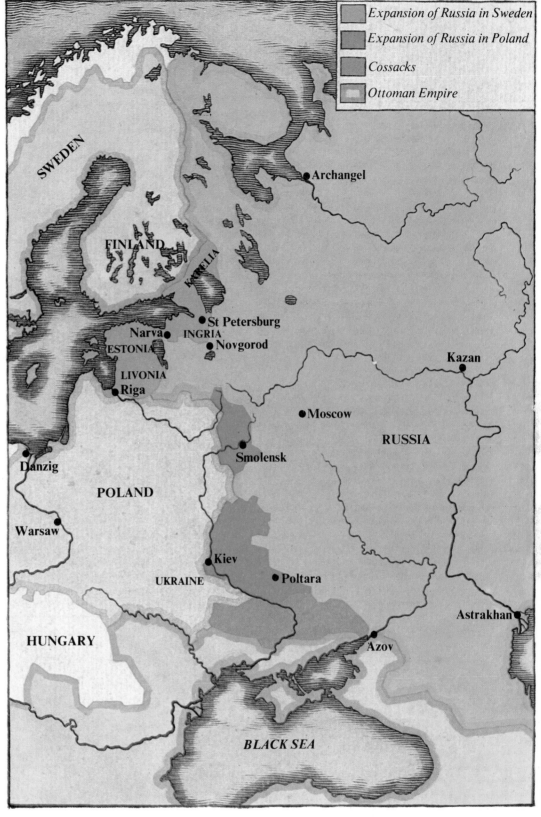

Military campaigns

Peter's reign was dominated by wars. During the entire period of his rule, from the downfall of Sophie until his death, only one whole year, 1724, was free from military activities. The needs of these very expensive wars determined not only his foreign policy but the domestic history of the reign as well. The great majority of his reforms were introduced with a view to making the country fight more effectively.

Above, the expansion of Russia during the reigns of Alexis I and Peter the Great.

Above left, the tsar's forces doing battle with the rebellious regiments of the Russian army known as the streltsy.

Opposite left, Sophie Alekseyevna (1657–1704).

Opposite top right, Peter the Great, Tsar of Russia (reigned 1682–1725), reviewing the Dutch fleet.

Opposite bottom right, the house in Saardam, in Holland, where Peter the Great stayed in 1697.

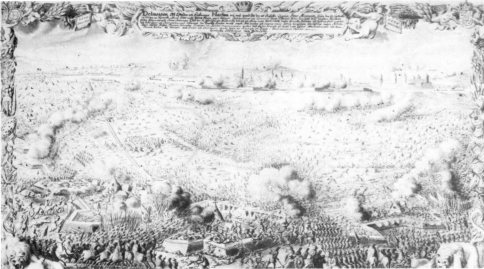

The military operations of the reign included campaigns against Turkey in 1695, 1696 and 1710–11 and a war against Persia in 1722–3. As a result of the campaigns against the Turks Peter gained and then lost the port of Azov on the Black Sea. In the Persian war he obtained territory on the western and southern shores of the Caspian Sea, lands which Russia lost soon after his death. These wars, however, were overshadowed by the great struggle against Sweden, which occupied the years from 1700 to 1721. Peter fought to gain territory on the Baltic which would give him an outlet to western Europe. In the struggle Russia was only one member—though certainly the most important member—of a coalition which included, at different times, Denmark, Poland, Brandenburg and Hanover. Each of these countries had its own ambitions and grudges against Sweden, which was still in 1700 the dominant Baltic power and a great European power as well.

At first Russia did very badly. She suffered an overwhelming defeat in 1700 at Narva, a Swedish fortress on the Gulf of Finland. In that battle a small army of Swedes under their young warrior-king Charles XII, a man of reckless courage and some military genius, defeated a Russian force perhaps five times as large. As a result of the defeat Peter for a time contemplated peace at any price. Soon, however, he recovered his nerve and set about reorganizing his army and building a fleet. His efforts were repaid in full measure in 1709 when, at Poltava in the Ukraine, the reformed Russian army, under Peter's personal command, inflicted a crushing defeat on the Swedes. It was the turning-point of the war. Charles XII took refuge in Turkey after his defeat. He later returned to Sweden but was never able to recover for his country her former dominant position. After his death in battle in 1718 peace became inevitable. The Treaty of Nystadt of 1721 recognized the changed power structure in the north. Russia gained from Sweden the Baltic provinces of Livonia, Esthonia and Ingria and a part of Karelia. Peter had obtained his window to the west, but it was at a heavy cost to the Russian people.

The Northern War was the great motivating force behind most of Peter's domestic reforms. He reorganized the army and created a navy in order to defeat Sweden; his financial measures were designed principally to secure enough money to pay for the vastly expanded military establishment; his administrative measures were intended to make the country's war machine more effective by strengthening the civilian government behind it; his encouragement of industrial development was chiefly designed to produce arms, equipment and clothes for his soldiers and sailors.

Peter began the war against Sweden with an army 35–40,000 strong, consisting mainly of inadequately trained volunteers. By the

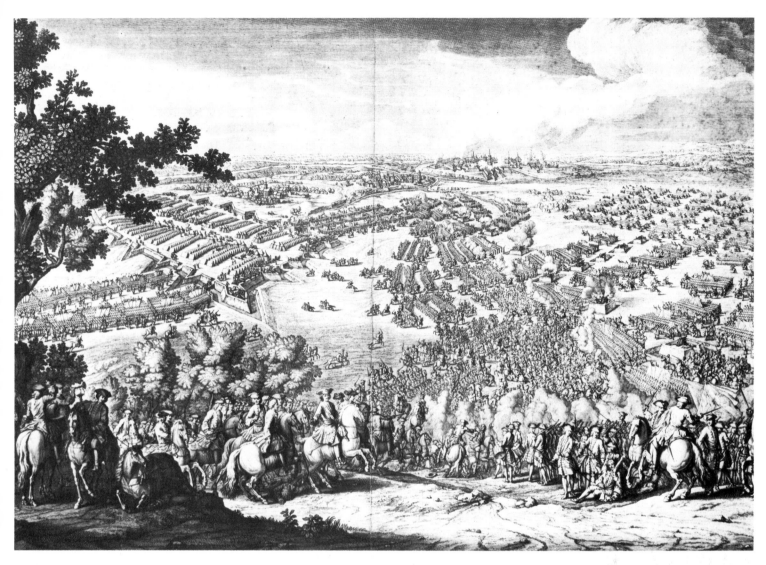

end of the reign it had developed into a comparatively well organized regular force of some 200,000 men. In 1703, when the conquest of Ingria gave him access to the Baltic, he began to construct a fleet there. When he died in 1725 he had about 800 vessels of all types manned by nearly 30,000 seamen.

Peter was always desperately short of money to pay for his ever-expanding army and navy. War expenditure rose from about 2,300,000 roubles in 1701 to 3,200,000 in 1710, and even in 1724, a year of peace, the maintenance of the army and navy cost the state well over 5,000,000 roubles. The additional revenue required to meet these growing military needs was raised by debasing the coinage and by hand to mouth methods such as the invention of ingenious new taxes, like those imposed on hats, beehives, smokestacks, private bathhouses and beards. State trading monopolies—on salt and tobacco, for example—were established and towards the end of the reign a poll-tax. The poll-tax, levied on individuals, replaced a tax on households as the basis of the system of direct taxation. This reform in particular brought considerable additional revenue to the government—revenue from direct taxation rose from 1,800,000 to 4,600,000 roubles after its introduction.

The burden of these additional taxes fell, of course, on the peasants, who also provided the great bulk of recruits for the armed forces. Peter's quest for military glory certainly brought no obvious gains to the rank and file of his subjects, only added burdens.

The tsar's administrative reforms, some of them directly inspired by military problems, were all at least indirectly related to the needs of war; greater efficiency in civil government would help to produce a more effective military machine. The reforms introduced were of the greatest importance in Russian institutional history. The provinces, into which the country was divided by a decree of 1707, lasted, with modifications, until the fall of the Empire, as did the Senate, which was established in 1711. This became the chief organ of administrative control in Russia and the highest judicial authority as well. The central administration itself was reorganized in 1717 by the creation of nine colleges, based on Swedish models, to replace the old *prikazy*. Some of these colleges lasted until the nineteenth century.

The confusion almost inevitably created by the introduction of so many major reforms in a few years, together with the lack of properly trained staff for the

Above, the Battle of Poltava, in the Ukraine, at which Peter the Great gained his revenge over Charles XII of Sweden, who was forced to take refuge in Turkey. This victory ensured that Russia would be a permanent force in northeastern Europe.

Opposite top, Peter the Great, who modernized the Russian army and navy and reorganized the state administration in order to be able to support his aggression, winning important victories over the Swedes, and also attempting to expand Russia in the southwest. National Maritime Museum, London.

Opposite bottom, the Battle of Narva in 1700, at which Charles XII of Sweden decisively defeated Peter the Great of Russia. The defeat led Peter to reorganize the army and build new defences in the north, and it encouraged him to modernize Russia.

133

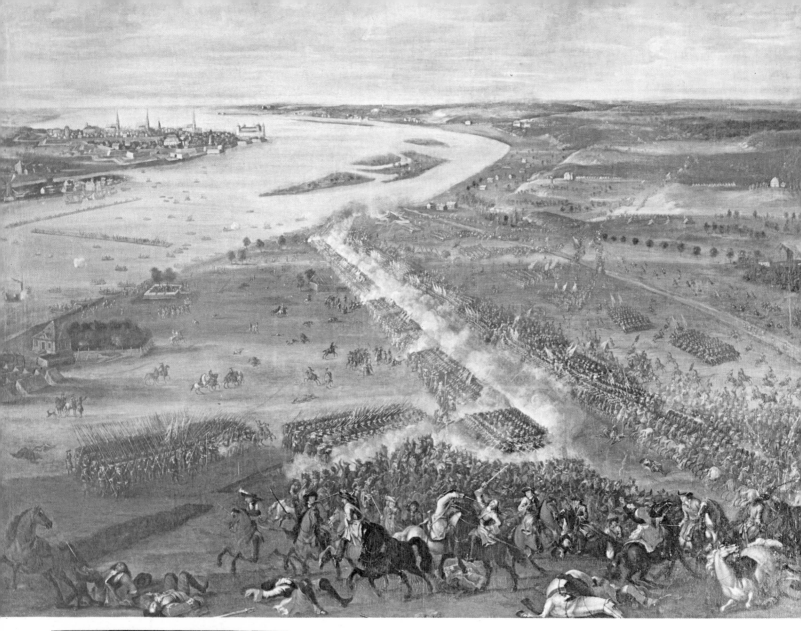

reign there were about two hundred large-scale industrial enterprises in operation. Among the most important of these were armaments works and foundries—notably the iron industry of the Urals—and textile mills, which produced cloth for army uniforms.

Nobility and the Church

The chief duty of the nobility in seventeenth-century Russia had been military service. This remained its principal function in Peter's reign, though he imposed the obligation with a vigour which had previously been lacking. He also began large-scale recruitment of the nobility into the newly created organs of civil administration. Noblemen may have been angered by the growing duties imposed upon them by the state, but they had compensations. In Peter's reign they were allowed to maintain and even to increase their already firm hold over their serfs. The serfs, in contrast, had nothing to brighten the gloom of their lives. They had not only to contend with the cruelties of their masters but were faced with ever increasing demands from the

state: demands for their bodies, to be used as cannon-fodder in Peter's wars, and demands for more and more of their meagre earnings in taxation. It is no wonder that frequent peasant revolts, especially in southern Russia, were a permanent feature of the reign.

Peter, therefore, treated his subjects, nobles and peasants alike, not as individuals but as assets at the service of the state, assets to be employed in any way he thought fit. The Church, too, was firmly subordinated to his control. The Russian Church had traditionally been subservient to the tsars, and the schism of 1667 had increased its dependence on the state. Until Peter's reign, however, it had at least had its own head, the Patriarch, who enjoyed vast dignity and prestige.

After the death of Adrian in 1700, however, Peter left the patriarchate vacant. In 1721 the office was abolished altogether and the government of the Church handed over to a holy synod, which was headed by a layman appointed by the tsar. After this reform the Church became, much more clearly than ever before, a department of state, a position which it was to retain until the Revolution.

new institutions, meant that the measures had less success than Peter hoped in producing administrative efficiency. Their long life, however, bears witness to their great importance.

The development of Russian industry under Peter was largely a result of the great and growing need of the army and navy for arms and equipment. By the end of the

A new capital

In addition to his major reforms Peter introduced many minor changes which had a significant cumulative effect on the appearance and behaviour of the upper classes in society. Members of the nobility were ordered to wear western dress and to shave off their beards, and women of the upper classes were encouraged, even ordered, to attend social gatherings—a fundamental breach of the traditional seclusion in which they had been kept until then. These reforms meant that the upper classes had been westernized in dress and appearance by the end of the reign. The peasantry remained largely unaffected. Peter's reign marked, in fact, the beginnings of a decisive split in Russian society between the nobility and the rest of the population. This tendency was accentuated by and indeed was partly a result of the foundation of St Petersburg in 1703 on the shores of the Gulf of Finland. The new capital, which became the mecca of the Russian nobility, was, by its very geographical position exposed to the influence of western Europe as Moscow had never been.

Peter's creation of a new capital was one completely original and very important contribution which he made to Russian history. There were other original policies, such as the establishment of the holy synod and the creation of a navy, but much of his work was a development, at an accelerated pace, of trends already established by his predecessors. This was certainly true of his policy of 'westernization'.

Peter died in January 1725, at the age of fifty-two, of complications caused by chronic venereal disease. He remains an enigmatic figure. He combined enormous energy and great intellectual curiosity with a propensity for extreme cruelty which can only be explained, not excused, by the general brutality of the age and country in which he lived. There is no doubt about his importance in Russian and, indeed, in world history. In the mid-1690s, when he assumed personal control of the government, Russia was at best a second-, at worst a third-rate power. At his death in 1725 she was, as a result of his efforts, unquestionably the dominant state in northern and eastern Europe and a power of first-rate importance in the continent as a whole. She has retained both these positions ever since.

Below, the Russian boyars or nobility of the seventeenth century, in their traditional costume; Peter abolished the rank of boyar, and tried to replace it with a nobility which owed services to the state in the civil service or the army.

Below left, Peter the Great himself cut off the beards of many of the nobles on the day after he returned from Europe in 1698, and then imposed a tax on beards. This attack on externals was generally understood to be the prelude to a revolution in Russian society. National Maritime Museum, London.

Opposite top, Charles XII of Sweden (reigned 1697–1718) winning control of the crossing of the River Dvina in 1701, prior to his conquest of Poland and installation of Stanislaus I as his puppet there in 1704. After consolidating his hold over Poland, he once more invaded Russia in 1708. Drottingholm Castle.

Opposite bottom, Charles XII of Sweden, who fought the Northern War of 1700–21 with Peter the Great in a struggle to determine control of the Baltic and whose eventual defeat meant the permanent decline of Swedish power. Sjoholm Castle.

ENGLAND, THE UNITED PROVINCES AND RUSSIA DURING THE SEVENTEENTH CENTURY

Date	England	United Provinces	Russia
1600			
	James I (1603–25)	Truce with Spain (1609)	Tsar Michael Romanov (1613–45)
	Gunpowder Plot (1605)	Oldenbarneveldt executed (1619)	
	Charles I (1625–49)	End of truce with Spain (1621)	
		Frederick Henry, Prince of Orange and stadholder (1625)	Treat with Poland (1634)
	War with Scotland (1639)	Capture of Breda (1637)	
	Long Parliament (1640)	Marriage of William II of Orange and Mary Stuart (1641)	
	Execution of Strafford (1641)		
	Civil War begins (1642)		
	Laud executed (1645)		Tsar Alexis (1645–76)
	Battle of Naseby (1645)	Succession of William II of Orange (1647)	
	Execution of Charles I (1649)	Treaty of Münster (1648)	Code of Laws (1649)
1650			
	Charles II defeated at the battle of Worcester; goes into exile (1651)	Death of William II; birth of William III (1650)	
	Cromwell lord protector (1653)	First Anglo-Dutch War (1652)	
	Death of Cromwell (1658)	John de Witt grand pensionary (1653)	War with Poland (1654)
	Restoration of Charles II (1660)	Treaty of Paris (1662)	
	Act of Uniformity (1662)	Second Anglo-Dutch War (1665)	
	Conventicle Act (1664)		
	Great Plague (1665)		
	Fire of London (1666)	Treaty of Breda (1667)	Russian Church council (1666–7)
		Triple Alliance (1668)	

Date	England	United Provinces	Russia
1670	Treaty of Dover (1670)	Third Anglo-Dutch War (1672)	Peasant's revolt (1670–1)
		Invasion by French (1672)	
		Murder of de Witt brothers (1672)	
		William of Orange hereditary stadholder (1674)	
	Popish Plot (1678)	Mary Stuart marries William III (1677)	Tsar Fedor (1676–82)
1680			
	Accession of James II (1685)	League of Augsburg (1686)	Tsar Peter the Great (1682–1725)
	Landing of William III (1688)		Revolt of the Streltsy (1682)
	Declaration of Rights: William and Mary, king and queen (1689)		
	Battle of the Boyne (1690)		Building of Russian fleet (1696)
	Triennial Act (1694)		Capture of Azov (1696)
		First Partition Treaty (1698)	Massacre of the Streltsy (1698)
	Act of Settlement (1701)	Alliance with Holy Roman Empire against France (1701)	War with Sweden (1700)
	Accession of Anne (1702)		Defeat at Narva (1700)
		Suspension of stadtholderate (1702)	
	Act of Union with Scotland (1707)		Founding of St Petersburg (1703)
			Victory at Poltava (1709)
		Peace of Utrecht (1713)	Peace of Pruth (1711)
	Accession of George (1714)		Execution of Tsarevich Alexis (1718)
			Peace of Nystadt (1721)
	Accession of George II (1727)		Death of Peter the Great (1725)
1730			

Chapter 15

Rebellions and Revolutions

In the 1640s and 1650s there was a great series of rebellions and revolutions in Europe. In May 1640 the people of Catalonia in the northeast of the Iberian peninsula rose in revolt against the Madrid government of Philip IV and his minister, the Count-Duke of Olivares. In January 1641 the rebels elected Louis XIII of France as Count of Catalonia in place of Philip IV, and the struggle continued until 1652 when the Spanish government recaptured the town of Barcelona and brought the revolt to an end. Portugal also rebelled in 1640 against the demonination of Madrid, and the Duke of Braganza, a scion of the old national royal House of Avis, was proclaimed king, a decision which was ratified by the Cortes, the Portuguese parliament, in January 1641.

The war between Spain and Portugal which followed lasted intermittently until 1668, when Portuguese independence was formally recognized. The third great rebellion against Spain did not come until seven years after the outbreak of the Catalonian and Portuguese revolts. In July 1647 a young Neapolitan fisherman, Masaniello, led a movement against the oppressive government of the Duke of Arcos, the hated Spanish Viceroy of Naples. The revolt, however, was short-lived. It lasted only until March 1648, when Spanish authority was restored.

Besides the three rebellions against Madrid there were revolutionary movements in England, France and the United Provinces. By far the most important of these, of course, was the conflict in England. This can be said to have begun in 1640 with the calling of the Long Parliament by Charles I, who was desperate for financial assistance against his rebellious Scottish subjects. The subsequent civil wars of 1642–8 led to the eleven years' interregnum which preceded the restoration of Charles II in 1660.

Less prolonged and of less permanent significance was the movement known as the *fronde,* which took place in France between 1648 and 1653. This had its immediate origins in general discontent at the financial exactions of Cardinal Mazarin's government. In its early stages it was headed by the *parlement* of Paris, which imposed a comprehensive programme of reform on the Crown. Later, however, the leadership was taken over by members of the nobility, who showed only too plainly that they were motivated by selfish ambitions. As a result, Mazarin, who twice went into exile during the struggle, was able to return permanently in 1653. The reform programme which the government had accepted under pressure in 1648 was quietly forgotten.

The upheaval in the United Provinces, led to the establishment there of the republican régime of 1650 to 1672. In 1648–9, after the end of the Thirty Years' War, the States of Holland demanded substantial reductions in the army. William II, stadtholder of most of the provinces of the union and captain-general of its military forces, went some way to meet those demands but refused to go as far as the States of Holland wished. William and his opponents in Holland became more and more estranged as the months passed and civil war seemed a real possibility, especially as both parties took measures which overstepped the bounds of strict constitutional legality. In August 1650 William made preparations for a military coup d'état directed against Amsterdam, the centre of the opposition, but the city immediately made concessions. The general outcome of the struggle was, however, still uncertain in October when William caught smallpox. The following month he died. In the reaction which followed, the forces of centralization in the republic were left leaderless and the republican era, under the dominance of Holland, began.

Despite very great differences in the duration and importance of these six revolutions, their origins had some common features. All were to a considerable extent reactions against the financial demands of governments which were engaged in expensive wars. Spain, France and the United Provinces all took part in the Thirty Years' War. Spain fought against the Dutch between 1621 and 1648 and in 1635 found herself at war with France as well, a struggle which continued until 1659. The enormous cost of military operations led Olivares in Spain and Richelieu and later Mazarin in France to multiply the financial demands which they made upon their peoples. In Olivares' case, he was particularly determined that the non-Castilian parts of the Spanish Empire should pay a fair share of the cost of the war. He therefore made substantial financial demands upon Catalonia. Portugal and Naples, demands which led directly to rebellions.

Similarly, in France Mazarin's desperate need for money to carry on the war against Spain led to a series of financial expedients which in turn sparked off the *fronde.* In the United Provinces it was a combination of William II's determination to renew the war with Spain after the peace of 1648 and Holland's equally firm resolution to disband as many as possible of his expensive troops which produced the revolutionary situation in 1650. In England it was Charles I's need for money for an army to send against his rebellious Scottish subjects which compelled him to summon the Long Parliament.

The rebellions and revolutions of the 1640s and 1650s were, however, more than just political and constitutional conflicts brought on by war and fought out between governments on the one hand and the people and representative institutions of their countries on the other. This kind of interpretation, which, in a sophisticated form, satisfied many past historians, is now seen to be too simple. It tells us part of the truth about the conflicts of the mid-seventeenth century, but, if we want to discover the whole truth, we must dig deeper.

One explanation which has been widely publicized and widely accepted in recent years is the Marxist interpretation. According to Marxists and to some other economic historians who accept their arguments, the 'general crisis' of the mid-seventeenth century, which produced so many revolts and revolutions, was basically an economic crisis. The conservative forces in the rebellions, they believe, represented 'feudal' interests, whereas the revolutionaries, in some of the revolts at least, represented the 'progressive' ambitions of the bourgeoisie, hampered in their economic activities by the dominance of restrictive and obsolete governmental systems. It was only in England, however—so the argument goes on—that the 'progressive' forces, representatives of nascent capitalism, were able to triumph completely. Thus, in England alone the old structure of government was shattered and, within the new freer forms which were established, rapid industrial advances possible later. Such an interpretation, which sees the English Revolution of 1640–60 as a necessary precursor of the Industrial Revolution of the eighteenth century, is, on the face of it, a plausible hypothesis. It gives a clear, general explanation of the mid-century revolts and specific reasons for the widely held assumptions that the conflict in England was much the most important of all the struggles.

There is, however, a grave weakness in the thesis. Little solid evidence can be advanced to support it. It is difficult, if not impossible, to demonstrate convincingly that the economic ambitions of the bourgeoisie were a significant motive force behind the revolutions of the 1640s and 1650s, and the supposition that the Puritan triumphs of 1640–60 in England directly aided the growth of capitalism there is only a theory. It has not been positively proved. The Marxist account is, therefore, an interesting hypothesis, but it can at best only add to our understanding of the mid-century crisis, not provide a total explanation of it.

Another ambitious interpretation less narrowly based than that of the Marxist is the recent thesis of Professor H. R. Trevor-

Roper, who argues that the mid-century revolutions were the culmination of a general social crisis which had been developing in western Europe since about 1500. The whole period from about the beginning of the sixteenth to the mid-seventeenth century should, he argues, be regarded as the age of 'Renaissance' society and the 'Renaissance' state. During these years, he maintains, the societies of most European states were dominated by the increasingly magnificent and expensive courts of their kings and princes and by ever expanding bureaucratic machines staffed by greedy officials. Only a small fraction of the cost of these great bureaucracies fell upon the princes whom they served. Much the larger share, probably well over three-quarters of the cost, fell upon the population at large. This was because the salaries and fees which officials were paid by their governments for prescribed administrative duties tended to be small and remain fixed. On the other hand, officials could expect tips or gratuities from clients who hoped, by such gifts, to oil the wheels of the administrative machine to their own advantage. Gratuities were generally accepted as a necessary evil, but the line between the legitimate profits of office and open corruption was hard to draw. It seems plausible that, as the sixteenth century wore on and the seventeenth century opened, standards throughout Europe declined. They certainly did so in England, where the situation under King James I, when any adventurer might hope to make a quick profit at the expense of the subject, was a far cry from the position in the middle of the Elizabethan period when the queen and her chief minister, Lord Burghley, husbanded the resources of Crown patronage in the general interests of the nation.

This expansion of courts and bureaucracies and the corruption which accompanied it was only possible, Trevor-Roper maintains, because the general expansion of the European economy in the sixteenth century made the expense bearable to the population as a whole. Even so, by the 1590s the cost of Philip II's wars produced everywhere in Europe a growing volume of complaint, and popular anger was very often directed against bureaucratic extravagances. If peace had not come in the first decade of the seventeenth century, the whole system might soon have cracked under the strain.

Court and country

In these circumstances, when war was resumed in the 1620s, governments with larger and larger military expenditure to meet had to make continually increasing financial demands upon subjects who had to find the money, amid the dislocations of war, out of the proceeds of contracting economies. The inflated Renaissance courts and bureaucracies then became intolerable financial burdens. The 1620s thus saw the creation of a revolutionary situation in which the main ingredient in many European states was the anger of the 'country'— those subjects who had no profitable contacts with the ruling courts and bureaucracies—at the demands and extravagances of their masters. The rebellions of the 1640s, Trevor-Roper believes, were fundamentally a result of this general resentment, though of course each revolt was sparked off by specific immediate grievances in its country of origin.

The Trevor-Roper thesis, brilliantly argued and presented, is open to detailed criticisms from specialists in the history of each of the individual countries concerned, but it surely adds to and deepens our knowledge of the mid-century rebellions. Tensions between 'court' and 'country' were certainly a very important factor in the history of early seventeenth-century Europe and though Trevor-Roper may be wrong in seeing them as the most important cause of the revolts of the 1640s his explanation of these conflicts as great social crises is a valuable and convincing complement to the more traditional stress on military and constitutional factors and to the theses of the Marxists.

The middle decades of the seventeenth century, the time of the rebellions, divide two different worlds. The reasons for the transformation of European life which took place at that time are many and complex. The political, constitutional, economic and social revolutions of the 1640s and 1650s—for the events of mid-century were all these combined—played a part in this transformation, but even more important were profound general changes in European thought. Basically, the world of 1700 was completely different from the world of 1600 because the seventeenth century saw a combined scientific and general intellectual revolution which had unparalleled consequences for human attitudes and, ultimately, for the physical life of man on earth.

Scientific and intellectual revolution

In the long run the scientific and intellectual changes of the seventeenth century were vital in producing our twentieth-century civilization with its generally accepted emphasis on rational calculations. We must remember, however, that, in the short term these developments produced a society in which to perhaps a greater extent than ever before, there was a profound gulf between the ideas and attitudes of the educated classes and of the ignorant multitudes. In previous centuries, although the gulf between educated men and the population in general was very wide, they shared to a considerable extent the same general assumptions about man and the universe.

Above, Johannes Kepler (1571–1630), the German astronomer who solved one of the important failings in the Copernican system by showing that the planets moved around the sun in ellipses rather than in circles. He published his findings in On the Motions of Mars *in 1609.*

Top, the trial of Charles I of England, conducted by the House of Commons in 1648. This event was the climax of the political upheavals in Europe in the 1640s.

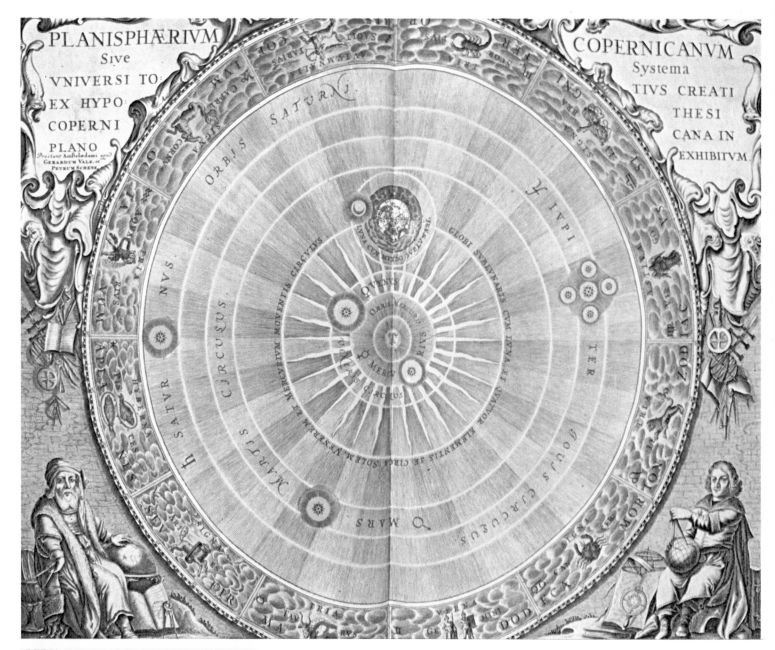

PLANISPHÆRIVM
Sive
VNIVERSI TO:
EX HYPO
COPERNI
PLANO
Prostant Amstelædami apud
GERARDUM VALK et
PETRUM SCHENK

COPERNICANVM
Systema
TIVS CREATI
THESI
CANA IN
EXHIBITVM.

CLARISSIMUS ET DOCTISSIMUS DOC
TOR NICOLAUS COPERNICUS TORU
NENSIS CANONICUS WARMIENSIS
ASTRONOMUS INCOMPARABILIS 1575

In the course of the seventeenth century this ceased to be true.

Between 1600 and 1700 the literate reading public of Europe fed itself on the flood of books in which those who were exploring the frontiers of knowledge propagated and sometimes even attempted to popularize their ideas. Of course, even the great majority of the educated men who read the books of the leading scientists and thinkers of the time did not fully grasp their arguments—how many men in the seventeenth century really understood the works of Newton?—but they absorbed enough to produce a radical change in their ways of thought. The profound difference between the educated and uneducated communities is one of the most fundamental and important facts of the time.

The great thinkers of the seventeenth century, with the notable exception of Leibnitz, rejected theological explanations of natural phenomena (that is, explanations in terms of an ultimate will and purpose which transcended scientific inquiry) and saw instead a universe which could be understood rationally by the analysis of carefully collected information. This was a change from a supernatural to a mathematical view of the universe. Mathematics was one of two fundamental sets of tools which gave man his new understanding of the universe. The other was the development of precision instruments, which could be used for assembling and measuring significant data. To take just one example, the telescope, invented in 1608 by two Dutchmen and improved and developed by Galileo and others, demonstrated beyond all doubt the validity of the Copernican system of astronomy which in the sixteenth century had rejected traditional views of the earth as the centre of the universe and postulated the idea that it revolved around the sun.

The growing emphasis on rational calculation received its greatest encouragement from developments in mathematics. The importance of mathematics in the seventeenth-century scientific revolution can hardly be overstressed. The century was not

138

only one of the greatest periods of progress in the history of mathematics, it was also the period in which mathematical knowledge and methods had the greatest influence on the growth of knowledge in other fields, and consequently on the general development of human life. It is difficult to say why there should have been a great period in mathematics at precisely this time. The main reason is probably the emergence of a number of mathematicians of genius, each of whom built on the work of his predecessors to produce general rules about mathematical truths which previously had been understood only separately and not in their interconnections.

Mathematics

The mathematical advances of the century were made on the broadest possible front, but perhaps the greatest single mathematical achievement of the period was the calculus. The calculus should not be regarded as a sudden invention. It was rather the completion and synthesis by two great mathematical minds, Leibnitz and Newton, of the work of a number of other men. Newton and Leibnitz worked independently of each other, and much ink has been spilled in discussing their relative shares of the credit. Whatever the verdict, it is certain that both deserve a great deal of praise for their work on one of the most practically useful instruments of calculation that has ever been devised by man. It provides the means of solving the most endless variety of problems which turn on the relationship between changing quantities and can in fact be used for almost all difficult calculations.

One of the mathematicians whose work was of great importance in the pre-history of the calculus was the Frenchman René Descartes, whose even greater fame as a philosopher will merit attention later. As a boy Descartes acquired a liking for mathematics, 'because of the certainty of its proofs and the evidence of its reasonings'. This love remained with him for the rest of his life and led to the production of his most important scientific work, the *Geometry* of 1637, in which he laid the foundations of analytical geometry. He showed that geometric problems could be put into algebraic forms and in this way introduced a system by which problems about space (that is, geometrical problems) could be solved by numerical calculations through the application of algebraic and arithmetical methods.

Descartes, in fact, was the originator of *l'esprit géométrique*, 'the geometric spirit', which stressed calculation and number as a key to understanding. He provided the basis for a world founded on measurements and his ideas dominated much of the thought of the later seventeenth and eighteenth centuries. Fontenelle, the greatest popularizer of seventeenth-century scientific developments, stated that, 'the geometric spirit is not so attached to geometry that it cannot be disentangled and carried over into other areas of knowledge.' By 1700 Descartes had a legion of disciples who applied his ideas and methods to politics, philosophy, literature, medicine and religion.

One area of Descartes' thought which produced difficulties was his attitude to the relationship between reason and experiment. He believed that men, after discovering a few fundamental principles as a result of observation, could reason out the whole structure of the universe from these basic ideas. Although he lost his earlier confidence in this method before he died, many of his followers ignored these doubts, especially when they applied his ideas to non-scientific fields. There were, however, many exponents of *l'esprit géométrique* who laid the very greatest stress on the importance of experimentation. In this respect they followed in the footsteps of Galileo rather than Descartes.

Galileo

Galileo can claim to be the 'father' of modern mechanics and physics and the founder of modern observational astronomy. His contribution to mechanics and physics was founded on his work on the theory of motion. In the course of experiments he examined with meticulous care the behaviour of freely falling bodies and of bodies moving horizontally on the earth's surface. In these experiments he anticipated two of Newton's three laws of motion, including the law of inertia. That law—the idea that every particle continues in a state of rest or motion in a straight line unless compelled by a force to change that state—is the real foundation of the modern theory of motion. Galileo was in fact, the first man to see that mathematics and physics, previously kept in separate compartments, should be joined together.

No less important was his astronomical work. In the spring of 1609 he learned of the recent invention of the telescope. He soon built models for himself, making improvements which ensured that his telescopes were the first which could be used for observing the heavens. By 1610 he was able to announce a series of fundamentally important astronomical discoveries, published under the title *Sidereus Nuncius*. He observed that the Milky Way was composed of a collection of distant stars, saw spots on the sun, discovered the satellites of Jupiter, observed the phases of Venus and found that the surface of the moon was irregular rather than smooth, as had previously been supposed. In 1611 he visited Rome and demonstrated his telescope to prominent members of the papal court. He was flattered by the cordial reception he received and this encouraged him, two years later, in his *Letters on the Solar Spots,* to raise openly the issue of the Copernican theory. He maintained that the movement of the

Above, Galileo Galilei (1564–1642), the Italian scientist whose invention of the telescope, discovery of the abstract principles of physics and demonstration of the truth of Copernicus' theories of the solar system can be said to have been the turning-point in the scientific revolution. Biblioteca Marucelliana, Florence.

Opposite top, an illustration by Andreas Cellarius in 1708 of the Copernican system of the universe, showing the sun at the centre with the planets, including Earth, orbiting it. By this time, Newton had dealt with the last problems inherent in Copernicus' ideas.

Opposite bottom, Nicholas Copernicus (1473–1543), the Polish astronomer whose book De revolutionibus orbium coelestium (1543) was the first to suggest that the Earth was not at the centre of the universe. Museum Historyczne Uniwerstytetu Jagielionskeigo, Cracow.

OPTICKS:
OR, A
TREATISE
OF THE
REFLEXIONS, REFRACTIONS,
INFLEXIONS and COLOURS
OF
LIGHT.
ALSO
Two TREATISES
OF THE
SPECIES and MAGNITUDE
OF
Curvilinear Figures.

LONDON,
Printed for SAM. SMITH, and BENJ. WALFORD,
Printers to the Royal Society, at the Prince's Arms in
St. Paul's Church-yard. MDCCIV.

spots across the face of the sun showed that the earth revolved around it. Copernicus was right.

In 1616, however, the theologians of the Holy Office declared Copernicanism 'false and erroneous' and the pope admonished Galileo not to defend its doctrines. In 1632 he openly violated this papal command by publishing his *Dialogues on the Two Chief Systems of the World*, a compelling plea for the Copernican system. The work was greeted with acclaim throughout Europe, but the Church authorities decided to prosecute him on 'vehement suspicion' of heresy. He was compelled to stand trial at Rome in 1633 and, under threat of torture, to recant his opinions in a formula in which he 'abjured, cursed and detested' his past errors. He was sentenced to imprisonment during pleasure—immediately commuted by the pope to house arrest for the last eight years of his life on his own little estate near Florence—and ordered to recite the seven penitential psalms once a week for three years. The sentence was comparatively mild by the standards of the time and no other eminent scientist of the century was forced to recant his opinions, but the fate of the aged Galileo illustrates the fact that scientific freedom was newly and not easily won in the seventeenth century.

Galileo's fate at the hands of the Inquisition must have discouraged writers who would have liked to challenge traditional views of the universe, and although scholars were well aware of the inadequacies of ancient cosmologies it was some years before the Copernican system was generally accepted. In 1686, however, there appeared a book which was more influential than any other in making Copernicanism fashionable. This was Bernard de Fontenelle's *Entretiens sur les pluralitiés des mondes*.

Fontenelle is a most interesting man. Born in 1657, he died in 1757, a month before his hundredth birthday. He was never a scientist of great originality, but he

kept abreast of all new scientific developments and corresponded with many European scientists. He was the great publicist of the seventeenth-century scientific revolution and recorded its achievements in innumerable books. Fontenelle presents a simplified version of Descartes' picture of the universe. This Cartesian cosmology—Descartes' ideas are described as Cartesian and his followers as Cartesians—accepted the basic Copernican thesis of the circulation of the earth around the sun and was also founded to a considerable extent on Descartes' theory of vortices. According to this, the whole universe consisted of a number of vortices fitting together like soap bubbles. In the centre of each vortex was a star. In the vortex containing the solar system the planets circled round the sun; some planets were surrounded by their own, subsidiary vortices containing satellites, like the moon. The whole universe was filled with a kind of celestial fluid, which kept the stars and planets in their places.

Fontenelle's book was popular but it was out of date the year after it was published, for in 1687 Newton's *Principia Mathematica*, one of the great scientific works of all time, appeared. Although the *Principia* was certainly Newton's masterpiece, it merely set the seal on a lifetime of scientific achievement. Isaac Newton was born in 1642 in the Lincolnshire village of Woolsthorpe. He went up to Trinity College, Cambridge, in 1661, taking his degree in 1665, when the university was closed because of the Great Plague. He thereupon returned to Woolsthorpe, where he remained until the spring of 1667. That year and a half, when he was twenty-three and twenty-four, was perhaps the most creative period in his entire life, as he himself recognized later, when he said that he was then in his 'prime . . . for invention, and minded mathematics and philosophy [i.e. science] more than at any time since.'

Newton

During that brief period, Newton made some epoch-making contributions to the history of science, including the foundations of the differential and integral calculus and the analysis of the composition of white light and the nature of colours, a piece of research which was the foundation of the technique of spectrum analysis. His great discovery was his conception of the force of gravitation extending from the earth to the moon.

Altogether, it was a series of scientific and mathematical advances unequalled in importance since the time of the Greeks. Newton's old Cambridge teacher, Isaac Barrow, himself a distinguished scientist, recognized his pupil's soaring genius and resigned the Lucasian chair of mathematics in 1669 so that Newton, then twenty-six years old, could succeed him.

Newton returned to the early work on light which he had done in 1666 and began researches which found final expression in his *Optics*, published in 1704. His theories about light gave rise to considerable controversy in his own time, notably with Robert Hooke, a fellow member with Newton of the Royal Society, and the protagonist of rival ideas on the subject. Hooke advocated a wave theory of light, according to which light consists of a series of pulses or waves transmitted through the ether pervading space. Newton, on the other hand, advanced a combination of wave and corpuscular theories. According to him, light consists of a series of corpuscles emanating from luminous bodies. These corpuscles give rise to waves as they pass through the ether. Newton's ideas have returned to fashion in our own time, in which there has been in scientific thinking a fusion of elements of both corpuscular and wave theories.

Newton set out the results of some of his early work on light in a paper which he presented to the Royal Society in 1672. The controversy which this aroused led him to explain his position. 'The best and safest method of philosophizing [that is, of conducting scientific enquiries] seems to be, first to enquire diligently into the properties of things, and of establishing these properties by experiment, and then to proceed more slowly to hypotheses for the explanation of them.' There could hardly be a clearer statement of the importance of the experimental method.

One very important by-product of Newton's work on optics was his invention of the reflecting telescope, a new form of the instrument which ultimately enabled very large telescopes to be constructed.

Important though Newton's work on optics was, his main claim to immortality rightly rests on his *Principia Mathematica*, begun in 1686 and published the following year. The fame it brought Newton inspired Alexander Pope to write his famous *Epitaph intended for Sir Isaac Newton*:

Nature and Nature's laws lay hid in night.
God said, Let Newton be! and all was light.

This tribute to genius should not, however, be allowed to obscure the fact that the *Principia* was a synthesis of advances made during the two preceding centuries and owed much to the researches of men like Leonardo da Vinci, Kepler, Galileo, Huygens, Hooke and Halley.

This is not, of course, to belittle Newton's achievement. It was he who produced the final proofs and in so doing created a picture of the universe as a rigid mechanism held together by absolute mechanical laws founded on the principle of gravitation, a principle which accounted for the movement of heavenly bodies, of the tides and of objects on earth. It was not until about fifty years later that Newton's explanation won general acceptance in preference to Descartes' theory of vortices. After that, however, Newton reigned supreme for some 200 years. It was only from the early twentieth century onwards, when Albert Einstein developed the special and general theories of relativity, that Newton's theory of the universe could no longer be regarded as final. The discovery that the mass of a body varies with its velocity changed the whole terms of reference of physics.

The publication of the *Principia* in 1687 marked a turning-point in the history of science in the short as well as in the long term. Nine decades of tremendously productive research were followed by thirty or forty largely barren years. It was as if the publication of Newton's masterpiece had exhausted the creative spirit of the age.

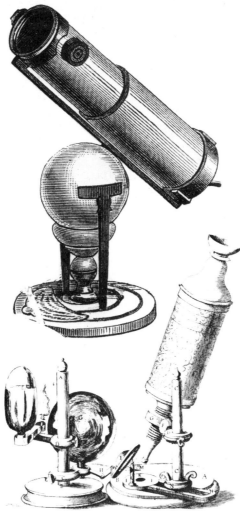

On first thoughts, this cessation of important discoveries seems surprising. There were many reasons why uninterrupted progress might have been expected. By 1700 European scholars formed an international community whose members exchanged information about their researches in voluminous correspondence and through the publication of learned periodicals. The new scientific learning was also slowly establishing itself in the universities, and, above all, *l'esprit géométrique* provided a favourable intellectual climate for continuing investigation and experiment. It also, however, provided a vehicle for the ideas of its founder, Descartes, and here perhaps lies a clue to the paucity of fundamental scientific discoveries between about 1690 and 1720. The authority of Descartes and Newton was so great that it cast a shadow over disciples who tended to feel that they had little to add to the words of masters, whose teachings they could only expound.

The eagerness of the generation of 1700 to apply the creative discoveries of the previous century to technology may also have left it less time for thinking about further fundamental advances. The years at the turn of the century saw many developments in applied technology: the improvement of pumps for mines, the application of the new mathematics and physics to the

problems of architecture, and the development of the steam engine are examples. Indeed, throughout the eighteenth century, engineers and other technicians continued the gigantic task of applying the 'pure' scientific achievements of the period 1600 to 1690 for the practical benefit of mankind.

Political philosophy

In the seventeenth century the influence of *l'esprit géométrique* made itself felt throughout the entire learned world. Almost all scholars shared the belief that the world could be understood by the aid of human reason and described in terms of mathematics. This belief influenced the style and content of their work in other fields, such as political thought, philosophy, literature, medicine and religion.

A name which can usefully be used to link seventeenth-century scientific and political studies is that of Sir William Petty, one of the early fellows of the Royal Society. Petty worked on figures of trade and population and expressed a firm belief in the benefit of applying the results to the problems of government. As such, he was the founder of what contemporaries called political arithmetic and we would call statistics. His ideas were to have a great future. The comparatively rudimentary calculations which he

made were developed in subsequent centuries into a sophisticated science which is the foundation of modern administration.

This general influence which the scientific spirit exercised on administrative and social problems can also be traced in the work of the three greatest political theorists of the century, the Englishmen Thomas Hobbes and John Locke and the Dutch Jew Benedict de Spinoza. All three shared the assumption that the same cause would always produce the same effect, one of the most fundamental of scientific theories.

Hobbes, who was born in 1588, grew to manhood and spent the middle years of his life at a time when the Elizabethan system of government was collapsing under the ineffective rule of James I and Charles I. When civil war broke out in 1642 the conflict turned largely on the question of sovereignty, on where, in other words, ultimate power in the English state lay. It was this problem of sovereignty which provided the central theme of Hobbes' most famous work, *Leviathan*, published in 1651, two years after England had executed her king. The title is metaphorical. Leviathan is the state and Hobbes chose the name because in the Vulgate version of the Book of Job we are told that no power on earth can compare with Leviathan. In that time of turmoil in England Hobbes turned, in fact, to the

idea of the supremacy in government of one selected man or assembly, preferably one man, who would exercise all legislative, executive and judicial power in both the secular and ecclesiastical fields.

Hobbes based his theory of the need for such a sovereign on a deterministic view of human nature. All human actions, he argued, were founded on self-interest. In such circumstances every man needed a guarantee of the good behaviour of his fellows, otherwise his life would be 'poor, nasty, brutish and short'. Such a guarantee could only be obtained by vesting all authority in a sovereign power which would be able to keep all men in order.

Hobbes' state was founded on a social contract. The ruler could treat his subjects in any way he chose as long as he was able to keep the peace, but 'the obligation of subjects to sovereign is understood to last as long as and no longer than the power lasts by which he is able to protect them.' These last lines explain why Hobbes' views failed to become an orthodox defence of monarchy. The Leviathan he conceived, with complete ability to overawe and at the same time protect its subjects, had seldom, if ever, existed. The arguments in *Leviathan* are, however, worked out with a rigid consistency which pays tribute to the scientific spirit of the age in which it was written.

Above, William Petty (1623–87), an English statistician who tried to set up a large-scale geographical survey and sought to establish the 'scientific' laws of political economy; such interests were typical of the intellectual milieu of Charles II's court in England, where the Royal Society was founded in 1661.

Above left, a Dutch astronomer of the second half of the seventeenth century. National Gallery, London.

Left, Thomas Hobbes (1588–1679), the English philosopher whose hatred of the English civil war led him to develop a political philosophy of absolute state power in his Leviathan of 1651; despite his conservative theme, his work was attacked for its materialist view of man and its denial of God as a formative influence in human society. National Portrait Gallery, London.

Opposite left, the Moon, according to a French book of 1685 describing the universe; the application of the telescope gave Europeans a new curiosity about the nature of the heavenly bodies and so brought the theories of Kepler and Newton to general prominence.

Opposite right, Christiaan Huygens (1629–95), the Dutch phycisist who discovered the pendulum clock. The accurate measurement of time was vital to the scientists of his day, who were much concerned with understanding the laws of motion.

Spinoza, one of the other two outstanding political theorists of the century, was also on the side of authority. He too denied any rights to individuals against the state. In his last work on politics, the *Tractatus Politicus*, published in 1677 after his death in the same year, he supported Hobbes' view that in a state of nature most men would strive for their own aggrandizement to the detriment of others. The only remedy was absolute government, which had the task of preserving the security and peace of its subjects. Unlike Hobbes, however, Spinoza saw that true peace was much more than just the absence of war. It meant, in fact, real concord among men, and a wise government, he argued, would preserve peace by granting, at its discretion, the maximum possible freedom to the people under its control, especially in matters of thought and religion.

John Locke had very different views from Hobbes and Spinoza. He was on the side of liberty rather than authority. It used to be thought that his most important work on political theory, his second *Treatise on Government*, which appeared in October 1689 (though dated 1690) was written specifically to vindicate the Revolution of 1688. We now know, however, that it was composed earlier in the 1680s. In it Locke gives his own theory of 'the true original extent and end of civil government'. Unlike Hobbes he assumed that man was naturally good and that he enjoyed inalienable rights to liberty and property which he retained when he made the original agreement which brought ordered society into existence. In making this 'social contract', in fact, men gave up their equality and natural 'executive' power with the specific objective of ensuring the preservation of their liberty and property. Rulers must therefore conduct their governments in the interests of their subjects. If they became tyrannical then the people were entitled to rebel and expel them from power.

Europe as a whole was at first more interested in Locke's philosophy than in his politics. Later on, however, in the eighteenth century, his political doctrines exercised very great influence abroad. He became the ancestor of much of the liberalism which played an important role in the life and politics of eighteenth-century America and France and is still such a powerful force.

Political theory, or political philosophy as it is sometimes called, can be regarded as a branch of philosophy as a whole, and two of the leading political theorists of the age, Spinoza and Locke, also wrote very important works of general philosophy. The seventeenth century is of the very greatest importance in the history of philosophy. In the words of Sir George Clark it 'contains the beginning of a chapter, the most abrupt of all the new beginnings since the rise of our philosophical tradition amongst the ancient Greeks'. The word 'philosophy' was used in the seventeenth century to mean what is now called science. We have

already discussed scientific developments and must now consider philosophy as the term is understood in our own time: the study of the ultimate problems which are raised in the search for truth and knowledge about man and the universe.

Medieval philosophical systems had been dogmatic: truth was the prerogative of authority, whether represented by the writings of Aristotle or the teachings of the Church. The new philosophy which developed in the seventeenth century was stimulated and indeed made possible by two great movements of thought, the Reformation and the scientific movement of the sixteenth and seventeenth centuries. The Reformation had little direct effect on philosophical speculation—it laid stress on faith rather than on learning and reason—but by flouting the authority of the Church in religious matters the reformers laid it open to challenge in other fields. The scientific movement, on the other hand, exercised a direct and powerful effect on philosophical thought. Copernicus, Kepler, Galileo and their successors presented new scientific views of the universe which led thinking men to speculate anew about the world and man's place in it. The influence of the new mathematics was profound—the greatest philosophers of the seventeenth century, with the exception of Locke, were all mathematicians of distinction.

Descartes

The man who can justly be called the 'father of modern philosophy' was a brilliant mathematician too. Descartes' methods were as important as the conclusions which he reached. The medieval schoolmen had gone about their work by systematically arranging all that was known about a subject and then arguing from the assembled material. That was induction, but clearly of a very different kind from the inductive methods based upon practical experiments which were later used by Galileo and Newton. Descartes, in contrast, stressed the importance of *deduction* in his principal philosophical works, like the French *Discours sur la methode*, published in 1637 and probably one of the two most influential books of the century (Newton's *Principia* was the other). His method was to begin by doubting everything and then to ask whether or not there was some truth which was so self-evident that it was not open to question. If he could find such a certainty he could then deduce other truths from it. It was clear, rational methodology, closely related to mathematics.

Descartes found his fundamental truth in the famous proposition, *Cogito, ergo sum*, 'I think, therefore I am', the idea that the processes which take place within the individual mind—such as understanding, calculating and doubting—prove beyond all question that the mind itself exists. From this starting point he went on to infer other

truths which, he maintained, necessarily followed. He constructed a universe which consisted of a world of experience and a world beyond experience. The existence of God, in the world beyond experience, was necessary because it was only from a being such as God that men could derive concepts which were outside their own experience: for example, eternity, immortality, omnipotence. The world of experience, the external world which men saw all around them, was not altogether as it seemed, because men's senses sometimes produced illusions about it. Still, it did have real qualities, which could be measured in mathematical terms.

In the Cartesian universe human reason was supreme. It led to a knowledge of God in the world beyond experience, and in the external world it seemed to make possible a mastery of man's environment.

Rationalists and empiricists

Descartes' works became the point of departure for both the opposing schools of thought into which philosophy divided during the seventeenth and eighteenth centuries, the rationalists and the empiricists. Those followers who stressed the rationalist side of his teaching and took the name 'Cartesians' were often men of considerable intellectual ability, though they were all far inferior mentally to another rationalist, Spinoza, whom we have already met as a political theorist but whose greater claim to fame is as a philosopher. Although far too distinguished simply to be labelled a Cartesian, Spinoza was in complete agreement with Descartes' methods and set out his own philosophical conclusions in the form of a deductive system in his greatest work, the *Ethics*, published in 1677.

Spinoza's philosophy is notoriously difficult to understand, but his conception of God, unlike Descartes', is not that of a pure spirit endowed with intellect and will. God, for Spinoza, combined attributes of matter and mind in a single substance, and was as much body as spirit. The physical laws which men knew were simply the operation of the divine mind: God and nature were one. Spinoza's philosophy, despite its frequent obscurity and difficulty, had a very practical purpose. It was designed to teach men how to live, as the title of his great work, *Ethics*, suggests. Only God was real, and all other beings and objects must be regarded in the context of eternity. This, however, did not preclude the need for human beings to try to live lives of virtue founded on reason and on intellectual love of God.

A few years after Spinoza's death John Locke arrived in Holland as a political exile. At that time he was already putting together the ideas which he published in 1690 as his *Essay Concerning Human Understanding*. Locke was the founder of a distinctively British philosophical school which exerted great influence on European thought in the eighteenth and nineteenth centuries, but he too owed much to Descartes, from whom he took his confidence in clear and distinct knowledge and his ideas about the fundamental distinction between mind and matter. However, he approached the problems of philosophy in a totally different way from Descartes. He used what he called a 'historical, plain method', an approach stressing the role of experience in the gaining of knowledge, in which he turned away from the construction of elaborate philosophical systems which had so preoccupied Descartes and Spinoza, to examine human ideas and their significance. In his *Essay* he took the contents of the individual mind and examined them one by one. The mind, he argued, was empty to begin with, but it soon filled up with simple data, impressed upon it by experience. It then worked upon these elementary ideas to form more complex thoughts. The whole of knowledge consisted of a collection and comparison of ideas.

Locke's work was much less ambitious in its aims than that of his predecessors. He

himself wrote 'it is ... enough to be employed as an underlabourer in clearing the ground a little, and removing some of the rubbish that lies in the way of knowledge.' He also makes much easier reading. His work has none of their difficulties of mathematical form and hard vocabularies of technical terms.

In any survey, however brief, of seventeenth-century philosophy, it would be wrong to omit the name of Leibnitz, a man of many-sided genius, mathematician, historian, theologian and politician as well as philosopher. He never worked out his philosophy in a single, comprehensive treatise, but his ideas were systematized by others after his death. According to Leibnitz the universe consisted of an infinite number of simple substances, each complete in itself, which he called 'monads'. The highest monads were the souls of men, but all monads were spiritual realities. Material things did not, in the strict sense, exist: it was only at the confused level of sense perception that they seemed to be real. Harmony among the monads was maintained by God, who, having an infinite number of possibilities to choose from, created the best of all possible worlds. This is Leibnitz's famous optimism, which was so ruthlessly caricatured by Voltaire in *Candide*.

Of course, despite his genius, he was a man of his times, limited in his ideas by his own concepts and those of his fellow scientists. Just as Newton did not anticipate the idea of relativity, so Leibnitz, even though he stressed that the monads were always changing, did not really understand that the essence of anything lies in its development in time: the idea of evolution.

Pioneers of medicine

The influence of the predominantly mathematical and scientific spirit of the seventeenth century can be seen in medicine, literature and painting no less than in political and philosophical thought. In medicine one school adopted Descartes' view that the human body is a machine. Prominent among these iatrophysicists, as they called themselves, was the Italian Giovanni Borelli, who was particularly interested in the physical laws which govern the body's movements. The greatest medical pioneer of the century, however, was the Englishman William Harvey. In 1628 he set out his discovery of the circulation of the blood in his *De Motu Cordis et Sanguinis*, a fundamentally important work which was the result of accurate observations and careful experiments.

Harvey revolutionized medicine by proving a series of closely interrelated points: that blood is propelled from the heart at regular intervals and in a constant stream, that the same blood circulates in both veins and arteries and that the heart propels only blood and not 'air' as well, as had formerly been supposed. He made other important

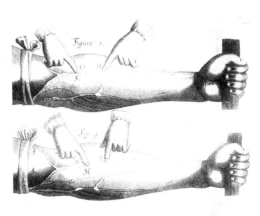

Above, the circulation of the blood, as illustrated in De Motu Cordis *of 1628 by the English physician William Harvey (1578–1657); this discovery was important in the development of modern medical science.*

Top, the title page of William Harvey's book of 1628 in which he outlined his theory of the circulation of the blood; his discovery owed much to the growing skill of surgeons in the previous century and also to the relaxation of the Catholic Church's ban on dissecting human bodies.

Opposite top, John Locke (1632–1704), the English philosopher whose theories of human knowledge led him to a political philosophy which was influential in justifying the Glorious Revolution of 1688; his belief that all men were born entirely ignorant, and that their ideas were the result of sensation and reflection, implied that society could only be organized for the benefit of all men equally. National Portrait Gallery, London.

Opposite bottom, René Descartes (1596–1650), the French philosopher and mathematician who is considered the founder of modern philosophy for his search for certain knowledge on which to base an understanding of the world. His system implied a sharp division between the material world and the world of ideas.

contributions to medical knowledge, especially in the field of embryology, and the new experimental methods which he used in his work were as important as the actual results he obtained. They pointed the way to the future, just as *De Motu Cordis* itself became the starting point for further research in physiology and anatomy, such as that of the Italian, Marcello Malpighi, Harvey's greatest immediate successor, who used the microscope to demonstrate the circulation of the blood in the capillaries.

In literature, the growth of the scientific spirit is revealed in stylistic changes which took place during the course of the century. Many early seventeenth century writers sought to impress by a difficult style—the poetry of John Donne and of his Italian and Spanish contemporaries is a good illustration of this—but as the years went by simplicity, lucidity and exactitude, mathematical ideals, became the fashion. They were exemplified during the century by the prose of Pascal and at its end by the works of Addison and Pope. The same kind of general tendency can be detected in painting. As the years passed there was a trend away from the Baroque grandeur and sumptuousness found in the early part of the seventeenth century in the works of Rubens towards the greater simplicity and restraint which characterized the art of Watteau at the end of Louis XIV's reign.

The Church opposes science

When we turn from art and literature to religion we find that the Church contributed little to the scientific revolution—in many ways it was a positive hindrance, witness Galileo—and that only one man made a front rank place for himself both as a defender of Christianity and a leader of the scientific revival. That was the Frenchman Blaise Pascal, a mathematician of great distinction who supported Jansenism in his *Lettres provinciales,* which appeared in 1656–7. His *Pensées*, published after his death in 1662, are fragments of a planned defence of Christianity.

The most important links between established religion and the scientific spirit in the seventeenth century are, in fact, to be found in the destructive effects which the latter had on the former. The Bible had previously been thought to be beyond criticism. Now, however, Cartesian sceptics argued that it should be subjected to textual analysis, just like any other document. Richard Simon, a Catholic priest, published several critical histories of the Old and New Testaments, works which revealed that the text of the Bible was full of difficulties of chronology and problems of vocabulary and meaning. His work was condemned by Catholics and Protestants alike, but, together with that of the great sceptic Pierre Bayle, it provided a great fund of arguments to support the Deists in the eighteenth century.

Indeed the end of the seventeenth and the beginning of the eighteenth centuries, the years roughly from 1680 to 1720, witnessed what has been aptly called a crisis in the European mind. Between these dates, large numbers of educated men, having absorbed the main ideas of the scientific revolution of the previous hundred years, began to question the very basis of traditional Christian teaching. Before 1680 only isolated thinkers had doubted that Christ was a Man-God who died on the cross for the salvation of mankind. After 1720 very many intelligent men questioned that belief. It was an intellectual revolution, a change from an attitude of mind which accepted traditional religious fundamentals to one which exalted scepticism and the secular spirit. The fact that the uneducated masses of Europe continued to adhere to old ideas only serves to highlight the change in attitude of so many intelligent men.

The new army

Besides vast political, social, scientific and intellectual changes, the seventeenth century also produced a military revolution. Professor Michael Roberts, one of the leading authorities on the subject, traces its beginnings back to the 1560s, but its main stages certainly came in the early seventeenth century and had profound effects not merely on military affairs in later years but on many other aspects of life as well.

In the mid-sixteenth century the dominant formation on west European battlegrounds was the Spanish tercio, or its equivalent. A tercio consisted of a square of pikemen and musketeers some 3,000 strong and epitomized the fact that infantry had replaced the heavy cavalry of the Middle Ages as the most important arm on the battlefield. The huge size of sixteenth-century infantry units made them difficult to manoeuvre quickly, with the result that tactics on the battlefield tended to be defensive rather than offensive. Commanders, in fact, usually avoided battles if at all possible.

The revolution which changed this situation took place in two stages between about 1590 and 1632, after an earlier, abortive start under Erik XIV of Sweden in the 1560s. The first stage, under the leadership of Prince Maurice of Orange, lasted until 1609, the second, under Sweden's Gustavus Adolphus, from about 1617 to 1632. Maurice returned to Roman models, with regard to both the size of his army units and their order of battle. His 'battalions' were about 500 strong—roughly the size of a Roman cohort—and he also favoured a linear order of battle as opposed to the square formation of the tercios. These changes made for much greater flexibility and manoeuvreability, but they did not win general acceptance in Europe, partly because they did not lead to any really striking successes against the tercios. It is notable that Maurice used the innovations chiefly in a

Blaise Pascal

defensive spirit. He fully shared the general contemporary dislike of battles.

This defensive attitude was completely changed by Gustavus Adolphus, who demonstrated the ability of the new linear formations to win successes in attack as well as in defence. He took over Maurice's smaller units but through a series of administrative and tactical reforms vastly increased their effectiveness on the battlefield. Junior officers and NCOs were given much greater responsibility and initiative on the field and musketeers and pikemen were linked together in the closest possible combination. This was greatly aided by Gustavus's exploitation of the salvo which he was the first to employ it at point blank range.

These changes, which were accompanied by important improvements in the mobility of the Swedish field artillery, demonstrated their significance in a series of victories during the Thirty Years' War, of which the Battle of Breitenfeld in 1631 was perhaps the most notable. The days of the tercio were numbered, and in 1643 the great Condé, then a young man, smashed once and for all the legend of their invincibility at the Battle of Rocroi. With that victory the military leadership of Europe, to which Gustavus Adolphus had aspired before his death in 1632, passed indubitably from Spain to France.

Changes in strategy

In the great battles of the Thirty Years' War, which marked the success of Gustavus' revolution, offensive tactics came back into favour after the long defensive interlude of the sixteenth century. At the same time, equally important strategic changes took place which transformed the whole scale of seventeenth-century warfare. In the sixteenth century, during the long Habsburg-Valois struggle, operations on several fronts

were common, but these were not usually planned in a systematic way. During the Thirty Years' War, however, with battles once more fashionable and hostilities ranging over the whole of central Europe, commanders began to look on the whole area of conflict as a single great theatre of war. Indeed, Gustavus himself planned to combine two types of strategy: offensive operations which were intended to defeat the enemy on the battlefield, and a gradual conquest of Germany by the systematic occupation of the country. His early death prevented any attempt being made to carry out the latter idea, but the grandiose nature of the scheme bears witness to the growing ambitiousness and scale of military operations.

The most noticeable result was a great increase in the size of armies. Philip II's Spain, the greatest military power in the later sixteenth century, had an army of

perhaps 40,000 men. Louis XIV's France, the leading military power of the seventeenth century, had 400,000 men under arms during the king's later years. Throughout much of Europe, in fact, the seventeenth century saw the permanent establishment of armies on a scale which had not been approached before. In the 1620s Brandenburg's army was less than 1,000 strong. In the early eighteenth century, in the reign of Frederick William I, it consisted of over 80,000 men.

Navies too grew rapidly in size. Spain, the greatest naval power of the sixteenth century, declined in importance at sea as well as on land during the seventeenth. By the end of the war of the Spanish Succession, indeed, she had almost no navy left at all. In any event, even at the height of her power in the sixteenth century she had never had a large, organized royal navy, maintained by the state for the purposes of war alone. Neither, of course, had her enemies. All depended, as

Above, the Battle of Rocroi in 1643, at which the French army decisively defeated the Spaniards. The seventeenth century saw a revolution in warfare that resulted in armies numbering more than 100,000 men and an improvement in fortifications against artillery. Musée Condé, Chantilly.

Opposite, Blaise Pascal (1623–62), the French philosopher who studied barometric pressures and invented the modern study of probability. His Pensées *were notes for a book outlining his belief that the scope of reason as a means of understanding the universe was limited – an unusual belief among scientists of his day.*

the Armada campaign had clearly shown, on large numbers of hired and commandeered merchantmen to supplement small nuclei of specialized warships. In the seventeenth century England, Holland and France challenged for the position which Spain had previously occupied. The three Anglo-Dutch wars and the threats which Colbert's naval building programme posed to both the maritime powers led to a considerable increase in the number and of great improvements in the construction of specialized warships and to significant developments in the administration behind them.

This vast growth in the size of armies and navies helped to increase social mobility. It is true that few of the leading commanders in the seventeenth century were of humble origin, but below the very highest ranks, and especially perhaps in naval and military administration, poor young men of intrinsic ability could readily make a mark which enabled them to raise their status in the world. Of more fundamental importance for the history of the times was the strain which the upkeep of these enormous forces placed upon the finances of European states. Rulers were always desperate to raise more and more money to improve their war machines or even simply to keep them going. It is very significant, as we have already noticed, that the immediate origins of the mid-century revolutions, which affected France, England, the United Provinces and the Spanish dominions, lay in the financial demands which the rulers of these territories made upon their subjects in order to pay for the upkeep of military forces. In short, the military revolution of the seventeenth century had profound social, financial and constitutional consequences.

The shape of the future

In 1715 the military, political, economic, religious and intellectual situation in Europe was very different from what it had been a century before. In the political and military spheres France had replaced Spain as the greatest European power. In 1600 the Spanish Empire, with possessions in four continents, was the dominant power. It is true that Philip II had failed to conquer England or to subdue his rebellious subjects in the northern Netherlands, but he passed on to his son Philip III in 1598 a much larger empire than the one which he had inherited from his father, the Emperor Charles V, in the 1550s. The seventeenth century, however, saw a steady reduction in Spanish power, which had been founded essentially on the strength of the Castilian heartland of the empire. The rapid economic decline of Castile from the early years of the century onwards led to growing financial demands on the periphery, which in turn helped to produce the revolts of the 1640s. Soon Portugal was irrecoverably lost and by the last years of the century an impoverished

Spain under the rule of a mentally subnormal king, Charles II, had sunk to the status of a second-rate power. In the early years of the eighteenth century, with a Frenchman, Philip V, on the throne, she began to recover some strength, but Spain was never again to be one of the greatest powers in Europe.

The Treaty of the Pyrenees in 1659, a landmark in the decline of Spain, also marked the rise of France to the position of the leading power in Europe, a place which she owed mainly to the work of the great cardinals, Richelieu and Mazarin, whose victories against both Austrian and Spanish Habsburgs in the Thirty Years' War strengthened the position of their country abroad, just as their work in domestic affairs laid some of the foundations for Louis XIV's rule at home. By the 1670s France, with by far the best army and diplomatic service in Europe, was also rapidly increasing her economic strength, particularly her industrial potential. It seemed that she was in a position to threaten complete domination of the continent. By 1715 that danger had gone. France remained the most powerful single state, but changes in the international situation from the 1680s onwards, and particularly the growing power of England, which under William III was constantly hostile to France, ensured that there was a balance of power in European affairs.

Indeed, the years from 1680 to 1715 saw the emergence of England, Austria and Russia as great powers, able to play very important roles on the eighteenth century European scene. The rise of England in the period 1688 to 1715 is demonstrated by the predominant role she played in the coalition which finally set limits to Louis XIV's ambitions in the war of the Spanish Succession. Under Marlborough, Britain's

armies inflicted the first serious defeats on the French military machine which it suffered during Louis' reign, and her navy, as large as the French and Dutch navies combined, dominated the seas. This growth in Britain's military and hence in her political power was accompanied by a relative decline in the importance of the United Provinces. William III, after he became king of England in 1689, made it clear that he regarded Britain as the senior partner in the alliance of the two maritime powers, and in 1715 it was already clear to informed observers that the United Provinces had begun that long decline in her political importance which took place during the eighteenth century.

Austria's star in the later years of the seventeenth century was by contrast in the ascendant. Her great victories over the Turks in the 1680s and 1690s, leading to the reconquest of Hungary, together with the huge possessions which she obtained in Italy and the Netherlands in 1713, made her very clearly a great power in 1715. Russia too, under the enormously energetic rule of Peter the Great, increased her strength by leaps and bounds at the turn of the century. By 1715 and still more by 1721 she had replaced Sweden as the predominant power in northern and northeastern Europe, where she exercised great influence in the vast but declining Polish state.

Russia's power rested on her large population and vast natural resources, the basic elements in the economic and hence in the potential political power of any country. Actual power, of course, depended on how far governments were able to use the skills and abilities of their people to develop the natural resources of the country in the service of the state. France, which had a numerous and relatively skilful population and considerable natural resources, was in 1700 more powerful than Russia, which had superior resources but a slightly smaller and very much less skilful population. The Ottoman Empire, if one considers its European, Asiatic and African provinces together, had many more people even than France, but its real power was limited by technological backwardness. The United Provinces, by contrast, concealed the disadvantages of a small country and population by exploiting the very highly developed skills and energies of its people and its natural geographical advantages at the centre of European trade routes to make itself the leading commercial and financial power of the seventeenth century. It was a remarkable achievement, but, in the nature of things, it was bound to be temporary. Once Britain, with a similarly favourable geographical position, a larger population and greater natural resources, began to concentrate more and more efforts on financial and commercial development the days of Holland's supremacy were numbered. In 1715 the United Provinces were still the leading commercial and financial power, but they were being rapidly overtaken by Britain.

In the seventeenth century, as the Anglo-Dutch wars showed, economic conflicts played an increasing role in international affairs, a tendency which continued in later years. Religious differences, in contrast, played a less significant part in the international relations as the seventeenth century wore on. The Thirty Years' War was the last great conflict in western and central Europe in which religion played a really important role, though of course the war between Austria and the Ottoman Empire in eastern Europe in the 1680s and 1690s had strong religious overtones. From 1648 onwards, in fact, the religious frontiers of Europe were fixed. After that date, although religion continued to play a very important role in the internal politics of states, as the treat-

ment of the French Huguenots and the career of James II in England showed very clearly, no European country changed its formal religious allegiance.

It was during these years too, however, that traditional religion, whether of the Catholic or Protestant variety, lost its hold over many educated Europeans. This intellectual revolution was preceded, accompanied and largely caused by the great developments in mathematics and science which characterised the seventeenth century and had ramifications throughout the whole field of thought. The intellectual climate among intelligent men was totally different in 1700 from what it had been in 1600.

These changes in thought were perhaps the most important of all the developments which took place during the period. It is traditional to see the great break in the century between the 1640s and 1650s, when so many political and social revolutions occurred. In the field of thought, however, the years 1680 to 1720 were crucial. It was in these years that great numbers of intelligent men who had absorbed the rudiments of the seventeenth-century scientific advances came to adopt a secular view of life and a sceptical attitude towards traditional authority which betokened a decisive breach with the past. It is perhaps at that time, rather than at any other, that we should place the dividing line between 'medieval' and 'modern' thought. The educated men of 1700 belonged in truth to a 'new Europe': they were the first generation to share a good many of the attitudes of the modern European mind.

Opposite, the formal gardens of an English country house at Stowe in Buckinghamshire, laid out in the 1690s; the passion for mathematical harmony overtook all the arts after the evaporation of the passions of the Baroque age.

THE CIVILIZATION OF THE SEVENTEENTH CENTURY

Date	Events	Arts	Sciences	Literature and philosophy	Date	Events	Arts	Sciences	Literature and philosophy
1600					1660				
	Accession of James I (1603)	El Greco: *View of Toledo* (1605)	Galileo: the telescope	Cervantes: *Don Quixote*		Restoration of Charles II	Rembrandt: *The Guild of Drapers*	Royal Society founded (1662)	Molière: *Tartuffe*
	Assassination of Henry IV (1606)	Birth of Rembrandt (1606) Monteverdi: *Orpheus*	Kepler (1571–1630)	Bacon: *Novum Organum*		Building of Versailles begins	Murillo: Decoration of the hospital of Coridad	Leibnitz: theory of movement (1670)	Milton: *Paradise Lost* (1667)
	Accession of Louis XIII (1610)	Rubens: *Last Judgement*	Harvey: circulation of the blood	Authorized version of the Bible (1611)					Pascal: *Pensées* (1670) Spinoza: *Ethics*
	Beginning of the Thirty Years' War		Harvey: working of the heart	Birth of Molière (1622) Birth of Pascal (1623) First Folio of Shakespeare published (1623)		Treaty of Nymegen (1679)	Sir Christopher Wren: Greenwich Observatory begun (1676)	Newton: theory of gravity (1682) Halley's comet (1682)	Bunyan: *A Pilgrim's Progress* (1678)
1630						Death of Colbert (1683)	Birth of Rameau (1683)		Leibnitz: *Systema Theologicum*
	Death of Gustavus Adolphus (1632)	Rembrandt: *The Anatomy Lesson* (1632)	Prosecution of Galileo (1633)				Birth of Watteau (1684)		Newton: *Principia Mathematica* (1687)
	Death of Richelieu (1642)	Inigo Jones' plan for Covent Garden Market	Birth of Newton (1642)	Birth of Locke and of Spinoza (1632) Donne's collected poems published (1633)			Birth of J. S. Bach and Handel (1685)		
					1690				
	Treaties of Westphalia (1648)	Van Dyck: *Portrait of Charles I*	Torricelli: the barometer	Corneille: *Le Cid* (1636)		William and Mary King and Queen of England (1689)	Purcell: *Dido and Aeneas* (1689)	Huygens: *Treatise on Light* (1690)	Birth of Voltaire (1694)
	Execution of Charles I (1649)	Velasquez: *Crucifixion*		Descartes: *Discours sur la méthode* (1637) Birth of Leibnitz (1646)		Treaty of Ryswick (1697)	Birth of Chardin (1699)	Newton: *Optics*	Congreve: *The Way of the World* (1700)
	Death of Cromwell (1658)	Mansart: *Val-de Grace* Rembrandt: *Portrait of the Artist*	Creation of the Academy of Sciences in Paris (1658)	Pascal: *Les Provinciales* (1656)		Death of Louis XIV (1715)	Birth of Boucher (1703)	Papin: experiments with steam	Leibnitz: theory of monads
					1720				

149

FRANCFORT

Offenbach

Seligenstadt

French Battery

Aschaffenberg

Dettingen

French Battery

Gens d'armes

HANAW

Cronbach

FRANCFORT
Aschaffenberg
Darmstat
Seligenstadt
Cronbach
Jommone
Miltenberg

Dettingen

The King

Part III

THE STRUGGLE FOR SUPREMACY

Introduction

The civilization of the eighteenth-century, despite the outstanding impact of English habits of thinking on scientific inquiry and philosophy on the age was continental in character. And apart from the rich contribution of the Austrian and German courts to music and the stage, the culture of the Enlightenment, taken as a whole, was French and its metropolitan centre was Paris. It was French fashions of taste and thought and of governmental and diplomatic habit which permeated the more provincial centres of Europe, especially the more backward parts of Europe where standards and practices were set not by a mercantile middle class but by 'enlightened despots' in touch with France and each other.

The civilization of the eighteenth-century was, indeed, continental in another sense. It was continent-wide. One must always guard against the tendency of historical perspective to see uniformities and to shade out disparities and in our case to accept the polite and the articulate and to discount the disparate, the turbulent, the primitive, indeed the barbaric, aspects of life in the rural society which Europe essentially remained. Nonetheless, Europe in the eighteenth-century was culturally more homogeneous than she had been since the Middle Ages and was to be again until the present.

'The concert of Europe' is a post-Napoleonic term which previous generations had not found it necessary to invent because its reality was assumed. The relations between states continued to be governed largely by dynastic assumptions and the room to manoeuvre by limited objectives in which an element of whim or fantasy was only partially displaced by Frederick the Great's intrusion of an element of *Realpolitik*. The limited objectives of diplomacy extended to wars fought by small armies of mercenaries and pressed troops drilled to formal manoeuvre in campaigns limited by the seasons and by a primitive organization of supply. The concepts of national mobilization and of ideological crusade had not yet been born. These objectives were limited by a social and political order which held so stable that trade between enemies could thrive and the gentry could travel through enemy country without any threat of molestation; social

communication among equals was unimpaired by war. This is not to deny that there were major shifts in the balance of forces such as the revolution in alliances of 1756 or that resulting from the inefficient but powerful new impact of Russia combined with the slackening hold of Turkey in eastern Europe. The latter, however, took place at the periphery of a Europe whose boundaries were extended to include a partially Europeanized Russia as part of the European system.

That system held not so much because of a common aristocratic and semi-feudal social order but because the personal rule of princes acquired new force from the rationalizing of administration: the erosion of medieval estates and privileges (including practices of self-government which were thought to be anachronistic) and the substitution of military, civil and judicial services responsible to the ruler. By such means the 'enlightened' despots of principalities

created for themselves both the fact and the notion of 'states'. Kosciuzko's Poland apart, however, this notion did not extend to that of the 'nation', and the threat of a revolution which was both French and ideological forced the despots of the Enlightenment into a reactionary defensiveness which, until national self-consciousness, was no match for the French revolutionary elan. Against this new force—which produced so cataclysmic an event, or series of events, that the map of Europe, politically, governmentally, socially and ideologically, was never the same again—the civility of the Enlightenment, so urbane and, in a measure, so well-intentioned, collapsed; and the civilization of the eighteenth-century, as proud and seemingly as established as that of the Roman Empire which was so much admired, was shown to be shallow and inadequate in its thinking, its practices and its capacity for change.

Chapter 16

Central and Eastern Europe in the late Seventeenth Century

Until the nineteenth century, an area considerably larger than the two present-day German states was occupied by the Holy Roman Empire—not an empire in the modern sense, or even a state, but a patchwork of some 350 territorial units owing allegiance to a Holy Roman emperor. The majority of the inhabitants were Germans, but the empire also contained the Czechs of Bohemia, the Flemings of the Spanish Netherlands and other non-Germans.

The empire was religiously as well as politically fragmented; and the hatreds of Catholic, Lutheran and Calvinist were the occasion of the terrible Thirty Years' War (1618–48), in which most of the European powers became involved. Germany was the main theatre of the war and at its close was physically and morally devastated. Although not all areas were equally affected, suffering and impoverishment were very widely distributed. Law and order vanished; trade was disrupted and often re-routed to avoid Germany altogether; and the population of both town and country fell catastrophically. In many areas the material and human losses were not made good until the early decades of the eighteenth century.

The political results were equally serious. For a time during the war it seemed that the Emperor Ferdinand II might be able to weld the empire into a unified state comparable with France or Spain. His failure entailed the creation of new weaknesses and—of much greater importance—the perpetuation of all the existing weaknesses. In an age when powerful and unified nation-states were coming to dominate Europe, and when the authority of governments was being asserted with increasing success by ever larger bureaucracies, the empire remained as it was: a quasi-feudal agglomeration of more or less independent units.

The lay and ecclesiastical princes, free cities and imperial knights whose territories made up the empire owed formal allegiance to the emperor, but the more powerful were entirely beyond his control. Imperial authority was backed neither by an army nor by the ability to levy taxes. The deliberative assembly, the Diet, was a wrangling, ineffective body; the judicial institutions of the empire were antiquated and notoriously slow. The exercise of imperial power was restricted to arbitrating in disputes between German rulers and occasionally between rulers and their subjects; and even this applied only to small or weak states.

The emperor did not inherit his office: he was elected by the most important princes of the empire. In the late seventeenth century the electors were the ecclesiastical rulers of Mainz, Trier and Cologne and the lay princes of the Palatinate, Saxony, Brandenburg, Bavaria, Bohemia and Hanover. Every candidate for the throne had to buy the electors' support with cash or concessions, so that any continuous growth of imperial authority was impossible to achieve in normal circumstances. In fact, the Habsburg family succeeded in monopolizing the imperial office: with one exception (1742–5), every emperor from 1438 until the dissolution of the empire in 1806 was a Habsburg. This provided the empire with its only element of effective continuity; and it was the resources of the Habsburgs' large hereditary possessions that sustained such authority as the emperor possessed.

For practical purposes, then, the largest German principalities were independent states, able to make alliances with each other or with non-German powers, jealous of their neighbours and hostile to the extension of imperial authority. A certain vestigial imperial or German sentiment could persuade the princes to rally to the emperor, notably in campaigns against the Turks; but it was always of brief duration. From 1681 there was even an imperial army of sorts, though it was mainly provided by the western states of the empire, which felt threatened by the aggressions of Louis XIV.

Indeed, the diplomatic history of these German states in the late seventeenth and early eighteenth centuries was largely one of reaction to French initiatives. Louis' insatiable ambition and over-confidence gradually united the empire against him. The powerful league of Rhine princes, formed in 1654 as a satellite of France, was dissolved in 1668. French success in the War of Devolution (1667–8), the Dutch War (1672–9) and the legalistic aggressions by which Louis 'reunited' border territories with France made it progressively more difficult for the French to buy off German states or to play upon their mutual suspicions; France, not the emperor, came to be seen as the main threat to their security. In 1686 the princes of Franconia and the Rhineland formed a defensive alliance, the League of Augsburg, directed against France; and within two years Brandenburg, Bavaria and Saxony had joined the league. From the beginning of the War of the League of Augsburg (1688), most of the empire took part in the long struggles against France that ended only in 1713.

This unity was as factitious and devoid of significance for the future as the larger unity of the European states against France. The

Above, a German woodcut of 1643 showing robbers attacking a horseman; the Thirty Years' War brought devastation to many parts of Germany and, in its wake, a threat of social collapse and anarchy.

Opposite, Madame de Pompadour, the mistress of Louis XV of France, with the Duke of Choiseul. Waddesdon Manor. The National Trust.

On page 150, the Battle of Dettingen of June 1743, an English victory in the War of the Austrian Succession. It was the last occasion on which an English king led his troops in battle.

Legend (on map):

POLAND

Boundary of the Empire ——
Ottoman Empire
Swedish possessions
Hohenzollern possessions
Spanish Habsburg possessions
Austrian Habsburg possessions
France and French possessions

Map labels: NORTH SEA, BALTIC SEA, DENMARK, HANOVER, RAVENSBURG, HOLLAND (UNITED PROVINCES), CLEVES, POMERANIA, EAST PRUSSIA, BRANDENBURG, SPANISH NETHERLANDS, MARK, SAXONY, SILESIA, BOHEMIA, MORAVIA, AUSTRIA, HABSBURG HUNGARY, TRANSYLVANIA, FRANCE, SAVOY, MILAN, OTTOMAN EMPIRE

customs duties levied at frontiers and along rivers drove away trade. Towns under princely rule were borne down by their rulers' exactions; the free cities, hemmed in on all sides by the territories of the princes, stagnated.

There were exceptions, notably Hamburg, Frankfurt and Leipzig; indeed, all generalizations about the empire—a miniature world of states and cities with varied resources and widely different socio-political structures—are subject to qualification. The situation of the peasants was even more various. In Saxony and western and southern Germany they were free and relatively prosperous. Elsewhere, and particularly in the northeast, they were still serfs, allowed to cultivate their holdings in return for various services, including work on the land which their lord farmed for his own use; and here the rigours of serfdom were if anything increased after the Thirty Years' War. Depopulation encouraged landlords to enlarge their own holdings, which entailed the imposition of greater labour services on a peasantry much reduced in numbers.

Thus all the facts of German life indicated prolonged backwardness, fragmentation and diversification. Germany was not to be united for two centuries, but the politics of central Europe were about to be transformed by the emergence of new forces, Religion gradually ceased to be a political issue; for most of the eighteenth and nineteenth centuries the main motif of German history was to be 'dualism', the domination of Germany by two states, the Habsburg dominions and Brandenburg-Prussia. This was foreshadowed by two developments in the late seventeenth century; the consolidation and extension of the Habsburg lands through the defeat of the Turks; and the forced growth of Brandenburg-Prussia under a succession of able Hohenzollern rulers.

Brandenburg-Prussia

The Electorate of Brandenburg was a poor, sandy, waterlogged land in north-east Germany. It had been ruled by the Hohenzollern family since 1415; under Frederick William, 'the Great Elector', it was to become the heartland of a formidable state.

The other Hohenzollern territories were scattered and difficult to defend. Only Pomerania, immediately to the north, was defensible; the duchy of East Prussia, for which the elector did homage to the king of Poland, was separated from Brandenburg by a wide belt of Polish territory; the duchy of Cleves and the counties of Mark and Ravensburg were in the distant Rhineland.

When Frederick William acceded in 1640, at the age of twenty, the Thirty Years' War was entering its final phase, and most of his possessions were occupied by foreign troops. He extricated himself from his difficulties by a combination of skill and good luck, and

less dramatic but more durable tendencies of the age reinforced the independence and power of the individual princes. The right of subjects to appeal to the emperor over the heads of their rulers was progressively curtailed. Several princes succeeded in weakening the representative estates in their dominions, or even in doing without them altogether, aping the absolutism of Louis XIV. Every petty ruler sought to emulate at least the trappings of the Sun King's greatness, building a miniature Versailles, making French the language of his court, creating a bureaucracy and maintaining a standing army.

The extra-imperial interests of the princes were emphasized by the dynastic ambitions that led them to seek thrones outside Germany, as when Augustus the Strong of Saxony became King of Poland (1697) and the Elector of Hanover became George I of England (1714). In the long run this kind of entanglement led to the neglect or over-exploitation of the German state concerned; and it was partly because Saxony and Hanover became involved in Polish and

British affairs that, as we shall see, Brandenburg-Prussia was able to become the leading German state.

German commerce had begun to decline in some places before the Thirty Years' War, and the war itself wrecked the German economy and left foreign powers in control of the mouths of the great German rivers. A highly centralized state like France, with large resources at its disposal, might have recovered fairly quickly; the hundreds of units making up the empire could not.

Division bred many weaknesses. The exactions of the princes were disproportionate to the resources of their states, which had to pay for the upkeep of a local court, a local bureaucracy, a local army. The burden was unevenly spread, since noble privileges were usually left untouched—a tacit repayment for noble acquiescence in princely absolutism. The means by which revenue was raised, though in accordance with the economic theories of the time, were inappropriate to a complex of small, impoverished states. Taxes, monopolies and excise duties discouraged manufactures:

154

with French support secured relatively good terms at the Peace of Westphalia (1648). Sweden took western Pomerania, with the vital harbour of Stettin which controlled the River Oder, but as partial compensation Frederick William received several secularized bishoprics adjacent to Hohenzollern lands. Only after Westphalia was Frederick William able to begin the task which occupied the rest of his life.

The Hohenzollern lands were not a state: they were separate entities which happened to be ruled by the same man; each was represented by its own Estates, preoccupied with local problems and averse to voting money for the defence of other Hohenzollern possessions. The essential achievement of Frederick William's reign was to make this dynastic complex into a unified state, the total resources of which were at the elector's disposal.

The Brandenburg Estates were dominated by the Junkers, nobles who farmed their lands for profit with serf labour, mainly producing corn and beer for sale. They were a working nobility, by no means very wealthy, and they had none of the thirst for adventure and glory characteristic of great aristocracies. In 1650 they refused the elector money with which to fight the Swedes in Pomerania: Pomerania was no concern of theirs. In 1652, when Frederick William demanded a general excise that would have ended the Junkers' virtual exemption from taxation, he had to be content with a compromise. The Junkers' control over their serfs was strengthened; the elector was to consult the Estates on all matters of importance; and in return he was to have a grant of 500,000 thalers.

In the event, what mattered was the money. With money Frederick William could raise troops; and with troops he could impose his will on his recalcitrant subjects. The war between Sweden and Poland (1655–60) gave him the opportunity and excuse to execute this policy. In the war itself he judiciously changed sides at the right moment, thereby securing the complete independence of his duchy of East Prussia; but the internal repercussions were even more important.

Everywhere the elector's soldiers recruited and collected the taxes he imposed; resistance was simply met by force. In Brandenburg alone, which had granted 500,000 thalers over six years in 1652, 110,000 thalers a month was being collected by 1659. The excise, which was gradually made compulsory for all the towns, became a permanent tax; and without the power of the purse the Estates became insignificant. The Junkers, secure in their control over the serfs and exempt from payment of the excise, quickly accepted the situation.

Elsewhere the pattern of events was similar. East Prussia, with a relatively wealthy nobility habituated to the anarchy of Poland, put up a stiffer resistance than Brandenburg. Only in the 1670s was all

opposition destroyed; the independence of the four locally elected governors was ended, and the duchy was integrated into the Hohenzollern state. The Rhineland territories preserved some independence, though they lost the exceptional liberties they had won earlier. They were simply too far away for the Hohenzollerns to control them autocratically.

It is difficult to assess how consciously Frederick William planned the development of the Hohenzollern state; but his rule undoubtedly possessed an inner logic, conscious or not. Given the scattered nature of the Hohenzollern territories, security could be gained only by strengthening the army. A bigger army had to be supported out of heavier taxes, which could be collected only by the army. Army and administration thus became closely identified. The General War Commissariat, created to organize supplies for the army during the Swedish-Polish war, took over the collection of taxes, and its officers became the most important executives of a centralized and militarized bureaucracy.

Above, Frederick William, elector of Brandenburg (reigned 1640–88), who won Brandenburg's independence from the Polish king, took Pomerania and created a unified and militarily strong Prussian state. Schloss Fasanenie, Fulda.

Opposite, the Holy Roman Empire after the Treaty of Westphalia in 1648.

155

The army, which had numbered less than 5,000 at the end of the Thirty Years' War, was 12,000 strong even after reductions made in 1660; and at Frederick William's death in 1688 a small population (about a million) was supporting a standing army of 30,000. The nobility increasingly valued state service as a means of advancement, developing an unshakable esprit de corps and unswerving devotion to the dynasty. Even under the Great Elector, army and state, officer and official were becoming synonymous.

The Great Elector had every interest in making his state prosperous, since prosperity entailed a larger tax yield. He encouraged immigration, granting favourable terms to Dutch farmers and Huguenot refugees from Louis XIV's persecution. He improved communications, building a canal that enabled barges to sail from the Oder to the Elbe via Berlin (thus avoiding the Baltic ports controlled by Sweden). A fleet of ten craft was equipped, and there were strenuous efforts to develop colonial trade—strenuous but misguided, since Brandenburg stood no real chance of competing with the maritime powers.

The negative side of Frederick William's economic policies (government regulation, heavy taxes and tolls) had much in common with that of his contemporaries; but its emphatic character derived from the need to support a disproportionately large army. Economic development was also inhibited by the disadvantages under which the towns laboured in competing with rural products sold by a privileged nobility. Recovery from the Thirty Years' War was slow, and Brandenburg-Prussia remained a poor land.

The army achieved its first notable success in the Dutch War by defeating the Swedes at Fehrbellin in 1675, though Sweden's ally,

France, bullied Frederick William into restoring his Pomeranian conquests. After this reverse the elector returned to the unheroic policy of taking subsidies from the seemingly invincible French. Only from 1685 did he ally with the emperor against France; and it was under his son Frederick (1688–1713) that Brandenburg took part in the great coalitions against France.

The wars brought the Hohenzollerns no acquisitions of any moment but Frederick acquired a new title. In return for his support in the imminent War of the Spanish Succession, the Emperor Leopold I agreed that Frederick should become King of Prussia, Prussia being chosen because it was outside the boundaries of the Holy Roman Empire. In January 1701 Frederick crowned himself and his wife with great pomp.

Frederick I of Prussia was not an outstanding king. Power was largely exercised by his ministers, while the king surrounded himself with ceremonial, spent lavishly, built palaces and patronized the arts. The Prussian Academy and the University of Halle were founded in his reign.

War and royal expenditure soon put Prussian finances in disarray, and it is likely that, had he lived, the king would have reduced the size of the army at the end of the war rather than sacrifice his pleasures. If this had happened, Prussia would have developed more normally, for better or worse; instead, his successor, Frederick William I, resolutely intensified the militarization of Prussia.

Habsburg lands

Although the Austrian Habsburgs failed to make the office of Holy Roman emperor an effective one, in the seventeenth century they prepared a new role for themselves by consolidating and extending their family possessions in central and southeastern Europe. From the eighteenth to the twentieth centuries they were to be most important as rulers of the state that it is convenient to call 'Austria'.

Its nucleus was formed when Charles V handed over the Habsburg lands in central Europe to his brother Ferdinand (1519–21) and Ferdinand secured his own election to the thrones of Bohemia and Hungary. But like the Great Elector's inheritance, the Habsburg lands were a dynastic complex rather than a state. In 1648, at the close of the Thirty Years' War, they comprised the German-speaking duchies of Upper Austria, Lower Austria, Styria, Carinthia, the Tyrol and Carniola; the kingdom of Bohemia, with Moravia and Silesia; and, outside the Holy Roman Empire, as much of the kingdoms of Hungary, Croatia and Dalmatia as the Habsburgs were able to defend against the Turks.

The process of state-building began early in the seventeenth century. Territories ceased to be apportioned among members of the

family, so that authority was concentrated in the hands of the emperor in Vienna; and the rights of the Estates were considerably reduced in the German-speaking lands. The crushing of the Bohemian revolt, which sparked off the Thirty Years' War, provided the opportunity for an even more forceful extension of Habsburg authority: the Protestant heresy was uprooted, the flourishing and self-assertive Czech towns ruined, and the Czech nobility replaced by Habsburg nominees (mainly German) who depended on the emperor for their continued security. The Bohemian monarchy, previously elective, became hereditary in the Habsburg family.

Although the servants of the emperor forged instruments of central control in the capital, they were never able to use them with the absolute authority of French or even Prussian administrators: there were too many differences of race, language and (in Hungary) religion, too many local laws, customs and institutions to permit the establishment of administrative uniformity.

The guardian—and beneficiary—of local privileges and immunities was the landlord. In the Habsburg lands, as elsewhere in central and eastern Europe, he was becoming more powerful—increasing his rights over the serfs, extorting more labour services from them, and successfully competing with the towns in selling the produce of his lands. Apart from the ravages of the Thirty Years' War, which had been terrible in the Habsburg lands north of the Danube, and the deliberate ruin of the Bohemian towns, the problem of depopulation had been accentuated by the emigration of persecuted Protestants. The backwardness of the Habsburg lands was perpetuated by neglect of the towns and by the drain of money, men and materials in the struggle against the two great enemies of the Habsburgs: France and Ottoman Turkey.

The Habsburgs' enemies

France and Turkey had been traditional allies since the early sixteenth century, just as France and the Habsburgs had been traditional enemies. At that time the Habsburgs seemed on the point of encircling and destroying France; from the mid-seventeenth century the situation was reversed. Spain, under another branch of the Habsburgs, was in decline; the Holy Roman Empire was weak and divided; Habsburg Austria seemed exhausted, remote and distracted by the Turkish menace. Louis XIV made France the greatest power in Europe, expanding her borders by a series of successful aggressions and even intriguing to become Holy Roman emperor.

Leopold I (1658–1705) was preoccupied with the struggle against the Turks in the first half of his reign and made no attempt to resist French aggressions until the Dutch War of 1672–9 (significantly, during a truce with the Turks). The great Austrian effort against France occurred only after the Turks had begun to retreat; from 1688 Austria took a most important part in the great coalitions that first checked and then humbled France.

The Turks were an even more pressing problem than Louis XIV. Their armies had menaced Europe for 200 years and had almost invariably defeated the armies of Christian states; only a strip of Hungary barred them from Vienna itself. Habsburg Hungary, hardly more than a quarter of the old kingdom, was effectively controlled by a turbulent nobility jealous of its liberties. The monarchy remained elective; the nobility claimed the right to resist the king if their privileges were infringed, legislated in their own interest through the Estates, paid no taxes and nominated the head of their own armed forces. Hungarian Protestants, plotters and nobles who believed their liberties threatened could look for protection to a powerful neighbour: Transylvania.

In origin Transylvania was a breakaway state from Habsburg Hungary. By 1648, thanks to the statesmanship of Bethen Gabor (1613–29) and Gyorgy Rakoczi I (1630–48), it occupied almost half the territory of old Hungary and was virtually independent of the Turks. Its Calvinist rulers tolerated Catholic and Protestant alike, adding an ideological element to the hostility of the devoutly Catholic Habsburgs.

The ambitious Gyorgy Rakoczi II led Transylvania to disaster. He joined the Swedish king, Charles X, in attacking Poland; and while he was being defeated there, the Turks invaded Transylvania. After a confused struggle Rakoczi was defeated and killed (1660), as was his successor Janos Kemeny (1662). The Turks overran Transylvania and prepared to attack Habsburg Hungary.

When they took the great fortress of Neuhausel in 1663, Christian Europe rallied to the defence of Austria with men and money—an indication that the medieval conception of a Christian community was still not entirely defunct; even Louis XIV sent 6,000 men. The subsequent defeat of the Turks at St Gotthard (1664), by an army under the imperial general Montecuccoli, was the first indication that military supremacy had passed to the Christian states.

The decisive nature of this event was obscured by the haste with which Emperor Leopold made peace—partly because Christian losses had been heavy, partly through caution and partly because he was becoming preoccupied with the Spanish succession problem. The treaty of Vasvar left the Turkish position in Hungary still unshaken.

The Hungarian magnates, incensed at what they deemed Habsburg treachery in not pursuing the defeated Turk, plunged into an orgy of incompetent conspiracy. Leopold made this the excuse for a military occupation of Hungary (1670), but the subsequent attempt to suppress Hungarian liberties, end toleration of Protestants and 'put the Hungarians into Czech trousers' was premature. Many Hungarians joined Imre Thokoly in northern Hungary, where, abetted by the Transylvanians and aided by the French, he conducted a ferocious and successful resistance. In 1681—just in time—Leopold realized his mistake and restored the Hungarians' lost liberties.

This action deprived Thokoly of much of his support and forced him to turn to the Turks, who were in any case preparing to march on Vienna. The Austrians appeared powerless to stop them, and in July 1683 the Habsburg capital was besieged by a great Turkish army. Again Europe came to the defence of Austria, all the more effectively since a great reforming pope, Innocent XI, ceaselessly exhorted and negotiated with the powers. Most of the German states sent contingents of troops and, largely through the pope's influence, in March 1683 Leopold secured the alliance of John Sobieski, King of Poland. In September, when Vienna was close to capitulation after a heroic defence, a cosmopolitan army of 70,000, commanded by Sobieski, swept down from the Kahlenburg and routed the Turks.

Vienna was saved, but the immediate fruits of victory were lost through dissensions among the victors. On this occasion Leopold decided to pursue his advantage. At Ratisbon (1684) he recognized all Louis XIV's gains since the War of Devolution in return for a twenty-year truce that left him a free hand in the east. The Turks were expelled from Hungary only after fifteen years of intermittent fighting, long periods of Austrian inactivity being enforced by the war against France (1688–97) which broke out despite the truce of Ratisbon. At last, in 1697, the brilliant Eugene of Savoy took command of the Austrian army and overwhelmed the last effective Turkish force at the Battle of Zenta. By the Treaty of Carlowitz (1699), the Turks ceded to the Habsburgs all of Hungary and Transylvania except Temesvar in the southeast.

The Danubian monarchy

The enlarged kingdom of Hungary became part of the Habsburg state in that the Hungarian Estates agreed to make the crown hereditary and renounced the right of insurrection (1686). But the Hungarians retained most of their privileges as well as their suspicion of the Habsburgs; despite the conciliatory tactics of the Austrians, there was a serious revolt under Francis Rakoczi (1703–11). Transylvania, where the tradition of independence was even stronger, was treated with equal moderation; it remained a separate Habsburg province, not subject to Hungary.

In the course of the eighteenth century it became clear that if the Habsburgs had

Below, an army from Brandenburg fighting the Turks in the seventeenth century; the Turks continued to be a real threat to the states of eastern Europe throughout the seventeenth century.

Opposite, Frederick I, Elector of Brandenburg (reigned 1688–1713), who won the title of King of Prussia in 1701 in return for his opposition to France and as a recognition of the reality of Brandenburg's power in eastern Europe.

failed to create a highly centralized state of obedient citizens like the Prussians, they had achieved a durable success. Despite its vicissitudes, the great Austrian-Bohemian-Hungarian bloc was to be one of the great European powers down to 1918.

Poland

The relief of Vienna was the last triumph of old Poland, and an appropriately chivalrous one. For although the largest state in Europe after Russia, late seventeenth-century Poland was manifestly in decline because of her antiquated political and social structure.

The monarchy was elective and therefore weak. Taxes and other important decisions required the approval of a parliament of nobles (the *Seym*) that was paralysed by increasingly strict application of the right of any member to use the 'free veto' which at once dissolved the *Seym*. In practice the local assemblies, also dominated by the nobility, were more powerful. Such a situation invited intrigues on the part of other states, while the Poles themselves, lacking any rational machinery for reaching decisions, frequently formed rival armed confederacies to forward the interests of the various factions. Civil war, or the threat of civil war, loomed at every crisis.

The nobles, who were the only beneficiaries of Polish 'liberties', resisted all reforms. About a tenth of the population was noble, though wealth and power were engrossed by a few great families, of whom the lesser nobility tended to become clients. The economy had been dominated by the nobility since the Turkish conquest of the Black Sea ports in the fifteenth century, which destroyed overland trade with the Baltic. In Poland, too, the position of the serfs was deteriorating, while noble privileges—above all the right of nobles to import and export without paying duties—made it impossible for the towns to flourish.

The impact of war on an anarchical and economically backward kingdom was bound to be disastrous; and Poland was almost constantly at war in the second half of the seventeenth century. In 1654 the struggle against the rebellious Dnieper Cossacks, which had dragged on since 1648, was transformed by the intervention of Russia; and the Russian example encouraged Charles X of Sweden to invade in the next year. In the course of the war the Swedes twice overran Poland, which was eventually saved by the help of Sweden's enemies, Denmark and Austria, and a volte-face by Brandenburg. At the Peace of Oliva (1660) Poland renounced her suzerainty over East Prussia; at Andrusovo, after seven more years' fighting against the Russians, she ceded the areas around Smolensk and Kiev.

The loss of territory was considerable, though mainly of areas that had long been in dispute; but the devastation caused by the war was much more serious. Before Poland could recover, she was at war with the Turks, who in 1672 invaded Podolia in southeast Poland. Despite John Sobieski's great victory at Chotin (1673), Podolia was ceded to the Turks in 1676.

The wave of national feeling provoked by the Turkish invasion led to the election of Sobieski as King of Poland (1673–96). He was a much more forceful ruler than his predecessors, John Casimir (1648–68) and Michael Wisnowiecki (1669–73), and it was he who led the Christian army that defeated the Turks before Vienna (1683). But he proved unable to cure Poland's internal ills; indeed, it can be argued that Sobieski became obsessed by his crusading zeal and sacrificed Polish interests to a war of which Austria was the main beneficiary.

The election of the Duke of Saxony, Augustus the Strong, as King of Poland (1697) inaugurated a long period of anarchy. Augustus's right to the crown was contested by the Prince de Conti and later by Stanislas Leszczynski, backed by Sweden. The civil war that ensued was ended only in 1717, with a treaty of exhaustion that solved nothing.

The Ottoman Empire

Turkish power, too, was declining, though the resources and manpower of the empire —stretching over North Africa, eastern Asia

Above, Augustus II of Poland (reigned 1697–1733), known as Augustus the Strong; he was unpopular in Poland and his aggressive policies towards Sweden provoked the Northern War of 1700–21, during which he lost his throne to Stanislaus I between 1706 and 1709. Barockmuseum Schloss, Maritzburg.

Above left, Charles X of Sweden (reigned 1654–60) fighting to hold on to Warsaw in 1656; he had taken much of Poland the previous year but was driven out by a combination of Polish resistance and hostility from Russia and Denmark. Drottingholm Castle.

Left, Medal struck to commemorate the treaty of 1686 between John III Sobieski of Poland (reigned 1674–96) and Russia. According to the treaty, Poland acknowledged Russia's authority over the eastern Ukraine, and thereafter John concentrated on an aggressive attack on the Turks. State Hermitage Museum, Leningrad.

Opposite, the relief of the Turkish siege of Vienna in 1683 by an army led by the King of Poland. The victory meant a permanent end to the Turkish threat in eastern Europe. Heeresgeschichtliches Museum, Vienna.

and the Balkans—enabled it to sustain catastrophic losses and even to make spasmodic recoveries.

The seventeenth-century crisis was at first sight of the sort that many states had passed through and survived. The sultan ruled as a despot, usually through a grand vizier; and the fate of the empire depended on the abilities of one or the other. Weak sultans were governed by household and harem intrigue, and the empire suffered accordingly: the administration became corrupt and incompetent, there were provincial revolts, palace revolutions and military setbacks—very much the pattern of Ibrahim I's reign (1640–48), and the early years of Mehmed IV (1648–87).

An able grand vizier could soon put this right. When Mehmed Koprulu took office in 1656, he conducted a brutal purge of inefficient and hostile officials, restored Ottoman finances by rooting out corruption, put down two dangerous revolts and re-invigorated the armed forces. The navy defeated the Venetians and recaptured Lemnos and Tenedos (1657), which had been lost under Ibrahim; the army invaded Transylvania, defeated Gyorgy Rakoczi II and re-established Turkish suzerainty.

But the revival left untouched the fundamental weakness of the empire: the Turks had failed to make a satisfactory transition from nomadic warriors to masters of a settled empire. Warriors held land in return

EMERGENCE OF THE GREAT POWERS OF CENTRAL-EASTERN EUROPE

Date	Brandenburg-Prussia	Austria	Russia
1640	Frederick William Elector (1640)		
		Peace of Westphalia ends Thirty Years War (1648)	
			War with Poland (1654–67)
1660	Peace of Oliva (1660)		
		Battle of St Gotthard (1664)	
			Razin's revolt (1670–1)
	Battle of Fehrbellin (1675)		
1680		Relief of Vienna (1683)	
		Reconquest of Hungary (1684–99)	
	War of the League of Augsburg (1688–97)		
	Frederick III Elector (1688)		Peter I the Great (1689–1725)
			Capture of Azov (1696)
			Peter in Europe (1697–8)
1700			Great Northern War (1700–21)
	War of the Spanish Succession (1701–13)		
	Frederick I of Prussia (1701)	Charles VI (1711–40)	Battle of Poltava (1709)
	Frederick William I (1713–40)	Pragmatic Sanction (1713)	Loss of Azov (1711)
		War with Turkey (1716–18)	
1720		Alliance with Spain (1725)	
		Treaty of Vienna (1731)	
		War of the Polish Succession (1733–5)	
		War with the Turks (1736–9)	
1740	Frederick I (the Great) (1740–86)	Maria Theresa (1740–80)	Elizabeth (1741–61)
	First and Second Silesian Wars (1740–5)	War of the Austrian Succession (1740–8)	War with Sweden (1741–3)
		Austro-Russian alliance (1746)	
	Convention of Westminster (1756)	Alliance with France (1756)	
	The Seven Years War (1756–63)	The Seven Years War (1756–63)	
1760			Catherine II the Great (1762–96)
	Alliance with Russia (1764)		War with Turkey (1768–74)
	First partition of Poland (1772)	First partition of Poland (1772)	
			Pugachev revolt (1773–4)
	Austro-Prussian War (1778–9)		
1780		Joseph II (1780–90)	
		Austro-Russian alliance (1781)	
			Crimea annexed (1783)
	League of German Princes (1785)		Charter of Nobles (1785)
	Frederick William II (1786–97)	War with Turks (1788–91)	War with Turks (1787–92)
		Leopold II (1790–2)	
	Prussia and Austria at war with revolutionary France (1792)		
	Second partition of Poland (1793)		Second partition of Poland (1793)
1800	Third partition of Poland (1795)	Third partition of Poland (1795)	

for military service, and both they and the sultan looked to plunder from successful warfare to supply much of their needs. Commerce was despised and left to European companies and non-Muslim subjects (Greeks, Armenians, Jews); even the administration of the empire was largely run by the 'Phanariot' Greeks of Constantinople.

Both the system and the outlook behind it were anachronistic. Expansion had effectively ended, and fighting on ravaged borderlands provided little plunder. Administrative negligence only increased the difficulty of raising taxes from peasants who rarely used money. The hereditary principle began to undermine military organization: landowners evaded service and passed on their holdings to their children, whether or not they were of military age or inclination; and the famous regular army of Janissaries ceased to be recruited from the sons of Balkan Christians and became a hereditary caste.

The Ottoman crisis was doubly serious because the West was making important technological advances. This superiority quickly became apparent in the conduct of warfare: in 1664, at the Battle of St Gotthard, European professional infantry and mobile field artillery smashed the Turkish cavalry. The Turks used unwieldy heavy artillery for siege operations, but the mystique—and social predominance—of the mounted warrior made it unthinkable for them to abandon battle cavalry. Social and cultural conservatism made decline inevitable.

Under Mehmed Koprulu's son, the able Fazil Ahmed (1661–76), Turkey managed to escape the consequences of St Gotthard and win fresh victories over weaker opponents: the Venetians were driven from Crete (1669) and Podolia was taken from Poland (1676). But Fazil Ahmed's successor, the grossly overconfident Kara Mustafa, led the Turks to the disaster before Vienna; and subsequent campaigns proved that, though the Turks might rally, European arms had acquired an unmistakable overall superiority. Two hundred and fifty years after the Turks had captured Constantinople, the Turkish threat to Europe disappeared, never to return.

Chapter 17

The Age of Reason

The Age of Reason or Enlightenment, the *siècle des lumières*, the *Aufklärung*: all terms commonly applied to the period from about 1715 to the outbreak of the French Revolution in 1789 and all expressive of a decisive shift in the way men thought. Until the Enlightenment, institutions and beliefs were largely determined by authority, custom and tradition, supported and sanctified by religious doctrine. Change could be justified only by appealing to the past, as Protestants appealed to Scripture and the practice of the primitive Church and English parliamentarians to the supposed liberties of the fifteenth century. The achievement of the Enlightenment was to substitute reason for tradition and the criterion of utility for authority and, in doing so, to create a secular humanitarianism and a secular conception of progress which have remained characteristic of modern man.

'The English philosophy'

Many of the ideas of thinkers and writers in the Age of Reason were not new, though they had previously been the property of the few. They had appeared in England as early as the 1680s, when John Locke (1632–1704) produced a political philosophy in which the government was a trustee for the people, who had the right to rebel if their trust was abused. His *Essay Concerning Human Understanding* examined the nature of the human mind and argued that ideas were not innate but derived from the experience of the senses. Both of these theories were subversive—of a divinely ordained human authority and of the religious idea of man as born in sin yet capable of distinguishing good from evil; they implied that the state should be rationally ordered for the benefit of its citizens and that man and society could be studied and altered.

The achievements of Sir Isaac Newton (1642–1727) held out the possibility of understanding the world by scientific investigation. They revealed a universe that functioned according to unvarying laws without divine intervention, making God a 'great watchmaker' who had created the universe, set it in motion and then withdrawn. Beliefs from which the apparatus of Christian dogma was absent—Deism, 'natural religion'—appeared in England very early in the eighteenth century.

England thus provided many fundamental elements of the thought of the Enlightenment, which in the eighteenth century was often called 'the English philosophy'. English influence was increased by the admiration felt for her 'free institutions', relatively fluid class structure and her policy of religious toleration, and all the more so since they were accompanied by a growing power and prosperity.

The *philosophes*

Just because of the greater freedom of English society, Enlightenment ideas never crystallized into a doctrine of opposition and attack. In France, an educated class as large as that in England confronted arbitrary rule, entrenched privilege and a powerful Church—all strong enough to oppress but no longer efficient or confident enough to suppress. It was therefore in France that the most articulate and rigorous criticisms of the old order were made; and it is the French writers called *philosophes* who epitomize the Age of Reason.

The *philosophes* were not an organized group and were by no means in complete agreement either theoretically or practically. They were not even 'philosophers' but rather popularizers and propagandists, explaining and applying scientific method—observation, experiment, generalization—to the different departments of human life and attacking prejudice, privilege and intolerance.

If they had no common programme, they did have many attitudes in common. The attack on religion occupied much of their energy—not unreasonably, since religion was the authority that justified all other authorities. They were in fundamental agreement in desiring a secular society in which men obeyed the law rather than an arbitrary power, in which there was freedom of speech, writing enquiry and dissent and in which cruelty was no longer part of judicial processes or punishments. Without necessarily being democrats or egalitarians, they disliked aristocratic privileges and the disabilities under which the peasants laboured. They shared an enthusiasm for practical improvements, whether industrial or political, akin to their devotion to the empirical methods of science and their contempt for metaphysics. Finally, almost all the *philosophes* assumed that, in principle, all men were capable of understanding the truth and wrote accordingly. It can be argued that their passion for lucidity, simplicity and order limited their profundity; whether or not that is so, it gave their writings an impact which can still be felt.

French society in the eighteenth century was an ideal one for the diffusion of subversive ideas. Paris was the intellectual

capital of Europe, and the Parisian salons, presided over by wealthy, fashionable and intelligent women such as Mme Geoffrin and Mme du Deffand, were arenas in which the ideas of the Enlightenment were tested and refined. They provided a receptive audience for manuscript works which the author dared not publish (frequently the case until the middle of the century) and a school for purity and clarity of language, the outstanding characteristics of eighteenth-century French prose.

The prestige of French literature facilitated the diffusion of the Enlightenment abroad. Under Louis XIV, France had become the cultural arbiter of Europe and French the language of polite society. Every German princeling built a miniature Versailles where only French was spoken and only French books were read. In the eighteenth century, France ceased to dominate Europe politically while retaining her cultural supremacy; but the salons replaced Versailles as the avant-garde of that culture. Both Frederick II of Prussia and Catherine II of Russia spoke French for preference, read the works of the *philosophes*, and claimed to be their disciples. Even as late as the 1770s, the great English historian, Gibbon, could assert that he thought and wrote best in French. Such was the European preoccupation with what the French did, said and wrote that the

German-born *philosophe*, Grimm, compiled a regular Parisian newsletter which circulated the courts of Europe.

Voltaire

In the 1720s the Enlightenment was still very much an underground movement, its attitudes expressed in published works only in indirect or ironical terms. Even at its height, criticisms of Church or state were guardedly phrased unless the work were published anonymously and/or abroad.

A full-scale attack on the Church appeared as early as 1697: Pierre Bayle's *Historical and Critical Dictionary*, published in Holland, provided ammunition against Scriptural history and theological dogmas that was still being used several generations later. Other published works were more cautious, notably Montesquieu's *Persian Letters* (1721), in which two Persian residents in Paris compare French customs with their own. The comparison implied not only that French society was riddled with absurdities and injustices but that its institutions had no universal validity.

At this date, however, the career of the greatest figure of the Age of Reason had already begun. François-Marie Arouet, known as Voltaire (1694–1788), was the universal genius of the age, by turns poet,

playwright, historian, scientific popularizer, anti-clerical polemicist and writer of picaresque or exotic 'philosophical' tales. His enduring fame rests upon his prose writings, which are unsurpassed models of clarity, economy and elegance, shot through with malicious wit and irony.

Voltaire knew the injustices of the existing order at first hand: he was beaten up by an aristocrat's bullies, some of his books were burnt by the public hangman, and much of his life was spent in flight and exile. During one such exile, passed in England, he wrote his *Lettres Philosophiques*, the most important piece of French propaganda for English thought and institutions.

Voltaire's best-known and funniest book is *Candide* (1759), one of the picaresque tales, in which the ingenuous Candide wanders the world, learning the hard way the inaccuracy of his tutor Pangloss's belief that this is 'the best of all possible worlds'. At last he determines to cultivate his garden —that is, to improve the world by practical activity. *Candide* was in part suggested by the terrible Lisbon earthquake of 1755, an event of some importance in generally undermining the doctrine of a beneficent providence.

Voltaire evidently came to the same conclusion as Candide, for his last years were spent in vigorous and often effective campaigns to right injustices. His most famous success was the rehabilitation of Jean Calas, a Protestant victim of the religious prejudice of the French law courts.

The great *Encyclopaedia*

By the middle of the eighteenth century, Enlightenment attitudes were becoming established and widespread. Many of the *philosophes*—Helvétius, Holbach, Morelly, Lamettrie, Condorcet—took up increasingly radical positions, formulating atheist, materialist, determinist and even communist systems. Lamettrie, for example, called one of his books *Man the Machine* (1747).

A utopian element was also becoming more pronounced: if man had not fallen, if he was formed by his sense-experiences, he could be improved by changing his environment; if he was capable of reasoning, he was capable of virtue and happiness. All mysteries would be revealed in time by science, all injustice abolished by reason and good will: earth could be made a secular paradise.

The epitome of the age was the great *Encyclopaedia*, which appeared in twenty-eight volumes from 1751 to 1772, despite sporadic attempts to suppress it. Its editor was Denis Diderot (1713–84), one of the most important *philosophes*, initially with the collaboration of the mathematician d'Alembert.

The *Encyclopaedia* was at once a monumental work of reference and a polemic against absolutism, Christianity and privilege. Almost all the great figures of the Enlightenment contributed, providing what amounted to a thinly disguised summary of 'philosophical' ideas. It was also a compendium of scientific and technical information, describing and illustrating in careful detail the craft and industrial processes that had previously been jealously guarded secrets—a fine example of the *philosophes'* enthusiasm for empirical science and the improvement of life by practical means.

Nations other than France contributed to the Enlightenment, though readers outside England and France tended to be more influenced by the French *philosophes* than by writers in their own countries. Such were the Italian Cesare Beccaria, whose *Of Crimes and Punishments* (1764) advocated a more rational and humane penal system, and the German dramatist and critic Gotthold Lessing (1729–81) who, like Diderot, attempted to create a realistic middle-class drama. The Scottish Enlightenment was of particular distinction and in David Hume (1711–76) produced an outstanding philosopher. Another Italian, Giambattista Vico (1688–1744), outlined an evolutionary historical philosophy that cut across such Voltairean simplifications as 'reason versus fanaticism', providing insights that were only developed later: a significant comment on contemporary preoccupations.

The most substantial achievements of the age were of another kind, resulting from the

Above, Voltaire (1694–1788) dictating while dressing; he was the epitome of the Enlightenment in his resolute and witty opposition to superstition and privilege; his book Candide *(1759) demonstrates that he was even able to satirize the rational and optimistic beliefs that he himself championed. Musée Carnavalet, Paris.*

Left, an engraving from Diderot's Encyclopaedia *(1751–72), showing a cutler's workshop and tools; eleven of the twenty-eight volumes of the* Encyclopaedia *were made up exclusively of such engravings of industry, which were based on drawings done by Diderot himself.*

Opposite, a gathering at the salon of Madame Geoffrin in Paris in 1755, including many of the most famous names of the French Enlightenment, such as d'Alembert, Rousseau, Diderot and Condillac. Château de Malmaison.

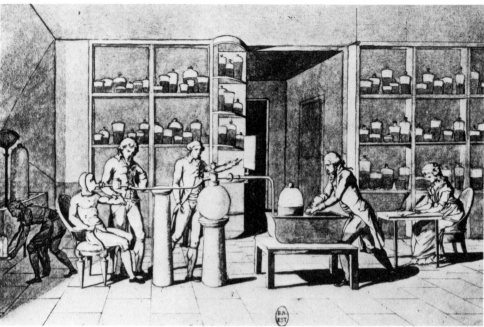

use of scientific empiricism to create mechanical 'Newtonian' models which operated according to immutable laws. This was particularly true of the study of man and society. Charles de Secondat, Baron de Montesquieu (1699–1755), already famous as the author of *Persian Letters,* was the effective founder of sociology and the study of comparative institutions. Despite its aberrations, his *Spirit of the Laws* (1748) represents the first attempt to analyse the interaction of religion, institutions, geography, climate and history in the formation of societies.

Similar developments were taking place in the study of history. In *The Age of Louis XIV* (1751) Voltaire abandoned the traditional narrative treatment of politics and war and presented a picture of French society as a whole, relating the manners, customs and beliefs of the period to the political, economic and administrative structure. The masterpiece of eighteenth-century historical writing was undoubtedly Gibbon's *Decline and Fall of the Roman Empire* (1766–88), a work of massive synthesis, written with urbane irony in rolling, balanced periods.

Experiments in improving agricultural and industrial production were one of the enthusiasms of the eighteenth century; and the larger questions of 'political economy' also became an object of systematic study. Theoretical advances were made by the 'Physiocrats' in France and, much more decisively, by the Scot Adam Smith. In *The Wealth of Nations* (1776) Smith analysed such fundamental processes as division of labour and provided the theoretical groundwork for the nineteenth-century belief in unfettered individual enterprise.

The natural sciences

Considerable progress was also made in the natural sciences, though the Enlightenment

was an age of solid advance rather than dramatic breakthrough. One example is the steady improvement of scientific instruments, which were essential to more exact and detailed research. Here it must suffice to mention the production of an accurate thermometer, to which the Swede Celsius, the Frenchman Réamur and the Danziger Fahrenheit all contributed.

Analysis and classification were characteristic activities of the Enlightenment scientist. In chemistry, the Englishman Henry Cavendish (1731–1810) isolated and described hydrogen, the Scotsman Joseph Black (1722–99) discovered carbon dioxide and another Scot, Daniel Rutherford (1749–1819), discovered nitrogen. Towards the end of the period, Antoine Lavoisier (1743–94), a French aristocrat, laid the basis for the modern system of classification into elements and compounds.

Biology too had its great classifier: the Swede Carl Linnaeus, whose *System of Nature* (1735) included some 12,000 living things, which were for the first time provided with precise names. The most influential and popular work of the period, however, was Georges-Louis Buffon's *Natural History* (1749–88), as much a work of literature as of science. Buffon, unlike most scientists of the day, had difficulties with the authorities, who censured his observations on fossils, which he rightly believed to be older than the date established for the creation of the earth by Biblical studies.

Other scientists' works can only be noted here: in electricity, for example, Pieter van Musschenbroek's Leyden jar (1746), Priestly's *History* (1767), Benjamin Franklin's experiments; in mathematics, Bernouilli, Euler, Lagrange. At the end of the period, the German-born English astronomer Sir William Herschel, also one of the great classifiers, made perhaps the most spectacular discovery of the age when he observed an unknown planet, Uranus (1781).

The impact of the Enlightenment

The Enlightenment created a climate of opinion in which 'the books that inspire benevolence are practically the only ones read' (Diderot). Pacifist sentiments began to be expressed among the educated classes; humanitarian feelings were manifested in disapproval of slavery, efforts to secure prison reform and the growth of Freemasonry as a secular religion of humanity.

Yet the immediate social and political results were negligible. The *philosophes* themselves looked to those already in power to introduce institutional changes. They admired and corresponded with the 'enlightened despots' of central and eastern Europe, and in France they cultivated the ministers and even the mistresses of the king. Such tactics could at best achieve only limited results; but all other avenues of advance were closed. The great monarchies contained no party, group or class to whom the *philosophes* could appeal in programmatic terms, which is probably the main reason why they never formulated a common policy and why not one of them produced a coherent political philosophy.

In the course of the century, however, Enlightenment attitudes did begin to appear outside the elite of court and salon. That is not to say that the works of the *philosophes* were read by the masses; but the diffusion of ideas, in a simplified and sometimes garbled form, can take place without popular acquaintance with primary sources. This was particularly true of France, but it could also be observed in most of western Europe before the French Revolution; and even as far away as Russia an intellectual minority disapproved of despotism and serfdom.

The *philosophes* did not think, and had no grounds for thinking, in revolutionary terms. Their ideas were to be one of the

elements that led to the French Revolution, but the Revolution was produced by a unique and perhaps improbable concatenation of circumstances and beliefs—the idealism generated by the American War of Independence, the quarrel between crown and nobility, the bankruptcy of the crown—which could not be foreseen in the mid-eighteenth century. Then, neither the resources nor the social structure of Europe were such as to promise rapid change.

Eighteenth-century society

Eighteenth-century society was still overwhelmingly agricultural, despite the growth of cities and the development of an urban middle class in western Europe. On the eve of the Revolution in France, the land of the Enlightenment *par excellence,* some twenty-two million out of a population of about twenty-six million were peasants. In central and eastern Europe the peasantry accounted for an even higher proportion of the population, towns were very small, and the only middle class of any importance was bureaucratic rather than mercantile. Only in Holland (properly called 'The United Provinces') had specific historical and geographical circumstances produced a mercantile society.

In the agrarian societies the dominant group was still the nobility. Nobles enjoyed great privileges, including tax exemptions and rights to payments and services from the peasantry; again, these tended to be very much greater in central and eastern Europe. They had a monopoly of the great offices of Church and state, even where (as in France) they wielded little collective political power.

There were wide differences in wealth and even status between nobles, since in most of Europe nobility was a matter of status—inherited by every child of a noble—rather than possessions; with the result that many were no more than small farmers, and a few were paupers. But when all the differences are allowed for, the aristocratic character of eighteenth-century Europe is undeniable.

The mercantile middle class was becoming increasingly prosperous and powerful in western Europe, particularly in England and France; and it is doubtless significant that it was in these countries, with a relatively large number of educated men and a rapid growth of literacy, that the Enlightenment was brought to birth and widely diffused.

The basis of middle-class wealth was trade, not industry, though the unprecedented expansion of trade in the eighteenth century provided the source of raw materials, the markets and much of the capital that made the Industrial Revolution possible. Trade between Europe and the rest of the world expanded continuously, and as Dutch maritime strength slowly declined a world-wide struggle began between France and England. Europe, North America, the West Indies and India were the main theatres of a conflict that continued in one form or another until 1815. Eighteenth-century governments if anything overestimated the importance of commerce and supported their merchants and colonists by subsidy and by force of arms. The wars of the period were not commercial wars, but commercial considerations powerfully influenced the way they were conducted. Hence the attention paid to the West Indies, the source of tobacco, sugar, coffee and dyestuffs. The Atlantic trade, of which the West Indies was the heart, brought prosperity to Liverpool, Bordeaux, Nantes and the other great ports of western Europe. Trade between European states, and with India, southeast Asia, the Mediterranean and the Levant, also expanded.

The commercial spirit touched life at many points. Commodities from overseas—tea, coffee, tobacco, muslins—changed European habits. Manufacturing areas in every mercantile nation became dependent on the prosperity of international trade. Merchants formed pressure groups that no government could ignore, and the wealthiest had little difficulty in marrying their children into the nobility.

Important as these developments were, they did not constitute a social or economic revolution. The harvest, not the trade figures, decided the happiness of nations. The most rigorous economic blockade could not reduce a nation at war: a bad harvest caused it to starve in peacetime. The agencies of transformation—rapid industrial growth and technological advance—were found only in England, and only very late in the century.

One fact that did make for change was population growth, which was substantial and steady in France, Spain and Italy and rapid (from about mid-century) in England, Ireland, the Low Countries, Scandinavia, Russia and parts of Germany. France remained the most populous country in Europe, with twenty-odd million inhabitants, until late in the century; then she was overtaken by Russia, whose population reached thirty-six million by the end of Catherine II's reign (1796). In England and Wales the increase in population (just over five million in 1700, nine-and-a-half million in 1800) was of great importance in providing the labour force and the market needed for an industrial revolution.

The agricultural revolution and the first phase of the industrial revolution in Britain are outside the scope of this book. They laid the foundations for a new kind of society, in which agriculture yielded pride of place to industry, the country to the town, the craft workshop to the factory. Even in Britain the transformation was effected only in the nineteenth century. The societies discussed in this book remained hierarchical and rural until the nineteenth and, in some cases, the twentieth century.

New modes of feeling

The consciousness of European man was changing more quickly than material reality. By the 1760s a new sensibility, in some respects hostile to the values of the Enlightenment, was beginning to manifest itself.

As inheritors of that sensibility we find the men of the Enlightenment 'rational' to the point of aridity: rather superficial and complacent in their belief in reason as the answer to all problems and lacking in warmth if not in light. This is partly an illusion created by the formal manners and polished conversation of the period: Voltaire, for example, fought intolerance and injustice with unmistakable passion. But it is also true that the *philosophes* were concerned with man as a social rather than an individual and unique being and that their writings display almost exclusively what may be called public feelings.

In the second half of the eighteenth century, the revulsion against reason, restraint and formality—already apparent somewhat earlier—became marked. The cult of sentiment, of spontaneous and passionate individual feeling, was the direct precursor of the Romantic movement, which is usually dated to the very late eighteenth and early nineteenth centuries. Indeed, most of the characteristics of Romanticism—love of nature, childhood, the remote and mysterious past, the exotic, the wild and irregular—appeared in some form quite early in the eighteenth century.

The new sensibility was expressed in many different ways. The English landscape garden replaced the formal French garden. A quasi-oriental style (*chinoiserie*) became the rage in furniture and interior decoration; Sir William Chambers built a pagoda at Kew. Ruins became collectors' items, and in 1747 the dilettante and letter-writer Horace Walpole—in many respects a typical figure of the Age of Reason—began to build himself a 'Gothick' house, Strawberry Hill. In painting, the graceful Rococo style of Wattau, Boucher and Fragonard gave way to Neo-classicism, in part a response to the growing cult of sentimental republican virtue—another of the obsessions of the age, given impetus by excavations at Pompeii and Herculaneum, which provided a wealth of information about everyday life in antiquity. In the 1760s, Greuze's oversweet paintings of maidenly distress and domesticity were acclaimed in France, where the attractions of the simple life prompted Marie Antoinette to play the sheperdhess in her dairy at Rambouillet.

Literature provided the fullest expression of the new attitudes in all their complexity. Here only a few landmarks can be indicated. In France, Galland published a translation of *The Thousand and One Nights* (1704–17) which gave a fillip to the taste for the exotic. In England, Edward Young's *Night Thoughts* (1742–45) were filled with a satisfactorily gloomy introspection, Thomson's *The Seasons* (1726–30) with an exalted love of nature, and Walpole's *Castle of Otranto* (1764) with supernatural horror in a mysterious 'medieval' setting. Thomas Percy, the Bishop of Dromore, collected and published old English ballads in his *Reliques* (1765), and the European vogue for the supposed poems of the Gaelic bard Ossian (in fact the work of their 'discoverer', James Macpherson) was such that they survived Dr Johnson's denunciations and were still being declaimed by Napoleon at the beginning of the nineteenth century.

Many of the extravagances of this 'pre-Romantic' period were somewhat tongue-in-cheek or were at least not felt profoundly enough to impinge on social mores. Horace Walpole lived in a quaint house and wrote a thriller; but his behaviour remained that of a cultivated English gentleman. That is not to say that fads and fashions are arbitrary: in this period they indicate (among other

things) a certain restlessness and dissatisfaction with the ordinary course of social life. But the dissatisfaction remained on the fringe of consciousness, not at its centre: it appeared in night thoughts rather than daylight actions.

The 1770s witnessed the brief emergence of the German 'Storm and Stress' writers, who displayed in their own lives an agonising inability to adjust to everyday realities that was to be one of the characteristics of full-blown Romanticism. Paradoxically, it was the most balanced—and by far the greatest—of the school, Johann Wolfgang Goethe (1749–1832), whose work had the most 'Romantic' impact: the suicide of the hero in *Young Werther* (1774) was imitated by many young men who fancied that they were profoundly introspective as well as unsuccessful in love.

Much more characteristic of the period, and probably much more deeply felt, was 'the cult of the heart'—of spontaneity, sincerity, love, sentimental virtue. Its special feature was that sincerity rather than actions increasingly became the criterion of virtue; hypocrisy became the worst of vices. In England, the heartless rake of Restoration comedy gave way to the likeable scamps of Fielding, Sheridan and Goldsmith. The new heroes got into scrapes hardly better than those of the rakes but were always saved by their transparent good nature.

A more religious morality was upheld by Samuel Richardson, whose multi-volume epistolary novels set all Europe weeping. *Pamela* (1740–41) and *Clarissa Harlowe* (1747–48), with their portraits of maidenly virtue under assault and protracted death-bed scenes, let loose a flood of sentimental novels, of which the most important was *The New Heloise* by Jean-Jacques Rousseau.

Society and the noble savage

Rousseau (1712–78) wrote few works, but every one made a profound impression on his own and following generations. He was the son of a clockmaker in Geneva, a city with powerful traditions of puritanism and independence, and both his social origin and place of birth influenced the attitudes of his maturity. So must his youthful experiences as a timid hanger-on, always on the fringes of good society.

Unlike the *philosophes*, Rousseau regarded the very existence of society as objectionable; it was not badly constituted, but bad in any form. In his first published work, the *Discourse on the Arts and Sciences* (1750), he argues that progress and society have corrupted man, that in his natural state man is virtuous and happy. Though he never used the phrase 'the noble savage', Rousseau is rightly associated with the idea behind the words, for it was largely the extraordinary eloquence of his prose that made the idea of unspoiled primitive man (already of literary commonplace) into a potent myth.

THE
SEASONS
BY
JAMES THOMSON
EMBELLISHED WITH ENGRAVINGS
FROM THE DESIGNS OF
RICH? WESTALL R.A.

R.Westall R.A.del.   Cha? Heath fc

—The Shepherds lyre the Virgins lay.
Hymn.

LONDON.
PRINTED FOR JOHN SHARPE, PICCADILLY,
1819.

Above, the title page of The Seasons, *by James Thomson (1700–48), a typical expression of the interest in the moods and lyricism of nature common in the romantic era.*

Above left, an engraving of Strawberry Hill, in Twickenham, Middlesex, which was built in 1747 by the English author Horace Walpole (1717–97) in a medieval style. Interest in exotic, curious and charming architecture and landscape replaced the formal and classical styles of the late seventeenth century.

Left, a painting of a scene from Pamela *(1740–41), the story of a maidservant and the son of her employer, written by Samuel Richardson (1689–1761); virtue and sexual morality was an important theme of eighteenth-century literature. Tate Gallery, London.*

The New Heloise (1761) was probably the most popular novel of the century, running to scores of editions. Like *Clarissa Harlowe*, it is written as a series of letters and now seems intolerably long and diffuse; but eighteenth-century readers were enchanted by extended descriptions of the struggle between passion and duty and by Rousseau's enthusiasm for nature, simplicity and children.

In *Emile* (1762), a tract on education thinly disguised as a novel, Rousseau takes the same line: the child Emile must be shielded from contact with society. Rousseau recognized that children were not miniature adults and that their capacities and needs differed at each stage of development. He insisted that the child must learn only what and when he needs to learn and that direct sensory experience was at least as important as learning from books. These doctrines were taken up enthusiastically, since the eighteenth century was one of growing emphasis on family life and the role of parents—not tutors or servants—in bringing up children.

The message of *The Social Contract* (1762), one of the most influential books ever written, is that the only legitimate foundation for political authority is 'the general will', not inheritance or force. The by and large passive and heavily qualified conception of popular authority proposed by Locke was now expressed in active terms. Rousseau understood that majority decisions might not be in the general interest (which is in fact one of the problems of democratic theory), and some of his speculations can be regarded as justifying dictatorship by a minority representing the 'true' will of the people. But despite its confusions and ambiguities, the central idea of *The Social Contract* is unmistakably that of government not only in the interests of the people—which an enlightened despot claimed to provide—but government directly answerable to their will.

Rousseau's posthumously published *Confessions* began the whole modern tradition of confessional literature. Here he attempted to tell the whole truth about himself, including his social failures, low actions and sexual peculiarities; unintentionally he also chronicled his growing persecution mania, which led him to believe that his friends and acquaintances were part of a vast conspiracy against him. The *Confessions* exhibit in its least attractive light Rousseau's assumption that sincerity excuses everything; but they also comprise a wonderful self-portrait, opening up a wide avenue by which man's knowledge of himself could be increased.

Reason, sentiment, revolution

The relationship between the rationalism of the Enlightenment and the new modes of feeling is complex and obscure. In some respects they were complementary: the attack on accepted beliefs and institutions, above all the attack on institutional religion, was certainly instrumental in the development of a new sense of individual uniqueness and new emotions towards man, society and nature. Even those who were consciously hostile to the *philosophes* absorbed much of their teaching: when Rousseau rejected the legitimacy of authority based on inheritance or prescriptive right, he was adopting the central position of the Enlightenment.

It would nevertheless be wrong to ignore the element of deliberate reaction against the Enlightenment in these emotions, especially since it became more prominent in the nineteenth century. In the immediate future, however, all the main currents of eighteenth-century thought and feeling were to mingle in the French Revolution, that amazing phenomenon which was at once rational, romantic, individualistic, utopian and severely practical.

Toi qui veux usurper le Sceptre du Parnasse,
Qui contre mes écrits parlas avec audace,
Sur toi de mes malheurs, ces poings me vengeront...
M'attaquer sur tes pieds! eh! bon Dieu! que diront
Les quadrupèdes tes confrères,

Te voyant des humains prendre ainsi les manières?
Mais, l'épée au coté, se battre en porte-faix!....
Pourquoi non? les brocards te causent des allarmes?
Un Sage, si tu l'es, ne s'écarte jamais
Des loix de la nature, et nos poings sont ses Armes

Chapter 18

The Enlightened Despots

During the eighteenth century, very considerable changes were introduced from above in the monarchies of central, southern and eastern Europe. The rational-humanitarian aspect of the changes and the fact that they were conceived and executed by monarchs or their chosen ministers (and not in response to public opinion) has made it natural to call this phenomenon 'enlightened despotism'. The image thus created, of the philosopher enthroned, was precisely that achieved by the sedulous self-advertisement of Frederick II of Prussia and Catherine II of Russia, the most glamorous rulers of the age.

In fact, 'enlightened despotism' was essentially the eighteenth-century phrase of a more extended process: the development of the modern state, served by a large bureaucracy, able to make heavy demands on the energies and resources of all citizens and intolerant of rival authorities. In this sense, eighteenth-century monarchs were imitators of French absolutism, concerned with the rationalization of functions, centralization and the destruction of class, regional and clerical privileges. Extensions of government activity and the increasing cost of waging war necessitated a larger revenue; and that in turn necessitated more civil servants, revision of the tax structure and measures to encourage agriculture, industry and trade.

But 'enlightened' is not an inappropriate description of this eighteenth-century phase of the process. Being well-informed and well-educated, monarchs and ministers could not avoid being influenced by the Enlightenment, and many characteristic measures of the period—freedom of speech and writing (albeit limited), abolition of judicial torture, codification of laws, various degrees of religious toleration—can scarcely be dismissed as acts purely in the interest of the state. Many extensions of state activity were in any case welcomed by the *philosophes*. They too hoped to see the wealth of nations increase and disliked privilege and clerical power, though their motives were different from those of the monarchs they admired.

Within the general pattern of 'enlightened despotism' there were numerous deviations and permutations. Frederick William I of Prussia greatly strengthened the state without being influenced by the Enlightenment. Catherine II proclaimed her 'enlightened' convictions but failed to translate them into action. Frederick II acquired religious scepticism from Voltaire, called himself the first servant of the state—and upheld aristocratic privilege in every sphere. It was, paradoxically, Austria—usually thought of as a highly conservative state—that produced the very type of the enlightened despot in Joseph II.

Enlightened despotism was confined to 'backward' Europe; the great mercantile states (Britain, France, Holland) were unaffected. The absence of a powerful middle class in central, southern and eastern Europe made the monarchy the initiator of change; but it also deprived monarchs of the effective support with which they might have curtailed noble privileges. As a result, the monarchy was in the last analysis dependent on noble support; and the price of that support was the perpetuation of privilege.

Despite the developments which have been described, the pre-industrial state had only limited instruments of control: there was no possibility of a state apparatus holding down a country without at least the acquiescence of the wealthy and socially powerful classes. 'Despots' and 'absolute' rulers could introduce only limited changes, though their limitations would seem less marked had the age of enlightened despots not been succeeded by the age of political and industrial revolutions.

The idea of 'the state'

The personal qualities of a ruler were still decisive: the most highly developed bureaucracies remained geared to personal control

Above, Frederick II of Prussia (reigned 1740–86) reviewing his troops; for him and his contemporaries war was the extension of the abstract art of diplomacy, and he believed that the army should be a professional body, independent of the rest of the population.

Opposite, an imaginary encounter between Voltaire and Rousseau, the two greatest exponents of Enlightenment thought; whereas Voltaire believed in reason and civilization, Rousseau advocated passion and freedom from artificial constraints on man's nobility.

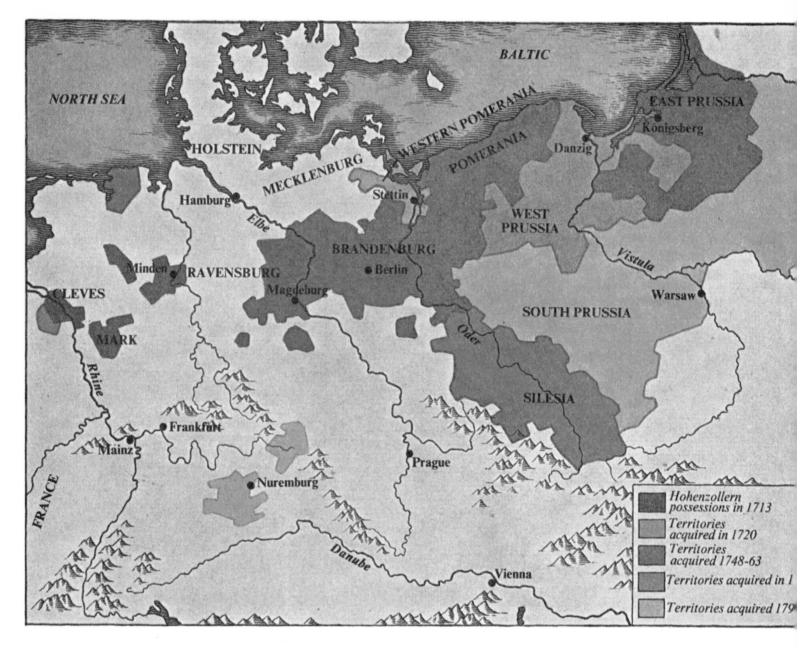

NORTH SEA

BALTIC

HOLSTEIN

EAST PRUSSIA
Königsberg

MECKLENBURG

WESTERN POMERANIA

POMERANIA

Danzig

Hamburg

Elbe

Stettin

WEST
PRUSSIA

Minden

RAVENSBURG

BRANDENBURG

Berlin

Magdeburg

Vistula

Warsaw

CLEVES

SOUTH PRUSSIA

MARK

Oder

Rhine

SILESIA

Frankfurt

Mainz

FRANCE

Nuremburg

Prague

Danube

Vienna

Hohenzollern possessions in 1713
Territories acquired in 1720
Territories acquired 1748-63
Territories acquired in 1
Territories acquired 179

by monarch or minister. If a ruler was feeble or entrusted the government to incompetents, the state stagnated or declined.

Nevertheless, in the eighteenth century, perhaps because administration was bureaucratized, the conception of monarchical government tended to become more impersonal. Kings increasingly thought in terms of state interests rather than family interests and identified themselves with the state rather than vice versa. On the other hand, when Frederick II (The Great) or Joseph II spoke of themselves as servants of the state, they meant the state and not the people; they remained very much masters of men. The idea of 'the state'—an abstraction for which any sacrifice could be demanded —came into existence even before technology and communications made its power all-embracing.

If the king were becoming the state's servant, he showed no sign of becoming redundant. The eighteenth-century conviction that a strong monarchy was the best form of government seemed to be supported by experience: republics like Holland and

Venice were declining, and the elective monarchies of the Empire and Poland were clearly incapable of governing effectively; only the constitutional monarchy of Britain provided a partial exception.

For most of the period, representative institutions were regarded as medieval anachronisms—obstacles to the unity and effectiveness of the state. The only enlightened despot to display any interest in representative institutions was Leopold of Tuscany (Leopold II of Austria) in the late pre-Revolutionary period, when the cult of Roman republicanism, the teachings of Rousseau and the practical success of the American Revolution had all combined to begin a revival of interest in representative government.

The French Revolution ended any possibility—and at best it had been only a possibility that enlightened despots might collaborate with this new force. Instead, monarchs were frightened into alliance with the nobility and the Church, and enlightened despotism passed into reaction pure and simple.

The 'drill-sergeant' king

Frederick William I of Prussia was far from the conventional idea of an enlightened despot. He was pious, uncultivated and subject to terrible rages in which he thrashed anyone within reach. Yet he gave the Prussian state a unique character, leaving his successor the means with which to make Prussia a power in Europe.

The army was the king's ruling passion. He hired or kidnapped men over six feet tall from all over Europe for his famous 'regiment of giants' at Potsdam. More significant was the increased size of the army, which by Frederick William's death comprised some 83,000 men, making it the fourth largest in Europe. It was supported by what was in fact one of the lesser European states in both population (about two-and-a-half million in 1740) and economic resources.

Like most European armies, it consisted of pressed men or mercenaries, many of them foreigners. Savage discipline and endless drills and reviews transformed it into

170

an efficient fighting force but did not prevent large-scale desertion. It was to remedy this that in 1733 Frederick William assigned to each regiment a Prussian district ('canton'), which was obliged to make up the regiment's numbers. Foreigners continued to be recruited in large numbers—even under Frederick the Great about a third of the total strength of the army was foreign-born —but the basis of a national fighting force had been created.

By providing peasant soldiers, the cantonal system speeded the transformation of the Junker class into a military service nobility. The king himself set an example by always wearing uniform. He created a cadet corps in Berlin for the sons of Junkers; membership became a much sought-after privilege that reinforced the attractions of a military career. The officer corps became the virtual monopoly of the nobility, and by 1740 the fractious Junkers, only half-tamed by the Great Elector, were devoted servants of the crown.

The other features of Frederick William's reign were bureaucratic control over the state and royal control over the bureaucracy. In 1723 the collection of taxes and crown revenues was concentrated in a new institution, the General Directory, which also supervised all the activities of provincial authorities through local committees. In the towns, elected local officials were replaced by salaried state officials. Bureaucratic control, originating in the need to raise large sums to support the army, became all-pervasive.

Royal control was maintained by a system unique to Prussia. Most rulers took decisions in council; Frederick William took them in his 'cabinet', alone with his secretaries, on the basis of reports submitted severally by his ministers. To avoid the concentration of power in the hands of any single official, the specialized 'colleges' into which the administration was divided never had a single head.

The main concern of king and bureaucrats alike was to increase revnue, most of which (about three-quarters) was used for the upkeep of the army. Frederick William made strenuous efforts to collect every sum that could possibly be interpreted as his due. He reformed the leasing arrangements for properties on the royal estates, on which about a third of the Prussian peasantry lived, and practised rigid economy. The measure of his success is that the income of the crown more than doubled during his reign.

Trade and industry continued to be strictly regulated, and immigration was encouraged by every possible means. Refugees arrived from France and Salzburg (from which Protestants were expelled in 1732), and many foreign recruits who joined the Prussian army settled in the Hohenzollern lands when they retired.

Despite Frederick William's idiosyncracies, the state that he created displayed

many essential characteristics of an enlightened despotism. The functions and powers of the bureaucracy grew; intermediate authorities—elected urban officials, guilds—were destroyed or emasculated; tradition was overridden in the interests of efficiency. But the Hohenzollern state also possessed unique features which derived from the maintenance of a disproportionately large army. Troops were billeted on the civilian population, and much local trade was concerned with supplying their needs; prices were fixed and enforced by garrison commanders; soldiers received a rudimentary education and staffed the lower grades of the civil service. Close government supervision accustomed the

Above, Frederick William I of Prussia (reigned 1713–40), who spent much of his reign building up the Prussian army and reorganizing the finances of the state in order to be able to support it. Yet he fought only one limited war during his reign. Schloss Charlottenburg, Berlin.

Opposite, the growth of Prussian and Hohenzollern power in eastern Europe in the eighteenth century.

citizen to obey soldiers or authorities that were military in origin or style; respect for the landlord blended with respect for the officer. Other states, it has been said, possessed armies; only the Prussian army possessed a state.

Frederick William accumulated troops and treasure, but he made little use of them. The solitary Prussian acquisition during his reign was part of western Pomerania, with the port of Stettin (1720), a reward for helping to end the Great Northern War. Because of Frederick William's diplomatic ineptitude, Prussian influence in Europe was negligible—in the event, no great misfortune, since the wars and diplomacy of the period were singularly wasteful and inconclusive.

The philosopher prince

It was Frederick William's successor who revealed Prussian might to an astounded Europe.

Frederick II (1740–86) had a troubled adolescence and young manhood. His addiction to the flute, books and elegant conversation enraged Frederick William, and relations between father and son reached breaking-point in 1730, when the eighteen-year-old Frederick decided to flee abroad.

His plan was discovered, he was imprisoned and forced to witness the execution of his confidant, Katte; and for a time his own life seemed in danger, In fact, he was kept under supervision while he performed routine administrative and military duties—an invaluable apprenticeship despite its punitive aspect. The incident was a valuable lesson in patience and self-control; henceforward Frederick obeyed his father without question.

Neither now nor later did he abandon his cultural pursuits. He was a skilful flautist, a competent composer, read voraciously, and poured out odes, tragedies, prose arguments and, in later life, histories and memoirs. All his literary works were written in French; he thoroughly despised German, which he wrote abominably. When his father allowed him more freedom, Frederick gathered about him a company of wits and scholars, while his correspondence with Voltaire provided Frederick with good literary advice and both correspondents with opportunities for relentless mutual flattery.

Those who expected Frederick to be a peaceable philosopher-king had mistaken his character. He absorbed the rationalism of the Enlightenment rather than its humanitarian idealism. As early as 1731 he was discussing the expansion of Prussia without reference to legality or diplomatic fictions. He regarded himself as the first servant of the state; but Frederick's state was an abstraction with strategic necessities and appetites: it was by no means synonymous with 'the people', whose welfare could in fact be sacrificed to its interests. If it did not

originate with Frederick, this impersonal conception of the state was first consciously formulated by him.

Frederick's first acts as king displayed his allegiance to the Enlightenment: judicial torture was abolished, censorship of the press ended and religious toleration proclaimed. The difference between Frederick's conception of kingship and his predecessors' was clearly shown in the deforestation of royal hunting-grounds for agriculture: the state came before royal pleasures.

Meanwhile, Voltaire hurried the king's *Anti-Machiavel* through the press, believing that Frederick might now prefer to suppress his criticisms of the great analyst of political ruthlessness. Events proved Voltaire right: Frederick's first major act of policy was to attack Austria without provocation.

The Austrian emperor, Charles VI, had been succeeded by his daughter, Maria Theresa. The disputed succession of a woman gave Frederick his opportunity: at the end of 1740, with 40,000 Prussian troops, he marched into Silesia, confident that although the powers (including Prussia) had formally accepted Maria Theresa's accession their greed would soon lead them to follow his example.

Frederick's calculations proved correct: his action began the War of Austrian Succession (1740–8). Prussia's part in it was limited to two relatively brief struggles against Austria (1740–2 and 1744–5), generally known as the First and Second Silesian Wars. Prussian victories astonished Europe and made it clear that she had joined the ranks of the great powers. Many of these victories—Chotusitz, Hohenfriedberg, Soor—were gained under Frederick's command. and even before the end of the war he had begun to be called 'Frederick the Great'. At its end, all the powers recognized Prussia's acquisition of Silesia.

Silesia was a wealthy and populous province, with a thriving woollen industry and

deposits of iron, coal and lead that were invaluable to a militaristic state. It is indicative of the limited aims (and means) of eighteenth-century rulers that this single acquisition was to be at risk for most of Frederick's reign.

This was in part a result of Frederick's methods. His wartime diplomacy—ceasing to fight when his French allies seemed about to overwhelm Austria, taking up arms when Austria grew too strong—had been successful; but they left him friendless. Maria Theresa burned to recover Silesia; Russia coveted East Prussia; and France, formally still Prussia's ally, no longer trusted Frederick.

The Seven Years War

Frederick was aware of his isolation; after the Second Silesian War he declared that henceforth he 'would not disturb a cat'. However, eight years of uneasy peace revealed Frederick's weaknesses as a diplomatist: a tendency to credit others with his own rationality and subtlety, and a temperament bias towards 'action'. In January 1756, alarmed by an Anglo-Russian rapprochement, Frederick signed the Convention of Westminster with Britain—which simply convinced France that she should accept Austrian offers of a defensive alliance. Believing that he was about to be crushed by a Franco-Russo-Austrian coalition, Frederick decided to move first.

In August 1756 he attacked Saxony, a strategically important state because its borders were only a few miles from Berlin. The Saxon army was defeated and incorporated into Frederick's forces and the resources of Saxony harnessed to Prussia's needs. In return for these advantages Frederick had precipitated war with Russia and Austria and—by attacking instead of waiting to be attacked—had ensured that

France would join them. Sweden also declared war, and Frederick found himself encircled by enemies determined to dismember his kingdom.

For Prussia, the Seven Years War was a struggle for survival only. Frederick's sole ally was Britain, which paid him yearly subsidies and maintained an army in western Germany. Despite brilliant victories—at Rossbach (1757) over a Franco-German army, at Leuthen (1757) over the Austrians, at Zondorf (1758) over the Russians—the coalition drove Frederick's armies back by sheer weight of numbers. Against this, victories brought only temporary relief; and there were as many defeats as victories. The king was tireless and endlessly resourceful and his army had the advantages of interior lines and unity of command; but the situation several times reached a point at which Frederick contemplated suicide.

From 1760 the war was mainly one of attrition, siege following siege, while both sides became increasingly war-weary. The coalition began to break up—possibly saving Frederick from ultimate defeat—with the succession of Frederick's fanatical admirer, Peter III, as Tsar of Russia. When peace was made in 1763, Prussia—including Silesia—remained intact.

Prussia had survived, thanks to Frederick's genius and determination; but even more of the credit lay with the army and bureaucracy created by his predecessors. In particular, the efficiency of the civil service provided a revenue proportionately greater than that of the other European states and actually as great as that of Russia.

In most respects Frederick was content to follow the same methods as his father. He attempted to keep down imports and encourage exports; waged tariff wars against Austria and Saxony; reduced internal tariff barriers; built canals; drained marshes; and established hundreds of new villages. Silesian ores were vigorously exploited. The production of silks and woollen cloths increased so rapidly that they became the chief Prussian export. There were inevitable conflicts between the state's need for revenue and the needs of production and inevitable defects in a system so highly regulated and inimical to initiative; but on the only meaningful basis of assessment—comparison with other states—Prussian economic policy worked well.

Frederick was an ubiquitous presence, supervising, directing, checking. Unlike his father, he interfered even in routine matters. He would set up specialized agencies, correspond with local officials over the heads of their superiors and set one official to spy upon another. Such methods did often get things done more quickly, but they disorganized the machinery of the Prussian administration and made civil servants reluctant to act on their own initiative. These defects were tolerable while the king was a man of exceptional industry and intelligence—that is, while Frederick was king—but inevitably he had no successor as a one-man state supervisor.

During the Seven Years War, Prussia was devastated by the hostile armies and population declined by about a tenth. Frederick redoubled his efforts: the peasants were kept going by credits and supplies from the war magazines; the currency was restored; a state bank was opened; the growing of potatoes and sugar-beet (preventatives of famine) was encouraged despite opposition from the conservative peasantry. Despite some dubious experiments, state regulation was conspicuously successful in bringing about economic recovery.

The social and economic privileges of the nobility remained untouched; indeed Frederick, unlike his father, preferred to appoint men of noble birth to posts of any importance. In this as in other respects, Frederick became less and less 'enlightened'; in fact, the only notable reforms of his reign

another matter: Frederick was enthusiastic in seconding the Empress Catherine's suggestion that Russia, Prussia and Austria should each take a slice of Polish territory. The first partition (1772) fulfilled one of Frederick's long-cherished ambitions: the acquisition of West Prussia. This territory contained a large German-speaking and Lutheran element, easily absorbed into a German state; and East Prussia, hitherto indefensible, was joined to the main block of Hohenzollern lands.

This was Frederick's last coup: henceforth his postures were defensive. The war between Prussia and Austria (1777) was a halfhearted affair, but Frederick succeeded in preventing Austria from acquiring a large part of Bavaria. Perhaps the crowning irony of his career was his leadership of the League of German Princes, formed in 1785 to oppose Joseph II's Bavarian exchange scheme. Frederick, the unscrupulous aggressor who had twice broken the peace of the Empire, now marshalled German opinion against the radical schemes of the emperor himself.

were judicial. His efforts to increase the peasant's security of tenure are perhaps another exception; but it is more like that they were prompted by concern for the availability of cannon-fodder.

Frederick's later years

Between the wars Frederick was still the patron of art and letters, for whom Knobelsdorff built the Berlin Opera House, the east wing of the palace at Charlottenburg and the Rococo palace designated by Frederick for relaxation—the famous Sans-Souci at Potsdam. Frederick wrote a long poem, *The Art of War* (extensively revised by Voltaire), and a *History of My Times* about the Silesian wars—the first of several such histories. Voltaire himself became a guest of Frederick (1750–3), though the king's treatment of him after they quarrelled indicated

that the tyrant was close to the surface in the philosopher-king.

The stress of the Seven Years War strengthened the misanthropic and conservative elements in Frederick's make-up. The brilliant young prince, the glamorous king, were gradually replaced by a bent figure in a shabby, snuff-stained coat, remote from other men in his dedication to the state.

The conservatism of Frederick's foreign policy was less a matter of choice. Prussia could not afford another war and had no friends. France and Austria remained allies. Britain, Frederick believed, had let him down. He made the only possible alliance open to him, with Russia (1764–80). Frederick had no wish to see Russia expand, and much of his diplomatic activity was in fact designed to prevent his ally from exploiting her victories over the Turks. Poland was

Frederick's legacy

Under Frederick the Great, Prussia became recognized as a great power and acquired the territory and population (over 5 million by 1786) to support her new status more effectively. In immediate political terms his aims and methods were justified by their success; but their long-term effects were more questionable.

The military aspect of the Prussian state was decisively strengthened. The prestige of the army became unshakeable, and its influence was felt everywhere in Prussia. Frederick has, with some justification, been accused of beginning the European arms race: after the Seven Years War the army remained at its wartime size of just under 200,000 men (about four percent of the population), and habits of obedience and belief in force as a method of solving disputes became deeply ingrained in the citizens. In this sense it is possible to blame Frederick and his father for some of the disasters of modern German history.

In the immediate future Prussia continued to expand: Frederick's successor, Frederick William II (1786–97), took part in the Polish partitions of 1793 and 1795. But the penalties of rigid structures and unthinking obedience were soon to be visited upon Prussia in the Revolutionary and Napoleonic Wars, in which Frederick the Great's army was smashed and the state itself almost destroyed.

Austria under Charles VI

The reign of Charles VI (1711–40) coincided in time almost exactly with that of Frederick William I of Prussia; but whereas Prussia steadily grew in strength, the Austrian Monarchy struggled with financial difficulties, military reverses and internal disaffection.

The early years of the reign were promising. The long War of Spanish Succession came to an end, and if a Habsburg no longer sat on the throne of Spain the Austrian branch of the family acquired most of Spain's possessions in Europe: the Spanish Netherlands, Milan, Naples, Sardinia. In the war against the Turks (1716–18) Eugene of Savoy crushed the Turkish armies and captured Belgrade; and when peace was made at Passarowitz (1718), Austria gained Temesvar and considerable territory to the south and east of Hungary.

The most pressing internal problem appeared to have been solved when agreement was reached with the Hungarians. The Rakoczi revolt ended in 1712, and Charles was able to negotiate a settlement that was satisfactory to the dynasty, if not entirely so to the state. The Hungarians continued to enjoy a very considerable degree of self-government and to pay little in taxes (the nobility paid nothing); but they accepted the succession of Charles's daughter and the principle that Hungary was an indivisible part of the Habsburg Empire.

The fact that Charles had no male heir complicated both his internal and external policies. In a declaration of 1713—the 'Pragmatic Sanction'—Charles willed all his dominions to his eldest direct heir, whether male or female; and over the years it became clear that he would be succeeded by his daughter, Maria Theresa (born in 1717). After he has secured the agreement of the Hungarians and his other, more tractable subjects, Charles formally promulgated the Pragmatic Sanction in 1724; but he still needed the acquiescence of the other great powers. This was necessary not because women were regarded as inevitably feeble rulers—though that conviction had not entirely disappeared despite examples to the contrary—but because Maria Theresa had possible rivals. Charles's elder brother, Joseph I, had left two daughters who had married the electors of Bavaria and Saxony; and it seemed likely that other powers would support their claims in order to weaken and possibly to dismember the Austrian Empire.

Charles's tortuous and otherwise ineffective foreign policy was primarily intended to avoid this contingency by securing international recognition of Maria Theresa. In this at least he succeeded: by the end of the War of Polish Succession (1733–5) all the great powers—even the hereditary enemy, France—had guaranteed the Pragmatic Sanction.

It was an ill-advised policy: in return for paper guarantees Charles sacrificed real advantages. Austrian strength and prestige. —the only real guarantees of the Pragmatic Sanction—steadily declined. Charles's wars exhausted Austrian finances yet produced military results that were at best unimpressive. In a new war (1737–9) against the Turks, they were disastrous: Austria was heavily defeated, and all the gains of Passarowitz were lost except Temesvar. The prospect of expanding overseas trade through the Ostend Company had been sacrificed to placate the maritime powers, and the small fleet built at Trieste was sold. Economic growth remained slow, and—as if to punish Austrian weakness with the maximum irony—the most rapidly developing province, Silesia, was lost as soon as Charles died.

Maria Theresa

As soon as Maria Theresa came to the throne, Frederick the Great attacked Silesia, and the electors of Bavaria and Saxony asserted their wives' claims to the Habsburg inheritance. By the summer of 1741, France, Bavaria and Spain had formed an alliance against Austria, and by October the ill-prepared Austrian army had to face a Franco-Bavarian force in Bohemia as well as Frederick's army in Silesia. The beginning of the War of Austrian Succession appeared to foreshadow the dissolution of the Habsburg state itself.

Above, Charles VI, Archduke of Austria and Holy Roman Emperor (reigned 1711–40), whose reign was mainly taken up with his unsuccessful attempt to become king of Spain, and to secure a peaceful accession of his daughter Maria Theresa to the Austrian throne on his own death.

Top, the Opera House of Berlin in 1742; Frederick himself was a skilful flautist and composer and was an eager patron of music, including opera.

Opposite left, Frederick II of Prussia (reigned 1740–86), known as Frederick the Great. He combined an interest in learning and music with a determination to expand Prussia to be the dominant state of eastern Europe. Schloss Hohenzollern.

Opposite right, Frederick the Great at the Sans-Souci castle near Potsdam, with a number of guests, including Voltaire, in the early 1750s.

At this crisis the twenty-three-year-old Maria Theresa behaved with courage and resolution, making a dramatic appeal to the Hungarian nobility which won their support. More immediately important, Frederick the Great effectively dropped out of the war: he had no wish to see his ally France destroy Austria and dominate Europe. The French and Bavarians were driven from Bohemia, and the initiative passed to Austria. The crisis had passed: the fortunes of war fluctuated, as Frederick again intervened (1744–5) to prevent an Austrian triumph; but the existence of Austria was never again threatened.

After the peace of Aix-la-Chapelle (1748), Austrian policy was almost exclusively directed towards revenging her defeat by Prussia and recovering Silesia. Even during the war Maria Theresa would have preferred to make peace with France in order to face Prussia alone; but she had been hindered by her British allies (who were only interested in fighting France) and by the French obsession with their traditional anti-Habsburg policy. Now she set about winning the friendship of France in earnest.

The architect of this policy was Prince Wenzel von Kaunitz, the outstanding diplomatist of his generation, who became chancellor of Austria in 1753. Kaunitz believed that the Bourbon-Habsburg struggle was no longer relevant to European politics and that only the destruction of Prussia could restore Austrian primacy in Germany. A new policy required a new partner. Britain had neither the desire nor the ability to intervene in eastern Europe, whereas the support of France, still the most powerful nation in Europe, would ensure victory, and French subsidies would keep the Russian (as well as the Austrian) armies in the field.

While Kaunitz negotiated with France, another of Maria Theresa's advisers, Count Ludwig Haugwitz, was organizing the military, administrative and financial reforms which might enable Austria to match the Prussian war machine. The army was subjected to a more rigorous training; conditions of service were improved; and administrative and tax reforms greatly increased revenue. Austria and Bohemia, the most docile Habsburg possessions, were the chief targets, and Austro-Bohemian institutions were streamlined and integrated. Now, as later, Hungary in particular was handled with tact. Maria Theresa had won the devotion of the Hungarian nobles in 1741 and she retained it by giving them preferential treatment and respecting their privileges.

Meanwhile, Kaunitz's diplomacy met with limited success. Austro-French negotiations were cordial but showed little sign of reaching a conclusion. Only Frederick the Great's miscalculations angered the French into making a defensive alliance with Austria (1756) and then brought them into the coalition against Prussia.

Kaunitz's diplomacy triumphed, but the Austrian and other coalition armies failed to give Prussia the coup de grâce; and Austria emerged from the Seven Years War with nothing to show for her expenditure of blood and treasure.

After the disappointment of the Seven Years War, Maria Theresa avoided adventures in foreign policy and determined upon a more thoroughgoing reorganization of her dominions. All internal policy was brought under the direction of a single Council of State; and a central bureau, the Directorium, controlled the administrative system. A beginning was made in efficient budgeting, while the functions of the provincial estates were largely taken over by royal officials, and further military reforms were introduced by the empress's son, Joseph.

Maria Theresa's agrarian reforms were more radical still. Their original motive was financial: a peasant who performed heavy services for his lord could not make his own land productive; so he could not pay much in taxes. But the investigations of royal commissioners revealed a degree of peasant misery that produced a genuine humanitarian revulsion in Maria Theresa, who was only with difficulty persuaded not to abolish serfdom entirely. Maximum labour services were established in successive provinces over a period of years (1767–78) and the result was a definite improvement in the lot of the peasantry. The direction in which the government hoped to move was made clear by their treatment of peasants on crown lands, who were freed from all servile obligations and became simple tenants. By and large, however, landowners failed to follow the government's lead.

These measures demonstrate the extent to which 'enlightened despotism' sprang from the needs of the state rather than the personality or convictions of the ruler. Nobody could have been less the received image of the enlightened despot than the pious, conservative, sturdily sensible but scarcely intellectual Maria Theresa; yet she proved willing to override custom and tradition in the interests of the state and to tax the clergy and dissolve monasteries in the face of papal opposition. She, much more than self-conscious Enlightenment intellectuals like Frederick II and Catherine of Russia, deserves a place among the enlightened despots.

The radical emperor

Maria Theresa's successor was her son, Joseph II (1780–90), who intensified the programme of radical reform. Joseph lacked his mother's caution and common sense; he was a doctrinaire Enlightenment prince who meditated profound changes in the structure of the state regardless of social, regional or religious difficulties. He proceeded at a pace that was dangerous in itself and madness

when combined with an adventurous foreign policy.

Joseph's hankering after military and diplomatic success became apparent even in his mother's lifetime. It was mainly he who convinced Maria Theresa that Austria should take part in the first partition of Poland (1772); and it was he who championed the Bavarian succession scheme which led to war with Prussia (1778), a fiasco that drained the Austrian treasury without achieving anything. Similar adventures were to ruin all Joseph's attempts at internal reform.

In the early years of the reign all went well. Administrative centralization was carried to its logical conclusion, and the empire was divided into administrative areas that ignored local and regional differences (a characteristic Enlightenment attitude, with both strengths and weaknesses). Equality before the law and religious toleration were introduced. The peasants were given personal liberty (that is, they were no longer forbidden to leave the estates on which they worked) and security of tenure for themselves and their descendants.

Joseph made the first sustained effort to end Austrian economic backwardness. No consideration other than utility was allowed to influence policy. For example, several hundred monasteries were dissolved because they were non-productive; as Joseph proclaimed (in the characteristic accents of the Enlightenment), 'orders which are absolutely useless to their fellow-men cannot be pleasing to God.' Internally, restrictions on trade were removed. The state ceased to subsidise industry, and the guilds lost much of their power to restrict production and commerce. External commercial policy remained mercantilist: tariffs were imposed on foreign goods in order to stimulate production in Austria, and Joseph concluded a number of advantageous trade agreements with other states.

Interference with the economic and social systems prevailing in the countryside—still, of course, the heart of the Austrian economy —went even further. During the 1780s a comprehensive census and land register was compiled for all Joseph's dominions; the feudal obligations of the peasants were swept away and replaced by fixed money rents; and finally, in 1789, a land tax representing twelve percent of yearly income was imposed on landowner and peasant alike, who now became equal before the tax collector as well as the law.

The magnitude of the changes introduced by Joseph—changes that would have transformed Austria into a modern state—was bound to arouse opposition. They quickly justified themselves in terms of economic growth and increased state revenue; but they offended most sections of the population in some respect—religious belief, regional independence, financial advantage, social superiority. Nor should the 'despotic' (as opposed to the 'enlightened') aspect of

Joseph's policies be ignored: the destruction of local liberties, the use of secret police, the imposition of German as the official language of the Habsburg dominions. Even without foreign entanglements Joseph would have encountered difficulties; military defeat completely destroyed his policies.

Joseph's early foreign policy failed; but its failure was not vital. The Austrian Netherlands were difficult to control and of limited commercial value, since the 1648 treaties had given Dutch shipping exclusive use of the River Scheldt. Joseph first attempted to force the Dutch to open the Scheldt and then elaborated a scheme to exchange the Austrian Netherlands for Bavaria, the acquisition of which would have enlarged the main block of Habsburg territory. But his Russian allies let him down, and in the face of French opposition and Frederick II's League of Princes (1785) Joseph had to abandon both his objectives.

His real misfortunes began with the war against the Turks (1788), into which he allowed himself to be led by Catherine. The war was a disaster: Russian strength proved an illusion and the Austrian armies again failed in the field. The exorbitant cost of the war wrecked Austrian finances, trade was disrupted, and prices rose steeply. New taxes to pay for the war made Joseph even more unpopular with all classes. The absence of the army made it impossible to suppress discontent, and Hungary and the Netherlands rebelled. Disillusioned, Joseph cancelled most of his reforms before he died, leaving the monarchy again in a state of crisis.

His successor, the able Leopold II (1790–2), had been an outstanding reformer as Duke of Tuscany and struggled to preserve some of the advances made under Joseph. He made peace with the Turks, managed to stabilize the internal situation and ·even

began to elaborate plans for constitutional reforms involving popular representation; but his death ended any prospect of continued reform. The increasing radicalism of the French Revolution panicked Leopold's successor into blind reaction: the Austrian experiment in enlightened despotism was over.

German reawakening

Eighteenth-century Germany remained provincial and backward. Limited agricultural advances were made, but, with the partial exceptions of Prussia and the Rhineland, industry was of minimal importance. Urban development was slow and the urban middle class small and uninfluential.

German artistic and cultural development was nonetheless remarkable. The princely craze for culture, initially prompted by envy of Louis XIV, led to court patronage of architects, musicians and writers. Catholic Germany and Austria produced a sumptuously decorative Baroque architecture that reached its apogee in spectacular churches and monasteries. The Germans became the leading musical nation with the appearance of the composers, Johann Sebastian Bach (1685–1750) and Handel (1685–1759) and the Viennese masters Gluck (1714–87), Haydn (1732–1809) and Mozart (1756–91); Vienna, where Beethoven lived and worked from 1792 as pianist and composer, was to be the musical capital of Europe right down to the late nineteenth century. Literature, though held back for a time by imitation of French models, produced a dramatist and critic of the first order in Lessing (1729–81) and a universal genius in Goethe (1749–1832), who was followed in the 1790s by a galaxy of talents. The foundation of Halle (1694)

Above, Joseph II, Holy Roman Emperor (reigned 1765–90) lending a hand at the plough. His primary concern was with the lot of the peasantry, and in 1781 he abolished serfdom and permitted the peasants to buy their own land.

Top, a view of Vienna in 1785, one of the main cultural capitals of central Europe at a time when the cities were vying with each other to attract the best artists and musicians.

PETRUS LEOPOLDUS
Imperator Romanorum &c.

and Göttingen (1736–7) began the European pre-eminence of German universities and the writings of Immanuel Kant (1742–1804) that of German philosophy. Culturally, if not yet politically, Germany had become one of the great nations of Europe.

Though Charles Albert of Bavaria had a brief moment of glory as Holy Roman emperor (1742–5), the political history of Germany was dominated by Austro-Prussian dualism. The German princes became, even more markedly than in the previous period, dependants and auxiliaries of greater powers. Some were even content to supplement their revenues by hiring out their troops, providing Britain in particular with a convenient method of responding to continental emergencies.

Such conditions did not offer much incentive to the would-be enlightened despot; and for that matter the smallness of most states precluded ambitious undertakings. The only prince who instituted radical reforms comparable with Joseph II's was Charles Frederick of Baden, who imposed a uniform tax on land and abolished serfdom. But 'Josephism', as the emperor's anti-clerical policies came to be called, was adopted by a number of Catholic rulers, including ecclesiastical princes.

Towards the end of the pre-revolutionary period, there were indications that Enlightenment attitudes towards politics and society had begun to filter down to a wider public. (In Austria this had been deliberately fostered by Maria Theresa and Joseph, who had encouraged the production of books and pamphlets attacking the privileges of landowners and clergy.) The abolition of serfdom and noble privileges, religious toleration and political freedom became widely discussed as news of the French Revolution arrived. Enlightened despotism, it now became clear, involved an internal

contradiction: to gain public support the despot had to spread enlightenment—which, however, led men to question despotism.

Even before the French Revolution, German rulers had become alarmed by the development of a German public opinion. Freethinkers had begun to be persecuted in Bavaria and Prussia; the limited freedoms characteristic of enlightened despotism had begun to be curtailed. Whether or not these events were part of a more general European 'revolutionary crisis', as some historians believe, is difficult to determine. After 1789, opinions in Germany (and everywhere else in Europe) were determined not by internal events but by reaction to the French Revolution.

Russia

By the time of Peter the Great's death in 1725, Russia had begun to emerge from the semi-oriental seclusion of previous centuries. Peter had imported Western technology and developed industries, created a large and formidable army and won for Russia a 'window on the West' in the Baltic provinces wrested from Sweden. To set the seal on his achievements he had built a new capital, St Petersburg, on the newly acquired coastline, where it faced Europe.

The work begun by Peter was far from complete. Russia was still technologically backward, with an almost wholly illiterate population engaged in agriculture and hunting. The furs and timber of the far north were still the chief source of wealth. Industry and overseas trade grew in the eighteenth century—particularly the iron industry in the Urals, which dominated the European market until coke-smelted British iron began to overtake it in the 1760s. But in general, capital remained short, techniques were

rudimentary and communications poor. Lacking another Peter the Great, and handicapped by the inherent disadvantages of a serf-economy, Russia continued to lag behind the West.

Even at the beginning of the century Russia was the most populous state in Europe apart from France, with more inhabitants than Austria and Prussia combined. It was this fact that enabled her to become a great power despite her backwardness (though, ironically, abundant manpower may have helped to perpetuate that backwardness by providing a temporarily adequate substitute for technological development). By the end of the eighteenth century the population of Russia, swollen by natural increase and acquisitions of territory, stood at thirty-six million, far surpassing that of France.

The majority of this population were serfs, engaged in cottage industries or agriculture, who paid rent in money or kind or worked so many days a week on their lord's land. The serf was little better than a slave: he worked, married and travelled as and when his lord determined and was liable to be sold and taken to his new owner's estates without his family. During the eighteenth century the serf's position deteriorated further as landlords increased their demands and strengthened their legal rights; ultimately, under Catherine II, they acquired authority to send serfs to Siberia as convicts without public trial. Not surprisingly, the eighteenth century was a period of peasant unrest.

By contrast, the position of the nobility was improving. As well as increased control over their serfs, they won greater personal freedom and a privileged status. Peter the Great had instituted compulsory state service for life, controlled their movements and forbidden them to divide their estates; but under his successors these measures were relaxed or reversed.

The tradition of state service remained strong, but a large section of the nobility took the opportunity to become a leisured class, comparable with—and imitative of—their Western counterparts. Only political power was denied them: in Russia too, privilege was a tacit return for noble acquiescence in the continuation of the autocracy. The only serious attempt to limit imperial power—the conditions imposed by the Privy Council on Anne when they offered her the crown in 1730—did not survive her accession.

Peter the Great's successors had little of his ability and none of his determination. Under Catherine I (1725–7), Peter II (1727–30), Anne (1730–40) and Ivan IV (1740–1), the government was an indolent autocracy largely at the mercy of opposing factions. The coup d'état that replaced Ivan IV by Peter the Great's daughter, Elizabeth (1741–61), began a period of relative stability, though the intrigues of lovers, favourites, ministers and diplomats were still the determinants of public policy. In the eyes of Western observers, habituated to dynastic stability and a bureaucratic absolutism, Russia continued to be a barbaric 'Eastern' state, ruled through the seraglio.

However badly governed, Russia had become a force in Europe, albeit an erratic one which was liable to be paralysed by a coup or change of ruler (as happened in 1741 and 1762) and which could often afford to take the field only with the help of subsidies from another power. The War of Polish Succession (1733–5) made it clear that Russia, not France, was now the paramount influence in Polish affairs. The war of 1736–9 against the Turks revealed that Russia was stronger than Austria, her ally in the struggle after 1737. Whereas Austria was forced to make a humiliating separate peace, Russia at least regained Azov, which Peter the Great had lost in 1711.

In addition, easy victories over Sweden

Above, Maria Theresa, Queen of Bohemia and Hungary (reigned 1740–80), and ruler of the Habsburg territories of Austria and the Netherlands.

Left, a view of Moscow in the late eighteenth century, which was increasingly, though to a lesser extent than St Petersburg, dominated by western fashions and culture.

Opposite left, Leopold II, Holy Roman Emperor (reigned 1790–92), who reversed many of the policies of his brother Joseph II in order to restore peace to his lands.

Opposite centre, Joseph Haydn (1732–1809), the Austrian musician who played an important role in the development of the symphonic form.

Opposite right, Wolfgang von Goethe (1749–1832), the German philosopher, poet and statesman who became the epitome of the civilization of Germany in the late eighteenth century, combining the classical and the romantic traditions.

(1741–3) showed that here too the balance of strength had altered decisively in Russia's favour. In the West fear of 'the Russian colossus'—a fear that was to become irrational and obsessive in many nineteenth-century statesmen—had already begun to be expressed. Frederick the Great warned his successors that it was imperative to 'cultivate the friendship of these barbarians'. As yet, circumstances—and ineptitude—prevented Russia from reaping the harvest of her victories.

The Seven Years War followed the same pattern. Russia took her part in a great European coalition, held East Prussia for the duration of the war and even briefly occupied Berlin (1760), making her status as a great power indisputable. But the war also revealed the eccentricity of the new tsar, Peter III (1761–2), who took Russia out of the war because he admired Frederick the Great too much to fight against him.

Much of our information about Peter is untrustworthy, since it derives from his wife, Catherine, who supplanted him. But, if not quite the ignorant lunatic described by Catherine, he displayed an eccentricity that was little short of madness in an occupant of the dangerous throne of Russia. Peter, the half-German Duke of Holstein, ended the war against Prussia, openly displayed his preference for his Holstein troops, paraded his Lutheranism and insulted the Orthodox Church.

The outcome was inevitable. Catherine won over the guards regiments and, abetted by her lover, Grigory Orlov (a guards officer), deposed her husband.

Catherine II

The new empress was even less Russian than Peter. Sophia of Anhalt-Zerbst, who had been renamed Catherine on her reception into the Russian Orthodox Church, was the daughter of a Prussian noble family. In 1745 she became the bride of Peter, at that time heir to the throne, as part of one of Frederick the Great's diplomatic manoeuvres.

Catherine's early years in Russia were dangerous and difficult, and on occasion she was almost caught in the web of intrigue and counter-intrigue that characterized Elizabeth's reign. In this hard school she learned political realism. Unlike Peter, she adopted Russian manners, learned the language and professed Orthodoxy. When her hour struck, she was able to put herself forward as the representative of the Russian people, Orthodoxy and the army. First Peter, then Ivan IV (who had survived in confinement since 1741) were murdered, and Catherine was able to remain the undisputed ruler of Russia until her death in 1796.

Before she became empress, Catherine educated herself in the philosophy of the Enlightenment, becoming familiar with the

Pierre III, assassiné par les ordres de Catherine II son épouse.

works of Bayle, Montesquieu, Voltaire and Beccaria. Later, when she corresponded with Voltaire, Diderot and others, she took the opportunity to picture herself as an enlightened ruler and Russia as a well-administered land of plenty. Catherine herself laid the basis for her European reputation and began to be called 'the Great' as a result of her own propaganda.

Russian realities were very different. Catherine toyed with schemes to create a legislative assembly and codify the laws and made some efforts to revive Peter the Great's educational programme; but at heart she cared more for the triumphs of war and diplomacy. Besides, any reform would jeopardize the tacit alliance between the autocracy and nobility. Catherine loved power too much—and for that matter shared too many aristocratic prejudices—to take the risk. Only in secularizing Church property—a measure foreshadowed by her predecessors—did she act in a manner of which *philosophes* and enlightened despots alike would have approved. One incident illuminates her real position. In 1769 she began publishing a journal designed to improve Russian manners and morals; but when the numerous periodicals that flattered her by imitation were joined by Nikolai Novikov's *The Drone*, which attempted serious social analysis, it was promptly suppressed.

The gulf between privileged and unprivileged was in fact deliberately widened. In the few months of Peter III's reign, the emancipation of the nobility had been completed. Under Catherine they were loaded with privileges, culminating in a Charter of the Nobility (1785) which confirmed all their gains over the century and

gave them a share in local government. Hundreds of thousands of state peasants passed into serfdom as gifts to her noble supporters from the prodigal Catherine, and many of the peasants in lands conquered by Russia also become serfs. The condition of the peasantry continued to deteriorate as masters increased their demands in order to set up manorial industries or share the pleasures of life in St Petersburg.

Catherine's court was more sophisticated than that of her predecessors. To superficial observers St Petersburg appeared 'the Athens of the North', for which foreign architects designed beautiful new buildings—the Winter Palace, the Hermitage, Tsarskoe Selo. Its society was dominated by the spirit of the Enlightenment in its more superficial aspects: use of French and displays of wit, cynicism and polished manners. In this respect, too, Catherine's reign was a pseudo-Enlightenment—a tribute to the French culture which contemporaries were prone to identify with the Enlightenment.

Pugachev

The great rebellion of 1733–4 can be regarded as the peasants' verdict on Catherine and previous rulers. The rebels were led by Emelian Pugachev, a Don Cossack adventurer who claimed to be the dead Peter III (a type of imposture frequently adopted by Russian rebels). Exploited serfs, persecuted members of the sect of Old Believers, discontented non-Russian peoples and all who resented control by distant St Petersburg joined Pugachev, who was soon in control of much of the Volga region.

At first the rebellion was not taken very seriously, but when Pugachev laid siege to Orenburg and repulsed a relieving force, Catherine ordered a full-scale campaign to be mounted. Orenburg was relieved, but Kazan fell, and for a time Moscow itself seemed threatened. The arrival of Russian forces released by the Russo-Turkish peace (1774) sealed Pugachev's fate. His followers were hunted down, areas which had supported him were subjected to terrible reprisals, and Pugachev himself was captured and executed.

Pugachev's rebellion increased Catherine's conservatism. Her reaction was to create a uniform system of provincial administration (1775) with which the nobility were associated. In theory at least it should have led to better government; but its main object was to increase control over the countryside. Repression and vigilance, not reform, was Catherine's formula for the peasant problem.

Catherine's conquests

Catherine's claim to greatness lies in her conduct of war and diplomacy: she made Russia more powerful, if not happier. At the beginning of her reign Catherine entertained Nikita Panin's scheme of a 'northern

alliance' with Prussia, Poland, the Baltic states and Britain against the French and Austrians; but, apart from an alliance with Prussia (1764), the plan came to nothing. Catherine proved wise enough to concentrate on the problems at hand: Poland and Turkey.

Agreement to 'maintain Polish liberties' was an important motive in the Russo-Prussian alliance; but, in spite of the election of one of Catherine's lovers, Stanislas Poniatowski, as King of Poland, the Poles continued to be troublesome. The activities of the Polish confederacies tied down a large number of Russian troops—a situation made the more serious by the outbreak of war between Russia and Turkey (1768).

Despite Russian commitments in Poland, the war was prosecuted with success. However, Austria was ready to fight rather than see Russia gain territory in the Balkans, while Frederick II—ally or not—was unprepared to back Catherine against Austria but very willing to reconcile all three parties at the expense of Poland. In effect, the first partition of Poland (1772) was Catherine's way of buying off Austria and Prussia and of compensating herself for the Balkan gains she had been forced to renounce.

The Turkish war was brought to a successful conclusion at Kutchuk-Kainardji (1774), though Catherine might have pressed for greater advantages but for the Pugachev rebellion. Russia acquired a foothold on the Black Sea and right of passage through the Dardanelles for her merchant shipping.

Above, a Russian embassy at the court of the Ottoman sultan in 1775; after the treaty of Kutchuk-Kainardji the Russians were able to begin to dominate their southern neighbour, a policy that would cause diplomatic problems to Europe throughout the nineteenth century.

Top, a view of St Petersburg in 1753; founded by Peter the Great earlier in the century, the city was by this time the centre of Russian society and cultural life.

Above left, Catherine the Great, Tsarina of Russia (reigned 1762–96), walking her dog in 1794; as well as her luke-warm attempts at reform on enlightened principles, she was concerned with the expansion of Russian authority.

Below left, the execution in 1775 of Emelian Pugachev, the Cossack whose rebellion of 1773–74 expressed the social strains of the growing Russian state. Pugachev was able to control the Ural region and take Kazan before being defeated.

Opposite, the murder of Peter III, Tsar of Russia (reigned 1762); his wife, later Catherine II, forced him to abdicate on the grounds of insanity, and may have ordered the murder a few days later.

The Crimea became independent of Turkey (the first step towards its incorporation into Russia), and Russia gained vaguely worded rights to make representations on behalf of the sultan's Christian subjects. (In the nineteenth century this clause was the pretext for repeated Russian interference in Ottoman affairs.) The Treaty of Kutchuk-Kainardji was a landmark in Russian history: under Peter the Great, Russia had gained access to the Baltic; under Catherine, she gained access to the Mediterranean.

The second half of the reign was a sort of repeat performance. When the alliance with Prussia lapsed, Catherine chose a new partner who would be of more direct help against the Turks: Joseph II of Austria. With Joseph's support she annexed the Crimea (1783); but characteristically she made no effort to help Joseph to reestablish Austrian supremacy in Germany. On this, as on other occasions, Catherine posed as the arbiter of Europe—a flattering and undemanding role—but refused to commit her forces outside eastern Europe.

In the 1780s she dreamed of overthrowing the Ottoman Empire completely and reestablishing the ancient Byzantine Empire (the 'Greek project'). In the war that began in 1787, Austria quickly collapsed; and though the Russian performance was better, it hardly justified such extravagant ambitions. At the Peace of Jassy (1792) the Sultan of Turkey accepted Russia's acquisition of the Crimea and ceded the rest of the northern shore of the Black Sea.

Catherine led the way in destroying the Polish state by the partitions of 1793 and 1795. Her troops did most of the fighting and she took the largest single share. Her partners, Austria and Prussia, were also engaged in the struggle against revolutionary France, in which Catherine had promised her aid. Whether she would have intervened on any scale is debatable: it seems more likely that she would have launched another attack on the Turks. Her death left the question open.

In Russia, the French Revolution was greeted with enthusiasm in some circles, influenced by the Enlightenment culture that Catherine had favoured. But from the fall of the Bastille in July 1789, Catherine herself loathed the Revolution, and any of her remaining pretensions to liberalism disappeared. Russian students in the West were ordered home; the imports of French books and journals—including Catherine's favourites—was prohibited. Novikov, whose *The Drone* had got him into trouble some twenty years before, was imprisoned as a subversive publicist and freemason. Alexander Radishchev, who can be regarded as the first figure in the great tradition of Russian literature of social conscience, was sent into Siberian exile.

Catherine's triumphs were bought at a high price. The cost of her wars was enormous, and she financed them by issuing ever greater quantities of paper money. This

rapidly depreciated, dislocating the whole Russian economy and wrecking many of the real industrial advances that had taken place. Other negative features—the growth of noble privileges, the deterioration in the lot of the peasantry—have already been noticed.

The positive features were by no means negligible. Russia gained six million new subjects (though not all of them accepted Russification with docility) and vast territories in the south. These were to become the granary of Russia, and made possible the population explosion of the nineteenth century.

The Baltic states

The conclusion of the Great Northern War (1721) marked the end of Sweden's bid for supremacy in the Baltic. Russia took Sweden's territories on the eastern shore of the Baltic, and Prussia acquired western Pomerania. It soon became apparent that they had also replaced Sweden and her old antagonist, Denmark, as great powers; and from the eighteenth century Scandinavia was on the periphery of international affairs.

The situation in the Baltic itself was stabilized. Sweden remained in control of Finland, Denmark of Norway. The Danes accepted the loss of what had become southern Sweden; the Swedes gave up their attempts to conquer Norway and reconciled themselves to paying the Danes customs duties for passage through the Sound. The two powers were comparable in population and resources, and the balance between them lasted the rest of the century.

The disasters of Charles XII's reign (1697–1718) had destroyed Sweden's Baltic empire and with it the justification for absolute royal authority. When Charles died leaving no direct heir, the aristocracy seized their opportunity: the crown was offered to Charles's sister, Ulrica, on condition that she accepted a constitution drawn up by the Swedish Estates. Her agreement initiated what came to be known as 'the Age of Freedom'. The council that ruled Sweden was selected and controlled by the Estates, which met regularly and took decisions by majority vote.

The 1720s and 1730s were dominated by Count Arvid Horn, whose policy of avoiding foreign adventures while Sweden recovered her strength resembled that of Walpole in Britain and Fleury in France. This unheroic policy led to the formation of the opposing 'Hat' party, which advocated resuming Sweden's traditional alliance with France and dreamed of recovering the lost provinces from Russia.

Horn and the 'Caps' were ousted in 1738; but, though the Hats managed to hang on to power until 1765, the period that followed was one of intense party conflict which gave foreign powers unlimited opportunities for interfering in Swedish affairs by intrigue and bribery. The overambitious policy of the Hats led Sweden into war with Russia (1741), from which she was fortunate to escape with only the loss of a strip of Finland, and to join the coalition against Prussia in the Seven Years War, with equally negative results.

After a brief period of rule by the 'Younger Caps', the twenty-five-year-old Gustavus III (1771–92) staged a coup, overthrew the constitution, and recovered most of the powers that the crown had possessed before the Age of Freedom. He introduced many of the reforms characteristic of the enlightened despot—abolition of judicial torture, religious toleration, freedom of the press, lifting of internal tariffs etc.

Noble opposition revived in the 1780s, provoked in particular by the king's heavy military expenditure, culminating in a fruitless war with Russia and Denmark (1788–90). With popular support Gustavus was able to reinforce and extend his powers by a second coup d'état (1789), but his triumph was brief: in 1792 he was assassinated by a group of nobles.

From the reign of Frederick III (1648–70), Denmark was ruled absolutely by his dynasty, the Oldenburgs. The old nobility was carefully controlled, and royal power was exercised through a new nobility and a civil service, of which many members were Germans who owed everything to the crown. During the eighteenth century, however, a series of weak kings allowed the royal council to engross more and more power—a trend briefly reversed by Johann Friedrich Struensee.

Struensee, a German, was the insane Christian VII's physician and the queen's lover. In 1770 he became virtual dictator of Denmark, broke the power of the council, and launched a programme of enlightened reforms. The pace at which they were introduced, and above all Struensee's attacks on noble privileges, led to his fall and execution (1772). But not all his measures were cancelled; and a few years later even more important reforms were initiated by Andreas Bernstorff, culminating in the effective abolition of serfdom in 1788.

Poland

Poland failed to overcome her difficulties until it was too late. Under the Saxon kings, Augustus II (1697–1733) and Augustus III

(1733–63), economic and social problems went unsolved, and the *Seym* was constantly sabotaged by use of the free veto. Foreign intervention became blatant, and the disputatious Poles easily formed the habit of appealing to outsiders. Interested powers—Russia, Prussia, France—corrupted members of the *Seym*, decided who should be king and violated Polish territory with impunity.

The full extent of Poland's weakness became apparent on the death of Augustus II. Stanislas Leszczynski, once Augustus II's rival, was elected by the Poles with enthusiasm. But Leszczynski was also the French candidate; and Austria and Russia had decided that the Saxon line should continue. A Russian army compelled the Poles to change their minds and drove Leszczynski from the country.

During Augustus III's reign Poland sank deeper into anarchy. Internal politics revolved around the struggle between two great families, the Czartoryskis and the Potockis, both of which attempted to form connections with the great powers. During the Seven Years War, Russia used Polish territory as a base from which to attack Prussia, and Prussian troops counterattacked across the border while the Poles themselves remained in a state of near civil war.

The long overdue reformation began under Stanislas Poniatowski, who became King Stanislas Augustus in 1764. Poniatowski had been one of Catherine II's lovers and was placed on the throne by Russia and Prussia; but he refused to be a puppet and had already made some progress towards reform when the first great crisis of his reign occurred.

Religious dissensions in Poland had provided a pretext for Russian and Prussian diplomatic pressure for several decades. Poland was a Catholic state but contained a large Lutheran minority (mainly German) in the northeast and an even larger Orthodox minority (mainly Ukrainian and Russian) in the east and southeast. Both had very limited civic rights and were subject to strong Catholic pressure. Their natural defenders were Lutheran Prussia and Orthodox Russia; and Frederick II and Catherine II—both religious sceptics—were quite prepared to exploit the issue.

Catherine first encouraged the 'dissenters' to form confederacies, then (1768) bullied the *Seym* into ending their religious disabilities. The reaction was swift: confederacies sprang up all over Poland and harried the Russians, who were further embarrassed by a border incident which sparked off the Russo-Turkish war of 1768–74.

Catherine solved her ensuing difficulties by joining Prussia and Austria in partitioning Poland. In 1772 about a quarter of the kingdom and more than a third of its inhabitants were taken over by new masters.

The first partition shocked the Polish nobility out of their complacent absorption in 'Polish liberty'. Encouraged by the king, the *Seym* passed a series of measures designed to modernize and strengthen the state, culminating in the constitution of 1791. The crown became hereditary; the free veto and confederacies were abolished; a centralized administration was set up; the system of taxation was revised and made more equitable; and the privileges of the nobility were reduced. Intellectual life quickened under the impact of educational reform, and even the Polish economy, half-strangled by concessions to Prussia and Russia, showed some improvement.

Catherine was less than ever inclined to allow a Polish revival. The constitution of 1791 decided her: in 1792 the conservatives, who had opposed the constitution, were stirred into activity, and Russian troops

again invaded. Poniatowski was forced to agree to a second partition (1793), Russia taking a huge slice of eastern Poland and Prussia a smaller area in the west. All that remained of the ancient kingdom was a small and defenceless state under Russian control.

The disappearance of Poland now seemed only a matter of time. The Polish leaders, partly inspired by the successes of 'the people in arms' during the French Revolution, decided to act before the Russian grip tightened; and in 1794 Poland rose in revolt.

The leader of the rebels was Tadeusz Kosciuszko, an enthusiast for liberty who had already fought in the American War of Independence. Under Kosciuszko the revolt took on something of the nationalist fervour that characterized Polish revolutionary activity throughout the nineteenth century. The peasants, promised their freedom, went into battle with scythes; and against all expectations they defeated the Russians at Raclawice.

Lacking help from outside, the revolt was nevertheless doomed to failure. Prussian troops arrived to support the Russians, and after a few months the redoubtable Suvorov took Warsaw. Kosciuszko was captured and later went into exile.

The failure of this gamble brought about the third partition that the Poles had striven to avoid: in 1795 Russia, Prussia and Austria completed the destruction of the Polish state.

The Ottoman decline

After 1700 the decay of the Ottoman Empire proceeded with seeming inevitability. The instability of authority at the centre, where seraglio intrigues continued to determine the fate of viziers, or prime ministers, (and sometimes of sultans), encouraged the ambitions of provincial governors and local warlords. In most of north Africa the sultan's authority became merely nominal, and from about 1750 to 1820 there were even semi-independent principalities in the Anatolian heartlands of the empire. The Balkan peoples grew uneasy under Turkish rule, and the Balkan bandit began to take on full heroic stature in legend and folklore.

Cultural and religious conservatism kept the empire backward, and maladministration, political disorder and epidemics made it poor. But what made eighteenth-century Ottoman stagnation more than an episode in the empire's history was the impact of the West, whose technological superiority was increasingly manifested in economic as well as military terms. Western factory products, especially western textiles, crippled the traditional handicraft industries, inhibited the growth of towns and perpetuated Levantine economic and technical inferiority.

It was hard for the Turks to learn from the West. They were by tradition a military race, and centuries of success in war appeared to justify contempt for commerce, administration, diplomacy and their Christian subjects. Intelligent Turks at least grasped the necessity of military reform; the unintelligent could not grasp even that. Several Turkish rulers attempted to refashion the army on western lines, but even the most sustained effort—made under Selim III (1789–1807)—achieved little against the opposition of the Janissaries and the protests of the faithful. Distrust of change had become ingrained.

This attitude might have been more difficult to sustain had the empire's international position declined more rapidly; but for most of the eighteenth century it was maintained with surprising success. The war of 1736–9 against Austria and Russia was, if anything, victorious: Azov was finally lost, but all the Balkan territories ceded at Passarowitz were recovered. Apart from a setback in Transcaucasia. Turkey held her own against her old eastern antagonist, Persia (also beginning to decline); and the long wars in Europe provided her with a breathing-space in the middle decades of the century.

The war of 1768–74, the loss of the Crimea and the war of 1787–92 revealed the full extent of Turkish weakness. They also revealed that the result of the 1736–9 war had not been fortuitous: Russia had replaced Austria as Turkey's main antagonist and, having occupied the northern shore of the Black Sea, was certain to attempt the penetration of the Balkans.

Two elements of the nineteenth-century 'Eastern Question' were now present in southeastern Europe: a decadent Turkey and an aggressive Russia. The diplomatic exertions of France on Turkey's behalf, and Austrian hostility to Russian gains in the Balkans, prefigured the jealousies and anxieties of the other powers, which were to complicate the Russo-Turkish conflict. It required only the eruption of Balkan nationalism in the nineteenth century to create a problem of European magnitude and labyrinthine complexity.

Above, Selim III, Sultan of Turkey (reigned 1789–1807), who tried to reform the Ottoman state along western lines, but was defeated by the conservatism of the Janissaries, who deposed, imprisoned and eventually assassinated him.

Opposite left, Stanislaus II of Poland (reigned 1764–95), who was put on the throne as a Russian puppet but who attempted to reform the Polish government and improve the condition of the peasantry. He was forced to abdicate after the third partition of Poland in 1795.

Opposite right, Tadeusz Kosciuszko (1746–1817), the Polish patriot who rebelled in 1794 against the second partition of Poland the previous year; after his defeat he went into exile in America, where he had earlier helped the colonies to win their independence from Britain.

Chapter 19
War and Diplomacy in eighteenth-century Europe

The period between the late seventeenth and late eighteenth centuries was one of diplomacy and warfare conducted without ideological passion. The wars of religious fanaticism had ended; the wars inspired by revolutionary or nationalistic ideologies had not yet begun. Before the French Revolution of 1789, diplomatic activity had a single motive: to advance the interests of the dynasty or state.

In this sense, eighteenth-century rulers were immoral or (more accurately) amoral. But the politics of self-interest do not necessarily cause more suffering than the politics of religion or idealism: and this was a period when self-interest in fact led to a diminution of the scope and intensity of warfare.

Most eighteenth-century wars were fought without antagonism and for limited objectives. The aggressor hoped to win a province; and if he was defeated he expected to pay with one. Monarchs respected one another's property, if only to avoid retaliation: towns were no longer sacked and soldiers were forbidden to loot and pillage. War became conventionalized—an occupation for professionals which for much of the time did not affect civilians. Trade between belligerents might well continue without interruption, and a gentleman could travel freely in a state with which his own was at war.

The bulk of almost every army was drawn from the dregs of the population, bribed or bullied into the ranks by recruiting sergeants. There were usually also large contingents of foreign mercenaries or soldiers conscripted in occupied territories. Such troops had to be endlessly drilled and savagely disciplined until they were more afraid of their officers than of the enemy. Naturally, when they got the chance, many of them deserted.

Desertion was a major problem for commanders, whose need constantly to supervise their own troops limited the striking power of their armies. Soldiers liable to desert could not be sent out in scouting parties, so information was inadequate. They could be deployed only in open country, so that freedom of manoeuvre was restricted and the line of advance irregular. Armies operating *en bloc* had to be supplied from large war magazines and could not

easily sustain long campaigns at a distance from their base area. Finally, large baggage-trains and poor communications further impeded rapidity of movement.

Even the greatest eighteenth-century commanders—Marlborough and Frederick the Great—only partly transcended these limitations. Decisive victories of the Napoleonic type, in which a mass national army penetrated deep into enemy territory, lived off the land and destroyed the opposing army with a single knockout blow, were unthinkable. Most wars involved long sieges, prolonged manoeuvring, set-piece battles and inefficient pursuit of a defeated enemy. In western Europe, defensive tactics were highly developed, and only minimal advantages were sought. Peace was generally made when one or both of the contestants were financially exhausted rather than defeated.

Diplomatic realities and illusions

Such conditions necessarily imposed limited aims; but statesmen did not always think so. The eighteenth century was a period of overelaborate and sometimes fantastic schemes: the improbable combination of Swedes, Jacobites and Spaniards projected by Charles XII's minister Goertz, the plans for dismembering France entertained by the Spanish queen, Elizabeth Farnese, and Charles VI of Austria, Panin's northern alliance, and Catherine's 'Greek project'.

In part, the prevalence of diplomatic fantasies resulted from uncertainty about the direction which European affairs were taking. Until the early decades of the eighteenth century, certain constant diplomatic factors had guided generations of rulers. The conflict between France and the Habsburgs had polarized European diplomacy for two centuries, offering other states the clear alternative of joining one side or

the other; and in eastern Europe, the struggle against the enemy of Christendom, Ottoman Turkey, was still older. Even the Swedish attempt to dominate the Baltic (and perhaps central and eastern Europe) dated back to the 1640s.

By 1713 the familiar patterns had begun to disappear. France, exhausted by Louis XIV's wars and ruled in turn by a pacific regent, a pacific minister and a feeble king (Louis XV), ceased to dominate Europe. With Spain no longer ruled by a Habsburg, and imperial power negligible, Austria became a mainly east-European power. The liberation of Hungary ended the Muslim threat to Christendom, and Turkey became more or less another member of the European state system. And at the battle of Poltava (1709). Sweden was once and for all destroyed as a great power by the armies of Peter the Great. The traditional alliances were no longer satisfactory, though it was more than half a century before they were abandoned. For at least a generation, Austria, Britain and Holland had combined to resist France, whose traditional allies were Sweden, Turkey and Poland. By 1748 the Dutch, like the Swedes and Turks, were no longer a force in Europe, while Britain and France were increasingly absorbed in a struggle for empire outside Europe. Even more important was the rise of two new states: Prussia, which rivalled Austria for primacy in Germany, and Russia, which established a virtual protectorate over France's old dependant, Poland.

The Franco-Austrian rapprochement of 1756 was the first drastic realignment prompted by the changed balance of forces. It was the prelude to an even greater change: the division of Europe into separate diplomatic spheres: the west, where Britain, France and Spain fought intermittently for colonies; and the east, where Russia, Prussia and Austria manoeuvred or combined to decide the fate of their weaker neighbours. Europe only became a single theatre of diplomacy and war with the French Revolution and its Napoleonic sequel.

The Peace of Utrecht

The War of the Spanish Succession (1701–13) was effectively ended by the Peace of Utrecht (1713). Its chief results were that France, though almost brought to her knees in the last years of the war, secured the Spanish throne for Louis XIV's grandson, who became Philip V; and that Spain lost all her European possessions, most of which were taken over by Austria. Thus Spain passed from the Habsburg family to the Bourbons, and Austria became the paramount power in Italy as well as acquiring the Spanish Netherlands. The Duke of Savoy gained Sicily and some territory in mainland Italy; and various other provisions were made to contain France and reward members of the anti-French coalition. Britain's gains were mainly colonial, but her retention of Gibraltar and Minorca increased her power in the Mediterranean and ensured future conflicts with Spain.

Peace-making and peace-keeping

In 1716 the Austrian armies under Eugene began a war against the Turks that culminated in the victorious peace of Passarowitz (1718). The most important event of 1716 was, however, the Anglo-French alliance, to which the Dutch also adhered (1717). Neither Britain's new Hanoverian king nor France's regent was entirely secure: and both countries were war-weary. They had a shared interest in maintaining European peace.

It was partly Anglo-French diplomacy that brought the Great Northern War (1700–21) to an end, though it did little to affect its outcome: Sweden ceded her eastern Baltic possessions to Russia and fell from the ranks of the great powers; Russia, as later became apparent, joined them.

Before the pacification of the Baltic had been completed, the western Mediterranean became the potential centre of a new European war. Under the direction of Elizabeth Farnese and her adviser, Alberoni, Spain attacked and captured Sardinia (1717) and Sicily (1718). The powers reacted swiftly. The emperor adhered to the British-French-Dutch system (Quadruple Alliance, 1718); and a few days later a British fleet defeated the Spaniards off Cape Pessaro. Philip was compelled to make terms by a French

Opposite top, recruiting for the army in Leipzig in 1726; wine and merriment were often sufficient inducement for men to sign up, and most European armies were well-drilled and professional.

Opposite centre, the Battle of Poltava in 1709, at which the Russians decisively defeated the Swedish army. State Hermitage Museum, Leningrad.

Opposite bottom, Europe in 1721.

invasion of Spain (1719). The immediate (and irrelevant) result of the crisis was that the Duke of Savoy was compelled to cede Sicily to the emperor in return for the poorer island of Sardinia, of which he became king. The self-imposed peace-keeping mission of France, Britain and Holland appeared to have succeeded.

In fact, nothing had been solved. Spain, fobbed off with promises of territory in Italy for Elizabeth Farnese's sons, remained dissatisfied. Charles VI of Austria, resenting his dependence on the maritime powers, attempted to get a share in overseas trade for Austria through his Ostend Company (1722). In 1725 Spain and Austria became allies—the outstanding geopolitical absurdity of a period marked by halfhearted attempts to adjust to changed conditions. Faced by a British-French-Prussian combination, Austria backed down. Spain fought a brief war against Britain (1727), unsuccessfully besieging Gibraltar, until French diplomatic pressure forced her to make peace. By the treaties of Seville (1729) and Vienna (1731), Elizabeth Farnese's son Charles became Duke of Parma and was recognized as heir to Tuscany. Charles VI abandoned the Ostend Company and collected British and Dutch guarantees of the Pragmatic Sanction, which had now become his chief diplomatic aim. The ultimate success of Spanish policy demonstrated that, in a period when the great powers were concerned to preserve peace, a second-class power could exploit its nuisance-value to make limits gains.

In the 1720s and 1730s British policy was directed by Walpole and French policy by Cardinal Fleury, men of similarly pacific outlook. While they stayed in control, Anglo-French relations remained good, though in the decade after 1731 Britain played little part in European affairs. The French war party, on the other hand, dragged the reluctant Fleury into yet another round of the Bourbon-Habsburg conflict.

The War of the Polish Succession

'War of the Polish Succession' is a misnomer for the conflict of 1733–5. France had no serious chance of opposing the Austro-Russian candidate, Augustus III; and she embarked on what was primarily a war against Austria in order to compensate herself for loss of influence in Poland.

The French overran Lorraine, but Italy, where France, Spain and Sardinia fought in alliance, was again the chief theatre of war. The Austrian armies suffered several defeats, and the peace terms were unfavourable to the Habsburgs. Stanislas Leszczynski, the unsuccessful French candidate for the Polish throne (and Louis XV's father-in-law), received Lorraine, which was to become French territory at his death; Francis of Lorraine, Maria Theresa's husband-to-be,

received Tuscany in compensation. Charles VI received Parma; Charles of Parma became ruler of Naples and Sicily. One major objective of Habsburg policy was achieved: France joined the other great powers in guaranteeing the Pragmatic Sanction.

The war was important for several reasons. Russia supplanted France in Poland; and in the virtual acquisition of Lorraine the French monarchy won its last great triumph before the Revolution. Franco-Spanish cooperation began an enduring pertnership that was geographically and dynastically appropriate—and, incidentally, the first permanent feature in European diplomacy since Utrecht. And the situation in Italy was stabilized: henceforward the south was to be ruled by a Bourbon dynasty and most of the north by Habsburgs. This arrangement too was sound and lasted without material alteration until the second half of the nineteenth century.

The War of the Austrian Succession

In the Turkish war of 1736–9 Austria lost all the territory outside Hungary that she had gained at Passarowitz, whereas her Russian ally was at least nominally victorious. The most serious aspect of this reverse was that Austrian weakness was revealed at a moment of dynastic crisis. The accession of Maria Theresa, Frederick the Great's invasion of Silesia, the invasion of Bohemia by a 'Bavarian' (in fact Franco-Bavarian) army and Spanish attacks on Habsburg possessions in Italy seemed to prefigure the disintegration of the empire. Austria's only ally, Russia, was paralysed by the crisis attendant on Elizabeth's accession and the simultaneous Russo-Swedish war. Even the German imperial crown was lost, for in January 1742 Charles

Albert of Bavaria was elected Holy Roman emperor—the first non-Habsburg to sit on the throne since 1438.

Then Austrian fortunes revived. Frederick the Great agreed to a brief truce (October 1741) which enabled him to occupy the rest of Silesia while the Austrian army rallied to defend Bohemia. Britain helped Maria Theresa with subsidies and began to form an auxiliary 'Pragmatic army'. In 1742 Prussia inflicted heavy defeats on Austria but made peace in return for Silesia, while the French and Bavarians were driven from Bohemia with heavy losses and Bavaria was occupied by Austrian troops.

In real terms this ended the War of the Austrian Succession. The Austrian monarchy was saved and Silesia lost; and what followed was a futile European war on the old pattern. Ties between Britain and Austria were strengthened, and in 1743 the Pragmatic army under George II defeated the French at Dettingen. In 1744 France declared war on Britain, entering the Anglo-Spanish colonial war that had been in progress since 1739. She also declared war officially on Austria and invaded the Austrian Netherlands. Frederick the Great, alarmed by Austrian successes, re-entered the war (1744–5) long enough to obstruct an Austrian invasion of France and then left it for good, still holding Silesia. In 1745 the French, under Maurice de Saxe, won the great Battle of Fontenoy over the British, Austrians and Dutch and in the next two years overran the Austrian Netherlands and part of Holland. Fontenoy was to be the military counterpart of the acquisition of Lorraine—the last great victory of pre-Revolutionary French arms but for the moment it seemed as if France was again 'the great nation' in Europe.

Faction and financial difficulties hampered the diplomatic exploitation of French victories; and France, like most of the other combatants, lacked intelligible war aims. When peace was at last made, at Aix-la-Chapelle (1748), it was on the basis of a restoration of all conquests. European or colonial. The imperial crown had already returned to Habsburg control on the election of Francis of Lorraine as Holy Roman emperor (1745). The only gainers at the peace were Elizabeth Farnese's second son, Philip, who became Duke of Parma, and the King of Sardinia, who was rewarded with territory for helping Maria Theresa.

All the same, the war registered important changes in the European situation. The Dutch were clearly no longer a great power. The emergence of Prussia signified that European wars would never again assume the aspect of straightforward Austro-French struggles for supremacy in Germany. Finally, the renewal of Anglo-French antagonism, based on commercial and colonial rivalry, became a permanent feature of European diplomacy until the end of the Napoleonic Wars.

Kaunitz made the decisive break with

diplomatic tradition. He initiated negotiations for an Austrian alliance with France. The French were sympathetic towards the idea of an understanding that would leave them free to concentrate on the unfolding colonial struggle against Britain but for that very reason were unwilling to participate in an Austro-Russian attack on Prussia.

Agreement was precipitated by a series of misunderstandings and miscalculations. A subsidy treaty between Britain and Russia (1755) convinced Frederick II that he should himself reach an accommodation with Britain. By the Convention of Westminster (January 1756) Prussia and Britain agreed to neutralize Germany: foreign troops were to be kept out and peace maintained. Frederick protested that the Convention did not affect the Franco-Prussian alliance, but Louis XV and his ministers regarded Frederick's action as the blackest treachery. Elizabeth of Russia, who had viewed the treaty of 1755 as a preliminary to attacking Prussia, was equally angry with Britain, and egged on Austria to bring France into an anti-Prussian coalition. As a result, France hurriedly concluded the first treaty of Versailles with Austria (May 1756). The diplomatic revolution had taken place.

The treaty was only a defensive one, however: each party agreed to help the other if attacked in Europe—a provision that kept Austria out of the Anglo-French colonial war, which had already begun (1755), but gave France the continental security she needed in order to win it. That, at least, was France's position in May 1756. Whether Austria could have tempted her into an aggressive war against Prussia remains in doubt; for Frederick, obsessed by the spectre of a French-Austrian-Russian coalition, determined to launch a preventive war. His attack on Saxony activated the defensive alliance between France and Austria and brought into being the coalition that he dreaded most of all.

The Seven Years War

The central drama of the Seven Years War in Europe was Prussia's fight to survive against the armies of Austria, Russia, Sweden and the German states, which has been sketched out in the section describing Frederick the Great's career. There were a number of reasons for the failure of the anti-Prussian coalition: Frederick's meticulous preparation, military genius, ruthlessness, resourcefulness and luck; suspicion and lack of coordination between his enemies, the Austrian preference for titles rather than talent in commanders; Russian slowness in mobilizing and intervening (1758); and, possibly decisive, the change of ruler that took Russia out of the war in 1762.

It is unlikely that Frederick could have survived until 1762 if France had been able to add her weight to the coalition. In this respect Frederick's British alliance proved invaluable. Under the elder William Pitt, Britain subsidized Frederick and undertook a holding operation in western Europe. From the British point of view the object was to frustrate a French victory in Europe and thereby prevent France from concentrating her resources on the colonial struggle. In pursuance of this policy, regular naval-cum-military attacks were made on the French coast; but Frederick's effective

Above, the Battle of Fontenoy in 1745 at which the French Count de Saxe defeated the British in the War of the Austrian Succession; such battles had little effect on the economies or fortunes of the nations concerned, beyond the territorial ambitions of their rulers. Château de Versailles.

Opposite, Stanislaus I of Poland (reigned 1704–09; 1733–35). who relied for his throne on Swedish support during the Northern War and regained his throne with French help in the 1730s; Poland, though a sovereign state, was never independent from foreign interference in the eighteenth century.

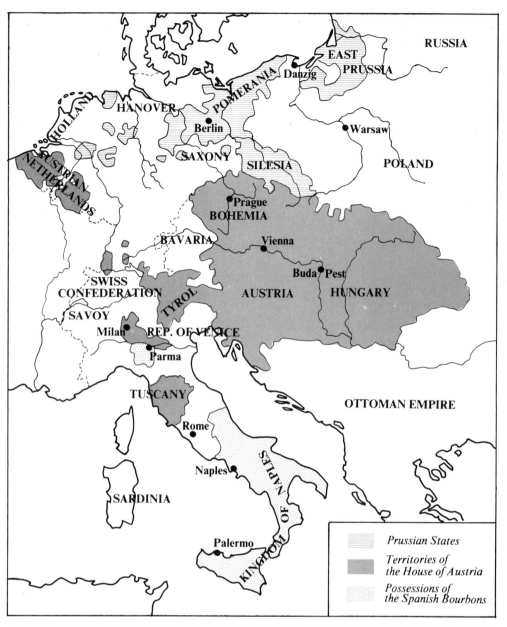

protection was the mixed army of British, Hanoverian and hired German troops maintained by Britain in western Germany. After his victory at Rossbach (1757), Frederick never had to face a French army; the French were contained and even defeated at Crefeld (1758) and Minden (1759) by the Anglo-German force under the command of Ferdinand of Brunswick.

British policy was triumphantly successful. By 1759 France was compelled to reduce her subsidies and other commitments to Austria, while British naval and colonial victories multiplied. The 'Family Compact' between France and Spain led to Spain's entry into the war against Britain (1762) but failed to shake British maritime supremacy. The war overseas was ended by the Peace of Paris (1763), and French withdrawal from the European war, following upon that of Russia, left Austria no alternative but to make peace with Prussia at Hubertusburg (1763). Britain's colonial gains were substantial; continental Europe, after seven years of exhausting struggle, remained as it had been before the war.

Two diplomacies

After 1763, France remained in close alliance with Spain and more loosely connected with Austria; but she carefully avoided continental entanglements. Lorraine became French in 1766, and France bought a rebellious Corsica from Genoa in 1768; for the rest, she bided her time until she could revenge herself on Britain. Britain, shunned by Frederick, was unable to find a continental partner. Though they were not always fully conscious of the fact, the western European powers had few interests and no influence in central and eastern Europe.

Russia, Prussia and Austria were equally preoccupied. The Prusso-Russian alliance (1764) operated to maintain the Polish and Swedish constitutions until the question of the dissenters embroiled Russia in Poland and led her into war with Turkey. While Gustavus III seized the opportunity to reestablish absolutism in Sweden, Austrian hostility forced Russia to forego gains in the Balkans and, with the connivance of Frederick the Great, led on to a three-way reconciliation based on the partition of Poland (1772). Russia was left free to make a highly advantageous peace with the Turks at Kutchuk-Kainardji (1774).

In the west, the American War of Independence (1775–83) enabled France and Spain, at last unhindered by continental commitments, to take their revenge on Britain. The thirteen colonies became independent, and Britain ceded some of her colonies to France and Spain. In Europe, the British navy was defeated in the Mediterranean and Minorca was lost; but a Franco-Spanish force failed to capture Gibraltar. The other powers were not involved, though Catherine II organized the League of Armed Neutrality (1780) to

Left, a firework display in London in 1763 given to celebrate the end of the Seven Years War; all the important gains made by Britain during the war were in India and America rather than in Europe.

Opposite top, central Europe in the early eighteenth century; the main areas disputed in the wars of the time were Italy and Poland.

Opposite bottom, the Battle of Minden in 1759, at which the English and Hanovarians defeated the French; the illustration demonstrates the reliance on troops of men marching around the battlefield in an attempt to outmanoeuvre the enemy.

oppose the British practice of searching neutral vessels on the high seas.

The resurrection of Austrian ambitions in central Europe prompted France to diplomatic if not military activity. Austrian claims to Bavaria provoked a brief and half-hearted Austro-Prussian war (1778–9) and aroused the hostility of France, which had no wish to see the Austrian border expand westwards. Completely isolated, Austria was forced to back down.

Joseph II continued the Austrian forward policy and, since Prussian hostility was inevitable and French friendship had been found wanting, allied with Russia (1781). But whereas Joseph wanted Russian backing in central Europe, Catherine viewed Austria as an ally against the Turks. Catherine got the best of the bargain: Austrian diplomatic pressure enabled Russia to annex the Crimea without difficulty (1783), but Russian help for Austria never went beyond verbal support. Joseph failed to compel Dutch agreement to the opening of the Scheldt and was equally unsuccessful in his scheme to exchange the Austrian Netherlands for Bavaria. France opposed both schemes, and Frederick the Great was able to crown his career by organizing a League of German Princes (1785) which effectively quashed the Bavarian project.

Into the age of revolutions

In the late 1780s two of the great powers were in a state of collapse. France was paralysed by the chronic financial difficulties of the crown and the violent opposition of the privileged classes to any kind of reform, Austria by military disaster against the Turks and rebellions in Hungary and the Austrian Netherlands.

The other powers took surprisingly little advantage of this situation, though Prussia, backed by Britain, did break the pro-French party in Holland (1787), which then joined a Prusso-British alliance (1788). Surprisingly Prussia let slip the opportunity of crippling or even destroying Austria, and Leopold II was able to make peace with the Turks and put his house in order.

Russia brought her war with the Turks (1787–92) to a victorious conclusion, despite a Swedish declaration of war. The hostility of other powers towards the Russian advance proved ineffective. Britain's prime minister, the younger Pitt, protested at the Russian seizure of Ochakov, thought about sending an ultimatum and then changed his mind. Eastern Europe remained the preserve of Russia, Prussia and Austria, with Russia very much the leader.

This was confirmed by the second and third partitions of Poland, the most enduring effect of which was to make the three great eastern powers partners in crime. Whatever their differences, they had a shared interest in holding down the Poles. The post-Napoleonic Holy Alliance was already prefigured and was to last in one form or another until the late nineteenth century. So, as we have seen, was the Eastern Question, posed by the decline of Turkey.

Elsewhere in Europe, diplomacy was dominated by a new phenomenon—the French Revolution, which ushered in a new age of ideological conflicts, created new diplomatic patterns and, in power-political terms, enabled France to reorganize her resources and resume her primacy in Europe.

Chapter 20

England in the Eighteenth Century

The eighteenth century saw the culmination of the great Anglo-French struggle for colonial empire. The outcome was profoundly affected by the domestic history of each country during the same period. France had undoubtedly greater resources, and both nations saw a large influx of commercial wealth. But whereas the British adapted their institutions to utilize such riches, the French were continually straining within the archaic straitjacket of the *ancien régime*. The result was that the most remarkable event of the century in each country was a revolution, but whereas the British upheaval was industrial that of the French was political. The French Revolution ultimately released the long-constrained energies of that nation, but by 1789 Britain had already won the duel for empire and had established an ever-growing hegemony of the world outside Europe.

The Glorious Revolution

On 5 November 1688 William of Orange landed in England, and a month and a half later King James II wisely fled the country. An observer of the time might have thought these occurrences were typical of the English. For over a generation, England had appeared to be one of the most unstable states in Europe. One king had been executed and another driven from his throne. The country had lurched wildly from monarchy to republic and back to monarchy again. A great civil war had been fought. It was anything but clear in 1688 that this chaotic phase was over, but it had in fact passed for ever. The next era would be one of great political stability compared with other nations. During this period, the English would show a positive genius for the creation and sensible use of their national wealth. Internal peace and orderly government would allow the nation to develop commerce, extend its empire and defeat its largest imperial rival, France. The wealth so accumulated would then be ploughed into manufacturing to create the Industrial Revolution. Thus England would eventually transform the world in a way that no single nation has ever done again.

The English accepted their new ruler with some misgiving. Though a Protestant the lean and tubercular Dutchman was not much more attractive personally than his predecessor. The best thing about him was his wife Mary, who at least was of pure Stuart lineage. They were to reign together as William III and Mary II.

As it was felt necessary to bridle somewhat the powers of the monarchy, the two new rulers did not ascend the throne without conditions. Before their arrival, a convention had met and produced a declaration of rights which was later converted into the Bill of Rights. By this it was maintained that parliament should be called frequently, while William was deprived of the power to maintain a standing army in time of peace on his own authority.

To all this the king agreed. Of course his freedom of action was somewhat limited, but then so was his interest. William was a constructive monomaniac. The sole driving passion of his life was his hatred of France. But at least this was not simply an empty obsession, rather he saw more clearly than others the magnitude of the threat to Europe of French hegemony. For aid against France he was willing to sacrifice some of his powers as a domestic monarch.

So England entered the War of the League of Augsburg which was waged until 1697. Despite few victories and many defeats, the great confederacy of European nations that William had scraped together was ultimately successful in curbing the expansionist activities of Louis XIV. Yet Englishmen at home became dissatisfied. They did not see the need for the fighting in quite the same lucid clarity as did their leader, and it certainly brought little in the way of glory. True, William decisively trounced James II in the Battle of the Boyne when the latter landed in Ireland, but the country was beginning to get restive.

William did little to counteract the growing mood of disenchantment with himself. Though he was willing perforce to share some of his power with parliament, he did his best to avoid placing much of it in the hands of a single political party. This annoyed the Whigs, who had done most to bring him to power. Between 1694 and 1698, in control of parliament, they forced themselves upon him, but their own avarice for power and place soon made them much disliked, while the king's popularity also continued to decline, especially after the death of Queen Mary in 1694.

More and more, politics fell into a state of confusion, and more and more political leaders began opening up secret correspondence with James, 'the king across the water'. By the time of the election of 1698, James II was hoping to return to his country not by conquest but as a result of dutiful recall by his loyal subjects. The election itself brought heavy gains for the Tories, led by the shrewd and devious Robert Harley, and these were pushed further in the election of 1700. Then, as the

House of Commons became more resolutely hostile to the king, the succession problem created yet another crisis. William and Mary had left no offspring, and all the many children of the heir apparent, the Princess Anne, had died. This necessitated an Act of Settlement, which stated that in the event of both William and Anne dying without heirs the throne was to pass to a member of the Protestant ruling family in Hanover, which was related to the Stuart house by marriage.

Meanwhile, in Europe, the dynastic ambitions of Louis XIV and the imbecility of the dying King Charles II of Spain had created a situation which raised the spectre of a future in which the mighty empires of both France and Spain would be ruled by a single monarch. In order to forestall this, William began laboriously to construct a new grand alliance, which was completed in September of 1701. In England the idea of a new war brought great consternation, but Louis XIV managed to play directly into the hands of his enemies. When James II died a few days after the alliance was negotiated, Louis stupidly recognized James' son, the 'Old Pretender' as King James III of England. This ended divisions in the country completely. And when William III died a few months later, the country cheerfully embarked on the war he had begun under the leadership of its new sovereign, Anne, and her general, John Churchill, Duke of Marlborough.

War costs money. Between 1688 and 1815, England was to fight no less than five colossal wars with her great enemy, France. The ultimate success of the British was owing in no small measure to the fact that in the very first of these conflicts they developed sophisticated methods of finance. King William's War of the Grand Alliance placed immense strains on the nation, but British business proved equal to the occasion. The most important expedient devised was the Bank of England. The new bank raised £1,200,000 from the public in twelve days and loaned it to the government at eight percent. So long as the interest was paid annually, the original loan was allowed to remain, and thus the National Debt came into being. The bank was incorporated and allowed to issue notes, although not at first as legal tender. Despite an early run on it, and a moratorium, the bank survived, prospered and was able to declare a dividend of twenty percent after the war. It proved to be one of the most important steps in England's march to world empire.

Whigs and Tories

The reign of the homely and rather inept Queen Anne was both enhanced and dominated by the War of the Spanish Succession, marked by the incomparable victories of the Duke of Marlborough. During the period domestic policies were noted for strife between the Whigs and the Tories, which

rose and fell in bitterness erratically, reflecting the fortunes of the war itself. At the beginning, however, the nation was united and led by a coalition government headed by the two great non-party ministers, Lord Godolphin and Marlborough himself. Behind the scenes the queen was greatly influenced by her intense friendship with the Whiggish Sarah, Duchess of Marlborough, though Anne's own bias lay towards the Tories, principally because of her love of the Church of England in its High Church form.

It did not take long for the early harmony to disappear, and discord erupted between the Tory-controlled House of Commons and the Whig-controlled House of Lords as early as 1702.

The high Tories now became more and more critical of the conduct of the war, but this proved to be a disastrously wrong move. Soon the Duke of Marlborough was winning victories of greater magnitude than the English had enjoyed for over a hundred years. The country was swept with patriotic ardour, and in the election of 1705 both the Whigs and a group of Tories—led by the too-clever Harley—who supported the ministry made substantial gains. For the next four years the Whigs steadily increased their position but at the same time managed thoroughly to overplay their hand. Their arrogant pursuit of power alienated the queen, who was also beginning to tire of the Duchess of Marlborough. In 1707 Abigail Masham, a relative of Harley's, began to replace Sarah in Anne's favour. This lured Harley himself into making a premature coup to secure the dismissal of Lord Godolphin. But Marlborough's threat of resignation temporarily ended the matter, and it was Harley himself who resigned.

Nevertheless, 1709 saw the beginning of the Whig downfall. In November, a controversy over the sermon of one Dr Sacheverell led many people, including the queen herself, to feel that Godolphin and the ministry were attacking the Church. Moreover, dissatisfaction with the seemingly interminable war was now rapidly increasing. Finally, the friendship between the queen and the Duchess of Marlborough broke down completely. In 1710 Robert Harley persuaded Anne to turn out Godolphin himself. The elections held later in the year resulted in a huge Tory majority.

Above, the Duke of Marlborough at the Battle of Malplaquet in 1709; despite this and other victories, Marlborough was not able to finish the war decisively and its expense gave rise to a strong Tory opposition. National Army Museum, London.

Top, Blenheim Palace in Oxfordshire, built by John Vanbrugh in the early eighteenth century and given to the Duke of Marlborough by the English nation in gratitude for his military services against Louis XIV.

Shortly afterwards even Marlborough was curtly dismissed, and the greatest English military hero since the Middle Ages retired to Holland. Anti-war feeling was sweeping the country, and the queen now created twelve Tory peers, to give that party control of both Houses of Parliament. After long negotiations, the Peace of Utrecht was signed in April 1713.

Yet the Tory triumph was to be a brief one. In December 1713 the queen became seriously ill and this raised the vexing problem of succession. Many Tories would have preferred to see James Stuart, the 'Old Pretender', called to the throne, and a leader of this group, the young Viscount Bolingbroke, secured the overthrow of Harley, now Earl of Oxford, on 27 July 1714. But instead of power going to Bolingbroke himself, it fell to the enigmatic Duke of Shrewsbury, a moderate Tory who gave the casting vote in support of the Hanoverian succession on the very day before Queen Anne died on 1 August.

One important aspect of her reign remains to be mentioned. The dead queen had begun by ruling over two nations and had ended by reigning over one. It had long been obvious that England and Scotland, separate kingdoms although ruled by the same monarch, must move either further apart or closer together. The English had been worried over Scottish loyalty, the Scots attracted by opportunities of participating in England's colonial empire. So, after some serious bargaining, the Scots gave up their own parliament and agreed to the Hanoverian succession. On 1 May 1707 the Act of Union was settled, and both Scotland and England merged into the United Kingdom of Great Britain.

George I

George Lewis, Elector of Hanover, the gross, concupiscent and somewhat vicious man who had become king of Great Britain, arrived in the country in September 1714. His reign was to mark something of a decline in the effective powers of the monarchy. It was not that any constitutional changes took place or that the new king was uninterested in British politics. But he was absent in Hanover for long periods, and he did not have the mentality to grasp the structure of the British system sufficiently to manipulate it. His accession to power, however, was remarkably uneventful, owing to the good management of Shrewsbury.

One thing that became rapidly clear was that the day of the Tories was over. Those who had any dealing with the Stuarts were brutally snubbed; even those who had not, like Shrewsbury, soon faded away. The Tory downfall was completed when Bolingbroke and the Duke of Ormonde fled to France and joined the court of the Old Pretender. This resulted in the abortive and mismanaged Scottish rebellion of 1715, after which most Tories seemed tainted with Jacobitism.

The hour of the Whigs had therefore arrived and was soon confirmed by their resounding election victory in 1715. Who would lead them? The man who quickly shouldered his way to the top was Marlborough's former general, Lord Stanhope. Stanhope's principal policy was to restore Britain's proper position in Europe after the diplomatic isolation which had arisen from the Peace of Utrecht, when Harley's Tory administration had abandoned the nation's allies in its indecent haste to end the war. In the next six years Stanhope worked towards this end, conducting a brilliant diplomacy.

But dissensions soon appeared within the Whig Party itself. Robert Walpole, the able chancellor of the exchequer, backed by Viscount Townshend, was intent on economy. The Earl of Sunderland supported Stanhope, whose diplomacy, with its expensive subsidies to various continental nations, was costly. The two factions had more or less fought each other to a draw when the whole country was rocked by the famous South Sea Bubble crisis. In 1720 the South Sea Company came up with a plausible proposal to take over the whole of the National Debt on remarkably favourable terms. This was eagerly accepted by Sunderland and resulted in a wild rise in the value of the company's shares, which had increased by 1,000 per cent in August of 1720. Then the inevitable reaction set in; the shares slumped, and thousands of people were ruined. A storm of indignation broke over the government, with charges of bribery and corruption. Walpole, who had earlier established public financial confidence with a sinking fund, was hastily called in to save the situation. He did his work well. By December 1720 parliament had accepted his schemes for reform and Walpole's prestige rose immensely. Then, at the same juncture, his rivals miraculously disappeared. Stanhope dropped dead during a debate in the House of Lords, and Sunderland, too, died shortly afterwards. Walpole and Townshend emerged supreme. The result was to be forty years of remarkably stable government.

Walpole and the supremacy of the Whigs

Robert Walpole was a man of great ability and a remarkable judge of character. He was also very greedy. Yet the greed of the new 'prime minister' (as Walpole was coming to be called)—especially his greed for power —would ultimately be to the nation's benefit, for Walpole wished to exercise his power in the directions in which he was most talented—those of finance and of building commercial prosperity. Fortunately, there was possibly no period in Britain's history when such talents could

bring greater national rewards.

It has been said that Sir Robert could never brook a rival and surrounded himself with mediocrities. This assertion is only half true. Certainly, he eliminated his rivals. Together, Walpole and Townshend managed to outmanoeuvre Lord Carteret, the last and most brilliant leader of Stanhope's faction, and edge him out of the government. But even Townshend, Walpole's brother-in-law and confederate, was deemed too much of a threat and was forced to resign in 1730. On the other hand, Walpole's 'friends'—Harrington, Hardwicke and especially the brothers Pelham, Henry and Thomas, Duke of Newcastle—were scarcely nonentities. Rather they were formidable men, but with limited capacity for leadership. Therefore they could greatly assist Walpole but were unable to challenge his own position until he was greatly past his prime.

Nevertheless, although Walpole swiftly emasculated his rivals, a strong opposition of Tories and discontented Whigs always dogged his footsteps. To these were eventually added the formidable talents of Bolingbroke, who had finally forsaken his Jacobitism and returned to England. Yet, for all of this, Walpole was able to keep his position intact for nearly twenty years. Not only did he usually have a parliamentary majority in his pocket but he also had the support of the monarchs. George I came to rely upon him; so did George II, while the latter's wife, Queen Caroline, proved to be the staunchest of all his many adherents.

Walpole also played parliament and Crown off against each other. The usually sound majority for Walpole in parliament was really the creation of the Duke of Newcastle. Newcastle was a dithering, eccentric and neurotic man, who lived in a state of constant agitation, often bordering on panic. But he possessed shrewd common

sense and made political patronage into a fine art. He was the man who knew everybody in all the constituencies, understood where money was to be applied in order to win elections and forced every civil servant in however minor a position to support the government with his votes and influence or forfeit his job. Even so, Walpole's hold on parliament sometimes failed, and on these occasions he was quite willing to use against it the considerable powers of the Crown—powers which George II did not have the skill to use in his own right.

Thus was set the pattern of politics for a long time to come. A Whig government, consistently but impotently opposed by the Tories, but occasionally in danger from other Whig factions which rose and fell around outstanding personalities and orators. Of course, parliament was the old unreformed parliament in which the House of Commons suffered from a proliferation of 'pocket boroughs', where the electorate was controlled by some landed magnate, and of 'rotten boroughs' which returned members although the constituencies contained no real electorate. It represented the lower classes hardly at all and even the upper classes most unevenly. Nor did representation even remotely relate to distribution of population. Yet, despite its peculiar nature, the British legislature was far more responsive to the wishes of the nation as a whole than that of any other European country. When Britain fell on more evil days in the reign of George III, a demand arose to reform its basic institutions; but in the mid-eighteenth century parliament's prestige was high, perhaps the highest it has ever been.

Under Walpole, the system certainly managed to work to the nation's benefit. Striving to maintain peace abroad, in domestic affairs he reformed the system of taxation, reduced the National Debt and

Above, George II (reigned 1727–60); he was a strong supporter of Walpole's government. National Portrait Galley, London.

Top, the Battle of Culloden in 1746, at which the English destroyed the supporters of Bonnie Prince Charlie and which led to permanent Scottish subjugation to English rule.

Top left, Robert Walpole (1676–1742), the leader of the Whigs in parliament and the king's first minister between 1721 and 1742. His control over the government was exerted through a cabinet of colleagues and relied more on his power in parliament than on the support of the king. National Portrait Gallery, London.

Opposite left, Queen Anne (reigned 1702–14) accepting the Articles of Union of the kingdoms of Scotland and England in 1707.

Opposite right, George I of England (reigned 1714–27), also Elector of Hanover, made king according to the Act of Settlement which was intended to bar the Stuarts from the throne. George himself was scarcely interested in England, but his Protestantism made him acceptable to most, and the Tory party, which supported the Stuarts, was eclipsed on his accession. Royal Collection.

increased commercial prosperity. He did suffer some defeats, notably his failure to impose an excise tax in 1733, but on the whole his long ministry succeeded in transforming the national outlook. By the time he retired, the political realities of the not so distant past—religious controversies, battle to the death between Whigs and Tories, the putting up and the casting down of kings, the possibility of great civil wars—seemed like memories of a bygone age. Perhaps the greatest tribute to his ministry occurred in the year of his death, when Charles Edward Stuart, the 'Young Pretender' landed in Scotland in the hope of capturing the throne for his father. Backward Scottish Highlanders would rally in numbers to the romantic banners of Bonnie Prince Charlie; the English would have none of him—to them he represented danger and the return of pointless strife.

After 1733 it became increasingly clear that Walpole's power was declining. With growing age, he began to lose his grip, and at the same time his enemies were waxing stronger. Eventually, even Walpole's friends were beginning to have their doubts. The crisis came in 1739 with the outbreak of the War of Jenkin's Ear against Spain. Walpole wished to avoid it, but the nation's mood was strongly bellicose and he was pushed aside.

Sir Robert's departure was followed by some turmoil. The brilliant Carteret succeeded him, but the miseries and failures of the war increased and Carteret, too, was turned out of office.

Yet no sooner had Carteret been removed than the nation had to reckon with rebellion and invasion. In 1745 Bonnie Prince Charlie landed in Scotland; the Highlands rallied to him and he had soon captured Edinburgh. But the 'Forty-five' was a forlorn hope without English support and this was not forthcoming. The invasion of England failed and King George's son, the Duke of Cumberland, slaughtered the Scottish army in the Battle of Culloden. The Highlands were ruthlessly scourged and subdued, and Charles Edward fled the country never to return again.

Meanwhile, Walpole's friends were re-establishing their power, and Henry Pelham, a sort of diminutive Walpole, now stepped firmly into the shoes of his great predecessor. It was natural that the Pelhams should wish to carry on Walpole's system, but one might wonder why the nation would want such uninspired leadership. Walpole's government without Walpole somewhat resembled an orchestra without a conductor. Yet somehow the brilliant alternatives to him in the House of Commons seemed dangerous. The orchestra, therefore, was willing to try to continue under the leader, so to speak, and Henry Pelham provided a sound, if dull, administration until his death in 1754, and then Newcastle himself carried on. But colonial conflicts

were already beginning to involve the country in yet another war. And when that, too, began to go badly, the foundations of the old system began to shake. It was then that the king called William Pitt to take command.

Methodism

John Wesley was born in 1703, the son of a Church of England clergyman. Oppressed by a deep sense of sin, he entered the Church himself but found little solace there until 1738, when he underwent a deep mystical experience. From this he emerged preaching the necessity of every individual to attain a personal and highly emotional relationship with Jesus Christ, his Saviour. Wesley never intended to break from the Established Church but hoped to transform it. The Church, however, resisted him bitterly, and connections were finally severed in 1784.

In the intervening years, Wesley had uncovered a dark facet of English life which had remained unremarked. Following its victory over the Puritans, the Church of England had more and more lost contact with the lower classes of the nation. The souls of the ordinary people were truly a house swept and garnished and now dominated by a massive purposelessness which so often found its outlet in gambling, cheap gin and in the more brutal sports of the day, such as cock-fighting and bear-baiting.

Preaching a violent mixture of damnation and salvation, the Wesleyan movement swept through England and indeed on to America. The Methodists were drawn from the poor but were extremely well organized, and in fact Wesley had without knowing it constructed a machine of great revolutionary potential. But it was not to be used for revolutionary purposes; Wesley had no wish to overthrow existing institutions. Nevertheless by the time he died Wesley and his God had enabled hundreds of thousands of people to find a vital core of meaning to their existence which had been lacking hitherto.

Wesleyan Methodism was but one of the illustrations of the growth and ferment in

Above, a cartoon of gamblers in The Hazard Room *by Thomas Rowlandson (1756–1827), done in about 1729. Victoria and Albert Museum, London.*

Left, a cartoon of stockjobbers by William Hogarth (1697–1764); the early eighteenth century was an age of commercial investment and saw several scandals, such as the South Sea Bubble in 1720. Guildhall Art Gallery, London.

Opposite, John Wesley (1703–91), the English evangelical preacher. He was opposed by the Church of England and set up the Methodist Church, gaining widespread support in the industrial regions of the north and of Wales. National Portrait Gallery, London.

the society that lay behind the stately facade of Georgian politics. From about 5,500,000 at the beginning of the century, the population of the country had risen to about 9,000,000 at the end. Throughout the century the majority of the people remained rural, but London, the largest city in Europe, doubled its population to over a million in the same period. Similarly, the seaport towns of Bristol and Liverpool began their remarkable rise in size and prosperity with the growth of colonial commerce, especially the slave trade. Moreover, the face of the land was changing and more people were being driven to the towns. New ideas about agriculture and stock raising led to much larger farms; commons and waste lands were enclosed, and many small farmers were forced to become agricultural labourers or to seek different work in the towns.

There was also much influx and change on the intellectual scene. Sir Isaac Newton, the nation's greatest scientist, died in 1727 after profoundly changing the whole of man's picture of the universe. Locke, Hume, Gibbon and Adam Smith extended the fields of philosophy, history and political economy. The fine arts boasted a galaxy of great names from Reynolds to Hogarth. Literature enjoyed a splendid age, and the century that opened with the acerbic satire of Swift and Pope closed as Jane Austen was beginning to write.

Behind all this lay the rising wealth of the commercial revolution which preceded the industrial one. Commerce in eighteenth-century England laboured under many hindrances, but from Walpole onwards England was blessed by a series of governments that put the increase of the nation's wealth before everything else. This dominance of the profit motive affected everything—commerce itself, agriculture, industry and also the institution of war.

Throughout the first half of the century agriculture and industry were moderately prosperous. They would become more so once it was demonstrated how more money could be made from them. For the moment, however, the best investment was trade and commerce, and it was there that the national energies were directed. Britain's trade was

increasingly colonial. The mercantile system had apparently paid off; the East India Company, the great consumer market in America, the African slave trade, above all, the sugar, rum and molasses trade of the West Indies—these all filled the nation's coffers.

Commerce also greatly affected British warfare. In an old Scottish folk song the English commander, Sir John Cope, challenged Bonnie Prince Charlie to battle with the words: 'I'll larn you the arts o' war.' On this occasion, Sir John was swiftly defeated. Nevertheless, despite this and dozens of other exceptions, Britain had a great deal to teach the Continental dynasts (of whom Charles Edward Stuart was a representative) about methods of waging war in the mercantile age. Of course the country was helped by its insular position, which meant that more concentration could be placed on the navy than on the army. Armies were expensive and their officers often incompetent. The navy was also expensive, but its value in relation to the greatest single producer of wealth that Britain had—the merchant marine—was indisputable. Britain could let other nations fight on the continent, while her navy swept

the commerce of her enemies from the sea and gobbled up their colonies. Of course, all this required qualities of leadership in which British governments were often sadly lacking. But when good management was available, as when the elder Pitt was directing affairs, half the world could be brought within Britain's grasp.

Pitt and George III

The political upheaval which marked the end of the long era of Walpole-Pelham domination is associated with the names of two men—William Pitt the Elder and George III. These two had much in common; both were naively idealistic, both hated parties and party politics; Pitt was mentally ill, and in the king's later days his mental faculties were gravely impaired.

Pitt, the member of a family which had made its fortune in the East India trade, naturally thought in commercial and colonial terms. He saw clearly that it was by concentrating on these spheres that the country might triumph in its great conflict with France. But he was too brilliant, too aloof, too erratic; indeed, any man who could say, 'I know that I can save the

country and that I alone can', must have been either a genius or a madman, and there was undoubtedly something of both in this remarkable man. It was only the disasters at the beginning of the Seven Years War that resulted in his call to high office. But when Pitt was lucid he saw much further than most people. A war-winning combination was quickly worked out—Newcastle kept matters quiet at home, while Pitt directed the conflict abroad. Soon the church bells of London were ringing for victory with a happy frequency.

In 1760, however, George II died, and the young and inexperienced George III ascended the throne. George, encouraged by his tutor, the Earle of Bute, had long looked forward to the day when he could rid the country of the greedy, self-seeking, corrupt men whom he thought were running it. In this group he included Pitt, since the latter was now collaborating with Newcastle. For the moment he did nothing but bring Bute into the ministry, but soon both Pitt and Newcastle were turned out. The king then called in Henry Fox to handle the grosser side of politics, and Fox forced all Newcastle's adherents throughout the land, from the highest to the lowest, either

John Wilkes Esq.r

Drawn from the Life and Etch'd in Aquafortis by Will.m Hogarth,

Price 1 Shilling. Publish'd according to Act of Parliament May y.e 16. 1763.

Left, John Wilkes (1727–97), the English reformer who criticized the king in a newspaper and whose expulsion from the House of Commons three times led to popular demonstrations on his behalf in London. His case accentuated the differences between the ruling faction and the mood of the country in the 1760s.

Opposite, The Election *by William Hogarth satirizes the effects of public elections and blatant bribery by the various factions. But relatively few elections were contested in mid-eighteenth-century England, especially in the county seats and the pocket or rotten boroughs. Sir John Soane's Museum, London.*

to support the new ministry or to forfeit their positions.

This 'massacre of the Pelhamite innocents' destroyed Newcastle's power, but it did not help the king much. Bute soon found that he lacked the resolution to remain prime minister; Fox did not have the ambition and the king was left alone. Nor could he get Pitt and Newcastle back again—they were estranged from one another and would not cooperate. For ten years there was great political instability marked by rapidly changing ministries. During this period the storm which was to rob Britain of much of her American empire was steadily growing.

Wilkes and Lord North

It was in 1770, with the emergence of Lord North as prime minister, that the country once again saw strong and stable government. Moreover, George III had at last learned, as neither of his predecessors had, how a king could still play a predominant role in British politics by building up his own party in parliament. Much of Lord North's support came not from the old Whig factions, but from a new group, the 'King's friends', who were willing to vote for the ministry that the king himself supported. But such halcyon days for king and parliament were not destined to last for long.

Even before North came to power, John Wilkes was challenging the whole system. Wilkes was a rather unsavoury character who nonetheless managed to leave important landmarks on the road to individual and national political liberty. Starting with criticisms about the Peace of Paris which ended the Seven Years War in 1763, over the next decade Wilkes, by his fierce audacity, managed to provoke a series of governments into persecuting him in ways that were sometimes constitutional, sometimes unconstitutional, but generally rash. Always fighting back, whether in jail, the law courts or in parliament, Wilkes not only established some fundamental principles of justice but also heaped great disrepute on several governments and on the whole unreformed system of parliament itself.

The Wilkes debacle was soon followed by the wars of the American Revolution, during which the ineptitude of government by the king and Lord North became increasingly evident. There were many triumphs and defeats for the ministry along this long road, but by 1783 the country was in desperate straits, fighting not only its own colonists but also France, Spain and Holland as well, and it had temporarily lost the vital command of the seas. In that year, the king's system collapsed, the Treasury benches were stormed, Lord North was driven from power and replaced as prime minister by the Marquis of Rockingham, an old associate of the now deceased Duke of Newcastle.

For the moment, however, it did not seem as though any national regeneration had taken place. Although some good work was done, notably Edmund Burke's reform of the Civil Service, a period of ministerial instability returned which culminated in the assumption of power by the cynical political coalition formed by Lord North and his arch-rival, Charles James Fox.

George III was by now quite distracted. Where could he find an honest man? The one he finally produced was the second William Pitt, the younger son of the former great minister. The king had chosen well. Only twenty-four years of age, Pitt, with one brief interruption, would rule the country until his death. At first he was in a minority in parliament, but in 1784 he won a great election victory. Pitt then set to work quickly, but many of his more important measures were forced into abeyance by the next great storm that broke over the country. In 1789, the French Revolution began. This not only profoundly altered politics within Britain itself but meant that once more the country would have to enter into another long struggle for

survival. When the Revolutionary and Napoleonic Wars finally ended, so did the world of the eighteenth century. The age of Walpole, the Pelhams, the Pitts and the Foxes had dissolved, and the era of Grey and Peel, of Gladstone and Disraeli, was about to begin.

The New Jerusalem

The closing years of this period saw the start of the most important changes ever to take place in Britain and perhaps in any other country. The colonial-commercial revolution of the early part of the century was followed, after 1760, by the beginning of the Industrial Revolution. Why this happened is a very complex question, and there were many contributory factors, such as the abundance of coal and the cheapness of water transportation within Britain itself. Basically it was a question of wealth; of having the wealth and of knowing how to use it. Above all, British business men saw industrial production as a better way of making money than such things as floating loans to governments or purchasing offices. Moreover, the British government supported

them wholeheartedly in this, and, unlike those of other nations, the upper classes did not despise investment in commerce and industry. For a hundred years the country had accumulated wealth through commerce, and commerce pointed in directions where more wealth could be made. For instance, if you were shipping Indian-made textiles from Britain for sale in Africa or the West Indies, it did not take much sense to understand that it would be a great saving to ship them directly from England and that immense profits might be made by any Englishman who could devise means of manufacturing textiles as cheaply and as efficiently as the Indians. Small wonder, therefore, that the capital was found to back the series of inventions that revolutionized the British textile industry in the eighteenth century. And, of course, once the Industrial Revolution began to gather momentum, invention begat invention. Soon Britain was well on the road to the new world of vastly increased industrial production and material prosperity as well as that of sweated workshops and child labour. In 1789, these unfamiliar and undreamed of horrors and benefits lay just beyond the horizon.

Chapter 21

The Reign of Louis XV

'I am leaving you, but the state will always remain.' So spoke Louis XIV, the grand monarch, on his death-bed. But would it? Cardinals Richelieu and Mazarin and King Louis himself had certainly created the most formidable nation in Europe. The terrible divisive elements of former centuries had been dissolved; the religious wars had ended, the power of the great nobles had been broken and the aristocracy as a whole reduced to impotence. Yet much of the substance of the newly great nation had been wasted on Louis' own wars and in the expulsion of the Huguenots. Despite the administrative centralization, a sound financial structure had not been achieved and the taxes were still concentrated on the poorer parts of the community. Nevertheless, there was still much to be optimistic about in 1715. The disastrous War of the Spanish Succession had not ended nearly as badly as might have been expected. The confused aims of the allies, a last victory by Marshal Villars, a skilful negotiation of the peace treaty had kept losses to a minimum at the treaties of Utrecht. France had been weakened but was undoubtedly still the most populous and the greatest power in Europe. The most urgent problem was that of the succession. The quality of absolute monarchies necessarily depends on the character of the monarch. The new king was a child of five.

Regency and *Polysynodie*

The extreme youth of Louis XV required a regency, and by custom the regent would be the man next in succession to the throne. This meant that power would fall into the hands of Philip, the Duke of Orléans, a man of many accomplishments and of good political sense. But Philip was also a person whose private life was marked by impiety and a total disregard of the obligations of his rank: he lived in the midst of a vast bevy of loose women and degenerates who staggered through an endless series of orgies and gargantuan drinking bouts in the fashionable underworld of Paris.

The old king had cordially detested Philip and in his will had attempted to reduce the regent to a cipher. Real power was to reside in a council made up of the royal bastards—Louis' sons by the Marquise de Montespan. But the nobility, long wearied by monarchial absolutism, looked to Philip as their champion and helped him to free himself from the dead hand of Louis XIV. All turned to the *parlements* as the repository of the French constitution. The *parlements*, basically aristocratic law courts (and not to be confused with the English parliament, the French equivalent of which was the Estates General), had kept their authority intact in theory under the grand monarch by not exercising it in practice, but they, too, now hoped that their hour had come. The dead king's will was duly and swiftly quashed.

Philip soon made other changes as well. The court was moved from Versailles to

Above, Philip, Duke of Orleans who acted as a regent during the minority of Louis XV and who attempted to restore the French economy by traditional means.

Opposite, William Pitt the Younger (1759–1806), the British Prime Minister whose ministries of 1783–1801 and 1804–06 saw Britain's development into the first industrial nation.

Paris, where the nobles would be more comfortable and the regent more free to indulge his tastes. Next came a major administrative reform. The nobility, who had placed Philip in real power, hoped he would dismantle the structure of royal absolutism. The regent's answer was the creation of the *Polysynodie*. Instead of the old system where all business was conducted by the king through his secretaries, a new organization came into being consisting of six councils, staffed largely by nobles. But the foundations of royal government, arduously created by Louis XIV, were not to be cracked so easily. After a generation in which they had been allowed to devote themselves only to war, the conduct of their own states and the petty intrigues of Versailles, the nobles found themselves unfit for anything else. They were unable to govern, and consequently government nearly came to a halt. The *Polysynodie* was about as bad a failure as it could have been. It was abolished, unlamented, in 1718.

Yet somebody had to govern. It was clear that the regent, preoccupied as he was with sex, wine and the nature of the universe, already had enough to do. But Philip did have a certain grasp of the problems of his country as well as a mind that was totally untrammelled by orthodox modes of thinking. When a young Scottish adventurer whom he had met in one of his nightly escapades announced that he could cure the ills of France, the regent paid attention.

In retrospect the career of John Law, emerging from a gambling den, briefly taking over the whole economy of France, then fleeing to Britain leaving ruin and disgrace behind him, seems like some monstrous sort of a confidence trick. Yet Law had real insight into some of the problems of the day. The main point, he realized, was that true national wealth depended on population and production. Money should not be an end in itself but merely a means of exchange to promote trade. France, without adequate credit facilities, could be outrun by lesser states like Britain and Holland, which had better developed their smaller resources. His remedy was a royal bank, which would use the king's credit to print paper money, which in turn would be used to finance the exploitation and the development of all of the country's undoubted resources.

Philip, pleased with such radical ideas, gave Law encouragement, and in 1716 the Scot was authorized to establish a private bank. This proved a great success, and a year later Law obtained control of the languishing Mississippi Company with its monopoly of the trade of Louisiana. This he reorganized into the Company of the West, and within two years Law's bank became a royal bank and his company had absorbed all of the other rather derelict colonial companies dealing with the trade of Senegal, the East Indies, Africa and China. Orthodox financiers were aghast and opposed him, but Law was not to be brooked.

When the farmers general, who collected all the indirect taxes of the country, attacked him, Law outbid them and gained control of the raising of taxes himself. His rise continued with breathtaking speed. He took over the coinage of money and then assumed the national debt, asking only three percent interest. Finally, he received the office of comptroller general of finances, bringing the whole of the French economy under his direction.

Law then sketched out a programme of badly needed reform. Direct and indirect taxation was to be reorganized in a unified system. All sorts of unnecessary offices were to be abolished, capital was to be advanced to manufacturers, and a large programme of public works begun. Most important, a new tax was to be introduced that would be paid by all classes of the community and from which the nobles and the clergy were not to be exempt.

But the foundation of Law's prestige was a shaky one, and the speculative nature of the Company of the West—renamed the Company of the Indies in 1719—was to prove fatal to his programme for reform. Much of Law's success was owing to the fantastic boom of the company's shares. In fact the company had good potential and given a generation or so of hard work might have paid off handsomely. But Law's agents issued propaganda grossly misrepresenting Louisiana, which was pictured as a veritable land of gold. Share prices began to rise amazingly. By the middle of 1719, there were such wild scenes of buying in the Rue de Quincampoix in Paris that police had to clear the streets because of bloodshed, while the shares were inflated to forty times their face value. This could not continue, given the discrepancy between the share values and the immediate real potential of Louisiana. By 1720 a panic had begun. Law attempted to stem it by means of

a controlled deflation, but now his enemies showed themselves. The *parlement* of Paris refused to register the edict cutting the value of all notes in circulation by one-quarter. Law's empire of paper money collapsed completely, and he himself fled the country.

Law's schemes for financial reform disappeared with their projector, but the failure of the miracle worker did not mean the fall of the regent. France, even under its old system of financial mismanagement, could still manage to stagger on so long as there was peace. And this was provided by the skilful diplomacy of the Abbé du Bois, Philip's old tutor. But in 1723 the regent died; the raffish epic of society to which he had given his name perished with him, and a new era began.

Cardinal Fleury and the old regime

Philip of Orléans was succeeded as regent by the next prince of the blood, the ugly and stupid Duke of Bourbon. The latter's one action of note lay in the field of royal matrimony. It was decided that it would be for the best if the young Louis XV were to marry and produce an heir to the throne as soon as possible. Therefore, his present fiancée, the five-year-old Spanish infanta, was bundled back to her homeland to the fury of the Spanish court, and Louis was quickly married to Marie Leczinska, a daughter of the ex-King of Poland.

Bourbon shortly afterwards brought about his own downfall by attempting to remove a potential rival—André Fleury, Bishop of Fréjus, and tutor to the king. But this incident brought together Louis' two most pleasing characteristics—an eye for talent and loyalty to his friends. The sixteen-year-old king stood his ground, dismissed Bourbon and made Fleury the virtual ruler of France. Not until nearly the end of his reign did the king again exert himself so decisively and to such good effect.

When Fleury, soon to become a cardinal, assumed the reins of government, few people other than the deposed Duke of Bourbon were upset or worried. After all, the new minister was a mild and inoffensive little man and at the age of seventy-three did not seem destined to pursue the arduous labours of government for very long. In fact he soon showed himself to posses great reserves of energy, determination and political skill, and he went on ruling the country for the next thirteen years. Strongly conservative, Fleury was not temperamentally suited to undertake any of the revolutionary changes needed to revivify the ailing structure of government. But by practising honest administration at home, and by cultivating peace abroad, he could at least stop decline, and this he managed to accomplish.

In the first place, he built up a strong team of assistants and gave them the security of tenure that was necessary for them to do their work well. D'Aguesseau was made chancellor and continued the vast work of legal codification. Maurepas built up the navy, and D'Angervilliers showed much industry in his long tenure as secretary of state for war from 1728 to 1740. Orry was an orthodox and efficient comptroller general from 1730 to 1746. Owing to this remarkable period of stability in the heads of departments, and to the abilities of the men themselves, Fleury's administration marked a period of peace and prosperity—the flowering of the old regime.

Given the precarious state of French finances, the sine qua non for the success of Fleury's policy was the keeping of peace. He was fortunate in that his long term of office coincided with the rule in England of the equally pacific Sir Robert Walpole. Towards the rest of Europe, he conducted a skilful diplomacy. Yet Fleury could not always have his own way, even in France. Here, his main obstacle was the old aristocracy who still persisted in seeing their main reason for existence in getting killed or in cutting heroic figures in foreign wars. He was therefore always dogged by the war party, which in his ministry centred around Chauvelin, the keeper of the seals. Eventually the hopes of the queen's father regaining his throne allowed Chauvelin to lead the country into war in the dispute over the Polish succession in 1733.

Even then, Fleury managed to keep the campaign to a minimum, secure some diplomatic triumphs and all the while give Chauvelin enough rope to hang himself. The latter was disgraced and dismissed in 1737. The nation had another breathing space, but it was not to last for long. The decline of Walpole changed the attitude of Britain, while the bellicose young nobles of France soon found a new, stronger leader in the Count of Bellisle. When Fleury died at the age of ninety in 1743, the country had stumbled into the much more ruinous War of the Austrian Succession.

Madame de Pompadour

Cardinal Fleury was not to be replaced. Like Louis XIV on the death of Cardinal Mazarin, Louis XV determined to be his own prime minister once his old tutor had passed from the scene. Unlike Louis XIV, however, he did not have the qualifications for such a rôle. Louis was intelligent enough, but he had an almost pathological lack of faith in his own judgment. Consequently, he rarely exercised it. The result was that councils would meet, the secretaries of state and the heads of departments would argue their points of view, the king would listen to it all in silence, and then the meeting would break up and the ministers struggle on as best they could without any sort of co-ordination. In the circumstances, government lost all sense of direction.

Perhaps it was a bad conscience about his own inability to govern that led Louis

to indulge so remorselessly and so compulsively in his other two main pastimes—hunting and women. Year after year, vast numbers of slaughtered animals filled up the royal larder and a long procession of mistresses wandered in and out of the royal bedchambers. Most of the latter were quick and easy conquests, whose time in the royal favour might last only a few nights or weeks, but in 1744 a woman of different calibre appeared on the scene. Jeanne Antoinette Poisson was the daughter of a servant in one of the great French banking houses and was married to the nephew of one of the farmers general. She understood the mysteries of high finance and of many other things as well. In September of 1745 she became Louis' recognized mistress and was given the title of Marquise de Pompadour. Then something curious happened. Louis and his new beloved failed as lovers but became close friends. For a quarter of a century, first as actual, then as titular mistress, Pompadour ruled the glittering society of the court.

It is with Pompadour that the elegance of the period is associated. An exquisite beauty, she wished to be surrounded with

Above, a masked ball at Versailles in 1745; the cost of the court was becoming an expensive luxury to the stagnant French economy. Musée du Louvre, Paris.

Top right, Cardinal Fleury (1653–1743) who acted as tutor to Louis XV and who attempted to restore the French economy by more traditional means.

Top left, Maria Leszczynska, who was the daughter of the King of Poland, and who married Louis XV in 1725. Painting by Maurice Quentin de la Tour, 1748. Musée du Louvre, Paris.

Opposite, John Law (1671–1729), the Scottish financier who won the support of the Duke of Orléans in 1716 to establish a national bank of France and give widespread credit. His scheme led to a wave of speculation and subsequent financial disasters.

objets d'art, and taste became everything. Armies of craftsmen—jewellers, goldsmiths, bookmakers, makers of porcelain, furniture and tapestries—laboured to meet the inexhaustible demand of the king's great mistress. Buildings were built and gorgeously decorated, musicians and artists patronized. It used to be thought that this was the extravagance that ruined French finances and hastened the Revolution. And it is true, of course, that the lavish French court, which plumbed depths of inanity as often as it reached heights of elegance, can hardly have presented an edifying spectacle to starving French peasants. Nevertheless, the country was basically rich enough to have carried such expenditure, vast though it was, with relative ease. To discover the ills of France, it is necessary to look further than the frivolous court.

Wealth and taxation

The story of France in the eighteenth century is by no means one of continuous decline. The population was certainly increasing. By mid-century it had reached about 22,000,000, and one European in every five was French. Wealth, too, especially commercial wealth, was on the upsurge. The wars of Louis XIV had proved destructive to overseas trade. But the period of peace after 1715 and Fleury's stabilization of the currency in 1726 had made new beginnings possible. Successful French diplomacy in the Ottoman Empire brought a large upsurge of trade with the Levant. At the same time the traditional export of wine and brandy from Bordeaux to the rest of Europe continued.

The most significant part of French commercial expansion, however, was her colonial trade. While the huge areas of Canada and Louisiana did not really amount to much economically, and while her trade in India showed but modest gains, France had discovered a fountain of wealth in the West Indies. Her sugar islands, Martinique, Guadeloupe and Saint Dominguéand the trade in slaves attendant upon them, were soon employing over 500 ships a year and causing great envy to the rival West Indian power of Britain. A rise in prosperity in such ports as Marseilles, Dunkirk, Le Havre and, above all, Nantes testified to the growing opulence of overseas commerce.

So wealth certainly came into France. But what was it used for? Much found its way into the hands of the great bankers and financiers like the Paris brothers. These men, who also farmed the indirect taxes, found that their easiest profit came from loans to the king to finance wars and to meet deficits. They did not invest much in commerce, despite its potentiality.

The picture regarding industry and agriculture was even worse for, with the population increase pressing on the land, revolutions in industry and agriculture

became necessary. They did not take place. The fact that the Industrial Revolution began in Britain in the eighteenth century and not in France does not testify to the greater inventiveness of the British but rather to the fact that the British were willing to capitalize the inventions. By 1789 there were some 20,000 spinning jennies in Britain and less than 1,000 in France. French industry did improve in the eighteenth century but at a modest rate, held back by the regulations of guilds and by state control. Even worse was a system, of an almost incredible number, of hindrances on domestic trade caused by internal tolls, customs and excise dues. This system produced both armies of smugglers and armies of officials attempting to prevent smuggling. Yet all efforts to change it came up against a blank wall of vested interests.

But the most glaring abuse in old France was the system of taxation. Louis XIV had created a centralized state administratively but left it to be financed by machinery that was positively medieval. The principal tax in France was the *taille,* a relic of fuedal times that was placed on people who did not perform military service. The sum to be raised by it each year was annually determined by the Council of Finances. The *taille,* and a few other direct taxes, were supplemented by an impossibly vast and complex system of indirect taxation, the proceeds of which were gathered by the farmers general. From the direct taxes the nobility were exempt and the clergy, immensely wealthy, were nearly so. With an income of between 100 and 200 million livres a year, the Church paid out a 'free gift' of two or three millions. Nor were the taxes levied or gathered with much sense of equity. Many people, locally and nationally, could secure exemptions. It was always the poor and defenceless sections of the community that bore most of the burden.

Under such a system, the structure of

French society was clearly in danger. Yet there was a surprising quiescence throughout the land. The peasantry, vast and inarticulate, caused surprisingly little trouble. Even during the Revolution, it was moved only once to radical action. The middle classes were more powerful and hence more dangerous to the established order; but middle classes are not by nature prone to really violent revolution. The working class seemed too small to count. If the French government could have managed to stagger on without financial crises, the old regime would probably not have ended in the holocaust that it did. But for the government to make ends meet, the system of taxation had to be reformed or involvement in wars had to be absolutely avoided. Astride both of these paths stood the aristocracy. The nobles were as eager as ever for warfare, but they would not give up their privileges, which included exemption from taxation. Thus they marked out the path of their own destruction, but for them the road to hell was not paved with good intentions.

During the days of Fleury's rule, the comptroller general of finances had been Orry. The latter's methods of extreme economy had succeeded in keeping things going, but the War of the Austrian Succession proved to be too great a strain and in December of 1745 Orry was dismissed. The man picked to replace him was Machault D'Arnouville, the former intendant of Valenciennes. The appearance of this icy but rigidly honest administrator in Louis' gay court again testifies to the king's good judgement of men. Working with great energy Machault somehow managed to finance the war—using every immediate expedient he could think of. But he was not content to rest on such laurels and as soon as peace returned he began digging towards the roots of all France's problems. In 1749 he produced his solution—the *Vingtième,* a tax of one-twentieth on all income without

exception. Then, as Machault began to organize the new administrative personnel necessary to collect it, the astonished forces of reaction began to prepare their resistance.

The *parlements* and the provincial estates at first refused to register the edict of taxation. However, the king compelled them to do so. Then the clergy took the lead in opposition. The campaign they waged was so powerful that at last the king began to waver. In his court, the *dévot* Catholic party, including the king's own daughters, pushed the claims of the Church. Pompadour gave her support to Machault, but in the end the bishops triumphed. In December of 1751 Machault gave up, and all hope of financial reform was lost for the time being.

Jansenists and *parlements*

It was in the 1740s that another problem began which caused much consternation throughout the country. It commenced as a religious struggle between the Jesuits and the Jansenists and was transmuted into a political conflict between the *parlements* and the king. By the mid-eighteenth century, Jansenism, as it had existed fifty years before, had more or less died out. But the name was still used to describe those who championed the Gallican rights of the Church in France against papal authority in Rome. Opposed to these were the Jesuits and the *dévot* party in the court, which included the queen. It was in 1713 that the pope had issued the famous Bull, *Unigenitus,* condemning supposed Jansenist proportions. But it was not until 1746 that the new Archbishop of Paris, Christophe de Beaumont, took the extreme step of threatening excommunication against those who refused to accept the Bull and began forbidding the last rites to those who had not obtained a ticket of their acceptance from a priest. At this point the *parlements* objected. The French *parlements* were law courts which

also had wide police powers over various matters such as religion, trade and industry, and morals. The most important of them was the *parlement* of Paris with a jurisdiction stretching over one-third of the country. Membership in all the French *parlements* was less than 2,000. Originally recruited from middle-class lawyers, heredity and money had since become the requirements of office. By the eighteenth century, the *parlements* were a stronghold of aristocratic reaction. In fact they were more reactionary than the king himself and wished only to replace his power with their own. But the people were not fond of the Jesuits nor of the *dévot* party, and by emerging as the protectors of Gallicanism the *parlements* could hope to gain much popular support.

When the Archbishop of Paris took his position on the Bull, *Unigenitus*, the Paris *parlement* threatened to imprison priests who refused to allow confession or to give the last rites. In 1735, when sacraments were denied to a seventy-eight-year-old nun, the *parlements* even threatened to bring the archbishop to trial. At this point the king intervened. In the court, Pompadour had been supporting the Jansenists, but Louis was more influenced by the bishops and by the *dévot* party.

The king now ordered the Paris *parlement* to cease its attack on the archbishop. Instead the *parlement* replied by drawing

Above, The Oyster Luncheon, *painted in 1737 by de Troy in pre-Revolutionary France; the French nobility were more concerned with sensual pleasures, and with protecting their own privileges, than with the well-being of the country as a whole. Musée Condé, Chantilly.*

Above left, Jean Baptiste de Machault d'Arnouville (1701–94), who attempted to tax the nobility and clergy in the late 1740s to pay for the War of the Austrian Succession but who had to abandon the policy in 1751. Musée de Versailles.

Opposite, the port of Bordeaux in the eighteenth century, one of France's largest ports, particularly enriched by its association with the slave trade.

up the *grandes remonstrances* of 9 April 1753. Remonstrances were a traditional right that the *parlements* had, but they usually delivered them to the king in private. In this case, they were printed and soon sold 20,000 copies. Now the *parlements* were claiming not only to be the protectors of the Gallicans and the Jansenists but were also debating the king's absolute power, sometimes using the arguments of Montesquieu and Locke; it was claimed that the king was a constitutional monarch bound by the fundamental laws of the realm of which the *parlements* were the guardians. Soon, placards were appearing reading 'Long live the *parlement*! Death to the king and the bishops.'

The king was not certain of what to do and, bedevilled by divided counsels, he pursued a wavering course. In May 1753, he exiled the members of the Paris *parlement* to other parts of the country. A year later, he was forced to bring them back, after no one would do business in the temporary royal court. They returned to bonfires and celebrations, and public opinion was greatly aroused. The struggle continued, in a tortuous way, over the next few years, but a truce occurred in 1757 when an attempt on the king's life briefly induced moderation on both sides.

The prestige of the king, which had suffered from his battle with the *parlements,* was soon to sink still lower. In the Seven Years War, a long series of defeats, inflicted by the British and the Prussians, brought the repute of the government to its lowest ebb. The country needed some sort of a saviour and Madame de Pompadour felt she could produce one. In 1758 a friend of hers, then at the embassy in Vienna, was hastily recalled, made Duke of Choiseul and created secretary of state for foreign affairs.

The indefatigable yet lighthearted Choiseul was perhaps not as great a man as he appeared at the time, but nevertheless he quickly set to work, re-establishing some measure of royal authority and of the country's prestige. Little could be salvaged from the war, but at the Peace of Paris Choiseul did as well as could be expected. French losses were grievous but not as bad as they might have been.

If he could not save one war, Choiseul could at least prepare for victory in the future. His foreign policy was sound, shoring up the Austrian alliance and creating the Family Compact with Spain. He then began to overhaul the army, buying out and retiring many officers and placing recruitment and equipment in the hands of civil servants. The artillery was integrated within the army as a whole; the better military schools were begun. More important, he rebuilt the French navy. The number of capital ships was doubled, and naval administration as a whole was overhauled. His term of office also saw two important accessions to French territory in Europe. In 1768, Choiseul purchased

Corsica from the Republic of Genoa, suppressing the nationalist rebellion of Paoli. Two years before, Lorraine had become incorporated within France as the result of the death of Stanislaus Lesczinski, although this was really a long-term result of Fleury's foreign policy.

Although Choiseul thus strengthened the military sinews of the nation as a whole, he did not take action at home to bolster the king's authority over the *parlements*. On the contrary, he believed in the necessity of coming to terms with them and gained much of his freedom of action from his cordial relations with the Paris *parlement*. And it was during his term of office that the *parlements* finally gained their victory over their most hated enemy—the Jesuits. In Martinique, a large commercial enterprise built up by a Jesuit priest went bankrupt and the creditors obtained judgment against the Society as a whole. With truly heroic folly, the Jesuits appealed to the *parlement* of Paris. That body immediately and gleefully proclaimed the Society responsible for all the debts incurred and then set up a commission to examine and report on the Jesuit Order as a whole. As a result, the *parlement* declared against them as strongly as possible, and it was decreed in 1762 that the Society of Jesus should be suppressed.

Louis XV, inspired by the *dévots*, attempted halfheartedly to protect the Jesuits. But in the midst of the defeats of the Seven Years War, he simply did not feel strong enough to challenge the *parlements*. In the end, he consented to a royal edict which abolished the Society and confiscated all its property.

The *parlements* and the king

With the suppression of the Jesuits, the overweening pride of the *parlements* was becoming boundless. They persisted in their obstruction of all types of financial reform. Following its victory over Machault, the Paris *parlement* waged war against successive comptrollers general, while the provincial *parlements* followed its example in respect to the royal intendants. By 1763, they had managed to get one of their own members appointed as comptroller general, and all further hope of financial reforms seemed permanently lost.

Then events in Brittany took them one step further. There a controversy over who had the right to build provincial roads grew out of all proportion and resulted in the arrest of the leader of the Rennes *parlement* by the royal governor. For the first time, all the other *parlements* in the country joined together in the support of Rennes and in denunciation of an act carried out with royal authority. Soon their statements were close to denying the sovereignty of the king. But then, with unexpected determination, Louis bestirred himself and suspended the *parlement* of Rennes. In 1766, in a *lit de justice* the king appeared before the Paris *parlement*, ordered it not to concern itself with the fate of its sister at Rennes and declared: 'I am answerable to no one. In my person alone resides the sovereign's power; from me alone my courts take their existence and authority.' Even Louis XV had at least been stung to action.

Given that Louis was at last contemplating action against the *parlements*, the position of their ally, the Duke of Choiseul, was necessarily weakened. The loss of his protector, Madame de Pompadour, who died in 1764 at the age of forty, does not seem to have hurt his standing, but his violent dislike of her successor, the ravishing beauty, Madame du Barry, did. Then, in 1768, Maupeou, a man known to be hostile

Date	England	France	Europe	Date	England	France	Europe
1600	Publication of Newton's *Principia* (1687) Accession of William of Orange (III) and Mary II (1689)		Peter the Great assumes the government of Russia (1689)	1725	Death of George I. Accession of George II (1727) Founding of Methodist Society (1730)	Réamur's thermometer (1730) *Corvée* (public works) instituted by Fleury (1733)	Death of Peter the Great (1725) War of the Polish Succession (1733)
	Battle of the Boyne (1690) Death of Mary II (1694)	French take possession of Nice and Savoy (1696)	War of the League of Augsburg (1697)		War of Jenkins' Ear (1739)	French East India Company established (1735) Famine in Paris (1740)	Accession of Frederick the the Great (1740) Accession of the Empress Elizabeth (1741)
1700			Death of last Habsburg, Charles II of Spain (1700) War of the Spanish Succession (1701)		Bonnie Prince Charlie (1745)	Pompadour becomes Louis XV's mistress (1745) Machault's *vingtième* tax (1749)	
	Act of Settlement—English crown to Hanover (1701) Death of William III Accession of Anne (1702)			1750	Death of George II. Accession of George III (1760)		Seven Years War opens (1756)
	Union of England and Scotland (1707) Dismissal of Marlborough (1710) Death of Queen Anne. Accession of George I (1714)	Papal Bull *Unigenitus* (1713) Death of Louis XIV. Accession of Louis XV. Regency of Duke of Orléans (1715) John Law's Bank (1716)	Battle of Blenheim (1704) Peter the Great's defeat of Swedes at Poltava (1709) Treaty of Utrecht (1713)		Expulsion of John Wilkes from the House of Commons (1764) James Watt's steam engine (1765) Hargreaves' spinning jenny (1767) Cook's first voyage (1768) Repeal of the Stamp Act (1776)	Suppression of the Jesuits (1762) Purchase of Corsica (1768) Birth of Napoleon Bonaparte (1769) Lorraine incorporated into France. Louis XV breaks the power of the *parlements* (1770)	Death of the Empress Elizabeth. Accession of Catherine the Great (1762) Peace of Paris (1763) Jesuits expelled from Spain by Charles III (1767) Linnaeus publishes his *Systema Naturae* (1768) First Partition of Poland (1772)
	South Sea Bubble. Rise of Walpole (1720)	Collapse of Law's financial system (1720) Death of Duke of Orléans (1723)	Treaty of Amsterdam. Russia as a European power (1717) Proclamation of Russian Empire (1721) Maria Theresa named as Habsburg heiress (1723)	1775	Cook's second voyage (1772) 'Intolerable Acts' (1774)	Death of Louis XV. Accession of Louis XVI (1774)	Cossacks' Revolt under Pugachev (1774)

to the powers of the *parlements*, was made chancellor. The following year, Maupeou's friend, the Abbé Terray became comptroller general. In 1770 Choiseul clashed with the new comptroller and lost. Louis supported Terray, and Choiseul was dismissed and stripped of all his offices.

Power now passed into the hands of Maupeou, Terray and the new secretary for foreign affairs, d'Aiguillon, who became known as the triumvirate. Maupeou quickly set to work against what he clearly saw was his greatest adversary and cleverly managed to provoke the *parlement* of Paris into an open rejection of the king's authority. On Maupeou's advice, the king acted. The magistrates of the *parlement* were exiled to remote counties. Their privileges and their offices were abolished without compensation. The huge territory under the jurisdiction of the Paris *parlement* was broken up into six areas, each of which was given a new royal court.

With one swift stroke it appeared that the king and Maupeou had struck off the head of the enemy. His part in the action made the chancellor decidedly unpopular, but then an ugly, bad-tempered little man like Maupeou would hardly have expected to be loved anyway. Following his victory, he then proposed a fundamental reform of the whole judicial system of France.

The downfall of the *parlements* at last opened the way for Terray to begin the much-needed financial reforms. Machault's old edict of 1749 establishing the *vingtième* was put into operation. At the same time, Terray ironed out many of the inequalities of the taxation system and came to a new arrangement with the farmers general which increased the yield of indirect taxes. New forces were clearly at work that in a few years might have ended many of the anomalies of the old regime. Such was not

to be. In April of 1774 Louis XV contracted smallpox. A month later he was dead.

The death of Louis XV did not end all attempts at reform. Yet under his successor, a better man but a weaker king, the aristocracy and the *parlements* were able to fight back, regain their position, and once again flout all further attempts at progress. Choiseul's efforts gave France a chance for victory in the next war with Great Britain, but in winning it the French monarchy lost everything. Once again the royal finances were overwhelmed and this time there was no remedy but to summon the Estates General, a ghost that had not been seen since 1614. In doing so, the king and aristocracy raised a spectre that eventually destroyed them all.

When the corpse of Louis XV was taken to Saint Denis for burial there were few signs of mourning. No mass had been said in Paris for his recovery. At the funeral, contemptuous shouts deriding the dead king's main interests were heard: '*Voilà, the pleasure of women*' and '*Taiaut! Taiaut!*'—the French equivalent of 'tally-ho!'—were the cries. From the point of view of the ordinary people, this was not unfair. Louis had done little enough for them. But the nobility who also rejoiced should have mourned him. Had he lived, the seedy old king might have just managed to break their power—and saved them in spite of themselves.

Above, Louis XV with his sister; Louis was probably not greatly interested in solving the problem of financing the government nor with France's loss of prestige in European politics. Palazzo Pitti, Florence.

Opposite, a meeting of the Paris parlement *in 1723, known as the* lit de justice, *so-called after the seat on which the king sat to attend its official sessions. The* parlement'*s authority was primarily judicial and was limited to a small area of France. Musée du Louvre, Paris.*

Chapter 22

The Western Mediterranean and Italy

The treaties which ended the War of Spanish Succession changed the western Mediterranean in two important respects: Spain lost her predominant position in Italy to the Austrian Habsburgs, and Britain became a Mediterranean power through her acquisition of Gibraltar and Minorca. The partial re-establishment of Spanish influence in Italy (1715–48) marked the end of territorial instability, since it was followed by alliances between all the great Mediterranean land powers. War at sea, where Britain was opposed by France and Spain, continued throughout the period, but its effects on the Mediterranean lands were slight.

Stability provided an opportunity for reform, and several more or less enlightened despots duly appeared. They had to combat peculiar difficulties: the fragmentation of the Italian peninsula into numerous small states; regionalism in Italy and Spain, created by geography and history; the numbers, wealth and privileges of the clergy in the traditionally devout Mediterranean lands; and psychological and economic inertia, induced in Spaniards and Portuguese by recently vanished greatness and long dependence on silver and gold from colonies in the Americas.

Italy was already a tourist's paradise, and the high court of the English aristocrat's 'grand tour'. The pleasures of Venice and the splendours of Rome could be enjoyed in a warm climate, and the more discriminating tourist relished the art treasures in which Italy abounded. Remains of Roman antiquity were still to be seen, and the hardy and serious-minded might risk being attacked by southern brigands to visit newly excavated Pompeii and Herculaneum.

What the tourist found picturesque was merely squalid in the eyes of intelligent Italians. The gap between rich and poor was even greater than elsewhere in Europe. Crime and violence were endemic, and law-enforcement corrupt and arbitrary. Economic fragmentation, clerical privileges, the dominance of the feudal nobility in the south, all aggravated the pressure of a growing population on the resources provided by a backward agriculture.

The states ruled by Italians failed to meet the challenge. Venice lived on her great commercial past and her tourist present; her trade declined, her fleet decayed and the fabled stability of her constitution became *rigor mortis*. Genoa, like Venice, practised neutrality as the only means of survival; her forces proved inadequate to control rebellion in wild and primitive Corsica, which was sold to the French (1768). The kingdom of Sardinia-Savoy, no longer able to profit by the quarrels of France, Spain and Austria, ceased to expand, remaining in the grip of a feudal nobility governed by an intermittently despotic king. The Papal States were worse governed still; a few reforms were introduced in the eighteenth century, but popes were hardly in a position to attack clerical privileges. Only in states attached to foreign powers—the villains of the nineteenth-century drama of Italian unification—was a serious effort made to cure Italy's ills.

Habsburg and Bourbon

The Habsburgs in the north were the most successful. Under Maria Theresa and Joseph, Lombardy (as the Duchy of Milan began to be called) became the most prosperous area in Italy, largely thanks to financial reforms culminating in a fixed tax on land (1757). Many of the Austro-Bohemian reforms were later introduced in Lombardy, including the reduction and regulation of feudal obligations, the suppression of monasteries and the partial abrogation of clerical tax exemption.

In Grand Duke Leopold (later Leopold II of Austria), Tuscany had perhaps the most enlightened ruler of the age. During his twenty-five year reign (1765–90), Leopold reformed the prison system, abolished torture and the death penalty, introduced tax equality, suppressed the guilds and (without complete success) struggled to diminish clerical privileges. The army was disbanded and the entire Tuscan navy (two ships) sold to Russia. But Leopold's most important achievement was to abolish all restrictions on trade, internal and external, including the internal tolls and customs barriers that survived from the age of Italian city-states.

Naples and Sicily provided more intractable problems. The Italian south was impoverished, infertile and malarial. Vast areas had not been brought under cultivation; almost all land was owned by the nobility, the Church and the king. The nobility, backed by armed retainers, existed in a state of feudal semi-independence, wielding powers of life and death over the peasantry. The Church was enormously wealthy and, like the nobles, exempt from most taxes.

The enlightened despot was not equipped to solve a problem of this magnitude; it is by no means solved today. Under Elizabeth Farnese's son Charles and (after 1759) his minister Tanucci, some clerical abuses were remedied, feudal obligations were reduced, the number of noble retainers was limited and an attempt was made to civilize and tame the nobility. The struggle to control the Church assumed an anti-papal aspect with the expulsion of the Jesuits (1767) and Tanucci's refusal to acknowledge the vague papal overlordship of Naples. Such measures made an admirable beginning, but only a beginning; and Naples was to be denied the generations of firm and enlightened rule that alone could have given her order and prosperity.

The papacy

Even in the seventeenth century, the papacy retained a not inconsiderable influence in international affairs, and, but for Innocent XI, Austria might not have chased the Turks from Vienna. In the eighteenth century this influence disappeared, along with the intense politico-religious quarrels that had sustained it. For diplomatic purposes, the pope was an insignificant Italian prince, with no army to speak of, whose territory could be violated with impunity.

The Church—and papal power over the Church—was regarded with increasing hostility by Catholic rulers. The papacy was constantly on the defensive. New concordats with Catholic powers increased the state's rights of appointment and taxation; monarchs dissolved monasteries and forbade the unlicensed publication of papal edicts. Habsburgs and Bourbons carried the war on the Church into Italy itself.

Catholic anti-clericalism was not new; nor was the struggle between Church and state. But it had entered a new phase of intensity with the development of bureaucratic state power and the state's growing need of revenue. And it was strongly coloured by the anti-clericalism of the Enlightenment, which tended to see the Church, and above all the Jesuits, as a sort of international conspiracy. For the Jesuits this meant temporary extinction. They were expelled from Portugal (1759), France (1764), Spain, Naples and Parma (1767). Finally, when the Bourbon powers united to coerce the pope, the order was dissolved (1773). This conflict, like so many others, was curtailed by the French Revolution, which united Church and king against the common enemy.

The revival of Spain

In the sixteenth century, Spain drew recklessly on the resources of her mighty empire in an attempt to dominate Europe and extirpate Protestantism. The legacy of that effort was a countryside drained of its manpower; an economy disrupted by the expulsion of heretical Jews and Moors and by the quantities of bullion that had poured in from the American colonies; a backward-looking, pious society, with a vast number of gentlemen (hidalgos) who considered most forms of work beneath them; and a mass of malpractices, useless honorary offices and antiquated institutions and regulations. The decline of Spanish power and prestige, visible throughout the seventeenth century, reached its nadir in the reign of the last Spanish Habsburg, the degenerate Charles II (1665–1700), and the subsequent War of Spanish Succession. At the end of the war the Bourbon dynasty (in the person of Philip V, grandson of Louis XIV of France) occupied another throne; but Spain had lost all her European possessions.

The disaster was less complete than it seemed. Spain was no longer obliged to overtax her resources by trying to defend the Netherlands, Milan and Naples; and the Bourbon administration displayed a reforming spirit that was, by Spanish standards, remarkable. Most of the credit belonged not to Philip V, but to his wife, Elizabeth Farnese, who controlled Spanish policy down to Philip's death in 1746.

Elizabeth was Philip's second wife, and her sons were unlikely to succeed to the throne; so she determined to carve out an inheritance for them in Italy. Over a period of years, she succeeded in making Charles King of Naples and Philip Duke of Parma. The triumph was dynastic rather than national, since these acquisitions were not under Spanish sovereignty; and Elizabeth's initial successes were gained through making Spain a nuisance rather than a terror to the great powers. All the same, Spanish prestige was undoubtedly increased.

When Philip arrived to fight for his Spanish crown (1701), he brought with him French experts who remedied some of the more obvious abuses. Their reforms played an important part in winning the war in Spain. Reform continued under Elizabeth, and for the same reason: an ambitious foreign policy necessitated an improvement in revenue and the creation of an efficient army and navy. Economic and fiscal reform did not go deep; energy and efficiency in exploiting resources, not structural change, was the rule; but the result was not unimpressive.

The death of Ferdinand VI (1746–59) brought one of Elizabeth Farnese's sons to the throne after all. Charles III (1759–88) was a competent and serious ruler, and at his accession he had already had twenty-five years' experience of governing Naples. Under Charles, as under so many supposedly enlightened despots, the needs of the state were paramount; but in attempting to satisfy those needs he instituted more fundamental changes than his predecessors.

Many of the reforms followed the familiar pattern of strengthening ministerial and bureaucratic control and ensuring efficient collection of revenue; but there was also a

and his ministers had no intention of introducing religious toleration, but they wished to complete royal control of the Church, which had been attained in most respects by the Concordat of 1753. Jesuits had been prominent in the riots of 1766, and Charles took the opportunity to subject the whole order to a biased enquiry whose findings gave him an excuse for expulsion. A reduction in the powers of the Inquisition completed the subjugation of Church to state.

Reform released energies which had been accumulating under the earlier Bourbons. With official approval, societies for economic improvement were formed in many Spanish towns. Despite colonial wars with Britain, which disrupted trade and brought the government to the verge of bankruptcy, the fruits of Charles's policies became apparent in the rapid industrial and commercial growth of the 1780s. An age of prosperity and expansion seemed to have begun.

Instead, the accession of a feeble king, ruled by his wife and her favourite, restored the rule of incompetence; and the French Revolution and Napoleon inspired crown and people alike with a reinforced attachment to the values of the past. Despite the achievements of Spain's enlightened despot, Charles III, the next century was to be one of internal paralysis and external impotence.

Portugal

Portugal lay in an even deeper slumber, despite the national upsurge that terminated the brief period of Spanish rule (1580–1640). Like Spain, Portugal looked back on a glorious epic of exploration, colonial empire and commercial expansion. In the eighteenth century their only relics were the gold and diamond mines of Brazil and the complementary Angolese slave trade.

sustained attempt to revitalize the economy. The Spanish Empire in America was reorganized and its commerce stimulated through reforms. As regards Spain, colonial trade ceased to be the monopoly of Cadiz and Seville and was opened to most Spanish ports and all Spanish nationals. The heavy sales tax that crippled commerce was drastically cut. Industry was encouraged by the abolition of guild restrictions and protected by tariffs, with the result that Spanish production of cotton cloths was surpassed only by that of Britain, and the silk and iron industries made considerable progress. There was no question of Spain becoming a great industrial nation, but Spanish manufactures at least took a respectable share of the internal and colonial markets.

The reform of agriculture, still the occupation of the overwhelming majority of the population, entailed a social revolution that few rulers were prepared or able to face. Charles attracted some foreign Catholic immigrants to work on uncultivated royal lands, distributed waste and other unused lands and introduced free trade in grain—a creditable record. But the deep-seated problems—farmers' lack of capital, unequal distribution of land, infertility, wasteful use of land for pasture instead of arable, ignorance and conservatism—remained unsolved.

The most dramatic event of the reign was the expulsion of the Jesuits in 1767. Charles

Brazilian gold bore up a state in which a small population (only about three million by 1800) supported droves of idle gentlemen and a priesthood whose wealth, privileges and numbers were probably in relative terms the greatest in Europe. Gold was also used to make up Portugal's balance of payments deficit, for whereas manufactured goods poured into Portugal, from Britain in particular, the sole Portuguese product for which there was any demand was port, one of the vices of the English gentry.

The only man who tried to change this state of affairs was the Marquis of Pombal, who dominated Portugal throughout the reign of Joseph I (1750–77). Pombal was consistently brutal in suppressing actual, potential or imagined opposition; he was a dictator first and a reformer second. An attempt on the king's life (1758) provided him with an opportunity to break the great noble families and move against the Jesuits. Jesuit property was sequestered and the order expelled (1759), an action that was to be imitated by the Bourbon courts. Portuguese obedience to Rome was withdrawn until the final suppression of the order.

These actions were performed in the interests of the state and Pombal's own power: neither noble privileges nor the religious monopoly of the Church was ended, and the works of the *philosophes* continued to be banned. Apart from his Brazilian policy Pombal's reforms were mainly designed to secure administrative and judicial efficiency, which had social implications only in so far as it entailed the abolition of sinecures. Much of his energy was employed in attempting to combat British domination of the Portuguese market —with inevitably limited success, since Portugal had not even the beginnings of a manufacturing economy able to supply her needs. Pombal's revolution was largely

political; and as such it was quickly reversed when the pious Maria I (1777–1816) succeeded Joseph.

With or without Pombal, Portugal remained a backwater of Europe. The great conflicts of the period concerned her directly only once, when Spain invaded in an unsuccessful attempt to close Portuguese harbours to the British (1762). One event made a European sensation: the terrible earthquake which destroyed Lisbon (1755). Lisbon, thanks to Pombal, was built again (and built better), but the shock—actual and psychic—was felt throughout Europe.

Above, Lisbon in the mid-eighteenth century, shortly before the great earthquake of 1755 which destroyed most of the city.

Top, the port of Seville in the eighteenth century; after losing its monopoly of Spanish colonial trade in 1718, the town suffered a chronic decline.

Above left, the expulsion of the Jesuits from Spain by Charles III in 1767; Charles was an 'enlightened despot' who saw the Jesuits both as enemies of the truth and as opponents of his complete control over his kingdom.

Opposite left top, Charles of Bourbon visiting Pope Benedict XIV (reigned 1740–58) at a coffee-house in Rome; despite Benedict's patronage of the arts, he was unable to restore the papacy to the majesty and respect of former times. Palazzo di Lapodimonte, Naples.

Opposite left bottom, Philip V of Spain (reigned 1700–46), the first Bourbon king of Spain, painted with his family by Van Loo. During his reign, Spain's economy began to develop more successfully than at any time since the sixteenth century. Museo del Prado, Madrid.

Part IV

NEW WORLDS TO CONQUER

Introduction

Less than five hundred years ago the cloistered universe defined by Ptolemy was shattered, as inquisitive explorers of the Renaissance reached out over unknown waters and found strange lands on the other side of a round world. Although it was not realized at the time, the European struggle for power on the North and South American continents had opened when Columbus, by linking a New World to the Old in 1492, laid the foundations of the Spanish overseas empire. Five years later the ambit of European ambitions was once again widened when Vasco da Gama rounded the Cape of Good Hope, establishing a route to the East that has been followed to this day. Ranged along the Atlantic seaboard, Spain, Portugal, France, Holland and England sought in turn to exploit the discoveries, and the colonial rivalries of these western powers occupy a significant part of seventeenth- and eighteenth-century history. As competition for overseas wealth gradually superimposed itself on the traditional pattern of continental relationships, European states had to revise their calculations on the sources of national power. Age-old policies of continental conquest and expansion inevitably conflicted with new and inviting dreams of riches to be found in ancient and vulnerable empires beyond the horizon.

Spain had the advantage of a head start, but she failed to develop a stable administrative and economic basis from which to exploit her new-found riches. Nonetheless, despite her decline from European heights, in part owing to the savage aggressiveness of rivals, her empire in Central and South America remained intact. Remoteness was probably the key to immunity, for the area of competitive colonization had shifted by the middle of the seventeenth century northward of the Caribbean. Successive Spanish governments continued a vain struggle to monopolize the commerce of resentful colonial dominions. Vast discoveries of silver, gold and diamonds brought settlers, soldiers and administrators, but embittered natives and corrupt officials combined to defeat the mother country's regulations. Only in the second half of the eighteenth century did Spain's governors cautiously relax trade restrictions and, like the Marquis of Pombal in Protuguese Brazil, try without success to eliminate excessive abuses that were to lead, early in the nineteenth century, to armed revolt and the establishment of independent Latin American republics.

Meanwhile, a small, fiercely ambitious and loosely federalized republic, recently relieved of Spanish control, sought command of the world's sea routes. In Indonesian seas the Dutch ousted the Portuguese and took over the greater part of their empire. Although far more businesslike than Spain, Holland had not the financial strength to maintain, in addition to a first-class navy, an army sufficient to withstand the invading forces of Louis XIV. By 1674 she had lost for a second time, and finally, her one strategic base in North America, New Amsterdam (New York).

Rivalry for empire became thereafter essentially a long-drawn-duel between France and England, which became, in the eighteenth century, a struggle that embraced Asia as well as North America. In America the French saw from the beginning the strategic points that are vital to this day. They recognized the possibilities of a great circle of river and lake stretching from the St Lawrence River to Lake Michigan and thence southward by the Mississippi to the Gulf of Mexico. A successful policy of encirclement would enable them to shut the British behind the Appalachian chain of mountains and would ultimately give France the continent.

But only the most constant support in terms of men and supplies from Europe could have made the grand project feasible. Without secure communications French possessions in North America were bound to be hostages of the British navy, which after the Battle of La Hogue gradually achieved an overall command of the seas. Determined to maintain her European hegemony, and at the same time to build a great overseas empire, France fell between the two stools of imperial dreams and continental attachments.

In North America, the issue was fundamentally one of manpower. Had 50,000 Huguenots been forced, like the Puritans, to take refuge in Canada (instead of being barred from that country), French ambitions might have stood a chance of fulfilment. Had a mere half of one percent of the French population of some 18,000,000 been persuaded to emigrate to Canada at the beginning of the eighteenth century, the colony would have gained the numerical strength which alone could justify imperial policies of expansion. Against the weight of more than 2,000,000 British settlers, hemmed in the Atlantic coastal strip east of the Appalachian Mountains, a French colony of under 50,000 in 1755 could scarcely fulfil the designs of its explorers and governors. That New France was able to endure as long as it did was principally owing to professional troops and good organization. Although unrecognized at the time, the beginnings of the 'Second Hundred Years War' for empire foretold the twilight of French American domination.

The rivalry of France and Britain revealed itself as dramatically in India as in North America. When the English East India Company was incorporated on the last day of the sixteenth century, the power of the Muslims in India was reaching its zenith under the Moguls, invaders of Mongolian origin who under Babur had in the early years of the sixteenth century swept through the passes of the northwest frontier into the plains below. Under sovereigns like Akbar, English traders could do no more than cling precariously to the coastline in little factories whose existence depended on the favour of the local ruler. The Portuguese had long retired before the competition of the Dutch, whose concentration on the East Indies archipelago alone enabled the English to stick to such mainland trading outlets as Fort St George (Madras), Fort William (Calcutta) and Catherine of Braganza's dowry gift to Charles II, Bombay.

As a consequence of mounting corruption and inefficiency, the Mogul Empire was tottering long before French and English rivals for the spoils launched their Lilliputian forces against its imposing hulk. When the last great Mogul emperor, Aurangzeb, died in 1707, both the power and the glory had departed, and the way was open for France and Britain to struggle for an oriental heritage that neither Muslim nor Hindu was capable of sustaining.

As in North America, so in India, France lost out to Britain. Less skilful in native diplomacy, the British were able to combine land and naval power effectively and allow to leadership an initiative that was denied the French paladins—Dupleix, Bussy, Lally and Suffren. In romance and wonder, the British conquest of a subcontinent with handfuls of European soldiers equals the Spanish triumphs in Central and South America. Nearly a million square miles containing some 200,000,000 people—an area embracing religions and customs reaching back to fabulous antiquity—fell to an English company's arms.

By the terms of the Treaty of Paris in 1763, practically the entire French Empire in the East and West had disappeared. Half the world, so it seemed to a later generation, had slipped through French hands like sand between the fingers. With the exception of some West Indian sugar islands and a few isolated posts on the Coromandel coast, France had been dispossessed of her imperial domain. Only if Britain, through some catastrophic upset of the balance of power, lost command of the sea, could France hope to wipe out her painful humiliation. As it happened, in 1778 a resuscitated French nation, subsequently joined by Spain, was in a position not only to challenge British superiority but for a moment actually to win command of the sea. Bereft of allies and occupied with powerful enemies elsewhere, Britain had neither the ships, the materials, nor the men to subdue thirteen rebellious American colonies some 3,000 miles away. Nonetheless, by the end of the Napoleonic Wars the second British Empire overseas had not only survived, it had grown and consolidated itself into a world-wide business concern, which for the greater part of the nineteenth century European nations were content to accept.

Unlike the Americas, where, with the exception of Mexico and Peru, no organized states offered serious resistance to European arms, both China and Japan were able to withstand, and until the nineteenth century even to reject, the advances of the acquisitive West. Although European traders had tried in the seventeenth century to breach the portals of China, they had little success. Apart from occasional loopholes like Canton, China remained impenetrable; her Manchu conquerors and rulers refused admission to the profit-seeking barbarians of the outer world except under humiliating restrictions.

The first openings had been made in 1521 when the Portuguese, who had occupied Malacca in 1511, sent a representative to Peking. Although expelled within a year, they were able in 1557 to establish a settlement in Macao, not far from Hong Kong. It remained a European lookout and trading entrepôt for the China coast long after the Portuguese commercial empire had succumbed to the Dutch, who (five years after founding Batavia) established their Formosan base in 1624. The Jesuits had begun to trickle in, led by the famous Matteo Ricci (1552–1610). But unfamiliar enthusiasm for converts resulted in their deportation to Macao. They returned in about the middle of the century to enjoy the favour of the new Manchu dynasty and to make their great contributions to scientific learning. The Jesuit success represented a unique partnership of East and West which was unhappily broken some fifty years later.

The Jesuits under St Francis Xavier (1506–52) had also introduced Christianity into Japan, and pioneer Portuguese traders were followed early in the seventeenth century by Dutch, Spanish and English. By 1620 it was estimated that some 300,000 Christians were living in the main Japanese islands. A few years later, however, a policy of national isolation was adopted, accompanied by a period of savage repression which saw the consolidation of Tokugawa rule. From about 1640 to the end of the century, a handful of Dutch and Chinese traders at Nagasaki represented Japan's only connection with the outside world.

Not until after the middle of the nineteenth century was Japan compelled to open her ports to foreign commerce and, with the collapse of the old feudal structure, to organize a national state on the Western pattern as the best means of ensuring freedom from Western domination and conquest.

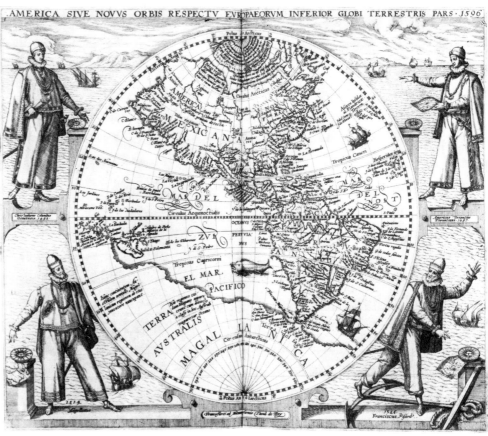

When Hong Kong fell to the British navy, and 'Treaty Ports' opened the way to European commerce in 1840–42, it seemed certain that China too would copy the manners and methods of the West. But the very nature of the Treaty Ports provoked reaction—they were in every case territorial concessions extracted by force, or the display of force, by the European nations strong enough to make a bid for influence in the Far East. The principal reason for establishing these bases was the pursuit of trade, the benefits from which seemed unlikely to be mutual. After the experience of the Opium Wars, the Chinese saw in foreign commercial enterprise the chief menace to her security and way of life. As subsequent events were to prove, their fears were more than justified. China had neither the will nor the aptitude of Japan for emulating and keeping step with the West. As a result China had to endure her 'century of humiliation' at foreign hands. The result was the rise of a bitter anti-foreign sentiment and, with the triumph of Communism, the closing of the doors once again. Today China remains the one civilization outside the boundaries of the present international order and one that is largely beyond Western comprehension.

Above, the Western Hemisphere as it was known, or imagined to be, in 1596; around the map stand the great sixteenth-century explorers, Columbus, Vespucci, Pizarro and Drake.

On page 212, an illustration of William Penn's treaty with the Indians of 1681, painted by Edward Hicks in the early nineteenth century. Thomas Gilcrease Institute, Tulsa, Oklahoma.

Chapter 23

America in the Sixteenth and Seventeenth Centuries

The discoveries of Columbus and the feats of Cortes and Pizarro excited the imagination of all Europe. Soon other nations were sending expeditions across the Atlantic in the wake of the Spaniards. Extravagant hopes of finding new kingdoms built of gold rapidly faded, but settlers quickly accommodated themselves to exploiting the more durable wealth of forest and soil. Throughout the seventeenth century Britain, France, Spain and Portugal steadily developed their colonies in North and South America. Competition inevitably brought friction, and by 1700 the European powers were already beginning a titanic struggle for the control of a hemisphere.

Latin America after the Conquest

There is no other event in human history quite like the Spanish discoveries and conquests in the western hemisphere. Unknown continents, hidden empires, fabulous wealth —it all seemed much more like fantasy than reality. But it was reality, and the Spanish monarchs were faced with the task of ruling over vast new lands, greater in area and more populous than Spain itself. How were the new territories to be governed?

It was the system first developed for ruling over conquered Spanish Muslims that the conquistadores now extended to the American Indians. By royal grants, specified numbers of Indian households were 'entrusted' to individual captains, officers and even foot soldiers in the conquering Spanish army. These grants were called *encomiendas*, and the *encomendero* who received one would then build his estate and maintain his family and his personal following from the tribute in produce and in labour that the Indians entrusted to him would be forced to pay.

Many such grants were of truly princely extent. Cortes, for instance, received a domain containing over 100,000 Indians and sprawling over 25,000 square miles. Pizarro's was equally magnificent, and the other Spaniards were rewarded in accordance with their ranks. But the *encomiendas* were basically allotments of people rather than feudal grants of land. Indeed, the conquistadores did not usually desire a rural life and,

in true Spanish fashion, began laying out cities and villages almost as soon as they had arrived. The *encomedero*, therefore, often lived in a town and simply informed the various Indian head men of his *encomienda* how much tribute he expected to receive. The headmen, or *caciques* as they were known, would then have the onerous duty of raising the produce and labour for their overlords, as well as a little extra to keep for themselves. This, then, was the manner in which the conquering Spanish army spread its authority over the native population of the New World.

Despite the great distance of the Indies from Spain, and despite their own relative ignorance about their new dominions, the Spanish monarchs were from the beginning quite determined that royal authority in those territories should be real and not merely titular. They therefore regarded the early adventurers like Cortes and Pizarro with extreme suspicion—as men who might be tempted into becoming over-mighty subjects.

Thus, in the wake of the conquistadores, came the king's men, who were to rule the two huge viceroyalties of New Spain and Peru on behalf of their royal masters.

In Spain itself, various organs of government were hastily established. The *Casa de Contratación*, or Board of Trade, was set up in Seville to supervise all commerce between the homeland and the new colonies. But the Casa was soon placed under the aegis of another, more powerful, body, the Royal and Supreme Council of the Indies, subject only to the king and created by Emperor Charles V in 1524. The Council, consisting originally of only four or five members, continued in existence until 1834 and throughout most of this long period was an efficient and hard-working body of high prestige.

In America the viceroys arrived to set the king's recently won domains in order. Antonio de Mendoza arrived in Mexico in 1535, after an unruly period marked by the

atrocities of the ferocious Nuño de Guzmán and by the attempts of Cortes to exercise real power. In his long administration of fifteen years Mendoza ruled well, consolidating Spanish imperial authority and attempting to protect the Indians from the abuses of many *encomenderos*. At a slightly later date, from 1569 to 1581, Francisco de Toledo played a similar role in Peru. Both men laboured ably to bring order out of a relative chaos and both men left behind them an established system of government that was hardly to be altered until the end of the colonial period. It was a cleverly designed system of checks and balances constructed to limit the accumulation of power in the hands of any one man or body of men and to ensure that royal authority was felt down to the very lowest levels of administration. In this it succeeded. The whole complex structure will be dealt with in a later chapter. For the moment suffice it to say that other colonial empires were more successfully administered from the point of view of the colonists, none better than the Spanish from the point of view of their kings.

The wealth of the Indies

It was the Spanish discovery of precious metals that first convinced the world that America was something more than just a colossal barricade astride the sea route to the Orient. And the wealth that was found there was truly astonishing, arousing the

cupidity and wonder of all Europe. Some alluvial gold was early located on the island of Hispaniola. After that came the accumulated treasures of the Aztec and Inca domains, then the discovery of the great silver mines. In 1545 took place the most stupendous mineral discovery ever made by man. At Potosí, in Bolivia, an actual mountain of silver was uncovered. And by 1558 the three most important mines in Mexico were in operation.

But the wealth of the Indies was by no means restricted to minerals. Pearls and cochineal were important, but in the long run agricultural produce proved the most valuable of all. Not only were numerous varieties of crops of both New and Old World origin grown throughout the Spanish Empire, but also cash crops for export. Cotton, tobacco, sugar and dye-woods eventually produced more money than the mines.

To bring such riches home, the Spaniards evolved their famous trading system. Once or twice a year, two great fleets, laden with European manufactures, would leave Spain for the New World. One of these would proceed to Vera Cruz, the chief port of New Spain; the other would sail to Nombre de Dios (or later to Porto Bello) on the north coast of South America, whence the goods it carried would be shipped overland to Peru. Then, laden with the produce of the New World, the southerly fleet would refit in the great fortified harbour of Cartagena before keeping rendezvous with the other,

returning from Vera Cruz, in the equally fortified Havana. From there, the combined fleet would continue, under escort of galleons, back to Spain. There were other trade routes as well; Peruvian silver went to the Philippines, and there was inter-colonial trade between Peru and New Spain. But, of course, it was the transatlantic fleets, laden with silver, which were the most famous and which aroused the greed of pirates, privateers and men-of-war from the time of Drake until the latter part of the eighteenth century.

The Church and the Indians

All European nations colonizing the New World claimed that one of the principal objects was the Christianization and civilization of the Amerindians, but only the Spaniards took this seriously. This was partially owing to the character of the Indians they encountered. Once settlers were fighting them for their lives, they

Above, the silver mines at Potosí, in Peru, which provided fabulous wealth for the Spaniards; the mines were worked by the Indians, many of whom died in the airless conditions underground.

Above left, the Aztec god Huitzilopochtli being worshipped, according to a Dutch book of 1671 describing the wonders of the New World.

Opposite, Mexico City in the sixteenth century; the city, which was built on a lake, had been the Aztec capital and was taken over by the Spaniards as their headquarters.

217

quickly lost all ideas of converting the red men. Even in the Spanish Empire, so-called 'wild' Indians, like the Araucanians of Chile, received short shrift. But the conquest of the great Aztec and Inca domains produced a different type of situation. Here, after a brief resistance, large populations of settled Indians were completely helpless and at the mercy of their conquerors. How should these people be treated? There were two main alternatives: that they should be forced to support their rulers and to labour for them in field and in mines—for if the Spanish settlers were clear about nothing else, they were determined to avoid manual labour—or on the other hand the Indians could be looked upon as a harmless people whose welfare had been entrusted to the Spaniards by God. The first of these points of view was generally adopted by the settlers; the second by the majority of the priests and missionaries. Between these alternatives, the Spanish monarchs vacillated, their consciences genuinely torn.

Even before the mainland conquests, the Spanish settlers had been committing atrocities against the Indians on the island of Hispaniola. As early as 1511 the Dominican friar, Antonio des Montesinos, had spoken out. Using the text 'I am a voice crying in the wilderness', he denounced his own congregation, declaring: 'You are in mortal sin for the cruelty and tyranny you use in dealing with these innocent people.' After the exploits of Cortes and Pizarro, the problem was immensely sharpened. Bishops like Juan de Zumárraga and Vasco de Quiroga gained control of the *audiencia* of New Spain and overthrew the atrocious rule of Nuño de Guzmán. Others denounced the *encomiendas*, which in fact if not in theory made Indians into slaves. Worse still was the *repartimiento* or forced labour system. Friar Motolinía described with horror the scenes near the mines of New Spain where, 'it was hardly possible to walk except over dead men or bones and so great were the numbers of birds and the buzzards that came to eat the bodies of the dead that they cast a huge shadow over the sun'.

The most heroic champion of the Indians was the great Bartolomé de las Casas. Born in 1474, las Casas had arrived in America as a soldier of fortune as early as 1502. He prospered and gained control of much land and many Indians, but at the age of forty, when ordained as a priest, las Casas came to feel that he had been taking part in a monstrous crime. A vigorous, astute man, he made most of his appeals directly to the Crown, which held supreme jurisdiction over both the Indians and the Church.

Through the influence of the Crown, las Casas and his allies gained significant victories for their cause. The Inquisition, although extended to Spanish settlers in the New World, was given no authority over the Indians. Their denunciation of the abuses of the *encomiendas* resulted in 1542 in a series of new laws for the Indies

promulgated by Charles V. These insisted that all forms of Indian slavery should be ended, while other provisions, if acted upon, would have virtually abolished the whole *encomienda* system. However, as might be expected, this called forth stubborn resistance from the settlers. In New Spain, even the conscientious Mendoza advised that the colony might be lost if the laws were enforced. In Peru, the clumsy attempt to institute them immediately made by the first viceroy, Vasco Núñez, resulted in a full-scale rebellion led by Gonzalo Pizarro, one of the two surviving brothers of the old conquistador. Pizarro was quickly defeated and beheaded and royal authority restored, but it was clear the new laws would have to be revised. In 1547, another series of decrees restored the *encomiendas* although curtailing rights of inheritance associated with them, but the prohibition of Indian slavery was allowed to stand.

In 1547, las Casas, aged 72, finally left America to battle against any reversal of policy and to argue against Juan Gines de Sepulveda, a theologian who was insisting that the Indians were an inferior people and were 'natural slaves' in the Aristotelian sense. Las Casas was immediately aroused. In the first place, he was in no way intimidated by Aristotle whom he described as a 'gentile burning in hell, whose doctrine we do not need to follow except in so far as it conforms with Christian truth'. In the second place, he claimed that even if one accepted Aristotle's ideas they did not apply to the Amerindians who were clearly rational beings. In 1550, las Casas and Sepulveda met in Valladolid in a great debate on the issue, and until it was decided Charles V forbade all further Spanish conquests in America.

The debate itself was a moral victory for las Casas, and Sepulveda was not allowed to publish his own doctrines afterwards. Yet the problem was never to be resolved by a clear edict from Charles V or from any of his successors. The Spanish monarchs were indeed in a cleft stick. Their consciences took the side of the Indians, but their minds could not forget the silver. And to the kings the wealth of the Indies had an important religious use—they saw themselves as the secular champions of Roman Catholicism, and the riches of the New World helped to create the armies with which they fought both Protestants and Turks. What they really wanted was a world that could never be—one where the Indian would not be exploited and would gently be led to Christianity and where the silver would mine itself. Since they could not have this, the kings temporized and attempted both to please the settlers and to protect the Indian. They failed in each case.

It was only in a land where no great mineral wealth was to be found that the Spanish Church in America was temporarily able to achieve its ideal. In the La Plata basin, from 1605 on, Spanish Jesuits built up a huge mission centre containing some 100,000 Indians. Here they constructed a benevolent, theocratic despotism where every aspect of the daily life of the Indians was conducted under the strict supervision of the priests. The Paraguay mission was the only really large area conducted under such principles, but numerous other missions on the frontiers of New Spain and Peru created similar communities on a smaller scale. The rigid and narrow paternalistic rule of the priests meant that these areas were hardly idyllic, but they certainly constituted a nobler form of experiment than that of the *encomienda*.

There was one curious way in which the dilemma of Spanish-Indian relations could be resolved—by the exploitation of a third race. Within a few years of the discovery of America the infamous Atlantic slave trade had begun. To relieve one people from oppression by oppressing another seems

strange logic, but the Spaniard of the time saw a difference. The American Indians he had conquered were clearly his own responsibility; but, owning no possessions in continental Africa, he was only indirectly concerned with the negro. He did not enslave negroes himself but merely bought people already captured by the Portuguese. The ageing las Casas and a few others raised their voices against the iniquity of such fine distinctions, but on the whole Spanish opinion in all circles was overwhelmingly indifferent to the plight of the negroes.

The enslaving of the negro, however, did not save the American Indian. Nothing saved the Indian. Shortly after the conquest, the whole population structure of New Spain began to tremble, to shake and, finally, to disintegrate. The main cause was disease. Smallpox, measles, consumption, malaria and yellow fever, all these were brought to the New World from the Old by Europeans and Africans and ravaged a people who had no natural immunities to them. Perhaps 25,000,000 Indians dwelt in New Spain in pre-conquest days. By the mid-sixteenth century this figure had slipped to 6,500,000; by 1580, it was perhaps 1,900,000. Whole villages died out, vast areas went out of cultivation, and the whole of New Spain seemed destined to become a desert. Finally, in the seventeenth century, this horrific population decline was halted and reversed, but the new population was

largely of mestizo, or half-breed, rather than of pure Indian stock.

Much of the cultural heritage of the Indians of New Spain disappeared even faster than the peoples themselves. By the mid-seventeenth century, it was at last clear that the Catholic missionaries were winning great successes in the conversion of this vanishing people. In their vast desolation of soul, the Indians turned to the new religion, although keeping many of their own customs and rituals. Soon only monuments to the past remained—and the great statues and temples built to the various gods of the old Aztec pantheon would stare dumbly through the centuries over the people whom they had not saved and who increasingly knew them not. The Indian heritage of the Mexican people would reassert itself in the nineteenth and twentieth centuries. At the end of the seventeenth it seemed to have been buried for ever.

Decline of Empire

The tremendous decline of the American Indian population, and consequently of the New World labour force, was naturally reflected in all facets of colonial life. But the problem did not stop there, for the whole of the Spanish Empire, in the Old World as well as in the New, underwent a truly precipitous decline. In the sixteenth century, Spain had not only been the greatest power in Europe but had had only one conceivable rival for world empire—Portugal, which was finally absorbed by Philip II in 1580. Yet, in less than eighty years, all the power and glory of the Spain of Philip II had

shrunk to the cardboard kingdom of Charles II—perhaps the most pathetic reversal of national fortunes in the whole of European history.

Of all of the manifold causes of the decline of old Spain, two stand out sharply: war and the lack of economic development. The seemingly inexhaustible stream of wealth from America encouraged the aggressive tendencies of the Habsburg monarchs, and their wars soon ate up that wealth and much more besides. Similarly, the inflow of silver at first stimulated the Spanish economy, but soon rising prices and costs ruined Spain as an economic competitor in Europe; Spanish industry first stagnated and then fell into complete decrepitude. Things were bad even at the end of the sixteenth century when silver imports from America were at their height, but soon the supply of silver began to dry up and Spain slipped from periodic to hopeless bankruptcy.

Everything seemed to work into a vortex spiralling downwards. Spanish mercantile policy, like that of the other European nations, had aimed at keeping the whole of the colonial trade in the hands of the mother country, but Spain simply could not manufacture the goods that the colonists wanted in exchange for their silver and agricultural produce. This increased costs enormously and encouraged smuggling by the English, French and Dutch. As Spanish power and commerce declined, so did the Spanish navy, and the smuggling could not be checked. By the seventeenth century, the Spanish concept of mercantilism had proved a complete failure.

In the New World, the depopulation at least solved the old controversy over the *encomiendas*. As the Indians disappeared so did the tribute on which the *encomienda* system was based. The new economic order that emerged was based on the *hacienda* and on peonage.

There was also a decline in government and administration in the Indies. Philip II had taken a close and consistent interest in his colonial empire; his increasingly weaker successors, Philip III, Philip IV and Charles II, cared less and less. More and more considerations of merit disappeared with regard to appointments, and offices were bought and sold like any other form of property. Nevertheless, the decline in the Indies did not proceed nearly so far, nor so rapidly, as the decline in Spain itself. Similarly, when a period of recovery came in the eighteenth century the Spanish possessions in the New World advanced much more rapidly than those in the Old.

Portuguese Brazil

By the Treaty of Tordesillas in 1494, Portuguese territory was to include all land within 370 leagues of a line drawn west of the Cape Verde islands. The Portuguese hoped that this area would contain the mythical continent of Atlantis. It did not, but in April 1500 Pedro Alvarez Cabral discovered, within the demarcation limits, the coast of Brazil and claimed it for Portugal.

Devoting most of her overseas energies towards the Indian Ocean, Portugal did little at first to develop her new colony. Indeed, she managed to keep possession of it only because it seemed so unimportant economically, producing little more than some dye-woods. Even so, English and especially French interlopers gave trouble but were finally evicted. Then came a modest boom in sugar cultivation. Portuguese sugar planters had long been prospering on the African island of São Tomé, but in the 1570s slave revolts led many of them to emigrate to Brazil. This greatly encouraged the Atlantic slave trade and also made Brazil look more attractive to alien powers. When, in 1580, the Portuguese Empire was swallowed by the Spanish this event not only demoralized Portuguese Brazilians, it also meant that Spain's enemies descended upon them as well.

Further French incursions were finally ended in 1615, but the Dutch were more successful. After a few abortive attempts in the early part of the seventeenth century, they gained a firm foothold at Recife in 1630. Within a few years they managed to gain control of some 1,200 miles of Brazilian coastline. The Dutch, particularly during the wise administration of John Maurice of Nassau, guaranteed the property rights and religious liberties of the Portuguese planters. The colony therefore prospered during the period of occupation, but when

Portugal freed herself from Spain in 1640 this provoked a nationalist reaction in Brazil as well. Revolts broke out against alien rule, and after fourteen years of warfare the Dutch withdrew.

Once again under Portuguese dominion, Brazil continued to prosper on the basis of sugar and cotton. It was not until the eighteenth century, however, with the discovery of gold and diamonds, that the colony was to attain its real importance.

North America

In the seventeenth century, the English, French and Dutch infringed the Spanish monopoly of the western hemisphere and eventually established colonies in the West Indies that were to grow rich on the labour of African slaves. Further north, attracted by the fur trade, the French founded an immense empire that stretched from Quebec to the Gulf of Mexico. The English moved more slowly so far as territory was concerned but much more rapidly with regard to settlement. By the end of the century, they had heavily populated the eastern seaboard of North America from Maine down to the Carolinas.

The Cabot voyage of 1497 had given England some claim to North America. That of Verrazano in 1523 did the same for France. Then, between 1534 and 1541, the French seaman, Jacques Cartier, made a remarkable series of voyages that carried him up the St Lawrence river as far as Montreal. Throughout the sixteenth century, a number of English navigators searched unsuccessfully for a northwest passage to Asia in the wastes of the Canadian Arctic. The purpose of all these early explorations was to find a sea route to the east or to discover rich Indian empires, thus duplicating the Spanish feats in Mexico and Peru. As such hopes faded, thoughts turned more

soberly to projects of colonization. During the last of Cartier's voyages Roberval, a French nobleman, brought out a party of settlers to Canada. But this attempt at colonization proved an ignominious failure, and twenty years later a settlement of French Protestants in Florida was cruelly exterminated by the Spaniards.

The next series of attempts was made by the English. The half-brothers Sir Humphrey Gilbert and Sir Walter Raleigh had experimented with planting settlements in Ireland and hoped to apply their experience to the New World. In 1583, Gilbert formally claimed Newfoundland for the English, but his attempt at settlement farther south was ended when storms wrecked his ships and Gilbert himself was drowned. Raleigh took up Gilbert's project and in the next few years three small groups of settlers were placed on or in the neighbourhood of Roanoke Island, in the area that he named Virginia. But all of them were to perish, and it was not until the next century that the English, French and Dutch established themselves successfully in North America.

Above, a Brazilian sugar mill of about 1640; sugar became the most important crop of the New World in the eighteenth century, as Europe's demand for it grew dramatically. Oliveira Lima Collection, Catholic University of America, Washington D.C.

Top, Sebastian Cabot (1483–1557), the Genoese sailor, towards the end of his life. He helped his father to discover Newfoundland in the 1490s and later explored the coast of South America.

Top left, an Indian village in Brazil in about 1640; the Indian populations of Central and South America fell dramatically in the sixteenth and seventeenth centuries. Oliveira Lima Collection, Catholic University of America, Washington D.C.

Opposite, negroes imported to work in the silver mines in the 1590s; it was discovered soon afterwards to be equally profitable to use these negro slaves on sugar plantations in the Caribbean and in North America.

French interest in the New World lagged for some time after Roberval's fiasco, but there were always those who thought of the possible profit that might arise from a monopoly of the fur trade. After an experiment in Nova Scotia, in 1608 Samuel de Champlain founded the city of Quebec on the St Lawrence river. With its citadel strategically built on the top of a cliff and commanding the one great river system penetrating from the Atlantic to the heart of the continent, Quebec was to be the stronghold of France in the New World.

Champlain was one of the greatest inland explorers of modern times. Driven by idealistic visions of empire, yet immensely practical as well, he pushed inland as far as the Great Lakes and southward down the Richelieu River, organizing the fur trade as he went. He also engaged deeply in Indian diplomacy and in 1609 formed the alliance between the French and the Hurons and Algonquins against the Iroquois, thus beginning the century and a half of conflict between the French and the latter formidable tribal federation.

At first, the fur trade was run in a haphazard manner, but in 1627, Cardinal Richelieu organized the famous Company of New France. The new association had great ambitions but was involved in immediate disaster. War broke out with England, and the buccaneering Kirke brothers both captured Quebec and destroyed the expedition bringing settlers and provisions in which the company had invested most of its initial capital.

Quebec was given back to France in 1632, and Champlain returned as governor. But the great explorer died three years later, and the Company of New France had been greatly weakened. It was reorganized in the 1640s, however, and began to show a profit. Nevertheless, the number of settlers in New France was miniscule, and the colony was soon racked by disastrous wars with the Iroquois. Not until the reign of Louis XIV did the fortunes of New France revive.

Raleigh's interests in the New World were eventually taken up by an organization which ultimately became known as the Virginia Company and was placed under the presidency of Sir Thomas Smyth, a great merchant adventurer. In 1607 Captain Christopher Newport took out a group of settlers on behalf of the company and near the mouth of Chesapeake Bay founded Jamestown, the first permanent English settlement in America. In the first year of its existence the new colony nearly perished through starvation and malaria, but the energetic Captain John Smith managed to keep things going, while his own life was saved, on the occasion of his capture by the Indian chief Powhatan, by the famous and timely intervention of Pocahontas, the chief's daughter, who later married an Englishman and came to England, where she died.

BEAUFORT SEA

GREENLAND

ICELAND

Yukon

Mackenzie

Great Bear Lake

Great Slave Lake

Lake Athabaska

HUDSON BAY

Nelson

JAMES BAY

Lake Winnipeg

NEWFOUNDLAND

GULF OF ST LAWRENCE

St Lawrence

NOVA SCOTIA

Columbia

Lake Superior

Lake Huron

Lake Michigan

Lake Ontario

Lake Erie

Great Salt Lake

Missouri

Ohio

Allegheny Mts

BERMUDA

CALIFORNIA

Colorado

Mississippi

Rio Grande

FLORIDA

BAHAMAS

GULF OF MEXICO

CUBA

HISPANIOLA

I. DES PINOS

JAMAICA

CARIBBEAN SEA

■	English
□	French
▨	Spanish

The Virginia Company had aspired to quick profits through the discovery of gold mines or from the production of wine and silk. These hopes proved illusory, but in 1612 a settler named John Rolph, who had married Pocahontas, began to grow tobacco. To the horror of King James I, the production of this 'vile weed' proved the salvation of the colony and the foundation of its future prosperity. The harsh but necessary period of stern military rule and of communal ownership of land was finally brought to an end. Settlers were given their own allotments and the government placed in the hands of a civil governor and council responsible to the Virginia Company. The colonists themselves were allowed representation in an elected House of Assembly. The establishment of this form of administration, which became a pattern for all the British colonies, was ultimately to be of immense importance.

223

The manner of their fishing.

A few Dutch traders and settlers had been active on the Hudson River since Henry Hudson had explored that area on their behalf in 1609. The original New Netherlands Company was slow in taking up any advantages, but the great Dutch West India Company, founded in 1621, began to activate matters. In 1626, Peter Minuit bought Manhattan Island from the local Indians; shortly afterwards an embryonic Swedish colony was swallowed up, and the New Netherlands came into being.

The settlement was basically a fur trading colony, centred around New Amsterdam (now New York), with its protective bastion at Wall Street and its acquisitive inhabitants straggling along the Hudson River. Trade with the Indians occupied most of their energy from the beginning, although there was also some agricultural settlement including grants of land over which the patron, or patroon, held manorial rights and where he wielded almost absolute power. By the time of the English conquest in 1664, there were about 7,000 souls in the New Netherlands, and a long period of good government under Pieter Stuyvesant had encouraged settlement. Even so, the colony had always been a minor concern of the West India Company and there were few Dutchmen who felt that their country had made a bad bargain when it eventually gave up all claims to the area in return for the confirmation of its rights in Surinam in South America.

At the same time that Virginia was finding its feet in the tobacco fields, a series of new English settlements with a radically different outlook from their southern neighbours were appearing in the north. The Pilgrims were a small and humble religious sect which had been driven from England by an intolerant establishment. Sailing in the *Mayflower* from Plymouth in September of 1620, they arrived off Cape Cod, Massachusetts, two months later. Far away from any government, they drew up their own political contract on board ship and indeed thus produced the first written constitution of any English-speaking people. They were diligent and hardworking and soon established the colony of New Plymouth.

This first English settlement in the north was soon followed by a much more important project. In England many Puritans found themselves despairing of the government of Charles I and were harried by the High Church party. A group of them managed to get a grant of land in North America and formed the Massachusetts Bay Company, under charter from the Crown. Ostensibly designed as a commercial organization, the new company had settlement in mind from the beginning. In 1629, all shareholders not intending to emigrate to America were bought out. A year later the vanguard, led by John Winthrop, sailed to found a new colony. Further emigration increased their numbers, and by 1640 there were some 14,000 Puritans in Massachusetts.

The Virginia Company was not destined to be as successful as the colony itself. Despite several reorganizations and schemes for raising capital, it began to founder financially. In 1624, King James I assumed royal responsibility for the colony; company rule had ended. Meanwhile, Bermuda had been discovered by accident when settlers going to Virginia were shipwrecked on the island. More important was the founding of Maryland in 1632, by Cecil Calvert, the second Lord Baltimore. Maryland, established on the side of Chesapeake Bay opposite Virginia, was granted as a proprietorship, and this gave Lord Baltimore wide feudal powers over the land. He hoped that the colony would be commercially successful and also a haven for his fellow Roman Catholics, and in a small way it proved to be both. Marylanders were soon cultivating tobacco, and economically the colony resembled a miniature Virginia. Roman Catholics were never in a majority among the settlers; however, there was no established Anglican Church and, distinct from their position in any other English dominions at the time, the Catholics enjoyed equal rights and freedom of religion.

The fact that Massachusetts was originally a company or corporate colony somewhat influenced its form of government. Governor, council and assembly were all elected in the way that shareholders might elect a chairman and a board of directors. This did not mean that Puritan Massachusetts was a democracy. The electorate was small and strictly confined to carefully scrutinized church members. The Puritans enforced their own brand of religious orthodoxy with rigid insistence, and those who dissented from it were persecuted almost from the beginning. Massachusetts was also fiercely determined to remain politically independent and had as little to do with the mother country as was possible.

The very intolerance of Massachusetts soon created new colonies. The Puritans rapidly drove out from their ranks people like Roger Williams, who believed in full freedom of conscience, and Anne Hutchinson, who followed her own mystical brand of theology. These two, and others like them, journeyed south, where Williams eventually founded the tolerant province of Rhode Island. Still others sought unsettled regions and brought into being the colonies of Connecticut and New Haven.

If the Puritans had so little tolerance for such godly radicals as Roger Williams and Anne Hutchinson, it may be imagined they had even less use for the more ruffian-like types of settlers. In nearby Quincy, a renegade lawyer called Thomas Morton had settled with a tough and lusty group of traders. There they sold liquor and firearms to the Indians and passed their leisure hours in drinking and in dancing with naked Indian girls around a maypole decorated, it was said, with obscene verses. The Puritans hastily packed Morton off to England, but the latter very nearly had his revenge. From the Crown's point of view Massachusetts had only been a sub-settlement in an area already granted to a body known as the Council of New England, under the presidency of Sir Ferdinando Gorges. Gorges had originally looked with favour on the Puritan settlements which he considered were under his jurisdiction. Later, influenced by Morton, he decided to take action against them. On Gorges' instigation, Charles I declared that he would take over New England as his father had taken over Virginia, and Gorges was appointed as first royal governor. But Gorges' ship was wrecked on the voyage to America, and then the outbreak of civil war in England ended forever any hopes of Charles I about strengthening his authority in the lands beyond the ocean.

The Red Indians

Conversion of the Red Indians to Christianity was always high amongst the avowed aims of all the European powers who colonized the New World. In practice, the Spaniards took this very seriously, the

French less so, the English and Dutch hardly at all. After the brief period of good relations established under the auspices of Pocahontas and her kinsmen, the settlers of Virginia were forced to fight a series of border wars with Indians who rightly feared that their hunting grounds were disappearing forever. The northern Puritans believed that they were God's chosen people come to His chosen land and treated the Indians as the Israelites had treated the Canaanites.

As for the Indians themselves, most were hunting and fishing people, practising a little shifting agriculture. They were fierce fighters, but they were soon outnumbered and were usually incapable of any widespread coordination of their efforts. Many were killed, more died through disease, and by the end of the century most had been pushed back from the seaboard to the Alleghenny Mountains. On the upper Hudson River and north of Lake Erie, however, lived more formidable and more settled tribes who had large villages and who cultivated maize. The more southerly of these were banded into a confederation, the famous League of the Five Nations, and were called by the French the Iroquois. They were often at war with their northern neighbours, the Hurons. The fur trade soon exacerbated this conflict, the Iroquois acting as middlemen for the Dutch, and later the English, on the Hudson River and the Hurons allying themselves with the French. The Hurons, less organized, were nonetheless more numerous and good fighters. Into their land, in the wake of the fur traders, came Jesuit priests, the spearhead of French diplomacy, and it briefly appeared that this area might turn into another Jesuit theocracy. Unhappily, an epidemic greatly reduced the Hurons, and a deep factional struggle between Christians and pagans grew up within their ranks. At this fatal juncture the Iroquois began their great offensive of the 1640s. The Hurons were virtually exterminated, the French fur trade came to a halt, and soon even the settlements of the St Lawrence were placed in peril. It was to be some time before the French were able to regain the initiative in North America.

The West Indies

The enthusiasm aroused by their mainland discoveries had diverted the interests of the Spaniards from the Caribbean. By the seventeenth century they had settled only the larger islands and even these very sparsely, while the numerous small islands of the sea were still virgin territory. In 1622 Thomas Warner discovered St Kitts. Three years later an English settlement under Warner and a French one under the Sieur d'Esnambuc were cooperating peacefully on the tiny island.

From St Kitts colonization spread. The English occupied nearby Nevis and Montserrat, while in 1625 John Powell discovered

Above, Cecilius Calvert, the second Baron Baltimore (c. 1605–75) who became proprietor of the colony of Maryland in 1632 and organized it as a refuge for religious refugees of all faiths. Enoch Pratt Free Library of Baltimore, Maryland.

Top, the first houses being built in 1607 at Jamestown, Virginia, the first successful English colony in North America; regular support for the new colony from Europe enabled it to survive. Library of Congress, Washington.

Opposite, drawing of Indian methods of fishing in Virginia, made by a member of Walter Raleigh's expedition of 1584; Indian hostility to the first colonists added to the hazards of the dangerous journey and severe winters. British Museum, London.

the larger more fertile and uninhabited island of Barbados. Meanwhile, d'Esnambuc had sent settlers to occupy the more important island of Martinique. France later added Guadeloupe and St Lucia to her list of possessions, and in 1635 a chartered company was formed to be responsible for the French West Indian colonies.

Prior to this, an attempt by English Puritans to found a settlement on the island of Providence had failed when the colony degenerated into a nest of pirates and was removed by the Spaniards. However, the idea of plundering the Spaniards on the one hand and trading illegally with their colonists on the other was by no means exclusive to the Puritans of Providence. In these fields it was the Dutch who first achieved success. In 1628, in the sea battle of the Matanzas, the Dutch admiral Pieter Heyn forever enshrined himself in the history of the Caribbean by capturing intact the Spanish treasure fleet. This fabulous success, which allowed the Dutch West India Company to declare a fifty percent dividend to every shareholder, set a goal for generations of other seamen but was only twice repeated during the colonial period. The Dutch also claimed island colonies for themselves—Curaçao, Aruba and St Eustatius. These, however, were mainly used as trading entrepôts where

Dutch goods could be sold illegally to Spanish colonists.

So far as the English and French islands were concerned, the main event which overtook them was the sugar revolution of mid-century. Once the knowledge of how to raise sugarcane was imported from Brazil, it transformed the whole economic basis of the area. By the 1650s most of the smaller islands had switched to sugar, Barbados leading the way for the English and Martinique and Guadeloupe for the French. Such a change was to have an immense effect on the demography of the West Indies. During the early period the islands had absorbed large numbers of white immigrants as small farmers. But sugar cultivation required much capital, large plantations, and huge labour forces. Soon large sugar planters were buying out the small tobacco farmers, while the white population of the islands fell dramatically and the number of negro slaves soared. This both encouraged the slave trade enormously and also brought much wealth to the white planters and ultimately to the merchants of France and England. It was not until the next century, however, that the two colossi of Caribbean sugar producers—British Jamaica and French St Domingué—emerged as the most important colonies in their respective Western empires.

The great Civil War in England temporarily ended the English monarchy and replaced it with the Commonwealth. At first, some of the English colonies, both in the Caribbean and on the mainland, retained royalist sympathies, but a Puritan squadron sent out from England soon brought them to heel. However, provinces such as Massachusetts, which gave lip service to the Commonwealth, were left virtually independent.

The accession of Oliver Cromwell to full power in England again focused events on the West Indies. Cromwell's policy harked back to archaic ideas such as a league of all Protestant powers against Catholic Spain, and a new assault on Spanish America was planned and given the grandiloquent title of 'the Western Design'. In the event, this resulted in one of the most thoroughly wretched expeditionary forces ever to leave English shores embarking upon the attempted conquest of Hispaniola in 1655. The Spaniards proved more than a match for their adversaries, but the disgruntled English commanders did manage to capture weakly garrisoned Jamaica as a sort of consolation prize. Cromwell was thinking in terms of a foreign policy half a century out of date, yet he accidentally stumbled in the direction of the future. Jamaica, little regarded at the time, was to become the sugar queen of Britain's mercantile empire a century later. In the meantime, the island proved to have a modest usefulness of a different kind—it provided a base for the buccaneers who now entered upon their heyday of plundering and pillaging Spanish shipping and settlement.

The term 'buccaneer' originated from a group of Frenchmen who lived by curing meat or *boucan* on the uninhabited coasts of Hispaniola. They were peaceable enough until the Spanish cruelly scattered their settlements and hunted them down like animals. Taking to the sea, the buccaneers exacted a terrible revenge. Soon joined by many English and Dutch adventurers, they built up large fleets and irregular armies. For a generation they terrorized the Caribbean; the most famous of them all was the Englishman, Henry Morgan—he who amassed a fortune by sacking three of the richest Spanish settlements, who forced prisoners to walk barefoot over hot coals in order to get them to reveal their wealth, who made captured monks and nuns advance ahead of his troops and be shot down by their fellow Spaniards, who led armies that slaughtered men and raped women throughout the whole of the Spanish Main. Eventually, by the Treaty of Madrid in 1670, the Spaniards agreed to recognize the English settlements in the Caribbean and the English agreed to suppress the buccaneers. Morgan was retired, knighted, created lieutenant governor of Jamaica and quietly allowed to drink himself to death.

Mercantilism

Mercantilism was an economic doctrine that provided the whole theory for imperial expansion up until the end of the eighteenth century. Basically, mercantilists believed that all the European powers were engaged in a life and death struggle over controlling the natural wealth of the world. Those nations that gained most of this wealth would wax ever stronger; those who were shut out from it would inevitably weaken and perhaps perish.

Early economists thought of natural wealth in terms of amassing precious metals and bullion. Later on the mercantile concept was widened to include commodities as well. The major aim was to build a self-contained state that could produce all it needed and could free itself from dependency on rival powers. This was the motivating force behind the European imperial expansion of the time, although matters rarely worked out exactly as planned. In the long run, geography and consumer demand rather than mercantilist theories dictated what was produced. In fact, the Europeans stumbled across commodities like sugar, tobacco, coffee, cotton, cocoa and indigo which proved capable of producing immense profits, even though the demand for them in previous centuries had been nonexistent or severely limited. Of these, sugar was the most valuable, and thus, for both the English

and the French, the West Indies became the focal point for their American empires.

By the end of the seventeenth century, the tiny island of Barbados was becoming the jewel in Britain's imperial crown, with a trade turnover greater than most of the much larger mainland colonies put together.

Mercantilism had many interesting implications. Since the wealth of the nation was the first consideration, it was taken for granted that the state would interfere heavily in overseas economic affairs. The Dutch showed the way with the development of the two huge, monopolistic, chartered companies, the East India Company and the West India Company, which were almost departments of the government itself. But the most famous legislative expression of the mercantile system was Britain's Acts of Trade and Navigation, begun in the mid-1650s. These attempted to lay down the principles that all important commodities produced in the colonies should be shipped directly to Britain and not to other countries; that all goods which the colonists bought in exchange should be shipped directly from Britain; that all shipping should be carried in British or colonial ships. Since mercantile commerce was overseas commerce, the system enormously enhanced the value of sea power and encouraged all nations to build large navies and merchant marines. Mercantilism also meant that colonies existed for the sake of the mother country and not the other way around. Thus the colonists, although expected to gain their fair share from the wealth of empire, were nonetheless politically and economically subject to the dictates of European governments.

Above, English sailors trading with the natives of the West Indies in the late sixteenth century; a hundred years later these natives had been swamped by European and negro immigrants, who had come to work on the sugar plantations. Conversely, the West Indies gave the disease syphilis to Europe.

Opposite, a chieftain in Florida in the sixteenth century showing settlers a column erected by earlier European explorers. In places where the Indians did not fear the loss of their hunting grounds, Europeans and native Americans often cooperated amicably. Chicago Historical Society, Chicago, Illinois.

The Stuart Restoration and further expansion

The return of the Stuarts to power in England in 1600 was accompanied by a new outburst of enthusiasm for colonial activities, of which the Navigation Acts were only one expression. A large new colony was planned immediately south of Virginia when, in 1663, Charles II issued a proprietary charter covering the territory which was to be known as Carolina. But this venture was chiefly noted for the absurd expectations of the proprietors of quick financial returns and for the ridiculously authoritarian constitution for the colonists drawn up by the philosopher, John Locke, mainly known for his anti-authoritarian political ideas. Most of the area remained uninhabited until the following century.

Nevertheless, other new English colonies came into being farther north along the Atlantic seaboard. In 1664, when England and Holland were at war, King Charles' brother, the Duke of York, organized the expedition which conquered the New Netherlands. The duke then turned this area into his own proprietary colony and renamed it after himself. Soon, however, he sold off the more southerly portions to another group of proprietors, and thus the separate colonies of East and West New Jersey came into being.

More important was the large colony established by the Duke of York's friend, William Penn. As a haven for his fellow Quakers, Penn acquired proprietary rights in what became Pennsylvania as payment for a debt owed to him by the Crown. When Charles II died and the Duke of York ascended the throne as James II, New York then became a royal colony. Pennsylvania, however, was a proprietorship until the American Revolution.

The Restoration era also saw the formation of two large chartered companies, with members and associates of the royal family among the shareholders. The Royal African Company was organized to put the slave trade on a better footing, while the Hudson's Bay Company was designed to exploit the wealth in furs available in the Canadian Arctic. The latter company was to suffer many vicissitudes during the following years of war with France, but in contrived to survive and is still operating.

Besides founding colonies, Restoration statesmen grappled with the problem of making royal authority more effective. The notoriously independent colonies of New England were eventually brought to heel by an English naval squadron and by their own fear of the French power growing up behind them. Ultimately, they acquiesced in acknowledging the sovereignty of the Crown and in promising obedience to the Navigation Acts. When James II became king, however, he attempted to push this trend still further. The former Puritan colonies were then deprived of their charters and forced to join together in the new Dominion of New England along with New York and New Jersey. However, the revolution of 1688 which drove James off the throne of England was immediately followed by the break-up of his embryonic Dominion. Nevertheless, William III did not allow the clock to be turned back completely. While New York, the New Jerseys, Connecticut and Rhode Island all regained their former status, Massachusetts remained a royal colony.

But the most remarkable development in the English American colonies had nothing to do with the deeds of Stuart statesmen: this was the astonishing growth of population. Through immigration and natural reproduction the number of English settlers had grown from the few hundred who landed at Jamestown to about 350,000 by the end of the century. This growth was to continue and was to be the most important single factor in deciding which power would ultimately rule in North America.

New France and the fur trade

In pursuit of the fur trade the French, as we have seen, had penetrated to the region north of the Great Lakes and allied themselves with the Huron Indians. But when the Iroquois hit back and destroyed Huronia, the whole existence of New France was placed in jeopardy. The threat of physical extinction had passed by the 1660s when a great Iroquois drive on Montreal was halted by the famous last stand of Adam Dollard at the Long Sault. Nevertheless, with the fur trade totally disrupted by the Iroquois, the colony must necessarily have withered unless help were forthcoming from France itself. This materialized in the reign of Louis XIV. Louis' great minister Colbert, was an avowed mercantilist and determined to retrieve the fortunes of the colony. Under his auspices the old and inefficient monopoly companies were replaced with a system of direct royal control, with a council headed by a governor, a bishop and an *intendant*. In 1665, the Marquis de Tracy arrived in New France with detachments of a crack French regiment—the first regulars who served in the colony. A year later, the French marched out to the Iroquois country and destroyed the villages and strongholds of the Indians. The latter avoided a pitched battle but were obliged to sue for peace.

Once this external threat was removed it was possible to overhaul the colony itself. The new system, with the governor as military and administrative head, the *intendant* handling economic and financial affairs, and the bishop dealing with the very important ecclesiastical side of life (for New France was a very Catholic colony), was designed to be a powerful 'troika' working to establish the settlement's welfare. Great strides were certainly made, particularly during the period of the zealous *intendant,* Jean Talon (1665–72), who devised methods of raising the population; there was a great increase in the area of land under cultivation and even the establishment of some modest industries.

Eventually, life in the colony took on a settled and permanent character. Its basis was the seigneurial system, a structure of feudal land-tenancy and of feudal dues, and despite its antiquated nature the system worked well. The seigneur acted as the local squire, magistrate, perhaps militia leader. But he was rarely much wealthier than his tenants and often worked in the fields with them. The tenants were assured of the full possession of land so long as they paid small dues and contributed minor labours, and they were free to sell their tenancies at will. Neither tenants nor seigneur had any political power—all this was invested in the council in Quebec.

Unfortunately, governor, bishop and *intendant*—designed to complement each other—might also oppose each other and paralyse administration. The most famous of the many such controversies was between Frontenac, the formidable governor who wished to extend the fur trade as rapidly as possible, and Laval, the greatest of the bishops, who was appalled at the way brandy debauched the Indians and brutalized life in the colony in general. It was inevitable that it should have been Frontenac's point of view that ultimately carried the day. To the government in Paris, if New France did not mean the fur trade, it meant nothing at all, for the sales of beaver pelts sustained the colony. But the fur trade was antipathetic to settlement; farmers ploughed land and cleared forests, thus driving away the Indians who trapped the beavers—and the beavers themselves who provided the furs. Moreover, many young men needed to work on the farms were drawn off into the more adventurous life of *coureurs de bois*—roaming the forests, trading, living with the Indians and on many occasions intermarrying with them.

It was the fur trade that also accounted for that other main characteristic of the French Empire in North America—its sprawling size. As old areas were denuded of furs new ones had to be found, so the empire expanded. Frontenac built a fort on Lake Ontario and by the end of the century the French were pushing towards Lake Superior. In the south, Marquette and Joliet reached the Mississippi in 1673; La Salle followed the great river to its mouth in the Gulf of Mexico in 1682, and Iberville founded a colony there in 1699.

But the occupation of this vast area inevitably led to conflict with the English settlers, who, their numbers steadily increasing, were already trickling over the mountains and eyeing the fertile lands to the west. In the whole of the French dominions in North America in 1700 there were scarcely more than 10,000 people. Thus, the fur trade

QUEBEC, *The Capital of* NEW-FRANCE, *a Bishoprick, and Seat of the Soverain Court.*

1. The Citadel. 2. the Castle.
3. Magazine. 4. y Recolets.
5. Ursulines 6. Jesuits. 7.
Cathedral of Our Lady.
8. The Palace 9. y Seminary
10. The Hôtel Dieu.
11. St Charles River.
12. The Common Hospital.
13. The Hermitage of the Recolets.
14. The Bishop's House. 15. The Parish Church of the Lower Town.
16. The Upper Town v. y Lower Town.
18. The Platform & Battery of Cannon.
19. The Isle of Orleans. 20. Point Levi.

created a huge empire for France and staffed it with men—hardy fur traders and their Indian allies—who could defend it with great skill and courage. But it also ensured that these men were very few in number.

The first conflicts

The War of the League of Augsburg which began in 1689 was mainly a European affair, but for the first time colonial fighting was of some importance. Indeed skirmishes occurred in America even before the formal declaration of war. The French had captured posts on Hudson Bay, while the Iroquois Indians, allied to the English, had annihilated the town of Lachine, six miles from Montreal.

When real war began, the old Count Frontenac was sent back as governor of New France. He immediately organized savage Indian raids against the frontier of New England. In 1690, however, the French were placed on the defensive. In May a New England force, commanded by Sir William Phips, easily captured Port Royal in Nova Scotia.

In August, Phips set out with 2,000 men and thirty-four ships against Quebec itself. But the expedition did not reach its objective until October. Nor did the French simply capitulate in the face of enemy power as Phips appears to have expected. Frontenac answered his demand for surrender 'from the mouths of my cannon', to use his own words, and after some skirmishing and shelling the New Englanders gave up and withdrew.

The French next launched an offensive in 1696. Frontenac himself commanded the

Above, Quebec in the mid-seventeenth century. The city became the administrative centre of the French province of New France in 1663, and was subject to regular attacks by both the Iroquois and the English until 1759, when it was permanently lost to the English.

Opposite left, the colony of New Amsterdam on the southern end of the island of Manhattan in the 1620s. The first colonists arrived there in 1624, and the island was bought from the Indians for a few trinkets two years later.

Opposite right, the seal of the city of New York, inscribed with the date 1664, the year in which the English won it from the Dutch. The colonies of New England had been founded in the 1630s and 1640s, and the conquest of New York, giving access to the Hudson River, increased English security in this region.

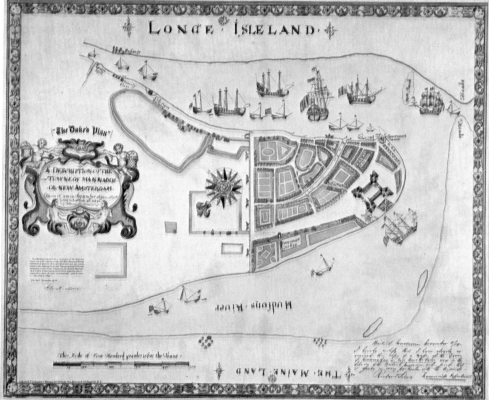

expedition striking at the Iroquois, while in an astonishing campaign the remarkable Sieur d'Iberville captured Pemaquid in Maine, attacked the English settlements in Newfoundland and in a single vessel bested three English warships on Hudson Bay.

In the West Indies the several operations of the war ended in a draw. Du Casse ravaged Jamaica but could not hold it. A French assault from St Dominguè on Spanish Hispaniola was halted by the Spaniards in the battle of Limonade, but an Anglo-Spanish counter-attack failed when the troops perished from disease.

The Treaty of Ryswick, which ended the war in 1697, made few alterations in the West Indies, but in the north the French gained some advantages. Nova Scotia was returned to them, and they kept all but one of the English forts on Hudson Bay. By separate agreement, the Iroquois promised Frontenac to remain neutral in future conflicts. So the first, rather small, clash of empires had seen the English somewhat worsted by their rivals. Ryswick, however, was not the end of the story, only the beginning.

Chapter 24

Colonial Conflict in the Eighteenth Century

Just as the seventeenth century had been an age of primitive empire-building, so the eighteenth was to be one of imperial conflict. The economic doctrine of mercantilism, which had provided the impetus for colonization, also greatly influenced the institution of European warfare. On the one hand, it helped to temper it. Commercial wars were much less ferocious affairs than religious or nationalistic ones. On the other hand, mercantilist attitudes made the occurrence of war much more likely. The necessity of controlling ever more of the world's natural wealth inevitably led to the desire to destroy or swallow up the colonies owned by rival nations. Fighting was conducted on a world-wide basis. In the War of Jenkins' Ear, Britain made a great assault on Spanish America and utterly failed. But against their more formidable French enemies, the English were ultimately successful. A long series of colonial campaigns, reaching their climax in the Seven Years War, saw Britain wrest from France control of both India and North America.

Latin America

The seventeenth century, as we have seen, was a period of catastrophic decline, both for Spain and for her imperial possessions. The following century, however, saw an upward trend; the new Bourbon dynasty, arriving in Spain in 1700 in the person of Philip V, brought more brisk, French-inspired ways of thinking to the decrepit empire. This trend continued for most of the next hundred years and found its best expression during the reign of Charles III, from 1759 to 1788. Charles was an enlightened despot, whose motto was 'Everything for the people, but nothing by the people'. Although not over intelligent, he was sincere in his good intentions and ailing Spain saw a marked, if only partial, revival in her fortunes.

This upsurge was also evident in Latin America. This was partially owing to natural circumstances. By 1700, the dreadful population decline had been halted and reversed and so gave hope that reforms would enjoy a measure of success. At the same time the secret report of two Spanish naval officers, Antonio de Ulloa and Jorge Juan, clearly

depicted the large amount of corruption and indolence that existed in Spanish colonial administration.

Latin America was much larger in the eighteenth century than it is today. Below the English and French settlements on the east coast of North America, almost the entire continent belonged to Spain and Portugal, who excluded all colonists but their own nationals. The only exceptions on the mainland were French Guiana (Cayenne), Dutch Guiana (Surinam), and the logwood-cutting camps of the British

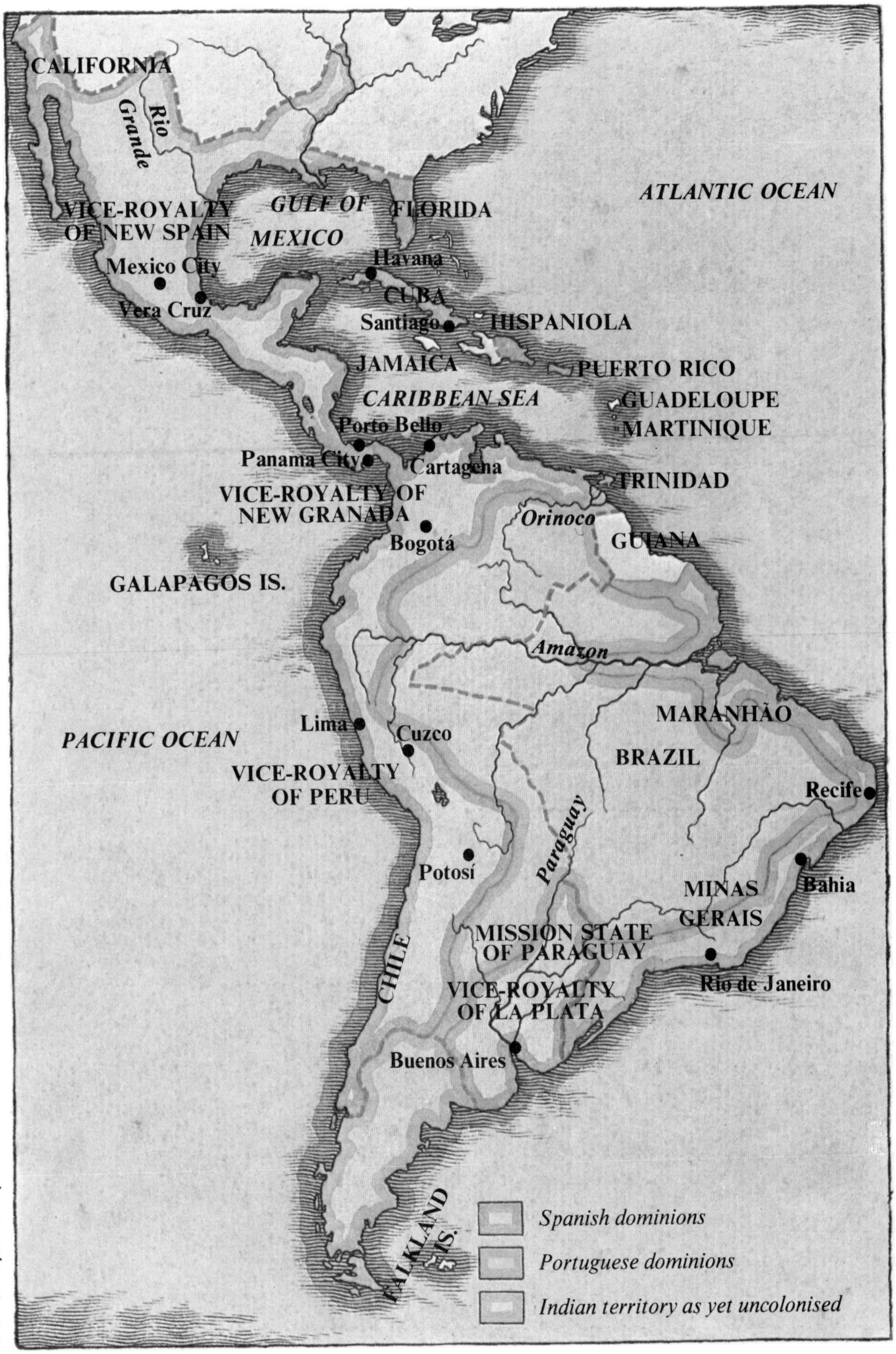

Above, Latin America in the late colonial period, at the end of the eighteenth century. Apart from Portuguese Brazil, most of Latin America was ruled from Lima, in Peru.

Opposite top, William Penn's Treaty with the Indians, painted by Benjamin West (1738–1820). The Pennsylvania Academy of Fine Arts, Philadelphia, Pennsylvania. Joseph and Sarah Harnson Collection.

Opposite bottom, a Dutch plan of the early 1660s showing the layout of Mannados or New Amsterdam, founded in 1647.

Map legend:
- Spanish dominions
- Portuguese dominions
- Indian territory as yet uncolonised

in Honduras, which the Spanish made a few attempts to evict. The Caribbean, a vital area because of its sugar, indigo and tobacco, was divided between France, Britain and Spain. It was one of the main theatres of colonial warfare.

The Portuguese share of Latin America was Brazil; all the rest belonged to Spain. And the area of Spanish sovereignty was still growing. Texas was permanently occupied (1720–22); Spanish colonists settled Upper California from 1769, founding San Diego, Monterey, San Francisco and Los Angeles; Spanish explorers penetrated further up the west coast in an effort to pre-empt the British and Russians. Spain acquired Louisiana (the territory east of the Mississippi) from her ally France as compensation for Florida, which was ceded to Britain in 1763 but regained in 1783. Thus, over the century, Spain even made a territorial profit from her dealings with her stronger rivals.

The keynote of the century in both Spanish and Portuguese America was expansion, in most senses of the word. Spanish settlers moved into Uruguay in the 1720s, founding Montevideo, and into Patagonia in the 1770s. The Portuguese expanded to the south and west of Brazil. Cities, above all Mexico City, grew in size and splendour; trade boomed; new sources of wealth were tapped; and wealthy colonials began to visit the Old World.

Much of this was made possible by reforms in Spain and Portugal; but their success in fact brought forward the date when the colonies would seize their independence. Mercantilist economics encouraged all states to exploit and restrict the development of their colonies. The fact that Latin America was ruled by states poor in resources and militarily weak made the growth of colonial self-confidence a dangerous phenomenon.

Administrative reform

In the years of the Bourbon era, many salutary administrative experiments with regard to the colonies were made at both metropolitan and local levels. In Spain itself, the year 1714 saw the creation of a new Ministry of Marine and the Indies.

This body proved much more modern and efficient than the old Royal and Supreme Council, which had done good work in its time but was now past its prime. The old council still remained, however, rather obstructing the work of its younger rival, but most of its powers were gradually shifted to the new ministry in the course of the century. Another improvement occurred when all of the administrative institutions regarding the colonies were moved from Seville to Cadiz, a much more satisfactory port.

In the colonies themselves dramatic changes also took place. In the course of the century, the huge and cumbersome Vice-Royalty of Peru was split into three. In 1717, modern Colombia and Venezuela were detached from Peru, and the Vice-Royalty of New Granada was created. To the south, the area comprising much of present-day Argentina, Uruguay, Paraguay and Bolivia was turned into the Vice-Royalty of La Plata in 1776, with its capital at Buenos Aires. This area, originally ruled from Lima, thousands of miles away and

232

behind the mountains of the Andes, now saw a period of rapid growth, testifying to the usefulness of the change. At the same time, the quality and ability of the viceroys themselves was improved, and in the late eighteenth century we have men like Bucareli and Revillagigedo, whose names and deeds are worthy to be compared with such notables from earlier days as Mendoza and Toledo.

Spanish government in the New World had originally been designed to ensure that royal authority was felt down to the lowest levels of administration. Its fundamental unit was the *cabildo* or town council. *Regidores*, or councillors, and *alcaldes*, or mayors, were the centres of power in their own small communities. They collected taxes, supervised police, sanitation and all the other duties of a municipality. The members of *cabildos* were ostensibly forbidden to use their positions for private gain, and all their acts were in theory reviewed, by higher officials.

Supervising the conduct of the *cabildos*, and of all other inferior magistrates, were the *audiencias*, or royal courts, whose judges were known as *oidores*—'those who hear'. The latter individuals were very highly paid, and their lives were circumscribed by rather monastic restrictions to guard against perversion of justice. Some ten *audiencias* had been created in the sixteenth century, each exercising many judicial, administrative, military and financial functions in its section of the empire. They were also designed to ensure continuity of administration and automatically took the place of a viceroy should he die or be recalled.

A viceroy was, of course, the direct representative of the king, and he lived in a palace with an establishment that many European monarchs might have envied. His powers were huge; so was his salary—in an effort to place him above corruption. His term of office, however, was generally short—in theory only three years. He was forbidden all private business, was not allowed to marry within his own realm and was always subject to instant recall from Madrid. He and all other officials were open to the periodic examinations of a royal visitor, who might appear when he chose, investigate all records and listen to complaints which anyone might bring. At the end of his term of office, every viceroy had to undergo a *residencia*, where a judge appointed by the crown would examine his whole record in public.

In some ways this cumbersome and complex structure of government had worked remarkably well. But during the lax period of the seventeenth century many abuses had grown up. The most important remedial measure of the eighteenth century was the introduction of the *intendencias*, again borrowed from French models. The greatest failure of the old system of administration had been the gap between the

extremely well paid viceroys and members of the *audiencias* on one hand and the local administrators such as the *alcades* and *corregidores* on the other. Owing to their small salaries, the latter had derived most of their income from bribery or exactions, while their pettiness and their distance from the seats of power had largely protected their corruption from investigation by the higher organs. Now, however, the viceroyalties were subdivided into dozens of *intendencias* ruled by professional administrators with good salaries. Beneath these were further subdivisions, administered by *sub-delegados*, who were appointed by the intendants. This extended to the majority of the populace at least some hope of real justice.

Economic revival and colonial defence

One of the reasons for the seventeenth-century decline of both Spain and the Indies was the tremendous falling off in the production of precious metals during this period. Similarly, the eighteenth century revival was accompanied by a remarkable increase in bullion production, especially in Mexican silver, greatly aided by the recoinage of the clipped and debased colonial currency undertaken in 1728 under the aegis of Philip V. Other factors as well—a decrease in the labour shortage, better mining techniques, and the more sensible management of the mining companies themselves—helped to double the Mexican silver output.

The Indies were also becoming important as exporters of other commodities. An increased demand for leather in Europe strongly stimulated the production of hides, taken from the wild cattle that roamed the pampas of the Argentine. Hitherto there had been little demand for meat, and the carcasses of these slaughtered cattle had been left for the vultures. But the discovery of huge salt mines near Buenos Aires meant that this area could begin to produce the

Above, a French indigo factory in the West Indies. Indigo, like many other vegetable dyes, was a valuable export to Europe until the nineteenth century.

Opposite left, Port St Jacques in Cuba in 1691; rich in both minerals and agriculture, this Spanish island was sought by the other imperial powers in the eighteenth century, but, apart from the years 1762–63 when it was held by Britain, the island remained firmly Spanish.

Opposite right, the title page of a history of the New World, published by Spain in 1730 as part of an attempt to revitalize interest in Spain's empire.

salted beef which was in such demand by the navies of the world. Agricultural exports, especially cash crops like coffee and cocoa, also saw an astonishing period of growth. Spanish lethargy had originally left the immense profits of sugar cultivation almost exclusively in the hands of other nations. But by the eighteenth century it was being grown in many places, both on the mainland and on the Caribbean islands. In Cuba, sugar production increased ten times within forty years. By the end of the century, that island was the greatest of the Caribbean exporters.

To manage their colonial wealth better, the Bourbons created a number of state monopoly companies modelled after the British and Dutch East India companies. The most important of these were the Honduras Company, the Havana Company, the Santo Domingo Company and the Caracas Company. But only the last-named was ever really an important success or paid good dividends.

The return of economic prosperity to the Spanish dominions was naturally accompanied by an important revival of trade and a significant growth of shipping. It was during the reign of Charles III that sensible attempts were made to increase this trend by the promotion of a freer trade within the Spanish Empire itself. In 1765 the monopoly of Cadiz was at last breached, and the Caribbean islands were opened to virtually unlimited trade with nine of the chief Spanish ports. This type of concession was later expanded, between 1768 and 1778, to all Spanish America excepting New Spain (Mexico) and Venezuela.

As her empire once again became so valuable to Spain it was necessary for the mother country to devote more thought and energy to protecting it. The old *encomienda* system had provided levies of soldiers to defend the empire in a manner similar to the Scottish clan system. But the decline of the Indian population on which it was based had led to the virtual disappearance of the *encomienda* by 1700. For a period, it was only detachments of regular soldiers that gave military protection to Spanish America. After 1760, however, a colonial militia system was introduced and organized with reasonable efficiency. Earlier,

a coastguard had been created in an attempt to end the huge illegal trade carried on between the Spanish colonists in the Caribbean and the foreign possessions there. Against smugglers, the *guarda costas* proved remarkably efficient, indeed almost too much so; the over-enthusiastic seizures made by their captains were among the chief factors promoting war with England in 1739.

To guard her trade and commerce with the colonies, Spain in earlier years had relied on the convoy system, on the vast complex of fortresses guarding the harbours of Havana in Cuba and Cartagena in Colombia and on her navy, at one time the finest in the world. In the seventeenth century, however, the convoys had ceased to sail, the fortifications had fallen into disrepair, the navy was virtually nonexistent. During the reigns of the Bourbons, new efforts were made in all three of these directions. In 1720, a 'project for Galeones and Flotas' was promulgated, ordering that regular convoys be resumed. But the system did not prove very adequate and worked only intermittently. It was abolished in 1789. The fortifications, however, were repaired to good effect—as the war of 1739 would show. Work on rebuilding the navy was begun in 1717 under Philip V. It was perhaps not as successful as the Bourbons had hoped, but within twenty years Spain could put some formidable fleets to sea.

Another important factor in terms of colonial defence was the alliance between Spain and France which existed for most of the century. France and Spain together could hope to equal or surpass British power at sea, and the Spanish Empire was secure from the French assaults on its territorial integrity that had occurred so frequently in the seventeenth century.

The War of Jenkins' Ear

The renewed attempts of Spain to strengthen her empire came none too soon. Her rich possessions always incited the cupidity of her enemies, and British statesmen were certainly giving serious thought to the prospect of seizing or destroying her dominions. Indeed, the Anglo-Spanish conflict which

broke out in 1739 was almost purely colonial in its origins.

One of Britain's chief gains at the Treaty of Utrecht in 1713 had appeared to be the *asiento* contract. This had assured the South Sea Company of the right to deliver 4800 slaves a year for sale in the Spanish colonies, to keep factors in several Spanish American ports, and to send one shipload annually of British merchandise to the Spanish trade fairs in the New World. It was expected that all this would be extremely lucrative. Yet great profits were not in fact forthcoming, and for one reason or another many of the annual voyages did not take place. Nevertheless, the Spaniards felt they, too, had grounds for complaint in that the British annual ships carried far more goods than the treaty had projected.

Worse still from the Spanish point of view was the constant smuggling of merchandise from the British Caribbean islands to the Spanish colonies. The introduction of the *guarda costas* somewhat checked this, but the over-enthusiastic seizures made by those vessels provoked great cries of rage in England against all sorts of real and supposed atrocities. Indeed the war of 1739 received its odd name when a Captain Jenkins produced his pickled ear in the British parliament, claiming it had been cut off by the Spaniards.

Relations between the two nations reached a crisis in 1738. The Spanish government wished to avoid conflict, as did Robert Walpole in England. Other British statesmen were, however, already mentally carving up the Spanish Empire. When negotiations foundered in 1739, the English decided to open hostilities with a surprise attack in the Caribbean.

British statesmen seemed sure that the Spanish Empire was ready to fall like some overripe fruit; but ideas differed about the best way to shake the great tree. Some thought in terms of conquering territory, others of seizing strategic ports. Others still surmised that the best idea might be to aid the Spanish colonists in seeking independence, because afterwards they were certain to trade mainly with Britain. In the end, much was left to the discretion of the commanders on the spot. Admiral Edward Vernon was despatched to the Caribbean

with one fleet; another was to follow, transporting a large army under Lord Cathcart. Simultaneously, Commodore George Anson set sail on an epic voyage to raid the Spanish possessions in the Pacific, equipped with dozens of proclamations urging the colonists to revolt. Vernon arrived at Jamaica in October of 1739; a month later, and without declaration of war, he stormed and took Porto Bello in Panama with only six ships.

The Spaniards now looked to their defences. One good fleet lay in Cartagena harbour under the astute command of Don Blas de Lezo; another commanded by Admiral Torres was on its way to the Caribbean. Then came an intervention. In 1740, a French fleet under the Marquis d'Antin arrived at St Dominguè. Though France was at peace with Britain, d'Antin had secret orders to attack; but before anything could happen sickness had ravaged the French and d'Antin sailed home. England and France remained at peace. Spain was left to make the best of her own resources.

It soon became clear that the first blow would fall on the great fortified harbour of Cartagena, on what is now the north coast of Colombia. There the one-eyed, one-armed, lame Don Blas de Lezo was skilfully preparing defences. But in March 1741 the British arrived in apparently overwhelming numbers—twenty-nine ships of the line, over a hundred smaller vessels and some 23,000 men, of whom 15,000 were sailors. Despite the massive fortifications of Cartagena, the odds seemed against Don Blas and his 4,000 defenders. Yet it was time rather than numbers that was of the essence. A stubborn and drawn-out defence could

allow Spanish America's two greatest weapons—malaria and yellow fever—to begin their deadly work.

The pattern of the campaign quickly became clear. The two admirals, Edward Vernon and Sir Chaloner Ogle, both old Caribbean hands, urged and themselves took quick action. But General Thomas Wentworth, who succeeded in command when Lord Cathcart died, proved constitutionally incapable of hastening matters. With the navy leading, the outlying Spanish forts were taken and the harbour entered, while Don Blas carefully withdrew. At last only a single castle remained to the defenders, but it was beyond reach of naval bombardment. Wentworth now began, with exasperating slowness, to make dispositions for attack. His men were soon dying off from disease while the admirals fumed about 'gentlemen of parade . . . trained to nothing but reviews'. At last Wentworth attempted to assault the fort but was repulsed with 650 casualties. By then hundreds of men were collapsing daily, and soon there were only 3,500 effective soldiers left of a force of 8,000. In May the British ignominiously withdrew.

Eyes now turned towards Cuba, but the Spaniards meanwhile had been hastening the reinforcement of Havana. With their

Above, an encounter between the ship of Commodore George Anson and a Spanish ship from Manilla during the War of Jenkins' Ear.

Top, the capture of Porto Bello in November 1739 by the English in the War of Jenkins' Ear; this commercial war was fought entirely in the West Indies and it helped to speed the decline of Spanish colonial power.

Above left, a satire on the treaty between England and Spain made by Walpole in 1738; the interests of commerce had overtaken the old fears of Catholicism.

Opposite left, the port of Santa Domingo, on the island of Hispaniola. Like the other Spanish colonial ports this stronghold against pirate attacks in the sixteenth century was opened to English and French shipping in the eighteenth century.

Opposite right, the city of Cartagena, in Colombia, painted in 1786. Formerly twenty-nine forts had protected its treasure houses, but by this time its importance to the economy of Spain and the politics of Europe had declined. Museo del Palacio Real, Madrid.

own forces so depleted, the British therefore decided to destroy Santiago on the southern shore of the island. The troops disembarked in July, but Wentworth again sat and deliberated about whether or not to advance. At last he decided to await promised reinforcements from England and again his men began to sicken and die. Finally, with over 2,000 dead or ill, he withdrew from the island in November.

When 3,000 British reinforcements did arrive at Jamaica, one last assault was planned against the Spaniards—a surprise landing at Porto Bello, followed by a rapid march across the isthmus to Panama City. On this occasion, Vernon, in bad temper, spoiled the surprise element, whereupon Wentworth refused to march.

When the remnants of the three successive disasters reached Jamaica for the last time, the irritation and lack of trust between the commanders had reached such proportions as to doom all further efforts. Vernon and Wentworth were either not speaking or were quarrelling: Vernon and Ogle became involved in a physical brawl with the governor of Jamaica; councils of war could not be held. At last the Duke of Newcastle recalled both army and navy. Meanwhile, in the Pacific, Commodore Anson had fared better, attacking Spanish settlements and spectacularly capturing the richly laden Manila galleon. But the loss of two-thirds of his men from scurvy precluded his efforts to raise the Spanish colonies in rebellion.

The campaigns of the War of Jenkins's Ear are little remembered today, yet they are extremely important in the history of both the western hemisphere and the world. During the Seven Years War, Britain had more success in wresting colonies from Spain, but the campaign she planned at that time was much more limited and less deadly in its scope. The Vernon-Wentworth expedition was the only one launched by Britain which might conceivably have destroyed or crippled the Spanish Empire and placed large areas of Latin America under British rule. The walls of Cartagena, the skill of Don Blas and the valour of his men and the mosquitoes that carried tropical diseases had all cooperated to preserve Spain's dominions intact.

The fall of the Jesuits

Within the Spanish Empire, the Roman Catholic Church in the colonies was well controlled by the Church in Spain, and virtually all of the most important positions in its hierarchy were in the hands of Spanish-born clergy. It was also immensely opulent in the things of this world. By now, too, most of the Indians had been converted to Christianity, although observers had felt that while they had lost their old faith they had not truly grasped the new. At any rate, during the eighteenth century the Church remained a bastion of the establishment.

The chief exception to this rule was the Jesuits. Through shrewd investments, the order grew rich, but not so its individual members, who remained poor and dedicated and worked under a rigid discipline. Following their secret investigation in the 1740s, Juan and Ulloa reported, 'one does not see in them the lack of religion, the scandals and the loose behaviour so common in the others.' But the Jesuits, through championing the Indians, had always been disliked by the settlers. In 1767 they fell foul of the Crown as well. Charles III, annoyed by an order which was more loyal to Rome than to himself, ordered their expulsion. Whatever the merits of the case against them in Spain, the expulsion of the Jesuits was something of a disaster for the colonies. Missions fell apart, schools declined, hospitals and houses of charity disappeared. Especially pathetic were the results in the huge mission centre of Paraguay. There the rigid, theocratic sway that the Jesuits had exercised over the Indians might not have produced the best of all possible worlds; it was far better, however, than the breaking-up of the missions, the sale of land to rich planters and the exploitation of Indian labour which followed it.

Land and labour

The decline and disappearance of the *encomiendas* in the late sixteenth and seventeenth centuries necessitated a new type of basic agricultural organization. They were in fact replaced by the *haciendas*, or great estates, and by the system of peonage. The *haciendado* was the landowner, the peons his labour. This was not a system enforced or devised by any laws but one which grew up informally. In theory, the peon was a free agricultural labourer who received wages for his work. And indeed, if he could somehow save any money, this was his position in reality. In fact most peons lived out their lives in a form of debt-slavery. They fell into debt for rent they could not pay, for clothing or food advanced them by their estate owner, for many other reasons; and their wages rarely overtook their debts. They were tied to the estate and could not go elsewhere. Soon, almost all of the settled land was divided up amongst the huge *haciendas* and one employer would not usually accept the services of a runaway from another. Moreover, debts were continuous and inherited from father to son. Thus, throughout much of the Spanish Empire, a great deal of the population lived in a serf-like state, bound to their *haciendas*, and were often bought and sold with them.

Although it was the Indians who suffered most from the iniquities of the colonial system, they constituted the least threat to Spanish rule. Ignorant, illiterate and with little contact beyond their immediate neighbours, they had scant hope of making any sort of organized resistance. Their occasional, small-scale revolts of desperation were easily crushed. On one single occasion, however, the vice-royalty of Peru was shaken to its roots.

José Gabriel Condorcanqui was a *mestizo*—one of mixed Spanish and Indian blood—who was also a direct descendant of the last great Inca. The Spaniards recognised him as the legal heir of the Incas and gave him the title of Marquis of Oropesa and a prominent position within the community. He may have been educated by the Jesuits, but his sympathies lay with his Indian relations. Taking the Inca name of Tupac Amaru, he carried the Indian cause to viceroys and governors. Unable to obtain any legal redress for the wrongs of his people, he raised a rebellion in November 1780. Thousands of Indians flocked to his banner; the authorities were unprepared, and briefly he found himself in control of a huge empire.

Naively believing that the local administrators were his only real enemies, Tupac called on the creoles to join in his revolt and proclaimed himself a viceroy ruling loyally on behalf of the Spanish king. After six months, however, regular soldiers and colonial militia dispersed his followers and Tupac himself was hideously tortured to death after witnessing the execution of his wife and family. But this only provoked another rebellion and more guerilla warfare. When it ended, over 80,000 Indians and settlers had perished. This, however, proved to be the one great, blind and hopeless revolt of the masses; the ultimate danger to Spanish rule came from the higher orders of society.

Creoles and *gapuchines*

The varied peoples of the Spanish Empire were grouped in six great divisions derived from race of origin. There were Negroes, mulattoes, Indians, *mestizos*, white Americans of Spanish descent and, lastly, Spaniards born in Spain. It was the growing enmity between the last two groups that caused the greatest hazard to Spanish rule. Those Spaniards born in America called themselves *americanos* and were called by others creoles. Those born in Spain were known as *peninsulares* or more derisively as *gapuchines*. The creoles had many reasons for their discontent. Politically, despite a few exceptions, they were consistently excluded by the Spaniards from the highest offices of Church and state. Economically, the creole wholesalers of Mexico and Lima resented the privileges of the Spanish shippers in Seville and Cadiz. In the army and militia, creole officers were slighted by those of Spanish birth. Most irritating of all, perhaps, was the social distinction. Invariably, people of Spanish origin, whatever their background, looked down on even the wealthiest creoles of good family standing as being uncultured provincials. The creole upper classes greatly resented this; they were

Little of true originality was produced, however, except for the poetry of Sor Ines de la Cruz, a nun with strange genius who became world famous.

Architecture, however, was a different matter, and here was found the most distinctive creativity of the Indies. The inspiration came from Alberto de Churriguera, a Spanish architect belonging to a school whose members extended the extravagance of the Baroque style to such extremes that they became known as 'the delirious fools'. In the colonies this extravagance was pushed even further, with predictably varying results, but it is generally agreed that Mexico now boasts perhaps as many masterpieces of the late Baroque as all the rest of the world put together. Indeed, it could be said that a gorgeous Mexican cathedral, wherein great men and ladies knelt to pray beside crowds of wretched and unshod Indian peons, provides the most apt symbol of the Spanish Empire as a whole—a breath-taking edifice, beautifully adorned, containing within its walls extremes of squalor and splendour.

Brazil

Compared with the glitter of the Spanish colonies, Portuguese Brazil appears more like some vast charnel house containing all of the vices of mankind, somewhat tempered by a certain tolerance and cheerful indolence. Urban life was neglected. Cities were small and unimportant and churches unimpressive. Illiteracy and cultural ignorance were colossal; no printing press was set up, few books were imported, no universities were built. Life was rural, centring on the *fazenda*, or plantation, which sprawled over huge areas. One was larger than the whole kingdom of Portugal itself. Here the planter ruled from his great house like an absolute monarch over his hundreds or thousands of subjects. Labour conditions were often atrocious.

Unlike the Spaniards, the Portuguese showed no qualms of conscience about the fate of the aboriginal inhabitants of the continent. From the beginning, Indians were brutally kidnapped and worked to death as slaves on the plantations. But there were never enough of them, and huge numbers of negroes were imported from Angola and West Africa. Theoretically, Brazilian society was divided into a rigid caste system based on race. In practice, however, it was usually economic status that made the difference. The mulatto off-spring of the planters and their slaves were often treated as whites and sometimes rose to high positions. And there were certainly plenty of mulattoes and *mestizos*. Miscegenation proceeded at an incredible rate. Quite unashamedly, the Portuguese planters displayed their large broods of white, coloured and illegitimate children as a proof of their virility. This tremendous racial mixing was only partially caused by a relative lack of

Above, a Brazilian mulatto, the child of a European father and a negro slave mother; mulattoes were often able to attain positions of importance in colonial Brazil.

Left, a Brazilian Indian; although he appears here to reflect the Enlightenment's interest in the noble savage, the Brazilian Indians never in fact received any such respect from the Europeans.

willing to respect the viceroys and the *oidores* but not the numerous minor Spanish officials. Between these groups a marked resentment grew. But the creoles did not have the type of political institutions, as the Americans in the British colonies had, through which to voice their grievances. Moreover, they were intensely loyal to the Spanish monarchy. And, in the last analysis, it was not until that monarchy itself fell into grave disrepute during the Napoleonic Wars that the New World decided to break with the Old.

Spanish American culture

Culture and the fine arts were respected in Spanish America. Mainly they took the form of provincial versions of the culture of old Spain, deriving a strange fascination from their setting in a new and luminous land. Although sporadic efforts were made to educate the Indians, these were usually discouraged on the correct assumption that they constituted a danger to the establishment. Culture, therefore, was mainly upper-class culture, but it was widespread. Books were in great demand in the colonies, almost from the beginning of the conquest, and printing presses were early established in the Indies. Soon a stream of literature about New World subjects enriched that of the Old. Universities, modelled after the famous Spanish institution of Salamanca, were founded at an early date. Classes began in the University of Lima in 1572 and in Mexico in 1663. Some twenty-five institutions of higher learning had been organized by the end of the eighteenth century. The fields of drama, music, poetry, painting and sculpture all aroused enthusiastic interest.

white women. Portuguese men had a positive preference for the exotic. Whereas Portuguese women were kept in seclusion and treated as an inferior species, a handsome mulatto mistress might obtain a position of power in the household. One contemporary observer noted 'Brazil is a hell for blacks, a purgatory for whites and a paradise for mulattoes.'

Portuguese colonial government was rather haphazardly modelled on that of Spain. An overseas council, set up in Lisbon, was somewhat analogous to the Supreme Council of the Indies. After Portugal itself became free from Spain in 1640, a viceroy was appointed to rule Brazil, but this position was soon dropped in favour of the less royal title of captain-general. Under the captain-general the vast area of the colony was subdivided into several captaincies, while in the north the state of Maranhão was ruled independently from Lisbon. Portuguese government, however, never attained the same degree of centralized authority and control as did its Spanish counterpart. How could it? Portugal was a tiny nation with a population of less than two million. In the seventeenth century, when the empire extended over large areas of Africa and the countries bordering the Indian Ocean, it has been estimated that there were only about 10,000 Portuguese active throughout the whole of it. As the eastern empire declined, however, interest in Brazil increased. This became especially true after the discovery of gold and diamonds in the early eighteenth century. When, in this era, the King of Portugal could describe Brazil as his 'milch cow', royal authority was effectively extended somewhat further. Yet by Spanish standards Brazil was always lightly ruled.

The beginnings of the history of the Church in Brazil commenced with the arrival of six Jesuit priests in 1549. In 1551 the Portuguese king was made Grand Master of the Order of Christ by the pope and given much the same exclusive control of the Church in his realms as the Spanish monarchs exercised in theirs. The growth of Church organization in Brazil was slow, but Roman Catholicism was always of great importance in the social development of the colony. The numerous secular clergy, however, quickly identified themselves with the planter class and came under the influence of the great estate owners as much as anyone in the colony. Again, the Jesuits were an exception. Alone, they saw their main duty in protecting and Christianizing the Indians. They learned Indian languages, built dozens of mission villages and generally protected their charges (sometimes behind barricades) from the rapacity of slave hunters. In doing so, they earned the antipathy of virtually all other white people in the colony.

It was in the seventeenth century that the Portuguese began to move inland from the coast. The absorption of the Portuguese Empire by the Spanish between 1580 and

1640 had one advantage for Brazil. The Spaniards allowed the colony's boundaries to be extended further westwards than the line originally drawn by the Treaty of Tordesillas. The initial agents for this expansion were the ferocious Paulistas of the south from the area around São Paulo. These wild men, usually of mixed Portuguese and Indian blood, began to roam the hinterlands, hunting down Indians whom they sold as slaves. Their horrible raids destroyed many Indian tribes, but they also opened up much country which was eventually filled by the *vaqueiros*—the cowboys and stockmen who came after them.

In the 1690s roaming Paulistas discovered large deposits of alluvial gold in the area that came to be known as the Minas Gerais. Soon the first great gold rush of modern times had begun. People flocked in from all parts of the colony and from Portugal itself. They came from all walks of life: planters

deserted their plantations, merchants their shops, priests their churches and monasteries. Soon these newcomers were fighting a civil war with the Paulistas—the War of the Emboabos. The Paulistas were defeated but pushing further inland eventually discovered diamond fields as well.

The Portuguese court rejoiced. With his new-found wealth the king was able to improve his political position by ceasing to call his parliament, while his display of opulence astonished Europe. In the long run, however, the gold rush brought little of lasting good to either colony or kingdom. In Brazil itself, it marked the blackest period of its history. Gold was everything; and to get it out thousands of Indians and negro slaves were viciously worked to death. Plantations were neglected. Agriculture declined and many observers of the time felt that the colony was ruined and would sink into barbarism. Nor did the quantities of gold shipped across the ocean bring much that was lasting to Portugal. It caused inflation, was squandered by the king, and ultimately almost all of it disappeared from the nation into the shrewder hands of the English and Dutch.

During the eighteenth century, Portuguese colonial administration saw one brief period of enlightened rule reminiscent of the era of Charles III in Spain. During the reign of Charles's Portuguese contemporary Joseph I, virtually dictatorial powers were given to the able and energetic Marquis of Pombal. Pombal's most important reforms took place within Portugal itself, but he also attempted to deal in a like manner with the colonies. In Brazil there was a further effort made to strengthen and centralize royal authority. At the same time, several monopolistic trade companies were incorporated in an attempt to encourage colonial commerce. Pombal was also interested in humanitarian ideas. Little was done for the negroes, but a serious attempt was made to establish equality for the American Indians. Not only was Indian slavery prohibited, but also all forms of forced labour. Intermarriage between Portuguese and Indians was encouraged and all, except negroes, were to be considered equal.

Pombal's reforms are more interesting for their intention than for their achievement. The attempt to improve administration mainly disappeared in the bogs of bureaucratic inefficiency. The chartered companies were never a great success, and the enlightened legislation regarding Indians fell into abeyance after Pombal's death. In the long run his most lasting reform was for the worst. He, too, suppressed the Jesuits, a measure which pleased the planters but, as usual, had catastrophic results for the Indians.

Brazilian colonial history was more notable for the number of revolts by the servile and oppressed classes than was that of the Spanish possessions, although none was as serious as the great rebellion of Tupac Amaru. Many negro slaves rose against their masters on isolated plantations, and thousands escaped to the backwoods where they sometimes formed independent communities. One of these, the so-called Republic of Palmares, maintained itself for a decade against bands of Paulistas hired by the captain-general to destroy it. One of the major factors leading to the expulsion of the Jesuits had been a three-year war against Indians who had been ordered to evacuate their mission villages when Brazil took over a piece of territory formerly occupied by Spain. But the most interesting uprising occurred in the late eighteenth century in the area of the Minas Gerais. There the mineworkers, outraged when the government attempted to raise its profits from gold by increasing their taxes and lowering their wages, found a leader in one Joaquim José da Silva Xavier, a jack-of-all-trades, who had at one time worked as a

dentist and was nicknamed Tiradentes, or 'the tooth puller'. After organizing the workers and voicing their protests, Tiradentes called for large measures of social reform including the institution of a university, the abolition of slavery, the establishment of factories and, most important, the independence of Brazil from Portugal. The armed rebellion which he led was, however, quickly suppressed. Tiradentes was beheaded in 1792 but became a martyr and subsequently a national hero.

By 1800, the colony of Brazil had staked out what are roughly the boundaries of the Brazilian nation of today, sprawling over half a continent. Much of it was, and is, unoccupied. Other areas proved rich in agricultural and mineral resources. Its history was marked by unheard of atrocities against Indians and negroes and yet also by a less rigid colour bar between races than proved typical in most of the western hemisphere. In the ranks of the upper classes, there was something of the same cleavage between creole Brazilians and people born in Portugal that existed in the Spanish dominions. On the other hand, these differences were muted by the relative lightness of Portuguese rule. Brazil, however, had grown into a much more important community than Portugal itself and was unlikely to endure a second-rate status for ever. In the end, the Portuguese American Empire, like the Spanish, fell as a direct result of turmoil in Europe. Yet in Brazil Portuguese power was to subside by means of a series of gentle collapses rather than disappear precipitately by spectacular revolution.

Above, the Marques of Pombal (1699–1782), the Portuguese statesman who tried to reassert Portuguese authority over Brazil, stimulate its economy and improve the conditions of the Indians. He introduced many similar enlightened reforms in Portugal itself.

Opposite, Tupac Amaru, the leader of a violent Indian attack on European rule in Bolivia in 1780. He was executed in 1782 and his revolt brutally suppressed.

Chapter 25

The Struggle for North America

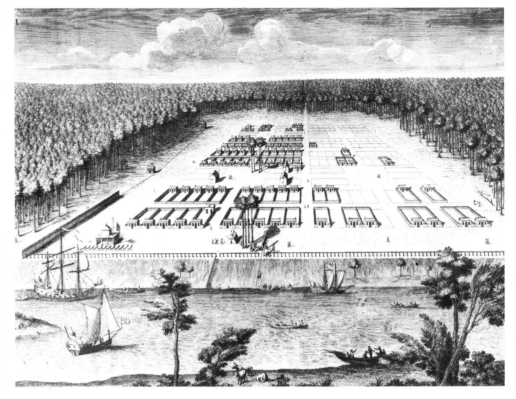

In America France, Spain and Britain struggled for the control of a hemisphere. Three factors can be named as most important in determining who won or lost in the American conflict—sea power, settlement and disease. The nation that controlled the sea could destroy harbours and capture islands with ease. More important, it could keep vital supplies from reaching the colonies of its rivals. On the other hand, areas that were well settled could support large bodies of regular troops and militia and were invariably difficult to subdue. The role played by disease has rarely been stressed but was of immense importance. Certainly malaria and yellow fever were prime factors in determining the course of warfare in the tropical regions of America.

In continental North America, disease was not of great importance, and here it was Britain that had both settlement and sea power working in her favour. Her colonists on the eastern seaboard were in such great numbers that, by the eighteenth century, there was no real chance of their being driven from the continent; it was simply a question of whether or not they could be contained. At the same time, the power of her navy made it easy for Britain to protect and nourish her own possessions while striking against the enemy either in the Caribbean or up the St Lawrence River.

France was somewhat, though not completely, lacking in all three essentials. Disease could protect her West Indian colonies from attack to a certain extent; in Quebec, she had a small area that was well settled: her sea power was by no means weak, especially when joined to that of Spain. But she suffered from grave disadvantages, and these would prove decisive in the event of major clashes with Britain. She attempted to make up for these as best she could. It was impossible to maintain large armies in North America because they could not be supplied, but she could and did send small bodies of very good troops and some excellent officers; she could build strong fortresses like Quebec and Louisbourg; she could practise Indian diplomacy astutely; she could count on a divergence of interests between the various British colonies and between the colonies and Britain herself. Lastly, she could hope that victories won by

her fine armies in Europe might counterbalance defeats in America. Yet, despite a gallant struggle, French weakness in sea power and settlement was ultimately fatal.

The British and French Empires

The Anglo-French duel for North American supremacy, which had begun in William III's time, continued for the next half century and reached its climax in the 1750s. During the same period, both empires continued to expand after their own fashion. For the English, growth was primarily demographic. Although the population of New France made the startling leap from about 7,000 to about 60,000 in this time, it remained absolutely dwarfed by that of the English colonies, which was rapidly pushing on towards the number of 2,000,000. Territorially however, driven by the needs of the fur trade, the French Empire continued to spread its borders west and south. In the score of years after 1720, a chain of forts, such as Niagara and Detroit, was built in the Great Lakes region, south into Ohio and Illinois territory and then far to the west when la Verendrye pushed deep into the Canadian prairies. In the extreme south, Iberville's brother, Bienville, founded New Orleans in 1718, and the French began moving up and down the River Mississippi in an attempt to connect New France with Louisiana.

British territorial expansion in the same period was more modest. In the north, Fort Oswego was built on the southeast shore of Lake Ontario, and Nova Scotia was conquered from the French. In the south, the uninhabited territory between Carolina and Florida was penetrated in 1733 when

General James Oglethorpe founded the colony of Georgia. This settlement was designed as a philanthropic venture which, it was hoped, would provide a new life for worthy but insolvent debtors. Such things as slavery and the trading of rum to the Indians were prohibited, but most settlers soon left the colony for the easier life of Carolina. In 1752 the restrictions were finally removed, normal colonial government instituted and the colonists granted 'the one thing lacking'—the introduction of slavery.

Even during wartime, the English colonists were inhibited from directing all of their energies against their French enemy by their quarrels and discords with each other. Moreover, trouble was brewing between the colonists and Britain herself over the question of how much political power should reside in the elected colonial assemblies and how much should be exercised from London. But one thing was clear: the English settlers were increasingly ready to burst the boundaries set by the Allegheny mountains and spill into the Mississippi valley where they would collide with the rapidly expanding French.

Spanish Succession and Austrian Succession

The War of the Leage of Augsburg had ended in 1694 with the French gaining certain advantages in North America. The War of the Spanish Succession (1702–14), which soon followed it, again saw colonial campaigns which were waged over thousands of miles along the eastern coast of the hemisphere. In the south, the French began well, their forces ravaging the settlements of England's Portuguese ally in Brazil. In the Caribbean, Iberville took the offensive once more, capturing St Kitts and Nevis before he died of fever. The English, however, soon recaptured the former island, although disease and stubborn French resistance ended their attempted conquest of Guadeloupe.

Further north, Governor James Moore of Carolina moved south into Florida and devastated a dozen Spanish mission villages. At St Augustine, however, Governor Zúñiga successfully defended the fort for seven weeks until Moore was forced to retreat. In 1706, it was the Carolinians who were on the defensive when a major Franco-Spanish expedition failed to take Charleston. The British then struck back, but two sorties against Pensacola also miscarried.

It was further north that the most important fighting of the war took place. Oddly enough, the exposed area of New York saw little action owing to the neutrality of the Iroquois Indians, who remained faithful to their treaty with Governor Frontenac. New England, however, suffered severely from raids by French Indians, the most famous of which was the sack of Deerfield, Massachusetts in 1707. But New England proved able to retaliate. Two militia attacks on Port Royal, Nova Scotia, failed in 1708, but two years later the energetic Francis Nicholson at last seized the ill-defended fort, and Nova Scotia fell into British hands.

In 1711, it was decided that Nicholson should advance overland to Montreal, while a major British amphibious expedition should strike down the St Lawrence River directly to Quebec. The military commander on this ill-starred venture was to be Brigadier Jack Hill, a brother of Abigail Masham. He commanded seven veteran regiments of British regulars, and the English Tories hoped he would win a great victory to offset the triumphs of the Whiggish Duke of Marlborough. He did not get the chance. The fleet transporting his men was commanded by Admiral Hovenden Walker, an old nonentity. Walker was not entirely destitute of all qualities of seamanship but was unfortunate enough to make the egregious error of attempting the ascent of the St Lawrence without good pilots. As a result, on the night of 23 August, many of his ships piled up on the north shore. Seven transports, one stores ship and about 900 men were lost, and English hopes of capturing Quebec ended in tragedy.

In the Peace of Utrecht, which ended the war, England made substantial colonial gains. Nova Scotia became hers, and her sovereignty over Newfoundland was recognized as well. All fur trading posts commanded by the French on Hudson Bay were given up, while in the Caribbean the island of St Kitts at last became a firmly established British possession. Finally, Spain granted to Britain the *asiento*—the sole right to carry slaves from Africa to the Spanish colonies—for a period of thirty years. Concessions such as these, however, owed less to the feats of British arms in North America itself than to Marlborough's splendid victories in Europe. But it was during this war that Britain emerged as the most formidable sea power in the world, and this was to have an inestimable effect on the future.

The major colonial theatre of operations in the War of Jenkins' Ear (which merged into that of the Austrian Succession, 1739–48) was the Caribbean, and the defeat of Britain's great offensive in that area has already been described. But there was also important fighting on the continent as well. In the south British forces, now commanded by Oglethorpe, failed twice more in attempts to take St Augustine. Nevertheless, in 1742, Oglethorpe, with only 600 men, skilfully cut to pieces a Spanish army of 3,000 intent on conquering Georgia.

This important defensive success was matched by an offensive victory in the north. Despite the loss of Nova Scotia, the French position in that area had actually grown stronger rather than weaker. On the island of Cape Breton they had built the huge fortress of Louisburg to command the Gulf of St Lawrence. Moreover, the majority of the inhabitants of Nova Scotia itself were still French Acadians (original settlers of the maritime provinces), who remained stubbornly hostile to their English rulers. Thus, the threat to New England from the area was at least as strong as ever, and in Massachusetts Governor William Shirley began to plan an audacious project— the capture of Louisburg itself. A force of 4,000 New England volunteers was organised under Sir William Pepperrell.

Fortune seemed to favour the efforts of the Americans. Louisburg was weakly garrisoned. From the far away West Indies, Commodore Peter Warren offered to escort and support the colonists with three warships. On the other side of the ocean, in Brest, the main French fleet which could have relieved the fort was blockaded by British squadrons. Lastly, as the attackers neared Louisburg, Warren managed to capture twenty French vessels which were heading for the fortress laden with provisions and ammunition. While attempts at direct assault failed, starvation soon took its toll and reduced the French garrison to surrender.

The French wasted no time in attempting to retrieve their fortress. However, one major fleet which slipped the British blockade was scattered by gales, while another was destroyed by Warren and Anson. A great naval victory by Hawke, off Rochelle in 1747, ended all French hopes of recapturing Louisburg by a feat of arms. But in the end it was returned to Louis XV at the Treaty of Aix-la-Chapelle, which ended the war; conquests by Maurice de Saxe in the Low Countries were useful bargaining counters. For once, the French land strategy had succeeded. Thus, the enterprise of the New Englanders had been largely in vain.

Opposite, the city of Savannah, the first settlement in Georgia, the year after its establishment in 1733; the colony was established as a buffer between the main British colonies and those of Spain in the south.

The final conflict

The great world conflict known as the Seven Years War actually began in America some years before the war was formally declared in Europe. In 1753, the advancing French built Fort Duquesne at the great river intersection where the Ohio River begins and where the city of Pittsburgh stands today. Upon learning of this the colony of Virginia, which also claimed the area, despatched a small force commanded by the young George Washington with orders to dispossess the French. Washington was surrounded and forced to capitulate to superior French forces, but the British government decided to support Viginia strongly. A year later, General Edward Braddock, with 3,000 British regulars under his command and with Washington as aide-de-camp, marched westwards to destroy Duquesne. But in the wilderness near the Monongahela River, Braddock led his forces to a signal defeat.

On 9 July a French force, much smaller than Braddock's advance group of 1,500 men, blundered into the British and its commander was killed. Jean Dumas, the French second-in-command, spectacularly reversed what should have been a French defeat. Splitting his men into two groups, and sending them into parallel ravines, he caught the British in a raking cross-fire. Braddock's van reeled back; his rear advanced; the main body of his men was

caught in a struggling melee into which the French continued to pour their fire. Braddock, as brave but less cunning than a bull, rode about the field shouting, had five horses killed beneath him and was finally shot down. Two-thirds of his men fell with him. Washington and the remainder hastily retreated into Virginia.

News from the north was not much better. Admiral Boscawen failed in an attempt to waylay a French fleet bringing reinforcements for Canada, and these fresh troops

were soon joined by an exceptionally able commander, the Marquis de Montcalm. Then, in 1756, war broke out on a full scale in Europe, and the British government faced a major political crisis. At last, England's sick genius, William Pitt, was called in to take direction of the deteriorating situation.

Pitt's war strategy was simple and direct. He wished to weaken France's position as a great power as much as was possible. But England would generally avoid facing France's large continental armies; that area

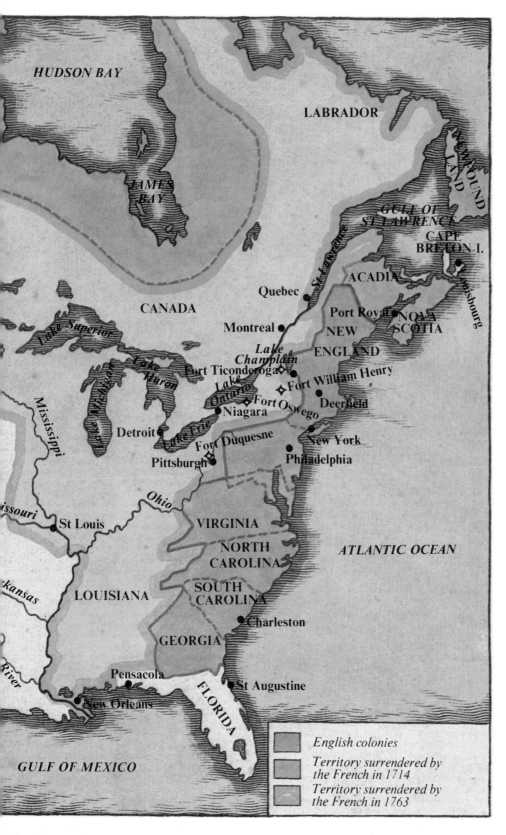

Above, Louis Joseph de Montcalm (1712–59), the French general who recaptured Lake Ontario from the English in 1756 and took Fort William Henry the following year. He was killed during the British capture of Quebec in 1759.

Left, the struggle for control of North America in the mid-eighteenth century. Britain's eventual success was mainly a result of superiority of numbers.

Opposite top, the capture of the French fortress of Louisburg, on Cape Breton Island, in Canada, by a force of New Englanders in 1745. Rivalry between France and England spilled over into North America, but events there were seen as of minor importance, and Louisburg was soon restored to France in exchange for Madras. National Maritime Museum, London.

Opposite bottom, the capture of the French citadel of Quebec by the English led by James Wolfe in 1759. The daring attack, made by scaling a cliff known as the Heights of Abraham, led to the collapse of French power in North America. National Army Museum, London.

Map legend:
- English colonies
- Territory surrendered by the French in 1714
- Territory surrendered by the French in 1763

of action would be left to Britain's powerful ally, Frederick the Great of Prussia, whose military machine would be primed with British money. Instead, Britain would concentrate on using her advantages at sea to the utmost. France's colonial empire was to be destroyed and her overseas commerce ruined. According to Pitt's grand strategy, the French navy would be blockaded in its home ports while British armies would be transported across the ocean to conquer North America. To achieve these ends, Pitt sketched out the campaigns himself. He also chose good men to execute them, removing senior but incompetent officers and promoting promising juniors. Men like Wolfe, Saunders and Amherst performed magnificently in the field, but the arm that reached across the ocean was unquestionably Pitt's.

Yet it took another year for matters to begin to improve. In 1756, Montcalm in a daring raid, seized the British fort of Oswego on Lake Ontario; in 1757, he ranged deep into New York, taking Fort William Henry,

where many of the British garrison were subsequently massacred by the Indians.

In 1758, however, came Pitt's great three-pronged attack. One British wing moved west towards Fort Duquesne, another north-east to besiege Louisburg, while the centre advanced up the Lake Champlain-Richelieu River route to attack the very heart of New France. The plan was only partially success-ful. The dying General Forbes cut his way across the mountains and occupied Du-quesne, while Louisburg eventually capitu-lated to Amherst and Wolfe after a long siege, but Abercromby's vital push in the centre was a failure. At Fort Ticonderoga, Montcalm, commanding in person, had built a huge redoubt of fallen trees. Aber-cromby, with a foolishness which ap-proached criminal negligence, sent his Scottish Highlanders to their deaths in direct frontal assaults. After losing 1,500 men, the British withdrew.

Not until 1759, therefore, did the great assault against Quebec take place. In June of that year a huge fleet commanded by Admiral Charles Saunders and conveying 8,500 troops, led by the thirty-two-year-old James Wolfe, moved up the St Lawrence. The British pilots, among whom was James Cook—later to be known as the greatest navigator of the age—plotted the course with scrupulous care, and at the end of the month, Saunders had reached Quebec with-out losing a single ship. But Montcalm proved resourceful in defending his great fastness, and Wolfe spent the summer deliberating on the best way to come to

grips with him. Finally, as the campaign season was drawing towards its close in September, he selected one of the least likely tactical plans on his list. Sailing down river at night, the British troops secretly landed and scaled the forbidding cliffs by a narrow path which was providentially almost un-guarded. Thus, at 6 a.m. on the morning of 13 September, both armies faced each other outside the walls of Quebec on the Plains of Abraham, and Wolfe and Montcalm pre-pared to meet a destiny that would be both historical and personal. The steady fire of the British regulars won the day over Montcalm's raw militia. Both commanders were killed. Quebec was quickly besieged and fell a few days later.

The great citadel had fallen, but the war was not yet over. Montcalm's second-in-command, the courageous Chevalier de Lévis, gathered together the still significant French forces in the area and retreated to Montreal. Saunder's fleet and many of the English were forced to depart before the St Lawrence froze over. Then, in April of 1760, Lévis, with a mixed force of 7,000 men, reappeared on the Plains of Abraham, challenged and defeated General James Murray's weakened garrison of 3,000. The British retreated inside Quebec and were in their turn besieged by the French. A month later, when the ice melted, a British squadron sailed up the St Lawrence to the relief of the fortress.

Lévis was forced to retreat again to Montreal but was determined to stay in the field. Perhaps the British, in spite of their

overshelming force, would make some terrible blunder. Even with Quebec lost, a French army still on its feet and fighting would make a great difference in a peace treaty if the war ended in the meantime. But Amherst, who had captured Niagara and Ticonderoga when Wolfe was taking Quebec, made no blunders. Up the Richelieu River, up the St Lawrence, down river from Lake Ontario—the British forces moved on Montreal from three directions. On 6 September 1759 Governor Vaudreuil ordered capitulation. Lévis burned his battalion flags in a last gesture of defiance. French dominion in North America had ended.

With the fighting in continental North America over, and with the command of the sea firmly in their hands, the British now turned with a vengeance to the West Indies. In that area opportunities for conquest had been suddenly increased, for Spain had foolishly and precipitously entered the war on the side of France. In 1759 Guadeloupe was taken, as well as some French slave-trading settlements in West Africa. Mar-tinique, however, successfully resisted a major British attack. But in 1762, two huge amphibious operations were aimed at both Martinique and Cuba. The former fell to Rodney and Monckton in February, the latter to Pocock and Albemarle in August. Finally, after France and Spain had hastily signed a treaty of peace, news came that a British expedition had captured Manila in the faraway Pacific as well.

Thus, the war saw most of Pitt's dreams

THE EUROPEANS IN AMERICA

Date	Latin America	North America	Europe
1500			Charles of Spain becomes Emperor Charles V (1519)
	The Conquest of Mexico (1521)	Giovanni de Verrazano reaches the coast of New York (1523)	
	Creation of Royal and Supreme Council of the Indies (1524) The Conquest of Peru (1531)	Jacques Cartier begins exploration of the St Lawrence (1534)	
	Mendoza's administration in Mexico begins (1535)		Ignatius Loyola first president of Jesuit order (1541)
	Las Casas achieves new laws for the Indians (1542) Discovery of silver mountain at Potosi (1545)		Council of Trent (1545) Disputation on the rights of the Indians at Valladolid (1550)
	Toledo's administration in Peru begins (1569) University of Lima founded (1572)	Sir Humphrey Gilbert claims Newfoundland for England (1583)	Portugal absorbed by Spain (1580) Death of Philip II of Spain (1598)
1600			English East India Company founded (1600) Death of Elizabeth I of England. Accession of James I (1603)
	Spanish Jesuits at La Plata (1605)	Jamestown founded by Christopher Newport (1607) Champlain founds Quebec, reaches Great Lakes (1608) The Dutch on the Hudson River (1609)	Gunpowder Plot (1605)
		John Rolph starts tobacco cultivation in Virginia (1612)	Assassination of Henry IV (1610)
	Raleigh in Guiana (1616)		Richelieu becomes Secretary of state (1616)
	The Dutch in Guiana (1620)	Pilgrim Fathers arrive at Cape Cod (1620)	
	The French in Guiana (1625)		Death of James I. Accession of Charles I (1625) Richelieu organizes Company of New France (1627)

Date	Latin America	North America	Europe
1630	The Dutch in Brazil (1630)	Founding of Maryland by Cecil Calvert (1632)	
	The Dutch leave Brazil (1640)		Portugal regains independence (1640) Execution of Charles I (1649)
		Capture of Jamaica by the British (1655)	
	University of Mexico founded (1663)	Carolina Charter (1663)	Restoration of Charles II (1660)
	Hudson Bay Company awarded royal charter (1670)		Treaty of Madrid (1670)
		Marquette and Joliet reach the Mississippi (1673) La Salle follows Mississippi to its mouth (1682) Hostilities between England and France (1689)	War of the League of Augsburg (1689) Treaty of Ryswick (1697)
1700		Sack of Deerfield by Indians (1707) Nicholson secures Nova Scotia for England (1710) Loss of Hill's fleet in the St Lawrence (1711)	Bourbon dynasty in Spain, Philip V (1700)
			Treaty of Utrecht (1713)
	Creation of Spanish Ministry of Marine and the Indies (1714) Creation of new vice-royalties of New Granada and La Plata (1717)	Founding of New Orleans by Bienville (1718) Founding of Georgia by Oglethorpe (1733)	
			War of Jenkins' Ear (1739) Treaty of Aix-la-Chapelle (1748)
		Montcalm seizes Oswego (1756) British take Louisbourg (1758) Wolfe captures Quebec and Montreal surrenders (1759)	Accession of Charles III of Spain (1759) Peace of Paris (1763)
	Expulsion of the Jesuits from Paraguay (1767) Rebellion of Tupac Amaru in Peru (1780) Rebellion of Tiradentes in Brazil (1792)		

realized. The same could not be said for the Peace of Paris, signed in February of 1763. By then Pitt had been driven from power, and negotiations had been carried on by the less imperially minded Earl of Bute. Britain's gains were great, but France's world power had only been weakened and she could still hope for yet another war of revenge. Nevertheless, Britain kept the huge areas of Canada and the eastern Mississippi valley as well as several small West Indian islands. Spain ceded Florida to the English, in order to get Cuba back, and was granted Louisiana as compensation by her French ally. After nearly a century of conflict, Britain was at last supreme in continental North America.

But Europe's disposition of North America, drafted in 1763, would last but for a season. The house that Pitt had built fell apart within twenty years through the spirit of colonial rebels. The great empires of Spain and Portugal similarly crumbled soon afterwards. Nevertheless, the long period of colonial conflict established some enduring realities. The vast areas where Spain, Portugal, France and England planted their progeny have kept, with modifications, the indelible stamp of their parent nations.

The collapse of the colonial empires did not alter these basic factors. However important the American Revolution may have been, more important still was the fact that the largest part of the rich North American continent was going to be inhabited by English-speaking peoples carrying with the their English cultural, political and economic heritage.

The impact on world history created by the development of the American hemisphere has been inestimable. This epic story, still unfinished, began with the European mastery of the oceans, the discovery and settlement of the New World. Conquest, colonization, slave-trading and imperial rivalry—all called into being new nations and new peoples ready to take their part in the succeeding age of national, industrial and ideological revolutions that has shaped our modern world.

Opposite, The Death of General Wolfe, *painted by Benjamin West. Despite personal illness, James Wolfe led the daring British assault on Quebec which took the city in 1759. Royal Collection.*

245

Chapter 26

The Far East

In the seventeenth century the Manchu conquerors of China created the largest and most powerful realm that had existed since the time of Mongol supremacy. Japan, under the Tokugawa shoguns, achieved internal peace and enjoyed a century of economic and intellectual development. In southeast Asia the kingdom of Siam grew in power and resources, while its neighbours and rivals, Burma, Cambodia and Vietnam, suffered from internal strife.

The rulers of these countries were strong enough to dictate the terms of such intercourse as they permitted with Europe. Visitors from the West recorded with admiration the magnificence of their capitals and the myriads of their armies. Nevertheless the foundations of Western domination were established over northern Asia and in the Indian Ocean at this time.

The Russian conquest of Siberia

In 1581 a Cossack adventurer, Yermak, crossed the Ural mountains and captured the town of Sibir, the capital of a local Tartar chieftain, and from this time the whole vast region between the Urals and the Pacific was called Siberia. Although Yermak himself subsequently met his death, by 1600 the Russians were firmly established in western Siberia, where they founded a settlement at Tobolsk. From here the Russians, few in numbers but equipped with firearms, pushed rapidly eastwards, subduing the scattered native tribes whom they encountered. They overcame the difficulties of travel by making use of the great rivers, much as did the contemporary French voyageurs in Canada. By 1649 they had reached the Pacific and founded the settlement of Okhotsk. They then turned southwards and by 1651 had explored Lake Baikal and established the town of Irkutsk. Thence they pushed eastward to found Nerchinsk in 1654 and to sail down the Amur River. Here, however, they came into collision with the Manchus and were for the time being checked.

The Cossacks were brave and hardy adventurers but fierce and ruthless in their treatment of the natives. These were held down by building a chain of *ostrogs—*

stockaded trading posts something like the frontier posts of the American West. The lure of Siberia lay in its wealth of fur-bearing animals, and the conquered tribes had to pay a tribute of furs to the Russian government. The illegal exactions of the Russian settlers were much heavier, and they inflicted the most savage penalties upon those who failed to satisfy their demands. In 1637 the tsar established a department of Siberian affairs at Tobolsk in an attempt to enforce order and justice, but many of the local officials were among the worst offenders.

Behind the soldiers and fur traders came peasants, who were mostly exiles seeking to escape from serfdom or political disorder in European Russia. Settlement grew slowly, but by 1700 there were some 250,000 Russians in Siberia and the vast region was becoming an increasingly valuable part of the expanding Muscovite Empire.

The contest for the spice trade

In the seventeenth century the maritime supremacy of the Portuguese in the Indian Ocean was destroyed by the Dutch and the English. The Dutch began direct ventures to the East Indies because they were excluded from the spice trade at Lisbon by Philip II. In 1602 the government of the Netherlands consolidated a number of concerns into a single Dutch East India Company. This company waged war against the Portuguese in Indonesia where they had previously monopolized the spice trade. In 1622 the Dutch founded Batavia (Jakarta) which became their headquarters. Malacca, the chief Portuguese settlement in Malaya, was captured by them in 1641, and they drove the Spaniards from the Moluccas, although they failed to expel them from the Philippines. In China the Dutch were defeated in an attempt to take Macao, though from 1623 to 1662 they held part of Formosa.

The English East India Company, which was organized in 1600, tried to secure a share of the spice trade, but although England and Holland had been allies against the Spaniards the Dutch would not tolerate English competition in the East Indies. In 1623 they seized the English trading post at Amboina and put to death most of the Englishmen there. The English East India Company could not match the resources of the Dutch one and eventually gave up the contest. By the end of the century the Dutch had reduced the native sultans to vassalage and had firmly established their empire in the East Indies.

In India the English company, despite opposition from the Portuguese and the Dutch, secured trading rights from the Mogul emperor Jahangir. But so long as they had no secure base of their own their position was precarious. In 1639 they secured a grant of land on the Coromandel coast from the local ruler and there founded Fort St George (Madras). On the west coast the Portuguese held Goa and also the island

of Bombay. In 1661, when King Charles II married the Portuguese princess, Catherine of Braganza, Bombay was part of her dowry. In 1667 Charles gave it to the East India Company and, under the capable administration of its first governor, Gerald Aungier, it grew from a neglected village into a thriving city, since it was secure from both Mahratta raids and the exactions of Mogul governors. Calcutta, which became the third centre of British trade and influence, was also a place of no importance until Job Charnock established himself there in 1686. After a period of hostilities with the Mogul governor of Bengal, East India Company control was finally recognized by Aurangzeb in 1691. Meanwhile the Dutch drove the Portuguese from Ceylon and wrested trading posts from them in southern India.

After the Dutch and the English came the French. In 1674 they secured a settlement at Pondicherry and another at Chandernagore in 1688. The French were active in missionary work and French missionaries went to Burma, Siam, Cambodia and Vietnam. For a time, during the reign of Louis XIV, the French seemed likely to secure political and commercial ascendancy in southeast Asia, especially in Siam, but their activities provoked a reaction which, together with the wars of Louis in Europe, checked the French expansion.

The Spaniards in the Philippines

The conquest of Manila by Legaspi in 1571 established Spanish power in the Philippine islands, but their hold upon the archipelago as a whole remained very limited. Much of the mountainous interior regions remained

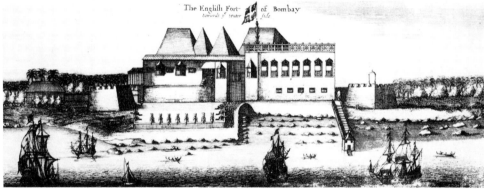

virtually untouched by them, while in Mindanao and Sulu they were held at bay by the fanatical converts to Islam whom they called Moros. The Philippines were governed by a captain-general, or governor, with subordinate officials. He was responsible to the viceroy of Mexico, since the Spaniards regarded the Philippines as an offshoot of their colonies in Latin America, which in many ways it came to resemble. As in Latin America, Spanish officers who had taken part in the conquest were given large estates, *encomiendas*, which they ruled as feudal fiefs. The Church also became a large land-owner, and the clergy, especially the friars, exercised great authority.

Chinese junks brought silks and porcelains to Manila which the Spaniards purchased with silver dollars brought from Mexico in the galleons from Acapulco, so that the Mexican dollar became a standard currency in the Far East. The Spaniards were nervous of the large Chinese settlement in Manila and they even massacred some of the Chinese on suspicion of revolt.

The Manchus

The country northeast of the Great Wall which was to become known as Manchuria consisted first of all of a southern part which had long been settled by Chinese, although it was still rather a colonial area. The plateau and steppe region to the northwest was the home of nomad Mongol tribes, while the mountain and forest region in the northeast was inhabited by Tungus tribes, of whom the Manchus were one group. Their chiefs were given high-sounding titles by the Ming and so encouraged to remain faithful tributaries. One such was Nurhachi, who was born in or about 1559. He proved to be

a leader of genius, who built up his power in a long series of successful campaigns until he had gained control over many of the tribes and in 1616 assumed the royal style. The Ming court, alarmed at the growth of his power, sent aid to his enemies. Nurhachi in reply invaded the Chinese-settled area of Manchuria. His army, divided into divisions or banners, defeated the Ming forces, took Mukden and overran most of Manchuria. Many of the Chinese there, sickened by Ming misrule, readily joined them. These were also organized in banners, there being ultimately eight Manchu and eight Chinese banners.

The Ming forces, aided by cannon made under the supervision of the Jesuits, managed to check the Manchu advance upon Peking by way of the Shanhaikuan pass. Nurhachi died in 1626 and his son endeavoured to outflank the Chinese defences by overrunning western Manchuria and Inner Mongolia. Some of the Mongol tribes were defeated while others allied themselves with the Manchu ruler, and in 1635 they gave him the state seal of the former Mongul emperors, thus recognizing him as the rightful inheritor of the empire

Above, the English fort at Bombay; the town was a Dutch possession from 1534 until 1661, when it was handed over to England. The English made it their foothold in the west of India, and also the headquarters of their East India Company until 1858.

Top, the town of Batavia on the island of Java, the headquarters of the Dutch East India Company from the early seventeenth century and the main base from which the Dutch kept their fierce hold over the profitable spice islands.

of Genghis Khan. The Manchu ruler now assumed the dynastic title of Ch'ing or Pure, which signified his intention to overthrow the Ming in China itself.

To meet the cost of the war against the Manchus the government greatly increased the land tax and other levies. This deepened the disaffection among the landowning class, while the peasantry were afflicted by drought and famine especially in north China. Among the consequent leaders of rebellion a Shensi peasant, Li Tzu-cheng, became pre-eminent. The imperial forces sent against him were defeated or else went over to him, and in 1643 he took Sian, the capital of Shensi. In 1644 he advanced on Peking which he captured and sacked. The Ming emperor committed suicide and Li proclaimed himself emperor. But the best forces the Ming still possessed were under the command of General Wu San-kuei, who was guarding the Great Wall. He elected to side with the Manchus rather than with the ex-brigand Li and made an agreement with the Manchu Prince Dorgun who was acting as regent for the infant grandson of Nurhachi. Consequently, Li was defeated and the Manchus entered Peking.

After the fall of the capital a relative of the deceased Ming emperor was set up in Nanking, but he was soon defeated and killed by the Manchus and their Chinese allies. Another prince of the Ming house held out, first at Canton and later in the extreme west of China. He was aided by the pirate leader, Cheng Cheng-kung, who for a while held much of the south coast. The Ming claimant to the throne in gratitude gave him a title of honour, which Europeans rendered as Koxinga. After he could no longer hold out on the mainland, Koxinga in 1661 established himself in Formosa, from which he expelled the Dutch. He and his son continued to wage war against the Manchus at sea. The conquest of southern and western China was accomplished by Wu San-kuei and other Chinese generals who had joined the Manchus. After years of fighting the last Ming forces were driven into Burma; but for a while much of the south and west of China was under the almost independent rule of Wu San-kuei.

The Manchu dynasty gave China good government, internal peace and increase of empire. Under the dynamic K'ang Hsi (1662–1722) and his successors, Yung Chang (1723–35) and the extremely able Ch'ien Lung (1736–96), the Chinese Empire reached the greatest extent in its long history. The lands adjoining China proper were brought firmly under control, the Mongols were crushed; the area northwest of China was organized as Sinkiang ('the new dominion'); the Tibetan Dalai Lama became a Chinese nominee; and the borders of Manchuria were stabilized by treaty with the Russians at the northernmost reaches of the Amur River. Formosa was conquered and integrated into the empire; Korea, Annam, Burma and Nepal acknowledged the suzerainty of the Celestial Emperor.

Internal peace ensured prosperity, for China was a rich, self-sufficient land. The area under cultivation was notably increased, and population rose steeply, reaching some three hundred million by 1800. No significant changes were introduced—which was, to the Chinese, entirely proper. Reverence for ancestors, for the past, for long-established practices, was a prime feature of the Confucian ethic, reinforced by the remarkable continuity of Chinese history.

Chinese conservatism was in fact becoming still more deeply ingrained. One of many fields in which this became apparent was literary activity, a great deal of which consisted in encyclopedic compilations of literary classics and an increasingly sophisticated apparatus of critical scholarship. The same tendency, already perceptible under the previous Ming dynasty, appeared in all the arts, with the partial exception of porcelain. (Though, significantly, the new decorations the Chinese discovered were mainly applied on export ware.) The skills of the past were employed to produce fine works of craftsmanship, often superbly executed in the great styles of the past; but creativity was absent.

Change is not, so to speak, compulsory: and attachment to the past has been the rule rather than the exception in history. Chinese indifference to new ideas was to prove disastrous in the nineteenth century, not because China was in some absolute sense 'in decline', but because her society was forced open by the aggressive, technologically advanced culture of Europe.

Much the same can be said of nineteenth-century Chinese political history. In his later years Ch'ien Lung leaned upon a favourite minister, Ho Shen, who seems to have carried financial corruption to the most extravagant lengths. The tangle of injustice and extortion produced by a corrupt civil service provoked the first revolts for almost a hundred years. Henceforward they were to be frequent until the end of the dynasty—and the empire—in 1912. The incapacity of Ch'ien Lung's successors indicates that the Manchus were following the pattern of previous dynasties: vigorous early emperors were succeeded by increasingly effete sovereigns, until an energetic usurper created a new dynasty—which followed the same pattern. Again, it was not so much a question of Chinese decline as of a period of weakness coinciding with the irruption of a dynamic society—the West—into the closed world of China.

The Jesuits in China

The one source from which the Chinese might have acquired new knowledge without loss of face was the Christian missionary. The overwhelming majority of missionaries were Catholics, of whom the most distinguished were the Jesuits. A Jesuit, Matteo Ricci, had been the first European Christian missionary in China since the Tang period (AD 618–907) and had commended himself to the Ming emperors as an astronomer and mathematician. Jesuits continued to act as scientific advisers under K'ang Hsi, who appreciated their reform of the Chinese calendar (a most important feature of Chinese religious life) and in 1692 issued what was in effect an edict of toleration.

The Jesuits proved equally adaptable in their attempts to convert the Chinese, whose eclectic approach to religion made them impatient of claims to their exclusive devotion and who were besides deeply attached to the rites honouring ancestors. To attack these was to attack the fundament of Chinese civilization, and Ricci and other Jesuits achieved some success by desisting, arguing that the Confucian ethic and filial piety were not incompatible with Christianity.

The question of 'the rites' was hotly debated within the Church, at least some of the opposition to Jesuit practice deriving from jealousy of the order within the Church. In 1715 the pope condemned the rites, later reinforcing his condemnation with the Bull *Ex Illa Die* (1742). The hitherto benevolent K'ang Hsi, who had backed the Jesuits, was deeply offended by this insult to Chinese culture. New Chinese decrees effectively prevented the spread of Christianity (1717), and Chinese Christianity went into a decline that was hastened by the papal dissolution of the Jesuit order (1773).

All questions of religion aside, it was a misfortune for the Chinese too. Contact with the Jesuits enabled the Chinese court to become familiar with the inventions of the Western barbarians without publicity and therefore without loss of face. Not that the conditions existed in China for an industrial revolution of the sort about to begin in the West; but the Chinese might at least have come to understand the extent of Western power and the workings of the Western mind. Since Europeans were no better informed, mutual incomprehension was responsible for much of the violence

MAKOU

Above, Matteo Ricci, a Jesuit priest, and Ly Paulus, a Chinese convert, who introduced Christianity to China between 1580 and 1610. Ricci encouraged intellectual contact between China and the West, and, although he was not able to win many converts to Christianity, he was held in great respect by the Chinese.

Above centre, Lord Macartney, who led the first British mission to China in 1793, in an attempt to win trading concessions. The emperor, however, had no interest in trade or any other contact with the 'barbarians'. National Portrait Gallery, London.

Above left, the Amboina massacre of 1623, in which the Dutch killed an English trading settlement on one of the islands of the East Indies, suspecting a conspiracy against their trading monopolies. This incident provoked the first break between the two Protestant countries, which had previously been united in their opposition to Spain and the Spanish Empire.

Left, Dutch ships in the Chinese port of Macao in the 1660s; in the previous century Macao had been the centre of the Portuguese monopoly of trade with China.

Opposite, Nurhachi (1559–1626), the Manchu leader who united the tribesmen of Manchuria and began an all-out attack on the Ming dynasty of China in 1618. The Manchus eventually won control of the whole of China in 1644.

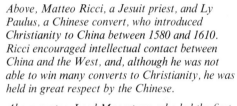

with which East and West met in the nineteenth century.

The Chinese conception of the world made other forms of contact impossible. Insulated for millennia by seas, deserts and mountains from states of comparable power and civilization, the Chinese had known only cultural inferiors—like the steppe nomads, who had sometimes overrun China, only to adopt Chinese speech and customs—and imitators like the Japanese.

Understandably, therefore, they had come to believe that their state was 'the state' and that Chinese culture was 'culture'. The emperor was the only ruler below heaven, though not all barbarians had yet submitted to him or mastered the ways of civilization. Of diplomacy, which presupposes the existence of more than one state, the Chinese had no conception.

When Britain sent embassies, they were greeted as tribute-bearing missions. The arrival of Lord Macartney (1793) and Lord Amherst (1816) was met with impressive ceremony and great politeness, though the question of whether the ambassadors would kowtow to the emperor (thus acknowledging Britain's tributary status) caused dignified wrangles. But there was no question of a permanent embassy: tributaries delivered gifts, heard the emperor's commands and took themselves off.

The China trade

Inability to establish diplomatic relations became increasingly irritating with the growth of trade with China, particularly to the British, who outstripped their commercial rivals in the eighteenth century. The China trade was extremely profitable but subject to strict limitations. The Portuguese in Macao, the British and other Europeans in Canton, existed in waterfront 'factories' sealed off from China. They dealt solely with a guild of Chinese merchants, the Hong, who were able to fix prices arbitrarily; official China ignored their existence. European representations failed to make any impression on the Chinese.

From their own point of view, the Chinese had good reasons. If diplomatic agreements were unthinkable, diplomatic regulation of trade was a still more absurd notion: merchants (even Chinese merchants) were a despised class, and the emperor could not participate in their activities. Furthermore, there was no place for foreign merchants within the structure of Chinese society: their presence on the waterfront was 'overlooked', and if they misbehaved the Hong merchants were punished. An imperial officer taxed the Hong, of course, so that the emperor was able to profit by the arrangement without being contaminated.

This attitude was reinforced by China's self-sufficiency. Europeans wanted Chinese silks, porcelain, tea; China wanted nothing from Europe. There was an important economic aspect to this situation: China had to be paid in bullion, which had been intermittently drained from the West since Roman times. The imbalance of trade between East and West led Europeans to wink at illegal traffic in the one commodity Chinese wanted: opium. From 1773 the East India Company had a monopoly of its manufacture and sold it to all comers: what they did with it was their business. By 1800 large quantities of the drug were being sold over the sides of the European ships in the Canton River.

The nineteenth century witnessed a tremendous development in the opium trade and increasingly direct participation in it by Europeans. Diplomatic redress was impossible without diplomatic relations; mutual incomprehension excluded moderation. Chinese notions of collective responsibility made it natural for them to blame all Europeans for the behaviour of a few; and an unfortified coast and a non-existent navy made threats or reprisals directed against the European merchant community the natural response to European self-assertion. The pattern of nineteenth-century conflict was already predictable.

Japan

Japan was closed to the West even more firmly than China. The Europeans who

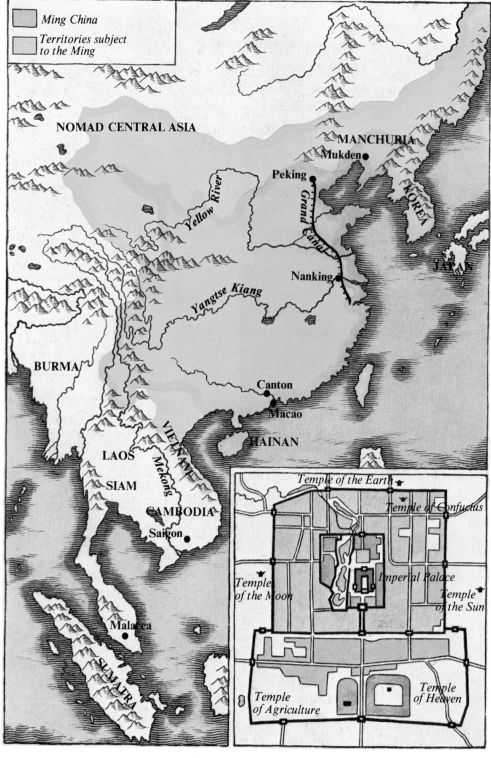

arrived from 1542–43 taught the Japanese to use firearms and build fortifications on the European model. They also brought Christianity, which enjoyed considerable popularity in the sixteenth century but became increasingly identified with political subversion and external aggression. The Japanese reaction was ferocious and extreme: by 1638 Christianity had been uprooted by force and Japanese ports shut to Europeans: even Japanese abroad were forbidden to return. Previously a roving people with a reputation as fearless soldiers and pirates, the Japanese became introverted and let a sizeable fleet and an expanding trade run down.

The only exception was trade with China and with the Dutch, who were allowed to operate from the islet of Deshima. They lived in cramped conditions and under close supervision of a sort that made the lot of Europeans in Canton enviable; and once a year they were brought to grovel at the imperial court. Through the Dutch, the Japanese acquired some knowledge of Western science, especially medicine, though by the early eighteenth century only two Dutch ships were arriving each year. Until the Industrial Revolution, Japan knew enough of the West to be certain that she remained secure against interference; and she wanted to know no more.

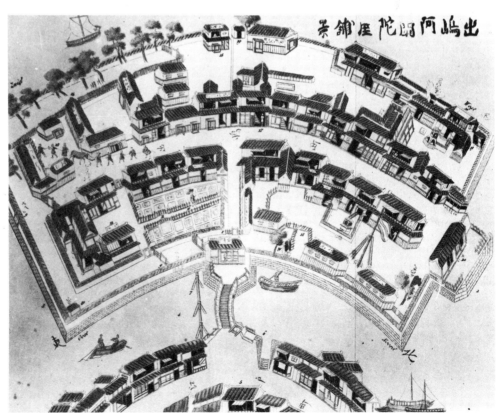

The Tokugawa regime

Isolation was not unfamiliar to the Japanese. The mountainous archipelago of Japan was most densely populated on the east coast, away from the Asian continent; even China was far away. Once in every few centuries the Japanese took some part in Asian wars, and their early history had been deeply influenced by the superior civilization of China; but extended contact was impossible, and Japanese society absorbed Chinese influences without losing its distinctive character.

Isolation, an agrarian economy and a regionalism created by the irregular topography of Japan had led to the development of a military feudal society in which central authority was hard to maintain for any length of time. Since the twelfth century, the real head of the Japanese government had usually been a shogun ('generalissimo'). The emperor was a ceremonial figure, deeply revered but powerless. However, the shogun might in turn be the puppet of a powerful noble house with a 'clan' of relatives and military retainers (the famous *samurai*). Japan easily became the battlefield

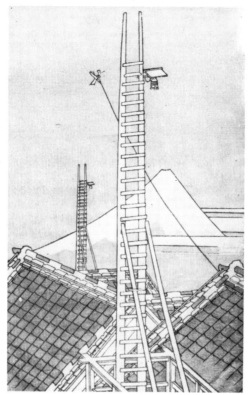

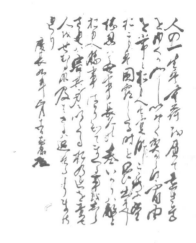

of rival clans, as was once more the case during most of the fourteenth and fifteenth centuries.

From 1603 to 1867 the shogunate was in the hands of the Tokugawa family, who greatly strengthened it. But, although Japan enjoyed a long period of peace under the Tokugawas, the price was high. Unity and stability—and Tokugawa power—could be maintained only by ceaseless vigilance. Access to the imperial court at Kyoto was rigidly controlled by the shogun. The great nobles were compelled to build villas at the effective capital, Yedo (later Tokyo), where their families resided permanently, as permanent hostages; noble fiefs were changed so that suspects were always neighbours of powerful loyal vassals; the nobility was coerced or encouraged to spend lavishly so that they should not become too powerful; travel was viewed with suspicion; and the country was filled with spies and spies on spies. The Tokugawa regime was as near a police state as pre-industrial technology allowed.

Extended peace aided the growth of a prosperous merchant class and a money economy, and these were accompanied, from the late seventeenth century, by the development of a sophisticated urban society. Yedo, with almost a million inhabitants, was in the forefront, swollen with officials, noble families and their servants, merchants looking for a good time, and an army of entertainers both reputable and disreputable, hawkers, beggars and hangers-on. A new kind of audience stimulated the production of a vigorous and realistic popular art, including the puppet and *kabuki* theatres for which Japan's greatest dramatist, Chikamatsu Monzae-

mon (1653–1725), wrote his works, and the great woodblock artists, of whom the most famous were Hokusai (1760–1849) and Utamaro (1754–1806).

Tokugawa decay

The contradictions inherent in the Tokugawas' policies became apparent in the eighteenth century. Without external enemies (for the outside world had been abolished), a military aristocracy could not exist unchanged during a long period of peace. The shoguns, on whom the whole system rested, were not always fit for their post; and, lacking military occupation, many *samurai* and some of the great nobles fell into dissipation and debt. Masterless *samurai* became something of a social menace, a privileged caste of unemployed who were disbarred from useful work and made quarrelsome by pride and poverty.

Though the population remained at about 30 million throughout the eighteenth and well into the nineteenth century, agrarian disorders became frequent from the 1780s. The peasant's lot was always difficult in mountainous Japan, where more than half the land was uncultivable and the work of years was liable to destruction by earthquake, flood or typhoon, but things seem to have become appreciably worse in the eighteenth century, probably because landlords attempted to solve their own difficulties by evictions and increased demands on the peasantry.

The last shogun to make serious efforts to restore stability was Yoshimune (1717–44), and his programme amounted to little more than a revival of regimentation. He also issued the first of many decrees

favouring debtors—for it was no part of the Tokugawas' intentions that merchants should become more powerful than their social superiors. Indeed, rigid maintenance of social distinctions had been one of the formulas of Tokugawa stability.

Other developments threatened the position of the Tokugawas themselves. They had encouraged Confucianism because it inculcated reverence for law and civil authority; but the Confucian cult of the emperor was less welcome to a military dictatorship. Revival of interest in Shinto, the indigenous religion of Japan, also fostered imperial sentiment, since it proclaimed the emperor's descent from the sun-goddess. From about the mid-eighteenth century a spirit that was at once deeply nationalistic and hostile to the shogunate became manifest. Other disquieting events, including the restiveness of the great feudatories in outlying areas (never effectively controlled by the Tokugawas), indicated that the 200-year-old police state could not endure much longer.

What would have replaced it remains a matter of speculation. The merchants— bankers and money-lenders rather than a mercantile or industrial middle class— would almost certainly not have done so. It is more likely that another cycle of feudal in-fighting would have commenced. In fact, Japan was to be wrenched out of her seclusion by the intrusion of Western ideas and technology, announced by the arrival of the American, Commodore Perry, in 1853. Unlike China, she proved capable of integrating them into her existing society, just as she had integrated Chinese culture a thousand years before. Post-Tokugawa Japan re-entered world history, but as a curious hybrid of old and new.

Siam

In the late sixteenth century Siam was conquered by the Burmese ruler Bayinnaung. But after his death in 1581 revolt in Burma against his son gave the Siamese prince, Pra Naret, the opportunity to reassert Siamese independence. In 1587 he defeated a Burmese attempt to take Ayuthia, the Siamese capital, and he also repelled a Cambodian invasion. In 1590 he became King Narasuen and inflicted further defeats upon the Burmese and Cambodians. The latter were for the time being crushed, and the former lost the provinces of Tavoy and Tennasserim. Narasuen, who is one of the great heroes of Siamese history, died in 1605. His immediate successors were less warlike and the Burmese were able to regain some of the territory they had lost.

The Siamese kings were ready to welcome foreign traders. They had already established relations with the Portuguese and the Spaniards and at the beginning of the century they admitted Japanese traders. A number of Japanese, some of them exiled Christian converts, were enlisted as mercenaries in the royal guard and for a time, under their leader, Yamada Nagamasa, played an important part in Siamese politics. The Dutch were allowed to establish trading posts at Patani in 1602 and Ayuthia in 1608. In 1609 the first Siamese embassy to visit Europe was received at The Hague. The English East India Company was given trading rights in Ayuthia in 1612 but found it difficult to compete with the Dutch and in 1622 withdrew from Siam for some years. During the reign of King Prasat T'ong, from 1630 to 1656, the Japanese, who had conspired against him, were driven out. These events left the Dutch in a position to monopolize the foreign trade, and this the Siamese naturally resented.

In 1657 King Narai came to the throne. As a curb to the aggressive Dutch, he welcomed the resumption of trade by the English in 1661, and he also showed favour to French Catholic missionaries, who in consequence mistakenly believed that he might be converted; in fact his real object was political. In 1675 a Greek called Constantine Phaulkon, who had entered Siam in the service of the English East India Company, rose to be superintendent of foreign trade and became very influential with the king. As the result of a quarrel with the agents of the English Company Phaulkon used his influence to promote French interests. A French embassy arrived in Ayuthia in 1685 and the Siamese sent representatives to Versailles in 1686. Meanwhile, Phaulkon had been converted by the Jesuits and he promoted an arrangement whereby French troops were to be stationed in Mergui and Bangkok, ostensibly for protection against the Dutch. The troops arrived in 1687, but a section of the Siamese nobility, headed by a general called Pra P'etraja, saw in this a menace to Siamese independence. In 1688 King Narai was taken ill and Pra P'etraja became regent. He immediately seized and executed Phaulkon. Then King Narai died and the regent succeeded him. Pra P'etraja then turned on the French; a number of them were killed and others had to leave the country. The result of this episode was that the Siamese attitude towards foreigners became less liberal. The trade privileges of the Dutch were curtailed and the English once again withdrew from Siam.

Burma

Upper and Lower Burma were reunited by King Anaukpetlun, but after his death in 1629 his successor Thalum, who removed the capital from Pegu to Ava, was faced with fresh revolts by the Mon people of the Irrawaddy delta region. He was a capable administrator, but his son Pindale, who ruled from 1648 to 1661, was incompetent. In addition to more trouble with the Mons and the Siamese, Pindale became involved in difficulties with China. In 1658 Yung Li, the last Ming emperor, was driven out of Yunnan into Burma. He was imprisoned and his followers then pillaged parts of Upper Burma. Pindale was deposed in 1661 and his brother, Pye, who succeeded him, had to placate the Manchus by surrendering Yung Li to them. His defeated soldiers then dispersed. For the remainder of the century Burma was at peace, but its rulers were weaklings dominated by their ministers.

Annam

The kingdom of Annam—the modern Vietnam—still remained under the nominal rule of the descendants of Le Loi, the national hero who in the fifteenth century had freed his country from Chinese rule. But in fact power had fallen into the hands of feudal noble families, among whom the chief contenders were the Trinh and the Nguyen. The Trinh held Hanoi and the Red River valley, the Nguyen dominated southern Annam. From 1620 to 1674 civil war raged between the two families. The Nguyen, who received some help from the Portuguese at Macao, were able to hold their own and in 1674 a peace was made which left the Nguyen as rulers of southern Annam. For the sake of trade the Nguyen tolerated Catholic missionaries, although there were occasional severe persecutions. It was the missionaries who invented a romanization of the written Vietnamese language, which is still in use.

The Nguyen rulers, especially after they had made peace with the Trinh, expanded their territory southwards at the expense of the Cambonian kingdom, weakened by wars with the Siamese and by internal strife. Consequently by the end of the century it had lost most of the country around Saigon to the Vietnamese.

Laos

The remote and mountainous region of Laos, which had fallen under Burmese control in the sixteenth century, regained its independence in 1591. From 1637 until 1694 it was ruled by King Souligna-Vongsa, with his capital at Vientiane. In 1641 the first European made his appearance, a Dutchman named van Wuysthof. He came on a trading mission, but because of the difficulties of communication nothing came of it. In 1642 Father Leria, an Italian Jesuit, came to Vientiane and remained for five years, but the opposition of the Buddhists prevented him from opening a mission. After his departure Laos remained untouched by European influence until the nineteenth century. After the death of Souligna-Vongsa succession disputes broke out and at the beginning of the eighteenth century Laos became divided into the kingdoms of Vientiane and Luang Prabang.

ASIA IN THE SEVENTEENTH CENTURY

Date	India	China	Japan	South-east Asia	The Russians in Asia	Date	India	China	Japan	South-east Asia	The Russians in Asia
1500				Conquest of Manila by Spaniards (1571)					Christian revolt. Shimabara (1638)		
					Cossacks cross the Urals (1581)			Li Tzu-cheng sacks Peking. Last Ming emperor commits suicide (1644)			
				Accession of Narasuen of Siam (1590)			Kandahar abandoned to Persians (1648)				Russians reach the Pacific (1649) Nerchinsk founded (1654)
1600			Battle of Sekigahara. Ieyasu master of Japan (1600)		Russians established in western Siberia (1600)					King Narai of Siam. New contacts with Europe (1657)	
		Matteo Ricci in Peking (1601)	Tokugawa Shogunate (1602)	Establishment of Dutch East India Company (1602)			Aurangzeb seizes throne (1660)				
	Death of Akbar Accession of Jahangir (1605)							K'ang Hsi becomes emperor (1661)		Constant Phaulkon becomes superintendent of Siam's foreign trade (1675)	
		Nurhachi in control of Manchuria (1616)		Siamese embassy to Holland, the first in Europe (1609)							
	Persian victory at Kandahar (1622)			Founding of Batavia (1622)			Mahratta wars (1681)			Execution of Phaulkon. Siamese self-isolation (1688)	
	Death of Jahangir Accession of Shah Jahan (1627)	Death of Nurhachi (1626)		New Burmese capital at Ava (1629)							Frontier between China and Russia defined (1689)
	Famine in India (1630) Building of Taj Mahal begins (1631)							Treaty of Nerchinsk with Russia (1689) Catholic missionaries given permission to preach by K'ang Hsi (1692)			
		Manchus assume dynastic title of Ch'ing (1635)				**1700**	Death of Aurangzeb (1707)				
	Kandahar regained from Persians (1637)			Establishment of department of Siberian affairs (1637)							

Chapter 27

The Mogul Empire and the Rise of British India

Upon the death of the Emperor Akbar in 1605 his son, Salim, succeeded. He took the title of Jahangir, which means Lord of the World. In 1611 he married a Persian lady, on whom he bestowed the title of Nur Mahal, or Light of the Palace. She was an ambitious woman who, with her brother, Asaf Khan, exercised great influence over the emperor. Jahangir was a competent ruler who continued the policy of toleration towards his non-Muslim subjects which Akbar had begun. His somewhat erratic character was well described by Sir Thomas Roe, who was in India from 1616 to 1619 as the ambassador of King James I. The emperor could be just and generous, but he could also be fiendishly cruel. This uncertainty of temper came partly from his nightly drinking bouts. He was a patron of the arts and was himself something of a painter.

While Jahangir won victories in Bengal and Rajputana, he suffered defeat at the hands of the capable Shah Abbas of Persia, who took Kandahar in 1622. Jahangir attempted to extend the conquests which Akbar had made in the Deccan, but the city of Ahmadnagar, ruled by a capable Abyssinian minister, Malik Ambar, long held out against him. His son, Prince Khurram, won a victory in the Deccan in 1616 and was given the title of Shah Jahan, King of the World, by his grateful father. Later, however, the prince became estranged from his father and from 1623 to 1625 was in actual revolt against him. This was because Shah Jahan had insisted upon marrying the lady of his choice and not the one selected for him by Nur Mahal. The revolt ended in an outward reconciliation between father and son, but in 1626 Mahabat Khan, a prominent general, rebelled against the dominance of Nur Mahal and her brother, and Jahangir was taken prisoner. The empress succeeded in freeing him, but in 1627 the humiliated emperor died.

Shah Jahan

Shah Jahan defeated and executed pretenders to the throne and in 1628 proclaimed himself emperor in Agra. He kept Nur Mahal in strict confinement until her death. Once he had secured his position he maintained the policy of general toleration and

was anxious to act justly towards all his subjects. But .his reform edicts had little effect in checking the avarice of the provincial governors and lesser officials. Shah Jahan, like his predecessors, tried to prevent civil and military appointments from becoming hereditary and in· this way to preserve imperial control over the nobles. But in a huge and loosely knit realm it was difficult to stop them from exercising a large degree of local authority, especially as the emperor, in times of foreign war or succession disputes, was dependent upon their loyalty. Moreover, the conquests and building projects in which Shah Jahan indulged had to be paid for by heavy taxation, so that the splendours of Agra and of New Delhi contrasted with the squalor and misery of the peasantry. From 1630 to 1632 a great famine, in which thousands died, afflicted Gujerat and parts of the Deccan.

Above, the Mogul Emperor Jahangir (reigned 1605–27) holding a portrait of his father Akbar. Jahangir encouraged both the Portuguese and the English to trade within his empire. Musée Guimet, Paris.

Shah Jahan was devoted to his empress, Mumtaz Mahal, the mother of all his children. When she died in 1631 he commissioned Persian and Indian architects and craftsmen to build the magnificent mausoleum at Agra known as the Taj Mahal, or Jewel of the Palace. Another architectural wonder, constructed in Agra, is the Pearl Mosque. While he thus beautified Agra, Shah Jahan set to work to build a new capital near the old town of Delhi. This he achieved during the ten years from 1638 to 1648, and he called the new city Shahjahana-bad, the city of Shah Jahan. The French traveller Bernier, who saw it in 1663, described New Delhi, as it was to become known, as built in the form of a crescent on the right bank of the Jumna River, with walls extending for six or seven miles and a population as great as that of Paris. The main streets, crowded with shops of all kinds, led to the royal square, beyond which was the fortified palace, a building which Bernier considered to be twice as large as any palace in Europe. Here was the great Hall of Audience, where the emperor appeared daily before his nobles and courtiers, all grouped in strict precedence. The emperor, seated on the Peacock Throne, so called from the golden peacock with outspread tail made of precious stones which crowned it, heard petitions from his subjects.

In Afghanistan, Shah Jahan fought with the Persian Shah Abbas II and managed to recapture Kandahar from him in 1637. But in 1648 the Persians surprised and again seized the town, and in the face of the superior Persian artillery the army of Shah Jahan was obliged to retire. Kandahar was abandoned and left in Persian hands. The emperor was equally unfortunate in his attempts to conquer part of Turkestan. He led an army across the Hindu Kush mountains but was soon in difficulties in the rugged terrain and harassed by the Uzbek tribesmen. Shah Jahan returned and sent Prince Aurangzeb to continue the struggle. But the prince and his military advisers saw that the country could not be held; they succeeded in getting the army back over the mountains into India, but at the price of heavy losses in men and equipment.

Shah Jahan was more successful in the Deccan. Malik Ambar died in 1626 and his unworthy son betrayed Ahmednagar to the Mogul armies. The city fell in 1633 and was annexed to the Mogul dominions in 1636. Aurangzeb, who was appointed viceroy of the imperial territories in the Deccan, waged war against the sultans of Bijapur and Golconda and would probably have conquered both kingdoms but for the jealousy of his brother Dara, who prevailed upon Shah Jahan to accept their offers of submission and payment of tribute in 1656.

The Succession War

Shah Jahan had four sons—Dara, Shuja, Aurangzeb and Murad. In 1657 the emperor was taken ill and could no longer attend the court audiences. At the time Dara, his eldest and favourite son, whom he wished to be his successor, was in Agra. The other three all held governorships away from the capital. When Shuja and Murad heard that their father was no longer seen in public they declared, and perhaps sincerely believed, that he was dead but that Dara was concealing this. Each proclaimed himself to be emperor and began to advance upon Agra. Aurangzeb, masking his own ambitions, joined forces with Murad. In May 1658 Dara was defeated at the battle of Samugarh, near Agra. Aurangzeb took the capital and proclaimed himself emperor in July 1658. He had his brother Murad condemned on a charge of breaking Islamic law by his drunken habits, and after three years of captivity Murad was executed. In 1659 the fugitive Dara was betrayed into the hands of Aurangzeb, who had him put to death. Shuja defeated near Allahabad, fled into Bengal and thence to Arakan, where he was murdered. By 1660 Aurangzeb, who styled himself Alamgir, Conqueror of the World, had crushed all opposition to his rule. He kept his father, Shah Jahan, a prisoner until the unfortunate emperor died in 1666.

Aurangzeb was an able general and a skilful diplomat. He was cold and reserved in manner and gained the admiration, rather than the affection, of those who came into contact with him. He was a devout orthodox Muslim who, as far as a Mogul emperor was able, followed the teachings of the Koran and lived a simple and indeed ascetic life. He knew the Koran by heart and made copies of it which he sent to Mecca and Medina, since his responsibilities as a ruler forbade his making the pilgrimage himself. Had he contented himself with ordering his private life in this fashion, the change from the profligacy of Jahangir and Shah Jahan might have been beneficial. But he allowed his religious beliefs to shape his policy towards his subjects. He appointed Muslims to office in preference to Hindus and he revived the *jizya*, or poll-tax, upon all who were not Muslims. Since these amounted to some three-quarters of the population of the empire, this policy caused widespread disaffection and revolt. It involved Aurangzeb in a long and ultimately unsuccessful war in Rajputana. The fierce warriors of this region, once reconciled to Mogul rule by the conciliatory policy of Akbar, had formed a most valuable part of the imperial army; now many of the Rajput forces became hostile to the Mogul Empire and their defection was a grave source of weakness.

Aurangzeb at war

During the first part of his reign Aurangzeb was mainly concerned with re-establishing the authority of the Mogul Empire in the north of India. In 1662 his army, under the leadership of an able general called Mir Jumla, defeated the Ahoms, who had taken advantage of the civil war in the Mogul Empire to invade Bengal. They were driven out again and Assam itself invaded, but the unhealthy climate proved fatal to many of the imperial soldiers including Mir Jumla himself. There were also wars with the Afghan tribesmen, especially the afridis, who in 1674 inflicted a defeat upon the Mogul forces. These Afghan frontier struggles absorbed many of the best troops of the empire at a time when they were needed elsewhere.

It was the great ambition of Aurangzeb to conquer the Deccan and to bring the whole of India under his sway. He was determined to extinguish the kingdoms of Bijapur and Golconda, both for political reasons and because their rulers belonged to the Shia sect among the Muslims, which he, as a Sunnite, regarded as heretical. But by the time he was able to turn his full attention to the south, a new enemy had arisen. The Mahrattas were a Hindu people who lived in rugged plateau country over-looking the southwestern coast. Here there were many natural hill fortresses from which the Mahratta horsemen could sally out to raid the lowlands and in which they could offer a desperate resistance to an attacker. The Mahrattas were united under a leader called Sivaji who became the terror of much of the Deccan and raided the Mogul territory there. In 1664 he sacked Surat, although he was repulsed from the foreign settlement there by English and Dutch resistance. By the time of his death in 1680 the Mahrattas had become a formidable fighting force.

In 1681 the emperor left his capital to take command in the Deccan, where he was to wage war for the next twenty-five years. He took Bijapur in 1686 and Golconda in the next year. But against the guerrilla tactics of the Mahrattas he could gain no decisive success. The huge Mogul army, which was swollen by hosts of camp-followers, especially when the emperor was present, could win pitched battles, but could not cope with a swiftly moving enemy who raided its lines of communication and constantly harassed it. In 1689 Aurangzeb succeeded in capturing Sambhaji, the son of Sivaji, and put him to death. But the Mahrattas continued the struggle and the Mogul army suffered heavily in attempts to invade their country and storm their hill fortresses. The aged but indomitable emperor fought on, but his troops became more and more discouraged. Aurangzeb was compelled to admit failure and to retreat to Ahmadnagar, where in March 1707 he died at the age of eighty-nine.

It was in Aurangzeb's long reign that the seeds of ultimate collapse began to appear. Aurangzeb was more intolerantly Muslim than his predecessors, and his policies produced a reaction in many sections of the Hindu community. Territorial expansion in itself merely made the empire more cumbersome. Moreover, there was a certain hardening of the arteries of the Mogul bureaucracy —lack of resolution and disregard for the importance of office. And once the empire began to deteriorate, it was unlikely that it would be regenerated by the Indian community. For all the years it had ruled the country, the Mogul dynasty was still an alien institution of Turkish origin. It had often commanded respect, rarely affection; if it were to be reformed, then reformation would have to come from the top or not at all.

On Aurangzeb's death authority at the summit became divided and vacillating. After a shaky period of palace revolutions, Muhammad Shah emerged as emperor in 1719. The new ruler was shrewd and crafty but unable to provide the leadership. During his twenty-nine years reign, he constantly mortgaged the future to keep possession of the present. Large areas began to break away from centralized control, giving only nominal allegiance to the fading Moguls. Nevertheless, in Muhammad Shah's reign, the rot proceeded behind a facade that was still impressive. But when he died in 1748 the facade peeled away, exposing the wreck within. Titular and puppet emperors would succeed one another for a further century, but after 1750 the real question about Mogul power was what would replace it.

Persians, Afghans and Mahrattas

That the withering Mogul Empire might be replaced by a European one seemed anything but likely at the time, and indeed the idea was not even considered. Instead, eyes turned to India's menacing neighbours, Persia and Afghanistan, and also to the formidable Hindu power of the Mahratta Confederacy.

The Persians were the first in the field. In 1710 the old Safavid dynasty of Persia was ended by an Afghan invasion, and it seemed that the Persian Empire would fall to rapacious neighbours; Afghans, Russians, Turkomans and Turks all seized a share. But in 1730 a new Persian military leader appeared on the scene in the form of Nadir Shah, who first posed as a champion of the Safavids and then claimed the imperial throne for himself. Rapidly defeating the Afghans and the Turks, Nadir then succeeded in driving out the Russians, and a campaign which began with the securing of his eastern frontiers led to the invasion of India. In 1739 he defeated the Moguls and sacked Delhi. Somewhat unaccountably, however, he then replaced Muhammad Shah on the throne and withdrew. Perhaps he expected to return, but after more wars in central Asia Nadir was assassinated in 1747. Persia disintegrated once more.

The Afghans now regained their independence and found their own military genius in Ahmad Shah. After consolidating his own mountain kingdom, Ahmad rode through the passes and sacked Delhi in 1756. Meanwhile, in India itself, the Hindu

Above, the Mogul Emperor Aurangzeb (reigned 1658–1707); his devotion to Islam undermined the basis of Mogul authority in India, which was founded on religious toleration and the employment of officials of all races and religions. Musée Guimet, Paris.

Opposite, the Mogul Emperor Jahangir on an elephant. The emperor was more concerned with the arts than with politics, but he granted important trading concessions to the Portuguese and to the recently founded English East India Company.

British and French

About two decades before the Battle of Panipat, it was becoming clear that a new relationship was developing between the Indian political powers and the Europeans who traded in the subcontinent. Previously, the Europeans had shown no interest in occupying Indian territory but had remained in their little trading factories and enclaves—the British in Madras, Bombay and Calcutta, the French in Pondicherry, the Portuguese in Goa and Diu—rather like frogs around the side of a pool. But what changed this situation was the increasing rivalry between the British and the French.

The English had arrived in India to find themselves competing with the Dutch and Portuguese; even the Danes and Germans had shown some interest in the area. But England had bested the Portuguese, while the efficient Dutch had devoted most of their trading activities to the Indonesian archipelago. The activities of the other nations had not amounted to much. The Moguls were in fact friendly to the English, and in the seventeenth century the East India Company's ships had often acted as the Mogul Empire's navy.

It was not until Colbert founded the French East India Company in 1664, and gained Pondicherry ten years later that England had a really serious competitor. The new company made slow headway at first, and by the beginning of the eighteenth century French interest in India seemed on the wane. But in the reorganization of colonial enterprises that took place after John Law's great débâcle, the French East India Company was put on a better footing. By 1740 it was quite a profitable concern, and besides Pondicherry and two other small posts on the mainland also controlled the very important islands of Mauritius and Réunion in the Indian Ocean. Mauritius, especially, with its good harbour and its strategic position astride the main trade route from Europe, provided an excellent base from which France could protect her own shipping and menace that of Britain in time of war.

However, it was not until 1744 that conflict actually came. Previously, even when their respective nations had been at war in Europe, the British and French settlements in India had remained at peace—partly because the Moguls wished it that way and partly because it was more profitable to do so. But when the War of the Austrian Succession broke out the British governor rebuffed the overtures of the French to maintain the peace. What the Moguls wished no longer counted, and the British, who had a small squadron in Indian waters, thought they might quickly destroy the factories of their rivals. This move was almost a disaster. The French governor of Mauritius, Mahé de la Bourdonnais, quickly improvised a little fighting

Mahrattas had begun throwing off the shackles of Mogul dominion as soon as Aurangzeb had died. Forming a confederacy and developing highly mobile military techniques, they spread right across central India to Orissa. Then, when the Afghans invaded, the Moguls called upon the Mahrattas for help. For a time, the Mahratta Peshwa drove back Ahmad Shah's forces, but this only made the Peshwa increasingly overbearing towards the Moguls. Soon the only thing that seemed in doubt was whether it would be an Afghan or a Mahratta emperor that replaced the great Mogul. But, in 1761, both of these competitors for the imperial throne unexpectedly eliminated each other. In the decisive battle of Panipat, fought in January of that year, the Mahrattas were thoroughly crushed by the Afghans. Then, at the height of their power, the Afghan soldiers mutinied over back pay and Ahmad Shah's forces withdrew from India when it seemed that the country was theirs for the taking.

fleet of armed merchant vessels, drove the British squadron away from the coast and attacked and captured Madras. This, however, was the extent of the French success. The arrival of a British fleet under Admiral Boscawen precluded any further French offensives, and although Boscawen failed to take Pondicherry Madras was returned to Britain in the Treaty of Aix-la-Chapelle that ended the war.

There now seemed to be no reason at all why commercial affairs in India should not return to their normal course, but in fact Joseph Dupleix, the French governor of Pondicherry, was about to upset the balance for ever.

Joseph Dupleix

During the war, Dupleix had fallen foul not only of the British but also of the local Indian ruler, the Nawab of the Carnatic. When the latter sent a large army against him, Dupleix easily defeated it with a small European-trained force. This significant event made Dupleix realize that it was now possible for Europeans to interfere far more in Indian political affairs than had been possible in the days of Mogul strength. If

by intrigue, diplomacy and small military campaigns the French could set up Indian puppet rulers who would support them, or if they could even control territory for themselves, then it would be possible for them to eject the English and monopolize the whole trade of the subcontinent. At first this conclusion seemed dubious. The expense of wars, subsidies and territorial administration would surely outweigh all the profits that might be made from eliminating the English. Such an idea would scarcely appeal to the commercially minded directors of the French East India Company. But Dupleix had an answer for that as well. Parts of India were very rich in agricultural produce, textiles and many other items. If the French could control such areas to the extent of levying and collecting taxes from the inhabitants, it would be possible to build a wealthy empire that would cost the company and the French government nothing.

In 1748 the deaths of the two most important Indian potentates in the south and the resultant succession disputes gave Dupleix the opportunity of putting his plans into operation. The French backed their own candidates and actively supported

Above, the Mogul emperor, now controlling little real power, granting to Robert Clive, the representative of the English East India Company, sovereign rights over Bengal in 1765. India Office Library and Records, London.

Opposite, the Mogul Emperor Shah Jahan (reigned 1628–58) with one of his sons. Shah Jahan spent most of his energy on his building programme at Agra and Delhi. Victoria and Albert Museum, London.

259

them. When the Nizam of Hyderabad attempted to interfere, Dupleix's intrigues resulted in the Nizam's murder and a great extension of French influence. When the new Nizam visited Pondicherry, Dupleix, in Muslim robes, was seated beside him on the throne and created personal governor of an area not much smaller than France.

The British company's officials, although disturbed by this train of events, could at first think of no riposte. But Thomas Saunders, a tough governor who took over command in Madras in 1750, began replying in kind. Chanda Sahib, the French candidate for Nawab of the Carnatic, soon found the British supporting his rival, Muhammad Ali. Shortly afterwards, opposing Indian armies, stiffened by British or French troops, were on the move and there was fighting throughout the Carnatic. This complicated pattern of warfare continued for three years and was made famous by the exploits of Robert Clive and Stringer Lawrence for the English and of the Marquis de Bussy for the French.

Dupleix himself was hopeless as a military leader, and when Bussy was forced to go north to Hyderabad to restore a position there that was becoming shaky the English gained the ascendancy in the south. It was now that Clive really came to the fore. Muhammad Ali had long been urging a diversion against Arcot, one of Chanda Sahib's principal possessions. The British were dubious, but when the young Captain Clive offered to make an immediate attack Saunders gave him his head. To everyone's astonishment, Clive's force of less than 300 easily occupied the city when the Indian garrison of 3,000 withdrew without fighting. Chanda Sahib quickly sent forces to besiege the place, but Clive held out for two months until relieved, so gaining the British their first considerable success. It was rapidly followed by others. Stringer Lawrence and Clive quickly cleared the whole of Arcot and then attacked Chanda Sahib, who was besieging a British force in Trichinopoly. In the ensuing engagement, several hundred French were captured, while Chanda Sahib was seized and put to death by an Indian rival.

Further north, however, the French were doing better. In Hyderabad, Bussy was quite successful in getting his candidate, Salabat Jang, installed as Nizam and in defending him against several rebellions. In return, Salabat made many concessions to the French, granting them the right to levy taxes and raise revenue in the Carnatic, which was nominally under his overlordship. This, in theory, was the fulfilment of Dupleix's policies, and the latter wrote an excited letter to the directors of the French East India Company stating: 'This affair, of the highest importance to the Nation deserves the closest attention, for it will dispense with the need of sending funds to India for your investment.'

Yet this was a triumph in theory only.

For the Carnatic, so freely given to the French by Salabat, was actually falling into the hands of the British candidate, Muhammad Ali, after the death of Chanda Sahib. Dupleix did his best to retrieve the situation. He now had difficulty in finding Indian candidates to support and even thought at one point of getting himself declared Nawab of the Carnatic. In the meantime his Indian allies besieged Trichinopoly again. Dupleix sent French reinforcements, but Stringer Lawrence, defending the city, held out through most of 1753. Dupleix then resorted to the desperate gamble of an assault with scaling ladders during the night. It came close to being a suprise success but in the end was a heavy defeat for the French, Dupleix losing about 400 of his regular troops.

Such events proved too much for the directors of the French East India Company. Dupleix's plans had been unorthodox in the first place and his dealings with his superiors cavalier in manner. His failure to fulfil his plans could have but one end. In 1754 he was recalled in disgrace. But he had set forces in motion that would not be stopped easily.

The Black Hole of Calcutta

For the moment an effort was made to turn back the clock. The English and French companies entered into negotiations and produced a treaty in 1754 that delimited spheres of influence. Fighting was to end and once again it was to be business as usual.

It was an Indian ruler who upset the new balance. In the northeast, Alivardi Khan, the Nawab of Bengal, had been increasingly disturbed by the European intrigues and fighting to the south. However, he had wisely remained neutral and contented himself with forcing the English and French in his own area to keep the peace. But when

Alivardi died in 1756, his successor, Sirajud-Dawlah, decided on more direct action. Europeans in Bengal were ordered to limit the military defences of their forts. The British in Calcutta refused, and Siraj attacked them. Decrepit old Fort William was easily overwhelmed, and 146 of the captured British defenders were then locked up in a tiny unventilated room where all but twenty-three stifled to death in one night. This incident—the Black Hole of Calcutta—was really a case of criminal negligence rather than of premeditated murder, but it provided the British with an emotional rallying cry and a cause to be avenged. In October Clive was ordered to retake Calcutta and given command of a force of 1,800 Europeans and sepoys, as Indians trained by Europeans were called. Calcutta was easily retaken in the following year, and Siraj was defeated and forced to sign a treaty confirming the rights of the company. It was at this point that the outbreak of the Seven Years War again transformed the situation.

The Seven Years War

As soon as news of the war arrived, Clive demanded permission from Siraj-ud-Dawlah to attack the French trading factories in Bengal. Siraj, however, now seriously worried at the growth of British power, began intriguing with Bussy in Hyderabad. Clive then determined that Siraj would have to be overthrown and in June 1757, with 3,000 British and sepoy troops, marched to Plassey where Siraj lay encamped with 50,000 men. Clive, brilliant, moody, reckless, spent the night before the battle in deep depression. So did Siraj. But in the morning they both determined to fight and in the ensuing curious encounter Clive suffered less than thirty casualties and Siraj only five hundred. Yet Plassey had the same result as a crushing and decisive victory.

Siraj's army fled precipitously, he himself was hunted down and killed, while Mir Jafar, a British candidate, became regent in his place. The British were masters of Bengal; if they could deal with the French, they might be masters of all India.

In the south, the French moved first. By early 1758, troop reinforcements had arrived at Pondicherry under the command of the Comte de Lally. In the late spring, Lally took the offensive and won several small victories over weaker English forces, capturing Arcot, Cuddalore and Fort St David. At sea, however, Admiral Pocock defeated a French fleet, and Lally's advance then bogged down. Bussy was now recalled against his will from the north, and he and Lally together laid siege to Madras. In Fort St George, however, Stringer Lawrence held out for three months until a squadron arrived from Bombay and broke the siege. The tide now turned, and following Bussy's enforced departure the French situation to the north began to deteriorate. Revolts broke out in Hyderabad, and even Salabat Jang, a French puppet for eight years, began negotiating with the British. He ultimately signed a treaty ceding some of his dominions to the East India Company. At the same time, the arrival of a large French squadron failed to shake Pocock's control of the sea, and in January of 1760 Eyre Coote heavily defeated the French forces in the Battle of Wandiwash. From then on the French were in retreat. At last, after a long siege, Pondicherry capitulated in January 1761. At the Peace of Paris in 1763, it was returned to France along with other minor settlements she had established in India before 1750. But French influence was now strictly limited to these enclaves; Dupleix's dreams of empire had perished for ever.

Clive

The war over and the French defeated, Clive, rich with gifts and bribes he had accepted from the Indian enemies of Siraj, departed for England. But he left behind him a Bengal where chaos, far from ending, was getting worse.

Clive's successor was Henry Vansittart, who at twenty-eight had already seen fifteen years in the company's service. Not nearly so weak a man as contemporaries claimed, Vansittart wished mainly to establish honest methods of trading. It was the actions of his subordinates that allowed matters to get out of hand. He took a rapid dislike to the incompetent Mir Jafar, deposed him and put Mir Kasim in his place. With the latter Vansittart concluded an agreement freeing external trade from duty but taxing all internal traders, English and Indian alike, at a rate of nine percent. Vansittart's own council repudiated this, however, and the English would neither pay the duty nor allow Mir Kasim to abolish it for Indians as well. Mir Kasim in a rage massacred 150

British merchants at Patna. The company then launched a military offensive and destroyed Mir Kasim's armies in the battle of Buxar.

This victory in a sense opened the road to Delhi, where a Mogul emperor still maintained a shadowy existence, and it brought to the surface divided counsels among the company's servants. Some became inflamed with grandiose ideas of empire; others, like Vansittart, wished to return to the old trading pattern; most of them simply wished to become rich. For the latter occupation, the times were propitious. The company's officers now wielded great power and accepted little responsibility. Huge sums were extorted or wheedled from the Indian potentates who in turn ground the peasantry with heavier taxes. Individuals became fabulously wealthy almost overnight. The East India Company, however, did not; indeed its profits fell as its servants ignored it and traded for their own interest. Soon Bengal was reduced to a state of misrule and anarchy as to make even Clive blanch when he returned.

Clive returned in 1765 with full powers to end the corruption. He opposed the abuses and the anarchy resolutely enough but had by no means solved the confusion when he departed again in 1767. More important for the future was the political system he left behind him. By a treaty with the nominal emperor Clive set up a dual system of government which left the Nawab of Bengal with only formal power. The crucial *diwani*, or right to collect the revenue, was granted to the East India Company in the rich territories of Bengal, Bihar and Orissa. The taxes in these areas could more than pay for the company's administration expenses there. Thus was the logic of Dupleix's system ultimately vindicated—but to the benefit of the British and not to that of the French.

Above, Joseph François Dupleix (1696–1763), the French East India Company official who built up a vast sphere of influence in the years around 1750, and whose independence and ambitions caused the French to call him home.

Top, Warren Hastings (1732–1818), his wife and servant, painted by Johan Zoffany. Hastings became governor of the British possessions in India in 1774 but was tried for corruption in the late 1780s. Victoria Memorial, Calcutta.

Opposite, Delhi in the eighteenth century; although it was now the main residence of the Mogul emperors, it was no longer the capital of India in any sense.

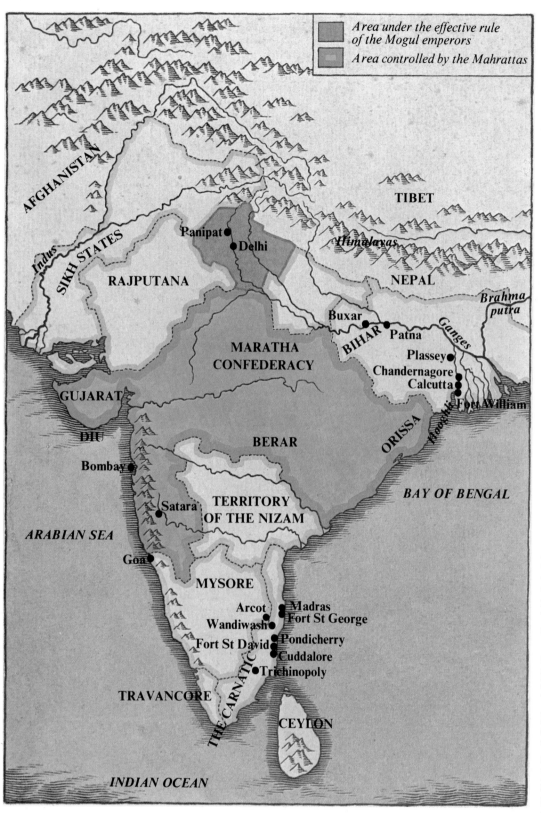

Area under the effective rule of the Mogul emperors	
Area controlled by the Mahrattas	

AFGHANISTAN

TIBET

Panipat
Delhi

SIKH STATES

Indus

RAJPUTANA

NEPAL

Himalayas

Brahma putra

Buxar

BIHAR Patna

Ganges

MARATHA
CONFEDERACY

Plassey
Chandernagore
Calcutta
Fort William

GUJARAT

ORISSA

Hooghly

DIU

BERAR

Bombay

BAY OF BENGAL

Satara

TERRITORY
OF THE NIZAM

ARABIAN SEA

Goa

MYSORE

Arcot   Madras
Fort St George
Wandiwash
Fort St David Pondicherry
Cuddalore
Trichinopoly

THE CARNATIC

TRAVANCORE

CEYLON

INDIAN OCEAN

Warren Hastings

The man who became governor of Bengal in 1772, and who was destined to mould the state from the territory that Clive had secured, was little known outside company circles. Small, steely and self-contained, Warren Hastings was to construct the framework of British India. Arrogant and opinionated, he could also show inexhaustible patience. He could stain his record by executing an inveterate Indian opponent for forgery, when forgery was a capital offence in England but not in India. Yet he thought more highly of Indians than many of the men who would follow him. 'Among the natives of India', he wrote, 'there are men of as strong intellect, and sound integrity and as honourable feelings as any of this kingdom.' It was Hastings' belief that British government should benefit the people of India culturally and materially in addition to filling the coffers of the East India Company.

He arrived in a province racked by famine, extortion and military troubles, with the Marathas on the borders. He attempted to tackle everything. The idea of dual government was abandoned. If the Company were to receive the revenue of Bengal, it must also take over the responsibilities of the internal administration. But Hastings' task was made inordinately difficult at the outset by an action of the British government.

Lord North's Regulating Act of 1773 was prompted by the misrule in Bengal and represented an attempt to bring Indian policy in the broadest sense under the control of parliament, although the East India Company would be left to work out details of administration. The Regulating Act promoted Hastings from governor of Bengal to governor-general in India and gave him powers over the presidencies of Bombay and Madras. Yet it also circumscribed him, giving real executive power to a council which could outvote him. In fact, the council was to obstruct Hastings consistently, especially when the opposition was led by Philip Francis, who wished to return to the system of combined rule. The Hastings-Francis rivalry was a long and enervating struggle lasting over six years, but in the end the governor's opponents 'sickened and died and fled'.

Once Hastings had thus outlasted his adversaries, he was able to get on with his work. Of great importance both to Bengal and to the East India Company were his successful commercial reforms, particularly the long-overdue ending of the private trade of the company's servants. Administratively, he began the arduous overhaul of the all-important revenue-raising system, although this task was not to be completed until long after he had departed from the scene.

Yet it was in the preservation of the state he was building that Hastings was to play his greatest role, for soon the British were encompassed on all sides. From the beginning Hastings was confronted with the problem of uneasy borders around Bengal and felt the necessity of making alliances with friendly Indian princes and of supporting his allies in their disputes. This was the policy that would point in future to the slow march of British territorial dominion across the whole of the subcontinent. The securing of borders would involve the conquering of fresh territory, but this in turn would mean new borders, new troubles, new conquests.

Nevertheless, Hastings was able to restrain this policy of reluctant empire-building for the moment so far as Bengal was concerned, though his unruly subordinate presidencies of Bombay and Madras involved him in grave trouble. Rash actions at Bombay provoked war with the Marathas, now finally recovered after Panipat, and led to the annihilation of a small British army. The situation at Madras was even worse; there, the policy of the presidency

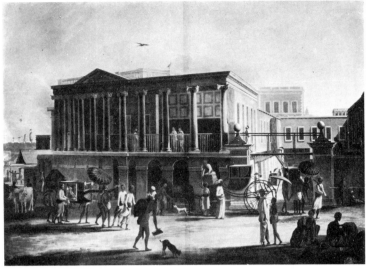

Above, a British factory in Calcutta in the 1790s;
the British used the great wealth that they won
from India both to enrich themselves and to
introduce European values and styles of art to
their empire. British Museum, London.

Above left, a European officer being entertained by
Mahadaji Sindhia, an Indian soldier who won
control of much of the area ruled by the Mogul
Empire in the 1760s and 1770s; the European
powers were able to exploit the political vacuum
that permitted such adventurers to rise to power.

Left, an Indian nabob or local ruler being carried
in a litter; the Indians were used to a rigid social
hierarchy, and the arrival of European overlords
made little difference to their way of life.

Below left, the reception in 1792 of Tipu Sahib,
the Prince of Mysore, by Lord Cornwallis; Tipu
Sahib had attacked British territory three years
before and was defeated by Cornwallis. He
rebelled again in 1798–99, and his kingdom was
shared between the British and the Nazim of
Hyderabad on his death. National Army Museum,
London.

Opposite, India in the late seventeenth and early
eighteenth centuries; as Mogul power declined,
the Mahrattas and others created virtually
independent kingdoms, and the Europeans were
able to exploit their rivalries.

INDIA: THE DECLINE OF THE MOGULS AND THE BRITISH ASCENDANCY

Date	Europeans in India	India	Neighbouring states	Date	Europeans in India	India	Neighbouring states
1600	English East India Company trading post at Fort St George Madras (1639)			1740			French take possession of Réunion and Mauritius (1740)
		Accession of Aurangzeb (1658)			Dupleix captures Madras from British (1746)		Assassination of Nadir Shah. Ahmad Shah assumes power in Afghanistan (1747)
	Founding of French East India Company (1664)		First Russian mission to Persia (1664)				
		Chittagong annexed by Aurangzeb (1666)			Madras returned to British. Treaty of Aix-la-Chapelle (1748)		
	Charles II grants Bombay to the East India Company (1668)				Clive seizes Arot. Dupleix recalled to France (1755)		
	French established at Pondicherry (1674)				Black Hole of Calcutta (1756)	Sack of Delhi by Ahmad (1756)	
	Establishment of English factory at Calcutta (1689)				Battle of Plassey (1757)		
						Battle between Mahrattas and Afghans at Panipat (1761)	
1700		Death of Aurangzeb. Accession of Muhammad Shah (1707)	Kandahar proclaims independence from Persia (1706)				The English establish trading post at Bushire on the Persian Gulf (1763)
		War between Sikhs and Moguls (1708)			Battle of Buxa. English in control of Bengal and Bihar (1764)	Massacre at Patna. Indian armies defeated at Buxar (1764)	
	English East India Company secures exemption from customs duties (1717)	Rise of the Mahrattas (1717)	Afghans secure independence from Persia (1706)		Clive leaves India (1767)		
					Dissolution of French East Company (1769)		The English at Basra (1770)
			Afghans invade Persia (1722)		Warren Hastings governor of Bengal (1772)		
		Hyderabad proclaims independence from Moguls (1724)	Shah Mahmud's reign of terror in Isphahan (1724)		Lord North's Regulating Act (1773)		Afghan power at its zenith Death of Ahmad Shah (1773)
			End of Safavid dynasty in Persia. Nadir Shah seizes throne (1736)	1785	Warren Hastings leaves India (1785)		
		Sack of Delhi by Nadir Shah (1738)					

provoked a really colossal confederation against the British of all important powers in the area—the Marathas, the Nizam of Hyderabad and Haidar Ali, the formidable ruler of Mysore—and led to the defeat of two British armies

It was at this juncture that the outbreak of the American Revolution allowed the French to begin intriguing again and ultimately enabled them to take direct military action. Yet Hastings overcame all difficulties. The governor of Madras was suspended, and proper military dispositions were made. Then superb diplomacy neutralized the Nizam and also the more important Maratha leaders. Haidar Ali went on fighting but died in 1782. By the time French arms actually arrived on the scene, there was little they could do. The fleet of the brilliant French admiral, Suffren, was fended off by the workmanlike British commander, Sir Edward Hughes. The famous Bussy arrived with an army only to find that the war had ended before he could launch an offensive. At the peace, the French were again returned their trading settlements which Hastings had overrun but again received nothing more. British dominion in India was more firmly established than ever when, in 1785, Hastings was replaced as governor-general by Lord Cornwallis.

The brilliant careers of Clive and Hastings ended in tragedy. Clive found no scope in England for his restless, unstable genius. His great years in India were investigated by parliament at the instigation of his enemies, who accused him of peculation. He was eventually acquitted but became morose and committed suicide in 1774. Hastings, expecting to be received as a hero on his return, found himself instead impeached by the House of Commons. The intrigues of Philip Francis had persuaded Edmund Burke to this course; Burke was sincerely but mistakenly convinced that Hastings was the author of many of the abuses he had been trying to suppress. The trial dragged on for eight years, during which Hastings was obliged to justify his achievements. He did this with tenacious dignity and in the end was acquitted—but his ordeal, which began in his vigorous middle age, left him an old man.

For Cornwallis, his successor in India, this course of events was to be reversed. He went to India from the humiliation of the surrender at Yorktown in the War of American Independence—and stayed to build a great career. Under him the state which Clive had conquered and Hastings had formed was to be fashioned into a practical administrative reality.

Chapter 28

Africa in the Eighteenth Century

European colonial and commercial rivalries were important in eighteenth-century Africa, but there the European presence was largely confined to the coast. This was partly because the interior of the continent held few obvious attractions and partly because penetration inland was precluded from large areas by the prevalence of malaria, sleeping sickness and yellow fever. On the coasts, however, the presence of the Europeans was becoming increasingly important. In the north, the rather disorganized Arab and Berber principalities were drawn into closer commercial relationship with Europe. In the extreme south, the Dutch were inadvertently laying the foundations of the one African state which would eventually have really significant numbers of white settlers. On the west coast, and increasingly on the east, the slave trade was of prime importance, but whereas the former area saw the heyday of European traffic in human beings in the latter region a weak European power was replaced by a strong Arab one.

The Mediterranean north

In those parts of Africa which bordered on the Mediterranean, the most notable characteristic of the period was the continuing decline of the Turkish Empire which was nominal ruler over much of the area. This created an effective political fragmentation, and the local scene in most regions oscillated between bouts of outright anarchy and periods of stern dictatorship. In Egypt, real power remained with the Mamelukes—former slaves from Georgia and Turkestan—but within their ranks individuals rose and fell with bewildering rapidity. Sometimes a strong ruler emerged, such as 'Ali Bey, who between 1757 and 1772 secured full control of Egypt and also occupied parts of Arabia and Syria, but too often the scene was one of chaos and decrepitude. Yet for all this, and for all its grave commercial decline, Egypt managed to retain a precarious independence both of Europeans and its nominal Turkish overlords.

In Tunisia and Algeria, conditions resembled those in Egypt, although with important local variations. The pashas, representing the Sultan of Turkey, were forced to delegate most of their powers to local beys and deys. These often fought among themselves, and the two states also warred against each other; but the European commercial presence was much stronger than in Egypt. Some rulers were violently xenophobic and turned the foreigners out; others, however, made important commercial concessions and signed treaties with the Europeans, especially with the French. More and more the once formidable fleets of pirates and corsairs that these areas had formerly supported gave way to normal shipping connections. This was also true of the huge and independent kingdom of Morocco. Despite its unwieldy size and a period of anarchy in mid-century, Morocco, especially during the reigns of Mulay Ismail (1672–1727) and Mulay Muhammad (1757–90), saw long periods of peace and order. Moreover, despite an inveterate dislike of the Portuguese, who controlled some of their coastal cities, the Moroccans were willing to come to terms with other Europeans. The Danes were given a monopoly of trade on the Atlantic coast, while the Dutch and French were very active on the Mediterranean.

East Africa

During the fifteenth and sixteenth centuries, the ancient, Islamized city-states of the east African coast, such as Kilwa and Mombasa, had been subdued by Portugal as part of the latter's strategy for dominating the entire maritime commerce of the Indian Ocean. During the seventeenth century, however, Portugal fell into decline, and many of the outposts of her eastern empire were commandeered by the English and the Dutch.

Above, Mulay Ismail, ruler of Morocco (reigned 1672–1727); Morocco was a virtually independent state which relied on capturing slaves by piracy for its wealth.

Top, Algerian pirates landing their slaves at Algiers in about 1700; the Europeans did not manage to assert their control over the southern coast of the Mediterranean until the nineteenth century.

Opposite, British officers watching a cockfight at Lucknow, in India, in 1786.

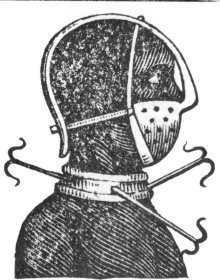

But neither of these powers was much interested in East Africa, and here the failing hand of the Portuguese was gradually displaced by Arabs from Oman, the principality that had claimed the trading cities before the Europeans arrived. Finally, in 1698, the chief bastion of Portuguese power, Fort Jesus in Mombasa, fell to the Imam of Oman after a two-year siege. In the early eighteenth century the Portuguese made some attempts to recover their lost supremacy but only met with further defeats. By 1730, their power had ceased to exist north of Mozambique.

Despite their victory over the Portuguese, troubles in Arabia itself kept successive imams occupied, and it was not for another century that Oman was able to occupy Zanzibar effectively and establish a firm hegemony over the coast. During the eighteenth century, therefore, each city-state was usually governed by a local Arab dynasty, although the predominance of the Mazrui family brought some measure of political cohesion. It was during this period

that the East African slave trade became a major factor, and great Arab caravans bought slaves inland to be sold eventually in the markets of Turkey, Arabia, India and Persia or to the French colonies of Mauritius and Réunion. Thus began the period when pipes sounded on Zanzibar truly made men dance in the region of the inland lakes.

The Dutch in the south

The most important European incursion in the history of Africa began on 6 April 1652, in the southern part of the continent. On that day Jan van Riebeeck dropped anchor in Table Bay with three ships and a small group of settlers. The Dutch East India Company had decided to make the Cape of Good Hope its chief provisioning station between Holland and the Indonesian archipelago. In the ensuing years more settlers came, including a few French Protestants. But throughout the whole period of Dutch rule the progress of the colony was slow, tortuous and trammelled by restrictions. The Cape was truly a company settlement, and the colonists were continually hedged in by the instructions given by the directors of the East India Company in Holland.

Nevertheless, the Dutch settlers were fortunate in their temperate climate, spectacular scenery and in the lack of competitors for the land. The only African peoples in the immediate vicinity, the bushmen and the Hottentots, were few in number. The tiny, Stone Age bushmen proved to be sly enemies and the Dutch did not hesitate to exterminate them or drive them back. Relations with the Hottentots were better. Despite some conflicts, a reasonably cordial understanding was established with many of these more sophisticated, cattle-raising and copper- and iron-working

people. Some of the Hottentots were willing to work on the Dutch farms; other labour was provided by negro slaves brought to the colony from West Africa. This latter factor was to increase in importance especially when the Dutch East India Company took the momentous decision in 1717 that slave labour rather than free was to be the basic rule for the settlement. The eastern part of the colony was expanding rapidly, and in 1776 Dutch frontiersmen met with westward-moving Bantu tribesmen in the region of the Great Fish River. First contacts were friendly, but by this time years of slave-owning experience had indelibly fixed in the minds of the settlers some very definite ideas about the place of the negro in the Dutch God's scheme of creation. The implications for the future were tremendous.

West Africa and the slave trade

There had been a slave trade in West Africa for centuries before the coming of the Europeans. South of the Sahara, in the vast grasslands area known as the Sudan, great civilized negro empires had grown up in medieval times. These states had long raided the forest areas for slaves, who were then transported across the desert for sale in the markets of Morocco. But the Sudan had been falling into increasing chaos and decline since 1590, and soon the flow of slaves was moving south to the ocean rather than north to the desert.

Throughout the eighteenth century, the harbours of the West African coastline, reaching from Senegal to Angola, was annually infested with European ships seeking to purchase slaves. The great and increasing demand for sugar in Europe had in turn created an insatiable demand for slave labour in Brazil and the West Indies, where the sugar was grown. So, to sweeten the beverages of Europeans, millions of Africans were kidnapped, branded, shipped across the ocean and worked to death on the plantations of the New World. Exactly how many were taken we shall never know. Perhaps 8,000,000 slaves arrived in America in the course of this century alone; perhaps 2,000,000 more died on the way.

The trade was very well organized, and the Europeans did not capture slaves themselves as a rule. Rather, the latter were captured far inland, in great slave-raiding wars, then sold through a series of African middlemen down to the coast, where Europeans acquired them from local chiefs in exchange for goods in demand in Africa, such as guns, copper and iron ware, rum and textiles. Trading methods varied widely from one part of the coast to another, and certain areas were generally considered the preserves of particular European nations. The English, for example, dominated the trade in the Gambia and Sierra Leone, the French in Senegal and Gabon, the Portuguese in Angola. But in other places, like the Niger delta and Dahomey, ships of several nations traded together. On the Gold Coast, where the competition was most keen, the British, Dutch and Danes had about twenty forts and large castles interspersed one with another.

Most of the European nations originally found it expedient to grant a monopoly of their share of the slave trade to large chartered companies with great resources of capital. The prototype of these was the Dutch West Indies Company, formed in 1621, which quickly asserted its power and drove the Portuguese from most of West Africa by mid-century. Other peoples— English, French, Danes, Swedes and even Germans from Brandenburg—all formed national trading companies in imitation of the Dutch. Few survived the intense competition. In the long run the British did better by abandoning the chartered Royal African Company, formed in 1672, which was losing much trade to 'interlopers'— English individuals or firms who illegally ignored the company's monopoly and got away with it. In 1750, the corporation was dissolved and replaced by a new association called the Company of Merchants. This body did no business on its own account but existed to facilitate the slave trade for all English merchants who wished to participate in it. Anyone could become a member of the company by paying a small annual subscription, and this abolition of monopoly proved advantageous. The English share of the trade steadily increased during the century, and by 1785 Britain was buying and selling more slaves than all other European nations combined.

Among the side effects of the slave trade was the influence it had on African political development. The tiny city-states of the Niger delta adapted traditional tribal institutions to the demand for slaves and created quite astonishing and complex commercial organizations. In other areas the introduction of firearms encouraged African tribes to expand their territories. In the interior of the Gold Coast, the Confederation of Ashanti steadily grew throughout the century, defeated its rivals and by 1800 was threatening the European position on the coast. Further east, under a series of strong and implacable kings, Dahomey began empire-building in the same fashion. Thus, the inhuman trade had created powerful vested interests in Africa and America as well as in Europe. The fight to abolish 'the abominable traffic' was bound, in these circumstances, to be both protracted and arduous.

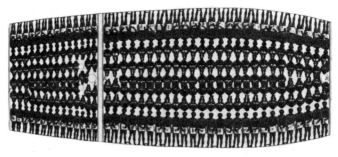

Above, British naval officers making a treaty with Africans in 1815. After the English outlawed the slave trade in 1807, they were to take a greater interest in the internal affairs of Africa. Bibliothèque Nationale, Paris.

Top, a diagram of the way in which slaves were packed into the ships that took them across the Atlantic in the 1780s. The slaves were rarely allowed on deck, for fear that they would mutiny, or jump overboard.

Opposite top left, the Hottentots or Khoikhoi people of southern Africa, who at first accepted the Dutch settlers in their sparsely populated land but later suffered enslavement and extermination.

Opposite right, a chain of slaves taken from the interior of Africa to the coast for shipment to the New World. The Europeans themselves did not round up the slaves – this job was left to the Arab traders and to the King of Dahomey, whose power was greatly increased by this trade with the Europeans.

Opposite bottom, an iron mask, and collar, shackles and spurs, all used by Europeans to restrain Africans taken for slaves in the New World. In addition to the human suffering it caused, the slave trade brought social instability to vast areas of central and western Africa in the eighteenth century.

Chapter 29

The Pacific World

At the beginning of the eighteenth century there were still vast areas of the globe of which Europeans knew nothing: the African interior, most of the Americas, the Pacific. The great exploratory achievement of the century was to chart the largest of these areas—the Pacific: an islanded expanse of water which covers about a third of the world's surface, framed by eastern Asia, the Americas and both polar regions and comprising a great diversity of climatic conditions, flora and fauna which—before the European came—supported widely different societies.

In the sixteenth century, Europeans established themselves in the East Indies (modern Indonesia) and the Philippines. The first European crossing of the Pacific was made by three Spanish ships commanded by Magellan, which went on to complete the first circumnavigation of the earth (1519–22). After this, Spanish voyages in the Pacific became frequent, and a regular trade began between Manila and Spanish America; but, though the Pacific was used as a waterway, little progress was made in charting or exploring it.

There were several reasons for this—the frequency with which great naval powers became involved in European wars, the secrecy with which any seemingly lucrative discovery was guarded—but the fundamental reason was navigational. A less than perfect ability to determine longitude did not prevent a ship from locating a sizeable land-mass; but it made it impossible to chart and rediscover the position of a Pacific archipelago. Hence the early Spanish explorers kept discovering islands and losing them again; Mendana discovered the Solomons on his first voyage (1567), only to miss them at a second try (1595) and end up in the Marquesas. The islands sighted by Quiros on his voyage in search of a southern continent (1606) were also 'lost'. And though Quiros's deputy, Torres, discovered a passage through the reefs and shoals separating Australia from New Guinea, the fact was not widely known for generations. It continued to be believed that Australia and New Guinea were part of the same land-mass, and even in 1768 Bougainville was not sufficiently convinced to make an attempt on the passage.

Terra Australis

Lack of progress in exploring the innumerable islands of Oceania is understandable; lack of interest in the island continent of Australia, close at hand, is at first sight inexplicable, especially in view of the European obsession with 'Terra Australis', the great southern continent that was believed to exist somewhere between the Cape of Good Hope and Cape Horn. Marco Polo had described its enormous wealth; Biblical interpretation supported Marco; and symmetry and sense required the existence of a land mass to balance those of the northern hemisphere and stop the earth toppling over.

There were, however, practical difficulties in pursuing the quest for the southern continent. Spanish ships came from Peru, Mexico or round the Horn—when the southeast trade winds lifted them steadily towards the Equator, so that they missed most of the actual Polynesian islands as well as the mythical Terra Australis—or sailed north from the Philippines to catch the westerlies that took them to Spanish America.

Nor were the Dutch better placed in New Guinea, though they were inhibited by more mercenary considerations. In 1605 William Jansz discovered New Holland (Australia), and the north and west coasts were soon fairly well known; but as they happen to be the least attractive areas of Australia and were inhabited by aborigines who seemed dirty, utterly primitive and poverty-stricken, there was no great incentive to explore further. This could not be the fabled Terra Australis.

The Dutch were right in this respect, as they discovered when a serious voyage of exploration was at last undertaken. In 1642, by sailing eastward from Mauritius so that the winds enabled him to stay in a high latitude (i.e. far south), Tasman proved that

there was no Terra Australis in the Indian Ocean. He reached what is now Tasmania and went on to New Zealand, Tonga and the Fiji Islands. It thus became clear that Australia was an island (though New Guinea and Tasmania were still believed to be parts of it), and it was the *known* southern land (Terra Australis *Cognita*). Belief in the southern continent (Terra Australis *Incognita*) remained unshaken, though its projected area was diminished; Tasman himself thought that New Zealand might be its northern promontory.

And there matters remained for more than a century. The Dutch East India Company, like the Spanish Council of State before it, decided that it had better things to do with men, ships and money than to search for the southern continent. Europeans became preoccupied with their wars, and when the British, the seafaring people *par excellence* in the eighteenth century, appeared in Pacific waters, it was as buccaneers (like Dampier) or predators on enemy shipping (like Anson). Only after the Seven Years War was Europe to begin its decisive irruption into the Pacific.

Cook

Credit for this achievement is rightly given to Captain James Cook. The Englishmen Wallis and Carteret discovered—or rather rediscovered—Tahiti and Pitcairn Island in 1767; and in 1768 a French ship under the command of Bougainville also visited Tahiti; but it was Cook's three great voyages from 1768 that literally put the Pacific islands on the map.

Cook (1728–78) was the son of a Yorkshire farmworker. He had run away to sea in his teens, worked on colliers on the east coast and then joined the service. His record was distinguished and of the most valuable kind for his future activities—charting the shoals of the St Lawrence during the Seven Years War and surveying the coasts of Nova Scotia; but his rise was slow, perhaps because of his humble birth. He was thirty-nine, and newly made a lieutenant, when he was given the command that made him famous.

He had all the requisite qualities. He was completely professional, popular, brave and audacious—though his courage and audacity were expressed in such a matter-of-fact executive thoroughness that they are easily overlooked. Like other eighteenth-century commanders, he kept order among his men—the disreputable haul of the press-gangs—by harsh discipline; but his scrubbing-brush-and-vegetables regime almost banished the seaman's worst enemy, scurvy.

The public (and genuine) objective of Cook's first voyage (1768–71) was to observe from a mid-Pacific station the transit of Venus across the face of the sun—in itself an important task, undertaken at the instance of the Royal Society. But when Cook left England in August 1768 it was with secret and quite explicit instructions to search for the unknown southern continent, to bring back specimens of Pacific flora and fauna, to cultivate the friendship of any natives he met and to take possession, in the king's name, of such territories as he discovered.

Cook's ship, the *Endeavour*, was an adapted collier: a slow but sturdy vessel whose shallow draught made her ideal for surveying in coastal waters. With him Cook had the most up-to-date navigational aids: the sextant, which made it possible to take astronomical readings despite the ship's motion, and accurate lunar tables with which to interpret the readings. On his second voyage Cook was to secure even better results by taking an improved chronometer that measured distances at sea. Thus it had at last become possible to navigate and chart the Pacific accurately.

The *Endeavour* also carried the naturalist Joseph Banks, an astronomer and an artist; and Cook's later expeditions were similarly accompanied. His were therefore the first scientific expeditions activated by an un-prejudiced curiosity, which extended to the human fauna, towards whose customs Cook and the scientists displayed a sympathy and tolerance worthy of the Age of Reason.

First voyage: the south Pacific

The *Endeavour* reached Tahiti via Cape Horn in April 1769 and stayed for three months—the first protracted contact between Europeans and Polynesians. The easy conditions of Polynesian life—and the absence of Western sexual taboos, of which the sailors took full advantage—made the island seem a paradise. The accounts given by Cook and others on their return lent credence to the myth of 'the noble savage'. In Tahiti itself, one of the effects of European contact soon appeared: half of Cook's men contracted the venereal diseases presumably brought by Bougainville's or Wallis's sailors. Nevertheless, apart from the Tahitian propensity to steal anything they could lay their hands on, relations between Europeans and natives were excellent.

After observing the transit of Venus—an activity almost prevented by the theft of the quadrant—Cook followed his secret instructions, sailing south and then west to New Zealand. He spent six months methodically charting the 2,400 miles of the coastline. The warlike Maoris, who had scared off Tasman, were handled with tact and remained friendly. By establishing that New Zealand consisted of two islands, Cook further diminished the possible extent of the legendary southern continent.

From New Zealand he sailed to Australia, making landfall at what was christened Botany Bay, in a part of the island continent that was far more inviting than the barren shores hitherto known: Cook called it New South Wales. Within a few years it was to be the home of English convicts and their keepers. The expedition explored the 2,000 miles of the eastern coastline, narrowly escaping disaster on the Great Barrier Reef, and observed the seemingly primeval landscape of Australia—the 'blackfellows' who seemed like the first men, the hopping kangaroo and flying fox (opossum). The final achievement of the voyage was a passage through the Torres Strait, virtually rediscovered after 160 years, which confirmed that Australia was a separate island from New Guinea. The *Endeavour* now returned via the Cape to England (1771), having circumnavigated the world.

The explorers' reception was a compound of scientific and literary enthusiasm. They had revealed the existence of an innocent world which had never known the Fall, mapped it and brought back a vast quantity of botanical, zoological and geological specimens and drawings, as well as native tools and clothing. The papers on which the naturalists Banks and Solander dried their specimens were, ironically, proof sheets for a commentary on Milton's *Paradise Lost*.

Second voyage: Terra Australis vanishes

Cook did not stay long to enjoy his fame. In July 1772 he set out on his second voyage with the *Resolution* and the *Adventurer*, both adapted colliers like the *Endeavour*. This time he followed Tasman's example and entered the Pacific from the west, determined to hold a course as far south as possible. And during the three summers (1772–4) of this second voyage, the *Resolution* ventured into the South Polar Sea, three times crossing the Antarctic Circle and once reaching as far south as latitude 71 degrees. By the end of the third summer it had effectively circumnavigated the Antarctic.

Above, the fruit of the plant Myrmecodia beccarii, *better known as ant house, found in Australia by Cook on his first voyage; the exploration of Australasia revealed many species of animals and plants previously unknown, and naturalists such as Joseph Banks were important members of the expedition. British Museum, London.*

Top, a tattooed Maori warrior, according to a member of Cook's first voyage. The Maoris had been established in New Zealand since the thirteenth century and had built up a series of strong and warlike kingdoms. British Museum, London.

Opposite, a sketch made by Captain Cook of Tolaga Bay in New Zealand. British Museum, London.

expedition's artist, Hodges, painted a picture which effectively conveys their remote, unreal presence. The exploration of the Oceanic islands alone would have justified Cook's second voyage; the circumnavigation of the Antarctic made it an epic. His return to England in 1775, again loaded with drawings and specimens, sealed his fame.

Third voyage: the Northwest Passage

Again he scarcely paused to enjoy it—which indicates that, for all his matter-of-factness, Cook suffered from the compulsive wanderlust attributed to the explorer in folklore. In 1776 he sailed to lay another myth: the Northwest Passage. Two centuries before Cook, Englishmen had tried to find a northwest passage from Hudson's Bay into the Pacific; now he was to seek it from the Pacific. There was also a political motive for the voyage: Cook was instructed to discover how much of the Pacific coast of North America was in Spanish and Russian hands.

On this, his last voyage, Cook sailed into every sizeable inlet along the Alaskan coast without finding the Northwest Passage, passed through the Bering Strait across the Arctic Circle and explored the Arctic coast of America, discovering and naming Cape North. Further south, he discovered Christmas Island (1777) and the Hawaiian Islands (1778); and it was to Kealakekua Bay in the Hawaiian Islands that he returned from the Arctic (1779) and met his death.

As in the previous year, he was welcomed as a god. His ships, the *Resolution* and the *Discovery*, left Kealakekua Bay for home, but were forced to turn back by two days of storm. The homage due to a god was repeated, despite the tiresome impropriety of

The fabulously wealthy southern continent had once and for all been proved a myth; below the southern oceans there were only walls of ice, numbing cold, gales and fogs. Cook thought that there probably was a land-mass centred on the South Pole; but the question of its existence seemed of little interest and incapable of solution. The hazards encountered by the *Resolution* understandably led Cook to believe that no explorer would be able to penetrate further. He wrote, the Southern Hemisphere has been sufficiently explored, and a final end put to the searching after a Southern Continent, which has at times engrossed the attention of some of the maritime powers for near two centuries past, and the geographers of all ages.

The wealth hoped for in Terra Australis *Incognita* did exist, though not in the form envisaged by readers of Marco Polo and Quiros. Cook's exploration of Tierra del Fuego, South Georgia and the Sandwich Islands revealed that the polar regions supported an abundance of wild life, including whales, seals and sea-lions. The existence of such prey was to bring large numbers of Europeans into the South Pacific within a few years of Cook's voyages.

Cook and his men recuperated from the rigours of Antarctica by spending the winters roaming the Pacific, discovering or rediscovering the Marquesas, the Society Islands, the New Hebrides, New Caledonia, Norfolk Island and many other islands. Perhaps the most fascinating rediscovery was Easter Island, on which great crumbling figures gazed mysteriously into the distance. The

the god's reappearance; but trouble blew up when some Hawaiians stole one of *Discovery's* boats. Cook had faced this situation before and made his standard response by taking hostages to compel the return of the boat. But this time something went wrong: Cook's men fired at some canoes and killed a chief. The Hawaiians attacked Cook's party on the shore. The explorer was stabbed in the back and fell face down in the water, and the incensed Hawaiians surrounded his body and cut it to pieces. A friendly native later brought some of his remains out to the ships, and they were buried at sea.

Pacific cultures

Cook and his men, like other Europeans, found it difficult to distinguish between the various peoples they encountered: 'Indians' were either happy, like the Tahitians, or miserable, like the natives of Tierra del Fuego, whom Cook described as 'perhaps as miserable a set of people as are this day on earth'. In the course of his three voyages, Cook became aware that Oceania contained a diversity of races and cultures; and the realization that the Tahitians took part in savage intertribal wars, practised infanticide and indulged in occasional human sacrifices disabused him of any idea that Pacific peoples were 'innocent'.

In fact, Pacific societies were the product of a long evolution, and even the least advanced had made a complex adaptation to their surroundings. They had elaborately regulated codes of social behaviour, extensive mythologies and highly developed skills. Among other things they produced striking drawings, paintings and objects for magic and ritual purposes. They were, however, inferior to Europeans in certain essential respects: they did not use metal, they

had not developed a system of writing, and they had no draught animals. They also took for granted many rites that were repulsive to the European moral sensibility; though it may be questioned whether the self-mutilation of the aborigine or the cannibalism of the islanders was crueller than what actually went on in European slave ships and prisons.

The Tasmanians and Australian aborigines were the most backward peoples in the Pacific: they were hunters and food-gatherers, like men of the Paleolithic (Old Stone Age) period. The Tasmanians, now extinct—or, rather, extinguished by the white man in the nineteenth century—were a dark-skinned, woolly-haired people, possibly of Papuan origin. Where they came from and how they reached Tasmania is unknown. As toolmakers they lagged behind the aborigines, since they had neither spears nor boomerangs. They probably numbered only 5,000.

Australia, too, was sparsely populated, with only a few hundred thousand aboriginal inhabitants, who had come to Australia from Asia before the two land-masses had separated. Australia lacked cereals and herding animals, which limited the possible development of the aborigine. But though his existence was a hand-to-mouth one, his few skills—making weapons, hunting, fishing, gathering berries and grubs—were developed to an extraordinary degree and ensured survival even in periods of draught. A complex kinship system linked the various clans within a tribe, and every tribe had its totem—a common ancestor, plant or animal —which was celebrated in ceremonies. All aborigines practised some form of initiation of the young at puberty (usually circumcision) which entailed the infliction of great pain. Aboriginal painting and drawing—on

Above, HMS Resolution, *one of the two ships taken by Cook on his second voyage. Mitchell Library, Sydney.*

Top, the inhabitants of Tierra del Fuego, as found by Cook in 1769. British Museum, London.

Top left, a bearded pensuin, recorded on Cook's second voyage. British Museum, London.

Opposite top left, the Resolution *and the* Adventure, *the ships that Cook took on his second trip to the south Pacific, in 1772–75, anchored off Tahiti. National Maritime Museum, London.*

Opposite right, Otoo, or Tu, the King of Tahiti, whom Cook met on his second voyage and for whom he had great friendship and respect. National Library of Australia, Canberra.

Opposite bottom, the island of Tahiti, depicted by a member of Cook's second voyage. British Museum, London.

271

bark, on the ground, in caves—ranged from extreme stylization to a vivid naturalism.

Melanesia

The peoples of Oceania were at the Neolithic (New Stone Age) level of development: that is they lived in permanent settlements, cultivated the land and had domesticated animals. All subsisted on 'garden' and tree products such as yams, coconuts and breadfruit.

But the differences between them were as important as their similarities. Oceania was inhabited by three distinct races, though there was inevitably a good deal of cross-breeding and cultural interchange. The Melanesians ('black islanders') were the least advanced, dark-skinned, woolly-haired peoples who had spread from New Guinea to the neighbouring islands (the Solomons, the New Hebrides, New Caledonia, part of the Fijis). The dense vegetation in most parts of Melanesia led to the development of isolated, widely different communities with separate languages.

The Micronesians ('people of the small islands') were predominantly Mongoloid, relatives of the peoples of eastern Asia. They had yellow-brown skins and straight black hair and were small and slight. Both racially and culturally they were more hybrid than the other Oceanic peoples, Polynesian influence being particularly strong. They occupied the Marianas, the Carolines, the Marshalls and the Gilbert Islands.

The Polynesians ('people of the many islands') were the latest arrivals in the Pacific. Where they came from remains in dispute: most scholars believe it was Asia, but Thor Heyerdahl has put forward a strong argument in favour of South America, proving by his famous Kon-Tiki expedition (1947) that it was possible to make a journey by raft from Peru to the Society Islands. Whatever their origin, the Polynesians were undoubtedly a remarkable seafaring people. According to the orthodox account, between the ninth and thirteenth centuries

AD they spread out from the Society Islands over a vast area of the Pacific, reaching the Hawaiian Islands, the Ellice Islands, New Zealand and Easter Island.

They were a Caucasian people, with good physiques, light-brown skins and straight or wavy hair, and occupied the most favoured areas of the Pacific (free from malaria, supporting the sweet potato, etc.). These facts largely account for the European prejudice which even now leads people to identify 'Polynesians' and 'South Sea Islanders'. However, it is true that they were most advanced of the Pacific races. Apart from their seafaring exploits (less in evidence by the eighteenth century), they made a sophisticated study of oratory, were skilled musicians and possessed an appealingly dignified code of manners. On his second voyage, Cook brought a Tahitian called Omai back to England, where he became a society lion with no difficulty at all, meeting George III and sitting for two romanticized portraits by Sir Joshua Reynolds. The less attractive side of Polynesian life included diseases (yaws, hookworm), cannibalism and a variety of murderous burial and sacrificial rites.

Easter Island deserves to be mentioned separately, since it has been the subject of much speculation. It is a thousand miles from the nearest Polynesian island (Pitcairn) and two thousand from South America; so that, whichever direction they came from, the Polynesians must have accomplished a great feat of navigation in reaching it. The island has two features of intense interest: the gigantic statues carved from soft volcanic rock, which in the eighteenth century were still crowned with hats carved from a different red stone; and wooden tablets carrying undeciphered writing or hieroglyphs—the only example in the whole of the Pacific. Both are now attributed to the Polynesians rather than to a 'lost' race, but the almost complete destruction of the island's population during the nineteenth century effectively terminated any oral tradition that might have provided more information on the subject.

The European invasion

Australia had few inhabitants, whereas the Pacific islands were densely populated, perhaps even overpopulated. Europeans were soon to reverse this situation by colonizing Australia and visiting a whole series of misfortunes on the islanders.

The explorers behaved well, exemplifying rational curiosity and a humanitarian enthusiasm which extended to providing friendly natives with seed, iron tools and domestic animals—the introduction of the pig greatly improved the islanders' diet. Cook set a high standard of conduct that was generally followed by his sucessors, of whom the best-known are the French commanders La Pérouse (1785–8), Freycinet (1818–19) and D'Urville (1826–9 and 1837–40).

All the same, the explorers were indirectly to blame for the coming disaster: they made the Pacific accessible to the European. Cook himself repeatedly expressed doubts as to the benefits of European influence on the natives, though he mainly thought in terms of a fall from grace on their part. Up to a point he was right: the islanders quickly became dependent on European tools and began to lose some of their old skills; and European firearms made tribal wars much more deadly.

The civilized attitudes of the eighteenth-century gentleman-officer-scientist were not shared by sailors and most other Europeans. The famous mutiny on the *Bounty* (1789) provided a clear warning: the mutineers, who have become heroes of romance for setting the tyrannical Captain Bligh adrift in an open boat, mistreated the natives and fought among themselves wherever they went (Tahiti, Tubai, Pitcairn).

The depredations of the European were to be on a much larger scale than this. The Pacific became the stamping ground of the escaped criminal, the deserter and the ne'er-do-well. Traders invaded the area, greedy for sandalwood, copra, pearls and *bêche-de-mer* (an edible sea-slug very acceptable to the Chinese palate). 'Blackbirders' kidnapped or

hoodwinked thousands of islanders to work in the sugar-cane fields of Queensland and the mines of Mexico and Peru. Whalers and sealers disrupted native society with alcohol, violence and disease, as well as destroying the wild life of the Antarctic. Missionaries resisted these intrusions but suppressed the island cultures, forbade singing and dancing and (regardless of climate) thrust the men of the islands into singlets and shorts and the women into 'Mother Hubbard' shifts. If the demoralized natives escaped kidnappers, press-gangs, alcoholism and venereal disease, they succumbed to European ailments against which they had built up no immunities.

Most of these developments were in full swing by the end of the eighteenth century. The most striking result was a catastrophic decline in population, visible by the mid-nineteenth century, when the European powers began to annex the island groups. Generally speaking, annexation improved the native's lot by giving him some sort of legal protection; but the damage had already been done. The booming trade in copra brought Chinese, Indian, Japanese and other immigrants into the Pacific in the nineteenth century. But the islanders themselves made a partial demographic recovery only in the present century, and the cultural adjustment is still not complete.

The fierce Maoris of New Zealand, in origin a Polynesian race, were slightly more fortunate. They were given to fighting among themselves and eating each other but proved capable of resisting the white man with remarkable success. The arrival of European traders enabled them to acquire firearms, which increased inter-tribal bloodshed but also put them on an equal footing with the European. When annexation inevitably took place (1840), the Maori race was still intact and able to secure relatively favourable terms.

The birth of white Australia

European governments were slow in annexing and settling the Pacific lands, partly

because of preoccupation with European events, partly because of a growing conviction that political control was unnecessary and burdensome. The single exception, Australia, was made only because Britain had lost her American colonies, and with them a dumping-ground for convicts. In 1788 eleven ships under Captain Arthur Phillip arrived at Port Jackson (later Sydney), just above Botany Bay, with a cargo of 717 male and female convicts and a New South Wales Corps raised in Britain to guard them. The eastern half of Australia was formally claimed by Great Britain.

Guarded chain-gangs of convicts continued to work in the new continent as before: the rigours of the British penal system were simply transferred unchanged to a new setting, except that uncertain supplies, rum and the unreliability of the New South Wales Corps made for greater confusion and hardship. For two decades Australia was governed despotically by naval commanders, who spent much of their time trying to suppress the traffic in rum and curtail the power of the

Above, a woman of New Holland, later known as Van Diemen's Land, or Tasmania, as recorded on Cook's third voyage. British Museum, London.

Top, the interior of a winter house found by Cook in one of the Aleutian islands, off the coast of Alaska; the roof was covered with turf. Peabody Museum, Harvard University, Cambridge Massachusetts.

Top left, HMS Resolution at anchor off Vancouver Island, Canada, on Cook's third voyage, on which he tried to find the western end of the north-west passage. British Museum, London.

Above left, an eskimo of Alaska, depicted by a member of Cook's crew. He is wearing a visor against the glare of the snow. Peabody Museum, Harvard University, Cambridge, Massachusetts.

Opposite left, the ceremonial presentation of a pig to Captain Cook in Hawaii in 1778; he was treated as an incarnation of the god of peace and happiness. Bernice P Bishop Museum, Honolulu.

Opposite right, a sketch of Hawaiian men dancing; Bernice P Bishop Museum, Honolulu.

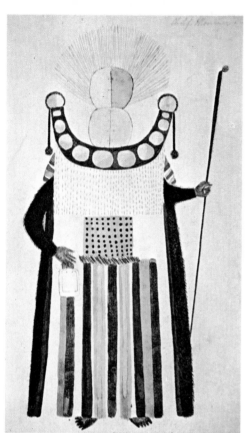

EUROPEANS IN THE PACIFIC

Date	The Pacific	Europe
1500		
	Balboa sights Pacific (1513)	
		Luther's 95 theses (1517)
	Magellan crosses Pacific (1520)	
	Mendana: first voyage (1567)	
	Sir Francis Drake in Pacific (1578)	
	Mendana: second voyage (1595)	
1600		
	Janszoon: 'New Holland' (1605)	Gunpowder plot (1605)
	Voyages of Quiros and Torres (1605)	
	Hartog explores western Australia (1616)	
	Tasman's voyage (1642–4)	English Civil War (1642–6)
	Dampier on north coast of Australia (1699)	
1700		
	Roggeeven discovers Easter Island and Samoa (1721)	
		Seven Years War (1756–63)
	Wallis and Carteret (1766–7)	
	Bougainville (1767–9)	
	Cook: first voyage (1768–71)	
	Cook: second voyage (1772–5)	
		American War of Independence (1775–83)
	Cook: third voyage (1776–9)	
	Voyage of La Pérouse (1785–8)	
	Australia: convicts at Botany Bay (1788)	
		Storming of the Bastille (1789)
	Bounty mutineers on Pitcairn (1790)	
	Australia: first free settlers (1793)	
	First mission on Tahiti (1798)	
1800		
		Battle of Waterloo (1815)
	Voyage of Freycinet (1818–19)	
	D'Urville: first voyage (1826–9)	
	Australia annexed (1829)	
		Great Reform Bill (1832)
	D'Urville: second voyage (1837–40)	
		Victoria becomes Queen (1837)
	New Zealand annexed (1840)	
1850	French begin island annexations	

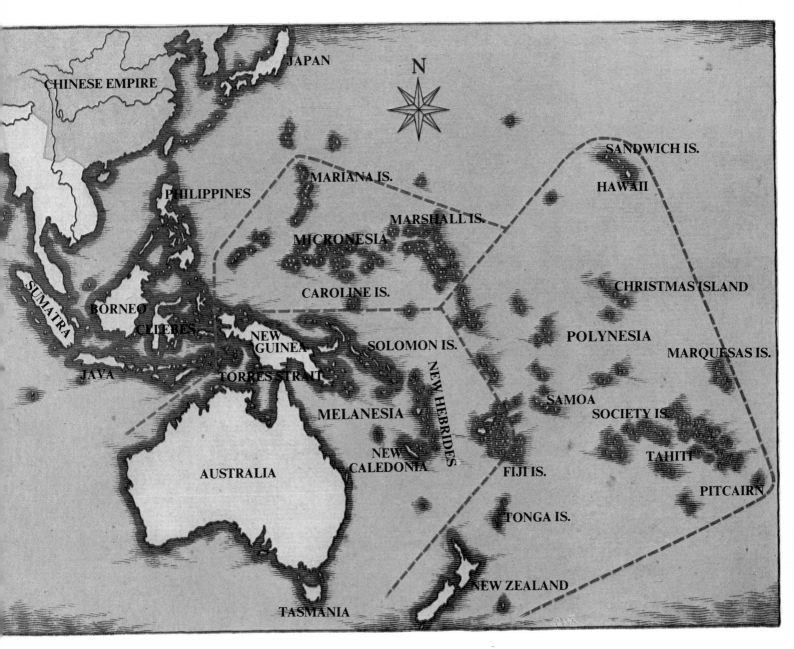

Top, Australasia in the eighteenth century.

officers of the Corps, who had become great landed proprietors. The aborigines were driven from their hunting-grounds and became pitiful hangers-on or retired further inland, where they killed and were killed by any white man they came across. The settlement of Tasmania began the process by which the white man rapidly destroyed the native population. There was an insurrection of Irish convicts (mainly political prisoners from the Irish rebellion of 1798) in 1804 and a 'rum rebellion' in 1808 against one of the governors, the unlucky Bligh of the *Bounty*. It was in many respects an unpromising beginning.

More constructive efforts were also being made. The first free settlers arrived in 1793. provided by the British government with tools and grants of land. The convicts too were given land when their sentences expired. Sheep-raising began in the 1790s. In 1798 George Bass discovered the strait separating Tasmania from the continent, and in 1802–3 Matthew Flinders completed the exploration of the south coast and circumnavigated Australia. The continent had

become a British preserve, and it was only a matter of time before it was annexed (1829).

The nineteenth century was to be one of continued hardship, dissension and exploitation (convicts were transported to Australia until 1867) but also one of settlement, exploration and eventual self-government. For better or worse, a new nation came into being in the South Pacific.

Above, convicts breaking stones in the English penal colony of New South Wales, established in 1788. Private Collection.

Top, Australasia in the eighteenth century.

Opposite left, a native of Tahiti wearing full mourning outfit, painted by one of Captain Cook's crew in 1770. British Museum, London.

Opposite right, Sydney Harbour in about 1810; the original colony of Botany Bay was soon overtaken by Sydney.

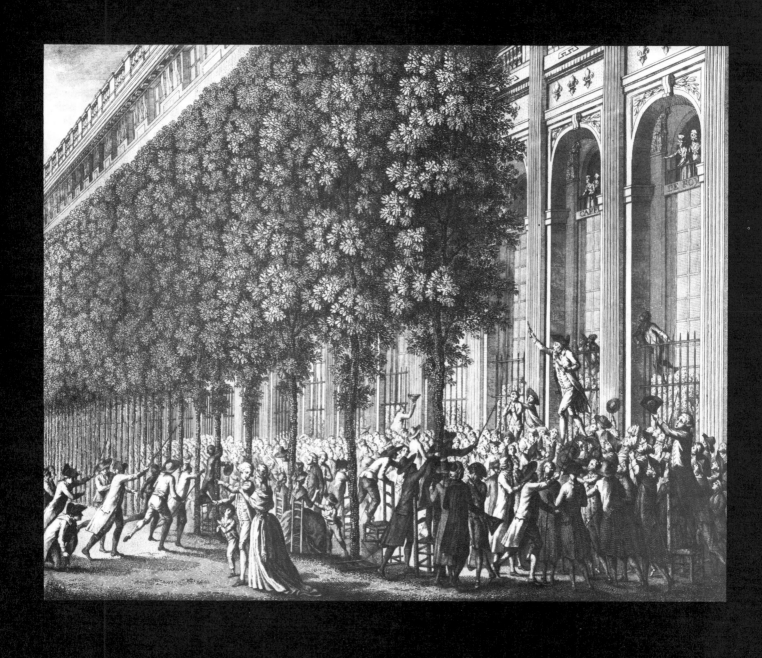

Part V

THE AGE OF REVOLUTIONS

Introduction

The second half of the eighteenth century is the classic Age of Revolution. There is more in revolution than transition of a particularly rapid and violent kind, and the revolutions in the western world—the Puritan revolution in England, the Russian Revolution, and the American and French Revolutions—have all had a constructive purpose and outcome. Indeed, it has been wisely said that a revolution is an unlawful change in the conditions of lawfulness. Revolution is always illegal, but its aim is not lawless. It begins by defying an older authority and ends by creating a new one, and so the American revolution concluded with the establishment of the new government of the United States, the French with Napoleon's organization of modern France.

There is good reason to treat the American and the French Revolutions together. It is true that France and the Thirteen Colonies were in many respects very different. France was ten times as populous, more urbanized and more civilized and much more troubled by the problems of wealth, poverty and privilege with which an old and complex society is often afflicted.

Yet events in the two countries formed part of a larger whole. It was French support that enabled the Americans to win a clear decision in their war of independence. That war was, in fact, one of the series of Anglo-French conflicts that ran intermittently from the time of Louis XIV to that of Napoleon. But in thus helping to dismember the British Empire, the French monarchy was only briefly to enjoy its moment of revenge. The expense of the American war turned its chronic deficits into financial paralysis and brought about a breakdown of the social order. The example of rebellion in America had a direct consequence in the French Revolution.

While educated Americans such as John Adams and Thomas Jefferson read mostly English books, they also shared in that European enlightenment for which French writers were the principal spokesmen. On the other hand, various of the French who became revolutionaries in 1789—Lafayette, Mirabeau, Condorcet, Brissot and Mounier —had long talked, thought or written about the American Revolution and the new American ideas.

The ideas shared in France and America were to inspire all the liberal and democratic movements of modern times. Some had been anticipated in England in the seventeenth century. Some were again expressed in demand for reform in England, Scotland and Ireland, which became audible at about the time of the American Revolution and made itself increasingly heard until the days of Gladstone.

Similar ideas existed in most other parts of Europe also. It thus happened that when, during the French Revolutionary and Napoleonic wars, the French occupied Italy or Germany, Holland or Poland, they found men in those countries who were willing to work with them. The Revolution 'expanded'. The French empire under Napoleon may have resembled the German control of Europe under Hitler in some ways, but certainly not in spirit. Napoleon appealed to the enlightened and progressive forces in Europe; Hitler loathed them. Hitler annihilated the Jews; Napoleon, while caring nothing for Judaism, insisted that the Jews receive equal rights.

The common fund of revolutionary ideas was mixed, various and internally conflicting. Some ideas fared better than others at different times and in different places, but it is easy to establish a general list. There was the principle of the sovereignty of the people, which sometimes meant national self-determination or independence and sometimes meant that ultimate authority must lie with the governed and not with the government, a governing class, or a ruling elite or family.

This principle passed into either republicanism or constitutional monarchy. It involved ideas of representation and limited government, which had existed in Europe since the Middle Ages but now took a more modern form. An equality among citizens, rather than a hierarchy of ranks and orders, was to be the base of representation. Liberty, an old ideal, now carried the ring of individual freedom.

There must be freedom of thought and expression, subject to the needs of public order, which at times, as under Robespierre or Napoleon, were construed to mean the silencing of political opposition. There must be freedom of religion. In the modern state people of any religion or of no religion should enjoy the same civic rights and have the same duties. There should be a written constitution, a document deliberately and rationally contrived and agreed upon, not a mere inheritance of familiar customs and practices.

Closely related was the idea of separation of executive, legislative and judical powers. All magistrates, from the king (if any) downwards, were to possess only a delegated function, and law courts were to be more rational, expeditious and humane. Men had rights, by nature and as citizens, to be specifically declared and secured against arbitrary power. The Americans and the

French issued many such pronouncements, and the French Declaration of 1789 was the most memorable document of the era.

But if the French and American Revolutions were alike in some of their ideas, they were also very different. The American was much milder and much less of a revolution. The ruling groups in America before the Revolution were less entrenched, less ostentatiously rich, less obstinate and less detested than in France. British rule was not really oppressive, and before 1776 the British governors and regiments in America were not considered as foreigners. They made themselves very objectionable, but there is a whole school of thought that has seen the American Revolution as a civil war within the British Empire, with discontented persons on both sides of the Atlantic opposing crown and parliament as they then existed. The ultimate cause of the rupture must be found in the fact that England and its colonies had developed in contrary directions in the four or five generations since the first settlement. Relatively speaking, the colonies were already 'democratic', whereas England was in the heyday of its landed aristocracy and the oddities of the unreformed parliament.

The American Revolution is remembered, in part, as the first successful case of colonial independence. It initiated the break-up of the first European overseas empires and was followed later by the Latin-American revolutions and by increasing autonomy for Canada and the British dominions.

It is sometimes seen also as a precedent for the twentieth-century, anti-colonialist revolutions of Asia and Africa. There are indeed parallels, and the Americans did reject a distant authority that was increasingly felt to be alien. However, the racial feelings and the deeper cultural differences that have animated the recent movements of decolonization had no part in the American Revolution, especially since at that time it was only the white Americans—then mostly of English or Scottish origin—who counted.

The French Revolution was vaster and more widely significant and became the prototype of revolution itself. It passed through a series of increasingly radical phases and was opposed by organized counter-revolutionary attempts. It developed a psychology of world liberation matched by the Austro-Prussian intervention to uphold the French king's authority in 1792. The result was the fall of the French monarchy, more civil struggle, more radicalization of the Revolution, the Terror and French military victories that went on interruptedly for twenty years.

In France, unlike America, the whole social structure was transformed. Old forms of income disappeared, such as the right to receive feudal dues and tithes, and also class privileges in taxation which were, in effect, a form of income. Much more real property changed hands, when lands and buildings, both in the towns and in the country,

belonging to the Church or to nobles who had fled abroad were bought up by peasants and the middle classes.

Changes in local government, including a new plan of municipal organization, altered the social relationships of gentry and common people, and proved more lasting than constitutional reforms at a higher level. The Church was revolutionized from top to bottom. Roman Catholics, Protestants, Jews and the non-religious received the same rights. So did free negroes. Slavery itself was abolished in the colonies in 1794, although soon restored. Marriage, the family, the schools and the selection and training of an educated elite were put on a new basis.

The economy was opened up by the abolition of guilds, regional tariffs and older forms of commercial law. It benefited from new technical schools, public museums, the awarding of prizes to inventors, decimal currency and the metric system. War itself was transformed. The army of the citizen soldier, resting on popular enthusiasm and promotion to the highest ranks according to merit (a phenomenon already seen in America but unknown in Europe), was now made more systematic in France, as befitted a country of 25,000,000 inhabitants at war with the powers of Europe.

All such developments heightened the national consciousness, or sense of membership, commitment, unity and common advantage, within the state. But the main immediate beneficiaries of the French Revolution were undoubtedly the middle classes, people in town or country who had, or could obtain, some property, education and social position. Many of the former aristocracy remained disaffected. The wage-earning and artisan classes received no lasting or tangible satisfaction.

The Revolution was marked by acute class conflict. The beginnings of a working-class movement in 1793 were soon put down. It is true to say that there was in the French Revolution no socialism of any developed kind, but when a revolutionary socialism appeared in the next generation it looked back to the French Revolution for precedent and encouragement. Since the end of the eighteenth century the idea of revolution, either belief in it or fear of it has been a permanent feature of our world.

Chapter 30

The American Revolution

The British colonies in North America in 1763 were not limited to the Atlantic seaboard. They stretched from the Hudson Bay Territory, Newfoundland, Nova Scotia and Quebec in the north down to the Florida keys in the south and across to the islands of the Caribbean, from Bermuda to Jamaica and from Dominica and St Vincent to Grenada. Britain also controlled Belize and the Mosquito Coast in Central America. France held the Caribbean sugar islands of Guadeloupe, St Domingue (Santo Domingo), Martinique and St Lucia (which some contemporary observers thought more valuable than empty Canada) and Cayenne in Guiana. Louisiana, Cuba and Hispaniola were Spanish possessions.

Nevertheless, it was Britain which dominated both the mainland and the Caribbean with 8,000 ships at sea and 70,000 sailors. Britain saw its American empire as maritime and its purposes as mercantile. America's raw materials—sugar and rice, tobacco and timber, furs and fish—precisely because they could not be produced easily (or at all) at home were the justification for the colonies' existence.

In exchange for all these things the colonies were given military and naval protection and trading bounties and were sold the manufactures, the cambrics, the necessities and the luxuries which they needed. The British Empire, like all empires, was founded for the profit of the mother country, not its glory. Without this motive, the Empire would not have existed.

The mainland colonies extended for 1,600 miles along the coast of North America and in 1763 hardly reached more than 100 miles inland. At each end there was a military or naval outpost: Newfoundland was a tiny settlement of 6,000, but its numbers were doubled in the summer as the Grand Banks were swept for cod and mackerel. Florida, won from Spain in 1763, was seen as a frontier against the Spanish-controlled west and against Spain's Indian allies—the Creeks, the Choctaws and the Cherokees. To the acquisitions of 1713—the Hudson Bay Territory, Newfoundland and Nova Scotia—there was added in 1763 the vast province of Quebec. Nova Scotia had been given a representative assembly in 1758 and by 1775 its population had reached a total of 20,000. Quebec, however, was French in character, unready yet for any form of representative government, with only nineteen Protestant families living outside Quebec and Montreal.

The British colonies, from Massachusetts to Georgia, varied greatly in character, government and economies. By 1763 the majority were under the direct rule of the Crown, except for Pennsylvania, Delaware and Maryland (owned by private families) and the self-governing provinces of Connecticut and Rhode Island, both of which had elective governors and legislatures. The governors, whether appointed or elected, had considerable vice-regal powers, even though they were in almost all cases now dependent for money on the grants made by the colonial assemblies. Whatever their powers and whatever their dependence on Britain for protection and trade, the colonial assembles were well-established and had all too frequently discussed the issues of taxation and representation along lines familiar in English history.

The social structure of the mainland colonies was aristocratic. Power in Virginia, in South Carolina and in the Hudson Valley lay with the long established families, and it was rooted in the land. The land owned by the Fairfax family in Virginia ran from the coast to the headwaters of the Potomac. Maine was all but a private holding of Sir William Pepperrell, the conqueror of Louisburg. Much of Georgia was owned by Sir James Wright. Even in Congregationalist New England, seating in church, like the lists of students at Harvard and Yale, went according to property and social class: it was 'property, virtue and intelligence' in that order. From these men of property the colonial councils were recruited. These were 'the friends of government'.

Yet colonial society was not a rigid one. The ease with which property was acquired weakened the sense of class division. George Washington, a protégé of the Fairfaxes, was ill-educated and largely self-made. So were John Macpherson, an enterprising ship-owner of Philadelphia, Benjamin Franklin, who owed everything to his pen and his printing press, John Hancock, the merchant-smuggler, and J. S. Copley, the artist. There was abundant opportunity to make one's way into the gentry.

Below these people were the 'middling sort' of clergy and shopkeepers, teachers and craftsmen, and beneath them, in turn, the large working class, many of whom made their way to North America by serving under contract for a term of years. Among the last group were numerous Germans in Pennsylvania and, particularly in the west and on the frontier, Scots-Irish.

The working class, too, included men of enterprise: Matthew Thornton of New Hampshire, who signed the Declaration of Independence; William Buckland, who built Gunston Hall; and Charles Thomson, Secretary of the Continental Congress. 'You may depend upon it', said William Allen, an American clergyman and author, 'that this is one of the best poor men's Country's in the World.'

It was, moreover, a growing country. If it moved west slowly before 1763, it pushed more rapidly in the direction once the French threat was removed. It was increasing fast in numbers: high birth rates and large families were the rule. The average number of children a family was 7·5 and the population doubled each generation. 'An old maid or an old bachelor are as scarce among us and reckoned as ominous as a blazing star', wrote William Byrd. The population in 1763 was almost 2,000,000 of whom approximately one quarter were German and Scots-Irish and approximately one-fifth negro. By 1775 it was 2,500,000. Fifteen years later, in 1790, when the first census was carried out, it was 3,929,214, of whom 757,208 were negroes.

The problem of the west

Very few contemporaries in 1763 foresaw or predicted independence for the British colonies. Some French observers did, of course, hope for trouble. 'Colonies are like fruits which cling to the tree only until they ripen', was the view of Turgot, the French statesman and economist. Benjamin Franklin, the most balanced and shrewd of observers, foresaw a world in which the weight of population and of economic power would lie on the American side of the Atlantic, although he did not want it to be a future of separate states. In the 1760s Franklin was an 'Old England man'. So were the vast majority of Americans.

There was no reason why in 1763 independence should have been contemplated. The colonies of mainland North America were English foundations, reflecting Old World values and institutions. The sea was their line of communication and their trade was linked profitably to Britain by the mercantile system. Their own land boundaries were moving very slowly inland and were menaced by fierce and unpredictable Indian tribes against whom Britain gave protection. The Iroquois of New York might be friendly but the Creeks, Choctaws and Cherokees were not, and there was an ugly war with the Cherokees between 1759 and 1761. In 1763, angered by the prospect of British rule and still more by the prospect of land grabbing by white settlers, the Ottawas rose under their chief, Pontiac. They were defeated in 1761 by Colonel Henry Bouquet, but not before they had captured every western post except Detroit and Fort Pitt and had killed about 200 settlers and traders. Moreover, they were defeated once again at the hands of British regular soldiers, obligingly paid for by the home government, and not by any colonial army. North America still seemed a vulnerable, sharply divided and dependent world.

To meet the Indian threat to the frontier communities and to placate the Indians, in 1763 the British government proclaimed that the land west of the Appalachians was an Indian reserve. In the reserve white settlement was forbidden and Indian traders were to be licensed. This liberal measure was largely the achievement of the Earl of Shelburne as president of the Board of Trade and was designed not only to reassure the Indians but to guarantee the fur trade. It had the further effect of confining the settlers to the coastal and inland areas, and it was hoped thus to discourage not only the westward movement but also the growth of population and thus of colonial manufacturing industry.

What was welcome to the Indians was repugnant to the colonists. Land settlers and frontiersmen saw in the proclamation a barrier to be overturned or to be ignored. It was an obstacle in their path to the good bottom land of the western river valleys and hence to profit. It was, they said, an infringement also of the 'sea to sea' clauses of colonial charters, which permitted steady expansion westward.

Many prominent colonists, like George Washington at Mount Vernon or Franklin in London seeking a charter for his land project in the Ohio Valley, resented interference with their plans. (Washington in fact ignored the restrictions altogether.) Moreover, the machinery for regulating Indian trade and the military posts established in the west to check further Indian rebellions imposed a heavy financial burden on Britain. The national debt stood at £133,000,000 in 1763, an increase of £60,000,000 in eight years. The extra cost of colonial defence would be crippling. The time had therefore come for a new policy. It was thorough and thoughtful as would have been expected from George Grenville, the first lord of the Treasury. Ironically, it was also the first stage on the road to revolution.

Above, the gaol of Philadelphia; by the mid-eighteenth century this was a flourishing town, larger than any English city other than London. It was to be the first capital of the United States.

Above left, a typical farm in Pennsylvania in about 1800, painted by Edward Hicks in 1845–48. Apart from Boston and Philadelphia, the American economy was still firmly agricultural, but the structure of the agriculture varied from colony to colony. Colonial Williamsburg Foundation, Virginia.

Opposite, an American immigrant family moving into Ohio in the eighteenth century; the opening-up of the West gave further impetus to the move to break all connections with Europe.

The Stamp Act

Grenville planned to station a standing army in America to guard the settlements not only against the Indians but against any resumption of French attack and considered it fair that the colonists should meet one-third of its cost. He sought also to enforce more strictly the Navigation Acts of 1651 and 1660, which had confined colonial manufactures to British or colonial shipping, and in 1764 passed the Sugar Act, by which the duty on sugar and molasses was reduced in order to make it easier to collect. The laws were to be enforced. To raise revenue to meet part of the costs of defence a Stamp Act was to be passed, imposing a duty on newspapers and pamphlets, cards and dice and legal documents. The Stamp Act was a device used in England since 1694. The taxes to be raised by it were much less severe than those in Britain. Colonial opinion was fully canvassed in advance and the colonial agents (appointees stationed in London) fully consulted, but no alternative plan was put up by them. Indeed, the speed with which some distinguished colonial figures, such as George Mercer of Virginia and Jared Ingersoll of Connecticut, accepted the posts of stamp distributors gave no indication of an approaching crisis.

In fact, colonial opposition was instant and all but uniform. In the Virginia House of Burgesses, Patrick Henry presented a series of resolutions, attacking the act and the king. 'If this be treason', he said, 'make the most of it.' In Boston Sam Adams organized a group which took the name 'Sons of Liberty' with the intention of preventing the sale of stamps by threats of direct action against those using them.

Eastern merchants boycotted British goods, and delegates from nine colonies met in City Hall, New York, in the so-called Stamp Act Congress, demanding repeal of the act and issuing a 'Declaration of Rights'. This claimed that since the colonists were not represented in Parliament they could not be taxed by it without their consent.

The fact that the British government expected no resistance to its proposals but met a massive protest is an indication of the gap dividing the Old World from the New. It was partly a matter of the geographical distance: 'Seas roll and months pass between the order and the execution,' said Edmund Burke. It was partly—and more fundamentally—a matter of national psychology. The New World was now peopled by many who had no ties of affection or concern with England and who, if they were English, were Dissenters and Nonconformists by religion and by situation. A distinct attitude was emerging—sombre, evangelical and hostile to the Church of England in religion, close to nature, self-dependent and socially fluid—that was utterly alien to the status-bound ways of England. Some 3,000 miles of isolation from Europe made real representation impossible. The same 3,000 miles made it not only impossible but increasingly unsought.

Many colonies were coming to be in practice independent states, as some perceptive governors like Sir Francis Bernard of Massachusetts and Robert Dinwiddie of Virginia recognized. One of the strands that was gradually being severed was the religious one: there was a mounting fear in the colonies of Anglicanism and of the imposition of religious control from London. As in seventeenth-century England, it was to be

but one step from 'no bishop' to 'no king'. Dissenting academics and the small schools which acquired the name of log colleges kept the memories of the Puritan Levellers of 1649 alive.

When Grenville passed his Stamp Act he had little notion of the mettle of the colonies. The saddest fact of all was that there were few in Britain who were aware of the extent of the differences between them and the colonists or who sensed that there was in the thirteen rival colonies a nation in process of birth. Those who did know were unconsulted and powerless.

Not for the first or the last time parliament bent before the storm. It did not accept the principle of 'no taxation without representation', since more than ninety percent of the home population was as much disfranchised as the Americans. Moreover, without any abrogation of sovereignty—indeed a Declaratory Act was passed asserting that parliament had complete authority to make laws binding the colonist 'in all cases whatsoever'—the government, now headed by the Marquis of Rockingham, repealed the Stamp Act in February 1766. This was partly a result of Franklin's skilful pleading at the bar of the House of Commons, still more because of the economic consequences of the boycott. However, the colonists felt that they had won round one of the struggle and celebrated with bonfires and the erection in New York of statues to King George III and William Pitt. Neither the mood nor the statues lasted long.

The challenge to authority

The colonists' choice of heroes—Rockingham, John Wilkes and William Pitt—was

significant. Grenville, with a lawyer's logic, had thought it both lawful and expedient to tax the colonies. Rockingham, one of the earliest of British party leaders, thought it lawful but not expedient. The Earl of Chatham, as Pitt became in 1766, thought it neither lawful nor expedient. He was, however, a frequent absentee from the government he headed in 1766–8, as a result of gout and temperament in equal proportions.

In 1767 his chancellor of the exchequer, Charles Townshend, sought to honour a rashly-given pledge to reduce the land tax at home by raising an American revenue, not from taxes but from duties on certain imports—tea, glass, paper and paints. He believed it was legitimate for parliament to impose such trade levies. With the revenue he would pay the salaries of colonial governors and judges and free them thereby from colonial control. To stop smuggling, vice-admiralty courts would be strengthened in power and increased in number.

These measures proved to be as unwelcome as the Stamp Act. In his *Letters of a Pennsylvania Farmer* John Dickinson distinguished between acts intended to raise revenue, which he saw as illegal, and those intended to regulate trade, which he accepted as valid. By this standard Townshend's duties on imports were plainly unconstitutional. At this point, indeed, the colonists began to abandon the distinction between internal and external taxes altogether and to take the primitive but very popular line that all taxes, however imposed, were bad and that government was best which governed least. The Massachusetts General Court issued a circular letter—the work of Sam Adams, James Otis and Joseph Hawley—appealing to the other colonies for common action and asserting that only Americans should be permitted to tax Americans. Governor Francis Bernard of Massachusetts branded it as seditious, but seven colonies endorsed it.

When John Hancock's sloop *Liberty* was seized for smuggling, a riot followed in which the over-efficient customs officials were mobbed and had to take refuge in Castle William on an island in Boston harbour. The Boston garrison was strengthened by two regiments of infantry, the 14th and 29th, in an atmosphere that Thomas Hutchinson, Bernard's successor, described as frankly revolutionary. Reports to parliament on the Boston situation in 1769 led both houses to resolve that 'wicked and designing men' were responsible and should be suitably punished.

To Sam Adams in Boston the situation was certainly explosive. By 1770 the movement was no longer led by the merchants of Philadelphia or New York, who were now cautious and not a little frightened of the forces they had unleashed. Effective leadership was now in the hands of the 'Sons of Liberty' in New York and the group organized by Adams and operating from 'The Green Dragon' tavern in Boston. To them the presence of British redcoats—'the lobsterbacks'—was both inflammation and pretext. In New York in January 1770 soldiers and civilians clashed round a liberty pole. There was bloodshed, but no fatalities, in this episode known as 'The Battle of Golden Hill'. In March in Boston the taunting and snowballing of soldiers, first by schoolboys and then by citizens, led to shots being fired, and five Bostonians, one of them a negro, Crispus Attucks, were killed. The soldiers were acquitted after a skilful and courageous defence by their counsel, John Adams. However, their presence was proving to be not a safeguard but an irritant and they were more often the victims than the masters of the local situation.

After 1770 the soldiers were carefully confined in Castle William, and the British government repealed the Townshend duties except for the penny a pound on tea, retained, like the Declaratory Act, to assert a principle that was increasingly being seen to be only a form of words. Ironically even this decision was taken in cabinet by the casting vote of the new prime minister, Lord North. Had it not been taken there might well have been no need in 1773 to aid the East India Company's tea trade and the history of the world might have been different. However, the colonists had also won the second round of the contest. Once again, under whatever guise, the government had retreated. Now the cause had martyrs too. For revolutions these are more necessary than issues and easier to identify.

Between the second and third rounds of the contest there came an interlude, a return of prosperity and a reaction against the radicals. The merchants abandoned their boycott, and Sam Adams lost control of the Massachusetts Assembly. Yet this was the period when he worked hardest to keep the cause alive, by writing pamphlets under a host of pseudonyms and by the organization of the 'Committees of Correspondence'. Governor Thomas Hutchinson described

Above, the people of Boston tarring and feathering an exciseman, while in the background cases of tea are thrown into the sea; Britain's determination to tax the colonies was the main immediate grievance of the colonists.

Top, the Boston massacre in March 1770, when British troops opened fire on a crowd protesting against new taxes; they killed three men and wounded two others. It was the first violence between the colonists and the British troops.

Above left, George III of England (reigned 1760–1820), whose determination to oppose any reforms in the American colonies contributed to the tension that led to the outbreak of hostilities in 1775.

Opposite, the trustees of the state of Georgia presenting the Indians who sold him land to the colony's trustees in London in 1734.

the Boston Committee as composed of 'deacons', 'atheists', and 'blackhearted fellows whom one would not wish to meet in the dark'. However, they began to emerge in each colony and to constitute an unelected but nevertheless representative body of those with grievances, providing a basis for intercolonial action, should the crisis ever come. Although there is no evidence that the colonists had serious grievances, Adams' great achievement was to maintain a feeling of unrest and to produce a machine for action. In 1773 the opportunity came.

The British government, alarmed at the near bankruptcy of the East India Company, allowed it to send tea to America without paying the duty of one shilling a pound, thus making it cheaper than smuggled tea. This certainly would have hit hard at smuggling and at the profits of those who, like John Hancock, traded in smuggled tea. Thus, the third round of the contest began, oddly enough, with a mass protest against cheaper tea.

In December 1773, three ships carrying cargoes of tea reached Boston. Sam Adams addressed a large crowd, estimated at 7,000, on the evils of drinking cheap and legal tea, and from this meeting a group moved to the docks disguised as Indians. They dropped 342 tea chests to the bottom of the harbour, stoving them in as they did so.

This action was difficult to justify and it was indeed condemned by all responsible colonial opinion, including John Adams and Franklin, and by many merchants. Moreover this time parliament was not prepared to yield. Since 1769 it had been considering an inquiry into Massachusetts. The rendezvous of the navy had already been moved from Halifax to Boston. Half-measures would no longer suffice.

In the spring of 1774 further measures were passed. The port of Boston was closed until the tea was paid for. The Massachusetts charter was annulled, and the governor's council was henceforth appointed by the king. Arrangements were made to quarter troops in occupied as well as empty dwellings. Officers or soldiers accused of crimes were to be sent to Britain for trial.

The Quebec Act was also passed. This was planned beforehand and was not intended as a punitive measure, but it was seen as such in the colonies. It killed all hopes of new colonies in the northwest by transferring to the province of Quebec the lands (and the fur trade) between Ohio and the Mississippi, in which Virginia, Pennsylvania, Connecticut and Massachusetts held interests. Moreover, and even more ominously as the colonists saw it, it gave to this region French civil law and the Roman Catholic religion. The regime provided was centralized, in keeping with customs of the province, and there was to be no jury trial. This was a liberal and intelligent measure, drafts for which had existed since 1763. However, Chatham, Burke, Barré and Fox attacked it as pro-French, autocratic and wicked, and the vehemence of their

attacks confirmed colonial suspicions. The timing, as distinct from the merits, of the measure was unfortunate. The colonists now feared the use of arbitrary power and the influence of the Roman Catholic and Anglican Churches.

There were now two firm positions. 'The die is cast', said King George III. 'The colonists must either triumph or submit.' Joseph Reed put it differently in a letter from the first Continental Congress to Lord Dartmouth. 'The people are generally ripe for the execution of any plan the Congress advises, should it be war itself.'

The First Continental Congress

The measures passed in 1774 marked the end of the period of economic and commercial grievance. The issues now were clearly political and were seen as such in the colonies. Resolutions of sympathy and supplies of food reached Boston. When royal governors dissolved assemblies that were loud in their expression of support for Massachusetts, the members promptly formed themselves into illegal provincial congresses. Indeed, in Virginia the call to the first Continental Congress went out from Hays' Tavern, just across the street from the Williamsburg capitol.

This congress, which met in Carpenter's Hall, Philadelphia, in September 1774, was a gathering of fifty-five diplomats from twelve colonies. Each colony except Georgia was represented. John Adams was greatly stirred by it: 'There is in this Congress a collection of the greatest men upon this Continent in point of abilities, virtues and fortunes. The magnanimity and public spirit which I see here make me blush for the sordid venal herd which I have seen in my own Province.'

Adams was especially impressed by the Virginians and not least by Washington— 'six feet two, and straight as an Indian'. Though not gifted either in speech or with the pen, Washington looked like a soldier and had experience of the west shared by few. He was still loyal to the king but was a critic of parliament. He never forgave being refused a colonelcy in the French and Indian War. An alliance of north and south—of radicals and merchants plus planters and 'sultans'—began to emerge.

The First Continental Congress was nevertheless evenly divided between radicals and moderates—'one-third Tories, another, Whigs and the rest Mongrels', said Adams. Joseph Galloway's plan for a Grand Council to be chosen by the colonial assemblies headed by a president-general and acting as a kind of third House of Parliament was rejected, although only by a single vote. John Dickinson wanted to move slowly: action should be taken 'peaceably—prudently—firmly—jointly', or, as he said later, 'procrastination is preservation'. There were,

however, other voices. The Declaration of Rights and Grievances demanded 'the rights of Englishmen', the repeal of the measures of 1774 and the dismissal of the king's 'designing and dangerous' ministers. And the 'Resolves' forwarded by Suffolk County, Massachusetts, denied all obligation to obey recent acts of Parliament, described George III as a sovereign 'agreeable to compact' and threatened armed resistance. The Continental Association was formed to bring pressure by boycott on British merchants.

In 1774 British authority in Massachusetts all but collapsed. County conventions and a provincial congress took over the functions of the legally constituted government. Minutemen were formed and in all colonies militia forces came into being. When Washington returned home after the Congress, he was offered the command of seven of the militia companies in Virginia. He put on the buff and the blue of Fairfax County and made it the colours of liberty on two continents. Newspapers now openly discussed independence and, as a contemporary put it: 'Sedition flowed openly from the pulpits.' Colonial governors stored arms, not always discreetly.

When a new parliament assembled at Westminster in November, it was fortified by an improved trade with Europe and prepared to be—at last—tough. 'The New England governments are in a state of rebellion,' said the king. 'Blows must decide.' In February Parliament recognized the fact of rebellion in Massachusetts, and in August acknowledged that this was equally true of all the other colonies. In April, General Thomas Gage, the military governor of Massachusetts, tried to capture Sam Adams and John Hancock and to seize the stores being assembled at Concord. Paul Revere, by trade an engraver and silversmith, by calling a patriot, gave the alarm to a whole countryside. At Lexington, while on the retreat, the redcoats were sniped at with deadly result from every hedgerow. They lost two hundred men and the Americans ninety-three. This was no war.

The Second Continental Congress

It was against this background that the Second Continental Congress met in May 1775. Sixty-five delegates were there, to be joined by five from Georgia in September. John Dickinson's petition, known as the 'Olive Branch' petition, was adopted, only to be scorned in London. In June, Washington was appointed commander-in-chief and set off to take command of the assembling New England militia outside Cambridge, Massachusetts. Before his departure he heard of the second open battle of the war. at Bunker Hill, where the British lost 1,150 out of 2,500 engaged. Nevertheless, Washington was appalled at the state of his

army and made slow progress in training it and forcing on it a genuine acceptance of rank and discipline.

With Washington in command of an army that was in name opposing not the king but his parliament, there were now, in a sense, two centres of resistance. Although quite devoid of legality, the Congress acted as the central government, raised troops, established a treasury, issued paper money and negotiated alliances with Indian tribes and European allies. It did so by means of about eighty committees with John Adams on a great many of them. However, it hesitated about independence. The majority of the population were still opposed to independence. They were still content to claim the rights enjoyed—or deemed to be enjoyed—by British subjects. But, with an army in being, the momentum of events now moved firmly towards separation. John Adams declared that every day and every post, independence rolled in on Congress like a torrent. Unless Congress acted swiftly, Hawley wrote to Sam Adams, a 'Great Mobb' would march on Philadelphia, purge Congress and set up a dictator.

Britain had declared the colonists to be rebels and proclaimed a blockade. Governor John Dunmore of Virginia called on the slaves to rise in rebellion. British attacks were made or planned against coastal towns like Norfolk and Charleston. Britain was seeking to raise mercenary troops—Germans certainly and Russians, too, it was rumoured. By May 1776 North Carolina, Virginia and Massachusetts had instructed their delegates in Congress to vote for independence. On 7 June, Richard Henry had introduced his resolution that 'these United Colonies are, and of right ought to be, free and independent States.' Because of the hesitation of Pennsylvania, New Jersey, South Carolina and New York a vote was postponed for three weeks.

It was however the existence of an army that was to prove decisive. The dashing and utterly unreliable Ethan Allen, at the head of his so-called Green Mountain Boys, seized Ticonderoga from a sleepy and incredulous British commander. An expedition to liberate Canada was planned, although it proved a failure. In March 1776, with Washington in control of Dorchester Heights above Boston, the British decided to evacuate the city. When they sailed away they took some 200 loyalist merchants with them. The war was now a civil war also. Behind the formal battles it was a struggle not only between the Old World and the New but over who should rule at home.

The army in the field was the arm of the civil Congress. In July 1775 the Congress had issued its 'Declaration of Causes of Taking Up Arms'. Americans it said, would die rather than be enslaved, but the declaration also stated that independence was not the goal. By July 1776 the hesitations were gone. Washington was partly won over in January 1776 by reading Tom Paine's pamphlet *Common Sense*. To Paine, who urged an immediate declaration of independence, the king was no God above the battle but 'the royal brute'. The pamphlet sold well. The note of republicanism was struck late, but it became the dominant theme. In the eyes of the colonists it was no longer parliament that was the tyrant but the king.

Independence

The aims now were separation and republicanism. Congress no longer claimed 'the rights of Englishmen' but 'natural rights'. When Thomas Jefferson, at the behest of Congress, drafted the Declaration of Independence, he claimed that thus far the American people had voluntarily associated themselves with Britain and had voluntarily acknowledged the same king. This king, by his despotic acts (twenty-seven specific charges were listed), had forfeited this allegiance. There was no reference at all to acts of trade or to parliament. This statement was prefaced by one of the noblest testaments of faith in liberty and in man's capacity for it which has ever been written:

We hold these truths to be self-evident, that all men are created equal; that they are endowed by their creator with certain unalienable rights; that among these are life, liberty and the pursuit of happiness. That,

Above, Thomas Jefferson (1743–1826), the chief drafter of the American Declaration of Independence and a protagonist of the rights of the small farmer against the aristocracy. His followers later developed into the Democratic Party of America.

Top, the second Continental Congress of 1775–76, at which the representatives of the colonies voted to accept the Declaration of Independence and which set itself up as the temporary government of the rebels.

Above left, George Washington (1732–99) taking command of the American army at Cambridge, Massachusetts, in 1775; despite the disorganization and indiscipline of the army, he was able to begin to attack the British positions by early 1777.

to secure these rights, governments are instituted among men, deriving their just powers from the consent of the governed; that, whenever any form of government becomes destructive of these ends, it is the right of the people to alter or to abolish it, to institute new government, laying its foundations on such principles, organizing its powers in such form, as to them shall seem most likely to effect their safety and happiness.

The same sentiments, without the same eloquence but with greater vivacity were expressed by an old soldier to whom John Adams talked many years later:

'Captain Preston, why did you go to the Concord fight, the nineteenth of April 1775?' The old man, bowed beneath the weight of years, raised himself, and turning to me, said: 'Why did I go?' 'Yes', I replied. 'My histories tell me that you men of the Revolution took up arms against "intolerable oppressions".' 'What were they?' 'Oppression. I didn't feel them.' 'What, were you not oppressed by the Stamp Act?' 'I never saw one of those stamps, and always understood that Governor Bernard put them all in Castle William. I am certain I never paid a penny for one of them.' 'Well, what about the tea tax?' 'Tea tax! I never drank a drop of the stuff—the boys threw it all overboard.' 'Then I suppose you had been reading Harrington or Sydney or Locke about the eternal principles of liberty.' 'Never heard of 'em. We read only the Bible, the Catechism, Wells' Psalms and Hymns and the Almanack.' 'Well, then, what was the matter, and what did you mean in going to the fight?' 'Young man, what we meant in going for those redcoats was this: we always had governed ourselves, and we always meant to. They didn't mean we should.'

These two views have, in their different ways, become the spirit of the Revolution. The American Revolution was the first successful act of rebellion by a new nation in modern history. The shots fired at Lexington Green and Concord bridge have echoed round the world. Almost all the independent states of Africa and Asia today, and many of the new nations in Europe, as part of the legend of their own independence find links with 1776. The statues that are grouped outside the White House in Washington are a reminder of those from other nations who then saw in the struggle for American independence a symbol and a portent of the struggle of other nations to be free. It is indeed impossible to calculate the consequences for the world that have followed from the events that took place on the narrow Atlantic seaboard in the years from 1763 to 1776.

The War of Independence

The Declaration of Independence was proclaimed on 4 July 1776. The day before, Sir William Howe seized Staten Island and led a British army ashore from the largest armada which had ever assembled in North American waters. New York was a loyalist centre, and it seemed possible to move up the Hudson Valley from New York to cut off rebellious New England from the other, less resolute colonies and to command the overland route to Canada.

The task of suppressing the rebellion, however distasteful, did not appear to be too difficult. The British had overwhelmingly superior numbers, outmatching the colonies by four to one in manpower and in ships of war by a hundred to one. Command of the sea—until the entry of the French—allowed them to strike at points of their own choosing. At times, trying to anticipate where the

blow would fall, Washington found himself 'compelled to wander about the country like the Arabs in search of corn'. Britain had superior credit, could hire foreign mercenaries and had a professional army and navy—even if a few of its senior officers like Lord Amherst and Admiral Keppel refused to serve against Americans. Against them were untrained, ill-clad, undisciplined and usually unpaid militia, led by officers who, with the exception of Charles Lee, Horatio Gates and Washington, had as little experience of war as themselves and little taste for it.

However, from the first it was for Britain a story of tactical successes left unexploited, of basic strategic errors and of some irredeemable disasters. Sir William Howe put his men ashore on Long Island with ease, defeated Washington's army and forced it to retreat across the Sound to Manhattan. He drove up the island with the same unhurried effortlessness and Washington made another hasty retreat over the Hudson and through New Jersey. The Americans lacked flour, clothing and money to pay their soldiers. Paine wrote in *The Crisis*: 'These are the times that try men's souls. The summer soldier and the sunshine patriot will, in this crisis, shrink from the service of their country; but he that stands it *now* deserves the love and thanks of man and woman.' Washington's view of events was more laconic: 'I think the game is pretty near up.'

At any of these points Howe could, it seemed, have destroyed the enemy army completely and captured its leader. That he failed to do so was overwhelmingly because he saw himself as an arbitrator and diplomat rather than as a soldier. If he pressed them a little more, they would surrender. The diplomat's role did not harmonize with the soldier's. After each tactical triumph he expected that negotiations would now begin. On the other hand, British morale was being steadily eroded by the procrastination and delays.

On Christmas night 1776, Washington carried through one of his cleverest manoeuvres of the war, and certainly the most psychologically effective. He crossed the Delaware with 2,400 men, surprised Colonel Rall and his still festive German troops at Trenton and took 1,000 prisoners. Colonel Rall paid for his card game with his life. Leaving his campfires burning to deceive the hurriedly summoned British reserves, Washington outflanked them and appeared at Princeton to strike again.

By the time both armies went into winter quarters—war was still a game played according to a gentlemanly, and seasonal, calendar—Howe's troops were no longer safe beyond the Hudson, and Washington had regained the advantage. If he failed to stop the transfer of Howe's forces in 1777 to Philadelphia, he at least managed to hold his own small force together.

Left, the Battle of Bunker Hill (June 1775) was one of the first engagements of the American War of Independence. Despite the eventual British victory, it proved a great boost to the morale of the Americans, whose defeat was primarily caused by a shortage of ammunition.

Opposite, a satire on the explosive impact of the Boston Tea Party of 1773; although unplanned, the incident brought the anti-British feeling in the American colonies to the surface and made militant resistance acceptable.

Left, the Declaration of Independence, formally adopted on 4 July 1776. The declaration combined an attack on the abuses of recent British rule with a statement of the rights of man and the principles of government; in these ideas Jefferson, who was mainly responsible for the document, was influenced by the ideas of the Enlightenment. Yale University Art Gallery, New Haven, Connecticut.

Left, an incident during the naval war in August 1776, when the British aimed for control of Lake Champlain and the Hudson River, to isolate New England from the other colonies.

The road to Saratoga

The winter of 1777–8 was the real testing time—one that tried not only men's souls but their stomachs. Valley Forge, where the American troops were quartered, was, said Washington, 'a dreary kind of place and uncomfortably provided'. 'Poor food—hard lodging—cold weather—fatigue—nasty clothes—nasty cookery—vomit half my time—smoked out of my senses—the devil's in't—I can't endure it,' wrote Surgeon Albigence Waldo. But the Americans did endure. They were now better drilled than ever before thanks to Friedrich Von Steuben, the Prussian soldier who had offered his services to Washington. Washington's greatest achievement was to keep an army in being at Valley Forge. He said afterwards that Howe could still have won the war had he attacked at that point. By October 1777, however, it was beginning to look too late for a British victory.

While Howe was taking Philadelphia and relaxing in its comfort, General John Burgoyne, with 7,000 men and a vast baggage train, was seeking to cut a path south from Canada via Lake Champlain and the Hudson Valley. The intention was to bring reinforcements to Howe (who, Burgoyne had expected, would come north to meet him), to cut off New England permanently and to divert Washington's attention.

However, Burgoyne's transport was inadequate. One of his raiding columns hunting for food in Vermont was destroyed by the Green Mountain Boys. A parallel force, which was to move down the Mohawk River to join him, gave up the attempt and went back to Canada. Meanwhile, the American force under Horatio Gates that blocked his path increased in numbers and in spirit day by day. By the end of September Burgoyne was outnumbered four to one. On 14 October he surrendered at Saratoga, abandoning arms and supplies and undertaking that his men would not serve any further against the Americans. This was not only a British disaster, it was a humiliation

and it proved to be the turning-point in the war.

Until the news of Saratoga the French had hesitated about giving open support to the Revolution. The French monarchy had no taste for governments that were overthrowing kings. However, any dissension in Britain's colonies was worth cultivating. On the outbreak of war, Congress sent to Paris a three-man team to act as negotiators for money, supplies and for an open, they hoped, alliance with France. The quest for foreign aid had been active from the start. The new nation wanted the commercial contracts with Europe which the colonial mercantile system had banned. And it not only sought them for themselves. Without foreign aid it could not long survive.

The three men who served as emissaries were the irascible and self-important Arthur Lee from Virginia, the wily merchant-politician Silas Deane from Connecticut (who proved to be in Britain's pay and passed everything on to the British government) and Benjamin Franklin, who became the principal agent and ambassador. During his years in Paris (1776–85), when he was already over 70, Franklin emerged not only as the architect of the alliance but as the favourite of the salons of Paris, admired and worshipped as both scientist and diplomat, man of affairs (both business and amatory) and, indeed, as Jean-Jacques Rousseau's 'natural man' made visible. There were Franklin rings, Franklin snuff boxes and even Franklin chamber pots. His wig, worn to hide his eczema, became a symbol of liberty. The old man was amused, and he not only enjoyed the experience but exploited it to his own benefit.

From the first the French were prompt with aid, 1,000,000 livres being given through the fictitious company, Rodrigue Hortalez et Compagnie. Spain proved equally generous. However, aid could not be openly avowed without inducing a declaration of war by Britain. The surrender of Saratoga led to the planning of a peace mission by Britain, and Franklin craftily allowed it to be known in Paris that

he favoured its prospects. France moved towards open intervention and in February 1778 the Treaty of Alliance was signed—the United States' first entangling alliance. France recognized the United States as independent and each country undertook not to make a separate peace. Each also undertook to treat the other commercially as a 'most favoured nation'.

Spain entered the war a year later not as an ally of the United States but as an ally of France. Its motive was the reconquering of Gibraltar, which the Spanish besieged for four long years. By 1780 Britain was also at war with Holland and with the League of Armed Neutrality (Denmark, Sweden, Portugal and Russia). The war was now a world war. It was fought in places as far apart as India and the Caribbean. The American naval commander, John Paul Jones, provisioned from Brest, raided the Scottish and Yorkshire coasts, and a French landing in Ireland was planned. The American theatre of war now became in British eyes little more than a side-show.

This dramatic transformation of the situation was a great relief for the Americans. French aid was in any event substantial. French gifts and loans amounted in the end to $8,000,000, a large sum for an eighteenth-century war. The entry of France also helped to guarantee the Dutch loans to the United States. With money there also came men and ships. After 1778 French fleets prowled the Atlantic coast, and Britain lost its naval preponderance. The operations of the French naval commander, the Comte d'Estaing, diverted British troops to the West Indies and speeded the evacuation of Philadelphia in 1778 and Newport in 1779. It was the appearance of a French fleet off the Virginian coast that sealed the fate of a British army under Lord Cornwallis at Yorktown in 1781. The siege of Yorktown itself was made possible by the presence alongside Washington's army of 9,000 regular French troops commanded by the Comte de Rochambeau, with the Marquis de Lafayette, one of the earliest and most fanatical of French volunteers, leading a

brigade. When General O'Hara, deputizing for Cornwallis—who feigned illness—surrendered his sword, he sought to surrender it to Rochambeau. Rochambeau refused and indicated Washington. Lafayette, for his part, never forgot his American experience and at the beginning of the French Revolution saw himself as playing a Washington. If his role in French history never in fact matched his own hopes for it, the French Revolution certainly owed much to the enthusiasm of those who had helped the American cause.

The Treaty of Paris

With the surrender of Cornwallis at Yorktown, the war was virtually over. King George III was with difficulty dissuaded from abdicating. Lord North resigned as prime minister in March 1782, Shelburne becoming first secretary of state and, on Rockingham's death, prime minister. At first Shelburne opposed the idea of independence but not for long.

With the merchant Richard Oswald acting as his emissary in Paris, negotiations were opened with Franklin in April 1782 and concluded in November of that year. Franklin broke his word in concluding a separate peace, but in the thick air of spying and counter-spying in Paris it was hardly possible for the French foreign minister, Vergennes, to be unaware of what was happening.

By the terms of the treaty Britain recognized the independence of the United States and accepted its western boundary as the Mississippi River. Britain conceded the right of navigation on the Mississippi and fishing rights off Newfoundland. Congress agreed to recommend to the individual states that they indemnify the loyalists and pay their debts to Britain. This was easy to say but hard to implement.

The United States won more by diplomacy than its victories entitled. If Saratoga and Yorktown were disasters for the British, this was in large measure because of their own folly. By 1783, however, Britain had

averted direct invasion, and Admiral Rodney's victory in 1782 off Dominica in the West Indies gave Britain additional bargaining power. Spain and France had not done particularly well out of the war. Spain regained the Floridas but not Gibraltar. France won some West Indian islands and a huge debt, the full interest on which would be six years in falling due. For the Americans it was a total triumph.

Yet by 1783 the evidence of triumph was hard to see. The new nation had not acquired a written constitution until 1781, the 'Articles of Confederation', drafted by John Dickinson. These provided for a single-chamber government in which each state had one vote. There was no president and no supreme court. The government was in form and in fact a federal union of unwilling members. Congress had no power to levy taxes, regulate commerce, raise an army or enforce the laws. In the last years of the war Congress had even been driven from Philadelphia when unpaid regiments rebelled.

Above, the capture of Yorktown and final surrender of the British forces under General Cornwallis in October 1781. The English were unable to fight against the combination of French and American soldiers and French blockade.

Top, the British embarking German troops to send to the American colonies in 1783.

Top left, Benjamin Franklin (1706–90), the American scientist, at the court of France, where he had been sent in 1776 to win recognition for the new republic. The French sent a fleet to support the Americans in 1778.

Opposite left, George Washington capturing almost 1,000 German troops under British command in December 1776 at Trenton, New Jersey. This was the first real American success of the war.

Opposite right, the surrender of General Burgoyne at Saratoga in October 1777, after the British had lost the support of their Indian allies and had been surrounded. After this defeat, the British had little real hope of winning the war.

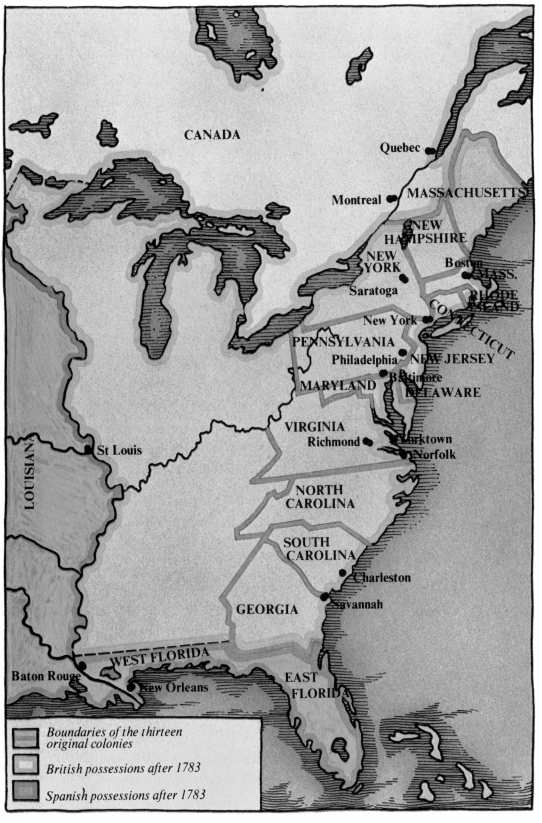

CANADA

Quebec

Montreal MASSACHUSETTS

NEW
HAMPSHIRE

NEW
YORK   Boston MASS.

Saratoga   RHODE
ISLAND

New York   CONNECTICUT

PENNSYLVANIA

Philadelphia NEW JERSEY

Baltimore
MARYLAND   DELAWARE

VIRGINIA
Richmond   Yorktown
              Norfolk

St Louis

LOUISIANA

NORTH
CAROLINA

SOUTH
CAROLINA

Charleston

GEORGIA   Savannah

WEST FLORIDA

Baton Rouge   EAST
New Orleans   FLORIDA

*Boundaries of the thirteen
original colonies*

British possessions after 1783

Spanish possessions after 1783

This period, from 1781 to 1787, was given
the name of 'The Critical Period' by the
American historian, John Fiske, in 1888,
and he attributed the difficulties to the lack
of real sovereignty in the existing government, that is, the government under the
Articles of Confederation, agreed on by
1781. The commercial crisis, however, was
not only a result of the Articles but the end
of the wartime boom and of the dislocation
of American trade that followed it. Congress
could have done little to affect this. Moreover, no direction by it to the states to
honour their debt or to treat the loyalists
sympathetically would have had much
influence, when there was no general wish
to do either.

However, the diplomatic achievements of
the period were considerable. The Treaty of
Paris and the Northwest Ordinances of 1785
and 1787 were remarkable by any standards.
The first of the Ordinances provided for a
system of land surveys based on townships
six miles square and subdivided into thirty-
six sections. The latter set out the stages
whereby a territory (5,000 inhabitants) and
finally a state (60,000 inhabitants) would be
established. Out of the entire territory of the
old northwest five states were in the end
formed: Ohio, Indiana, Illinois, Michigan
and Wisconsin. In them freedom of religion,
trial by jury and due process of law were
guaranteed, slavery was forbidden and the
newly-created states were seen and treated
as equal in importance to the original
thirteen. The west was peopled fast. This
generous and far sighted provision, essentially the handiwork of Thomas Jefferson,
was to prove almost as significant as the
constitution itself. It was its federal character
as much as its republican constitution that
made the United States in the nineteenth
century the 'last best hope of man'.

The constitution

Nevertheless the political weaknesses of the
Articles pointed to a need for revision.
James Madison of Virginia persuaded his
state to discuss with Maryland their common interest in the navigation of Chesapeake
Bay and the Potomac. The Mount Vernon
Conference in 1785 established the need for
a wider agreement and all the states were
invited to Annapolis in 1786 to discuss inter-
state commercial regulations. Five states
sent representatives—New York, New
Jersey, Virginia, Pennsylvania and Delaware.

Alexander Hamilton, the brilliant young
West Indian-born lawyer who had served
as Washington's aide-de-camp, moved a
resolution to invite all the states to meet the
following year to revise the Articles. Fifty-
five men, representing all the states except
Rhode Island, met in the Philadelphia State
House in May 1787. They decided on a
totally new document and they hammered

There was no power to enforce even the
Treaty of Peace. Moreover, Congress could
not enforce uniform import duties against
foreign countries or prevent the customs and
boundary wars of state versus state. For
money it relied on issues of paper, which
depreciated fast—'not worth a Continental'
is still a phrase in use in the United States.
Some states printed their own paper money
and other states refused to honour it. When
in Massachusetts creditors foreclosed on
the properties of the debt-ridden farmers,

about 1,500 of them, led by Daniel Shays,
seized the arsenal at Springfield and closed
the courts.

The economic situation was worsened by
the exclusion of the new state from the
British Empire and the loss of trade with the
West Indies. British markets, bounties and
guarantees were also lost. Britain retained
the fur posts, claiming that loyalists had not
been indemnified or debts to British merchants repaid. There was no matching
power of retaliation available to Congress.

Above, Alexander Hamilton (1755–1804), the New York lawyer who supported a strong federal authority, both in the debates on the Constitution and during the 1790s when he served as Secretary to the Treasury and as a supporter of Thomas Jefferson.

Left, George Washington in his masonic regalia; his future political power was based primarily on his great success as a military leader. Henry Francis du Pont Winterthur Museum, Delaware.

Opposite, the North American Atlantic seaboard after the independence of the United States.

out agreement on its through the long, hot summer. They ended by drawing up a constitution, 4,000 words in length, for a farmer's republic of 3,500,000 people. The same document, amended only occasionally and mainly in inessentials, is still the binding form of government for a vast cosmopolitan society of more than 200,000,000 people living across and beyond a continent. The Founding Fathers were remarkable men. Thomas Jefferson called them an assembly of demi-gods.

There was much on which the delegates agreed: a written constitution, the separation of powers, the need for the federal government to be strong and to have the power to declare war and make peace and to tax and regulate commerce. There was much on which agreement was reached only slowly by careful compromise. Perhaps the most serious basic political disagreement was on the issue of representation. The large states, whose case was presented by Edmund Randolph of Virginia, favoured a bicameral legislature, with representation in each

based on size of population. There was also to be a single executive and judiciary, both chosen by the legislature. This caused bitter feeling, for the disparity of the states in size was striking. Delaware had 60,000 people and Rhode Island 68,000. On the other hand, Virginia, which then included Kentucky, had 750,000, of whom 300,000 were slaves. Massachusetts, excluding Maine, had 380,000, very few of whom were slaves.

New Jersey countered the Virginia plan with its own, presented by William Paterson: a legislature of one house, elected by the states regardless of population and with an executive consisting of more than one man elected by Congress. After a month's debate agreement was reached on a compromise— the 'Connecticut compromise'—providing for equal representation of each state in the Senate, while maintaining the principle of representation by population in the House of Representatives.

This system is still in force, although, until the 17th Amendment of 1913, the Senate was elected indirectly by the state

legislatures and not directly by the people. Yet fears of rivalry between great and small states proved largely illusory. Maryland, a small state, and Virginia, a large one, shared on the Chesapeake a common economy of tobacco plantations and slave labour. Connecticut and Massachusetts had similar commercial interests. The rivalry of state against state has never been as important in American history as the clash of sectional interests.

The second major compromise appeared at this time to be less important but was to have far-reaching consequences: how were slaves to be counted both for representation and for taxation? The northern states, with businessmen's logic, wanted slaves excluded from representation, since they were neither citizens nor voters, but included for tax purposes, since they were property. In other words, they themselves had few slaves, and they wanted it both ways. The south disagreed: it did not want to be taxed without some matching representation. In the end the 'three-fifths' compromise was reached. A slave was counted as three-fifths of a person for purposes of both taxation and representation. It was also agreed that there would be no interference with the importation of slaves until 1808. Slavery was not yet the emotional issue it was to become. Even the revolutionary fires of the French Revolution that led to Toussaint l'Ouverture's rebellion in Santo Domingo sparked few fires in the United States. The most bitter attack at the constitutional convention came in fact from Virginia. As masters on their deathbeds often freed their slaves, as did Washington, slavery was expected gradually to die out.

There was one other basic compromise: on the election of the executive. There were many among the Founding Fathers who distrusted 'the people' and opposed direct election. It was therefore agreed, in the closing stages of the convention, that the president and vice-president should be chosen by an electoral college, equal in number to the number of senators and representatives, meeting in each of the states and forwarding the names of its choice to the federal government. The college still survives, weakened by the growth of political parties, as a curious relic of eighteenth-century political mechanics. It makes it possible for a president to be elected who (as in 1888) has fewer popular votes than his opponent. Furthermore, since a president must have an absolute majority of electoral college votes and not merely be head of the list, it is possible for the choice of president to be thrown to the House of Representatives, voting by states, as was done in 1824. The system is a reminder that, although the three branches of government were nicely balanced by the compromises of 1787, only one half of one branch, the legislature, was directly elected. The president chose the judges, and he himself was indirectly elected.

In all the states there was also a property qualification for the suffrage. As a result it has sometimes been said that the Founding Fathers feared democracy rather than favoured it. Certainly, there were those among them, like Alexander Hamilton and Gouverneur Morris, who thought the constitution a 'weak and worthless' document. Nevertheless, Hamilton himself rendered immense service by the campaign he waged in New York to secure the ratification of the constitution in the New York state convention and also by writing, with John Jay and James Madison, the series of masterly articles in its support known collectively as *The Federalist Papers*.

It is true that the majority of the delegates at Philadelphia were beneficiaries of the Constitution—investors, land speculators, merchants and slave owners. Moreover, the document was not submitted directly to the people and contained no bill of rights. Indeed, to meet this criticism a bill of rights was added to it, in the shape of the first ten amendments, ratified in 1791. In other words, the constitution was not perfect, like any other product of the hand of men, and a bitter civil war was to be fought in 1861 over the interpretation of it. Yet it was a remarkable document. Its ambiguity, as James Madison, the fourth president of the United States, said, was the price of unanimity. The Founding Fathers knew that paper constitutions would only survive if they were brought to life and made workable by men and women. The American nation has been built up in 1787 and since not by federal or judical enactments but by the common life lived and chosen by its members.

Much of the anxiety that the convention might have aroused was removed by the general awareness that, whatever the form of election, George Washington was likely to be the universal choice for president. With John Adams as his vice-president, Washington took his oath of office on the balcony of Federal Hall, New York, in April 1789. He chose Jefferson (who had succeeded Franklin as ambassador in Paris) as his secretary of state, Hamilton as secretary of the treasury and Henry Knox (a Massachusetts bookseller turned general) as his secretary of war.

Washington's contribution to the presidency was immense, since all the decisions he took set precedents. He brought dignity and decorum to the office: a coach and four, weekly levees and an address to Congress similar to the British sovereign's speech from the throne. Both the Senate and Supreme Court, he discovered, refused to grant advice before negotiation of treaties or legal cases, so presidential initiative was increased and presidential authority heightened. The judiciary was organized, with a chief justice and five associate justices. Washington's administration was also distinguished by the work of his two brilliant secretaries, Hamilton and Jefferson.

Hamilton believed that the new federal government would be strong only if its credit was thoroughly established. Nations—like individuals—must pay their debts. He therefore recommended to Congress that the national debt, both foreign ($12,000,000) and domestic ($24,000,000), should be paid at face value and that the federal government should accept and meet the debts contracted by the states. He proposed to do this by funding the debt, that is, by offering a new loan. There was no opposition to the payment of the foreign debt but much to the payment of the domestic one, since speculators (mainly northerners) had been buying up government bonds at cut rates and thus stood to gain appreciably. Moreover, those states like Virginia, which had already begun to meet their obligations, objected to the indirect aid being given to their less generous or less wealthy rivals. However, Hamilton had his way, in part by agreeing to placate the south by locating the planned national capital (then spoken of as the 'federal city') on the banks of the Potomac and near Mount Vernon. This device by Hamilton won the support of the moneyed class for the constitution and the federal government.

Hamilton also set up a national bank, although Jefferson and Madison opposed what they saw as a monopoly and a threat to the state banks. He also proposed an excise tax and a higher tariff to encourage manufacturers, and again he had his way.

Hamilton and Jefferson

Policy-making was one thing; implementation was another. Hamilton's excise tax ran into difficulties. He had urged an excise tax on distilled liquors in part to impress upon the western frontiersmen the powers of the federal government. These men had for a long time been accustomed to convert their corn and rye into whisky, since in this form it was easier to transport over the mountains and more readily saleable. They resented the tax bitterly and in 1794 in Western Pennsylvannia they offered resistance to the federal collectors, in what was known as the 'Whisky Rebellion'. Hamilton called out the militia and, at the display of force, opposition melted away. Hamilton never lost the reputation of having engineered this deliberately and he showed a disposition throughout his career to be over-assertive in government.

Gradually a division on both political and personal matters appeared between Jefferson and Hamilton. The latter was a supporter of strong federal government, of manufacturers, of 'the rich, the well-born and the able' and of the British connection; the former was an advocate of states' rights, freedom for the farmer and support for France. Jefferson began his period in office as an admirer of France and as a sympathizer with the French Revolution. He cooled in these views, partly because of the undiplomatic exuberance shown by the French ambassador, Edmond Genêt.

In 1793, misreading the American scene and invoking the alliance of 1778, he assumed US support for revolutionary France, equipped 'revolutionary' ships to raid British shipping and planned 'liberating' armies that were to march into the Spanish-owned west. In April 1793 Washington issued his neutrality proclamation. In August the cabinet voted to ask the French government to recall Genêt.

Robespierre retorted by asking in return for the recall of Gouverneur Morris, the arch-Tory minister of the United States to France. In the end Genêt persuaded the US government not to send him back and wisely settled in the Hudson Valley.

Foreign policy divided the two emerging parties as much as economic issues. Broadly, Jefferson and the Republicans were pro-French and the Hamiltonians pro-British. Paradoxically, however, New England and the seaboard towns, normally anti-British because of their trading rivalry, were now pro-British, fearing revolution, French privateering and 'popery'. The Virginian planters, usually pro-British, were now pro-French, because of their taste for Parisian ways and a dislike of Yankee capitalism and Hamilton's excise taxes. From now on the rivalry of parties covered a more fundamental division between sectional interests.

When war between France and Britian began in 1793, American neutrality was inevitably threatened. Britain was still in occupation of the fur posts and proposed to continue to occupy them until the debts left unpaid in 1783 were settled. Britain began to seize US shipping engaged in trade with the French West Indies and to impress US sailors into British service. Although pro-French feeling in the United States declined after Genêt's excesses were revealed (Jefferson himself resigned office in December 1793), nevertheless, Washington was alarmed at the prospect of war with Britain in alliance with a terrorist revolutionary regime in Paris. He was still more worried at the rising tide of war feeling: militia were drilling on village greens and harbours were being fortified.

Accordingly, in 1794 Washington sent Chief Justice John Jay to London to try to settle his disputes with Britain. Jay succeeded in averting war but only at the expense of American national pride. The Jay treaty secured a British promise to evacuate the northwest posts and to submit the boundary and debts question to commissions. However, the United States had to surrender its position on neutral rights. It was given a few concessions in the British West Indies and agreed to open its own ports without restrictions to British shipping. The treaty was as a result extremely unpopular. Jay was burned in effigy, Hamilton stoned in the streets and Washington began now to feel biting public criticism for the first time.

The treaty was in the long run a step towards the use of arbitration in the settlement of disputes. It stimulated the settling of disagreements with Spain, and the 1795 Treaty of San Lorenzo allowed Americans the right of navigation of the Mississippi and of depositing and transferring foodstuffs at New Orleans. These were major commercial concessions. However, it also widened the breach between Federalists and Republicans and Washington signed it only with reluctance. Hamilton himself resigned office in 1795.

Despite these tensions and despite the emergence of two distinct parties in Washington's second term, Washington's presidency was to be as significant in foreign policy as in domestic. This policy, developed further by the Monroe Doctrine of 1823, left the United States neutral towards Europe after 1793 and thus able to profit from the twenty-five years of war into which

Above, John Adams (1735–1826), a lawyer from Boston who was a leader of the American cause. He is shown here in his role as ambassador to Britain in 1785–88, and later he became the second President of the United States (1797–1801), adopting a conservative policy. Fogg Art Museum, Harvard University, Cambridge, Massachusetts.

Opposite, the Constitution of the United States, signed in Philadelphia in September 1787; based on the principle of the sovereignty of the people, it aimed to balance the power of the executive, legislature and judiciary, and to compromise on the question of state independence versus federal authority.

Europe was plunged by the French Revolution and Napoleon. By the time that struggle was over the United States was a strong and distinct society, which could afford to be indifferent to Europe.

Nevertheless, Washington's second term was far from happy. He was distressed by the feud between his two lieutenants and by the rising spirit of party (the contemporary word was 'faction'). He was bitterly attacked in the popular press despite forty-five years of public service and found it distasteful. He made it plain in 1796 that he did not want a third term of office and this too became a precedent. Washington's farewell address was a comment and a confession. He deplored the 'baneful spirit of party', though to no avail. He stressed the need for union as 'the main prop' of American liberty, and he urged his fellow countrymen to shun foreign connections and permanent alliances. He was happy to retire at last to 'his own vine and fig tree' at Mount Vernon, where he died suddenly in 1799 from a chill caught while riding round his farms in the rain.

John Adams

The advice of the farewell address was ignored in the bitter partisanship of the four years of John Adams' presidency (1797–1801). Since his opponent, Jefferson, had the second highest vote in the 1796 election, the latter became vice-president and thus the two leading figures in the administration were in opposite parties. What was worse, Hamilton, the leading federalist thinker and planner, conspired against Adams and had great influence over Adam's chief cabinet officers. Adams, though honest and high-minded, was vain and prickly. He, with some justice, disliked Hamilton as much as

Hamilton with less justice, disliked them. It was a miserable four years.

Adams had one achievement to his credit. Despite the tensions between the United States and revolutionary France as a result of French interference with US commerce, and despite the obvious attempt by Talleyrand and his agents to solicit bribes from the US negotiators in 1797, Adams ignored public opinion and succeeded in keeping the peace with France. However, he was unable to prevent Congress, under Federalist control, from exploiting anti-French feeling and passing in 1798 four acts that were obviously intolerant and which in the end strengthened the Republicans rather than the Federalists.

The Naturalization Act extended the residence period of aliens seeking citizenship from five to fourteen years, thus hitting at the Republican party to which foreigners tended to flock. The Alien Act authorized the president to deport any aliens whom he considered dangerous. The Alien Enemies Act empowered him to deport the aliens of any country with which the United States was at war. Finally, the Sedition Act made it possible to punish by fine or imprisonment anyone publishing any 'false, scandalous and malicious writing'. Under this Act ten republican editors were convicted or punished.

The intent was clearly to silence all opposition, and this gave Jefferson and Madison their chance. In the Kentucky and Virginia Resolutions, they set forth the Republican or states' rights view—that the federal government was created by the states and might be criticized by the states if it exceeded its powers. They claimed, in fact, that, as the constitution stated, power remained with the states or with the people. In the presidential election of 1800, Jefferson and Aaron Burr, each with 73 votes in the Electoral College, defeated Adams and

Charles C. Pinckney. The final choice of president was made by the House of Representatives, which, after thirty-six acrimonious ballots, chose Jefferson.

To prevent a recurrence of such a tie in the future, the twelfth amendment was passed in 1804 to allow for the election of president and vice-president on separate ballots. Jefferson, highly cultivated, idealistic and liberal, moved into a still uncompleted presidential mansion (not yet the White House), in a far from completed federal city (not yet Washington), to preside over a tenuously united United States. Nevertheless, the year 1800 marked, in mood, in direction and in consequences a real revolution.

THE FORMATION OF THE UNITED STATES

Date	North America	Great Britain	France	Date	North America	Great Britain	France
1765		Rockingham becomes prime minister (1765)		1785			Affair of the queen's necklace (1785)
	Repeal of Stamp Act (1766)	Earl of Chatham forms government (1766)	Corsica ceded to France (1768)		Philadelphia Convention: Establishment of federal government (1787)		Dissolution of Assembly of the Notables (1787)
			Birth of Napoleon Bonaparte (1769)		Franco-US alliance (1788)	Impeachment of Warren Hastings (1788) Regency crisis (1788)	Recall of Necker (1788)
1770	Boston 'Massacre' (1770)	Lord North prime minister (1770)			George Washington first president (1789)		Summoning of the Estates-General: outbreak of the Revolution (1789)
	Boston Tea Party (1773)	Royal Marriages Act (1772)	Accession of Louis XVI (1774)	1790	Creation of a national bank		Civil Constitution of the Clergy (1790)
	Quebec Act (1774) First Continental Congress (1774)	Warren Hastings governor-general of India (1774)	Turgot controller-general of finance (1774)		Jefferson founds the Democratic Republican party (1791)	Canada Act (1791)	
1775	Outbreak of war (1775) Battle of Bunker's Hill (1775)						Abolition of the monarchy (1792)
	Battle of Trenton (1776) Declaration of Independence (1776)	James Cook's third voyage to the Pacific (1776)	Fall of Turgot (1776)			Britain and France at war (1793)	
	Lafayette in America (1777) Surrender of Burgoyne at Saratoga (1777)	Death of Earl of Chatham (1778)	Necker director-general of finance (1777) Abolition of serfdom in the royal domains				Fall of Robespierre (1794) Formation of the Directory (1795)
1780		'No Popery' riots in London (1780)			John Adams president (1797) Death of George Washington (1799)	Naval mutinies (1797)	Establishment of the Consulate (1799)
	Surrender of Cornwallis at Yorktown (1781) Treaty of Versailles:		Dismissal of Necker (1781)	1800	Washington becomes the capital of the United States	Act of Union with Ireland (1800)	
	Britain recognizes independence of American colonies (1783)	Pitt the younger prime minister (1783) Government of Indian Act (1784)	Calonne controller-general of finance (1783)				

Chapter 31

The French Revolution

The French Revolution was neither the only nor the first of the disturbances that shook the old order in Europe in the late eighteenth century, but it was the most spectacular and the most important. It broke out in one of the largest, most populous and powerful of European countries and one which was for many the very centre of culture and civilization. In its principles and its practice it went much further than the American Revolution both politically and socially. Moreover, unlike the American Revolution, the French Revolution was propagandist and aggressive, challenging the old order outside its boundaries with armies as well as ideas.

In twenty years of war it carried revolutionary ideas throughout the length and breadth of Europe, and no place it touched was quite the same thereafter. Its influence extended even to places where its armies never set foot and persisted long after the event, and it found an echo in those movements of nationalism and democracy—liberal, radical and even socialist—which dominated so much of the politics of the following century. For generations it provided the very image or idea of revolution, for those who dreaded it as well as for those who desired it.

There is no single, simple explanation of this great episode, if only because the Revolution itself was not a single, static event. It was a dynamic series of events, whose development depended upon the interaction of a variety of forces and circumstances. Undoubtedly the most important of these factors was the middle class bourgeoisie), and it is possible to see the Revolution simply as a major episode in the onward march of the conquering middle classes. They represented the new forces in society, growing in numbers, importance and ambition and increasingly out of sympathy with the existing values and institutions (political, social and economic), which were still geared to the conditions and needs of a bygone age. They provided most of the leaders of the Revolution, the men who dominated its assemblies and committees. They compiled the indictments against the old regime, and in the 'Declaration of the Rights of Man' they proclaimed the principles of the new order. It was they who shaped the new institutions and it was they who

emerged in the end as the major beneficiaries of the subsequent regime.

Even so, the Revolution was not purely a battle of the middle classes against aristocracy and absolutism. Without the activity of humbler elements of society, the peasantry and the urban lower classes, the Revolution would not have followed the course it did. The fate of middle-class revolutionaries often depended on, and their policies were often conditioned by, the role of these other groups, which were driven on by discontents and aspirations which did not always coincide with those of the middle classes.

The situation, for example, which led to the summoning of the Estates-General, and which was to give the middle-class spokesmen their opportunity was not primarily the doing of the bourgeoisie or its popular

Above, Marie Antoinette (1755–93), with her children; she opposed Necker and Turgot in their attempts to reform the finances of the monarchy, and her lack of sympathy with the French people aggravated the unpopularity of the crown. National museum, Stockholm.

allies. It was the product of the difficulties of the monarchy and the ambitions of the aristocracy. By 1973 'royalists' and 'aristocrats' might appear to the popular mind as the two great enemies of the revolutionary ideals of liberty and equality, but in the 1780s the most obvious conflict in France was between the crown and the aristocracy. And it is this which explains the outbreak of revolution, even if thereafter there was a realignment of the forces involved.

The old order

The absolute monarchy of eighteenth-century France marked the peak of the crown's ascent to authority. Internal rivals to its political power had been reduced to submission in the seventeenth century. Nobles who had once challenged the crown in battle now waited on its pleasure. The palace of Versailles, the splendours of the court it housed and the royal power it symbolized—all these served as models to other continental rulers to be admired and imitated. Theories of divine right and absolutism reflected the crown's triumph. According to the absolutist theory, all the powers of the state—legislative, executive and judicial—rested with the king himself. 'It is in my person alone', said Louis XV, 'that sovereign power resides . . . it is from me alone that my courts derive their authority . . . it is to me alone that legislative power belongs completely and exclusively.'

There was no constitutional check on the king's powers, no body of elected, representative people with which he must work or to which his servants needed to answer. Hereafter, no doubt, the king would have to answer to God, but on earth he was God's agent and wielded his powers by divine right. 'The royal throne', the seventeenth-century theologian Bossuet had claimed, 'is not the throne of a man but of God himself.'

By the 1770s, however, the practical weaknesses of the crown were as important as its vast theoretical claims. This was partly a matter of character. Louis XIV's successors were weaker individuals, and the administration lacked the effective direction and coordination which only a dedicated monarch, or a chief minister with his steadfast backing, could provide. There was, moreover, a real decline in the profession of kingship ('le métier du roi'). But the main weakness was the chronic inadequacy of the monarchy's finances. Its money troubles were not the result of extravagant favours and pensions lavished on idle courtiers, though these were an extra burden. They were mainly the price paid for the long series of increasingly expensive wars that France had fought over the last 100 years. The annual interest due on the debts incurred in these was now swallowing about half the royal revenue. Current military costs, also an increasingly heavy item, took another quarter. It was only in peacetime, and then

with luck, that the monarchy could stumble along just on the right side of bankruptcy.

Financial difficulties were a symptom as well as a cause of weakness. They did not reflect any dwindling in the resources of the country but rather the crown's inability to draw on these resources more fully, to increase them or to reorganize the tax system so as to make it more productive. Important groups and regions enjoyed privileges, exemptions in taxation, and some of the more recently acquired provinces, the so-called *pays d'états*, had successfully claimed the right to negotiate their own contributions to taxation. Many towns, or groups within the towns, were either exempt from the *taille* (the most important direct tax) or arranged to pay it on easier terms. A previous royal device for raising money—the creation and sale of offices—had by now resulted in a horde of hereditary, irremovable office-holders, exempt from certain taxes.

Indirect taxation was contracted out to private companies, the farmers-general, and the country itself was divided by a network of natural barriers where these customs dues and tolls were levied. The Church owned about ten percent of the land of France and its revenues were large; but its contribution to royal revenue was limited to its own occasional 'voluntary grant'. The nobility, owning about twenty-five percent of the land, was exempt from the *taille* and, although not exempt from other direct taxes—the *capitation* and the *vingtième*—it often secured a favourable assessment for these. The taxes were collected efficiently enough but the drawbacks of this undergrowth of vested interest were not only that they represented a loss in revenue but also that the tax burden bore all the more heavily on the poor, increasing their hardship and discontent. Moreover, internal customs hindered the growth of domestic commerce and the expansion of the nation's resources. In fact, the chief beneficiaries of the system of tax collection were the farmers-general themselves.

By the middle of the eighteenth century there were signs that royal ministers were fully aware of this deplorable state of affairs. There were schemes for reforming the fiscal system, for persuading the privileged classes to give up some of their tax immunities and for cutting away some of the tangle of local barriers and particular interests which restricted the growth of the nation's wealth.

However, every attempt to introduce such reform met fierce protests from the beneficiaries of privilege, especially the nobility. Tax exemptions had a monetary value which was important to many impoverished country nobles. They were a valuable mark of social status, which mattered to them all. Nor were the nobles keen to sacrifice their cherished rights to please an absolute monarchy, which had excluded them from what many considered their historic right to a share in political power. Indeed, in the eighteenth century

there was an aristocratic resurgence as the nobles moved to the counter-offensive against royal absolutism. By the 1780s the crown's financial plight had become the aristocracy's opportunity.

The main spokesmen of the resistance to reforms and of the attack on absolutism were the *parlements*, especially the *parlement* of Paris, the most important of a dozen in the kingdom. They were essentially courts of law and the special preserve of the judicial aristocracy, the *noblesse de robe*. In one important respect their powers were more than judicial: all royal decrees had to be registered with them and they could present protests before registration took place. Although the king could then override their protests, these were nevertheless an important weapon of resistance, one used to great effect. Any scheme which affected privilege called forth the protests of the *parlements*.

With the cooperation of the local estates in Brittany and Languedoc and the assembly of the clergy, they thwarted moves for more fiscal equality in the early 1750s and again in 1763. During the 1760s they backed the estates of Brittany in a long resistance to the royal representative. In the course of this conflict they asserted that only the Estates-General, the old assembly which had not met since 1614, could ratify new taxes. Louis XV, in a burst of energy during his last years, had overriden the *parlements* and then suppressed them so that his ministers could get on with reform programmes. However, Louis XVI, in one of the first and most misguided acts of his reign, restored the *parlements*. They then resumed their campaign of obstruction up until 1788.

The effect of this conduct on the part of the *parlements* was not only to thwart useful reforms and to prop up the system of privilege but also to bring absolutism into growing disrepute. Although their resistance was inspired by petty self-interest, they presented it as the defence of liberty, constitutionalism and law against the onslaught of a despotic crown. When the king set their objections on one side, and still more when he suspended the *parlements*, it merely seemed further evidence of the tyranny in action.

The terms in which they framed their protests helped to make familiar notions of limited monarchy, representative institutions, fundamental laws and the rights of the nation. Their own interpretation of these was, in fact, narrow: liberty meant their privileges and representative institutions a body dominated by the nobility. Yet they were liked by the common people. This was partly because of skilful publicity and well-organized demonstrations, but it was also because the attack on despotism struck a popular note. Liberty and representative institutions, although in a wider sense than the *parlements* contemplated, had attractions for many who found themselves outside the privileged orders.

The social order

In this political conflict the aristocracy might feel that popular opinion was with them against despotism. Social discontent, on the other hand, made for a different alignment of forces.

Society under the old regime was still essentially aristocratic: prestige and pre-eminence in the social hierarchy were accorded to those of noble birth or possessing titled rank and landed estates. These distinctions enjoyed official legal recognition in the traditional concept of society as consisting of three estates: the clergy, the nobility and the rest, the first two orders being entitled to special privileges.

Some of the nobility's privileges were honorific, like the right to carry a sword. More materially, they were exempt from paying the *taille* and favoured in other aspects of direct taxation. A noble land-owner was entitled as *seigneur* to exercise jurisdiction in manorial courts and to retain the fines imposed. He was also allowed to hold certain monopolies in his manor, such as the winepress, whose users had to pay him a fee. Finally, he was entitled to a variety of feudal dues, in the shape of money payments —some annual and some occasional—as well as services from the peasantry.

Within the nobility there were differences and distinctions, such as those between the few thousand great ones who frequented the royal court at Versailles and the lesser, often hard-pressed, provincial nobles. There was a further distinction between the older nobility 'of the sword' and the office-holding, judicial nobility 'of the robe'. But by contrast with all non-nobles, the small group of perhaps 400,000 had this distinction in common: all held by law a superior, privileged position in society.

There were signs, especially from the mid-eighteenth century, that they were maintaining this position more exclusively and exploiting it more thoroughly. The *parlements* tried to restrict entry into their ranks to those who were already of noble descent. From 1781 most commissions in the army were open only to those who could prove that they stemmed from generations of nobility. They appropriated more and more of the better posts which had before been open to non-nobles, especially those with money. By the 1780s all the bishops, all the intendants (provincial administrators) and almost every one of the royal ministers were nobles. In the countryside, perhaps under the pressure of rising costs of living, they began to exploit their seigneurial rights more strongly, even to the extent of resurrecting old, unenforced ones and claiming payment of arrears.

The Third Estate, the non-privileged order, comprised more than ninety-five percent of the French population. They were not nobles and they were not clergy but they might be anything else. The Third Estate was a legal category and not a social

or economic class. The wealthiest and most progressive element covered a wide and ill-defined range of comfortably-off townsmen. They flourished especially in such activities as finance, commerce and industry, administration and the liberal professions. They were the chief beneficiaries of the remarkable commercial expansion of France during the eighteenth century.

Between the 1720s and 1780s foreign trade had trebled, colonial trade multiplied five times, industrial output doubled, prices rose and profit margins increased. The great ports of Marseilles, Nantes and Bordeaux enjoyed an unprecedented prosperity. In towns and cities a rush of building projects —elegant town houses, public squares and gardens, promenades and parks—bore witness to the new wealth. Only big financiers, organizing the loans for central and local authorities, or the great tax farmers could outdo in fortune the merchant-princes of the foreign and colonial trade.

Industry, like domestic trade, suffered from the hindrances that impeded economic activity under the old regime—the internal tariff barriers, government regulations and guild restrictions. Even so, large-scale enterprises based mainly on a domestic system were appearing.

The administrative and professional groups, the holders of small offices in the courts and the bureaucracies, and the lawyers, doctors and writers could not match the wealth of the businessman, but they were far more numerous and included a mass of talent—educated, articulate, enlightened and ambitious. From this section more than any other came the leadership in the Revolution, the men who dominated its assemblies and committees, shaped its legislation and conducted its policies.

These middle classes, growing in size and wealth and conscious of their importance

Above, a cartoon of the ancien régime: *the priest who prays for all, the soldier who fights for all, the peasant who works for all and the lawyer who feeds off all. Nevertheless, lawyers played a large part in the Revolution.*

to the country, were not likely to tolerate indefinitely old systems, institutions and values which barred them from a share in power, hindered their freedom of industry, restricted economic enterprise and relegated them to an inferior social status. Yet they were slow to act in independent opposition to the privileged orders. Many of them not only aspired to reach these social heights themselves but for a long time had enjoyed opportunities to do so. The crown had often drawn its servants from these sections of society rather than from the feudal nobility. Wealthy bourgeois had benefited from the royal practice of creating offices for sale, for these could confer noble status. They might marry their children into the families of needy nobles or use their wealth to get their son a promising position in the judiciary or the administration. They might buy land together with seigneurial rights and to that extent live like lords.

From the mid-eighteenth century the growing exclusiveness of the nobility hindered advance through these traditional channels and probably increased social resentment. Everywhere, according to the politician Antoine Barnave, privilege barred the path to all but trivial careers. Georges Danton complained of a system which gave educated men no opportunity to show their talents. Even so, the injured self-esteem and frustrated ambition of the middle classes were slow to transform themselves into weapons of revolution. Only when it became apparent that the aims of the aristocracy did not include any abandoning of their privileged position did the middle classes break away and strike out on their own.

Below the minority of comfortable bourgeoisie came the vast majority of townsfolk. In Paris they accounted for well over 400,000 of the city's population of half a million. They ranged from small tradesmen and shopkeepers, workshop masters, craftsmen and journeymen down to labourers and domestic servants, paupers and

vagrants. These were the common people, a collection of small-income groups including wage-earners. There was little development as yet of a distinct wage-earning proletariat and virtually no organization of workers.

Most workshops were on a very small scale. Masters, themselves craftsmen, worked alongside their few employees, and journeymen often lodged with their masters. Masters and men together resisted the attacks of big employers on the guild regulations which protected the crafts. As small earners, whatever their activity they easily felt the pinch of rising prices, especially of bread, and their normal collective response to this was not strikes and wage demands, but food riots, calls for price controls and action to improve the town's supplies of grain. In this respect they lived in a different world from the bourgeoisie, who were strangers to this kind of economic distress.

Most Frenchmen, however, were not townsmen at all. More than eighty percent of the population were rural; and the great majority of them were peasants. They were free individuals—there was very little serfdom left in France—and in this respect they were better off than the peasantry of many other countries. Many of them, perhaps a quarter, had come to own their land. Others were tenant-farmers on a rent or sharecropping basis. Many (in Normandy perhaps thirty percent) were little more than landless labourers. Except in the case of a fortunate minority their conditions, even if better than at earlier times, were oppressive. Even those who held land had so little that they needed to supplement their earnings. Most got little benefit from the rising prices of foodstuffs, since few had much surplus for sale. The population rose by about 6,000,000 (or thirty percent) during the eighteenth century, and this increased the competition for land, encouraged the subdivison of holdings, swelled the ranks of the landless and checked advances in wages. In addition, the peasants bore the full weight of royal taxes—the *taille* and the salt tax. They paid tithes to the Church and dues to the lord of the manor. They also faced increasingly heavy pressure from those with a more commercial approach to agriculture. Progressive landlords threatened to depress the poorer peasantry still further by enclosing common land and by depriving them of traditional rights, however desirable this might be for agrarian advance. Finally, their *seigneurs* squeezed harder for feudal dues—the most detested burden of all, as the complaints and conduct of the peasants in 1789 were to show.

These discontents acquired an additional significance with the growth of public discussion of critical ideas about man, government and country. The *philosophes*, whose writings provided much of the material for discussion in salons, literary clubs and philosophical societies, were concerned with far more than politics, and their political notions did not always agree.

Not revolutionaries in the normal sense, they nevertheless encouraged a revolution of rising expectations and helped to undermine confidence in the existing order. Inspired by the triumph of physical science in discovering the grand, simple laws of nature, they favoured a similar rational approach, questioning all traditional beliefs, customs and institutions. Their writings encouraged this critical attitude.

Their chief target was the Church as the stronghold of irrational belief and superstition, insisting on blind, unquestioning obedience to apparently absurd dogmas and preventing by censorship and persecution the spread or even the holding of other opinions. The powerful attacks by the *philosophes* on this bulwark of tradition helped to weaken the hold of traditionalism in general. Above all they were concerned with freedom, the essential condition of the better society they hoped for: freedom to question, to hold opinions and to communicate them by speech and writing. In conditions of freedom rational man, as they understood him, seemed capable of great achievements.

Louis XVI

The reform of institutions from above would not have been impossible, but it would have been extremely difficult. The crown would have had to prove itself a despot equipped with a vigour and ruthlessness of which it had as yet given no evidence, in order to rouse feelings against it. Moreover, the 'despot' would need to be magnanimous enough to admit limitations on his own authority.

All this called for a mixture of authority and finesse, in which the new king, who came to the throne in 1774, was sadly lacking. Louis XVI was a well-meaning young man who wanted to be liked. He had simple tastes and was not very fond of the glittering round of court life. Rather shy and awkward, fat and not very lively, he preferred the harmless pleasures of eating, hunting or tinkering at his work bench. He would have done well, Madame Roland thought, in some obscure position in life. The business of government and administration bored him. He lacked the strength of character to stand by a subordinate against the untiring pressures, intrigues and influences around him. He showed no personal initiative of his own at all.

His queen, Marie Antoinette, was shallow and fickle and did nothing to offset his weaknesses. She had many enemies, through no fault of her own, but her indiscreet behaviour gave them opportunities for campaigns against her which lowered still further the reputation and popularity of the monarchy.

Louis XVI's earliest actions, designed to show his goodwill, were misguided. He brought back the *parlements* and dismissed the ministers who had got rid of them. This was a popular move but it proved disastrous for the prospects of reform. It cancelled out the otherwise promising appointment of Turgot as controller-general of finance. Turgot was a devoted servant of the crown, an experienced administrator who had achieved impressive results as *intendant* of Limoges and a disciple of progressive economic thought. He believed that the way to increase national wealth was to abolish the internal barriers which limited the circulation of goods and the restrictions which hampered industrial enterprise. He also believed that the way to improve royal finances was to make all landed proprietors pay taxes. His measures embodied this: he freed the internal market in grain, abolished the privileges of the guilds and substituted a general tax on land for the peasants' obligation to do road work. He transformed an annual deficit of 21,000,000 livres into a surplus of 11,000,000.

The opposition to these reforms was fierce. The *parlements* protested, declaring that Turgot's attack on privilege threatened the whole existing social structure. Louis ignored them, but the vested interests persisted in their opposition. The queen's circle murmured against Turgot; other ministers undermined his position. Despite Turgot's pleas to Louis to hold firm, to stand by him and to ride out the storm, Louis dismissed him in 1776. In doing so he sacrificed his best, if not his last, opportunity. Turgot was quick of tongue and temper, but he had ability and integrity, and these were qualities in short supply in 1776.

In the next confrontation with the privileged opposition, the crown's needs were once more desperate and its position more precarious than ever. Within ten years the monarchy was bankrupt, and its weakness was the aristocracy's opportunity to force its demands for a share in power.

The crucial development was the French intervention in the American Revolution. The French government obtained what it had sought since 1763—revenge for its defeat by Britain in the Seven Years War. It was, however, to prove the most expensive act of vengeance in French history. This was partly because association with the American cause stimulated the fashionable notions of liberty and representative government. Much more important was its shattering effect on the weak royal finances.

Turgot's successor as director of the Treasury was Jacques Necker, a Swiss banker. Since he was a Protestant he was not made controller-general of finance or a member of the royal council. Necker financed the war from loans, raised often at eight or ten percent interest. This not only sent the total debt soaring but required an even greater share of the annual revenue for paying the interest due on the debts. The charges had more than doubled since 1774 and were swallowing more than half the state income. An annual budget deficit had never been unusual, but it was now more

than double the deficit which Turgot had faced.

Retrenchment would make little impression on this, nor could borrowing go on at such a rate. Moreover, existing taxes could not be fruitfully increased, especially since the economy had slumped since the late 1770s and those whose tax burden was

Above Louis XVI (reigned 1774–92), who attempted to institute long-overdue reforms; his dull personality was not adequate to deal with the mounting crisis that faced him.

Opposite, a French peasant woman, weighed down with the burden of supporting the Church and the nobility, both of which were exempt from taxation.

already heavy were suffering a decline in real wages. The only solution was to recast the tax system so that all paid, regardless of status. The sole fiscal reform which would meet the crown's need inevitably involved an attack on the existing social system of privileged orders.

This was the essence of the programme proposed by Calonne, who was controller-general from 1783 to 1787. The ending of the American War hid the real position for a time, as did an excellent harvest and a trade treaty with Britain. For a time Calonne lived in a false boom, built roads and harbours and raised big loans. In 1786, however, he reverted to Turgot's policy. He proposed to replace the *vingtième*, in which the nobility were favoured, with a new tax on all land regardless of the status of its owner. To stimulate productivity internal barriers were to be abolished. There were to be new local assemblies to help to advise in taxation, which would be based on land-owning not social status: wealth, not birth and rank, would be the measure. Moreover, they were to be controlled by the royal agent, the *intendant*.

The new tax would ease the crown's finances, by providing a permanent broad-based tax on all land. The composition of the new assemblies would check the social exclusiveness and political pretensions of the privileged nobility. They would also give greater opportunities to wealthy, local middle-class men to play a role. They would increase the efficiency and uniformity of administration and they would, under the *intendants*, be acting as agencies of the crown. At the same time the removal of economic barriers would at once promote a greater unity within the kingdom and provide more incentives to economic enterprise.

The retreat from absolutism

For these same reasons the policies could expect opposition from both the defenders of the existing system and the critics of royal despotism. Calonne hoped to avoid this by summoning a handpicked assembly of notables drawn from the high nobility, the men of the *parlements* and the leading clergy. If careful explanation and persuasion could win their approval beforehand, subsequent opposition from the *parlements* might be less automatic and less effective.

The notables disappointed these hopes. Some were ready to give up their tax privileges, but even they were not convinced of the need for new taxes, nor were they keen on assemblies which ignored distinctions between the three estates and looked like institutions to strengthen the ministerial authority. When Calonne tried to appeal to a wider public, he lost whatever influence he had had with these notables, and Louis was persuaded to dismiss him.

Calonne's successor, Loménie de Brienne, an ambitious cleric and one of Calonne's leading critics in the Assembly of Notables,

had no more success. For all his criticism of Calonne, Brienne's own proposals were only a slightly modified version of his predecessor's. Despite Brienne's standing with the notables, the Church and the queen, his proposals were rejected. The notables had done nothing to relieve the financial position. By defending privilege and the status quo they had angered the Third Estate. Real reform could come only from some higher body, preferably the Estates-General, which had last met in 1614.

Thwarted in his first approach, Brienne turned next to the traditional method: he brought forward his decrees to be registered by the *parlement* of Paris. The result of this was the appearance in full force of the revolt of the nobility. The two driving forces in the *parlement*, the one concerned to preserve privilege and the other aspiring to a check on despotism by constitutional means, had both been encouraged by the rebuffs already delivered to the monarchy by the notables. They refused to register the tax proposals and demanded the summoning of the Estates-General as the one body competent to agree to a tax on land. Months of conflict came to a head in May 1788. The *parlement* issued a manifesto denouncing arbitrary government, arrest and taxation and asserting the rights of the Estates-General in matters of taxation. Brienne sent troops, arrested leaders, had all the *parlements* suspended and proposed to transfer their powers of legislation and appeal to a new set of tribunals.

Far from settling matters, this act provoked the biggest demonstrations witnessed so far. The *parlements* were seen—far from accurately—as a barrier against tyranny. In Paris and the provinces the despotism of ministers was denounced. The Assembly of the Clergy protested, as did the leading nobles. Hundreds of pamphlets appeared championing the Paris *parlement*. Riots broke out in provincial cities. In Brittany, where provincial feeling was always strong and the local Estates were flourishing, the machinery of resistance was highly organized. Elsewhere, as in Dauphiné, where the local Estates had long since died out, campaigns were begun to restore them. At Grenoble popular riots prevented troops from removing the local *parlement*, and a hastily summoned provincial Estates refused to pay the new taxes until these were sanctioned by the Estates-General.

Faced with this widespread protest the government gave in. The notion of new tribunals, along with other projected reforms, was abandoned. Brienne resigned and was replaced by Necker; his last act was, in fact, to declare the nation bankrupt. The crown agreed to summon, in May 1789, the Estates-General. In September 1788 the *parlement* of Paris was restored amid popular acclaim. The privileged classes, with wide popular support from members of the Third Estate, had forced absolutism to retreat. To accept the Estates-General was

to admit the right of a representative body to a share in power and thus to a permanent limitation in the authority of the crown. However, the successful aristocratic revolt to end the autocratic power of the crown had merely opened the way to a revolution that was to end the power of the privileged aristocracy. As the French writer, François de Chateaubriand, later said: 'the patricians began the Revolution and the plebeians completed it.'

The common front of nobility and commoners against absolutism had hardly won its victory in the summer of 1788 when it began to distintegrate. The reason for this was the Third Estate's discovery that the nobility's intentions were very different from its own. Once it became apparent that the nobility's idea of a constitution was one which ensured its own predominance and perpetuated the existing system of inequality of status, the Third Estate denounced its former allies and struck out on its own. 'Despotism and constitution', wrote an observer, 'are now minor questions. The war is between the Third Estate and the other two orders.'

There had already been signs of this division of interests, notably in Brittany, even at the height of the common resistance to Brienne. But the great revelation of how narrow the aristocracy's aspirations were came with the announcement by the *parlement* of Paris, just after its restoration, that the Estates-General should meet in its ancient form. Each Estate was to return the same number of representatives, each was to meet separately and each was to vote separately.

This would condemn the Third Estate to permanent inferiority and impotence. Since two of the three orders were privileged, vote by order would mean that the Third Estate could always be outvoted by two to one and certainly would be on anything which touched the privileged status of the other two Estates. Royal absolutism would be exchanged for a constitution dominated by privileged orders. In seconding the nobility's demands for a constitution, the middle classes had not meant to revive a medieval relic which would perpetuate the concept of stratified estates and enshrine their own inferiority. They added to the protest against absolutism their own clamour against privileged status. The Revolution was to be about equality as well as liberty.

The indignation at the Paris *parlement*'s announcement was immediate and widespread. The *parlements* lost their traditional popularity, and the privileged orders in general became the major target of denunciation. In a great outpouring of pamphlets and petitions the Third Estate proclaimed its own ideas and demands. These were that the Third Estate should have as many representatives as the clergy and nobility together (the 'doubling of the Third'), that all the orders should meet in a single assembly and that voting should be by individuals, with the decision going by majorities. In such a mixed assembly the Third Estate would be powerful, since its representatives could expect support from the more liberal nobles and from the poorer clergy.

The general mood is well illustrated in the best-known of these pamphlets, *What Is the Third Estate* by the Abbé Siéyès. It was useless, he said, for the Third to be represented under the ancient forms: 'Its presence would only consecrate the oppression of which it must be the eternal victim.' It would prolong the 'odious injustice' whereby, whatever a man's talent, industry and public service, the path to honours and high position would stay closed to him and be open only to the privileged orders. He went further when he dismissed the aristocracy as a tiny (and useless) minority. The Third Estate represented the nation: 24,000,000 commoners mattered more than 400,000 of the privileged. The Third Estate was 'everything'. So far it had been treated in practice as if it were 'nothing'. It demanded in future to count for something.

There were the beginnings also of organization to promote the Third Estate's views. Liberal aristocrats like Lafayette enlightened *parlement*. Men like Adrien Duport and Hérault de Séchelles, clerics like Talleyrand and Siéyès, and even princes of the blood like the Duke of Orléans associated with the 'patriotic' party.

One request, for the doubling of the Third Estate's representation, was conceded by the king in December 1788. He did not say whether the orders should sit and vote together, but it seemed as if the crown were coming down on the side of the Third Estate's demands.

The Estates-General

The preparations for the coming assembly of the Estates-General added to the air of excitement and expectation. In thousands of meetings throughout France men assembled to elect the representatives of their order for their district and to discuss and draft the lists of grievances (*cahiers*) they would take with them to Versailles. The nobility, like the clergy, chose their representatives directly, but the deputies for the Third Estate were chosen indirectly. Most Frenchmen over the age of twenty-five could vote in a local assembly, but they usually picked electors who proceeded to a higher meeting of electors which actually chose the deputies.

This process favoured the men of some eloquence, education and local standing, especially as these same meetings had to discuss and draft the list of grievances. It favoured the urban, professional middle class: men like Maximilien Robespierre in Artois and Antoine Barnave and Jean Mounier in Dauphiné. Of the 610 deputies, about two-thirds were lesser office-holders

J.'somm' du Tier-Etat.

or lawyers, and another five percent came from other professions. About thirteen percent were from commerce, manufacture or finance and about ten percent were farmers.

The general list of grievances of the Third Estate was mainly the work of this middle-class group. Some of the demands of the peasantry and poorer people were neglected or glossed over. But they do reveal the line of divergence between the middle classes and the privileged orders. The grievances submitted by all the orders usually denounced arbitrary government, demanded a constitution, a representative body to control taxation, freedom of the individual and the press and the abolition of internal customs barriers. But the nobility, though sometimes ready to give up its tax exemptions, still insisted on its honorific privileges and on its special status—the retention of the system of separate orders. For its part the Third Estate demanded complete civil equality: the nobility was to lose all its privileges and its special status.

There was in all this another opportunity for the king. The alliance of people and nobility had broken down. The groups which had so often sabotaged ministerial plans for reform were unpopular with the spokesmen of the Third Estate. By his agreement to meet a representative body in order to discuss reform and by his concession which enabled the representation of the Third Estate to be doubled, Louis had won popularity and trust. An alliance of crown and people on a basis of moderate reform was feasible. But it was expecting a great deal of a monarch whose whole upbringing and outlook were cast in a traditional mould

Above, Jacques Necker (1732–1804), the French financier who introduced reforms of government finances in the 1770s and 1780s but who was shackled by opposition within the court. His dismissal in July 1789 prompted the storming of the Bastille.

Top, a craftsman and a washerwoman drinking the health of the Tiers État, *whose voice was to be heard for the first time in 175 years when Louis XVI summoned the States-General in 1789. The* Tiers État *included all those who were neither noble nor clergy.*

to throw over the nobility and join with a collection of provincial lawyers and bureaucrats. It was too much for a monarch as indecisive as Louis XVI, who was surrounded by influences favouring the established system.

As the Estates-General assembled in May 1789, the hopeful deputies of the Third Estate were soon disillusioned. The traditional ceremonies underlined their inferior status: they had to wear black, enter by a side door and go bareheaded, while the other orders wore hats. They were received in a different room. When Necker announced that the Estates should meet separately, not in a common assembly, disillusion was complete. On this vital point the king had agreed with the privileged orders.

Recognizing that to accept this was to accept the defeat of their hopes, the deputies of the Third Estate determined to ignore it. They embarked on a tactic of passive resistance and began a war of nerves. They refused to take any step, however small, until the other orders should join them. For weeks no business at all was transacted. On 17 June they went further and took a clearly revolutionary step: they proclaimed themselves to be, not the mere representatives of the Third Estate, but the National Assembly. On 20 June, finding their normal meeting

hall locked, they adjourned to a nearby tennis court and took an oath not to disperse till a constitution had been finally established.

On 23 June they carried their defiance still further. Louis, addressing all the orders in a special session, outlined important reforms but said that the ancient distinction of the three orders would be preserved in its entirety and ordered the estates to assemble in their separate halls the next day. The deputies of the Third Estate sat firm. 'The nation when assembled', declared Jean Bailly, the president of the Third Estate, 'cannot be given orders.' 'We will not leave our places', said Mirabeau, 'except at the point of a bayonet.' Many of the clergy including the Archbishop of Paris (from fear) and Talleyrand, Bishop of Autun (from calculated enthusiasm), had already responded to the Third Estate's exhortations to join them. So did about forty of the nobles, including the Duke of Orléans. Louis, perhaps alarmed at the growth of unrest in Paris, yielded. On 27 June he instructed the First and Second Estates to merge with the National Assembly.

The Third Estate had won its war of nerves with the king and the nobility. Henceforth, there were no representatives of the Estates of France, only representatives of the French nation.

Despite their impressive defiance the position of the middle-class deputies remained precarious. The royal orders of 27 June did not mark the conversion of Louis to their ideas but merely a temporary expedient. Recalcitrant nobles and court circles were urging him to use force. He began to summon regiments to Paris and Versailles. He dismissed Necker and replaced him with a court favourite, the Baron de Breteuil. It looked as if the last argument of kings was to be used against the upstart deputies. What saved the day for the National Assembly was the appearance of new forces in this complex movement. And these forces had their own interests and aspirations which made them invaluable but disturbing and uncertain supporters of the middle class in the Assembly.

The beginning of the Revolution

It was the intervention of the people of Paris that thwarted any royal plan for using force. This was not merely a gesture of solidarity. Economic distress caused by high prices and shortage of food was particularly acute. The price of bread in Paris was acute. The price of bread in Paris was double

the normal rate. Wide popular unrest over this had shown itself in demonstrations, so that when the political crisis of July arose the Parisian people were already in the streets in an angry mood. Feelings about politics might not have brought them out in such strength or worked on them with such effect had it not been for these economic grievances. Time and again during the Revolution food shortages and rising prices would appear as the great driving force behind popular discontent. Yet, although high prices could provoke riots, these would have had no more significance than they had had in the past but for the political situation.

The Parisians were kept in touch with the latest developments as news and rumours came through from Versailles. The great distributing centre was the Palais Royal, a favourite public resort, where every night orators and agitators, in particular Camille Desmoulins, addressed the crowds. They warned the people of aristocratic schemes to launch troops against Paris and urged them to take up arms. Excited and alarmed, the crowds surged through the streets seeking weapons, which they found in the Hôtel de Ville and the Hôtel des Invalides.

On 14 July they converged on the Bastille in the Faubourg Saint-Antoine. It

was thought to contain weapons. Also it was suspect as the stronghold from which the royal troops would attack, and its guns were trained on the streets. In panic the small garrison opened fire. The angry crowd, supported by rebellious soldiers with artillery, forced the governor De Launay to surrender and killed him. 'This is a revolt', said the king. 'Sire', replied a courtier, 'it is not a revolt, it is a revolution.'

The fall of the Bastille had important consequences. The king had lost control of Paris. At the same time, the body of electors who had chosen the deputies for Paris and who had continued to meet thereafter threw out the old city authorities and set up themselves as the municipal council—the Commune. They established a militia, the National Guard, both to resist any aristocratic plots and to check excessive popular disturbances. Its commander was Lafayette; its badge the tricolour.

Throughout the towns of France similar new bodies took over from the old authorities and set up similar national guards. Meanwhile, on 17 July the king had recalled Necker and had visited Paris where at the Town Hall he accepted the national cockade: the red and blue of Paris with the white of the Bourbons in between. The most intransigent nobles began to flee from France.

Above, the storming of the Tuileries, in Paris, in August 1792 marked the decisive takeover of the Revolution by the Parisian mob. Shortly afterwards a republic was declared and the king was tried for treason. Château de Versailles.

Top left, the opening of the Estates-General in Versailles in May 1789; the country expected the meeting to recognize the new authority of the Tiers État and to institute sweeping reforms, but instead the superior status of the nobility and Church was confirmed.

Above left, the 'tennis-court oath' of June 1789, when the representatives of the Tiers État, who had now declared themselves to be a National Assembly, swore not to disperse until a constitution had been agreed.

Opposite left, the arrest of the governor of the Bastille after it had been stormed on 14 July 1789; he was killed shortly afterwards. The event acquired psychological importance as the first act of violence against the government in the Revolution.

Opposite right, General de Lafayette (1757–1834), the French hero of the American War of Independence, who organized the national guard and attempted to reconcile the two sides in Paris in 1789–92; eventually he was forced into exile because he supported the monarchy. Musée Carnavalet, Paris.

303

The same month another popular force made its weight felt in the Revolution. In the years before 1789 the position of the masses of the peasantry had worsened, with the growing pressure of population and the more rigorous exaction by *seigneurs* of their dues. In the economic recession and the bad harvests of 1788 the peasantry suffered badly, and the surviving lists of grievances of rural assemblies indicate the nature of their many complaints: enclosing landlords, tithes, heavy taxes and, above all, the seigneurial dues.

From early in 1789 there was widespread unrest, and attacks on grain stores and convoys took place. The peasants had expected good news from Versailles and when none came rumours spread: the aristocrats were not only conspiring to prevent improvements but they were planning to launch armed vengeance against the peasants, and the instruments of the aristocrats were to be the brigands. This legend was strengthened by the movement of unemployed labourers and vagabonds. Such rumours spread like wildfire creating panic armong the peasantry over large areas. The 'great fear' resulted in a wave of peasant

uprisings, in which they attacked châteaux, destroyed the manorial records of the detested seigneurial dues and overturned enclosures. Many believed, or pretended to believe, that they were acting in the king's name.

The middle classes in the Assembly were alarmed. Such widespread disorders and attacks on property were not to their taste. Yet they had no forces which could put down disorders on such a scale. The only way to restore peace to the countryside was to make swift concessions. This was the underlying reason for the destruction of the feudal regime by the Assembly on 4 August. One deputy proposed the surrender of feudal rights and an orgy of sacrifice followed, as one after another tax privileges, tithes, seigneurial rights and the privileges of provinces and cities, guilds and corporations were offered up. It was an impressive occasion, but essentially it was the recognition of an accomplished fact. Indeed, the Assembly later stipulated that the peasants should redeem the seigneurial dues. But this could never be enforced. Just as the action of townspeople throughout France had thrust aside the municipal authorities of the

old regime, so the action of the peasantry had destroyed some of the traditional structure in the countryside.

Yet another popular movement in Paris during October set the seal on the revolutionary triumphs of 1789. Once again it was brought about by a combination of economic distress and political excitement. The latter sprang from revived suspicions of the king's intentions. Louis had stubbornly refused to give his assent to the decrees in which the Assembly had embodied their abolition of feudalism on 4 August. Some deputies felt he needed another push. Their impatience was reinforced by alarm early in October, when a regiment was called to Versailles and at a welcoming banquet drank royal toasts and trampled on the tricolour cockade. The orators of the Palais Royal were quick to pass on this ominous news to their excitable audiences and to suggest thwarting such aristocratic plots by removing Louis from the poisonous atmosphere of Versailles to the pure patriotic air of Paris.

The food shortages had not been eased. There were riots and angry denunciations of the authorities, especially by the housewives of Paris. It was during a demonstration by the women at the Hôtel de Ville that someone suggested that they march to Versailles to petition the king and the Assembly for bread. Several thousand women made the twelve-mile journey. The Assembly arranged that their petition for bread should reach the king and suggested that political demands—his assent to their decrees—be added. Further persuasion appeared in the shape of 20,000 Parisian National Guards under Lafayette, presenting the demand of the Paris Commune that Louis should return to Paris. On 6 October, accompanied by cheering crowds, Louis made the journey from Versailles, to be followed in a few days by the National Assembly.

'It is finished', wrote Desmoulins. 'The aristos are at their last gasp, the patriots have triumphed.' It was not finished and Desmoulins would not live to see the end. The alliance of the middle-class Assembly and the common people of Paris was to prove uneasy and unstable. Indeed, the Assembly in Paris soon took severe measures, including the imposition of martial law, to check the excessive energies of the people.

Nevertheless, Desmoulin's optimism was understandable. The aristocracy's plans for the future of the constitution and of society had been defeated; their attempts to bring in armed force had been thwarted; and many of them had fled the country. The Assembly, backed, however fortuitously, by the people, had triumphed. The king was in Paris under their eyes. The people were calm, partly because of sterner disciplinary measures but also because the Assembly improved the flow of food to Paris and because the next harvest was good. They could proceed to reshape the institutions of France along the lines of middle-class aspirations.

The National Assembly

Between 1789 and 1791 the National Constituent Assembly carried through a great reconstruction of French institutions. Not all its measures were permanent or satisfactory: some worked poorly; some were quickly abandoned. The decision-makers were essentially men of the middle classes, who dominated the Assembly, together with some 'patriotic' nobles and clergy. For this reason their vision was often limited to the boundaries of a comfortable middle-class liberalism. Nevertheless, much of what ultimately survived from the Revolution was the work of these years, and it represented a radical change in every aspect of life in France.

In its 'Declaration of the Rights of Man and Citizen' (August 1789), the Assembly proclaimed the principles on which the new order should be based and rejected those of the old Regime. Liberty and Equality—'men are born and remain free and equal in rights'—was the negation of arbitrary government and aristocratic privilege. Social

Above, the women of Paris marching to Versailles in October 1789.

Left, the nobles in the Estates-General renouncing their privileges on 4 August 1789; this concession to popular feeling came too late to affect the course of the Revolution.

Opposite top left, the fall of the Bastille, drawn by an eyewitness; the Parisians were supported by rebel detachments from the army, who brought artillery.

Opposite top right, the Parisian mob carrying the head of the governor of the Bastille in a demonstration outside the Hôtel de Ville on 14 July 1789; the capture of the Bastille involved the loss of royal authority in Paris.

Opposite bottom left, the mob in the salon of the Tuileries palace in Paris in August 1789.

Opposite bottom right, the lynching of Joseph François Foullon, the French intendant of finances whose severity was hated by the people. He was killed on 22 July 1789, one of the first victims of the Revolution.

distinctions were to be based on public usefulness only, not on inherited status. Public offices were to be open to all on a basis of talent, not reserved for a privileged few on a basis of rank. There was to be freedom of opinion, of speech and of writing and freedom from arbitrary arrest and imprisonment. Popular sovereignty—'the source of all sovereignty resides in the nation'—was a total reversal of the previous theory of royal sovereignty.

These principles, though fatal to the old order, were not meant to imply extreme measures of democracy in the new era. Equality meant equality before the law and a career open to talents, not a levelling out of economic inequalities. The fact that men had a natural right to property did not foreshadow some great redistribution: it meant

that the individual property owner had a right not to be deprived of it. When the Assembly did contravene this 'sound and inviolable right', it was always with excuses and usually resulted in compensation for the affected person. Nor did popular sovereignty mean universal suffrage. The Assembly wanted to keep power in responsible, educated, middle-class hands. Hence, while all citizens enjoyed civil rights, only those paying a certain sum in taxation were classed as 'active citizens' and given the right to vote in national or local elections. Even most of the 'active' citizens could vote only in primary assemblies, the election of deputies coming at a later stage and being confined to voters with a higher tax qualification. Some deputies, notably Robespierre, protested at this creation of a new aristocracy of wealth and managed to obtain some modifications, but the main distinctions remained.

In a variety of measures the Assembly carried through the destruction of the old regime which was implied in their declaration. Decrees like those of August 1789 swept away large numbers of the old privileges in shoals. The National Assembly was to a certain extent merely recognizing facts already accomplished by the peasantry. They defined some seigneurial rights as legitimate property rights which the peasants should purchase from the lord. However, since the peasantry never recognized this fine distinction, in practice a great host of feudal and seigneurial dues and obligations and payments were abolished. Serfdom was also abolished where it still lingered on. All tax privileges and exemptions of provinces, towns and corporations as well as privileged groups were suppressed, as were tithes. Hereditary nobility and titles were abolished: all men were now citizens. The old venal offices were swept away (a generous gesture from an Assembly nearly half of whose members held such offices), although all holders were to be compensated for their loss. The old *parlements* were abolished and the judges compensated for the loss of proprietary rights in their seats.

Among the most radical and enduring of the institutional changes was the reform of local government. The Assembly struck at the most disagreeable characteristics of its old structure. Local government was a confused patchwork of complicated divisions, overlapping authorities, differing institutions and areas of special jurisdictions and particular immunities, in which *seigneurs*, priests, village notables and royal officers all had a hand. The confusion was itself the result of the system of unequal privilege and fostered barriers and divisions by its stress on provincialism. Moreover, the royal authorities were imposed from above and controlled from the central government.

The Assembly aimed to replace this by a more uniform and rational system, embodying equality of treatment and the elective principle. France was divided into eighty-three departments, subdivided into 374 cantons, which were in turn divided into communes. All the 44,000 communes had equal status, similar powers and similar authorities, elected in each commune by the active citizens. This was also the case with cantons and departments, although in these larger units the governing council was elected indirectly in stages.

The reform was not an immediate success. All the authorities were too short of money to carry out effectively their administrative responsibilities. Moreover, there were conflicts between the departmental authorities

and those of the communes: in the former, indirect elections produced councils of more wealthy and cautious citizens, whereas in the communes direct election in a small area produced more radical, lower-middle-class councillors. In their desire to avoid the objectionable centralization of earlier days, the Assembly established no clear links between the local authorities and the central government. In time, however, under pressure of emergency, strong links were forged, and the leaders of France then had an administrative machine which could carry their commands through France with an efficiency no absolute monarch had ever known.

In their judicial reforms the Assembly achieved a notable success. The old system had been chaotic and confused, with a variety of courts ranging from the seigneurial courts and special ones like the ecclesiastical courts to the sovereign courts—the *parlements*. All, including the *parlements*, were swept aside. A simpler, uniform system of courts, geared to the new local government units, replaced them. The new judges and justices of the peace were to be elected. Again privilege suffered, for many of these courts had been the embodiment of privilege. Venal judicial offices were abolished, although compensation was to be paid.

Judicial procedure was reformed in enlightened and humane ways. Arbitrary imprisonment was forbidden. The accused was innocent till proved guilty, trials were to be public and juries were introduced in criminal cases. Barbarous practices and punishments such as torture, branding and breaking on the wheel were abandoned. The death penalty was retained, though some like Robespierre argued for its abolition. Even here privilege was abolished. Previously aristocrats had enjoyed the distinction of being beheaded whereas commoners were hanged. In future all would be beheaded. The deputy, Dr Guillotin, recommended, although he did not invent, the new machine for this purpose, which was named after him.

In their economic legislation the Assembly mainly favoured the progressive, individualist approach and dismantled many of the controls and restrictions of the old regime. They introduced a uniform system of weights and measures. They abolished the system of local tolls and internal customs barriers, although these free trade notions stopped at the national frontier. The guilds and corporations, obstacles to individual enterprise, were suppressed. New types of association, the trade unions, were as unacceptable as the old ones. The le Chapelier law prohibited associations of workmen.

Reform and the Church

Whatever such measures might do eventually to increase the national wealth, they were of little help with the immediate financial problems. The Assembly had to devise a new tax system to replace the inadequate, unequal one of the old regime. They proposed to do this with three taxes, the main one falling on all landed property. These taxes were not very productive in the still disordered condition of France, nor would they clear the great debt inherited from former days. There was no question of repudiating this debt. The deputies were financially orthodox, and the middle classes from which they were drawn included many bondholders. Indeed, they had considerably increased the national debt by paying compensation to those whose offices had been abolished.

The solution was to confiscate the vast property of the Church, which the Assembly argued could be seized, since it was not private property and since it was supposed to promote purposes like education which the state would henceforth discharge. The sale of Church property would replenish the Treasury and, pending its sale, the property provided backing for the issue of a paper currency, the *assignats*. As Church land was sold, *assignats* to this value would be called

Above, a dance held on the site of the now-demolished Bastille, on the anniversary of its fall, 14 July, 1790. Musée Carnavalet, Paris.

Top, the wholesale attack on privilege and rank inspired by the events of 4 August 1789, when the nobility and clergy voted to abandon the feudal rights traditionally due to their rank.

Above left, the abolition of tolls paid on goods moving into and out of Paris in May 1791; the high price of bread and other basic foodstuffs had contributed to the frustration that had been voiced in 1789.

Opposite left, the march of the women of Paris to Versailles in October 1789; they captured the king and queen and took them to the Tuileries to prevent a counter-revolution.

Opposite right, the first victims of the French Revolution – de Launay, the governor of the Bastille and Foullon, the intendant of finances.

307

in and destroyed, so that inflation would be avoided.

The move had important consequences. It worked well at first, but in time the temptation to print *assignats* in excess of the resources backing them was too great. The resulting inflation contributed to that economic distress which underlay so much of the popular unrest throughout the revolutionary years. The main purchasers of Church lands seem to have come from the middle classes and the wealthier peasantry. These great beneficiaries became hardened in their resistance to any attempts to put the clock back to 1789 and equally determined to oppose any radical attempts to put it too far forward.

The move also played a part in one of the most fateful acts of the Assembly, its reorganization of the Church. As the state had commandeered its wealth, the money for the upkeep of the Church would have to come from state funds. Most deputies were soaked in the anti-clericalism of the philosophers and believed that the Church needed a thorough overhaul, the more so if it were to be supported from public money. In the Civil Constitution of the Clergy in July 1790, the Assembly redrew diocesan and parish boundaries, made bishops and parish priests subject to election and dissolved many of the religious orders. They demanded that all clergy take an oath of loyalty to the constitution including these last arrangements. Even the clerics in the Assembly, good 'patriots' till now, hesitated to do this before some religious authority—the papacy—had approved of this secular scheme. After nine months' delay, the papacy condemned the Civil Constitution in March 1791. Nearly all the bishops and most of the French clergy had already refused the Assembly's command to take the oath, and the papal pronouncement confirmed their resistance. The 'non-jurors' were deprived of their posts, which were given to compliant, 'constitutional' clergy, but in many districts, especially in northern and eastern France, parishioners stuck by their clergy and ignored the 'constitutional' ones. In addition, the 'non-jurors' became identified as counter-revolutionaries, with a potential support among devout parishioners, so an extra bitterness and alarm was injected into the whole revolutionary situation, which was increasingly precarious.

The threat to the monarchy

Meanwhile, in their major task, the framing of a new constitution, the deputies experienced their fiercest divisions. The reactionary right, consisting of sullen nobility, had gone by August 1789. All the members of the Assembly hereafter could call themselves patriots. Moreover, they all agreed that France should have a constitutional monarchy, with a loyal executive directed by a popular legislative assembly. But on the precise powers of that executive and its relations with the assembly there were differences. Some wanted a strong executive, feeling that a weak one would lead to the spread of disorder. In particular, they felt that the crown should have the right to veto legislation and that royal ministers should sit in the Assembly to ensure coordination of both branches of government. The majority, however, were too distrustful of the executive to invest it with large powers. They believe that a powerful executive was the main danger to the individual liberties they prized. They feared, too, that a royal veto would be used to destroy revolutionary legislation and suspected that ministers in the assembly would become the means whereby a crafty king would dominate it.

On every issue, the opponents of a strong executive—with Barnave and Robespierre their most cogent spokesmen—carried the day. Jean Mounier and Pierre Malouet, the leaders of the 'strong' monarchy men, had given up in October 1789, in protest at the way in which popular intervention had been allowed (or used) to sway the decision on the veto. Only Mirabeau, the *déclassé* noble, forceful, clever, ugly and dissipated, remained as a powerful voice for a strong royal executive. Mirabeau's ability and vigour, together with his leading role in the events of 1789, gave him great personal influence in the Assembly. Even Mirabeau's weight, however, could not overcome the Assembly's distrust of a strong monarchy, nor indeed was the king willing to act on advice from so prominent a revolutionary.

When the constitution was finally agreed in September 1791, Louis XVI, now King of the French by the grace of God and the will of the nation, was chief executive, but with very limited powers. He could choose his own ministers but they were not to be drawn from, nor could they sit in, the Assembly. He could not initiate legislation. He could not veto the Assembly's legislation completely but merely delay it for a time. He could not dissolve the Assembly. The latter, as the elected representatives, embodied the sovereignty of the people and the general will of the nation.

Even before the constitution was completed there were ominous developments for the future of constitutional monarchy. Louis XVI was never reconciled to his position from the summer of 1789, and his dislike of it increased after the Civil Constitution of the Clergy. Mirabeau's death in April 1791 removed the one influence which might have countered the more hot-headed schemes of Marie Antoinette. She argued that the royal family should escape from Paris to the northeast frontier near Metz, where the army commander was sympathetic to the royal cause. From there Louis could issue an appeal which would be answered by the *émigré* nobility congregated across the frontier and, it was hoped, by the queen's brother, the Emperor Leopold, with Austrian forces. On the night of 20 June 1791, the Queen's admirer, Count Fersen, smuggled the royal family out of Paris. But Louis was recognized at Saint-Ménéhould, caught at Varennes and brought back under heavy armed escort to Paris.

Within the capital there had for some time been signs of anti-monarchical feeling. This was not apparent in the Assembly (where all were monarchists whatever their differences over its powers) nor in the favourite club of the deputies, the Jacobins. But other less reputable clubs, with small subscriptions and a lower-class clientele, especially the Cordeliers, had fostered more radical notions among the Parisian populace. Many of these were discontented with decisions

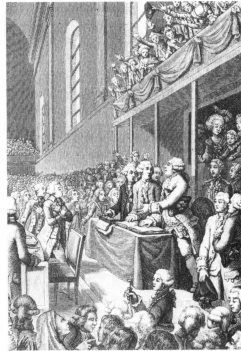

like the restrictions on suffrage. In these circles the flight to Varennes confirmed their worst suspicions of the king and provoked open demands for a republic. The Cordeliers Club demanded that France be no longer a monarchy.

The Assembly, while angered at Louis' move, was uncomfortable at this surge of popular republicanism. To depose Louis might bring foreign armies down upon them. Nor did they care for the social implications of republicanism, championed as it was by demagogues and the town populace. Barnave argued for an end to the Revolution before it degenerated into a general attack on property. Hence the members of the Assembly clung to the monarchical constitution, saving their faces with the fiction that Louis had been abducted on 25 June, so that his 'flight' was not evidence of any ill-will on his part.

The effect was to reveal only more clearly the deep rift within the ranks of the Third Estate. The popular Parisian demand for Louis' removal was not stifled. On 17 July great crowds assembled in the Champs de Mars to sign a petition against a monarchy. The municipal authorities, who shared the outlook of the Assembly, sent in the National Guard who opened fire, killing about fifty people. This was followed by a fierce repression. Ringleaders were arrested and popular papers suppressed. The Champs de Mars marked the end of the notion of a solid Third Estate in Paris. It was the opening conflict between the comfortable rulers and the *sans-culottes*, as the Parisian lower-class republicans were called.

The Assembly hastily finished drafting their constitution, obtained the king's agreement on 16 September and dissolved. A new Legislative Assembly would be elected to work the institutions they had devised.

The bulk of the members of the Assembly,

as they broke up in September 1791, might well feel that, with all the changes they had made since 1789, the work of Revolution was accomplished. The evils so loudly denounced in 1789—despotism and legal privilege—had been overthrown. France could now proceed to a more normal and much more satisfactory regime with its new institutions and new social order. Yet within about twelve months their main work, the constitution, was overthrown. Many of those who had shaped it, revolutionary heroes in 1790, were regarded as renegades, and the Revolution had moved into a new stage, which was repugnant to them.

Such optimistic expectations had been unrealistic even in 1791. The constitution itself had weaknesses which only goodwill and cooperation could overcome. These were unlikely to be forthcoming from a monarch who had shown such dislike for his role and persisted in hoping for foreign assistance to restore him to his true position. The flight to Varennes had added to the popular suspicion of the constitution and stimulated the hankerings after republicanism which increased the difficulties of working it. Moreover, the constitution had laid down that none of the members of the present Assembly should be eligible for the new body. Thus the new deputies lacked colleagues with any experience.

The Legislative Assembly

The main forces impelling the Revolution further forward emerged clearly only in the course of the new Legislative Assembly from October 1791 onwards. These forces were: first, the struggle for power within the ranks of the middle-class revolutionary politicians; second, the mounting pressure of the common people of Paris, intensified by

Above, the Marquis de Mirabeau (1749–91), the early leader of the Tiers État *in the Estates-General; he sought to establish a constitutional monarchy on the English model but never won the support of Louis or Marie Antoinette.*

Top, Louis XVI's speech to the nation of 4 February 1790; he had little interest in establishing a workable compromise with the revolutionaries.

Top left, a caricature of the funeral of the Church, in recognition of the decision of November 1789, according to which ecclesiastical property was expropriated by the nation.

Opposite left, looting the houses of the nobility in Paris in November 1790; by this time a large proportion of the nobility had already gone into exile.

Opposite right, a magic lantern show of the abuses of the Church, for the entertainment of the Parisians.

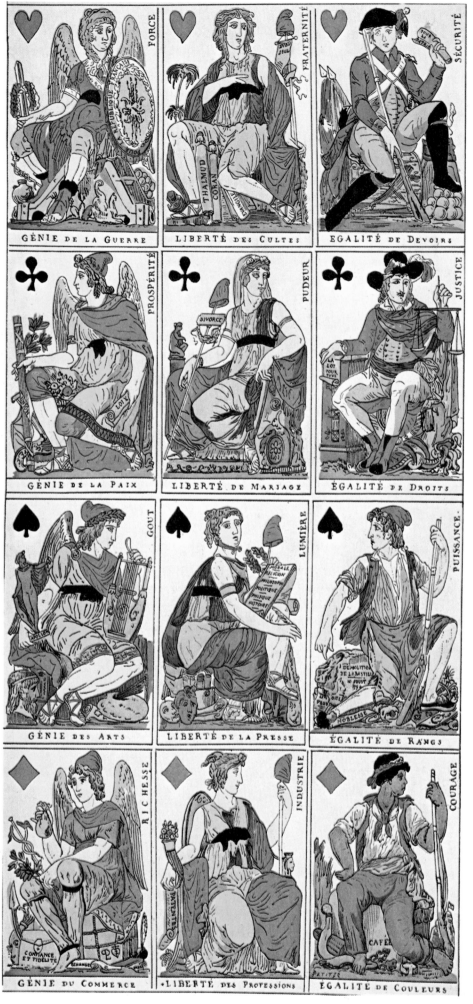

GÉNIE DE LA GUERRE

LIBERTÉ DES CULTES

EGALITÉ DE DEVOIRS

GÉNIE DE LA PAIX

LIBERTÉ DE MARIAGE

ÉGALITÉ DE DROITS

GÉNIE DES ARTS

LIBERTÉ DE LA PRESSE

ÉGALITÉ DE RANGS

GÉNIE DU COMMERCE

LIBERTÉ DES PROFESSIONS

EGALITÉ DE COULEURS

economic distress and political discontent with their middle-class rulers; and third, the advent of war in 1792. The effect of these forces was heightened by the interaction between them. Thus politicians in their conflicts were ready to exploit the fears and hopes of the Parisian people.

War transformed the situation. It stimulated the hopes of those who disliked all that the Revolution had done and intensified the fear and determination of the revolutionaries. It contributed to the inflation and shortages which fostered Parisian grievances and made more tense the atmosphere in which rumours of conspiracies and treacheries flourished. It presented politicians with massive new problems, in meeting which they had to make moves and sanction measures that took them far beyond the intentions of 1789 to 1791. And the monarchy, discredited and disliked, might have managed to survive in peace, but in the desperate days of war it was among the first casualties.

The war itself, however, was not a thunderbolt hurled by a malevolent providence against innocent, unsuspecting revolutionaries. It was in fact provoked by revolutionary politicians in pursuit of power. The Legislative Assembly, like its predecessor, was not divided into organized parties with coherent policies. There were no divisions of social or economic class, since the vast majority were, as before, from the same comfortable middle classes. Politically, most were connected to no special group, though they all wanted to maintain the gains so far made by the Revolution and would support those who seemed most likely to ensure this. Of those who were committed, the majority group were constitutional monarchists, supporters of the 1791 constitution, and the ministers were at first their associates.

In the National Constituent Assembly these had formed the more 'popular' element, members of the Jacobin club and advocates of a weak executive against the right-wing spokesmen for a strong monarchy. But in the new Assembly the constitutional monarchists appeared as the 'right' wing. Significantly, they had seceded from the Jacobins and set up their own club, 'The Feuillants'. The other main political group, a minority at first, continued to frequent the Jacobins (or the Cordeliers) and to attack the Feuillant ministers from a more popular and vaguely republican standpoint.

The leading spokesmen of the left were the Brissotins (later known as Girondists), the circle grouped around J. P. Brissot. His main activities before 1789 had taken place in the twilight world of popular agitation and inflammatory journalism. He had been a frequenter of the Palais Royal, had run an extremist journal since 1789 and had played a part in organizing the demonstration on the Champs de Mars. A fluent, rhetorical speaker, he was ambitious and an intriguer, though not without a naive idealism. His

associates included some of the most eloquent orators of the Revolution, Pierre Vergniaud, Armand Gensonné and Gaudet, all deputies from the Gironde. In his struggle for power and the limelight, Brissot was ready to work recklessly on popular fears and passions.

From the beginning the Brissotins preached a violently militant line, demanding ruthless action against internal enemies of the Revolution, such as refractory priests, and against external dangers. By 1792 the numbers of *émigrés* massing on the frontier, especially at Koblenz, was a source of alarm in Paris. Austria and Prussia had both expressed sympathy with the French king. This was in fact a substitute for action, not a prelude to it, but the revolutionaries did not appreciate this. Consequently Brissot's urging—'if you wish with one blow to destroy the aristocracy, the refractory priests, the malcontents, then destroy Koblenz'—struck a sympathetic note. So did Vergniaud's argument that they should attack first, not wait to be attacked. They saw such a conflict as 'a war of peoples against kings', a triumphant crusade in which the forces of liberty would brush aside the effete, mercenary armies of Europe and be welcomed by the oppressed peoples. Moreover, war would consolidate the Revolution internally. Opponents would be seen and dealt with as the traitors they were and the people would be roused to new revolutionary ardour. 'We need war', declared Brissot, 'to consolidate freedom, to purge

Above, an attack on the Tuileries palace, the residence of the king and queen, in February 1791; republicanism had not been strong in 1789, but the intransigence of the monarchy made it soon appear to be the only solution.

Top and above left, the arrest of Louis XVI at Varennes in June 1791, after he had tried to flee abroad to organize support against the revolutionaries. This failure meant the imminent downfall of the monarchy.

Left, Jacques Pierre Brissot (1754–93), a journalist who led the Girondist faction, arguing for the need for a revolutionary war to liberate the rest of Europe from monarchy. He was executed by the Jacobins.

Opposite, playing cards depicting the various benefits that the Revolution would confer: prosperity, might, wealth, good taste, industry, enlightenment, modesty, religious understanding, security, justice, power and courage.

311

away the vice of despotism.' War would also bring triumph to the war party, the Brissotins.

The policy paid handsome dividends. The Brissotins carried the Assembly to a man. They held the majority in the Jacobins Club against the criticism of a small group which included Robespierre, who feared that war might strengthen the position of the crown and make more enemies than friends abroad. The king, too, was confident that war would work to his advantage, and so he was prepared to agree to a war policy. The Feuillants ministers were dismissed, being replaced by sympathizers of the Brissotins, and in April 1792 war was declared on Austria.

The Revolution gathers momentum

The immediate effects showed how misleading had been the easy optimism of the Brissotins. The French forces were desperately short of officers, more than sixty percent of whom had abandoned their commissions, and of trained men, equipment and supplies. They broke and ran at the first contact with the Prussian and Austrian forces. Only the excessive caution of the aged Prussian commander, the Duke of Brunswick, hindered a swift advance to Paris by the Prussians and Austrians.

Popular fear and anger over the military danger was exacerbated by an economic

grievance. The *assignat* began to depreciate rapidly. By June 1792 it was down to about half its face value. Bread prices rose and provision merchants were suspected of hoarding supplies till prices rose still higher. The Brissotins diverted this popular wrath from themselves by accusing the court of treachery, all the more vehemently when Louis dismissed their friends from the government. Their behaviour encouraged a new wave of popular intervention which in its first stage took the form of a demonstration at the Tuileries and forced Louis to restore the Brissotin ministers.

Now, however, the Brissotins had helped to summon up a force they could not control. Alarm and excitement rose higher as the enemy invaders advanced, as rumours spread of counter-revolutionary plots and as Brunswick threatened a 'memorable vengeance' on Paris if the royal family were harmed. Demands for the deposition of the king mounted. The Brissotins, who were fonder of the people as an emotive phrase in debate than as a reaility in the streets exerting its own rough pressures, hesitated. Agitation—now that it had served their purposes—ought to stop. Hoping that provincial forces might offset the Parisian ones, they summoned national guardsmen from other towns to Paris. But these men, the so-called *fédérés*, merely swelled the ranks of the Parisians, providing them with extra forces and a rousing new march, the 'Marseillaise'.

Other politicians were now bypassing the Brissotins. Robespierre in the Jacobin Club supported the popular cause by demanding a National Convention elected by universal suffrage to frame a new constitution. Popular feeling in Paris had by now an organizational basis of its own in the meetings in the forty-eight sections, the electoral divisions of Paris. In July these went into permanent session, so that meetings could be held any time. They began admitting 'passive' (that is, voteless) as well as 'active' citizens. Thus the lesser shopkeepers and tradesmen, the master-craftsmen and artisans and the small people of Paris in general could congregate to frame their own demands and provide local leaders. By August, forty-seven of the forty-eight demanded that the Assembly depose the king.

On 9 August they made their own move. Representatives from almost thirty of the sections moved into the Hôtel de Ville, where the municipal authorities of Paris sat, and proclaimed themselves the new 'revolutionary commune'. Under their direction, on the following day crowds from the sections and contingents of *fédérés* moved on the Tuileries.

After a savage conflict, which cost the attackers 400 lives and the defenders, mainly Swiss Guards, about 800, the Tuileries was taken. The royal family had fled to the Assembly building which offered Louis personal protection. But the intervention of the

people had killed constitutional monarchy and the Brissotins were compelled to recognize this. They suspended Louis, set up a provisional executive council including the non-Brissotin but highly popular Danton and arranged elections for a National Convention to draft a new constitution.

All this took place against a background of crisis abroad and at home. Longwy (22 August) and Verdun (2 September) fell to the Duke of Brunswick; Lafayette went over to the enemy. The road to the capital was open. On 2 September the Commune issued a panic-stricken call: 'To arms! The enemy is at the gate!' Between 2 and 10 September some 1,400 priests and prisoners were killed.

It was no time for political reflection. Indeed, there were few voters in the election for the Convention. Many were excluded by law, and some excluded themselves out of fear. It is probable that this Convention represented the will of only some seven out of a hundred of the population as a whole.

The Convention

The first months of the new assembly were marked by a fierce struggle for power among the revolutionary politicians. Two small active factions fought to command the support of the majority of deputies, the 'Plain', who were concerned to hold the ground gained by the Revolution but were

Above, the execution of Marie Antoinette on 16 October 1793.

Top, Marie Antoinette facing her accusers in October 1793. Found guilty of treason for secretly encouraging the Austrian invasion, she was executed the following day, 16 October.

Top left, a 400 livres note of 1792, decorated with the name of the Republic and its symbol, the Jacobin cap.

Centre left, the massacre of the nobility in Paris in September 1792 and of other people arrested on suspicion of sympathy with the Austrian invaders.

Left and far left, royalist prisoners and women killed during the days of early September 1792, when a great wave of fear swept France that the revolution was being betrayed, by an alliance of royalists and Austrians.

Opposite top, the idyllic and pastoral ancien régime contrasted with the violent and militaristic revolutionary age, in two counter-revolutionary satirical prints.

Opposite bottom, the fatherland in danger in July 1792; the readiness of the Austrians to interfere on behalf of the king encouraged the revolutionaries to execute him after the Austrian defeat in September.

not committed to any particular political group. The first of the active factions were the Brissotins, more generally known at this stage as the Girondins. They were at first the dominant group, controlling the executive committee and holding the majority in the Convention. Their old 'right-wing' antagonists of the Legislative Assembly, the constitutional monarchists, had gone from the scene, but they were themselves attacked by the small radical group known, from the high seats which they occupied in the Convention, as the 'Mountain'. Their main spokesmen were Robespierre, Marat, Billaud-Varennes and, later, Danton.

It is not easy to see sharp contrasts of political or social principle between these two contending groups. Socially, both were the same kind of substantial middle-class deputy who bulked as large in the Convention as in its predecessors: lawyers and office-holders, doctors, businessmen and merchants. Both were strong believers in the rights of private property and subscribed to enlightened notions of economic liberalism and laissez-faire. Politically they were republican and agreed, as the first act of the Convention, to the abolition of the monarchy, the declaration of a Republic and the

dating of a new era from this, 'Year I'. Both were also determined to save the Revolution and carry out the war energetically. Their leaders belonged to the Jacobin Society, though the Mountain retained the name, while Brissot's group became known as the Girondins. The main differences lay in their attitudes towards the popular movement in Paris and the suspicions that they had of one another.

The *Sans-Culottes*

The Parisian movement was an important element in the power balance at this stage. It had actually shown its strength in the summer and remained influential in the Commune and active in the sections. The *sans-culottes*, the backbone of the popular movement, were not the dregs of Paris; they comprised the small masters and their journeymen, small shopkeepers and tradesmen and clerks and wage-earners. They were not a proletariat, indeed they were not a well-defined social or economic group at all. They consisted mainly of poor people who suffered when prices rose and food was in short supply. As a result, they demanded economic controls of prices and supplies

and the punishment of hoarders and profiteers. They were credulous and excitable. susceptible to rumours of plots and treason and were informed by popular journals like Marat's *Ami du peuple* or Hébert's *Père Duchesne*. They were exploited, but they were not a passive instrument. Above all, the *sans-culottes* were zealous patriots, republicans and revolutionaries, although they had a rough and ready common man's attitude to democracy compared with the more sophisticated approach of the better educated but often just as zealous middle-class representative. They showed a positive pride in *sans culottisme* as against the knee-breeches of the more refined classes and also favoured the more democratic usages like 'citizen'. They were suspicious of wealth, elegance and fine gentlemen and even maintained that the Convention only contained 'fine talkers who eat well'. The poor people practised a kind of direct democracy in their sectional assemblies and felt strongly about their rights as the 'sovereign people' to control their representatives, to make their wishes known in a forceful way and to 'insurrect' if need be. They had oversimplified views, looked for traitors when things went wrong and demanded quick solutions.

There was much in this of which no group
in the Convention could really approve:
their crude manner, the disrespect which
they often showed for the dignity of the
nation's elected representatives, their unenlightened demands for economic controls,
their indiscipline and disorder. But the
Jacobins were realistic enough to appreciate
that this was a power to be reckoned with, a
force which could aid the revolution as well
as promote the Jacobin cause. Some, like
Robespierre and Marat, may have had a
genuine sympathy with many of their
notions, but all were ready, in an emergency,
to submit to the demands of the *sans-
culottes* for some of the time, whatever their
reluctance and reservations. And as the
leading Jacobins were deputies for Paris,
they were readier to excuse the conduct of
their constituents and able to maintain
contacts with the movement.

The Gironde on the other hand were
more hostile and less flexible in their attitude
since they were alarmed at these popular
manifestations, which were already out of
control by the summer. Their distaste was
enhanced since the Jacobins, their rivals for
power, were associated with them. Their
electoral background reinforced this for, as
deputies from the moderate provinces, they
obviously had an interest in resisting the
pretensions of Paris to dominate the revolution and in opposing a movement which
posed a threat to order and property.

The struggle between the two factions was bitter. Charges and counter-charges over the activities of the previous summer, the behaviour of the Commune and the September massacres served the purposes of each group which strove, by every possible method, to discredit the other side. The Girondins denounced the Jacobins for trying to establish a dictatorship of Paris over the rest of France. The Jacobins interpreted Girondin references to the rights of the other eighty-two departments as a federalist scheme to disrupt the unity of the republic and their attacks on the popular movement as evidence of their desire to save the benefits of the revolution for the wealthy.

On the question of the fate of the deposed king, the Jacobins took the popular line, insisting on his death; the Gironde, on the other hand, clung to more moderate elements and delayed and evaded. This merely incensed popular suspicions, especially when the discovery of Louis' correspondence with the Austrians left no doubt of his treason. Indecisive and divided the Girondins lost, the Convention voted for death, and on 21 January 1793 Louis XVI went to the guillotine.

The enemy at the gates

The perpetual wrangling produced disorder and confusion in the assembly, but there was one consolation; the war was going well. It was because of this success, especially after halting the enemy advance at Valmy in September, that the Gironde managed to maintain a majority in the Convention. In the same month, French armies occupied Savoy and Nice, and in October French forces crossed the Rhine and took Frankfurt. In the following month, Dumouriez, the Girondins' favourite general, defeated the Austrians at Jemappes and entered Brussels.

In November and December the exultant Convention issued a provocative challenge to the established order in Europe. They offered assistance to all people wishing to regain their freedom; order the abolition, in all territories occupied by the French, of tithes and feudal dues; stated that existing authorities were to be replaced by elective bodies and that royal properties should be confiscated. French officials were to work with them to arrange the support and supplies for the French forces.

In January 1793 Danton proclaimed the doctrine of natural frontiers: France should extend to the Alps, the Pyrenees and the Rhine and international agreements, scraps of paper signed by unrepresentative monarchies, should not stand in the way of the rights of the nation. In February the Convention welcomed Brissot's move to declare war on Britain and Holland and, in March, on Spain. Soon France was at war with almost all the powers of Europe—'all the tyrants of Europe' as Brissot put it, except Switzerland and Scandinavia.

From early 1793, however, the situation rapidly deteriorated and a new crisis even more alarming than that of the previous summer developed. Dumouriez, far from pressing on to invade Holland, was defeated at Neerwinden. Worse still, blaming the politicians for his defeat, he tried to march his armies against Paris and, unsuccessful in this, deserted to the enemy along with most of his staff. The Austrian forces pushed over the border on to French territory and behind them came the *émigrés*. Further south, other French armies were forced back from the Rhine. At the same time civil war broke out in France itself. A move by the Convention to raise a levy of 300,000 men met stubborn resistance in some regions, especially in the Vendée. Here the religious measures of 1791 had already created unrest and an attempt to conscript the peasantry brought on an open revolt which local nobles were quick to exploit. Not surprisingly the rebel armies, having employed to advantage the difficult terrain they knew so well, soon established control of this region.

News of defeat, treason, invasion and counter-revolution poured in on Paris where agitation exacerbated economic distress. Financing the war effort had promoted inflation; the *assignat* had fallen to about one third of its face value, and food prices had risen sharply from early in the year. Extremist agitators, like the radical priest Jacques Roux, gathered a large following as they voiced popular demands for controls on prices and currency, for requisitioning food supplies and for tough measures against hoarders and speculators. Jacobins as well as the Girondins disapproved of the activity of these *enragés* or wild men. They distrusted their influence over the *sans-culottes* and disliked their unenlightened

programme of economic controls, as well as their petitions, their deputations and demonstrations to put pressure on the assembly and the violence of their language, which showed little respect for politicians of any kind. But it was the Gironde, still the dominating element in the assembly, and the most outspoken in denouncing both the notion of economic controls and the activities of the *sans-culottes*, who were most blamed for the Assembly's indifference to the people's demands.

The Girondins became the target of more determined onslaughts as military setbacks added alarm to discontent. They were especially damaged by the defection of Dumouriez since he had been so closely associated with them. They seemed as reluctant to respond to popular demands for drastic measures in this emergency as to those for economic controls. True the Assembly did take steps in March which were to be of great importance. They strengthened the executive by establishing a Committee of Public Safety, set up a Revolutionary Tribunal and began to reassert central direction by sending deputies out on mission to the localities.

In all this it was the Jacobins who took the initiative, especially Danton. The Girondins aired dislike of a strong executive, the more so since it was being pressed by popular demands and advocated by the Jacobins. The latter openly aligned themselves with the *sans-culottes* and not only intensified their longstanding criticism of the Girondins but also declared that the Revolution could only be saved with the help of the people. In May, they championed the popular economic demands about which they had been silent before. At the same time the sections denounced the Girondins as hindrances to the determined action needed to save the Revolution and demanded that the Assembly should purge these guilty men. By May, three-quarters of the sections had submitted such demands and threatened to act themselves if the Convention refused. Another popular revolution was in the making.

Revolution and insurrection

The revolution took place between the 31 May and the 2 June. The Girondins, desperate because of constant criticism, took action which only confirmed popular distrust and hurried on the insurrection. They tried unsuccessfully to have Marat condemned by the Revolutionary Tribunal, set up a Commission to enquire into the recent conduct of the section and arrested popular agitators like Hébert, whom they were later forced to release. The Girondins also talked of dissolving the Commune and summoning a new Assembly in the provinces. In short they appealed to their constituencies against Paris, threatening to annihilate the capital if the insurrections continued so that men would 'search the banks of the Seine for signs of the city'.

The effect of all this heightened popular fury and hurried on popular insurrection. At the end of May, delegates from the sections set up a central revolutionary committee which directed operations from 3 May. On 2 June, the Assembly was surrounded by *sans-culottes* and national guards: 'We have come to demand, for the last time, justice on the guilty.' The deputies, prevented even from leaving the Assembly, had to submit to this force and accept a Jacobin motion to expel about thirty of the leading members of the Girondins.

The expulsion of the Gironde, followed as it was by the departure of many alarmed deputies, gave the Jacobins control of the Convention. However, they were in a desperate situation, for the threat of foreign invasion was mounting. The Austrians from the north and the Prussians from the Rhine continued their advances and took three major fortresses in Italy. In the south, Spanish forces crossed the Pyrenean frontier and in the southeast the Piedmontese pushed back in Savoy.

Within France the rebellion of the Vendée was still dominant in the west and seemed likely to move against Paris. To this was now added a widespread outburst of protest from the provinces against the events of 2 June. Over sixty of the eighty-three departments denounced the highhandedness of the Parisians who presumed to interfere with the elected representatives of the nation.

Important cities like Bordeaux, Lyons, Marseilles and Toulouse went beyond protest, turning out local Jacobins and encouraging armed resistance. This stimulated forces elsewhere hostile to the revolution to emerge. In Toulon a royalist faction secured control and handed over the port, along with a large part of the French fleet, to the British. In Paris, the popular hero Marat was assassinated in July by the Girondin sympathizer Charlotte Corday. In these circumstances moderates no less than Jacobins felt that only resolute and ruthless action would serve.

At the same time the Jacobins were under constant pressure from below, from the *sans-culottes* who had put them in power. The Jacobins had promptly drafted a democratic constitution in June which along with universal suffrage, direct elections and the referendum recognized society's obligation to provide work for the able-bodied, relief for the needy and education for all. But this, though promising, was not to be implemented immediately.

With the news of defeats and betrayals, mounting inflation and disrupted food supplies popular tension grew. Throughout July and August, the assembly was bombarded with requests from the sections for effective legislation on prices, for stiffer laws against aristocrats and hoarders and for severe punishments against offenders.

The clamour reached a peak early in September with large-scale demonstrations and a mass march on the Assembly. The Jacobins, apart from any special sympathy for a more 'popular' revolution, recognized their crucial importance. These demonstrations represented a danger in that they might, in an excess of furious impatience, sweep away the whole Convention, Jacobins and all; but they also represented, despite their drawbacks, the most zealous forces which the revolution possessed at this desperate time. It was only in order to keep their support that the Convention introduced price controls on food and a wide range of consumer goods, levied a forced loan on the rich and sanctioned the establishment of 'revolutionary armies' to forage for food. The demonstrators also wanted strict laws against suspects and hoarders of food and revolutionary justice meted out against offenders. Now, under the twin pressures of

Above, the murder of Marat in his bath by the aristocratically-born Charlotte Corday in July 1793. She was later guillotined.

Top, the massacre of some 6,000 citizens of Lyons in December 1793 after a brief counter-revolutionary rising, which had required a two-month siege to break. The city was then deprived of its name, being known as Ville-sans-nom.

Opposite, Georges Jacques Danton (1759–94), an early advocate of the French Revolutionary Wars and radical opponent of the monarchy; he later criticized Robespierre for his dictatorship, was tried for conspiracy and executed. Musée Carnavalet, Paris.

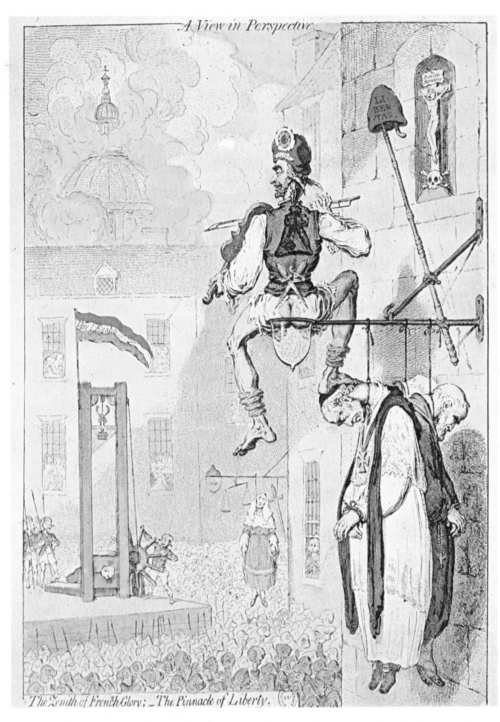

A View in Perspective

The Zenith of French Glory; — The Pinnacle of Liberty.

which, month after month, returned the same twelve Jacobins to the Committee, and debate dwindled.

In earlier regimes the assemblies had been the centres of activity, where the main struggles had been fought out in long verbal battles. Ministers had been shadows. Now that the executive committee was the centre of the real work, the Assembly had to listen to the Convention's explanations and pass the decrees they required. The committee wielded enormous powers over the whole field of domestic and foreign policy, though police matters were left to another body, the Committee of General Security. Earlier ideals of decentralization likewise were abandoned as the Committee steadily strengthened the central government's grip over all local institutions.

In December the respresentatives on mission, hitherto vested with wide powers to eliminate trouble makers, were brought directly under the Committee, their authority limited to carrying out the Committee's policies. The local institutions and departments were bypassed, the smaller cantons and communes made the big units. In each of them the central government appointed national agents who were supposed to report to the government every ten days. The Paris commune had its powers restricted. The 'revolutionary' armies of *sans-culottes*, invaluable in the summer, were disbanded, the committees of the sections put under central government and their leading officials paid or transformed from popular spokesmen to government agents. And along with executive power went ruthlessness. In September 'Terror' became the rule as the processes of revolutionary justice were made more swift and summary and the instruments—revolutionary tribunals and committees—used more fiercely.

The Committee of Public Safety

The direction and the driving force of revolutionary government came from the Committee of Public Safety, the twelve-man team which, with very few changes, ruled France for twelve crucial months. All deputies and Jacobins, they were mainly men of that provincial urban professional middle class which played the major role in all the revolutionary assemblies. Hérault de Sechelles, the chief architect of the Jacobin constitution of 1793, was an exception; he was a former aristocrat and parlementaire. Lazare Carnot, mainly responsible for the organization of the armies of the revolution, was a former captain of engineers; Claude Prieur de la Côte d'Or, another military engineer, worked closely with Carnot.

Robert Lindet, a lawyer from Normandy, had the special task of supervising supplies and provisions and was assisted by Pierre Louis Prieur de la Morne. Jeanbon Saint-André, a Protestant clergyman and once

a national emergency and popular clamour, a new kind of revolutionary government began to take shape and each successive stage was to bring about a new alignment of forces.

The climax of the Revolution

The twelve months from July 1793 to July 1794 saw the Revolution at its most dramatic. Under the rule of Robespierre and the Jacobins it reached its peak of effective government in the Committee of Public Safety, of ruthlessness in the Reign of Terror and of radicalism in the alliance of Jacobins and *sans-culottes*.

In these circumstances the Jacobin leaders recognized that only the most resolute and ruthless action would be effective. Besides, they had no intention of putting their new democratic constitution into operation; it was for show and for the future, not for immediate use. Its suspension was made official in early October when the Convention decided that the government was to be revolutionary, that is of an emergency character, until the coming of peace.

The main instruments of revolutionary government were already in existence from the spring; the executive committees of Public Safety and General Security and the Revolutionary Tribunals and Committees. What the Jacobins did was to wield them with a new determination and ability. The Convention remained legislative authority and appointed the main Executive Committee of Public Safety by monthly election. But previous notions of a weak executive and the separation of powers were dismissed, for the Jacobins dominated the Convention

a sea captain, now concerned himself primarily with reshaping the navy. Bertrand Barère from Toulouse, another lawyer, acted as a kind of public relations man for the Committee, expounding and defending its policies in the Convention. Billaud-Varennes, who had been many things in his time, including both a pamphleteer and a teacher, and Collot d'Herbois, actor and playwright, were both extremists with a strong influence in the Commune and the sections. Both were appointed after the extremist agitations of early September, probably to reassure the popular forces and to strengthen the Committee's connections in that important region.

Georges Couthon, a crippled lawyer from the Auvergne, and Antoine Saint-Just, a twenty-five-year-old law graduate, both spent much time on special missions. Couthon, a gentler man than some of his speeches suggested, and Saint-Just, cold and arrogant, were also the close associates and admirers of the dominant figure of the Committee, Maximilien Robespierre.

It was Robespierre, the lawyer from Arras, who came to seem the embodiment of the revolutionary government. He was in his early thirties, a small man, not much over five feet, with a thin, pale face and a harsh voice. He was always neatly dressed, fastidious in his tastes and reserved and withdrawn in manner. A bachelor, he lived in modest lodgings, indulged in little social life and had few friends. He was no demagogue and could hardly have looked less like a *sans-culotte*, but he inspired popular trust because of his incorruptibility.

By his adherence to principles and his constant praise of the common man, he had established a reputation as a zealous revolutionary, a formidable parliamentarian and a popular hero. Likewise his criticism of the constitution in 1791, his opposition to Brissot in the Jacobin Club in 1792, and his championship of the Mountain and the popular cause in the Convention had all kept him prominently in the public eye. Despite this, he had no official supremacy in the Committee, nor was he its dictator. The people in the Committee worked harmoniously as a body and met daily, from early morning till late at night. All those who were in Paris came along and took part in discussions, and if they agreed on the policies signed the documents. Dissenters abstained. They were determined men, set on saving the republic from counter-revolution at home and outside enemies, and all were ready and responsible for whatever measures were needed to achieve this end.

It was here, in the Committee and the Convention, that Robespierre had a stronger influence than any other politician. On the Committee he assumed no special 'department' and never went on any mission to visit the armies or the provinces. He was thus constantly on the spot, assiduous in Committee attendance and free to brood over

general policies and to make speeches in which he discoursed on the principles and character of the true Republic. He was the Committee's most conspicuous spokesman in the Assembly and the Jacobin Club, and his integrity and dedication were never in doubt: 'He will go far', Mirabeau had prophesied, 'he believes what he says.'

The Terror

The new regime showed its resolution in its vigorous onslaughts against the counter-revolutionary forces within France. Its

Above, a revolutionary poster, proclaiming liberty, equality and fraternity and demonstrating the unity of interest between the people and the army. The Jacobins, whose symbol was the cockade cap, insisted on the need for radical reform and the efficacy of naked power.

Opposite, an English satire on the excesses of the French Revolution, suggesting that the fine rhetoric of the politicians meant little more than a violent attack on the Church. English support for the early days of the Revolution soon evaporated.

great weapon was terror, the use of fierce intimidation to destroy or deter the republic's foes and reassure its supporters. Hitherto terrorism had flared sporadically in the shape of lynch law, as in the prison massacres of 1792. From September 1793, when the Convention had decreed that 'terror was the order of the day', it became official government policy. There should be no restraint, said Saint-Just, for 'between the people and its enemies there is only the sword'. In the same month the Law of Suspects decreed the immediate arrest of all persons suspected of disloyalty, a crime it defined in broad and vague terms, and the Revolutionary Tribunal was reorganized to deal more effectively with the increasing number of those accused of treachery.

Under the terror about 40,000 people were executed and many times that number imprisoned. It was concerned with disloyalty wherever found, not with social class, and the victims came from all walks of life. About ten percent of them were nobles, six percent clergy, fifteen percent middle class and the great majority poorer classes and peasantry. Some were executed under the economic laws against hoarding and speculation, but the majority suffered for broadly political reasons, armed rebellions, voting against recruitment or advocating counter-revolutionary opinions.

The weight of the new regime also made itself felt in those districts which had risen in rebellion. Throughout the autumn Government armies steadily reduced the rebel centres. Marseilles surrendered in August, Bordeaux and Lyons in October, and Toulon was recaptured in December after an artillery bombardment from an 'officer of outstanding merit', the young Napoleon Bonaparte. In the Vendée, insurrection continued to smoulder for years, but

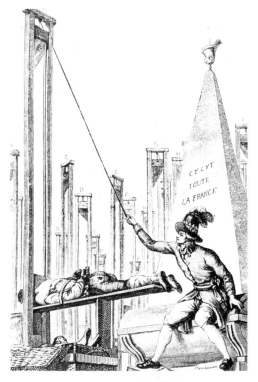

the main rebel armies were scattered in October and December by experienced republican troops. Behind the armies came the deputies on mission to punish the rebels. In Lyons the guillotine did not work fast enough for Collot d'Herbois; he called in firing squads to its aid, and then cannon. The victims were herded in batches, mowed down by cannon fire and shovelled into graves. The houses of the wealthy were destroyed and the name of Lyons struck off the map: 'Lyons made war on liberty, Lyons no longer exists.' At Toulon, Barras and Fréron used firing squads for mass executions: 'Every day since our entry, 200

Toulonnais have been shot.' In the Vendée, Carrier executed Republican vengeance by drowning 2,000 rebels in the Loire, and having another 3,000 shot. Jacobins on the local revolutionary committees throughout France acted as agents, unearthing and denouncing suspects.

Throughout these same months when they were suppressing the internal enemies of the Republic, the Jacobins also had to conduct the war against invading armies on several fronts. Their achievement was astonishing and novel, a great drive to mobilize the nation's manpower and resources for the war effort. 'The Republic',

declared the Convention in August, 'is a great city in a state of siege: France must become one vast camp.' It proclaimed a *levée en masse* (mass mobilization); young men would go to the front, married men see to weapons and food and women make clothing and do hospital work. In fact the first age groups recruited, eighteen to twenty-five, produced barely half a million recruits.

To feed and equip new forces on this scale, the government had to play a bigger role in directing the economy. Under Lindet, a central food commission saw to the supply and distribution of food according to the needs of the armies and the regions of the country. Under Claude Prieur the munitions industry was directly controlled by the government. State factories were established, buildings commandeered, labour and materials requisitioned. Carnot speedily fashioned a new army and each unit of raw

men was seasoned with a few veterans. New tactics were introduced to make the most of their advantages of great numbers and high zeal. New young generals were promoted, and celebrated names made their appearance—Jourdan, Hoche, Pichegru, Bonaparte. By early 1794 France had a million men under arms and a dozen armies in the field. The Austrian advance from the north had been checked at Wattignies, the Spaniards driven back over their frontier, the Piedmontese pushed out of Savoy and the Prussians thrown back across the Rhine.

By the spring of 1794 the national emergency was receding, but the regime became more dictatorial, not less. Terror, instituted as a weapon against the counter-revolutionary enemies of the republic, was now wielded against the revolutionary critics of the government. Prominent among these were the left-wing extremists, linked

with the popular agitator, Jacques Hébert, who ran a notorious journal, the *Père Duchesne* and was influential in the commune, sections and popular societies of Paris. For the Hébertistes the revolution was still not popular enough. They wanted more measures to ease the social and economic hardships of the *sans-culottes* and more ruthless repression of those who exploited them. Even though inflation had been checked, prices remained high, wages were never high enough and controls never a complete success. They championed more direct action by the people, more scope for popular bodies to terrorize their enemies and more power for the people's revolutionary armies.

The Committee's response to this was increasingly cold. The Jacobins were more radical than other middle-class politicians, had more sympathy with the popular movement and were ready to make concessions.

They had introduced economic controls, abolished without compensation the remnants of seigneurial rights, made land purchase easier and furthered schemes for free education. Robespierre and Saint-Just had sponsored a large scheme for distributing the property of suspects among needy patriots, but they would not champion the interests of the *sans-culottes* exclusively, still less allow the control of the revolution to pass into their hands.

The Jacobins

The Jacobins' economic ideals were basically different from the *sans-culottes*: they envisaged a free enterprise economy, not one which, like that of the old regime, was choked with controls and restrictions. They were ready to introduce some controls, but these were merely temporary measures to meet the exigencies of a siege economy and the exceptional demands of a wartime emergency. They did not represent, as the *sans-culottes* were reminded, a desire to champion the exclusive interests of a particular class, by the fact that wages and prices were to be contained and labour strictly disciplined. Again the extremist campaigns were alarming and alienating the middle classes, and Jacobism needed to hold the support of these as well as of the *sans-culottes*.

Jacobins preferred to stress the unifying aspects not the divisive ones of class. For them the touchstone was the quality of man's patriotism and republicanism rather than his occupation or income. They had a suspicion of great wealth and a preference for the modest property-owner, but they did not intend any large redistribution of property, since this to them, as to the men of 1789, was an inviolable right. The Jacobins' dislike was directed mostly at the bad Republican rather than at the prosperous property owner. Moreover, the Jacobins now saw the scene from the point of view of a government. Popular pressure against earlier regimes, which the Jacobins had denounced as incompetent, selfish and reactionary was praiseworthy; against their own regime which was effective, enlightened and looked with wisdom to the best interests of all Frenchmen, it was unnecessary and undesirable. Democracy, explained Robespierre, did not mean that all the people in a vast gathering could participate directly in decisions or that a myriad of small discontented groups could blithely pursue their own fancies regardless of the rest. It meant that they returned delegates to an assembly which made decisions on their behalf; and, in practice, the revolutionary government's advance towards ever more centralized control was running quite counter to that more direct democracy in which the *sans-culottes* indulged. The independent activities of the sections, of 'revolutionary armies' and of unofficial terrorism, became objects of disapproval to an authoritarian

regime which desired prompt obedience and no rivals. It was ironic; no one had clamoured more loudly for, or done more to help to install, an effective government than the *sans-culottes*, but effective government meant a curb on *sans-culotte* freedom.

The Hébertiste movement was all the more unwelcome for adding to its usual activities a new campaign for dechristianization. The Jacobins generally, it is true, had little regard for traditional religion; they were enlightened rationalists and staunch anti-clericals. The Convention had readily adopted in October 1793 a new Republican calendar, with natural names for the months and a ten-day week: this broke the religious pattern of the year, obliterating Sundays, Saints' days and religious holidays. But unofficially the movement went further. In Paris, promoted by Hébert and the Commune, it spread into attacks on the clergy, compelling them to resign. Churches were plundered, ceremonies prohibited and statues destroyed. Mock processions aped those of the despised religion. The Commune closed down the churches or used them for secular celebrations, and busts of Voltaire and Rousseau were set up in place of statues of the saints.

The government feared this 'religious terror' would only upset much of their support and give counter-revolutionaries further arguments for discarding the revolution. In November 1793 the Feast of Reason was celebrated in Notre Dame with Reason represented by a woman of the streets, wearing a cap of liberty.

Robespierre in particular disliked it since he believed in God and insisted that there was an important place in the revolution for religion. He deplored impiety with the strongest epithet a revolutionary could use:

Above, the adoration of the goddess of Reason, in the form of an actress, in the nave of the cathedral of Notre Dame; this atheistic religion was opposed by Robespierre, who had its founder, Jacques Hébert, executed.

Opposite top, the siege of Toulon in 1793, after the royalists had given the city up to the English. The siege was notable for the part played by the young Napoleon Bonaparte in recapturing the city.

Opposite bottom left, the bombardment of Lyon by the Republicans in October 1793; at this stage royalist groups had won control of large areas of south and west France, and severe repression was needed to restore republican authority to these regions.

Opposite bottom right, the festival of the regeneration of nature, in August 1793. After the abolition of Christianity by the Revolution, several alternative religions were established, including the cult of Reason, set up by Hébert, and the cult of the Supreme Being, instituted by Robespierre.

'Atheism is aristocratic!' This proved to be an additional source of confusion at a time when the enemy was moving steadily nearer.

The downfall of Robespierre

To halt the drift towards atheism and social disruption a deistic religion was devised—the cult of the Supreme Being. But there were other dangers, for the Hébertistes by their speculation had emptied the Treasury and weakened the state. Desmoulins in *Le Vieux Cordelier* mounted a counter-attack on them not only for their atheism but also for their treachery. Moreover, the Committee of Public Safety was now afraid that it would lose power to the Commune and to the Cordeliers Club which the Hébertistes dominated. Danton for his part wanted the machine of Terror dismantled, the end of controls and a negotiated peace. When in March, therefore, the Hébertistes threatened an insurrection on the model of that of June or September 1793, Robespierre and Danton arranged for their arrest and execution. Six days later Danton, Desmoulins and Hérault went to the guillotine (April 1794) on a charge of conspiracy with foreign financiers. It was an easy action to perform, but it was also significant, for this was the Terror at its height, the summit of Robespierre's dominance. It was to last for just three and a half months.

On 22 Prairial (10 June 1794) Robespierre persuaded the Convention to pass a law which deprived prisoners of the aid of defending counsel and made death the sole punishment. He also sought to control wages in a desperate effort to control the economy. Yet the need for such terror and discipline began to seem more and more unnecessary as foreign armies retreated and France's frontiers seemed secure. In May Pichegru beat the Austrians, in June Jourdan routed Coburg at Fleurus, the British fell back into Holland and the Austrians to the Rhine. There was a growing fear of Robespierre and a bitter hatred of his parade of civic virtue and his pride in his own incorruptibility. The cult of the Supreme Being was as unpopular as the cult of Reason, and the great procession in his honour from the Tuileries to the Champ de Mars, organized by the painter David on 8 June, alienated many.

The climax approached when Robespierre recalled many representatives on mission who now began to fear for their lives. However, the real break occurred on 8th Thermidor (26 July 1794) when he rashly spoke in the Convention of defending himself by one last act, namely the removal of a group of enemies whom he did not specify by name. The next day he was shouted down and arrested. He went to the guillotine on 10 Thermidor (28 July): eighty-seven members of the Commune soon followed him.

The Thermidorians

It is wrong to describe the Thermidorian reaction as the end of the Revolution, but it was certainly its climax. Barère and Barras assumed that the government would continue intact, for 10 Thermidor was for them but a 'partial commotion'. Within a month, however, the apparatus of the Terror was abandoned; the law of 22 Prairial was repealed; within six months the regulation of wages and prices was scrapped; within nine months the surviving Girondins returned; within a year Barère himself and his colleagues were on their way to Devil's Island. The Thermidorians when joined by the released Girondins and a few royalists emerged as a 'republic of proprietors', led by Barras and Fréron, Cambon and Siéyès. They said that they sought a return to 'the principles of 1789' but swept along by the tide, the Jacobins were hunted down and the Jacobin Club closed. A new terror, but of a different political complexion, had been unleashed. However, press and theatre were free again; and in the salons the style was set by Thérésa Tallien and the widow Josephine Beauharnais. However, as prices rose, so did unemployment, and in March and May 1795 popular insurrections erupted, with demands for the re-enactment of the Law of the Maximum and the 1793 Constitution—'Bread and the Constitution of 1793'. For a moment the

Above, the army of the Prince of Condé (1736–1818), made up of French counter-revolutionary activists; the army fought for the Austrians until 1797 when Condé joined the Russians. It was dissolved in 1801.

Top, the closing of the Jacobin club in July 1794, as a result of hostility to the severity of the Reign of Terror.

Opposite top, the Battle of Fleurus in southern Belgium, where the Austrians were decisively defeated by the revolutionary armies. It was the first battle in which balloons were used for reconnaissance. Musée de l'Armée, Paris.

Opposite bottom, the arrest of Robespierre in July 1794 by members of the Committee of General Safety; in the struggle he tried to shoot himself and was wounded in the jaw. He was guillotined shortly afterwards.

Date	Internal history	Foreign policy	Events in Europe	Date	Internal history	Foreign policy	Events in Europe
1789	Meeting of the Estates-General (5 May) Oath of the Tennis Court (20 June) Storming of the Bastille (14 July) Abolition of privileges (3–4 August) Declaration of the Rights of Man (26 August)		Act of Union in Sweden Revolt of Austrian Netherlands Establishment of Belgian Republic	1792	Storming of the Tuileries (10 August) September Massacres (2–5 September) First session of the Convention (20 September) Abolition of the monarchy (21 September) Trial of the king (11 December)	War with Austria (20 April) The Brunswick Manifesto (25 July) Battle of Valmy (20 September) Battle of Jémappes (6 November) Conquest of Belgium	Treaty of Berlin between Austria and Prussia Accession of Francis II of Austria Assassination of Gustavus II of Sweden End of Russo-Turkish War
1790	Civil Constitution of the Clergy Priests required to swear allegiance to the Civil Constitution	Repudiation of the Family Compact	Austrian forces overthrow Belgian Republic Pope condemns Civil Constitution of Clergy End of Russo-Swedish War Accession of Leopold II of Austria	1793	Execution of the King (21 January) Rising in La Vendée Committee of Public Safety Constitution of the Year I	Annexation of Nice (31 January) War with Britain (1 February) Battle of Wattignies (16 October) Bonaparte recaptures Toulon from British (19 December)	Formation of First Coalition against France Meeting of Polish Diet Second Partition of Poland
1791	Flight of the king Constitution approved by Constituent Assembly and ratified by the king Legislative Assembly meets	Ultimatum to the Elector of Trier Avignon annexed to France	Austria and Turkey sign treaty of peace Declaration of Pillnitz Turkey defeated by Russia				

'Furies of the Guillotine' reappeared. These were ruthlessly suppressed, and in June 1795 the Parisian *sans-culottes* finally ceased to be a major factor in Revolutionary politics. What Generals Pichegru, in April, and Menou, in May, did to the mob in the *faubourgs* of Paris, General Napoleon Bonaparte with a 'whiff of grapeshot' did to the Parisian Royalists when they rose in October. Significantly the *sans-culottes* did not rise with them, for they were finished politically and the Revolution now became safe for the men of property.

Dominated by the Thermidorians, the Convention completed a new Constitution, the Constitution of the Year III, in August 1795. It was designed for the propertied classes and was largely the work of Boissy D'Anglas. A single-chamber assembly was now seen to be dangerous so the Legislature was now to consist of two houses—a Council of Five Hundred aged thirty or over which was to initiate legislation and a Council of Ancients numbering 250 who had to be over forty and married, presumably because this made them more responsible, which had the right to veto. Executive authority was vested in five Directors elected by the legislative councils—each holding office for five years. They could neither sit in the Councils nor initiate laws, but they controlled the army and the police, the civil service and foreign affairs. The departments were left as they were, but each was controlled by a commissioner appointed by the Directory—a forerunner of Napoleon's prefect. The deputies were chosen by an elaborate system of indirect election, and property qualifications were needed for the primary and secondary assemblies. And though liberty of speech and of worship were spoken of as sacrosanct, the press was tightly curbed, and political clubs and the right of insurrection were forbidden. The attempt was clear: to create a balanced government in order to prevent the dictatorship of an assembly, a committee or of a single man. Its very rigidity proved to be its undoing.

Chapter 32

From Revolution to Empire

In retrospect, the Directory is inevitably seen as an interlude between the Revolution and the inevitable dictatorship. And the post-1799 Bonapartist press destroyed what little was left of its reputation. It saw itself, of course, quite differently, as the end of an ugly road. Although Barras was unscrupulous, immoral and lazy, the rest were men of some worth. Fearing dictatorship, of one man or of a mob, they set up a mixed government. Also, to guarantee continuity and stability and to prevent new waves of unrest from left to right, they stipulated that 500 of the 700 legislators must come from the Convention itself. Those who were re-elected were known as 'perpetuals' who saw themselves carrying on the Revolution against royalism, continuing the war and enforcing the October 1795 decrees against clergy and *émigrés*. Because they feared dictatorship, annual elections were prescribed, but these only served to guarantee unrest, dissension and disorder.

The new members were moderates who wanted an end to the war and a constitutional government. A few of them were monarchists; many more would have settled for limited constitutional government. Generals Menou and Pichegru made no secret of their royalism.

The Directory could perhaps have survived this political division. It could not survive economic chaos and corruption. There was wild inflation because the *mandats*, issued in April 1796 to replace the *assignats*, had soon fallen to one percent of their face value. The state was internally bankrupt by September 1797, and all classes suffered. The Directory was in part induced to continue the war not for frontier defence, but in order to draw the treasures of foreign countries into France. Thus Napoleon took 750,000 francs and part of his portrait gallery from the Duke of Modena, 21,000,000 francs from the kingdom of Naples and 20,000,000 francs and the promise of more from the pope. Had the war stopped, the French army of a quarter of a million men would have had to be paid from State funds, and these were totally inadequate. It lived on foreign grain and foreign gold.

To financial chaos was added corruption. Many of the supplies Paris required from

the provinces never arrived because of smuggling and inefficient administration. Bridges and roads fell into disrepair and the Paris mobs lived on doles. Bids for peace from Britain met a request from Barras for £500,000 before negotiations began; Talleyrand made a similar request in the XYZ affair when John Adams made overtures in 1798.

In this context, the Babeuf conspiracy is understandable. Ever since 1798 'Gracchus' Babeuf had advocated an agrarian law for the common sharing of goods. He was the first and perhaps the sole French Revolutionary socialist. In the winter of 1795–6 he planned to overthrow the Directory by force in a conspiracy joined by ex-Jacobins; his plan was based on a series of radiating groups and depended on the rising of the *sans-culottes*. Again, as in 1795, they failed

Above, the Battle of Aboukir, or the Battle of the Nile (August 1798), an important English victory in which Nelson destroyed the French fleet and virtually ended Napoleon's attempt to win control of the Middle East and to cut Britain off from India.

Top, Napoleon dismissing the Council of Five Hundred on 18 Brumaire (9 November 1799); by this act he overthrew the government of the Directory and set up the Consulate instead.

Opposite top, a meeting of the Directory in 1796, which was soon accused both of inactivity and of corruption.

Opposite bottom, the festival of the foundation of the republic celebrated on 22 September 1797; this re-enactment of Roman chariot races emphasizes how much the revolutionaries modelled themselves on the example of the Roman republicans.

to respond. A police spy reported the plot in May 1796 to Carnot and, as a result, Babeuf and some forty of his associates were either shot or guillotined. The same fate overtook the conspiracy of the royalist Abbé Brottier in January 1797. But Babouvisme was to live on in the writings of his friend, the Tuscan Philippe Buonarroti.

In the 1797 elections there came an influx of royalists into the Assembly and the great mass of 'perpetuals' was eliminated. Pichegru was elected President of the Five Hundred and Barbe-Marbois, another royalist, President of the Ancients. Measures were passed favouring priests and the relatives of *emigrés*, but in the Directory the two pro-royalists, Carnot and Barthélemy, were still outnumbered, and the Triumvirate, fearing a royalist coup, appealed to the generals to save the Revolution. Napoleon, who had swept through northern Italy in 1796 and was forcing its treasure back into France, had by the spring of 1797 driven the Austrians north from the Piave and Isonzo, when he responded to the call; so did Hoche at the head of the Army of the Sambre-et-Meuse. Augereau, Napoleon's lieutenant, marched on Paris; Barthélemy and Pichegru were arrested; the Councils were purged of over 200 deputies, and sixty-five were exiled to the 'dry guillotine' of Guiana. Carnot, the only lucky one, escaped to Switzerland. The date was 18 Fructidor (7 September). It was the first of the coups, and the beginning of the heavy indebtedness to Napoleon.

The rise of Napoleon

From now on, the Directory dominated over the Legislature and severe measures were taken against priests and returned *émigrés*. In the coup d'état of 22 Floreal (11 May 1798) the Directors annulled the elections of their opponents and nominated their own deputies. Blessed by good harvests, the price of grain fell for the first time in a decade. But in fact the Directory, despite a powerless legislature, faced a rising tide of unpopularity, because of religious persecution, the Law of Hostages which provided that relatives of *émigrés* might be seized as hostages and because of the maritime war with Britain which had forced up prices and kept tariffs high. The law of Conscription of September 1798 made all unmarried Frenchmen between twenty and twenty-five liable for service, but it was bitterly unwelcome and evaded. Added to this the French armies in 1799 met defeat at Stockach, Magnano and Novi.

Meanwhile, fortune favoured Napoleon. In 1797 he had formed the Ligurian Republic (Genoa) and the Cisalpine (Lombardy). At Campo Formio he obtained a guarantee from Austria of the Rhine as the boundary of France, thus securing Belgium and acquired a bridgehead at Mainz. Venice was given to Austria and in June 1797 a Venetian fleet in French service seized the Ionian

Islands and aroused Napoleon's eastern ambitions. With an invasion of Britain a very risky enterprise, and with his power rising dangerously, the Directory resolved to attack Britain through the east and saw the Ionian Islands as a base against Egypt. In May 1798 Bonaparte sailed from Toulon with 35,000 men, took Malta in June and landed at Alexandria in July.

This only further alarmed the Directory and to make matters worse the Belgian Provinces suddenly revolted. In the April 1799 elections, two-thirds of the government candidates were defeated and Siéyès replaced the senior director, Reubell. Siéyès wanted a new constitution and, with the support of Barras, he carried through a parliamentary coup, offering as justification the defeats on the frontiers and the rallying cry of *la patrie en danger*. The other three directors were

persuaded to resign, and the new Director, Ducos, joined Siéyès and gave him the majority he sought. Siéyès was backed by a group who were to prove themselves in a distinct way perpetuals—Murat, Talleyrand and Fouché. Siéyès then looked for a general sympathetic to the cause of the Republic in danger. He approached Joubert, but was killed at Novi. As for Moreau and Bernadotte, they refused. At this juncture—when in fact the tide was turning on the French frontier, since in September Masséna had defeated Suvorov in Italy and the Duke of York was defeated in Holland—Napoleon landed at Fréjus. His campaign in the east had not been a success: he had been blocked by Sir Sidney Smith at Acre, and he had abandoned his troops on the Nile, who now saw him as a deserter. But his landing and his timing were providential, and he had

about him the glamour of victory and a Jacobin past. He was, he liked to say, the child of the Revolution. He was also to be its destroyer.

The Consulate

Napoleon's plans almost went awry. The Legislature was persuaded to meet at Saint-Cloud on the grounds that the Paris mob was unreliable. However, when Napoleon appeared in person, with his grenadiers massed outside, there were many protests about military dictatorship, and such was the poor impression that he made that he was shouted down. It was only his brother Lucien, presiding over the Five Hundred, who saved the day by summoning the troops to drive the legislators from the hall. A remnant of this body declared the Directory abolished and a provisional consulate of Ducos, Siéyès and Napoleon established, until such time as a new Constitution could be drawn up. It was the 18 Brumaire of the Year VIII (9 November 1799).

But Siéyès had made a mistake. He had expected Napoleon to select his senior officials along Washington's lines and to play the role of a president above politics. In fact Bonaparte made himself the First Consul and the power-house of the state. In December 1799 yet another Constitution appeared, the Constitution of the Year VIII. Siéyès and Ducos were persuaded to resign and were replaced by silent allies in Lebrun and Cambacérès. All three were to hold office for ten years and be re-eligible, but only the First Consul could appoint and dismiss officials and promulgate laws: the second and third had only a 'consultative voice'.

The Council of State was the key to the

system. This constituted the group of experts and officials who prepared the laws and ran the government. It was the same with Napoleon as it had been with an earlier *grand monarque*: the Council was the inner bureaucracy, appointed, dependent, ultra-conscientious, loyal and efficient. It appointed prefects and mayors and through them Paris governed France; local government was bereft of its powers and died. In and around the Council were the lieutenants of the Master: Talleyrand, foreign minister (1799–1807), Berthier, war minister (1800–07) and Fouché, police minister (1799–1802 and 1804–10). No other institution matched the Council. The tribuneship could not initiate measures and was abolished in 1807

Above, the return of Napoleon from Egypt in 1798; despite the defeat at the Battle of the Nile, the expedition had captured the imagination of the French in its bold strategic intentions.

Top, Napoleon's fleet capturing Malta in 1798 from the Knights Hospitallers, as a first step to establishing French superiority in the eastern Mediterranean.

Opposite top, the French armies taking works of art from Venice to Paris in 1797, before handing the city over to Austria.

Opposite below, Napoleon's army crossing the Alps in 1800, surprising the Austrians and defeating them at the Battle of Marengo.

and the Legislative Body of 300 members had no powers of debate. It was true that the Senate of eighty members, all over forty and appointed for life, had powers to annul laws, but this power waned, and in the Year XII the Senate was nominated by Napoleon and no longer limited in number. In theory there was universal suffrage, but in fact the Senate nominated the members of the assemblies from a 'national list', itself chosen from 'departmental lists' and from communal lists in an elaborate system of indirect election.

The Press was tightly controlled, and education became a department of state. Even the salons were disciplined and Madame de Stael was banished from Paris. This was absolutism as naked, centralized and thorough as Louis XIV could have wished. He would have found it familiar and acceptable. The prefects were his *intendants* but more powerful, and they are still there. Napoleon was not only the child of the Revolution but also the heir to the best in the government of the Bourbons.

The *condottiere*

There is a curious anomaly about intense nationalism; it is apt to be felt most sharply on the perimeter of the nation. Thus Hitler, the great pan-German, was born across the frontier in Austria; Stalin, who was an autocrat of all the Russias in the line of the Tsars, was born in Georgia; and Napoleon, perhaps the greatest of all Frenchmen, was born French only by accident and raised on the fringes of France.

Perhaps the truest description of him was that he was neither truly a nationalist nor a revolutionary but that he was at heart a *condottiere* of genius, a leader of men. His methods were always more Italian than French, the leanings always Machiavellian. The advice he gave Eugene he followed himself; base your statecraft on dissimulation and strive only to be feared.

Napoleon Bonaparte was thirty on 18 Brumaire. He was born in 1769 in Ajaccio, Corsica, a year after Genoa had sold its stormy island to France. Only a few months before his birth, French troops had crushed the Corsican rebellion led by Pasquale Paoli. Bonaparte was the second son in a large family of the lesser nobility, and there were four brothers and three sisters, all dominated by their formidable mother, *née* Litizia Ramolino, Madame Mère. His father saw him from the outset as a man of genius: he was lean and pinched in appearance but with a piercing hawk-like gaze, great will-power and intensity. He went with a scholarship to the military school at Brienne and the École Militaire in Paris, and he went with a purpose; to free Corsica. He studied hard with this intent and was utterly out of tune with the rich sons of the nobility around him who had come there by easy roads and with no such design. He was commissioned a second lieutenant of artil-

lery in 1785; and he read assiduously, not least Rousseau and the *philosophes*.

Like Caesar before him and like Hitler after, the army was his ladder, his tool and his passion. He wrote a tract or two, but his weapon was the sword, not the pen. He exploited the Revolution and saw it as his cause and made it at once Corsican and French. In 1792 and 1793 he tried to seize Ajaccio for the Revolution, only to be defeated by Paoli fighting for Corsican independence and prepared to call on monarchists and anglophiles as allies. In 1793 the Bonaparte family was expelled from Corsica, and the France of the Revolution now became his own cause—apart, that is, than himself. His batteries helped to expel the British from Toulon in 1793, and his commander, du Teil, gave him most of the credit. By the age of twenty-four he was a brigadier. On Robespierre's death, he lost his mentor, so he attached himself to Barras, the least reputable of the Directory. Vendémiaire and the 'whiff of grapeshot' brought him the command of the Army of the Interior, the rank of major-general and the hand of Josephine de Beauharnais, one of Barras' discarded mistresses. He may well have loved her for a while, if he had room for any other passions than war. She may have grown in her fashion to love him, for there was an incandescent quality here and immense physical magnetism. However, four days after the marriage, Napoleon was on his way to Italy. The victories of 1796— Lodi, Castiglione and Arcole—and of 1797 —Rivoli—to name only the most important of the twenty-six battles won in twelve months made him a revolutionary hero at a time of economic discontent and political frustration and, in a military sense, were his greatest achievements. He dominated northern Italy as far as Rimini, occupied Florence and Leghorn, compelled the British to evacuate Corsica and merged Milan, Modena and Bologna into the Cisalpine Republic. At Campo Formio the Machiavellian emerged: he gave much of the Venetian Republic to Austria, in return for the Ionian Islands, an advance base for a campaign in the East. To the Corsican, the Venetians, like everyone else, were expendable. And there followed the Egyptian campaign.

Napoleon rendered immense service to France. But the Napoleonic legend, which via Louis and Napoleon became a legacy and via Boulanger, Pétain and de Gaulle a heavy liability, is bound up with the autocrat and the adventurer and battles won on foreign soil. The idea of *La gloire* in French history goes back, of course, long before Brumair, but the first, overwhelming image of Napoleon is of the conqueror.

Originally this was not his intention, for, on becoming First Consul, he had offered terms of peace to Britain and to Austria, the surviving members of the Second Coalition, only to have them scorned, for the Austrians were now dominant in North Italy except for Genoa, which they were besieging. Napoleon dispatched Moreau across the Rhine and he drove the army commanded by Kray back to Ulm. He himself crossed the St Bernard Pass, entered Milan and struck at Melas's army in the rear. Genoa had already surrendered, its streets piled with corpses from disease and famine. But at Marengo (June 1800) the tide had turned. Helped by Desaix's corps—and by Desaix's own death in action—Napoleon won back North Italy in a single day and the Austrians again abandoned Genoa, Piedmont and Milan. By July, Moreau occupied Minden and in December had won the Battle of Hohenlinden, Brune and Macdonald's joint army then moving on Vienna. The emperor was forced to make peace at Lunéville on 9 February 1801. Lunéville destroyed all

Above, the Battle of Marengo, fought in June 1800, was an important victory for Napoleon, destroying the Austrian threat to France from north Italy and beginning an attack on Habsburg power that led to the abolition of the Holy Roman Empire in 1806. Château de Versailles.

Opposite, Napoleon Bonaparte (1769–1821), painted by Gerard; Napoleon's genius was to take the chaos of France during the 1790s and turn its energy entirely to his own will.

that was left of the Holy Roman Empire, which Voltaire had said was neither holy, roman nor an empire. Austria ceded to France all territory west of the Rhine, including Belgium, and also recognized the independence of the new republics, the Cisalpine and Ligurian in Italy, the Batavian (Holland) and the Helvetic (Swiss), all of which were formed in the image of France. The Adige became the frontier between France and Austria in North Italy, and Austria accepted the right of France to intervene in Germany in the affairs of the princes. The minor states of Germany were now as much at the mercy of Napoleon as they had been the puppets of Richelieu 160 years before. To save herself, Vienna abandoned Germany: and this too was to be a bitter legacy. The Tsar Paul became the friend of France and revived the Armed Neutrality of Russia, Sweden and Denmark against Britain. In March 1801 Spain ceded Louisiana to France and plans were made for a great empire in the Caribbean. But the assassination of Paul in March allowed Alexander I to make peace with Britain: and Nelson's victory at Copenhagen destroyed Napoleon's attempt to wreck Britain's trade with the Baltic and the North.

By 1802 Britain had lost almost all her allies. If she had averted a direct French invasion and thwarted Napoleon in Egypt, the National Debt had doubled and there was starvation. She controlled the sea but seemed powerless to stop France on land: it was a war of whale versus elephant. And so a truce was made at Amiens in March 1802. France had withdrawn from Egypt in 1801; she agreed to restore Malta to the Knights and to evacuate Naples. All of these were but a recognition of facts. Britain surrendered all her own conquests except Trinidad, which had been Spain's, and Sri Lanka, which had been Holland's. 'A

peace which all men are glad of', said Sheridan, 'but no man can be proud of.' It was a triumph as well as a truce for Napoleon, and even if it was short-lived, it was the first time that France had been at peace in a decade. It was the high point of Bonapartism. In August he made himself a Consul for life, in a plebiscite that gave him 3,500,000 votes, against only 8,300 who had the courage to say 'No!' The new constitution gave him the right to choose his successor and to amend the constitution, to make treaties and to dissolve the Assemblies.

Thus fortified he looked west. A French army was sent to Santo Domingo and the negro revolutionary Toussaint l'Ouverture was seized and sent to France and execution. But his followers fought a bloody war against the new Imperialism, and what they failed to do yellow fever abetted for there were over 20,000 French deaths within a year. These facts, and the fear of a revival of war with Britain, led to the abandonment of the dream and the sale of Louisiana to Jefferson's emissaries. Thwarted in the west, Napoleon turned back to Europe. He became, in his own person, president of the Cisalpine Republic and master of Lombardy, which was renamed the Italian Republic. He annexed Piedmont, Elba and Parma and strengthened his French forces in Holland and Italy—all in denial of the terms of Lunéville. In April, he sought to close to British commerce all the ports which he controlled. He published reports that indicated a resumption of the war in the east. Britain protested, and in May 1803 the war was resumed—the War of the Third Coalition. More than ever it was the land giant versus the mistress of the seas.

War brought with it the threat of internal sabotage, treason and plot. Napoleon claimed that the Count of Artois alone was maintaining sixty assassins in Paris. In Feb-

Above, the Battle of Copenhagen in April 1801, in which the British fleet of Hyde Parker and Horatio Nelson destroyed the Danish fleet, shortly after Denmark had joined the League of Armed Neutrality. According to this its members – Prussia, Russia, Sweden and Denmark – refused to allow the British to search neutral vessels.

Opposite, Napoleon Bonaparte at the Battle of Arcole in 1796, in a painting by Antoine Jean Gros. The battle represented an important victory over the Austrians in Italy. Musée du Louvre, Paris.

ruary 1804, the plot of Georges Cadoudal and General Pichegru to murder Napoleon and restore Artois (the later Charles X) was discovered. A month later, the young Duke of Enghien was kidnapped by French troops on the neutral territory of Baden, brought to Paris and executed on the false charge of having been involved in the Cadoudal-Pichegru plot. And so, in May 1804, and in the interests of the state, Napoleon became emperor. This time 3,500,000 were for and only 2,500 against. On 2 December 1804, the Corsican heir of all the Bourbons took the crown of Charlemagne from the hands of Pope Pius VII and put it on his own head. And as David's canvas portrays, a stiff and high ceremonial settled on the parvenu court. The Legion of Honour had been established in May 1802. There were grandiloquent titles, and all the Bonapartes were honoured: Joseph was Grand Elector and Louis Grand Constable—and these were but preludes to even greater honours, for all of Napoleon's brothers, except Lucien, later became kings. Sixteen generals became Marshals of France, and Murat, the ally of Vendémiaire, became Grand Admiral. Napoleon was to create, honour and endow princes and senators: 31 dukes, 388 counts, 1,090 barons and 1,500 knights were created in a great hierarchy designed to make even

chivalry and pomp instruments of his statecraft. The Court was to cut Napoleon off in some measure from the nation, but around this particular throne were men of outstanding ability and of outstanding loyalty and devotion.

The First Consul

But behind the general and the pomp and pageantry of empire lay the achievement: in law, the Church and education.

These were the 'blocks of granite' on which he believed his power rested. In the three years from 1800 to 1803, the Paris years, he carried through most of his reforms. It was as if Louis XIV had been reincarnated with a team of outstanding talent—Talleyrand, Cambacérès, Lebrun Gaudin, Portalis and Thibaudeau.

In the codes of law drawn up by his Committees between 1804 and 1810, Napoleon drew heavily on the legislation of the Constituent and Legislative Assemblies. A uniform Civil Code had been a dream since Louis XIV, for there were no less than 360 local codes in existence, but until Napoleon all efforts to introduce one had failed. Napoleon himself participated directly in the discussions and his influence and vigour

were vital. Indeed, he took greater pride in the Civil Code than in all his forty battles. The Code Napoleon was promulgated in March 1804 and it expressed in law the first principles of the Revolution: equality before the law, including the equal distribution of property among sons and daughters, though it was possible to leave a little more to one child if the family contained several children; freedom to work and to worship; freedom of conscience and the secular character of the state. It defined a modern property law freed of all manorial or seigneurial features, and it aimed to make the law uniform, understandable, rational and lucid, in contrast with the customary laws of France and England. In some ways it was strongly conservative for it put marriage and the family (not merely divorce) on a civil basis of the Old Regime. It encouraged firm parental authority both in family and state, for the cohesion of the family group was itself the basis of the cohesion of the state. The father's control in the family was made absolute; a wife was seen as subject to her husband and could not acquire or sell property without his consent. The principle of divorce was admitted—for adultery, cruelty and for grave criminal offences—but once only.

The Civil Code proved the most durable

part of Napoleon's handiwork and it was carried throughout Europe by his armies. In France and beyond, it stood the test of time. It was reinforced by a Code of Civil Procedure, a Commercial Code, which was the least durable of the enactments, and by Criminal and Penal Codes. Yet valuable as they were, the Codes were essentially comprises between the Old Regime and the Revolution, between the authoritarianism of Rome and the liberalism of customary law. Though equality was proclaimed, most of the provisions of the Civil Code were devoted to the protection of property. In the Criminal Code, though penalties were carefully prescribed, they were far from liberal: capital punishment, imprisonment or deportation for life, branding and slavery in the colonies were firmly established: the jury system was tightly curbed and used for judgement but not for accusation, and the juries themselves were chosen by prefects. While accused persons were tried in public and allowed to speak and to use counsel, they were not allowed to hear the case against themselves as it was being assembled in the preliminary investigation: there was no system of habeas corpus: the Codes were authoritarian in temper and far removed from the spirit of the *philosophes*. They were well designed to detect crime and to ensure

fast and speedy trial: but there was no attempt to see the law as a barrier against arbitrary executive power. And in economic terms the Codes said little about wages and conditions of work: it was property, not labour, that was sacrosanct. Employers were given freedom so that the economy should boom, and in wage disputes the master's word was taken against the worker's: in the Penal Code, the le Chapelier Law of 1791 was reintroduced and associations, whether of masters or of workers, were forbidden.

Yet, however illiberal they were, the Codes were immensely valuable. In them the permanent shape of the Revolution became clear: the objective was a secular state based firmly on a peasant proprietor class: the protection of private property mattered as much as did equality: but, since all men had equal rights, there was a genuine chance for the 'men of talent' to find their own way to property, fame and fortune.

Napoleon's own taste also emerged clearly: the taste for order and for 'men of talent' not for the common man. Here again he was in the tradition of the Old Regime. Like Louis XIV, Napoleon chose his servants from diverse backgrounds and, as Louis had been frightened by the *fronde*, so Napoleon had seen enough of the *sans-culottes* and of the extravagances of the

Above, Napoleon giving the insignia of the imperial eagles to his armies, according to an engraving after a painting by Jacques Louis David. Napoleon's success was always based on the enthusiasm he could summon up from the army.

Opposite, the coronation of Napoleon in December 1804 as Emperor of the French. Although the pope was present to perform the coronation, Napoleon snatched the crown from his hands and placed it on his own head to symbolize his independence from the Church. Musée du Louvre, Paris.

Directory to judge them harshly. Also, much in the same way as Jefferson, the democracy he sought was that in which able men would rise rapidly to the top. It was to be equality to allow the flourishing of unequal talents of unequal men. And what the Codes did in law, Fouché did in practice at the Ministry of Police: it was a regime that offered a widening of opportunity and also an extension of censorship and repression. By 1810 each department had a single newspaper, tightly controlled by the prefects, and by 1811 all the Paris newspapers had been confiscated.

The same spirit permeated the educational system. Primary education remained in local hands and was seriously handicapped by lack of funds. The secondary schools of the Directory were replaced by *lycées*, advanced secondary schools in which military drill and style were curiously married to a classical curriculum. By 1814 this had become and was to remain one of his great achievements. But it was, of course, masculine. As he wrote in 1807, 'what we ask of education is not that girls should think, but that they should believe.'

In 1808 an Imperial University was set up, the Grand Master of which was the educational autocrat of the whole system. A degree from the Imperial University became a prerequisite for teaching. There was even for a time an Imperial Catechism, to teach loyalty to the emperor. Napoleon also gave new life to those creations of the Convention which were its most valuable legacy: the École Polytechnique, set up in 1795 to train engineers, the École Normale Supérieure, to train teachers, and the Institut de France. Much was done to encourage industry and applied science with technical schools,

rewards for invention and industrial exhibitions. But again the intention was clear—education was a department of state, and its watchwords were training, discipline and centralization. Some of its discipline lasted a very long time.

Central to the Napoleonic strategy were good relations with the Church. If he could secure this he would, at one blow, weaken both royalists and revolutionaries and gain the support of the great number of faithful Catholics. The clergy, he said, would join the police in generating contentment. To him, the arch-secularist, religion was necessary not for its own sake but for his, as a further buttress to loyalty and sentiment. 'In religion', he said, 'I do not see the mystery of the Incarnation, but the mystery of the social order.' 'If I were governing the Jews, I would restore the Temple of Solomon.'

The Concordat concluded with the pope in 1801 and sanctioned in 1802 was, again, primarily his own handiwork. All bishops were required to resign their Sees and the bishoprics were regrouped so that there were now ten archbishoprics and fifty bishoprics. Napoleon nominated them and they were consecrated by the pope. The clergy took an oath of obedience to the government and got in return, as good servants of emperor as well as God, a fixed salary. The bishops were given absolute authority over them but ecclesiastical property, confiscated in the heyday of the Revolution and bought by the *bourgeoisie* and the peasants, still remained in the hands of its purchasers. Roman Catholicism was recognized as the 'religion of the great majority of Frenchmen, but equal rights were granted to other faiths—a basic principle of the secular state which was

unknown anywhere before the Revolution.

In other words, the spirit like the mind was disciplined in Napoleon's service, and the Church, like the schools, became a Department of State. The *Journal des Curés*, the only clerical newspaper to appear after 1806, carried his imprimatur, sermons were strictly censored and there were to be no papal bulls, papal legates or investigations from Rome. But if it was to gain little for Pius VII, at least most of the religious orders returned, as did the Sabbath and the Gregorian calendar. Also the Concordat ended Gallicanism.

Yet when the quarrel with Rome came it was not over these issues. The strongly Gallican spirit in France long pre-dated Napoleon; his attempts to exploit it for his own purposes had the effect of driving his clerical opponents into ultramontanism; that is, they recognized the pope as the supreme head of the Church. Pius VII disliked the extension of the Code Napoleon to Italy, since it authorized divorce; Napoleon despoiled Rome of the Legations of Bologna and Ferrara, which he added to the kingdom of Italy, and he handed over Ponte Corvo and Benevento to Bernadotte and Talleyrand respectively. Pius objected to Joseph Bonaparte's accession to the throne of Naples, and in 1806 he refused to expel the enemies of France from the Papal states. In May 1809 Rome was annexed by France; in June Pius excommunicated Napoleon and the pope was arrested in the following month and imprisoned in Fontainebleau.

In the end the pope returned to Rome as a result of the allies' triumph at Leipzig, and his steady resistance undermined all Napoleon's efforts. Napoleon found that it was his own unbridled ambition and not the Concordat which succeeded in alienating many Catholics, for he tied Church and state so closely together that their alliance has been a continuous source of tension and danger to France. However, the Concordat survived the quarrel and remained in force until 1905.

Law, Church and education were, then, the instruments of this enlightened despot and far more successful and durable than those of his eighteenth-century precursors, mainly because of his own abilities and his organizing and technical efficiency. However it is only fair to add that the success of Napoleon's reforms was a result not only to his own talents but because the Revolution had swept away all the interests, privileges, habits and established groups whose opposition had blocked similar changes since the time of Louis XIV. Absolutism ensured order and it came close to guaranteeing prosperity.

In 1800 the Bank of France was established with the sole right of issuing banknotes. There was active state interference in industry, laws to regulate the supply of food and for the registration of workers with the police. The wars with Britain were cala-

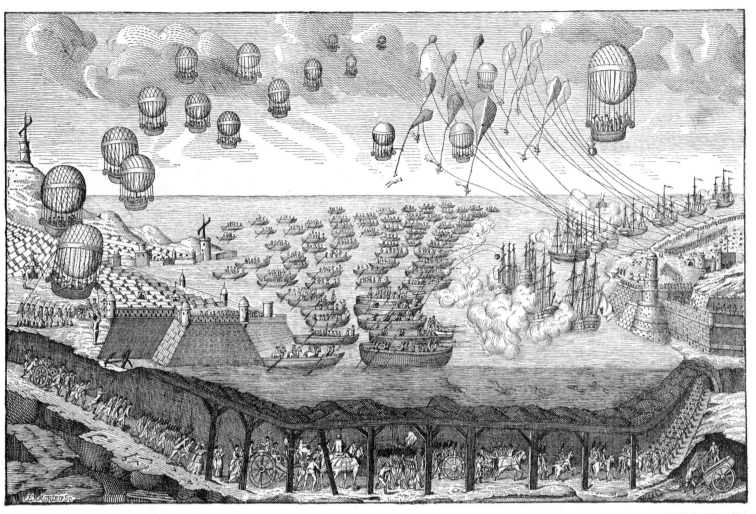

Above, Napoleon accepting the surrender of the city of Ulm in September 1805. This victory was a triumph for Napoleon's tactic of quickly encircling the enemy. Château de Versailles.

Top, an engraving of Napoleon's invasion plans of England before the Treaty of Amiens in 1802; Napoleon actually began building a tunnel under the Channel, but his invasion plans required superiority at sea, which he never fully won.

Left, the Battle of Trafalgar in 1805, a decisive victory for the British over the French navy; British control of the Atlantic and Channel proved a crippling blow to Napoleon's strategies. Musée de la Marine, Paris.

Opposite, the Battle of Austerlitz in Moravia, in December 1805, at which Napoleon won his greatest victory, sweeping aside the combined armies of the Austrians and the Russians. Château de Versailles.

mitous to trade but a stimulus to industry. The wool and silk trades prospered: the government paid its bills promptly, helped by foreign treasure brought in by the nation's armies; the French peasant who in 1789 kept only nineteen out of every one hundred francs he earned kept seventy-nine after 1800.

Indeed, Napoleon's regime was based on the support of two classes, the workmen, whom Napoleon feared and who gave him an illogical devotion, and the peasantry. The last were the great beneficiaries of the Revolution who, having profited from it, rejoiced now to see its excesses curbed. By 1810 there were seven million rural proprietors in France, which was all but self-sufficient as its agriculture flourished. It was of course, after Russia, the most populous state in Europe: some 26,000,000 aginst divided Italy's 17,000,000, Britain's 15,000,000 and Spain's 11,000,000. France's armies had battle experience and, at least until the disastrous Russian campaign of 1812, almost unlimited numbers. The army poised to cross the Channel in 1805 had 200,000 men, of whom more than half had war experience. This was a strong, cohesive and disciplined state. In the years of the Consulate, Napoleon gave it the stamp of his own authority and energy, his realism and detail, his respect for order and his scorn for abstract rights. The student of Rousseau had progressed a long way in a decade. So also had the Revolution.

The Empire to Tilsit

The years of the Consulate revealed a ruler of outstanding ability who had turned from war to peace. However, after the collapse of the Treaty of Amiens, the old image was restored, Napoleon as Attila the destroyer. The state he commanded was so strong and the cause he was thought to champion so explosive and popular that for a decade he swept through Europe as the Goths had done twelve centuries earlier. As a result, the war of the Third Coalition was total war of a kind unknown before.

It began with the attempt to invade Britain. Nelson's blockade of Villeneuve's fleet at Toulon and Collingwood's blockade of Ganteaume's fleet at Brest prevented the assembling of the transports: Villeneuve escaped to the West Indies and returned to be checked at Finisterre. He put in to Cadiz to refit and Nelson, prowling the Atlantic in baffled pursuit, was able to overtake him at Trafalgar in October 1805, and by his victory end the risk of invasion and give Britain supremacy at sea which was to last for a century. It was only these ships which stood between Napoleon and possible world dominion. In the meantime Pitt had created a Third Coalition of Britain, Alexander of Russia, Austria, Sweden, Sicily and Naples, while Prussia equivocated.

To meet the Austrian danger Napoleon broke up the armed camp and the 200,000

veterans of the Army of England were dispatched east in seven divisions under the ablest commanders in modern history: Ney, Marmont, Davoust, Augereau Soult, Lannes and Bernadotte. With them went Murat with the cavalry and Bessières with the Imperial Guard of 10,000 men. They covered 200 miles in a fortnight, faster than Austria or Russia believed possible and before either of them had time to plan their defence. As a result Mack was surrounded, overwhelmed and surrendered with 25,000 men at Ulm in October. The following month Napoleon entered Vienna.

Napoleon now found that his lines of communication were extended, and therefore the Allies, not least an impetuous Tsar, resolved to attack. The result of this was that Napoleon won what was his greatest victory—Austerlitz, north of Vienna, on the anniversary of his coronation. His losses were 9,000 out of 70,000; the Austrians and Russians lost 30,000 out of 80,000. Partly it was speed of movement: partly great tactical skill: most of all brilliant leadership with plans communicated frankly to all his men in advance. 'It is by speaking to the soul that men are electrified.' Austria made peace and Russia hurriedly withdrew into its own territory. Ferdinand pulled back to Sicily, safety sheltered by the British fleet and in January 1806 Pitt died, broken by thirteen years of war. By the Treaty of Pressburg Austria surrendered all her Italian possessions— some of them the ancestral estates of the Habsburgs. The Holy Roman Empire was formally abolished.

Napoleon now organized an array of satellite states: his brother Joseph was made King of Naples and Louis King of Holland. The Confederation of the Rhine was set up as a pro-French barrier in Europe and it made a defensive alliance with France: 63,000 Rhinelanders fought in French armies.

Prussia at last decided to move, only to be destroyed at Jena and Auerstedt in October 1806. Napoleon then marched through Berlin, from which city he issued the Berlin Decrees enforcing the Continental System and a blockade of Britain by the whole of

Europe. He demanded the surrender of all Prussian territory, first west of the Elbe, then west of the Vistula. Frederick William III fell back into East Prussia hoping for Russian help. By December 1806, Napoleon was in Warsaw.

At last Russia moved again. Eylau (February 1807) was a drawn battle with heavy losses on both sides. And though each member of the Coalition talked of action, no common action was taken. At Friedland in June the Russians were overwhelmed and driven across the River Nieman. The two rulers, the emperor and the tsar, met in July 1807 on a raft moored in the river and signed the Treaty of Tilsit.

Tilsit was the climax in the Napoleonic story: the high point of empire. The two emperors divided Europe between them. Napoleon dominated the West, from the Nieman to the Channel. Prussia was heavily despoiled when her Polish acquisitions became a grand duchy of Warsaw which Napoleon gave to the King of Saxony: her lands west of the Elbe went to form a new kingdom of Westphalia, given to Napoleon's brother Jerome: her army was to be limited in size and she was to close her ports to British trade. Alexander for his part recognized France's acquisitions and ceded the Ionian Islands: he was urged to take Moldavia Walachia from the Ottoman Empire and was promised French help in the attempt. After the destruction of the Holy Roman Empire, the Ottoman was to suffer in a similar manner. Thus both rulers agreed to fasten the shackles of the Continental System on Europe, to keep British and neutral shipping from trading with Europe and to isolate, blockade and finally to destroy Britain.

Chapter 33

The Fall of Napoleon

At the close of 1807 the weaknesses of the Continental System were still not apparent. Napoleon reigned supreme. Europe was at his feet, and no one could have prophesied that within seven years his great empire would lie in ruins, his attempts to bring about the collapse of Great Britain's financial and commercial prosperity having alienated influential opinion within the areas he already ruled and helped to bring about his downfall.

In spite of three defeats at the hands of the French in little over ten years and the great expansion of Napoleonic power, by 1808 the Austrians were again ready to attempt to defeat the ruler of Europe. Their natural desire for revenge and their hatred of Napoleon were stimulated by the events in the Iberian peninsula. In November 1807 French troops conquered Portugal, causing the Portuguese royal family to flee to Brazil, and in March 1808, when a French force marched on Madrid, an internal revolt forced the Bourbon king, Charles IV, to abdicate. Napoleon soon gave the Spanish throne to his brother Joseph. The Habsburgs had good reason to fear a ruler who could deal so summarily with the royal families of the Iberian peninsula. Moreover, the Spanish people were demonstrating that resistance to the French was possible. In May 1808 the population of Madrid rose against the new French rulers, and the French found themselves drawn into extensive guerrilla warfare.

If Austria could wage war successfully her previous losses could be restored, and there was a growing belief in the country that the Austrian army was now much stronger and might well be capable of defeating Napoleon. Since the disasters of 1805 the leadership in reforming the Austrian army had been taken by Archduke Charles, brother of Emperor Francis, and by the new chancellor, Count Johann Philip von Stadion. The reforms had produced a marked improvement in the regular army, which was augmented by the creation of an enthusiastic reserve army by 1808. Stirred by the events in Spain, the Austrians were again becoming ready to risk combat with the French.

Napoleon was quickly discovering that it was easier to create a great empire than to maintain it. In the summer of 1808 he condemned the Austrian rearmament and once again arranged to meet Tsar Alexander in an effort to cement Franco-Russian friendship before embarking on an expedition which he hoped and expected would crush Spanish resistance. His meeting with the tsar at Erfurt was unproductive. Alexander avoided making any major promises to Napoleon, showing far less admiration for him than he had at Tilsit in 1807; he gained an ally in the French statesman Talleyrand, who now showed himself willing to work secretly against Napoleon. Both Alexander and Napoleon were accustomed to daily flattery and found it difficult to compromise their dignity by yielding supremacy.

Although Napoleon took personal command in Spain late in 1808, his efforts produced no conclusive result, and early in 1809 he returned to Paris to prepare for a campaign against the Austrians.

In the early months of 1809 Napoleon waited for Francis I to make the first move. In Austria troops were flocking to the colours with considerable enthusiasm, but the Austrians could expect little aid from outside. The other German states either remained neutral or indeed actually fought on the side of the French, and Great Britain could offer no direct aid. She did promise a diversionary movement in the north, but the

Opposite, the meeting of Napoleon and Alexander I, Tsar of Russia, on a raft in the River Niemen at Tilsit, in June 1807; at the meeting they agreed peace between their empires and Russia promised Napoleon help in the event of further war between France and Britain.

Below, Napoleon crossing the River Danube before the Battle of Wagram in July 1809; his artillery proved too strong for the Austrians, who were forced to sign another armistice shortly afterwards. Wellington Museum, Apsley House, London

disastrous Walcheren expedition came too late to be of any use even in diverting French attention from the main scene of operations.

The campaign began early in April 1809 when Archduke Charles advanced into Bavaria. Napoleon reacted with speed and confidence. By mid-April he had arrived in the vicinity and at the battles of Abensberg and Eckmühl drove the Austrians back. On 12 May the French entered Vienna and a week later crossed to the north bank of the Danube to attack the Austrian army. In the two-day battle of Aspern and Essling the Austrians succeeded in repulsing the French forces; they withdrew to the island of Lobau. Losses had been severe on both sides; the French suffered nearly 20,000 casualties and the Austrians themselves several thousand more.

After this bloody engagement there was a pause in the campaign while both sides attempted to strengthen their armies. Early in July, after being reinforced by Eugène Beauharnais, Napoleon once again crossed to the north bank of the Danube. He had with him an army of approximately 170,000 men to meet an Austrian army of more than 30,000 fewer. The French attack at Wagram was launched on 6 July, and although Napoleon carried the day it was no Austerlitz. The Austrians put up a stubborn resistance, and both armies suffered severely. On 12 July the two sides concluded an armistice

and prepared to make peace. Instead of gaining revenge, Austria was now in danger of additional losses.

While the main armies clashed near Vienna, the people of the Tyrol took up arms against the Bavarians, who had gained that area at the Peace of Pressburg in 1805. Under Andreas Hofer the Tyroleans waged a brave struggle. Innsbruck was taken in the spring, and even after the Austrian defeat at Wagram the uprising continued until the end of the year. Hofer was eventually captured, tried by the French and executed.

Other signs that Napoleon faced increasing disgust at his attempt to control the whole of Europe came from Germany. The Duke of Brunswick raised volunteers to fight the French, took Dresden and after the Austrian defeat at Wagram managed to escape with his army northwards across Germany, to be taken off in British ships. This force, whose death's head insignia became famous, later served in the Peninsula. In Prussia Major Friedrich von Schill attempted to organize a military uprising against the French. He took Stralsund in May but was killed when the town was stormed by the French and the Danes. It was becoming all too clear that many in Europe regarded Napoleon as a tyrant to be overthrown.

Yet, for all the heroics, and in spite of the greater Austrian enthusiasm, Napoleon had

won, and in October 1809 he forced the Austrians to sign the Treaty of Schönbrunn. It was a harsh peace. Napoleon never learned the value of moderation in victory. Francis I was shocked by the loss of more than three-and-a-half million subjects. Salzburg was given to Bavaria, west Galicia to the Grand Duchy of Warsaw, and Austrian possessions between the Save River and the Adriatic were taken by France and made part of the Illyrian Provinces. Austria would clearly not rest content until some of this territory had been regained, and this humiliating settlement planted the seeds of future wars. It was obvious that Metternich, the new Austrian chancellor, would wait for an opportunity to weaken France and restore Austria's fortunes, although to help Austria he was prepared to work with Napoleon until the right moment for revenge.

Having again preserved his power by military victory, Napoleon now turned to marriage in an attempt both to secure the future of his dynasty and to ensure future Austrian cooperation. It now appeared that his first wife Joséphine was too old to bear him a son, and Napoleon craved not only immediate power but also the creation of a legitimate dynasty. Napoleon gave consideration to both a Russian or an Austrian marriage, and on returning from his victory over Austria he made the definite decision to divorce Joséphine. Joséphine had no choice: in December 1809 she had to consent to Napoleon's wishes, and the French Senate was necessarily obliged to follow suit.

With Napoleon casting around for a future empress, Metternich seized upon the opportunity to ensure Austria's temporary safety; available as an offering was Marie

Louise, daughter of Austrian emperor Francis I. The possible religious objections were overcome by Napoleon's pressure on the hierarchy of the French Catholic Church: it was agreed that the marriage to Joséphine could be annulled. The marriage to Marie Louise took place by proxy in Vienna in March, and civil and religious ceremonies took place in France at the beginning of April. In an effort to create a legitimate dynasty Napoleon was prepared to use every possible illegitimate device, and it soon appeared that the abandonment of Joséphine had proved a success: within a few months Marie Louise was pregnant. The birth of a son, the King of Rome, in March 1811 for a time gave purpose to the whole hurried divorce and remarriage, but the joy was short-lived.

Prussia

While Austria yet again attempted to overcome Napoleon, Prussia seethed under the humiliation of her 1806 defeat. The French troops who occupied Prussia after the victory of Jena left only after the Prussians agreed to pay a huge cash indemnity and to maintain their army at no more than 42,000 men. Napoleon's unwillingness to deal more leniently with his defeated opponents in this case, even more than his harshness towards Austria, helped to produce internal changes which contributed to his eventual downfall. Prussians who had little faith in reform were eventually persuaded to accept it as the only means by which a national revival could be engendered and the hated Napoleon be defeated.

The key figures in the Prussian revival were the king, Frederick William III, and his ministers Hardenberg and Stein. After the events of 1806 the king had to acknowledge that the great army and system created by Frederick the Great were not enough to cope with a revivified France under the leadership of a military genius. Inspired by Hardenberg and Stein the king was prepared to force reform measures on often reluctant aristocrats.

The most practical and tangible reform here, as in Austria, was in the army, and this improvement depended on the leadership of two soldiers—Scharnhorst and Gneisenau. An attempt was made to modify a system which had depended for its discipline on the imposition of frequent punishments; aristocratic birth was no longer to be the sole attribute for promotion, and an attempt was made to induce a Prussian national pride in the army. Also, by training and then discharging bodies of men it proved possible to avoid the absolute limits on the size of the army established by Napoleon.

A far-reaching internal reform was set in motion by the edict abolishing serfdom in October 1807. The ensuing land reform gave the Prussian peasants a much firmer stake in the land. Without the crisis brought about by Napoleon's overwhelming victories, this could hardly have occurred at so early a date. Much less far-reaching as a reform, but of significance, was the establishment of a

Opposite and above, Napoleon and Marie Louise, whom he married and made empress in 1810. She was made duchess of Parma, Piacenza and Guastalla by the Congress of Vienna in 1816.

Centre, the marriage between Napoleon and Marie Louise, the daughter of the Emperor of Austria, in Paris in 1810. Napoleon's intention in this marriage was more to gain acceptance for his rule than to establish a permanent peace with Austria.

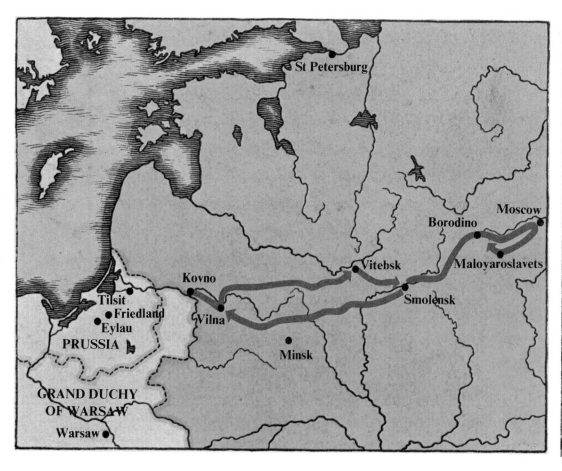

degree of municipal independence by allowing the local election of town officials.

A distinctive feature of the Prussian revival after 1807 was the burst of intellectual and cultural nationalism. Ultimately, this was probably more important for future German history than for the age of Napoleon. The most important figure in this nationalistic revival was Johann Gottlieb Fichte, who in his famous lectures at Berlin in these years preached the necessity of a Germanic revival; a revival which would be based on patriotic virtue and a sense of a mystical German past. This was hardly the theme to fire the peasants, but it did create a ferment among the Prussian intellectuals. This group were also influenced by the activities of the *Tugendbund* ('League of Virtue') formed among professors at Königsberg. These men hoped to achieve a moral regeneration of the nation.

More practical in its results was the reform of the Prussian educational system inaugurated by Wilhelm von Humboldt. At the core of the reforms was the intention to create a national system of education, and a structure was established which culminated in the new foundation of the University of Berlin.

Although the German states of this age were fragmented and subject to the political and military whims of Napoleon, they had a remarkably fruitful intellectual and cultural life. In Prussia a strong emphasis was placed on moral regeneration and the creation of a vague sense of a Prussian and German soul, but elsewhere the flourishing cultural life was less tied to nationalistic reform. At

Weimar Duke Charles Augustus had gathered around him the most distinguished philosophers and writers in Germany, and Goethe made the city famous throughout Europe. To the south Beethoven thrilled Vienna. To many Napoleon's first victories in Germany had seemed a deliverance, a blow by which feudal privilege and archaic law were to be swept away. As the years passed, however, the development of tyranny and the constant demands for men and money alienated even those who had been his friends.

Europe under Napoleon

Although Austria and Prussia retained their identity and even found a new burst of national enthusiasm under the crushing defeats inflicted by the French, much of Europe either quite happily accepted French rule or had neither the power nor the allies to make resistance possible. Those areas closest to France were under the greatest domination by the French system.

Holland had been given to Napoleon's brother Louis Bonaparte in 1806, and French administration had not been particularly onerous for the Dutch; indeed the French law and government had been an improvement over the old Dutch system and had helped to unify the country. The chief possibility for real conflict, as in so many areas of the French empire, was the attempt to exclude British trade by the introduction of the Continental System. As a major commercial people, the Dutch found the attempts to restrict their trade

intolerable. Louis showed himself willing to compromise and allow loopholes in the Continental System to placate his people, but in 1810 Napoleon deposed him and annexed Holland. He also annexed the Duchy of Oldenburg and the Hanseatic towns of Bremen, Hamburg and Lübeck to extend his control along the German coastline. Denmark was not annexed, but it obeyed the Continental System.

Sweden was going through turmoil in the period following the French-Russian agreement at Tilsit. After that settlement the Russians had occupied Finland, and following further difficulties the Swedish king Gustavus IV was deposed, and his elderly uncle replaced him as Charles XIII. As he had no heirs, a group of Swedish officers suggested that the throne should be offered to Napoleon's Marshal Bernadotte. After obtaining Napoleon's permission, Bernadotte accepted in 1810. He quickly espoused the cause of Sweden, and the French emperor was soon to discover that the elevation of his marshal had made Sweden anything but a satellite.

Napoleon was more fortunate with his intervention in the affairs of Switzerland. By the 1803 Act of Mediation he had moved to unify Switzerland and to guarantee the reforms brought about in that country by the French Revolution. Napoleon took for himself the position of Mediator of the Swiss Confederation. The Swiss were to maintain their neutrality throughout the decline of Napoleon's power, although their territory was violated when an Austrian army marched across their borders in order

Above, the Battle of Borodino, outside Moscow, in September 1812; the battle opened the way for Napoleon's occupation of the Russian capital but did not give Napoleon the decisive victory for him to subdue Russia.

Left, Moscow in flames in September 1812; it is probable that after the city had been occupied by Napoleon, Russian patriots set fire to it to force the French out.

Opposite, Napoleon's invasion of Russia and his retreat in 1812; the enormous distances involved in this invasion proved too much even for his well-organized supply system.

to obtain a convenient route for the invasion of France.

Napoleon's dreams of reconstituting the whole map of Europe were clearly revealed by his attitude towards the Poles. His position was complicated by his attempted friendship with Russia after Tilsit. The Russians were extremely reluctant to accept any measures which might revive Polish nationalism. Yet, in spite of Russian fears, Napoleon in 1807 established the Grand Duchy of Warsaw out of Prussian Poland. The King of Saxony was made Grand Duke of Warsaw, and in 1809 it was enlarged with Austrian territory. Napoleon had taken on an impossible task if he hoped both to

encourage Polish national aspirations and at the same time retain the friendship of Tsar Alexander.

In 1810 Napoleon still ruled a great empire and had satellites throughout Europe, but weak spots were becoming apparent. The was in the Iberian peninsula continued, costing French lives and giving the British a foothold on the continent. Throughout Europe, and even in France, there was discontent both at the enforcement of the Continental System and at Napoleonic exactions. The French emperor himself was becoming more tyrannical. He was less willing to accept advice, made more arbitrary decisions and showed little willingness to ap-

pease any groups within his empire. If Napoleon hoped to establish a dynasty and to create a Europe under French leadership, then the time had come for consolidation and accommodation, not fresh adventures, more requisitions, more fighting and more deaths. Yet Napoleon could not be satisfied, and the cracks in the empire that appeared in Spain and in the enforcement of the Continental System were soon to broaden and undermine the foundations of the precarious and ramshackle structure that he had built from military victory.

Russia

In the five years after Tilsit the French and the Russians maintained an uneasy peace that could hardly be called friendship. The meeting of Alexander and Napoleon at Erfurt in the autumn of 1808 did nothing to cement a firm alliance between the two nations. The tsar had hoped by his agreement with Napoleon at Tilsit both to hurt Great Britain and to advance Russian ambitions in eastern Europe, but he quickly developed resentment against the overbearing power of the French emperor.

A continual source of irritation was Napoleon's promotion of the grand duchy of Warsaw. Alexander was particularly disturbed when Austrian Galicia was added to the duchy after the defeat of Austria in 1809. Although Napoleon maintained that he had no intention of creating an independent Poland, Russia had ample reason to distrust French assertions. Napoleon himself showed little concern to placate the Russian tsar. In December 1810 he annexed the duchy of Oldenburg, although the heir-apparent was married to Alexander's sister Catherine. Napoleon's affront to her husband ensured that there would be an influential advocate of an anti-French policy with immediate access to Alexander.

Tsar Alexander had also become increasingly irritated by Napoleon's arrogance and found it difficult to accept him as the arbiter of Europe. Alexander's own ego was such that he would view with satisfaction any diminution of the Napoleonic glory.

In practical terms, however, Russia's reluctance to enforce the Napoleonic Continental System became the major point of contention between France and Russia. Throughout 1810 Napoleon continued to hope that his restrictions on British trade would bring Great Britain to disaster, but Alexander showed great reluctance to make Russia an economic satellite of the French. In December 1810 he issued a *ukase* (order) which restricted the importation of French luxury goods and opened Russian ports to other shipping. It was clear that Alexander was ready to separate himself from the French connection as soon as the chance arose, and in 1811 the two powers began to prepare for war.

Napoleon well knew the difficulties and dangers of a campaign into the depths of Russia, and he was determined that his army for this enterprise would be the greatest he had ever assembled. By the spring of 1812 he had gathered in Poland more than half a million men for his campaign. Less than half of these troops were French, for Napoleon's armies were bolstered by troops from allies, satellites and conquered countries all over Europe; even Austria and Prussia had no choice but to provide troops for the campaign. Fired by the prospect of a great military victory, Napoleon, as the months passed, showed less and less willingness to allow for all the dangers which would beset any army plunging into the interior of Russia. Rational thoughts of enforcing the Continental System or ensuring that Russia would not join the British were submerged in grandiose dreams of glory and empire.

At the beginning of the conflict, Alexander could place in the field nothing like the force assembled by Napoleon: the Russian tsar had not many more than 150,000 men to meet the initial French advance. He had, however, achieved two diplomatic successes before the war began;

in April Napoleon's old subordinate Bernadotte, now heir to the Swedish throne, had reached an agreement with Russia, and in May the Turks had concluded a peace.

On the night of 23 June Napoleon's army began to cross the Niemen river into Russia. He was in high hopes that he could quickly bring the Russians to battle, defeat them and force Alexander to sue for peace. Apart from Napoleon's main army, separate wings of the attack were sent towards Riga and St Petersburg, and in the south the Austrians advanced under Prince Karl von Schwarzenberg.

Napoleon's hopes of bringing the Russians to battle were frustrated in the early days of the campaign. The French advance stirred unexpected depths of resistance in the Russians. The ruling classes, fearing the wholesale changes and reforms instituted by Napoleon elsewhere, naturally had no desire to accept any quick French victory. Moreover, even the Russian people, who logically might have been expected to welcome the possibilities of general changes in their condition, responded to the threat to their tsar and to mother Russia. With a primitive religious fervour they, like their rulers, were prepared to suffer great hardship to resist the desires of the French emperor.

The difficulties of maintaining discipline and of supplying Napoleon's motley army proved impossible to overcome. There was no great victory to maintain morale, and throughout the campaign the desertion rate exceeded all expectations. Within a week the French were in Vilna, but already there had been difficulties in maintaining the flow of supplies. After more than two weeks' delay, the French pressed on, reaching Vitebsk by the end of July. Still there had been no major battles, although the French had encountered severe resistance from the Russian rearguard. Again Napoleon delayed for two weeks.

The Russian retreat, and their destruction of all that might aid the French, was producing great consternation among the French generals. As the French army advanced further and further from its base, an increasingly large number of troops had to be detached to protect the lines of communication, and the task of supplying the main army became extremely complicated. Already Napoleon's generals were advising retreat, and Napoleon himself seemed unable to decide on the best course to pursue. Although he ignored his generals and continued to advance, his thrust into Russia lacked the inspiration of his earlier campaigns. His very anxiety to ensure that he had a large enough army to preclude defeat had given him a force incapable of rapid action.

Napoleon's main hope now was that he would be able to meet the defeat the Russians at Smolensk. He hoped and expected that there the Russians would make a stand and that by defeating them he could

force Alexander to sue for peace. For two days his artillery bombarded the city, but on the night of 17 August the Russian general Barclay de Tolly withdrew along the road to Moscow with his army. Junot, who had been sent around Smolensk to prevent the retreat, failed to arrive in time. Yet again the Russians escaped.

The Russians simply did not have the army to make a stand at Smolensk, but in spite of this weakness it was becoming increasingly difficult for Barclay to defend his constant withdrawal. Although Napoleon feared more than anything else that he would be unable to bring the Russians to battle, Russian politicians were urging a battle to save Moscow. Alexander was persuaded to remove Barclay and replace him with Kutuzov, who had made his reputation against the Turks. It was understood that Kutuzov would fight to stop the French advance.

A week after entering Smolensk Napoleon's army again pressed on towards Moscow. Kutuzov had determined to make his stand at the Moskva River, and his army entrenched itself near the village of Borodino. On 5 September the French encountered the Russians. Believing that he did not have the resources to risk dividing his army to flank the Russian position, Napoleon decided that it would have to be taken by a direct frontal attack. The attack was launched on the 7th.

In spite of all Napoleon's hopes of a huge army in Russia, his actual force for the attack amounted only to some 120,000 men; the Russians had slightly more in the field. All day the French surged into attack against the Russian positions. This was no brilliant strategic victory on the part of Napoleon but a struggle of bloody attrition. By the end of the day the French were in possession of the field, but they had suffered some 30,000 casualties; Russian casualties were over 50,000. All the talk of French

glory, and of justice and unity for Europe, were revealed in their true light in the reality of tens of thousands of dead and dying, sacrificed to the vanity and ego of a brilliant Corsican soldier of boundless ambition. Borodino was not the victory he needed. Although the Russians had lost practically half their men as casualties, they had not been routed or annihilated. There was still a Russian army.

Moscow, however, was now open to the French, and Napoleon still hoped for Russian emissaries to announce that Alexander was suing for peace. But nothing happened. Kutuzov retired beyond Moscow, and Napoleon entered the city on 14 September. It was a strange sight. Many civilians had followed the Russian army, and the French troops marched in through deserted streets. On the same night fire broke out—it was never certain whether by accident or design. In the following days fire gutted the city, and the French troops wandered through the deserted houses seizing valuables soon to be destroyed or discarded. Napoleon desperately needed a Russian request for peace. He had driven deep into the heart of Russia, but it was now September. Winter was near. Soon the snow would come.

The retreat from Moscow

For over a month Napoleon waited for the tsar to seek peace, but there was no news. There were no letters seeking terms, there were no emissaries. There was to be no peace with the French despoilers. When Napoleon finally decided in the middle of October that he would have to retreat, it was too late. He still had more than 100,000 men, but he had to find food and shelter before winter set in. Even before he began the retreat the task seemed practically hopeless. Morale was

low, there was a shortage of food, there was far too little warm clothing for an army retreating at the beginning of a Russian winter, and the Russians were ready to fall on the hated French.

An immediate problem that faced Napoleon was that the road he had travelled from Smolensk to Moscow had been pillaged by the passage of the armies; there was no food and little shelter. The French army would have had far more chance of survival along the road further to the south which ran towards Kaluga, but Kutuzov's army was blocking that alternative route. Napoleon decided to try to force his way along that road, and on 19 October the French army of some 100,000 moved southwards out of Moscow. Napoleon had left men to blow up the Kremlin, but their inefficiency saved all the important buildings. The retreating army moved slowly, burdened not with essential supplies but with loot from the Russian capital. When the Russians checked the French at Yaroslavetz on 24 October, Napoleon decided that he dare not risk attacking the whole Russian army and turned north to return by the route along which his army had advanced.

The first test of the French army was the long march along the devastated road to Smolensk. It was already obvious that the French faced complete disaster. Although it was not yet bitterly cold and there was little snow on this section of the march, the French troops were already exhausted and hungry. They entered Smolensk on 8 November. There was little food, not nearly enough for the whole French army, which was rapidly becoming more an undisciplined mob than an organized force. They marched on from Smolensk after several days' rest. The French rearguard under Ney was separated from the main army. In desperate fighting it rejoined Napoleon, but Ney lost over 7,000 out of a total force of 8,000 men.

It now seemed possible that the whole campaign would end at the Beresina River. Three Russian armies amounting to over 120,000 men were converging on the crossing. The only bridge had been destroyed, but the French engineers moved to the north and succeeded in building two temporary bridges across the icy water. Even yet it seemed that the whole French army might well be annihilated. On 26 and 27 November the army began to cross, but on the 28th troops on both banks and those crossing the river were under heavy fire from the Russians. Amid scenes of horror hundreds were thrown into the water, and on the next day the French destroyed the bridges, leaving thousands of stragglers on the east bank. Yet 60,000 troops had crossed the Beresina; this had seemed impossible a few days before.

In the following two weeks many thought they would have been better off drowning in the Beresina. The temperature fell to well below zero, and the French troops, already exhausted by the marching, the fighting and

the lack of food and warm clothing, collapsed on every side along the way. Desperately the survivors struggled on to Vilna, hoping that there they would find food and shelter. They found some, but not nearly enough, and by this time the army was a rabble. In the middle of December Marshal Ney crossed the River Niemen with the last of the rearguard. Over 500,000 men had been used on the Russian campaign: fewer than 50,000 could be reassembled in Polish territory.

Napoleon was no longer with the remnant of his army when it crossed the Niemen out of Russia. On 5 December, after previously dictating a bulletin announcing his defeat, he set out with all possible speed for Paris. The reason for his haste was to re-establish his position in France and to demonstrate that he had not died on the Russian campaign. He had heard of the conspiracy of General Claude François de Malet, who for a brief time had remarkable success in Paris by the simple expedient of announcing that Napoleon was dead. Although Malet was soon taken and shot, Napoleon was shocked to discover that no one had rallied around Marie Louise and his son, the King of Rome. He travelled rapidly to Paris to establish his own position and that of his dynasty, arriving at the French capital on 18 December.

In 1808, when Napoleon had been at the height of his achievements, it had seemed that the only blemishes on the whole fabric of French European power had been the uprising in the Iberian peninsula and the discontent caused by Napoleon's determination to crush the British through the use of the Continental System. By 1812 these minor blemishes had become gaping holes. Enforcement of the Continental System had caused resentment through much of Europe and in France itself and had helped to send Napoleon on his disastrous expedition into Russia. The little regarded uprising of the Spaniards had in four years been transformed into a major conflict, which was constantly draining French troops and resources.

In 1812, while Napoleon pushed into Russia, Wellington had defeated the French at Salamanca in July and for a time occupied Madrid. The French had found it impossible to suppress the Spanish uprising and throw the British from the peninsula. With the loss of a huge army in Russia, Napoleon was now at bay.

It is difficult to summon sympathy for the French emperor in 1812. The thousands upon thousands of men who had died or had been maimed on the battlefields of Europe

Above, the French army retreating from Moscow in the winter of 1812–13; it suffered equally from hunger, cold and the enemy's guerrilla tactics, and the campaign cost Napoleon almost 500,000 casualties.

Opposite, Napoleon's armies crossing the River Beresina, in central European Russia, in November 1812. The French lost 20,000 men and only narrowly escaped total annihilation or capture by the Russians. Musée de l'Armée, Paris.

had perished largely because of Napoleon's overwhelming ambition and his refusal to set reasonable limits to his power. In Russia there had been too large and unwieldy a French army, it had been inadequately supplied, and no proper precautions had been taken against the dangers of campaigning in a Russian winter. The emperor returned neither frost-bitten nor hungry, but men from all over Europe were left frozen in the snows of Russia.

The turn of the tide

Such had been the effect of Napoleon's crushing victories since 1805 that even after the disasters of 1812 those European powers who had suffered from his military genius were reluctant to send their armies into the field against him. Many did, however, take the opportunity to sever the French alliances into which they had been forced.

The Prussians, who had been engaged on the northern wing of the advance into Russia, hated the French for earlier humiliations, and on 30 December General Yorck, who had commanded the Prussian contingent on the Russian invasion, signed the Convention of Tauroggen with the Russians. Frederick William of Prussia was still undecided whether to throw his country fully

into the conflict against Napoleon, but once he was sure that the Russians intended to press on into Germany against the French he was willing to sign an agreement with Alexander; this was accomplished by the Treaty of Kalish on 27 February. In the middle of March Frederick William formally declared war against France.

While a variety of European powers were trying to decide what to do, the Russians in the first months of 1813 were advancing to the Elbe. The French under Eugène Beauharnais left garrisons in key Prussian defence points, but the main body of troops had no choice other than to retreat while the Russians moved into Germany.

This steady advance of the Russians helped to bring another country on to the side of Napoleon's opponents. Since assuming the control of Sweden, Bernadotte had shown no inclination to act as a satellite of Napoleon. In spite of Napoleon's desires, the Swedes had not taken part in the invasion of Russia in 1812. At the beginning of March 1813 Bernadotte agreed to join the allies, and his troops soon entered Germany to swell the number of France's enemies. With the Russians and Prussians facing the French in Germany, the Swedes soon to join them and the British firmly established in

the Iberian peninsula, Napoleon had both to raise men as quickly as possible and attempt to placate his allies and the neutrals.

Through the early months of 1813 Napoleon set about the task of raising another army. In response to the emergency he used extreme measures to raise men, including calling up the conscripts for 1814. Inevitably, the constant demands for men caused resentment in France and ensured that it would be difficult to create the enthusiasm of the early Revolutionary days in an effort to preserve the Napoleonic empire.

In the middle of April 1813 Napoleon left Paris to join Eugène in Germany. He still had hope, and he still had allies. Although Russia and England had been joined by Prussia and Sweden, Austria was still in doubt. It was not that Napoleon's father-in-law had any love for him but rather that Metternich did not intend to risk defeat and that he feared the Russians as well as the French. In spite of British and Russian hopes, Austria bided her time. The various states of the Confederation of the Rhine also feared to desert Napoleon until they were quite sure that his fangs had been drawn, and Denmark threw in her lot with the French emperor. As there were also Italian and Polish troops in the French army, the struggles of 1813 cannot be explained simply in terms of patriotic nationalists intent on throwing off the French yoke. In reality, the rulers of the various European states, big and small, were still pursuing their own personal and political ambitions. There were expressions of nationalistic sentiment, particularly in Prussia among the intellectuals, but most important for Napoleon was to convince the traditional rulers of Europe of his power. If Napoleon could demonstrate that he had the military skill and resources to win battles in his old decisive manner, then the European rulers would again have to reach an accommodation with him.

When Napoleon took command at Erfurt late in April he had available some 200,000 men: this was more than the Russian and Prussian forces combined. However, the more time that passed without the French winning a decisive victory, the more this advantage would diminish. The first engagement took place at Lützen (Gross Görschen) near Leipzig at the beginning of May when the Russian General Wittgenstein's force met Ney. Both sides suffered heavy losses and the allies were forced to retreat, but the French had not won a decisive victory.

The French again attempted to transform the situation at Bautzen on 20 May, this time with Napoleon in direct command: once more the fighting was fierce, again the French won, but still no army had been annihilated. On 4 June Napoleon agreed to an armistice, presumably hoping that this would be to his advantage, allowing him time to bring up additional troops and in taking away the enthusiasm of the allies for continuing the advance. It was a miscalculation. Although Napoleon used the armistice (which lasted into August) to increase his force in Germany to over 400,000 men and strengthened his cavalry in the hope of taking better advantage of his victories, the allies profited greatly from the pause.

The main blow to Napoleon during the armistice was the commitment of the Austrians to the allied cause. In June at Reichenbach Great Britain agreed to supply Prussia and Russia with subsidies, and Austria, Prussia and Russia signed an agreement by which it was decided that the three powers would present a list of demands to Napoleon: the duchy of Warsaw was to be broken up, Prussia was to regain her 1806 boundaries, the Illyrian provinces were to be restored to Austrian control and the Hanseatic towns were to be given their independence. Metternich was the guiding spirit behind these proposals. Even if Napoleon would not accept these terms, and their rejection seemed extremely likely, Metternich could well hope that their rejection would help to unite opinion against the French emperor.

Metternich met Napoleon in Dresden, and although Napoleon promised no concessions it was agreed that a conference would be held in Prague. The conference lasted from the middle of July until near the middle of August, but there never seemed

any real chance of success. Napoleon would not yield to the ultimatum of the Reichenbach allies, and on 12 August Austria, who had received promises of British money, declared war on France. Two days later Napoleon accepted in substance the Metternich proposals, but it is doubtful whether he would ultimately have abided by them, and in any event the allies were now ready to move in for the kill.

For Napoleon to maintain his power it was essential that he should move swiftly to defeat the separate allied armies before they could act in coordination to move westwards across Germany. There were three main allied armies on the German front: the Prussian Marshal Blücher commanded just over 100,000 Prussians and Russians in Silesia, Bernadotte commanded over 120,000 Swedes, Prussians and Russians in the north, advancing from Prussia, and in the south the Austrian Marshal Schwarzenberg had nearly 250,000 men under his command. When the campaign began Napoleon centred his forces in the region of Dresden: he hoped he could beat the allies separately, but appeared undecided whether or not to commit the mass of his army in the hope of achieving decisive victory. The Russian disaster had left him uncertain of the quality of

Above, Gebhard Leberecht von Blücher (1742–1819), the Prussian general who helped to defeat Napoleon at Leipzig and led the Prussian troops on their entry into Paris in 1814. His intervention in the Battle of Waterloo in 1815 won the day for the allies against Napoleon. Wellington Museum, Apsley House, London.

Opposite, the Battle of Leipzig of October 1813, at which the Russians, Austrians and Prussians routed Napoleon and drove him back to west of the River Rhine; Napoleon was forced to abdicate six months later. Historisches Museum, Frankfurt-am-Main.

his troops and also perhaps unwilling to take the risks that once would have seemed natural.

Instead of moving decisively, Napoleon detached smaller forces against the allied armies, and the French suffered defeats: at Grossbeeren by Bernadotte's army and at Katzbach by Blücher's. When Schwarzenberg attacked Dresden late in August Napoleon won a victory on the 26th and 27th but suffered exceedingly heavy losses, and lost all advantage from it when three days later Vandamme's army of 10,000 men was forced to capitulate at Kulm.

By September 1813 Napoleon was in dire trouble. He had won no decisive victory, he had lost a great many men, the allies were receiving reinforcements, and the French now faced encirclement as the increased allied armies combined against them. Under this pressure Napoleon retreated to Leipzig. He decided that here he would make his stand. As the ring tightened the allies were hardening in their war aims. By the Treaty of Teplitz on 9 September Prussia, Russia, and Austria agreed to fight for the restoration of the 1805 boundaries of Prussia and Austria and for independence for the states of southern and western Germany. A month later Bavaria agreed to join the allies.

When the Battle of Leipzig begain on 16 October Napoleon had 160,000 men; the allies had twice that number. It was a three-day struggle. On the first day Napoleon attempted, unsuccessfully, to rout Schwarzenberg's forces. On the 17th both sides desperately attempted to reorganize and reform, and the allied army was stiffened in the course of the day by the arrival of numerous reinforcements. On the 18th the battle was decided. The Saxon troops left Napoleon to join the allies, and Bernadotte's troops arrived. That night the French flight into and through Leipzig began, and it continued on the next day. It was a scene of chaos. Napoleon and many of his troops crossed the Elster River by the bridge, but this was blown up too soon, and many French troops were left in the town. The French had been routed, and they fled westwards across Germany.

The collapse of Napoleon's empire

After Leipzig Napoleon's empire was in ruins. At the end of October some 60,000 French troops fought their way through the Bavarians at Hanau to cross the Rhine. All over Europe there was a rush to join the allies. The German states deserted Napoleon, by mid-November Holland was in revolt, and the Italians were up in arms. In the Iberian peninsula Wellington's victory at Vittoria on 21 June had forced the French to retreat into France. By the end of the year Wellington was invading from the south.

Even yet the allies presented peace terms rather than advancing across the Rhine into France. Again Metternich was the instigator of the proposals, and as in the case of the earlier offer at Prague there were ambiguities clouding the suggested terms. It appeared from the Declaration of Frankfurt, which was agreed on by the allies in November, that they were prepared to offer the French their 'natural frontiers' of the Alps and the Rhine and to leave Belgium to France, but this was not specified in so many words.

Metternich, as earlier in the summer, had mixed motives. Undoubtedly he was hoping that whatever settlement was eventually decided upon would not so crush France as to upset completely the balance of power in Europe; Austria feared Russia almost as much as Napoleon. Yet if Napoleon accepted negotiations on Metternich's terms he had good reason for believing that he would have difficulty obtaining all he wanted in actual treaties; England was in no mood for generous concessions. If Napoleon turned down the offer of negotiations, then it could be argued that his overweening ambition had prevented France from accepting peace on the basis of her early Revolutionary victories.

Napoleon, as so often in 1813, appeared not quite sure how to proceed. In December he replied agreeing to negotiations on the basis of the allied offer, but by then this was no longer enough. The British government had made it quite clear that it was not prepared to accept a peace which gave France a firm stake in the Low Countries. Moreover, Alexander had the ambition of leading his armies in an invasion of France.

The invasion of France

Late in December 1813 the allies began to cross the Rhine to invade France. Napoleon was desperately trying to raise an army to meet them, conscripting any men who had avoided the army in previous years and calling on those who should have been conscripted in 1815. He had lost hundreds of thousands of men in eighteen months, and many of those veterans who were still under arms were cut off in fortresses scattered all the way across Germany. It seemed that all that could save Napoleon now was a mass uprising and a burst of nationalistic fervour of the kind that had been seen at the start of the Revolutionary wars. But the French people had suffered too much in the previous five years to defend with passion a ruler who had become increasingly arbitrary from the time that his empire had reached its greatest extent. In January 1814, all his efforts not withstanding, Napoleon could put into the field only some 60,000 men to meet the invaders.

The allied invasion was made in overwhelming force. First across the Rhine were the Prussians under Blücher, who invaded northeastern France; in addition the second army, led by Schwarzenberg, violated the neutrality of Switzerland to invade France further to the south, Bernadotte's force was advancing into the Netherlands, and in the south Wellington's army was continuing its steady penetration.

Napoleon first concentrated his efforts against Blücher's army and then turned against Schwarzenberg. Of necessity Napoleon led an army of manoeuvrable size, and at this moment of disaster his military genius was at its greatest. On 29 January he met Blücher's Prussians at Brienne and routed them, but he suffered a reverse at La Rothière three days later on 1 February and lost many men. At La Rothière the allies simply had too many troops, as Blücher's Prussians had linked up with a force from the south.

After La Rothière Blücher advanced rapidly into France, making the mistake of scattering his army along the valley of the Marne. Napoleon took full advantage of this, and in a series of engagements in the first two weeks of February inflicted repeated defeats on Blücher's forces. He then quickly moved against Schwarzenberg and forced that army to retreat in engagements culminating on 18 February. In less than three weeks, with a much inferior force, Napoleon had hit again and again at the allied armies. Schwarzenberg was ready to order a full retreat, but the British and Russians were not dissuaded by the military reverses.

While the armies were clashing on French soil in February, a series of negotiations

Above, the Battle of Salamanca in Spain in July 1812, at which the British under Wellington defeated the French army; by the following year he had driven the French out of Spain altogether. National Army Museum, London.

Opposite top, Napoleon crossing the Rhine in 1812, pursued by the allies.

Opposite bottom, the Battle of Badajoz, in southern Spain, in 1812, when Wellington drove out the French armies, which had occupied the town since the previous year. Badajoz was a centre of Spanish nationalist opposition to the French, and it had withstood a French siege in 1808–09.

La Restauration de la Statue d'Henri quatre Le jour de l'Entrée de Louis XVIII Le 3 May 1814.

were carried on between France and the allies at Châtillon. There never seemed any real chance of success in these negotiations. At first Napoleon had empowered his emissary Caulaincourt to make any possible peace, but his victories early in February then made him reluctant to accept even the best terms the allies were now likely to offer him. With their armies actually in France the allies were prepared to offer few concessions to the French emperor: they now intended that France should return to her pre-Revolutionary boundaries. The leadership in bolstering the allied determination was taken by the British Foreign Minister Lord Castlereagh.

On 1 March 1814, the allies signed the Treaty of Chaumont. Great Britain, Austria, Russia and Prussia agreed to fight to enforce France's pre-Revolutionary limits and to make no separate peace while Napoleon refused to accept this settlement. Great Britain agreed to subsidize the other powers while the war continued. Apart from sharing the burden of the military operations she promised to add an additional five million pounds a year to be divided among the other three powers. The allies also made a number of other agreements regarding the postwar territorial settlement: Holland and Belgium were to be combined under one monarchy, Italy was to be divided, and Swiss independence and neutrality were to be guaranteed as well.

After Chaumont it was clear that there

was to be no turning back. On 7 and 9 March the relentless Blücher, who had never had Schwarzenberg's doubts about the necessity of crushing Napoleon in France, met Napoleon's army in bitterly fought battles at Craonne and Laon. Although Blücher could claim no clear victories, Napoleon was by now so badly outnumbered that there was little he could do. He did take Reims, but at the battle of Arcis-sur-Aube on 20 and 21 March he was outnumbered by over three to one. Still he thought of attack, and planned to move against the allied lines of communication. The allies captured a letter telling of this and determined to march to attack Paris and ignore what was left of Napoleon's army. On 17 March Napoleon had made a last effort to secure a negotiated peace when he sent new instructions to Caulaincourt, but though he was now much nearer to accepting the allies' demands, the

allies were in a position to impose any peace they desired. They no longer felt any need to conciliate Napoleon. His gesture was ignored.

As the allies closed rapidly on Paris, the Empress Marie Louise and Napoleon's son left the capital. On the 30th there was fighting outside Paris, Marchals Marmont and Mortier trying to defend the capital with fewer than 30,000 men against some 200,000 on the side of the allies. Although Napoleon was rapidly approaching the city, nothing could be done to save it. On 31 March Tsar Alexander and King Frederick William of Prussia were able to enter the city.

Napoleon's abdication and exile

Napoleon would have been willing to see still more deaths and destruction in an effort to save his position, but more reasonable men prevailed. Talleyrand wanted to protect France, not Napoleon, and he persuaded Alexander that the soundest course would be the restoration of the Bourbons. The French Senate met at the beginning of April, quickly established a provisional government and announced the deposition of the emperor. On 6 April, at the urging of several of his marshals, Napoleon signed his act of abdication. His efforts to have his son recognized as emperor failed.

The fate of Napoleon was settled formally by the Treaty of Fontainebleau on 11 April. By this treaty Napoleon renounced the throne of France. He would now be emperor only of the island of Elba and would be granted two million francs a year. The Empress Marie Louise was given Parma and Piacenza in Italy, and Joséphine was given an annuity of one million francs. For a man whose ambitions had brought death and suffering to millions it was hardly a harsh settlement, but for Napoleon the fall was great. On the 12th he attempted unsuccessfully to commit suicide by taking poison.

On the 20th the ruler of Elba had an emotional parting from the Guard and set off for his island. His journey was an ignominious one and for a time the fearful emperor was disguised in Austrian uniform. He was taken to Elba on a British frigate. He arrived on 4 May, the day after Louis XVIII had arrived in Paris.

Louis XVIII

The new king now had the immediate tasks of signing a peace treaty with the allies and establishing a new government with himself as king. The Treaty of Paris was signed on 30 May 1814. France was given her 1792 boundaries, and most of her colonies were returned to her. On her part she recognized the independence of the German and Italian states, of the Netherlands and of Switzerland. Although other general principles were agreed on by the allies, it was resolved that the precise settlement would be decided upon at a congress in Vienna.

In an effort to establish a government that would be acceptable to a country which had passed through both the Revolution and the rule of Napoleon, Louis XVIII incorporated liberal features into his royal regime. The charter which he issued in June in principle promised representative government (through two chambers—one hereditary, one elected), freedom of the press and permanence for the land reforms of the Revolution. But in practice many found that Louis XVIII had learned too little from the Revolution and from the death of his brother, Louis XVI. The French people feared that the liberties granted to them would gradually be eroded. More important for Louis' immediate power, he also alienated the army by showing more favours to old courtiers than to the Napoleonic veterans. A France which had seen the world-

shaking reforms of the Revolution and the imperial glory of Napoleon could hardly be expected to greet the mediocre government of Louis XVIII with any enthusiasm.

The Congress of Vienna

While France attempted to accustom herself to her reduced state, the victorious allies met in Vienna to decide the future of Europe. This famous gathering which lasted from the autumn of 1814 to June 1815 had representatives from all over Europe; the real power, however, lay in the hands of Great Britain, Russia, Austria and Prussia. The negotiators were distinguished: Alexander came in person to represent Russia, Castlereagh acted for Great Britain, Hardenberg and Wilhelm von Humboldt for Prussia and Metternich for Austria. In view of the reason for the Congress it was remarkable that Talleyrand, who came to Vienna on behalf of France, should also have exercised such influence on the proceedings of the Congress; that he did stemmed in large part from the jealousies and dissensions which beset the victorious powers.

The eventual territorial settlement arranged by June 1815 followed the lines already established in the agreements made by the powers when advancing against Napoleon. The settlement was reached, however, only after major quarrels between the powers; these quarrels were to help to inspire Napoleon to a new effort.

Prussia gained massively by the settlement, obtaining a large part of Saxony together with territories on the Rhine. That Saxony survived at all was because of the vigorous efforts of Great Britain, Austria and Talleyrand. Germany, apart from Austria and Prussia, was organized into the Germanic Confederation of thirty-nine states and cities; they controlled their own internal affairs but ceded some powers in external affairs to the Confederation. Although Alexander did not obtain all he wanted, much of Poland came under Russian control. Holland and Belgium were united as the Kingdom of The Netherlands under

Above, the entry of the allied armies into Paris in 1814; by this time France was drained of resources, both of money and of manpower, by twenty years of war throughout Europe. Korrermuseum, Dresden.

Above left, the arrival of Napoleon at St Helena, his second place of exile, in October 1815; he was kept a virtual prisoner on the island, where he dictated his memoirs, until his death in 1821.

Opposite left, Louis XVIII, King of France (reigned 1814–24), the brother of Louis XVI; he was restored to the French throne by the allies in 1814 but had to abdicate briefly in 1815 when Napoleon returned from exile in Elba. Victoria and Albert Museum, London.

Opposite above right, the return of Louis XVIII to Paris, in May 1814; his restoration of some of the abuses of the ancien régime, *and his disavowal of the glory that France had won under Napoleon, quickly lost him the support of most of his people.*

Opposite below right, The Congress of Vienna of September 1814, at which princes from all over Europe met to re-establish the status quo. *Kungl Bibliothek, Stockholm.*

The Hundred Days

the House of Orange, and Switzerland was established as a confederation of cantons. Italy remained a collection of independent states, and Venetia and Lombardy were given to Austria. Napoleon had been defeated, but his reshaping of Europe left its mark on the peace settlement in 1815.

In late 1814 and early 1815 the situation in France and in Europe proved particularly favourable to the exiled Napoleon. In France Louis XVIII had done little to endear himself to the French people, and many looked back longingly to earlier days. In Vienna the allies showed signs not only of dissension but even of resorting to war. The greatest argument had been over Saxony, but Poland had also helped to drive a deep rift between the victorious powers. Prussia hoped at Vienna to annex the whole of Saxony, while Russia hoped for Poland. Their efforts to force their territorial demands on the Congress had by the end of 1814 pushed Great Britain and Austria together and had persuaded them both to enter a closer relationship with the defeated French. Early in January 1815 Great Britain, Austria and France signed a secret treaty pledging themselves to resist Prussian and Russian demands. The signs of discontent in France and of tension in Europe were keenly watched by Napoleon.

Since arriving at Elba Napoleon had shown little inclination to sink into a pleasant retirement. He ran the little island like an empire in miniature, although he had no empress. Marie Louise would not join him with their son, and she was able to find consolation elsewhere. At Elba Napoleon was supplied with information from the mainland of Europe and knew of the difficulties in France and at Vienna. He also had reason to complain that Louis XVIII had not paid the annuity agreed on. Yet, of course, it was not for the sake of an annuity that he was prepared to make another dramatic throw. It was power and glory that drove him; an insatiable hunger that could not be assuaged on the little island of Elba.

On 26 February 1815, Napoleon set sail for the mainland. He had fewer than a thousand men with him, but he had all the confidence of a man who had ruled Europe. On 1 March, after good fortune had helped him to avoid the British navy, he landed on the mainland. The whole episode was in the balance until he reached Grenoble, where he was welcomed with enthusiasm. From there support flocked to him, and Napoleon was again willing to encounter the combined

powers of Europe. On 20 March he entered and took command of Paris. The king had fled.

In Vienna the news of Napoleon's landing had arrived by 7 March. The allies acted promptly. Napoleon was declared an outlaw, and on 25 March the four main powers signed an alliance by which they promised to fight until their old enemy had been completely defeated. With foreign powers quickly combining against him, Napoleon felt that his main hope was to appear as the liberator of the French people. To rally the French nation behind him he attempted to create a liberal façade such as he had never felt to be necessary when he had dominated Europe.

Late in April he issued the so-called Additional Act, which tried to embody liberal reforms, including two chambers, freedom of the press and promises of a reign of liberty for French citizens. The whole plan was so clearly dictated by necessity that it aroused no enthusiasm. In general, Napoleon's attempts to arouse the French people during the Hundred Days achieved little success. The reality was not the promised liberties but rather the certainty of more war and more deaths. Napoleon's advantage was that his veterans were now in France rather than scattered in garrisons throughout

Europe, and in essence it was on these veterans that Napoleon depended. He soon had assembled an army of nearly 250,000 men, and when he moved to attack the allies he used half of these as a striking force.

A major problem confronting Napoleon in the spring of 1815 was a lack of allies. One possibility was Murat, King of Naples, who had earlier deserted Napoleon. But Murat made his move too early, in March, when he attempted to arouse Italy against the Austrians. As a result, by the time Napoleon was ready to move he had already been defeated and had fled from Italy. Napoleon would have to depend on the army he could raise in France, and he was certain to be greatly outnumbered.

At Vienna the allies planned for three armies to invade France. More than 250,000 Austrians, Bavarians and Russians under Schwarzenberg were to cross the upper Rhine; more than 150,000 Prussians under Blücher were to attack across the lower Rhine; and Wellington was to command more than 100,000 British, Hanoverians, Dutch and Belgians in the Low Countries. Wellington, who had driven the French out of Spain, had earlier in the year replaced Castlereagh as the British representative in Vienna. He was now to fill a more active role.

The Battle of Waterloo

Before the general plan of attack on France could unfold, the actual course of events was precipitated by Napoleon. He was determined to strike before the allies could assemble and drive into France. He wanted to take the offensive, defeat Wellington and Blücher and then engage the largest army under Schwarzenberg. To achieve maximum effect he would have to attack before Wellington and Blücher had combined their forces.

Napoleon left Paris on 12 June. He commanded some 125,000 men and knew quite well that he would have to strike quickly. Wellington had under his command approximately 90,000 troops, consisting of British, Germans and Dutch-Belgian forces. Blücher commanded about 125,000 Prussians; they were strung out along the Sambre and Meuse rivers, resting their right on Charleroi. Wellington's force was to the right of the Prussians, although troops were assembling as far north as Brussels. They hoped to combine for an attack into France, but the French forestalled them. The allies were not in prepared defensive lines and indeed were vulnerable as they were attempting to assemble for their own advance.

The French crossed the frontier on 15 June. Napoleon's first hope was to split the allies, rout them, and drive on to Brussels. Quickly the French drove the Prussians from Charleroi and occupied the town. Napoleon now pushed on with the main part of his army in order to engage the Prussians, while Ney was ordered to advance towards Wellington's force. Wellington moved slowly and was able to assemble only part of his army at Quatre Bras. Napoleon

Above, the Battle of Waterloo in June 1815; despite France's exhaustion after twenty years of virtually continual warfare, it was a remarkable measure of Napoleon's popularity that he could raise an army of 75,000 even though he had been in exile for a year.

Opposite, the entrance of the allied forces into Paris in March 1814, after what appeared to be the final collapse of Napoleon's ambitions. The emperor was exiled to Elba but returned to France less than a year later to stage one final bid for glory, an attempt that ended at Waterloo in June 1815.

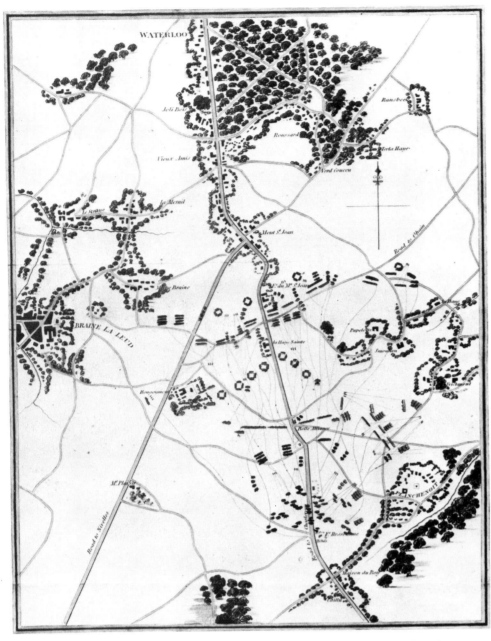

did not achieve the complete victory that he needed. The Prussians were concentrated at Ligny, and Napoleon drove them from the field on the afternoon of the 16th after bitter fighting. Ney was also able to force the allied army to retreat at Quatre Bras, but neither there nor at Ligny were the allies pursued and annihilated. The Prussians retreated in good enough order to keep in contact with Wellington's force and were ready to support him if necessary.

Wellington's army retreated towards Brussels, and Napoleon, believing that he had effectively knocked out the Prussians, detached Grouchy with 33,000 men to follow their retreat, while he prepared to attack Wellington with 74,000 men. He had divided his army on the false assumption that the Prussians were retreating away from the British.

Napoleon came up to Wellington's troops on the evening of 17 June; they were drawn up near the village of Waterloo at Mont Saint-Jean. Wellington had the assurance of Blücher that if necessary the Prussians would come to his aid. Napoleon was confident of success. He had 74,000 French veterans against Wellington's polyglot army, which was slightly inferior in numbers but markedly inferior both in cavalry and artillery, and Napoleon believed that the Prussians were incapable of taking part in the battle. Indeed, he expected that Grouchy's force of over 30,000 would be able to detach itself from the defeated Prussians and come to his aid. His only immediate problem was that the heavy rains had left the ground wet and heavy, but he hoped to solve this difficulty by delaying his attack on the morning of 18 June. The delay was far more important than Napoleon realized.

Napoleon believed that he could defeat Wellington with a direct frontal attack, and he finally sent his troops into action at 11.00 a.m. For the next five hours his infantry threw themselves with great bravery against the allied lines, but with equal bravery the allied troops held their ground. At 4.00 p.m. Napoleon decided to use his cavalry, and the British troops faced the awesome sight of massed French horsemen thundering down upon them. The squares held, and Ney re-formed his men, threw in more cavalry, but was again unable to break the British squares.

From 4.00 to 6.00 p.m. charge after charge failed; 15,000 horsemen were unable to sweep the infantry aside. By 6.00 p.m. Napoleon was very near failure, for the Prussians were now arriving on the field (Grouchy never arrived). In a desperate attempt to break through Wellington's army, Napoleon at last threw in the Guard. All their tradition and bravery was not enough, they too failed, and with Wellington's troops now moving forward and increasing numbers of Prussians throwing themselves into the battle the French began to crack and finally fled in panic. Now the allied cavalry were flung into action and pursued the fleeing Frenchmen. It was a complete rout. The losses were great. Wellington suffered nearly 15,000 casualties, the Prussians 7,000. The French never formed to assess their losses, but their casualties certainly exceeded those of the allies.

The last act

Napoleon fled from the battlefield, arriving in Paris on the 21st. After so many deaths, so much tragedy, he still talked of raising another army, of madly continuing the fight, as if the French desired nothing more than to pour out their blood in a desperate attempt to maintain Napoleon and his relatives in grandeur. Led by Fouché, the minister of police, the Chambers held firm for their own rights against Napoleon's suggestion that only a dictatorship would save the country. On 22 June Napoleon again abdicated and proclaimed his son as French emperor. It was no use. The Prussians entered Paris on 7 July, and Louis XVIII followed them on the next day.

Napoleon now hoped that he would be able to seek sanctuary in America or even find asylum in England, but the British government decided to place him on St Helena, far away in the South Atlantic. He died there on 5 May 1821. His complete reversal of fortune helped to build his legend, and in his own writings and conversation he attempted to give reasonable explanations for the many vagaries of his career.

Europe had been profoundly changed because Napoleon lived. Some of the changes had been clearly desirable, but the transformations had taken place at an incredible cost in human suffering. The Corsican adventurer had gloried in war. He had been a military genius, but part of his strength had been his very callousness, in the manner in which he was not repelled by the killing. Europe had been shaken out of her complacency. Many reforms in law and government had been brought by the French armies; many others had been induced by the desire of European states to reform to resist Napoleon. In 1815 Europe tried to recover its stability and rebuild forms of

government that were doomed, but they were doomed more because of the French Revolution than because of Napoleon.

Across the Atlantic, in the New World, the return to stability attempted in Europe was never possible, for there the changes of the Napoleonic years and of the previous generation were irreversible. In North America the success of the experiment in republican government had been in doubt since independence from Great Britain had been obtained in 1783; after 1815 it was in doubt no more. In South America the European wars had given the possessions of Spain the opportunity to emulate the British colonists to the north and break away from

Europe. Their attempt at independence still seemed in some doubt in 1815, but in reality they had begun a move for separation which could not be stopped.

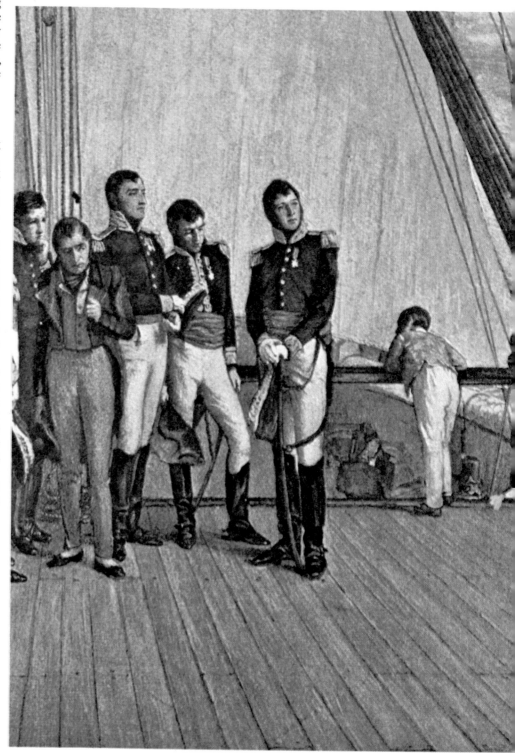

THE COLLAPSE OF THE FRENCH EMPIRE

Date	French Internal Politics	External Politics	Battles	Date	French Internal Politics	External Politics	Battles
1808		Franco-Russian conference at Erfurt Invasion of Spain	French defeated at Vimeiro	1812	Annulment of the Concordat The pope at Fontainebleau Second conspiracy of Malet	Russian campaign Retreat from Russia	Smolensk, Borodino Burning of Moscow Crossing of the Beresina
1809	Imprisonment of Pope Pius VII Napoleon excommunicated	Treaty of Schönbrunn	Battles of Corunna and Talavera Austrians defeated at Wagram	1813	Concordat of Fontainebleau	General coalition against France Joseph Bonaparte driven from Spain	Lützen and Bautzen Rout of the French at Leipzig
1810	Measures strengthening the emperor's dictatorship Napoleon's marriage to Marie-Louise Disgrace of Fouché Publication of the Penal Code	Peace with Sweden Annexation of Holland Decree of Trianon		1814	Fall and abdication of Napoleon Recall of Louis XVIII Declaration of Saint-Ouen	Campaign in France Congress of Chatillon Treaty of Chaumont Congress of Vienna	Brienne, la Rothière, Monterau, Laon, Arcis Surrender of Paris
1811	Birth of the king of Rome	Annexation of the German coast lands of the North Sea	Defeat of Marshal Masséna at Torres Vedras in Portugal	1815	Napoleon returns to France Louis XVIII flees and returns after Napoleon's abdication and banishment to St Helena	Napoleon escapes from Elba Allied troops defeat French army	French victories at Ligny and Quatre Bras Napoleon finally defeated at Waterloo

Left, Napoleon on board HMS Bellerophon, *the ship to which he surrendered after Waterloo in June 1815. Despite his hope for asylum in England, he was taken to exile in St Helena, a south Atlantic island*

Chapter 34

Independence Movements in Latin America

In the age of Napoleon the Spanish and Portuguese possessions on the American continent were divided into five huge areas of rule: the Viceroyalty of New Spain, which extended through modern Mexico and central America, the Viceroyalty of New Granada in the north of South America, the Viceroyalty of Peru on the west, the Viceroyalty of La Plata on the southeast and the Portuguese possession of Brazil. These great administrative divisions were, however, only lightly superimposed on settlements isolated from each other by immense distances, towering mountains, impassable jungles and interminable plains. The population was less homogenous than that of North America. At the very top was a small ruling elite sent from Europe. The local ruling class was the creoles, the colonial-born Spaniards or Portuguese, but there was also a large downtrodden Indian population, as well as the *mestizos*, who were half-European, half-Indian and a large population of negro slaves, particularly in Brazil, where there were also many mulattoes.

The creoles were the leaders in the movement for independence. Although they lorded it over the majority of the population, they also had a variety of grievances against colonial rule. One obvious grievance was that the highest positions of political and social power were denied to them by the *peninsulares*, the native-born Spaniards, who looked down upon the creoles as inferior.

More practically, the creoles began to look longingly at the prospects of trade outside the Spanish imperial system. The United States had waxed rich economically since breaking out of the British imperial system in the Revolution, and the creoles also thought of the prospects of trade expansion. Moreover, the creoles complained of taxation and the general economic subservience of the colonies.

In spite of underlying grievances it took a series of developments outside Latin America to produce widespread uprisings. The intellectual base for revolution had been laid in the eighteenth century. The ideas of the European Enlightenment had been influential throughout the New World; the emphasis on political and religious freedom and on the natural rights of man held a

particular fascination for Latin American intellectuals. The American Revolution also had a profound effect in stimulating ideas of independence and reform in Latin America. Not only had the North American colonies achieved their independence from Great Britain, they also had succeeded in forming a political union.

Of more direct impact on the Latin American colonies was the French Revolution and the turmoil which ensued in Europe. At first the Revolution appealed to many intellectuals, but as in North America the excesses and violence which followed the earlier constitutional phase brought fear to many creoles; they had no desire to see a social revolution which would produce an uprising of *mestizos*, Indians or perhaps even slaves. Many wanted more control of the political and economic policies for their own regions and a higher social position, but they were not asking for complete equality for the rest of the population.

Perhaps more important in Latin America than the egalitarian ideas of the late eighteenth century was the manner in which the wars of the French Revolution and Empire revealed the extent of the decline of Spain. Buffeted by France and Great Britain, Spain revealed only too plainly how far she had declined from the great power that had established a world-wide empire.

After 1796, and the conclusion of an alliance with France, the Spanish had great difficulty in maintaining connections with Latin America. It was painfully apparent to the creoles that Spain could do little against British naval power. Also, direct British influence was made possible by their occupation of the island of Trinidad in 1797: the British now traded extensively with the Latin American colonies. Spanish naval power reached a low point in 1805 when most of their navy was destroyed by the British at Trafalgar; it now seemed that the Spanish had little or no ability to defend or control their Latin American colonies.

In June 1806 a British expedition captured Buenos Aires without Spanish interference. By August, however, the inhabitants themselves had defeated the invaders. In the following year another British force occupied Montevideo, but in the early summer the British were repulsed when they attempted

to take Buenos Aires and withdrew from the whole region. These episodes gave the local inhabitants confidence in their ability to defeat a European expeditionary force and revealed yet again that the Spanish had no real means to defend their colonies in the New World.

The catalyst for revolution in Latin America was Napoleon's intervention in the Iberian peninsula in 1807 and 1808. In late 1807 French troops invaded Portugal with the object of closing her ports to British ships and British goods. The royal family, with thousands of Portuguese aristocrats, sailed to Brazil before they could be taken by the French. They arrived in the New World in January 1808.

Next Napoleon intervened decisively in Spanish affairs. In May 1808 he deposed the Bourbons and gave the Spanish throne to his brother Joseph. This intervention was to bring Napoleon a bloody war against Spanish insurgents, but even before the Spanish uprising could affect the Latin American colonies the colonists had reacted to the deposition of the Spanish monarchy.

The French emissaries who were despatched to Latin America to bring news of the takeover were rejected by the colonists. Indeed, the first assertion of independent action was in favour of the Bourbons against the French usurpers. Once, however, this

degree of independent action had been taken it was only a short time before the possibilities of struggling for full independence became apparent. There was to be no unified, coordinated action, but circumstances had simply left much of Latin America to its own devices.

Simón Bolívar

There had been a number of revolts in Latin America in the second half of the nineteenth century, but the possibilities of creole demands for independence had been revealed most clearly in the career of Francisco de Miranda, who was born in Caracas in 1750. As a young man he travelled extensively in Europe and the United States and eventually settled in England. He dreamed of the liberation of Latin America and in 1806 led an abortive expedition from the United States against Venezuela; when this early attempt at revolution failed he returned to England but was soon involved again in the early efforts to free Venezuela.

With the development of Spanish resistance to the French, Latin American creoles in a number of cities formed local juntas, emulating the Spaniards fighting against Napoleon who had formulated these local committees to organize the struggle against the French. The juntas in Latin America

Above, the proclamation of the independence of Venezuela in July 1811, with Francisco de Miranda as head of the new republic. He was unable to maintain his authority, especially after the chaos caused by a severe earthquake the following year, and it was left to Simón Bolívar to complete the work of making Venezuela independent.

Opposite, Franciso de Miranda (1750–1816), the Venezuelan revolutionary who learned his radical ideas during the American and French Revolutions. Despite leading the revolution in Venezuela in 1810–12, he surrendered to the Spanish and was eventually deported to Spain.

became more interested in independence than in supporting the Bourbons against France. These local revolutionary movements began in widely scattered areas in Latin America in 1810 and they inaugurated the first phase of the struggle for Latin American independence. For the most part these first uprisings were unsuccessful, although they were to persist in some regions until 1816.

In northern South America the independence movements in Venezuela and in New Granada (Colombia) were entwined in the years from 1810 to 1816. In Venezuela the local inhabitants had refused to recognize French rule in Spain in 1808, and in the following year some argued for separation from Spain. In 1810 a local junta was formed in Caracas, and though some argued that this was to protect the rights of Bourbon Ferdinand VII the movement quickly became more extreme. In July 1811 a congress declared the independence of Venezuela from Spain.

The leadership of this early Venezuelan movement was taken by the most important of the revolutionaries, Simón Bolívar. Bolívar was born in Caracas in 1783 and like his compatriot Miranda had travelled extensively in Europe. In 1810 he was sent to England in an attempt to obtain aid for the Venezuelan revolution. This effort failed,

but at the end of 1810 Bolívar returned accompanied by Miranda (who had been living in England). Miranda became commander-in-chief of the insurgent forces. He had a difficult task. There was internal opposition to the revolution, and the Spanish General Juan Domingo Monteverde had successfully reconquered large areas of the country.

Another blow to the patriot cause was the great earthquake of March 1812, which was felt far more severely in the rebel than the loyalist areas of Venezuela and caused great damage and many deaths. Looked upon by many as a judgement of God, it reduced support for the rebellion. In July 1812 Miranda capitulated to the Spanish and was then seized by Bolívar and his supporters who argued that he had betrayed the cause. He was turned over to the Spanish and died in prison in Spain in 1816.

Bolívar now led the revolution in the north, and, with the uprising in Venezuela for the time being crushed, he went to Cartagena in New Granada to aid the revolutionaries in that region. Cartagena had risen in revolt, and a junta had been formed there in the spring of 1810. A few months later there was a revolt in Santa Fé de Bogotá. After fighting briefly in New Granada, where there was considerable internal turmoil in the next few years, in

1813 Bolívar crossed the Andes with a few hundred men to attempt to revive the revolution in Venezuela. For a time he was remarkably successful, and in August 1813 he entered Caracas.

The renewed success in Venezuela was only temporary. Loyalist forces soon recovered lost ground, retook Caracas and Bolívar fled to New Granada. Again he succeeded in temporarily improving the position for the revolutionaries in New Granada, but the whole northern revolution was now in jeopardy, as in April 1815 General Pablo Murillo arrived from Spain with 10,000 troops. For a time Bolívar had to exile himself to Jamaica and Haiti, and his attempt to re-establish himself in Venezuela in 1816 was a failure. In 1815 and 1816 Murillo crushed the revolution in New Granada.

In Chile as in New Granada there had been considerable internal dissension. The creoles had taken the initiative in forming a junta in 1810, but any feeling of unity was soon dispelled by the development of a more radical movement under José Miguel Carrera. Many of the creoles placed more faith in their leader Bernardo O'Higgins, and the split between Carrera and the O'Higgins forces severely hampered the revolutionary movement in Chile. The victory of the loyalists at the battle of Rancagua in October

1814 temporarily quelled the Chilean revolution, and many patriots fled to Argentina.

In the viceroyalty of New Spain the movement for independence took a somewhat different form from that in other areas, in that at first it deeply involved the Indian inhabitants of Mexico. The creoles of Mexico were planning what appears to have been a more typical rebellion in the autumn of 1810 but were forestalled when their plans were discovered by the authorities. One of the planners, Father Miguel Hidalgo y Costilla, decided to go ahead immediately, and on 16 September 1810 in Dolores he urged the inhabitants of the region to rise in rebellion and invoked the name of the Virgin of Guadalupe in support of his cause.

Hidalgo's revolt met with initial success, won extensive support from the most downtrodden classes in Mexico but soon began to alienate the creoles. His decision to restore lands to the Indians and to abolish slavery was hardly likely to appeal to prosperous Mexican landowners. In January 1811 Hidalgo and his unruly followers were defeated by loyalist troops. Hidalgo was soon captured and was shot in July 1811.

After Hidalgo's death the leadership of the Mexican revolution was assumed by another priest, José María Morelos. Like Hidalgo, Morelos urged the abolition of slavery and the end of social and racial injustice. Mexican independence was declared in November 1813, and a constitution was drafted a year later, but in 1815 Morelos was captured and shot. The struggle continued, but soon only isolated bands fought for independence while most of Mexico was again under Spanish control. Efforts at resistance in the rest of New Spain, in central America, were mainly under the leadership of José Matías Delgado, but by 1814 there was little overt resistance, and the area needed a more general collapse of Spanish rule if it were to win its independence.

The only area of Spanish rule which was able to proceed reasonably steadily towards separation without major setbacks was the viceroyalty of La Plata. At Buenos Aires the inhabitants had demonstrated their strength in victories over the British in 1806 and 1807, and in May 1810 a junta of creoles was formed there. Although this junta was to have more success in maintaining itself than those in most of the other Latin American colonies, it encountered difficulties when it tried to unite the distant regions of the huge Viceroyalty.

Attempts were made to win control of what became the modern countries of Bolivia, Paraguay and Uruguay, but in each area the Argentinians were unsuccessful. Montevideo was for a time taken by an Argentinian army, but the people of

Uruguay showed a marked reluctance to place themselves under the rule either of Argentina or of their other large neighbour, Brazil.

In spite of its failure to unify the outlying regions of the viceroyalty of La Plata, the Buenos Aires junta did manage to maintain itself as an independent body. Mariano Moreno was its first important leader, but he was forced out and from 1811 the government was in the hands of a triumvirate. In spite of many quarrels, a declaration of independence was finally agreed on in March 1816 at Tucumán. Yet, in spite of the success, the influence of Argentina on the uprisings in the rest of Latin America was less by example than by the fighting qualities of José de San Martín. With Bolívar he was the key figure in the final success of the Latin American independence movement.

San Martín

San Martín was a creole, born in 1778 in what is now northern Argentina. He had travelled to Spain as a boy and had served in the Spanish army for some twenty years. In 1812 he returned to Buenos Aires, and offered his services to the revolutionary government. By 1814 he was the military leader of Argentina, and he revealed that he had ambitious plans not only for the independence of Argentina but also for the freeing of South America from Spanish rule. His strategy was based on the assumption that the vital stronghold of the Spanish position in South America was in Peru, and that the Spanish would have to be beaten there, where they were strongest. To achieve this he decided that it would be necessary to invade Chile from Argentina, conquer it for the patriots and then launch the attack on Peru. In 1814 he obtained an appointment as governor of the province of Cuyo in western Argentina.

From 1814 to the end of 1816 San Martín organized and trained his invasion army. It consisted of Argentinians, refugee Chileans and adventurers from as far away as Europe. He was supported by Bernardo O'Higgins, who had already fought the loyalists in the earlier phase of the Chilean revolution. When at last he was ready to move in January 1817, San Martín had an army of some 5,000 men. In two detachments they made a remarkable march over the Andes into Chile, losing a great many horses and mules but few men.

On 12 February San Martín's force completely defeated the Spanish at the battle of Chacabuco and entered Santiago. San Martín could have been ruler of Chile, but he stood aside in favour of O'Higgins. Southern Chile was still controlled by the loyalists, and in March 1818 the patriots suffered a severe defeat, but as the royalists advanced northwards San Martín defeated them at Maipù on 5 April 1818. San Martín now turned his attention to Peru.

Efforts at a revolutionary movement within Peru itself had achieved little success in the years after 1808. Creole attempts at uprising had been quelled by the Spanish troops, and in 1814 and 1815 an Indian uprising was crushed. If the Spaniards were to be thrown out of Peru, it needed an outside force, and after his success in Chile San Martín immediately began organizing for invasion.

San Martín's immediate needs were financial support and a navy. He succeeded in obtaining some financial support by journeying to Buenos Aires, and to command his navy he was lucky enough to secure the services of Admiral Lord Cochrane, who had been dismissed from the British navy, though his dismissal was not directly related to his qualities as a sailor. The navy consisted of ships bought or seized by San Martín or O'Higgins; with Cochrane in command it was powerful enough to carry and protect San Martín's force on its invasion of Peru.

In September 1820 San Martín landed with over 4,000 troops in southern Peru. He did not wish to risk his force in a direct attack on the coast near Lima, and after recruiting more men and attempting to raise the country to arms he moved north beyond Lima along the coast. All the time he was attempting to win over more of the Peruvian population to the rebel cause, and he also began negotiations with the Spanish authorities in an attempt to arrive at a satisfactory settlement. Although these negotiations were unsuccessful, the growing resistance in Peru caused the Spanish to withdraw from Lima into the mountains in July 1821.

Left, the Battle of Chacabuco of 1817, at which San Martín surprised and routed the Spanish army in Chile, following a dramatic march through the Andes. The victory ensured the independence of Chile.

Below, the Chilian navy in action against a Spanish frigate at Callao in 1821; the Chilean admiral was Thomas Cochrane, Earl of Dundonald, a former British commander who later assisted the Greek navy against the Turks.

San Martín entered Lima a few days after the Spanish withdrew, and on 28 July he proclaimed Peruvian independence. San Martín became 'Protector' of Peru, although the Spanish still held much of the country. As in 1820–21 impatient supporters urged him to attack immediately, but San Martín preferred to wait and to use the time to win more inhabitants from their allegiance to the Spanish. The chance for more decisive action came in 1822 with a meeting between the two great liberators—San Martín and Bolívar.

Bolívar's triumph and disappointments

The low point in Bolívar's efforts to liberate northern South America had been reached in 1815 and 1816. In March 1816 Bolívar had again journeyed to Haiti after making little impression on the Spanish in Venezuela. In 1817 he determined to try again and this time to attempt a different strategy with new allies. He decided to ignore Caracas and to concentrate on the valley of the Orinoco. There he allied himself with José Antonio Páez, leader of the *llaneros*, the wild horsemen who inhabited the plains of the Orinoco region.

Bolívar also gained assistance at this time

from the British. Several thousand recruits arrived from Great Britain in the years after 1817, and as many of them were veterans of the European wars they were a great aid to his army. Bolívar established a base at Angostura (Ciudad Bolívar) on the Orinoco and there carried out the detailed planning necessary for his new strategy: he had resolved to attack up the Orinoco, across the Andes and strike against Bogotá in New Granada.

In spring 1819 Bolívar began an epic march with several thousand men. It involved trekking for hundreds of miles in rain and heat, and then up 13,000 feet into the Andes in icy cold. The horses did not survive the journey, many men died, but Bolívar reached New Granada with an army. On 7 August 1819, Bolívar met and defeated the loyalist army at the Battle of Boyaca, and on the 10th he entered Bogotá. Bolívar was now anxious for union in Latin America, and later in the year Gran Colombia came into being; it combined Venezuela with New Granada and the Presidency of Quito (modern Ecuador), although Quito was still under the control of Spain. Bolívar was appointed president of the new country.

Bolívar still had to win control of Venezuela. This was mainly accomplished by his victory over royalist forces at Carabobo in

June 1821. Later that month Bolívar entered Caracas, and, although the last Spanish forces in Venezuela were not defeated until 1823, Colombia and Venezuela were now effectively freed. In August 1821 a constitution for the combined Colombia–Venezuela was drafted—Bolívar became president and Francisco de Paula Santander vice-president. Bolívar had no intention of stopping at his successes of 1819 to 1821; he now wanted to carry the revolution farther south and to expand his concept of South American union.

In the Presidency of Quito (Ecuador) there had been unsuccessful uprisings in the immediate aftermath of Napoleon's intervention in the Iberian peninsula; an attempt to establish a creole junta in 1809 had failed, and efforts at achieving independence in the next few years were similarly unsuccessful. In 1821 General Antonio José de Sucre was sent by Bolívar to lead an uprising in Ecuador. He landed at Guayaquil, marched towards Quito and in May 1822 won the Battle of Pichincha and with it the revolution in Ecuador. Bolívar reached Quito in the next month, and Ecuador became a part of Gran Colombia, along with Venezuela and New Granada.

In July 1822 the two great South American liberators, Bolívar and San Martín, met at Guayaquil. The actual details of their

conversation are unknown, but after the meeting San Martín determined to retire from the area to avoid any basic divisions between himself and Bolívar. His active role in the independence movement had ended, and he went to Europe, where he died in 1850.

Bolívar now had the task of ending Spanish control of large areas of Peru. He did this with the major aid of General Sucre. The main battles were fought in 1824; in August, at Junin, Bolívar and Sucre won the first major victory, and in December at Ayacucho Sucre won the battle that ended any effective Spanish control of major areas of Peru; the few remaining Spanish troops could easily be defeated.

Upper Peru (Bolivia) also achieved its independence as a result of the 1824 victories. There had been uprisings there in the years after 1808, and Argentina had taken an active interest in attempts to free the area from Spanish control, but Bolivian independence did not come until 1825. Sucre became the first president.

Mexican independence

After the executions of Hidalgo and Morelos a sporadic struggle continued in Mexico, the Spanish administration attempting a policy of conciliation after 1816. The major effort at revolution in the following years was made by Francisco Xavier Mina. Mina was born in Spain in 1789, had fought first against the French and later against the Spanish regime of Ferdinand and after going to England had decided to attempt an expedition to Mexico. He obtained some support in the United States and eventually landed in Mexico in April 1817. He won some success but in the autumn was defeated, captured and shot.

After this renewed failure, the turning point in the Mexican Revolution did not come until after 1820. Decisive here was the change of affairs in Spain. Napoleon's intervention in 1808 and the temporary deposition of the Bourbons had created the opportunity for liberalization in Spain. The organization of patriotic juntas to combat the French led to the calling of a representative body, the *Cortes*. In 1812 a constitution was adopted which tried to provide for more popular government through an elected *Cortes*, with the king as a constitutional monarch.

The Bourbon restoration which brought Ferdinand back to the Spanish throne in 1814 also produced an attack on the acts of liberalization. Ferdinand abandoned the constitution of 1812 and crushed liberal ideas. In 1820 there was a revolution in Spain, in which the king as a result of

Above, the Battle of Ayacucho, in December 1842, at which the Peruvian nationalists under Sucre defeated the Spaniards and secured Peruvian independence. The battle also represented the final success of the Latin American revolution against European rule.

pressure, restored the constitution of 1812. Ferdinand later disavowed the measures of liberalization and called in other European powers to restore his power in 1823. By that time, however, the developments in Spain had inspired action in Mexico.

The 1820 Spanish revolution convinced the conservative Mexican creoles that the time had come to press for independence as a means of preserving their own power. As their military leader they settled on Agustín de Iturbide. Iturbide was a prominent creole and had fought against the revolutions of Hidalgo and Morelos. He had proved himself to be a ruthless, conservative figure, and the creoles had good reason to believe that with Iturbide leading the struggle for independence there was no danger of any radical reforms.

At the beginning of 1821 Iturbide joined with the rebels in southern Mexico, who had maintained the struggle against the Spanish government. Iturbide and the rebel leader, Vicente Guerrero, reached an agreement at Iguala on 24 February 1821. The 'Plan of Iguala' called for an independent Mexico in which there would be a monarchy, with a European ruler, in which the position of the Roman Catholic Church would be maintained and in which there would be equality between creoles and native-born Spanish. Iturbide and Guerrero amalgamated their forces, and for the time being the divergent groups in Mexico united behind the movement for independence.

On 24 August 1821, the Spanish viceroy signed the Treaty of Córdoba by which Mexico was declared independent; the 'Plan of Iguala' was to be followed in forming the new government. The Spanish government, however, refused to honour the agreement of its viceroy, and, instead of a Spanish Bourbon prince, Iturbide was elected as Emperor Agustín by a national congress in May 1822. Agustín I had a short reign. In the following year he was forced to flee the country. He returned in 1824 but was captured and shot.

Central America

Central America did not suffer the intense fighting that characterized the independence movement in much of the rest of Latin America. There had been some agitation under Delgado after 1808, but after 1814 there was little activity in the movement for separation until an impetus was given to revolutionary ideas by the Mexican reaction to the Spanish revolution of 1820. In September 1821 a declaration of independence was issued in Guatemala City.

In the first years of Central American independence from Spain, the main issue was whether or not the whole area should be part of Mexico under Iturbide. With the fall of Iturbide, a firm decision was taken for separation. On 1 July 1823 a constitutional assembly from the five provinces of Central

America declared that the region was independent as the 'United Provinces of Central America'. In 1825 Manuel José Arce became the first president of the United Provinces. He was soon to discover the enormous difficulties and problems of maintaining a unified government.

Brazil

The independence of the huge Portuguese colony of Brazil was achieved in a manner very different from that of the Spanish colonies. This was as much because of force of circumstance as any inherent difference between the Spanish and the Portuguese possessions.

The first decisive step in Brazilian independence was the invasion of Portugal by the French late in 1807 and the flight of the Portuguese royal family and many of the nobility to America. The convoy carrying the royal family and its supporters arrived in Brazil late in January 1808. Regent John, acting in place of his mother, the mad Queen Maria, became ruler of Brazil, and in March 1808 he established his court at Rio de Janeiro.

John quickly moved to inaugurate reforms in the colony he was now to rule directly. Of greatest importance for Brazilian prosperity was his decision to throw the colony open for the ships and goods of all nations, though he also tried to stimulate local industry. His reforms extended into the cultural and social sphere: he established a national library, museums and medical schools and made a variety of attempts to create a less provincial atmosphere in his capital.

On the death of Queen Maria in March 1816 the regent became King John VI and seemed quite willing to remain in Brazil. However, his rule was meeting with increasing opposition. Some resented the power of the Portuguese nobles, others voiced republican sentiments, and nearly all objected to increased taxation. In 1817 a revolt broke out in Pernambuco, but it was suppressed within the year, and it took another basic change in European events for Brazil to alter its government.

While the Braganzas lived in Brazil, power in Portugal was exercised by a regency. In 1820, in the aftermath of the Spanish Revolution, the government of the regency was overthrown, and the Spanish

constitution of 1812 became the rallying-point of the Portuguese revolutionaries. They now wanted John to come back to Portugal and rule as a constitutional monarch on the basis of the 1812 constitution.

In Brazil the Portuguese developments produced a new demand for liberalization and forced John to accept the Spanish constitution of 1812 for Brazil as well as Portugal. At first John intended to send his son Pedro to Portugal, but fearful of the new demands in Brazil he sailed for Portugal himself in April 1821, leaving Pedro to rule in Brazil. It soon became clear, however, that the Portuguese liberals who had forced the changes in 1820 were not liberal in their attitude towards Brazil. They showed no inclination to respect Brazil's desire for greater independence and also ordered Pedro to return to Portugal.

Many Brazilians now sought to achieve independent status under Pedro, and the leadership in this movement was taken by José Bonifácio de Andrada e Silva, a scientist of marked abilities in government. Dom Pedro announced in January 1822 that he would stay in Brazil, and Bonifácio became his most important minister. On 7 September 1822 Dom Pedro declared Brazilian independence, and in the following month he became emperor.

As there were still Portuguese garrisons in Brazil, it was now necessary to expel them, and for this Dom Pedro called on the aid of Admiral Lord Cochrane, who had done so much for the success of San Martín's expedition against Peru. By the end of 1823 the Portuguese had been driven from Brazil, and the country had achieved its independence with the aid of the Portuguese royal family.

Foreign recognition

By 1824 the Latin American colonies of Spain and Portugal had effectively separated themselves from Europe. There were still some fears that there might be attempts to renew European control, but these were effectively ended by the attitude of the United States and of Great Britain.

The United States could really do little in these years to keep European forces out of Latin America, but she did use her influence to encourage Latin American independence. Many in the United States were delighted to see their neighbours to the south follow their example in throwing off European rule, and others were delighted at the prospect of additional trade opportunities. The United States delayed recognition while the issue in Latin America still seemed in doubt and while the United States was still anxious to secure Spanish agreement to the cession of the Floridas, but after this was accomplished in 1821 the United States government in 1822 accepted the principle of recognition for the new countries of Latin America. In December 1823, in the Monroe Doctrine, the United States indicated her own special interest in maintaining a Latin America free from European interference. The lack of American power to enforce this idea was made somewhat irrelevant by the attitude of Great Britain.

Since Great Britain was anxious to develop and expand her trade connections with Latin America and had no desire to see a renewed expansion of European influence in the area, her interests in this matter coincided with those of the United States. When it seemed possible in 1823 that the European powers in the Holy Alliance would help Spain to regain her lost colonies, England at first hoped to act in concert with the United States to prevent this. But the United States preferred to make an independent statement. With the British navy in command of the Atlantic, the Latin American powers were safe from any new attempts by the European powers to recapture the area.

By 1825 the huge provinces of the Spanish Empire in Latin America had already been shattered by separatist movements from within as well as by uprisings against Spain. Some still had high hopes of general unity, but within fifteen years the modern states had been created in their general outlines.

Left, Agustin de Iturbide, the Mexican revolutionary, receiving the keys of the city of Mexico in September 1821; after winning control of the country suddenly in the previous year, he became emperor (1822–23) but his conservative policies led to a further revolt against his rule.

Opposite, José de San Martín (1778–1850), the liberator of Chile and Peru from Spanish control. He served as protector of Peru from 1821 to 1822, when Bolívar persuaded him to give up the country. San Martín then retired to exile in Europe.

On page 370, a slave market in Rio de Janiero in the 1820s; slavery continued in Brazil until the 1880s, when its abolition led the plantation owners to overthrow the emperor.

On page 371, Pedro I, Emperor of Brazil (reigned 1822–31) at his coronation. Pedro was the son of the exiled King of Portugal, who declared Brazil's independence from the mother country. National Library of Australia.

The most imaginative effort to achieve unity in Latin America was that of Bolívar, who in his years of victory over Spain had formed Gran Colombia (consisting of the modern states of Venezuela, Colombia and Ecuador) and had dreamt that he would be able to include Peru and Bolivia in one mighty nation. In a few years after his victory over the Spanish he saw his dreams crumble. The distances were vast, the terrain formidable, there were entrenched local interests, and a general gulf existed between creoles, *mestizos*, Indians and slaves. The Congress of Panama in 1826, in which Bolívar placed so much hope, was an abject failure, and by the time of his death in 1830 Gran Colombia was breaking apart.

The Mexican Empire under Iturbide met a fate similar to that of Bolívar's, although it had never promised as much. On Iturbide's fall in 1823 Central America broke away and for a time remained united as the 'United Provinces of Central America'. But by 1839 this had collapsed into its constituent parts of Guatemala, Honduras, E. Salvador, Nicaragua and Costa Rica. Panama was a part of Colombia until 1903. Other attempts at unity were equally disappointing; an attempt to link Peru and Bolivia after 1835 soon failed, and although Argentina and Brazil at times had hopes of annexing Uruguay these ambitions had failed completely by 1828.

The problems of independence

The problems of nineteenth-century Latin America were immense. Unity had proved impossible, and now a variety of different countries was attempting to establish stable relations with each other and the outside world and at the same time to achieve political stability and economic prosperity. Whether their aims also included racial and social equality depended on the outlook of particular individuals. Although some of the revolutionaries had hoped for equality as well as independence, many of the creoles had merely fought for the right to control their own affairs not to change the whole political, social and economic structure of their countries.

Democratic constitutions were numerous in nineteenth-century Latin America, but there was little democracy in practice. There had been little tradition of self-government in the colonial period, and too often an autocratic system was readily transferred to the independent countries, the creoles used their political power to enhance their position within a still aristocratic society. Many remained poverty-stricken and oppressed. The turmoil and warfare in and between these newly independent nations soon allowed the *caudillos*—the opportunistic, military dictators—to take over many governments.

The economic dislocation of the struggle for independence severely hindered the development of prosperity, and in many areas it was the middle of the century before steady economic advance began. Yet, even with the coming of greater Latin American prosperity, wealth was heavily concentrated in a few hands. Huge landowners dominated the countryside, aristocratic creoles the urban centres. Although the Roman Catholic Church at first suffered from the revolutions, it maintained its dominant position, and in many areas there were bitter struggles with the clergy. For many the fine hopes of independence vanished in suffering and despair. Revolution after revolution, and constitution after constitution, still left the mass of the people illiterate, impoverished and subject to the vagaries of innumerable petty dictators.

The Brazilian Empire

By far the largest of the independent Latin American states was Brazil. It was also unusual because it was Portuguese in origin, the revolution having produced a splintering of the colonial area of government, and independence having evolved gradually through the cooperation of the Portuguese royal family after their flight from Europe; in addition the country was governed as a monarchy until 1889.

The Brazilian Empire lasted from 1822 to 1889. There were three distinct periods: the rule of Pedro I from 1822 to 1831, the Regency from 1831 to 1840, and the long reign of Pedro II from 1840 to 1889. The reign of Pedro I was a tumultuous one of internal revolt and foreign war. In spite of the effectiveness of his first chief minister, José Bonifácio, Pedro became unpopular. He was more autocratic than those who had helped to place him in power expected, was extravagant, and his reputation was hurt when he was obliged to recognize the independence of Uruguay in 1828. The main political achievement of this period was the constitution of 1824 which served, with modifications, as the basis of government until 1889.

Although the constitution of 1824 gave extensive power to the emperor, including the right to appoint the presidents of the various provinces, it did allow popular participation in government and attempted to protect individual liberties. Ultimately, however, the nature of the government depended upon the emperor, and it seemed for a time that the system established in 1824 would be short-lived.

The pressures on Pedro I increased throughout his reign. He exceeded the ample powers given to him by the constitution, and his immorality became so notorious

that it offended even his tolerant subjects. Clearly, he had been more successful than most of his contemporary South American rulers in maintaining the unity of his nation and in promoting its advance, but his unpopularity was such that in 1831 he was forced to abdicate in favour of his son, the future Pedro II, who was only five years old.

The Brazilian regency lasted from 1831 to 1840, and during this period Brazil was in danger of breaking up as the country was disrupted by civil war. Partially because of good fortune, partially because of the dedication of individual men in the government, Brazil survived and in 1840 Pedro was declared of age. In July 1841 he was crowned.

Brazil was remarkably fortunate to have Pedro II as its ruler from 1840 to 1889. Not the least of Brazil's debts to José Bonifácio was the two years he spent as the first tutor of Pedro II. He set a standard that was continued throughout the regency, and by the time he assumed the throne Pedro II was extremely well-educated. As he had the intelligence to make use of his education, he became a tolerant ruler, modest and moral in his life, and capable of appreciating the changes that were occurring in nineteenth-century Europe. He encouraged innovation and scientific endeavour as well as acting as a patron of cultural activities.

The initial problem confronting the new

emperor was a continuation of the internal dissension which had plagued the regency. A number of revolts were crushed in the early years of his reign, and by 1845 there was peace in Rio Grande do Sul, an area which had long been in a state of disruption. After the failure of an uprising in Pernambuco, Brazil settled into a period of calm which again accentuated the difference between this former Portuguese colony and many of its Spanish-speaking neighbours.

The ending of major internal uprisings did not bring complete peace to Brazil, for in the 1850s and 60s the country engaged in two foreign wars. In 1851 and 1852 the Brazilians combined with Uruguay and Argentinian revolutionaries in overthrowing the Argentinian dictator, Manuel Rosas, and between 1864 and 1870 Brazil combined her forces with those of Argentina and Uruguay in fighting Paraguay. Although the sufferings of Brazil were slight compared with those of Paraguay, she lost many dead. As in earlier Brazilian struggles a key factor in bringing about the conflict was the argument over possible external control of Uruguay. The country survived these foreign entanglements without severe injury.

The huge country of Brazil was relatively sparsely populated in the nineteenth century, but from little more than five million inhabitants in 1830 Brazil had grown to some

Above, the port of Buenos Aires in 1858; disputes over the authority that the city wielded over the rest of the country led Buenos Aires to secede from the rest of Argentina between 1853 and 1862.

Opposite, the city of Buenos Aires, the capital of Argentina, in 1847.

eighteen million by the end of the century. The Brazilian population at the beginning of this period was composed of those of Portuguese ancestry, negroes, Indians and those of mixed race. Immigration was only slight in the first half of the century, but after 1850 increasing numbers crossed the Atlantic.

Another immigration that continued until the middle of the century was that of negro slaves. An act to end the foreign slave trade had been passed as early as 1831 but it was not effectively enforced until the early 1850s. After the middle of the century there was growing sentiment among liberals for the ending of slavery itself. They were helped by the support of the emperor, who had freed his own slaves, and who was strongly in favour of abolition. At last in 1871 the Rio Branco law provided that all children born of slave mothers would now be free. Pressure for total abolition continued, and in 1885 all slaves over sixty were freed. The final act came in May 1888 with the abolition of all slavery. There was no compensation for the owners.

As the internal disorders died down by the end of the 1840s, the economy of the country began to advance rapidly. Brazil had great natural resources, and although they were not properly tapped the country advanced spectacularly compared with most South American nations. Coffee became increasingly important in the second half of the century, sugar and tobacco were also grown extensively, and there was a very large cattle industry. The southern area of Brazil was particularly stimulated by this economic advance, and the province of São Paulo became of major importance in the Brazilian economy.

There was also a marked increase in industry and general commercial activity in the second half of the century. Financial stability was promoted by the foundation of the Bank of Brazil in 1853. Manufacturing increased at this time, and there was considerable expansion of transport and communications facilities. These were stimulated

by foreign capital which was attracted by the comparative stability of this Latin American nation. The most important of the Brazilian speculators was Ireneu Evangelista Mauá, who established a banking fortune and invested in all aspects of Brazil's expanding economy.

The construction of railroads began in the 1850s, and by the end of the empire in 1889 there were over 6,000 miles of track. Steamship lines and a telegraph service were also developed. Most of Brazil was still undeveloped and there were still incredible problems of communication, but against the background of most other Latin American nations the advances appear remarkable.

Despite all these advances, Brazil remained a country of large landowners, rich aristocrats and numerous poor people. Although Pedro II was greatly interested in education, most of his people were still illiterate at the end of his reign. For the future of the empire, however, it was more important that Pedro began to lose the support of influential groups and that a republican party began to gain strength.

In the 1870s the government alienated many Catholics by siding with the Freemasons in a dispute with the Church. The government had already lost the support of many of the great landowners because of the partial abolition of slavery in 1871, and lost others because of total abolition in 1888. A third area of vital support was lost by the emperor's attitude towards the army. Pedro II was no militarist, and many officers had begun to feel that the military would receive greater recognition under a different type of government. With many of the military, the Church and the great landowners alienated and liberals demanding a republic, the empire came to an end in 1889. A bloodless army revolt forced Pedro II to abdicate. He died in Europe in 1891.

The republic established in Brazil in 1889 at first provided little stability. In 1891 a constitution based on that of the United States was put into effect, but until near the end of the century Brazil was again beset by internal revolts; whatever the constitution the country was for a time ruled by the military. It was not until 1898 that it was again possible to restore something approaching normal conditions and to begin to rebuild the economy. In the early years of the new century the country again began a steady economic advance.

Spanish Latin America

Any discussion of the ex-Spanish colonies in Latin America in the nineteenth century is complicated by their lack of uniformity and the internal chaos that existed for so many years in these countries. Although it is possible to group them for convenience into certain divisions—the Rio Plata countries of Argentina, Uruguay and Paraguay the two Andean groups of Chile, Bolivia and Peru and Venezuela, Colombia and Ecuador, and the former New Spain area of Mexico and Central America—the countries within any one group frequently had little in common with adjacent states and pursued their own ambitions. For many of these years, the history of these Latin American countries is a sorry tale of internal turmoil, bloodshed and despotism and frequently costly and senseless external conflicts. Bolívar's dream all too often became a nightmare in nineteenth-century Latin America.

Argentina

From the beginning of the independence movement in 1810 to the end of the 1820s it proved impossible to establish a unified Argentina. Some hoped that Uruguay and Paraguay would form part of a great nation, but even the unity of Argentina itself was not possible. Buenos Aires attempted to make itself the centre of a unified nation, but the outlying provinces, led by their *caudillos,* refused to recognize its leadership, and by the 1820s had effectively separated themselves, after a series of wars, from the control of the Buenos Aires region.

The development of the power of Buenos Aires came with the rise to prominence of Juan Manuel de Rosas. Rosas was born in Buenos Aires in 1793 but had spent years ranching, an experience that helped him greatly in winning the respect and support of the *gauchos,* the hard-riding horsemen of the Argentinian plains. In 1829 Rosas became governor of the province of Buenos Aires, and soon became one of the most powerful *caudillos* in Latin America. He served three years as governor but then left Buenos Aires to fight the Indians in the south. In 1835, when Buenos Aires politicians persuaded him to take power again, he inaugurated a dictatorship. Although he was still officially governor only of Buenos Aires, he also dominated the rest of the Argentinian provinces.

Rosas' rule lasted from 1835 to 1852. These were years of tyranny, brutality and

murder. Rosas exterminated his rivals and ruled by terror. He discouraged immigration, showed a total lack of imagination in his economic policies and engaged in a variety of foreign quarrels. He was finally brought down by a combined army of Argentinian opponents, Brazilians and Uruguayans in 1852. He fled to England and died there in 1877.

The main Argentinian opponent of Rosas, Justo José de Urquiza, became President of

Argentina in 1853 under a new constitution based on that of the United States. The confederation united all the provinces except for the most important one of Buenos Aires, which remained independent. When Buenos Aires finally joined the other provinces, after Urquiza had retreated from the forces of General Bartolomé Mitre in 1861, it was essentially on her own terms. In 1862 General Mitre became president of the now united Argentina, and he rapidly began to

Former Spanish territories
*British, Netherlands, French
Former Portuguese territories

develop a more prosperous nation, encouraging immigration and stimulating the economy. Progress slowed in 1865 when Argentina joined in the war against Paraguay, but when Mitre's term ended in 1868 he had done much to establish a unified and prosperous country.

The 1870s brought rapid advance economically in the newly unified Argentina. At last Argentina was free from internal and external struggles, and under the presidencies of Domingo Faustino Sarmiento (1868–74), Nicolás Avellaneda (1874–80) and Julio A. Roca (1880–86) seemed to be achieving prosperity. Sarmiento reflected his own background as a teacher and writer encouraging education. He was a forward-looking politician, encouraging immigration and promoting the national economy, particularly in improved communications.

Sarmiento's successor, Nicolás Avellaneda, having first put down a revolt by Mitre, who objected to the manner in which Sarmiento had helped to defeat Mitre's own candidacy, continued the economic advances. Cattle ranching, long of vital importance, was expanding rapidly, and wheat was becoming of increasing importance. Moreover, in the last years of his administration, Avallaneda's minister of war, Julio A. Roca, extended the area that could be farmed in the south by waging a war against the Indians in that region. These campaigns helped to create Roca's political career.

One of the last and most important acts of Avellaneda's government was the federalization of the city of Buenos Aires. This was done against the will of the province of Buenos Aires and was a major issue in the 1880 campaign for president, in which Roca was supported by the existing administration. When Roca won, Buenos Aires attempted to resist the desires of the other provinces but soon capitulated. The last stage in political unity had been achieved.

The prosperity of the 1870s continued into the 80s, but there were now more signs of weakness in the economy, as first President Roca and then President Miguel Juárez Celmán allowed, or even connived at, public corruption. The inflated economy of the 1880s brought great profits to many, as the long-established foreign trade in hides had now, with the development of refrigeration, expanded into trade in meat. By the 1880s Argentina, with its extensive foreign trade in beef, mutton and wheat had changed remarkably from the pre-1850 country of Rosas. This boom period came to an end in 1889 with a major economic crisis.

In 1890 a rebellion against the government was crushed, but with opinion firmly against him President Celmán soon resigned, and Vice-President Carlos Pellegrini took over. His policy was caution and honesty. In spite of his avowals, the election of Luis Sáenz Peña in 1892 inaugurated a period of political turmoil and internal dissent. In 1895 Peña resigned, and his vice-president, José Uriburu, took over. Not

until 1898, when Julio A. Roca was elected to serve once again as president, did order return and the nation regain its prosperity. Those who wanted political reform were not satisfied, however, and in the new century the Radical party grew rapidly in strength. In 1916 it ousted the long-established ruling elite.

Uruguay

The small country of Uruguay, which was created from the region known until 1828 as the Banda Oriental, was a region of almost constant turmoil in the nineteenth century. Logically, Uruguay seemed destined to become part of one of its large neighbours, Argentina or Brazil, but in reality their rivalry allowed Uruguay to achieve a precarious independence, which in the twentieth century developed into a more prosperous stability.

The struggle for Uruguayan independence began in 1811 under the leadership of José Gervasio Artigas, a gaucho who had gained military experience in the Spanish army. His struggle for independence was complicated by the necessity of winning freedom not only from the old Spanish rulers but also from Argentinian revolutionaries, who hoped to make the region and its main city, Montevideo, dependent upon Buenos Aires. Another difficulty was the Portuguese royal family, who after they came to America hoped to add the region to their domains. The precarious independence won by Artigas collapsed, and he fled to Paraguay where he died in 1850.

From 1821 Uruguay was controlled by Brazil, but in 1825 the Uruguayan Juan Antonio Lavalleja entered the country with a tiny group of compatriots—the 'immortal thirty-three'—to wage war for independence

Above, Justo José de Urquiza (1801–70), the Argentinian politician who opposed the rule of Rosas and became president of the confederation of Argentina in 1854; nevertheless he was unable to prevent the temporary autonomy of Buenos Aires province.

Above left, Juan Manuel de Rosas (1793–1877), the Argentinian dictator who, as governor of the province of Buenos Aires between 1829 and 1832, and again between 1835 and 1852, was able to rule the entire country. He suppressed all opposition ruthlessly and planned to extend his rule over Paraguay and Uruguay.

Opposite, Latin America in the early nineteenth century, showing the dates in which each region won its independence.

against the Brazilians. He was supported from Argentina, and a Brazil–Argentina war ensued which was finally settled, with the aid of British pressure, in 1828. The peace treaty which was signed in August 1828 gave a Brazilian and Argentinian guarantee of the independence of Uruguay. Although her powerful neighbours were still to interfere in the country, never again was Uruguay in such danger of being annexed.

From this time until the first decade of the twentieth century Uruguay was the scene of constant tumult, revolution and internal division. The initial struggle (in the 1830s) was between the partisans of the first president, Fructuoso Rivera of the Colorado party, and Manuel Oribe of the Blanco party, who became president in 1835. The Colorado party, which claimed progressive ideas, and the Blanco group, which was more conservative, were rallying-points for rival factions in the following years, although any true liberal–conservative division was completely obscured by the continual struggles of a variety of *caudillos*. It was the twentieth century before a president could take office without the constant fear of being violently overthrown.

In spite of the political turmoil, Uruguay began to make some economic and social advance, particularly from the 1870s. The population, which had been only 70,000 in 1830, had reached nearly 1,000,000 by 1900, aided by the immigration of thousands of Europeans. Stock raising was by far the most important economic occupation of the country, although political turmoil prevented development of the refrigeration facilities essential for a successful export trade until long after Argentina had acquired them. Similarly, it was not until the 1870s that definite progress began to be made in education. Few observers in nineteenth-century Uruguay would have dared prophesy the degree of success achieved in the twentieth century.

Paraguay

Paraguay had a disastrous nineteenth-century history and has remained one of the most backward and isolated of the Latin American nations. Its population, largely Indian mingled with Spanish, suffered incredibly in the nineteenth century.

The first efforts at Paraguayan independence came in 1811, when the Spanish were overthrown and a junta established. The Spanish had previously resisted the efforts of the Argentinian revolutionaries to absorb the area. By 1814 the country was in the control of José Rodríguez de Francia, a lawyer of mixed Portuguese and Spanish creole parentage. By 1816 he was established as dictator for life.

The Francia regime was a strange one. Francia was dedicated and frugal but also cruel and ruthless. He totally crushed oppo-

sition in Paraguay and then isolated the country from foreign influences, preventing immigration and allowing only limited trade. His country suffered none of the chaos prevalent in much of Latin America at this period and its agricultural development was promoted, but there was no freedom, no education and no refreshing outside influences.

Francia, a man of whom little is known, created his own little island in the middle of South America and kept all the power in his own hands. His death in 1840 brought turmoil for a short time, but by 1844 Carlos Antonio López was installed as president for a ten-year term. López and his son were to dominate the nation until 1870. López, like Francia, ruled as a dictator, but the nature of his rule was similar to that of other Latin American rulers. He opened the country to foreign contacts and pursued an ambitious foreign policy, in 1852 helping to bring down the Argentinian dictator Rosas.

On the death of López in September 1862 control of Paraguay was taken by his son, Francisco Solano López. He soon made the Paraguayans realize how fortunate they had been under the moderate dictatorship of his father. The young López was a cruel, ambitious incompetent who inflicted suffering on his country to an extent that has rarely been experienced in any nation. He sought foreign glory and as a result of his ambitions led Paraguay into a war against Brazil, Argentina and Uruguay simultaneously. The Paraguayan war lasted from 1865 to 1870, and more than half of the Paraguayan population of 500,000 was dead at the end of the conflict. Fewer than 30,000 men were still alive and López had been killed. Paraguay was defeated and was forced to pay an indemnity.

After 1870 the main political change was

that the dictators succeeded each other with great rapidity. No political stability was achieved, and Paraguay entered the twentieth century as a sorry example of man's ineptness and cruelty. Economic and social progress had been slight, communications were atrocious, most of the population lived in primitive conditions, and there was general illiteracy. Wealth was confined to a very small minority.

Chile

The elongated nation of Chile, stretching along much of the Pacific coastline of South America, achieved a notable degree of stability in the nineteenth century. In the colonial period Chile had been overshadowed by Peru, but in the nineteenth century the area was to achieve more success than its neighbours.

The internal struggle for power in Chile began as early as 1810, but it was not until 1817 and 1818, when San Martín invaded the region, that independence was won from Spain. The first leader was Bernardo O'Higgins, whose Irish father had risen to be Viceroy of Peru. Bernardo was illegitimate—his mother a Spanish creole. He governed as a progressive dictator, but was forced out in 1823. In the years to 1830 Chile appeared to be drifting into total disorder. General Ramón Freire held power until 1827, but for the next few years there was a rapid change of rulers.

An advance towards stability in Chile came in 1830 with the victory of the conservative group known as the *Pelucones*. This group had been contending for power with the liberals, the *Pipiolos*. The most important architect of the new regime was Diego Portales, who set up a conservative

Above, one of the main streets of Santiago, capital of Chile, in the mid-nineteenth century, showing the customs house and the Jesuits' Church. British Museum, London.

Above left, the sinking of a Brazilian gunboat by Paraguayan boats using torpedoes, during the War of the Triple Alliance, in 1865.

Left, Bernardo O'Higgins (1778–1842), the Chilean revolutionary whose father was Irish and who was supreme director of the country from its independence in 1818 until 1823.

Opposite, fighting in Uruguay during the War of the Triple Alliance of 1865–70, when Paraguay's aggression was opposed by Brazil, Argentina and Uruguay. By 1870 Paraguay was devastated.

ruling clique of landowners and clergy, and effectively stifled both military and liberal opposition.

The constitution of 1833 was a conservative document, placing considerable power in the hands of the president and establishing Roman Catholicism as the official religion. Although this was not what South American liberals had hoped for, Chile did not have the tyrannical, brutal rule inflicted on so many other areas in these years. Under the presidencies of Joaquín Prieto, Manuel Bulnes and Manuel Montt from 1831 to 1861, Chile advanced steadily economically, and there was some progress in education.

In 1861 the liberals were at last able to take over in Chile, the government having alienated some of its supporters by a quarrel with the Church and the abolition of primogeniture (inheritance solely by the eldest son). Liberal rule from 1861 to 1891 wrought no radical changes, but the conservative system created by Portales was slowly modified, even though the presidents were still in a position of great power. The prosperity of the nation continued to increase, and its boundaries were enlarged by the War of the Pacific with Peru and Bolivia between 1879 and 1883.

The liberal regime ended in 1891 when President José Manuel Balmaceda, who had come to power in 1886 and had carried out an extensive programme of public works, was opposed when he went further than most Chilean presidents in attempting to rule outside the constitution. Balmaceda was overthrown, and from 1891 the Chilean Congress was better able to control the power of the presidents as parliamentary rule came to Chile. There were still many poor, many who played no part in government, but compared with much of Latin America Chile had achieved a reasonable measure of success as an independent country by the beginning of the twentieth century.

Peru

Peru had been a centre of Spanish power in Latin America. The Spanish had exercised a tight control over the largely Indian and *mestizo* population, and not until San Martín's invasion in 1820 and 1821 and the victories of Bolívar and Sucre in 1824 were Spanish hopes in Peru crushed.

Bolívar had been invited into Peru in 1823 to unite the revolutionaries and drive out the Spanish, and he ruled as a virtual dictator until he left the country in 1826. The government he had placed in power was overthrown in the following year, and the period from 1827 to 1844 was filled with conflict and struggles for power among warring factions. Between 1835 and 1839 a Bolivian, Andrés Santa Cruz, united Peru and Bolivia in a confederation, but this collapsed. No stability was achieved until

Ramón Castilla came to power in 1845.

Castilla was a *mestizo* of Indian, Spanish and Italian forbears. He was the main force in Peruvian politics from 1845 to 1862, serving as president from 1845 to 1851 and from 1855 to 1862. Between his terms in office the country was ruled by José Rufino Echenique, a far less able leader, who was overthrown by Castilla in 1855. Castilla brought far more political stability than had been known earlier, and the country also advanced economically and socially during his rule. Guano exports increased greatly, communications were improved and slavery was abolished. Constitutional revision took place, culminating in the conservative constitution of 1860 which was to be the basic document until 1920. The president was given considerable power, and Roman Catholicism was made the official religion of the country.

After Castilla Peru again had difficulty achieving any real political stability, and few presidents were able to serve out their terms in peace. Only President Manuel Pardo between 1872 and 1876 achieved moderate success, but his administration foundered financially. The 1860s and 70s were also marred by foreign entanglements. A brief war with Spain produced no major disasters, but the War of the Pacific (1879–83) against Chile was a crushing blow. Although allied with Bolivia, Peru was unable to protect even her own territory. Lima was occupied and the economy suffered a major setback.

In the aftermath of the war, military leaders struggled for control of the country, and it was not until 1895, when Nicolás de Piérola came to power, that a modicum of stability was achieved. Even then the majority of the Peruvian people were not represented in the government.

Peru had been the heart of the Spanish empire in South America, but its progress in the nineteenth century was extremely limited. The country was unable to achieve a progressive and responsible government, and there was no great economic advance. Guano was of importance, but Peru had

lost its nitrate assets in the war against Chile. There had been some advance in the development of railroads, but the profits helped the British, who owned them, more than the Peruvians. All in all, the Peruvian experiment in independence had been a major disappointment.

Venezuela

Bolívar's hope that Venezuela would become part of his great confederation had been shattered at a very early date. The key figure in the early history of Venezuela was José Antonio Páez, a general under Bolívar, who was left in command in Venezuela when Bolívar went south to conquer new lands. Páez was a llanero, a cattleman from the great Venezuelan plains. He exercised a peculiar fascination over Venezuela's large *mestizo* population, although his rule in effect benefited the white minority.

Venezuela withdrew from Bolívar's confederation in 1829 and in 1830 drafted a constitution and made Páez the first president. He was to dominate the politics of the country until 1846, and even returned as late as 1861 to rule until 1863. Although Páez was basically an autocrat, he allowed a certain degree of freedom, restored the prosperity of a country badly hurt by the wars of liberation and attempted to encourage Venezuelan trade. It was not a democratic regime, but for the most part it was a reasonable one.

The collapse of Páez's power in the mid-1840s was brought about by the Liberals, but in reality power still rested with a narrow group of Venezuelans, and from 1846 to 1858 control of the country was in the hands of José Tadeo Monagas and his brother José Gregorio Monagas. Apart from the abolition of slavery in 1854, this was no liberal regime, and little was accomplished for the mass of the population.

The fall of the Monagas regime in 1858 precipitated some twelve years of turmoil in Venezuela, although Páez did come back and attempt to restore order in the early

1860s. For the most part these were years in which *caudillos* struggled for power, ignoring the interests of the great mass of the population. The turmoil ended with the rise to power of Antonio Guzmán Blanco in 1870. He controlled the country until 1888.

Guzmán Blanco put himself forward to the people as a man sympathetic to their aims and ideals. In reality, he ruled ruthlessly, spent a great deal of money and indulged his remarkable vanity in extravagant living. Yet, for all this, he was an able ruler who made a definite attempt to develop his country. He was able to create economic prosperity by encouraging exports (particularly coffee), improving communications, attracting foreign capital and generally providing the stability necessary for economic advance.

The rule of Guzmán Blanco did little, however, to break down the great gulf in Venezuela between the privileged few and the mass of the poor and deprived. Indeed, his rebuilding in Caracas served to emphasize the physical distinction between the prosperous few and the poverty-stricken masses in their rural hovels.

After the fall of Guzmán Blanco stability was again lacking in Venezuela. It was won back, but at a terrible price in cruelty and oppression, under Cipriano Castro from 1899 to 1908 and under Juan Vicente Gómez from 1908 to 1935. For most in Venezuela, Bolívar's dreams of liberty and freedom proved illusory.

Colombia

Bolívar's attempt to include what is now Colombia in his unified state of Gran Colombia had failed by 1830. As in Venezuela, settlers of European origin were in a minority; the majority of the population was *mestizo*.

In the 1820s the dominant political figure in the region was Francisco de Paula Santander. He was forced to flee the country in 1828, and the secession of Venezuela and Ecuador brought an end to Gran Colombia. In 1832 a constitution was adopted at Bogotá for the state of New Granada. Santander, who returned in 1832, became the first president. In his years of rule to 1837 he provided an orderly and honest government and promoted the economic and educational well-being of his population.

In spite of Santander's efforts to establish a firm basis of government, the next fifty years brought internal turmoil and constant struggles for power. The country (which became the 'United States of Colombia' in 1863) was racked by interminable arguments between liberals and conservatives. There was some advance—slavery was abolished in 1851—but the failure to agree on basic policies prevented the country from achieving any steady progress economically, socially or politically. In the 1860s and 70s the liberals controlled the country, and by the constitution of 1863 they allowed considerable local autonomy, though they alienated many by their attack on the Catholic Church.

A conservative regime returned to power when Rafael Núñez was elected president in 1880. He had received liberal support, but once in power he created a new party—the Nationalist party—which became a major conservative force. He was president until 1894 (except between 1882 and 1884) and codified the principles of his regime in the constitution of 1886. This ended local autonomy, and created a highly centralized system and also gave back to the Church the position it had lost under the liberals. A concordat with the pope in 1887 completed the re-establishment of the position and power of the Church. Núñez built so carefully that the conservatives were to hold power in Colombia until well into the twentieth century.

Economically and socially Colombia made little progress in the nineteenth century. In 1900 communications were still poor, agriculture was primitive, and even coffee had not yet achieved a position of great importance as an export. These difficulties were compounded by a civil war from 1899 to 1902 in which the liberals attempted to overthrow the conservatives and were defeated only after a major struggle which brought great destruction and many deaths. To add to Colombia's troubles, in 1903 Panama became independent as a result of the intervention of the United States. In view of its nineteenth-century record, Colombia was to make surprising progress in the twentieth century.

Ecuador

Early attempts to establish the independence of Ecuador had failed in the years after 1809, and the region did not establish its independence from Spain until 1822. The union of Gran Colombia existed for a few years, but in 1830 Ecuador became independent. Juan José Flores, a Venezuelan who had served under Bolívar, became the first president of the independent state, ruling until 1835 and again from 1839 to 1845.

The constitution of 1830 gave considerable powers to the president, and Flores used them to establish an autocratic regime. His main opponent was the liberal Vicente

Rocafuerte. In 1834, to avoid being overthrown, Flores agreed that Rocafuerte would be the next president. In his term, which ran from 1835 to 1839, Rocafuerte liberalized the government and attempted some progressive reforms. Flores returned to power in 1839 and in 1843 changed the constitution to extend his term, but was overthrown in 1845. There followed a time of chaos.

Order returned in 1861 when the conservative Gabriel García Moreno, an aristocrat of Spanish ancestry, came to power. He was in control of the country either in person or through his unfluence until his assassination in 1875. García Moreno's rule was remarkable because of the extent of the power he was prepared to give the Catholic Church. He gave it a monopoly of religion in the constitution of 1861 and then allowed it to control all education. Although García Moreno ran the country as a dictator, he was honest and made a determined effort to stimulate the economic development of the country. On his assassination in 1875 Ecuador sank into twenty years of turmoil.

When the Liberals came to power in 1895 their dominant figure was Eloy Alfaro, who was president from 1895 to 1901 and from

1906 to 1911. Alfaro attempted to limit the power of the Church, practised religious toleration and removed clerical privileges. He did not achieve any massive changes in the country, but he did improve communications and attempt to bring Ecuador a little more into the modern world. At the beginning of the twentieth century the mass of the Ecuadorian people, who totalled some one-and-a-half million, still lived as their ancestors had lived. Power and wealth were held by a tiny white minority.

Mexico

Mexico was the most heavily populated of the newly independent Latin American nations, and only Brazil was larger in area. The difficulties in achieving a stable government were numerous. Many of the creoles who wanted to separate from Spain wanted even more to prevent the *mestizos* and Indians creating a social revolution. Even among the ruling elite there were sharp differences—some were enthusiastic for a loose federalism, others for a centralized state. These conflicting views plunged Mexico into a turmoil from which the country

scarcely emerged until the dictatorship of Díaz more than fifty years after the achievement of independence.

The collapse of Iturbide's hopes of establishing an empire in Mexico came in 1823, and in the following year a constitution was adopted which embodied the ideas of the federalists, who opposed a highly centralized system. Within little over ten years, however, this constitution was replaced by a centralized dictatorship under the leadership of Antonio López de Santa Anna.

Santa Anna was the most important political leader of the first thirty years of Mexican independence. He was a creole who had gained military experience in the Spanish army, and he assumed power in 1834. Santa Anna was a ruthless, unscrupulous power seeker, and until 1855 he had a decisive role in Mexican politics, even when he was not serving as president.

The immediate effect of the abolition of the federal state system was the secession of Texas from Mexico in 1836. The Americans who had settled in that area since 1820 now decided to fight to separate themselves from Mexico; many hoped that they would then become a part of the United States. Santa Anna was completely defeated in Texas in 1836, Texas achieved de facto independence and after much effort was finally accepted into the United States in 1845.

In May 1846, after a clash between Mexican and United States troops, the United States declared war on Mexico. The basis of the difficulty was ownership of the northern Mexican possessions. Although the United States had grievances against Mexico for non-payment of claims, the basic reason for the war was United States pressure on the northern regions of Mexico. The Mexicans defended their country fiercely, but the war was a disaster for them. The United States won a complete victory. At the Treaty of Guadalupe Hidalgo in February 1848 Mexico had to agree to almost the modern boundary between the two countries. The size of Mexico had been nearly halved.

Santa Anna had ruled as a dictator, raiding the national treasury and bringing misery to the mass of the Mexican population. Even after the disasters of the Mexican war, he regained power once again in 1853 and ruled the country until forced to flee in 1855.

The fall of Santa Anna inaugurated a twenty-year effort at liberal reform, which brought more turmoil to this troubled nation. In this period the Indian, Benito Juàrez, dominated the government. First serving under President Juan Alvarez, Juàrez himself ruled the country for much of this time. The liberals took firm measures against the Church, expelling the Jesuits and reducing the size of Church land holdings. The constitution of 1857 provided for freedom of speech and of the press, restored the federal system and limited the powers of the president. The liberal reforms led to civil war, and although Juàrez was victorious (bringing far stricter measures against the Church) he found himself with a major problem in foreign policy.

In 1861 Great Britain, France and Spain agreed to intervene in Mexico to secure the payment of debts owed to their citizens. It soon became clear that France wanted more than the payment of debts. Napoleon III, beset with dreams of grandeur, had decided to establish an empire in Mexico. England and Spain withdrew, but the French troops entered Mexico City in 1863. The United States could do nothing as she was torn by the Civil War. In the same year a hereditary monarchy under the Habsburg archduke,

381

Ferdinand Maximilian Josef, brother of the Austrian emperor, was established. He arrived in Mexico in 1864. Juàrez continued the fight, and Maximilian was deserted when, under American pressure France withdrew her troops. Without French support Maximilian could not maintain his government. In 1867 he was captured and shot.

Juàrez now ruled the country until his death in 1872, and even then his policies were continued until 1876. The end of the Juàrez era was brought about by the mestizo Porfirio Díaz, who had led Mexican armies in the war against France and Maximilian. In 1876 he led a military revolution against the government and assumed the presidency. With the exception of the years from 1880 to 1884, when he continued to rule behind the scenes, Díaz held office until 1911.

Díaz brought order and peace to Mexico, although he ruled ruthlessly. He restored the position of the Church and attempted to achieve Mexican prosperity by stimulating economic activity. This involved improving communications, encouraging foreign capital, developing mining and manufacturing and establishing a stable financial system. Yet, though Mexico was now more prosperous and stable, only a small minority within the country and the many foreign investors obtained the benefits of this prosperity. The great mass of the people were

untouched by the improvements. The rural areas were poverty-stricken, had few schools and no say in how they were governed. Mexico achieved greater stability and prosperity under Díaz, but most of the Mexican people did not share in the improvements.

The Central American states

For a time after the achievement of independence, it seemed possible that the five modern countries of Guatemala, El Salvador, Honduras, Nicaragua and Costa Rica would achieve some unity, but these hopes nursed by the revolutionary generation such a short time before.

The collapse of the 'United Provinces of Central America' was not surprising. Its five parts thought of themselves as distinct units, there were massive problems of communication and local leaders were desirous of enhancing their own political careers. The total population of the region was something between one and one and a half million. Most of these were Indians, many were *mestizos* and there was a small minority of creoles. After the collapse of the United Provinces in 1839, there were other attempts at unity, but none of them was successful. Separate, impoverished, the countries of Central America were the scene of constant turmoil in the nineteenth century.

The dominant political figure for over twenty-five years after the break-up of the confederation was Rafael Carrera, a *mestizo* who controlled Guatemala from 1840 to 1865. He was a dedicated conservative who allied himself with the Church and exerted great political influence on Honduras, El Salvador and Nicaragua as well as on his own country. In 1840 and 1855 he helped to turn out the liberals in Honduras, and in the 1840s and 50s he also intervened in El 1840s and 50s he also intervened in El Salvador to support the conservative faction.

The first change to a liberal regime in Guatemala came in 1871 under Justo Rufino Barrios. His ideas were more liberal than those of Carrera, but his rule was still autocratic. He controlled the country tightly until his death in 1885. Little progress had been made in Guatemala by the turn of the century. Economic development was slight, and most of the population was poor and illiterate.

Honduras, Nicaragua, and El Salvador had similarly unfortunate experiences in the nineteenth century. Honduras was poorer than Guatemala, and developed little. Nicaragua was beset with liberal–conservative quarrels, and in the 1850s an American adventurer, William Walker, was even able to take over the country for a time after being invited in by the liberals. In the latter part of the century the clash continued, but

Nicaragua made great progress in agriculture, bananas and coffee becoming of increasing importance.

Tiny El Salvador, only some 13,000 square miles, experienced the same turmoil as the rest of Central America and sank into obscurity for much of the nineteenth century.

Costa Rica was unlike the rest of Central America in that the majority of its population was of European origin. Its history for much of the nineteenth century was also less tragic than its neighbours, and it suffered less from dictators and adventurers than did the other Central American countries. All in all, however, Central America could hope for little while so many of the people of the area were impoverished and illiterate and political fragmentation prevented the desired economic cooperation.

The history of Latin America in the nineteenth century demonstrated quite clearly that independence from European control did not in itself create enlightened, democratic and prosperous regimes. A colonial heritage of autocracy, racial and social gulfs, a lack of economic development, the failure to achieve unity, a problem of terrain and climate and the intolerance and cupidity of individuals combined to produce a Latin America which fell far short of the high hopes nursed by the revolutionary generation such a short time before.

Above, the Battle of Rivas in the war between Costa Rica and Nicaragua in 1856. An American adventurer, William Walker, had made himself President of Nicaragua earlier in the year, but this defeat at the hands of his neighbours led to his surrender to the US fleet the following year.

Opposite, a Mexican delegation at the court of the Archduke Maximilian of Austria in 1863, offering the crown of Mexico. He found little sympathy with his new lands, relied entirely on French support for his authority and was expelled from the throne and killed in 1867.

Part VI

EUROPE AND NORTH AMERICA IN THE NINETEENTH CENTURY

Introduction

When in 1815 Louis XVIII returned for a second time to the throne of the Bourbons it seemed that an ugly and violent chapter in European history was at last closed. Although the French had again revealed their political instability by the enthusiasm they had shown for Napoleon Bonaparte when he escaped from Elba in March 1815, he was now safely incarcerated on St Helena deep in the South Atlantic and could not escape again; and the very moderation of the peace terms on which the British foreign secretary, Lord Castlereagh, insisted seemed to promise an opportunity for good sense to prevail after the twenty years of conflict. These hopes were reinforced by the conciliatory mood of Louis XVIII. He was declared king 'by the grace of God', and he graciously presented a royal charter to his grateful people. But he was wise enough to include in it the concession of those civil rights and rights to property which had been the permanent result of the Revolution and which had been won the hard way. The hope was for constitutional government on British lines.

Yet the form was clear: the watchword of the Congress of Vienna was 'legitimacy', even if the case for the restoration of the legitimate rulers and their descendants was that it was in the people's best interests. 'The principle of legitimacy', wrote Talleyrand to Louis XVIII, 'must be held sacred in the interest of the people themselves, because legitimate governments can alone be strong and durable, whereas illegitimate governments, relying upon force only, fall to pieces the moment that support fails them, and then the people are delivered over to a succession of revolutions of which no one can foresee the end.'

And so, for a variety of reasons, the Concert of Europe was born. The French foreign minister, Talleyrand, wanted to restore the pre-revolutionary map of Europe and get the best possible terms for France. Metternich dreaded a new wave of revolution lest it further weaken the diverse and chequered Habsburg Empire. Hardenberg of Prussia shared his fears. Alexander I of Russia, alternating between moods of repression and liberalism, sought a union with his fellow rulers 'as members of a single Christian nation' and opposed whatever might thwart

it. And Castlereagh's objective was primarily to re-create a power balance in a Europe torn and destroyed by a generation of war so that his island empire could absorb her widely scattered conquests to which there could now be no European challenge. Along with 'legitimacy' went the 'compensations'. And by them Britain did well indeed. She dominated the key strategic points – and the coaling stations for the coming age of steam – on all the oceans. For two generations she was the political and industrial pacesetter for the world.

It is easy now in retrospect to see how false were some of these assumptions and how short-lived the post-1815 stability. Yet the Holy Alliance and the conferences of the post-1815 years saw for the first time a genuine attempt to manufacture by diplomacy a European concert of power. It was for a purpose: the suppression at source of the first signs of unrest. Revolutions were put down by force, at speed and by foreign intervention: 1819 in Germany, in 1821 in Italy, in 1823 in Spain, in 1830 in Italy, in 1831 in Poland and in many countries in 1848–9. In 1830, in 1848 and in 1870 the barricades were raised in Paris; and throughout the period unrest and violence were endemic in Russia. There was no peace. When Metternich fled in 1848, there was still his replica, Schwartzenberg, to reign in his place. But, except in 1827 in Greek waters and in 1854 in the Crimea, there was no war in Europe either. The diplomats relied on the exhaustion of Europe, on the passiveness of a heavily rural society and on military force. And from their experiences they could hardly have acted otherwise. They ignored however the social and economic forces, the fact that the movement of armies carried with it the movement also of ideas, the growth of population, the development of railways, telegraph and postal services, the appearance in each country of a middle class that was the product of city life, commerce and schools, that would now break

the aristocratic pattern permanently and begin to grope towards an Internationale of trade. Metternich was intelligent, shrewd, every inch a realist, utterly devoid of Alexander's mysticism. He recognized, and was right to do so, the fragile character of human society. His ideal was limited but in its way noble. He laboured hard to maintain the equilibrium of Europe; as he wrote in 1824, Europe 'has acquired for me the quality of one's own country'. He was remarkably successful. He held the fort until 1848. But he ignored the three new creative and disruptive elements that were to make the years between the fall of Napoleon I and the rise of Bismarck so exciting; the industrial revolution and the forces of nationalism and socialism.

The industrial revolution was of course very uneven in its impact. Europe as a whole was still rural: serfdom was abolished in France in 1789 and in Prussia in 1807. But the effects of the abolition were varied. If small peasant farms became characteristic of western Europe, in the lands east of the Elbe a large, landless, agricultural labouring class was produced. And in Russia in 1815 there were still 16,000,000 serfs on the Crown lands alone. Serfdom brought acute problems to the Tsars, who had great difficulty in finding any solutions.

It was to this overwhelmingly rural world that the industiral revolution came. It came first in Britain and spread to western Europe: it was British capital and companies which applied steam to transportation on land and sea in France as well as Britain, so that a spider-like spread of railway lines appeared on the map of Europe between 1830 and 1870; coal and factory production boomed because of the use of steam engines. Ghent and Brussels, Liège and Lille, Namur and the Ruhr, Manchester and Glasgow became industrial centres of textiles, metallurgy, coal and steel.

The results were evident in the population boom – there was a fivefold increase in the British population between 1814 and 1914, and London grew from 875,000 to 2,000,000 in the years from 1800 to 1850 and to 5,000,000 by 1900; Cologne and Paris doubled in population in the same period; in 1800 there were 22 towns in Europe with more than a population of 100,000; by 1850 there were 47. There was also a series of cholera and typhus epidemics which led to a campaign for a public health service. Interest grew in wider and larger markets (hence the emphasis on the Empire of Britain and on the Union of the German States), state education and scientific invention and the development of joint stock companies. Napoleon was in nothing quite so farsighted as in his commercial code, which was adopted throughout most of western Europe; he was far more modern-minded than Metternich or Castlereagh.

Industrially, Britain was half a century ahead of Europe. She produced 10,000,000 tons of coal in 1800, 56,000,000 tons a year by 1850. This process did not occur in France until the years of the Second Empire: coal and iron production trebled between 1850 and 1870. And by 1871, aided by victory, Germany was, by rapid scientific training, outdistancing France. By 1871, though few appreciated this, British dominance was over. Between 1850 and 1910 iron production trebled in Britain, rose sixfold in France, but twenty-sixfold in Germany.

The same forces were at work in agriculture, with improvement in farming techniques, the abandonment of the fallow land system, the use of fertilizers, the specialization of crops and the cross-breeding of cattle.

And behind all these developments was money, not least in London, Paris and Amsterdam. Krupp was typical of one aspect of the industrial growth. What in 1826 was a near-bankrupt household business had become by 1870 a vast, private, paternalist empire of steel and bronze and guns, with pension schemes, hotels and stores – and no trade unions. The five Rothschild brothers from the Frankfurt ghetto managed the banking houses of Frankfurt, Vienna, London, Paris and Naples. When the transfer of funds over such distances was dangerous they could act as one, speedily and with confidence and trust. They invested shrewdly, especially in railways and shipping. They became barons of the Austrian Empire and assisted Disraeli over Suez, but they never overcame either envy of their skill or prejudice against their race. Yet, as their careers showed, it was possible to climb up the greasy pole, whatever your origins, your accent or your race. It was easier in Britain than in Europe. Or rather it was not easy at all: but it could be done.

Metternich's vision of Europe had a certain nobility – seen at least in the light of the problems of today. But it foundered, as did the fortunes of the Habsburg house he served, not only on indifference to economics but on ignorance of the emotional force of nationalism. So did the cause of aristocracy. The early nineteenth century was held together in its internationalism by the existence of a class whose manners were stylized, whose language was French and whose loyalties were less to territory and nation than to a sovereign. The chancellor of the German Empire in 1894, Hohenlohe, had a brother who was an official of the Emperor Joseph of Austria, another on service in Prussia and yet another at the Papal Court in Rome. Their loyalties were personal. The coming of the bourgeoisie meant the emergence of nationalism. Honour now became national, and nations began to take offence, to meet challenges that had been seen until then as purely personal. And the nationalism itself passed from the romantic and cultural force that it was to Chateaubriand and Mazzini to a hard, scientific, military force – a product of Darwin. The test of national honour by 1870 was conflict, and the national concept was in the process

brutalized, coarsened and devalued. Nationalist symbols and legendary grew, not least in Britain and the United States. But of its emotional power there could be no question. Loyalty was no longer to king or lord, class or creed, but to the republic one and indivisible. It became synonymous with notions of the rights of men and the career open to talent. It would be defended not by a professional class of warriors but by all its citizens. And it was for export. Belgium won its independence in 1830; Italy as a nation became more than a 'geographical expression'; each component part of the Austrian Empire struggled for self-determination; poets and historians kept alive the sparks of independence in Prague and Budapest, Belgrade and Athens. Greece won its independence and the map of the Balkans became a jigsaw of ever-changing boundaries. Every little language felt that it had to have a country all its own. Nationalism was a force that later both Bismarck and Hitler could exploit. And beyond nationalism was imperialism and the notion of the raj. By 1870, with the Suez Canal cut and a quick road open to India, an imperial age was about to be born. But the major force that emerged in these years was, in Europe at least, Socialism itself. Before long class would compete with nation for loyalty and allegiance, and some of the most difficult tensions and problems of our time would come to birth.

Three thousand miles away, on the other side of the Atlantic, a not dissimilar sequence of events had taken place. The United States had spent the first two thirds of the nineteenth century establishing its own nationhood, defining its own particular national characteristics that distinguished it from the European nations who had originally peopled it. Having established, in the Monroe Doctrine in 1823, its claim to its own sphere of influence, it could safely ignore events in Europe, its attention taken up with pushing its settlements ever further to the west.

The second main geopolitical problem inherent in the very establishment of the United States had also resolved itself by the last third of the century. This was the conflict, most importantly but not exclusively over slavery, between the rapidly industrializing and heavily populated North and the agricultural, more sparsely inhabited South. The Civil War had been bloody and bitter, but once the armies had withdrawn from the field the nation reunited remarkably quickly, social attitudes and an element of nostalgia perhaps excepted.

Now, the United States slowly took up its position as a world power whose rapidly growing economic and political strength could no longer be ignored by the major European nations. These may have reached the peak of their power only as late as the years between 1870 and 1914; but, not far behind, though scarcely noticed, lay the United States, which rapidly came to supplant them.

Above, London warehouses as depicted by the French painter Gustave Doré (1833–83): at the start of the nineteenth century the economies of western Europe and the United States were primarily agricultural. By the end they were primarily industrial, industrialization bringing with it the unplanned growth of big cities and of an urban proletariat.

Opposite, Tsar Alexander I, Francis I of Austria and Frederick William II of Prussia concluding the Holy Alliance, 26 September 1815. Though the document espoused Christian principles, it joined the three most powerful autocracies of central and eastern Europe in an alliance armed at self-preservation.

On page 384, Liberty Guiding the People *by Eugène Delacroix (1798–1863): this painting, executed in 1831 in the aftermath of political revolution in France, might be said to symbolize one of the nineteenth century's main aspirations, a popular yearning for national liberty. Though these hopes had by and large been fulfilled in western Europe by three quarters of the way through the century, central and eastern Europe, not to mention Europe's overseas territories, had to wait until the twentieth century. Musée du Louvre, Paris.*

Chapter 35

The New Europe

A man born in 1815 might reasonably have expected to live until 1870. Had he done so, he would have witnessed more changes – political, economic, industrial and social – than in any comparable period in history. While the Europe of 1870 was recognizably modern, that of 1815 was still in many respects medieval. After more than twenty years of revolution, war and destruction the old order was restored by the victors of Waterloo, and the deep cracks which had seemed to be breaking up the structure of European society in 1789 were temporarily pasted over. Except in France, the lot of the peasant had scarcely changed, and the land which still formed the basis of the European economy continued to be tilled in the same laborious way that it had been for centuries past. But the apparent continuity with the past was only superficial, and from about 1830 onwards scientific progress and social change accelerated spectacularly. Developments in industry, commerce and trade brought vast new wealth to western Europe but at the same time created a rootless working class and an intellectual protest that was ultimately to shatter the old order so carefully reconstructed in 1815. The lasting revolution was to be an economic, not a political one, its home in England, not in France.

At the beginning of the nineteenth century Europe remained essentially agricultural, and as in all agricultural societies life was directly affected by the state of the harvest. The absence of any permanent crop surpluses seriously hampered economic development: seasonal and annual crises, traceable to weather conditions, inadequate commercial organization and transport systems were followed at the end of the wars by a long period of falling prices which afforded no encouragement to change of any kind. With a few exceptions, agricultural techniques remained backward and unchanging. Great aristocratic landowners, uninterested in the processes of farming, were content to draw rents from their tenants and to value their estates in terms of the social status and political power that they conferred. Small farmers, though they might have the will to experiment and make changes, could rarely command the capital necessary to do so.

Throughout most of Europe, cultivation was still by the primitive methods of the Middle Ages. For lack of fertilizers land had to be kept fallow one year in every three, and much still lay in uncultivated waste: seed was sown 'broadcast' by hand, reaping was by scythe and threshing by flail. Crop yields were low, and undernourished animals, left to fend for themselves on rough pastures and commons, prevented any progress in scientific stock-breeding. The absence of developed communications and means of storing food compelled each country – and, often, each district – to be as self-supporting as possible, and it was only in a few luxury foods such as spices, sugar, coffee and tea that there was any important foreign trade.

Yet the first half of the nineteenth century was to see impressive agricultural progress, spurred on by growing populations and increasing demands for food. Change had begun in England in the previous century, where 'improving' landlords had enclosed scattered holdings into compact farms, had introduced new rotational systems based on the use of root crops and had greatly increased the size and weight of animals by selective breeding. Such practices became more widespread during the Napoleonic Wars and enabled England not only to survive the French blockade but to feed a population that grew threefold, from 6,000,000 to 18,000,000, during the century 1750–1850.

By the 1840s steam-ploughs and steam-threshers were coming to replace the labour of man, manure and artificial fertilizers (discovered by the German chemist Liebig) were enriching the soil and increasing yields, while the drainage of heavy clay lands, made possible by the mass production of non-porous pipes, was bringing ever more land under the plough. Altogether these changes meant a fundamental break with the past and a new concept of landownership for profit rather than pleasure.

Outside England there were two main types of agriculture in Europe. In France, the Low Countries, Switzerland and Northern Italy the suppression of feudal servitude had emancipated the peasants but had resulted in a pattern of small and medium-sized farms which were economically unable to take advantages of the new and costly agricultural techniques.

Elsewhere in Europe, vast manorial estates remained typical. In Southern Italy the landowning aristocracy practised absenteeism, leaving the management of their estates to stewards who let them out to tenant-farmers, often at exorbitant rents. Spanish lords also leased out their lands but were restricted by the *Mesta*, the powerful association of sheep farmers who monopolized vast areas of pasturage and were opposed to the development of arable farming.

In Prussia and eastern Europe the Napoleonic reforms were also abandoned soon after Waterloo, and peasants who had acquired land were now often compelled to restore part of it. On some Prussian estates. however, there was evidence of agricultural improvement on the English model, in contrast with the medieval conditions that still prevailed in Russia. Here, the land was owned entirely by the Crown and nobility; landowners kept back part for their own use and let the rest to serfs in small plots in return for payments and obligations of many kinds. Although Russia was the largest exporter of wheat in Europe, it was at the expense of a population that permanently lived close to starvation level. This contrast between eastern and western Europe, based on the different systems of land-ownership, resulted in glaring economic divisions which were to survive until recent times.

Industrial Europe

The new Europe – the Europe of machines and factories, railways and steam-engines – was hardly evident in 1815. Only in England, where industrialization had been growing at an increasing pace since about the middle of the eighteenth century, were the changes clearly visible. Here, a small population had

responded to a great overseas demand by mechanization, first of the spinning and weaving of textiles, next of the manufacture of iron and steel, and then of the actual means of power. Whether the British people had any peculiar inventive skill over other nations is doubtful: it is more likely that the industrial revolution began there because of a particular combination of circumstances – economic, social and political – that could not be found elsewhere at the time. But the fact was the discoveries of Hargreaves (the spinning jenny) and Arkwright (an early spinning machine driven by water power), of Watt (the steam engine), Cort (a process for purifying iron) and a score of others were not only turning England into the wealthiest and most powerful nation in the world but were ultimately to start a revolution throughout Europe, the consequences of which are still not fully worked out.

Britain, admittedly, had certain natural elements which favoured her early industrialization – coal and iron in great quantity and easily accessible, an old-established cloth industry which supplied a basis of organizational knowledge and experience, a vast colonial market for her goods, a developed banking system and a political structure that encouraged freedom and individual initiative. Before 1830, industrialization in France made only slow headway, delayed by poor communications and banking institutions and by the continuation of protectionist policies that only hampered progress. Here, the pace of change quickened noticeably after the accession of Louis Philippe: the iron industry developed rapidly under iron masters like Schneider at Creusot and Wendel in Lorraine, the number of steam engines in use doubled within six years, while the number of power-looms in Alsace and Normandy increased sevenfold between 1830 and 1848.

In Germany, the 'take-off' into industrialization was even slower. In 1830 the Ruhr was still a predominantly agricultural region, and Krupp, the great armament manufacturer of the future, employed only nine workers: such industrial centres as existed were situated close to the iron-fields of Saxony, the Saar, Upper Silesia and Bohemia. Only towards 1840 did the more intensive exploitation of coal fields and steam power indicate the real beginnings of technological advance. In Belgium, too, money from the aristocracy was by now beginning to stimulate the heavy industries in the valleys of the Meuse and Sambre.

Elsewhere in Europe there was, as yet, little sign of industrial progress. Some Italian cities were famous, as they had been for centuries past, for high quality workmanship in silk, leather and precious metals, but these were small-scale craft industries carried on in much the same way as they had been since medieval times. Here, as in Germany and other European states, the development of trade was seriously hampered by political divisions and the survival of local monopolies controlled by guilds and city corporations.

In spite of such impediments, it is likely that total European industrial output doubled between 1815 and 1848. Yet the progress of early capitalism was uneven, marked by booms and slumps which implied an inadequate adaptation to the market forces of supply and demand. Most countries attempted to protect their economies by complicated systems of tariffs and import restrictions which only served to keep down the total level of international trade. Such ideas were increasingly coming under attack from economists like Ricardo, Say and Mill who, deriving their theories from Adam Smith's *The Wealth of Nations* (1776), argued that wealth would be greatly increased if each country concentrated on producing what it was best fitted for by nature (whether food or manufactures) and then exchanged freely with all other nations. In the absence of artificial controls, production would always adjust itself to demand through the agency of the price mechanism.

Free trade found its first expression in England, where a gradual process of tariff or Customs duty reduction was begun in the

Above, opening-day (7 December 1835) on the first German railway, from Nuremberg to Furth: railways played a significant role in the commercial, industrial and social revolutions of the nineteenth century, easier travel and communication of all kinds quite literally helping to develop national consciousness.

Above left, Justus von Liebig (1803–73) in his laboratory: the founder of agricultural chemistry, Liebig was one of the century's greatest chemists.

Opposite, view of Normandy by Jules Dupré (1812–89): outside England, the industrial revolution only took place well into the nineteenth century, and national food distribution had to await the construction of extensive railway systems.

1820s by Huskisson and continued by Peel in the 1840s. Its most spectacular success came in 1846 with the repeal of the Corn Laws and the removal of the protection from wheat imports which farmers had long enjoyed: England would hereafter buy her food in the cheapest markets of the world and live by her manufactures.

The transport revolution

Industrialization required a fast and efficient system of communications for the movement of men, materials and goods. During the latter half of the eighteenth century, England had already made important developments in mobility by the construction of canals for the movement of heavy goods and the improvement of road surfaces for the transport of passengers. On the turnpike roads of Brindley, Telford and Macadam stagecoaches could carry twenty passengers at speeds of up to fifteen miles an hour.

The decisive change came with the steam locomotive, first successfully developed by George Stephenson in 1814. Originally, it was seen merely as a means of speeding up the transport of coal from mines, and the first railways, such as the Stockton to Darlington in England and the Saint-Etienne to Andrezième in France, were intended solely for industrial purposes.

But by 1830 Stephenson had produced a locomotive which could travel at thirty miles an hour, and the use of steel rails, automatic brakes and improved coaches made people aware of the railway's great potential for passenger transport. A 'railway mania' in England resulted in the formation of hundreds of private companies, some of them economically unsound but many paying handsome dividends to shareholders. By 1850 almost all the principal towns had been linked by some 6,000 miles of rail, the average cost of which had been £56,000 per mile.

In other countries, development was retarded by distrust and the opposition of vested interests. Hostility came from landowners, coaching establishments and innkeepers – above all, sufficient capital was not forthcoming from investors, who preferred to put their money into land or safe government securities. Despite campaigns led by the banker Péreire and the economist Chevalier, the French network really only began after 1837, the first line, Paris to Saint-Germain, being sponsored by Baron Rothschild. Although it was an immediate success, there were still only 2,000 miles of French railways in 1848.

Railway construction followed in Belgium, Germany, Italy and in many countries throughout the world, often directed by British engineers and carried out by British workmen. In Germany the railway had a particular importance in the development of the *Zollverein* – the customs union by which Prussia was gradually forging a nation out of a collection of independent states: in 1850 Germany had some 3,500 miles of track and a great continental line from Aachen to Hanover and Berlin.

The economic and social effects of railways was revolutionary. Journeys were shortened from days to hours; the cost of moving goods was halved and the market for them vastly expanded; perishable foods in particular received a new mobility and could now be transported into the rapidly growing urban centres in good condition. Railways broke down the isolation of centuries and compelled people whose horizons had previously been bounded by the village to think in terms of the nation: although they were a socially binding force it is probably true to say that they were a nationally divisive one.

But it is not in dispute that steam locomotion – whether by land or by the new steamships that were now crossing the Atlantic in seventeen days instead of forty – was one of the most powerful forces shaping modern civilization. Where the rail was laid, telegraph systems were constructed alongside, news and letters could be carried cheaply and swiftly, and national daily papers became possible. The new mobility that was thus given to the movement of ideas was at least as important as that conferred on people and goods.

The conquering bourgeoisie

Rich and poor there had always been, but industrialization tended to exaggerate the differences between plenty and want, to make the extremes more conspicuous, more exposed to public envy and concern. In countries which had not yet felt the impact of industrial change, the traditional two-tier system of aristocratic landowners and landless peasants persisted – in Southern Italy and in parts of Prussia and Russia, where social and political influence was still exclusively in the hands of a tiny territorial aristocracy.

However, in the industrially developing parts of Europe a third, middle class was rapidly rising to power and wealth, a class distinguished by its manipulation of capital rather than by ownership of land. These were the bankers and merchants of the new professions that complex financial undertakings and business relationships called into existence. At the extremities they merged imperceptibly into the classes above and below them; there was no single middle class, rather an infinite series of gradations. What characterized them, and distinguished them sharply from their social inferiors, was the ownership of capital or means of production on which they could employ others to work or the possession of special professional skills usually derived from some form of advanced education.

At the summit of the middle classes, barely distinguishable in wealth from the landed aristocracy, was the financial elite – a relatively few great families whose business lay in the use (to some the abuse) of money. These were the banking and financial houses, which dealt in money-lending on a grand scale, government credit, the discounting of bills of exchange and speculation in mining and the precious metals.

A general shortage of currency (still based on gold and silver) at a time of expanding trade, as well as the inadequate development of banking facilities, favoured such activities and their concentration into a few hands. Banking houses like the Barings in England, the Hopes in Amsterdam and the Rothschilds, with a family network extending through five European capitals, rivalled the wealth and influence of dukes and princes. The Jewish origins of some prevented their complete social acceptance, yet others were ennobled, became leading patrons of the arts and were famous for their lavish entertaining and hospitality.

Below the merchant princes were the upper middle-classes – the owners of textile factories and iron-works, the leading members of the professions and public administration, the army officers and diplomatic officials. Socially they were of mixed origins. Government service and army were still recruited mainly from the younger sons of nobility who, because of the rule of primogeniture, would not succeed to their fathers' estates: patronage assured them of remunerative sinecures, the actual work of which was done by poorly paid clerks. But in the ranks of the industrialists were found members of the nouveau riche, men of often humble origins who had carved their way to fortune by hard work, thrift and an unusual degree of intelligence or good fortune.

These various elements had in common the enjoyment of a degree of affluence which enabled them to educate and provide for their children and provided them with fine houses in the fashionable quarters and suburbs of the towns, armies of domestic servants who relieved their wives of all the household duties. Above all, they shared a

thirst for political power, a dislike of the aristocracy and a distrust of the working classes, a belief in free trade and free enterprise as the keys to economic success both for themselves and for the nation.

In the more advanced countries of western Europe they were already making a bid for power and, beginning to break the domination of the landed gentry. In England the middle classes were enfranchised by the Reform Act of 1832 and through the newly formed Conservative Party of Robert Peel won a remarkable success with the abolition of the Corn Laws in 1846: similarly the accession in 1830 of Louis Philippe, 'the bourgeois king', was the beginning of a period of increased power and influence for the French middle classes.

There were no overnight revolutions. Aristocratic power remained deeply entrenched, and even in England it was not until 1880 that middle-class members constituted a majority in the House of Commons: the important thing was that a shift in economic power was gradually bringing about a major political change and was causing a mounting attack on the aristocracy, its power and privileges.

The disinherited

In his famous work *Das Kapital*, first published in 1867, Karl Marx stated his belief that industrialization inevitably tended to divide society into two opposing groups of employers and employees, those who possessed capital and those who did not, and that the issue between them could be resolved only by revolution. To many observers in the first half of the nineteenth century his gloomy prediction seemed fully justified.

Above, Punch *cartoon of 1843 entitled* Capital and Labour, *a surprisingly acid comment on the structure of society.*

Opposite right, contemporary print depicting the three locomotives that took part in trials held in 1829 by the Liverpool & Manchester Railway: Stephenson's Rocket *won hands down. The Liverpool & Manchester, opened in 1830, was the world's first modern railway, that is, the first to operate on its own account regular passenger services hauled entirely by steam locomotives.*

Opposite left, power-loom for weaving carpets on show at the Great Exhibition, 1851: the industrial revolution had started in Britain, and in 1851 she was still the world's leading industrial power, though she would not remain so for long.

Even in the wealthy western countries of Europe, agricultural labourers, who still constituted the majority of the population in 1815, lived in destitution and semi-starvation, existing on a diet of bread, cheese and vegetables, with meat a rare luxury. Meagre wages were supplemented by the earnings of wives and children as soon as they were old enough to work at field-labour or domestic occupations like spinning and weaving.

In England the land enclosure movement had created a class of landless labourers entirely dependent on the wages paid by farmers. Elsewhere in Europe, small peasant farms had remained, but under such difficult conditions that the tenants had a constant struggle to escape from the extortions of landlords and moneylenders. Riots and risings were common occurrences in Russia, southern Germany and Ireland and were not unknown even in the 'peaceful' English countryside.

All over Europe there was a steady migration into the towns. Whether men felt dispossessed from the land or attracted by the greater opportunities of town life is difficult to say, and it is still impossible to draw up an accurate balance sheet of the gains and losses which such a transition involved. In factories and mines wages twice and three times as high as those of the agricultural labourer could be earned. On the other hand, workers had to submit to the impersonal discipline of the mill, to accept a working day of fourteen or fifteen hours, often in overheated and insanitary conditions, and to live in crowded slums shut out from the familiar peace and beauty of nature.

The employment of children from the age of five of six upwards in such conditions was a new a special evil which ultimately excited public concern and control, but the inhuman conditions under which thousands of men and women had to work – the tyranny and brutality of petty masters and overseers, the disease and early death that factory life often brought about, the drunkenness, immorality and prostitution that were all too common in the industrial town – seemed to pass almost unnoticed.

In England, Belgium and France the spontaneous reaction of workers to such conditions was often to break the machines that appeared to be depriving them of their livelihood. These 'Luddite' risings, like the sporadic strikes which were a common feature of early industrial society, were suppressed with great severity – none more so than that of the Lyons silk-weavers, which resulted in a thousand deaths. In the absence of effective trade unions such actions were doomed to failure. The only form of workers' associations which had any success in the period were the peaceful friendly societies formed by skilled craftsmen to insure themselves and their families against sickness and unemployment.

But almost from the beginning the growth of industrialization produced its critics. By the 1820s and 1830s the heightened contrast between wealth and poverty was leading some to question the very foundations of the new society and to propose, in the name either of Christian charity or social justice, fundamental reforms and new political systems.

Reformers and utopians

One of the most significant protests to develop from within the Church itself was the Liberal Catholic movement which began in France in 1829 under the leadership of the clerics Lamennais and Lacordaire with the support of the young peer, the Count of Montalembert. Totally opposed to the *ancien régime* and the control of the Church by the state, they urged through their journal *L'Avenir* freedom of conscience, of the press and education, the sovereignty of the people, universal suffrage and freedom of association. Considered dangerous to authority, the movement was condemned by the French government and by the pope in an encyclical of 1832. Nevertheless, the ideas survived and found expression in the work of a young student, Frederick Ozanam, who founded the Society of St Vincent de Paul for mutual aid and charity.

From outside the established order, and aiming at the overthrow of the capitalist

system as a whole, came a stream of socialist writings. Most of the early work was utopian and unrealistic, the product of the imagination of philosophers and intellectuals who were remote from practical politics, although their ideas contributed importantly to the later foundations of socialism.

One of the earliest was the Count of Saint-Simon (1760–1825), a ruined nobleman who became a violent critic of a social order based on competition and the exploitation of the most numerous class by a tiny minority of privileged owners. His conclusion was that it would be necessary to suppress this class, whose possessions and capital would thus revert to the state, the only legitimate owner. Society could then be reorganized and new classes constructed on the basis of ability, not wealth.

In place of the power of Crown and Church there would be the power of the creative sections of the population – intellectuals, bankers, industrialists, workers – all inspired by a common faith in service and progress.

Saint-Simon's influence was greater after his death than during his own lifetime. Two of his disciples, Enfantin and Bazard, tried to establish a small community in accordance with the principles of the master 'to each according to his ability, each man's ability to be judged by what he achieves', but, like many similar ventures, the project failed because of internal disputes and a law-suit brought by the state. Saint-Simon's significance lay in his challenge to a system which, to nearly all men, had seemed God-given and eternal and in the influence of his philosophy on his contemporaries and successors.

Among these was the English socialist, Robert Owen (1771–1858), who conceived a society in which all power would belong to the working classes, organized into co-operative societies which would both own and control the instruments of production. The son of a draper, Owen had a successful career as an employer in the cotton industry and then as manager of the largest cotton mills in Scotland, at New Lanark. It was during his time there as one of the few enlightened employers of the period that he developed his basic socialist principles: man is not good or evil by nature but largely as a result of the environment in which he grows up; and second, that the machine is not something to be feared and destroyed but to be encouraged for its power to lighten human labour and create vast new sources of wealth. However, to ensure that this wealth was fairly distributed among those who created it, Owen believed that the machine (including all the instruments of production) would need to be publicly owned and controlled and taken out of the hands of private capitalists. These shattering views were published in his *New Moral View of Society* as early as 1813.

Although he had important effects on the development of management, education and cooperation, as a practical socialist Owen was no more successful than Saint-Simon's disciples. A socialist community in the United States, inappropriately named 'New Harmony', collapsed after a few years, and Owen's Grand National Consolidated Trade Union (1834), which was to have taken over British industry after a general strike, was defeated by the combined action of government and employers.

Similar ideas were developed by another French socialist, Fourier. The state was to disappear and give place to self-governing socialist communities, each of about 2,000 people, which would be free associations in which all could devote themselves to the occupations of their choice. In this way, each would find personal fulfilment and happiness. Again, in the theory of Louis Blanc (1811–82), all private industries would be incorporated into social workshops, where workers would choose their employers and share the profits. Proudhon (1809–65) attacked the existence of private property ('property is theft'), the institutions of law and the state, even the sovereignty of the people ('universal suffrage is a lottery'). In his philosophy there was to be no system of government at all: he was the apostle of anarchy.

The very diversity of these views indicates that socialism was not, and could not be at this time, a political party with a well-defined programme. Its main theorists had been intellectuals and philosophers, often of aristocratic or middle-class background, remote from the hopes and aspirations of ordinary men. However, towards the end of the period socialism began to pass from the scholar's study to the mines and factories, as reformers began to organize the working classes for more effective political action.

In Paris in 1836 the Federation of Just Men was founded by a group of emigré German revolutionaries, of whom a tailor, Weitling, was the leading figure. In 1847, at the Federation's annual congress in London, the name 'Communist League' was adopted. It was on this occasion that Karl Marx and Frederich Engels drew up the *Communist Manifesto* (published 1848), which was to prove the most influential political document of modern times.

The triumph of science

But to many contemporaries it was not so much the development of new political ideas or the artistic achievements of the Romantic Movement that characterized the age as the spectacular advances in scientific knowledge and application. The origins of the scientific revolution lay much further back in the seventeenth century, when men had first begun to observe, measure, analyse and deduce laws from the natural world around them, but at this time science was still part of philosophy, the intellectual pursuit of gentlemen-scholars for its own intrinsic interest.

By the nineteenth century scientific knowledge had come to provide the very basis of industrial and technological progress, the life-blood of the new age, no longer the pastime of gifted amateurs but the activity of professional scientists and researchers.

The new science rested fundamentally on basic mathematical theory, which was greatly advanced by a group of scholars from many countries. One of the characteristics of the new knowledge was that it did not observe national boundaries but was developed by men of many countries, often working closely with each other by the exchange of ideas through meetings and publications. Thus Gauss, a professor at Göttingen University, did pioneer work in applying mathematical theory to electricity and magnetism; the Frenchman Monge largely established descriptive geometry, while Laplace demonstrated the stability of the solar system. The Norwegian Abel worked on mathematical astronomy and le Verrier, on the basis of pure calculation, discovered the existence of the planet Neptune which was only observed several years later by telescope.

Similar fundamental research was being pursued in physics which had developed little since its laws had been first established by Newton. Now, Biot and Arago made the first accurate measurements of the density of the air. Gay-Lussac discovered the laws of expansion of gas and Carnot defined the laws of thermodynamics (the science of the relations between heat and mechanical work) on which the Englishman James Joule later based his work.

Although these discoveries were the necessary basis for many new applications, their immediate contribution to human life and work sometimes seemed remote. Not so with the development of electricity, which, from early in the century, began to be used for a variety of purposes. In 1800 the Italians Volta and Galvani constructed the first electric battery: within a few years discoveries by the Dane Oersted, the Frenchman Ampère, the Englishman Faraday and the German Ohm had defined the laws of electromagnetism, established the idea of induction and expounded the mathematics of electrical currents. By the 1840s the electric telegraph, invented by Morse and Steinheil, was in use in England, France and in some other countries.

Discoveries in one branch of science frequently led to developments in others. Electrolysis was used to isolate new chemical substances such as potassium, magnesium, sodium, chromium and aluminium, many of which were to have highly important industrial uses. Similarly, the discoveries in organic chemistry by Chevreul and Liebig led to the development of artificial fertilizers and to much new knowledge about the chemistry of food. Already at the beginning of the nineteenth century Dalton and Avogadro were outlining the first modern theories of atomic structure.

Biologists, meanwhile, were investigating the nature of the cell, the fundamental element in the tissues, which was discovered in 1830. Advances in medicine and, in particular, the discovery of anesthetics were beginning to make treatment and surgery safer and more practicable, though until after the middle of the century hospitals continued to be places in which patients often died of diseases other than those with which they entered.

More fundamental research still was being undertaken into the nature of the earth itself. Detailed study of rocks enabled geologists to reconstruct the principal stages in the evolution of the earth's crust, while the examination of fossils by Cuvier laid the foundations of the science of paleontology. From here it was a short step to the posing of questions about the origins of man. Some of Cuvier's pupils remained convinced of the unchanged nature of species since their original creation, yet, to others, the discoveries of fossil remains, some of them closely similar to *homo sapiens*, seemed to argue some kind of evolutionary process from which modern man had developed. Why had some prehistoric animals disappeared from the earth while others had survived in changed, though recognizable form? Lamarck and Saint-Hilaire suggested a theory of evolution of species under the impact of changes in heredity and environment upon which Charles Darwin was later to build. Such views were, of course, irreconcilable with the teachings of the Christian church about the special creation of man and opened a long controversy between science and religion.

But the spirit of scientific enquiry was not confined to the exploration of matter. To many people in the early nineteenth century science was all-important and all-embracing, a tool that could unlock all doors and expose all secrets. Scientific method could be applied to history, to the civilizations of the past as readily as it could to physics or chemistry. It was in this spirit that Champollion deciphered the meaning of hieroglyphics and thus founded the study of Egyptology, while excavations in Greece and Mesopotamia began the modern study of archaeology. It was this profound belief in the power of science that gave to the age so much of its confidence, its sense of purpose and of the inevitability of progress.

The romantic age

Running parallel with the scientific movement of the day, in some ways complementary but in others contradictory to it, was the romantic movement. Its origins lay in the violent upheavals of revolutionary France and the Napoleonic era, which gave rise to changes in the ways of life, attitudes, tastes and feelings of a whole generation.

Napoleon had ultimately been defeated by the traditional monarchies and aristocracies of Europe, and romanticism found its first expression in writers wishing to affirm their anti-revolutionary faith. Romanticism was a philosophy of protest against prevailing circumstances, changing as the circumstances changed. Thus, the early writings of the exiled Chateaubriand showed a fiercely conservative outlook, and both the young Alfred de Vigny and Victor Hugo proclaimed themselves fervent monarchists. It was natural that among subject peoples conquered by the sword of France writers and poets should make themselves the champions of national feeling. They were anxious to assert their difference and individuality, to demonstrate their own distinct culture, language and literature. To oppressed peoples, history is a lifeline and a bulwark against the destruction of a nation's individuality.

But after 1815, the re-establishment of conservative monarchies throughout Europe and the absolutist policies of the Holy Alliance no longer satisfied romantic spirits eager for personal liberty and freedom. Some, like Victor Hugo, returned to the liberal camp and the literature of protest. Others retreated from the real world into a world of nature that had never been, endowed with sublime beauty, solitude and melancholy. The Germany of Goethe and Schiller was the principal home of literary romanticism, but England was also brilliantly represented by the poets Coleridge, Byron, Shelley and Keats and the historical works of Sir Walter Scott. Young people in many countries were fired with enthusiasm for the supposedly Celtic poems of the ancient bard Ossian – in fact, written by a Scotsman, James Macpherson, about 1760 – and Lamartine could write, 'Ossian was the Homer of my early years.' Romantics, no less than modern artists, were not uncommonly subject to self-deception.

In many European countries, however, romantics constituted an uninfluential minority desperately seeking to express their views against strongly entrenched, classical schools of literature. In France particularly they had to struggle to get their works published or produced on the stage, as did Lermontov against the forces of reaction in Russia. In such countries, where absolutist regimes had been re-established after the overthrow of Napoleon, romantics tended to be regarded as near revolutionaries, troublemakers, purveyors of anti-government literature, opponents of order, authority and religion. Some, it is true, were no more than wayward, angry young men; a few were wicked or depraved. But the death of Byron at Missolonghi, fighting for the independence of Greece against the despotic Turk, and the premature end of Lermontov, killed in a duel, symbolized the generous ideals, the courage and selflessness of the romantic spirit at its best. Such ideals were to find different, more positive outlets in the revolutions of 1830 and 1848.

England after Waterloo

In 1815 England came triumphantly to the end of a war in which she had been involved almost continuously for twenty-two years. In a real sense it was her victory. Although at the end, at Waterloo, the English armies had done little more than hold the line until the arrival of Blücher and the Prussians, England had been at the centre of the coalitions which ultimately defeated Napoleon and had provided the money and the war materials on which the armies were raised. Above all she had kept the seaways open and free from French domination. But victory had not been gained lightly. The long war left a crippling debt, an economy that had been subject to violent fluctuations and a working population which had been denied many freedoms in order that the enslaved of Europe should be freed. In some respects, the postwar difficulties and hardships were more acute than the wartime ones had been.

The England of 1815 remained, socially and politically at least, essentially the England of the eighteenth century. Despite the Industrial Revolution, which was rapidly changing the basis of Britain's economic wealth from land to industry and trade, all real power still remained in the hands of a territorial aristocracy numbering no more than a few thousand families. They represented the view – once arguable but by now irrelevant – that those who owned the land of Britain should control its destinies and public affairs. Since the 'Glorious Revolution' of 1688 Britain's system of government had been a parliamentary monarchy, with effective control of national policies in the hands of the two Houses of Parliament rather than the crown. The power of the monarchy had since been reduced further by the insanity of George III and the emergence of powerful parliamentary leaders like Chatham and Pitt. The peers of the realm had hereditary seats in the House of Lords where, together with the lords spiritual, they formed a solid bulwark not only against revolution but against reform. Although most legislation was now initiated in the lower chamber, the lords could always reject, delay or amend it out of recognition. In local affairs they also wielded immense influence through their appointment to the magistracy and county administration: their control of local justice and the administration of poor relief could be relied on to ensure a docile, even servile, rural population.

In theory the House of Commons, with members elected by the counties and boroughs of the four kingdoms, was a more representative body. But here, too, the right to vote and the right to election of a member rested on a property qualification which enfranchised a mere 150,000 out of a population of more than 15,000,000. Once flourishing centres such as the ancient port of Aldeburgh in Suffolk still sent more than

one representative to the Commons even though they were now reduced to small villages or hamlets (in Aldeburgh's case through coastal erosion sinking the city beneath the sea). In many 'pocket' and 'rotten' boroughs electors were sufficiently few for their votes to be bought or commanded, and it was common practice for wealthy young men seeking a political career to buy a parliamentary seat at a price of £5,000 to £6,000. Of 658 seats in the Commons only about fifty were actually fought by rival candidates.

By no stretch of imagination, then, could Britain's parliamentary system in 1815 be described as democratic. The privileged members of both Houses divided themselves between the two great parties, Whigs and Tories, the differences between which were by now all but lost in history. Originally, Tories had stood for the rights of the Crown and the Anglican Church, Whigs for parliamentary government, freedom of conscience and moderate reform. But both parties consisted of landowners equally devoted to the maintenance of the existing class structure and equally remote from the new centres of power that were beginning to reshape English society.

England in 1815 presented a strange contrast of the old and the new. In the countryside, where more than two-thirds of the population still lived, there was much that was traditional and unchanging: ways of life, methods of agriculture, food, dress and habits were still almost medieval, especially in the remoter parts of the West and North. But, by contrast, in the Midlands, Lancashire and Yorkshire industrialization had

made rapid progress during the wars, spurred on by the demand for guns and munitions, ships, clothing and army supplies of all kinds. Vast new centres of population sprang up as rural dwellers were attracted by the opportunities and earnings of industry. Within the first half of the century Birmingham trebled in size, Manchester quadrupled, Bradford increased no less than eightfold. This rapid and unplanned growth of cities created immense problems – of accommodation, sanitation, local government and recreation – whose solution lay far in the future. More immediately, it showed up the inadequacies and inequalities of a parliamentary system which gave two seats to a 'rotten borough' of a score of voters but denied representation to a great new city like Manchester.

But in one respect, at least, England had an advantage over other European countries. Here there was no impassable gulf between the aristocracy of birth and the aristocracy of wealth: the two met and mingled, their sons were educated together in the public schools, their families not infrequently intermarried. Robert Peel, the son of a successful Lancashire cotton manufacturer, could become an MP at twenty-one and, ultimately, prime minister; Richard Arkwright, the wandering barber who invented (some said stole) the idea of a water-powered spinning frame, could be knighted and created lord-lieutenant of the county of Nottinghamshire, an office usually reserved for a territorial lord. Industrialization offered to some glittering prizes of wealth and social mobility unknown to previous ages. To others, perhaps a majority

Above, The Election at Eatanswill, *a satire on the bribery and corruption common in elections before the 1832 Reform Act.*

Above left, portrait by Thomas Phillips of Lord Byron (1788–1824): both his writings and his fervent belief in political liberty (he helped Italian revolutionaries and joined the Greeks fighting for independence from Turkey) made him an inspiration to many European writers and poets, and his name is still commemorated in Greece today. National Portrait Gallery, London.

of the population, it offered misery heightened by the evidence of wealth about them.

At the end of the war England entered upon a long depression which brought to many even greater hardship than the war had done. Industries lay depressed with the sudden cessation of wartime demand, agriculture no longer enjoyed the protection that Napoleon's blockade had brought and began to contract, while European countries, impoverished after years of conquest and exploitation, could not afford to resume their former level of trade. It was, in fact, twenty years after 1815 before British exports recovered to their previous level. Added to the existing problems of unemployment and low wages were some half a million demobilized soldiers and sailors, suddenly thrown on to a labour market that could not absorb them. The years from 1815 to 1820 were among the darkest in English history when many feared, with some cause, a repetition of the events which had torn France apart in 1789.

Radicalism – an extreme form of politics which advocated fundamental reform of the constitutional and financial system – grew to brief importance under such popular leaders as Cobbett and Hunt. In their hatred of industrialization they preached a naive 'back-to-the-land' philosophy which seemed attractive to populations of former peasants exposed to the insecurities of town life. Significantly, the cause of the 'Peterloo Massacre' in Manchester in 1819, when a defenceless crowd was charged by squadrons of cavalry, was a speech by Hunt, not on the problem of wages or unemployment, but on the subject of land reform.

Most labour movements in the first half of the century had this strong agrarian background. A majority of the new town dwellers were peasants by origin, unaccustomed to

the regularity of factory work and the overcrowded life in slums and tenements. They tuned instinctively to solutions that offered simpler, better understood relationships in which men seemed to be something more than mere instruments of production. Working people gave their support to Radicalism, not because they understood or even cared very much about abstract democratic principles but because it represented a protest against the unacceptable conditions of life. To its few middle- and upper-class supporters it was much more – a progressive, democratic demand for a government responsible to the popular will and an administrative system based on efficiency rather than privilege.

To such suggestions the governments of the day responded with severe repression. The Tory party remained in office from the end of the war until 1830, first under Lord Liverpool, later under the wartime hero, the Duke of Wellington. Their belief was that the British constitution was perfect and that any attempt to disturb it must be put down firmly. Trade Unions were illegal until 1824 and even after that striking was still a criminal offence, public meetings and meeting-places required to be licensed and newspapers were subject to a crippling stamp duty of five pence a copy. Together with such measures went a crude system which paid a meagre dole to labourers whose earnings were inadequate to support their families (the Speenhamland System of poor relief) and which had the effect of impoverishing whole areas of the country.

In 1820 the mad George III was succeeded by his son, the former prince regent, who had been notorious as a beau and a rake. For many years now he had deserted his wife, Caroline of Brunswick, in favour of a succession of mistresses. Caroline had finally left England in 1814 to live abroad, and

George, the regent, had appointed a commission to investigate her conduct. Its report appeared in 1819, full of supposedly scandalous revelations about the intimate life of the Princess Caroline. She, however, refused to be divorced and published an open letter defending her own conduct and attacking that of George. In June 1820 she set sail for England to be crowned alongside her husband.

On her progress to London, and in the capital, Caroline was received by enthusiastic crowds who saw her as a wronged and innocent victim of a degenerate king. Divorce proceedings opened at Westminster in July, and the private lives of the British monarchy were exposed to the tales of lackeys and ladies-in-waiting. Public regard for the Crown had not been at a lower ebb since the Civil War of the seventeenth century, and there were many who predicted a republican future for the country which had developed the concept of constitutional monarchy. The court was unable to reach a decision, but ultimately Caroline was induced to yield by the payment of a handsome pension: one of the most ugly chapters in the English monarchy closed with an unseemly bribe.

The postwar depression and public disorder of the period between 1815 and 1820 had shown up the inadequacies – indeed, irrelevancies – of both political parties to the changing needs of the time. But after 1824 Tory policies began to receive a new direction at the hands of a group of enlightened young politicians – Canning at the Foreign Office, Peel at the Home Office and Huskisson at the Board of Trade – who appreciated the necessity of reshaping policies in the light of Britain's changing economic conditions and world role.

Middle-class reform

'Enlightened Toryism', which Sir Robert Peel was later to develop into the new Conservative Party, gave the government a fresh lease of life. Its appeal was particularly to the rising class of merchants and industrialists, who were favoured by reductions in the tariff system and by modifications to the Corn Laws. Under the Corn Law of 1815, passed in response to pressure by the landed interest, the import of foreign wheat was totally prohibited when the English price was less than eighty shillings a quarter. Whether it had very much effect on the price of wheat is debatable, but it certainly acted to the disadvantage of exporters who wished to sell to countries like Germany, Hungary and Russia who had little else but wheat to offer in exchange. The Corn Laws therefore constituted a serious hindrance to the expansion of world trade, from which Britain, as the greatest exporting nation, suffered particularly. By various acts in the later 1820s a sliding scale was substituted for the total prohibition, so that duties on imported

Gent.　　No Gent　　& Re gent!!

wheat remained high when the English price was low and vice versa. These measures at least opened the way for the ultimate repeal of the Corn Laws in 1846.

Other reforms by the enlightened Tories were of benefit to the population as a whole. Peel, as home secretary, began to modernize the penal system by abolishing the death sentence on several hundreds of petty offences. At the same time, his establishment of the Metropolitan Police made the detection and punishment of crime more effective. In 1828 the Test Acts, which had debarred Nonconformists from the holding of public office as MPs, magistrates, etc., were repealed and, more significant still, Catholic emancipation was passed in the next year. This issue was forced by the 'election' of the Irish Catholic leader, Daniel O'Connell, for County Clare, and rather than face what might have been a civil war in Ireland the prime minister, Wellington, acceded to the demands of Catholics to be treated as equal citizens. After more than two centuries of persecution religious toleration was finally established in Britain.

Catholic emancipation did not solve the problem of Ireland. Tenants of English landlords, forced to pay tithes to the English Church and subjected by the Act of Union of 1800 to English political domination, the Irish now asserted their claims to absolute independence.

O'Connell and his Young Ireland party renewed their agitation. Monster demonstrations were organized, particularly between 1843 and 1847, and there was even an abortive attempt at revolution in 1848. But Ireland was crushed by poverty and exhausted by famine. In 1846 the potato crop on which the majority of the population depended was hit by blight, and thousands starved to death. Between 1841 and 1851 a million Irish – many of them the most intelligent and resourceful part of the population – emigrated to England and America. For the time being political issues were merged in national calamity.

Meanwhile, in England, agitation for parliamentary reform had been growing with an uneasy alliance between Whigs, Philosophical Radicals and some sections of the working classes. In 1830 the hated George IV died and was succeeded by William IV, of no great intelligence though more amenable. Revolutions in France and Belgium had some influence in England: in 1830–1 there was a large-scale rising of agricultural labourers throughout the eastern and southern counties demanding higher wages, fairer rents and an improved system of poor relief. Events were converging towards a major political change.

In the general election of 1830 the Whigs were returned to power under Lord Grey. Their first act was to introduce a measure for parliamentary reform, which passed into law in 1832 only after numerous amendments and an initial rejection in the House of Lords. Although always known as the 'Great Reform Bill' its provisions were modest enough and far less than the Radicals had hoped. It abolished the separate representation of small towns with less than 2,000 inhabitants and left towns with 2,000 to 4,000 with only one member; 143 seats were then available for distribution among the great new cities and among those counties which were not adequately represented.

Manchester and Birmingham for the first time received their own members of parliament, but even after 1832 an ancient borough of 2,010 inhabitants could still return its own representative. The other main provision of the Act was the extension of the franchise to householders in the towns rated at £10 a year and to £50 a year tenant farmers in the country – essentially the urban and rural middle classes: the electorate was thus increased to 600,000 voters. The Act did not enfranchise the working classes nor make voting secret. Parliamentary participation was still to rest on the possession of property as an indication of worth and responsibility. The Reform Act in no way converted English government into a democracy, though it was the first and in some ways the most decisive step in that process.

Above, meeting of the Birmingham Political Union in 1832: Political Unions – Birmingham's was one of the first and most important – were formed to press for parliamentary reform; the demands of some radical members for economic and social reform remained unfulfilled.

Above left, Cruikshank cartoon dating from 1816 satirizing the rakish life led by the Prince Regent.

Opposite, cartoon by George Cruikshank (1792–1878) of the Manchester Heroes *of the Peterloo Massacre in 1819: economic depression after the Napoleonic wars led to a series of popular protests throughout the country, of which the meeting that led to the 'massacre' was one of the largest. In the 1820s the economy revived, and the threat of revolution, so feared by the established order, vanished.*

The new poor law

The next task of the Whig government after the reform of parliament was reform of the poor law. A system which paid a dole to all and sundry, which encouraged the idle and discouraged the diligent and which acted as a deterrent to labour mobility was totally unacceptable to the 'practical' principles which inspired middle-class Whigs. In 1832 a Royal Commission, headed by the great classical economist Nassau Senior and the lawyer Edwin Chadwick, was appointed to investigate the existing provisions for the .poor and to make recommendations for their reform.

Senior accepted the pessimistic view of the Reverend Thomas Malthus that population would inevitably outstrip the resources necessary to feed it unless kept down by 'natural checks'. Poverty was inherent in society, but pauperism could be eradicated by suitably stringent forms of relief. Under the Poor Law Amendment Act of 1834 the payment of doles, at least to those fit to work, was to cease: in future, the only form of relief would be in workhouses where conditions would deliberately be made 'less eligible' (i.e. more unpleasant) than those of the poorest paid free workers. Here, husbands and wives would be separated, fed on the sparsest diet and made to labour at the most uncongenial tasks. Behind the outward cruelty, however, there lay the hope that these measures would force up the level of wages, make labour more mobile and, not least, bring down the cost of poor relief. In this last respect the act was a marked success. As Carlyle commented cynically, 'If paupers are made miserable, paupers must needs decline in multitude. It is a secret known to all rat catchers.'

In a broad sense, the Amendment Act was in tune with the general philosophy of the Whigs of removing antiquated restrictions and bringing about greater freedom. The Municipal Corporations Act of 1835 reconstituted the local government of boroughs, establishing elected councils in all towns above the size of 25,000 inhabitants. More important, an Act of 1833 abolished slavery in the British Empire, so completing the work begun by Wilberforce who had earlier succeeded in stopping the slave trade in 1807. In the same year, 1833, the great East India Company was deprived of its monopoly of trading with the East and the gateway was thus opened for a remarkable expansion of British trade in India, China and Japan. All these measures were, in effect, advancing the cause of Free Trade, which became the guiding philosophy – almost the religion – of the Liberal Party later in the century.

The beginning of the Victorian Age

William IV died in 1837, to more or less universal indifference. England remained a monarchy, but for more than a century the

English people had had no feeling for their kings except amusement or contempt. A young girl of eighteen was now to regain the affection and respect that kings had forfeited.

For nearly two-thirds of a century (1837–1901) Victoria was to unite the people and the monarchy in an intimate, almost mysterious, relationship. Although she came to learn her position as a constitutional monarch very well and did not, after the first few years, attempt to intervene in party political issues, she was often able to represent the views and interests of the people to the government and hence to play an important part in the shaping of policy. In her simple, naive way she exercised a moral, moderating influence on politics, restraining the hot-headed, encouraging the timid and the humane, steadfastly opposing repression either at home or abroad.

Victoria had been an extremely unlikely

successor to the throne of England. The problem had presented itself during the lifetime of George III, when the royal family comprised seven princes, two of whom succeeded as George IV and William IV. But none of them had any children – at least, any legitimate children capable of succeeding to the throne. The Duke of Kent, who was deep in debt, agreed 'in the interests of the kingdom' to contract a 'reasonable' marriage. He left his mistress to marry a German princess, Victoria of Leiningen, a member of the distinguished Saxe-Coburg family. Of this union Victoria was born in May 1819.

The future queen was brought up strictly, seriously, even humbly for a person of her rank. At eighteen, she was intellectually unprepared for her role, though imbued with devotion to her task and a deep desire to raise the status of the monarchy from the ignominy of previous reigns. Political intrigue developed early around the young

queen whom every politician thought to influence, but Victoria acted mainly on the counsel of Lord Melbourne, the Whig prime minister after 1834, who offered wise and palatable advice on English constitutional practice. Victoria's marriage to her cousin, Prince Albert of Saxe-Coburg, also added strength, intelligence and moral purpose to the new monarchy.

In some important respects, the long reign of Victoria instituted a new kind of monarchy, one of the many adaptations that nineteenth-century England was obliged to make. Monarchy in the past had been associated with rural England, with the territorial aristocracy and the 'gentlemanly' pursuits of farming, sport and leisure. Such a role would have been impossible for the queen anyway, but, particularly through her husband, she chose to identify herself much more with urban and industrial interests, with the new sources of activity and wealth that were transforming England into a middle-class society. The royal court was still as magnificent as ever, there were still rural retreats in Scotland and the Isle of Wight (no longer Brighton), but the energy and moral purpose, the devotion to work and good causes of the royal couple were new characteristics of the monarchy, closely in tune with the principles of bourgeois life. The queen's unsophisticated taste in literature, music and interior decoration was mirrored in thousands of suburban homes,

Above, the reformed House of Commons meeting in 1835: ironically, in view of the vehement opposition to reform, the first parliament elected was, according to the diarist Greville, 'very much like every other parliament', and the south and the landowners maintained their dominant position. National Portrait Gallery, London.

Left, an early photograph, taken by Roger Fenton in 1854, of Queen Victoria (1819–1901) and Prince Albert (1819–61): the royal couple, who were married in 1840, were devoted to each other. Prince Albert had a difficult role which he fulfilled well, promoting especially industrial and social reform (the Great Exhibition of 1851 was his idea) and the arts.

Opposite top, painting by Benjamin Haydon of a meeting held by the Birmingham Political Union, 16 May 1832. Birmingham Museum and Art Gallery.

Opposite bottom, Bridewell prison, London, in 1808. Social reform, particularly of the system of poor relief and of the prison system, took a high priority among nineteenth-century radicals. Many debtors found themselves imprisoned in Bridewell and thus unable to pay off their debts.

and the extensive yet virtuous domestic life of the monarchy served to set a seal on the Victorian preoccupation with family, hearth and home.

The reshaping of the monarchy to essentially middle-class standards and ideals was only one of many adaptations that English institutions had to make in response to economic and social changes. By the 1870s complete free trade had been established except for a few duties kept for revenue purposes only. Recruitment to the expanded Civil Service had been established on competitive principles in place of privilege. The powers of local authorities had been enlarged to include responsibility for public health and, in part at least, for housing. More important still, in 1870 the state reluctantly accepted a duty towards popular education by instituting a system of public elementary schools. Although the composition of parliament was still unrepresentative of the changes taking place outside it, even here the beginnings of a modern party system were discernible, with stronger party discipline and greater concentration of authority in the hands of the cabinet. This development became marked only later during the great ministries of Gladstone and Disraeli.

The middle classes had made substantial gains in the early years of the queen's reign. But Victorian prosperity rested on a wide substructure of poverty in the working classes, for whom it must often have seemed that England had nothing to offer except unending toil, a slum dwelling and a pauper's grave. After the Reform Act of 1832 the alliance between the radicals and the middle classes collapsed; the workers were still unenfranchised and unrepresented and felt betrayed by those whom they had supported. Now there seemed no one to take their cause.

The saddest plight of all was that of the factory children, forced to work at the age of six or seven from five in the morning until seven or eight at night. Many were too exhausted to eat, some were maimed and even killed by the machines they tended. Industrialization in its early stages required cheap, amenable labour, and women and children could often perform the routine tasks it demanded with little or no training.

Direct political action by the working classes had, for the time being, been tried and had failed. Some improvements were to come, however, from philanthropists and humanitarians concerned for the sufferings of the poor and especially for the welfare of children. Lord Shaftesbury was particularly successful in compelling the investigation of conditions in factories and coal mines, which formed the necessary basis for the legislative control of employment which began in the Factory Act of 1833.

Robert Owen had already demonstrated at the New Lanark Mills, contrary to all popular belief, that humane factory management could reduce hours of work, pay higher wages and still make handsome profits. As an enlightened capitalist employer Owen was an outstanding success, as a socialist philosopher and educational theorist brilliant and inspiring, as a practical political leader an utter failure. His schemes for co-operative production and, more ambitious still, for the great Grand National Consolidated Trade Union (1833–4) intended to 'nationalize' British industry and run it socialistically, collapsed under the united attack of government and employers. The enduring memorial to Robert Owen, symbolic alike of his inspiration and failure, is the case of the Tolpuddle Martyrs (1834), sentenced to seven years transportation for having dared to form a trade union.

The Chartist challenge

The failure of Owen's schemes for a socialist millennium was to revive the agitation for direct political representation. The lawsuits which had struck at the trades unions, the harshness of the new Poor Law and the limited success of the Factory Act of 1833 all served to indicate to the worker that legislative policy would continue to be made regardless of his interests so long as he continued to be excluded from parliament.

In 1836 the London Working Men's Association was formed to campaign for parliamentary representation. It was, in itself, a moderate movement of working-class intelligentsia, deriving much of its programme from late eighteenth-century radicalism, but it quickly became caught up in much more violent agitations in the Midlands and North, particularly against the new workhouse 'bastilles'. In 1837 'The People's Charter' was formulated – a demand for six democratic reforms the most important of which were manhood suffrage, secret voting and the payment of members of parliament.

Chartism was the major working class movement of the first half of the century, dominating the stage from 1837 until 1848. Although outwardly a political movement, seeking to persuade parliament of the justness of its demands by the presentation of monster petitions, its root cause were economic and social discontent, and its main support came in the two major periods of depression and unemployment, 1839–42 and 1847–8. As one of its leaders, Joseph Stephens, put it, 'Chartism was a bread and cheese question, a knife and fork question.' It's appeal, especially after 'physical force' leaders like Feargus O'Connor took over command from those who advocated only moral persuasion, was to the hungry and destitute, the unemployed and the underemployed, the sweated workers and the casualties of industrialization.

Petitions presented in 1839 and 1842 were unheeded by parliament. The last, of 1848, which purported to contain six million signatures, was examined and found to include less than two million, many pages in the same hand and including such unlikely supporters as the Duke of Wellington and Mr Punch. The charter was laughed out of existence in an atmosphere of near hysterical relief.

Chartism failed for many reasons – because its aims were over-ambitious, because it was badly led, lacked funds and influence, and, not least, because it was firmly opposed by the ruling classes who alone might have championed it in parliament. Nevertheless, it has rightly been regarded as the first mass movement of an identifiable working class, and its very existence helped to draw attention to what Disraeli called 'The Condition of England Question'. Gradually a social conscience was aroused on specific evils, which found expression in legislation regulating the hours and conditions in factories and mines, the removal of street refuse, the conduct of common lodging houses and the adulteration of food and drugs.

In general, however, the mood of the mid-century was one of unbounded optimism and confidence in Britain's progress. After the depression of 1848 England seemed to move on to a new plateau of prosperity which began to bring gains, not only to the employing class, but to all sections of the community. The 'Golden Age', if it had not already dawned, was imminent.

The triumph of free trade

Britain's economic success in the middle of the century was in no small part a result of her adoption of a policy of Free Trade. It fell, ironically, to the lot of Peel, the leader of the Conservative Party from 1841 to 1846, to initiate the process of abandoning the Corn Laws in 1846. By so doing he acted against the wishes of the landed gentry which had helped to vote him into office and left his party split and in the wilderness.

Peel had become gradually convinced of the necessity for a free trade in corn, partly as a social reform which could cheapen the cost of bread to the working classes, partly as an economic measure which would enable Britain to sell more manufactured goods to countries which could only pay in food and raw materials. These and other arguments had been forcibly put by the Anti-Corn Law League under its founder, Richard Cobden, a Manchester industrialist of humble origins who had made a fortune in the cotton trade. The success of the League was in direct contrast to the failure of Chartism. It was efficiently organized and well led; it had the support of the middle classes and of many MPs, it used methods of propaganda such as the distribution of millions of pamphlets through the new penny post to ensure that its message was heard throughout the land. The campaign was a masterpiece of persuasion, essentially modern in its use of the mass media and its deliberate enlistment of influential support.

It seems that Peel had been convinced of the necessity for total removal of the Corn Laws by 1842 or 1843 and that thereafter he was only awaiting the right occasion. This came in 1846, with the Irish Famine, when thousands more would have died if the free import of wheat had not been allowed. Repeal was carried through parliament by a minority of the government (the 'Peelites')

Above, meeting of the Anti-Corn Law League at Manchester, 1841: this highly effective middle-class pressure group, whose aims were to abolish the duty on imported corn and extend Free Trade, achieved total success within seven years, a telling contrast with Chartism, whose aims were too extreme to gain any parliamentary support.

Above left, the National Convention of the Chartist movement, held in London in February 1839: the Convention – the first major gathering of the movement – revealed divisions between radicals and moderates that were never solved; these, combined with irresolute leadership and lack of contact with the nascent trade union movement, meant that the Chartists never became a force for effective political change. Most of their demands for parliamentary and electoral reform were enacted, however, within the next three quarters of a century.

Opposite, interior of a mid-nineteenth century doll's house, a perfect reproduction of the comfortable and solid though somewhat unimaginative style set by the royal family and followed by many of the more prosperous of their subjects. Bethnal Green Museum, London.

with the support of the Whigs and against the bitter opposition of the landowning Tories. It opened the way for the establishment of complete freedom of trade in the next decade.

By sponsoring repeal of the Corn Laws Peel split his party and committed political suicide. The young Disraeli made his reputation at this moment by denouncing his leader as a betrayer and putting himself at the head of the protectionist Tories. Gradually he welded a new Conservative party out of the ruins, dedicated to social reform at home and expansion of the empire abroad. 'Peelites' ultimately amalgamated with some of the Whigs to form the new Liberal party, of which Gladstone, the natural heir and successor of Peel, was to become the leader. Liberalism stood, above all, for Free Trade and free enterprise, for democratic reform and for a policy of peace abroad. These two great leaders were to dominate British politics until almost the end of the century.

The British Empire

With the War of American Independence (1776–83) the first British Empire had come to an end. But during the nineteenth century a second British Empire was constructed partly by acquisition, partly by conquest, partly by treaty, which was greater than the first – greater, indeed, than the world had ever seen – and which was at once her pride and the envy of other nations. Much of it had come by conquest at the expense of France and her allies, Spain and Holland, during the Revolutionary and Napoleonic Wars – huge areas in India and Canada, Ceylon and the Cape of Good Hope, many of the West Indian islands and strategic possessions in the Mediterranean like Gibraltar, Malta and the Ionian Isles. But there was little deliberate plan about the development of the empire – it has even been said that it was born 'in a fit of absence of mind'. A large empire, and the ability to maintain it and the sea routes between it, was a symbol of the power and status of the mother country. Some territories supplied useful products and raw materials, some provided substantial outlets for British manufactures, but in general the second British Empire came into being not so much from economic or military reasons but rather because of a rather ill-defined pride of possession often combined with genuine religious and humanitarian impulses.

The special pride of the Victorian Empire was India. By the end of the Napoleonic War Britain was firmly established in the territories of the Ganges and of the Deccan in the south but did not yet hold the whole sub-continent. The struggle against the Mahratta chiefs (1817), the conquest of the territories round the Indus and the war against the savage Sikhs of the Punjab occupied the first half of the nineteenth century. Then followed the task of governing and administering these vast dominions, a task accomplished on the whole with efficiency and honesty by the Indian Army and the Indian Civil Service, which was reconstituted on modern lines even before the reforms in home administration. For many functions the East India Company continued to act as the agent of the British government until 1858.

Protection of sea routes also assumed a major importance in the far-flung British Empire. St Helena, the Cape of Good Hope, Mauritius, Aden (acquired 1839), Ceylon and Singapore (1819) all became impregnable bastions and barriers to the colonial ambitions of other European powers.

Elsewhere, where outright conquest failed or seemed too costly, Britain contented herself with establishing a protective belt around her dominions. After the failure of the conquest of Afghanistan in 1842, the British army confined itself to fortifying the mountain passes of the Northwest Frontier. To the north of India the Himalayas provided a natural barrier capable of repelling any invader, while to the northeast Burma was at least partly occupied after two campaigns in 1826 and 1852.

India also served as a base for the domination of the Far East. The old East India Company had always claimed the monopoly of trade with all lands east of the Cape of Good Hope, though its success had been virtually confined to the mainland of India. Now, the search for ever wider markets was to open up the formerly closed countries of the Far East which had for centuries sought to insulate themselves against the influence of the West. The Opium War of 1840–2 forced China to open five ports to British trade, including the great cities of Canton and Shanghai, and to cede the island of Hong Kong, a trading centre and strategic port in the Pacific. In 1857 trade was opened with Siam, in 1858 with Japan.

In India and the Far East the motives of imperialism were economic and military, sometimes religious and philanthropic. It was never intended that British people should settle permanently in tropical and subtropical latitudes, where they were exposed to a harsh climate, endemic diseases and sudden, even violent, death. Countries which were so inhospitable, poor and already over populated offered little attraction to the English emigrant.

On the other hand, the mother country herself seemed to offer few prospects of health and happiness to many of those who laboured in the early days of industrialization, and there were parts of the empire – South Africa, Australia, New Zealand and Canada – where the climate was acceptable, where farmland could be had cheaply or even free, and where a man of energy and purpose could be master of his own destiny. There was a steady and continuous stream of emigrants from Britain, amounting, during the course of the century, to no less than twenty million people. Britain's human export, many of them men and women of above average intelligence and initiative, was perhaps her most important and enduring gift to the world.

To many, the Cape of Good Hope, acquired from Holland in 1815, seemed to offer the most attractive prospects. The original Dutch settlers, the Boers, were gradually pushed further back into the interior as more settlers arrived from Britain. Isolated and unprotected, they were unable to oppose the abolition of slavery in 1833, though this threatened to deprive them of the black labour force on which their agricultural economy depended.

In 1833 the Great Trek took the Boers from one side of the River Vaal to the other, into Natal. When this was annexed by Britain in 1844, the Boers trekked again, and Britain now recognized as independent the Republics of Transvaal and The Orange Free State. For the time being the issue seemed to be resolved – the diamond mines had not yet been discovered.

At the other end of the world Australia, remote and open, seemed less attractive to settlers and until the middle of the century was used primarily as a convict settlement. But the success of many ex-prisoners as sheep farmers, the availability of free land and the discovery of gold in 1851 soon began to exert a magnetic effect on emigrants. Rich lands also awaited the settler in New Zealand, where the warlike Maoris were defeated and pushed back into the hills. In Canada, especially in the state of Quebec, the situation was different. Here, English colonists encountered an existing white population of French descent, hostile to British domination and acutely aware of their distinct origins and culture. Little by little the French were swamped by continued migration, though they continued jealously to preserve their own customs and ways of life.

The spread of the 'white empire' posed new problems for the home government. The 'black' colonies, it was argued, constituted an 'empire in trust': they required the benefits of English law and firm government, of Christianity, educational and philanthropic provision generally and of military protection from more ruthless exploiters. In return for such benefits, England had a right to expect loyalty, trade concessions and treaty rights. But the lesson of history was well understood – that the attempt to impose such conditions on emigrated Britons had lost us the American colonies, the most highly prized pearl of the first British Empire.

It required little imagination to see that the new 'white' colonies must be treated differently and, in particular, be given a substantial measure of control over their own affairs. The new policy was initiated in 1847,

when Canada was granted a large degree of autonomy, her own parliament and a responsible minister, while Britain remained primarily responsible for foreign policy and defence. The process of self-government was thus begun which finally culminated in the Statute of Westminster of 1931.

The American colonies had been lost by England's attempt to control their trade and economic development. Now, Britain gradually abandoned her old colonial system by which the colonies had been obliged to trade only with the mother country. In 1825 Canada was permitted to trade with foreign countries, and in 1849 the repeal of Navigation Acts brought free trade to all the colonies. By this time, the 'white empire' was firmly linked to Britain not by political bonds but by common language and civilization and by unquestioned loyalty to the Crown. Queen Victoria's adoption of the title 'Empress of India' was symbolic of the

Above, British troops taking Cape Town in 1806: the colony, founded by Dutch settlers in 1652, was taken and lost several times before finally settling in British hands in 1815. The conflict between settlers of Dutch and British origin persisted throughout the century, flared up in the Boer War (1899–1902) and still exists today.

Top, view of Government House, Calcutta, executed by J. B. Fraser, c.1825: British rule in India, at least until the last decades of the nineteenth century, was generally dedicated and enlightened and certainly avoided the exploitation, of both people and resources, that characterized European dominion elsewhere.

Opposite, the Corn Law Repeal Hat, manufactured by one W. Marriott, a South London hatter and supporter of Free Trade.

403

new role of the monarchy and of the strange power which a small island had to control the destinies of two hundred and forty million people throughout the world.

Britain's achievement

To other European countries in the first half of the nineteenth century Britain's success seemed remarkable and phenomenal. When thousands of foreign visitors attended the Great Exhibition in Hyde Park in 1851 they were impressed, even overwhelmed, by the industrial products and mechanical ingenuity of the British, as by the colonial pavilions displaying the resources of her far-flung empire. Designed, in the Prince Consort's words, 'to illustrate the point of industrial development at which the whole of mankind has now arrived', it in fact demonstrated for all to see the immense wealth of Britain and the great lead which she enjoyed over all other nations.

Yet it is important to remember that this position had been only recently acquired and, in the perspective of history, was comparatively short-lived. In 1800 France had been the 'great power', the conqueror of Europe, master of a vast empire, home of a

philosophy that seemed destined to swamp the world. By 1870 Britain's position was already coming to be challenged by newly industrialized nations, Germany and the United States, who seemed to possess in a marked degree the characteristics of industry and initiative of which Britain had thought herself the sole repository. Observers at the International Exhibition at Paris in 1867 were now struck not so much by the British contribution as by the remarkable progress of other countries.

Britain's tenure of unchallenged world leadership was, then, comparatively brief. She achieved it partly through the natural talents of her people and the abundant natural resources of her land, partly through the absence of any substantial rival. France after 1815 was defeated and exhausted, her economy virtually prostrate after a quarter of a century geared to war needs. Germany and Italy did not yet exist as nation-states and would not do so until the processes of unification had been completed in 1870, while the United States of America, 'united' in name, were not so in any real sense, as the Civil War of the 1860s was to demonstrate. None of these countries could yet command the political stability which seemed to be a

necessary condition of economic growth.

It would be a gross over-simplification to say that Britain in the nineteenth century chose to have an industrial rather than a political revolution. The evolution of democratic institutions went on alongside economic and social changes, often impelled by those very changes. On the continent political change frequently occurred which was not rooted in the economic fabric of society but was much more the product of philosophical ideas and intellectual ferment. Neither Robert Owen nor the Chartists ever brought Britain close to revolution, though Britain was the home of the first industrial proletariat and, in the Marxist logic, should have been the first to experience an open class war. The fact was that industrialization enriched as many – perhaps more – than it impoverished and in the course of time raised standards of living infinitely higher than they could ever have been under a rural economy. New wealth created new classes and new political parties which responed in a practical way to the pressures for change. In Europe such evolutionary change was often impossible, and there was no alternative to a sudden and violent overthrow of an existing regime.

GREAT BRITAIN IN THE EARLY NINETEENTH CENTURY

Date	Great Britain	British colonies	Scientific progress	Date	Great Britain	British colonies	Scientific progress
1815	Corn law (1815) Widespread distress and economic depression Peterloo Massacre (1819)	Revolt against British rule in Ceylon suppressed (1817) Singapore founded (1819)	First steamship crosses the Atlantic (1819)	1835	Death of William IV; accession of Queen Victoria (1837) Chartist petition rejected by Parliament (1839)	Great Trek in South Africa; Orange Free State republic founded (1836) Rebellion in Canada (1837) Boers defeat Zulus at Blood River (1838) Act of Union in Canada (1840)	Samuel Morse develops telegraph (1837) Daguerre discovers daguerrotype process (1838)
1820	Death of George III; accession of George IV (1820) Cato Street Conspiracy (1820) Canning foreign minister (1822)	Gold Coast becomes a crown colony (1821) Britain acquires Malacca (1824)	Stephenson builds first iron railway bridge (1823) Stockton-Darlington railway opens (1825)	1840	Robert Peel prime minister (1841) Chartists riots in Lancashire: second Chartist petition to Parliament rejected (1842) Bank Charter Act (1844)	New Zealand becomes a separate colony; Maori insurrection (1841) South Australia a crown colony (1841) Natal becomes a British colony (1843)	First use of general anaesthetic in an operation (1842) First screw-steamer crosses the Atlantic (1843)
1825	Duke of Wellington prime minister (1828) Sliding scale of duties on imported corn (1828) Catholic Emancipation Act (1829) Death of George IV; accession of William IV (1830)		Niepce makes photograph on a metal plate (1827) G. S. Ohm defines electrical current, potential and resistance	1845	Repeal of the Corn Laws (1846) Failure of Chartist Movement (1848) Famine in Ireland	Responsible government in Canada (1846) Establishment of Orange River Sovereignty (1848) Annexation of Punjab (1849)	Sewing-machine invented (1846) Aneroid barometer designed (1847) Steam threshing machine invented (1850)
1830	Whig government under Earl Grey (1830) Reform Act (1832) Abolition of slavery in British colonies (1833) Robert Owen's Grand National Consolidated Trades Union (1834) Tolpuddle Martyrs (1834)	Revolt in Jamaica (1831) Falkland Islands become a crown colony (1833) St Helena a crown colony (1834)	Construction of first US railway (1832) Faraday's laws on electrolysis (1834) Samuel Colt patents his revolver (1835)	1850			

Above, Derby Day: *William Frith's (1819–1909) painting, completed in 1858, captures the exuberance and prosperity of mid-Victorian Britain when her industrial and imperial might was unrivalled. Tate Gallery, London.*

Opposite, interior view of the Great Exhibition of 1851.

Chapter 36

The Springtime of Nations

The political history of Europe between 1815 and 1870 is largely the history of the undoing of the attempt by the victorious allies to reconstruct the old order throughout the lands once conquered by France. In this sense, the results of the French Revolution were enduring. In the face of strong liberal and nationalistic movements, it proved impossible to turn the clock back to repressive government, and the peoples of Europe – whether in Germany, Austria, Italy, Greece or in France itself – constantly erupted into open revolt against governments which denied them the principle of democratic participation. The real 'challenge of the nineteenth century' was, then, the challenge of revolution – the necessity of reconciling the legitimate liberty of the individual with the ordered government of the state.

The peace treaties of 1815 had been designed not only to reorganize and make safe the frontiers of Europe, to punish France and reward her opponents, but also to conserve the firm position of tradition, order and religion against any possible return of revolution. It had been envisaged that there would be regular meetings of the four great powers – England, Prussia, Austria and Russia – to maintain these principles against any attempt at disturbance. But from about 1820 onwards, what has been called 'the Metternich System' had to defend itself constantly against a mounting and double attack from liberalism and nationalism. These concepts were in theory distinct, though in practice frequently unified.

Liberalism was largely the heritage of the ideas spread by the French conquests (civil and political liberty and equality, the sovereignty of the people and the right to democratic government). It had the support of many of the middle classes, who were hostile to rule by the minority and to the continuing powers and privileges of aristocracy and they found ready allies for their cause among the growing body of industrial workers in the cities.

Nationalist feelings owed less to the French Revolution itself, more to the spirit of patriotism which the Napoleonic conquests had awoken in many peoples not previously remarkable for their national loyalty. It was also the case that the peace treaties of 1815 had divided populations with little consideration for such feelings, so that, for example, the Rhineland was given to Prussia and many Italians found themselves part of the Austrian dominions. Also, the policy of the allies of maintaining tiny principalities throughout Europe – inspired partly by a fear of powerful states – took no account of this growing sense of nationhood and desire for unity among peoples who shared a common language and culture.

The first congress planned by the allies was held at Aix-la-Chapelle in 1818 and was concerned exclusively with French affairs. It was decided that occupation troops could now be evacuated and that France under the re-established Bourbon monarchy of Louis XVIII was sufficiently stable to join the Quadruple Alliance. But in Germany revolutionary agitation had already begun, led by a student body, the *Burschenschaft*, who in the course of a demonstration had burnt reactionary literature and other symbols of militarism. The rulers of three German states – Bavaria, Baden and Wurtemburg – were sufficiently alarmed to grant democratic constitutions to their peoples. Shortly afterwards, the assassination by a student of the journalist Kotzebue, a Russian agent who had been leading a campaign

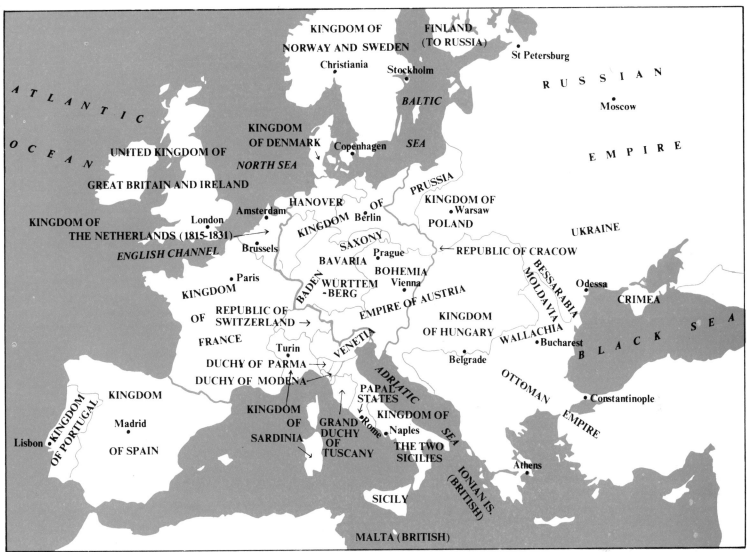

The map labels (as printed on the map):

KINGDOM OF NORWAY AND SWEDEN · Christiania · Stockholm · FINLAND (TO RUSSIA) · St Petersburg · RUSSIAN EMPIRE · Moscow · BALTIC SEA · KINGDOM OF DENMARK · Copenhagen · NORTH SEA · ATLANTIC OCEAN · UNITED KINGDOM OF GREAT BRITAIN AND IRELAND · London · Amsterdam · HANOVER · KINGDOM OF · Berlin · PRUSSIA · KINGDOM OF POLAND · Warsaw · UKRAINE · KINGDOM OF THE NETHERLANDS (1815-1831) · Brussels · ENGLISH CHANNEL · SAXONY · Prague · BOHEMIA · REPUBLIC OF CRACOW · BESSARABIA · MOLDAVIA · Odessa · CRIMEA · Paris · KINGDOM · BADEN · BAVARIA · WÜRTTEM-BERG · Vienna · EMPIRE OF AUSTRIA · KINGDOM OF HUNGARY · WALLACHIA · Bucharest · BLACK SEA · OF · REPUBLIC OF SWITZERLAND · FRANCE · Turin · VENETIA · Belgrade · OTTOMAN EMPIRE · ADRIATIC SEA · DUCHY OF PARMA · DUCHY OF MODENA · PAPAL STATES · Constantinople · KINGDOM OF PORTUGAL · Lisbon · KINGDOM · Madrid · OF SPAIN · KINGDOM OF SARDINIA · GRAND DUCHY OF TUSCANY · Rome · Naples · KINGDOM OF THE TWO SICILIES · Athens · IONIAN IS. (BRITISH) · SICILY · MALTA (BRITISH)

against liberal and nationalistic ideas, determined Metternich, the chancellor of Austria, to act. At Vienna in 1820 the German princes outlawed the *Burschenschaft*, imposed press censorship and brought the universities under strict control, though Metternich was unable to persuade the South German rulers to withdraw the recently granted constitutions.

In Spain, the restoration of the despotic King Ferdinand VII had brought to power a party which represented the deepest reaction. The country was now plunged into one of the unhappiest episodes in her unhappy history.

During Spain's struggle for independence against the French it had been shown that the local parliaments or *cortes*, where liberals were usually dominant, could produce enlightened and effective policies, but after the restoration of Ferdinand the *cortes* were ignored, thousands of liberal patriots were branded as French sympathizers, a strict censorship was imposed and despotic rule and corruption triumphed everywhere. The only resort left to liberals was to form secret societies against the government and to engage in plots, which always failed.

In 1820 in Cadiz, however, a much more serious situation arose. An army of 20,000 men had been assembled to be sent to South

America to suppress revolution in the Spanish colonies there. Colonel Riego led many of the troops in revolt, demanding a liberal constitution. Successful in Andalusia, insurrection spread quickly to the provinces of Galicia and Catalonia, and the king was forced to adopt the constitution and to dismiss his unpopular ministers.

The apparent victory of the Spanish liberals now spread revolutionary ideas across the Mediterranean to Italy. Italy in 1815 was, in Metternich's famous phrase, merely 'a geographical expression'. She was a collection of independent states – Piedmont-Sardinia in the north, Parma, Modena, Tuscany and the Papal States in the centre and the kingdom of the Two Sicilies in the south. Austria possessed the kingdom of Lombardy-Venetia and wielded great influence in the affairs of many of the states. Everywhere there was censorship and police suppression of any attempt at liberal agitation. As in Spain, middle-class liberals had formed secret societies, known locally as the *Carbonari*, because their members met in the woods like charcoal burners.

Yet, at the news of the Spanish insurrection, army officers in Naples called out their troops in revolt in July 1820, and their leader, General Pepe, forced Ferdinand I of Naples to accept a democratic constitution

Above, Europe after the Congress of Vienna, 1815, called to settle European affairs after Napoleon's defeat: among the territorial changes were the establishment of the German Confederation, the union of Poland with Russia, the union of Norway and Sweden and the unification of the United Provinces and the Austrian Netherlands (Belgium) as the Netherlands.

Opposite top, contemporary illustration of the murder of August von Kotzebue (1761–1819), 23 March 1819, by Karl Ludwig Sand, a student at the University of Jena: Kotzebue had attacked the Burschenschaft, *quarrelled with Goethe and published anti-Romantic works.*

Opposite bottom, one of Goya's (1746–1828) etchings for his Disasters of War *series, done between 1810 and 1820, a foretaste of the bitter hostility and violence that was to surround Spanish politics in the nineteenth and twentieth centuries.*

similar to that granted in Spain. To many it seemed that this pattern of events marked the beginning of the end of autocracy.

Metternich's fear was that revolution would now spread through the whole of Italy. In 1820 the emperors of Austria and Russia, the king of Prussia and French and English representatives met at the Congress of Troppau in Silesia. Metternich converted the tsar to the idea of armed intervention against liberal movements, despite opposition from Castlereagh (the English foreign secretary) and the French delegate, who saw it as a move to increase Austrian influence in Italy.

At the Congress of Laibach, in January 1821, armed intervention was agreed on. Austrian troops dispersed the forces of General Pepe and entered Naples: the constitution was abolished and liberal leaders executed. But meanwhile revolutionary ferment had spread to students and army officers in Lombardy, with the object of freeing their state from Austrian domination. The king, Victor Emmanuel I, who had been restored by the allied powers in 1814, was hated by the liberals because of his reactionary policies and now abdicated in favour of his brother Charles Felix (1821). He lost little time in calling in the Austrians, who easily defeated the liberal forces at Novara.

The tide was also turning towards reaction in Spain. The liberal reformers who had secured the constitution from Ferdinand VII had no experience of government and did not succeed in maintaining order or in putting reforms into practice. Plots and risings occurred ceaselessly, giving Ferdinand the opportunity to call in outside help. The so-called 'Holy Alliance' of Russia, Austria, Prussia and France, formed in theory to conduct the affairs of Europe in accordance with Christian principles but in fact as an instrument for maintaining the status quo,

was more than willing to respond. The Congress of Verona (September 1822) was thus called to deal with the Spanish question.

Canning, who had succeeded Castlereagh as the British foreign secretary, declared himself strongly opposed to intervention in the internal affairs of Spain or her rebellious South American colonies. In officially recognising their independence Britain was, he announced, 'calling in the New World to redress the balance of the Old'. His message was lost on the other European powers. France was especially anxious to suppress revolution so close to her borders, as well as to demonstrate the military might of the restored Bourbon monarchy. Approval was given by the congress (Britain having withdrawn) to her intervention, and in April 1823 a French army of 100,000 entered Spain and quickly defeated the rebels at Cadiz and elsewhere. The repression which followed throughout the next ten years was more ferocious even than that in Italy, the liberal leader Riego and his comrades being mercilessly hunted down, shot and massacred. Until 1828 French troops continued to garrison fortresses throughout Spain in order to buttress the repressive policies of the Spanish minister of justice, Francisco de Calomarde.

For a few years in the 1820s the forces of reaction in Europe seemed triumphant: Italy and Spain lay prostrate under the heel of foreign autocratic domination. But in 1830 the Paris Revolution and the replacement on the French throne of the Bourbons by the 'bourgeois king' Louis Philippe caused reverberations throughout Europe which seemed to echo the storming of the Bastille by the Paris mob forty years earlier. Exiled *Carboneria* in Paris not unnaturally looked for French assistance in a new attempt to rid Italy of the hated Austrians. Secret revolutionary societies were again

active in Lombardy, the Papal States and throughout central Italy.

Revolution in fact broke out in Modena in February 1831, quickly spreading to Parma, Bologna and the Romagna. In March an unlawful assembly at Bologna proclaimed the union and independence of the rebel provinces. Again, however, Metternich was master of the situation. He persuaded Louis Philippe that two of the Bonaparte princes were in the movement and that it therefore constituted a danger to the security of France. Austrian armies suppressed the rebels in Parma and Modena. In Bologna the rebels were either dispersed or arrested. Louis Philippe himself sent an expeditionary force to occupy Ancona.

By now the *Carbonari* had been thoroughly discredited by their repeated failures and their apparent inability to organize effectively. The spirit of revolt in Italy was kept alive, however, by writers and propagandists, many of them in exile. By far the most influential was a young Genoese, Guiseppe Mazzini, who founded a movement in Paris in 1832 known as 'Young Italy'. Its aim was a democratic republic, free of foreign domination: its slogan 'Unity and Republic, God and People, Thought and Action'. Mazzini's romantic personality attracted many followers, but his vague idealism was hardly what the situation demanded. More realistic policies were advocated by the Abbé Gioberti, who proposed a federation of the Italian states under the papacy by the historian Balbo, who gave to Piedmont the role of unifying Italy, and by Count Cavour, premier of Sardinia, who foresaw the necessity of defeating Austria militarily before independence could be achieved. All these ideas and aspirations were eventually to fuse in the *Risorgimento*.

Germany and Poland

In 1815 Germany, like Italy, was a mere 'geographical expression'. It consisted of thirty-nine independent states, some powerful like Prussia and Bavaria, others no more than tiny principalities, though equally proud of their separate identities. As yet there was little thought of national unity, though, as elsewhere in Europe, democratic thought had gained ground during the Napoleonic period.

The events of 1830 led to renewed demands for liberal reform in several states, and the rulers of Saxony, Bavaria, Brunswick and Hesse-Cassel were made sufficiently uneasy to grant constitutions to their peoples. The *Burschenschaft* was also re-formed in universities throughout Germany. As always, Metternich was alarmed at these stirrings of independent thought and, supported by Prussia, was able to get rigorous measures adopted by the Diet of Frankfurt (July 1832) including press censorship and the banning of unauthorized clubs and meetings. The writings of Heinrich Heine, Georg

Büchner and others were banned as subversive, and pressure was put on France to expel the large number of political refugees who had gathered there.

In fact, the idea of German unity was making progress in quite a different way. Prussia took the first step by founding the *Zollverein* or customs union, allowing the free passage of goods between states instead of the heavy tolls formerly charged. As a free trade measure it was a spectacular success, greatly increasing the level of commerce and economic activity generally: one state after another joined, until by 1834 nearly all had done so. More than this, however, the *Zollverein* facilitated the movement of people and ideas in Germany, undermined local prejudices and demonstrated the growing leadership of Prussia in German affairs.

Liberalism had an even harder struggle in Poland. This unhappy country had often been the subject of dispute and division among the powers, most recently in 1815 when the Duchy of Warsaw had been created a separate state and made part of the dominions of Russia. In theory it was endowed with its own parliament voting laws

and taxes, as well as its own army, though this was under the command of the Tsar Alexander's own brother, the brutal and authoritarian Grand Duke Constantine. The tsar's promise of a liberal, constitutional regime showed no sign of fulfilment.

In the other parts of Poland – Galatia, which had been ceded to Austria, and Posnan, which had been given to Prussia – there existed assemblies which were only partially representative of the people. Polish patriots, many officers and intellectuals had long been meeting together in secret societies, awaiting the moment to rise in support of unification and independence. At the news of the revolution in France in 1830, Constantine foolishly ordered the mobilization of the Polish army, and rumour quickly had it that he intended to use Polish troops to suppress the French liberals. The Poles in Warsaw rebelled, the Diet proclaiming the independence of the country and the deposition of the tsar in January 1831.

In spite of sympathy from France, none of the powers intervened to help the Poles, and the rebellion was soon crushed by the Russian army. There followed a more than usually severe repression, with mass hangings and deportations. Universities were closed, lands were confiscated and Russian was made the official language of the country. Thousands of Polish émigrés fled to France where they continued to hold up the torch of freedom.

The birth of modern Belgium

Only one of the many revolutions of 1830 was, in fact, successful – that of Belgium. In 1815 this little state had been given to the Netherlands – before that she had been, in turn, ruled by Spain, Austria and France. Although the union of industrial Belgium with agricultural Holland had been an economic success, there was almost nothing in common between the two countries. Belgians spoke French (or Flemish), not Dutch; they were Catholics, not Protestants; they were in outlook liberal, not authoritarian. Moreover, the constitution was heavily weighted against them, with the Dutch William of Orange as king, only one Belgian minister out of a cabinet of seven, and fewer than 300 officers out of an army of 2,000.

In 1830 an alliance of Catholics and liberals rose in revolution, set up a provisional government and proclaimed the independence of Belgium. Everything now depended on the attitude of the great powers, particularly that of Britain whose traditional policy it was that the Low Countries should not be under the control of a strong and possibly hostile country. For this reason Britain opposed the offer of the Belgian crown to the Duke of Nemours, son of Louis Philippe of France. At the conference of London (December 1830) the powers formally recognized the independence and – significantly for the future – the neutrality of Belgium. The crown was accepted by a German prince, Leopold of Saxe-Coburg-Gotha, who became King Leopold I. Holland, who had still not accepted the situation, attacked the new country the next year, but England and France quickly came to her aid and forced the Dutch to withdraw. Holland officially recognized the existence of Belgium in 1839.

The crisis of 1848

The historian De Tocqueville wrote in 1848, 'Here begins again the French Revolution – this is exactly the same.' In fact, the events of 1848–9, though more widespread, violent and spectacular, were much more akin to those of 1821 or 1830 than to the localized events of 1789. As before, there was the same mixture of liberal and nationalist aspirations, but a third element was now significant for the first time in the social conflict bred by industrialization. By 1848 many European cities had sizeable working classes which had been almost non-existent at the time of the French Revolution – populations of factory workers condemned to be the slaves of machines, confined to miserable lives in tenements and slums, who were beginning to demand a voice in their own destiny. Significantly, in Paris in 1848 the workers actually rose against the liberal middle classes, so opening a new chapter in the history of revolution which was to end in the accession to power of Napoleon III, the nephew of the former emperor. In the events of the mid-century, social and economic issues were fundamentally more important than the purely political.

More immediately, the events of 1848 had their origin in the Irish potato disease of 1845–6. This spread to the continent, causing an acute shortage of wheat which doubled prices in 1846–7 and resulted in food riots in France, Germany, Belgium and Italy. Commercial crises developed, as the banks used up stocks of gold to pay for wheat and could advance no more credit: there were numerous bankruptcies and a general lack of commercial confidence which resulted in heavy unemployment. While prices rose eighty to a hundred percent, wages were cut by an average of twenty percent.

The events of 1848 are confused and complicated; political demands are inextricably mingled with the social discontent, and there is an interaction or chain process which seems to sweep the infection across Europe, invading first one country, then the next. Revolution occurred first in Italy in January 1848, then in France in February, next in Vienna in March. By June the tide was running at its height, by the end of the summer it was already on the ebb.

In Italy the immediate cause of revolution was a combination of the economic crisis and the election of a liberal pope, Pius IX, from whom a lead in liberal reforms was expected. By the end of 1847 the whole peninsular was in ferment, and independent risings shortly broke out in widely separated states – in Sicily, demanding her independence from the kingdom of Naples, and in Lombardy in the north, where a boycott of Austrian tobacco sparked off bitter street fighting in Milan. Rulers were sufficiently alarmed to give way to demands for democratic constitutions in Naples, Tuscany and in Piedmont, where Charles Albert invited the revolutionary, Balbo, to join the government. In the Papal States Pius IX accepted laymen as cabinet ministers, and he too proposed a new constitution.

The most serious fighting was in Milan, where the revolution took the form of a truly national struggle against the Austrians. After five days of bitter street warfare (18–22 March) Austrian troops were forced to evacuate Milan, while in Venice, the other Austrian possession in northern Italy, the garrison was forced to capitulate by the patriots, led by Daniele Manin and Niccolo Tommaseo. The dukes of Parma and Modena, puppets of Austria, were also replaced by provisional governments.

With independent revolutions occurring throughout the peninsula, it seemed that the time had come for some state to take the leadership in the movement for unity and independence. The state of Piedmont in the northwest was ruled by Charles Albert and he and Count Cavour, who was then his chief minister, believed that it was Piedmont's destiny to lead an Italian crusade which would rid the country of the foreigner and unite the states under the Piedmontese dynasty. Piedmont entered the war on 24 March without any alliance from an outside prince or, indeed, the other provisional governments of Italy. For a time it seemed that Charles Albert's calculation was justified. Volunteers flocked in from Rome, Tuscany and Naples, and Manin collaborated by organising the defence of Venice.

At first there were early successes against the Austrians at Goito and Peschiera. Soon, however, the alliance began to falter. There were suspicions that Piedmont had territorial ambitions on other states and that her part in the movement was not entirely unselfish: Pius IX decided to withdraw the papal forces on the ground that the pope could not engage in war against Austria, the protector of the Catholic faith. Two more members of the alliance, Naples and Tuscany, quickly followed suit. Piedmont and Venice now remained alone against the might of Austria.

In Austria-Hungary, the ancient empire of the Habsburgs, the problems were complex. In the capital, Vienna, the revolution was primarily one of students and middle-class liberals in opposition to the absolutist régime of Metternich, the chancellor. Elsewhere nationalism was the main impulse and democracy only a secondary issue. The empire in fact covered a vast territory, inhabited by peoples of widely different beliefs, language and culture, and the motives of their protest were often obscure.

While Austria herself was largely German in language and customs, Hungary was mainly Slav. In theory a separate kingdom, she shared the common rule of the Habsburgs and was in most respects subservient to Austria. For many years there had been a movement for national independence in Hungary, led by some of the great landowners in what was still primarily a peasant country. There was also a body of liberal rebels led by men like Louis Kossuth and Ferenc Deák working for democratic reform and the development of a modern economic system. The fact that even Kossuth was less liberal in his attitude towards the Romanian and Croat minorities within Hungary was something that Metternich was subsequently able to exploit.

Bohemia was also a centre of national feeling in the empire – though she had not

existed as an independent state since the seventeenth century and had since undergone a long process of Germanization. The Czechs had experienced a national reawakening led by poets and historians like Jan Kollár and František Palacký, and already by 1845 the Diet of Prague was showing opposition to the rule of Vienna.

In many parts of the empire, therefore, nationalists were waiting for the signal to rise. The day after the Paris revolution, on 12 February 1848, the students of Vienna began attacking the government forces, and after a few days of bitter fighting Metternich was forced to flee to safety hidden in a laundry van.

The Emperor Ferdinand granted freedom of the press and of assembly and promised a constitution. When published, it was thought insufficiently liberal, and a general insurrection then took place in May, at which Ferdinand now agreed to government by a constitutional assembly elected by universal suffrage. Vienna was firmly under the control of the students and the National Guard, formed by the middle classes to defend the revolution.

Elsewhere in the empire the revolution also seemed to be successful. In Hungary, led by Kossuth, independence was gradually being won, as the country gained the right to have its own army and financial system. In Prague a provisional government had been formed under the historian Palacký and a pan-Slav congress had met with a view to uniting the scattered Slavs of the empire into one state.

In Germany, too, there had been outbreaks of students, workers and peasants from February onwards, in the Rhineland in the north as well as in several southern states. Some rulers granted free speech and the right of constitutional assembly, abolished feudalism and the status of serfdom. The old King Louis of Bavaria abdicated in favour of his son Maximilian, while in Berlin a bloody riot in March forced King Frederick William IV of Prussia to withdraw his forces and promise a universally elected government. Tendencies towards national unity were also becoming noticeable. At Frankfurt an assembly of 600 delegates drawn from all parts of Germany agreed on the election of a constitutional parliament to prepare the way for a new, unified government for the whole country. This hopeful experiment in fact never had much likelihood of success. The parliament consisted mainly of notables and intellectuals, the commercial and business interests holding aloof. It soon showed itself to be a powerless debating chamber, quite impotent as an instrument of government.

Nevertheless, the very extent of the revolutions throughout Germany, Austria and Italy served to indicate the imminent break-up of the old Habsburg Empire. That it was able to survive the crisis was in no way due to the monarchy but to the loyalty of the professional army in the face of disaster.

In spite of the Viennese rising, Field Marshal Radetzky, the Austrian commander, decided to send his army first against the Italians. The Piedmontese army was attacked and defeated at Custozza (July 1848), Milan was occupied and Piedmont forced to accept an armistice. Already, two of the objectives of the *Risorgimento* had failed – to unify the Italian states under the head of the House of Savoy (Piedmont) and to involve the papacy in the national struggle. But there still remained Mazzini's ideal of a republic which would sweep away all incompetent monarchies.

Mazzinians were strongest in Rome itself, where many refugees had fled from other states, and in November 1848 Count Rossi, Pius IX's anti-democratic minister, was stabbed. The Pope left the city in the hands of Mazzinians, who established a republic there in February 1849. Both Florence and Venice, under Daniele Manin, also proclaimed republican constitutions. New hope dawned of an Italy freed from both foreign oppressors and tyrannical rulers. Mazzini himself was triumphantly welcomed in Rome in March, and his lieutenant, Giuseppe Garibaldi, organized the army there.

This growth of republican feeling alarmed Charles Albert of Piedmont, who saw his chances of leading the Italian movement slipping away. Breaking the armistice, he re-entered the war but was utterly defeated by the Austrians at Novara and abdicated in favour of his son, Victor Emmanuel. Austria now invaded the smaller states of Parma, Modena and Tuscany and restored the dukes there. At the same time, Ferdinand of Naples regained control of Sicily.

In Rome, the success of the republicans now began to alarm foreign powers, in particular, France. The Catholic party there wished to support the Pope, while national interests were in favour of a military success which would limit the power of Austria in the peninsula. An expeditionary force of 7,000 men which arrived at Civitavecchia was beaten back by Garibaldi's amateur army, but with the help of reinforcements the French army entered Rome in July 1849, and Mazzini was forced to flee. Resistance continued only in Venice but, worn down by famine and disease, she too capitulated in August. The heroism and sacrifice of the Italian patriots had seemed to be in vain. Only in one state – Piedmont – did there remain a ray of hope. Though militarily defeated the new king, Victor Emmanuel, refused to abandon his constitutional regime. Advised by his minister, Cavour, he reflected on the lessons of 1848–49 and planned for the future.

What Radetzky had done in Italy, Marshal Windischgraetz was to do in Austria. He was a man of the sternest principle, once having declared that 'Blood is the only remedy for all the ills of the century – communism, radicalism, impiety and atheism.' Prague was bombarded, besieged and forced to submit to a military dictatorship in June 1848. The imperial cause was helped by the disunity of the rebel states, and particularly by the enmity between the Croats and the Hungarians. Hungary, under Louis Kossuth, had now come to the point of open rebellion against Austria, and the emperor cunningly gave command of the opposing army to the Croat 'Governor' Jellachich. At the news of the war against Hungary, the Viennese liberals again rose in revolt, hanged the Minister of War and forced Ferdinand to flee the capital.

In October Windischgraetz laid siege to Vienna, while the Croat army prevented aid coming from Hungary. Eventually the city fell and the democratic leaders were shot and their supporters arrested in great numbers. The emperor, now somewhat discredited by his weak handling of the situation, was, however, persuaded to abdicate in favour of his nephew, the Archduke Francis Joseph in December 1848.

From September 1848 Kossuth had headed the revolutionary government of Hungary and led the army of resistance against Austria. There was, however, an obvious limit to the capability of largely untrained volunteers against what was probably the best army in Europe, and despite all their efforts the Hungarians could not prevent Austrian and Croatian troops from entering the country in February 1849. By the spring, however, Kossuth had almost miraculously driven the enemy forces from the country and proclaimed the independence of Hungary and deposition of the hated Habsburgs in April 1849.

The emperor now entered into negotiations with the tsar, Nicholas I, for assistance. Nicholas was only too ready to help Austria in return for a free hand in the East against Turkey and immediately put an army of 130,000 men at the disposal of his ally. This meant virtual annihilation for the rebels. Kossuth resigned and sought refuge in Turkey. The last Hungarians capitulated at Vilagos in August 1849, and bitter reprisals followed against the patriots and all who had aided them. For the time being Francis Joseph had patched up his tottering empire: he was to live long enough to witness its virtual collapse.

At Frankfurt, the constituent parliament from all parts of Germany continued to debate the formation of a unified empire in place of the thirty-nine independent states. After endless discussions the hereditary crown of the new empire was offered to King Frederick William IV of Prussia, in spite of the protests of Austria and of the south German states who disliked the idea of a Protestant sovereign. There was, in fact,

little choice in the matter. Prussia was incomparably the strongest of the German states, had re-established firm government in her own country and had demonstrated her ability to lead through the idea of the *Zollverein*. The only other possible contender was Bavaria, who had considerable influence over the Catholic states but was less powerful economically and militarily. But although Frederick William would have dearly liked an imperial crown, he was unwilling to accept one 'from the public streets, like that of Louis Philippe, a crown of rubbish made of clay and mud'. His chief minister, Bismarck, a firm believer in the divine right of kings, supported his decision.

Frederick William's rejection proved to be the death-blow for the Frankfurt Parliament. The Prussian deputies withdrew, and there was now no hope of effective leadership. But in numerous other German states – the Palatinate, Baden-Baden and Saxony – there were risings in the summer of 1849, and, significantly, these were much more working-class movements for social and economic reform than middle-class demands for nationalism or liberalism. The young Karl Marx, who was publishing the *Rhine Gazette* in Cologne at this time, learned much about the dynamics of the class struggle from a situation in which the middle classes increasingly allied themselves with the nobility in fear of the prospect of proletarian revolution.

But although Frederick William had refused the offer of an imperial crown from the people, he had not renounced the ambition of German leadership on his own terms. He now negotiated with the kings of Saxony and Hanover a scheme for unity to which twenty-eight of the German states were ready to agree: a congress at Erfurt was planned to settle the final arrangements. He had, however, to face the jealousy and distrust of outside powers. Austria, who had now crushed her Hungarian revolt, strongly opposed this growth in the power of Prussia, as did the tsar. Saxony and Hanover were persuaded to withdraw from negotiations, and Prussia continued her plan with only the northern states.

Austria had decided that Prussia must be humiliated and that her own leadership of German affairs should be unchallenged. Schwarzenberg, the new chancellor of Austria, devoutly believed that there could be no Reich (German commonwealth) without Austria and sought an occasion to break up the league of princes which Prussia was sponsoring. The opportunity arose over Hesse-Cassel, where the tyrannical duke had recently been deposed: Prussia supported his subjects, Austria demanded his restoration. For a while the rival armies of Prussia and Austria faced each other poised for war, but two days later at Olmutz Prussia gave way and accepted all the Austrian demands including the dissolution of the proposed union.

By 1850 there seemed little left of 'the year of revolutions'. Austria had apparently re-established firm government in her empire and prestige among the German states. Democratic and nationalist movements had equally failed to take root, and the sufferings of the peoples of Europe seemed to be in vain. The enduring results were a liberal constitution in Piedmont and the abolition of feudalism in Austria and Germany. Moreover, two men had emerged from the crisis who were to become central figures on the European stage during the next twenty years. These were Cavour in Piedmont and Bismarck in Prussia. Under their leadership, the course of German and Italian unification was to take a new and decisive turn. But for the immediate future, the attention of Europe was drawn to the East, where similar nationalist aspirations were beginning to open great cracks in the once powerful Turkish Empire.

Opposite, Field Marshal Joseph Radetzky (1766–1858): commander in-chief in Lombardy from 1831, he was forced to leave Milan in 1848 but reoccupied the city a few months later. He was governor-general of Lombardy and Venetia until the year before his death.

Below left, Charles of Albert, king of Piedmont, enters Pavia, 29 March 1848.

Below, Louis Kossuth (1802–94), leader of the Hungarian revolution and for a short time governor of the independent Hungarian state declared in 1849: in exile in Great Britain and the United States during the 1850s he attracted a considerable following as a freedom-fighter, but after twice staging unsuccessful risings against Austria in the 1860s he spent the rest of his life in quiet retirement in Italy.

The Eastern Question

At the beginning of the nineteenth century the Turkish Empire, despite an already long history of decadence, still remained a vast conglomeration of states placed at the crossroads of three continents, Europe, Africa and Asia. Her territories covered the great peninsula of the Balkans and extended eastwards into Asia Minor and westwards along the North African coast as far as Algeria. Yet it was not so much the strength as the weakness of the Turkish Empire that produced the Eastern Question of the nineteenth century. Her declining power and supposed imminent collapse roused the territorial ambitions of both Russia and Austria. Britain was also concerned since she had no wish to see a strong power in this area which might endanger her trading routes to India and the Far East.

But the European powers were also interested in the affairs of the Orient on religious grounds. The Turkish Empire, officially Muslim in faith, contained substantial minorities of Christians within its borders who were regarded as *raia* (no more than cattle). They were subject to many special disabilities, taxes and dues which made them very much the most profitable subjects of the empire. Only if converted to Islam could they become full citizens, but the Turks, who wanted to keep the Christians weak and vulnerable, did not encourage

such additions to Allah. In general, the Christians maintained their beliefs as members of the Greek Orthodox Church, of which Russia regarded herself as the protector.

For many years groups of rebels – half-patriots, half-brigands – had sought independence of the Turkish yoke. Here, too, the French Revolution had spread ideas of democracy and independence, and in the disturbed conditions of war bands of Serbian *haidouks* and Greek *palikares*, forerunners of modern freedom-fighters, had begun to attack the hated Turkish army. Ever since 1804 the Serbs had been rebelling under their leader Kara George and had suffered terrible reprisals. In 1815 revolution broke out again, led by Miloš Obrenovich, but this time the sultan acted with more prudence, fearing the possibility of Russian intervention on the side of the Serbs. Obrenovich was granted the title 'Chief of the Serbs' and made a pasha, responsible for the government of the province. The Turkish Empire had unwittingly taken the first step towards its own dissolution.

The awakening of Greece

'Come, children of the Hellenes, the hour of glory has arrived. . . . Macedonians, rise up like wild beasts: spill the blood of all tyrants.' This song, based on the 'Marseillaise', appeared in 1797 at the beginning

of the movement for Greek independence. In fact, the Greeks were among the most favoured subjects of the Ottoman Empire, allowed to practise their religion under their own Patriarch, holding four of the great offices of state, and largely monopolizing Mediterranean trade with their great merchant fleet. It was this measure of freedom and power that gave the Greeks their desire for more, that magnified their sense of injustice and reminded them of their former glories.

Significantly, the movement for independence sprang from the wealthy merchant communities spread around the Mediterranean shores and islands, traders who could command between them 600 ships manned by 17,000 sailors. In the great Turkish city of Constantinople Greeks dominated the *Phanar* (the business quarter) and furnished numerous of the sultan's administrators. In Odessa on the Black Sea Greeks had formed a secret society, the *Hetairie*, to prepare for revolution. Throughout the ports and the islands a secret network was gradually built up, linking the Greek communities together in a dream of freedom.

For the rich Phanariots of Constantinople and the Anatolian Greeks who dreamt of 'The Great Idea', time stood still after 1453. The great social, economic and intellectual upheavals of the West bypassed them. The Renaissance, the Reformation and the Industrial Revolution never touched them.

Towards the end of the eighteenth century some Greeks were pitchforked from the past into the hardy ideals of contemporary Europe. The writings of eighteenth-century French liberals and revolutionaries were translated for (if imperfectly understood by) the merchant circles of Smyrna and the Greek *Frontisteria* of Dimitsana and Trebizond. Their effect was devastating.

In 1821 Alexander Ypsilanti, a general of Greek origin who was in Russian service, was appointed military leader of the movement. The time seemed propitious, as the sultan was occupied with a revolt of the Pasha of Janina, who was trying to establish his own dynasty in Albania. Ypsilanti called on the Greeks to rise in March 1821 and the Archbishop of Patras launched an appeal for independence. The campaign was, in fact, ill-led and failed to receive the expected outside support from Russia; the rising in Walachia was easily crushed by the formidable Turkish janissaries (soldiers, originally forming the sultans's guard). But at sea, on the islands and in the Morea, bitter guerrilla fighting continued which the Turks could not suppress.

By the beginning of 1822 the whole of the Morea was in Greek hands, and deputies of the rebellious districts, meeting at Epidaurus, proclaimed the independence of the Greek nation. A National Assembly, presided over by Alexander Mavrokordatos, voted the first Hellenic Constitution in

euphoric recollection of the democracy of classical times. In savage revenge for their defeats, the Turks seized the island of Khios, where they perpetrated horrible cruelties on a defenceless people – 23,000 inhabitants were killed and 47,000 carried off into slavery. Two daring Greek sailors, Canaris and Miaoulis, set fire to the Turkish fleet in the roads at Khios and incurred the lasting gratitude of their people.

The situation was now transformed by the intervention of Egypt's powerful army and navy on the side of the sultan. The brilliant but unscrupulous Mehemet Ali, an Albanian Muslim who had been tax gatherer, tobacco merchant and commander of the Albanian contingent in the Ottoman army, had recently expelled the Turks from Egypt and set himself up as pasha there. He now offered his efficient army and navy to the sultan for the suppression of the Greeks in exchange for Crete and the provinces of Syria and Palestine.

Egyptian armies quickly overran the Morea while her fleets dominated the Aegean. European opinion was appalled to discover that hundreds of Greeks were being sold as slaves in the markets of Cairo, but the mutual rivalry between the powers and the belief that 'legitimate' governments must be maintained at all costs prevented any joint action. Austria and Britain remained highly suspicious of Russian ambitions in the Balkans, and, equally. Tsar

Below, the Balkans and the Near East in the nineteenth century: at the root of the 'Eastern Question' was the problem of the future status of the European territories controlled by the decaying Ottoman Empire. Disputes over these territories were largely responsible for the Crimean War, 1853–56 (the main battlefields of which are shown in the inset), which checked Russia's influence in southeast Europe.

Below left, Marshal Radetzky on the battlefield of Novara, where he defeated the Piedmontese for the second time in less than a year. Heeresgeschichtliches Museum, Vienna.

Opposite, Austrian troops under Marshal Radetzky leaving Milan after the March 1848 uprising: the Piedmontese immediately declared war on Austria but were twice defeated, and within eighteen months the status quo *had been restored throughout Italy, all hopes of unification squashed. Museo del Risorgimento, Milan.*

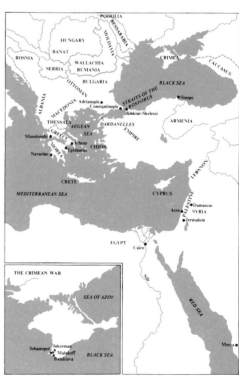

415

VEDUTA DEL CAST. D'ACROPOLIS DALLA PARTE DI TRAMONTANA

Alexander had no wish to offend two such powerful nations.

Metternich commented at the Congress of Laibach in 1821, 'Over there, on the other side of our eastern frontiers, three or four hundred thousand people hanged, butchered, impaled . . . all that hardly matters.' Not all accepted his counsel of despair. From all over Europe democrats and patriots flocked to the cause of Greek independence, inspired more by the vision of what had once been Greece than by the realities of the savage conflict. The French Colonel Fabvier offered his sword to the rebels, the great poet Byron joined Mavrokordatos at Missolonghi, only to die of fever two months later (1824).

Village by village, the Egyptian armies extinguished the flame of Greek independence. Missolonghi fell heroically in 1826, the last defenders setting fire to the powderkegs and blowing themselves up with their attackers: a year later Athens was forced to surrender. There remained in Greek hands only a few islands where the rebellion had begun six years before.

Unlike the issue of Italian independence, Greek independence ultimately succeeded because the European powers came to her aid. The invitation to intervene was made by George Canning, the British foreign secretary, who viewed Greece as the original home of European civilization. France accepted out of sympathy, Russia because she also wished to win independence for her fellow Slavs in Serbia. Austria and Prussia were not interested in supporting a rebellion against a lawful authority, even if it were an authority as unworthy as that of the Turk.

In the Treaty of London (July 1827) Britain, France and Russia agreed to mount a 'peaceful' naval blockade on Turkey which would force her, if negotiation failed, to recognize the rights of self-government of her Greek subjects. As the Turkish and Egyptian fleets, under the command of Ibrahim, son of Mehemet Ali, were at anchor in the roads of Navarino, the allied fleet drew near to make a show of strength. On 20 October 1827 what was intended as a naval manoeuvre erupted into war. A chance shot fired at the French flagship was taken to be a hostile act, and within a few hours of bitter fighting the Turkish and Egyptian fleets were destroyed. The Triple Alliance was now inevitably drawn into war by the outraged sultan, and the politicians at home were forced to uphold the actions of their commanders in the field. The Greeks owed their freedom to the mistake of a Turkish sailor.

Charles X sent a strong French force to the Morea. Russian troops attacked in the Caucasus and on the Danube, while a British fleet was sent to Alexandria. By 1829 Russia had entered Adrianople, and the sultan was forced to sue for peace. The mixed motives of the allied intervention were demonstrated clearly enough in the peace settlement. By the Treaty of Adrianople (1829) Russia acquired strongholds in the Caucasus and Armenia, two ports on the Black Sea and the right for her merchant ships to pass freely through the Straits of Bosporus and trade with the Turkish Empire. The sultan also recognized the independence of Serbia and of the Romanian provinces of Moldavia and Walachia. The recognition of Greek independence came almost as an afterthought, and only partially, for the new state was not to include Thessaly or Crete and excluded many Greek-speaking peoples. In 1832 the crown of the little state was offered to a Bavarian prince, who became King of Greece as Otto I.

The issue of Greek independence, in itself relatively insignificant, was of profound importance for the future of Europe. It demonstrated on the one hand the chronic weakness of Turkey, 'the sick man of Europe', on the other the might and ambition of Russia for influence in the Balkans. It marked, too, the virtual end of the autocratic government of Europe by congress and Holy Alliance, as it did the increasing participation of Britain in the affairs of the Near East and in support of liberal movements generally.

The Egypt of Mehemet Ali

Mehemet Ali was by birth an Albanian, whose family had settled in Macedonia. He was working as a successful tobacco merchant when conscripted for military service in Egypt against the Napoleonic armies, where he showed great courage and daring. Having reached high office in the army, he had himself declared Pasha of Cairo by popular consent after the departure of the French. Now he gradually gained control over all the sources of power and wealth – the land, the army, commerce and trade. Ali was the classic example of the unscrupulous adventurer, clever, treacherous, always awake to the main chance and his own advantage.

After establishing himself in Egypt he turned to a policy of expansion, seizing the holy cities of Mecca and Medina, conquering the Sudan and founding the city of Khartoum. The Egyptian army, manned mainly by Albanians, was made the most modern and efficient fighting force in the Near East, and it was typical of his Machiavellian way of conducting affairs that his method of expelling his Mameluke mercenaries was first to invite them to a banquet and then to have them killed.

The more positive aspect of his policies lay in modernizing the antiquated institutions of Egypt. Agricultural techniques were improved, cotton spinning and sugar refining industries established, harbours equipped and a modern merchant fleet founded. Foreigners were encouraged to bring Western knowledge to Egypt, and young Egyptians of promise were sent to study in London and Paris.

Above all, Mehemet Ali wished to legitimize his rule, to make lawful the independence that he already possessed in fact. By 1830 he was sixty-one (Mehemet Ali, Napoleon and Wellington were all, by a strange chance, born in the same year) and needed to make his title hereditary so that it could pass to his son, Ibrahim. He also demanded Syria from Sultan Mahmud as the price of his military assistance against Greece and as compensation for the loss of his fleet at Navarino. When Turkey refused, Ibrahim invaded Syria in 1832, seizing Acre and Damascus and overrunning the Taurus.

Ibrahim's army decisively defeated the Turks, commanded by the Grand Vizer Pasha Rashid, at Konieh. Again, the sultan had to look for outside aid and in desperation turned to the Russians who had so recently been his enemies: 'A drowning man clutches at a serpent', Mahmud is reported to have said. Again, the European powers became alarmed at the likely increase of Russian influence in the Balkans, and Britain, France and Austria all put pressure on the sultan to make concessions to Mehemet Ali and end the conflict; in the Treaty of Koutaieh (1833) Turkey agreed to cede Syria to the rebel. However, the sultan also signed the secret Treaty of Unkiar-Skelessi with the tsar by which Russia guaranteed the safety of Turkish territory in return for the closure of the Dardanelles to all foreign ships. Under this agreement the Black Sea would be virtually a Russian lake, denied to the trade of the world, and Russia would have established a practical protectorate over the Turkish Empire.

When the terms became known Britain felt her interests particularly threatened, and Palmerston, the Foreign Secretary, promised British aid for the reorganization of the sultan's armed forces: in return, he negotiated a trade agreement by which Turkey lowered her tariffs to a nominal amount. British forces were also permitted to occupy Aden, key to the Red Sea, to prevent further expansion of Mehemet Ali's power.

Under the aggressive leadership of Palmerston, the British Foreign Office was now anxious to extend still further British influence in the Turkish Empire as a counterbalance to that of Russia. For his part, the sultan had never accepted the independence of Syria except under duress, and in 1839, encouraged by Britain, he sent a strong army against Ibrahim. It was crushingly defeated at the Battle of Nezib, while shortly afterwards the Admiral of the Turkish fleet treacherously handed it over to the Egyptians.

Mahmud did not live to witness these tragedies. At the point of collapse, as it seemed, his empire passed into the hands of a seventeen-year-old boy, Abdul Medjid.

The new sultan had, at least, a sensible awareness of his country's failings and a genuine desire to reform. He began his reign by launching the *Tanzimat*, a programme of reform and modernization which was to include a properly organized system of taxation and regular military recruitment: its good effect was, however, to some extent nullified by the apathy and reaction of the old guard.

It was Britain who now intervened to save Turkey from Mehemet Ali. Russia, Austria and Prussia were all in favour of a mediated settlement of the Eastern Question, France alone now supporting Ali. By the Treaty of London (1840) a ten-day ultimatum was delivered to him, under which he was to receive Egypt as a hereditary title and Palestine for life but was to give up his other conquests and his fleet to the sultan. This the pasha refused, supported by Louis Philippe and his minister Thiers. A leading French newspaper at the time declared, 'France should remember that, although alone in her position, she could resist the rest of Europe.' In the event, however, France was quite unprepared to take on a war against the three strongest powers of Europe. Palmerston, in a typical display of what has come to be known as 'gunboat diplomacy', sent a fleet and small expeditionary force to Syria, which was sufficient to persuade Mehemet Ali to submit. At the Conference of London (1841) Egyptian independence was ratified by the powers, subject to the payment of an annual tribute to the sultan and a limitation on the size of the Egyptian army. Although his greater ambitions had failed, Mehemet Ali's original dream of establishing an Egyptian dynasty had been realized.

At the same time, the powers came to an agreement over the Black Sea in the Straits Convention by which the Bosporus and the Dardenelles were to be closed to the warships of all nations. This agreement, cancelling the terms of Unkiar-Skelessi, was a triumph for Lord Palmerston, as was the Treaty of London as a whole. He had now prevented the future growth of the Egyptian army, halted the expansion of French influence in the Turkish Empire, and stopped Russia from converting the Black Sea into a private lake from which her warships could dominate the Eastern Mediterranean. In 1841, it seemed, the Eastern Question had been answered.

The dispute over the Holy Places

Under its new sultan the Ottoman Empire made some progress towards constitutional reform and the westernization of her archaic

Above, Mehemet Ali (1769–1849), Viceroy of Egypt from 1805: adventurous and ambitious (he founded the dynasty that ruled Egypt until 1952), he was the first major nationalist leader outside Europe, drawing on European culture and technology while attempting to assert an independent national identity.

Top, the Battle of Navarino, fought on 20 October 1827 in the Bay of Navarino in the southwest Peloponnese.

Opposite, the Turks attack the Acropolis, Athens, during the Greek War of Independence: Greek national aspirations slowly revived during the eighteenth century, revolt broke out in 1821 and the Greeks became the first subjects of the Ottoman Empire to attain full nationhood.

inevitably involved in the dispute, since Russia regarded herself as the protector of the Greek Orthodox faith and Roman Catholics tended to look to France as theirs. During the Revolutionary and Napoleonic Wars France had been in no position to honour that role, but by 1850 there were good political reasons for the new government of Louis Napoleon to do so.

At the end of 1850 Louis Napoleon's government, anxious to win support from the French Catholics, made official protests about the custody of the Holy Places. Ali Pasha, the Turkish foreign minister, attempted to avoid offence to either side by establishing a mixed commission to try to reach agreement. As this did not satisfy anyone, it was very soon replaced by an all-Muslim commission. This eventually suggested a compromise by which Catholic monks were to hold the key of the main door of the church of Bethlehem but not the right to hold divine service there and a complicated arrangement by which the Christian sects were to follow each other in a kind of rota in the Sanctuary of the Holy Virgin. Such a solution was, of course, only likely to produce further quarrels in the future.

The 'Sick Man of Europe'

In a situation in which the host country, Turkey, was unquestionably weak – some thought on the point of death – the policies and postures of the European powers were all-important. For her part, Russia had ambitions to expand southwards into the Balkans and control of the Black Sea; equally, Britain regarded this as a threat to her Eastern and Oriental interests. It was also significant that British public opinion, especially that part of it represented by the jingoistic policies of Palmerston, was strongly anti-Russian and regarded Nicholas I as evil, despotic and treacherous.

Nicholas believed, however, that he might reach an agreement with Britain, and it was in this hope that he declared to the British Ambassador, 'We have on our hands a sick man . . . let us reach an agreement to divide his inheritance.' He suggested that Britain should take Egypt to safeguard her route to India and that Russia should receive Moldavia and Walachia, Bulgaria and Constantinople, which would be made a free port. The moment for such a surgical operation seemed to the tsar opportune. France was on the point of re-establishing the empire after the coup d'etat of December 1851, which gave Napoleon III dictatorial powers, and Austria was still feeling indebted to Russia for her help against Hungary in 1849.

Prince Menschikoff, the tsar's aide-de-camp, was sent to Constantinople with a demand for immediate satisfaction in Jerusalem and a treaty which would grant Russia a virtual protectorate over the

institutions. Revolts in the Lebanon and in Bosnia were dealt with firmly but with clemency, and the vigorous application of the measures of the *Tanzimat* was beginning to bring progress to a country which had seemed rotten with decay.

A new and explosive crisis was, however, soon to develop. For centuries there had been dispute between the Greek Orthodox and the Roman Catholic churches as to which monks should have guardianship of the Holy Places in Jerusalem, Nazareth and Bethlehem. Historically, the Catholic monks had had custody, but in the seventeenth

century Orthodox monks had succeeded in ousting their rivals. On several subsequent occasions there had been open fighting between Greek pilgrims and Catholic monks, even in the Church of the Holy Sepulchre in Jerusalem.

In a sense, the problem of the Holy Places was a trivial ecclesiastical dispute which need never have grown to critical proportions. Turkey recognized that the great sanctuaries of the Christian world should be under Christian care, and to her it was a matter of indifference which sect was given that privilege. But political issues were

20,000,000 Orthodox subjects of the sultan. Before replying, Abdul Medjid consulted the British ambassador to Turkey, Lord Stratford de Redcliffe, who was held in special respect as a known friend of Turkey and implacable enemy of Russia. In the event, Redcliffe advised acceptance of the tsar's demands, and throughout the negotiations, contrary to what was once thought, urged moderation on the sultan. Nevertheless, Medjid rejected Russia's demands, probably on the calculated risk that, whatever the British ambassador was bound to advise officially, the British government could be relied on as an ally if necessary.

Britain and France continued to look for ways towards a negotiated peace, but in 1853 Russia occupied the principalities of Moldavia and Walachia and Turkey gave an ultimatum for her withdrawal within one month. The first shots were exchanged between Russia and Turkey in October 1853, and a month later the Turkish fleet in the Black Sea was destroyed off Sinope. Russia's refusal to compromise had, it seemed, made war inevitable, and public opinion in Britain and France moved strongly in favour of early intervention on the side of the friendless Turk. In 1854 the two countries concluded a treaty of alliance with Turkey by which they agreed to defend Ottoman territory and not to seek any advantage for themselves. War with Russia was officially declared in March.

The Crimean War

By the time that plans had been made and armies assembled Russia had already been driven out of Moldavia and Walachia by Turkey unaided. The war was therefore conceived as principally a naval exercise, the point of attack being the great Russian naval base of Sebastopol in the Black Sea. A combined force of about 50,000 men was landed in September 1854 after the allies had won the Battle of the Alma and encamped near Balaklava. Meanwhile Sebastopol had been heavily fortified and resisted a long siege through the cold of the Russian winter. The necessity for the war – if 'necessity' it had ever been – had now largely disappeared with the evacuation of the principalities. Why the particular target of Sebastopol was selected was never very clear, nor what strategic advantages would follow from its capture. It is likely that all that was in mind was some blow inflicted on Russian pride.

The Russians made two attempts to break through the allied lines – at Balaklava, where the Light Brigade was wiped out by the Russian guns, and at Inkerman, but cholera and frostbite took a far greater toll of the invaders than the enemy. The Crimean campaign soon became a public scandal for the gross inefficiency of its conduct, the mistakes of its military leaders and the neglect to ensure appropriate clothing, supplies and medical services for the troops.

France had to recruit another 140,000 men for the campaign, while Piedmont supplied an expeditionary force of 15,000 so that she might take a place alongside the powers in any future disposition of European affairs.

A new general attack was launched in the summer of 1855, and in September a French division under General Mac-Mahon at last succeeded in taking the fort of Malakoff and breaching the defences of Sebastopol. The city surrendered shortly afterwards, and the new tsar, Alexander II, was prepared to sue for peace. Though Palmerston, who had now become British prime minister, was in favour of a vigorous continuation of the war to some more dramatic victory, he was

Above, the Charge of the Light Brigade at the Battle of Balaklava, 25 October 1854: the Charge (the Brigade lost a third of its men dead or wounded) served only to highlight the inefficiency of the military command. The resulting criticisms led to radical reforms of the army.

Top, the British lines at Sebastopol. The Crimean War was the first recorded by photography and the first reported by war correspondents.

Opposite, Delacroix's painting Greece Expiring at Missolonghi, *painted in the aftermath of the Greek defeat there: the Greek struggle for independence caught the imagination of writers and artists throughout Europe. Musée des Beaux-Arts, Bordeaux.*

persuaded by Napoleon III that honour had now been fully satisfied and that a lasting peace in the Balkans could be made. 'The Empire is Peace' Napoleon had said on his accession. France had already lost 100,000 men in the Crimea, 85,000 of them killed by disease.

The peace treaty, signed in March 1856, decreed that the Black Sea was to be neutral (neither Turkey nor Russia being allowed to maintain a war fleet there), that Moldavia and Walachia were to be independent (Moldavia being enlarged by the addition of part of Bessarabia from Russia), that there should be free navigation of the Danube and that Russia was to resign her protectorate over the Orthodox Church in Turkey. In return, the sultan promised to confirm the privileges of his Christian subjects.

The treaty thus secured for the allies all the aims for which they had professed to enter the war. For the time being, Russia was humiliated and crippled; France, for the first time since 1815, was restored to the rank of a great power; little Piedmont, represented by the brilliantly able Count Cavour at the conference table, was able to air publicly the wrongs of Italy at the hands of Austria. The empire of the Turk had been once more propped up, and the 'sick man's' illness halted, if not cured. Finally, the Treaty marked a considerable expansion of French influence in Turkey, evidenced by the establishment of a French lycée there and a considerable export of French capital.

In fact, the Peace of Paris solved none of the long-term problems of the Balkans. By 1870 Russia had renounced the Black Sea clauses of the treaty, and the powers had acquiesced in her faithless act; Moldavia and Walachia formed the independent kingdom of Romania in 1866, so confirming the break-up of the Ottoman Empire which had been begun by Greece. Above all, Turkey remained weak and impotent, a prey to internal crises and to foreign ambitions which were to carry within them the seeds of the First World War.

Chapter 37

Russia: the Years of Conflict

nations which would preserve the peace of Europe in accordance with Christian principles. We have already seen how this well-intentioned scheme became an instrument for the suppression of all reformist movements, a mere buttress for the maintenance of despotism and privilege. In Russia itself the tsar's policy was now no less illiberal: students were forbidden to study abroad, foreign teachers dismissed, and all the apparatus of a police state was erected in an attempt to prevent any criticism of the government or its policies.

The period between 1815 and 1870 also witnessed revolutionary changes in the eastern world no less far-reaching than those in the west. Russia, convulsed by her defeat in the Crimean War, passed from autocracy to a more liberal regime under Alexander II, who freed the serfs and established a process of modernization and westernization. When the forces he had unleashed seemed to be passing out of control, reaction returned and his reign ended in repression and terrorism. But despite her internal difficulties Russia continued to pursue an expansionist foreign policy.

Russian history in this period is to a considerable extent the history of the tsars and the tsarinas who ruled the country with autocratic power: 'the people' seem shadowy, unsubstantial figures, moved here and there, like pawns, at the whim of rulers and nobles. Under Peter the Great and Catherine II Russia had been brought into western political life, though no concessions had been made to those democratic ideas which had exploded in France in 1789. On Catherine's death her son, Paul I, a mentally unbalanced tyrant, ruled for only five years until his assassination in 1801. With the accession of Alexander I hopes for reform revived. In particular, the tsar's minister, Speranski, was a great admirer of Napoleon and wished to introduce a representative system into Russia as a first step towards a constitutional monarchy.

But any progress towards liberalization was soon dashed by the French invasion of Russia in 1812. Napoleon and all that he stood for was now the arch-enemy, and the Russian nation suddenly became united in a determined effort to repel the invader and resist the spread of subversive ideas. Speranski was sent into exile and his enemies promoted to high office. One in particular, Arakcheyev, an extreme opponent of any change, was largely instrumental in turning Alexander's views from liberalism to autocracy. Under the influence too of the extremely pious and visionary Julie de Krüdener, the tsar became increasingly aloof from political life and inclined towards a well-meaning but vague form of mysticism.

It was in this spirit that, after the final victory of the allies in 1815, Alexander conceived the Holy Alliance – a union of

The Decembrists

In an unexpected and unintended way, however, the ideas of the French Revolution were to have profound effects in Russia. Russian armies had fought Napoleon in Europe and had been stationed in France after his defeat. Soldiers of all ranks returned to the homeland full of liberal ideas, convinced that Russian government and institutions were backward and corrupt. The effects of European culture and attitudes were most marked on the young officer class who, despite the aristocratic origins of many, seemed suddenly to have developed a social conscience and humanitarian instincts.

Freemasonry, made illegal during the reign of Catherine II, was now revived and became a focus for liberal thought and discussion. Secret revolutionary societies multiplied throughout the country, including some of the highest nobility like Prince Paul Trubetskoi among their members. But such societies were mainly debating arenas for intellectuals, hardly action groups. Some advocated the establishment of constitutional monarchy, some a republic, others, like the United Slavs, a union of Slav peoples beyond the confines of Russia. Among the more extreme of the revolutionaries, however, some positive plans were being formulated. Men like Ryleiev and Colonel Pestel, son of a former chief of police, were among the strongest advocates of a republic, prepared even to assassinate the tsar and the royal family as the principal obstacles to their plans.

The death of Alexander I in 1825 posed a problem of succession, since the tsar left no direct heir. He chose to grant the crown to his second brother, Nicholas, but this was disputed by his elder brother, the Grand Duke Constantine. Ultimately, Constantine was persuaded to renounce his rights to the throne, but the whole occasion had provided an opportunity for the revolutionaries to take advantage of the uncertainty. On the morning of 14 December 1825, many officers who were members of the secret societies raised a body of troops in the belief that Constantine, who was being held prisoner in Warsaw, would not agree to a renunciation. The rebels formed up in Senate Square, St Petersburg, where the new tsar

Opposite top, contemporary photograph of French trenches and, on the horizon, the fort of Malakoff.

Opposite bottom, the signatories of the Congress of Paris, 1856, convened to settle the Eastern Question at the end of the Crimean War.

Autocracy and orthodoxy

For the thirty years of his reign Nicholas remained an implacable enemy of liberalism and the principal buttress of conservative ideas. He had come to the throne 'at the cost of the blood of my subjects', as he wrote to his brother Constantine, drawing from this experience a profound fear of any concession that might seem to encourage revolution. At the same time, he was acutely conscious of the responsibilities of his office, was hard-working and devotedly attached to the army and its iron discipline. These were hardly endearing qualities, and the new tsar's regime quickly became a byword in the West for severity and inhumanity. De Tocqueville described it as 'the cornerstone of despotism in the world' and the Marquis de Custine in 1839 wrote that 'the Russian government has substituted the discipline of the camp for the order of the city: a state of siege has been made the usual state of society.'

Nor did the church escape the strict control of the government. A colonel of the Hussars was appointed to the holy synod (ecclesiastical assembly) and was given powers greater even than those of the patriarch, the nominal head of the Orthodox Church. The watchwords of the regime – 'orthodoxy, autocracy, nationality' – were officially proclaimed by Count Uvarov, the minister of education.

The enforcement of such precepts required a ruthless and efficient police state, which effectively muzzled press and public opinion, banned secret societies, trade unions and all expressions of opposition to the state. An ardent nationalism and pride in Russia was to be impressed on the young, and it was in keeping with this that foreign travel was made almost impossible and French tutors and governesses – supposed sources of disaffection – placed under strict supervision.

There were, however, some more positive aspects of the Russian dictatorship. Speranski was recalled to complete the massive codification of Russian law and in 1830 the Complete Collection of the Laws of the Russian Empire was issued, which brought together some thirty thousand promulgated over the centuries.

Nicholas was also anxious to reorganize the cumbrous administration of the empire and planned new central and local institutions which would bring greater efficiency into the archaic structure of Russian government. The only practical outcome of these plans was, however, the creation of a new government department – the tsar's 'personal chancery' – which was responsible among other things for the police régime. Nicholas saw public order as the necessary condition of social progress. Once efficient government was established throughout his vast dominions, freedom and civil liberties could follow, the serfs could be emancipated from bondage and the subject peoples of the empire given control of their own affairs. Any hopes of such a gradual relaxation of

Nicholas was to come to take his oath, but they were dealt with swiftly and efficiently. Artillery opened fire on the barricades, the rebels dispersed and arrests followed. The same pattern was repeated in the south, at Kiev, where loyal troops again suppressed the insurrectionaries. A trial of prisoners was carried out with apparent meticulous justice: 121 of the accused were brought before the High Court, where they defended themselves with great courage. Pestel declared at his trial, 'My greatest fault is to have tried to reap the harvest before I had sown the seed.' He and another were hanged, the rest of the conspirators being deported to Siberia.

Pestel's words were an apt comment on the failure of the Decembrists' rising as a whole. They had planned insufficiently, had counted on greater support from the people and had not imagined that so many of the troops would remain loyal to the tsar. But in one vital respect the rising of 1825 was significant. For the first time in Russian history members of the aristocracy had been allied with workers against the interests of their own class and had been involved, not merely in a squabble over the succession, but in a fundamental attempt to change the nature of the state. The Decembrists left both a legacy and an inspiration to the revolutionaries of the future.

Above, painting, dating from the 1830s, of the December uprising in St Petersburg, December 1825: the uprising, a military conspiracy that had originally planned to assassinate the tsar in May 1826, misfired, initially because of his death in November the previous year and then because of the collapse of the plotters' morale.

Left, contemporary print of the Russian royal family: flanking the heir to the throne, the Grand Duke Alexander (who as Alexander II ruled 1855–81), are the Emperor Nicholas I (ruled 1825–55) and the Empress Alexandra. Nicholas' regime was socially and intellectually repressive; though Alexander was more liberal – the serfs were emancipated, elected provincial assemblies were established – he too mercilessly put down a Polish revolt and severely repressed all signs of revolutionary activity at home.

Opposite, Tsar Alexander I of Russia (1777–1825, ruled 1801–25): a liberal at the beginning of his reign, he became increasingly pietistic and reactionary, founding the Holy Alliance in the hope of resisting revolution in Europe. Royal Society of Medicine, London.

lords continued to regard their serfs as chattels to be bought and sold, exchanged or pledged at the bank as security for a loan, brutally punished or imprisoned if they dared to offend. A police report of 1827 stated, 'the peasants await their liberation as the Jews await their Messiah.'

The tsars faced an impossible choice of policy – to modernize the institutions of Russia and so liberate forces which might overthrow their regime or to try to maintain their autocracy in spite of the mounting pressure for change.

In particular, the promise of public education, made necessary by the increasing industrialization of Russia as well as being desirable on social and moral grounds, tended to whet the appetite for economic and political changes which the tsars were totally unwilling to concede. Nicholas's policy of limited and hesitant liberalism was to prove quite inadequate to resolve the country's problems.

The intelligentsia

Leadership in the movement for the re-organization of Russia now increasingly passed to the intelligentsia of students and teachers. As educational opportunities widened some young men from the lower classes began to find their way into university, and it was largely from such students, inspired by German romantic philosophy, that the revolutionary lead now came. Contempt for riches and conventions, hatred of tyranny and a somewhat mystical yearning for progress were its main characteristics, though it was sometimes also mixed with a strong sense of patriotism, the belief that the Russians were a chosen people and should go their own way independently of western influences. Whatever their ideological differences, the intelligentsia were, however, all agreed on one thing – that, as Herzen expressed it – 'the Slav race will take the initiative in the Renaissance of humanity.'

These attitudes were clearly reflected in the cultural developments of the new Russia. Already the poet Alexander Pushkin (1799–1837) had begun to free Russian literature from classical and French influences, showing that English and German writers were models more akin to Russian traditions: another, Lermontov, wrote the epic *Heroes of our Time* in a style closely similar to that of Byron. During the reign of Alexander I Pushkin wrote a number of what were soon to become classic works – *The Prisoner of the Caucasus*, *Eugene Onegin* and *Boris Godunov*. But it was the work of a new writer, Gogol, that marked a decisive turning point by using literature to take up a moral standpoint. 'The writer', he said, 'should make judgments in the service of humanity', and, especially in his *Dead Souls*, he daringly attacked the shortcomings of Russian society and administration. The same period also saw the emergence of Ivan Turgenev, whose masterpiece was *Fathers and Children*.

policy were shattered by the revolution in France in 1830 and its repercussions in Russia, where the military garrisons in Novgorod rose in a revolt reminiscent of that of the Decembrists five years earlier. Although easily suppressed, the renewed threat of revolution brought to an end any move towards a more liberal policy.

In fact, Nicholas saw his greatest danger in the subject peoples who had been annexed to the empire after 1815 – the Finns and Swedes of Finland, Germans, Estonians and Latvians in the Baltic provinces, the Poles, Lithuanians and Jews of Poland, the Georgians of Transcaucasia – none of whom had any sense of loyalty to the Russian crown and might be expected to seize any opportunity to shake off alien control. At the end of 1830, after revolutions in France, Belgium and Italy, the Poles rose in revolt, and the Grand Duke Constantine, military governor of Warsaw, was forced to flee, Polish officers and landowners fought bravely for a year against the might of Russia, inflicting and receiving heavy losses, but by September 1831 Warsaw had been subjugated and the rebels captured or dispersed. Thousands were exiled to Siberia and the last vestiges of Polish freedom were suppressed: for all practical purposes Poland disappeared, to be absorbed into the tsarist empire.

The new Russia

But not even Russia could remain unaffected by the changes that were transforming western Europe. During Nicholas's reign Russia underwent the first stages of an industrial revolution, much of it necessarily initiated by the state in the absence of a sufficiently large and wealthy middle class. The tsar himself drew on a map with a ruler the route of the railway line from St Petersburg to Moscow, work on which began

after 1838, though no line yet connected Russia with the West. Much road development also took place, enabling the freer movement of goods and people. At the tsar's accession in 1825 Russia had 5,000 factories employing 200,000 workers: within ten years there were already 10,000 factories with 500,000 employees and economic growth was to continue apace. In her vast domains Russia had most of the raw materials necessary for industrialization, while her large population provided at once a ready labour force and a potentially huge market. Already she was able to replace previously imported products like textiles with her own manufactures.

But, as elsewhere, industrialization brought about social change and social problems. The growth of industry and trade offered opportunities for middle class manufacturers, merchants and professional people generally. Equally, it created a new urban working class alongside the serfs of rural Russia. Nicholas's deliberate policy was to encourage this new middle class and to ally it firmly to the monarchy. A class of 'notable citizens' was created with special privileges, who were to hold important positions in the civil service, commerce and the professions. But despite this development, significant for the future, Russia remained essentially a two-class society, with all real power monopolized in the hands of some 120,000 landed nobles. Russia was still a land of farms and villages and, with few exceptions, the towns were no more than overgrown market centres for the surrounding countryside, with wooden houses, unpaved streets and a total lack of sanitary provision. In 1838 there were 11,000,000 serfs, subject to laws which made them virtually the slaves of their lords, compared with the mere 80,000 free peasants, the numbers of whom grew only very slowly. Most

The work which caused the greatest sensation was, however, Nicholas Turgenev's *Russia and the Russians*, published in France in 1847 where the author had fled after the December Revolution. The book was a bitter denunciation of the evils of serfdom and the vices of the tsarist regime. Such works had a limited, and necessarily secret, circulation among the Russian intelligentsia. With a strict press censorship and police supervision they ran a terrible risk, and in 1849 all the members of one political and literary club – the Petrachevists – were arrested and the leaders sentenced to death. As they stood on the scaffold awaiting execution, the tsar's pardon was proclaimed. The event left a lasting impression on one of the condemned men, Feodor Dostoyevsky, who in *The Idiot* described the mounting panic on the scaffold and the cruelty of the delayed reprieve: the nature of their offence had been officially described as a 'conspiracy of ideas'. For this, Dostoyevsky was deported to a prison camp in Siberia where he wrote his *The House of the Dead*.

The Russian intellectuals of the 1840s were not revolutionaries thirsting for direct action against a corrupt state so much as artists and idealists who used the political scene as the dramatic background for their canvas. But the intellectual ferment they created, and the public criticism that they levelled at the tsarist regime, was to take on a deeper significance in the next decade when the power and authority of Nicholas I was to suffer its first great defeat.

The consequences of the Crimean War

'War', wrote Karl Marx, 'is the forcing-house of democracy.' In victorious Britain, the ineptitude of the conduct of the Crimean campaign brought reforms to the army and the civil service based on promotion by competition and ability in place of wealth and privilege. In defeated Russia, the consequences were even more far reaching. The Treaty of Paris, signed in 1856, marked, for the time being at least, the end of Russian ambitions of territorial expansion and the reversal of the steady growth of influence in Western affairs which had been built up for long centuries past. For thirty years Nicholas had been the greatest champion of counter-revolution in Europe, the arch-enemy of any change towards more liberal policies in the conduct of affairs. Dying at the beginning of 1855, he did not live to see the complete collapse of his system.

The Russian autocratic regime had been able to command the loyalty and submission of its subjects so long as it was militarily successful. Once defeated in the field, the faith in Russian supremacy which had silenced the voices of the critics was broken. The Crimea came as a shattering and traumatic experience to the armies which still

Above, illustration from an 1890s edition of Fyodor Dostoevsky's (1821–81) The House of the Dead.

Top, Mikhail Lermontov (1814–41): A Hero of Our Times, described by the author 'a portrait composed of the vices of all our generation', is a work of social and political criticism, whose hero, Petchorin, wastes his life aimlessly, scornful of the court, yet remains cut off from the ordinary people by his European education.

Top left, view of Moscow in the early nineteenth century.

Opposite, Russian and Polish cavalry clashing during the Polish uprising in 1830: Nicholas I easily but severely repressed the revolt, absorbing the nation into his empire. Only in 1918 did an independent Poland come into being, for the first time since the eighteenth century, and that state too has once again suffered Russian imperialism. Muzeum Wojska Polskiego, Warsaw.

rested on their laurels of 1812. To be beaten was bad enough, but to be beaten on her own soil by the two great liberal powers, France and Britain, assisted by the despised Turk, was catastrophic. The Crimean War was widely interpreted as a failure for autocracy, a success for liberalism. Russia experienced an agonized period of guilt and self-analysis, during which an outpouring of literature passed secretly from hand to hand, criticizing all those who had been involved in the conduct of the war but chiefly the Tsar himself. 'Awake, oh Russia', proclaimed one of the pamphlets; 'Awake from your long sleep of apathy and ignorance. Arise, prepare yourself, and demand before the despot's throne that he render account for the disaster that has befallen the nation.'

The abolition of serfdom

Nicholas had once said, 'My successor will do what he pleases: I myself cannot change.' In many respects it was the epitaph of the old regime. His son, Alexander II, came to the imperial throne at the age of thirty-seven, intelligent, tolerant, well-prepared for the role he was to play. In the manifesto in which he announced to the Russian people the end of the Crimean War, Alexander stated that internal reform was necessary. A government which protected itself by silencing public opinion, a people of whom the majority were still bound by serfdom – such things were incompatible with a modern state and largely explained the defeat of the armies in the field.

The key to reform was, however, to be gradualness. Little by little a greater degree of freedom was given to the press, the universities and to public opinion in general. There was much discussion of the need for modernization of Russian institutions along Western lines, for the development of railways, banks and industrial companies and for the improvement of education and agriculture. Pressure for change was kept up by Russian exiles, of whom the revolutionary leader and writer, Alexander Herzen was among the most outspoken in his journal *Kolokol* (*The Bell*).

Shortly after his accession the new tsar announced that he intended to emancipate the serfs, though not immediately. In fact, the problem was an exceedingly delicate one and was examined in great detail by a Secret Committee for the Amelioration of the Situation of the Peasants, which was set up in 1857. Were the serfs to be freed with or without possession of their lands, and if granted land rights were they to have free possession or some kind of tenure? If, on the other hand, emancipation were not to carry land with it, would it not merely weaken the position of the peasants and possibly create a vast and dangerous rural proletariat?

Influenced by liberal advisers, Alexander II chose to grant freedom and land. Provincial land committees were established to investigate the problems locally and to report directly to the tsar, who presided over the Central Committee. Alexander also toured the provinces personally, appealing for a spirit of generosity and conciliation among the great noble landowners. On 19 February 1861, the sixth anniversary of his accession, the tsar signed the manifesto announcing the greatest reform in Russian history.

By this bold measure, 47,000,000 peasants were granted personal liberty – 21,000,000 the serfs of lords, 20,000,000 of the Crown, and the rest a mixed body of servants and workers. The actual terms of the emancipation were, however, complex and not as generous as many had hoped. The peasants were granted freehold possession of their houses and the ground immediately surrounding; the farmland on which their livelihood depended was assigned to the collective ownership of the *mir* or village council, which then granted to the peasants the use of specific parts. A clear indication of the fact that the land was not his own was that the *mir* was charged with making a periodic redivision of the property; even the *mir* was not the owner in the fullest sense since it was still subject to certain seignorial rights reserved by the lords. In fact, the reform satisfied no one. The lord, deprived of his forced labour, now had to hire workers or hand over all his estates to the *mir*. Equally, the peasant believed that the land he tilled should have become his and felt cheated by any survival of the lord's authority.

But in one respect at least, the institution of the *mirs* was an outstanding success. They introduced to the Russian people the idea of local self-government, free from the control of the former lords. They administered, judged and kept order on the democratic principle of equality in a society which had formerly been sharply divided into those who had rights and those who had none. The village *mirs* were grouped together into larger units, the *volosts* (cantons), above which again were elected municipal corporations. Thus, the Russian peasants were given a complete system of local self-government, which ensured that, for the first time, the voices of the poorest and meanest of the tsar's subjects could be heard. In 1864 the same principle was extended to the major units of provincial administration, the districts and the provinces, which were given the right to elect councils (*zemstvos*) by universal suffrage and charged with responsibility for roads, schools, hospitals and provisions against famine. In these important regional assemblies the nobility were more strongly represented, yet nevertheless this new system of local government proved to be one of the main instruments that brought the nobility and the peasantry into contact and alliance with each other in the pursuance of common interests. The building of thousands of schools and the modernization of agricultural techniques were two of their more important achievements. The growing number of towns also received a measure of self-government when the merchant corporations and craft guilds were allowed to elect representatives to the municipal council (*duma*). It seems, however, that Alexander was conscious of the possible dangers of allowing too much power to these democratic bodies. *Zemstvos* and *dumas* were never permitted to take joint action: the tsar was to remain the sole link between the two.

Another major reform, undertaken between 1862 and 1865, was the reorganization of the system of justice. The courts were increased in number and modelled on Western lines: juries were established, secret trials, torture and corporal punishment abolished. The most important principle was that the judiciary was to be separated from the executive arm of government and so freed from royal control. As in the British constitution, the judges were to be independent and able to arrive at their decisions without fear or favour.

In the early years of Alexander's reign a new spirit of freedom and conciliation seemed to be moving through Russia. The country which had once sought to suppress public opinion now seemed anxious to stimulate criticism and change. Press censorship was eased, control of the universities was relaxed, and many scholarships were granted in order to spread higher education among those formerly excluded on the grounds of cost. To many it seemed that a new Russia, freer and greater than the old, was about to be born.

The chief beneficiaries from these more enlightened policies were the intelligentsia and students, but far from drawing them into alliance with the tsar the new taste of freedom served only to alienate them from his regime. In recognition of the growing danger, Alexander went back on some of his earlier reforms after 1861, for example by forbidding the universities to admit women or any student who could not subscribe to the orthodox religion. As the country began to take steps towards a more modern, industrialized society, the social problems of the towns and their inhabitants increasingly forced themselves on the public's attention and the intellectuals turned for guidance and inspiration to the writings of the French socialists and to Hegel, Marx and Engels.

Increasingly, the younger and more educated classes came to see revolution as the only means of creating a new world in which there would be no distinctions of rank or wealth, no nobles or serfs but a classless society in which each man would be free to give of his talents to the common good. This idealism was compounded of many elements – liberalism, socialism, and not least a devout religious faith which still inspired many young Russians as it had their fathers for generations before. Dostoyevsky in *The Possessed* described the atmosphere of mysticism which hung around the revolutionary intelligentsia. The organization necessarily had to be secret, for despite his liberal sympathies the tsar could never have tolerated a body the whole object of which was aimed at the foundations of his power.

In 1861 Nikolai Chernyshevsky, a publicist and critic, founded the most influential of these secret societies, 'Young Russia', which had the support of most of the intelligentsia and was in close contact with Russian emigres abroad and with political prisoners exiled to Siberia. In the next year, Chernyshevsky was himself arrested and deported to the prison camps, but others were soon willing to follow the lead he had given, and in 1863 the society 'Land and Liberty' took up the struggle. In a climate of opinion that now regarded any public criticism of the régime almost as treason, it was impossible that these dissentient elements could form a constitutional opposition party as they might have done in western Europe: their only recourse was direct action and terrorist activities against the state.

The hopes of the young Russian revolutionaries were raised by the growth of national feeling in Poland. Since the revolution of 1831 this poor country had suffered under the harsh yoke of Nicholas I, who had tried to stamp out all vestiges of independence. But under the more liberal régime of Alexander II Polish hopes for political independence and for the recovery of the lost Lithuanian provinces revived. Increasingly 'Young Russia' saw the expression of its own hopes in the struggle of the oppressed Polish people.

The Polish insurrection

To the Polish people, the blunders and prevarications of the Russian government seemed a mockery. A strong nationalist spirit had persisted there ever since the abortive rising of 1831, strengthened by a fervent Catholic faith which further separated the Poles from the Russian Orthodox Church. The seeming impossiblity of any kind of peaceful negotiation with their Russian masters led, in the absence of any organized Polish army, to the outbreak of guerrilla warfare in 1863. Within a short time fighting had spread to the whole country, and the Russian army was taking bitter reprisals against the civilian population, ostensibly for harbouring the rebels. Once again, the sympathy of the European powers was not translated into action. Abandoned to their fate, the Poles now lost all remnants of independence, and Russia was allowed officially to absorb the state into her dominions. By 1866 resistance had been crushed: Russian was made the official language, and the former kingdom was carved up into ten regions forming part of the vast tsarist empire.

In effect, the Polish insurrection hindered rather than helped the liberal cause in Russia. Although some of the young revolutionaries hailed it as a bold blow for

freedom, the more general reaction in Russia was to condemn the Poles as ungrateful rebels and to rally public support solidly behind the government in its policy of 'pacification'. Liberal opinions, once tolerated and even encouraged, now came to be condemned as unpatriotic. The turning point in attitudes occurred in 1866 when a young student, Karakozov, unsuccessfully attempted to assassinate the tsar. The government was able to take advantage of the public alarm to put down all supposedly subversive movements. The members of the secret societies were tracked down and hundreds deported. The liberal experiment in Russia was at an end.

The 1860s therefore form a decisive decade in Russian affairs. A definite break had occurred between liberal opinion and government policy: there could be no accommodation between the two, no steady progress towards a liberal constitution. From the time of Karakozov war was declared on the tsar and all his policies, and terrorism became the order of the day. In 1881, fifteen years after the first attempt on his life, Alexander II died at the hands of an assassin.

Above, Russian peasants greeting Alexander II in front of the Winter Palace in St Petersburg, 19 February 1861, the day of their emancipation.

Top, public reading of the statutes emancipating the serfs on an estate near Moscow: though emancipation was in many respects the beginning of the end for the old autocratic regime, making further reforms almost inevitable, many peasants were worse off than before and were still tied by debt to their village.

427

Date	France	Russia	Other European countries	Date	France	Russia	Other European countries
1815	Restoration of Bourbons; Louis XVIII	Holy Alliance (1815)	Battle of Waterloo	1845	Affair of the Spanish marriages	Occupation of Danubian provinces	Revolutions in several countries (1848)
	The Ultra-Royalists come to power	Nicholas I tsar (1825)	Holy Roman Empire becomes German Confederation under Austria		Revolution in Paris (1848)	Start of Crimean War (1854)	Campaigns of Garibaldi in Italy
	Chambre introuvable	December uprising (1825)			Election of Louis-Napoleon Bonaparte as president	Alexander II tsar (1855)	Crimean War (1854)
			Uprising in Greece (1822)			Liberation of the serfs in the royal domain (1858)	
	Assassination of the Duke of Berry (1820)	Capture of Erivan (1827)	Independence of Serbia		Military expedition to Rome (1849)		
	Expedition to Spain (1823)				Coup d'état of 2 December (1851)		
	Accession of Charles X (1824)				Establishment of the Second Empire (1852)		
	The Liberals are elected				Assassination attempt by Orsini (1858)		
	Capture of Algiers and Oran				Franco-Sardinian alliance		War between Austria and Sardina (1859)
1830	July Revolution in Paris	The Polish revolt (1830)	Independence of Belgium (1830)	1860	Acquisition of Nice and Savoy	Emancipation of the serfs (1861)	Bismarck comes to power in Prussia
	Louis Philippe becomes king	Russians take Vassorie (1831)			Intervention in Mexico	Creation of the *zemstvos* (1864)	Sadowa—Prussia defeats Austria (1866)
	Treaty with Abdul el-Kader (1834)	Treaty of Unkair-Skelessi (1833)			Liberal concessions (1867)	Attempted assassination of Alexander (1866)	Opening of the Suez Canal (1869)
	Capture of Smala from Abdul el-Kader (1843)	Straits Convention (1841)	Victoria Queen of England (1837)		Ollivier ministry		
	French Moroccan War (1844)				War against Prussia Sedan	Municipal reform	
				1870	Fall of the Empire		

To some extent, the return of ruthless repression at home was compensated by a successful policy of expansion which helped to buttress the prestige of the tsarist regime. By the late sixties middle-class liberals had been alienated by the policy of stern despotism, and the more extreme revolutionaries had turned to the new philosophy of nihilism, a creed which challenged every aspect of the old order while having nothing positive to offer in its place. Against this mounting opposition, the government of the tsår had two popular causes to offer – the unification of the peoples of the empire and the conquest of central Asia.

In the Caucasus, the primitive mountain people, Muslim in faith and owing allegiance to the Imam Schamyh, had resisted Russian advance for twenty years; they were finally defeated in 1859. Between 1865 and 1868 Turkestan, to the east, was overrun after the capture of Tashkent and Samarkand. Further east still, the crumbling Chinese empire was forced to cede the maritime province in which Russia founded Vladivostock, the 'key to the East', in 1860. For many people, Russian despotism again seemed to be justified by its military success, though externally her expansion was watched with growing concern by Britain and, before long, by the new and ambitious power of Japan. Conquest alleviated but did not cure the ills of Russia.

The economic development of Russia

Terror and autocracy might also have been compensated by the material progress of the Russian people, by economic and industrial developments and by a rising standard of living which could have brought prosperity comparable with that enjoyed by some western European countries. Russia was vast and populous, rich in material resources largely unexploited, and with a people noted for their hard work, imagination and inventiveness. Precise statistics on the Russian economy in the 1860s are not available, but it is likely that at this time some ninety percent of the people lived in villages, only ten percent in towns. Russia was predominantly agricultural, with rather more than half her 260 million acres now in the hands of peasants. But the average size of holdings was only eight to nine acres per household, and many were too small to support a large family. The land was still divided up into tiny strips, often widely scattered, as it had been in Europe in the Middle Ages, one-third of it allowed to lie fallow and unproductive each year.

The consequence of this was that modern methods of farming – the use of agricultural machinery, rotational systems and fertilizers – were almost unknown on most Russian farms. Even scythes, one of the simplest of all agricultural tools – had to be imported, and the primitive ploughs in use did little more than scratch the surface of the land. Despite the great fertility of her 'black earth' Russian wheat yields were only half those of Austria and France and one-third those of England.

Whether or not Alexander II's reforms produced any measurable change in the standard of life of the Russian peasant is doubtful. Just before the First World War the *Encyclopaedia Britannica* (eleventh edition 1910–11) commented:

The present condition of the peasants – according to official documents – appears to be as follows. In the twelve central governments they grow, on average, sufficient ryebread for only 200 days in the year – often for only 180 and 100 days. The peasantry are impoverished, and in many parts live on the verge of starvation for the greater part of the year.

Although technically emancipated, the serfs were free only in name. They bore the brunt of Russian taxation, both direct and indirect, and were also taxed by the *zemstvos* on which they had only indirect representation. For the most part they lived in huts of wood and mud with earthen floors and usually with no water supplies or sanitation: the single room was shared with pigs and poultry, and infectious diseases took a tremendous toll of human life. Even at the beginning of the twentieth century the Russian deathrate was the highest in Europe – thirty per thousand per year compared with sixteen per thousand in Britain – and one child in every three died during its first year. In 1914 only twenty-one percent of the whole population could read and write, and the figure would have been smaller still in the 1860s. Count Witte, the prime minister in 1905–6, commented:

The peasants are free from the slave-owners. But they are now slaves to arbitrary power, legal disabilities and to ignorance. The peasants have ceased to be private property. . . . That is all that remains of the reform of 19th February, 1861.

There was little more evidence of progress in the Russian towns than in the countryside. Although St Petersburg and Moscow were centres of culture and fashion for a few thousand nobles and rich bourgeois, the great majority of town dwellers lived in conditions no better than their country brothers. They were crowded into insanitary shacks and tenements and forced to labour at sweated trades, hardly yet affected by mechanization, for a mere pittance. Rich material resources of coal and metals had scarcely begun to be exploited, and as late as 1914 only about one-thenth of the country had been geologically surveyed. Coal production was only one-twenty-seventh and iron-ore production only one-twelfth that of the United States of America. This state of industrial backwardness was to some extent actively encouraged by the crown and nobility, who feared the growth of a powerful urban proletariat as a possible source of change – even of revolution. Ultimately, as the events of 1917 were to demonstrate, their fears were amply justified.

Chapter 38

France from the Restoration to Napoleon III

The French Revolution bequeathed to its birthplace a heritage of problems – political, social and economic – which successive governments strove vainly to solve. To reconcile liberty with order, to give effect to the democratic principles for which Frenchmen had fought while re-establishing the necessary authority of the state taxed the energies and imaginations of statesmen and politicians for more than half a century, and to achieve this while at the same time providing the conditions of economic growth and military power ultimately proved an impossibility. Monarchy, republic and empire all fell victims to the same enemies from within, and in this sense the eventual consequence of the French Revolution was the humiliating defeat of French arms on the battlefield of Sedan.

The restoration of the Bourbons

The last Bourbon king had fallen victim to the guillotine. Now, in 1815, Louis XVIII was restored to the throne, brought back 'in the baggage of the allies' after more than twenty years of exile. The new king was intelligent enough to know that the *ancien régime* could never be re-established, that the middle classes were prepared to accept a monarchy only if the essential freedoms of the Revolution were confirmed. Thus at the outset of his reign, Louis XVIII was brought face-to-face with a fundamental philosophical problem which demanded immediate and practical solution.

Although intelligent, cultured and refined, Louis XVIII was ill-equipped to provide such an answer. His long exile had taught him to be patient and amenable and to accept the position of a constitutional monarch which was the condition of his restoration; on the other hand, he had no intention of playing only a nominal part in affairs of state. Unfortunately, his closest associates, led by his brother the Count of Artois, were more royalist than he himself and were not prepared to make concessions to the principles of 1789.

Under the new constitution of 1815 the king was the head of state and the executive power: he had the right to choose his own ministers, who were not responsible to the parliament. The latter was to consist of two houses – an Upper Chamber nominated by the king and a Chamber of Deputies chosen by an electorate limited to men over the age of thirty who paid at least 300 francs a year in taxes. There were less than 100,000 voters in all, and the working classes were totally excluded from political power. Moreover, even the 'democratic' Chamber of Deputies could only discuss legislation and vote taxes: since they had no executive power there was no means of enforcing their decisions unless the king also agreed.

Yet, despite its very limited nature, the constitution was regarded as revolutionary by many of the nobility and clergy, who dreamed of a restoration of real power to the ancient pillars of the state. They had influential leaders like the Count of Artois, the Count of Villèle and the writer Chateaubriand, as well as their own organ in the *Gazette de France*.

Ranged against them were those who benefited from the new constitution – essentially the middle classes and professionals who had been brought into political competence, supported by a few enlightened nobles. These 'Constitutionalists' were led by the historian François Guizot and expressed their views in the *Courrier Français*. To their left stood a more extreme group, led by Benjamin Constant and the veteran Marquis de Lafayette, who had no faith in the constitution and were uneasy at the excessive influence of emigrés and clergy in the new government. These 'Independents' drew most of their support from the lower middle classes: their objective was a more democratic constitution in which the elected chamber would have real power.

One of the king's promises on his restoration had been an amnesty for all those Frenchmen who had supported Napoleon at the time of the Hundred Days, but in the country as a whole anti-republican feeling was running high. In several cities known Bonapartists were assassinated by mobs, and in the first post-war election the Ultra-Royalist party surprisingly won a majority in the Chamber of Deputies. Louis, who had not dared to hope for such support, described it as 'The Unknown Chamber'.

The king was now urged – probably not wholly against his will – into a policy of repressive conservatism. Talleyrand, the moderate prime minister, was replaced by the royalist Richelieu. Eighteen high-ranking officers who had fought with Napoleon at the end – including the once-popular hero Marshall Ney – were condemned and shot, while a general purge of the courts, the universities and local government removed some 9,000 from public office. Finally, the Bonaparte family, and all those who had had any part in the execution of Louis XVI, were banished from France.

But if the royalists wished to restore the *ancien régime*, the king knew that to do so would lose him his crown. Making an astute appraisal of the political feeling of the

Above, Louis XVIII (ruled 1814–24): Louis' reign was a time of reconciliation for France, brought about as much by an improving economic situation as by the king's moderate, efficient and honest government.

country, Louis dismissed the chamber in September 1816 and held another election in which the Royalists lost many seats and the Constitutionalists gained a small majority. For the next four years France was to experiment with more liberal policies.

The old king now had an opportunity to show his wisdom and shrewdness in steering a middle course between the two extremes of reaction and reform. Though he never became a popular figure – the memories of France's departed glories and the bitter pangs of Waterloo were too strong for that – he succeeded ably in maintaining peace and prosperity while paying off the country's war indemnity and liberating her soil from foreign armies. Under the new prime minister, Décazes, the electoral law was altered in order to reduce the influence of the great landowners over their tenant voters, military conscription was replaced by a volunteer army of a quarter of a million and, again to reduce aristocratic power, officers were selected by competitive examination and promoted by seniority and merit. Finally, in 1819, press censorship was abolished, and in future cases concerning publications were to be tried by jury in the assize courts, no longer by special tribunals appointed by the government.

One of the unforeseen results of this general relaxation of control was a large increase in the circulation of liberal newspapers, and in the 1819 elections the Independents gained considerable ground. Décazes, alarmed at the strength of the forces he had unleashed, brought his programme of reforms to an end, dismissed several of his most liberal ministers and increasingly allied himself with the Right. Groups of extreme anti-clericals had formed themselves into secret societies on the model of the Italian *Carbonari*, and in 1820, when there were revolutionary outbreaks in Pied-

mont, Naples, Spain and Portugal, there were disturbances in France culminating in the murder of the king's nephew, the Duke of Berry, by a Bonapartist fanatic. Under pressure from his own family and the country, Louis dismissed his friend Décazes. The Ultra-Royalists quickly seized power in the council, appointing one of their own number, the Count of Villèle, as president.

There now followed the undoing of much of Décazes' patient reconstruction. Villèle, the puny little member for Toulouse, was a shrewd administrator who understood clearly enough the realities of political power. In order to halt the progress of the liberals he abolished the new electoral law and, moreover, introduced double voting rights for that quarter of the electors who paid the most taxes: political competence was to rest upon economic foundations, not on abstract principles of justice and equality. As a result, the liberals lost heavily in the elections of 1820, and Villèle completed their defeat by reimposing censorship of the press and the hearing of cases by special tribunals: in this way the publication of most opposition journals was stopped.

Villèle's policies relied in part on a renewed energy and spirit in the Roman Catholic Church, which through a determined onslaught on the schools and universities was attempting to reconquer areas of French life which had lapsed into paganism during the Revolution and subsequent war. Villèle strongly supported the *Congrégation*, an association dominated by the Jesuits, and placed the universities under the supervision of the bishops.

But despite the attacks on them, the opposition continued a vocal criticism of the government and its policies. The fifteen members of the left in the Chamber of Deputies included some outstanding orators like Benjamin Constant and General Foy,

while secret presses continued to pour out broadsheets and songs denouncing the government and the Jesuits. In the universities student demonstrations against control by the Church were often violent, especially when popular professors like Guizot and Victor Cousin were suspended from their duties.

Among some of the more extreme revolutionaries the belief grew that Villèle's regime could only be ended by armed insurrection. Republicans like Lafayette and Cousin formed secret *charbonneries* with cells of twenty members directed by a high command. Badly organized and idealistic, they were no more successful than their Italian counterparts and had little support from the public at large. The ease with which their local risings were put down indicated that the government had the situation well in hand and that they constituted no real threat to the authority of the Ultras. But in September 1824 the old king died and was succeeded by his brother, Charles X, who in a few months was to destroy what little credit the French Crown had left.

Charles X

Where Louis had been shrewd, moderate and easy-going, Charles was unintelligent, stern and autocratic. At sixty-seven he was the epitome of the *ancien régime*, proud, haughty and unbending, a staunch adherent of the Church and an implacable enemy of paganism and reform. 'I had rather chop wood', he had once said, 'than reign after the fashion of the King of England', and his coronation ceremony was symbolically performed at Reims with the full pageantry of medieval rites. One of his first acts was to increase the penalties for sacrilege, and it rapidly became clear that Charles intended to put the clock back to 1789. His abolition of the National Guard, who had demonstrated in favour of constitutional reform, and his granting of compensation to the emigre nobles were especially unpopular. In the Chamber, Constitutionalists and Liberals allied together in a powerful opposition headed by Guizot and in the next elections won a majority of 250 seats against the government's 200. Villèle had no alternative but to give his resignation to the king in January 1828.

Charles was now faced with an unmanageable Chamber and a seemingly impossible situation. To gain time, he first appointed a Constitutionalist, Martignac, who completely failed to win the support of the deputies. Increasingly, the feeling grew that the king was planning a coup d'état to overthrow the constitution and restore the *ancien régime*. This view seemed to be confirmed the following year when he dismissed Martignac and appointed Prince Polignac, one of the original emigres and a man who had refused to swear allegiance to the Charter of 1815: one of his stranger

The glorious days of 1830

The political crisis of 1829 had resulted in important regroupings of the parties, the Republicans growing in strength and, more important, a new party led by the Duke of Orléans emerging in the forefront of affairs. This was a party of moderate Royalists, anxious to safeguard the interests of the middle classes and having the support of influential men like Talleyrand and Adolphe Thiers. Their ideal was a constitutional monarchy like that of England, where power was shared between the sovereign and the houses of parliament.

Faced with growing opposition in the Chamber of Deputies, Polignac now dismissed parliament and prepared for an open conflict. On 25 July 1830, royal ordinances were issued which limited the freedom of the press, dissolved the Chambers and altered the electoral law. Although the king had authority under Article 14 of the Charter to do this, it was clearly a provocative gesture, especially as the new electoral law limited the franchise to those who paid land tax or property tax and so deliberately excluded many professional and businessmen who were known liberal supporters.

It was the journalists who reacted first, on 26 July, by issuing a declaration that they would continue to publish newspapers without the required permission.

Next day, workers from the poorer quarters of Paris erected barricades in the streets, but the final spark to the revolution

delusions was that he received direct guidance from the Virgin Mary.

was given on the 28th, when the government announced that the hated General Marmont, who had betrayed Napoleon in 1814, had been given command of the royal armies. There followed three days of disorder and fighting, when thousands of Parisians of all classes marched through the streets with tricolour flags at their head. Students of the Polytechnic had previously seized several army barracks and distributed arms to the population. Those royal regiments which had not gone over to the rebels were quickly overcome, and after the capture of the Louvre and the Tuileries Marmont, defeated, evacuated the capital.

The revolution of 1830 was over before most French people realized what was happening. The events had happened entirely in Paris, so that the royalist strongholds in the provinces were unable to move until it was too late. But in some ways the strangest part of the revolution was its outcome. Its leaders had been mainly Republicans or Bonapartists, anxious to establish in France either a presidential constitution or a second empire under one of the children of Napoleon. In fact, the result was neither of these but a bourgeois monarchy under Louis Philippe, the head of the House of Orléans, who as a young man had fought in the revolutionary armies and had subsequently known sorrow and poverty. The Orléanists, essentially the party of the middle classes and professionals, were able to turn events to their advantage partly because they were better organized than their political opponents, partly because a constitutional monarch who would accept the Chamber and honour the tricolor

Above, the Count of Villèle (1733–1854), President of the Council under both Louis XVIII and Charles X from 1822 to 1828: efficient, hardworking and illiberal, Villèle encouraged Charles in his attempts to return to a more autocratic style of government.

Left, painting by L. L. Lecomte of fighting in the rue de Roman, 29 July 1830. Musée Carnavalet, Paris.

Below, Charles X (1759–1836, ruled 1824–30): unsympathetic and reactionary, he went back on his promise to maintain the political gains of the Revolution and soon met increasing unpopularity.

Opposite, Louis XVIII returns to Paris, 8 July 1815, after Napoleon had once again gone into exile, this time for good. Musée Carnavalet, Paris.

represented a middle way which the majority of French people could support. It was therefore relatively easy to persuade the two Chambers, on 30 July, to send a deputation to Louis Philippe offering him the crown, in much the same way that William of Orange had been invited to take the English throne in 1688. The Parisian mob, at first somewhat hostile, were won over when Louis Philippe appeared on the balcony of the Hôtel de Ville, draped in a tricolour flag, and warmly embracing Lafayette, 'the grand old man of the revolution', who had announced his adherence to the Orléanists.

Meanwhile, Charles X made a last bid to rescue the situation for the Bourbon dynasty, abdicating in favour of his young grandson the Duke of Bordeaux and suggesting that Louis Philippe should act as Regent until he came of age. This Louis refused, and after further threatened attacks by the Paris mob Charles escaped to England. The throne of France was officially offered to Louis Philippe by the two Chambers on 9 August.

The July Monarchy

There could hardly have been a greater contrast between the new king and his Bourbon predecessors. To outward appearances he was the personification of the petty bourgeois – a shabbily dressed man who loved to stroll through the streets of Paris with his umbrella under his arm, a devoted father of five sons and three daughters, a man of simple tastes and no pretensions. Behind this very ordinary exterior there also lay much courage and resolution, a sound business sense and a determination to raise the authority of France from the low levels to which Charles X had reduced it.

Louis Philippe accepted a constitution considerably more democratic than that of 1815. By a series of amendments, the

king no longer had the power to promulgate ordinances having the force of law, press censorship and double voting were abolished, and in future the choice of prime minister was to lie with the two Chambers. Thus parliamentary supremacy over the legislative function was clearly and absolutely established. By additional clauses, the National Guard was permitted to choose its own officers, the hereditary peerage was abolished and the Chamber of Peers opened to the middle classes, and the property qualification for the vote in the Chamber of Deputies was lowered from those paying taxes of 300 francs a year to those paying 200 francs thus doubling to 200,000 citizens.

The new king's policy was clearly to try to steer a middle course between the two extremist groups, the Republicans and the

Bonapartists. Like all compromises, it satisfied few people. The Republicans regrouped under the leadership of such men as Carrel, the lawyer Garnier-Pagès and the chemist Raspail and through the now free press launched a campaign for universal suffrage. Again secret societies sprang up to prepare the ground for the next general election. Even within the Orléanist party, differences of opinion appeared between the more conservative leaders like Casimir Périer and Guizot, who believed that reform had now gone far enough, and liberals like Laffitte and Lafayette, who wished to continue reform towards an even more democratic constitution. Louis Philippe had to choose between the two: he chose the liberals under the leadership of Laffitte, 'the king of bankers and the banker of kings'.

One of Laffitte's immediate problems was the trial of Charles X's former ministers. Justice seemed to require that they should be punished for the injuries they had inflicted on the French people: the more extreme elements demanded their execution, the upper house contented itself with sentencing them to life imprisonment. Widespread demonstrations had accompanied the trial, and early in 1831 there was a wave of violent anti-clericalism when Roman Catholic priests were insulted and attacked. In an attempt to win popularity, Laffitte lowered the taxes on alcoholic drinks, which only had the result of producing a budget deficit of forty million francs.

Louis realized that the situation demanded a firmer hand. Dismissing Laffitte, he appointed Casimir Périer, another banker but an authoritarian of more conservative views, determined to suppress public disorder. Within a few months the budget was again balanced and the new minister could turn his attention to a serious situation which had appeared in Lyons, the centre of the great French silk industry. In November 1831 the weavers, wretchedly paid and housed in miserable slums had taken up arms against their employers, and had occupied the town after two days of bloody fighting against the police and the army. Whatever the rights or wrongs of the situation, Louis Philippe's government could not allow such a threat to public law and order to continue, and General Soult was ordered to march on the city.

The army regained possession of the city on 5 December, the silk workers then being disarmed and treated as rebels: if anything, their conditions subsequently grew even worse. It was thus clearly demonstrated, early in the new reign, that the rights of the property-owning middle classes were to be regarded as paramount and that the Revolution of 1830 had served merely to confirm the power of the bourgeoisie, leaving the workers as excluded from political participation as they had been under the Bourbons.

The stirrings of the Lyons proletariat had hardly been suppressed when a new threat to the monarchy appeared. In 1832 the Duchess of Berry, widow of the murdered Duke and mother of Prince Henry, the heir of Charles X, landed in the Vendée, western France, in an attempt to rally support for her son's cause. In the event, she drew few followers and was arrested shortly afterwards in Nantes. At least the episode demonstrated that royalist opposition to Louis Philippe was no longer a serious threat.

More disturbing was the growth of the Republican movement. In June 1832 there was a serious rising of Republicans against the government, when over 800 died in bloody street fighting. Two years later another insurrection, inspired by the Society for the Rights of Man, resulted in the deaths of a further 300 rebels in Lyons. Such risings could be put down with relative ease because the army remained loyal and because the National Guard, essentially a middle class body, could always be relied on for support, but they demonstrated an inherent weakness in Louis Philippe's regime that it was not firmly based on the respect and affection of all classes of Frenchmen.

In 1835 an attempt on Louis' life served as the pretext for laws directly aimed at the Republicans. One imposed severe penalties for attacks on the monarch, including the caricatures of Louis Philippe by Honoré Daumier and other artists which had been circulating; the other officially outlawed Republicanism and laid down special rules for the trial of political offences.

Within about four years, therefore, Louis Philippe's government, now under the leadership of conservatives like Guizot and Thiers, had brought the liberal experiment to an end, though at least that had established firm government. For the time being, the Republican menace was halted, both in the Chamber of Deputies and in the country at large, and for a few years France was to enjoy a period of calm during which economic expansion and a growth in prosperity seemed to justify the political conservatism of the July Monarchy.

Guizot's ministry

For some years after 1835 Louis Philippe virtually ruled France himself. Technically, a series of puppet ministers presided in the Chamber, and the middle classes, enjoying a period of unusual economic growth and prosperity, were for a while content to allow him to hold the reins of power. In the elections of 1839, however, the prime minister Molé, was defeated, and after some months of hesitation Louis gave the leadership to Guizot, a distinguished academic historian who was a staunch royalist and conservative. To Guizot the constitution of 1830 was perfect: the art of the politician was to make it work, to give the monarch a position of real influence in government while allying the representatives of middle class wealth and culture solidly behind the throne.

But the first task of any government, Guizot believed, was to maintain order. He inherited a confused situation in which Republican and dissident elements, secret societies and subversive literature constituted a serious threat to public order and to France's economic development, and in the very year of his taking office 700 rebels belonging to one of the secret societies known as 'The Seasons' occupied the law courts and police headquarters in Paris. Precisely what they intended to do is not clear, though it seems that they hoped to overthrow the constitution and establish a republic. Guizot's new government dealt with them easily and effectively, surrounding the rebels and arresting the leaders Barbès and Blanqui, yet the episode demonstrated the continued and growing attraction which the idea of a republic had for many Frenchmen.

The other strong current of opposition opinion was Bonapartism. As the years went by, the tyranny and oppression of the empire was forgotten, only its glorious victories before which the powers of Europe had trembled were remembered. Historians,

Above, portrait by Hippolyte Delaroche of François Guizot (1787–1874): his refusal to extend the franchise and to make any concessions to radical thinking led to his overthrow in 1848.

Top, army and silk weavers facing each other on the Place des Bernardines, Lyons, 22 November 1831: the revolt was bloodily crushed, as was a further rising sixteen months later.

Opposite top right, the Parisian crowd attacks the Louvre, 29 July 1830.

Opposite top left, four of the leaders of the 1830 Revolution: from left to right Jacques Laffitte, Casimir Périer, the Marquis de Lafayette and Marshal Gerard.

Opposite bottom, Louis Philippe (1773–1850, ruled 1830–48), the 'citizen king', portrait by Franz Winterhalter. Château de Versailles.

poets and pamphleteers, combined to venerate the Little Emperor, to reinterpret his defeat during 'The Hundred Days' and to record his reminiscences and conversations from his exile in St Helena. It was symbolical of this process of rehabilitation that in 1840 his ashes were brought back from St Helena to be given honourable burial at Les Invalides in Paris, the funeral carriage being followed though, by an immense crowd. As yet, it was too soon for the Bonapartists to overthrow the strong government of Louis Philippe.

The head of the Napoleonic house was Louis Bonaparte, nephew of the great Napoleon and son of Napoleon's brother who had once held the throne of Holland. He was a strange, studious young man, convinced of his imperial destiny and unabashed by the utter failure so far of his attempts to seize power in France. Already in 1834 he had unsuccessfully tried to win over the garrison of Strasbourg. Now in 1840, when he landed at Boulogne, the French army, instead of rallying to his cause,

merely captured and imprisoned him in the fortress of Ham. Yet, in retrospect, the origins of the Second Empire are discernible plainly enough in the events of 1840.

For the next six years Guizot's conservative ministry continued to resist all political change. Industry and agriculture prospered, and in 1842 plans were drawn up for the construction of a huge railway network converging on Paris. The philosophy of 'grow rich, pay taxes, and you too will enjoy the vote, gradually brought a few more Frenchmen into democratic competence, and in the elections of 1846 the government was overwhelmingly returned to power. In all outward appearances at least 'the bourgeois king' was more secure than at any time since his accession.

The revolution of 1848

The beginning of the trouble was an economic crisis, caused by a failure in the wheat and potato harvests in the autumn of 1846. As prices soared, bands of starving

people began looting the bakeries, spreading terror throughout the countryside, while in the towns factories closed and the number of unemployed multiplied alarmingly. At the same time, the disclosure of a series of government scandals gave the opposition their opportunity to demand changes in the electoral system and the lowering of the property qualifications for the franchise to 100 francs. Unwisely, but predictably, Guizot refused all pressure for change. The opposition leaders now decided to put the issues before the public, organizing mass meetings at which they exposed the government's failures to large and enthusiastic audiences of workers. Republicans like the journalist Louis Blanc and the author Alphonse de Lamartine quickly came to the forefront, campaigning for universal suffrage and the improvement of economic conditions.

'The wind of revolution is blowing', wrote de Tocqueville. The storm burst on 22 February 1848, when Guizot refused permission for a public banquet to be given

by the Republicans. A protest demonstration turned into a riot when a frightened army patrol fired a chance volley into the crowd. By the 23rd the National Guard had joined the rebels and Louis Philippe's dismissal of Guizot came too late to retrieve the situation. As in 1830, arms were seized from the barracks and barricades erected in the streets, but, as in 1789, it was the 'Marseillaise' that was on everyone's lips. After some skirmishes with the remaining royal troops the crowd marched to the Tuileries were Louis abdicated and shortly afterwards fled to England.

The speed and easy success of the revolution startled even the Republicans. Their problem now was to make sure that the victory was not wrested from them. To do this meant excluding the deputies from any share in the success. The crowd took possession of the Chamber, Lamartine reading out the names of the new government to the Parisians who crowded into the benches and galleries. The Republic was then officially proclaimed from the Hôtel de Ville.

Louis Philippe's government had given France for eighteen years an unaccustomed measure of peace and prosperity, but ultimately it failed because it was not broadly based on the popular will. By devoting itself to the avarice of the middle classes it had alienated that growing body of workers on whom the wealth of France depended, and they, in anger and despair, had ended the life of a monarchy which had either treated them with contempt or ignored their very existence. Now these same workers were flushed with success, but unorganized, inarticulate, an easy prey to the demagogue who could promise all.

At the same time as Lamartine was proclaiming the new Republic, another group had strong supporters in the crowd. These were the Socialists, followers of Louis Blanc and Albert, who had derived their ideas from earlier French philosophers like Saint-Simon, Fourier and Proudhon and were now advocating fundamental economic, not merely political, changes. At the meeting at the Hôtel de Ville they had tried to substitute

Above, the proclamation of the Second Republic at the Hôtel de Ville, painting by J.-J. Champin. Musée Carnavalet, Paris.

Left, members of the Provisional Government, formed on 24 February 1848, an uneasy mixture of republicans, such as Lamartine and Ledru-Rollin, and socialists, such as Albert and Louis Blanc: after the shattering socialist defeat in the April elections and the bloody suppression of the June uprising, power returned to the propertied classes, and in December Louis Napoleon Bonaparte was elected president. Four years later he became hereditary emperor.

Opposite top, Napoleon Bonaparte's funeral cortege in the Champs Elysées, 15 December 1840. Bonapartism remained weak throughout Louis Philippe's reign, though it revived rapidly after 1848.

Opposite bottom right, Louis-Philippe's throne being burnt by the Parisian crowd, 25 February 1848.

Opposite bottom left, cartoon by Honoré Daumier (1808–79), the celebrated painter and caricaturist, of Louis Philippe fleeing to England; the king travelled as plain 'Mr Smith'.

The National Workshops

The first general election to be held under conditions approaching manhood suffrage was, therefore, a shattering defeat for socialism. It illustrated, perhaps, the victory of common sense and practicality which has rescued France from more than one crisis, for it was clear enough that a country on the brink of economic disaster was hardly the place for utopian experiments. The government had urgently to find money, yet with the future so uncertain the policy of raising loans by the issue of government bonds was a miserable failure. Appeals to French patriotism were in vain, yet to increase the level of taxation was equally unthinkable. There remained the possibility of reducing government spending.

For this reason, if for no other, Louis Blanc's idea of cooperative production was doomed. He and other Socialists had advocated the setting-up of National Workshops, where workers would both own and control the processes of production and would divide the profits among themselves. Initially, the state would provide the capital to buy premises, machines and materials, but thereafter workers would be free to run their own affairs independently of their former capitalist masters. Part of the profits would be set aside to purchase more workshops, so that ultimately the whole of the nation's economy would be socialist.

Obviously, such ideas held great attraction for the poor and unemployed of the French cities, but equally clearly they faced immense problems of finance and organization. It was, to say the least, unlikely that the middle classes who had sunk their fortunes in industry would voluntarily renounce their ownership, and the new minister of public works, who himself opposed the whole idea, was easily able to wreck any chance of success that the National Workshops might have had. Although work of a kind was certainly provided for the unemployed, he made no attempt to select men for tasks according to their skill and no attempt to create work which could show a profit. Men were directed into planting trees or digging trenches which they then filled in again. Workers soon became disheartened, abandoned their support of the Socialists and spent their time either in idleness or fruitless political agitation. The National Workshops had skilfully been turned into objects of public ridicule and scorn.

Meanwhile, reaction was setting in in the government. All real power was concentrated in an Executive Committee of five members which, although it contained Republicans like Lamartine and Arago, had no Socialist representative. In May an armed demonstration resulted in the arrest of the Socialist leaders Barbès, Blanqui and Albert and the closure of the revolutionary clubs, while one of the first acts of the newly-elected Assembly was to order the closure of the National Workshops. Workers were

the red flag of socialism for the tricolour of the republicans, but Lamartine had rushed forward and in a famous speech had condemned their emblem as the flag of blood and hatred. He was not, however, able to prevent the inclusion of the socialist leaders in the new government.

The Republicans knew clearly enough that the immediate cause of the revolution had been the economic crisis and the miserable poverty of many of the working classes, but even if they had wanted to exclude the proletariat from power there was no way of doing so. Universal suffrage which had been proclaimed and would now enfranchise nine million pople instead of a quarter of a million. Freedom of the press and of public assembly resulted in the appearance of hundreds of revolutionary newspapers and political clubs. For the first time, it seemed, a new working-class consciousness had emerged, in which they were no longer content to accept the leadership of middle-class liberals but wanted a complete reconstruction of society on their own terms. To outside observers like Marx and Engels, publishing their Communist Manifesto at this time, it seemed that the hour of the proletarian revolution had struck.

In the uneasy situation the new government played for time, appointing a special commission to enquire into working conditions in industry, which resulted in a substantial reduction of hours. But there were growing signs of a rift between the middle classes and the socialists over the timing of the general election, the one urging delay, the other pressing for immediate action. Popular discontent was further heightened by increases in taxation made necessary by

the government's critical financial position.

In fact, the postponement of the elections favoured the Socialists rather than the Republicans. Lamartine and his followers believed that people instinctively recognized the truth when it was presented to them and that propaganda was therefore wasted on intelligent and discriminating human beings. More realistically, the Socialists knew that many of the French working classes were poor and illiterate and believed that they were entitled to a period of instruction to remedy the effects of their political inexperience. Demonstrations and mass meetings were therefore organized throughout France, sometimes attended by as many as 100,000 to listen to renowned speakers like Louis Blanc. On some of these occasions public order was only kept by the National Guard, and a growing rift became apparent between the two groups who had so recently been allied to bring about the revolution.

On 23 April for the first time millions of Frenchmen went to the polls. The results were as the Socialists had feared. France was still a predominantly rural country, and the strength of socialism was almost entirely among the exploited working classes of the towns. The peasant was traditional and conservative in outlook, a staunch supporter of property and order and suspicious of the Parisian trouble-makers. The newly-elected Assembly was moderate and middle class, hardly dissimilar from that of Louis Philippe's closing years. Of 900 Deputies only 100 were Socialists, fewer than the 130 Royalists of the extreme right: the rest were moderate Republicans, pledged to suppress disorder and to restore financial stability to France.

given the choice of two unattractive alternatives – military service in Algeria or work draining the mosquito-infested swamps of Sologne in central France. For the middle classes, it seemed a good way of removing a disorderly mob from Paris, but the men of the National Workshops who had once dreamed of being their own masters had no intention of accepting either. Once more the barricades went up in the streets of Paris, but this time Republican was against Socialist.

For a while it seemed that the government forces were taking little action. In fact, General Cavaignac first cut off the infected areas of the city like the Latin Quarter and then made organized attacks; only after several days of very bitter fighting did these become successful. Middle-class opinion had been outraged by accounts of the brutality of the rebels, such as the fatal injury of the Archbishop of Paris who had tried to intervene in the dispute, and the Assembly now wreaked terrible vengeance; 10,000 Socialists were executed, a further 15,000 imprisoned. In future the Socialist working class and the Republican middle class, who had once fought together behind the barricades, were divided by the blood spilt in June 1848. The inevitability of the class war, which Karl Marx had predicted, seemed to be amply justified by the turn of French events.

The return of Louis Bonaparte

With public order re-established so dearly, the first task of the Assembly was to prepare a constitution. That this was to be a Republican one was never in doubt, but beyond this there were almost as many opinions as deputies. Ultimately, a constitution resembling in some respects that of the United States of America was agreed, its main principle being to establish a president with executive power sufficient to guarantee public order. He was to be chosen by universal suffrage for a period of four years – long enough, it was hoped, to make his mark but not to establish a dynasty. As the legislative arm there would be a single National Assembly, also elected by universal suffrage, though the precise relationship between the Assembly and the president was not clearly defined. The principle of 'the right to work' was specifically not mentioned: it was replaced by 'the freedom to work'.

The presidential elections took place in December. A number of candidates entered the lists – Lamartine, the revered writer and Republican, Cavaignac, the general who had saved Paris from the mob, two Socialist leaders and, finally, Louis Bonaparte, returned from England where he had quietly been waiting for the call. He was elected at the head of the poll by a majority of more than four million votes.

By a series of unlikely chances – the early death of Napoleon's own son, then that of his elder brother, killed during *Carbonari* violence in Italy – Louis had become the heir to the Bonapartist succession and legend. Although possessing few of his uncle's qualities, he had lived a life of some daring and adventure in Switzerland and Italy, had twice before made a bid for French power and had escaped from his final imprisonment in the fortress of Ham to England in 1846. Here he waited until the events of February 1848 brought him rushing back to France. At forty he was still hesitant and timid, a poor orator who fumbled his speech as a newly-elected deputy, but he had the name of Napoleon which still passed in every Frenchman's memory for discipline, power and military renown.

There could be no mistaking the relief with which the French electors turned to a candidate who had the advantage not only of the name but of having been apart from the vacillations and shabbiness of French politics in recent years. Here, it was thought, was a president who would be above politics, who could be loved at home and respected abroad. Louis was elected overwhelmingly, polling 5,400,000 votes compared with 1,400,000 for Cavaignac: the rest were far behind, at the very bottom the poet Lamartine with a mere 20,000.

Elections for the Legislative Assembly were held a year later – in·May 1849. The result was a major defeat for the moderate Republicans and a victory for the Conservatives, but also significant was a substantial gain for the extreme Republicans led by Ledru-Rollin. The strange situation was already occurring that out of a republican revolution had emerged a president who was a prince and an Assembly elected by universal suffrage which was solidly conservative and which, indeed, contained many royalists. One of the first acts of the new government was to send a French expeditionary force to Rome, not to support the republic of Mazzini, but to overthrow it. Ledru-Rollin and others who had attempted an insurrection against the campaign were sent into exile.

It soon became clear that the Republic and its president were no democrats or tolerators of free thought. The spread of socialism, it was believed, had originated with teachers of 'advanced' ideas in schools and colleges, and in order to prevent such people from practising the Falloux Law of 1850 was passed, limiting the right to teach to those who held a university degree. An even greater restriction followed in May 1850, when the parliamentary franchise was made conditional on having lived in the constituency for three years and having never had any crown conviction, even for the most trivial offence. This removed the franchise from 3,000,000 of the former 9,000,000 voters: in particular, it hit at Socialists and extreme Republicans, many of whom had been technically guilty of political offences and were precisely the people who never

Above, Louis Blanc (1811–82): Blanc had long opposed competitive industry and favoured co-operative workshops and had set out his ideas in L'Organisation du travail (1840). Though the provisional government did establish a form of National Workshops, they were little more than a means of providing unemployment relief and certainly did not realize Blanc's own aims. Even these failed and after the June days he fled to England.

Opposite, the Archbishop of Paris faces a firing-squad during the June days. The June days were a virtually spontaneous outburst of almost leaderless popular fury, partly stimulated by the closure of the National Workshops. The uprising lasted two days, was brutally put down and left the republicans and socialists bitterly divided.

stayed long in the same place. The Assembly had very effectively removed political power from their opponents without incurring the unpopularity of restricting the franchise by a property qualification.

Louis Napoleon was sufficiently astute to let it be known that he personally disapproved of the measure and thus could continue to stand as the representative of freedom and equality. It seems likely that he was already preparing the ground for his coup d'état, the seizure of power by which he could again make Bonapartism a reality. In retrospect, there is an inevitability about the course of events.

The elected president found himself in a chamber in which he had no personal following and from which he could expect no support; he was by temperament a liberal and a nationalist, yet he was forced to acquiesce in conservative policies at home, even to support the pope against the Republicans in Italy. The constitution stipulated that the president should hold office for four years and was not eligible for re-election. The nephew of Napoleon, who had risked all to return to France, was unlikely to accept such transitory power.

The president now carefully prepared the ground. First, the military governor of Paris was dismissed on a pretext and replaced by one of his own supporters. The Africa Corps, on whose loyalty he could depend, were also quartered in the capital. He next undertook a series of tours throughout the provinces, rallying support at mass meetings in which his supporters had been carefully planted to lead the cry of '*Vive l'Empereur*'. Finally, he began a campaign to alter Article 45 of the constitution to allow the president to serve for a further term of office of four years. In doing so, Louis Bonaparte probably calculated on the Assembly's rejection; if so, his prediction was justified. His amendment to the constitution was finally rejected in July 1851.

From this time, an open conflict had really become inevitable, but the president still chose his time carefully. The selected date was to be 2 December, the anniversary of his uncle's coronation as Emperor of France and of his great military victory of Austerlitz. On the evening of the 1st, he gave a splendid reception at the Elysée Palace, where he was seen to be unusually charming and courteous. At one point, however, he slipped away to give instructions to an inner circle of conspirators – his half-brother Morny, Maupas the Prefect of Police, and Saint-Armand the military commander. During the night the plan was put into effect – occupation of the Assembly, arrest of all the principal leaders who might have organized resistance, including Thiers and Cavaignac, and military occupation of strategic points in Paris. An announcement was made dissolving the Chamber of Deputies and re-introducing universal suffrage.

When Paris awoke the next morning, the takeover was already accomplished. A few deputies tried to resist, objecting that the president had broken his oath, had violated the constitution and was therefore deposed. Few took any notice, and those like Victor Hugo who tried to urge the people to take up arms against a tyrant found no support. Parisians had suffered and died at the barricades only three years before and had gained nothing from their middle class allies. Louis Napoleon was seen as a democratic deliverer who would restore the Rights of Man and again make France respected throughout the courts of Europe.

The coup d'état succeeded brilliantly in a city overcome by lethargy and bored by the succession of civil disorders. One of the few instances of courage occurred when the deputy Baudin was urging the workers to help him to build a barricade, and one of them called out: 'Do you think we are going to get ourselves killed to protect your twenty-five francs a day?' (The official salary of a deputy). Baudin replied: 'Stay there, my friend, and you will see someone killed for twenty-five francs a day.' Shortly afterwards he was killed at the barricade. On 4 December there was shooting on the boulevards, which terrorized Parisians, and armed risings in the provinces which were put down with terrible severity. In all, some 1,200 innocent citizens were killed in the coup, 10,000 more deported, and sixty deputies, including Victor Hugo, expelled from France. Louis Napoleon's seizure of power was thus achieved by fraud, duress and murder, yet it also had the overwhelming backing of the French people. On 21 December a national plebiscite was held, and by 7,350,000 votes to a mere 650,000 France expressed her approval of the prince-president's acts.

A new constitution became immediately necessary and was quickly drawn up. The President of the Republic was to hold office for ten years. Under him was to be a Council of State, a silent body whose debates were never made public but which had the crucial role of proposing legislation to the Legislative Assembly. There was also to be a Senate of dignitaries and notables. The new constitution thus approached that of a monarchy, giving considerably greater power and security to the president than would be usual under a republic.

Clearly, Louis' position was now firmly established, but would the European powers accept a Bonapartist on what had, for all practical purposes, become the 'throne' of France?

Louis Napoleon, elated with success, had already observed to the Sardinian Prime Minister, 'Now I can do what I want, I shall do something for Italy', and it was the fear that a revived Bonapartism in Europe might reawaken nationalist feelings among subject Italians, Poles, Hungarians and Slavs that most alarmed the rulers of Austria and Russia. Even in Britain, where there was admiration for the president's liberal and democratic ideas, there was also concern that a Bonaparte was again in command in France, placed there by the force of arms and known to be looking for military glory. His frequently asserted claim that 'the Empire is Peace' seemed genuine enough, however. Britain recognized the new president, Russia and Austria remained suspicious but had no way of intervening.

Precisely a year after the seizure of power, on 2 December 1852, a hereditary

Empire replaced the Republic which had had nothing republican about it except its name. In a strange calm a new empire was born and a new figure stepped onto the European stage. Still not acceptable socially, the new emperor was not permitted to marry into any of the legitimate royal families of Europe but in January 1853 took as wife a beautiful young Spanish countess, Eugénie of Montijo.

The aristocratic empire

For the first few years of his reign the emperor ruled personally and with a strong hand. Normal political life practically ceased: the opposition was either cowed or exiled, and the few who, like Victor Hugo, dared to raise their voice against 'the Little Napoleon' made no headway.

The press was effectively muzzled, and any criticism of the emperor quickly resulted in suppression. Even elections, which had been the great national preoccupation of recent years, ceased to be of much interest when only loyal candidates were able to stand. The local prefects kept a complete control over the conduct of election campaigns, to such good effect that when opposition candidates tried to present themselves they found it impossible to hire halls for meetings or to find printers who would publish their literature. Prefects openly canvassed for the 'official' candidates, factory owners warned their workers to 'vote properly'. Political passion had, for the time being, been suffocated.

In some respects the France of the early empire seemed to turn back to the attitudes and values of Louis Philippe. If political life was sterile and unrewarding, at least in the new stability of domestic conditions one might make money and enjoy oneself. It was an era of heavy investment and great banking development, the government leading the way by financing enormous public works, road and railway building programmes. Paris itself was to be reconstructed, the Prefect of the Seine, Baron

Haussmann, being commissioned to prepare plans to build the most magnificent capital in Europe, a city to dazzle the foreigners who had scorned the elected emperor.

Great new boulevards were cut through the heart of Paris, at once giving a plan and symmetry to the capital which it had never had before and, in the process, destroying many of the slums which had disfigured it. The wide roads with their tarmac surfaces were beautiful and impressive: at the same time, they made army manoeuvres easier and deprived Parisians of the paving-stones which rebellious mobs had been accustomed to fling from behind the barricades. Haussmann's remodelling of Paris therefore had many motives – economic, social, aesthetic and military. Not least important, it provided employment for those evicted from the National Workshops and gave immense opportunities to investors, speculators and businessmen of many kinds.

Paris in the 1850s was a city of feverish activity and frivolous gaiety, admirably

Above, the fashionable Boulevard des Italiens. Musée Carnavalet, Paris.

Top, contemporary print depicting Felice Orsini's attempt to assassinate Napoleon III and the Empress, 14 January 1858: after the assassination – Orsini had been disgusted at Napoleon's failure to assist Italian unification, which the Emperor had supported as a young man – Napoleon's interest in Italian affairs revived.

Top left, Victor Hugo (1802–84): a Napoleonist until 1848, Hugo was elected to the National Assembly in 1848 and again in 1849 but fled the country after the 1851 coup.

Opposite right, the Emperor Napoleon III and Eugénie in their wedding costume.

Opposite left, deputies being arrested during Louis Napoleon's coup d'état, 2 December 1851: popular in the provinces, Napoleon met scarcely any resistance in Paris, still smarting from the violence of the previous few years.

439

reflected in the popular light operas of Offenbach, *The Tales of Hoffmann* and *La Belle Hélène*. The reputation of Paris as a city of easy virtue, if not positive wickedness, dates especially from this period, when the emperor of the French could devote time to playing Blind Man's Buff or, less innocently, to his mistresses.

For many of the working class, too, times were good, with regular employment, booming trade and rising wages. For that growing section who now had some margin of income over necessary expenditure there were new pleasures, new recreations, great new stores like 'Bon Marché' where customers could find all that they needed at moderate prices under one roof or could simply come to stare.

The countryside also shared in the prosperity of the capital. Roads and railways brought a new mobility to people and goods, enabling farm produce to be sold profitably in the growing towns and bringing the benefits of civilization to formerly remote areas. Agriculture was still the mainstay of the French economy, some two-thirds of the whole population still living on the land and cultivating their small peasant farms. For them, the political events of the last few years had been remote, almost irrelevant, but now they could take pride in a revived empire and share in the benefits of a programme of national development. Even the sandy wastes of the Landes area in western France came to be planted with fir trees to provide pit props for the expanding coalmines, while in the Alps the daring project was begun of driving a tunnel through the heart of Mont Cenis.

But for the Second Empire to become a complete reality it needed to spread its wings beyond the confines of France and establish a colonial hegemony. It was in pursuance of such an object and in the face of ridicule and scepticism by Britain, that in 1859 work was begun on cutting the Suez Canal in Egypt. A sea route to India and the East could bring back the Mediterranean into importance in world trade, could revive the great ports of southern France and begin to move back

the balance of maritime power from the British-dominated Atlantic. With these great purposes in view the foreign policy of the empire was bent towards extending French influence throughout the Mediterranean world – intervention in Italian affairs, the pacification of Algeria and the defence of the Holy Places in Palestine which involved her in a victorious war against Russia. With the signing of the Treaty of Paris in 1856, France had successfully reasserted her place in the conduct of European affairs.

The Orsini affair

For the first few years the reign of the new emperor was undisturbed by the political crises which had come to be regarded as almost the normal condition of French life. The opposition party made some small gains in the elections of 1857, though insufficient to constitute any real threat to the security of the government which was bringing an unaccustomed measure of order and prosperity to the country. In 1858, however, a more serious event occurred. As a young *Carbonari* before his accession to power, Louis Napoleon had vowed that he would help the Italians to liberate their country from the Austrians: now, as emporer, he was more prudent and cautious, seeming to betray his Italian friends. One of the most extreme of the Italian nationalists, Orsini, was driven to make an attempt on the emperor's life, his bombs killing or wounding over a hundred people. Napoleon himself escaped injury.

The 'Orsini Affair' was, however, influential in shaping French attitudes. At home, the attempt provided the government with good grounds for tightening security by permitting the prefects to deport any suspect by simple adminstrative order. Over 300 Frenchmen were so exiled on evidence which would scarcely have satisfied a court of law. France quietly acquiesced in a policy which some regarded as a move towards autocracy, even dictatorship, on the part of an all-powerful emperor.

The liberal empire

Unaccountably, however, Napoleon suddenly retracted his policy and proceeded to introduce a series of liberal reforms. In fact, it seems likely that it was the growing opposition from Catholic and the industrialists, who had formerly supported the regime, that forced the change. Increasingly, Napoleon had to seek an alliance with the political left as the right deserted him.

The Catholics he had offended by insufficiently backing the temporal power of the Pope in Italy. Industrialists were claiming that the Free Trade Treaty signed with Britain in 1860, which allowed the passage of goods without duty between the two countries, would ruin the French economy. Napoleon, ahead of his people, had become a confirmed free trader, impressed by the success of the policy in England, but most French industrialists believed that their continued prosperity depended on maintaining the protection afforded by the tariff system which their goods enjoyed in the home market. Now the two disparate groups made common cause in resentment against the dictatorial aspects of the regime which they had once been only too ready to support.

The Catholics were the first to launch an open attack against the emperor in the columns of the influential Catholic newspaper *L'Univers*. The government responded by suppressing the religious society of St Vincent de Paul. But the chief power of the Church lay in its control over the schools, and the Minister of Education now decided to attack this. His real desire – to establish a system of state elementary schools throughout the land – proved impracticable, but he did set up the lycèes (secondary schools) for girls in direct competition with the convents and himself planned a course of ethics and morals to replace instruction in religion. The great struggle between church and state – a central issue in European politics since the Middle Ages – had been reopened.

The emperor therefore had to fall back on his old enemies, the liberal Republicans, and in order to gain their support concessions were required. An amnesty was granted for many political offenders, freedom of speech was allowed to deputies and the right of publication of parliamentary debates. In the general election of 1863 the opposition polled two million votes, and Thiers, the liberal, was returned to office. The new policy also made a greater appeal to the working classes, and trade unions were granted the legal right to strike in 1864. Two years previously, permission had been granted for a delegation of working men to go to London to meet English workers: out of this meeting was born in 1864 the International Working Men's Association which, under the influence of Karl Marx, was to become a powerful force in international socialism.

Once again, the pattern of events which had shaped French history ever since the revolution of 1789 reasserted itself. Autocracy could survive so long as the people were content: when opposition appeared, concessions had to be made which only served to demonstrate how little freedom the people really had and it whetted the appetite for more.

In other ways, too, the strength of the regime was ebbing. The strong men of 1848, including the emperor himself, were now older and feebler than they had been twenty years before. Foreign affairs had not gone with the flair and success that an empire seemed to demand, and, in particular, France had been obliged to watch with growing concern the rise to power of Prussia and her overwhelming defeat of Austria on the battlefields of Sadowa in 1866. The policy of concession in no way abated the mounting opposition to the regime, which became increasingly dangerous as Republicans and Socialists sank their former differences and became reconciled in a common opposition to the policies of the Empire. The failing power of the government was amply demonstrated in the elections of 1867 when, despite all efforts to gain support, its majority was drastically reduced and the combined opposition of Catholics, Republicans and Socialists polled more than 3,000,000 votes. Further concessions to the freedom of the press and of assembly followed in a desperate attempt to curry favour.

For the last two years of his reign the emperor was the subject of ridicule, even public dislike. One of the consequences of the now free press was an outpouring of satirical comment on Napoleon and his government, most brilliantly handled by the journalist Rochefort in *La Lanterne*. By 1869, when in fresh general elections the opposition polled almost half the total votes, the situation had become extremely dangerous; either the Empire must make some drastic bid for popularity or must quickly fall.

At this critical point in French affairs, help suddenly came from an unexpected quarter. One of the Republican opposition to be elected was Emile Ollivier, at first a bitter critic of the emperor who later came to support him. By 1869 he found himself prime minister. His responsibility, as he saw it, was to the Assembly rather than to the emperor, and here he gradually built up a powerful group of moderate liberals which became known as 'the Third Party'.

By 1870 it seemed that a parliamentary Empire modelled on the lines of the British political system might at last become a reality. A new constitution was framed on liberal principles, submitted to a national plebiscite, and accepted, to the immense relief of the emperor, by nearly 6,000,000 votes. The Republican-Socialist opposition was crushed, and the Empire seemed even more secure, and rooted in popular support than it had been in 1852. 'On whichever side we look,' declared the new prime minister,

'there is an absence of troublesome questions; at no moment has the maintenance of peace in Europe been better secured.' Precisely one month later a war broke out which was to sweep away Ollivier, Louis Napoleon and the Empire and to result in the appearance of a powerful, united Germany on the stage of Europe.

Above, Émile Ollivier (1825–1913), the liberal deputy chosen in January 1870 to head a parliamentary government under Napoleon: he was dismissed seven months later in the wake of Prussian victories in the Franco-Prussian War.

Opposite, rebuilding the rue de Rivoli in Paris, 1859: as Prefect of the Seine département from 1853, Georges Haussmann (1809–91) was responsible for rebuilding Paris; he installed a sewerage system and the water supply, built a new opera house and created the Bois de Boulogne.

441

Chapter 39

The United States, 1800–1865

When the United States achieved independence from England in 1783 she was beset with numerous problems. Most important was the need to establish a form of government which would effectively unite the thirteen colonies scattered along the eastern edge of the North American continent. Vital also was the need to pursue a foreign policy which would prevent the European powers from taking advantage of American weakness to win control of large areas of the new country.

A massive step towards achieving national unity had been taken when the new constitution had been put into effect in 1789, but even yet the United States was vulnerable to foreign powers. Although her economic prosperity was increasing rapidly, the United States had extremely weak military forces, and many of her citizens were opposed to any increase in military power. The outbreak of the wars of the French Revolution gave the United States the opportunity to take advantage of European divisions but also posed the danger that the extensive American maritime commerce would involve her directly in the wars.

In the 1790s the United States first had a crisis in her relations with Great Britain which almost led to war and then from 1798 to 1800 engaged in an undeclared war at sea against the French. Fortunately for Thomas Jefferson, who was elected president in 1800, he took office in March 1801 at a time when American foreign relations had improved strikingly as a result of a temporary cessation of the European wars.

Thomas Jefferson

When Jefferson assumed the presidency in 1801 he had long been a towering figure on the American scene. If he had never been president, his name would still have lived as the author of the Declaration of Independence. His career as governor of Virginia had not been successful, but as a legislator in that state his achievements were massive. They included the Virginia statute for religious freedom, the codification of the law (including reforms in the laws of inheritance) and a passionate espousal of the expansion of educational opportunity.

As secretary of state in President Washington's first administration, Jefferson had become leader of a group who were to form the Democratic-Republican party. It was as leader of this party that Jefferson came into office in 1801. The Federalists, who under the inspiration of Alexander Hamilton had held office in the 1790s, had accomplished the major task of welding a nation from disparate states, but it was Jefferson and his Democratic-Republicans who were prepared to show the faith in popular government that had been expressed in the American Revolution.

Although Jefferson was obliged in practice to modify some of the ideas he had expressed in his public writings and letters, the influence of his philosophy of government was to be felt throughout the nineteenth and into the twentieth century. Jefferson expressed a belief in democratic majority rule, tempered by a respect for the rights of the minority. He also believed in the subordination of military to civil authority, in strict economy in government and in an educated electorate. He felt that a healthy nation was based on a strong group of active, educated yeoman farmers. He distrusted cities and urban mobs and hoped that the United States would be governed by a natural elite, an elite that would be given the opportunity to rise to the top through education and which would be elected and supported by an educated electorate.

Jefferson disliked slavery but as a slave-owning Virginian was unsure whether the negro was equal in body and mind to the white man. But for his time and place,

Jefferson demonstrated a remarkable belief in man's capacity to govern himself. When it is remembered that he was also an active scientist, architect and inventor it is clear that few nations have ever been blessed with a man of his calibre to guide their early years.

The Democratic-Republican victory in 1800 inaugurated a period of rule which lasted until the break-up of the party in the late 1820s. The years from 1801 to 1825 were those of the 'Virginia Dynasty'. All three presidents in these years were from Virginia: Jefferson until 1809, James Madison for two terms until 1817, and James Monroe from 1817 to 1825. The Federalists never held control of the national government again after 1801. This failure was not only because of the greater faith of the Democratic-Republicans in the democratic process but also because the best ideas of the Federalists were adopted by the Democratic-Republican party.

As president, Jefferson soon discovered that he could not in practice grant the individual states the freedom he had argued for in theory and that his advocacy of strict construction of the constitution had been far more practicable for a party in opposition than for a party in power. He did not make any basic changes in conducting the executive branch of the government.

Jefferson's first term was a triumph. The pause in the European war from 1801 to 1803 meant that American ships could sail the seas unmolested, and the increased trade produced increased revenue from the customs. Jefferson's secretary of the treasury, Albert Gallatin, was thus able to eliminate

the excise taxes long opposed by the Democratic-Republicans, balance the budget and even reduce the national debt. He was aided in this by the cuts in the military forces which accorded well with the general Jeffersonian philosophy of government as well as finance.

Not all went as well as Jefferson hoped. He was obliged to fight a short and exotic naval war against Tripoli to protect American shipping in the Mediterranean, and at home he was ultimately rebuffed in an attack on the Federalists entrenched in the federal judiciary. But the setbacks were overshadowed by the triumph of the Louisiana Purchase, a triumph which owed as much to luck as to judgement.

The Louisiana Purchase

The American settlers who since the Revolution had been advancing across the Appalachians into the Mississippi Valley depended for their economic well-being on an export trade down the Ohio and Mississippi river systems to the Gulf of Mexico. This was the only practical way to find a market for bulk produce, but the trade was made difficult by the presence of the Spanish. They owned the territory west of the Mississippi, New Orleans and a strip of land eastwards along the Gulf through the southern parts of modern Mississippi and Alabama and the whole of modern Florida. From 1795 the United States had the right to ship goods through New Orleans and deposit them in that port before export, but this working relationship was threatened after 1800.

In 1800 Spain ceded the Louisiana Territory to France in exchange for warships and for territory in Italy. This Louisiana Territory was a vast area west of the Mississippi River, stretching north and northwest to the Canadian border and the Rockies. France had dreams of re-establishing her New World empire, and Louisiana would be the source of supplies for the sugar-rich West Indies. This French dream was to collapse within a few years. Since the 1790s the island of Santo Domingo had been in revolt. The slaves, believing that they too should share in liberty, equality and fraternity, had risen against their masters, and in the years after 1800, led by the great leader Toussaint L'Ouverture, they resisted French efforts to restore control. A whole French army was wiped out by yellow fever, and by 1803 Napoleon was ready to cut his losses and withdraw from the complicated New World situation.

Although France did not take over Louisiana from the Spanish in 1800, rumours of the change in ownership reached the United States in 1801, and by 1802 Jefferson knew that instead of impotent Spain the France of Napoleon was about to control the outlets of the United States on the Gulf. This fear was increased in the autumn of 1802 by the news that the right of deposit at New Orleans had been suspended. Although this action had been taken by Spain, it was naturally assumed that France was responsible. The Westerners now cried for war and the capture of New Orleans. To avoid military action Jefferson decided to attempt to buy access to the Gulf. In 1803 James Monroe was sent to join American

Above, New York street scene in the early nineteenth century. New York Historical Society.

Opposite, the Capitol building, Washington, in about 1800: Washington was designated the nation's administrative capital in 1790 not least because its geographical position meant it could be claimed by neither north nor south. The government moved there in 1800, but construction work proceeded very slowly. The Capitol was extended in 1851 when chambers for the Senate and House of Representatives were added.

minister Robert Livingston in France with instructions to buy at least New Orleans and if possible the Floridas. Nothing was said about the vast area of the Louisiana Territory, although Jefferson showed a definite interest in the region at this time by sending Lewis and Clark to explore all the way west to the Pacific.

In France Napoleon had decided to sell the whole of Louisiana. Napoleon in 1803 did not want to send another army to Santo Domingo. It was clear that the war with England would soon be renewed (England declared war in May), Napoleon needed money for a European campaign, and he could not defend New Orleans against the British fleet. Although the American envoys had been empowered to spend no more than $10,000,000 for New Orleans and the Floridas, they agreed to pay $15,000,000 for New Orleans and the whole Louisiana Territory, with no mention of the Floridas. When Jefferson heard the news he had qualms regarding the constitutionality of the transaction, but his cabinet persuaded him not to ask for a constitutional amendment. The territory of the United States had been nearly doubled and the foundation laid for expansion westwards to the pacific.

Maritime problems

United States foreign policy in the years from 1805 to 1812 was dominated by the dangers presented to American ships and seamen by European maritime warfare. Jefferson's triumphant first term was succeeded by a second term of major disappointments, and James Madison, who had done so much to frame the American government, had to serve as president in a time of foreign crisis which ill suited him. These were decisive years in the experiment of American independence, for once the United States had weathered this crisis it was not until the American Civil War that the United States was again in such danger.

The basic problem confronting the United States in these years was her desire to trade at a time when Europe was engaged in general war. By her 1807 Orders in Council Great Britain declared that United States ships could trade with the possessions of Napoleon if they first came to England to be licensed. By his Berlin and Milan Decrees of 1806 and 1807 Napoleon declared Great Britain in a state of blockade and announced that neutral ships which obeyed British regulations would be liable to seizure. In theory, American ships were liable to be seized whatever they did. In practice, both sides were anxious for some trade and connived at a variety of evasions. Their safety depended however, on the whims of Great Britain and France.

Although Napoleon inflicted some damage on American commerce, the British were for the most part in command of the seas, and the weight of their restrictions was felt much more heavily, particularly as Great Britain was the old enemy of the Revolution. Moreover, the British particularly infuriated American opinion by their practice of impressment. Many British deserters found service in American merchantmen, and the British claimed the right to stop these ships and seize any British deserters found on board. British captains, if they lacked hands to man their ships, also frequently removed American seamen. Several thousand Americans were impressed, and this practice was viewed as a particular outrage by American citizens who had fought a revolution to establish their freedom from Great Britain.

In the years after 1803, as the war between Great Britain and France became more intense, difficulties at sea increased, and in June 1807 a crisis which seemed likely to lead to war developed between the United States and Great Britain. In stopping an American frigate, the *Chesapeake*, to search for British deserters, the British *Leopard* fired into her, killing American seamen. Many Americans demanded war, but Jefferson took steps to avoid it. His motivation was mixed. As a practical man he knew that the United States possessed extremely weak military forces, indeed he had reduced their effectiveness during his administration and had no desire to risk the gains of independence in a risky war against Great Britain. As an idealist, Jefferson had long maintained that the United States should demonstrate to the decadent powers of Europe that countries could attain their ends without war. His solution to the dilemma in 1807 was to adopt the idea, used by the American colonies before the Revolution, of economic coercion as an alternative to war.

In December 1807, at Jefferson's request, Congress passed an embargo, which confined all American ships to port and prohibited all exports. Earlier Congress had passed a non-importation law against selected imports. Jefferson hoped that British industry would starve for lack of American cotton and that British manufacturers, who depended so heavily on the American market, would force their government to remove their restrictions on American commerce to obtain a renewal of American trade.

Jefferson's experiment in economic coercion failed because in 1808 Great Britain was not prepared to make concessions which might aid France, even though these would also ease the plight of the manufacturing districts. Moreover, Jefferson was unfortunate in that Napoleon's invasion of the Iberian peninsula threw open the Spanish and Portuguese colonies in Latin America to British goods and helped to offset the losses in trade to North America which resulted from the embargo.

Shortly before he left office in March 1809 Jefferson repealed the embargo, and in the next three years the United States floundered. The main measure of economic coercion had failed. The alternative was war, but with the country divided, and with inadequate military forces, it seemed likely that war would only add to America's problems. Also France's hostility made it unclear whether the United States should fight one, both or neither of the great European belligerents.

Uncertain of how to proceed, the United States first followed the embargo with a weaker method of economic coercion (the Non-Intercourse Act against Great Britain and France) and then in 1810 threw open her trade, promising, however, a friendly neutrality to that power which would remove its restrictions on American commerce. Napoleon took advantage of this offer (although in reality still seizing American shipping), and early in 1811 the United States resumed non-intercourse against Great Britain.

The War of 1812

Having failed to acheive her ends by peaceful means, the United States at last began to move towards war. This policy reversal was made easier because since 1807 the British in Canada, fearing an American invasion, had supplied and organized the Indians on the frontiers of the United States. This gave another grievance to Americans, who became convinced that Great Britain would not respect American ships and seamen unless compelled to do so by an American invasion of Canada.

From 1810 an enthusiastic group of young men in Congress – the War Hawks – began to press for war to save national honour and to force Great Britain to respect American maritime rights. Their leader was young Henry Clay of Kentucky. This move for war met determined resistance from the Federalists, who wanted to continue trading and who believed with good reason that American commerce would suffer still more if war was declared. They also feared Napoleonic ambitions more than they disliked their old colonial enemy, Great Britain.

Eventually, however, in June 1812 the Democratic-Republicans, led by young men from the West and the South, obtained enough votes for war. Ironically, two days before the United States declared war, the British government had intimated in London that the Orders in Council would be withdrawn; this news was not known in the United States for several weeks.

The Federalist opposition continued into the war itself. Many in New England would give no support to the war effort, and many even supplied the British in Canada. In December 1814 in the Hartford Convention the New Englanders discussed the possibility of extreme action, possibly even secession. Eventually, however, they settled for a list of proposed constitutional amendments designed to restrict the power of the South.

American strategy in the war was to invade and conquer Canada and to use this as a pawn to force maritime concessions from Great Britain. Many thought, wrongly, that the conquest of Canada would be accomplished with little difficulty. Even those who argued for war were prepared to admit that the United States had little hope at sea. The tiny American navy was overshadowed by the great British naval power. Forgotten even in America was the fighting quality of individual American ships and the numerous merchantmen that could be fitted out as privateers to raid British commerce.

In the first year of the war the British public was shocked, and that in the United States surprised, by American victories over British frigates in single-ship engagements – the *Constitution* over the *Guerrière*, the *United States* over the *Macedonian* and the *Constitution* over the *Java*. These were great morale boosters for the American people, but by the summer of 1813 British ships were placing a tight blockade around the American coast and for the rest of the war effectively controlled American trade. American privateers still escaped, however, and until the end of the war seized British merchantmen.

Above, illustration from the diary of an expedition member of Lewis and Clark holding a council with the Indians.

Top, the US frigate Constitution *engaging the* Java *off the coast of Brazil, December 1812: after her masts and rigging had been shot away, the* Java *surrendered. This was one of several engagements in which the young American navy performed brilliantly against the far more experienced British. US Naval Academy, Annapolis, Maryland.*

Opposite left and right, William Clark (1770–1838) and Meriwether Lewis (1774–1809), who were sent by Jefferson to explore the territories acquired by the Louisiana Purchase: their expedition, which took eighteen months, reached the Pacific and blazed a trail in the northwest that settlers were soon to follow.

The 'new nationalism'

The year 1815 was a turning point in American as well as in European history. The miraculous survival in 1814 and the news of the remarkable victory at New Orleans sent a surge of enthusiasm through the American people. The founding fathers had been convinced that in creating a new republican nation they were setting an example for the rest of the world, that they were showing the world that a nation could be safe, prosperous and democratic. Now, after 1815, as American prosperity increased, a belief in the ultimate greatness of the United States became very strong among the American people. A surge of nationalism swept through the country, and although eventually the national spirit faced a major clash with growing sectionalism in the South the years after 1815 saw an enhancement of national power.

The Democratic-Republicans now showed themselves willing to use the power of the federal government in a manner which they had attacked when earlier proposed by the Federalists. In 1816 they conceded that the developing American industry needed protection by placing a moderate tariff on imports, and they also completely reversed Jefferson's earlier stand when they agreed to charter the Second Bank of the United States. Some Democratic-Republicans, particularly those from the West, also argued that the federal government should spend money on internal improvements to improve the nation's communication system. Congress was almost evenly split on this proposal, and Presidents Madison, Monroe and Jackson all vetoed internal improvement bills on the grounds that they believed such expenditures unconstitutional.

As the Democratic-Republicans espoused an increasing number of policies that had once been Federalist, they gradually became the completely dominant party. James Monroe became president in 1817 after an easy victory and three years later in 1820 won re-election with only one electoral vote cast against him.

The enhancement of federal power that took place in these years was aided considerably by the attitudes and decisions of John Marshall of Virginia, who was Chief Justice of the Supreme Court from 1801 until 1835. Marshall consistently interpreted the American Constitution and the relationship between the central government and the states in such a manner as to enhance federal power. Although he was roundly criticized, particularly in the southern states, his work endured and was a most important ingredient in creating a powerful central government.

The power of the federal government was developing rapidly in the first three decades of the nineteenth century, but the problems that confronted it were also increasing with remarkable speed. Indeed, the question was

The invasion of Canada failed disastrously. All the efforts of 1812 and 1813 produced only slight inroads into British territory. By the close of 1813 the United States faced a tight blockade around her coasts and the prospect of heavy reinforcements for the British military forces. As the power of Napoleon collapsed in the spring of 1814 the British had ships and troops ready for transfer to America. In 1814 it was no longer a question of the United States conquering Canada in order to force a change in British maritime policies; the United States was now in danger of defeat and dismemberment. That she managed to avoid this fate was, like the Louisiana Purchase, the result of chance just as much as of good management.

In August it appeared all was lost for the United States. After landing in Chesapeake Bay a British force routed the Americans at Bladensburg, marched into Washington D.C., and burned the public buildings. With its trade shattered, the country was bankrupt and unable any longer to meet the interest on the national debt. In the New England states some people were talking of secession, and veteran British armies were preparing to invade in the north and south.

The sudden change in affairs was so remarkable that it seemed to the Americans that their nation was blessed by divine providence. In September the British left Washington and tested the defences of Baltimore. It held firm. The British commanding general, Robert Ross, was killed in a skirmish, and although the British navy bombarded Fort McHenry it resisted attack and inspired the writing of the song that eventually became the American national anthem. The British army decided not to attack and withdrew to the fleet.

In this same month of September 1814 ten thousand British troops marched south along Lake Champlain. It seemed that nothing could stop them, but at the naval battle of Plattsburg Bay on Lake Champlain the American fleet totally defeated the British. The British army, fearing that its line of communications could now be severed, halted the invasion and then withdrew to Canada.

The repulse of the British was decisive because in Ghent British and American commissioners were discussing the terms of peace. The British had been delaying, hoping and expecting that news of major victories would force the Americans to grant large territorial concessions in any peace treaty. When the news of the British withdrawals arrived in Europe, it helped to persuade the government to make peace. On 24 December 1814, the Treaty of Ghent was signed. There were no major changes in the treaty; it merely brought the war to an end. The main reason for fighting had disappeared with the end of the war in Europe.

Although the war was over, one major and important battle was still to be fought. There was no way for the British to stop the army that was already assembled to attack New Orleans. The British failed to advance swiftly when first landing near the city in December, and by the time they finally attacked on 8 January it was against entrenched American positions and troops well commanded by Major-General Andrew Jackson. As the British advanced across the flat ground they were shattered by the American fire. When they withdrew their total casualties amounted to over 2,000; the Americans had suffered little more than seventy. The British commander, Wellington's brother-in-law Edward Pakenham, had been killed.

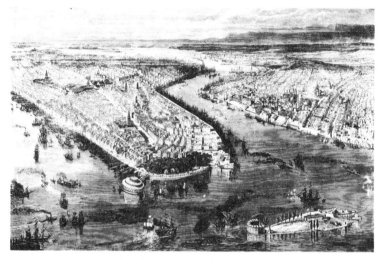

arising whether the powers of the central government could increase rapidly enough to cope with the problems presented on the one hand by a nation that was constantly expanding in size and on the other by an area of the nation – the South – that was becoming particularly sensitive to its own particular problems. The westward advance of American pioneers, while helping to create a nation that spanned the continent, also complicated the organization of an efficient national government and accentuated the already serious difficulties with the South.

Westward expansion

In the years from the beginning of the seventeenth century to the Revolution the American people had pushed inland only as far as the Appalachian mountain barrier. In the years immediately before the Revolution they were just crossing into the modern states of Kentucky and Tennessee. Although

it had taken 150 years to move 200 miles inland, within 100 years after the Revolution a network of states and territories extended across the whole 3,000 miles of the American continent.

From its inception the American government had decided not to establish a colonial regime beyond the Appalachians but rather to create new states which would enter the Union on an equal basis with the older states. Under this arrangement the thirteen original states were soon outnumbered by the new admissions of the nineteenth century: five new states were created before 1815, another six by 1821, seven more between 1836 and 1850, and five more between 1858 and 1864.

This expansion was made possible by a remarkable increase in the American population. From nearly 4,000,000 in 1790 the population increased to over 9,600,000 by 1820, to over 17,000,000 by 1840, and to over 31,400,000 by 1860. The great natural increase was aided by the immigrants who poured into the United States during the

Above, Austin, Texas, in 1840: Texas was admitted to the Union in 1845; its rich farmlands soon attracted settlers from the east.

Above left, view of Manhattan from the south, 1855: New York was the destination of almost all immigrants to the USA, among whom Germans and Irish predominated during the first decades after independence.

Top, James Monroe (1758–1831, president 1817–25): he recognized the independence of the Spanish American republics and in 1823 laid down in the Monroe Doctrine that 'the American continents ... are henceforth not to be considered as subjects for future colonization by any European power.'

Top left, the Battle of New Orleans, 8 January 1815, at which American forces, commanded by Major-General Andrew Jackson, later to become president, defeated the British. The War of 1812 was the last occasion on which the United States had to defend itself on its own territory against foreign intervention.

Opposite, Oliver Perry capturing a British naval force on Lake Erie during the War of 1812.

447

nineteenth century, attracted by the prospect of land, economic prosperity and a degree of religious and political freedom unknown in much of Europe. As in colonial days great numbers of immigrants came from England, Scotland, Wales, northern Ireland and Germany, but during the first half of the nineteenth century they also entered in increasing numbers from Scandinavia and from southern Ireland.

In the years after 1815 the younger sons of farmers pushed west to find new lands and new opportunities. The new states they established pressed the federal government for expenditures on internal improvements and for more liberal land policies, and many in the east resented these new areas which were reducing the power of the older states, attracting eastern population, and asking for larger expenditures of federal tax money. This east-west division was complicated by an increasing rift between northern and southern areas of the Atlantic seaboard and by a different type of western expansion north and south of the Ohio River in the Mississippi Valley.

The South and slavery

Although indentured servants had been a more important labour force than slaves in early colonial days, slavery had become an integral part of the American scene by the time of the American Revolution. Of an American population of nearly 4,000,000 in 1790 some 700,000 were slaves. The great majority of these slaves were employed on the plantations of the southern states.

In 1808 Jefferson's administration abolished the foreign slave trade but did not interfere with slavery itself nor with internal trade in slaves. The desire of many in the South to retain a system of slavery was strengthened in the first decades of the nineteenth century by the opening up of the rich lands of the southwest and the expansion of the British cotton market. Those who had once thought that slavery was likely to be economically unprofitable on old, worn-out tobacco lands were hopeful of rich profits from the cotton lands of Mississippi and Alabama, and even the upper South could profit from this by selling slaves to the new areas.

Slavery had already been extended into Kentucky and Tennessee in the Revolutionary period, and after 1800 increasing numbers of slaves were taken into the lower southwest to what is now Mississippi and Alabama and after 1803 to Louisiana. This movement grew after 1815 and produced great problems of future political allegiance. There was no doubt that the southerners expanding south of the Ohio River would be able to take slaves with them, and even within the bounds of the modern state of Louisiana it was clear that slavery would be allowed to continue, but for the vast area of the Louisiana Purchase north of

Louisiana there was considerably more doubt. In the Northwest Ordinance of 1787 slavery had been prohibited between the Ohio and the Mississippi Rivers, and some in the north were beginning to question the desirability of the further expansion of a slave system.

The question involved far more than simply the continuation or restriction of the expansion of slavery. It had major political and economic implications. Those states who had large numbers of slaves were engaged for the most part in the production of extensive agricultural surpluses for sale overseas and in the north. The economy of the South was much less diverse than that of the northeastern and middle states. Accordingly, the Southerners wanted to avoid high tariffs and generally feared too great an addition of power to the central government, which if too powerful might threaten slavery itself and with it the whole social system of the South.

In view of this, the extension of slavery to newly created states became of great importance to the southern states, for they wanted to be quite sure that they could not be outvoted in Congress. In the House they were falling behind, because northern population was growing more rapidly than southern, but in the Senate, where there were two senators from each state regardless of size, they could hope to maintain a balance.

The first major crises on the question of the expansion of slavery arose in 1819 when Missouri applied for admission to the Union, and representative James Tallmadge of New York proposed an amendment which would provide for the gradual abolition of slavery in the new state. At this time there were thirteen slave and thirteen free states in the Union, and the issue of slave expansion was debated bitterly both in

Congress and in the country at large.

The compromise that was eventually worked out after extensive debate did not remove the causes of difficulty but merely delayed the clash. It was agreed that Missouri could enter the Union as a slave state, but that Maine, which had long wanted to separate from Massachusetts, would be admitted as a free state. In the future, the dividing line between slave and free states west of the Mississippi would be set at 36° 30′.

The quarrel over the admission of Missouri to the Union made it quite obvious that the old parties were falling apart and that sectional splits were posing a major threat to national unity. These tendencies became particularly clear in the presidential election of 1824. Although the Federalists could present no real opposition to the Democratic-Republicans, the latter party had four candidates in the race, representing different sections of the country: John Quincy Adams of Massachusetts, William H. Crawford of Georgia, Henry Clay of Kentucky and Andrew Jackson of Tennessee. Adams had made a brilliant reputation as secretary of state, Crawford was the natural successor to the Virginia dynasty, and Henry Clay was becoming increasingly prominent as a spokesman for a policy of economic nationalism; his 'American System' called for high tariffs, federal expenditure on internal improvements and a strong Bank of the United States.

Andrew Jackson was a new type in the race for the American presidency. A Tennessee settler, he had made his local reputation as a lawyer and politician but achieved national fame as an Indian fighter and a legendary reputation as the victor over the British at the Battle of New Orleans. As a plantation owner and leading Tennessee figure, he was never the man of the people that his backers proclaimed him to be, but he was able to win general national support.

Although Jackson gained the most electoral votes, no candidate had an absolute majority in the 1824 election, and so it was thrown into the House of Representatives. There Henry Clay gave his support to John Quincy Adams, who was second in electoral votes, and Adams gained the presidency. John Quincy Adams, son of the second president, was a man of many talents, but he had an unfortunate presidency. His opponents charged him with making a 'corrupt bargain' with Clay, and the Jacksonians immediately began to make preparations for the 1828 election. The Democratic-Republican party had fallen apart, and out of the supporters of Jackson arose the Democratic party of the 1830s.

In the 1828 election Jackson gained popular support because of his military reputation, but he also had influential backing from the new entrepreneurs of the west who were anxious to end eastern dominance and special Southern strength through the vice-presidential candidate John

C. Calhoun and the assumption that a Tennessee plantation owner would be sympathetic to the Southern point of view. Jackson won a resounding victory in 1828, and to the easterners long established in government positions in Washington his victory was looked upon as a disaster: a backwoodsman was to end the rule of eighteenth-century aristocrats. This feeling was increased at his inauguration when his supporters crowded noisily and tumultuously into the White House.

The Jackson era

Andrew Jackson showed himself more willing to enhance the powers of the presidency than any earlier president. He used his veto power more regularly and showed himself quite willing to contend with Congress, the federal judiciary and the individual states. Instead of placing full reliance for advice on his official cabinet, he formed an unofficial 'kitchen cabinet' out of his most ardent supporters; they gave him the support of men who were entirely dependent on him for their power. In general, Jackson showed himself far more willing than any previous president to reward his followers with the spoils of office, even to the extent of removing previous office holders to make room for them.

Jackson's first term proved a surprise to many who had supported him in 1828. The Maysville veto in 1830 disappointed those

who had hoped that he would be willing to overcome any constitutional qualms concerning the expenditure of federal funds on internal improvements. But his major difficulties with his former supporters came from the South. Although the South had shared in the nationalistic enthusiasm of the immediate post-1815 years, disillusionment set in during the 1820s. The struggle over the admission of Missouri, Marshall's Supreme Court decisions and in particular the tariff question produced an increasing development of Southern sectionalism and resistance to federal policies. South Carolina assumed the leadership in this movement not only because of the calibre of her politicians but also because of the decline in her prosperity owing to the competition of the new, rich cotton lands of Alabama and Mississippi.

In 1816 many Southern congressmen, including John C. Calhoun, overcame their deep-seated hostility to commercial restrictions and in the cause of national prosperity voted for a moderate protective tariff. In the 1820s, feeling that national policies threatened Southern prosperity and a way of life, Calhoun led the Southerners in intense opposition to high tariffs. The increase in 1824 was strongly opposed, and in 1828 the tariff forced through Congress over Southern opposition was christened 'the tariff of abominations'. Calhoun anonymously wrote *The South Carolina Exposition and Protest* in which he argued for the

Above, illustration by the British caricaturist George Cruikshank of the celebrations at the White House on President Andrew Jackson's inauguration day: Jackson (1767–1845, president 1829–37) brought a new style to the presidency, one more in line with life on the western frontier than in the old-established eastern states.

Opposite, illustration entitled 'Selling Females by the Pound' from a book on slavery published in 1834: the South had primarily a one-crop, labour-intensive economy, and its advocacy of slavery rested at least partly on economic grounds.

doctrine of nullification: individual states would have the right to reject those laws of the federal government which they thought unconstitutional.

It was soon apparent that the alliance that had elected Jackson could not hold together once he was in office. Calhoun men in the cabinet soon clashed with the followers of Secretary of State Martin Van Buren, the New York politician who had done so much to build support for Jackson in that state and region. Tension between Jackson and Calhoun increased rapidly as it became clear that Jackson had a concept of national power which accorded ill with Calhoun's hopes for the South.

Indicative of the tension in the administration was the social crisis over Secretary of War John H. Eaton's marriage to Peggy O'Neale, a young woman who had been seen with Eaton before her sailor husband had died. Mrs Calhoun led the group who snubbed this daughter of a Washington tavern-keeper. Jackson's own wife Rachel had been attacked during the 1828 campaign, shortly before she died, and Jackson took up the cause of the Eatons. With such stresses and strains, it was not surprising that in 1831 Jackson reorganized the cabinet and reformed it without the Calhoun men.

The full crisis came in 1832 when Congress again passed a tariff much higher than that desired by the South. In November a South Carolina convention declared the tariffs of 1828 and 1832 'null and void'. Calhoun resigned as vice-president, and Jackson faced the greatest threat to federal power the country had yet known. He rose to the occasion in a manner which belied his own southern origin. He asked Congress for a Force Bill and made it clear that if necessary he would invade South Carolina to enforce the law.

Open hostilities were avoided by the desire, both in Congress and in South Carolina, to avoid if at all possible an open clash and by the efforts at compromise led by Henry Clay. In the spring of 1833 both the Force Bill and a compromise tariff bill passed Congress. The compromise tariff, called for a gradual reduction in duties over the next nine years. Once again, as in the Missouri Compromise, the ultimate problems had been left unsettled. This was made particularly clear when South Carolina rescinded her nullification of the tariffs but nullified the Force Bill, an important symbolic gesture even though the bill had by now become unnecessary.

The other major issue that beset Jackson in the election year of 1832 was the re-chartering of the Second Bank of the United States. Since Nicholas Biddle had become president of the bank in 1823, this institution had assumed a vital role in the nation's finance and general economy, acting as a restraining force on local banks and gaining great power through its function as the government bank of deposit. The bank had made a great many enemies who for various reasons desired to see its power reduced.

Many of the rising financiers and entrepreneurs in the west and other regions of the country resented the power of the old-establishing ruling clique. To oppose the bank they formed a strange alliance with two very different groups: farmers who resented the restraining influence of the bank and who as debtors would have been happy if the local banks had created an inflationary situation and another group (Jackson leaned to this argument) who put their faith in hard cash and felt that banks merely lived on the work of others.

During Jackson's first term Biddle became fearful for the future of the bank and increased his lobbying activities. Some of his actions, such as advancing loans to congressmen, were of a dubious nature. Biddle was also involved in the political complications of Jackson's first term.

As the Democratic Party came into being under Jackson its main opposition at first was the alliance of Henry Clay and John Quincy Adams, men who in the 1832 election ran as the National Republicans. They supported the 'American System' of Henry Clay, and in looking for an issue for the 1832 election they seized upon the bank. Clay persuaded Biddle to apply for a recharter of his bank in 1832, although the old charter did not have to be renewed until 1836. In this way the Clay group hoped to force Jackson to take action which would hurt him in the 1832 election.

For a time everything proceeded as planned. Congress passed a recharter bill, and Jackson vetoed it with a ringing attack in which he charged that the bank was a monopoly which allowed the rich to oppress the poor. The National Republicans were delighted. They believed that Jackson could be defeated on this issue. Henry Clay ran for president as a National Republican and Jackson as a Democrat. There was also a third party – the anti-Masons – who originating in western New York as a rural movement distrusting the foreign and the unusual, had been used by the politicians as an anti-Jackson movement in a number of northeastern states. For the first time national political conventions nominated the candidates, and it soon became clear that Jackson had an excellent sense of popular attitudes. He won an easy victory.

In his second term Jackson's weaknesses in economic policies became more apparent. Rather than waiting for the bank to expire naturally, he determined to attack it directly by ending its function as a government bank of deposit. He began to distribute federal funds to a variety of state banks – the 'pet banks' – and essentially destroyed the effectiveness of the United States Bank as a check on local banking.

The American economy and the panic of 1837

The American economy had taken tremendous strides since 1815. In spite of a setback in 1819, the constantly expanding population, the abundant natural resources and a government which gave internal peace and opportunity combined to bring a flourishing economy. American shipping was still to be seen all over the world, and the large export trade in tabacco was soon surpassed by the cotton trade as the rich cotton lands of the southwest opened up in the years after 1815.

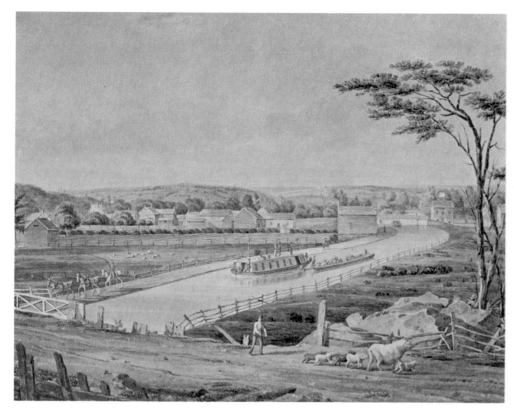

The real American industrial revolution was not to occur until after the Civil War, but already in the first decades of the century New England and the Middle States were laying a solid base for industrial expansion, particularly in textiles and the iron industries. Internally, communications had grown at a rapid rate. Before 1815 the country depended on river traffic and inefficient roads, but between 1816 and 1840 a whole network of canals (aided by the development of steamboats) boosted the economic expansion of the nation. The success of the Erie Canal (connecting the Hudson Valley and the Great Lakes), which was completed in 1825, inspired states to begin canals which could never hope to have the same trade and revenue potential. States borrowed money, confidently expecting to repay it by revenue earned from the finished canals. Many underestimated the costs of upkeep and were also placed in a difficult position by the steady growth of railroads in the 1830s. These were to expand with great rapidity in the following decades: by the end of the 1860s they spanned the continent.

In the late 1820s and in the early 30s the United States was in a boom period. Foreign commerce flourished, states feverishly built canals, railroads were beginning to be constructed, settlers poured west and land was being sold at an ever-increasing rate. As revenue flowed in from the tariff and land sales the nation had a strange new embarrassment: an excess of money. The national debt was rapidly being paid off (it was repaid by 1835), and yet even though facing a surplus the government had difficulty in reducing its revenue. The compromise tariff could not be tampered

with, and the price of public land could not be reduced without infuriating those easterners who already objected vehemently to the ease with which the eastern states were deprived of population.

In 1836 the government took steps to deal with the surplus. Henry Clay had long argued that his should be distributed to the states for them to use for internal improvements. This had been objected to on the grounds that it was unconstitutional, but in 1836 it was agreed that all funds over five million dollars in the Treasury on 1 January 1837 would be distributed to the states in four instalments. To avoid constitutional difficulties this would be a loan not a gift. The decision meant that federal funds on deposit all over the country would have to be transferred. In the summer of 1836 the Jackson administration also acted to curb the inflationary situation. Lands bought from the government would have to be paid for in gold and silver not banknotes.

By early 1837 there was a great pressure for specie (payment in coinage), and with the obvious signs of instability in the American economy foreign creditors began to press for payment of all outstanding obligations. The general pressure was too much to bear. Banks all over the United States suspended specie payments in the spring of 1837, and the financial panic that followed led to a prolonged depression whose effects were not thrown off until the 1840s. Then the economy again leaped forward.

The panic of 1837 inevitably delivered a blow to the fortunes of the Democratic Party, but fortunately for Jackson's supporters the election for president in 1836 took place in an atmosphere of continued

Above, view of the waterfront at Cincinnati, Ohio, in 1843, already an important manufacturing centre: the Ohio (on which Cincinatti stands) and Mississippi Rivers were important waterways, along which settlers travelled westwards and goods eastwards.

Top, iron works alongside the Erie Railroad in upstate New York: railroads played an enormous part in opening up the interior and in the growth of industry. The 1850s were the boom decade – more than 21,000 miles of line were built, bringing the total to over 30,000 – and by the 1860s a fully developed network was in existence in all the states east of the Mississippi.

Above left, View on the Erie Canal by J. W. Hill, 1830–32: opened in 1825, the Canal linked the Atlantic and the Hudson River with the Great Lakes, so opening up a new, fast route to the west. New York Public Library. Stokes Collection.

Opposite, The American Slave Market, 1852: for many southerners – though by no means all – slaves were a commodity to be bought and sold like any other. Chicago Historical Society, Illinois.

prosperity. Jackson had welded together an effective party while the opposition had difficulty in cementing a political alliance. By 1836 both anti-Masons and anti-Jackson southerners had joined with the National Republicans to form a new Whig party (named from its opposition to 'King Andrew I'), which was to exist into the early 1850s.

The basic weakness of the Whig party was its diversity and a lack of unified beliefs. The Southern plantation owners who joined the party because of their hatred of Jackson were also opponents of Clay's economic policies. In 1836 the Whigs ran several candidates, hoping to throw the election into the House of Representatives, but with the support of Jackson, and with a country not yet beset by economic difficulties, the Democrats won under their candidate, Martin Van Buren.

Van Buren had a most unfortunate presidency dominated by the economic distress of the country, and the Whigs were in an excellent position for the 1840 election. Their candidate was William Henry Harrison, a man in his late sixties, who had come to national fame as the victor over the Indians at Tippecanoe in 1811 and as a general in the war of 1812. Learning from the Jacksonian techniques, the Whigs ran Harrison as a western man of the people in the 'log cabin and hard cider' campaign. To gain southern support John Tyler of Virginia was given the vice-presidential nomination. The Whig candidates ran under the banner of 'Tippecanoe and Tyler Too.'

The panic was too great a liability for Van Buren to overcome, and the Whigs took office. Within a month Whig hopes were shattered by the death of the president and the succession to the presidency of John Tyler. It soon became all too apparent that while Tyler was anti-Jackson he was certainly no Clay Whig. The resulting clash caused a bitter intra-party fight, which made the administration ineffective.

The Democrats had emerged from the 1830s as a reasonably coherent party. The Whigs, however, never really succeeded in obtaining unity and depended more on those who disliked the Democrats than on policies that could be supported by the whole party. They entered the election of 1844 with the legacy of an administration of intense internal fights and at a time when the Democrats were better sensing the mood of the electorate in regard to the rapidly developing problems in foreign relations.

Foreign policy and the American Indians

In the years after 1815 there was a dramatic change in the relationship between the United States and foreign nations. In the first thirty years of American independence the United States had been in constant danger and had devoted much of her energy to avoiding entanglement in the European wars. After 1815 there was no general war involving Great Britain, the European continent, and general maritime blockades for another hundred years. Not until the First World War were American ships again to be beset with the problems they had experienced after 1793.

After 1815 the United States, without major interference, was able to expand over much of the North American continent and to begin to extend her general influence through Latin America as well. Instead of being in danger herself, the United States posed a threat to those powers who held territory adjacent to her in North America. The basis of this expansion was the rapid increase in the American population and the determination of American citizens to seek a better life on new lands to the west.

To the inhabitants of the United States the presence of vast, rich, undeveloped lands acted as an irresistible lure. To many it was a vast 'empty' continent ready to be cultivated by those who had the energy to build a new life.

In reality, of course, not even the undeveloped lands within the actual bounds of the United States were empty; they were occupied by a variety of Indian tribes who had no desire to yield their lands to the American pioneers. Before 1815 the American government argued that American expansion would benefit the Indians, because as they yielded their land the Indians would be given the benefits of American civilization and would be assimilated within the American nation. After 1815, as it became clear that most Indians did not want to accept American civilization, an increasing number of Americans accepted the argument that the Indians were doomed, that they would be swept aside and would eventually disappear as obstacles in the path of progress.

When in the 1830s the Indians east of the Mississippi River were moved to lands west of the river it was still argued by some that this would help to save the Indians, but others were now more ready to accept the argument that the Indians were an inferior race, destined to be engulfed in the advancing stream of American civilization. Although the Indians fought fiercely to prevent the American advance, it was a futile fight. Not until after the Civil War was the American government again to think as seriously of the possibility of assimilation as they had before 1815.

Apart from sweeping aside an aboriginal population, the Americans had the problem of land in the possession of other nations in their rapid advance across the American continent. Though the land immediately

west of the Mississippi had been bought from France in a stroke of fortune in 1803, and other purchases proved possible later in the century, possession of much of what is now the United States had to depend upon diplomatic pressure and war.

The possessions of Spain in East and West Florida had been desired by some in the United States since the Louisiana Purchase in 1803. Jefferson attempted to buy West Florida and placed severe pressure on the Spanish government. In 1810 a revolution at Baton Rouge gave part of the area to the United States, and during the War of 1812 American troops occupied and kept possession of Mobile.

After John Quincy Adams became secretary of state under Monroe in 1817, he made determined efforts to secure the Florida region and resisted a cabinet attempt to censure Jackson when he led troops across the Spanish border in pursuit of the Indians. In 1819 the Spanish, realizing that they had no way of protecting the Florida region, yielded to American pressure and, under the Adams-Onis Treaty, sold it for $5,000,000. However, this money was not to leave the United States but was to be used to pay claims of American citizens against the Spanish for damage suffered to their property in the European wars. As part of the agreement the United States acknowledged Spanish ownership of Texas, and Spain ceded to the United States any claim she had to the land north of California on the Pacific coast.

The Monroe Doctrine

John Quincy Adams, more than any other American statesman during these years, envisaged a United States which would own much of the North American continent and would also extend her sphere of influence throughout Latin America. His chance to assert positively the hopes of the United States came both because of the situation on the distant northwest coast of North America ('the Oregon country') and because of the situation in Latin America.

In the early nineteenth century several powers had hopes of controlling the North American coast north of California. Spain's long-lasting claims were given up in the Adams-Onis Treaty of 1819, but the United States, Great Britain and Russia continued to have an interest in the region. Britain and the United States had claims based on exploration, while Russia, who had advanced into Alaska in the eighteenth century, was anxious to extend her control down the west coast of North America. In 1812 a Russian post was established north of San Francisco, but Russia's attempt to assert a claim to the region was resisted by Adams in the early 1820s.

The various regions of Latin America that had been in revolt from Spain since the Napoleonic wars were anxious to secure recognition from other powers. The United States sympathized with the aspirations of the area, both because of a supposed similarity with her own Revolution and because of the opening of new trade opportunities, but had delayed recognition in the years after 1815 because of her desire to obtain the Floridas from Spain. After that transaction was completed, however, the United States rapidly moved to recognition, even though there was some fear in the early 1820s that the Holy Alliance powers of Europe would come to the aid of Spain in recovering her Latin American colonies. In 1823 the United States also made a general assertion of the principles she was trying to uphold on the American continents by issuing the Monroe Doctrine.

The occasion for the issuance of the Monroe Doctrine was a British request that the Americans should join in a declaration in opposition to any European efforts to help Spain to restore her power in Latin America. John Quincy Adams turned down the British request but persuaded the American government to act unilaterally and assert the position of the United States. Accordingly, in his annual message of December 1823, President Monroe incorporated a statement summarizing the American position.

President Monroe declared that the United States would view as unfriendly acts any new colonization by the European powers on the American continent or any attempt to change the forms of government: as the United States did not wish to interfere in European affairs, European powers should not interfere in the western hemisphere. In 1823 the United States did not have the military power to enforce her desires, but as Great Britain, who controlled the Atlantic, did not want any major European interferences in the New World the general principles could be upheld.

The interests of the United States and Great Britain were not in accord, however, on the Pacific coast north of California. Russia had agreed to withdraw from this region in the mid-1820s, but Britain and the United States both maintained their claims and merely agreed that for the time being the area would be open to citizens of both countries.

While John Quincy Adams and the American government asserted the general principles upon which the United States was acting, American settlers continually advanced the bounds of actual settlement. From 1821, with Mexico now independent from Spain, Southerners and their slaves began to move in increasing numbers into Mexican Texas. For much of the period this movement received Mexican encouragement, although for a time Mexico tried to stop the immigration as she realized the dangers it posed to the region. By 1835 over 25,000 Americans had crossed into Texas. They attempted to gain greater independence while the Mexican leader Santa Anna pressed for centralization. The friction led to open warfare. The American government did not involve itself officially in Texas, though individual Americans gave aid.

Santa Anna advanced into Texas early in 1836 and in March helped to arouse Texas resistance when his army, after meeting great opposition, stormed the Alamo in San Antonio and killed all the defenders (under 200), including the famous frontiersmen Davy Crockett and Jim Bowie. The Mexicans continued their advance, but on 21 April 1836 at San Jacinto the aroused Texas, led by Sam Houston, completely defeated the Mexican army and captured Santa Anna. He was freed after promising to acknowledge Texan independence but later broke the promise.

Andrew Jackson would have liked to incorporate Texas into the Union – this was strongly desired by the Texans – but he did not wish to provoke war with Mexico and also had to contend with the resistance of northerners who did not want to see an addition to the power of the slave states. Accordingly, Jackson merely recognized Texan independence before he left office.

Manifest Destiny

By the 1840s the long-established American interest in expansion on the North American continent had erupted into a popular surge of enthusiasm usually described by the phrase 'Manifest Destiny'. Americans' confidence in their destiny and mission reached reached new heights; not only was the United States clearly intended to expand to the Pacific, it was also argued that this would help bring about a new age of democracy and republican government in the world. The American advance would expand the area of freedom, it was argued, and if Mexicans blocked the way they, like the Indians, would be overwhelmed.

In the election of 1844, when the Whigs were already in dire trouble because of their internal splits, the Democrats began to take advantage of the new national enthusiasm and helped to guide it. James K. Polk, the Democratic candidate, was prepared to take strong action to accomplish American aims, both on the Pacific coast and in the southwest. The slogan of 'Re-annexation of Texas and the reoccupation of Oregon' stirred American blood and helped to elect the Democrats.

The first practical result of the Democratic victory was that lame-duck President Tyler, before handing over to his successor, considered he now had a popular mandate to

annex Texas, and this was done by joint resolution of Congress in March 1845. A formal treaty for annexation was avoided as this would have needed a two-thirds majority in the Senate and would have met opposition from the northeasterners.

American pressure on the Pacific coast and on the southwest had been made possible by the activity of American traders and settlers in those regions. In the previous decades American traders had settled in the ports of Mexican California, and an overland trade had been built up from the central Mississippi Valley states to Mexican Santa Fe by way of the Santa Fe Trail. In the 1840s the trade interest was followed by that of the American pioneer farmers who travelled the Oregon trail across the Continent. They set out west from the vicinity of Independence, Missouri, trekking along the Platte into the Rockies and then over to Oregon, or perhaps by a southern cut-off to California.

In the early 1840s several thousand pioneers found their way across the continent to Oregon, following missionaries who had arrived there a decade earlier, enabling the American government to reopen the Oregon question with Great Britain. Although extravagant claims had been made to an area extending northwards as far as

the southern boundary of Alaska, actual control of the region was rather different. British fur trading interests had long held effective control over the region between the forty-ninth parallel and the Columbia River, and American settlers had moved only into the region south of that river.

President Polk exerted strong pressure on the British government, at first arguing that he wanted the boundary at 54° 40'. But, eventually, in the Oregon Treaty of June 1846 he accepted the line of the forty-ninth parallel as the boundary to the Pacific (Vancouver Island was given to the British). The boundary was not what Polk had originally demanded, but he actually won control of an area that the British had previously dominated. As other United States-Canadian boundary problems had been settled in the Webster-Ashburton Treaty of 1842, British-American relations from now on improved markedly.

War with Mexico

California and the southwest presented a more difficult problem for the American government, as Mexico had no desire to give up this section of her country. Since the 1820s the United States had been urging Mexico to sell portions of this region, but Mexican-United States relations became bitter after Texas obtained her independence. Mexico believed, with good reason, that the northern regions of her country were in imminent danger from the advancing American pioneers, and the United States complained of Mexican intransigence in refusing to negotiate and also of the Mexican failure to pay claims of American citizens for the loss of their property in the frequent Mexican revolutions.

When the United States annexed Texas in 1845, Mexico broke off diplomatic relations, and many Mexicans urged war against the United States. Polk was still anxious to secure what he wanted by negotiation and in November sent John Slidell to try to obtain Mexican recognition of the annexation of Texas. He was also to secure recognition of a Rio Grande boundary between Texas and Mexico and to try to buy New Mexico and California.

The Mexicans refused to negotiate with Slidell, and in the spring of 1846 tension between the two countries erupted into open conflict. American troops were ordered into the disputed territory immediately north of the Rio Grande, and Polk resolved to ask Congress for war. His task was made easier by the news that Mexican and United States troops had clashed north of the Rio Grande. On 13 May 1846, the American Congress declared war on Mexico.

The Mexican War was a complete victory for the United States. While American troops took possession of New Mexico and California, General Zachary Taylor invaded the provinces of Mexico south of the Rio Grande. His victory at the Battle of Buena Vista in February 1847 won control of the region for the United States. By that time New Mexico had been taken by an American force which marched overland from Fort Leavenworth, and California had already been conquered by a combination of internal revolt and American troops.

In March 1847 the American government took more direct steps to end the war. Polk, who was becoming increasingly concerned at General Taylor's growing popularity, had placed Winfield Scott in command of an army which was landed by sea at Vera Cruz. The Mexicans put up a stubborn and brave resistance, but in September the United States troops took Mexico City.

Polk had sent Nicholas P. Trist with Scott's army to conduct peace negotiations,

The growth of sectionalism

The years between 1820 and 1850 brought a marked deterioration in American national unity; in particular the South became a distinct section, dedicated not only to the preservation of slavery, but also to distinct economy and a whole way of life. The 1830s were decisive years in the creation of a solid South. Although there was opposition to slavery before 1830, it was the foundation of William Lloyd Garrison's newspaper *The Liberator* in 1831 that marked the real beginning of a radical abolitionist movement in the North.

In the following years hundreds of abolitionist societies were formed in the northern states. Their periodicals and other publications poured abuse upon the Southerners, depicted the worse cruelties of the slave system and demanded that the institution should come to an end. Although those involved were a small minority of the northern population, their arguments produced a strong reaction in the South. Instead of Southerners arguing that slavery was a necessary evil, as many had done in the years following the Revolution, they began to maintain that slavery was a positive good, that the negroes were an inferior race who were happier in their slave condition than if free, that their lot was better than that of the northern factory workers, and that slavery had been the basis of all great civilizations. They also showed fear that northern arguments would inspire slave insurrections: a rising led by Nat Turner in 1831 had resulted in the deaths of fifty-five white and had sent a shudder of fear throughout the South.

With tempers inflamed by the argument over slavery, the other basic issues separating North and South were contested far more vehemently. The acrimonious tariff struggle between President Jackson and South Carolina in the early 1830s was followed after 1836 by another argument over the admission of Texas. The North feared a major addition to slave power if that region were annexed to the United States.

Underlying the whole quarrel was the continued Southern desire to maintain enough votes in Congress to block any undesirable political, social or economic legislation. This was becoming more difficult as the population of the free states continued to grow more rapidly than that of the South, giving the South an increasingly weak position in the House of Representatives and making it all the more important for the Southern slave system to control new states and provide new Senate votes.

and, although Polk had ordered him to return, Trist signed the Treaty of Guadalupe Hidalgo in February 1848, and Polk decided to submit it to the Senate. The treaty gave California and New Mexico to the United States and acknowledged the Rio Grande as the boundary of Texas. The United States agreed to pay $15,000,000 for these areas as well as to assume $3,250,000 in debts owed by Mexico to Americans.

It was a crushing defeat for Mexico, made all the more galling because early in 1848 gold had been discovered in California. In 1849 thousands of Americans made their way to the goldfields overland, by the way of Panama, and around the Horn. This discovery was ultimately to lead to the expansion of the mining frontier over the whole region of the Rockies.

The American enthusiasm for Manifest Destiny was to continue into the 1850s, and there was talk of annexing Cuba, but the only addition of territory was by the Gadsden Purchase from Mexico in 1853, which gave to the United States a strip of land in the southwest suitable for a railroad route to the Pacific.

In 1783 the United States had been bounded by the Mississippi on the west, the Great Lakes on the north and Spanish territory to the south. Within seventy years the country had assumed her modern dimensions on the North American continent, with the exception of Alaska which was bought from Russia in 1867. Not only had these areas come under the sovereignty of the United States, her settlers were also rapidly advancing throughout the continent: by 1850 California was a state, Oregon a territory and Mormon settlers had established the nucleus of a future state by the Great Salt Lake. It now seemed that the only threat to the development of the United States into one of the greatest powers in the world was internal dissension, for now the threat of civil war was becoming ever greater.

The compromise of 1850

The war with Mexico produced an immediate crisis in the relations of North and South. Nationalistic enthusiasm had produced general support for the conflict at the beginning of the war, but northern Whigs soon expressed their opposition to a war of conquest and to any further extension of slavery. As early as 1846 representative David Wilmot of Pennsylvania had introduced into Congress the Wilmot Proviso, which stated that slavery should not be permitted in any of the territory obtained from Mexico.

While American armies conquered a huge addition to the territory of the United States, Congress argued about the Wilmot Proviso, which did not have enough votes to pass the Senate. Some were now contending that slavery should be allowed to expand into any area that wanted it, others maintained that the Missouri Compromise line of 36° 30′ should be extended to the Pacific. But what would happen to California, an area that was already asking for admission to the Union?

In the 1848 presidential election both candidates played down the basic issue, and military hero Zachary Taylor was able to win the second and last Whig presidential victory. His opponent Lewis Cass had become known as an advocate of the idea that the territories should decide for themselves whether or not they would have slavery, but he laid little stress on this in the election. Ominous for future unity was the third party – the Free Soil party – who ran ex-President Martin Van Buren on a platform against the future expansion of slavery. Taylor's victory had been based on both Northern and Southern votes, but it was now clear that it was becoming increasingly difficult for either main party to hold together such bipartisan support.

Taylor urged California to apply for admission to the Union and was willing to abide by the state's decision whether or not to be slave or free; in late 1849 California formed a free constitution and applied for admission. The South, fearing that all the land acquired from Mexico would be free, bitterly opposed the admission of California on these terms, and in 1850 Congress engaged in an impassioned debate on the future expansion of slavery. The eventual solution was devised by Henry Clay, now near the end of his long career, and was pushed through Congress after the death of President Taylor had brought Vice-President Millard Fillmore to the presidency.

The Compromise of 1850 consisted of a number of measures passed in the hope of giving some concessions to both North and South. Many on both sides voted for those measures they liked and were prepared to abstain when those measures they did not like were voted upon. By the compromise California was to enter the Union as a free state, New Mexico and Utah were to be organized as territories with no specification whether they were to be slave or free, the slave trade (but not slavery) was to be abolished in the District of Columbia, and a stricter Fugitive Slave Law was enacted. In addition, Texas was compensated for ceding her claims to part of New Mexico. The

compromise pleased neither side. Southerners objected to restrictions on slavery anywhere in the West, and northern abolitionists protested against the harsh Fugitive Slave Law, and insisted that the future expansion of slavery should be prohibited.

The increasing emotional impact of the issue of slavery was well demonstrated by the phenomenal success of Harriet Beecher Stowe's novel *Uncle Tom's Cabin*, which was published in 1852. This melodramatic depiction of slave life moved millions of northern citizens as a book, in serial form and as a play. As the North became more stirred by the moral implications of slavery, and as the South became convinced that it was losing political power, it became impossible to maintain political compromises.

The Compromise of 1850 collapsed within four years. The election of 1852 was fought between a Democratic party still anxious to maintain the unity of its Northern and Southern wings and a Whig party that was finally falling apart. The undistinguished Franklin Pierce of New Hampshire won an easy victory over Whig Winfield Scott. Pierce had a tumultuous presidency, and once again the fiercest arguments came over the westward expansion of slavery.

Although American settlers had pushed all the way to California and Oregon in the 1840s, there had long been a reluctance to advance on to the Great Plains. With good reason it was feared that the lack of timber and an uncertain water supply would present problems unknown in the eastern half of the continent. Yet, as the more desirable areas were populated and pioneers still looked for land, the adventurous began to encroach upon the Plains, and in the 1853–4 session of Congress a bill was introduced for the organization of the area west of Iowa and Missouri as Nebraska Territory. Although settlers were moving into this region, the bill also stemmed from the ambitions of Senator Stephen A. Douglas of Illinois.

In the 1850s there was a new breed of politicians in Congress. After the deaths of Clay, Calhoun and Webster, in both North and South some politicians had less patience for compromise. Men such as Senator Charles Summer of Massachusetts poured scorn upon their enemies. Of the new group of prominent political leaders, Democratic Senator S. Douglas appeared the most anxious to achieve compromise and preserve national unity; in his case it was bitterly disputed whether it was patriotism or personal ambition that led him to take this course.

As chairman of the committee on territories, Douglas introduced the bill to organize Nebraska Territory. He was interested not only in the settlers in that region but also in a trans-continental railroad. Since the 1840s there had been talk of such a link, and in the 1850s it was a major political issue; there was great competition from those areas seeking to be the eastern terminal of the railroad. Douglas was pressing for Chicago – he had a personal interest in the Illinois Central Railroad and in land speculation as well as a Senator's interest in his own state – but he realized that the area through which the line would pass needed a form of governmental organization if the railway was to be more attractive to Congress.

The question of Nebraska Territory sent Congress into turmoil. Nebraska would presumably enter as a free state, and to meet Southern objections it was agreed that the region would be divided into two territories: Kansas and Nebraska. Douglas also agreed that instead of the line of 36° 30′ dividing slave and free areas, as decided in the Missouri Compromise, 'popular sovereignty' would prevail in the territories. Douglas argued that, rather than Congress making the decision for an area, it would be more democratic for each area to decide for itself whether or not to have slavery. The advantage to Douglas was that this would also meet the wishes of the Southern section of his own party and help his presidential ambitions.

In spite of Northern objections, the Kansas – Nebraska Act was pushed through Congress, repealing the Missouri Compromise and allowing the territories to decide for themselves on the issue of slavery or freedom. From that time on there was little respite in the steady slide into Civil War.

There was no doubt that Nebraska would be a free area, but from 1854 until the Civil War the situation of 'bleeding Kansas' constantly aggravated relations between the North and South. Both Northerners and Southerners attempted to arrange the migration of pioneers who would vote Kansas slave or free, and the general turmoil was increased by the opportunists and criminals always attracted to the edge of the frontier. They speculated in land and ambushed and burned for personal rather than national motives.

The Republican party

The Kansas – Nebraska Act also helped to bring about the final disintegration of the Whigs and to create the new Republican party, a Northern party composed of ex-Whigs, Democrats who opposed Douglas and the Kansas – Nebraska Act and the old free-soilers, all uniting on opposition to the expansion of slavery. A third party, the Know-Nothings, appealed to prejudice, opposing Catholics and immigrants, and tapped the nativistic tradition in American politics, i.e. the tradition favouring those actually born in America. The Republicans spread quickly throughout the old northwest and New England, and the Whig party, which was a national party however disunited, was now replaced by a sectional party.

The bitterness of the Republicans was increased by the situation in Kansas. Soon two governments existed – one pro-slavery, one for freedom – and violent incidents multiplied. After a pro-slavery group had attacked the town of Lawrence, the unbalanced John Brown, with his sons and friends, murdered a group of Southern sympathizers. The breakdown of order even spread to Congress itself. In the Senate in 1856 Charles Sumner launched a vituperative personal attack on Senator Andrew P. Butler of South Carolina. Butler's nephew, Congressman Preston B. Brooks, heard about it, entered the Senate and beat Sumner on the head with his cane. Brooks was censured by the House but after resigning was swept back into Congress by his district in South Carolina.

In the 1856 election the Democrats nominated the mediocre James Buchanan while the Republicans, already strong enough to contest the presidency, nominated the national hero, soldier and explorer John C. Frémont. Ex-president Fillmore ran on the Know-Nothing ticket. Buchanan won, but it was ominous for the South that Frémont obtained 114 electoral votes to Buchanan's 174 and Fillmore's 8.

The Dred Scott decision

Buchanan's problems began immediately, for in March 1857 the Supreme Court, which had a majority of Southerners, declared in the Dred Scott case that the Missouri Compromise was unconstitutional. Slaves were property and the constitution protected individual rights of property. By this decision the Supreme Court made it clear that neither the federal nor the territorial government could constitutionally exclude slavery.

The Dred Scott decision brought impassioned arguments in the North, but it was also a crushing blow to Douglas, for the decision went further than his popular sovereignty in satisfying the Southerners; according to the Supreme Court an individual's ritht to own a slave was protected by the constitution, and even a democratic majority could not outlaw slavery in a territory. Douglas was placed in an even more difficult position when President Buchanan decided to ask Congress to admit Kansas to the Union under the provisions of the 'Lecompton Constitution'. This was a pro-slavery constitution supported by only part of the Kansas population and never voted on by all the people of the territory. Although this did not pass, it further divided the Democratic Party. The dilemma was revealed dramatically in Douglas's senatorial re-election campaign in Illinois in 1858. His opponent was Abraham Lincoln.

Lincoln was the son of a pioneer farmer, who, after his famous son's birth in Kentucky in 1809, moved on into Indiana and finally into Illinois. Lincoln became a lawyer

in the 1830s, although for the most part he was self-educated. He also became a Whig and served one term in Congress after his election in 1846. He was a competent state-level politician but was not at all well known as a national figure.

In the 1850s Lincoln began to take a strong stand against the further expansion of slavery, although he was not at this time an abolitionist. He soon became an important figure in the new Republican party and in 1858 ran for the Senate against Douglas in Illinois. The debates the two engaged in received major national attention, and although Douglas won Lincoln obliged him to choose publicly between popular sovereignty and the Dred Scott decision. At Freeport Lincoln forced him to answer whether or not the people of a territory could exclude slavery. Douglas answered that they could and in so doing alienated the Southern Democrats, who wanted Douglas to accept the Dred Scott decision.

The last years of Buchanan's administration brought a breakdown of responsible government. The division between Northern and Southern extremists was such that Congress had difficulty in conducting any of its business. Tension reached a high point when in the autumn of 1859 John Brown led a small group of followers into Virginia to attack the federal arsenal at Harper's Ferry. He wanted to arm the slaves and begin a revolt. After they had seized the arsenal the attackers were themselves besieged, Brown was captured, quickly tried and hanged. In life Brown was a fanatic; in death he became a martyr to the cause of freedom. His act was a fitting prelude to the climactic election of 1860.

When in the spring of 1860 the Democrats met in Charleston to nominate their candidate for president, the logical candidate, Douglas, could not obtain the votes for the nomination. Neither North nor South would compromise, and the Southern delegates walked out. The Democrats tried again in June at Baltimore, again failed to agree and eventually the Northern and Southern wings of the party nominated separate candidates: Douglas for the North, John C. Breckinridge of Kentucky for the South. As the Southerners had been unwilling to accept even the moderate Douglas, they now created an opportunity for the sectional Republicans. In May the Republicans nominated Abraham Lincoln for president, choosing him over the more extreme William H. Seward of New York. For the South the vital section of the Republican platform was that which opposed slavery in the territories.

A third party – the Constitutional Union party – attempted to hold the nation together with an appeal for national unity, but their candidate – John Bell of Tennessee – had no chance of success. Lincoln won the election with 1,866,000 popular votes; Douglas had 1,383,000, Breckinridge

848,000, and Bell 593,000. Although a minority president in terms of popular votes, Lincoln had an absolute majority of electoral votes.

Secession

The victory of Lincoln could not be accepted by the South. In half a century they had lost the dominant position in the nation. Between 1789 and 1825 Virginia had provided all the presidents but one, and Southerners had dominated public office, so much so that some in New England had thought of secession. In 1860 the North elected a president from a party which unalterably opposed the extension of slavery. With no possibility of expansion, the South would be outvoted in Congress, policies would be

adopted against Southern wishes, soon perhaps the institution of slavery itself would be threatened, and the South would be faced with a massive economic loss and a general social readjustment. By withdrawing from the Union many in the South hoped to preserve intact their economic and social system.

The first Southern state to act was South Carolina. In December 1860 she seceded from the Union and by the beginning of February had been joined by Mississippi, Florida, Alabama, Georgia, Louisiana and Texas. At Montgomery, Alabama, in February 1861 the seven seceding states set up the Confederate States of America. President Buchanan vacillated, and although various compromise plans were suggested there seemed no way to reunite the Union save by a swift use of force.

When Lincoln was inaugurated in March 1861 he asserted that he did not intend to interfere with slavery in existing states, but it was no use; the seceding states had no intention of returning. It was still not clear how Lincoln would proceed to his task of reuniting the nation, but action was precipitated by the situation of the federal forts in the South. On 12 April, just as reinforcements were arriving, the Confederate forces bombarded Fort Sumter in Charleston harbour. The fort surrendered two days later. Lincoln now called for 75,000 volunteers, and with this threat of force Virginia, Arkansas, Tennessee and North Carolina also seceded from the Union. Although Kentucky and Missouri had great numbers of Southern supporters, they did not officially leave the Union.

The Civil War

The discrepancy in force between the United States and the Confederacy was very great. The North had over four times the free population of the seceding states, by far the largest industrial development and the most extensive railroad system. She also had the naval power to blockade Southern ports. Southern hopes were based on the knowledge that a stalemate would benefit the South and that it was the North's task to wage a positive, offensive war. The South was also hopeful of foreign aid, particularly from Great Britain, the main consumer of Southern cotton. These hopes proved illusory. Although relations between Great Britain and the United States were strained at the beginning of the war, the strength of anti-slavery opinion in Great Britain was such that any suggestion of joining with the South met with great opposition.

At the beginning of the war the Confederacy gained a false confidence from the ease with which it resisted Northern armies. The politicians pressed the Northern army into action before it was ready, and this produced disastrous results on the main eastern front of the war: the stretch of country between Washington D.C. and the Confederate capital of Richmond, Virginia. At the first Battle of Bull Run in July 1861 the Northern armies were completely defeated. The elderly Winfield Scott was now removed from command, and George B. McClellan replaced him.

Until the spring of 1862 McClellan devoted his attention to the organization and training of the 'Army of the Potomac'. He then attempted to attack Richmond by having his main army of over 100,000 men landed by sea on the peninsula between the James and the York rivers while another force of over 40,000 advanced overland from Washington D.C. The campaign failed. In a running seven-day battle at the end of June Confederate General Robert E. Lee, aided by Stonewall Jackson, forced McClellan to retreat. Lee, who had served in the regular army before the war, had returned to his native Virginia to join her fight. He proved to be a masterly defensive general.

Throughout 1862 the Northern armies continued to suffer defeat on the Washington-Richmond front. In August Lee and Stonewall Jackson overcame the Northern armies at the second Battle of Bull Run, and Lee advanced into Maryland. In September he was obliged to withdraw after the bloody, indecisive Battle of Antietam in which total casualties amounted to over 20,000 men.

Even though Antietam was indecisive it enabled Lincoln to take a decisive step in the conduct of the war. The abolitionists had been urging the freeing of the slaves, and

Lincoln knew that he could also ensure British neutrality if he took the step of fighting for the end of slavery. He did not wish to appear to be freeing the slaves out of desperation, but after the partial victory of Antietam he issued the preliminary Emancipation Proclamation; the final proclamation was issued in January 1863. Yet, though the Confederacy was denied foreign intervention, it still seemed she could save herself, for 1862 ended in disaster for the North when General Ambrose E. Burnside threw his troops into suicidal attack against the Confederate positions at Fredericksburg and lost over 10,000 dead and wounded.

The first eighteen months of the war had seen the complete failure of the main Union effort to drive south from Washington

against the Confederate capital. There was extensive criticism of Lincoln and much disaffection in Northern areas. It was as well for the Union that other pressures on the South were weakening her resistance. Particularly effective was the blockade, which ruined Southern commerce. Also Northern naval forces eventually combined with land forces to split the Confederacy.

Union troops in the Mississippi valley were at first more successful than those in the east, and in April 1862 General Ulysses S. Grant won the Battle of Shiloh, with terrible losses, and forced the Confederate troops to retreat. In the same month a naval squadron under the command of David G. Farragut captured New Orleans and pushed up the Mississippi. In the next year

the Northern armies slowly fought their way south to join up with the naval forces on the Mississippi and split the Confederacy. On 4 July 1863, Grant took Vicksburg, and a few days later the North had succeeded in winning complete control of the Mississippi River.

The first days of July 1863 were the turning-point in the history of the Confederacy, for while Grant was preparing to take Vicksburg Lee was making a decisive move which he hoped would end the war. In May, Lee and Stonewall Jackson (who was killed) defeated Northern forces at Chancellorsville. Lee now decided to advance into Pennsylvania and by a decisive victory force the North to concede that the South could leave the Union.

From 1 to 3 July Lee met the Northern army of General George Meade at Gettysburg. The slaughter was immense, and on the third day Lee sent General George E. Pickett's men in wave after wave against the Union line. They could not break it, and Lee withdrew southwards. From July 1863 it became increasingly obvious that the South had lost the war, but unfortunately for future relations between the two sections the desperate struggle continued for nearly two more years. Lincoln could now quiet his critics, and in 1864 he won re-election over the Democratic candidate General George B. McClellan.

In 1864 and 1865 the federal armies plunged deep into the South to bring the Confederacy to its knees. The Northern armies in the Mississippi Valley were repulsed for a time at Chickamauga in September 1863, but in November after the Battle of Chattanooga the Southern forces retreated into Georgia. In 1864 the Northern armies moved to split the Confederacy again by driving into Georgia to Atlanta and then to the sea, while further north General

Grant, who had been transferred to command on the Washington-Richmond front, attempted to advance south towards Richmond.

There was intense fighting throughout the spring and summer of 1864. In May and June Grant fought a series of battles in the Wilderness and encircled Richmond, which was well defended by a series of trenches and fortifications. It was the following year before he could force Lee's army to withdraw from these positions.

General William T. Sherman and his

THE UNITED STATES AND LATIN AMERICA, 1800–1870

Date	United States	Mexico and Argentina	Rest of Latin America	Date	United States	Mexico and Argentina	Rest of Latin America
1800	Presidency of Thomas Jefferson (1801–09) Louisiana Purchase (1803) Presidency of James Madison (1809–17)	British occupation of Buenos Aires (1806)	Unsuccessful revolt by Miranda in Venezuela (1806) Abortive attempt at independence in Ecuador (1809)	1840	Presidency of W. Harrison (1841) Presidency of J. Polk (1845–49) Britain gives up Oregon (1846) Conquest of California (1847) Gold rush in California	Rosas dictator of Argentina Argentina at war with Paraguay (1845) War between Mexico and United States (1846–48) Treaty of Guadalupe Hidalgo (1848)	Reign of Pedro II begins (1840) Carlos López president of Paraguay (1844) Overthrow of Flores (1845) Castilla president of Peru (1845)
1810	War with Britain (1812–14) Presidency of James Monroe (1817–25) Spain cedes Florida to USA (1818)	Beginning of Mexican struggle for independence (1811–15) Argentina independent (1816)	Venezuelan independence proclaimed (1811) Spain reconquers Venezuela (1814) San Martin liberates Chile (1818) Greater Colombia founded (1819)	1850	Clay compromise (1850) Foundation of Republican party (1854) Lincoln-Douglas debates (1858) John Brown's raid (1859)	Revolt of Urquiza in Argentina Urquiza defeats Rosas at Caseros (1852) Secession of Buenos Aires (1853) Dissolution of the Order of Jesuits in Mexico (1855) New Mexican constituion (1857) Civil war in Mexico—Juárez against Miramón (1858) Buenos Aires rejoins Argentinian federation (1859)	Abolition of slavery in Colombia (1851) and Venezuela (1854) Fall of Monagas regime in Venezuela (1859)
1820	Missouri Compromise (1820) Monroe doctrine (1823) Presidency of J. Q. Adams (1825–29) Presidency of Andrew Jackson (1829–37)	Mexico independent (1821) Mexico a federal republic (1824) War between Argentina and Brazil (1827–28)	Peru independent (1821) Final liberation of Venezuela (1821) Liberation of Ecuador (1822) Brazil independent (1822); Pedro I emperor (1822–31) Bolivia a sovereign state (1826) Uruguay a sovereign state (1828)	1860	Election of Lincoln Secession of eleven Southern states (1860–61) Formation of the Confederate States of America (1861) Lincoln proclaims the emancipation of the slaves (1863) Surrender of General Lee (1865) Assassination of Lincoln (1865) Military occupation of the South	Juárez President of Mexico (1861) Bartolomé Mitre President united Argentina (1862–68) Maximilian Emperor of Mexico (1864) Maximilian executed (1867) Juárez re-elected president of Mexico (1867)	Liberal regime in Chile (1861) Argentina, Brazil and Uruguay at war with Paraguay (1865–70)
1830	Beginning of Abolitionist movement First Mormon Church (1831) Republic of Texas established (1836) Presidency of Martin van Buren (1837–41)	Santa Anna President of Mexico (1833–35) Rosas governor of Buenos Aires (1835) Santa Anna defeated by Texans at San Jacinto (1836)	Venezuela and Ecuador separate countries (1830) Pedro II Emperor of Brazil (1831–89); regency established Brazilian separatist movement in Rio Grande do Sul (1835–45) Flores assumes power in Ecuador (1839) Chile destroys Bolivian-Peruvian federation (1839)	1870			

armies from the Mississippi Valley had more dramatic success. Atlanta fell in September, and Sherman marched to the sea, taking Savannah in December. He was now able to turn north, and in the spring of 1865 the Confederacy collapsed. In April Lee was finally forced to retreat from Richmond; on 9 April at Appomattox he found there was no way of retreat and surrendered to Grant. Other small forces soon capitulated, and the war was over.

The cost of the war

The North had lost 359,000 dead, the Confederacy 258,000 dead. Much of the South had been devastated: plantations ruined, fortunes lost, railroad tracks torn up, cities destroyed. The Union had been preserved, and the slaves had been freed, but a monumental task of reconstruction and a deep legacy of bitterness and hatred remained. To climax the tragedy, on 14 April Lincoln was shot at Ford's theatre in Washington D.C. The nation faced the task of reconstruction without its great leader. Andrew Johnson of Tennessee became president.

Yet, even after this great war, the United States was ready to become one of the most powerful countries in the world. Although hundreds of thousands had been killed and maimed, Northern prosperity had suffered no severe injury. Industrial development, railroad construction and commerce were leaping forward. The South would remain a problem, but the vast unified United States spanning the North American continent would quickly press forward to new heights of prosperity and strength. A unified nation which offered a combination of political and religious freedom and economic opportunity attracted even more millions of immigrants from Europe in the years after the Civil War. To judge the advantages possessed by the United States, even after a bloody conflict, one had only to turn to South America to view the sad history of a fragmented continent which had obtained its independence from Europe but which had failed to obtain either the prosperity or the freedom of which some of the early revolutionaries had dreamed.

Opposite top, Yankee volunteers marching into the South: the north's assertion of its political and cultural way of life soured relations between the two parts of the Union for decades.

Opposite bottom right, a refugee family leaving the war zone, their belongings loaded on a cart: the armies of both North and South left a trail of destruction behind them, though none was exceeded by the devastation and looting of Sherman's army as it marched across Georgia in 1865.

Opposite bottom left, the United States during the Civil War, 1961–65: the final victory of the northern states preserved the Union, but at the cost of more than 600,000 dead.

Part VII

THE BALANCE OF POWER

Introduction

The nineteenth century had no monopoly of nationalism and imperialism – they seem to be as old as the earliest, organized human societies. But it was in the nineteenth century that the search for power and glory, the essential element in nationalism and imperialism at any time, was intensified by forces largely unknown in previous ages. Historians may debate which of these forces was the most influential in the promotion of nationalism and imperialism, but there is little doubt about what, in the main, they were: challenging developments and discoveries in science and technology which placed into men's hands – particularly into white men's hands – powerful agents for both construction and destruction; profound changes in the economic and social systems of Europe and America; the tensions of democracy; severe threats to the traditional faiths; and the agonizing search for new ones.

By the second half of the nineteenth century, Europe and its white offspring overseas were well advanced in the process of transforming themselves into areas in which new nation-states, flush with the enthusiasms and pretensions of novelty, co-existed uneasily with the older countries. Impelled by the new and often ill-understood forces of the century, both the old and the new nation-states of Europe found that the customary means of preserving their freedom of action by balancing their power, the one against the other, were no longer adequate; and, in the process of discovering new ones, changed not only themselves but the world overseas – white, black, brown and yellow.

The relations of white men with the old civilizations of the East, particularly in the second half of the nineteenth century are especially significant. By this time, the wheel which Europe had set in motion in the thirteenth century with such ventures as Marco Polo's journeys across Asia was coming full circle. The awe of white men at the power and the wealth of the East was being replaced by the East's respect for the power and wealth of white men.

In this process, the United States of America, that part of the New World upon which Europeans had stumbled accidentally in the fifteenth century in their search for the lands and riches of the East, was to play an important part. Indeed, it could be argued that the arrival in Tokyo Bay of the American naval expedition under the command of the militantly-minded Commodore Matthew Perry in 1853 was as important an event in the relations of white men with the non-European world as Columbus' voyage to the Caribbean in 1492.

Even within Europe, the remarkable growth of American political, economic and technological strength had a disturbing effect. The powers and peoples of Europe rarely acted in any sphere (political, economic, social or ideological) without some consideration of the American position.

Even the literature and language of the imperialism of the late nineteenth century reflected this. When, for example, Hilaire Belloc, the Anglo-French writer, produced in 1898 his satirical poem, *The Modern Traveller*, on the advances of the British Empire in tropical Africa, the famous couplet which he assigned to an English adventurer facing a crowd of hostile Africans,

Whatever happens, we have got
The Maxim gun and they have not

would have been impossible had not the inventor of this weapon been one Hiram Maxim, a gentleman of American origins. Hiram's brother, Hudson, an expert on explosives, also gave his name to a means of destruction – maximite (a high-explosive bursting powder for use in torpedoes), which helped to change the fate of nations and empires in Europe and in Europe's spheres of influence elsewhere. And when Rudyard Kipling produced his celebrated poem on the responsibilities of imperialism, he was stimulated by the American victory in the Spanish-American War of 1898, which made them heirs to the remains of the Spanish Empire in the Pacific and the Caribbean. Addressing his poem to these new American imperialists, Kipling declared that they must also take up 'the white man's burden'. This hypnotic and deceptive expression, indeed, might never have been coined if Kipling had not kept the United States constantly in mind.

Yet the core of what the great English writer, John A. Hobson, called 'the new imperialism', of the late nineteenth and early twentieth centuries, remained European.

It was promoted, in particular, by the challenge to the conventional balance of power in Europe by the unification of the German and Italian nation-states in the 1870s. The new Germany precipitated the new imperialism. The overthrow of the French Second Empire by the leaders of German nationalism, the Prussians, at the Battle of Sedan on 1 September 1870 was an ignominious defeat for the nation which had produced Napoleon I.

His nephew, the French emperor Napoleon III, who had all of his uncle's pretensions but little of his power and ability, was taken prisoner. The French nation – especially its army, with its ambitious officer class – could seek consolation in the extension of its overseas empire. Not for nothing did the English imperialist, F. D. Lugard, himself an ambitious army officer actively engaged in extending British territory in tropical Africa, say in 1893 that the Franco-Prussian War was indisputably linked to the scramble for Africa by the powers of Europe. Strangely enough, it was the pretensions of Napoleon III and his Second Empire, before its debacle in 1870, which launched the term 'imperialism' into the popular speech of Europe. But, in the last thirty years of the nineteenth century, the term was to acquire a variety of meanings which owed little to the Second Empire.

Most of all, perhaps, under the influence of the socialists and Marxists, the term 'imperialism' came to signify economic rather than political pressures behind the overseas expansion of the white nations. Undoubtedly, there were very important economic pressures behind the new imperialism. But there were also powerful political forces at work – if, of course, it is ever possible or realistic to attempt to disentangle political and economic elements. The new nationalism, in all its complexity, was one of them. And, as the influential German philosopher, Friedrich Nietzsche, who died at the beginning of the twentieth century, pointed out, there was the basic human drive of the will to power, flowing into the new European expansionist channels.

There was also an element in the new imperialism which can be too easily overlooked: disgust at the achievements and values of Europe and a desire to escape to the so-called 'uncivilized' lands overseas. Arthur Rimbaud, the French poet who served in the army of the Paris Commune in 1871 but who deserted France in disgust at the Western world, to wander in Asia and Africa for the remaining sixteen years of his life, exemplifies this tendency. There was a *fin de siècle* pessimism about such men, which the Jewish-Hungarian writer, Max Nordau, discussed pungently in his *Degeneration* of 1895. Nordau was an ardent Zionist who believed that the Jews should accept the offer of land by the British in their new possession of East Africa. For Nordau's pains, an attempt was made on his life by a Jew who was opposed to the scheme to found a new Zion in East Africa. It was psychological and political problems of this sort which made the pattern of the new imperialism more complex.

To complicate this even further, there were the reactions to the new imperialism and nationalism of Europe in the overseas lands to which they penetrated. In 1896, for example, the Ethiopian emperor, Menelek II, defeated the Italians at Adowa, forcing them to sign a treaty recognizing the absolute independence of his country. Nine years later, a resurgent Japanese nationalism,

having learnt well the industrial and military techniques of the West since Commodore Perry's visit half a century before, defeated the Russians and stripped them of some of their empire. Within a decade, the imperial pretensions of two white nations had been defeated by two 'coloured' countries. The new imperialism of Europe continued to search 'wider still and wider': but it was now less sure of itself, since it was compelled to consider the threat of what the new, cheap, popular press called the 'black peril' and the 'yellow peril'. The age of European dominance, apparently at the peak of its power at the beginning of the new century, could already be seen drawing to a close.

Chapter 40

Cavour and Bismarck

While the Westerners were pressing into the Far East, the European balance of power was changing. In 1871, after its crushing victory in the Franco-Prussian War, a triumphant and united Germany declared the Second Reich. The year before the Italians had occupied Rome and completed the formation of modern Italy. Two countries which had been disunited since the Middle Ages now took their places as great powers. They had achieved this under the leadership of two great men. Cavour and Bismarck, at the expense of Habsburg Austria.

Both nationalist movements were supported by businessmen, who sought wider markets for the products of the rising industrial system. The flourishing new bourgeoisie were also champions of liberal institutions, which gave them the voice in government needed for their commercial interests. Yet unification came about in very different ways in Italy and Germany. In one country liberals and democrats allied behind the monarchy of Savoy. In the other the Prussian army united the nation by smashing the power of France. In Italy the new constitution was essentially democratic. In Germany liberalism made little headway against the ruling militarist caste.

Italian unification

In many ways, however, the movements for Italian and German unification were very similar. They went on side by side from 1850 to 1870. Neither resembled in any way the popular uprisings of 1848. What happened was that one of the states within each country became strong enough to dominate and finally unite all the rest. Both these states, Piedmont in Italy and Prussia in Germany, were opposed to the Austrians. Both their leaders, Cavour and Bismarck. made masterly use of a new form of 'power politics'.

However, unlike the Germans, the Italians did not gain unity by surrendering to their own army. The Piedmontese army played an important part in fighting the Austrians, but they were greatly helped by popular unrest, guerrilla warfare, and the work of amateur generals like Garibaldi. After the war was

over, Garibaldi retired to his farm on Caprera.

Indeed the diffidence of the Garibaldians created marked difficulties. Romantic supporters of unity like his 'Redshirts' did little to organize an Italian state after 1870. This was left to the hardheaded statesmen of Piedmont. But at least unification here had a likeable spontaneity which saved it from the domination by the military which was the price of Bismarck's success.

Before 1848 the Italian patriot, Guiseppe Mazzini, had dreamt of a republic ruled from Rome, in which the power of the papacy and the individual princes would be broken and cast aside. The defeats of 1848 showed the weakness of his hopes. Republicanism, as he saw it, not only antagonized the Austrians but also horrified the Vatican and the rulers of the Italian states.

Mazzini's idealism was too extreme and impractical, and only a minority followed him. The alternative plan of the Abbé Vincenzo Gioberti, for an Italian confederation under the pope, was equally unworkable. Italy, especially northern Italy, was an Austrian sphere of influence. Even under the liberal Pius IX, the papacy could hardly afford to usurp the powers of the Habsburgs, its principal supporters.

As the 1850s opened, both the Mazzinians and Gioberti's 'neo-Guelphs' were discredited. Hopes turned to a third plan of liberation, that of accepting the leadership of the constitutional monarchy of Savoy, or Sardinia-Piedmont, which had already shown itself moderately liberal. Perhaps if

Savoy renewed the attack on Austria, it could join with Lombardy and Venetia to form a kingdom of Northern Italy. Beyond this Italian patriots worked out very little. They thought vaguely of organizing some form of federation between the north, the Papal States and Naples in the south. At least this seemed to be a more realistic proposition than Mazzini's republican pipe dreams.

After 1848, Italy, like the rest of Europe, moved into a phase of reaction against liberalism and nationalism. Even the once-idealistic Ferdinand of Naples had become an arbitrary despot. His kingdom of the Two Sicilies remained the most backward in Europe, its peasants too miserable even for revolution. When Mazzini's followers arrived in Naples in 1857 to try to organize a revolt against Ferdinand, there was no support for them, and they were easily wiped out by the Bourbon troops.

In Rome, Pius IX had been restored but now lived in terror of all liberal experiments. The constitution he had granted in 1848 was not restored; he was protected by a French garrison; and power passed increasingly to his diehard conservative secretary of state, Cardinal Antonelli. The rulers of Parma, Modena and Tuscany had become Austrian puppets.

Like Austria-Hungary itself, Lombardy-Venetia, which was still ruled directly from Vienna, had become a police state. After the 1848 revolt alone Metternich's officials there sent 4,000 rebels to prison and 1,000 to the gallows. In London, Mazzini continued to

dream impracticable dreams. The Austrian police crushed his network of Italian revolutionary committees in 1852. Yet he tried to raise the standard of revolt in Milan the very next year. The authorities acted swiftly, and forty republicans died on the gibbet. In the northern Italian states at least, not even the most optimistic patriots could see any solution but the leadership of Savoy.

Victor Emmanuel and Cavour

In 1849, after the bloody Austrian victory over the Piedmontese at Novara, Victor Emmanuel II came to the throne of Savoy. The new king was a homely little man, with an incongruous set of bushy black whiskers. He enjoyed great popularity in his capital of Turin, where he was nicknamed *il re galantuomo* ('the cavalier king'). His good public image was probably linked with his enthusiasm for trimming the privileges of the clergy, who were much less revered in the north of Italy than in Naples for example. This in itself produced a long series of quarrels between Victor Emmanuel and Pius IX. The man who was to make him king of Italy, Camillo Benso, Count Cavour, became a member of the cabinet in 1850.

Cavour had been born in Turin forty years earlier. He was unusually cosmopolitan for an Italian aristocrat. His mother was Swiss, and he himself was educated in France. Afterwards he travelled in England to study its politics and agriculture, before returning to Piedmont to edit the constitutionalist newspaper, *Il Risorgimento*. He had also spent a short time as an officer with the Piedmontese engineers, before losing his commission because of his liberal views.

Once in the cabinet, his rise was meteoric. First appointed minister of agriculture, marine and commerce, he became secretary of the treasury within a few months. After a very short spell out of office, he replaced D'Azeglio as prime minister only twenty-five months after taking his first cabinet post. From 1852 until his death in 1861, aside from a few months in retirement on his estate, he ruled Piedmont.

When his first government was formed, Cavour was forty-two, rich and one of the most popular men in Italy. The people of Turin called him 'Daddy Camillo'. He quickly launched a programme of reform. Unpopular convents were suppressed to the profit of the government. The army was modernized by La Marmora. Above all, Cavour aimed at interesting foreign businessmen in Piedmont's survival and success. British investors sank money in his railway expansion. Communications with France were improved, particularly when work on the Mont Cenis Tunnel started, to bring the magnates in Paris closer to those of Turin.

These measures raised the flagging hopes of Italian nationalists, who deserted Mazzini to follow the Sicilian exile, La Farina, now a champion of unification under the Piedmontese. Cavour was pledged to oppose Austria, and it was only a matter of time until he provoked a crisis. All he lacked for the struggle was a strong ally.

Above, Count Camillo Cavour (1810–61), Prime Minister of Piedmont from 1852 to 1861 (except for a short break in 1859): one of the foremost architects of Italian unification, he worked ceaselessly for it, dying only a few weeks after the first Italian parliament had proclaimed the new king. Pinacoteca di Brera, Milan.

Top, Victor Emmanuel (1820–78), King of Savoy from 1849: he was proclaimed the first King of Italy in 1861, though the whole nation was finally united only in 1870, when the French occupation of Rome came to an end. Museo del Risorgimento, Milan.

Above left, the uprising in Naples; on 29 January 1848 Ferdinand II was compelled to grant a constitution.

Opposite, cartoon by Daumier entitled Le Reveil d'Italie *(Italy Awakes) depicting Italy as Gulliver being jerked awake by the Lilliputians: it needed forty years of political agitation and armed uprisings to achieve unification.*

Piedmont-Sardinia in 1858
Acquired in 1859
Ceded to France in 1860
Annexed in 1860-1
Acquired in 1866
Annexed in 1870

He found such an ally in France. Napoleon III still had the vestiges of a liberal reputation as a result of his youthful involvement with the *Carbonari*, the romantic republicans of the years after the Napoleonic Wars. He was known to sympathize with the Italians. However, he was somewhat chary about unification, since this would inevitably lead to papal opposition. Even worse, it would offend groups of important Catholic voters in France.

Napoleon was no match for the brilliant diplomacy of Cavour. His master-stroke was to send a handful of crack Piedmontese troops to help the French and British in the Crimean War against Russia. La Marmora and his men gained much of what little credit was to be had from this disastrous campaign, and Cavour was invited to the peace talks in Paris in 1856. Napoleon, as usual clumsily anxious to appear as the champion of nationalism, denounced the oppression of northern Italy in front of the astonished Austrian delegates. Naturally they refused to discuss the subject, but Cavour had gained exactly what he wanted. He had drawn attention to his cause, Piedmont had appeared as a European power, and the other powers had been warned of the general importance of the Italian situation.

Piedmont now went from strength to strength. The whole nationalist movement was swinging over to constitutionalism. In Lombardy-Venetia, even the Mazzinian leader, Daniele Manin, the hero of the 1848 rising against the Austrians, gave support for unification under Victor Emmanuel shortly before his death in 1857. The flamboyant Garibaldi, who had been Mazzini's right hand man in 1848, offered his sword to Piedmont as its reputation for liberalism improved. Loyalty to Victor Emmanuel

grew stronger throughout the north Italian states, including the Austrian ones.

On the other hand, Mazzini lost support as fast as Cavour gained it. Indeed he sponsored the abortive rising of 1857 in Naples to prevent the loss of his republican followers to the monarchists of Turin. If the Bourbons had been defeated in the Two Sicilies, republicanism would have swept through the whole of Italy. After the miserable failure of this revolt, however, the Mazzinians, with their warm, romantic idealism, became a voice in the wilderness. Only success could succeed, and in the 1850s all the successes were Cavour's.

Cavour meanwhile continued trying to inveigle Napoleon into an alliance. '*Italia fara da se*' ('Italy will go it alone'), the slogan of 1848, had become outmoded, and Napoleon's help was essential for the attack on Austria. However, Cavour's hopes for an alliance were set back by the 'Orsini Plot'. One January evening in 1858, when Napoleon and the Empress Eugénie were on their way to the Paris Opera, they narrowly escaped assassination at the hands of an Italian refugee, Felice Orsini.

The concern of this most misunderstood of emperors for those injured by Orsini's bomb shows better aspects of his character than those stressed by critical historians. In the long run, Orsini's attempt actually helped the cause of unification. His appealing letters to the emperor, and his dignified call for help to Italy from his scaffold, increased French sympathy for the nationalists. After the first violent protests to Turin, Napoleon accepted his would-be murderer's advice to 'do something for Italy'. Cavour and he met secretly at the little resort of Plombières in July.

In fact neither Cavour nor Napoleon was interested in uniting Italy. Napoleon had no

wish to antagonize Pius IX, and Cavour shrank from having prosperous Piedmont saddled with the backward southern states. However, they agreed that after war with Austria, a kingdom of northern Italy should be formed, in exchange for which France was to gain Nice and Savoy. Princess Clotilde of Piedmont was to marry Napoleon's cousin. It was vaguely agreed that all Italy was to become a federation under the pope. Piedmont, however, was to go to war with Austria only on a pretext which would justify French intervention on her side. This conspiratorial bargain became the basis of a formal treaty in January 1859.

Cavour at once prepared to set Piedmont on a war footing. He floated new loans, had Garibaldi organize groups of guerrillas, and began to mass troops on the Lombard frontier. A much more difficult problem, however, was preventing Napoleon from changing his mind about the whole plan. As soon as the possibility of war became real, characteristically he began to talk vaguely in favour of an international conference on Italy. It had dawned on him that Paris bankers, and the conservative and clerical parties who supported him, were firmly opposed to French involvement.

Fortunately for Cavour, Napoleon's mind was made up for him by an Austrian blunder. In April Vienna delivered an ultimatum demanding Piedmontese disarmament. After it had been rejected, on the 26th, war was inevitable. Cavour's delight was expressed in his famous (and probably rehearsed) comment '*Alea iacta est*. [The die is cast.] We have made history – so now to dinner!' France dutifully entered the war against Austria.

When the French crossed the Alps and joined with the Piedmontese a month later, they were slightly outnumbered by an

Above, in March 1860 a plebiscite produced an overwhelming majority in Tuscany for annexation to Piedmont: here, Tuscan leaders are shown handing King Victor Emmanuel the statute of annexation. Museo Storico Topografico, Florence.

Left, the two Emperors – Napoleon III of France and Francis Joseph I of Austria – meet after the Battle of Solferino: the terms offered to Austria, despite her technical defeat, were relatively easy; she had to cede Lombardy but retained Venetia and thus a presence in the peninsula.

Opposite right, the Battle of Solferino, 24 June 1859. The truce concluded between France and Austria a few weeks afterwards led to Cavour's temporary retirement, though Italy's relations with France improved within a few months.

Opposite left, Italy and her neighbours during the Risorgimento: the kingdom of Italy was proclaimed in March 1861 after half a century of uprisings, and complete unification was attained in 1870.

Austrian army of 200,000 men. The first set battle of the war was at the small market town of Palestro, where the personal bravery of *il re galantuomo* was so striking that he was made an honorary corporal in Napoleon's zouaves. The Austrians fell back, and were defeated more decisively at Magenta. But although the allied monarchs rode into Milan in triumph, the Austrians under General Benedek simply fell back on the virtually impregnable fortresses of the Quadrilateral, which controlled the basin of the River Po.

They struck back at the French savagely on 24 June at Solferino, checking the advance of Mac-Mahon and the Piedmontese. Although this was one of the bloodiest battles of the century, and the tales of its slaughter prompted the foundation of the international Red Cross, it was in effect a draw. Control of northern Italy still lay in the balance.

The gentle Napoleon was horrified by the carnage he had witnesses. He was escorted vomiting from the battlefields of Magenta and Solferino. The imperial linen was even offered to augment first aid supplies. After Solferino, he took the first chance of making peace. In fact there were good reasons for the French to draw back. Mac-Mahon's shattered troops were unlikely to make much impression on the Quadrilateral. At home, anti-war feeling was growing – even the Empress Eugénie supported it. Prussia was moving forces up to the Rhine, to emphasize her leadership of the German states.

In Italy itself, the nationalists were doing rather better than Napoleon wished. In Tuscany, Cavour's agent, Ricasoli, deposed Grand Duke Leopold II in favour of a provisional government which offered the crown to Victor Emmanuel. Modena and Parma also fell to the rebels. Worst of all, the papal legate was forced to flee for his life from the Romagna. The rage of Napoleon's clerical supporters made it impossible for him to support Italian nationalism any further. In mid-July the French and Austrians signed the Peace of Villafranca. Napoleon and his army returned across the Alps hated by the Italian nationalists. They seemed to have deserted when the Austrians were on the verge of total defeat. Cavour's hopes for a kingdom of northern Italy had apparently come to nothing. He resigned and returned to his estates.

Cavour did not remain out of office for long. When he formed a new government early in 1860, however, French opinion, partly because of the stability of the provisional government in Tuscany, had changed. It was also clear that a restoration of the expelled rulers of the Italian states would be impossible. Secret negotiations between Cavour and Napoleon reopened, and it was agreed that Piedmont should expand into central Italy. Lombardy had already been given to her at Villafranca, and she was now to gain Parma, Modena and Tuscany. Savoy and Nice, however, were to go to France. Napoleon's condition was that these moves should be preceded by plebiscites to avoid the appearance of disregarding nationalist feelings. Naturally all the Italian population consulted declared overwhelmingly for union with Piedmont. In Savoy the ballot, whether rigged or otherwise, demanded annexation to France by 130,538 votes to 235, and the same decision was reached in Nice by 24,448 votes to 160.

Although the kingdom of Northern Italy was now declared it appeared that Napoleon had been well rewarded for his half-hearted pains. The remaining absolutist princes were appalled at the disregard for

471

the rights of their colleagues in the north and moved even further to the right. The papacy remained doggedly opposed to liberalism, perhaps partly because Napoleon had now moved over to attacking it. Soon after Villafranca he had sponsored a French pamphlet calling for the removal of the secular power of the Vatican.

In Naples, the Bourbon government was if anything even more wedded to its ancient traditions of reaction. Indeed northern and southern Italy might as well have been two separate countries. The north had become an industrial state characteristic of modern Europe. Its financiers and businessmen flourished and had a voice in the affairs of the state. But the kingdom of the Two Sicilies had changed little since the Middle Ages, its agriculture was still feudal, and it was quite without industry. Overseas trade and the modernizing contacts which went with it were also lacking.

Certainly, feudalism had been technically abolished in 1818, even on the island of Sicily itself. A small proportion of aristocratic land, and a number of church fiefs, had even been put on the market. But the peasantry, who lived by subsistence farming, had little money, and those who did buy holdings soon went bankrupt. The old feudal magnates at once moved in to buy land which had theoretically been confiscated from them.

In the end the system remained essentially unaltered, except that a few of the tiny Neapolitan middle class managed to buy land and began aping the ways of the aristocracy. Even in 1860, the miserable people of the Two Sicilies were dominated by a handful of backward-looking barons. Cavour would certainly have avoided liability for this archaic and poverty-stricken land if it had not been forced on him by the romantic nationalist Garibaldi.

Giuseppe Garibaldi

Garibaldi was fifty-four in 1860. In his teens he had been a sailor on the route to the Black Sea and the Levant. He left the sea out of enthusiasm for Mazzini's 'Young Italy' movement in the 1830s. After being condemned to death by Charles Albert, Victor Emmanuel's father, in the Piedmontese rising of 1834, he was pardoned and emigrated to South America. He fought for the insurgents of Rio Grande Province against the Braganza emperor, Dom Pedro I of Brazil. In the Uruguyan War of Independence against Argentina, which was eventually successful, he fought at the head of a battalion of Italian volunteers.

When the dramatic news of 1848 reached Uruguay, the Italian community in Montevideo collected money to send Garibaldi home, and he sailed for Europe with his young American wife, Anita Ribeiros. After fighting at first for his old enemy the House of Savoy, he went to the aid of the Mazzinian revolutionaries in Rome. When Pius IX was restored by Oudinot's French soldiers, he fled to New York, where he worked briefly as a candlemaker before going back to sea. His wife had died during the flight from Rome.

Garibaldi returned to Nice, the town where he had been born, in 1854. Like most Italian nationalists in these years, he came to see unification under Piedmont as being

the only realistic hope. He and his irregulars, the 'Hunters of the Alps', gave the war of 1859 a note of glamour which impressed all Europe. Next year he and his redshirted volunteers, the 'Thousand', prepared to sail for Sicily to assist a revolt against the Bourbon government. With little expectation that this would succeed, but glad to cause trouble in the south, Cavour helped to equip the expedition. However, its success was so dramatic that Piedmont became deeply involved in Naples and was eventually pushed into absorbing it.

Garibaldi landed at Marsala in May 1860. Although the peasants showed little enthusiasm and the landowners none, he had proclaimed Victor Emmanuel King of Italy and taken Palermo in a month. Unfortunately it was no easier for a liberal to improve the lot of the peasants than it had been for the Sicilian nobles. Their only interest was in land, and as the insurrection spread they rose savagely against their masters – just as the French peasants had done in 1789.

No concessions could stop civil war from spreading throughout Sicily. Not even Garibaldi had any brief for anarchy of this sort. The unfortunate aristocracy now saw the 'Thousand' as the only force which could save them, became nationalists overnight and flocked to the banner of Piedmont. Hundreds of bewildered peasants were shot or thrown into the dungeons of the Bourbons. Yet Garibaldi's advance continued through the island. Messina fell at the end of July, and the Redshirts prepared to cross the straits and threaten Naples itself.

Francis II, King of the Two Sicilies, wavered. He offered a new constitution to try to fob off the revolutionaries. However, he was probably not as frightened as Cavour, who had visions of an embarrassing Mazzinian revolution sweeping through the

south. He frantically ordered Garibaldi not to begin the advance on Naples. He dreaded a revolt in Rome which would bring foreign intervention.

Garibaldi's nationalism was much more uncompromising. With his romantic vision of ancient Italy reunified, diplomatic complications were meaningless. Nor did he see the difficulties of uniting north and south. Cavour did not want Naples, because his first concern was for Piedmont. Garibaldi did want it, since his first care was for Italy.

Garibaldi went ahead with his plans. He crossed the Straits of Messina, defeated the Austrians on the Volturno and sent Francis scuttling from his capital to Gaeta. Cavour now had to intervene. He soon gained the approval of Napoleon, who could easily be persuaded that anything was better than a republican Rome. Cavour's agents stirred

Above, Garibaldi's followers in action.

Top, Garibaldi's volunteers, the 'thousand', embarking for Sicily: they needed only three months to take the whole island. Museo del Risorgimento, Milan.

Top left, Giuseppe Garibaldi (1807–82): his romantic patriotic zeal did much to further Italian unification. Museo del Risorgimento, Milan.

Opposite top, the Neapolitan royal family attending a hunt: ruled by the house of Bourbon until 1860, when the city fell to Garibaldi, Naples was still an undeveloped feudal society, its economy and lifestyle quite remote from that of the industrializing north. Galleria d'Arte Moderna, Florence.

Opposite bottom, life in rural Sicily, as recorded by Chierici in his painting Gioie di una madre. Galleria d'Arte Moderna, Florence.

south. Cavour had never wanted it and knew that forging a new Italy from the disparate north and south would be as difficult as the tasks he had already accomplished. The Two Sicilies were far removed from the brave new world of the industrialized kingdom of Northern Italy.

Cavour died eleven weeks after his master had been proclaimed King of Italy. Even today, the slums of Naples show that the gigantic task he began has not been accomplished. In the 1880s and 1890s, hundreds of thousands of southern Italians flocked to the United States and Latin America in search of a better world. Joseph Conrad's novel *Nostromo* gives a fine picture of the life of such emigrant labourers.

At home, life in Naples and Sicily went from bad to worse. The romantic liberalism of Garibaldi's Redshirts had done very little for the southern peasantry. Although unification meant that the markets of northern businessmen expanded into the Two Sicilies, its economic needs were modest. Disgruntled merchants complained that the only things they could sell to the peasants were rosary beads. Southern life therefore had to be standardized to create a need for northern merchandise. The peasantry were ruthlessly taxed to pay the salaries of the officials who were to do this, yet gained few benefits from unification.

The first Italian governments, not surprisingly, were northern and shrank from spending money in an area with little business potential. As for the southern barons, their position was left all but untouched. They still controlled local government, and the new officials from Turin did little to help the peasants against their masters. In fact, the new government bought the loyalty of the magnates by guaranteeing their ownership of the land and their control over the peasants. Indeed they were net gainers from the revolution, since they had the assets to buy up land which Garibaldi in his sincerity had distributed among the peasants.

Although redistribution of land was begun again in 1861, with the compulsory breaking up of the greatest fiefs, the barons did what they had done after 1818 and quickly repossessed their land. The only difference was that they were now joined by

up rebellion in the papal states, and massed troops on its borders. On the pretext of defending liberal movements which the pope was attacking in Umbria, the Piedmontese then defeated the surprisingly stubborn papal army at Castelfidardo.

Meanwhile, Garibaldi had taken Naples. Cavour's army marched south to join him, carefully avoiding Rome itself. Although Garibaldi had at first said that he would hand Naples to Victor Emmanuel only if Rome was taken first, he handed over power to the Piedmontese army peacefully. After the inevitable plebiscites, which must have been meaningless in peasant areas at least, Naples, Sicily and the occupied areas of the Papal States were annexed by the kingdom of Northern Italy. The first parliament of all Italy met in Turin in February 1861. The following month it was announced that 'Victor Emmanuel II assumes for himself and his successors the title of King of Italy.'

The kingdom of Italy

The outlook for the new kingdom was not very bright. Though Cavour had taken his chances when they came, he had not wanted unification at this stage. He still had to pay the Piedmontese army and to complete his communications system. Pius IX remained steadfastly opposed to the new regime. Worst of all was the backwardness of the a sprinkling of rich middle-class business-men, many of them northern. They too found it easy to cheat the simple and usually illiterate peasantry, who found themselves perilously placed tenant farmers – exactly the position they had occupied since the tenth century. Not only this, but all classes in the south had to meet national taxes geared to the prosperity of Italy as a whole and unrelated to their small means.

The hope of industrializing the south under the new regime soon faded. What tiny amounts of capital were available were leeched off to the north, for no corresponding return. Little was spent on communications and irrigation in Naples and Sicily, where they were most needed. Perhaps worst of all, the self-confident north soon removed tariff barriers which were essential for the protection of infant industries in the south. Low-priced imports now came not only from Piedmont and Tuscany but from Britain and France. The modest family and craft concerns of Naples were destroyed.

Disillusionment with the government of united Italy partly explains the prevalence of banditry as a way of life in the mountain areas of the south. There is a great deal of glamour about our modern picture of the Sicilian bandit. But this does not hide the fact that he was often a man who had found that even with the utmost initiative it was not possible to make a living within the limits laid down by well-heeled officials from Turin. Although there was no leadership to mount a real organized resistance, the bandits were also encouraged by Bourbon agents trying to disrupt the government of the new nation. Indeed the latter was often goaded into clumsy measures of repression, which made the bandits public heroes and bred violent hatred of the north. Italy was not able to solve the problem of Naples in the nineteenth century.

Rome and Venice

After Cavour's death, his successors continued the policy of centralization in the north. But all their efforts could not hide the fact that Turin was not the natural capital of Italy. The country could only be fully united from the centre, from Rome, which was still occupied by a French garrison determined to defend Pius IX's rights. There was also the haunting fear that Garibaldi or some other extremist might do something rash to create a crisis over Rome or the *Italia irridenta* still under Austrian control.

After Garibaldi had been narrowly prevented from invading the Austrian Trentino, in the north, by the personal order of Victor Emmanuel, he gathered a group of alarmingly determined volunteers in Palermo and attacked Rome in August 1862. Although he was captured by the Italian army before he was able to attack the French, his expedition seriously compromised the new

Piedmontese government of Rattazzi at home and abroad. Successive governments fell, and after long negotiations with Napoleon a temporary Roman settlement was reached. The French agreed to a staged withdrawal of their troops, while the Italians were to symbolize their renunciation of Rome by moving their capital from Turin to Florence.

Although the deal over Rome horrified nationalists throughout the country – not least those of Turin – they were more encouraged by gains made in 1866 by the government of La Marmora, the hero of the war of 1859. Part of Bismarck's preparation for war against Austria had been to ensure that France would stay neutral by an agreement made at Biarritz. To guarantee trouble for the Austrians on their southern frontier, he also formed an alliance with the Italians. But although Bismarck crushed the Austrians easily, Victor Emmanuel's troops were heavily defeated at Custozza and the little Italian navy destroyed off Venice, at Lissa. The only successful actions in this disastrous war were the skirmishes led by the inevitable Garibaldi on the borders of Venetia. Nevertheless, at the Peace of Vienna a much-humbled Austria, with a very ill grace, disgorged Venetia. After the usual plebiscite, it became Italian.

But Italy had not yet been united, even by the end of 1866. Rome was still in the clutches of Pius IX, or Pio 'No, No!', as the London *Times* called him. In the north-west, Vienna still controlled Trieste and the Trentino. Naples and Sicily were still not fully subdued. During the war Palermo itself had revolted against the oppression of its overlords in the north.

The Roman problem seemed insoluble. The functions of church and state in the Holy See were bewilderingly interwoven.

Above, voting in Naples during the plebiscite held in October 1860 on annexation to the kingdom of Italy: the vote in favour was practically unanimous. Private Collection.

Opposite right, Garibaldi's triumphant entry into Naples, 7 September 1860: in political manoeuverings during the weeks after the fall of Naples, Garibaldi failed to retain power in the south and had to abandon his hopes of a march on Rome.

Opposite left, painting by Ignazio Alfani of one of Garibaldi's Redshirts departing for battle. Museo del Risorgimento, Florence.

While the Italian government were debating the niceties of this situation, Garibaldi again raised the standard of revolt in Rome itself, in September 1867. Garibaldi was captured and, as usual, sent back to Caprera. However, he escaped in time to fight against a French division which was landed at Città Vecchia, forty miles north of Rome. They defeated and captured him at Mentana. Although European opinion turned very much against Napoleon's intervention, the French garrison remained in Rome.

Within Italy, the republicans were beginning to gain ground. Opinion was turning very much against a régime which would do nothing for Rome. It is even doubtful whether the kingdom of Italy would have survived if it had not been handed to Rome by the crisis of the Franco-Prussian War of 1870. The French garrison was withdrawn for other duties, and Napoleon was deposed. Victor Emmanuel could argue that he had no obligations to the new Third Republic.

The Italian army swept into Rome in September. Pio Nono made no consessions and considered himself a prisoner in the Vatican until his death in 1878. Indeed it was only with the Lateran Treaty of 1929 that Italian difficulties with the papacy were settled through the creation of the Vatican City State. Again, Trieste and the Trentino remained Austrian until 1918. But in 1870 Rome declared sweepingly for unification with the rest of Italy. The House of Sardinia-Piedmont now ruled over a united country from the capital of the Caesars.

Germany

German unification was to change the course of European history even more dramatically than the emergence of the kingdom of Italy. The Battle of Sedan, which had given the Italians the chance to seize Rome, upset the balance of power in the West. The traditional Europe had been dominated on land by France and Austria and at sea by Britain. It was replaced by a new state system, with the massive land power of united Germany precariously balanced against Britain and her continental allies. This balance survived until the disaster of 1914 and re-emerged under Hitler. After the Second World War, yet another system of international relations took its place, Soviet Russia replacing Germany as the main threat to the other countries of Europe.

After the failure of the 1848 revolutions, Germany, like Italy, remained as disunited as she had been since the Middle Ages. However, the number of independent states left had been reduced to thirty-eight, and all were members of an extremely weak confederation. Its nominal head was the Habsburg emperor of Austria, and all states sent members to a central though powerless diet or parliament in Frankfurt. Certainly German liberals had developed a sense of common nationality. But the individual princes,

from the emperor in Vienna downwards, were jealous of their privileges. All resented Austrian domination, but this did not mean that they would listen to any plans which would threaten the integrity of their little statelets.

As in Italy, the 1848 failure had disillusioned the intellectuals who had led it. They drifted away from republicanism towards the strongest power which had shown any liberal inclinations – Prussia. Even here, hopes of success were low. After 1848 Austrian pressure had brought all the German states, including Prussia, into line against liberalism. Frederick William I was now an old man. The Prussian government was controlled by mediocre and thoroughly conservative ministers. Although second only to Austria within Germany, Prussia was still a second-rate power.

Yet the groundwork of future Prussian greatness was being laid. More than any of the neighbouring states, Prussia had gained from the *Zollverein* or German Customs Union. Formed under Prussian domination, this had defeated all other attempts to create free trade areas within Germany by the end of 1833, after which most of the other states joined it. Key seaports like Hamburg, however, remained outside. More significantly, Austria remained aloof and was excluded even when the *Zollverein* was re-organized and strengthened in 1853. Prussian businessmen were given the opportunity of extending their interests throughout a wider area of Germany, and industrialization was speeded up. Another important effect of the union was that the

German railway system came to be centred on Berlin, a factor which was eventually to give Prussia considerable advantages in time of war.

During the decades before German unification, quite apart from the *Zollverein*, industrialization went on apace. The contry's vast mineral resources were tapped, and production was revolutionized by complexes like that of the great ironmaster Alfred Krupp. Britain was no longer the only country with an industrial landscape. Germany was not spared the ugliness of industrialization, the dirt of its sombre factories and the misery of its poorest workers.

However, German society adapted readily. The hard-working middle classes were quick to adopt new methods, quick to reinvest their profits, and quick to make their businesses large and modern enough to compete with any others in the world. Even the solid, old-fashioned *Junkers*, who had ruled the villages and countryside of Prussia since the Middle Ages, were affected. They began to invest the profits from their land in industry or look for easier profits underneath it. Trade was not looked down on by the north German aristocracy, in spite of the Prussian love of military display, and industrialization was all the easier for it.

Prussia's modernization was encouraged by its ruling house, the Hohenzollerns. William I came to the throne in 1861, at the age of sixty-four. Not an original man, the new king was a competent administrator and, like most of his family, devoted to the army. The Berlin government was heavily

weighted towards soldiers, and the equivalent of secretary of state was the military strategist von Moltke, the uncle of the general of the First World War. In 1862, however, the government faced serious opposition to its plans for extending conscription from two to four years. It fell in September. The Kaiser's new prime minister was Count Otto von Bismarck.

Although Bismarck became the greatest diplomatic genius of the century, he was the most human of statesmen. Apart from unifying Germany, he invented his own favourite drink, the black velvet, a mixture of champagne and stout. The most important man in Europe was also a man whose unreasonable greed for pickled herrings made his old age a hell of indigestion. He was born in 1815, into a good Brandenburg *junker* family. They had always been modest landowners, with generations of service in the Hohenzollern armies behind them. Bismarck's sophisticated mother was an exception for a Bismarck wife, and her experiments in Berlin salon life had very nearly ruined the family by the time her son Otto came of age.

He was a strange mixture of brilliance and eccentricity. One moment he would be a great hearty giant of a man, the next an obnoxious and moody bore. Athletic and startlingly clever when he chose to work hard, he was proud of being a *junker* and proud of being a Prussian. As a young man he was known as a madcap, a fearless horseman and a massive drinker, and yet he worked frantically to set his family's affairs in order and pay off his mother's debts.

There was not the slightest trace of the revolutionary about Bismarck. Like other landowners, his main interest was in preserving the position of his estates, his class and his country. He opposed emancipation of the Jews and saw the vicious Prussian game laws as a bastion of society. No doubt it was because of his conservatism that he became a member of the united Prussian Diet in 1847. In the same year he married his gentle Lutheran wife Johanna von Puttkamer.

Bismarck lost no time in earning a reputation as an arch-reactionary. He struggled for counter-revolution in 1848. Bismarck had little sense of German nationality. He always thought in terms of Prussia annexing the other German states rather than true unification. But he was not foolish about his patriotism. When Austria humiliated Prussia in the Olmütz agreement of 1854, he spoke very sensibly against the hotheads who wanted to march on Vienna forthwith. He shared the feeling that honour was worthless for its own sake with his master Frederick William and was rewarded well for his loyalty. He was Prussian delegate to the weak Frankfurt Diet throughout the 1850s and then became ambassador successively to St Petersburg and Paris.

Later Bismarck made full use of the experience these posts gave him. He realized that Austria was the real obstacle to Prussian supremacy in Germany. He also had an opportunity to work out the way in which Napoleon's dreaminess laid him open to being duped by talk of liberalism and nationalism. He himself was not troubled

Above, the Krupps works in the mid-nineteenth century.

Opposite, 1852 cartoon from Kladderadatsch *(the German satirical journal) showing Prussia trying to persuade recalcitrant non-members to join the* Zollverein.

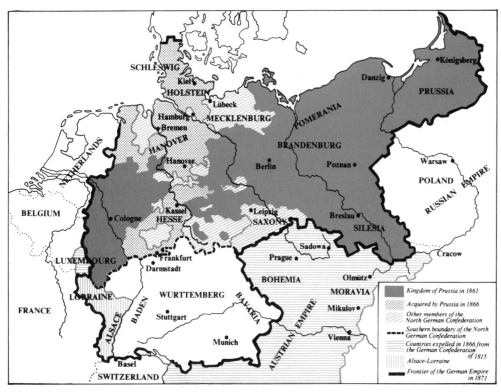

by platitudes of this sort. A real opportunist, his political life was never hampered by any set of ideals.

His first concern was his own career, his second the welfare of the Hohenzollerns and his third the greatness of Prussia. For the sake of all three objectives, he turned his powerful mind towards bringing Germany under the overlordship of Berlin. Unification for him had nothing to do with progress or change. He feared and hated both, though he would use their supporters when he could. Because of his flexibility, he was able to dupe those more idealistic than himself and seize all possible opportunities of increasing Prussian power.

Strangely enough, Bismarck hated force. He may have spoken about blood and iron, but he detested the clumsiness of actually using them. Yet he knew that his brilliant diplomacy would only be effective if backed by real military power, and he knew that this military power would eventually have to be used or the impregnable position he wanted for Prussia could not be gained without it.

His real genius appeared not in fighting wars against Denmark, Austria and France but in outmanoeuvring those who might have objected to such wars. His first task was to leave Austria without friends outside Germany. He won the regard of Russia by appearing as the only European statesman willing to help in the tsar's savage repression of the Polish revolt of 1863. After the Convention of Alvensleben, where Bismarck agreed not to give sanctuary to any refugees from Poland, he could rely on Russian friendship. France and Italy were the other two powers which might have been expected to object to Prussia's taking over German leadership from Austria. We have already seen how Napoleon was won over

at Biarritz and La Marmora persuaded to join in the war which led to the disasters of Custozza and Lissa.

Schleswig-Holstein

War with Austria eventually broke out over rival claims to the Danish duchies of Schleswig and Holstein. Both belonged to the Danish royal family but contained substantial German minorities anxious to join the German Confederation. When Christian IX was crowned in Copenhagen in 1864, he created a European crisis by announcing that he intended to incorporate Schleswig, Germans and all, into Denmark. Austria and Prussia together attacked the Danes on behalf of the German Confederation, and Christian was forced to give up both duchies. They were temporarily put under joint Austro-Prussian control.

Probably Bismarck had not thought out the implications of this situation. However, when he attempted to discredit Austria by questioning her administration of Schleswig, Vienna accepted the challenge. Francis Joseph had now promised Venetia to the Italians and thought they would not fight. The past record of the Habsburg army was good, and the southern German princes resented Prussian control of the *Zollverein* and suspected Bismarck's intrigues. It was Austria, not Prussia, which declared the war which would decide who was to lead Germany.

The Austrians had underestimated the brilliance of von Moltke and his army. Prussian discipline was splendid, and Austrian territory was invaded with bewildering speed. The power of the Habsburgs was smashed once and for all on 3 July 1866 outside the Bohemian town of Sadowa. The

news of the Austrian collapse galvanized Europe. Although Napoleon moved troops up to the Rhine, he could not act decisively on behalf of Austria when he had pledged himself so often to support liberalism and the rights of nationalities. Italy herself was crushed at Custozza, the British admired the Prussians and were unlikely to intervene in far-off Eastern Europe, while Russia had been bought off at Alvensleben. Bismarck was left to make peace in his own way.

In fact the Peace of Prague was most statesmanlike. Bismarck realized that a humiliated Austria would become an even more bitter enemy of future Prussian ambitions. The Habsburgs only lost their stake in the duchies and Venetia, both of which were commitments they could well do without. However, Prussia's gains within Germany were enormous. She absorbed Hanover, Schleswig, Holstein, Frankfurt, Nassau and Hesse. The weak confederation was swept away.

With Austrian power broken, Bismarck was also able to form a North German Confederation, under Frederick William's presidency, including all the states north of the River Main. As president, the King of Prussia was to appoint a chancellor – Bismarck – and to be advised by a council consisting of the rulers of the various states. A central parliament or Reichstag was to be elected by universal suffrage. Economically, this was a great advance over the *Zollverein*, since control of currency and trade was to rest with the central government. Other aspects of policy, like foreign policy and control of army and navy establishments, were centralized, although the sovereign states still dealt with internal affairs. Apart from the confederation, twenty-five million Germans were now ruled from Berlin.

The French response

Napoleon III, as he gazed across the Rhine and the Main to Berlin, was alarmed by what he saw. His efforts to construct a nationalist Europe had simply set the

Above, Field-Marshal Helmuth von Moltke (1800–91): he served in the Prussian Army for 66 years, becoming Chief of the General Staff in 1857, and was responsible for the successful campaigns against Denmark, Austria and France in 1864, 1866 and 1870 that led to unification.

Above left, the Battle of Custozza, Lombardy, 24 June 1866, at which Austrian forces, led by the Archduke Albrecht, defeated the Italians, allies of Prussia: Austria's victory brought her no benefits.

Left, Prussian troops advancing at the Battle of Sadowa, 3 July 1866, the chief battle of the Austrian-Prussian war: peace was signed three weeks later, and from now Prussia replaced Austria as the major central European power.

Below left, William I (1797–1888), King of Prussia from 1861 and Emperor of a united Germany from 1871, opening the Reichstag of the North German Confederation: the Confederation, formed in 1867, which Bismarck governed as Chancellor (the two assemblies had little power), was a union of virtually all Germany north of the River Mainz so designed to facilitate the membership later of the southern German states. Prussia was the dominant power.

Opposite right, Otto von Bismarck (1815–98), as portrayed in a photograph taken in 1863: Chief Minister of Prussia from 1862 and Imperial Chancellor from 1871 to 1890, he was a dominant figure in German unification and also in the establishment after 1870 of Germany as a world power.

Opposite left, Germany in the mid-nineteenth century.

Hohenzollerns in place of the Habsburgs as a threat to French security. His response was a written demand for territory to compensate France for Prussian gains. Bismarck (in private) contemptuously dismissed the note as an 'innkeeper's bill' and sat back to let the unhappy Napoleon make a fool of himself in the eyes of Europe. Although he at first did this with the simple intention of weakening French prestige as much as possible, he delightedly saw Napoleon's blunders push the south German states into alignment with Prussia.

First Napoleon asked successively for the Rhineland and part of Belgium but was assured their cession was politically impossible. Finally he lowered his sights to trying to buy Luxembourg from the King of Holland. The grand duke at once appealed to the North German Confederation, and Prussian detachments were moved in to support him. Bismarck took good care to make Napoleon's floundering public, and the German states became united in hostility to France. The most which was conceded was a guarantee of Luxembourg's neutrality and the withdrawal of Prussian troops.

· In his old age Bismarck recorded that he avoided a war at this time because, although he had decided that a conflict with France would be essential to unification, he wished to give his military reforms time to make the Prussian army unbeatable. But it is not likely that he thought of war or even unification until 1870. By then Napoleon's extraordinary bungles had left all the German princes clamouring for Prussia to lead them to battle. Bismarck then seized the opportunity of destroying the French threat on the Rhine, annexing the border states for his master the King of Prussia and thus 'unifying Germany'.

To do him justice, Bismarck did ensure that the Prussian army became the most efficient fighting machine in Europe. Arms were poured into Berlin's new dependencies and the increasingly friendly states of southern Germany. The French were much worse off. Recruitment had dropped, while conscription did not affect the rich and faced serious public opposition. Plans for mobilization were antiquated and ineffective. It was probably because they knew this that the general staff put so much pressure on Napoleon to guarantee the Rhine frontier against Prussian expansion. Indeed they were frightened and second-rate men compared with Bismarck's purposeful generals. Occasional reforming officers like Marshal Niel, who tried to reorganize the weak National Guard while war minister, ran up against solid opposition in the purblind Corps Législatif.

The pressures on Napoleon to bluster against Prussia were increased by the unstable nature of French politics. The empire was under heavy attack from the republicans and in May 1870 granted a new constitution. Control of affairs had really passed out of Napoleon's hands. He is something of a

tragic figure in these last months of the régime, ill, muddled and scared. All his advisers misjudged the real power of Prussia. The Empress Eugénie, the new prime minister, Émile Ollivier, the foreign minister, the Duke of Gramont, all gave the wrong advice to a man who was incapable of making up his mind for himself. The Second Empire faced its last crisis without decisive leadership.

The French response to the 'Hohenzollern Candidacy' for the throne of Spain gave Bismarck the chance to fight a war on exactly the terms he wanted. After the 'Glorious Revolution' of 1868 sent the Bourbons into exile from Madrid, the liberals led by General Juan Prim y Prats began what the Spanish press called a 'lottery of kings'. The Kaiser's cousin Leopold von Hohenzollern announced he would become a candidate in June 1870. Gramont, for once with the support of all parties, announced belligerently that France would consider foreign control of the Spanish crown a threat to her security.

However, the Kaiser, who had always been opposed to harrying the French through Madrid, eventually persuaded Leopold to withdraw. Matters would have ended there if Napoleon's final stroke of folly had not given Bismarck the opportunity he wanted. The Kaiser was on holiday in the Rhineland resort of Ems when Benedetti, the French ambassador, brought him a demand from Paris that Prussia should humiliate herself by refusing to renew the candidacy. He replied politely that he approved of the withdrawal and had nothing to add to it.

Bismarck had never dreamt the French would play into his hands in this way. He at once published an edited version of Kaiser Wilhelm's telegram telling him of Benedetti's demands. The 'Ems telegram' brought the countries to the brink of war. Its text

gave the impression that the ambassador and the Kaiser had exchanged mutual insults in an interview which closed with Benedetti being refused a further audience.

Ollivier at once moved towards war, which he announced he could now wage lightheartedly (d'un coeur léger). France declared war against Prussia on 19 July. Not even the wildest optimist in Germany could have expected France to take on this responsibility. She had no allies while the Prussians had no enemies. Even Alexander II had been friendly with the Hohenzollerns since the Kaiser entertained him at Ems in May.

Sedan

The Franco-Prussian War surprised Europe not by being so short but by not being even shorter. Although Leboeuf, the French war minister, reassured doubters by claiming that his preparations were complete down to the last gaiter-button, more important aspects of planning had unfortunately been neglected. The first French troops at the front were outnumbered two to one. The famous French *chassepôt* was as good as the German rifles, but unfortunately Leboeuf had not ensured that all his men had one. The German artillery was immensely superior. Worst of all, the French General Staff had no member who could match the brilliance of von Moltke.

His first army pushed a French army led by Mac-Mahon, the hero of the war of 1859, out of Alsace. A second army under von Moltke's own leadership advanced towards the great fortress at Metz, routing five army corps under General Bazaine. They re-formed in Metz itself, and the Germans surrounded the city. Thanks to Bazaine's half heartedness – or treachery – this French army of 173,000 remained out of action until the end of the war.

However, Mac-Mahon had redeployed round Châlons and might have presented the Prussians with a serious threat if the dithering Napoleon had not arrived at the front to direct the French defence. He ordered Mac-Mahon to try to relieve Metz, the very plan which was easiest for the Germans to counter. The rescuing forces were themselves surrounded by the Germans at Sedan, on the Meuse. After two attempts to break through the German ring, Napoleon offered to surrender on 2 September. The emperor became a German prisoner, and Moltke and the Kaiser marched unopposed towards Paris. Seventeen days later, they had placed the capital under siege. It appeared that the war had practically come to an end.

In fact France had not yet been defeated, although the fall of the empire had become inevitable. The Third Republic was proclaimed in Paris the day that news of the surrender at Sedan arrived. After tentative attempts to open negotiations with Bismarck, the provisional government's minister of the interior, Léon Gambetta, set about placing France on a footing of all-out national warfare.

On 7 October he himself left Paris by balloon, to sail across the German lines and rally support in the provinces. He and the Bonapartist d'Aurelle de Paladines formed a new army on the Loire and regained Orléans, while General Faidherbe checked the rather surprised Germans in the north.

Although Gambetta never managed to lift the siege of Paris, and Bazaine remained ineffectively cooped up in Metz, France's temporary recovery was startling. It could not last. The two sections of Gambetta's Loire army were defeated at Loigny and Le Mans, and the heroic Faidherbe at Saint-Quentin. In Paris itself, the Germans did not bother to waste men in a frontal attack, but simply sat down and waited for surrender. In the end the poorest Parisians genuinely faced starvation, while even the most fashionable restaurants were reduced to feeding their patrons on the inmates of the Tuileries Zoo. Paris could not have lasted much longer even if Bismarck had not ordered a bombardment which claimed 400 civilian casualties.

On 23 January 1871, Jules Favre, the Republican foreign minister, began to negotiate an armistice. When a new National Assembly was called, it declared overwhelmingly for peace and appointed the veteran statesman Adolphe Thiers as its plenipotentiary or 'Chief of the Executive Power' in negotiating with Germany. Meanwhile, Paris itself was on the verge of revolting to form the 'Commune'. In March radical rebels, some of them socialists, seized the city. Late in May Mac-Mahon, himself a thinly disguised royalist, reconquered it block by block against bitter resistance. Indeed the Third Republic's first task at home was the bloody suppression of the 'communards' in its own capital.

The Peace of Frankfurt

Since unification of Germany had suddenly become a practical possibility, Bismarck had to make peace on the terms which would make that unification as smooth as

possible. Anxious to appear as the protector of the southern German states, he could easily argue from Napoleon's erratic behaviour that Germany's neighbour was violent, greedy and irresponsible. Germany thus had to gain a frontier which would make French attack impossible (or, alternatively, make a German attack on France easy). This was why Bismarck demanded that the peace of Germany should be guaranteed by giving her the area on the left bank of the Rhine round the fortresses of Strasbourg and Metz. He argued that in German hands these would be used defensively, as a guarantee of peace. He warned Prussian diplomatic officials, somewhat unconvincingly, that 'in twenty wars we have never been the aggressors against France, and we claim nothing from her but the security she has so often threatened.' The beauty of this standpoint was that its appeal to the south German states made the prospect of unification under Prussia a reality.

When the final peace settlement was signed at Frankfurt in May, Alsace-Lorraine

Left, William I, General von Moltke and Bismarck in the Prussian lines during the siege of Paris: Paris did not prove an easy target as the imperial armies had expected and withstood a siege from 19 September 1870 to 28 January 1871, its population facing starvation and, from early January, nightly bombardment.

Centre, William I, King of Prussia, is proclaimed Emperor of Germany in the Hall of Mirrors in the Palace of Versailles, 18 January 1871, the final scene in Prussia's long struggle to control a united Germany.

Bottom, Jules Favre, foreign minister of France, and Otto von Bismarck signing the Treaty of Frankfurt, 10 May 1871. Under the Treaty France ceded Alsace and most of Lorraine to Germany and agreed to pay an indemnity of five billion francs; the former provision provided a lasting grievance, the second was met within a few years.

Opposite, painting by Adolph von Menzel of William I, King of Prussia, leaving to join the army in the field, 31 July 1870: within six months he had been crowned emperor of a newly united Germany. Nationalgalerie, Staatliche Museen Preussischer Kulturbesitz, Berlin.

was ceded to Germany, and it was agreed that German troops were to remain in eastern France until an enormous indemnity of 5,000 million francs was paid. The disgrace of these losses was keenly felt in France. The Mayor of Strasbourg died of shock on hearing the news of the peace. Although the people of Alsace-Lorraine were given the option of taking French citizenship, relatively few did so. Far more became settlers in Napoleon's great colony, Algeria. Later the *colons* became the most French of French exiles. Although Alsace and Lorraine were duly absorbed into the Second Reich, Bismarck's mistake was not to see that this ultimate humiliation would produce a France unlikely to rest until it had reversed the Peace of Frankfurt. This was one reason why the Europe he constructed slid so easily into the First World War.

The new German Empire was not very liberal and not very nationalistic. Even in the Catholic south, German life was standardized on a Prussian model, not a true German one. Although a constitution was granted, power remained where it had always been in Prussia, with the small class of *junkers* under the Hohenzollerns, themselves the principal *junker* family. But Bismarck had taken his chances and made Prussia the greatest power on the continent. The German princes were united under the Hohenzollerns on Hohenzollern terms because of the enormous success of the Peace of Frankfurt. It was no accident that the Second Reich was proclaimed on 18 January 1871 in the *Galérie des Glaces* of the Palace of Versailles, at a point when it was clear that France would give all the concessions necessary to win over the German princes to Prussia.

Even so, the organization of the empire in the preceding months had perhaps been Bismarck's most difficult task. He himself had probably wished to avoid a union with the decadent popish south when the war broke out, and although his own ideas changed during the autumn by no means all German rulers wished to bind themselves to Prussia. Several princelings, particularly the more powerful rulers of Baden, Würtemburg and Bavaria, proved stubborn about surrendering their privileges. Louis II of Bavaria was only won over by being allowed to retain control over his army, post office and railways. He also gained a secret pension of £20,000 per year (taken from the revenues of the exiled King of Hanover) and a promise that the Bavarian brewing industry would be protected by a reduced duty.

The greatest problem of all was to win over the Kaiser. He was unimpressed by the new-fangled idea of becoming Emperor of Germany. His interests were Prussian and not German, and unlike Bismarck he saw no reason for disguising Prussian greatness with the fiction of a nationalist empire. He distrusted popular power and was only converted when Bismarck managed to persuade Louis of Bavaria to write to him on behalf of the princes of Germany begging him to accept the crown. Even at the ceremony in the *Galérie des Glaces* he shook hands with all the dignitaries present except Bismarck. The chancellor had had him proclaimed as 'Emperor William' instead of 'Emperor of Germany', a subtle difference which avoided the implication of true kingly power over Germany.

The balance sheet

Ten years before, no one had dreamt that Piedmont would unite Italy or that Prussia would unite Germany. Neither Bismarck nor Cavour had been an exception. Their early aims had been limited but had expanded as the weaknesses or blunders of other powers gave them opportunities to increase their strength, which they faultlessly seized. The result was the emergence of the united countries German and Italian liberals wanted, although they were ruled respectively by soldiers and businessmen rather than by intellectuals.

For Europe as a whole, the result of the rise of Germany and Italy was revolutionary. Unfortunately Bismarck's successors failed to see that he had used force in 1870 as an adjunct to his diplomacy. Since they still possessed the world's finest fighting organization, they fell back on using it to gain whatever they wanted. This was the more dangerous since France also looked forward to the war of revenge which would give her back Alsace-Lorraine. The result was the war of 1914.

Although greatly different, both Germany and Italy gave new opportunities to industry and to the rising middle classes. The businesses which profited from the large new national markets mass-produced more and more new inventions. Many of their products were later sold in the widening markets of Asia and Africa. Partly for this reason, partly because of the desire for prestige connected with very new nationhood, Germany eventually began the 'scramble for Africa'. Italy also came to play a part in annexing territory overseas. At the same time, the expansion of the working class at home produced new social theories which brought the industrial states to the verge of revolution.

Chapter 41

The Modernization of Europe

Europe changed dramatically in the later nineteenth century. Nationalism upset the traditional relations between its states, and imperialism eventually extended its rule throughout the world. Neither, however, had effects as far-reaching as developments in industrial and intellectual life. As industrialization speeded up, in old and new nations alike, business units increased in size. Europe moved into the age of trusts, cartels and monopoly capitalism. Its need for machinery also gave an immense stimulus to inventiveness. The scientific and technological revolutions had even more startling results than the industrial one.

By 1900, modern medicine, electrical power and even the petrol engine, were accepted as part of European daily life. But at the same time as scientists were meeting the needs of the business world, it was creating new forces which would challenge it. Industry required labour, and as its workers were gathered together in Europe's growing cities they began to consider new theories of society which rejected the capitalist system which employed them. Karl Marx is as much a figure of the nineteenth century as Count Cavour.

Sir Lewis Namier, one of the greatest historians of our century, has called 1848 the year of the revolution of the intellectuals. These intellectuals were defeated by monarchists throughout Europe. The result was profound disillusionment with the hope of changing the social and political structure from within. It now seemed more realistic to abandon piecemeal reform. There was an increase in the numbers of socialists, who planned to substitute the rule of the community for the rule of kings and capitalists alike.

The most advanced of them, Karl Marx, tried to apply the laws of science to his interpretation of society. His *Communist Manifesto* was actually issued during the 1848 revolutions and thereafter rapidly made converts. Marx's prophecy that proletarian revolution would erupt throughout the world still remains to be fulfilled, but his theories of class structure have deeply affected all the modern 'social sciences'. Some disillusioned intellectuals went even further than Marx and abandoned the study of society and its ills completely. Some even joined the ranks of the great scientists and inventors of the nineteenth century. Their discoveries made changes in the life of the West – and the world – which had never been dreamt of by the men of 1848.

The physical sciences

By the nineteenth century, most elements known to modern science had been discovered. The next task was to classify them. In 1869 this was done by the Russian researcher Dmitri Ivanovich Mendeleev. He was of Siberian birth, the fourteenth son of a schoolteacher, and rose to be professor of chemistry at the University of St Petersburg. It was already known that matter was composed of atoms grouped into molecules of different formations, in turn linked in varying ways. Mendeleev grouped the elements according to their atomic weights ranging from the lightest (hydrogen) to the heaviest (mercury). This classification provided the groundwork for modern chemistry and may have been the most important work by a nineteenth-century scientist.

Equally significant progress was soon made by physicists. The whole field of astrophysics had been opened by the research of two German scientists, Kirchhoff and Bunsen. In their research on the physical properties of light, they developed the technique of spectrum analysis, which in turn was applied to chemistry. This not only made it possible to locate elements like rubidium but also led to the discovery of helium in the matter composing the sun before it had been isolated on earth.

In 1850, another German, Rudolf Clausius, who became professor of chemistry at Berlin at the age of twenty-eight, demonstrated the connection between heat and energy. His findings were supported by William Thomson, Lord Kelvin, the foremost British scientist of the age. In 1861–2, another Scot, James Maxwell, professor of physics at Aberdeen and later London, postulated the electromagnetic nature of light. Twenty years later the existence of the electromagnetic waves of which he had written was experimentally proven, and the discovery was eventually applied to radio transmission. Modern organic chemistry had been founded by the research of the French scientist Jean Baptiste Dumas on the chemistry of the alcohols. The next step was to apply all these advances to industry.

Biology and medicine

The nineteenth century also saw advances in biology and medicine, as both were taken into the laboratory. The theories of Claude Bernard first suggested that the body represented a complete and interdependent mechanism, to which experimentation could be applied as successfully as in any other branch of science.

Above, Robert Bunsen (1811–99), who, in addition to his pioneering work with Gustav Kirchhoff on spectrum analysis, can claim credit for several inventions, among them a galvanic battery and the Bunsen burner.

Opposite, French cartoon of 1870 showing Bismarck's dominant position in Europe.

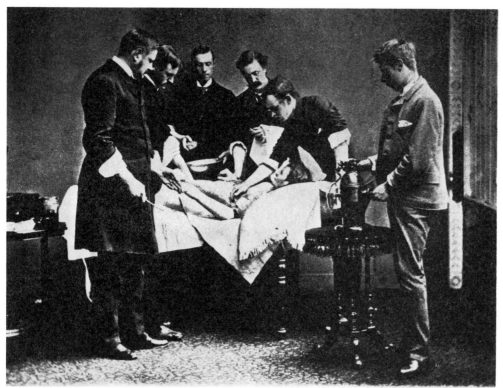

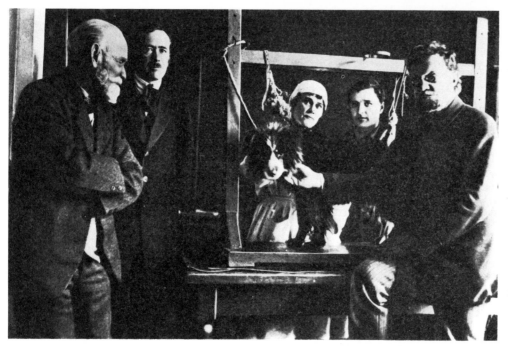

worked from the classification of species carried out by the great eighteenth-century Swedish naturalist Carl Linnaeus, Darwin rejected his assumption that the species were immutable and had been created in their current form.

Darwin argued that life had begun at the lowest possible level and that only those species which had come to terms with their environment had survived. This constituted his law of survival of the fittest, which governed the selection process by which humanity had emerged as the highest form of existence. In turn, not all humans would survive. Influenced by the gloomy theories of Thomas Malthus, Darwin was obsessed by the thought that as population outstripped world resources only the fittest would manage to survive. But it was not a pleasant thought to be descended from an ape, or something worse. Darwin was ostracized. Churchmen throughout the world were horrified and wrote learned treatises to defend the biblical account of the seven-day creation.

They had little success in refuting Darwin's startling heresy. The revolution in scientific attitudes went on apace. However, the discoveries which would have made Darwin's case unassailable went unnoticed. The researches of Gregor Mendel, a monk from Moravia in Czechoslovakia, were only recognized in 1900. Mendel had spent the years between 1858 and 1866 studying generation after generation of garden pea plants. He discovered that their hereditary characteristics appeared at set intervals between generations.

From this he was able to evolve 'Mendel's Laws' on heredity. Not only plants but animals and humans transmitted their characteristics by heredity, these characteristics changing slowly to meet new conditions in the way Darwin had suggested. Thirty years later the Dutch scientist Hugo de Vries discovered Mendel's work and confirmed his findings. The science of genetics had been founded.

At the same time, Pavlov's dogs were making history. This Russian biologist found that once they were accustomed to having a bell rung immediately before feeding time, the dogs salivated on hearing the bell even when no food was forthcoming. This research produced the theory of 'conditioned reflexes', which was the first step towards the development of psychology as we know it.

Also towards the end of the century, Sigmund Freud and his English popularizer Havelock Ellis began to write on the psychology of sex and the importance of sexual motivation in human behaviour. Since it could be argued that psychological as well as physical characteristics were likely to be passed down from generation to generation, the stage was now prepared for the controversy that was to last a long time among the great scholars over the importance of environment versus heredity.

Louis Pasteur (1822–95) was perhaps the most influential of all. He used his training as a chemist and his skill with the microscope to solve practical problems for vintners, brewers and dairymen. Examining spoiled wine under the microscope, he found living organisms in addition to the yeasts which produced fermentation. He concluded that these 'bacteria' caused decay and also spread infection in animals and humans. He was able to develop the process of 'pasteurization', in which heating of liquids for a prolonged period destroyed the infection-carrying bacteria they contained. He also found that the risk of infection among domestic animals could be reduced by inoculating them with weak strains of bacteria.

It was a short step onwards from his discoveries to develop antibiotics to fight the micro-organisms which cause human diseases like tuberculosis. Joseph Lister, professor of surgery at Glasgow and later Edinburgh, applied these theories to surgery. At King's College, London, he was able to reduce fatalities during operations through the use of antiseptics. Pasteur's work had begun a medical revolution.

Against the background of these discoveries, Charles Darwin was working on the most controversial of all theories of biology – the theory of evolution. His *Origin of Species* was published in 1859, after long years of research he had begun in 1831 on a round-the-world voyage as naturalist on the survey ship HMS *Beagle*. Although he

Left, caricature of Charles Darwin (1809–82) produced at the time of the publication of his Origin of Species *in 1859: his theory of evolution through natural selection, which met enormous resistance for many decades, provoked a fundamental change in scientific method and thought.*

Opposite top, an operation in progress during the mid-nineteenth century: the work of Louis Pasteur (1822–95) and Joseph Lister (1827–1912) had a revolutionary effect on surgery and laid the foundations for the development of bacteriology, thus making possible for the first time the defeat of diseases such as typhoid, diptheria and cholera.

Opposite bottom, Ivan Pavlov (1849–1936) with his colleagues and one of his dogs: his research on dogs produced theories of behaviour applicable in general to human beings.

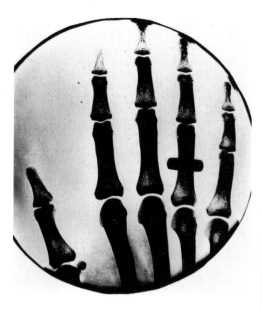

The new science

The most revolutionary findings of all, those of early atomic physics, were made in the last years of the century. In 1895, the German scientist Wilhelm Roentgen, who had studied under Clausius as a student, discovered X-rays. Three years later an even greater triumph came with Pierre and Marie Curie's isolation of the first known radioactive element, radium. The research of the Curies stimulated the work of Ernest Rutherford on the structure of the atom. This in turn looked forward to the time when the atom would be split and atomic energy harnessed, for better or worse.

The whole structure of science was changing. New subjects were being examined even in the most traditional of universities. 'Laws' of science which had been accepted for centuries now became the butt of scholarly ridicule. The data available was expanding with alarming rapidity, and scientific methods of study changed accordingly. Now, scientists would propose a hypothesis which they accepted as the best possible approximation to the truth. They expected future experiments to suggest a better hypothesis, when the first one would be discarded. And its value would not have been explaining an aspect of nature so much as in suggesting new areas of research. The German writer Max Weber even suggested that society should be studied through constructing hypothetical 'ideal types', against which its actual conditions could be measured. It is on his work and that of other scholars of his generation whom we would now call 'social scientists' that the new subject of sociology has been built.

The applications of science

The nineteenth century did not make its scientific discoveries for their own sake. Science was to be applied to technological advances, which could be used in the dominant industrial system of the West. But

in spite of the discovery of new metals and new sources of power, the late nineteenth century was still the age of steel and coal.

Steam was still the main source of energy used in industry and communications. It had improved immensely since the days of Watt and his kettle, because of the use of the compound engine, which increased efficiency by using steam that once heated was repeatedly recycled. Again, the invention of the Parsons' steam turbine made long distance ocean transport faster and more reliable. By the middle of the century, the great private steamship companies, plying from Liverpool, Southampton, Cherbourg and Le Havre to New York, were making enormous fortunes for their owners. By 1900 the ships used had become floating hotels, carrying their passengers in unparalleled luxury.

The steam turbine was also adapted to generating electricity in power stations. Electricity had not yet replaced steam as a source of industrial power, but the nineteenth century was the time of the inventions which made its harnessing possible. A clumsy electric motor had been invented in Belgium as early as 1869; twelve years later the brilliant German businessman, Werner

Siemens, had the first electric streetcar running in Berlin. More important for industry was the success of the French engineer Deprez in transmitting electrical power by means of high tension wires, the forerunners of the lines of pylons which march across the landscape.

Power could now be distributed cheaply from central generators to industries hundreds of miles away. Factories would soon be able to move away from the coal mines towards the markets they served. On the whole this meant that they were no longer confined to the most unattractive localities. Since the first experiments in harnessing hydro-electric power had also been made, the basic components of the system of electrical power on which modern industry depends had been invented by the end of the century.

Soon it would also be possible to use electricity outside the factory. No nineteenth-century invention now seems as indispensable as Edison's humble domestic electric lamp. In international communications, the first ocean cables had been laid as early as the 1850s. On the completion of the transatlantic cable – under the direction of the physicist Lord Kelvin – New York

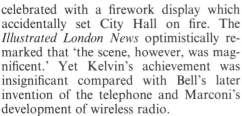

Above, Magnus Volk's Electric Overland and Submarine Railway, the first electric railway in Britain, it started operations along the Brighton seafront in 1883.

Left, the electric tramway at the Paris Electricity Exhibition, 1881: electricity soon became the prime source of power in industry but had only a marginal impact on transport, being chiefly used for urban streetcar networks, until electric locomotives began to be introduced on a large scale in the 1950s.

Below left, the opening of the Kaiser Wilhelm Canal (now known as the Kiel Canal), 21 June 1895: the canal was primarily built for strategic reasons, to give the German fleet rapid access from the Baltic to the North Sea, and reduced the journey by several hundred miles.

Opposite right, Pierre and Marie Curie (1859–1906 and 1867–1934), who in 1898 isolated radium: their discoveries, along with those of Röntgen, Antoine Becquerel (who discovered radioactivity) and Ernest Rutherford, completely altered the way in which scientists viewed the physical world.

Opposite left, an X-ray of a human hand taken in 1907: Wilhelm Röntgen's discovery of X-rays in 1895 marked an important advance for medical science.

celebrated with a firework display which accidentally set City Hall on fire. The *Illustrated London News* optimistically remarked that 'the scene, however, was magnificent.' Yet Kelvin's achievement was insignificant compared with Bell's later invention of the telephone and Marconi's development of wireless radio.

But the nineteenth century was not to feel the full impact of electricity. The same was true of early experiments with the internal combustion engine. It was first used in commercially available motor cars in 1885, when the German firms of Daimler and Maybach, and Benz, both offered models to the public. In the same year, Gottlieb Daimler even produced the first recognizable motorcycle. By the turn of the century, improved with the invention of the pneumatic tyre by Dunlop and Michelin, the motor car was known throughout Europe. The French manufactured it most enthusiastically,

largely through the firms of De Dion, Panhard and Peugeot.

But the motor car was still an aristocrat's toy in 1914. Even with the application of Rudolph Diesel's heavy engines to some areas of marine transport, little inroad was made into the supremacy of steam as a motive power. In the year the First World War began, ninety percent of all Europe's fuel for industry and transport came from coke and coal.

A shrinking world

As the output of industry increased, the long-distance transport which carried its wares improved to meet its demands. By 1914 the Kiel and Panama Canals had been added to Suez as the world's greatest artificial waterways. Steel-hulled, screw-driven ships had taken over the greatest share of

the world's ocean transport. Railway communications also improved, especially in the United States, where the Atlantic and Pacific coasts were linked in 1869. On 10 May, Union Pacific Locomotive No. 119 chugged up to Promontory Summit, Utah. It carried the company chairman, Dr Thomas C. Durant, to a ceremony at which he and Leland Stanford, President of the Central Pacific, tapped gold spikes into the final section of transcontinental track.

No European achievement in railway building equalled this. Nevertheless, the continental rail system expanded dramatically from about 1850 onwards. In many cases construction went on under the supervision of British engineers. The greatest plan of all was the completion of the Trans-Siberian Railway, which carried its first train in 1904. The mastermind behind it was the Russian minister of finance, Count Sergei Witte. The long journey from Moscow to Vladivostock, once one of several months, could now be made in favourable conditions in just under a fortnight. Trains in general became swifter. Lighter but more powerful engines and more comfortable coaches carried their passengers more cheaply and comfortably than ever before. The danger of accidents lessened as steel rails were substituted for faulty iron ones.

Competition between railway lines remained, with a resulting wastage of capital investment. But duels like the one between the North British and the Caledonian on the run from London to Scotland meant that schedules were pared and passengers were treated with unfailing consideration. The last years of the nineteenth century and the first of the twentieth were the heyday of the European railways.

Though few Europeans could afford to travel on the ocean liners or the great transcontinental railways, more modest advances affected the whole population. Even the poorest began to use the bicycle to release themselves from the monotony of town life. Again, the expensive Daimlers and Le Dions of 1900 were not far removed from the

Model T Ford and Baby Austins manufactured a generation later – or indeed from the Vauxhalls and Buicks of 1970. Soon the bicycle would be replaced by the mass-produced motor car.

It was only after 1900 that the lighter-than-air balloon gave way to the aeroplane. Even then, the dream of flying in machines heavier than air had fascinated inventors for so long that it was difficult to have any faith that it was possible for anyone to do so. The flight of the Wright brothers on the lonely shore at Kitty Hawk, North Carolina, attracted little attention, in their own country or elsewhere. At the end of 1903 Orville Wright's clumsy monoplane, built in his brother's own workshop, staggered through its first flight. Two years later the same machine stayed airborne for thirty-eight minutes. Yet the Brazilian aviator Santos-Dumont, when he made the first European flight in 1906, in a machine rather similar to a box kite, genuinely thought he was the first man to fly in a craft heavier than air. However, at least Santos-Dumont's achievement created some interest.

There was even greater popular enthusiasm when Blériot crossed the English Channel between Calais and Dover in his neat little monoplane in 1909. After this flying came to have an enormous glamour in the public eye, which made the Royal Flying Corps one of the most difficult services to enter during the 1914–18 war, though the military possibilities of aircraft were at first little understood. During the first part of the war they were considered one of the frills of the armed services.

On the other hand, it was well understood that the new invention would soon have commercial possibilities. Even the modest Wrights had been primarily businessmen. They flew in sober three-piece suits, starched collars and neat ties. The only article of city dress they left on the ground were their bowler hats. In the last few years before the war, other speculators began to build, improve and sell aircraft. Though the United States War Department had

originally scorned the Wright's toy, governments soon began to buy aeroplanes. Certainly early critics considered that the heavier-than-air machine, like the balloon, would be useless except for reconnaissance. They considered the problems of shooting or bombing from vehicles travelling at the breakneck speed of 60 mph to be insuperable. Nevertheless, this startling invention of the early years of the century was soon to revolutionize warfare. It would also have the greatest effect of all on international communications.

The world economy

As communications within and between the nations improved, it became possible for industry and agriculture to specialize. Produce could now be carried cheaply and quickly from one end of the world to the other. To take three examples, Ontario could concentrate on growing wheat, the Scottish border towns on producing woollens, the Ruhr on producing steel. Each area could provide the world with its speciality and avoid wasting time on producing the general necessities of life. These could readily be shipped from other regions in turn devoted to exporting other commodities. Another result of the improvement in communications was that it now became economical for both Europe and America to import raw materials from the

under-developed areas absorbed by 'new imperialism'. Specialization became the keynote of the world's economic life, as steam and steel reduced the area and widened the scope of the world market.

In the late nineteenth century, industry quickly adapted to the use and to the manufacture of the new inventions. Communications improved its sources of raw materials and expanded its markets, and factories in turn throve on creating the materials required for these communications. At the same time, advances in the processes of production increased industrial output. For instance, Europe's production of steel had increased and made cheaper ever since 1855, when Sir Henry Bessemer invented the converter which made steel by passing air through molten cast iron. A greater advance came with the Siemens-Martin process, using furnaces fired with superheated gas, which permitted the production of larger quantities of highly tempered steel.

Advances in mining made it possible to exploit mineral-bearing areas like Pennsylvania and South Africa. Huge new deposits of increasingly important metals like copper, tin and zinc were discovered in Russia, Canada, the USA and even West Africa. Lighter metals, which were to be of the first importance in twentieth-century industry and technology, were added to the traditional ones. Aluminium, for instance, had first been isolated in the laboratory in 1854 by two scientists working independently,

the Frenchman Sainte-Claire Deville and the German Friedrich Wöhler, professor of chemistry at Göttingen. The latter also isolated two other metals, beryllium and titanium, which were later put to use in making light alloys of steel.

In industrial terms, however, a more important discovery came in 1886 when the American Charles Hall evolved the method of producing aluminium economically by electrolysis. It had long been known that steel could be hardened through the addition of tungsten. Duralumin, a light and hard substitute for steel, was first produced in 1908 by combining aluminium, copper, manganese and magnesium. The basic metals used in modern technology were now available, and metal production bounded ahead. One hundred and fifty times as much steel was produced in 1913 as in 1850.

Industry also began producing articles which had previously been unknown and which sent Europeans all over the globe to find raw materials. For instance the infant automobile and aero industries were indirectly responsible for the devastation of the Belgian Congo. After the invention of the pneumatic tyre by Michelin and the introduction of vulcanization by Goodyear, world demand for rubber became insatiable. The one staple which the Congo could produce was crude rubber, and its unfortunate population was decimated by the refusal of European factors to accept tribute in anything else.

Above, the smoking chimneys of Stoke-on-Trent, the centre of England's china manufacturing, a scene that was repeated in every industrial centre in Europe and North America.

Opposite top right, the P & O Company's liner Himalaya *in 1895: the opening of the Suez Canal in 1869 considerably reduced sailing time to India, the Far East and Australia.*

Opposite top left, construction work in London on the world's first underground railway: the line, which ran between Paddington and Farringdon Street, was opened on 10 January 1863. Other major cities were slow to follow London's lead and waited until the early twentieth century to inaugurate a rapid transit system, though the first line of the elevated railway in New York started operating in 1867.

Opposite bottom, planting the first pole of the overland telegraph at Darwin, September 1870: the line ran 1800 miles to Adelaide, mostly across barren wilderness, and, once linked with a cable from Darwin to Java, put Australia in telegraphic communication with London.

491

With less disastrous results, the huge British textile industry searched for new sources of raw cotton once its main supplies were cut off by the American Civil War. India had always grown cotton in moderate amounts, and by the end of the century a substantial amount of Lancashire cotton was coming from Egypt, now effectively a British colony. Improvements in dyeing and patterning processes meant that more and more cotton prints could be produced to sell throughout the world. The British woollen industry had expanded in the early nineteenth century using the fleeces of Cheviot sheep which landlords had used to stock the Scottish Highlands after enclosing their estates and expelling their tenants during the Clearances. It now expanded even further to absorb the fine wool produced in Australia after the introduction of the Merino.

Widespread use of synthetic fibres would have to wait for the great chemical manufacturing complexes of our own century, but the textile industry was now far removed from the old era of craft production controlled by small businessmen. Textiles, like most other enterprises, were moving into an age of mass production when the great captains of industry effectively elbowed lesser men out of the economy. More and more men who would once have owned their own businesses sank to being employed by others.

The same was even true of farming itself, traditionally the preserve of men with little capital. The specialization made possible by improved communications was profitable, but in the first instance it was also costly. Australian sheep farming was only one area where the capital needed to begin farming was enormous. In other branches, new machinery and effective fertilization made yield higher, though this also meant that a larger unit had to be cultivated to give an economic return on capital invested. Once again the small man went to the wall.

The process was accelerated by the fact that competition could now be felt thousands of miles away from the places where crops were produced. Until subsidies and tariffs were introduced, for instance, it became uneconomical for European farmers to grow wheat, since North American imports could be sold so cheaply. The smaller producers were forced out of the market, while larger ones diversified the crops they grew or began to clamour for tariff protection. Even then, much European farming sank to being a form of glorified market gardening. The fruit farming of Britain and the Low Countries is a case in point. Even the French wine industry falls partly into this category, although it seemed likely to be wiped out by the scourge of phylloxera after 1868, until the European vine was saved by grafting it on to hardy Californian stocks. In agriculture in general, small farmers who failed had the choice of working for other farmers, moving into the towns or emigrating.

At all levels, units in the world economy grew larger. Free competition destroyed competition as the great industrial trusts swallowed one another up and became monopolies. Even if this did not happen, competition between huge concerns meant that the small businessman could not survive. By the end of the century companies had appeared in Europe which carried out every stage of the production of whatever article they made. In turn such companies raised capital for their enormous operations through borrowing from the bankers' trusts which dominated the new phase of 'finance capitalism'. The bankers' return for investing in any given company was to claim a number of its directorships. Great financial houses like Morgans, Barings and Rothschilds thus came to have a finger in most industrial pies and could effectively control the operations of the business world as a whole.

The only direction in which they could not control it was in its tendency to manufacture too much for its own good. Overproduction was the bane of the mature capitalist system of the nineteenth century. Each time the bulk of commodities on the market outran world demand, a slump resulted. The years 1877, 1893, 1907 and 1929, to mention the worst examples, saw disasters of this kind. Nothing could be done to curb the seesaw boom/bust pattern of business life until governments intervened to prevent overproduction. Meanwhile the industrial nations frantically searched for new markets to absorb their surpluses.

The slumps which caused industrialists so much worry had even worse effects on the masses of working men who had been gathered to work in the new factories. At each recession large numbers of them were left without jobs and the division between employers and employed appeared harsher. Industry was now controlled by a very few entrepreneurs. Small businessmen had become wage-earners, and farmers who had failed to withstand growing competition moved into the towns to join them. All became slaves of the factories, a solid 'proletariat' at odds with the captains of industry. In the *Communist Manifesto*, Marx argued that in this class capitalism had created its own ultimate enemy, the force which would overthrow it. For the present, however, the proletarian worked on at his monotonous task: 'He becomes an appendage of the machine, and it is only the most simple, most monotonous, and most easily acquired knack that is required of him.' Yet this humiliated workman, Marx thought, would be the revolutionary of the future. Eventually there would be a slump from which capitalism could not recover, since it would have no further markets to absorb its surpluses.

Later Lenin argues that the 'new imperialism' had postponed this final crisis by annexing territory which would become new fields for investment and salesmanship –

but after these had been used up, he maintained, the revolution would come. After prolonged slump, the proletariat, organized by alienated middle-class leaders, would turn on their masters and destroy the capitalist system.

Undoubtedly the speeding up of European expansion overseas was to some extent connected with the need to find wider and wider market areas. Yet the final crisis which Marx and Lenin prophesied has not come about. What they underestimated was the flexibility of the system they criticized. They could not look forward to the time when the liberal English economist John Maynard Keynes would advise governments to spend as much money as possible, even if this involved increasing public debts, to guarantee markets for their national industries. Nor could they imagine that the capitalists would ever change their nature to the extent where they would deliberately pay high wages so that their workmen could buy enough to prevent industry falling on hard times.

Marx would have been even more astounded if he could have been transported to the world of the 1960s. In his own time no one had thought of sophisticated advertising devices which make it possible to sell articles which rational enquiry proves to be useless. No one had thought of the even more sophisticated practice of selling articles which must be replaced regularly because they have been specifically designed to fall to bits as soon as decently possible. The capitalist system actually had a great deal more strength and adaptability than Marx had imagined. The structure of industry which emerged in the West in the late nineteenth century survives in our own day.

Until the appearance of Keynes' startling theories, however, European and American industry had its troubles. The saving grace was that many businessmen quickly developed an acrobatic knack of making money out of their own difficulties. When fears of overproduction, or perhaps hints of diminishing gold supply, led to alarm on the stock exchanges, nothing was simpler for those who had reserves of money than to buy shares at low prices and then to sit back to wait for conditions to improve. There was no capital gains tax in the 1890s. From making profits out of stock exchange fluctuations, it was a short step to engineering them. False rumours could start panic among speculators as well as true ones, and exactly the same profits could be made by buying cheap and selling dear. By these means and more honest ones, the numbers of extremely rich men increased.

There were more millionaires in America than anywhere else – from having twenty in 1840 the USA could count over four thousand in 1900. The size of individual fortunes increased too. John Jacob Astor, in the forties, had been worth a miserable seven and a half million. The great Scottish-

American steel magnate Andrew Carnegie, whose money founded several of the greatest British public libraries, including the Mitchell Library in Glasgow, died in 1919 leaving five hundred million. Exactly the same was happening in Europe. Marx was certainly right in arguing that the gulf between rich and poor had increased, although he was wrong in prophesying that it would go on increasing.

The rise of the industrialists also meant that the relation between farm and factory changed. Until the nineteenth century, perhaps even until the end of the nineteenth century, the richest men in Europe had been landowners. The increase in the size of business units, however, made it possible for men like Krupp in the German steel and armaments industry, Michelin in the French rubber industry or Morgan in American banking to amass fortunes undreamt of by earlier generations.

As for the legions of labourers required to man the factories, they were provided partly by draining off the population of the countryside. Farmers who did not survive the worsening conditions of competition in agriculture naturally sought a better livelihood in the growing industrial towns. It was only for very few that the hope of riches was ever fulfilled. The lure of the city meant that by the end of the century the characteristic European was coming to be a townsman rather than a peasant, though this development did not go ahead at a uniform speed. France, for instance, retains much of her rural character up to the present day. Only half her population were town-dwellers when the First World War began. Britain had reached this proportion as early as 1851. Even so, France was highly urbanized compared with the backward countries of Eastern Europe.

The new industrial complexes were also helped to find adequate labour by the population explosion of the latter part of the nineteenth century. Europe had a population of 293 million in 1870 and 490 million in 1914. This rise resulted not from change in the birth rate but from a startling increase in life expectancy. The death rate fell as hygiene improved and medical research concentrated on preventing disease rather than dealing with it once it had arrived.

Europe's growing towns created many difficulties for those responsible for governing them. Not the least was that the workers who lived in the towns began to combine in efforts to improve their condition, in ways which threatened the supremacy of their employers. A more immediate problem, however, was that of health. The more enlightened European governments and local authorities had to set about dealing with the risks created by filth and overcrowding in the massive cities of the new industrial world. The most important pioneer of the new science of urban administration was the British 'philosophic radical' Edwin

Chadwick. Pasteur's work afterwards made it clear that the removal of slums was extremely urgent.

By the end of the century it was agreed that towns should be planned to give their inhabitants at least reasonable amounts of light and space. It was recognized that the risk of infection meant that sewage and garbage disposal and the provision of uncontaminated water supplies were services which had to be provided for the public good, whether by central or local authorities. Some advanced towns set magnificent examples – Berlin almost doubled in population in the nineteenth century and yet had the most modern sanitary services in Europe. As the pattern of growth combined with more rigid health precautions was repeated in every city, so the old cycles of recurrent epidemics like typhoid and cholera gradually disappeared. At the same time, the role of the state in governing citizens' lives for their own good widened. European civil services swelled and on the whole became more efficient. Traditional groups of government employees were joined by a new and continually expanding class of trained local government officials.

Above, engraving of Parisian slums towards the end of the nineteenth century: measures to improve public health began to be put into effect during the second half of the nineteenth century, but slums such as these survived well into the twentieth century.

The rise of the proletariat

As the city populations swelled, the differences between those who owned businesses and those who worked in them sharpened. More significantly, as workmen were crowded together, they became aware that they had common interests and shared grievances against the captains of industry who controlled their lives. A true mass working class had now appeared. As a mass electorate, it was to revolutionize European politics after the First World War. In the late nineteenth century, sections of the workers set about expressing and organizing their opposition to the capitalist system. Strike action became more militant, and genuine socialist parties appeared throughout the West. The Socialists' First International, founded prematurely in 1868, had collapsed by the seventies. But the formation of the Second International in 1889, and the frequent congresses it held from that time onwards, signalized the organization of the proletariat as a force in world politics.

The international socialist movement, pledged to destroying capitalism, had itself been produced by the changing industrial order. This also involved a great expansion in the city-dwelling middle class. Its new members were men whose education was good, whose salaries were comfortable and whose posts depended on the prosperity of the great industrialists. But the fact that ownership was now concentrated in such few hands diminished their opportunities of rising up the scale.

The characteristic middle-class man of the nineties no longer owned his own small business but was employed in someone else's large one. He might also be a professional man disturbed at the low reward given to his specialized skills relative to industrial incomes or a humanitarian genuinely distressed at the misery he saw in the working population around him. Unlike the workers, none of these groups had the slightest intention of destroying the capitalist system. This would have been to take the bread out of their own mouths. But they did set out to try to mitigate its abuses. It was they who were most enthusiastic about improvements in the conditions of work in industry. Above all, they used their votes to bring pressure to bear on those richer and more powerful than themselves, entering into temporary alliances with workmen for this purpose.

This was the liberal impulse as it emerged in the later part of the century, giving rise to the organization of the great European liberal parties, the best example of which is the British one. All such parties, incidentally, were strongly patriotic and did much to sweep their countries into overseas expansion at the time of the 'new imperialism'. Socially, however, they were far more wedded to the existing system than even the most conservative trades unions and labour parties which were emerging throughout Europe at the same time.

The most effective bargaining counter which the workers possessed was their labour. They had everything to fight for. Working conditions were miserable, hours outrageously long, pay low and security or hope of advancement nonexistent. Although many dreamed of a new socialist order where these abuses could not exist, others joined the liberals in working for short-term improvements of their position. But where the liberals trusted in the political mechanism, the workers' hope was to force concessions through direct action. They therefore set about organizing strong labour unions to use the weapon of the strike most effectively. In doing so, they could be sure of some middle-class support. In the nineties, they were even encouraged by the Catholic Church, which cast aside its traditional conservatism in an enlightened attempt to win the poor away from the atheistic assumptions of socialism.

But the first problem of the trade unions was that not only their strikes but their existence were illegal in most European countries. Collective bargaining could also be defined as conspiracy in restraint of trade, and it was only gradually that the unions gained protection for their funds and had the rights of striking and picketing recognized.

Trade union history in each European country followed different lines according to the political structure and industrial sectors involved. In Britain, the Trades Union Congress, the first of its kind, initially met in Manchester in 1868. Its success in extorting legal recognition of its status and the right to strike from Gladstone and Disraeli inspired trade unionists throughout Europe. But the TUC remained a relatively conservative body dominated by skilled workmen.

When the 1875 recession threw thousands out of work, unskilled labourers also formed their own unions. The 'new unionism' was deeply influenced by socialist thought and developed political goals. At the Edinburgh Congress of 1896, British unionists called for a nationalization of mines and railways. Though this generation of leaders did not achieve anything so startling, their ties with the Parliamentary Labour Party, which worked in partial alliance with the liberals after its foundation in 1893, produced much of the legislation on working conditions which was fought for. The Liberal government further conciliated the Labour Party by providing for limited but compulsory National Insurance against sickness and industrial injury. By 1914, it seemed that the representation of the British working-class electorate through parliament had enabled them to lobby for advances in the conditions and security of their labour.

Although no other country had a union movement as successful as the British one, all show comparable developments during this period. In Germany, for instance, the union movement was well represented in the *Reichstag* through the Social Democrat Party. This had more seats than any other single party by 1912. Because of this success, both genuine revolutionary socialism and straight concentration on collective bargaining were underplayed in Germany. German unionism also had undertones of nationalism disturbing to socialists elsewhere. The Gotha Programme of 1875, for instance, stirred Marx to violent opposition because of its admission of the need for a 'people's army', presumably to fight nationalist wars. With the successes gained at the polls, there seemed no need for revolution or even forceful direct action in industry. Indeed the bulk of German unionists were opposed to the socialists.

When the German equivalent of the TUC first met in 1890, its general secretary, Karl Legien, even argued that the hope of organizing a general strike was a delusion. Its inevitable failure would destroy the patient advances made by previous generations of trade unionists. In 1906 the Social Democrat Party itself took exactly the same standpoint. If this was socialism, it was not the form envisaged in the *Communist Manifesto*. Indeed Marx, Engels and later Lenin, spent much of their time denouncing German 'revisionists'.

Syndicalism

France's trade unions or *syndicats* were much more radical than those of Germany. The recognition of trade unions by Jules Ferry's brilliant government of 1883 was followed in 1886 by the formation of the Fédération Nationale des Syndicats. This was strongly Marxist and suspicious of previous labour activity through the existing political machinery, though its leader Jules Guesde did not extend this ban to the Fédération itself. But early progress was slow. Ferry's law of 1884 forbade the formation of unions among state employees, who included the important railway workers. There was bitter and sometimes violent opposition to unions at all levels of French society. At the end of the century less than 600,000 French workers held union cards.

Much of this weakness was a result of disunity. The unions not only included men like Guesde but those interested in using them as workers' friendly societies, which could administer funds or relief during periods of unemployment or sickness. These were the aims of the Bourses de Travail set up in 1887 and federated five years later, though they could also be used as bases for much more radical anarchist or 'syndicalist' agitation. Although the Bourses joined in a new national organization, the Confédération Générale du Travail (CGT), in 1902, this division was to bedevil unity in the French movement for many years.

The more radical unionists also made the creation of any wide workers' front difficult because of their tactically wise refusal to accept any concessions from bourgeois or 'opportunist' politicians. They felt that any such acceptance could only weaken the genuine radical labour opposition. In fact French statesmen in general were still haunted by memories of the radical 'Commune' of 1871, and any concessions made were moderate. They were also badly received. When the socialist Alexandre Millerand became secretary of commerce in 1899, his sell-out to bourgeois politicians was seen in labour circles as direct treachery. Not even his creation of a new labour department, his extension of minimum wage and maximum hour legislation to all public employees and his institution of the eleven-hour day restored his good reputation.

The French labour movement, then, was more militant than those of Britain and Germany. In 1906, the CGT reaffirmed its faith in the general strike in the Charter of Amiens. By this time it had been deeply influenced by the 'syndicalism' of Georges Sorel, which involved use of the trade unions as training units to prepare for violent revolution. Indeed the movement had none of the encouragement to work through existing institutions given to the Social Democrats by their success in the *Reichstag* or to the British Labour Party by its success in extorting acceptable legislation from the Liberal Party.

In 1914, the CGT strongly opposed labour participation in the 'fratricidal' conflict. No other major European labour organization was far enough divorced from the nationalism of the middle classes to be able to do the same. French labour, on the other hand, was forced by the conservatism of the levels of society above it to reject contacts with the middle class completely. It was only in Italy and Spain, where the franchise was narrow enough to make hopes of constitutional reform faint, that other labour movements rejected all reform from above and followed France in a leaning towards syndicalism and anarchism. At the other end of the scale, the most backward unionism of all was that of Russia, which was legally recognized in 1906 but at once forced underground by tsarist police methods. In 1914, few could have foreseen that it would be in imperial Russia that the first socialist state would be founded.

International socialism

In nineteenth century socialist circles, Karl Marx now seems the most influential and purposeful figure. His assumptions about the structure of society influence most modern scholars, and the *Communist Manifesto* and his *Das Kapital* still provide much of the ideology of the underdeveloped nations which have gained their independence since that era. However, this should not obscure the fact that Marx was by no means unchallenged as the leader of socialists of his own generation. First, Marx was firmly in opposition to cooperation with bourgeois, clerical or aristocratic socialists, far less with liberals – 'the people, so often as it joined them, saw on their hindquarters the old feudal coats of arms, and deserted with loud and irreverent laughter' – thus the *Communist Manifesto*. Yet the feudal coats of arms were not enough to make all workers reject the gains they could make through such alliances. Much more serious opposition to Marxist socialism came from the anarchist wing of the labour movement. This became very clear when socialists tried to unite in launching the First and Second Internationals.

The First International, officially entitled the International Working Men's Association, was formed in London in 1868. It drew support from all parts of the labour movement, but in spite of the disunity this caused it made rapid gains and had about 800,000 members by the end of the decade. An increasing number of these members were Marxist socialists, who were gaining at the expense of the followers of Pierre Joseph Proudhon. Proudhon was the self-educated son of a French barrel-maker, who had become a printer by trade. He had won a large section of European labour over to a belief in attacking capitalism through workers' education and the formation of worker-owned cooperatives. The threat of the Proudhonites, however, was not as great as that of the anarchists.

The leader of the anarchist attack on the Marxists was Count Mikhail Alexandrovich Bakunin, the greatest of the Russian aristocratic revolutionaries. A complete nonconformist among nonconformists, one of his leaders in the Paris revolt of 1848 had exclaimed of him – 'What a man! The first day of the revolution he is a perfect treasure, but on the next day he ought to be shot.' It is

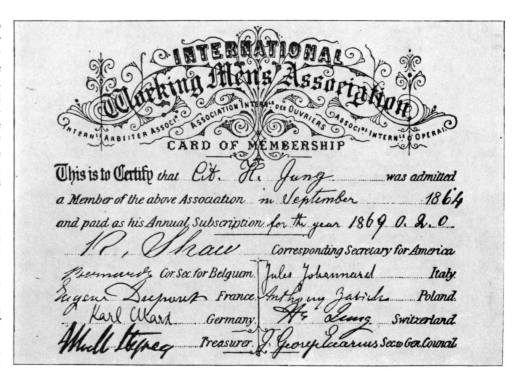

Above, Count Mikhail Bakunin (1814–76), Marx's chief opponent in the First International: Bakunin believed not in the dictatorship of the proletariat but in the destruction of all state organization and appealed not to the industrial proletariat but to the peasantry and workers of the less industrialized nations.

Top, membership card of the International Working Men's Association for the year 1869.

likely that Turgenev modelled the character of the dedicated revolutionary Insarov in *On the Eve* on his close friend Bakunin. After 1848, he spent eight years in jail in Saxony. The Saxons handed him over to the Russians, who in turn sent him to Siberia. Predictably, he escaped, via China, and sailed from Yokohama in Japan to the United States and thence to London.

His hopes of replacing all state agencies with self-governing workers' communes horrified Marxists, who thought in terms of rigidly centralized proletarian revolution. But his ideas appealed in countries where there was little hope of revolution as Marx understood it and less of constitutional gain. When Bakunin and his followers appeared at the 1869 Congress of the International, they received strong support from Swiss, Spanish and Italian delegates but were spurned by the French, Germans and British.

Bakunin clearly intended to cut the International loose from the 'German authoritarianism' of Marx, and he and his friend Nechaev worked hard to gain support. The confused network of even more confused secret societies they formed are bitterly satirised in Dostoevski's *The Possessed*. The anarchists were expelled from the International in 1872, but their opposition was so great that the organization fell apart. Although Marx cleverly moved the remnants of the International's headquarters to New York, it was dead by 1874.

Bakunin died in 1876 and Marx in 1883, but the European labour movement remained as disunited as ever. However, at least the trade unions made steady progress, and the earliest socialist parties were founded in the eighties. In 1889 delegates from all the European nations met in Paris to form the Second International. Among them were the Scottish socialist Keir Hardie and the German 'revisionist' Eduard Bernstein. Their programme was simple. They announced that they would work for universal suffrage and better working conditions and hold a one-day token strike on May Day of each year. What they did not do was provide any permanent organization or office, and this was only set up in Brussels in 1900.

The Second International had learned enough from past experience to try to exclude anarchists, although its inaugural meetings were frequently interrupted by the Italian Bakuninite Dr Merlino, who sneaked in, in various disguises and abused the organizers at most of the sessions. Anarchists or no, the International continued to waste effort in bitter disagreements. Even when it was formed in Paris, there were two rival conferences to celebrate the centenary of the revolution of 1789. The regular Marxist/trade unionist one eventually formed the International, while the other one was a meeting of 'possibilist' or opportunist socialists ready to work through existing parties. Yet all these elements had to be incorporated in the International if it were to remain a working force.

LE CONGRÈS SOCIALISTE

The new threat was not anarchism but 'revisionism'; the assumption that working-class prosperity and growing capitalist strength had now indefinitely postponed the revolution. The new role of the labour movement was thus to have wages raised and force concessions on suffrage and working conditions from liberal politicians.

Since the British were fully integrated into the International, because of the peculiar form of their socialism, the main spokesmen for the revisionists were the Germans. Their leaders Eduard Bernstein and August Bebel became the main opponents of the orthodox Marxists. Given German success in liberal politics, it was easy for them to illustrate their arguments from their own experience. Sure of their success through constitutional means, they even stuck to the damaging slogan, 'the general strike is general nonsense!' The Marxists were championed by the Frenchman Jules Guesde, now leader of the Parti Ouvrier Français (POF), so that the argument fell partly along nationalist lines. Each annual conference of the International ended in a violent exchange of insults connected with this division of policy.

However, the national socialist movements were in many cases divided internally as well. Even in Britain, where the working class vote apparently made revolution unnecessary, the Social Democratic Federation remained independent from the Labour Party and took a revolutionary position. The situation was far worse in France, where socialists had been debating Millerand's betrayal in joining the Waldeck-Rousseau cabinet in 1899. Guesde's attacks on the relatively mild Jaurès, with his belief in constitutional action, produced conflicts which reduced the movement's meetings to what Briand called 'annual scissions'

In Russia, Lenin's chief opponent in the years before 1917 was the revisionist Karl Kautsky. Indeed Kautsky replaced Bernstein as the European leader of the revisionists. The International was still prostrated by this disagreement when its unity finally disappeared in debate over the question of whether socialist parties should support their governments in the First World War.

Hopes of organizing a European revolution against the masters of the industrial system had faded. Socialist goals had not been abandoned, but it was increasingly felt that these could be reached by peaceful methods. In the first decade of the century, socialist parties and trade unions had become genuine powers which could exert genuine pressure within the capitalist structure of society. The future lay not with violent revolutionaries but with Bernstein's revisionists, or so it seemed until the stress of war made the Bolshevik revolution of 1917 possible.

Meanwhile, revisionism was all the more attractive because it did not involve abandoning national loyalties. The 1912 Conference of the International rejected a French resolution that the weapon of the general strike should be used to prevent a capitalist war. This involved an admission that direct and violent action had been given up in favour of 'evolutionary socialism'. But it also made it clear that for a majority of European socialists loyalty to the small unit of the state came before loyalty to the wider unit of the working class. The long fragmented Second International finally collapsed under the additional strain of the 1914–18 war. It was hard to talk of class brotherhood when socialist politicians from Britain and Germany had voted for taxes to fight against one another.

Clerical liberalism

The difficulties of the Second International were not wholly its own fault. The increasingly liberal capitalist system had simply acted to give timely concessions which would dampen the ardour of a large section of the socialist rank and file. The working-class vote and the improvements in conditions of labour in the factories were reforms which blunted the revolutionary impulse. Yet they left the essential structure of European society unchanged. There was still a class of very rich men in control of industry and with real power over the lives of the great mass of those poorer than themselves.

Changes were being made so that the position of the upper-middle and even middle classes might be preserved from attacks from below. This is nowhere more evident than in the attitude of the churches towards reform. The Catholic Church in particular began to campaign for concessions to labour after the death of Pio Nono in 1878. No doubt there was sincere humanitarianism in the new radicalism which appeared among churchmen. But they also hoped that workmen could be kept close to Christianity by diverting their attention from the appeals of atheistic socialists.

Pius IX

Prior to this, however, the Catholic Church had passed through an extraordinary period of medieval reaction during the long pontificate of Pius IX. Although he had become pope as a relatively young man, it had only taken two years of exposure to the startling radicalism of the Italian nationalists to drive him into dogged opposition to all reform, political or theological. After his flight from Rome in 1848, he became one of the most important supporters of the old order in Italy and throughout Europe. His conservatism deeply affected his theology. In 1854, in the Bull *Ineffabilis Deus*, he took it upon himself to outline the doctrine of the Immaculate Conception. This meant reviving a mystical aspect of Catholicism which was naturally under attack in an increasingly scientific age.

Even more archaic was Pius' insistence on reaffirming the doctrine of papal infallibility, a standpoint also open to rational doubt. Finally, he succeeded in antagonizing nationalists throughout the Catholic world through his 'ultramontane' assumptions on the power of the papacy over the individual national churches. Until his death in 1878, he was involved in a bitter struggle with the 'Gallican' Catholics, who insisted that each bishop should be given a degree of independence within his diocese.

Vatican attitudes to reform in general during Pius' pontificate were summarized in his encyclical *Quanta Cura* and his *Syllabus of the Principal Errors of our Age* (1864). Nationalism, liberalism, socialism, doctrinal revision and above all the toleration of these errors were roundly condemned. European liberals were horrified, and their opposition in some cases merged with that of the Gallican faction, who denied papal infallibility in matters of dogma. These they considered should be settled only by councils of the church. It was in response to the conservatism of Pius IX that Bismarck launched his *Kulturkampf* ('struggle of civilizations') against the Vatican.

Catholicism was not alone in reacting so strongly against the rapid changes of the modern world by attempting to shut them out. If anything the Protestant churches found themselves under even more severe attack from the new scientific thinkers, particularly those who accepted Darwin. Later, some clerical theorists were to adapt to the post-Darwinian world by arguing that the Protestant Christian nations had survived as being the fittest and that their duty was to rule other races and religions – including the Catholics – who had been less blessed in the struggle for existence. A rationalization for supporting the capitalist system was also provided by 'Social Darwinism', since it apparently proved that those who became richest were those who had been most able to adapt to the conditions of modern life and at the same time were the most scrupulous in applying religious ideals to their business life.

The first Protestant reaction to Darwin, however, was much more critical. His removal of God from the history of the world provoked ministers into a horrified rejection of his heresies. Their first instinct was to combat his ideas by falling back on fundamentalism and arguing that since the literal reading of the Bible contradicted the *Origin of Species* Darwin's conclusions were wrong if not actually sinful. The same kind of uncompromising opposition to a new intellectual movement appears in both Catholic and Protestant responses to the rise of socialism. At first it was regarded as an atheistic system which had to be attacked root and branch.

It was perhaps because of such a frontal attack was failing so conspicuously that the churches set about offering counter-attractions to socialism. If social reform could not be avoided, the most constructive plan was to carry it out freed from its atheistic connections and under the supervision of liberal churchmen. This was most obvious in the case of the Catholic Church, under Pius IX's brilliant successor, Leo XIII. Encouraged by this versatile and charming man, liberal Catholics who had been repressed by Pio Nono turned to destroying the appeal of socialism by improving the conditions of the working class in the Catholic nations of Europe. Working along with the rising liberal parties, they also organised extensive programmes of workers' education, which were intended to spread the belief that substantial reform could be achieved without abandoning religion.

Leo XIII himself set the new liberal Catholicism in perspective. His Bull *Immortale Dei* of 1885 allowed French Catholics to cooperate with the Third Republic, which had previously been disavowed by the Vatican. With more far-reaching effects, the Bull *Rerum Novarum* called for concessions to the new mass working class: 'The more that is done for the benefit of the working classes by the general laws of the country, the less need will there be for special means to relieve them.' The new pope even encouraged the Catholics of southern Germany to conciliate Bismarck in the hope of destroying the appeal of the *Kulturkampf*. It was only after Leo's death in 1903 and the election of Pius X, that Rome began to retreat from its position as a major force in international liberal politics. Pius X, like Pius IX, spent the rest of his life waging war against 'modernism', excommunicating large numbers of liberal Catholics to do so. Unlike Leo XIII, he was quite prepared to abandon the working classes to the socialists. Since his own theology was not far removed

Above, Pope Pius IX (1792–1878, elected Pope 1846): his reign saw the incorporation of all the papal lands into the new kingdom of Italy, only the Vatican City enclave remaining under the Church's control.

Opposite, magazine report of the 1900 Congress of the Second International, held at Paris: among the participants were, top left and top right, the German socialists Karl Liebknecht (1871–1919), who was murdered during the German Revolution, and August Bebel (1840–1913), leader of the Social Democrats in the Reichstag, bottom right, Jean Jaurès (1859–1914), founder of L'Humanité, who was assassinated a few days before the outbreak of the First World War, and, bottom left, Alexandre Millerand (1859–1943), at that time minister of commerce.

from that of the thirteenth-century scholar St Thomas Aquinas, it is not surprising that his Bull *Pascendi* condemned 'modernism' as 'the synthesis of all other heresies'.

The Protestant churches were not so unfortunate as to pass through such a period of reaction. In Britain middle-class nonconformists formed the backbone of the Liberal Party and by and large remained in it until its collapse after the First World War.

The expansion of Europe

Protestant and Catholic churches alike shared the strengthening missionary impulse which sent their most devoted clergymen to the corners of the earth. No doubt this filtered off many of the most enterprising young men in Europe's theological colleges and diverted their attention from more radical movements at home. But the missionaries of the late nineteenth century were also centrally important in the 'new imperialism'. In one sense this simply involved the annexation of the heathen part of the globe by the Christian part. Indeed all the rapid changes which have been described here reinforced the burst of European expansion overseas after 1884. The changing Church produced evangelical missionaries, the rising population provided emigrants. A strengthened industrial system, working through the new nation states, began to look overseas for new markets, sources of raw materials and opportunities for profitable investment. Medical improvements made life in the tropics tolerable, while Europe's new technology made light of primitive resistance. Better links by rail and sea provided the communications essential to expanding empires. The net result, over the space of a few years, was the extension of Western rule throughout the world. It may even be that the rivalries which the nations formed overseas were important causes of the Great War.

Even the critics of the new industrial order had a part to play in the history of the expansion of Europe. When the colonies of the 1900s became the emerging nations of the fifties, their ideology was largely drawn from European socialist thought. All in all, the late nineteenth century was the time when the world became recognizable as the one we live in today.

THE MARCH OF THE NINETEENTH CENTURY

Date	Politics in the West	Industry, labour and technology	Politics in the wider world	Date	Politics in the West	Industry, labour and technology	Politics in the wider world
1815			Raffles acquires Singapore (1819)	1868		First Trades Union Congress (1868)	Meiji Restoration in Japan (1868)
			British occupation of Rangoon (1824)			Suez Canal opened (1869)	
		Stockton & Darlington Railway (1825)				Mendeleev's classification of elements (1869)	
			British claim all Australia (1829)			First electric motor (1869)	
	Revolutions throughout Europe					American transcontinental railroad track completed (1869)	
1830		Darwin's voyage on the *Beagle* (1831)			Hohenzollern candidacy Franco-Prussian War, Battle of Sedan		Massacre of Catholics at Tientsin
		Opening of Lyons-Saint-Étienne line begins French railway construction (1831)		1870	Rome capital of a united Italy		
	English Reform Act (1832)	Faraday invents dynamo (1832)			Second Reich proclaimed (1871)		Livingstone and Stanley meet at Ujiji (1871)
	Emancipation of slaves in British colonies (1833)	Robert Owen founds Grand National Consolidated Trades Union (1834)			Communards rule Paris (1871)	Anarchists expelled from International (1872)	British buy Suez (1875)
	Formation of *Zollverein* (1834)		Great Trek (1836)			Gotha Programme for German labour (1875)	Queen Victoria becomes Empress of India (1876)
			Opium War breaks out (1839)		Leo XIII becomes pope (1878)		
1840	English Corn Law Repeal (1846)		Treaty of Nanking begins 'Era of Concessions' (1842)			Edison electric lamp (1879)	
	Pius IX becomes pope (1846)	Elias Howe invents sewing machine (1846)		1880			De Brazza extends explorations in the Congo
	Year of revolutions (1848)		California annexed by USA (1848)			Siemens electric tramcar in use (1881)	Boer revolt breaks out (1881)
	Victor Emmanuel takes Piedmontese crown (1849)		Livingstone's first journey (1849)				British bombard Alexandria and occupy Egypt (1882)
1850	Cavour takes office (1852)	Great Exhibition in London (1851)	Taiping Revolt begins (1851)			Death of Marx (1883)	Germans seize Togoland (1883)
	French Second Empire proclaimed (1852)				Berlin Conference on colonies (1884	Parsons steam turbines applied to shipping (1884)	Berlin Conference prepares for partition of Africa (1884)
	Outbreak of Crimean War (1853)		Commodore Perry arrives in Japan (1853)				Mahdists take Khartoum (1885)
	Garibaldi returns to Italy (1854)	Isolation of aluminium (1854)				American Federation of Labor founded (1886)	Gold discovered in Transvaal (1886)
	Paris Peace Conference (1856)	Bessemer Converter introduced (1856)	'Arrow' War (1856)				French Indo-China is organized (1887)
	Orsini Plot (1858)	Brunel's *Great Eastern* built (1858)	Indian Mutiny (1857) Peace of Tientsin ends 'Arrow' War (1858)		Negro slavery ended in Brazil (1888)	Second International (1889)	
	Pact of Plombières (1858)	Atlantic Telegraph Cable laid (1858)	French take Saigon (1858)	1890	British Parliamentary Labour Party founded (1893)	World slump (1893)	*Union Coloniale* formed in France (1893)
	First Austro-Italian War (1859)	*Origin of Species* published (1859)					Sino-Japanese War (1894)
1860	Garibaldi's Sicilian campaign		Russia seizes Vladivostock			Confédération Générale du Travail founded (1895)	
		Siemens-Martin smelting processed perfected				Marconi wireless telegraph invented (1895)	Jameson Raid increases Anglo-Boer tension (1896)
	Russian serf emancipation by Tsar Alexander II (1861)					Röentgen discovers X-rays (1895)	French annex Madagascar (1896)
	First Italian parliament (1861)					French annex Madagascar (1896)	Fashoda Incident (1898)
	American Civil War breaks out (1861)						USA gains Hawaii, the Philippines, Puerto Rico (1898)
	Cavour dies (1861)		Speke proves his and Burton's findings on source of Nile (1862)		Spanish American War (1898)		Outbreak of Boer War (1899)
	Bismarck takes office (1862)			1900			Boxer Rebellion
	Polish revolt (1863)		Cambodia becomes a French protectorate (1863)				Peace of Vereeniging ends Boer War (1902)
	American emancipation proclamation (1863)				First Russian Revolution (1905)	Orville Wright's first flight (1903)	
	Prussia fights Denmark over Schleswig-Holstein (1864)	Pius IX promulgates *Syllabus Errorum* (1864)			First *Duma* (parliament) meets in Russia (1906)	Trans-Siberian Railroad completed (1904)	Russo-Japanese War (1904)
		First International (1864)			Algeciras Conference strengthens Anglo-French ties (1906)	Charter of Amiens (1906)	
		Lister introduces antiseptics (1865)			Anglo-Russian Entente (1907)	Santos-Dumont makes first European flight (1906)	
	Austro-Prussian War, Battle of Sadowa (1866)		Rholfe crosses the Sahara (1867)		Second Moroccan crisis (1911)	Stock market recession (1907)	British and Russian zones in Tibet, Afghanistan, Persia settled (1907)
	Roman Revolt (1867)				Sarajevo and First World War (1914)	Blériot crosses the Channel (1909)	French occupy Casablanca (1907)
	North German Confederation formed (1867)						

Chapter 42

The New Imperialism

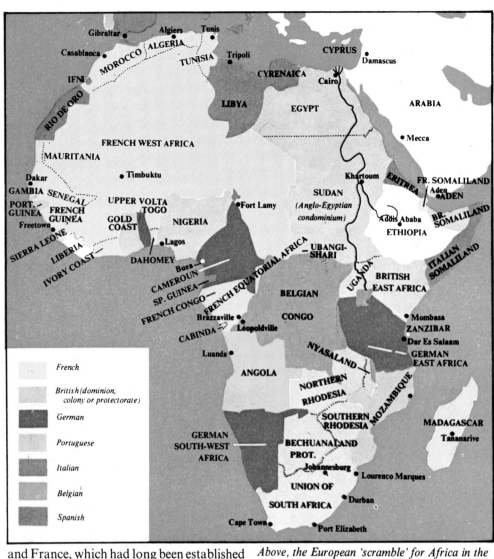

At the end of the nineteenth century, the overseas policies of the Western nations changed dramatically. Where they had once struggled to gain concessions and bases for trade, they now set about annexing swathes of territory in Africa and Asia. New anxieties were created with the rise of new nations. Bismarck's united Germany played a central part in the scramble for Africa. In 1898 the United States took its place as an international power by seizing Puerto Rico and the Philippines from Spain.

The old imperial powers, Britain and France, also annexed whatever territory they could. All the Western nations joined in a mad rush to seize unexploited land, often just to prevent other powers getting it. Patriotic enthusiasm supported all annexations, which were also linked to the advances in business and technology which made it essential to find foreign markets. Thus it was that in western Europe patriotism and industrialism combined to produce the 'new imperialism'.

Europe, Africa and Asia

Whatever was new about the new imperialism, there was also much about it that was old. Europe had been expanding ever since the Crusades or even earlier. The great Portuguese and Spanish colonists had first blazed the trail to Asia, Africa and the New World. The rise of the Dutch in the seventeenth century ruined both their empires, and the Dutch were pushed to the wall in their turn by other powers. We have already seen that the British and French were the dominant nations in China in the first part of the nineteenth century. They also had colonies in the West Indies and Africa, while the British ruled over Canada, India, Australia and New Zealand. Indeed the history of modern Europe may be seen as a constant struggle between the powers for an empire overseas.

After about 1880, however, the kind of empire which the powers wanted changed. New nations and new industries sought markets and territory overseas, and all Europe became involved in their ambitions. The pace of expansion quickened, its characteristics changed. Nations like Britain

and France, which had long been established in Africa, now had to widen their interests to protect themselves from interlopers and each other. In West Africa, for instance, the British had previously been content with owning a few coastal forts. By the end of the century they had annexed all of modern Nigeria and Ghana and had consolidated their settlements in Sierra Leone, and Gambia. Africa was soon dismembered. Asia was only saved from the same fate by a delicate balance between the interests of Japan, now a modern industrial state, and the individual Western powers. America absorbed the remnants of the Spanish Empire. The twentieth century dawned on a world in which little territory was not owned by Japan, the USA, the nations of Europe or, as in the case of Latin America, their offshoots.

Historians have found it difficult to explain this sudden burst of expansion. Clearly it is linked with the new needs of industrialism and with the rise of nationalism. After 1850, too, European population rose sharply, and emigration increased. In the middle of the century peasant emigrants, for instance the Irish displaced by the potato blight or the Scandinavians and southern Germans, flocked to the USA and Latin America. After about 1880 a new wave of emigrants left the poorer parts of southern

Above, the European 'scramble' for Africa in the second half of the nineteenth century: by 1912 only Ethiopia and Liberia were free from European domination or influence.

Italy and eastern Europe. Communications had improved and cheapened, and the attractions of the New World as described by shipping companies and American emigration agencies were great.

For others, however, the New World had less glamour. Many adventurous young men from the educated classes of the nations involved in the new imperialism set out as explorers and in the end became the administrators and engineers who opened up the Asian and African territories annexed by the West in the eighties and ninties. Rising scientific curiosity and the eagerness of such men to travel in unknown areas meant that this was also the period when the parts of the world which remained unexplored were first visited by Europeans. The drive towards exploration was all the stronger since so many Europeans were interested in bringing Christianity to black, brown and yellow heathens. It is difficult to imagine how the new imperialism would have arisen without the scientific and missionary impulses which encouraged exploration.

The greatest explorer of all, David Livingstone, well illustrates the complexity of motive of his generation of imperialists. Born in Scotland, he painstakingly scraped money together while working in a Lanarkshire cotton mill to begin his education and eventually to go to Glasgow University. By the time the London Missionary Society sent him to Africa he had a medical degree as well as strong interests in botany, zoology and astronomy. A committed abolitionist, he believed that opening Africa to Protestant missionaries would crush the slave trade. This continued in West Africa in spite of the efforts of the British West Africa Squadron to capture slavers and flourished more than ever through the East African depot in Zanzibar. He made three main journeys through unexplored Africa from 1849 onwards. On the first he crossed the continent, exploring the course of the Zambesi, and on the second he discovered Lake Nyasa.

The activities of explorers had become good press, and the whole of Europe and America followed the last journey, which he began in 1868. When he went missing, the *New York Tribune*, a paper which had fought against American slavery and was now the organ of the Republican Party, sent its ace reporter Henry Morton Stanley to look for Livingstone. The search took three years. In 1871, at Ujiji, on Lake Tanganyika, the reporter met a very sick and weary Livingstone with a handshake and the famous though superfluous question, 'Dr Livingstone, I presume?' Racked with fever and worn out by his labours, poor Livingstone was found dead by his bearers only two years later, in 1873.

Stanley himself continued the work of exploration, still sending his despatches back to the *Tribune* when he could do so. Travelling from Zanzibar in the east, he reached

the headwaters of the Congo and followed it down to the coast. Soon afterwards King Leopold of Belgium tried to expand his interests in the Congo, which together with the sudden intervention of Germany precipitated the 'scramble for Africa'.

Livingstone and Stanley were not the only great travellers of this period. In 1880 the French explorer de Brazza sailed up the Ogooué River from the coast of Gabon, cut across country to the Congo, and founded the post of Brazzaville, later the capital of the French Congo. Before Stanley, Livingstone and Brazza had showed the way into Central Africa, even more attention had been given to trying to discover the sources of the Nile. The riddle of this river had puzzled scholars for generations.

In 1858 the Royal Geographical Society of London sponsored the expedition of Burton and Speke, which discovered the Great Lakes – Tanganyika, Victoria, and Albert. Unfortunately the scholarly world could not believe that the controversy over

the source of the Nile had been settled, and Speke was denounced as a charlatan when he claimed that the river flowed out of a huge lake system in Central Africa. In 1862, however, he was able to prove his point by marching round Lake Victoria Nyanza, finding the outlet of the Nile and descending it as far as the first cataract. Since the successive expeditions of Mungo Park, Hugh Clapperton, and the Lander brothers had revealed the course of the Niger by 1830, European knowledge of Africa's main river systems was now complete.

In the late 1860s, the land routes across North Africa and the Sudan were also covered by two Germans, Gerhard Rholfe and Gustave Nachtigal. Rholfe trekked from Tripoli to Conakry in Guinéa in 1867. Nachtigal's achievement was to find a route from Libya to Lake Chad, turn eastwards to Khartoum and return home down the Nile. The names of such explorers became household words throughout Europe. More important, their work provided enough

knowledge of Africa to make penetration possible.

The interior of Asia received less attention from explorers than Africa. However, the imagination of Europeans was stimulated by travel accounts like that of the colourful medical missionary to China, Charles Gutzlaff. After 1870 even more attention was attracted by the voyages of the German traveller Richthofen. Another exploit was Garnier's exploration of south east Asia. He sailed up the Mekong, discovered the dramatically beautiful ruins of the Khmer palace at Ankgor Wat and penetrated into China's Yunnan province. The European public heard as much of the heroism of explorers in Asia as it did of those in Africa. The French poet Rimbaud reflected their enthusiasm when he wrote *Le Bateau ivre* ('The Tipsy Boat'). Indeed Rimbaud himself died while exploring part of Abyssinia. The publicity given to explorations no doubt helped to prepare European voters for later annexation of African and Asian territory.

The motives for imperialism

There were other factors behind the new imperialism as well as enthusiasm for the exploits of missionaries and explorers. Sometimes events proceeded almost by accident, with ambitious young men on the frontiers of European expansion annexing territory without orders from above. For instance the forward policy of the French in Indo-China was partly moulded by the enthusiasm of Gallieni. A similar case was the initiative of the British officer Frederick Lugard in seizing territory in Uganda.

However, it is unlikely that such men would have received the backing of their governments if deeper forces had not been at work. Sometimes these arose in the territory which was to be conquered and not in Europe. In West Africa, for instance,

traders had to appeal to their governments to move in when the local states on which they had previously relied for protection collapsed under the strain of generations of slave trading. The Boer War was also fought partly for internal reasons. Again, the Russian advance into Manchuria, where tsarist troops eventually clashed with the Japanese, was dictated partly by the need to find a frontier which was settled and stable on the other side. There were also direct economic motives for expansion. V. I. Lenin, the great leader of the Russian revolution, maintained that it arose because capitalism had to find new areas for investment to escape from the problem of over production at home.

Nevertheless, whatever economic interests were involved, the missionary factor in the new imperialism cannot be overestimated. No doubt some of the enthusiasm of the missionaries was linked with improvements in education which meant there were more young ministers than there were parishes for them to find jobs in. But the missionary movement was now given new scope among the tens of millions of heathens living in the vast new territories discovered by men like Livingstone and Garnier. The middle classes who had risen because of industrialization were fervently interested in missions, probably with complete sincerity.

The hope of spreading Christianity was linked with changing attitudes to race. It now appeared possible to fit the non-European races into the framework of *The Origin of Species*. If human history, like natural history, was governed by the survival of the fittest, the races of the West, with their advanced technology, had obviously survived most effectively. Clearly, therefore, their Christian duty was to extend their humane leadership throughout the world. This theory of the 'white man's burden' is best expressed in the poems of the great imperialist poet Rudyard Kipling and the popular novelist Rider Haggard. A

Above, the coffee harvest on the plantation at St Austin's Mission, Nairobi, 1902: imperial expansion was motivated by a complex mixture of national self-aggrandizement, commerce and evangelical zeal.

Above left, Gustav Nachtigal (1834–85), the pioneer German explorer: in addition to his Sahara expedition, he also annexed Togoland and Cameroun for Germany in 1884.

Opposite, illustration from a contemporary account of the Pierre de Brazza's (1852–1905) expedition to the Congo: here the explorer is shown treating with native chiefs.

STANLEY IN AFRICA

IMPERIAL FEDERATION. MAP OF THE WORLD SHOWING THE EXTENT OF THE BRITISH EMPIRE IN 1886.

generation of British schoolboys grew up reading these works.

Yet Lenin's theory of a link between capitalism and imperialism is of some importance. As technology advanced, the naval strength of the powers increased, especially in the cases of Japan and Germany. Influenced by the great American theorist Alfred Thayer Mahan, they all considered it essential to have large navies to protect their overseas interests. These interests in turn expanded, as industrial Europe demanded more and more raw materials and produced more and more goods for which markets had to be found. Spokesmen like Joseph Chamberlain in Britain or Jules Ferry in France could argue that new territory had to be found overseas to stave off the recurrent slumps which plagued the European nations. There is no single cause which explains the new imperialism. But it may be closely linked to the rapid changes in European industry, technology and ideas described in the last chapter.

By no means all Western statesmen were in favour of the new imperialism. Bismarck tried to keep Germany out of involvement in Africa and Asia, though his successors reversed this policy. In France, Jules Ferry was ably opposed by nationalists determined to concentrate on revenge against Germany. As for Britain, it has recently been discovered that Lord Salisbury, who was prime minister during the years when Britain annexed most of her new territory, spent his spare time in the sixties writing anonymous anti-imperialist articles for the *Saturday Review*. 'Love of Empire', he concluded, 'is inevitably a love of war.' Joseph Chamberlain and his followers were usually at odds with liberal and conservative leaders alike.

Chamberlain's group were usually called the 'jingoists'. The name comes from a popular song written during the Russo-Turkish War of 1878:

We don't want to fight,
But by jingo, if we do,
We've got the men, we've got the ships,
We've got the money too.

Chamberlain himself was the son of a Manchester manufacturer, the grandfather of the later prime minister, Neville Chamberlain. Convinced of Britain's destiny as an imperial race, he was less disposed than other statesmen to lose sleep over international complications which might be caused by an aggressive policy outside Europe. He was not alone in his assumption that God was on the side of the empire and that other nations and above all other races were less favoured. The age of the new imperialism was brash, self-confident and in some ways devout. Chamberlain was its most typical mouthpiece. It was partly as a result of his cavalier attitude to foreign affairs that Britain became involved in the Boer War.

Although the new imperialism was certainly responsible for creating trouble with other powers, Britain's worst colonial troubles of the nineteenth century came in the old empire and not in new territory. As early as 1857 the precious possession of India had burst into revolt in the Indian Mutiny. Revolt swept across central India and the middle section of the Ganges, destroying everything European which stood in its way. Although they announced loyalty to the old Mogul emperor Bahadur Shah, the mutineers lacked organization or any real plan. Bengal and most of southern India remained loyal. At the end of the year, the relief of Lucknow by General Campbell made it possible to disperse the huge numbers of rebels.

Although relations between Britons and Indians had been poisoned for generations, Indian government was reorganized under the Indian Civil Service. India was still Britain's richest possession and the key-point in imperial strategy. It was defended against the French by the British annexation of Burma in 1886 and against the Russians by an agreement over Tibet and Afghanistan in 1907. India's communications were also guarded by a line of way-stations stretching from London to Bombay, Gibraltar, Malta, Cyprus, the Suez Canal, British Somaliland, Aden and Bahrein.

Again, the British controlled the approaches to the Indian Ocean from their foothold in South Africa, while the maintenance of stability in Egypt, as the Canal Zone, was simply essential to them. These were the interests which led them into taking control of Egypt and fighting the Boer War.

The British on the Nile

The building of the Suez Canal had been a French enterprise, directed by Viscount Ferdinand de Lesseps. Indeed Egypt became very much Frenchified in the 1860s. In 1875, however, the Khedive of Egypt, Ismael Pasha, faced bankruptcy as a result of his speculations in railway-building. Since the French had their own troubles at the time, Disraeli was left to bale him out of his difficulties by buying the khedive's personal shares in the Canal. Disraeli actually received the news that the shares were on sale while dining with Baron Lionel de Rothschild, a fellow-gourmet and another Jew who had broken into the circle of the European aristocracy. The four million required for the transaction were promptly raised from him. Britain became the principal shareholder in the Canal. Further complications arose when Ismael Pasha subsequently cancelled the interest on international Egyptian debts. The British

THE LION'S SHARE.

and French accordingly formed a consortium to make him manage his money more sensibly. Among other economies, they had 2,500 army officers put on half-pay. These men joined with the masses of peasants suspicious of Western influence and crushed by taxes from Alexandria. When the Europeans responded to their criticism by deposing Ismael Pasha and installing his son Tewfik Pasha, they forced the whole Egyptian Civil Service into alliance with the discontented elements.

A series of disturbances followed. The French did not intervene, although their North African interests were expanding with the consolidation of Algeria. The British shelled Alexandria on their own initiative and landed an expeditionary force to restore order and take over the government. They were left in control of the Canal and the Egyptian capital. To consolidate their position, always thinking in terms of protecting the route to India, they found themselves forced to expand further and further inland. Ismael Pasha had never managed to bring the Sudan fully under control or stamp out the slave trade there.

In 1882 conditions deteriorated completely when a holy war or *jihad* was begun by a Muslim prophet calling himself the *Mahdi* or 'chosen one'. 'Chinese' Gordon, who had helped to train the Manchu troops to fight the Taiping, had already advanced to Khartoum on the White Nile. The Mahdi's hordes took the city in 1885, killing all its defenders, including Gordon, a few days before a relief force arrived. The British could not leave the hinterland of Egypt under Mahdist control, although the Mahdi himself died a few months later. It was only in 1898, however, that the 'dervish' troops of his successor were defeated at Omdurman. Egyptian troops led by British advisers took control of the Sudan. Egypt and the Canal were now safe.

The Boer War

By a coincidence, the British general at Omdurman was Kitchener, later the hero of

the relief of Ladysmith in the Boer War. The more general connection between these two conflicts is close. Control of the Cape was as essential to the protection of India as the Canal itself. Cape Colony, which had been taken from the Dutch during the Napoleonic Wars, controlled the entrance to the Indian Ocean. Its change of ownership, however, did not remove the Dutch population. From 1835 to 1837, the Afrikaans-speaking farmers of the Cape set out on the 'Great Trek' northwards, led by Piet Retief and other heroes of Boer history, to escape British rule. On reaching the rich grasslands they wanted, against bloody opposition from the Zulu *impis*, they formed the little republics of Transvaal and the Orange Free State, which were recognized by Britain in 1852 and 1854. Bitterness between Britain and the old-fashioned Calvinist Afrikaners, was increased by Sir Bartle Frere's unsuccessful attempt to re-annexe the Transvaal in 1881, after the Zulu War.

The hatred of the Afrikaners for those who wished to upset their way of life was further increased by the gold strikes of 1886 in the Witwatersrand. Boer society was threatened by the arrival of modern-minded businessmen and engineers, the *Uitlanders* or foreigners. A much worse threat was the covetousness of the great British imperialist Cecil Rhodes. The head of De Beers Mining Corporation and prime minister of Cape Colony from 1890 to 1896, he dreamt of a line of British territory from Cape Town to Cairo. This would link the Suez route to India with the Cape one and would make the British Empire in India impregnable.

Since a strong Boer Transvaal stood in the way of this plan, Rhodes tried to force it into a British-dominated federation ruled from Cape Town. He then harried the Transvaal by annexing the territory around it. When its president, Paul Kruger, stood firm, he took the part of the dissident Uitlanders and then mounted the disastrous Jameson Raid on Johannesburg on their behalf. It failed dismally and enabled the kaiser to make capital out of British blunders by denouncing this attack on the 'infant republic'.

Chamberlain fully supported Rhodes' plans and in spite of Salisbury's doubts he went ahead to provoke the Boer War, Britain's greatest conflict since the American Revolution. This unnecessary war broke out in 1899, after Sir Alfred Milner, the British High Commissioner at the Cape, made impossible demands on behalf of the Uitlanders. The superb irregular cavalry of the Transvaal and the Free State gave an excellent account of itself. The first British reinforcements were outfought but recovered ground after Lord Roberts, or 'Bobs' as his men called him, took command. His most successful generals were Kitchener and Sir John French, the future hero of Ypres.

After bitter guerrilla warfare, Kruger signed the Peace of Vereeniging in 1902. Given the brutality of the war, the settlement was statesmanlike. The British actually gave £3,000,000 in reparations to make good the damage done by their scorched earth policy. In 1906 Campbell-Bannerman's liberal government gave self-government to the Transvaal and the Orange Free State. Four years later they united with Cape Colony and Natal to form the Union of South Africa, the federated unit of which Rhodes had dreamt. With Egypt, Burma

and South Africa under British control, the
safety of India was guaranteed.

British interests in Africa were not confined to Egypt and South Africa. Spurred
on by the activities of other powers, Britain
joined in the 'scramble for Africa' after the
Berlin Conference of 1884. Kenya, Uganda,
Nigeria, the Gold Coast, Gambia and
British Somaliland were all annexed during
this period, not to mention swathes of
territory like Bechuanaland, Zululand, Pon-
doland and Rhodesia itself, which were
seized in the south under Rhodes' influence.

The French in North Africa

The Joseph Chamberlain of the Third
Republic was Jules Ferry. He too carried his
aggressive policies against strong opposition
from both left and right. By the nineties,
however, his ideas had been taken up by a
pressure group in the Chamber led by the
Algerian-born deputy Eugène Etienne. He
cooperated with two bodies out of doors,
the *Comité d'Afrique Française* and after
1893 the *Union Coloniale*. Indeed it was only
after 1890 that France made her main gains
south of the Sahara.

France's first commitment in Africa, of
course, was to Algeria. Although she had
defeated 'Abd el Kadar by 1845, the first
programme to dispossess the tribesmen of
their land did not come until 1871, when the
first *colons* from Alsace were settled. This
produced a serious uprising. It only brought
confiscations which were given to new
bodies of settlers. Although Algeria technically became part of metropolitan France,
its franchise was narrow, and rule still lay
effectively with a governor appointed in
Paris.

The impossibility of winning the loyalty
of its tribesmen did not prevent the French
from turning their attention to Tunisia,
which became their protectorate in 1881, in
spite of the ambitions of the newly united
Italy there.

The last part of French North Africa to
be annexed was Morocco. Constantly in a

state of disorder, its independence was a standing threat to the Algerian border. In 1903 Colonel Louis Lyautey was sent in to restore stability, and Morocco became a French sphere of influence after Casablanca was occupied in 1907. In spite of strong German suspicion of France, the powers recognized a French Moroccan protectorate in 1912. Lyautey's wise administration and the defeat of the fierce nomadic Tuaregs on the Algerian frontier ensured that North Africa was firmly under French control by 1914.

West Africa

Although other annexations were going on throughout the world, no area shows the rivalries of the imperialist powers better than West Africa. Although control of forts at Lagos, in the Gold Coast (Ghana) and Sierra Leone made the British strong in the area, the French had maintained trading stations on the Senegal since the great days of the slave trade in the eighteenth century. They also had interests in modern Guinea and the Ivory Coast, though they had not carried out any inland penetration.

It was Senegal which first became a real French colony. The greatest of the French colonialists, Louis Léon César Faidherbe, became governor there in 1853. In his first few years in office, he attacked the Senegalese traders who levied an exorbitant 'tribute' on all trade passing down the Senegal. He also checked the expansion of the Muslim leader Al Hajj 'Umar, whose strong state on the upper Niger was threatening to extend into the Senegal Valley. During tours of duty which went on until 1886, Faidherbe re-modelled Senegal. Its Islamic population became loyal citizens of the Republic, and the Senegalese riflemen came to be one of the crack units of the French Army.

Faidherbe, and other French leaders, began to dream of a French Empire which would stretch from Senegal across the Sudan to the Indian Ocean. This would also link up with the new territories in North Africa. On the other hand, it could not avoid clashing with the plans of Rhodes and the British to secure communications from Cairo to the Cape.

Equally difficult was the subjugation of West Africa itself. Al Hajj 'Umar was not

THE RHODES COLOSSUS
STRIDING FROM CAPE TOWN TO CAIRO.

the only Islamic leader who waged the *jihad* against the French. His son Ahmadu Bello, ruling a state of great sophistication which dominated the western Sudan, was only finally defeated in 1893. After this there was still resistance from Samori, the most like-able and least cultured of these Muslim princes, which went on until 1898. Indeed the European advance in West Africa was at least partly governed by the behavious of the strong Islamic states which stood in its way.

The scramble for Africa

The advance was also moulded by the relations of the powers with one another. King Leopold's interests in the Congo and the intervention of the Germans created fears that if territory were not seized soon, it

would no longer be available. Between 1883 and 1885, the Germans annexed Togo, Kamerun, German East Africa (Tanzania) and German South West Africa. In 1885, the Congress of Berlin, called by Bismarck, in effect laid down the rules for the partition of Africa. Although it also gave the Belgian Congo recognition and access to the sea, this alarmed the French into seizing the French Congo to the north of Leopold's state. Sir George Goldie, a director of the Royal Niger Company, was alarmed by the German and French advance into seizing Nigeria, which had been brilliantly subdued by Lord Lugard by the end of the century. The French advanced into Guinea, the Ivory Coast, and eventually Dahomey. To keep them out of the Gold Coast, the British pushed their long-standing grievances with the kingdom of the Ashanti to a conclusion in 1896.

Meanwhile British concern over German interests in modern Tanzania produced a similar policy in East Africa. Salisbury had Kenya declared a British sphere of influence in 1886, and it became a protectorate in 1893. In 1890 Lugard had arrived in Kampala with his one maxim gun, and had taken the part of the Protestants or *wa-ingleza* (the English party) against the *wa-franza* (the French party), Catholics converted by Lavigerie's famous White Fathers. The Imperial British East Africa Company then opened up the territory, and it too became a protectorate in 1894. The last power to enter the scramble was another new one, Italy, which managed to satisfy its hunger for national greatness by seizing Eritrea, on the Red Sea, and part of Somaliland in 1889.

Unfortunately this first stage of the scramble did not solve the problem of conflict between British and French imperial ambitions, which cut directly across one another. In 1896 the French, long humiliated by Germany at home and determined to compensate by seizing the kind of empire they wanted abroad, sent Marchand from the Congo to forestall British Cape-Cairo ambitions by annexing the headwaters of the Nile. Marchand and his tiny force sailed up the Ubangui River on their little steamer, the *Faidherbe*. When it could go no further, they dismantled it and dragged it through the jungle, in the hope of being able to re-launch it on the Nile. After two years of travel, they reached the station of Fashoda, on the Nile. Four days later it was approached by Kitchener, with a greatly superior British force, fresh from the victory of Omdurman.

A full-scale conflict was only avoided by the courtesy and tact of these two soldiers, who agreed that until orders arrived the British flag should fly over the town and the French one over the fort. Even this did not prevent a major international crisis. Only the threat of war persuaded Delcassé, the French foreign minister, that Marchand's troops should be withdrawn. Once the crisis blew over, however, the main barrier to Anglo-French understanding had been removed. From now on the two nations gradually moved together to become allies in the First World War.

China and southeast Asia

While the European nations were dividing the spoils of Africa, they continued the expansion of the earlier part of the century in the Far East. To protect India against the French advance in Indo-China, the British annexed Burma in 1886. However, French penetration had been greatly slowed up by the disaster of 1871 and by Garnier's discovery that control of the Mekong would not give the expected access to China's markets.

Attention now turned to the Red River and the Gulf of Tonkin. Although Hanoi was taken in 1873, the state of Annam

(north Vietnam) was surprisingly strong, and the ancient city could not be held. The only result of further attempts to take Hanoi was a disastrous reverse in 1883. This provoked Ferry and the French jingoists to a firmer policy. After bombarding Foochow, outside Canton, to discourage Chinese protests, the French finally annexed Annam. It was soon pacified, while neighbouring Laos became a protectorate a few years later. Although Siam remained independent, Britain and France had now divided all of mainland southeast Asia between them.

China itself was a little luckier. Although the Manchus were constantly humiliated during the era of concessions, they did at least remain in possession of the bulk of their land, if only because the mutual jealousies of the powers kept them cautious about annexation. Nevertheless, such scramble as there was in China was again triggered off by German action, when Admiral Tirpitz took the port of Kiaochow in 1897. Russia at once grabbed the precious warm-water harbour of Port Arthur, the French took Kwang-chow in the south and the British bullied the Chinese into granting a lease of Wei-hai-wei.

In 1898, the Americans also gained a foothold in the China Sea by conquering the Spanish Philippines. Anxious to gain further advantages in China, John Hay, the American Secretary of State, confirmed the delicate balance of Western interests by announcing (untruthfully) that the powers had agreed to his 'open door' policy. Any concession gained by one Western power was now to be open to all. In the next year, 1900, the powers actually cooperated in putting down the Boxer Rebellion. Fanatical anti-Western rebels besieged the Peking diplomatic community in the British legation. Eventually the siege was lifted by an international task force. This action confirmed first that the powers could not fully dismember China against each other's interests, second that the Manchus had become powerless and finally that America had become a world power.

Part VIII

DEMOCRACY AND THE NEW IMPERIALISM

Introduction

The closing years of the nineteenth century and the opening ones of the twentieth are from one angle best thought of as an epilogue, from another as a prologue. During the last decade of the nineteenth century contemporaries placed almosy equal emphasis on *fin-de-siècle* and on 'newness'. During the *belle époque* which ushered in the twentieth century there was an obvious contrast between surface glitter and structural disturbance. There were, indeed, many symptoms of violence before the greater violence of the First World War shattered the old world for ever.

In these years, ways of working, living, thinking and feeling were all transformed as a result of industrial development. The first great changes had taken place during the late eighteenth century with the exploitation of coal, iron and steam, but it was not until the 1840s, 50s and 60s that the railway, symbol of industrial progress, completed the British industrial revolution and intro-

duced industrial revolutions in other countries. Factories and furnaces were visible signs of a new dispensation. So, too, were industrial cities and regions. There were invisible signs also – new feelings about 'class', 'mobility' and the prospects for further technological and social advance. The transformation, moreover, was not confined geographically to a few countries where economic progress was most rapid: it affected countries which remained primarily agricultural, setting the terms of their relationship with the rest.

This great transformation is not easy to chart, for the history of industrialization is concerned not so much with events as with processes. There were spurts and lags and different chronologies of growth, disturbance and adaptation in different countries. By 1914 the processes were still incomplete. Many of the new techniques developed between 1870 and 1914 had not been fully exploited; many of the innovations had not left their impact on daily life. We can, nonetheless, trace back to the world before 1914 the origins of what we now take for granted – not only material comfort of a kind never before enjoyed but 'welfare states' in which governments intervene in the working of the market and large business organizations.

In the long run, industrialization meant greater wealth. Between 1870 and 1900, as many countries industrialized, world industrial production increased nearly four times. Between 1900 and 1914 the amount of world trade in manufacturing goods doubled. In consequence, there were marked improvements in standards of living along with the aspirations which went with them. Yet in the

short run, as industrialization proceeded, there were fluctuations in income and employment from year to year and wide disparities in every year in the distribution of wealth both within and between countries. These fluctuations and disparities were traced quantitively by men who developed the study of statistics, extending it to cover social as well as economic indices – birth and death rates, for example, or industrial accidents alongside figures relating to prices, wages and profits.

Between 1870 and 1914 there was rather less confidence in the rhetoric of industrial progress than there had been in mid-Victorian Britain, the pioneering industrial country. In Britain itself, where the early lead was beginning to be thought of as something of a handicap, businessmen were worried by foreign competition and by smaller profit margins: at the same time workers, skilled and unskilled, were becoming more organized, the latter for the first time in history. Critics of society as it was and as it was becoming complained not only of continuing poverty in the midst of plenty but of the wastes of early industrialization. In continental Europe, trade-union and political movements refused to accept the logic and authority of the profit-making industrial system. For every new opportunity which industrialization afforded there were parallel problems. The social costs of industrialization were difficult to measure, and those changes in the physical environment and in human relations which could not be measured quantitatively stimulated both intellectual argument and moral and political protest.

As many of the new techniques and innovations discovered before 1914 transformed the texture of daily life only during the 1920s and 1930s – electrical power, automobiles and wireless are obvious examples – so many of the criticisms of nineteenth- and early twentieth-century industrialization which were voiced before 1914 became effective in social and political terms only much later. There were time lags in experience and response, particularly in political response, as well as in the history of invention. In the meantime, the technology behind industrialization continued to change. Britain which at first was the 'workshop of the world' had established its lead on the basis of coal and iron – 'carboniferous capitalism'. Germany and the United States forged ahead in 'the age of steel'. 'The age of steel' is itself an inadequate label since there were striking developments in steel technology which now makes the early age of steel seem as distant as the age of iron.

There were differences also in organization and in scale. The British industrial revolution had depended on the free initiative of individuals: in later industrial revolutions the state counted for more. So, too, did science. Individualism itself proved inadequate to direct large-scale industry, and the development of industry depended increasingly on organizational efficiency. The industrial growth not only was uneven but the experience associated with industrialization varied as it progressed at different times in different countries. By 1914 Japan was the one Asian country to have undergone an 'industrial revolution', a distinctive experience which must be considered in relation to the developments in nearby China at that time and to the progress of the industrial revolutions which preceded and succeeded Japan's.

The experience of individual countries must always be studied within a bigger frame than that which they themselves provide. As a result of developments in transport and finance, an international economy came into existence between 1870 and 1914 within which Europe, with its growing population and its developing technology, played the dominant role in the world. By the First World War sixty percent of all manufactured goods were exported from three European countries, and although Britain was no longer the workshop of the world London still remained the centre of international economic transactions. Britain's share in world trade was declining, yet it was still the great trading country. It continued to provide both international economic services and a huge market, a free trade market for foreign goods. It served, in a phrase of J. M. Keynes, as 'the conductor of the orchestra'. As the world's largest creditor country, it never exploited its position to accumulate such large stocks of gold that it drained the resources of other countries within the gold standard system. Smaller countries could afford to let London

lay down the rules. Free movements of capital, stable exchange rates and the 'legal order' of the gold standard were thought by many to be essential aspects of any international economic network, and though there were rumblings from below and complex pressures which pointed to fundamental disturbances in the future, the system held until 1914.

There was irony in the fact that the collapse of the system in 1914 and during the years of unanticipated attrition which followed would not have been so catastrophic had not industrialization affected warfare as much as the making of wealth. The skills which had been applied to the making of machines and of consumer goods had been capable of being applied also to the making of weapons of destruction. The scale of destruction between 1914 and 1918 – and the scope of the organization which was necessary to wage war successfully – depended on the record of technical and economic progress before war broke out. It is apparent, moreover, that before 1914 industrialization played a larger part in influencing the fortunes of states in their rivalry, often ancient rivalry, with each other, a rivalry grounded in fear and mistrust, than it did in remodelling their internal forms of government. In administration even more than in politics old ways persisted after industrialization had posed new issues and demanded new remedies.

Below, saluting the flag in a New York school in the 1890s; especially between the 1860s and 1920s, the USA really was a new world for millions escaping poverty and oppression in Europe.

Opposite, members of the international relief force sent to Peking in 1900 to quell the Boxer rising and maintain western influence pose for the camera outside a photographer's studio.

On page 508, French soldiers occupying a railway station during a strike of railway workers, 1910: the years before 1914 were marked by increasing trades union activity, as organized labour came to realize its strength.

Chapter 43

The Growth of Democracy in Britain and France

Britain was the pioneer of the new industrialism. Since the late sixteenth century England had been renowned as a rich and powerful trading nation. During the seventeenth and eighteenth centuries she had fought a series of wars and thereby acquired a great commercial and territorial empire overseas, which left her trading rivals in western Europe far behind. British manufacturers seized the opportunity to produce for an almost unlimited market abroad as well as for Britain's own rapidly growing population.

The lead was given by enterprising manufacturers of cotton goods. In the second half of the eighteenth century improvements in textile machinery raised output dramatically. New steam-driven machines and the men, women and children who worked them were concentrated in factories. Other British industries followed suit in the quest for profitable inventions and profitable ways of organizing labour. In the nineteenth century trade was freed. Raw materials for the factories and food for the growing number of town-dwellers could now be imported cheaply. Railways revolutionized Britain's communications, while her trading competitors were much slower to change. Until the latter part of the century she had no rival in supplying and fostering mankind's demand for manufactured goods. By 1850 Britain had become, in the familiar phrase, 'the workshop of the world'.

The social cost of pioneering such a change was high. The entrepreneurs who organized industrial change made their fortunes out of it, while the early generations of factory workers had less cause to be grateful. Although it is possible that many of them were marginally better fed, better clothed and better housed, they had to adjust themselves to an entirely new and alien way of life: to the harsh and monotonous grind of factory discipline, to grim and cheerless factory towns, to the ever-present fear of losing, through no fault of their own, a job which was essential if the still greater tyranny of the workhouse were to be avoided. For these pioneers it was a bleak age.

Living conditions were much more obviously man-made than in an agricultural society, and it seemed reasonable to demand that the makers and upholders of industrial society should better these conditions. From the late eighteenth century onwards discontented workers organized themselves to win enough power to back up their demands. They often came into violent conflict with authority. As agricultural workers were suffering from an equally man-made transformation of the countryside in the interests of large-scale farming, they too erupted at times in protest. Down to the 1840s it seemed at least possible that the price of pioneering industrialism could be social revolution.

Yet despite the mounting fears of the propertied classes this point was never reached. Britain was to remain one of the few states, like America and Japan, where the social tensions brought by industrialization did not lead to political breakdown.

Compared with their more self-conscious successors in the rest of the world, the British industrialized slowly and casually, and the problems of social change emerged correspondingly slowly. There was no swift and sudden build-up of tension such as was induced by tsarist Russia's hectic pace of industrialization at the end of the nineteenth century. As pioneers the British had no precedents to guide them, but their political system, like that of America and the Scandinavian countries, proved remarkably responsive to the new era. It was a flexible system, which allowed more freedom of action for those seeking change than was usual in most countries at any time. Political societies, trade unions and polemical literature could flourish just sufficiently to act as a safety valve. Enterprising families could share power with the ruling aristocracy after a generation or so's apprenticeship in accumulating the necessary wealth and land.

The ruling classes contained enough able, intelligent and enlightened men to edge parliament in the direction of timely concessions to the middle and working classes. Reforms made in the first half of the nineteenth century left many people dissatisfied, but they bred optimism about the political system's capacity for changing both itself and the conditions in which people lived. It was significant that many of the reforms were the work of Sir Robert Peel, son of a cotton magnate and the first prime minister from the new manufacturing class.

By the 1850s more people than ever before were experiencing the rewards of industrialization in the form of higher earnings and a greater variety of goods to buy with them. The rewards were still scanty, and dismal poverty remained the lot of millions, but industrial society was at last accepted as a means and not a bar to progress.

The British could look back on the previous 100 years as a remarkable success story. They had pioneered an industrial revolution and had made themselves the most prosperous nation in the world. They had made enough political and social changes to avoid the revolutions which engulfed most of Europe in 1848 and could claim to be the most stable state in the world. And they controlled such a vast territorial and commercial empire and had beaten off so many challenges from their greatest rivals, France and Russia, that they could claim to be the most powerful nation in the world.

Palmerston and Britain's world role

The rewards of industrialization were, therefore, not only material ones. It had strengthened immensely the economic power which underpinned Britain's world role. Emotional satisfaction in the greatness of Britain's power was freely available to millions of her people who had to be content with a meagre share of her new wealth.

The symbol of this greatness was Lord Palmerston, who between 1830 and 1865 was the most influential figure in the conduct of Britain's foreign policy. He is the only British foreign secretary whose name is still familiar the world over, epitomizing breezy, cocksure diplomacy. Palmerston had style, and his boisterous handling of international business matched his own rakish and full-blooded private life. He breathed a self-confidence which was very reassuring to a generation perplexed by the hazards and uncertainties of industrial society. International problems, at least, could be made to look simpler by applying superior naval and military force. Power remained the most popular criterion by which a country earned respect and admiration. Palmerston proved that Britain had more power at her disposal than any of her rivals.

He used that power with great skill in furthering what most of his fellow countrymen would have agreed were the nation's interests: the security of its empire, the development of its commerce and the spread of the British kind of constitutional government. He used British forces to ensure the triumph of constitutional government in Spain and Portugal in the 1830s. In 1839–42 and again in 1856–8 he used war to force the Chinese empire to trade according to 'Western' rules. He used both diplomacy and war to prevent Russia from gaining control over the Ottoman Empire, Persia and Afghanistan, an area crucial to the long-term defence of British India.

Admittedly, in these and other cases Palmerston provided only temporary solutions. Constitutionalism never prospered in Spain or Portugal. The consequences of rousing the Chinese giant so rudely and unceremoniously are still working themselves out. The climax of his Eastern policy, the defeat of Russia in the Crimea in 1854–6, merely diverted Russian imperialism to Central Asia well out of range of British sea power. But his dramatic and skilful improvisations abroad, though often criticized, contributed towards a national unity and pride badly strained by the developments at home.

Palmerston was a dangerous model for statesmen in other countries exhilarated by the power industrialization had placed in their hands. The most famous incident of his career was a trivial one. In 1850, he sent an ultimatum and a naval squadron to Greece to extract compensation for one Don Pacifico, whose property had been destroyed in a riot and who claimed to be a British citizen. His critics claimed this was outrageous bullying. Palmerston retorted that a British citizen anywhere should get the same protection once afforded to citizens of the Roman Empire. This was splendid rhetoric and is testimony of his effect on national morale. A *pax Britannica* was an illusion, however, for other powerful empires were soon to come into being as industrialism spread. They, too, would seek a world role of the kind which Palmerston had made so glamorous and successful.

Gladstonian liberalism

The 1860s and 70s were decades in which most European governments were experimenting with modernization with the centre of authority shifting away from absolute monarchy. The timing is explained by the common experience of revolution in 1848 and a great series of mid-century wars. Both exposed dangerous defects in the states involved and offered serious warnings to others.

Although her economy was the most advanced in the world, in other respects Britain was badly in need of modernization. The constitution, the civil service, the legal system, education, the army, even the navy no longer answered the needs of an industrial society with world-wide commitments. The third quarter of the nineteenth century was to bring radical reform of the country's main institutions.

The most burning issue was that of parliamentary reform. The first reform of parliament in 1832 had scarcely affected the predominance of the landed gentry in the House of Commons. But it was the thin end of the wedge. It whetted the appetites of those who wanted a really sweeping change in the way the British people were represented in parliament. By the 1850s there was wide agreement among political leaders that further reform was inevitable in such a rapidly changing society. There was equally wide disagreement as to what form it should take.

During this same period party politics were in a state of flux. Sir Robert Peel's Conservative Party had split in 1846 over his decision to repeal the Corn Laws, which for decades had protected British farmers from having to compete with cheap grain imports. Because of the potato famine in Ireland, Peel got rid of this last big barrier to free trade. During the next twenty years Peel's opponents in parliament built a new Conservative Party – a conservative

section of the party, under the growing influence of Benjamin Disraeli. In the same years a new Liberal Party was emerging as a complex alliance of great Whig landowners, supporters of Peel on the Corn Laws issue and radicals. Its leader was William Ewart Gladstone, who as chancellor of the exchequer introduced a remarkable series of budgets which cut tariffs and reduced government expenditure. British politics in the 1860s and 70s were dominated by the rivalry between Gladstone and Disraeli.

By the 1860s both parties were alarmed by the scale of popular agitation for parliamentary reform. The result was Disraeli's comparatively radical measure of 1867, the Second Reform Act, which gave the vote to all male householders in towns. This meant that most urban voters would in future be from the working classes.

Above, Punch *cartoon, captioned 'A Bad Example', of the two great political rivals of the 1860s and 1870s: on the left, William Ewart Gladstone (1807–98), four times Liberal prime minister, reformer and a fervent opponent of repression, and, on the right, Benjamin Disraeli (1804–81), twice Tory Prime Minister, an enthusiastic reformer at home and imperialist overseas.*

513

Disraeli's hopes that these new working-class voters could be rallied in support of the Conservatives proved premature, and a general election in the following year returned the Liberals to power. Between 1868 and 1874 Prime Minister Gladstone's government enacted a series of overdue reforms: voting in parliamentary elections was at last made secret; a start was made in providing elementary education for all; the law courts were reorganized on simpler lines for the more efficient administration of justice; recruitment to the civil service was open to anyone who could pass a competitive examination. The army, after its poor showing in the Crimean War was thoroughly reorganized: country regiments were established; flogging was abolished together with the practice of allowing officers to purchase their commissions. Thus many of Britain's institutions became more democratic and efficient.

The principle of democracy was relatively new to British politics. The idea that every citizen was entitled to the vote and that a government's authority should rest on the consent of the majority of the people had been pioneered in France and America. Though political democracy was not a by-product of industrialization, it was in industrial areas that the working classes could most effectively organize themselves to demand political rights. The direct involvement of the whole population in politics, therefore, tended to follow in the wake of industrialism.

After the Second Reform Act it was only a matter of time before full parliamentary democracy was obtained in Britain. The Franchise Act of 1884 and the Redistribution Act of 1885 were logical extensions of the principles recognized in 1867. The Franchise Act gave the vote to working men in rural areas, just as its predecessor had enfranchised the towns. The Redistribution Act remapped the constituencies so that each member of parliament would represent roughly the same number of people. Representation of the British people in parliament still fell somewhat short of universal male suffrage, and none of the nation's women won the vote until after the First World War, but Britain now had a mass electorate of some 5,000,000 voters.

Both the composition of parliament and the style of British politics changed with the coming of democracy. The composition of parliament changed slowly, however, and working-class candidates initially got little support from the predominantly working-class electorate. This was partly because of the aristocratic and middle-class politicians who so quickly saw the need for a new style of politics. Gladstone in 1879–80 and the Birmingham radical Joseph Chamberlain in 1885 sought out the new electorate by personally campaigning throughout the country in support of their programmes. They set a fashion which other political leaders were obliged to follow. After 1867, both Liberals

and Conservatives groped their way towards new ways of organizing their parties so as to mobilize as much support as possible on polling days. The modern party 'machine' was coming into existence.

Because of the larger electorate, the drift of public opinion was much less predictable than in the past. The popular press helped to organize public opinion and projected the views of its owners. The *Daily Mail*, one of the first of the dailies deliberately aimed at millions made literate by the Education Act of 1870, was founded by Alfred Harmsworth in 1896. It was selling nearly a million copies a day by the end of the century. Dramatic and simplified presentation of the more emotionally charged issues of international affairs made politics seem exciting and relevant to the electorate, even when its material interests were being neglected. As in the days of Palmerston nationalist sentiment had a unifying effect.

The ruling classes in Victorian Britain had brought off a remarkable feat of political engineering. Political stability in an age of social and economic revolution was rare. For a while the history of the nineteenth century seemed to confirm a widespread belief in the possibility of steady and peaceful progress; but as the century wore on, doubts about the future became more prominent and there was apprehension about the future shape of British government and society now that the balance of political power had shifted from the middle to the working classes. Phrases like 'a leap in the dark' and 'shooting Niagara', used about the Reform Bill of 1867 expressed the sense of uncertainty. Demands for social and economic equality seemed likely to follow the winning of political equality. How could it be accommodated without wrecking the whole Victorian scheme of things, which assumed that everyone would find his proper level in society by the use of talent and energy and that the interests of the whole community would regulate themselves in the long run? Reality did not justify these gloomy predictions of 1867, however, and the newly franchised classes proved far from revolutionary in their demands.

There was apprehension as to the future of the British Empire. It remained the envy of its rivals, who saw it as the secret of Britain's power and wealth, and expanded dramatically between 1882 and 1890 when Britain won the lion's share in the partition of Africa. The financial coup through which Disraeli increased her stake in the Suez Canal in 1875 was of tremendous importance to Britain because of the value of the canal in reaching India. The British were, nevertheless, aware of the empire's vulnerable foundations. The unity of the United Kingdom itself was threatened by Irish discontent; and further threats to the empire multiplied in the later nineteenth century as Russia, France, Germany and America made spectacular gains in Africa and Asia. The task of providing against such threats became increasingly onerous, expensive and uncertain success. Britain's survival as a world power seemed at stake.

There was also apprehension about the economy. Though much of the nation became more prosperous and the rate of industrialization accelerated, progress was less smooth in the last quarter of the nineteenth century. It fluctuated enough for businessmen in the 1870s and 80s to talk gloomily and prematurely of the 'Great Depression'. British agriculture suffered from the rising imports of cheap foreign grain from America and Russia. British manufacturers had to compete with rivals from America, Germany and other newly industrialized states. In the face of such competition British industry adapted itself with only partial success, and Britain ceased to be the workshop of the world. Her future role in the international economy was obscure.

Trade unionism

The rise of trade unionism, the formation of a Labour party and the growing acceptance of the idea that the state should make itself responsible for the welfare of its poorer citizens proved again how well the British social and political system could adjust itself to change.

British workers had pioneered trade unionism during the first half of the nineteenth century. It was a long, slow process of trial and error. There was never any shortage of men willing to experiment in how best to wring better wages and conditions of work from their employers, and their persistence in face of repeated failure was eventually rewarded. By the middle of the century a booming economy and a shortage of skilled labour created the right conditions for successful agitation. The experience of previous decades enabled union leaders to take advantage of them.

The Amalgamated Society of Engineers, established in 1851, set a new standard for the movement with its large membership, ample funds and nationwide organization. The economic benefits of trade unionism were made apparent to an ever-growing army of industrial workers.

But they had not yet won respectability. The courts denied their legality, and the law did not protect their funds from absconding treasurers. In the 1860s the principal union leaders entered politics and agitated for the extension of the vote to working men. Union support was given to sympathetic parliamentary candidates, while at the same time a growing number of trade unionists stood for parliament themselves. The unions' case was forcibly put to the Royal Commission on trade unions, which reported in favour of legalizing them.

In 1868, the Trade Union Congress first met to provide a national forum for discussing labour problems, and in 1871 it set up a parliamentary committee to lobby M.P.s. This political activity proved effective, and the legislation enacted by Gladstone's government in 1871 and by Disraeli's government in 1875 reflected the new climate of opinion by making the unions a recognized British institution with legal status.

Only a minority of mostly skilled and 'respectable' workers were yet represented by trade unions, and to many workers the unions had become too respectable. In the 1880s and 90s a 'new unionism' developed, with a new generation of union leaders like Ben Tillett and Tom Mann, who organized the great mass of unskilled workers. Their tactics were more aggressive, their political thinking often socialist. The great London dock strike of 1889 won the dockers the sixpence an hour they demanded, and the 'dockers tanner' marked the triumphant arrival of the 'new unionism'.

The Labour Party

The 'new unionism' swelled the ranks of the labour movement, but it also made trade unionism less acceptable to middle class opinion. This was at a time when trade unions generally found themselves under renewed fire. Employers' associations increasingly resisted their activities, encouraged by the success of their counterparts in America. The courts tended to decide against the unions in test cases; even the legality of picketing, essential to the success of strikes, was again in doubt. Trade unions were blamed for the decline in competitiveness of British industry because they raised costs and resisted innovation. The position they had won for themselves after so many decades of struggle no longer seemed secure.

By the end of the century the union leaders were conscious of their political weakness. Since the 1860s they had counted on being

Above, members of the Matchmakers Union, 1888.

Opposite, membership certificate of the National Union of Gas Workers & General Labourers.

able to persuade the Liberals and, more indirectly, the Conservatives to look after their interests in parliament. Since 1885 working-class men elected to parliament had sat with the Liberals as 'Lib-Labs'. A new political party to represent working class interests, however, had been regarded as impracticable and unnecessary. Now even the most moderate union leaders were not so sure.

The demand for a new party had sprung from the revival of British socialism after 1880. The most influential of the various socialist groups formed at this time were the Social Democratic Federation and the Fabian Society. The Social Democratic Federation, led by H. M. Hyndman, was a Marxist organization too addicted to the idea of violent revolution to have a wide appeal to British workers. The Fabian Society, whose most famous members were Bernard Shaw and Beatrice and Sidney Webb, rejected revolutionary Marxism and believed in 'permeating' the existing parties with socialist ideas. Though the SDF and the Fabian Society were both predominantly middle class in leadership, the socialism they propagated spread to a small but enthusiastic section of the working classes. To many of them an entirely new political party seemed the obvious way of realising social and economic equality.

In 1893 representatives of various socialist societies and labour clubs met in Bradford to found an Independent Labour Party. Its programme was broadly socialist, but its prime aim was to attract as much working class and especially trade union support as possible for a parliamentary party working for the general interests of labour. Its leading light was the Scottish miner, Keir Hardie, who in the previous year became the first working man to sit in parliament independently of the main parties.

Although the ILP had little success at the polls, its activities helped to swing trade union opinion. In 1889 the Trades Union Congress decided to investigate ways of establishing a distinct group in parliament. In 1900 the unions joined with the ILP, the SDF and the Fabians to set up a Labour Representation Committee. Its secretary was Ramsay MacDonald, later to become the first Labour prime minister.

Many union leaders still remained unconvinced, but what convinced them was the Taff Vale Case of 1901. In that same year the House of Lords upheld a claim by the Taff Vale Railway Company against the Union of Railway Servants for damage to railway property done by its members in a strike called by the union. The union was ordered to pay £23,000 in compensation, which caused much resentment among trade unionists who regarded the judgement as an overt attempt to suppress strikes. In the general election of 1906 the strong feelings aroused by the Taff Vale case helped to return twenty-nine MPs to constitute the new Labour Party.

The problem of poverty

Through trade unions and the Labour Party the more energetic of the new voters had organized themselves for industrial and political action. Gradually the older parties came to see the wisdom of anticipating some of Labour's demands and began to tackle the worst evils of poverty.

Nineteenth-century liberalism had believed that the state should interfere as little as possible in the lives of its citizens. The best goods and services would be produced, to the benefit of all, if everyone pursued his own interests and knew that if he did not help himself no one else would. Charity and legislation like the poor laws and the factory acts reflected the belief of the upper classes in the virtues of hard work.

By the end of the century, however, it had become clear that leaving the system to regulate itself meant too high a cost in human suffering. Investigators like Charles Booth in London and Seebohm Rowntree in York produced startling figures of the extent and depths of poverty in a country which was renowned for its creation of wealth. The realization that nearly a third of the people of London, the richest city in the world, lived in misery, squalor and hopelessness shocked public opinion. With socialism putting forward radical solutions to the victims of poverty, who could now vote, both Conservatives and Liberals had cause to reconsider the perils of letting the state interfere with the economy.

But traditional ideas died hard, and the Liberals and the Conservatives were cautious about social reform. Disraeli had in his younger days written eloquently of the 'two nations' into which the country was divided by the poverty line; but during his second administration (1874–80) a relatively moderate programme of social legislation was attempted: a factory act for the further protection of women and children, a public health act and an act enabling local authorities to do away with slums.

But between 1885 and 1905, when Britain was governed almost continuously by the Conservatives, his successors, Lord Salisbury and Arthur Balfour, accomplished little except in the field of education. Elementary education became free in 1891, technical education was belatedly developed when its value to Britain's trading rivals was demonstrated and Balfour's Education Act of 1902 re-organized both elementary and secondary education on more efficient lines. In the long term no social reform could be more important than making education available to the whole of the nation's children, but the problem of ensuring their health and well-being deserved equal priority.

What was to become the 'welfare state' took shape after the Liberals came to power in 1906. Already, during the second half of the nineteenth century, enterprising municipal governments had made many of Britain's cities cleaner, healthier and pleasanter to live in through schemes for slum clearance, sanitation, transport services and the supply of water, gas and electricity. During their long spell as the minority party many Liberals had come to accept that the state should take direct responsibility for the welfare of its citizens. In the election campaign of 1906 (the first one for the Labour Party) they denounced the Conservatives for their incompetency in the Boer War and appealed to the country with a platform which called for the enactment of measures favourable to organized labour and a programme of social legislation. The Liberals won a considerable majority and thus began a new era for Great Britain, replacing the liberalism of Gladstone with the radicalism of men like David Lloyd George, who had a much deeper concern for the economic and social welfare of the masses.

Despite the opposition of the House of Lords, the Liberals succeeded in enacting the Workingmen's Compensation Bill and the Small Holdings Bill of 1907 which authorized the County Councils to acquire land suitable for small holdings and to sell or lease it to agricultural labourers or other persons desiring a small stake in the land. The most important legislative achievement of 1908 was the passing of the Old Age Pension Act, which provided for the payment of small pensions to people over the age of seventy whose yearly income did not exceed £31 10s. In the summer of that same year Lloyd George, who had been made chancellor of the exchequer, visited Germany and made a study of the German system of state insurance against sickness, accidents and old age. Deeply impressed by what he saw, he introduced his National Insurance Bill in 1911, which brought in a national insurance scheme to insure the working population against sickness and, to some extent, against unemployment. The British were at last doing what the old-fashioned paternalist government of the German Empire had done twenty years earlier.

Lords and suffragettes

The 'leap in the dark' towards democracy had been less hazardous than the old ruling classes had feared. Enough of the new mass electorate were as aware of the possibility of progress as the middle classes had been after 1832. Yet the slowness with which the two traditional political parties accepted the idea of actively promoting some redistribution of wealth put a strain on this belief in the years before 1914. Many trade unionists began to rely more on massive industrial action than on their representatives in the House of Commons, and a great wave of strikes hit the country in 1911–12. The railways and the docks were at times paralysed, and there were violent clashes with police and troops. But the strike movement died away, and syndicalism – the use of strikes to promote class struggle and political change – did not become the philosophy of the British labour movement.

The fundamental issue of this period was that of curbing the power of the House of Lords, which because of its hereditary character was not subject to popular control, was always dominated by the Conservative Party and hence obstructed a good deal of Liberal legislation. After 1906, although the Liberal government had won a massive majority for the first time since 1880, the Lords continued their wrecking tactics.

The long awaited clash between the Commons and the Lords came in 1909. The Liberal prime minister, Sir Henry Campbell-Bannerman, was forced to retire in 1908 and was succeeded by Herbert Asquith, who was in turn succeeded as chancellor of the exchequer by Lloyd George. Because of the cost of old-age pensions and other social legislation and the great increase in naval expenditures brought about by the competition with Germany, Lloyd George was immediately confronted with an enormous national deficit. In his 1909 budget he proposed to make use of the older forms of taxation such as the income tax, inheritance tax, luxury taxes on liquor and tobacco; but in addition he proposed to use the expedient of imposing a supertax on larger incomes. Another ingenious form of raising revenue was a tax on the sale of land, which was of course bitterly opposed by the landowners, many of whom were in the House of Lords. For six months this budget, the object of which was to wage war against poverty, was hotly debated in parliament. The Lords defied constitutional precedent by rejecting it after it had passed the Commons; but Lloyd George and his colleagues were not averse to a fight on this issue and managed to win the ensuing general election. Deferring to the popular mandate on the budget, the House of Lords finally passed it.

With the struggle over the budget out of the way, the Liberals turned to the central issue of curbing the power of the Lords. In April 1910 the Asquith government introduced the Parliament Bill, which abolished the right of the Lords to veto a money bill and established the procedure that any bill, other than a money bill, if passed in three successive sessions of the Commons was to become law, despite the veto of the Lords,

Above, suffragettes under arrest in Hyde Park, London: the 'votes for women' movement became increasingly militant between 1906 and 1914, though without making much impression on official attitudes. Female suffrage – granted to women over thirty in 1918 and to those over twenty-one ten years later – came about as a result rather of the crucial role on the home front played by women during the First World War.

Top, an old woman evicted from her south London home just before the First World War: by now old-age pensions and the national insurance scheme had laid the basis of the welfare state, but few municipalities recognized a duty to house their citizens.

Opposite, pupils at a London infants school in the late nineteenth century: only in the last decades of the nineteenth century was a national system of primary education established, and secondary education did not become compulsory until 1944.

provided two years had elapsed between the first reading of the bill and its final passage.

Only after another general election in 1910, which was in reality a referendum on the Parliament Bill, and a threat that the king would be asked to create enough Liberal peers to swamp their Conservative majority, did the Lords give way. An obvious anomaly in the British democratic system was removed and the House of Lords, like the Crown, became an appendage to the British system of government. The drama and high feeling of this major constitutional crisis were less important than the fact that it was peacefully and democratically resolved.

Another colourful constitutional issue of these years was the fight to win women the vote. As with most of the other emerging democracies, sex was more important than class in determining who should be excluded from the franchise. In 1903 Mrs Emmeline Pankhurst founded a movement which campaigned with ever increasing militancy to extend the vote to women. At first, her supporters confined themselves to heckling, but failure to get results turned the extremists to window-breaking, arson and other attacks on property. The campaign made female suffrage a more urgent political issue than it otherwise would have been, but the 1914 war intervened, and women's role in it proved their case more conclusively than suffragette militancy.

The Irish question

Grudging acceptance of social reform, hesitancy over women's suffrage and the reactionary stand of the House of Lords suggested that the ruling classes had difficulty in adapting themselves to democracy. Nevertheless, they did adapt themselves, and the impatient violence of the strikers and the suffragettes was a passing phase.

The real threat in the half century before 1914 was to the political unity of the United Kingdom and to Britain's ability to defend her overseas empire and the homeland from external attack. The first of these threats stemmed from failure to solve the Irish question.

Britain was a multi-national state in a century which was an age of nationalism. Though the Scots and the Welsh found close political union with the English profitable, the Irish did not, apart from the Protestant minority in the north of the predominantly Catholic island. Very few were bent on full independence, however, and the search for a form of union which would satisfy both the Irish and the rest of the British had been a major issue in British politics throughout the century.

The search failed. The turning-point was the great famine of 1845–9. Ireland had a rapidly expanding population which its primitive agriculture could not support. About half the Irish depended for their survival on the potatoes they grew. Crop failures were frequent and usually local, but in 1845 the whole country was affected by potato blight. It was in response to this crisis that Robert Peel repealed the Corn Laws and took more direct relief measures. In 1846 blight struck again, followed by a further failure in 1848. The result was famine, which Peel's successors handled disastrously, and in the wake of the famine came typhus and other diseases. Something like a million of Ireland's 8,000,000 people died from starvation or disease, and about the same number were forced to emigrate to America. The horror of these years bred deep and lasting bitterness. It would have taken an unusually imaginative statesman to bridge the gulf between the Irish and the rest of Britain.

Gladstone was such a statesman. Sooner than his fellow politicians he realized the scale of the problem and the danger of leaving it unsolved. From the time he first became prime minister in 1868 until he retired from public life in 1894 he made repeated efforts to reconcile the Irish to inclusion in the United Kingdom. He could have won over the Irish, but he failed to win over the English to the concessions he believed they had to make.

British complacency about Ireland was shaken, however, in the 1860s by the activities of a revolutionary nationalist organization, the Fenian Brotherhood. Public opinion accepted that something had to be done. Gladstone's early measures of reform combined with coercion won general support. In 1869 he disestablished the Anglican Irish Church, to which a resentful Catholic majority had hitherto been forced to pay tithes. His Land Act of 1870 tackled Ireland's basic problem by trying to prevent landlords from exploiting the poor tenant farmers who formed the majority of the population. Although it was an important first step towards solving the land problem, the Land Act was not enough and provided no security for fair rent, fixity of land tenure or for the free sale of land to Irish tenants.

In 1881 Gladstone put through another Land Act which recognized dual ownership of the land and created a land commission to mediate between landlord and tenant, thus contributing greatly to the solution of the agrarian problem.

By this time the Irish Nationalists in the House of Commons were demanding Home Rule for Ireland, and in 1875 Charles Stewart Parnell, who was soon to assume the leadership of the Nationalist Party, won a seat in the House of Commons. He also accepted the presidency of the Land League in Ireland, which had been organized to unite peasants and politicians against landlordism and which employed violent methods of reprisal against anyone who took over land from which a tenant had been evicted. One of their most effective methods of coercion was boycotting, named after a Captain Boycott, the despised English land agent of a large landowner in County Mayo.

By 1885 Gladstone, whose second Land Act of 1881 had proved inadequate, had become convinced that Home Rule was the only way to solve the Irish problem. His conversion split the Liberal Party, opponents of Home Rule allying themselves with the Conservatives as the Liberal Unionists. The most important of the Liberal Unionists was the great radical Joseph Chamberlain. It was clear that the majority of people in Britain were unsympathetic to Home Rule and apart from a brief spell (1892–5) the Liberals were out of office until 1906. The Irish Nationalist Party, too, which had been a dominant force in British politics in the 1880s, declined in influence after 1890 when Parnell was forced out of the leadership after being named as co-respondent in a divorce suit.

The Lords had frustrated two Home Rule bills introduced by Gladstone, though because of the restrictions of the Parliament Act of 1911 they could merely delay the third Home Rule Bill passed for a second time by the Commons in 1913. By this time, the prospect of Home Rule had precipitated a crisis in Ireland. The Protestants of Ulster, under the leadership of Sir Edward Carson, announced their determination to oppose Home Rule. This marked the beginning of the antipathy and religious hatred which still persists in Northern Ireland.

Asquith's Liberal government found itself faced by the threat of open rebellion on the part of Protestant Ulster. A force of Ulster Volunteers was formed, and in the south similar military organizations appeared to oppose it. Civil war seemed imminent in Ireland. The Conservative opposition in the House of Commons was strongly sympathetic to the Ulster cause. In March 1914 several officers of the British Army at Curragh, a large military base near Dublin, declared that they would resign their commissions rather than join in military measures against Ulster. The Home Rule Bill was due to be passed for the third time in May 1914, and Britain seemed on the verge of civil war. She was saved from such a disaster by involvement in another: on 4 August 1914 Britain entered the First World War. The Home Rule Bill was enacted as law in September, but to satisfy the Ulster Protestants a suspensory bill was passed by Westminster to delay the execution of Home Rule until the end of the war.

Threats to the British Empire

The cause of preserving the political unity of the British Isles was in the end lost. After a period of revolution and savage repression during the First World War, independence was conceded to all of Ireland except Ulster when a treaty was signed in 1921 setting up an Irish Free State. The war of 1914 did however stave off the other major threat of the preceding fifty years – the danger of attack on the British Empire and on the British Isles themselves.

A great expansion of the empire had been accomplished in the last fifteen years of the nineteenth century. A thrilling sense of global power gripped the British people as it did so many nations at this time. The British Empire was incomparably greater than any other and comprised some four hundred million people, about a quarter of the world's population.

Disillusion soon followed, however, when the empire's weaknesses became increasingly obvious. It was too vast and sprawling to be easily defended by a nation of 40,000,000, traditionally averse to conscription. It was safe as long as other powers were weak or inactive, but the renewed imperialistic interests of the European states and the United States put the empire at risk.

Britain's hasty acquisition of so much African territory was stimulated by fear that France, Germany and Italy would seize strategic areas of a continent which lay between Britain and her Asian possessions. The Fashoda crisis had ensured control of the Nile valley and hence Egypt and the Suez Canal. Even more important to communications with India however was the Cape of Good Hope. Between 1899 and 1902 Britain tried to crush a possible threat to her domination of South Africa in a war against the republics of Transvaal and the Orange Free State, which were inhabited by Boers of Dutch descent. A nerve-wracking and humiliatingly long struggle against a small nation of farmers ensued; and when victory came, imperialism had turned rather sour.

The Boer War occurred when fear about Russian expansion in Asia was at its height. Though backward Russia had more cause for alarm, as the Crimean War had shown, her defeat in the Crimea was followed by a burst of modernization and by a vast extension of her frontiers in Central Asia. In the 1890s Russia tried to industrialize rapidly and close the gap between her power and that of Britain and Germany. Russian advances in Asia seemed likely to give her predominance in China, and Britain, who had felt her hold on India uncertain as a result of the Indian Mutiny (1857), foresaw the balance of power in Asia shifting to Russia's advantage. Britain allied herself with Japan in 1902. Russian encroachments in Korea and Manchuria aroused the apprehensions of the Japanese, who precipitated war by attacking the Russian fleet at Port Arthur. In less than seven months Japan startled the world by defeating Russia and proving her strength as a new imperialistic power.

Imperialist fervour in Britain and anxiety about the empire's future combined to

Above, evicting a peasant from his holding: the poverty-stricken Irish peasantry's resentment of prosperous English absentee landlords was just one contributory factor in the unstoppable demand for Home Rule and the dissolution of the Union of England and Ireland.

Opposite, illustration from an 1857 edition of the Illustrated London News *of Irish emigrants leaving home: between 1841 and 1861 the population of Ireland fell from over 8 million to 5.8 million, the result of death from starvation or disease and of emigration, mostly to the USA.*

produce plans for strengthening it by closer political and economic links. Joseph Chamberlain, colonial secretary between 1895 and 1903, worked towards expansion in Africa and for imperial federation; but self-governing colonies like Canada and Australia were bent on greater independence, not tighter control. Chamberlain then tried in 1903 to foster unity by adopting the idea of a preferential trade agreement within the empire. This meant restriction of free trade with other countries, long regarded as one of the keys to Victorian prosperity. Chamberlain's resignation to campaign for tariff reform split the Conservative Party and paved the way for the Liberals' return to power in 1906. The empire remained vulnerable and beset by dangerous rivals.

The German challenge

Although much of the alarm about the future of the British Empire was premature it underlined the difficulties of holding together such scattered possessions. Without command of the sea, Britain herself would be open to blockade and invasion. The British had often before been jittery about the strength of their navy, but the great development of the German fleet at the beginning of the twentieth century offered the first real challenge to Britain's security since the time of Napoleon.

Industrialization in the second half of the nineteenth century had made Germany the richest and strongest state in Europe. By building a navy to match her army, Admiral von Tirpitz hoped to make Germany a world power. Britain's Admiral Fisher responded with a revolutionary battleship, HMS *Dreadnought*, which was launched in 1906 and made all existing battleships obsolete. Other navies followed suit, while the British strove to consolidate their lead.

This was a triumph for British technology, but the cost of the naval arms race was high, and finding the money to pay for such Dreadnoughts as well as social security had been the reason for Lloyd George's controversial budget of 1909. The Germans were simultaneously experiencing political conflict over the taxes needed to finance their armaments drive. Industrialization had made war vastly more expensive.

Though Germany never succeeded in outbuilding Britain in warships, it was believed in government circles that Germany was a major threat to the British Isles. Britain cleared up outstanding overseas disputes with France in 1904 and with Russia in 1907 in an attempt to reduce her international commitments, and she was to cooperate more and more with these two powers, who had already allied themselves against Germany. Gradually Britain was drawn into plans for participation in a European war which was generally thought to be in the offing; hitherto she had intervened in continental politics only occasionally and without lasting commitment. Talks with the French over the use of the small professional army, which the Liberal war minister R. B. Haldane had so effectively reformed after 1906, signalized the British government's growing acceptance of positive action to check Germany. Whatever the justification, it came to mean involvement in the 1914 war with its appalling cost and human sacrifice.

The balance-sheet of industrialism

Industrialism had made Britain the giant of nineteenth-century states, but she could not sustain the role once industrialism had spread. British industry only partially managed to meet the challenge of new and enterprising foreign competitors. There was

a decline in the growth of British industrial production at the very time when newcomers like Germany and America were setting a particularly gruelling pace. Even if the British economy had responded satisfactorily, the boost which industrialization gave to the power of rival states still would have strained Britain's capacity to defend her empire. The global character of the empire gave her more rivals than anyone else, and coping with the problems of defence in an age of industrial giants drew Britain into two world wars in the first half of the twentieth century. The cost of victory in both eventually convinced her that the task was beyond her strength.

On the other hand, the British surmounted the difficulties presented to all societies experiencing industrial change, and in the area of social legislation they outdid all except the Scandinavian states. The stresses of social and economic revolution and international crisis did not prove too much for what were on the face of it obsolete and inappropriate institutions. The monarchy, the aristocracy and parliament adapted themselves sufficiently and survived. Power was exercised in a restrained and civilized fashion which had no parallel among the other industrial giants. The demand for political change was expressed in an equally restrained and civilized way. This was an even more remarkable achievement than pioneering the industrial revolution, though its impact on the course of world history has, of course, been negligible in comparison.

The fall of the second Empire in France

France moved much more slowly than Britain towards urban industrial society. In about 1870 when a majority of the British lived in towns, less than a third of Frenchmen did. But, together with the Belgians,

the French were the first to adopt British methods of production, and in the nineteenth century they experienced the social tensions which usually accompany economic change. Although France was less industrialized than Britain, the strain of social tensions was greater because the French were deeply and bitterly divided as to the merits of the different kinds of monarchy and republic they had experimented with since 1789. There was a greater temptation than in Britain to remedy discontent by changing the political system rather than by individual reforms. Between 1815 and 1870 there were two monarchies, two republics and an empire. Thus, while France's economic development was comparatively unspectacular, it gave rise to political instability and violent change.

Napoleon III, whose regime was the outcome of revolution in 1848, tried to accelerate industrial progress by establishing a railway network and encouraging freer trade, which helped to make France a considerable industrial state, far behind Britain but ahead of the rest of Europe. Although change bred discontent, Napoleon used plebiscites to show that the majority of Frenchmen accepted his régime. He might have withstood the turbulence of French politics better than his predecessors but for his dangerous meddling in foreign affairs.

A series of diplomatic defeats was followed in 1870 by war with Prussia. The Prussian army was in general better equipped and organized than the French and very much better led. Napoleon's armies were quickly overwhelmed near the frontier, and the Prussians marched on Paris. His regime was too shallowly rooted to withstand military defeat, especially as he had made the mistake of personally commanding the army and being captured by the Prussians at Sedan. On 4 September 1870 revolution broke out in Paris and a republic was proclaimed.

In the revolutionary wars at the end of the eighteenth century the First Republic had saved France from the invader. The Third Republic was expected to perform the same miracle and for a brief moment seemed to be doing this. The most colourful personality in the provisional republican government was a young lawyer, Léon Gambetta. When the Prussians beseiged Paris at the end of September 1870, he escaped by balloon to organize resistance in the provinces. The large and enthusiastic volunteer forces which he mobilized disconcerted the Prussians, prolonged the war and restored French self-respect, even though the Prussian grip on France was never seriously shaken. After an agonizing four months under siege, the Government of National Defence signed an armistice for three weeks, ignoring the protests of Gambetta. Paris surrendered. The rapidly elected National Assembly agreed to negotiations with Bismarck at Versailles, which were to involve making peace with Germany at the cost of losing Alsace-Lorraine.

Although the new republic had failed to save France from the invader, it did save the country from social revolution – a prospect feared more than defeat by most Frenchmen. The elections of February 1871 produced a highly conservative National Assembly, the majority of whom favoured a return to some form of monarchy. Adolphe Thiers, a veteran politician, who had warned Napoleon III against war with Prussia, became head of state and was entrusted with negotiating peace. Most of the country wanted peace, even on humiliating terms. Paris did not and was seething with discontent. It had borne the brunt of the war, and its staunchly republican citizens resented the arrangements for peace made by the monarchist assembly. When the National

Assembly while still sitting at Bordeaux tried to deprive the National Guard of its pay and its weapons as part of the return to peace, Paris rose in revolt.

The Prussian occupying forces now witnessed a second siege of Paris conducted by troops of the French government. The professional revolutionaries, who haunted the political underground of Paris, took control of the insurrection. They represented various brands of republicanism and socialism, but they were united in their hatred of the wealthy bourgeoisie, the Catholic Church and the remnants of the old aristocracy. They dominated the emergency municipal government, elected on 26 March 1871, and called themselves the Commune, after a similar body in the French Revolution. Although the revolutionaries were in a minority, the government and its supporters saw the Commune as a threat to property and the social order. As defenders of both they attacked the Commune with savage determination, and after bitter street fighting and the slaughter of some 20,000 Communards the Commune was overthrown.

The main troops of the insurrection had been the industrial workers who had been saved from starvation by their service in the National Guard during the Prussian siege of Paris. Little had been done by any regime to alleviate their harsh working conditions, and it was not surprising that they looked to the revolutionaries for salvation. Their earlier protest in 1848 had also been brutally crushed. This second blood-bath in a generation intensified class hatred and provided European socialism with a legend of great emotional force. Thiers' triumph was in the long run to undermine the social stability it was meant to secure.

Its most dangerous opponents destroyed, the government could concentrate on recovering from defeat by the Germans.

The peace treaty was harsh. France had to pay an indemnity of five thousand million francs, to accept the presence of German troops until it was paid and to surrender the provinces of Alsace and Lorraine with their one and a half million inhabitants and rich resources. In addition, France had to adjust herself to a period of weakness and isolation. Prussia's victory in 1870 had enabled her to form a German Empire out of the confederation of Northern German States who had fought side by side with the South German states against France. Germany was in the middle of an industrial revolution which was quickly to consolidate her position as the strongest power in Europe. France's prospects of revenge and the recovery of Alsace-Lorraine seemed remote.

Nevertheless, French revival was swift. Thiers was a reassuring figure to the conservative-minded majority of Frenchmen, and he reinforced their confidence in him by avoiding innovation and experiment. This made it far easier for Thiers to raise the large public loans needed to pay off the indemnity, and as a result the French had the satisfaction of seeing the evacuation of German troops from her soil by 1873. France's renewed financial strength allowed her to begin rebuilding and modernizing her army by the mid-1870s. Although France was a long way from winning security and revenging the loss of Alsace-Lorraine, the Third Republic got off to a good start in the eyes of its citizens and of Europe.

Republic or monarchy?

It was by no means clear, however, that the Republic would survive. After the defeat of the Commune, a monarchy seemed likely to emerge. Thiers' career as a minister had been in the service of King Louis-Philippe, who

had been overthrown in 1848, and the National Assembly elected in February 1871 was predominantly monarchist.

Those who favoured a return to constitutional monarchy were divided as to who should be king. Some supported the Orleanist dynasty in the person of Louis-Philippe's grandson; others supported the old Bourbon dynasty and the grandson of its last king, Charles X, whom Louis-Philippe had supplanted in 1830. The Bourbon candidate would not accept the tricolour as the flag of France because of its revolutionary origins. His supporters knew that this attitude would make him unacceptable to the overwhelming majority of Frenchmen, but they would not switch their allegiance to an Orleanist while a Bourbon candidate was available. This deadlock was to destroy the prospects of monarchy in France.

Time was on the Republican side, and by-elections showed that the monarchist majority of 1871 was a fluke. Thiers himself quickly realized that a republic would divide the French less than any other regime provided it was conservative and not radical in its policies. The monarchists were of course incensed and insisted that Thiers be replaced as president by Marshal Mac-Mahon, who was to prevent any irrevocable decision about France's future form of government until the monarchists had agreed on who should be king. They left it too late. France could not go on indefinitely without an agreed constitution. In 1875 constitutional laws were finally agreed by the Assembly, but they were couched so as to avoid calling the regime a republic. Then a deputy named Wallon introduced the word in an amendment, which, because of quarrels in the monarchist ranks, got through by a majority of one. The Republic was no longer provisional – it was formally in being.

The first parliamentary elections under the new constitution took place early in 1876. The royalists secured a slight majority in the senate and the Republicans secured a majority in the Chamber of Deputies. A constitutional crisis now gave the Republic a chance to establish itself. Marshal Mac-Mahon dismissed the new Republican ministry, appointed a royalist prime minister, and held fresh elections in 1877 with the government using all the means of pressure at its disposal to secure a monarchist majority. They failed, Thiers and Gambetta joining forces in a successful campaign for the Republic. Mac-Mahon accepted the verdict of the electorate and resigned. Support for any kind of monarchy faded, and the Third Republic survived until 1940.

One reason why the Republic won such wide support was that during the decade 1879–89 the moderate republicans controlled the Chamber of Deputies and the good sense of its leaders compared favourably with the behaviour of the squabbling monarchists. Republicanism had freed itself from its revolutionary associations and represented the interests of the propertied classes in a country where landowning peasants predominated. Its conservatism and respectability made it popular.

The only drastic change contemplated concerned Republicanism's old enemy, the Catholic Church. Anti-clericalism was one of the strongest emotions uniting Republicans. One of their ablest leaders, Jules Ferry, was determined to end the Church's control of education. The nation's children were to grow up as loyal citizens of the Republic; they must not be taught by a church traditionally favourable to monarchy. The education laws of 1880–1 went a long way towards ensuring this. But this was the extent of the radicalism of the moderate Republicans.

In contrast with the governments in Britain and Germany, the Third Republic gave low priority to social reform. Although the slow pace of industrialization in France made it seem less urgent, she could not isolate herself from the effects of rapid change elsewhere. The world slump in the 1870s eventually affected France, and massive exports of cheap grain from America hit hard at her agricultural economy. By the 1880s, there was a good deal of discontent about the Republican regime which had failed to cushion people against the effects of world competition.

Disenchantment with the Republic was expressed through support for the colourful General Boulanger, who was made minister of war in 1886. The enemies of the Republic pictured him as a new Bonaparte leading a revitalized France to revenge against Germany. In 1887 the respectability of the Republic was shaken when the president had to resign after charges of corruption were brought against his son-in-law. Supported by various right-wing groups like the League of Patriots, Boulanger became a candidate for election to the Chamber of Deputies wherever by-elections occurred, the last being a constituency in Paris in January 1889. Paris crowds, discontented with the Republic, urged him to seize power, but his hesitation allowed the Republicans time to close ranks. Boulanger fled the country and committed suicide two years later.

Although Boulanger had proved a paper tiger, the remarkable support he had so easily won was a grim warning to the Republicans. The old royalist threat of Bourbon and Orléans was fading fast. The Napoleonic tradition was very much alive.

It was some of Boulanger's supporters who unearthed the Panama scandal. Ferdinand de Lesseps, who had won fame a generation earlier by building the Suez Canal, had been trying since 1881 to build a Panama canal linking the Atlantic and Pacific Oceans. The scheme proved a costly failure, and in 1889 his Panama Canal Company went bankrupt. In its final efforts to stave off bankruprcy, the company had tried to raise money by methods which needed parliamentary approval. In 1892 it was revealed that many deputies, including some ministers, had

been bribed to vote for the company's proposals. Two Jewish financiers had arranged the bribery.

The scandal severely damaged the Republic's reputation and gave further substance to the allegations of corruption made by its opponents on the Right. The way in which the scandal was used, moreover, confirmed that a new 'right' was emerging in France. Its leaders were strongly nationalist and anti-semitic; it charged the Republic with allowing Jewish and other alien influences to corrupt the nation and its traditions.

The Dreyfus Affair

The battle between the new French Right and the forces of Republicanism was joined over a miscarriage of justice in the French army. The army did not directly play at politics and saw itself as the loyal instrument of whatever government the democratic process threw up. But its upper ranks were dominated by men who would have preferred a royalist and clerical form of government. Republicans, therefore, viewed the

Above, General Georges Boulanger (1837–91), appointed war minister in 1886, leaving Paris in 1887 for a provincial command: he did, amid popular protests, indeed return, as the slogans fixed to the locomotive proclaimed he would, and almost staged a coup d'état in 1889, drawing back, to the disappointment of his supporters, at the last moment.

Opposite, the statue of Napoleon Bonaparte in the Place Vendôme, Paris, overthrown by Communards: the Commune's most constructive achievement was the myth of a genuinely socialist society it left behind it, reinforced by the viciousness with which it was repressed; in reality it had neither the time nor the ideological strength to establish anything remotely like an ideal society.

army with the same suspicion and dislike as they did the Catholic Church. Their suspicion and dislike were raised to fever pitch by the Dreyfus Affair.

In 1894 Captain Alfred Dreyfus was convicted of spying for Germany and condemned to life imprisonment on Devil's Island, the notoriously harsh penal settlement off the coast of South America. At first, the case seemed uncontroversial except for the stimulus it gave to anti-semitism. Dreyfus was the first Jew who had succeeded in becoming a staff officer. His apparent treachery seemed to justify the more usual practice of excluding Jews and fed the flames of the campaign against French Jewry currently being waged by the journalist Edouard Drumont.

In 1896 Colonel Picquart, the newly appointed head of counter-espionage, discovered that Dreyfus was innocent and that the real spy was another officer called Esterhazy. The army now made the fatal mistake of trying to suppress Picquart's evidence. Through Picquart the story reached political circles, and a small but influential group began to campaign on behalf of Dreyfus. The army hastily court-martialled and acquitted Esterhazy and posted Picquart abroad. The reputation of the army was held to be more important than the fate of Dreyfus.

In their anxiety to avoid a scandal the army authorities had made things worse. Public opinion was initially anti-Dreyfus, and the government had no desire for a row with the army; but a brilliant press and parliamentary campaign by the Radical politician Georges Clemenceau, the novelist Zola and others eventually forced a re-examination of the case in 1898. The minister of war discovered that documents to put Dreyfus's guilt beyond doubt had been manufactured by an intelligence officer, Colonel Henry, who was arrested and committed suicide. The establishment of Dreyfus's innocence seemed only a matter of time.

But much more than the fate of Dreyfus was now at stake. So little solid evidence had been available to the public during the controversy that it was possible to believe whatever one's prejudices seemed most likely. To most monarchists, Catholics, nationalists and anti-semites, it was obvious that a corrupt group of Republicans was trying to help a Jewish traitor to escape his just deserts. To the more radical and anti-clerical Republicans, as well as to the socialists and others on the far Left, it was equally obvious that the reactionary forces in the Church and the army had condemned an innocent man as part of their campaign to undermine the Republic. The debate about Dreyfus became an occasion for releasing pent-up political emotions. Settling the guilt or innocence of Dreyfus would also mark a propaganda triumph for either Right or Left.

The Right could hardly win. They had the disadvantage of having backed the wrong horse in the Dreyfus case itself. Although the army condemned Dreyfus again at a re-trial in 1899, he was quickly 'pardoned' and freed; his formal rehabilitation was eventually arranged in 1906. Moreover, most Frenchmen continued to back the Republic, which meant not so much the Dreyfusards who so passionately defended it as the more conservative Republicans who had governed France moderately and unspectacularly for the past thirty years. The Republican governments during the years of controversy had initially trusted the army's version and gradually moved over to a more sceptical attitude. This was probably in tune with the great majority of French voters. The Right, therefore, lacked mass support. They were divided, too, as to what they wanted in place of the Republic.

The Republicans, on the other hand, again showed their ability to unite when the regime was in danger, as during the height of the crisis when the nationalist writer Déroulède attempted a futile coup. A strong Republican ministry emerged which took effective counter-measures. The Republic had lasted longer than any other regime since the French Revolution in 1789. The frequent changes of government and the mediocrity of so many of its politicians made it look deceptively weak and unstable. The Dreyfus Affair showed that the Republic had formidable enemies but it also showed that the Republic could prove more than a match for them.

Anti-clericalism

The coalition of the moderate and radical republicans in the Chamber of Deputies which Premier Waldeck-Rousseau had formed in 1899 survived the Dreyfus crisis. In this coalition known as the 'Bloc' the radicals had the edge over the moderate opportunists or progressists, who had enjoyed predominance during the 1880s and had tried to reconcile hostile elements to the Republic. The passions revealed by the Dreyfus Affair made the task seem too difficult, and the radicals, who believed in 'Republicanizing' France, were now given their head. The minister of war was given control of army promotion to ensure that loyal Republicans got preference. Above all, there was a return to the anti-clericalism of the early years of the Republic.

Many Catholics in France had long desired to end the ancient feud with the Republic, but they were in a minority. Even when Pope Leo XIII lent his support to the idea of reconciliation in the early 1890s, the response from most Catholic bishops in France was cold. Hatred of Republicanism and all it had stood for since the French Revolution was too deeply rooted. The vision of France united by liberal Catholisism and moderate Republicanism quickly faded, but after the Dreyfus Affair the Republic and the Church seemed set on a collision course.

Between 1899 and 1905 a new offensive against the Church's power was launched, and most of the rich and influential religious orders were dissolved and their schools closed. The death of Pope Leo XIII in 1903 made reconciliation even more remote, because his successor, Pius X, was uncompromising and tactless and offended even sympathetic Republicans. Relations between the Vatican and Paris deteriorated to such an extent that diplomatic relations were broken off.

In 1905 the French government took the final step of scrapping Napoleon's Concordat with the Pope, which had been the basis of church-state relations since 1801. State and Church were now completely separated, and the Church lost its official status and its revenue from the state. When the Pope refused to accept the Separation Law the Church's property was confiscated.

Thus the Church lost its ability to intervene in politics, as it had done in the Dreyfus Affair, and a further step had been taken towards consolidating the Republic. The Church's loss of wealth was not altogether detrimental to spiritual life, and its influence was still exerted in less provocative fashion. Both sides benefited from the lowering of tension which separation brought.

Industrial development

With so much time and energy devoted to anti-clericalism, the ruling Republican parties had little time to spare for social reform. Even the radicals, who talked of it, did little when they had the chance. Electoral backing for the Republic might have been fatally undermined if it had decided to tax the peasant majority for the sake of the proletarian few. Income tax, for example, was not introduced until the First World War.

French industry continued to expand, but not enough to make the industrial population a majority, nor enough to put France on a par with Germany, Britain or America. France suffered from certain disadvantages, having fewer natural resources, like coal and iron, than her rivals and a slower rate of population growth. There was no urge to overcome these disadvantages, since the French economy as it stood supplied the needs of too many Frenchmen. France could not only feed herself but was the third

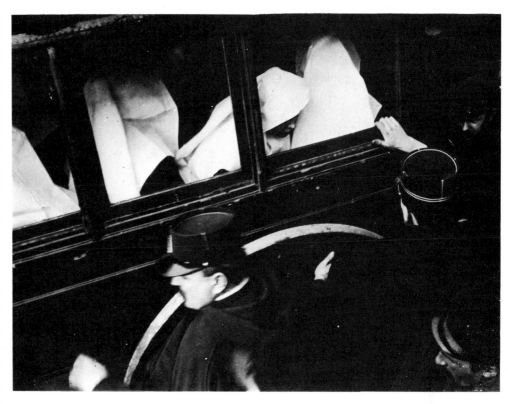

largest grain exporter in the world. Her reputation for manufacturing luxury goods like furniture, silks, jewellery, cosmetics and fashionable clothes was unsurpassed. The traditional preference for a family business of a size the family could directly manage continued to appeal to most industrialists. Sacrificing the good life in the quest for ever greater profit would have been alien to another French tradition. The sort of attitude which helped to build the giant firms of Germany and America was rare in France; and for peacetime government to urge the development of large corporations in the interests of national strength, as had happened in tsarist Russia, was alien to the political thinking of the Republic.

Hence there was a growing number of industrial workers destined for a long time to remain a minority of the electorate. In contrast with British and even German workers they saw little prospect of improving their conditions by conventional political methods. While the British and German labour movements became increasingly absorbed into the existing political system in the years before 1914, French workers became more revolutionary in their approach to politics. France had too little industrial development for her security in Europe but too much for domestic peace.

The revival of French socialism

The defeat of the Commune in 1871 had shattered the French socialist movement and destroyed thousands of its most militant supporters. Within a few years it had begun to revive, and in 1880 an amnesty for the Communards who had been sent into exile stimulated interest.

Above, nuns leaving their convent after the passing of the Separation Law, 1905: anti-clericalism had been a continuing theme of French politics since the Revolution of 1789; now that separation had been achieved it lost much of its potency.

Opposite, contemporary drawing of the crucifixion of Captain Alfred Dreyfus (1859–1935): General Mercier, the Minister of War, who willingly accepted the fabricated evidence against Dreyfus, is offering him a sponge soaked in vinegar. The Dreyfus affair split the country into two bitterly hostile camps and brought into the open the extensive anti-semitic feelings latent in France, as elsewhere in Europe.

As in the earlier pariod of French socialism the movement was deeply divided as to
doctrine. The principal difference among the
Socialist leaders, as in the rest of Europe,
was between the Marxists and the 'reformists'. The Marxists, led by Jules Guesde, saw
their task as preparing the workers for their
role in the revolution which would overthrow capitalism. The reformists wanted
pressure through conventional political
channels to win immediate reform of working conditions and a gradual transfer of
power to the working classes.

Socialists of all kinds did well at the polls
in 1893 after the Panama scandal had shaken
the Republic. The forty-nine socialists
elected included Guesde and the two ablest
of the reformists, Jean Jaurès and Alexandre
Millerand. In 1899 Millerand became minister of commerce in the Waldeck-Rousseau
government formed to ward off the challenge
to the Republic during the Dreyfus case.
Despite his success in carrying reformist
principles into practice by securing a minimum wage and reduced working hours for
public employees, his acceptance of office in
a bourgeois government scandalized a large
section of the movement.

Socialists overcame their differences sufficiently in 1905 to form a united socialist
party. Guesde's influence was strong, and
cooperation with the radicals in government was ruled out. But the old divisions
were never far below the surface, and on the
eve of the 1914 war French socialism lost its
most attractive and powerful leader when
Jaurès was assassinated. The parliamentary
socialists had made themselves a force in
French politics, but their hopes of real power
remained slight.

The record of the organized socialist parties was not such as to impress workers in
search of rapid and fundamental change.
France's underprivileged citizens had a long
tradition of revolutionary violence to secure
quick results. The bloodshed of 1848 and
1871 had deepened class hatreds and engendered the distrust of bourgeois political
leaders, which included most of the parliamentary socialists. They were sceptical
of winning socialism by parliamentary
methods and they did not want to wait for
the distant revolution promised by the
Marxists. The gulf between the trade unions
and the socialist parties, in sharp contrast
with developments in Britain and Germany,
further weakened French socialism.

When trade unions, or *syndicats*, were
legalized in 1884, they saw themselves less as
organisations to improve working conditions than as agents of revolutionary change.
Syndicalism, as their programme came to be
called, relied on a general strike to paralyse
capitalist society and enable workers to
seize power. The *syndicats* would then be the
units of the future socialist society based on
producer-cooperatives. The syndicalist doctrine was formerly adopted in 1892. It was
re-affirmed more explicitly in the Amiens
Charter of 1906, after syndicalists meeting

in a trade union congress at Amiens had defeated those who wanted cooperation with the parliamentary socialists.

Between 1906 and 1909 the syndicalist creed was put into practice with a wave of strikes culminating in an abortive general strike. Trade unionists were a small proportion of the French population – half a million at the turn of the century rising to a million by 1909 in a country of 39,000,000 – but concentrated in the major towns they could cause a good deal of disruption. Prime Minister Clemenceau's government acted ruthlessly against the strikers, and there was a lot of violence. When further strikes broke out in 1910, Clemenceau's successor, Aristide Briand, who in his early days had advocated syndicalism, mobilized the railwaymen who had paralysed communications and forced them to do their jobs in uniform. Syndicalism was spectacular in action, but it failed.

Doctrinal disputes among the socialist politicians and violence among the trade unionists were only to be expected in a country which industrialized slowly and whose politicians felt no urge to anticipate trouble by social reform. The prospect of a socialist majority seemed so remote that any programme of action could be shown wanting by its opponents, thus producing endless

debate in the chamber. A feeling of impotence among politically conscious workers in France was bound to be strong and often explosive. Also for a time the anarchists felt driven to violence, which in the 1890s took the form of bomb outrages and political assassination. The pattern was repeated in many other countries of Europe as part of the price of slow industrialization unaccompanied by adequate social reform.

The problems of empire

Under the Third Republic France built the second largest colonial empire in the world – Indo-China, Madagascar and vast areas of northwest Africa, including Tunis and Morocco, were conquered or made protectorates. The acquisition of an empire became an important way of compensating the French people for the humiliation of the 1870 defeat. Frustrated soldiers and other men of action could find fame and fortune by carving out an empire. The emphasis on North Africa was natural for a state doubtful of its security and anxious about its Mediterranean flank.

In theory the French favoured the assimilation of their colonial subjects, by which they would gradually come to share the

Above, contemporary illustration of a march through the mining villages of northern France during the April 1906 miners' strike.

Opposite top, strikers on their way to a meeting in central Paris, 1909: though the left was in power after 1905, the division between parliamentary and industrial socialism was never overcome.

Opposite bottom, Jean Jaurès, the French socialist leader, speaking at a demonstration against the three years' law, a proposal to increase the period of conscription from two to three years, May 1913 (the law was passed in July): on 31 July 1914 Jaurès was assassinated on his return from an unsuccessful attempt to maintain international socialist unity by persuading German socialists to strike rather than mobilize.

benefits of French citizenship and absorb the values of French civilization. One of France's most distinguished colonial administrators, Lyautey, summed up the ideal by declaring that France was a nation of 100,000,000 inhabitants. As the empire became more vast, the idea of an immense nation ceased to be a practical possibility, and the concept of assimilating a native elite to cooperate with the French in the work of government tended to take its place.

In any case, for most Frenchmen the empire was of secondary importance to affairs in Europe. Dreams of revenge or fears of another German invasion were always in the last resort more important than imperialist expansion overseas. Both the ministries of Jules Ferry were brought down because he was alleged to have diverted France's energies overseas – in 1881 by taking Tunis and in 1885 by conquering Indo-China. In 1882 the French government declined to join Britain in an expedition to Egypt, which marked the beginning of Britain's long predominance over the Nile valley and the Suez Canal. The Fashoda crisis of 1898 showed that the French were to regret their decision – their withdrawal from the possibility of war showed that the reasoning behind the decision of 1882 still held good. Despite its vast imperial gains, the Republic had discarded the Napoleonic tradition of foreign adventure on a grand scale, and the new French Empire was won with little risk of conflict with other powers.

France and the German threat

The 'German question' haunted the Third Republic throughout its history. The phrase had its origins in the German invasion of 1870 which was to be repeated in 1940 and destroy the Republic. France's dilemma after 1871 was that no French government could think of abandoning Alsace-Lorraine for ever, yet Germany's military superiority and her astounding industrial and commercial development were so great as to make avoidance of war a prime necessity.

Neither security against a further invasion nor revenge for the last one could be obtained without allies, and for the first twenty years of its existence the Third Republic was isolated. The German chancellor, Bismarck, was determined to keep France in isolation and had negotiated alliances with Austria-Hungary, Russia and Italy. The only other major European power was Britain, whom the French regarded as an enemy second only to Germany.

France's chance of breaking out of isolation came in 1890 when Bismarck fell from power and his successors tried to reduce and simplify Germany's obligations. They incautiously dropped the Russian alliance, leaving Russia isolated and threatened by the same two states whose power menaced France – Germany and Britain. An alliance between France and Russia was an obvious

BIBL. DE
L'OPERA
16,061

SAISON RUSSE 1909

OPERA ET BALLET

BAKST

move, because Germany would hesitate to face a war on two fronts.

What stood in the way was the tsar's hatred of republics and the fact that Paris was a centre for Russian revolutionaries in exile. He was gratified, however, by the arrest in Paris in May 1890 of a large group of these revolutionaries, which signalized a change in French government policy. Moreover, since 1888 Russia, desperately in need of foreign capital, had been floating loans very successfully in Paris with the active encouragement of the French government. The makings of an *entente cordiale* were present.

A dramatic colonial agreement in 1890 between Britain and Germany convinced both Paris and St Petersburg, wrongly as it happened, that their two main enemies were on the point of making an alliance. In July 1891 a French naval squadron visited Kronstadt, Russia's Baltic fortress. During the festivities Tsar Alexander III gave startling proof of Russia's new policy by standing bareheaded while a Russian band played the 'Marseillaise', the battle hymn of the French Revolution. Negotiations followed, and in January 1894 a defensive

alliance was signed. The ecstatic welcome given to the Russian fleet when it visited Toulon in October 1893 was a measure of the French relief at emerging from isolation. A further diplomatic success for the Republic came when Britain not only settled her differences with France and Russia but was drawn into ever closer cooperation with Germany in the years before 1914.

In all the Republic had enjoyed remarkable political success. It had beaten off its enemies at home and had built a coalition against Germany which enabled France to survive invasion in 1914 and win back Alsace-Lorraine at the end of the war.

The Republic did a great service by surviving so long, and within its political framework most of the French nation enjoyed a steadily growing prosperity. Nevertheless, it failed to solve two fundamental problems. Like all the other European states France could find no answer to the problem of surviving in a world torn by imperialist rivalry except by fragile alliances of the kind likely to provoke war. Moreover, France could not afford even a successful war like that of 1914–18, which exhausted her and made her all the less able to withstand the renewed

German challenge in the 1930s. The Third Republic also failed to unite the nation, and a dangerously substantial minority wanted a change in the whole system. Hostility from the Right persisted under the powerful influence of Charles Maurras, whose nationalist paper, *Action Française*, first appeared in 1899. The ruthlessness with which the Republican parties dealt with strikers embittered still further the socialist Left, whose numbers were bound to increase as industrialization proceeded.

Consequently, the Republic always had an air of the provisional about it despite its long life. In terms of both French history and the history of the world, the Republic is most likely to be remembered for the extraordinary array of painters who worked in France during these years. The exhibition by Impressionist painters in 1874 signalized a revolution in art, and by 1914 Paris had seen a succession of revolutionary developments in painting. Monet, Toulouse-Lautrec, Degas, Renoir, Cézanne, Van Gogh, Gauguin, Matisse, Picasso and many other great painters contributed to this astonishing artistic ferment. France's writers at this time were almost equally fertile in creating new literary forms, such as the symbolist poetry of Rimbaud and Mallarmé and the naturalistic fiction of Zola and Maupassant. It was in Paris that Diaghilev's Russian ballet and Stravinsky's music made their revolutionary impact. Paris was more than ever the cultural capital of Europe. The bold experiments of its creative artists were in strange contrast to the cautious and conventional acts of its statesmen; but both were responses to the same bewildering new world of industrial civilization.

Chapter 44

Russia: Prelude to Revolution

While the British and the French were pioneering industrialization and political democracy, Russia remained the most backward of all the major European states. She was ruled by an autocratic emperor, and about ninety percent of her inhabitants were peasants, who were either serfs and the private property of a small class of landed gentry or state peasants controlled by the government. They eked out a miserable existence by primitive agricultural methods and were at the mercy of the landlord who owned them. There were few towns, and in 1851 only about eight percent of Russia's 67,000,000 people lived in them. Although industry did develop in Russia in the first half of the nineteenth century, it was a slow growth and the gap between Russia and western Europe was widening all the time.

Just how wide the gap had become was brought home to Russia's rulers by the Crimean War. The war is remembered in Britain for the inefficiency with which it was fought and organized by the British army commanders: the futility of the charge of the Light Brigade, the scandalous provision for the wounded and the work of Florence Nightingale are the best known episodes. For Russia it was one of the greatest humiliations of her history. Since the time of Peter the Great, Russia had been renowned above all for her formidable army, and between 1815 and 1854 she was thought to be invulnerable. When the tsar's armies failed to dislodge the comparatively small and poorly led armies of Britain and France from Russia's soil, the shock was tremendous.

It was clear to the new tsar, Alexander II, who came to the throne during the war, that Russia's failure was a result of her economic backwardness. Like Peter the Great, who in the wake of defeat had introduced western European civilization into Russia, Alexander II proceeded to do the same. He freed the serfs from bondage in the hope of revitalizing Russian agriculture; he gave Russia an enlightened legal system; he created new organs of local government, the *zemstvos*, with elected members; he made the army more efficient and humane; he reformed Russia's finances. By instituting these changes he hoped to bring about conditions favourable to business enterprise and industry, which had given Britain and France a decisive edge over Russia in economic and military strength.

Alexander II wanted economic change without political change, however, and did not propose to give up any of his power to elected parliaments. He wanted to make the old autocracy work better so that Russia could regain her position as a great European power. Between 1855 and 1917 the tsars strove to catch up with their European rivals in military and economic strength, while at the same time trying to preserve autocratic government.

After such a long period of stagnation, Alexander's reforms stimulated a demand for much more sweeping changes; but Alexander's determination to preserve autocracy led to the growth of a revolutionary movement which was to undermine and finally supplant the tsar in 1917.

The middle class in Russia was small and insignificant, in striking contrast with most western European countries. Resistance to tsardom was led by discontented and conscience-stricken members of the intelligentsia – students, authors, teachers, doctors and so on – most of whom were of noble birth. One of them, Alexander Herzen, waged a propaganda war against the tsarist regime from exile. He initially greeted Alexander II as the 'Tsar-Liberator' but was quickly disillusioned and gradually inspired a younger and more radical generation than his own to seek change through revolution.

Student revolutionary societies were formed in the early 1860s. As they were suppressed, others emerged more militant and better organized, aiming not merely at overthrowing autocratic government but at establishing peasant socialism. Village communes in Russia ran their own affairs on roughly democratic lines, and Herzen had hoped the commune would be the unit of a peculiarly Russian kind of socialism, which would make it unnecessary for her to go through an industrial revolution, whose results in western Europe had horrified him. The movement aimed at this was known as 'Populism'.

Populists were at odds as to how best to bring about their revolution. In the 1870s thousands of young people went off to the countryside to bridge the gulf between the educated classes and the peasantry and to incite the peasants to revolt. The movement was a dismal failure which simply demonstrated that the gulf between the peasants and the educated Russians was too wide to be bridged so easily. Though hopes of a great mass uprising faded, hopes of overthrowing tsardom were kept alive. In 1876 a revolutionary society called 'Land and Liberty' was formed to organize a systematic campaign of propaganda in town and country. Its more impatient members saw a short-cut to success in terrorism.

The Land and Liberty movement was encouraged by the case of Vera Zasulich, who in 1878 had shot and wounded the

Opposite, Moulin Rouge *by Henri de Toulouse-Lautrec (1864–1901). Art Institute of Chicago, Illinois. Helen Birch Bartlett Memorial Collection.*

the repressive system of Nicholas I was restored. In the face of rising discontent among the educated classes Alexander II had, on the morning of his assassination, finally given his approval to a scheme for introducing some elected representatives into the work of central government. This might have been the first tentative move towards a breach in autocratic government and might someday have led to a constitution. It was quietly buried. Opposition to the government could still be expressed only through revolution, and it was only a matter of time before a new and wiser generation of revolutionaries was to emerge.

Russian expansion

While the regime was fighting off revolutionaries within Russia, it was experiencing mixed fortunes in its struggle to revive Russian power abroad. Between 1864 and 1884 Russian troops conquered a vast region of Central Asia, partly controlled by the principalities of Khiva, Bokhara and Khokand and otherwise occupied by nomadic tribes. These conquests brought Russia's frontiers in line with those of Persia and Afghanistan, beyond whose borders lay the British Empire. The battle for influence over these two unstable buffer states was now more urgently waged than ever. British nervousness increased, but there was no chance of a new Crimean War to warn the Russians off because Turkey was now anti-British and would not let British warships and troops through the Dardanelles into the Black Sea. British sea power was helpless to check Russia, as became clear in 1885 when the two nations came to the brink of war.

military governor of St Petersburg because he had ordered the flogging of a political prisoner. Her acquittal by the jury in defiance of the evidence showed the state of public opinion.

In 1879 'Land and Liberty' split over the question of terrorism, the terrorists forming a new society, called 'The People's Will', which believed that the assassination of the tsar would bring down the regime. This small group of men and women, hunted by the police, made numerous attempts to kill Alexander II and finally succeeded in March 1881, when bombs thrown during a street procession fatally wounded him.

The assassination did not bring down the regime, however, and Alexander III, who succeeded his father, ruthlessly repressed the revolutionary movement. Populism was crushed for a decade. Many of Alexander's reforms were watered down, and much of

Although British fear for her Indian empire was an agreeable form of revenge for Russia's Crimean defeat, she was still very vulnerable in regions less remote than Central Asia, as she realized during two great crises in the Balkans from 1875 to 1876 and again from 1885 to 1887. Both times Russia had tried to use rebellion against the Turks to bring Bulgaria under her influence, because Bulgaria was an excellent base for striking at the straits of the Bosporus and the Dardanelles, which, especially since the Crimean War, Russia had regarded as the key to her back door. To maintain her position in the Near East Britain was able to organize enough opposition among the powers to make Russia climb down. In 1878 Russia was particularly incensed at having to abandon a valuable peace treaty, which had cost her a year's bitter fighting. From these two crises Russia learned that she was still not strong enough to contemplate a European war.

In 1890, she lost her only remaining ally when the German emperor, William II, decided not to renew the treaty with Russia which had been negotiated by his former chancellor, Bismarck. Alexander III had little alternative but to ally himself with

France, although such an alliance might increase the risk of Russia having to fight Germany, now the strongest power in Europe. The conquest of vast regions of Central Asia made a spectacular triumph, but the diplomatic buffetings Russia received in Europe reminded her rulers that she lagged far behind the advanced industrial powers.

Industrialization in the 1890s

Russia's backwardness was underlined again in humiliating fashion when famine struck in 1891. The inability of the authorities to deal with the situation and organize food supplies made Russia the target of sneering remarks abroad, especially in Germany. Alexander III's pride was badly hurt by these comments and other evidence of Russia's low international standing. He was impressed by the arguments of Sergei Witte that only rapid industrialization would enable Russia to become a world power in keeping with her vast population and resources.

Witte came from a family of German origin which had long been in the service of the Russian state. He had worked his way up to an important post in the administration of Russia's railways, which were belatedly transforming the country's notoriously bad communications. He came to the notice of Alexander III and went to St Petersburg as minister of communications. In 1892 he became minister of finance, a post whose responsibilities were so wide as to make him virtual overlord of the whole Russian economy. He held the job until 1903 and presided over a massive drive by the Russian government to industrialize the country and thus acquire the immense power which industrialization had conferred on rival states like Britain and Germany.

Witte believed the task was an urgent one because of the intense competition for empire and influence among industrialized nations in the late nineteenth century. Russia had to equip herself to join the imperialist race to carve up the world or become a prey to the imperialists like Turkey or China. Russia could not wait for private enterprise to do the job, so the state must take the lead. Russia had too little capital, so foreign loans were sought. As mentioned earlier, great quantities of Russian government bonds were absorbed by the French market for the construction of the Trans-Siberian Railway and the equipment of the army. This investing was one of the factors which encouraged the alliance between France and Russia in 1894. In 1897, to stop the fluctuations in the value of the currency, Witte made gold the standard of Russia's monetary system and thereby created a further inducement for capitalists to invest in Russian enterprises.

Something like an industrial revolution was launched in Russia in the 1890s. Great

new industrial regions sprang up in the Ukraine with its coal and iron ore and in the Caucasus with its petroleum. Older industrial regions like Moscow and St Petersburg witnessed great expansion and modernization. Coming late in the day, Russian industrialization was able to take advantage of the latest machinery and techniques.

Although Russia achieved a quite extraordinary rate of economic growth in these years and was on the way to becoming a major industrial power, she was still essentially a peasant society. In 1900, there were only about 3,000,000 industrial workers out of a population of 133,000,000; these workers were concentrated in a few parts of the country, including politically important areas around St Petersburg and Moscow. If industrialization brought more discontent than prosperity, as it usually did in its early stages, these 3,000,000 workers could be a grave danger to the tsarist regime.

Lenin and Russian Marxism

Trouble for tsardom as a result of industrialization had been prophesied by George Plekhanov ten years before Witte began his work. Plekhanov had been one of the 'Land and Liberty' revolutionaries who refused to believe that terrorism would bring down the regime. After the assassination of Alexander II had proved him right, he had abandoned

Above, factory workers in 1888: because of its late start, Russian industry missed out the small units that had characterized the early industrial revolution in western Europe and went immediately into large-scale production.

Above left, the Nadezhdinsky iron and steel works, 1898: rapid industrialization in the last years of the nineteenth century could do little to alter the agricultural base of the economy.

Top, the Trans-Siberian Railway at the point where it crosses the River Volga: construction of the railway, nearly 6,000 miles long, started in the early 1880s and was completed in 1904. The line would, it was hoped, strengthen the Russian military strength in the Pacific, help internal migration and attract trade.

Opposite top, the assassination of Tsar Alexander II (1818–81, tsar from 1855), 13 March 1881 at St Petersburg: Alexander had been responsible for a programme of domestic reform including improvements in the legal system, education and local administration and, most important, the emancipation of the serfs in 1861; his heir, Alexander III, made no attempt to continue his father's policies.

Opposite bottom, the ringleaders of the assassination are executed, 3 April 1886.

Opposite centre, Gregory Guerchouny, one of the organizers of the assassination of Alexander II and a member of People's Freedom, which had already made at least seven unsuccessful attempts on the Tsar's life.

Populism, with its belief in a peculiarly Russian brand of socialism, in favour of Marxism. From exile in Switzerland, he argued that Russia would pass through the same stage of capitalism as the West and that the Russian revolution would be the work of the proletariat not the peasantry. Revolutionaries must await the coming of industrialization and prepare the workers for their future role.

In 1883 Plekhanov formed in Geneva the group called 'Liberation of Labour', the forerunner of the party which was to rule Russia after tsardom collapsed. As Plekhanov had predicted, its propagandist literature attracted a growing number of workers. When Russia's main cities became swollen by masses of harshly exploited and resentful factory workers, revolutionaries turned to them as the source of the explosion which would destroy tsardom.

The most remarkable of Plekhanov's disciples was Vladimir Ulyanov, one of whose underground pseudonyms was Lenin. Lenin had been born in 1870 at Simbirsk, on the Volga, the son of a local school inspector. His elder brother, Alexander, was hanged in 1887 for his part in a students' plot to assassinate the tsar. Lenin qualified as a lawyer in 1891 and at about the same time was converted to Marxism. He quickly became an important writer and organizer in the revolutionary movement in St Petersburg and, later, in exile.

Although a Marxist party, the Social Democrats, was founded in Russia in 1898, it was not until 1903 that representatives of all the various Russian Marxist groups met in Brussels and later in London to plan the new party's future. A split developed over whether the party should be restricted to dedicated professional revolutionaries or open to all active sympathizers, Lenin favouring restricted membership. His supporters were in the majority during the latter part of the congress because of a walkout by another group, and they took the name of 'Bolsheviki' (members of the majority). His opponents, led by Martov, incautiously accepted the name Mensheviks (members of the minority). The two factions in the Social Democratic Party continued to quarrel over most issues until 1912, when Lenin formed his Bolsheviks into a separate party.

Plekhanov and most other Russian Marxists were prepared to wait until capitalism produced the same conditions in Russia as existed in the more advanced industrial states. Lenin believed that the Russian revolutionary movement should adapt itself to Russia and that the small and backward proletariat should be guided by an elite of professional revolutionaries drawn from Russia's intelligentsia. After the Revolution of 1905, Lenin came to see the peasants as a valuable ally. The Russian masses in town and country alike could be a powerful force for revolution if properly harnessed. Lenin's blending of Populist and Marxist thought proved to be a successful formula

The picture of the eighth attack of port Arthur. The Flag-Ship Russia was destroyed by the torpedo of our navy, and Admiral Makaroff drowned.

for the Bolsheviks' seizure of power in 1917.

Even though the Bolsheviks eventually succeeded the tsars as the rulers of Russia, their chances of achieving this succession in the early years of the twentieth century looked no better than those of their rivals, the Mensheviks, the Socialist Revolutionaries and the liberals. The Socialist Revolutionaries were in the old Populist tradition but they accepted that industrialization could not be reversed and were anxious only to keep it in its place. The peasants were to play the key role in the coming revolution and in the new society that revolution would bring. Russian liberals, who aimed at a constitutional government on western European lines, had had valuable administrative experience in the *zemstvos* set up by Alexander II. They too began to organize themselves for political action at a national level.

At the turn of the century Russia's first political parties were taking shape. It was at a time when a world economic crisis was shaking Russia and halting the remarkable growth of the nineties. The peasants had been taxed to the limit, and peasant revolts became common for the first time since the emancipation of the serfs by Alexander II. The threat of these revolts together with a wave of strikes signalized a new stage in the tsar's battle for survival. Liberals, Socialist Revolutionaries and Social Democrats all sensed the approach of a great national crisis.

Empire in the Far East

During the period of growing political agitation, industrial strife and peasant revolt, Russia got involved in a war with Japan. Alexander III had confined his wars to central Asia, but his son, Nicholas II, who succeeded him in 1894, was less cautious and allowed himself to be drawn into two disastrous wars, the second, from 1914 to 1917, marking the end of the monarchy in Russia. The war fought in 1904–5 provided a dress rehearsal. In each case Nicholas seems to have gambled on victory restoring his popularity – in each case defeat meant revolution.

Like the unrest at home, the war with Japan resulted partly from Witte's industrialization programme. Russian expansion in the Far East was itself nothing new, since Russians had reached the Pacific in the seventeenth century and Siberia had gradually been colonized. Alaska, too, was part of Russia until its sale to America in 1867. Between 1847 and 1860 Russia extended her frontiers at China's expense, a gain which was to be a source of conflict between the two powers a century later. In the 1890s Russia became more ambitious. Witte believed that Russia could capture the vast Chinese market for her manufactured goods, which would further stimulate industry. Between 1891 and 1903, when the Trans-Siberian Railway was being built, China

began to turn to Russia for financial and political aid and in return was forced to allow Russia substantial economic concessions and military bases in Manchuria. Witte's scheme was working well. China looked like becoming a victim of Russian economic imperialism.

By disregarding Japanese interests in the Far East, however, Nicholas II and his ministers overplayed Russia's hand. When Japan went to war in 1904 to counter Russian expansion, there was an outburst of patriotism in Russia very reassuring to her harassed rulers. The shortsighted government failed to take advantage of the public mood to win over moderate opinion by a few timely concessions, relying instead on false hopes of victory.

The Revolution of 1905

The year 1904 brought political ferment at home and humiliating defeat by the Japanese on land and sea. The regime could still have averted the danger of revolution by conceding even limited participation in the work of government to an elected assembly. But Nicholas II believed it his sacred duty to pass on his autocratic power to his heirs. The unyielding attitude of tsardom was dramatically expressed in the events of 'Bloody Sunday'.

One Sunday in January 1905 a peaceful demonstration took place in St Petersburg when Father Gapon, an Orthodox priest, led a deputation of unarmed workers to petition the tsar at his Winter Palace. Gapon had organized a workers' union in St Petersburg with government aid in an attempt to keep labour relations under control. The petition to be delivered on 22 January had

Above, troops firing on demonstrators outside the Winter Palace, St Petersburg, on Bloody Sunday, 22 January 1905: though disturbances including a general strike and mutiny in the armed forces continued throughout the year the tsarist regime came through by and large unscathed, though a constitution was granted and a parliamentary assembly, the Duma, established.

Opposite, Japanese painting of a Russian warship exploded by a mine during the Russo-Japanese War, 1904–05.

resulted from strikes and general discontent among workers in the capital and contained a demand for the redress of grievances and for the convocation of a national parliament to be elected by the people. The march had not been forbidden by the authorities, but when the workers reached the Winter Palace they were fired on by troops and hundreds were killed or wounded.

Bloody Sunday destroyed popular faith in the tsar. Belief in the tsar as the father of his people was strong among millions of Russians who had traditionally attributed their sufferings to the gentry and to the tsar's advisers rather than to the tsar himself. Many of the workers who marched to the Winter Palace carried religious icons and pictures of the tsar.

Since Russia was an autocracy, the whole moral authority of the government rested on trust in one man, the tsar. In the months that followed Bloody Sunday it became clear that the government's authority throughout the country was collapsing. Strikes spread to all the industrial centres of Russia and involved white-collar workers as well as workmen in factories. In St Petersburg and elsewhere workers set up soviets (councils) to organize public services and act in general as alternative centres of authority. Peasant unrest affected many provinces, and for the first time the peasants began to organize themselves and transformed their *mirs* into petty republics. Then began the process under socialist leaders of organizing the republics into the giant federation called the Peasant's Union. Local government leaders and the professional classes added their vigorous support to these activities. Political protest was publicly voiced as never before in Russia.

Disaffection spread to the army and navy, the most spectacular demonstration being the mutiny of the battleship *Potemkin* at Odessa in June 1905, where street fighting raged for several days. The *Potemkin* crew,

however, failed to win the support of the entire Black Sea fleet; mutiny, immortalized in Sergei Eisenstein's film, ended in anticlimax with the crew sailing off to internment in Romania. It was, nevertheless, an alarm signal to the government. In August 1905 when the war ended with victory for the Japanese, the fate of the tsar's regime depended on troops who had been demoralized by defeat.

Nicholas had attempted after Bloody Sunday to restore his authority with gestures of conciliation. He agreed to the establishment of an elected assembly, but one which would have no real power and would exclude members likely to be hostile to the government. This gesture was rejected by even the most moderate opponents of the regime. In October, when the St Petersburg Soviet was formed, a railway strike was followed by a general strike which paralysed the cities of the empire. Practically the whole of Russia was in revolt.

At this point Nicholas II consulted Count Witte, who had been dismissed in 1903 after criticism of his industrialization policy but had been recalled in 1905 to negotiate the best possible terms in the peace talks with Japan. Witte saw only two alternatives open to the tsar: military dictatorship or the granting of a constitution. Though Nicholas preferred military rule, his most trusted generals regarded this as too risky; and therefore he accepted Witte's advice to grant a constitution.

Witte then drafted a manifesto, which announced the end of centuries of autocratic rule. Russia was to be a constitutional monarchy, whose parliament, the Duma, could veto legislation and supervise the activities of the tsar's ministers. Civil liberties, like freedom of speech and assembly, were to be guaranteed. The October Manifesto marked the failure of the tsarist bid to weld the new forms of economic power to the old autocracy.

The manifesto split the revolutionaries. The majority were prepared to accept it, but the Soviets were determined to secure a democratic republic. The Soviets grew in size and authority and appeared an admirable instrument of revolution to Social Democrat leaders like Leon Trotsky and Lenin, who had returned from exile. Strikes, mutinies and disorders in town and countryside continued to break out during the remainder of the year. Right-wing organizations added to the chaos by terrorizing non-Russian nationalities, especially Jews, who had long been victims of tsarist persecution and were understandably prominent in the ranks of the revolutionaries.

As the weeks went by it became clear that the revolutionaries were losing control over their supporters. The crisis had dragged on too long and the workers had borne the brunt of a struggle which no one seemed to know how to bring to a satisfactory climax. Calls to strike met with less response. Although the loyalty of many army units remained doubtful, the government felt safe enough to arrest the leaders of the St Petersburg Soviet. A summons to insurrection was answered in Moscow, where savage fighting ensued during December 1905, but this was a final despairing effort. Punitive expeditions against the centres of peasant revolt continued, but the Revolution of 1905 was over.

The constitution promised by the October Manifesto was set out in the Fundamental Laws of May 1906. The tsar kept most of his old power over the armed forces and foreign policy. He could rule by decree when the Duma was not sitting; and ministers were responsible to him, not to the Duma. Legislation had to be approved not only by the Duma but also by the tsar and an extremely unrepresentative upper chamber, half of which was chosen by the tsar himself. The Duma did not even have full control over the budget, the right most prized by any parliamentary assembly. The promised

guarantees of civil liberty were hedged around with exceptions. The constitution violated the whole spirit of the October Manifesto. The tsar and his advisers believed they they had won and that there was no need to keep faith with revolutionaries.

How fully the authorities had regained control of the country was shown when the new Duma made its first challenge. Elections for the Duma took place in March and April 1906. The old tsarist belief had prevailed that the peasants were loyal when not being led astray by agitators; therefore the government had framed an electoral law reasonably representative of an overwhelmingly peasant society. This proved to be a complete miscalculation of the state of peasant feeling, and the free elections produced an overwhelmingly radical Duma. The leftwing of the Liberal Party – the newly formed Constitutional Democratic Party, usually known as the Kadets – was the most successful of the rash of political parties which had sprung up and which took their seats when the Duma was first assembled in May in the Taurida Palace in St Petersburg. The Social Democrats and Socialist Revolutionaries had boycotted the elections because they refused to sit as deputies in a Duma created by the tsar. During the first few months of the Duma there were chaotic parliamentary manoeuvrings and clashes between the government's ministers and the Kadets and their colleagues in the Labour parties. Nicholas, disappointed in the character of the Duma, dissolved it, whereupon the Kadets called on the people to refuse to pay their taxes until the restoration of the Duma. There was no response to this appeal. After the upheaval of the previous year most Russians found voting for their first parliament a sufficiently revolutionary experience.

Eventually the government allowed new elections, thinking that they now had more influence over the voters. The second Duma

which met in March 1907 was even more radical than the first however and was dissolved by the government in June. By altering the electoral law, the government the third Duma in 1907 and in the fourth five years later.

Stolypin and the peasant problem

Even before the 1905 revolution it had been widely recognized that something would have to be done to improve the lot of the peasants. They had been freed from serfdom in 1861, but they had generally got a raw deal over the distribution of land, and they had had to pay a high price for it by instalments. The population was increasing so fast that there was, in any case, too little land to go round.

From 1906 to 1911 the Tsar Nicholas' principal minister was Peter Stolypin. Stolypin's career as a provincial governor had won him a reputation for pitiless suppression of peasant uprisings, but at the same time it had given him a deep appreciation of the peasant problems and a determination to solve them. Stolypin believed that the regime would be safe from revolution only if it could win the loyalty of the peasantry, who constituted the great majority of the Russian people.

In common with others who had studied the peasant question, Stolypin saw the village commune as the chief obstacle to a healthy agriculture and a contented peasantry. When the serfs had been emancipated by Alexander II, it was decided that the land allocated to them in each village was to be owned not by individual peasants but by the commune. The self-governing commune distributed the land periodically in strips to ensure that each household had its fair share. Stolypin had observed that communal ownership of the land offered no

incentive to the enterprising peasant to improve strips of land he might only hold temporarily. Moreover, the commune regulated its affairs by majority decisions, and the enterprising were not likely to be in a majority in a generally illiterate and hidebound society.

Stolypin believed that if peasants were allowed to own a piece of land and pass it on to their heirs they would have a stake in society. Like the French peasants they would then be inclined to be conservative because of their property interests. Between 1906 and 1911 Stolypin put through laws which allowed the head of a peasant family to withdraw from the commune with his own land, not in strips but a solid field, which thereafter would be his property to sell or pass on to his sons. During the period of Stolypin's premiership, something like two or three million individual farms were created in this way. Other measures intended to secure more arable land and raise

agricultural production were also put into effect; a credit system for buying land was established and the colonization of Siberia begun.

Stolypin's ambition to create a nation of conservatively-minded peasant proprietors loyal to the tsar would have taken a very long time to fulfil. What he called his 'wager on the strong' set in motion a revolution in agriculture just as Witte had precipitated an industrial revolution.

In 1911 Stolypin was assassinated while attending a gala performance in the opera house at Kiev. His strong and constructive government in the aftermath of the 1905 revolution had given the regime a misleading appearance of stability. The economy recovered, and industrialization proceeded at a slower but very impressive pace. Agrarian reform was at last under way. The revolutionary movement was in disarray, and tsardom seemed to have won its struggle for survival.

In fact, it had won no more than a breathing space. It had survived because enough of the army had remained loyal and because its opponents had been doubtful as to how to use the revolutionary crisis to win political power. In the next crisis things would be different. Even an impotent Duma would serve as an alternative centre of authority more convincing than the palace. The revolutionaries knew that they had a new weapon in the workers' soviets, which they could use to advantage in a crisis. Though the question of who should rule Russia remained undecided, there was wide agreement that it should not be the tsar.

Nicholas' unsuitability as a ruler was recognized even by the supporters of an absolute monarchy. The influence of Gregori Rasputin at the tsar's court was one of the major factors which contributed to this feeling. Rasputin was a Siberian peasant, who posed as a mystic monk with strange healing powers. A number of such religious quacks haunted the imperial court at the invitation of the Empress Alexandra, who hoped they might be more successful than doctors in healing her haemophiliac son. Rasputin earned her unshakable devotion by being able to halt Alexei's bleeding, apparently by hypnotism. Unfortunately, Rasputin was given to vices and orgies which scandalized St Petersburg. There were wild rumours about his relations with the empress and a feeling of alarm about his influence on decisions of state. From 1912 onwards he was attacked by members of the Duma and eventually by people who had supported the dynasty throughout its troubles.

The tsar was unlikely to survive the next great crisis, and with Nicholas II at the helm such a crisis was only too probable. He was a poor judge of men and events, disliked his ablest advisers, Witte and Stolypin, dismissing Witte as soon as the revolutionary threat had subsided and threatening Stolypin with dismissal. After 1911 Nicholas governed under the influence of his even less judicious wife and of ministers congenial to them. His chances were slight of being able to steer Russia successfully through a period of rapid social and economic change and mounting international tension.

The Lena goldfields massacre of 1912 began a new period of strife at home. Police killed hundreds of workers protesting against intolerable conditions while the government ostentatiously approved the police action. A wave of industrial unrest followed when Mensheviks and Bolsheviks seized their opportunity to revive the cause of revolution. How near Russia was to a new crisis on the scale of 1905 is open to dispute, but the symptoms were ominous. Moreover, the tsar was facing a crucial challenge to his traditional role as defender of the Slav nations as Austria-Hungary, supported by Germany, prepared to destroy the power of Serbia, Russia's Balkan ally. Another diplomatic humiliation at a time of domestic tension could be fatal for the regime. When the moment of decision came in July 1914, the tsar took up the challenge. The result was a war of unprecedented disaster.

Above, patriotic postcard issued in 1916 of Tsar Nicholas II, who became supreme commander of the Russian armies in September 1915.

Above left, Nicholas II (1868–1918, tsar 1894–1917) with the Tsarina Alexandra and his family: a weak and autocratic man, he could find no glimmer of sympathy or understanding for his subjects' desire for change.

Below left, the Duma in session: the four Dumas between 1905 and 1916 managed to achieve some reforms but are perhaps more remarkable for being the only democratically elected assembles ever in Russia.

Opposite top right, a Russian village in the 1890s: the peasantry was numerically such a dominant sector of society that both the revolutionaries and the tsarist regime attempted to engage their support, the latter by limited reforms after 1905. In the event neither succeeded.

Opposite bottom right, Gregori Rasputin (1871–1916) with some of his court followers: his sinister influence on the royal family was yet one more factor that helped to discredit it.

Opposite left, Peter Stolypin (1862–1911), prime minister from 1906 until 1911: cautious reform was the hallmark of his administration, accompanied by social reaction, including the introduction of a property qualification for the franchise and the encouragement of anti-semitism.

Chapter 45

Asia in the nineteenth century

At the time of the Crimean War, which resulted in the momentous revolutions of Russian political and economic institutions, China and Japan were also forced to adjust themselves to the fact of western military superiority. China's response was slow and ineffective, while Japan responded with a revolution from above, but a revolution carried through more systematically and successfully than in Russia. These differing responses shaped the history of Asia during the nineteenth and twentieth centuries.

In the mid-nineteenth century about half the world's population lived in Asia. They were mostly peasants, and Asia's industrial activity was confined to hand-made quality goods. Half Asia's population had come under European and American rule by the end of the nineteenth century. They bought the cheap manufactured goods produced by European and American factories, and they were exposed in time to democratic and nationalist ideas which bore fruit in the independence movements of the twentieth century. Little native industrialization developed, however, even in India, where British rule revolutionized communications by a vast railway network. Even though the British provided a background of law and order, the traditional way of Indian life offered no stimulus to private enterprise. Moreover, the European rulers had no interest in promoting competition for their home industries and looked on colonial territories as profitable markets and a great source of raw materials for their own factories.

For Asia the most important effect of the industrial revolutions was the strengthening of the nations which had already built empires in Asia and those which were ambitious to do so. The British, the French and the Russians extended their empires, and the Americans and the Germans entered the imperialist fray in the later years of the century. The older imperialists in Asia – the Spaniards, the Portuguese and the Dutch – were less active, but they were not in the forefront of industrialization. The aggressive imperialism of the others had alarming implications for the few remaining independent Asian states. Persia, Afghanistan and Siam were the weakest, but they maintained a precarious existence as buffer states

– the first two between the British and Russian empires, Siam between British India and French Indo-China. It was China and Japan whose position was most changed by the spectacular increase in power of the alien empires which surrounded them.

The Chinese Empire had towered over the rest of Asia for centuries. It was a huge and powerful centralized state on which had been based one of the world's greatest civilizations. Medieval Europe had borrowed extensively from Chinese science and technology, which was then the most advanced in the world. Europe's own scientific revolution of the sixteenth and seventeenth centuries had enabled her eventually to outstrip China, but it was not until the nineteenth century that China had cause to be disturbed by the results. Until then, the Chinese emperors had seen themselves as the centre of the world order. They treated the small squabbling western European states which had built commercial empires in Asia with the disdainful tolerance that a quiet giant might display towards noisy pygmies. Serenely confident of their cultural superiority and invulnerable strength, the Chinese refused to negotiate with European governments on equal terms. The most they would concede was limited trading privileges on the coast or at the border.

Japan had been strongly influenced by Chinese civilization but, politically speaking, was a very different sort of state. Its emperor was a figurehead, and real power lay with a warrior aristocracy headed by a shogun, or generalissimo. While China disdained the 'barbarian' world of Europe, Japan was afraid of it. The activity of European traders and missionaries during the

sixteenth century had proved unsettling to Japanese society. From the seventeenth century onwards Japan's ruling class forbade contacts with the outside world, except China and Holland, the latter having been more discreet in its use of the trading connection than other Europeans.

The challenge of the west

Between 1833 and 1860 Great Britain forced China to abandon her traditional attitude to the outside world and to accept a code of international behaviour convenient to European and American trading interests.

The demand for Chinese tea, porcelain and silks was high, and British merchants had secured the largest share of this lucrative trade. China was largely self-sufficient, and the Chinese government had never regarded foreign trade as important to the empire. Foreign merchants were restricted to the ports of Canton and Macao and forced to operate under highly unfavourable

conditions. The merchants put up with these in view of the vast profits to be made, but at the same time they pressed the British government to negotiate with the Chinese for improved trading conditions. British representatives who travelled to Peking in 1793 and 1816 were rebuffed by the emperor, who saw no need to make concessions to a state which had nothing to offer her in return.

The situation changed when foreign traders found there was an almost inexhaustible demand for opium in China. By the 1830s over half of British exports to China consisted of opium. Importing opium at Canton was banned, but by providing local mandarins with lavish 'presents' it was possible to smuggle the drug past the officials whose job was to exclude it. Their salaries were small, the profits of the trade vast. In effect, British merchants soon found that they could sell as much opium in China as they could carry there.

The effects on the Chinese population were disastrous. Early missionaries record that even the crews of coasting junks took it in relays to go into a drugged stupor. Apart from the cost of the trade, it was clearly ruining the health of the people. In 1839 the Tao Kuang emperor decided to appoint a high commissioner to deal with the situation at Canton. The man he chose was a capable official, Lin Tse-hsü, the Viceroy of Hunan. Much to the surprise of British merchants, he forced them to hand over all the opium in their possession and afterwards had a million *chin* (about 4,000,000 pounds) of it destroyed in lime pits dug on the banks of the Pearl River.

This energetic action soon brought war. Commissioner Lin continued to blockade Canton forcibly against the opium smugglers, and in the summer of 1840 a strong British naval force, some of it steam-powered, appeared off Canton. After sealing up the port, it took the nearby city of Tinghai, thus reducing the imperial defences to confusion. Officials had expected nothing less than the enormous strength of the Royal Navy. After some negotiation, it went on to bombard Canton.

The emperor had little to set against the greatest sea power in the world. Although resistance went on until 1842, the outcome was never in doubt, except in the minds of Chinese officials. Lin's mistake would have been even more disastrous if it had not been for China's enormous size. Although the prohibition of opium in Britain itself did not prevent Queen Victoria's government from protecting those who smuggled it into China, the cost of genuine conquest and annexation would have been prohibitive. After British troops advanced up the Yangtse River to Nanking, the Tao Kuang emperor sued for peace, and the Opium War ended with the Treaty of Nanking of 1842.

This was the first of the 'unequal treaties' between China and the West, and it gave British merchants all the concessions they wanted. This was not purely protection for their sordid opium smuggling but genuine trading equality, without the humiliating assumption of Chinese superiority. The Co-Hong was abolished, and British merchants given free trade rights in five ports, most importantly Shanghai and Canton. Hongkong was ceded to Britain, and an indemnity of £5,000,000 paid. The kowtow, with its implication of paying tribute, was no longer to be demanded.

Similar treaty rights were granted to the Americans and French immediately afterwards. The Opium War made it clear that the Chinese could no longer hope to stave off the power of the West. It may even be seen as the most important turning-point in 2,000 years of Chinese history.

Above, the ceremonial signing of the Treaty of Nanking, 1842, which gave Britain a dominant position in trade with China.

Opposite top, Gillray cartoon satirizing Lord Macartney's (1737–1806) embassy to China, 1793, to ask for free trade and diplomatic representation: the Chinese received Macartney as the representative of a submissive state, their assumption of the superiority of their own culture paralleling that of western imperialists only a few decades later.

Opposite bottom, Chinese sketch of a British sailor during the Opium War 1839–42: as a result of the war, the Chinese were forced to grant trading concessions to western merchants, the first dent in their deliberate refusal to recognize western military and commercial power.

The Taiping revolt

Few Chinese realized the significance of what had happened, and modern Chinese historians call the time which followed 'the twenty precious years when China stood still'. But Manchu power had declined drastically. In their difficulties the many enemies of this foreign dynasty banded together against them. The most formidable threat they had to face was that of the Taiping, which has been seen as the first modern nationalist movement in China. It also had many of the characteristics of a traditional peasant revolt. In either case, it kept the imperial troops at bay for thirteen long and bloody years, from 1851 to 1864.

The prophet of the Taiping was Hung Hsiu-ch'üan, a Cantonese student who had failed to pass civil service examinations. Embittered by his failure and neurotically ambitious, he was nevertheless an inspiring leader with an ability to put forward an appealing and coherent programme of reform. A smattering of mission Christianity appears to have been enough to convince this highly unstable character that he had been divinely chosen as the redeemer of China.

When he began to agitate among the discontented Hakka or immigrant population in southern China, his claim, probably sincere, was that he was the younger brother

of Christ. Yet he was much more than a simple revivalist. His message included demands for a series of radical social reforms, including improvement in the inferior status of women and equal distribution of land and all other property – which naturally appealed to a peasant population frequently on the verge of starvation. There was also to be a return to simplicity in religion, with opium, alcohol, tobacco and prostitution forbidden. Even the long pigtail worn in Manchu China was to be replaced by short hairstyles.

In 1851 Hung was proclaimed leader of the *T'ai-p'ing t'ien-kuo*, or 'Heavenly Kingdom of Absolute Peace'. He had launched the greatest peasant revolt in modern history, which aimed incidentally at removing the European influence which the decadent Manchu had encouraged. The Taiping took Nanking in 1853, while Shanghai fell to other rebellious sects. The Manchu were powerless.

Only the Westerners could save the dynasty. By 1862 the imperial troops had been well trained by advisers like 'Chinese' Gordon and joined with European mercenaries in the 'Ever-Victorious Army' which hurled back the Taiping offensive. In 1864 the revolt collapsed, and Hung died by his own hand. His disunited followers simply broke up into bandit gangs.

This does not disguise his achievement

in showing the way in which China was eventually to defeat the West. Where Hung had whipped up mass nationalist enthusiasm, with a bastardized form of Western religion, future leaders would copy Western industry and education and, finally, Western armaments. The lessons of the ill-fated Taiping were well learned by the Chinese revolutionaries of the present century, particularly Sun Yat-sen and the Kuomintang.

The 'Arrow' War

While the Taiping revolt dragged on, Western merchants were still engaged in the humdrum work of increasing their profits. Unfortunately they had still found no answer to the main problem: that the Chinese did not wish to buy anything manufactured in the West. Convinced of the quality of their wares, the merchants put this down to the ill will of the Chinese leaders and the backwardness of their people. Their solution was to push further and further inland and to put pressure on the central government in Peking itself. These were the aims of the 'Arrow' War, named after a British-owned junk which was very properly impounded by Chinese officials after sheltering a local pirate.

This insult to the flag, in 1856, produced swift action. The British and French took Canton in the following year, and Chinese

Above, a British merchant trading at Canton: the western presence in China had little impact at first, but gradually, as trading increased, accompanied by missionary and military activity, the authority of the Chinese administration was undermined.

Left, the Far East in the mid-nineteenth century.

Opposite, the British gunboat Nemesis, *one of the first ironplated warships built, attacking Chinese junks during the Opium War.*

resistance collapsed much faster than in the Opium War.

At the Peace of Tientsin in 1858, Britain and France were given sweeping new privileges. Eleven new ports were opened, and free navigation on the Yangtse granted. The commercial heartland of China now lay exposed. Foreign merchants were also given rights of special jurisdiction, which protected them from Chinese civil and even criminal law.

The wretched position of the Manchus soon became even worse. After new brushes, Lord Elgin advanced on Peking and sacked the beautiful Manchu Winter Palace. The subsequent Treaty of Peking gave the Westerners legations in the Chinese capital, which had always been refused in the past. Now they could deal directly with the imperial government, in order to extort whatever privileges they wished. China had surrendered to the West.

unwanted mouths in overloaded families.

When rumours got round that the priests were killing and even eating them, the result was the destruction of all mission property by a hostile mob, which also murdered all the Frenchmen who fell into its hands. The Chinese authorities gave ample satisfaction but nothing could improve the misunderstanding and bitterness between the races. Such incidents were many during the long era of concessions. They looked forward to the nationalist revolutions which produced the independent China of our own century.

The transformation of Japan

As in China, the Western challenge came to Japan at a time when the old order was already being undermined from within. Since the early seventeenth century the shogunate had been in the hands of the Tokugawa family. They had given Japan two and a half centuries of internal peace by maintaining strict control over the great feudal lords, the *daimyo*, and their military retainers, the privileged warrior class called the samurai. But in a period of peace the samurai had been encouraged to become men of learning as well as warriors. This proved dangerous, when samurai scholars began to question the legitimacy of Tokugawa rule and whether it was time for the emperor himself to resume power. The study of European books, which could be imported so long as they did not propagate Christianity, aroused doubt about the wisdom of isolating Japan from the world.

In addition, an important and wealthy merchant class had grown up, town life developed (Yedo, the future Tokyo, had a population of a million in the eighteenth century), the manufacture of Japanese handicrafts was flourishing. Merchant financiers were gaining control of the Japanese economy which was becoming more capitalistic, and Japanese society was changing with it.

The threat from America and Europe hastened the political revolution. With its prestige badly shaken by the country's helplessness, the shogunate faced mounting opposition from the *daimyo* and samurai, especially those from Choshu and Satsuma in western Japan. When, in 1867, a fifteen-year-old boy succeeded to the throne as the Emperor Meiji, the shogun Keiki restored to him power over the state, hoping that he would become the leading figure in the new regime. Opponents of the shogunate were determined to prevent any such compromise from taking place and intended to drive the Tokugawa family from power altogether. A group of samurai, led by Saigo Takamori of Satsuma, proclaimed in January 1868 a provisional government in the name of the emperor. Keiki's forces resisted, but were defeated. The imperial court moved into the shogun's castle at Yedo, which in future was to be known as Tokyo. The Meiji restoration was complete.

The European nations could now trade in China on their own terms. The old Manchu hope that the distasteful outer barbarians could be isolated in a few ports was finally dispelled. Much of coastal China had effectively become a European colony, and her major cities were open to any foreigner who wished to visit them. Western *hong* or trade compounds multiplied, even hundreds of miles inland. The Chinese themselves were treated with contempt, as a subject race which had been conquered in open warfare. Some parts of the European compounds even carried notices reading 'No dogs or Chinamen'.

The Chinese themselves adopted the bad habits of the West and distrusted its good ones. European diseases became rampant outside the borders of the concessions. It probably made little difference to the Chinese peasant whether he was oppressed by a Manchu or a European – both were foreigners. But the humiliated gentry and scholarly classes naturally distrusted a civilization which seemed to be superior in nothing but its weapons. Europeans seemed crude, vulgar and incomprehensible.

Indeed the Western population of the Treaty Ports constantly ran the risk of 'incidents' with the hostile Chinese population. Perhaps the worst was the massacre of the French Catholic missionaries at Tientsin in 1870. In this case the fathers were somewhat tactlessly gaining converts by buying infants who would normally have been exposed as a way of getting rid of

Although there was a restoration in form, the real rulers of Japan were a group of young and vigorous samurai bent on a revival of Japanese power by a revolution from above, which they accomplished with skill and determination. They abolished feudalism after convincing the principal *daimyo* that this was in the interests of the state. They created a conscript army, following the French example, to replace the warrior class to which they themselves belonged. With this army they were able to crush a samurai rebellion led by Saigo Takamori himself, who believed that reforms destructive of samurai traditions were damaging to Japan. The samurai reorganized the state's finances according to Western practice and built up a national network of schools and universities aimed at turning out loyal, patriotic and efficient citizens from all classes of society. They westernized their legal system in an attempt to bypass the unequal trade treaties to which they had agreed and which gave the foreigners control over tariffs and exempted them from jurisdiction by Japanese courts.

In addition to these radical measures, the young samurais brought about an industrial revolution. Because Japanese merchants were slow to risk their capital in industrial ventures, the government built railways, introduced postal and telegraph services, took over control of the mines and shipyards, set up model factories and lent money to men who were willing to invest in factories. The samurai reformers did everything possible to speed Japan towards the industrialization which their travels abroad had convinced them was the secret of national greatness and imperial expansion.

The samurai oligarchy were less enthusiastic about the political institutions of the West. Most of them believed that rapid modernization must have priority and that representative government and democratic institutions might get in the way. Only after a number of samurai rebellions did the oligarchy accept the idea of a Japanese constitution. In 1881 a constitution was promised, and in 1889 it was finally proclaimed, modelled on the Prussian one, with the emperor keeping control of foreign policy and the armed forces and being largely independent of parliament in money matters. Parliament was to be elected by only a small fraction of the population. The rights of the subject were only vaguely outlined in the constitution, which was not unlike the one which Nicholas II granted to the Russian people in 1906. Nevertheless, while the tsar continued to exercise power with disastrous results, in Japan the emperor allowed the samurai leaders who had emerged after 1868 to govern in his name with conspicuous success. When political parties were formed in the 1880s, however, Japan's leaders found it increasingly difficult to subdue them.

Within twenty years Japan had acquired the basic apparatus of industrial civiliza-

tion, and with it came the inevitable demands for democracy. Even a small, illegal socialist party had emerged by the early years of the twentieth century. Like the Prussians and the Russians, the rulers of Japan staved off the demand by a very limited constitution and also by a spectacular foreign policy. The extraordinary success of their foreign policy enabled them to preserve the 1889 constitution until 1946, apart from the introduction of universal suffrage in 1925.

Asia's lesser lands

Meanwhile the Westerners themselves were systematically annexing the smaller kingdoms which controlled the approaches to the China Sea. Both France and Britain were intent on seizing as many possessions as possible without actually dismantling China itself. The British had the advantage of a base in their huge Indian Empire and at the same time were driven by fears that any other power might gain land with strategic control over the approaches to the Indian Ocean.

As early as 1819, the colourful adventurer Stamford Raffles occupied Singapore. The British were now entrenched where they could control all traffic to and from the Far East. Next they turned their attention to Burma, a country torn by internal conflicts. Anxious as always for their Indian interests, and bent on securing the approaches to China, they took advantage of frontier incidents to intervene. Rangoon was occupied in 1824 and by 1852 the whole of southern Burma was under British control. Fifteen years later they gained territory further up the Irrawaddy, and by 1885 the whole of northern Burma had been annexed. Across the frontier from them was Yunnan province – in China.

Above, Commodore Matthew Perry (1794–1858) landing at Yokohama, with his officers and men, 8 March 1854: except for a few Dutch traders, Japan had been closed to all westerners since the seventeenth century. Now, after an initial period of uncertainty, Japan adapted well to the influence of the West, borrowing many of its better institutions but managing to retain much of her traditional identity.

Opposite top, an attack on Canton during the 'Arrow' War.

Opposite bottom, the guard at the British Legation at Peking, 1863: though she never officially became a colony, by the 1860s increasing western influence on Chinese government and society meant that effectively China was being colonized.

became the main aim of French policy in southeast Asia in the 1860s.

In 1863 Cambodia became a French protectorate. Much to the disgust of the French government, however, the great explorer François Garnier then returned from an expedition up the Mekong to announce that the river did not in fact go anywhere near the prosperous parts of China. It now seemed that the road to the Chinese market was by way of the Red River, which runs into the Gulf of Tonkin.

After they had recovered from the disaster of the Franco-Prussian War, the French began the search for an inland route into China all over again. By 1885 Tonkin, Annam, and Laos had joined Cambodia and Cochin-China as French dependencies. In 1887 all were reorganized as French Indo-China.

The only southeast Asian state to survive was Siam (or Thailand), which profited from the mutual distrust of the French and British. Wedged between Burma and Indo-China, it became a sort of buffer state or no man's land, where neither of its great Western neighbours could annex land without risking a major conflict.

The South Seas

Europe's stranglehold on the Far East became complete with the occupation of the islands of the South Pacific. Because they lacked the obvious wealth of China and Japan, missionaries were more important in exploring or even annexing them than merchants or soldiers. This is not to say that conflicts with the Polynesians, or between rival groups of missionaries, did not produce incidents which might involve governments at home.

After Captain Cook's exploring voyages, the great British missionary societies, especially the London Missionary Society and the Anglican Church Missionary Society, sent mission after mission to the South Seas. Their impulse was almost wholly religious, although some businessmen hoped that they could sell endless bales of Manchester cotton to the islanders once the missionaries had convinced them that nakedness was sinful. Working from the British settlement in Australia, missionaries soon founded posts in Tahiti, Fiji, the Marquesas and the New Hebrides. American missions became active in Hawaii.

However, Catholic missionaries soon appeared on the scene too. After the voyages of Dumont d'Urville in 1826 and 1827, the French government gave its support to missions in Tahiti, Samoa, the Marquesas and New Caledonia. The Protestant and Catholic missionaries soon quarrelled. In Tahiti, their spectacular squabbles produced a full-scale international incident between the British and French in 1844. Although the French responded well to Palmerston's fury at their activities, they retained the

Apart from constant border troubles with Burmese rulers, the British advance had been speeded up by fears of French activities in South-East Asia. When France joined in the race for China and Chinese markets, she at once began to consolidate her power in Indo-China. French missionaries and traders had always been prominent in Siam and Vietnam and, indeed, they had made every effort to get government assistance from Paris to advance their claims. Whether their interest was in Bibles or cashbooks, they agreed that they would have greater scope with the help of French gunboats.

However, for many years southeast Asia was too far away for French governments with plenty of problems at home to wish to become involved there. Only the empire of

Napoleon III, proclaimed in 1852, set enough store by French prestige overseas to consider a forward policy worthwhile. Vietnamese distrust of Christians continually led to incidents involving French missionaries, one of which provided the pretext for an attack on Hanoi. Annam (north Vietnam) was forced to cede what became Cochin-China, the first French colony in southeast Asia.

Cochin-China included the Mekong Delta, which the French believed would provide a waterway into China, thus short-circuiting the traditional trade-routes to the treaty ports of the empire. If they could gain control over the whole course of the Mekong, the profits to be made at the expense of other European powers would be fabulous. This

Society Islands, and Napoleon III was also able to annex New Caledonia in 1853. It became a colony for French convicts, similar to the British penal colony in Australia or the Siberian settlement in tsarist Russia.

The atmosphere of the Pacific islands in the early years of settlement – their beauty, calm and richness – is nowhere better described than in Herman Melville's *Typee* or in Joseph Conrad's much later *Victory*. Both novelists had roamed through the South Seas. Melville had nothing good to say of the missionaries, and indeed the islands were changing by the time he wrote. Like everywhere else, they had business possibilities. For instance, Hawaii, although independent until 1898, was under the control of American businessmen by the 1850s. The impact of the Europeans on the simple islanders was disastrous.

Japan defeats China

Japan won her spurs as a great power by defeating both China and Russia during ten momentous years of war and diplomacy, the bone of contention between the three countries being Korea. The kingdom of Korea was one of the states bordering China which acknowledged Chinese suzerainty by paying regular tribute to Peking. Burma, Siam and Laos were other such states. Korea's main frontier was with China, but it also touched the south-eastern tip of the Russian Empire near Vladivostock, and Japan lay only a hundred miles away by sea. Since the sixteenth century Korea, which had been strongly influenced by Chinese civilization, confined her relations with the outside world to China, Meiji Japan was determined to prise Korea open in the same way as she herself and China had been. In 1875 an incident involving Japanese warships off the Korean coast led to a threat of war from Tokyo. The Korean government gave way and signed a commercial treaty opening three of Korea's ports to Japanese traders. China did not intervene, but in the years that followed her foreign minister, Li Hung-chang, tried to re-assert Chinese influence in the Korean capital, Seoul.

A battle for predominance over Korea now began. Within Korea rival political groups looked either to Peking or to Tokyo. China seemed to be in a stronger position and held off growing Russian as well as Japanese penetration. Russia began in 1891 to build the great Trans-Siberian Railway. Japan saw this as the opening move in a Russian programme of imperialist expansion in east Asia and concluded that she would have to act quickly if she were to realize her own plans in the region. The Japanese government had for a long time been under pressure at home to take a more aggressive line. Despite governmental attempts to muffle them, Japan's new political

parties were giving trouble in parliament, and the government leaders realized that a victorious war would unite the nation and serve the national interest by forestalling Russia.

A pretext for war was easily found. Rebellion broke out in Korea in 1894, which, like the Taiping Rebellion in China, sprang from a religious movement. The Tong Hak was a society which aimed to preserve the spiritual traditions of the East against Western influences by reconciling Buddhism, Confucianism and Taoism. It became politically-minded and appealed to the country's oppressed peasantry. When the Korean army failed to crush the rebellion both China and Japan sent in troops, but China refused Japan's idea of joint action to reform Korea. At the end of July 1894, Japan set up a pro-Japanese government in Seoul, sank a ship carrying Chinese reinforcements to Korea and attacked the Chinese forces already there. China was taken by surprise.

Japan was overwhelmingly victorious on land and sea. The Chinese navy was defeated, enabling Japanese commanders

Above, the Battle of the Yellow Sea, 1894, during the Sino-Japanese War.

Top, Japanese troops landing in China in 1894: the rapid westernization of Japan in the second half of the nineteenth century was accompanied by an increasingly aggressive imperialism, culminating in the total defeat of China and Russia within ten years.

Opposite, late nineteenth-century painting illustrating the increasing westernization of Japan.

547

to pour troops into Korea and into China's neighbouring province of Manchuria. By the spring of 1895 Japanese armies were marching on Peking. Li Hung-chang promptly made peace. The Treaty of Shimonoseki was a landmark in Asian history, when China, which had grudgingly accepted the military superiority of the West, was now forced to realize that the western formula for success had transformed her small island neighbour into a major threat. The contrast between the response of the old order in China and the new order in Japan to the challenge of the West was now tragically revealed.

The powers close in on China

The terms of the Treaty of Shimonoseki called for China to pay a large indemnity to Japan for the cost of the war, grant Japan further trading rights, give up the islands of Formosa and the Pescadores and surrender to Japan the southernmost part of Manchuria, the Liaotung peninsula. This area contained the important naval base of Port Arthur, and its occupation would put Japan within striking distance of Peking.

The provisions of the treaty did not please Russia, who planned to dominate Manchuria herself and immediately launched a diplomatic rescue operation to save China from having to cede the peninsula. France, as Russia's ally, agreed, while Germany was only too pleased to encourage Russia in adventures so far away from the German frontier. Japan had found the war exhausting, despite her victory, and was in no position to resist the pressure from Europe. She gave up her claim to the peninsula.

China now had to pay the price of her rescue operation, which was higher than that extorted by the Japanese. Apart from Britain, the powers did not take Japan too seriously and assumed that her easy victory simply proved how ripe China was for domination. The Chinese who had been reluctant to import foreign capital and skill for the sake of rapid modernization now had no alternative but to seek foreign loans, which inevitably extended the European grip on China. A defensive alliance with Russia in 1896 was bought at the cost of allowing Russia to build a section of the Trans-Siberian Railway across Manchuria. This not only shortened the route for Russia but was a step towards her economic domination of Manchuria.

The other powers now closed in on China. In 1898 Germany seized Kiaochow Bay on the grounds that two German missionaries had been murdered in the area. Russia took the Liaotung Peninsula and Port Arthur, which she had just forced Japan to give back to China. France and Britain also obtained naval bases and forced China to grant long leases to these territories. The powers began to bargain with one another over their 'spheres of influence' in China, so

that they could exploit the country without coming to blows. America, realizing she was being left out of the territorial scramble, tried to persuade the other powers to accept an 'Open Door' to their spheres of influence so that all foreign commercial interests could share. She got a dusty answer.

Although China seemed on the verge of partition, she survived, as the Ottoman Empire survived, because her enemies were too much at odds among themselves. Britain and Japan were determined to prevent Russia from getting the lion's share of China. They succeeded.

The Boxer uprising

At first, events seemed to favour Russia. The aftermath of the scramble of 1898 was a fresh upheaval inside China, which was to bring foreign troops again to Peking. When the turmoil subsided, Russia seemed a step nearer her ambition of becoming the dominant power in Asia.

The upheaval known as the Boxer Rebellion was a popular movement directed against foreigners and, more especially, against Christians. It got its name from a secret organization whose name was translated as The Society of Harmonious Fists, popularly known as Boxers, which had previously attacked the Manchu dynasty and now redirected its attention towards western imperialism and Christians. The ill feeling aroused among peasants in northern China against European commerce and the acquisition of territories there was surreptitiously encouraged by the government.

For a few months in 1898 it had seemed that China might at last have started on the road to radical reform. The Emperor Kuang Hsu, horrified by the disasters to China which had marked his reign, was won over to proposals for modernization. The most influential of the reformers was K'ang Yuwei, who had managed to reconcile modernization in the western manner with the doctrines of Confucianism. Between June and September 1898 the emperor and his advisers introduced important changes. They hoped to reform the civil service examination system, which was the heart of the Chinese tradition of government, and

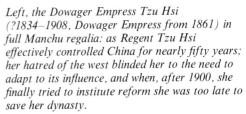

make it relevant to the problems of the day and not just based on the study of ancient texts. Peking University was founded. Army reorganization was set in motion. And many sinecures were abolished.

The emperor's 'Hundred Days of Reform' touched too many vested interests. Though she had supposedly retired, Empress Tz'u Hsi continued to exercise a controlling influence over affairs and now organized a palace revolution which ended with the emperor in prison, his advisers in exile or dead, and the reforms mostly countermanded. The triumph of reaction seemed complete.

It was Tz'u Hsi and her supporters who saw the Boxer rebels as a means of driving out the foreigners. In 1900, the Boxers seized Peking and besieged the foreign legations there. The German ambassador and other diplomats were murdered, and the Boxer policy of slaughtering Chinese converts to Christianity went into action.

With the lives of their ambassadors endangered, China's enemies got together an international brigade of Japanese, Russian, British, American, French and German troops. A smaller force had previously been repulsed, but in the summer of 1900 Peking was captured and the legations relieved. Tz'u Hsi and her supporters fled from the capital, and Li Hung-chang was recalled to make peace with the invaders.

By the 'Boxer Protocol' of 1901 the powers forced China to punish officials deemed responsible for the anti-foreign movement, to pay a large indemnity and to agree to the stationing of foreign troops to police the legations and the route between Peking and the sea. China's humiliation was complete.

The foreign intervention to suppress the Boxers finally discredited the Manchu dynasty. At last Tz'u Hsi realized the inevitability of the reforms she had tried for so long to suppress. She and her successors tried to make up for lost time: systems of communication and education were to be modernized, reforms in the civil service and the army were planned more systematically than before; a constitution similar to Japan's was projected. It left the emperor with wide powers, but, whereas the Japanese emperor had god-like prestige, the Manchu dynasty was non-Chinese in origin, had

kept its separate identity and by the beginning of the twentieth century had lost its prestige altogether. The last-minute effort to enact reforms merely emphasized the corruption of the dynasty and had come too late to save China from foreign exploitation. The Manchu dynasty was soon to go down to revolution.

The Boxer affair also strengthened Russia's position in Manchuria, which she occupied as part of the foreign 'police action'. Her 'arrangements' to evacuate her troops after the rebellion had been crushed contained loopholes which she fully exploited. In 1903 Russia evaded her undertaking to withdraw and thereby made it quite clear that she envisaged Manchuria becoming a Russian protectorate. Japan might have been willing to concede Russian control over Manchuria provided Russia had accepted Japanese predominance in Korea. The independence of Korea had been stipulated by the Treaty of Shimonoseki in 1896, and Japan was sufficiently versed in imperialist terminology to assume that other powers would understand this was a prelude to Korean dependence on Japan. Russia showed no such understanding, and her rulers were to pay as heavily as had China's for underestimating Japanese power.

The battle for east Asia

Japan's principal aim was still to establish her control over Korea. Her victory in 1895 had merely brought Russia into the field as her main rival. Both Japan and Russia

alienated the Koreans by their clumsy attempts to assert themselves by direct interference in Korean politics. There were rumours in Tokyo and St Petersburg that factions in both governments favoured a deal between the two governments at the expense of Korea.

Ito Hirobumi, the Japanese statesman responsible for the 1889 constitution, worked for an alliance with Russia whereby the two countries would share power in east Asia. He was opposed by Yamagata Aritomo, founder of the new Japanese army, who believed that sooner or later Japan would have to fight Russia for supremacy in east Asia.

Yamagata's view was the more popular, since Japanese resentment over the move by Russia, France and Germany to deprive her of the spoils of war in 1895 had been deep and bitter. Her indignation had been all the greater in 1898 when Russia forced China to lease her the Liaotung peninsula. The desire for revenge against Russia was also influenced by the popular feeling that Japan's historical mission was to lead Asia against the European intruders – a viewpoint which was to inspire Japanese policies especially in the years before 1945. But the principal emotion was Japanese pride in the achievements of its army and navy and willingness to trust them in settling accounts with Russia. The prestige of the armed forces gave them a strong voice in the cabinet, where officers controlled the military ministries.

As the conviction grew that war with Russia was inevitable, Japan began to make preparations. This time she took care that

they were diplomatic as well as military preparations. There was one, and only one, obvious ally. Britain was Russia's main rival in Asia and was openly alarmed at Russia's designs on China and Korea. Britain had dominated China's trade in the nineteenth century, but her prospects for the future had been dimmed by the success of her rivals in extracting economic concessions from China in the 1890s. The power Britain feared most was Russia. If Russia gained economic predominance over China and used it to secure a controlling influence over Chinese policy, the balance of power in Asia would shift decisively against Britain. She tried and failed to do a deal with Russia, she tried and failed to mobilize German support against Russia. For Britain too the obvious ally was Japan.

After a last-minute attempt by Ito to secure an alliance with Russia had failed, Britain and Japan came to terms. According to the terms of their alliance of 1902, if Japan should become involved in war with Russia, Britain would try to prevent any of the power from siding with Russia. Japan's fears of a coalition against her as in 1895 were relieved, and she had the satisfaction of being accepted as an equal by the greatest of the imperialist powers. For their part, the British had never shared the scepticism of other states about Japan's real strength. They knew the potentialities of an island nation with a strong navy, and their opinion of the Japanese navy was high. The consequences, however, of underwriting Japanese imperialism in Asia had more far-reaching consequences than Britain could possibly imagine, and forty years later her

own empire in Asia was to face a mortal blow from her former ally.

Japan's triumph

Throughout 1902 and 1903 Japan continued to negotiate with Russia. Time was on Russia's side. The Trans-Siberian Railway was nearing completion, and Russia would soon be able to bring her full weight to bear in the Far East. This was exactly the situation Japan feared, and it soon became evident that the Russians did not intend to give Japan the free hand in Korea which she demanded.

By the end of 1903 Japan had decided to fight, and her surprise attack on the Russian fleet at Port Arthur in February 1904 was the signal for war. In order to transfer her troops freely from Japan to Korea and Manchuria, the Japanese hoped to be able to keep Russia's fleet in Port Arthur and Vladivostok. Her plan was to inflict an early heavy defeat on Russia, since Russia's resources were vastly greater and Japan could not expect to win a war of attrition. She hoped for a rapid triumph of the sort she had enjoyed against China.

Japan's calculations worked, though only just, and her troops quickly seized control of Korea, invaded Manchuria and besieged the Russian forces in Port Arthur. In August 1904 at the Battle of the Yellow Sea the Japanese admiral, Togo, drove the Russian fleet back into Port Arthur while another Japanese naval victory kept the Vladivostok squadron in port. From that point on Japan kept control of the sea, and Russia lost the

chance to threaten Japanese communications. The siege of Port Arthur lasted nearly a year, and both sides suffered heavy losses. Russian attempts to relieve the base failed. After a massive Japanese assault under General Oyama in January 1905, the Russians surrendered Port Arthur.

News of the defeat struck a great blow at tsarist prestige and was an important motivation for the Revolution of 1905. The civil strife within her borders sapped the Russian government's will to fight and two more Japanese victories made Russia abandon the struggle. In March 1905, Japan won a great and costly battle at Mukden. This was followed in May by Admiral Togo's annihilation of the Baltic fleet, which had sailed around the world in a desperate attempt to recapture for Russia the initiative in the war. Japan was finding the war dangerously exhausting and suggested mediation, to which Russia agreed.

The Treaty of Portsmouth gave Japan the right to dominate Korea with control over the Liaotung Peninsula, Port Arthur and the southern part of the railway the Russians had built in Manchuria. She was also given control of half of the island of Sakhalin.

Japan's victories in 1895 and 1905 showed how a nation's power could be dramatically increased even in the early stages of industrialization. Like the Franco-British victory over Russia in the Crimean War, the Japanese victory over China showed that a small nation could defeat a large one provided its economy was more advanced. But Japan and Russia had reached similar stages in their advance towards industrialization – both were well on the way to becoming

Above, an incident during the 1904–05 Russo-Japanese war.

Opposite, Boxer print of foreign prisoners being brought before a military court, 1900.

industrial societies, though in 1914 both were still more agrarian than industrial. The difference between the two countries was that the Japanese political system, after the Meiji restoration, was more likely than the unreformed tsarist system to turn out efficient military and civilian leaders. Victory was, however, as dangerous for Japan as it was for imperial Germany. It concealed the long-term weaknesses of the state and bred a feeling of over-confidence. The Treaty of Portsmouth set Japan on the dangerous road to Pearl Harbor and Hiroshima.

The Russo-Japanese war was an important landmark in world history. An Asian state had defeated one of the great powers of Europe, heralding the end of a world order dominated by Europe. The economic and military power stimulated by industrialization had ceased to be a monopoly of the white-skinned peoples of the world.

Sun Yat-sen

Revolution from above had made Japan a major world power and its more energetic and adaptable leaders had forced the old governing class to accept a modern outlook. Conversely, in China the grudging acceptance of social and political reforms by the governing class opened the way to revolution from below. The aftermath of the Boxer rebellion saw an outpouring of revolutionary propaganda from Chinese outraged by a regime which had allowed China to suffer the humiliation of foreign invasion.

In 1905 the T'ung Meng Hui was formed and served to unite revolutionary societies all over China, attacking the Manchu dynasty for its failure either to learn from the West or to resist its encroachments. The T'ung Meng Hui was primarily made up of students who had been abroad to study, and their leader was Sun Yat-sen.

Sun Yat-sen, the son of a peasant, was born in 1866 near the Portuguese commercial centre of Macao in southern China. He acquired an elementary education on western lines from an Anglican school in Hawaii and continued his schooling in Canton and Hongkong, eventually qualifying as a doctor. During these years he became aware of the need for some sort of revolution against the corrupt rule of the Manchus in China.

The failure of the Manchu government to assert itself against France in 1885 convinced Sun that they should be overthrown. In 1895, after China's defeat by Japan, a revolutionary society led by Sun was foiled in its plans to seize Canton and challenge the regime. This was the first of ten attempts by Sun to rid China of the Manchus before their eventual downfall in 1911.

During his travels in Europe and America Sun achieved unintentional publicity for his cause when in 1896 the Chinese legation in

London involved itself in an international incident by holding him prisoner for ten days. More important was the influence on him of European socialism and of radical thought in America.

By the time he founded the T'ung Meng Hui (Alliance Society) in 1905, Sun had organized enough rebellions – all unsuccessful – to earn him a nationwide reputation and to give the revolutionary movement the rudiments of an ideology. The 'Three Principles of the People' which he planned to realize through revolution were: the unity of the Chinese nation, a democratic and republican form of government and a redistribution of land to benefit the peasants. He foresaw this revolution coming about after a period of military rule, which would uproot the old order, and a subsequent period of local self-government, which would serve to teach the nation the meaning of democratic government. The introduction of democracy on a national level would complete the revolutionary process. This was Sun's attempt to apply an assortment of Western ideas to the Chinese situation.

The spread of revolutionary ideas to the army proved to be crucial to the success of Sun Yat-sen's plans, which as yet seemed obscure to the peasants of China. The revolutionaries were forced however to act before they were ready because the discovery in October 1911 of their headquarters in Hankow led to a disturbance. Troops at the neighbouring town of Wu-chang made a rather desperate bid to start a rising. Hankow was seized, a provisional government was proclaimed and a general call to revolt was issued.

The Manchus were sufficiently alarmed by the uprising to recall Yuan Shih-k'ai, who had been summoned before by Tz'u

Hsi in 1898 at the time of the hundred days of reform. Yuan agreed to take command if the Manchus would offer some compromise political solution. The dynasty eventually agreed to a British style constitutional monarchy and made Yuan prime minister.

Meanwhile, the revolutionaries had established control of southern China as firmly as Yuan controlled the north. Sun returned from exile to become president of the provisional government in January 1912 and soon realized that Yuan was too strong to be ignored. He, therefore, offered to step down and arrange for Yuan to become president of a Chinese republic if Yuan would get rid of the Manchu dynasty. As Yuan was aiming throughout to secure supreme power for himself, he fell in with Sun's proposal. The Manchus found themselves without support, and they agreed to the abdication of their emperor, a boy of six. In February 1912, the last of the great Chinese dynasties came to an end. The revolutionaries had achieved their aim of establishing a republic.

The rest of Sun's revolutionary programme, however, was as far from realization as ever. Yuan was bent on using the revolution to make himself ruler of China, not to make her democratic or socialist. And once the Manchus were gone it soon became clear that Yuan was their real successor.

In 1913 a parliament was elected under the new republican constitution. Sun organized a new party, the Kuomintang, in an attempt to fight the elections and unite the forces of republicanism which were divided as to the future course of the republic. The Kuomintang was successful in the elections but almost immediately clashed with Yuan over the conditions of a foreign loan. The parliamentary struggle turned into a rebellion, which Yuan crushed. The Kuomintang was dissolved, Sun went back into exile and Yuan made himself dictator. He died in 1916 after trying unsuccessfully to make himself emperor. China fell under the control of a number of 'warlords' or military leaders who had taken advantage of the breakdown of the old order to carve out little empires for themselves in the provinces. Thus she entered a period of conflict and turmoil which continued until the triumph of Mao's communist movement in 1949.

Left, the heads of decapitated offenders hanging for all to see during the 1911 Chinese Revolution.

Opposite, Sun Yat-sen (1867–1925), founder and leader of the Kuomintang, the Chinese nationalist party, and briefly president of the new Chinese republic in 1912: his life was spent trying first to overthrow the Manchu dynasty and then to combat the warlords.

Chapter 46

The United States Industrialization and Imperialism

Of the dramatic events of the years 1895–1905 in Asia none was more momentous than the intervention of the United States, which until then had counted for little in world affairs. Her rise to power had been noticed with alarm only by the British with their imperial interests in North America. Europeans were quick to realize the significance of Prussia's victories against Austria and France in the years between 1866 and 1870. Prussia, transformed into the German Empire, would henceforth be the leading power in Europe. The significance of the American Civil War, however, fought between 1861 and 1865, did not seem so important to the Europeans. This was a war which showed, nevertheless, more clearly than any of those yet fought in Europe how wars were to be waged in an age of industrialism. Moreover, the victory of the northern states meant that the United States of America would survive as an entity, whose fast developing industries and expanding population would contribute to making her a leading world nation by the end of the nineteenth century. America's role in Asia at the turn of the century marked her emergence as a world power.

While the Civil War decided the question of America's unity, it left unsettled the question of what sort of state America was to be. The war had been fought because the southern states of the federation felt that they were a minority, unfairly discriminated against by the federal government in Washington and more specifically by the northern states, who favoured the maintenance of unity in the territories of the United States. The fundamental issue between North and South was that of negro slavery, which the South regarded as essential to their economy and way of life. The North saw the eventual disappearance of slavery as an inevitable part of economic and social progress much as critics of serfdom did in Russia in these same years.

In 1860 the new Republican Party elected Abraham Lincoln as president. The party had been formed to advance a programme of high tariffs and economic development on a national scale. The radical wing of the party, to which Lincoln did not belong, was very anti-slavery and anti-southern in sentiment. The South saw the election of Lincoln as a

challenge to their future, however, and the secession of ten southern states from the union in 1861 precipitated the Civil War.

The war of southern independence, which lasted for four years, involved battles as great and devastating as those of Napoleon. It was not until the southern armies had been greatly weakened by divisions among themselves that the Confederate general, Robert E. Lee, finally surrendered to General Ulysses Grant at Appomattox on 9 April 1865. The industrialized North had defeated the agrarian South.

Reconstruction

During the course of the struggle, President Lincoln had used his wartime powers to abolish slavery in the Confederate states by the Emancipation Proclamation of 1863, but the victors remained at odds as to what that emancipation was to mean in practice. Lincoln gave his first priority to healing the wounds of the Civil War for the sake of

national unity. As long as the South abandoned plans to break up the federation he was prepared to be conciliatory over working out the practical consequences of freeing the slaves. Though he was assassinated in April 1865 in the last days of the war, his successor, Andrew Johnson, had much the same attitude. He was opposed, however, by radical Republicans in the Senate and the House of Representatives, who believed that the North should use its victory to impose efficient government on the South and make its leaders conform to the democratic political principles which America had long proclaimed.

The radicals had their way in the aftermath of victory, when most people in the North felt that the South should pay a heavy penalty for such a bloody and costly war. In the South Reconstruction entailed the establishment of freed slaves as effective citizens, whose votes could be used to elect new legislatures in each of the southern states, where it was hoped that democratic state constitutions would be adopted. In

THE CONSTITUTIONAL AMENDMENT!

GEARY
Is for Negro Suffrage.

STEVENS
Advocates it.

FORNEY
Howls for it.

McCLURE
Speaks for it.

CAMERON
Wants it.

The LEAGUE
Sustains it.

They are rich, and want to make

The Negro the Equal
OF THE POOR WHITE MAN,
and then rule them both.

The BLACK Roll
CANDIDATES FOR CONGRESS
WHO VOTED FOR THIS BILL.

THAD. STEVENS
WM. D. KELLEY
CHAS. O'NEILL
LEONARD MYERS
JNO. M. BROOMALL
GEORGE F. MILLER
STEPHEN F. WILSON
ULYSSES MERCUR
GEO. V. LAWRENCE
GLENNI W. SCHOFIELD
J. K. MOORHEAD
THOMAS WILLIAMS

THE RADICAL PLATFORM--"NEGRO SUFFRAGE THE ONLY ISSUE!"
Every man who votes for Geary or for a Radical Candidate for Congress, votes as surely for Negro Suffrage and Negro Equality, as if they were printed on his ballot.

particular, Reconstruction entailed the enforcement of the Fourteenth Amendment to the American constitution, which abolished slavery everywhere in the country and made the national government the guardian of every person's right to 'life, liberty and property'.

Radical leaders like Thaddeus Stevens worked for a more democratic and humane system of government in the South. At first these radicals enjoyed a good deal of success, but reform was obtained only by the unscrupulous use of authority which enhanced the bitterness between North and South. This might not have been so important if the reforms could have been made permanent, but popular enthusiasm for reform in the North faded in time; after the withdrawal of the last federal troops from Louisiana and South Carolina in 1877 the southern states had again something like home rule. The radicals had failed.

Negroes in the South were left insecure, third-class citizens by the failure of radical reconstruction. Immediately after the Civil War secret societies like the Ku Klux Klan dedicated themselves to keeping negroes in as subservient a position in society as they had endured under slavery. Klan intimidation often took the form of horrifying cruelties and lynchings. By the end of the century southern legislatures had found more systematic methods of keeping negroes 'in their place' – like the use of poll taxes to deprive them of their right to vote and the segregation of public transportation and schools.

Although the negroes were little better off as freemen than as slaves, they could at least escape to the towns in the North, where racial discrimination was less blatant. A small but important negro middle class emerged, and negro education developed

under the leadership of men like Booker T. Washington, who saw no future in political action and concentrated on educating negroes to improve their economic well-being. The failure to force or persuade the South to emancipate the negroes after the Civil War postponed the settlement of a problem which was to survive into the second half of the twentieth century and prove a source of weakness and embarrassment when America aspired to the leadership of a world whose people were mostly coloured.

Emigration

Although the Civil War left divisions in American society which still persist, America did succeed in dealing with the problem of immigration. Over 30,000,000 immigrants poured into the United States from every European country and some Asian ones during the nineteenth century. National minorities did not prove a danger to America as they had to most European states, and immigrants were quite easily integrated into American society.

Most of Europe industrialized too slowly to support the continent's rapidly rising population, and land hunger drove millions to the spacious American plains and cities. Political, religious and nationalist oppression drove millions of others to the comparative tolerance and freedom of opportunity offered by America. Between the Civil War and 1890 most of the immigrants were German, Irish, British and Scandinavian. Between 1890 and 1914 they came mainly from Italy, Austria-Hungary and Russia. As immigration mounted, many Americans demanded some restrictions,

"ONE VOTE LESS."—*Richmond Whig.*

Above, cartoon by Thomas Nash, published in the New York journal, Harper's Weekly, *after an incident during the 1868 presidential election, in which a black was killed because he tried to vote.*

Left, election handbill produced in about 1866 (the constitutional amendment referred to is the fourteenth, which guaranteed negro suffrage): advocated by the radical wing of the Republican Party, negro suffrage was an unpopular cause even in the North and became non-existent in the South after the withdrawal of Federal troops.

Opposite, a family of freed slaves on a South Carolina plantation, 1862: a few blacks were granted their freedom by enlightened owners, but the vast majority had to await the end of the Civil War; then lack of economic strength and the hatred of the whites meant that freedom brought meagre benefits.

especially when Chinese and Japanese immigration became prominent on the west coast. But there were few restrictions until after the First World War. Generally speaking, Americans were proud of their tradition as the land of the free to which the victims of less enlightened governments fled; and the booming American economy was hungry for all the cheap skilled labour Europe could provide.

The opportunities for hard-working and enterprising men in American industry largely explains why most immigrants were quite easily assimilated. Immigrants were likely to be above average in enterprise, and in a society which admired those who raised themselves to wealth by their own efforts many immigrants climbed high in the social scale within a generation or so. America's educational system overcame the language problem and indoctrinated the newcomers' children in the rights and duties of American citizens. The Democratic and Republican party machines were hungry for voting fodder, and although organizations like Tammany Hall (the famous Democratic political machine in New York) were notorious for corruption they made the town immigrant feel an active citizen and involved him in political life. Corrupting 'hand-outs' at least alleviated poverty when immigrants were finding their feet in a society which did not believe in welfare services.

Immigration on this vast scale enriched not only industrialization but America's scientific and artistic development as well. For example, Andrew Carnegie, by origin a poor Scottish immigrant boy, built up one of the largest steel producing companies in the world. The German born physicist, Albert Einstein, who emigrated to America in the 1930s, revolutionized the scientific world with his theory of relativity.

Nevertheless, people who wanted to restrict immigration argued that the slum conditions to which immigrants came and in which the unsuccessful ones stayed bred crime and corruption and lowered the standards of city life. The United States tried to maintain an industrial society which left individuals to sort out their own destinies and had little sympathy for failure. The prospects of success were high enough to gratify the expectations of most of her new citizens.

Railroads

Though at the beginning of the nineteenth century America had been a thoroughly agrarian society, between 1830 and 1860 industrialization developed rapidly. Because of the high labour costs American industrialists eagerly adopted labour-saving machinery from the other side of the Atlantic and improved on it. American workers, who were generally better educated than those in Britain and other European countries, eagerly accepted the new machines as easing their tasks. By the time of the Civil War America had become second only to Britain as a manufacturing country.

As in Russia, the size of the country made the transportation of goods a major problem which could best be solved by a network of railways. In Russia industrialization began only when the construction of railways was started while America had become an important industrial power before the big trans-continental lines were laid down. The first of these lines, begun in 1863, was the result of two separate enterprises, one starting from Chicago as the Union Pacific Railway, the other, the Central Pacific, driving east from California. In 1869 the two lines came together in Utah after their

promoters had overcome phenomenal difficulties by brutal determination and often by shady financial operations. Other lines stretching across the American continent followed in the next twenty years.

As in other countries America's great railway network was an immense stimulus to industry, and American industrialists rose to the challenge of providing the coal and steel needed in such huge quantities. As the network developed, the costs of transporting raw materials, agricultural produce and manufactured goods fell. Apart from the economic benefits, the railways, together with the simultaneous development of telegraphic and telephone communications, helped to supply a sense of unity especially valuable in such a sprawling and scattered nation.

The triumph of capitalism

Although the urban population remained smaller than that of the countryside until after the First World War, the most striking feature of American history between the end of the Civil War and 1914 was the staggering growth of industry. By the time she entered the First World War in 1917, the US had outstripped every other industrial nation in terms of manufacturing output, and she could claim the highest per capita income in the world. As the leading industrial state America was to become the most powerful as well as the richest of the great powers.

The big business corporations which emerged during the late nineteenth century dwarfed those of Europe. The United States, even more than Britain, offered unrivalled opportunities for building great industrial empires. Remarkable and ruthless industrialists, like John D. Rockefeller, and Andrew Carnegie, emerged. They saw the

world of business as evolving through an endless struggle in which the fittest survived; and both Carnegie and Rockefeller, who survived as the fittest in their industries of steel and oil, saw it as their duty to use their enormous wealth to benefit the community at large. They became philanthropists on the same giant scale as their industrial enterprises. The Rockefeller Foundation continues to finance projects for the benefit of society, and Carnegie's fortune still promotes educational enterprise in Scotland as well as America.

The great issue in American politics in the ten years after the Civil War was the extent to which Reconstruction could impose on the defeated southern states the necessity of liberty and equality for all its citizens. General Grant, the North's hero in the Civil War, became president in 1868 and backed the radicals in their zeal to reform the South.

After the presidential election of 1876, however, when a congressional electoral commission had to decide the winner, a more conservative conciliatory mood descended on the Republican Party and the country as a whole. The new president, Rutherford B. Hayes, favoured an end to the strife with the South, and this seemed to be in tune with the rest of public opinion.

With the decline of radical influences in the Republican Party, both the main parties became conservative in their approach to the problems of government. The Republicans,

who won every presidential election between 1860 and 1912 except for those in 1884 and 1892, emerged as a middle-class party with a good deal of working class support. The Republicans bore some resemblance to the British Liberals and were similarly in tune with the spirit of industrialism. In the late nineteenth century they became increasingly linked to the interests of big business. Republican presidents in this period saw their role as ensuring efficiency in the rather limited work of central government, allowing private industry to develop to the nation's advantage.

Similarly, the Democrats, who elected only one president in these years (Grover Cleveland) but who frequently had a majority in both houses of congress, had a narrow view of the scope of central government. The experience of radical Republicanism left the South solidly Democratic during the following hundred years, and the Democrats in the South defended the rights of the old landowning class. The Democratic Party was also the party of the farmers, who believed that their interests were being sacrificed to the growing power of big business. Above all, the Democrats were for states' rights and against the power of the federal government in Washington, and they saw the presidency as a means of protecting the states. Their future role as the reforming party of Franklin D. Roosevelt's New Deal was still very distant.

Above, a railway construction crew by their locomotive: the years between the Civil War and the end of the First World War were the heyday of American railways; the transcontinental link was completed in 1869 and the network covered the entire country, increasing from 35,000 miles in 1865 to 254,000 in 1916, when one worker in every twenty-five was a railway employee.

Opposite right, the completion of the first transcontinental rail link, Promontory, Utah, 10 May 1869.

Opposite left, Italian immigrants at Ellis Island, the reception centre in New York Harbour for immigrants from Europe: more than twelve million people entered the USA through Ellis Island between 1892 and 1924, when mass immigration ended and immigrants were inspected in their country of origin.

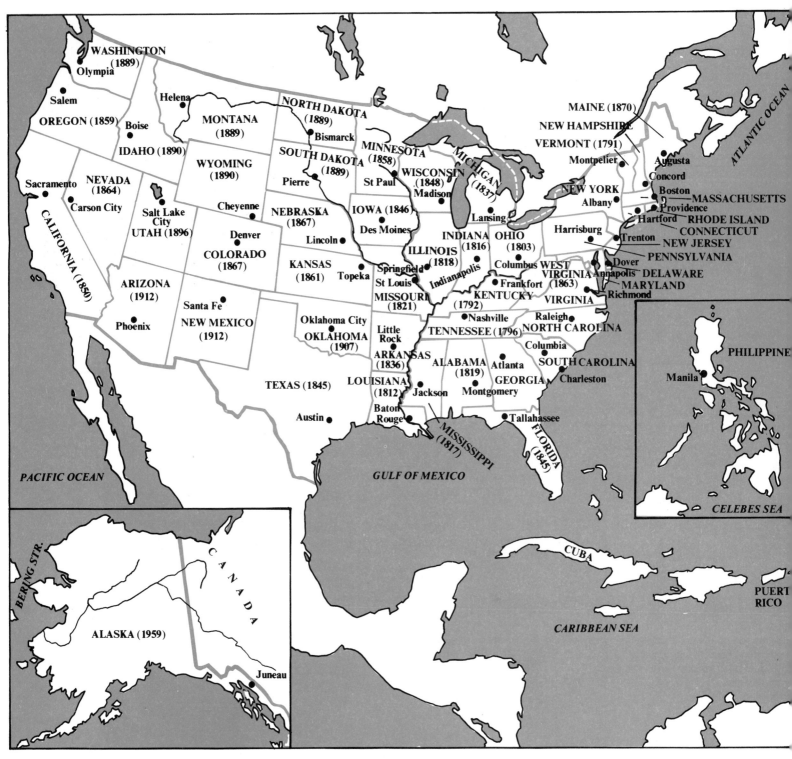

The presidents in these years of conservatism were worthy and efficient men but left no great mark on American society. While Abraham Lincoln's name became known the world over, Hayes, James Garfield, Chester Arthur, Grover Cleveland and William McKinley acquired little fame outside America. Two of them were assassinated: Garfield was succeeded by the sound but unspectacular Chester Arthur, but McKinley, who was shot by an anarchist in 1901, was succeeded by his dynamic vice-president, Theodore Roosevelt. With Roosevelt's accession the United States had for the first time since 1865 a leader of world stature to coincide with her emergence as a world power. Roosevelt's energy, which

alarmed many of his fellow Republicans, was to bring an end to the era of conservatism.

Roosevelt came to power at a time when strong minorities were becoming openly discontented with the way the country was run. Both industrial workers and farmers had grievances against the system; and although they failed to change it, their behaviour was turbulent enough to draw attention to the need for reform.

Industrialization in the United States was not accompanied by a rapid growth of trade unionism, and employers were in a stronger position than those in Europe in these years. Millions of immigrants supplied them with an ever-growing labour force accustomed to a lower standard of living and, therefore,

initially less demanding. The prevailing philosophy in America favoured rugged individualism which saw trade unions as disrupting the process by which free enterprise created wealth. Middle-class opinion was hostile to organized labour; the farming community had little interest in or sympathy for the problems of factory workers; and the courts were likely to find against them in disputes. The more militant workers, especially those with experience of labour politics in Europe, tended to become despairingly violent when peaceful pressure failed. Incidents like the riot in the Haymarket, Chicago, in 1886, when over a hundred people were killed or wounded, further alienated public opinion and discouraged

Above, a child labourer in a southern cotton mill, c.1900: organized trade unionism was slow to develop in the USA and never achieved the political power it held in Europe.

Above left, Henry F. Farny, The Song of the Talking Wire: *the telegraph and railroads marked the advance of the frontier across the western states, bringing to an end the traditional Indian way of life. The Taft Museum, Cincinnati, Ohio.*

Left, chromolithograph after The Lost Bet, *a painting by Joseph Klir, 1892: the incident portrayed resulted from a wager made between a Republican and a Democrat in Chicago during the 1892 Congressional elections, each promising to pull the other through the streets in a wagon if his candidate lost (the Democrat won). By now the party machines controlled every aspect of political life, especially in the big cities.*

Opposite, the growth of the United States of America: after the Spanish-American War of 1898, the USA gained the Phillipines, Guam and Puerto Rico; Cuba was also ceded by Spain and ultimately became a US protectorate.

the average worker from pressing for the establishment of unions.

The mainstream of the American labour movement abandoned any attempt to play politics in the manner of European workers. The Knights of Labour, founded in 1869, aimed at building a nation-wide labour organization for all kinds of workers. It proved too big, unwieldy and lacking in discipline to outwit employers willing to use a private army of hired detectives to break up strikes. However, smaller unions of skilled workers in particular trades had more success. The most influential leader thrown up by this kind or organization was Samuel Gompers of the Cigarmakers Union. A Londoner by birth, Gompers built up his union into a closely knit and disciplined one with a national fund and welfare benefits. In 1886 a number of these smaller unions joined together to form the American Federation of Labour, with Gompers as president and the dominating personality in the federation until 1924.

Samuel Gompers believed that there was no point in trying to challenge the entrenched Republican and Democratic parties by creating a separate labour party. He was hostile to socialism and worked to secure high benefits for his members within the capitalist system instead of trying to replace the system or even to change it. He tried without success to organize the labour movements of the world in a new non-socialist International. In America, however, Gompers' programme had wide appeal. Despite periodic depressions, prosperity was too obviously increasing for many American workers to be attracted by ideas of revolution or even radical political change. The American labour movement was to develop firmly on the lines laid down by Gompers.

In the period before the First World War, however, the American Federation of Labour represented only a fraction of American workers. Long hours and insecurity for the majority were not countered by effective trade unionism or state welfare provisions. A number of spectacular, violent and unsuccessful strikes towards the end of the century made more of an impression on public opinion than the ultimately more

significant work of Gompers. Although industrialists were able to withstand the demands of frustrated workers, their brutal methods in the 1890s helped to swing influential sections of society to greater sympathy with the workers' problems. This sympathy was one aspect of the Progressivist movement which Theodore Roosevelt came to represent.

The Populist Party

It was a curious fact that in the most flourishing industrial society in the world the farming community seemed a more powerful political force than the industrial workers. Farmers had a more deep-rooted grievance to express. While workers in the towns wanted to reform industrialization in their favour, the farmers opposed the capitalist system as a whole. For example, they opposed the railway owners who disregarded the rights of farmers in areas through which their railways passed. During periods of economic depression the farmers blamed high interest rates and an inadequate supply of credit on the east coast financiers, who wanted to impress foreign investors by establishing the gold standard in the United States. In 1892 the farmers formed the Populist Party.

The Populists denounced the capitalist system as immoral, and, in particular, they demanded a reform of the currency to allow an unlimited amount of silver coinage to augment the gold supply. Both Republican and Democratic party leaders were agreed on the need for the gold standard because an industrial economy had to have a 'sound' currency if it were to attract foreign investors. A depression in the mid-1890s intensified debate on the issue, and the propaganda of the Populists began to have its effect. In 1896 the Democrats split on the currency question and nominated as their presidential candidate for that year William Jennings Bryan, whose splendid and emotional tirade against conventional financial wisdom contained the famous words, 'you shall not crucify mankind upon a cross of gold.'

By persuading the Democrats to adopt their policy, the Populists enjoyed a remarkable triumph. But their triumph was short-lived when Bryan lost the election to the 'sound money' Republican candidate, William McKinley. The immense wealth of America's great banks and corporations was enlisted by the Republicans to counter Populist propaganda and the powerful oratory of Bryan. Moreover, the country was recovering from the depression, and prosperity was returning.

Whatever the merits of the gold standard the importance of which was probably exaggerated, Bryan's defeat was a significant event in American politics. Agrarian America had been defeated by industrial America. The radical Populist movement was backward-looking and romantic and

had some affinity with the very different Russian populist movement in its hostility to industrialism. By the end of the nineteenth century in the United States the future lay with industrialism. The campaign of 1896 was a brilliant rearguard action, but afterwards Populism faded, and the Democratic Party did not revive until 1912.

Progressivism

The farming protest had failed and trade unionism was slow to develop. A socialist movement under Eugene Debs attracted widespread interest but never became a serious contender for political power. The failure of populism and socialism did not mean that public opinion was complacent, however, for at the turn of the century an influential reform movement grew up known as Progressivism.

Progressivism arose from a growing distaste for the way in which the giant corporations pursued their aims without regard for the interests of the community as a whole. For many intellectuals the idea of the 'survival of the fittest' turned sour when they saw some of the triumphant survivors. The older generation of American capitalists were offended by the newer, more ruthless brand of tycoon and resented their success. 'Muckraking' journalists highlighted the seamier side of big business with stories of corruption and all sorts of abuses and helped to convince middle-class opinion that American society was getting out of control.

Not that Progressivism sought any radical change. Its followers aimed to make politics more democratic and to make businessmen responsive to public as well as private interests. They also favoured a limited amount of labour legislation to limit working hours, to compensate workmen for injury – the kinds of provisions which were becoming standard practice in most industrial societies. Some Progressives traced the causes of corruption and the evils of social and political life to immigrants and alcohol, and they started campaigns to restrict immigration and to prohibit the sale of alcohol. The more liberal side of the movement worked for the right of women to vote.

This moderate, mainly middle-class movement did something towards cleaning up the corruption in American political life. One important achievement was the adoption of 'primary' elections in many states in response to the demand that party voters should be directly involved in the nomination of party candidates instead of leaving it to corrupt party 'machines'. In general, the achievements of Progressivism matched its modest aims.

Progressivism gained from the assassin's bullet which ended McKinley's presidential career and put Theodore Roosevelt in the White House. 'T.R.', as he was affectionately referred to, was an energetic, colourful, restless figure with wide-ranging interests

and many enthusiasms. By the time he became president in 1901 he had written several books, worked on a cattle ranch and seen public service as assistant secretary of the navy, governor of New York State and vice-president of the United States. In everything he did he took a positive approach to the job and attacked corruption and inefficiency with gusto. Characteristically, he had found organizing the navy too tame during the war with Spain in 1898 and had instead played a dashing role as colonel of the 'Rough Rider' volunteers in Cuba.

Roosevelt was an appropriate president for an age of Progressivism and imperialism, very different in style from the conservative administrators of previous decades. He believed in using his office to ensure that the big corporations behaved themselves in a more public-spirited way and directed his administration to investigate monopolistic 'trusts' in the major industries. In an unprecedented extension of his executive office, Roosevelt intervened in a major coal mining strike in 1902 to get both sides to accept arbitration. In addition, he instituted federal control over the rates charged by the railways; he put through a pure food act which current scandals had proved necessary. Conservation was another interest of the indefatigable Roosevelt, who tackled the problem of protecting America's forests, rivers and natural resources from exploitation by private concerns.

Roosevelt was in office from 1901 until 1908, having been returned in 1904 with massive popular support. Even as interpreted by Roosevelt, the presidency did not carry enough power to do more than tinker with the problems which both he and the

Above, Colonel Theodore Roosevelt (1858–1919) and his 'Rough Riders' on San Juan Hill, Cuba, during the 1898 Spanish American War.

Opposite top, troops protecting a train during the Pullman strike in 1894: George Pullman (1831–97), in many respects a beneficent employer who had built a model village for his employees, cut wages and sacked workers during the 1893–94 economic depression but refused to lower rents. His employees struck, but, though Pullman cars were boycotted nationally and two-thirds of the railway system came to a halt, the strike was eventually broken.

Opposite centre, a Nebraska farmstead in the late 1880s: agriculture experienced a boom period in the last decades of the nineteenth century, as the rich soil of the Plains states was put under the plough, its products shipped east by the newly-built railroads; many small farmers, unable to cope with the development of agricultural capitalism, turned to the Populist movement to express their grievances.

Opposite bottom, ranchers and cattle, 1902: though the myth still endures, the reality of the wild west – the cowboy roaming the plains, driving his stock hundreds of miles to slaughter – lasted for only about twenty years, homesteaders then putting the Plains under cultivation and ranchers introducing industrialized methods of stockfarming.

Progressives saw as urgent. But he made regulation of the jungle warfare of American capitalism a popular cause to which future presidents would return.

Imperialism in Latin America

Roosevelt's approach to international affairs was as flamboyant as his approach to domestic problems and far more widely appreciated. Like the rest of the world's industrial powers, the United States was seized with imperialist fervour at the turn of the century.

During the nineteenth century she had taken the obvious course of extending her frontiers within the north American continent. The Indian wars between 1862 and 1886 resulted from the intrusion by white settlers on the hunting grounds of Indian tribes like the Sioux and the Cheyenne. After numerous Indian attacks on the settlers' camps had been savagely repulsed, America's Indian population was persuaded or compelled to settle peacefully in areas allocated to them by the federal government. War with Mexico in 1846–8 had forced the Mexicans to recognise US sovereignty over Texas and to cede New Mexico and California, where gold had been recently discovered. Settlers had moved steadily west during the century, and Americans were told by the historian Frederick Jackson Turner in 1893 that this moving frontier was the secret of their dynamic national character. By the end of the century the frontier was 'closed' – the great plains, where the cowboys and the pioneer farmers had left their legends, had become settled regions.

As in Britain and Germany, the achievements of the age of industrialism were so obvious to the eye, and the changes it wrought so rapid, that an exhilarating sense of national pride and confidence characterized the period. The United States now looked for fresh fields to conquer with her immense economic and military power. Alfred Mahan's *Influence of Sea Power upon History*, published in 1890, strongly influenced American – and European – opinion as to the need for naval bases and colonies in the quest for national security and power. As in Britain, the popular press sensationalized international issues and aroused resentment and alarm at European encroachments or interventions in Asia and even Latin America.

Pacific naval bases like Midway and Pearl Harbor had already been acquired before the imperialist movement got under way. It was the war with Spain in 1898 which released imperialist passions in America. Spain was an especially suitable victim, a European intruder in America's global backyard who possessed Cuba and the Philippines. She was also a reactionary colonial power, whose presence was hated by those she ruled. The United States had ample opportunity to experience the mixed

emotions of national interest and sincere self-righteousness which were the hallmark of imperialism in the industrial age. In 1895 the US had strongly supported the Cubans in their revolt against Spain, which had dragged on despite brutal repression by the Spanish colonial administration. American opinion was angered by events so close to her shores, and the idea of a liberating war grew popular. They mysterious explosion which destroyed the American battleship *Maine* in Havana excited feelings still further. In April 1898 Congress was practically unanimous in agreeing to war.

The ease with which victory was won was predictable enough given Spanish weakness and distance from her Cuban colony. The defeat of Spain's troops in Cuba and of her navy in the Philippines was very gratifying to American national pride. By August 1898 peace was being negotiated; Spain evacuated Cuba and handed over Puerto Rico and the Philippines to the United States. The annexation of the Philippines, whose population had rebelled against Spain and in the meantime set up their own government, caused much soul-searching and debate and was considered by some to be an act of colonialism. The misgivings were sincere enough, but imperialistic fervour was stronger than the feeling that Philippine self-determination should prevail. The argument of a civilizing mission, so familiar to European ears, eventually proved adequate to convince the Senate to ratify the treaty signed in Paris in 1898. Cuba was evacuated but only after the Cubans had accepted limitations on their freedom to manage their affairs which made the island something like an American protectorate.

This was also the year when the industrial powers began closing in on China. In 1899 the United States secretary of state, John Hay, made his famous 'Open Door' proposal to the other interested nations, hoping to keep China open to US economic penetration.

Dollar Diplomacy

American imperialism had thus been already launched in dramatic style when Roosevelt became president, and he himself had

played an important part in both the planning and the fighting of the war against Spain. Roosevelt was a convinced imperialist on both moral and political grounds. He accepted the idea that the era in which he lived was witnessing the carve-up of the world by the most civilized nations and believed it America's duty to join in the work of civilization. If she did not, she would fall behind in the race for power and influence in world affairs.

Although Roosevelt was a whole-hearted imperialist, he was not a greedy one and concentrated on emphasizing America's world image and her areas of influence. His only really spectacular international coup concerned the Panama Canal. When de Lessep's attempt to build a canal linking the Pacific and Atlantic oceans had collapsed in financial scandal, the US proposed to take over the project. In 1901 they at last got rid of the treaty by which they had agreed to share construction of the canal with Britain and internationalize it. Colombia, through whose territory the canal was to pass, put off ratifying an agreement by which America would get perpetual control of the canal area in Panama. Roosevelt, angry at the hitch, helped to engineer a revolution in Panama which declared itself independent of Colombia. The US government made payments to both the Republic of Colombia and the new Republic of Panama and got control of the Canal Zone in return. Even though Roosevelt's action was strongly criticized at home, he had secured effective control of the future Panama Canal, which was opened for traffic in August 1914.

After British, German and Italian intervention in Venezuela on a debt collecting expedition, Roosevelt, to forestall future ventures of this kind, enunciated his corollary of the Monroe Doctrine. The Monroe Doctrine, as proclaimed by President Monroe in 1823, had declared European colonization or intervention in the Americas to be acts unfriendly to the United States. In 1904 Roosevelt argued that if America's neighbours provoked other powers by failing to live up to their international obligations, it would be necessary for the US herself to act as an international policeman in the American continent. In 1907 the United States intervened in Santo Domingo in fulfilment of Roosevelt's doctrine and left again when her mission was completed.

On the world stage Roosevelt mediated in the Russo-Japanese war and in so doing notified the other powers of America's interests in the fate of east Asia. In 1906 Roosevelt agreed to support a conference to settle the dispute between Germany and France over Morocco and sent American representatives to the conference at Algeciras. In 1908 he sent the US fleet around the world to demonstrate her naval power. The voyage boosted American morale and was more significant than perhaps the rest of the world appreciated.

Although Roosevelt was a moderate imperialist by the standards of the time and had little blood on his hands, the decade after 1898 was a landmark in world history, signalizing the arrival of the richest and potentially the strongest state in the world.

The Republican split

When Roosevelt's term of office ended in 1908 he was succeeded by his secretary of state, William Howard Taft, who had been Roosevelt's choice but who lacked his predecessor's skilful political touch. Taft moved away from the Progressivist stance of the previous administration at a time when the tide of public opinion was still flowing strongly that way.

His administration was to become memorable for an event quite removed from politics. In 1909 the Ford Motor Company in Detroit, Michigan, produced the Model T, the first cheap, standardized car to be constructed on an assembly line. This method of production brought the motor car within the reach of the average man's pocket and inaugurated a worldwide expansion of the automobile industry.

When he left office in 1908 Roosevelt had gone on a big-game expedition to Africa and then a triumphal tour of European cities. He returned to the US to find the Republican Party threatened with a split over the 1912 presidential nomination. Encouraged by the enthusiasm with which he was greeted, Roosevelt challenged Taft for the presidential nomination in 1912, but the Republican convention was controlled by the conservatives who nominated Taft. Roosevelt led his supporters out of the convention and organized his own Progressive Party, also known as the 'Bull Moose' party. He stood for re-election on a platform of reform in industrial and political life.

In the three-sided electoral campaign which followed, Roosevelt and Taft faced the Democratic candidate, Woodrow Wilson, who won a great victory over his rivals. As always, American voting habits did not favour third parties.

Wilson was an academic who had specialized in law and history and had worked out theories about the nature of the presidential office and how it could best be used for reform. While he lacked Roosevelt's boisterous personality, Wilson had great political skill. After entering office in 1913 he immediately called for a series of reforms which he had called the New Freedom in his presidential campaign, such as anti-trust measures, and he reorganized the national banking system by the Federal Reserve Act of 1913. His interventions in Latin America were also in the Roosevelt tradition. Moderate reform and moderate imperialism distinguished America on the eve of the First World War.

Wilson's dilemma

The outbreak of war in Europe in 1914 took Wilson by surprise. He had so far concentrated his attention on domestic politics rather than international affairs, and his knowledge of European problems was sketchy. Almost immediately his friend and confidant Colonel House was sent by Wilson to see if the United States could help to resolve the conflicts among the European powers. House reported more optimistically than the situation warranted, and war was declared by the various angry nations before he had returned to Washington.

There was no question of the United States doing more than declaring her neutrality in a struggle so remote from her shores. Wilson hoped that she would eventually be able to restore peace, as Roosevelt had done between Russia and Japan in 1905.

It was impossible for the United States to remain an aloof and impartial bystander. The Allies needed her great wealth of raw materials, munitions and manufactured goods; and American industry was eager to supply them. They also wanted to prevent these goods being sold to the enemy. Inevitably Wilson was soon involved in trying both to protect domestic interests and seek international accord; and gradually the threat to United States interests grew to such an extent that it submerged the wish to mediate and remain neutral. Only after the United States had altered the course of the war by sending its armed forces to support the Allies was Wilson able to pursue his role of peacemaker.

Above, Sitting Bull (c.1831–90) the Sioux chief, in about 1885: his death at the hands of Indian police led to the Massacre of Wounded Knee.

Top, an Indian camp on a reservation: deprived of their former lands and their buffalo, the staple of their economy, destroyed, the Indians were confined to relatively small reservations providing an inadequate living; full legal rights and citizenship were only granted in 1924.

Opposite, US troops in Santo Domingo: the years around the turn of the century saw US imperialism confidently exercised in the Caribbean and Latin America, as the nation, internal expansion now complete, turned its attention to international events.

Chapter 47

Nations in Turmoil

Bismarck's German Empire was, like the America of Roosevelt and Wilson, characterized by moderate reform and moderate imperialism. German development had in some ways paralleled that of America as she experienced a steady growth of industry in the first half of the nineteenth century and then in the second half expanded at such a remarkable rate as to become one of the wealthiest and most powerful states in the world. Germany, like America, was a federation of states with different traditions, and these and other sources of discontent brought internal divisions which the empire's rulers never succeeded in healing.

In other respects the German Empire was a very different kind of state. Bismarck and his successors faced greater problems than any American president after the Civil War. German unity was achieved by war in the same decade that American unity was being confirmed by war. While the Americans could fight out their own quarrels remote from the interference of other great powers, the Germans were in the heart of Europe, where every change was anxiously watched by fearful neighbours. The historical experience of the German people set them on an entirely different political road from the Americans, although their economic development was similar.

By the nineteenth century the number of German states had been reduced to thirty-nine, Austria and Prussia predominating. Austria had a German dynasty and was the traditional leader among the German states, although it was divided into seventeen provinces and encompassed many nationalities besides Germans – Czechs, Poles, Slovenes, Italians, Croats, Serbs and a large community of Jews settled mostly in Vienna. In the first half of the nineteenth century the idea of drawing the German states together into one great central European empire began to have increasing appeal to the small number of politically educated Germans. Ideas of nationalism were in the air, and the economic advantages of a united Germany without commercial and other barriers became obvious as trade and industry developed.

These ideas were realized when the King of Prussia, under the inspiration of his brilliant and forceful minister, Otto von

Bismarck, challenged Austria over Germany in the 1860s. Prussia defeated Austria in 1866, and formed the North German Confederation. After her defeat of France, Prussia was able to go a stage further and draw the southern German states into her orbit. In January 1871, a German Empire was proclaimed, which united all Germans except those living under the Habsburg dynasty in Austria.

Although the new empire was a federation of the various German states, for all practical purposes it was a Prussian empire which Bismarck had created. Until his fall from office in 1890 Bismarck was the real ruler of Prussia and Germany because of the trust placed in him by Emperor William I and because of his immense prestige as the most successful statesman in Europe. The empire's constitution, however, made the emperor the key figure in political life, and in 1888 there came to the throne a man determined to use his power. William II became the emperor of Germany in fact as well as in name by getting rid of Bismarck in 1890. But whether the emperor or his chancellor ruled, the most influential class in Prussia was the *junkers*, the old landowning aristocracy from east of the river Elbe. They were prominent at court, in the army and in the civil service, and they were looked on by all the emperors as the mainstay of their regime. Bismarck was, of course, himself a *junker*, though of a rather eccentric kind. The *junkers* and their king dominated Prussia, and Prussia dominated Germany, with the result that the most dynamic industrial state in Europe was controlled by one of the most reactionary of the old European aristocracies. In this respect Germany was closer to Russia than Britain and totally remote from the United States.

Germany was also very different from Britain and the US in the strategic problems imposed on her by geography. Access to the sea and the power to control it allowed Britain and America feel secure during the upheavals of industrial change. Japan, once she had built a modern fleet, had a similar advantage, but Germany was hemmed in on all sides by other major powers. Although she was stronger than any one of them, a coalition of France, Russia and Austria-Hungary would be very formidable. The only other European power surrounded by enemies was Poland, which had been carved up by her neighbours. Prussia had come close to the same fate more than once and had come to trust in militarism as the only way of guaranteeing her survival. Even after the establishment of the German Empire with its huge resources and proven strength, her rulers felt uneasy about the dangers surrounding them.

They differed about what should be done to make Germany safe. Bismarck suffered nightmares about coalitions, but his remedies were restrained. He tried to impose discipline and unity at home by a combination of comparatively mild repression and moderate reform. Abroad he tried to make sure that Germany was always a member of a powerful coalition and thus unlikely to be a victim of one. His successors abandoned his moderation with calamitous results.

The more thoughtful members of the German aristocracy had long realized that they could play off the new middle-class employers against the new lower-class industrial workers. Bismarck had studied the way in which Napoleon III in France had used universal suffrage to bolster the existing social order. The *junkers* favoured the idea that the masses were conservative when not led astray by agitators and when their conditions were alleviated by a fatherly system of government – the same thinking which had influenced the Russian tsar after the 1905 revolution.

As usual, Bismarck put the idea into practice with more imagination and boldness than other statesmen. The *Reichstag*, the lower house of the imperial parliament, was elected by universal suffrage, an arrangement which had been adopted by the North German Confederation, whose constitution served as a model for the empire's. The confederation had been set up in 1867, the year when Britain had cautiously enfranchised better-paid workers in towns and the tenant farmers in rural districts. Bismarck could afford to be bolder than Disraeli. The composition of the British House of Commons determined who governed Britain, while the more democratically elected *Reichstag* had little real power. Ministers in the government were responsible to the emperor not to the *Reichstag*, which could resist legislation but had little control over the budget or the army. Moreover, the granting of universal suffrage in a country so divided as Germany created numerous political parties which the government could manipulate as it wished. The upper house of the imperial parliament or the *Bundersrat* was designed to represent the states and not their people and was composed of delegates appointed and recalled at pleasure by the state governments which they represented.

The various states making up the federation also had their own assemblies, the Prussian *Landtag* being the most important of these bodies. It was elected by giving equal representation to three classes of electors – roughly the wealthy, the rather less wealthy and the rest. This kind of franchise produced a safe assembly of *junkers* who were ever ready for a coup d'état to end the limited democracy which Germany had. One of them got a standing ovation from his colleagues in 1910 when he declared: 'The King of Prussia and the German Emperor must always be in a position to say to any lieutenant: "Take ten men and shoot the *Reichstag*".'

The middle class in Germany, which had become so prominent with the rise of industrialization, was also unwilling to fight for greater democracy. Its fear of socialism, and the pleasure which so many of its members took in gaining even limited access to the privileges of the old nobility, meant that it was firmly on the side of the emperor and his government. The governmental system in the empire was democratic enough to allow pressure to be brought successfully in exceptional cases, but the government's overriding interest was for industrial growth and the creation of as much wealth as possible. Organized labour had absolutely no chance of putting fetters on capitalism.

Thus Bismarck's semi-democratic system worked by removing the one issue which had traditionally united the mass of German people against the old ruling class – the desire for an elected assembly. Employers and employees could now fight among themselves while the emperor and his *junkers* held sway.

The *Kulturkampf*

Bismarck's main aim was always to hold together the old Prussian state in face of threats from within its borders and from its foreign rivals. In the 1860s his victories over Austria and France had united the nation in nationalist fervour at a time when German liberals were bent on turning Prussia into a genuinely parliamentary state. Because Bismarck knew that further wars would be dangerous, he had to ensure Prussian unity without them – a task made more difficult in the new empire which had extended Prussian power but given it more internal enemies. This expansion had greatly increased the proportion of Catholics in a predominantly Protestant country. While religion had long been one of the forces which united Prussia, Bismarck was now haunted by the divisive effect of the Catholics, who felt as much loyalty to Rome as to Berlin. His fears were confirmed when the Catholic Centre Party emerged as the second strongest in the elections to the *Reichstag*. They were led by a particularly skilful politician, Ludwig Windthorst, whom Bismarck detested.

In 1871 Bismarck undertook to subject the church, both Catholic and Protestant, to the authority of the state and make the latter supreme in both political and religious matters. In 1872 the campaign was extended to expel the Jesuits from the empire. In May 1873 Dr Adalbert Falk, who had been made Prussian minister of public worship (schools and churches were administered by individual states not by the empire), introduced a number of anti-Catholic measures known as the May Laws. The Prussian government was to have the right to veto church appointments, to supervise the education of the clergy, to control the church's discipline over its clergy and generally to restrict the church's freedom in various other ways. In 1875 grants to the Church were cut off in those Sees which resisted the new laws, and by 1877 many bishoprics were vacant, the bishops having been imprisoned or driven into exile, and many parishes were without priests for the same reason.

Bismarck's attack on the Catholics and his speeches against the Centre Party in the *Reichstag* were popular among German liberals. Pope Pius IX's denunciation in 1864 of progress, liberalism and contemporary civilization had been followed in 1870 by the dogma that papal decisions on matters of faith and morals were infallible. The Catholic Church was seen as the enemy

Above, cartoon from an 1875 number of Kladderadatsch *depicting Bismarck's conflict with the Catholic church.*

Opposite, drilling at barracks as depicted in a painting of about 1880: though the Second Reich was a parliamentary semi-democracy, the army, along with the bureaucracy and the landowners, remained a strongly conservative and authoritarian influence.

of reason and progress, and Bismarck's war was described as a *Kulturkampf*, or struggle between rival cultures.

Resistance from Germany's Catholic clergy was strong. Fines and imprisonment were imposed over and over again but without persuading the bishops and priests of the need to conform to Falk's laws. The more they resisted, the more Bismarck and German Protestants and liberals were convinced there was a plot against the empire inspired by the pope and Catholic France. It was at this time that the royalists in France had high hopes of a restoration of monarchy, and Bismarck believed that a monarchy would start a war of revenge against Germany. In 1875 there were signs that Bismarck was preparing for such a war, perhaps even by attacking France first. This 'war in sight' crisis moved other powers to make clear their position to a preventive war against France. Bismarck's exaggerated belief in the Catholic and French danger had brought him failure at home and humiliation abroad.

The campaign against the Catholics proved futile. The Centre Party was not destroyed and the Catholic Church was not intimidated. After five years of *Kulturkampf* Bismarck began to have second thoughts. The death of Pope Pius IX in 1878 and the conciliatory attitude of his successor Leo XIII gave him the chance to come to terms and wind up the affair. Falk resigned in 1879. The May Laws went into disuse or were repealed over the next few years, and by 1883 the *Kulturkampf* had died away.

The socialist threat

One of Bismarck's reasons for deciding that the Catholic threat to the empire's unity was less deadly than he had supposed was that he had sensed another more serious threat from German socialism.

In the 1860s, with Germany's industrial revolution in full swing, two workers' parties had been formed. The German Working Men's Association was founded by Ferdinand Lassalle, who believed in the peaceful achievement of socialism through political democracy. When the working-class votes were in a majority they could usher in socialism. Bismarck was interested in Lassalle's ideas as a means of diverting working-class political energies into peaceful channels, and he had secret talks with him. Lassalle was killed in a duel in 1864, but his followers continued to work for his ideas. A rival Marxist party was formed in 1869. Karl Marx had sent Wilhelm Liebknecht to Germany to organize labour there, after the foundation of the First International socialist movement in 1864. By 1869, with the help of August Bebel, Liebknecht had organized enough support to set up the Social Democratic Working Men's Party. In 1875 they united with Lassalle's group at the Gotha Congress to put forward their programme,

which was a mixture of Marx and Lassalle.

Bismarck was even more alarmed by international socialism than by international Catholicism. He thought in terms of an alliance of conservative powers to act against revolutionary conspiracies. He was determined to get the Reichstag to pass laws persecuting the social democrats. Here he ran into difficulties, as the National Liberals were suspicious of measures which might be a precedent for repressing liberalism as well as socialism. One of the advantages Bismarck could gain from ending the *Kulturkampf* was the support of the Centre Party for his anti-socialist legislation.

Bismarck's campaign was assisted by the occurrence of two attempts on the emperor's life in 1878. Though the would-be assassins were not socialists, Bismarck used the incidents to paint a picture of the empire threatened by revolutionary agitators whose propaganda drove people to violence. The anti-socialist law of 1878 banned public meetings and other open political activities by socialists.

Like the Catholics, the Social Democrats were strengthened by the persecution, which was too mild to achieve its purpose. Bismarck had exaggerated the threat to Germany's unity.

After Bismarck was forced to resign in 1890 the anti-socialist law was dropped. The Social Democratic Party was reorganized in 1891 with a full-blooded revolutionary programme on Marxist lines, which seemed to confirm Bismarck's worst fears and to prove him right. But the revolutionary ardour of the German Social Democrats was of the surface variety. A booming economy convinced German trade union leaders that they could win high benefits for their members within a capitalist system. In elections to the *Reichstag* the Social Democrats went from strength to strength until in 1912 they were the biggest single party. This seemed to suggest that with time they might become so powerfully supported in the country as to force concessions from the regime; but behind the revolutionary slogans and despite provocative action by employers and the government, the Social Democrats gradually became part of the 'establishment'.

The change of climate was summed up in the writings of Eduard Bernstein, an influential German socialist, who put forward his revisionist Marxist theory. Bernstein argued that socialism would not arise from the breakdown of capitalism as Marx had predicted. Capitalism had learned how to adjust itself to major crises. As capitalism led to a wider distribution of wealth, social tensions would die down and society would move towards socialism as the most reasonable and ethical way of living. Bernstein became an arch-villan to orthodox Marxists, and 'revisionist' is still their deadliest term of abuse.

Although Bernstein's views were officially denounced, the Social Democrat Party moved steadily towards his position in

practice. With more tolerance on the part of the government they would have been more easily reconciled to peaceful change. As it was, Bismarck and his successors helped to keep the revolutionary wing of the party alive.

Bismarck's failure to suppress socialism or the Catholic Church showed that he was never at his best in pursuing negative policies. In foreign affairs his greatest triumphs had been the result of bold and aggressive action, notably the wars of the 1860s. His later attempts to ward off a French war of revenge by keeping France isolated were much more clumsy and in the end unsuccessful. Similarly, in Germany itself Bismarck's genius was displayed not in the *Kulturkampf* or the anti-socialist law but in his bold adoption of universal suffrage in 1867 and the welfare legislation of his later years.

Bismarck realized that the best antidote to the socialism he feared was for the state to provide enough welfare services to take the edge off the German workers' appetite for change. The old idea of the ruler being the father of his people and alleviating their sufferings was still as strong as the liberal idea of people providing for themselves by enterprise and initiative. Bismarck could, therefore, depend on support from the *junkers* for state welfare schemes.

He began in 1881 with a bill providing for accident insurance. The National Liberals opposed the legislation as being socialist and were deaf to arguments that welfare measures would divert the workers from wanting power to redistribute wealth themselves. Eventually Bismarck got his measures through: a bill providing for sickness insurance was passed in 1882, and his accident insurance bill went into effect in 1884. In 1889 he introduced an old-age insurance law.

Although Bismarck's welfare legislation was in the old paternalistic spirit, the measures proposed were in tune with the needs of an industrial age. It was a statesmanlike and imaginative programme, valuable in itself and a precursor of the twentieth century welfare state. Other nations copied

it or drew inspiration from it, and the British later followed the German example.

By introducing 'state socialism' after his anti-socialist law, Bismarck failed in his main purpose. The working class was not converted from socialism, and the continued persecution of the Social Democrats convinced them of the enmity of the old ruling class. Even though socialism survived as the favourite creed of the German industrial workers, it was less of an immediate threat to the regime. It would have been even less of a threat if Bismarck had simply stuck to his legislative programme for old age pensions and industrial insurance. His creative statesmanship paid off in the age of democracy and industrialism.

Restrained imperialism

Just as Bismarck had some success in his bid to satisfy German socialist yearnings, he also managed to satisfy nationalist urges by his adoption of imperialistic tactics overseas. Although he preserved the old regime in Germany by a popular and victorious foreign policy, after 1871 he could not afford to risk the empire's destruction by further adventures. He sensed that the moment of easy victories was over because Germany was now the strongest power in Europe – and, as the strongest, the most likely to arouse hostile coalitions. He therefore spent the next twenty years building up coalitions himself and trying without much success to persuade the rest of Europe that Germany had got all she wanted.

A new outlet for German nationalism was found in overseas expansion, as agitation grew for an active colonial policy. Books and pamphlets glorifying imperialism proliferated throughout Germany to satisfy the popular belief that an empire was something no great power should be without. Bismarck was not himself swayed by these arguments and was sceptical of the value of colonies; but the growing membership of colonial societies after 1882 showed that it was a popular cause. By supporting an imperialistic foreign policy Bismarck could perhaps rekindle the spirit of national unity shaken by his campaigns against the Catholics and Social Democrats.

In 1882 he promised protection to a German trader, Lüderitz, if he could acquire territory in southwest Africa not already claimed by another power. This was the first step in a dramatic imperialist campaign which brought Germany a sizeable African and Pacific empire in a few years.

Bismarck embarked on this with less careful preparation than he had devoted in the past to major international ventures. In 1884–85 he got involved in an unnecessary quarrel with Britain over German ambitions in southwest Africa by failing to make his policy clear; but he soon adjusted himself to this new and unfamiliar field of international politics. There was still plenty of room to expand in Africa and the Pacific without offending France, Italy or Russia; and the only power he risked quarrelling with was Britain, the least dangerous opponent for Germany. Between 1885 and

Above, drawing dating from about 1890 of the restaurant at the Berlin Zoological Garden, favourite dining-spot of Berlin's haute bourgeoisie.

Opposite, woodcut dating from 1890 entitled The Blessings of Old Age Pensions and Sickness Insurance: *Bismarck's social welfare legislation, pioneering measures in this field, was extended after his retirement, so that by 1914 German workers were better protected than those in any other country.*

1890 Bismarck established a satisfactory working relationship regarding imperial questions with Lord Salisbury, the British prime minister. He found his new overseas interests useful weapons in blackmailing the British to side with him in European affairs.

The acquisition of a German colonial empire was a popular move, and the spectacular exploits of explorers like Karl Peters excited the imagination and pride of the German public. Imperialism also resulted in increased influence in international relations, as the interests of the other powers shifted outside Europe. The colonies however proved of little economic value, and the Germans began to feel cheated and jealous of the other powers who seemed to have got more than their fair share of the spoils. This attitude was dangerous. Bismarck had been able to keep German nationalism from demanding more than Germany could safely try to get. His successors were less cautious.

Bismarck's successors abandoned his moderate imperialistic policies because the immense increase in German strength brought about by industrialization made moderation seem less necessary. That their neighbours – especially Russia – were eventually acquiring the same amount of power from industrialization also made a quick and drastic solution to Germany's strategic problems seem all the more necessary.

The lead which Germany had built up over countries like Russia, France and Austria-Hungary during the second half of the nineteenth century was remarkable enough strongly to influence her rulers. Her population grew rapidly from about 40,000,000 in 1870 to 66,000,000 in 1913. By the early 1880s there were roughly as many Germans engaged in industry as in agriculture and by 1907 there were nearly twice as many. German production of coal, iron and steel – key industries in the industrial revolution in the nineteenth century – leapt to quantities comparable with the output of Britain though well behind that of America. Alfred Krupp had already built up his steel works at Essen into one of the major establishments of its kind in the world. Germany became a major shipbuilding country more or less from scratch. In the newer electrical and chemical industries, whose power to speed up production and create new materials and goods was so great as to constitute something like a second industrial revolution, Germany was particularly advanced. The automobile industry was pioneered by men like Gottlieb Daimler, who patented his small high-speed internal combustion engine and in 1890 founded the Daimler motor car company. Germany had not merely caught up with the pioneer of industrialism, Britain, but she was in the van of progress towards the science-based industries of the twentieth century.

Prussia had played an important part in initiating Germany's industrial revolution. In the first half of the nineteenth century, the Prussian government created a customs union, the *Zollverein*, to remove the barriers to trade produced by so many German frontiers. In order to improve transportation between her widely scattered provinces, Prussia encouraged the establishment of a network of railways, which were eventually to be nationalized. The value of technical education was realized by Prussia early in the century, and this farsightedness was to pay rich dividends later on. After Prussia's acquisition of Schleswig-Holstein in 1866, the Kiel Canal was built linking the North Sea with the port of Kiel and the Baltic. Prussia's annexation of Alsace-Lorraine after the war with France in 1870–1 brought in important iron-ore deposits.

Once the state had overcome political resistance to economic growth, there was a ready response from private enterprise. Joint-stock companies blossomed in the middle of the century, and later on Germany, like America, became the scene of giant industrial undertakings. The big companies tended to cooperate more and more towards the end of the century, drawing together in associations known as 'cartels' to fix prices, share out the market and avoid over-production. The great German electrical combine AEG was an example of a successful cartel. As in America the banks were important to industrial growth, as they supplied credit to investors, helped to organize cartels, financed overseas projects and became involved in the running of industries by being represented on management boards. Capitalism flourished in the

Prussian state, controlled as it was by a pre-industrial monarchy and aristocracy. By 1914 Prussian leadership had contributed much towards making the German empire, together with America and Britain, the three most industrialized and powerful nations in the world.

William II and Germany's world role

In 1890 Bismarck was forced to resign his chancellorship after a quarrel with the young Kaiser, William II. His successors as chancellor – Caprivi, Hohenlohe, Bulow and Bethmann-Hollweg – were men of lesser ability and easily manipulated by William II, who was intelligent and imaginative but impetuous and easily persuaded of the value of dramatic departures in policy. William II was to prove himself too much infected by nationalist fervour to be able to use it in the calculating and cautious manner of Bismarck.

As soon as Bismarck had resigned, William II's government began the blundering course which was to lead them to the disasters of the 1914 war. They refused to renew their alliance with Russia, and they signed the Heligoland treaty with Britain. The alliance with Russia had always been regarded by Bismarck as crucial to German security. He knew that France would always be an enemy as long as Germany controlled Alsace-Lorraine but that Germany could feel confident of defeating France if she were isolated from and unallied with Austria-Hungary or Russia.

To make sure there was no link between Vienna and Paris Bismarck had negotiated an alliance with Austria-Hungary in 1879 which was to last down to the First World War. An alliance between Paris and St Petersburg Bismarck knew could be even more dangerous. Although Russia was suspicious of Germany and frequently at odds with Austria-Hungary, Bismarck had succeeded with great difficulty in forming a Three Emperors' Alliance with Russia and Austria-Hungary between 1881 and 1887. When his two allies quarrelled over the Balkans, he made a separate Reinsurance treaty with Russia. It was this latter treaty which William II refused to renew in 1890.

William's motives were sound. Bismarck's policy was complicated and difficult to operate. It was not easy to remain friendly with two powers who disliked one another so decidedly as did Russia and Austria-Hungary. The only alternative was to ally with Britain. A combination of Germany, Austria-Hungary, Italy (who had joined the other two in 1882) and Britain might be enough to deter both France and Russia. Even though Bismarck had tried and failed to make an alliance with Great Britain, William II and his ministers went on believing they would succeed. They therefore followed their rebuff of Russia by making a major colonial agreement with Britain, allowing big concessions in Africa in return for the island of Heligoland, which the British had controlled since the Napoleonic Wars. The Heligoland Agreement was spectacular enough to convince Russia and France that Britain must have for all practical purposes joined the Triple Alliance. Russia began to move towards the fateful step of an alliance with France. France had emerged from isolation, and Bismarck's policy was in ruins.

William II's Germany never overcame the problem presented by the Franco-Russian Alliance which his policy had done so much to bring about. Although Britain's growing difficulties made her look at times with favour on an alliance with Germany, what she wanted more was an ally to help combat her chief colonial rivals, France and Russia. Germany could not risk a war on two fronts with France and Russia, knowing that British help in such a war could be of little value. Though there was no real basis for an alliance, William II maintained his belief that the British would eventually be forced into an agreement on Germany's terms.

Imperialist emotion was, moreover, continuing to grow in Germany in the 1890s, and William II was infected by it. The new generation in Germany thought in global terms like the British, the Americans and the Russians. Germany was becoming less worried by the prospect of what would happen in Europe and more concerned by the thought of being dwarfed by the great world empires. Thus there developed a feeling that Germany must assert herself on the world stage more boldly than in the Bismarck era. A few colonies were not enough – after 1898 the Kaiser's foreign policy was geared to the acquisition of 'spheres of influence' and an overseas empire.

Hence Germany enthusiastically engaged in the battle for concessions from China. In 1898 Admiral Alfred von Tirpitz set in motion his plans for a great fleet. German financing of the Baghdad railway project from Constantinople to the Persian Gulf was one of many signs of German influence in the Ottoman Empire. In 1905 Germany made clear her interest in the decaying state of Morocco.

Germany's world policy got her into far more difficulties than would have been involved in handling Austro-Russian relations in the Balkans. Tirpitz's naval programme alarmed Britain so much that she decided Germany was a greater threat than either France or Russia. The agreements reached between Britain and France in 1904 and between Russia and Britain in 1907 shifted the balance of power and made Germany's position in Europe more hazardous than ever before. German backing for Austria-Hungary in the Balkans and her growing influence in the Ottoman Empire worsened her relations with Russia. When the consequences of a world policy proved to be growing isolation, the Kaiser was strongly criticized. The Moroccan crisis of 1905–06 showed how isolated Germany was, and her reputation was further damaged by revolt against German rule in South West Africa. The Catholic Centre Party, which since the end of the *Kulturkampf* had supported the government in return for valuable concessions, now opposed the government and joined the left wing parties in refusing funds for the colonial war and demanding a reform of colonial administration.

In 1907 Chancellor von Bulow held a general election which was dominated by the question of Germany's world policy. Nationalist and imperialist societies worked hard on the electorate, and their arguments made a considerable impression. Von Bulow's claim that the government was being prevented from making Germany a world power by meddling from the opposition parties was sympathetically received. The Social Democrats, who had been attacked as 'anti-national', were shattered and lost half their seats in the *Reichstag*.

The appeal to nationalism had succeeded. The electorate was clearly responsive to the idea of Germany as a world power, and the Social Democrat advance had been checked. There was no doubt that nationalist and imperialist sentiment was strong in all sections of society. In the years that followed despite intensified industrial trouble the government maintained its ability to rally the nation with an expansionist foreign policy.

This was a dangerous consolation. Crisis succeeded crisis among the European countries, and Germany's leaders became ever more nervous and frustrated as the hostility

Opposite, Gottlieb Daimler (1834–1900) being driven in one of his earliest vehicles: he and Karl Benz (1844–1929) can be said to have invented the motor car, though many other engineers, from Europe and the USA, made immediate improvements.

than a quarter of the population. The next largest nationality were the Hungarians, who until 1848 gave most trouble to the Habsburg rulers. In 1848, however, when revolution engulfed most of the European states, the other nationalities showed themselves ambitious for greater freedom or even independence.

Although the Habsburg Empire nearly disintegrated as a result of the uprisings of 1848, it did not finally break up until 1918, towards the end of the First World War. In the seventy intervening years the emperor, Francis Joseph, who had succeeded to the throne in 1848, desperately tried to keep his empire together. He failed because he fought three wars and lost them all. If he and his ministers had been less obsessed with the problems of nationalist minorities, or more successful in solving them, they might have seen more clearly that economic backwardness was the secret of Habsburg weakness.

The empire survived in 1848–9 because the army was strong enough to crush the Czech and Italian rebels and to recapture Vienna and because the Russian army helped to defeat the Hungarians. Francis Joseph tried in the 1850s to follow up the victory over the rebellious nationalities by a system of direct rule from Vienna. German civil servants and German police were set to rule over the non-German nations, and national rights and privileges were swept away. The minister of the interior, Alexander Bach, was charged with the 'Germanization' of the empire, which became known as the Bach system.

It is possible that if the Habsburgs had been able to concentrate on maintaining this centralized absolutism for a generation or so national resistance might have died away. But the Habsburgs could not hope for enough time to make the Bach system work, and like the Prussians they were surrounded by enemies only too anxious to exploit their difficulties. Their only friend was the Russian tsar, who believed that monarchs must stand together against revolution, but they lost Russia's friendship by exploiting her difficulties during the Crimean War.

In 1859 war came with Piedmont and her ally, Napoleon III's France. The stake was Habsburg control of Italy, and defeat would mean that Habsburg control in the Italian peninsula would be confined to Venice. It would also mean that a united Italy could come into being – another probable enemy on the frontier. Austria's defeat, which was largely a result of the disaffection of the Magyars and Slavs, encouraged the Hungarians to resist the Bach system at a time when the Habsburg government was in no position to persist with it.

A state of emergency followed during which Francis Joseph was forced to consider the advisability of establishing a federal state system of rule, allowing each nationality within the empire the autonomy

of France, Russia and Britain grew. Since Bismarck's time the influence of the army in politics had greatly increased. The army thought in terms of a future war which would finish Germany's enemies in Europe once and for all. Political leaders dreamed of a Europe after such a war in which the German frontiers would be extended so far as to make her secure against all possible enemies. Once secure in Europe, Germany could take her proper place on the world stage. In 1914 they succumbed to their dreams.

The Habsburg Empire after 1848

Both Germany and Russia ruled over other nationalities, notably the Poles, who were kept in subjection by discriminating tactics.

The presence of active political nationalists like the Poles was disturbing to governments bent on national unity. Bismarck tried to 'Germanize' the Polish provinces of the empire, and the tsars tried to 'Russify' their various non-Russian groups, from whom many of the leading revolutionaries were to come.

Neither Germany nor Russia, however, had to deal with nationalities as various as those comprising the Habsburg realm – Germans, Hungarians, Czechs, Poles, Croats, Italians, Ruthenians, Romanians, Slovaks, Serbs and Slovenes – no one national group outnumbering the others. Though the Habsburg dynasty was German in origin, and Germans were the predominant group in their empire, in terms of numbers the Germans amounted to less guaranteed by its historic constitutions. The 'October Diploma' which restored the old local diets was issued by Francis in October 1860, but its terms satisfied nobody, and another constitution was announced in February 1861 (the 'February Patent'). This returned to something like centralized government, but with a representative assembly in Vienna.

Although Austria had become a constitutional state, this was bound to be a temporary arrangement because of the Hungarians' hostile attitude. The prospect of a new war was looming up, this time with Prussia. Francis Joseph knew that to enter another war with the Hungarians ready to revolt would be like fighting with one hand tied behind his back. He opened negotiations with the most realistic and statesmanlike of the Hungarian nobility, Francis Deák, but before a compromise could be reached war with Prussia broke out in the summer of 1866.

The Compromise of 1867

The first of Francis Joseph's wars, in 1859, had destroyed Habsburg power in Italy and forced him to realize that a compromise with the Hungarians was essential. The second disastrous war for the emperor was fought for the leadership of Germany and was quickly won by the Prussian armies, directed by Helmuth von Moltke. Considering the ease of the Prussian victory, Bismarck's terms were mild – Prussian domination of northern Germany and the transfer of Venice to Italy, which had been Prussia's ally in the war.

After the signing of the peace treaty, Francis Joseph resumed negotiations with the Hungarians, knowing that he was in no position to haggle with Deák over terms. The Compromise worked out between them provided for a unique political system whereby Hungary should have her own constitution but accept the Habsburg emperor as the King of Hungary. Although the Compromise was far less than many Hungarians demanded, it was far more than Francis Joseph would have consented to before the war with Prussia. The essential feature of the Compromise, which was formally accepted in 1867, was that it gave the Habsburg Empire three governments. The central government consisted of the emperor and three common ministers – for foreign affairs, the armed forces and finance. Austria's government was based on the February Patent, with the emperor as a constitutional monarch and a complicated system of representative assemblies in Vienna and in the provinces to be elected by an even more complicated voting procedure. The kingdom of Hungary was also a constitutional monarchy, with a two chamber parliament elected in such a way as to assure Hungarian predominance. County assemblies were to have nominal control over local

matters and were again to be Hungarian dominated. The emperor still had very considerable power in practice, though he would find it hard to have his way in Hungary without parliamentary support.

This 'dual monarchy' of Austria-Hungary survived until the end of the First World War. It made the Hungarians and the Germans the ruling nationalities within the empire at the expense of the Slavs, who in numbers made up nearly half the total population. Count Gyula Andrássy, who helped Deák negotiate the Compromise, is reported to have said to Francis Joseph: 'You look after your Slavs and we will look after ours.'

Although Andrássy's remark sounded sinister, both the Austrian and Hungarian governments at first approached the question of the other nationalities within their territories in a liberal enough fashion. Francis Joseph was above all concerned with the survival of his dynasty and had no special affection for the Germans in the Austrian half of the empire. They made up only a third of the population there, and the emperor was alarmed at the allegiance many of them showed towards the new German Empire to the north. He was inclined to support demands for special rights from the Poles and the Czechs especially, the most advanced of the Habsburg Slavs. From Budapest, Deák and his colleagues gave a measure of autonomy to the Croats, and introduced laws to enable the various nationalities to use their own languages as far as possible in their dealings with officials.

Within a few years the two parts of the empire diverged in their approach to the nationality question. In Austria, Francis Joseph continued to experiment with laws to avoid tension between the Germans and the Slavs. Czechs and Poles were prominent in Count Eduard Taaffe's ministry, which was in office from 1879 to 1893. One of Taaffe's successors as premier was Count Badeni, a Polish landowner. In 1907 universal suffrage was introduced in Austria. Although the Germans and Czechs still

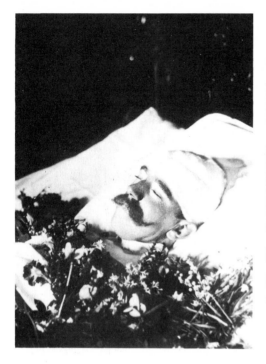

remained bitter enemies despite all attempts at compromise, the Habsburg dynasty remained remote from the squabbles and persisted in their efforts to reach a settlement.

In Hungary the moderates who had negotiated the Compromise were soon replaced by Kálmán Tisza's Liberal Party, which won the election of 1875 and stayed in power for the next fifteen years. Tisza, who was a powerful orator and a ruthless and able politician, used his gifts to consolidate the supremacy of the Magyars in their half of the empire. By means of education laws he tried to force the children of other nationalities to learn the Magyar language, and the government took steps to uproot other languages and cultures. Before long Magyar was made the official language of the government – to be used in railways, post offices and schools. This process of Magyarization was resisted by the Slavs and Romanians, but it stimulated demands among still more extreme nationalists for a complete break with Vienna. Francis Joseph countered these demands by backing the popular idea of universal suffrage. This would have swept away the Magyar nobility, who had kept power in their own hands.

The Yugoslav problem

The nationality question took a new and dangerous turn for the Habsburgs when states surrounding the empire began to cast acquisitive eyes on areas of the empire inhabited by their fellow nationals. Italy had never given up hope of bringing those Italians still under Habsburg rule into the kingdom of Italy. Romania, independent since 1878, wanted Transylvania where Romanians were subject to Hungarian rule. Most dangerous of all was Serbia who saw

herself as the Piedmont of the Balkans, and hoped to unite the South Slav people under the Serbian monarchy in much the same way as Piedmont had united Italy. As so many of the South Slavs lived in Austria-Hungary such a programme could only be accomplished at the expense of the Habsburgs. It was determination to stop Serbia fomenting revolution in her South Slav provinces that decided the Dual Monarchy to try to destroy Serbian power in the Balkans. The assassination in June 1914 of the heir to the Habsburg throne by a Serbian student gave her a pretext. After delivering an unacceptable ultimatum to the Serbian government and insisting that the government was behind the assassination at Sarajevo, the Austrians declared war on the Serbs on 28 July and thus precipitated the First World War. Francis Joseph's third war brought an end to the empire, whose various nationalities would found their own small independent states.

Such a drastic solution was probably unnecessary. Although there was serious discontent in Austria-Hungary, as in every other state, only a minority of extremists wanted to break up the empire. What most of the nationalists wanted was more privileges within the empire. Probably no solution satisfactory to all nationalities, Germans, Hungarians, Slavs and Romanians, could have been devised, but the empire could probably have staggered along until growing prosperity did its usual work of reconcilation.

What was fatal to the empire was the prolonged world war which its economy was too undeveloped to stand. Industrialization had been making impressive strides in Austria in the middle of the century, but the depression of the 1870s had shaken confidence, and the interests of the landowners generally got priority over those of the industrialists. There was also the fact that

Hungary was much poorer and much more decidedly an agricultural society. Steady progress had been resumed in the years before 1914. A sizeable working class had established itself (about twenty percent of the population), and there was a flourishing Social Democrat Party favourable to change within the empire. Welfare legislation similar to Germany's had been introduced. Within a generation Austria-Hungary might have become sufficiently industrialized to risk an aggressive foreign policy. But the persistent tensions of dealing with rival national groups seems to have worn down the patience and nerve of the empire's leaders. They gambled on war as they had done in 1859 and 1866.

Vienna

Despite its failure, an air of romance still clings to the Habsburg Empire. Although Francis Joseph was not a romantic figure, his beautiful wife, Elizabeth, who rebelled against the formalities of court life and was eventually murdered by an anarchist, had the makings of a tragic heroine. Their son, Rudolph, died with his mistress, Marie Vetsera, in mysterious circumstances in his hunting-lodge at Mayerling. However the most attractive thing about the empire was the flourishing artistic and intellectual life centred around Vienna, which since the middle of the eighteenth century had been the musical capital of the world. Gustav Mahler, Anton Bruckner, Richard Strauss, Arnold Schoenberg, Alban Berg, Johann Strauss and Franz Lehar are just a few of the composers who worked in Vienna during the latter part of the nineteenth century and the early twentieth. It was in Vienna that Sigmund Freud developed his revolutionary techniques of psychoanalysis during this same period.

There was unfortunately a darker side to Vienna. The worst manifestations of nationalism naturally occurred in an empire so divided. Demagogues whipped up nationalist emotion, more especially anti-semitic emotion. They were studied by one particularly apt pupil in the years before 1914 – Adolf Hitler was a subject of Francis Joseph and the formative years of his political education were spent in Vienna.

Revolution and repression in Spain

In 1808 the French emperor Napoleon I had invaded Spain and placed his brother Joseph on the throne. After the French army had been driven out by British troops commanded by the Duke of Wellington, the Spanish Bourbon dynasty was restored. In 1814 King Ferdinand VII returned to the throne.

Spain for the most part was a poor and backward country, whose peasant population were devoted to the old monarchy and the Catholic church. As Ferdinand VII intended to be an absolute monarch he could rely on the support of the church and the mass of the population. Unfortunately for him, an important minority of the Spanish people were bent on preventing a return to absolute monarchy. They included aristocratic landowners, army officers, manufacturers, municipal clerks, lawyers, journalists; and they had all been influenced by the ideas of the Enlightenment which had spread from France and Britain in the eighteenth century. When Ferdinand made clear his determination to crush the forces of liberalism, which had become prominent in the fight against Napoleon, he was faced with resistance from people whose position in society made them dangerous opponents.

Spain's colonies in South America were in revolt. An army to reconquer them was assembled at Cadiz. A group of young army officers exploited the reluctance of the troops to leave for service in America, and led a revolt against Ferdinand. Their principal leader was Rafael del Riego. In January 1820, Riego, an officer in the army encamped near Cadiz, proclaimed the constitution which a liberal assembly had drawn up in 1812 to be in effect. This constitution reduced the king to a cipher.

Riego's *pronunciamento* was the first of many revolts by politically minded army officers in nineteenth-century Spain.

Gradually Riego's attempt to stir up southern Spain spread to the north where liberals and their local armies began to proclaim the constitution of 1812. When riots broke out in Madrid, Ferdinand gave in and announced himself ready to accept the constitution. Because he was never sincere about the new government, Ferdinand was closely guarded by the rebels until 1823, when French troops invaded Spain as part of an international rescue

operation to restore Ferdinand's power. fearful of the spread of liberalism. The French troops were welcomed by peasants equally nervous of liberalism, and the revolution was crushed. Ferdinand had ignored the advice of his rescuers to concede a limited constitution and spent the last ten years of his reign in chronic bankruptcy, suppressing any further attempts at liberal reform.

The Carlist Wars

Before Ferdinand's death in 1833, he had firmly supported his wife's desire that their only child, Isabella, should succeed to the throne in preference to Don Carlos, Ferdinand's brother. This he agreed to even in the face of Salic Law which disputed the right of women to rule. Don Carlos and his supporters were prepared to fight for the throne. The queen, Maria Cristina turned to the liberals for help as the most fervent opponents of Don Carlos, who was a convinced absolutist. A protracted war was necessary to determine the issue.

In the civil war which raged between 1834 and 1839 the advantage lay with the liberals and the infant Isabella. The Carlists commanded a great deal of support in the poorer parts of the countryside, while the monarchy and the liberals had the resources of the big towns, which were prospering during this period because of the industrial development in Catalonia and other areas. Isabella's cause attracted the support of Great Britain and France, who were very conscious of being constitutional states in a continent dominated by absolute monarchies. Money, supplies and volunteers therefore were organized to ensure the triumph of liberalism in Spain. Britain and France formed an alliance with Spain and Portugal, which was experiencing similar troubles. Fighting

Above, an incident in Barcelona during the 1835 uprising: though Isabella's claim to the throne was supported by the liberals, when once she became queen her reign was notably repressive. Museo de Historia de la Ciudad, Barcelona.

Opposite left, the Crown Prince Rudolf (1858–89) on his deathbed at Mayerling.

Opposite right, the Ringstrasse in Vienna, 1891.

in difficult country dragged on until 1839, but there was little doubt as to the outcome.

Carlism continued to find loyal adherents especially in the Basque region, but its inability to prosper even in the chaotic political conditions of nineteenth-century Spain showed how weak it really was. The rest of Isabella's reign down to 1868 was marked by instability and revolutions. In 1834, Maria Cristina had proclaimed a constitution as the price of liberal backing. The liberals were divided over the constitution – the Moderates, who were primarily aristocrats and the wealthy middle class, accepted it, while the Progressives, who represented the less well-to-do sections of the middle class in the towns, wanted a return to the more democratic constitution of 1812. Both groups of liberals looked for support to the army, which held the key to power in Spain. Liberalism in these years entailed the prevention of a return to absolute monarchy, experimentation with different constitutions and the encouragement of economic expansion.

For most of Isabella's reign, therefore, Spain was ruled by politically-minded generals acting in the name of either the Moderates or the Progressives. Between 1840 and 1843 the Progressive general Espartero was in power. He was overthrown in favour of the Moderate general Narváez, whose brand of liberalism was summed up in his alleged deathbed remark: 'I have no enemies, I have shot them all.' In 1854 an army revolt was accompanied by a popular rising from below which alarmed Moderates and Progressives alike. Another general, O'Donnell, emerged to try to unite the less extreme members of both parties, and his ascendancy lasted, on and off, until 1863. During these years foreign capital had enabled Spain to build a railway network and exploit the mineral wealth, which was her principal economic asset. The sale of church and common land helped to increase the number of prosperous peasant farmers. These economic developments, however, only complicated Spain's political life further by increasing the number of people whose lives had been disrupted by change but failing to increase the standard of living of the majority of Spanish people.

Republican interlude

The monarchy continued to play an active part in the petty politics, court intrigues and corruption which characterized Isabella's reign. Isabella herself became unpopular and like her mother found relief from the political tensions thrust upon her since infancy in a colourful love life. This scandalized Spanish society and caused discontent to be centred on the monarchy as much as the politicians and the generals. In 1868 navy and army leaders overthrew the dynasty, resulting in Isabella's exile to Paris. Then the leading revolutionaries, General

Francisco Serrano and General Juan Prim y Prats, hunted Europe for a democratically-minded king, which Prim declared was like looking for an atheist in heaven. After innocently sparking off the Franco-Prussian war by offering the throne to a relative of the King of Prussia, they found a suitable candidate in Italy. A son of the Italian king became Amadeo I of Spain.

Amadeo was well suited to the role of being a constitutional monarch in an orderly political system, but the chaos of Spanish politics placed him in an impossible position. To the left of the liberal parties the Democrats and the Republicans had emerged. O'Donnell's attempt to find a compromise between the Moderates and Progressives had produced a party of Liberal Unionists. The revolution which overthrew Isabella had been led by a coalition of Liberal Unionists, Progressives and Democrats whose ablest leader was Prim; but after his assassination the coalition broke up. Amadeo found himself shunned by the more conservative elements in Spanish politics, yet unable to unite the groups which had called him to the throne. After ruling for two years, he gave up the task as hopeless and abdicated in 1873.

Radical elements in the *cortes*, Spain's parliament, were strong enough to proclaim the First Spanish Republic, but this was to last less than two years. Its supporters were mainly interested in trying to make Spain into a federal state. Strong regional feelings, most notably in Catalonia and the Basque area, had always resisted centralization from Madrid. The geography of the country made communications difficult, and the uneven distribution of wealth among the various regions resulted in jealousy and rivalries. There was considerable support for federalism, though no agreement on what form it should take; but when federalism was endorsed by the *cortes*, the provinces set about running their own affairs without waiting for elections. A new Carlist revolt flared up. Chaos and violence forced republican leaders to abandon the idea of federalism and concentrate on restoring order. They were alarmed, too, at the propaganda of the First International, which took the opportunity to sow the seeds of revolutionary socialism in Spain. Spain's fourth president in less than a year, Emilio Castelar, abandoned federalism and assumed dictatorial powers to re-unify the country. Under him and his successor, Serrano, the republic swung steadily to the right.

Opinion in the country swung in favour of restoring the monarchy. Isabella's son, Alfonso, came of age in 1874 and succeeded to the throne at the end of the year.

The leading statesman of the restoration was Cánovas del Castillo, who did much to win acceptance for the idea that political life should be orderly. The constitution of 1876, which survived for nearly fifty years, provided for a limited monarchy in which ministers were responsible to the *cortes*.

Alfonso was not anxious to put the dynasty at risk again, and followed Cánovas' advice to use his powers sparingly and let parliamentary government work. Cánovas led the Liberal-Conservatives, a party formed from Moderates and Liberal Unionists. Práxedes Sagasta founded the Liberal Party out of the old Progressives. Cánovas aimed to make these two parties the governing parties of Spain in the way Conservatives and Liberals governed Britain. Since Spanish electoral conditions were less likely to produce the 'swing of the pendulum' which made British parties confident they would get their turn of office, Cánovas, Sagasta and Alfonso collaborated to give each of the two parties its turn. The feeling that neither would try to influence the king to exclude the other from power and that power would alternate between Liberal-Conservatives and Liberals made revolution and army support unnecessary. Spanish politics entered a period of order and stability. When Alfonso died in 1885, his widow acted as regent for their son until 1902. The succession passed smoothly to Alfonso XIII.

In the years after the restoration Spanish liberalism had some notable achievements in securing more religious freedom than Spain had ever known, trial by jury and universal suffrage. But in a predominantly peasant country this did not bring democracy. It only established the conditions within which local party bosses and priests had to work in their efforts to shape opinion. A growing number of people were demanding more freedom and by the end of the century anarchism and socialism were attracting considerable support from the Spaniards.

Anarchism flourished more in Spain than in any other European country. Ideas of peasant socialism brought to western Europe by the Russian revolutionary Bakunin took firm root among the poverty-stricken peasants of Andalusia in southern Spain. Anarcho-syndicalism spread from France to Barcelona and the other towns of Catalonia, where industrial workers looked to the general strike for salvation. The terrorist wing of the anarchists was active in Spain at this time as in other European states and gave the movement dramatic publicity with its bombs and assassinations. Cánovas was among the victims. Socialism grew more slowly than anarchism. A socialist party was founded in 1879 and was influenced by the rigidly orthodox French socialist, Jules Guesde. A socialist trade union was set up in 1882. Socialism was strong in the industrial areas of northern Spain, which were beginning to rival Catalonia in importance. Spain's first serious strikes occurred there in the 1890s.

Spain's vanishing empire

The successive Spanish governments were unable to divert public opinion by managing any spectacular manoeuvres abroad.

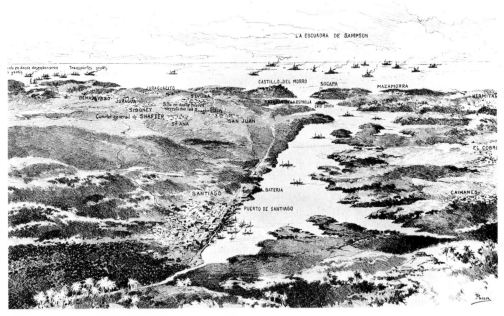

Spanish imperialism was persistent but largely unsuccessful. O'Donnell had won plaudits in the 1860s by a victory against Morocco, although it brought no concrete gain. Spain still hoped that she might regain something from her lost colonial empire in Latin America. She joined in an international debt collecting expedition to Mexico in 1861, but it led to nothing else. She got involved in a minor and inglorious war with Peru in 1864. An unexpected success came in 1861 when Santo Domingo asked to return to Spanish rule, but the inhabitants had regretted their move by 1865, and Spain withdrew in face of a revolution.

The only important colonies remaining to her after the achievement of independence by her Latin American colonies in the first quarter of the nineteenth century were Cuba, Puerto Rico and the Philippines. Although Cuba and Puerto Rico had remained loyal during the wars of independence, the Cubans became increasingly embittered by Spanish rule. A civil war broke out over liberal reforms in 1868, and the fighting continued for ten years. In 1895 a fresh revolutionary outbreak led to ruthless repression followed by offers of partial self-government which came too late. The continued strife was one of the causes of the Spanish American War.

That war which began in 1898 was a great blow to Spain, whose people still harboured delusions about their country's strength. With the loss of Cuba, Puerto Rico and the Philippines, Spanish prestige was at its lowest ebb. National unity under the Bourbon dynasty became more difficult to visualize as regional discontent grew. Anarchist and socialist influence among the slowly expanding urban population increased. A general strike in Catalonia in 1909 was accompanied by the killing of Catholic clergy. Brutal repression and the execution of the anti-clerical writer, Francisco Ferrer, embittered feelings still further. On the eve of the 1914 war, Spain's weakness, backwardness and disunity were breaking through the orderly façade of constitutional government.

Portugal

Events in Portugal followed a remarkably similar pattern to those in Spain. The aftermath of the Napoleonic wars brought dispute over the kind of constitution which should be adopted. In 1826 the throne passed to an infant girl, Maria, and her uncle, Dom Miguel, played the same sort of role as Isabella's uncle, Don Carlos, in Spain. Maria was actually overthrown in 1828, and Miguel made himself absolute monarch. Like Don Carlos, he was defeated during the 1830s by Maria's supporters, aided by the British and French. Maria was restored and reigned until 1853.

Thereafter, similar developments to those in Spain occur only in a different order. A party system like that of Cánovas developed, the conservative Regenerators agreeing to alternate with the liberal Progressives. After Carlos I came to the throne in 1889, his extravagant and scandalous behaviour lowered the reputation of the monarchy. In the face of rising discontent, Carlos suppressed parliamentary government in 1906 and gave dictatorial powers to João Franco. Then in 1908 Carlos and his eldest son were assassinated, and his second son, Manuel II, reigned for only two years. A republican

movement which had been gathering strength since the 1880s received the support of the army in 1910. When a cruiser in the Tagus River shelled the royal palace at Lisbon, Manuel fled into exile.

A republic was proclaimed which offered no immediate remedy for the chronic insolvency and economic backwardness which had characterized Portugal, like Spain, in the nineteenth century. The idea of syndicalism began to be accepted by the small working class in the towns, and Lisbon experienced a general strike in 1912.

In one respect Portugal's history in this period diverged considerably from that of Spain: while Spain lost most of her overseas empire and made only minor gains in northwest Africa, Portugal greatly expanded her African possessions by developing Angola and Mozambique. She avoided a clash with Britain, comparable with the Spanish-American war when in 1890 she gave way to a British ultimatum designed to prevent her linking the two territories together. In Portugal's case imperialism was not enough to save the monarchy.

Italian Unification – the disappointed hopes

'Italy is made, all is safe', Cavour was reported to have said in 1861. Cavour's skill in exploiting events which his own state of Piedmont was too small to control had been largely responsible for the expulsion of Austria from the Italian peninsula and the creation of a united Italy. He had used Napoleon III's desire to revise the map of Europe in France's favour to secure an alliance with France against Austria. After the war of 1859, Austria controlled only Venetia. When Garibaldi and his thousand Redshirts seized southern Italy – to the surprise of everyone, including Cavour – it was Cavour who made sure that his own monarch, Victor Emmanuel of Piedmont,

was the beneficiary. The kingdom of Italy was proclaimed in 1861, Piedmont dominating the kingdom as surely as Prussia dominated the German Empire, which was established ten years later.

Italy had been united by a combination of spectacular warfare, tortuous diplomacy and nationalist propaganda of the more idealistic kind. The Italian unification was one of the most heroic and glamorous episodes of nineteenth-century history and gave Italy many admirers abroad, especially in Britain. The aftermath of unification disappointed Italian hopes, however, for within a generation Italy was being treated in patronizing fashion by the other European states.

It took only ten years to round off the work of unification. In 1861 only Venetia and Rome, held by Austria and the Pope respectively, remained outside Victor Emmanuel's kingdom. In 1866 Italy got control of Venetia, having allied herself with Prussia in the latter's duel with Austria. In 1870 Italian troops entered Rome and made it the capital of the new Italy. Nevertheless the way in which these gains were made was ominous. In the war of 1866 the Italian army and navy were defeated by the Austrians in contrast with the overwhelming victory of the Prussians. Venetia was won by Prussian not Italian arms, and Rome was occupied in 1870 only because the Pope's protector, Napoleon III, had had to withdraw his troops to meet the Prussian invasion of France. Again, Italy owed her success to Prussian arms.

Italy's role in international politics became more depressing as the years went by. Italians had no sense of greatness abroad to compensate for their even more depressing inability to solve the country's basic social and economic problems. The tragic contrast between the fairly prosperous north and the dismally poor south, and the widening gap between rich and poor, continued to provide distressing evidence of how little unification

had achieved. Italy had been made, but her future was far from safe.

The guerrilla leader, Garibaldi, and the revolutionary thinker and organizer, Giuseppe Mazzini, had wanted to involve the whole Italian people in the work of unification. But the Piedmontese politicians with whom the real power lay were not democrats. They were ultra-cautious liberals who believed it best to let Italy develop at her own pace within the framework of a constitutional monarchy and a national parliament.

Italian politics, therefore, were played between a small electorate and politicians who had very limited ideas of reform. Cavour, whose vision might have brought wider changes, died in 1861, and his colleagues of the more conservative kind dominated the political scene from 1861 to 1876. Quintino Sella was the ablest of them, and his skilful handling of the nation's finances by a scheme of rigorous taxation and the reduction of government expenditure balanced the budget. By 1876 results were beginning to show in the form of completed unification, increased revenue, a reformed army and navy, a virtually newly created merchant marine, railway building and the beginning of industrialization. But the cost to the Italian people was heavy. High taxation was not accompanied by any measures to alleviate the immediate hardships it produced. Voters became impatient of waiting for long-term results.

In 1876 the Right were defeated and replaced by the Leftist groups who brought no radical change into the government of the country. The first prime minister under the new Left regime was Agostino Depretis, who was in power from 1876 to 1887. He was a man of moderation and political skill, who extended the franchise by widening the age and tax qualifications; during his time in office some ineffective welfare legislation was also introduced. Otherwise the political groups known as the Left did little to justify their claims in opposition, and Depretis

Above, Pope Pius IX blessing the French troops of the Papal Guard withdrawn by Napoleon II for service against Prussia: now that the papacy was unprotected, Italian troops entered Rome and the Papal States declared in favour of union with Italy, completing national unification.

Above left, revolutionary troops at the Royal Palace during the 1910 revolution: Manuel II fled to London and a republic was formed under the presidency of Theofilo Braga.

Opposite top right, Maria II of Portugal (1819–53): periodically threatened with overthrow during her reign, Maria nevertheless maintained the good name of the monarchy and kept her country together, unlike Isabella in Spain.

Opposite top left, plan of the harbour of Santiago da Cuba in 1898: in the war that year against the USA Spain lost the last remains of her once great empire and faced national humiliation as a result.

Opposite bottom, the bodies of Catholic clergy killed during the so-called 'Tragic Week' in Barcelona, 1909, a popular uprising directed against conscription for the North African campaigns.

became best known for his success in influencing elections by various corrupt methods and for his skill in organizing coalitions in parliament to support his policies. The latter technique was known as 'transformism', because contending groups were transformed into government coalitions.

Parliamentary government therefore disappointed many Italians as being slow, dull and corrupt. But the politically conscious classes on whom both Right and Left relied for support wanted a middle course between the clericalism and reaction of the old Italy and the radical and socialist ideas which were emerging. A cautious liberalism was probably all Italy could hope for at this time. The political system was self-regulating in that the principal bar to the majority of Italians taking part in politics was the literacy test. As literacy spread with the needs of a developing economy, so more of the nation would participate. The high ideals and hopes which had inspired unification made most Italians expect too much too quickly.

Crispi and Italian imperialism

Between 1887 and 1896 the most important figure in Italian politics was Francesco Crispi. Crispi was more radical than most of his colleagues on the Left, and when he succeeded to the premiership this was expressed in reform of the legal system, the prisons, public health and in a strongly anti-clerical policy, which included the abolition of compulsory religious education. Relations between the Italian government and the pope, who had been confined to the Vatican since the annexation of Rome, became worse.

Crispi's period in office was most notable for his aggressive policy overseas. Ever since unification Italy had been regarded as a great power by most of the other European countries; but in fact Italy lacked the means to maintain her new status. There were few natural resources, and the lack of coal and iron were especially detrimental. The Italian coastline was so vulnerable that friendly relations with Britain, the principal naval power, were an essential aspect of her foreign policy. It soon became clear that Italy's chances of winning control of the Trentino, the Italian-speaking area still held by the Habsburgs, were slight. Since the upheavals of the years between the Crimean War and the unification of Germany, Europe had settled down to a period of stable frontiers. Italy would have to look elsewhere if her appetite for additional territory were gratified.

The obvious course was to expand into North Africa and increase her standing as a Mediterranean power. As a result of the French annexation of Tunis in 1881, on which Italy had fixed her eyes, she began to quarrel with France, and in the following year allied herself with Germany and her old enemy, Austria, to form the Triple Alliance.

Crispi stuck firmly to this alliance and to close relations with Britain, which he tried unsuccessfully to turn into an alliance. Using this combination as a shield against France, he set out to build an empire for Italy in Africa. What was left of North Africa was technically part of the Ottoman Empire, whose further dismemberment Italy's allies were anxious to prevent. Crispi marked out the Red Sea coast as the area for Italian expansion. In 1887 Italian activities led to war with Ethiopia, the most powerful of the African states, in which Italy fared badly. Crispi had agreed to back the contender for the Ethiopian throne, Menelek, and claimed he had agreed to make Ethiopia an Italian protectorate. When Italy tried to realize this claim, Menelek took up the challenge and the Italian army suffered a disastrous defeat at Adowa in 1896. Crispi was forced to recognize Ethiopian independence and to confine Italian ambitions to the coastal colony of Eretrea.

The disaster at Adowa ended Crispi's career, and Italy's basic military weakness thirty-five years after unification was exposed in humiliating fashion. Britain had, of course, suffered humiliating defeats in Africa and Asia, but Britain could afford them. Italy could not, or believed she could not.

Crispi's successors prepared the next colonial conquest more carefully. They aimed to get Tripoli, the Turkish province lying east of Tunisia on the African coast. After years of diplomatic soundings, the Italians finally declared war on Turkey in October 1911 confident that no other European power would intervene. Italy's victory over the Turks and her acquisition of Tripoli encouraged the forces of Italian nationalism, although the victory reflected Turkish weakness rather than Italian strength. For Italy imperialism had proved to be a more difficult way of raising morale at home and prestige abroad than it was for the more industrialized European nations.

Economic backwardness contributed to Italy's inglorious foreign and imperial policy, and conversely the excessive attention which the government paid to foreign affairs diverted their energies from the task of promoting economic progress. At the time of unification the mass of the Italian peasantry lived in a state of continual poverty and insecurity. Industry did not begin to make strides until the 1880s and even then developed in slow and troubled fashion. The railway network which was built after unification, had begun by then to open up a nationwide market. Significantly, an armaments industry was an early achievement.

As in Spain, both anarchism and socialism flourished in an essentially peasant society with small concentrations of industry. Anarchist ideas imported by the Russian revolutionary Bakunin had the same appeal to the peasants of Sicily as they had to those in Andalusia. Syndicalism was popular with Italian workers as with those of France as

Spain. Orthodox socialism was promoted initially by journalists and intellectuals, and a socialist party was founded in 1892 which, though it accepted a Marxist interpretation of Italy's development, was less clear about how it might revolt against the evils of capitalism.

Peasant uprisings in Sicily in the 1890s were savagely suppressed by Crispi, and laws against anarchist and socialist organizations introduced. In 1898 there was street fighting in Milan, and socialist leaders were severely punished for agitation. King Umberto of Italy was assassinated by an anarchist in 1900. In the early years of the twentieth century there were widespread strikes in the northern industrial towns. By 1914, when election returns showed the growing strength of socialism, Italy was again in the grip of strikes and riots.

Giolitti

These years of industrial and agrarian unrest was also the period when Italy was moving towards parliamentary democracy. In 1903 Giovanni Giolitti became prime minister and for more than a decade was to dominate Italian politics. He tried to bring about a mood of reconcilation and consensus in Italian political life. He made concessions to the Catholic Church, which had been bitterly opposed by the Liberals in the past; he introduced laws to improve working conditions and cut food taxes in a bid for socialist support. Socialists were invited to join the government. In 1912 he extended voting rights to something approaching manhood suffrage.

Italy was at last undergoing an industrial revolution, and in the long run this would have brought benefits to a large enough section of the working class to give them some faith in a system which was no longer inclined to use authoritarian methods against industrial unrest. But Giolitti's policy of conciliating all important sections of opinion also entailed the pacification of

Left, the assassination of Umberto I, 29 July 1900: like many other nations, Italy experienced widespread strikes and unrest in the early years of the twentieth century.

Opposite, view of the street-fighting in Milan, May 1898: sharp rises in the price of bread had led to the demonstration, which was suppressed with unnecessary brutality, at the cost of fifty lives and hundreds of arrests.

strident nationalists, who were demanding the aggressive foreign policy Italy could not afford. They were granted the war with Turkey in 1911–12, but the cost of this resulted in increased taxation at home and further industrial trouble. Without a long period of peace Giolitti's policy for neutrality in the struggle between capital and labour had little chance of success. Parliamentary government had not worked sufficiently well to convince the majority of politically conscious Italians that it was unquestionably the best system. The only way to establish parliamentary government on a firm base was to associate it with prosperity at home. This took time and, with so much industrial strife, nerve. Italy's involvement in the First World War provided momentary relief from the wave of industrial and agricultural strikes, but it was eventually to create the inflammatory situation which heralded the rise of Fascism and the dictatorship of Mussolini.

The new Balkan states

The impact of industrialism on the relatively primitive and undeveloped states in the Balkans was even more disturbing than its effect on the highly organized agrarian nations of China and Japan, Spain and Italy, Russia and Austria-Hungary. After most of the Balkan nations had won their independence from the Ottoman Empire during the nineteenth century, they risked becoming dependent instead on the wealthy and powerful states of Europe. What

affected them most was not industrial development in their own countries, which remained very small, but the unavoidable influence of a foreign industrial civilization on their way of life.

The growing weakness of the Turks and the rise of nationalism among the Balkan Christians brought revolt and liberation: Greece became independent in 1830; Serbia, Montenegro and Romania were recognized as independent in 1878, (although they had effectively thrown off Turkish rule long before then); Bulgaria declared her independence in 1908, although in practice she too had been free for over twenty years. The Muslim Albanians freed themselves in 1912. Turkey had been driven almost entirely out of Europe.

The price of independence was high. The Balkans remained a turbulent area whose rulers saw territorial expansion as a prime duty. In order to militarize their new states, rulers had to get loans from the larger European countries, who frequently attached burdensome conditions to their agreements. Taxation was another source of revenue, but one which made for discontent. To pay their taxes the peasants had to raise enough money by producing for the European market or by borrowing at high rates of interest. The situation which resulted upset the age-old patterns of village life and added the complication of political instability. Success in foreign adventure became urgent

but very much dependent on the backing of an industrialized nation. All the new Balkan states found their independence limited by their need of the industrial world.

The Greek kingdom remained under foreign tutelage throughout the century. Her monarch was chosen according to the wishes of the great powers, who on three occasions prevented her from making war

and saved her from the consequences of defeat by Turkey in 1897. Her finances were subject to international control after this war had reduced her to bankruptcy. The economic backwardness which was responsible for Greek impotence was scarcely tackled by her political leaders, who conducted a dangerous foreign policy appropriate only to powerful and wealthy states.

Serbia, Montenegro, Romania and Bulgaria were rather more independent than Greece because they could play off Russia and Austria against one another. Between 1905 and 1907 Serbia successfully defied the attempt by Austria-Hungary to wage a tariff war against Serbia to induce her to return to Austrian control. The rivalry between the European powers encouraged the Balkan states to expand and thereby risk both their own survival and the peace of the rest of Europe. Thus the imperialistic designs of the powers in the Balkans pushed the small nationalistic states into imperialist projects of their own with disastrous results in 1914.

The Young Turks

In its struggle to survive during the nineteenth century the once-great Ottoman Empire had introduced a remarkable amount of reform based on western European examples, the high point of which

EUROPE, ASIA AND THE UNITED STATES – 1848–1914

Date	Western and Central Europe	Russia and Asia	United States	Date	Western and Central Europe	Russia and Asia	United States
1850		Taiping Rebellion		1890	Bismarck dismissed		Sherman Anti-Trust Law
	Great Exhibition in Britain (1851)					Great famine in Russia (1891)	
	Second Empire in France (1852)						Populist Party (1892)
		Crimean War (1853)			Trial of Dreyfus (1894)	Franco-Russian alliance (1894)	
	Bessemer steel (1856)	Arrow War in China (1856)				Sino-Japanese War (1894)	
		Indian Mutiny (1857)					Marconi invented wireless telegraph (1895)
			First oil well drilled (1859)				Venezuela boundary dispute (1895)
1860	Kingdom of Italy (1861)	Emancipation of Russian serfs (1861)	Outbreak of Civil War (1861)		Diesel's heavy oil engine manufactured (1897)		
	British make first all iron warship (1861)		Gatling machine gun (1861)		French quick-firing artillery (1898)	China leases territory to Powers (1898)	Spanish-American War (1898)
	First International (1864	Polish rebellion (1863)	Emancipation Proclamation (1863)		Tirpitz's first naval law (1898)	China's Hundred Days of Reform (1898)	
	Whitehead's self-propelled torpedo (1864)					Russian Social Democrat party formed (1898)	
	Siemens-Martin open-hearth steel (1866)		Lincoln assassinated (1865)		Bernstein's revision of Marxism (1899)		
			Fourteenth Amendment (1866)	1900	First Zeppelin launched	Boxer uprising	
	Battle of Sadowa (1866)		Transatlantic cable laid (1866)		Labour Representation Committee		
	England's Second Reform Act (1867)		Purchase of Alaska (1867)			Commonwealth of Australia (1901)	Theodore Roosevelt president (1901)
	Austro-Hungarian Compromise (1867)					Russian Socialist Revolutionary party formed (1901)	
	First volume of Marx's *Das Kapital* (1867)		British North America Act (1867)			Japan allies with Britain (1902)	
	Nobel manufactures dynamite (1867)	Meiji restoration in Japan (1868)	First transcontinental railroad completed (1869)		Serbian revolution (1903)		Wright brothers' flight (1903)
1870	Dogma of papal infallibility				Franco-British Entente (1904)	Russo-Japanese War (1904)	Panama independent (1903)
	Establishment of German Empire (1871)				Separation of Norway from Sweden (1905)	Bloody Sunday and the October Manifesto (1905)	
	Paris Commune (1871)				Separation of church and state in France (1905)		
	First Spanish Republic (1873)		Alabama settlement (1872)		British launch *Dreadnought* (1906)		
	Gotha congress of German Social Democrats (1875)					Russo-British Entente over Asia (1907)	
	Constitution of Third French Republic (1875)				Annexation of Bosnia-Herzegovina (1908)	Young Turk revolution (1908)	
	Restoration of monarchy in Spain (1875)	Midhat Pasha's Turkish constitution (1876)	Bell's telephone (1876)		Lloyd George's People's Budget (1909)		Ford's Model T car begins mass production (1909)
	Congress of Berlin (1878)	Russo-Turkish War (1877)		1910	Portugal a republic		
	Austro-German alliance (1879)					Assassination of Stolypin (1911)	
1880		Assassination of Alexander II (1881)				Chinese revolution (1911)	
	Fabian Society (1883)				First Balkan War (1912)		Woodrow Wilson elected president (1912)
	Gladstone's Franchise Act (1884)					Coup in Turkey by Enver Pasha (1913)	Federal Reserve Bank Act (1913)
	Maxim gun (1884)						Opening of Panama Canal (1914)
	Daimler's petrol engine (1885)	Penjdeh crisis (1885)	Canadian Pacific Railway completed (1885)		Assassination of Francis Ferdinand. Outbreak of First World War (1914)		
	Benz's first motor car (1885)	Indian National Congress (1885)	American Federation of Labor (1886)				
	Second International (1889)	Japanese constitution (1889)	First Pan-American Congress (1889)				
			Brazil becomes a republic (1889)				

was the proclamation of a constitution in 1876 by the Turkish statesman, Midhat Pasha. The adequacy of the reforms to enable the empire to cope with its problems was doubtful, but the movement was abruptly ended by Sultan Abdul Hamid. The Ottoman Empire reverted to a further period of stagnation and tyranny.

In 1908 a revolutionary organization, the Young Turks, which had strong support in the sultan's army, made its bid for power. The sultan hastily revived Midhat's constitution to save his throne, but his endorsement of a counter-revolution in 1909 led to his disposition and replacement by a puppet sultan. The reformers were at odds over the future form of the empire. After military disaster at the hands of Italy in 1911 and the Balkan states in 1912, power was seized by the extreme nationalists among the Young Turks. Although their movement was to end in a brutal dictatorship, they initiated many valuable reforms in education and municipal government in the meantime and pointed the way to Turkey's westernization by

Kemal Ataturk after the First World War. Like her former Balkan subjects Turkey developed in response to the challenge of the industrialized nations of Europe.

By 1914 this challenge was being faced in every part of the world. It had been taken up vigorously and successfully by America and Germany and later by Japan and Russia. With Britain and France they formed a new aristocracy among the nations. Elsewhere the response was slow and uncertain. In Austria-Hungary, Italy, Spain and Portugal political and social conditions were not conducive to rapid change, and the gap widened between them and the leading powers. Far less enviable was the position of countries like China, Turkey and the Balkan states as they struggled to avoid becoming the victims of a new and potent kind of imperialism. The great industrial states were often reckless and irresponsible in using the wealth and power they had created. In 1914 they turned their strength against one another.

Opposite top, Midhat Pasha proclaims the constitution at Constantinople, 1876, the culmination of a series of administrative reforms over the previous two decades. The constitution failed to survive the succession of the Sultan Abdul Hamid II.

Opposite bottom, delegates from the Young Turks and the Balkan Committee are received personally by the Sultan Abdul Hamid, who restored the constitution in Turkey on 24 July 1908.

Part IX

THE FIRST WORLD WAR: CAUSES AND CONSEQUENCES

Introduction

The Great War of 1914–18 still appears as a cataclysmic event, even though well over half a century has elapsed since it ended. The great powers of Europe had avoided war with one another for some forty-three years. In August 1914 they seemed to stumble into it unintentionally. Everyone thought that the battle would be short and that they would be 'home in time for Christmas'. In fact the war was to last for four years and people were driven by events to abandon their optimistic and consoling misapprehensions. Instead they persuaded themselves, with equal fallaciousness, that they were engaged in the last general conflict, a 'war to end wars'. Certainly no government expected, or was adequately prepared for, the extravagant sort of warfare in which it found itself embroiled.

Naturally enough, the causes of this surprising and unwanted war have, ever since, been a matter of controversy among both politicians and historians. Even today, the relative importance of the different policies, conflicting interests, circumstances and personalities which contributed to its outbreak remains in dispute.

The most intractable conflict of all was the Balkan rivalry between Russia and Austria-Hungary. Britain, France, Italy and even Germany had repeatedly shown that over colonial disputes they were all, in the end, prepared to seek a settlement without war. The French desire for revenge against Germany for 1871, and for recovery of Alsace and Lorraine, had never quite died, but it had died down. But the clash between the two ancient dynastic empires of Russia and Austria-Hungary seemed to be beyond compromise. Linked as it was with rival hot-headed nationalist movements in the Balkans on the one hand and through the system of great alliances with the fears and tensions of Europe on the other, here was the flash-point of the explosion.

The Great War (as it was called throughout the 1920s and 1930s) began, then, as a civil war in Europe. Only in 1917 did it become more genuinely a world war. But for various reasons the conflict was, from quite an early stage, worldwide in its repercussions and its future consequences. This came about because of the vast colonial empires of the major European powers,

which collectively dominated world trade, and not least because the war released the momentous new world force of the Bolshevik Revolution in Russia. The new idealism which crept into allied statements of peace-aims, notably through President Woodrow Wilson's 'Fourteen Points', roused the hopes of disunited nationalities. The victory of the western maritime powers of Britain, France, the United States, Belgium and the Commonwealth proclaimed a new world made 'safe for democracy'.

What most wrecked these hopes, highest at the moment of the Paris peace conference of 1919, were the uncontrollable effects of the war on the pre-war world economy. It was not simply that vast wealth and millions of lives had been destroyed or that individual countries, notably Great Britain, had now lost their lucrative overseas investments and become debtor-nations. What mattered most in a material sense was that the pre-war economy, the fabric of international trade and investment, was hopelessly disrupted and dislocated. With the central market of Germany temporarily gone, the Russian market closed, industrial production everywhere distorted by wartime needs, Europe needed more drastic and deliberate reconstruction than was possible in the desperate conditions of the immediate post-war years. Politics, as Maynard Keynes pointed out, seemed destined to frustrate economic recovery at every point. It created a host of new states whose frontiers often made little economic sense, it exaggerated attempts to exact monetary reparations from Germany, it insisted on the repayment of war debts, and it sought too hasty a return to 'normalcy'.

Economics, as it were, had its reprisals on politics. The resulting unemployment

of the inter-war years, the slumps induced by the shrinkage of international trade, the revulsions of inflamed nationalism, especially important in Italy and in Germany, ruined hopes of democracy's survival in the worst-hit countries. Militant, ruthless authoritarian movements arose during the 1920s and were quick to learn from the successful Bolsheviks the potency of a single-party state monopolizing all the resources of modern terror, propaganda and state power. The dictatorships of Mussolini in Italy and of Hitler in Germany were, in a real sense, consequences of the Great War.

Indeed, fascism was perhaps the chief beneficiary of the war, for it could hardly have gained power and flourished so much without the war's aftermath. But another beneficiary was communism, and not only because the collapse in war of both the tsarist regime and the liberal provisional government which succeeded it in 1917 opened the door to Lenin's Bolshevik Party.

Communist agents and propagandists exploited fully the conditions of unrest and distress which prevailed after the war. They saw in them the best guarantee of a world proletarian revolution. It took nearly two decades to prove that the fears their methods aroused did far more to help fascism than to promote communism. Repeatedly, communist agitation was the perfect excuse for fascist coups, and weak parliamentary democracies did not give place to proletarian dictatorship, only to fascist dictatorship.

Economic crisis, then, gave rise to political crisis, and to revolution, during the inter-war years: and political crisis gave rise to international crisis and eventually to a second world war. The new League of Nations was gravely weakened from birth

by the exclusion of Soviet Russia and Germany and by the abstention of the United States, its chief sponsor. We cannot but speculate whether it might have succeeded more but for the mounting challenges of Italy, Japan and Germany. Perhaps it could have achieved fuller international cooperation in social and economic affairs, but still without succeeding in its ultimate purpose of preventing war. But once aggressive military movements were in complete power in Japan, Italy and Germany and these three powers even drew together in common cause under the misleading title of the 'Anti-Comintern Pact', a major war was probably inevitable. The collapse of the League of Nations as a peace-keeping organization and the inertia of its major props in Europe, Britain and France increased the probability.

In these ways, there are certain links of cause and effect between the two world wars. It would be oversimplifying to see them entirely, as Winston Churchill once suggested, as parts of one 'Thirty Years' War' or as one great German challenge to the rest of Europe. The strongest evidence to the contrary is the role in contemporary history of China and Japan. Both during and after the Great War, Japan progressively rose to a position of supremacy in Asia. It was above all, as the author shows, China's chronic division and weakness that made this possible.

The shifting balance of power in the Far East is as much a part of world history, helping to explain the drift of events during the inter-war years, as is the rise of fascist dictatorships in Europe. It has even been suggested, with some reason, that the Second World War should be seen as having begun not in 1939, parochially, with a German attack on Poland but in 1937, when Japan embarked on full-scale war against a disintegrating China. In the same sense, China's communist revolution is probably the most important single event amid the complex aftermath of the Second World War.

Since 1945 the serious study of so-called 'contemporary history' (i.e. twentieth-century history) has become both fashionable and respectable. Much harm was done by the ignorance and the myths about the peace settlement of 1919 and the Allied treatment of Germany in the 1920s, and it is entirely to the good that research and better perspective have now made possible more objective accounts of those years.

There is little doubt that, just as the causes of the First must be looked for in the whole sequence of events from at least 1871 onwards and in the unique situation which they had produced by 1914, so historians will trace the origins of the Second back to the events here chronicled. History never divides sharply into separate phases, and it is wise to recall how small a part conscious human intention plays in determining the outcome of great events. Nobody went to war in 1914 to precipitate a communist revolution in Russia, or to set up a League of Nations, or to provide a home for the Jews in Palestine, yet these were among its most important consequences. The moral to be drawn from this period is, perhaps, that modern warfare is not only an exceptionally extravagant mode of action but also a most unreliable and uncontrollable means of achieving one's aims.

Chapter 48

The Approach to War

For most of its history, the continent of Europe has been more often at war than at peace. Viewed against this background, the four years of war which followed August 1914 were less remarkable than the forty-three years of peace between the great powers of Europe which had preceded them. What was most surprising about the great age of European imperialism in the later nineteenth century was not the national rivalries which it inevitably produced but the success with which these rivalries were contained. For centuries past, wars had been fought in Europe to decide the ownership of a few hundred square miles of territory. During the thirty years after 1871, the great powers of Europe divided between them more than ten million square miles of the earth's surface without once coming to blows among themselves.

Within Europe itself, the most serious and persistent source of tension during the half century before the First World War was the Balkan rivalry between Russia and Austria-Hungary. This rivalry was an inevitable consequence both of the geographic position of these two powers and of the progressive disintegration of the Turkish Empire in the Balkans. What was remarkable was not that this rivalry gave rise to a series of international crises but that these crises were so often settled without recourse to war.

The long period of peace between the great powers of Europe was partly produced by the even distribution of power between them during the later nineteenth century: a balance eventually disturbed by the enormous growth of German strength. But it was a consequence also of the fact that the great powers had learned a self-restraint unthinkable only a century before; Europe, in short, had become more civilized. By 1909 a generation had grown up which, for the first time in European history, thought of warfare as a thing of the past. Even when Europe finally went to war, many believed that they were doing so for the last time, that they were fighting a war to end all wars.

The alliance system

There had been no war between major European powers since 1871. The Franco-Prussian War, concluded in that year, had been one of the turning-points in the history of nineteenth-century Europe. It had ended two centuries of French supremacy on the continent of Europe and, at the same time, had enabled Bismarck to complete the unification of Germany under Prussian leadership. The war changed Bismarck himself from poacher to gamekeeper. For a decade he had used war ruthlessly for the aggrandizement of Prussia. But in 1871 he suddenly discovered a new role as the chief defender of the peace of Europe. The new state of Germany, Bismarck believed, was 'a satiated power' with no further territorial ambitions. France, on the other hand, robbed by Germany of Alsace-Lorraine, would 'regard revenge as its principal mission'.

The main object of Bismarck's diplomacy, therefore, was to preserve the position Germany had won and guard against the danger of a French war of revenge. He relied at first on an informal understanding between the three great continental monarchies – Germany, Russia and Austria-Hungary – to keep the French Republic in its place. That understanding, however, broke down in 1878 because of Austro-Russian rivalry in the Balkans. From 1879 onwards, Bismarck began to replace the informal understanding of the 1870s by a series of formal (and sometimes overlapping) alliances – with Austria from 1879, with Russia from 1881, with Italy from 1882 – all concluded with the same aim of keeping France isolated, and therefore powerless.

Great Britain became increasingly convinced during the later nineteenth century that its 'splendid isolation' from European alliances was a tribute to its strength. France, on the contrary, never regarded its own isolation during the twenty years after the Franco-Prussian War as less than ignominious. The first chance for France to escape from this isolation came soon after Bismarck's fall from power in 1890. With Bismarck safely out of the way, Kaiser William II rashly decided to allow the alliance with Russia to lapse. Hitherto, though Russia had sometimes tried to frighten Bismarck by threatening to ally with France, it had never seriously intended to carry out its threat. The Russian court, in particular, had an almost physical horror of the French Republic which it regarded as an inherently subversive institution. The future Tsar Nicholas II, the last of the Romanov dynasty, declared in 1887: 'May God preserve us from alliance with France. . . . It would mean the invasion of Russia by revolution.'

Russia's diplomatic estrangement from Germany in 1890, however, was accompanied by a growing financial dependence on France. Russia in the late nineteenth century was at one and the same time an underdeveloped country and a great military power, increasingly conscious that its future as a great power depended upon the modernization of the Russian economy. This, in turn, required massive foreign investment, investment which was available only from France. It was, above all, its dependence on French investment which persuaded the Russian government to conclude, by stages, an alliance with France which was finally ratified in 1894.

By 1894, therefore, the four great powers of continental Europe were already grouped in two rival alliances. Germany, Austria-Hungary and Italy were joined together in the Triple Alliance (though Italy was neither a great power nor, by 1902, an effective member of the Triple Alliance). France and Russia were united in the Dual Alliance. The making of these two alliances was later blamed by many as the root cause of the First World War. It was, said Jagow, the German foreign minister, in his final meeting with the British ambassador in August 1914, 'this damned system of alliances' which had dragged Europe into war.

At the beginning of the twentieth century, however, there still seemed no real likelihood of war between the Dual and Triple Alliances. The two major rivalries which divided these alliances – France's desire for revenge against Germany, Austria's rivalry with Russia in the Balkans – had both receded into the background. No French statesman of any consequence still dreamed of a war of revenge against Germany. Austria and Russia both seemed determined to abide by the agreement which they had made in 1897 to put the Balkans 'on ice'. To most European statesmen at the beginning of the twentieth century, the only serious threat of European conflict seemed to lie in the imperial rivalries between Britain and her future allies in the First World War, France and Russia. And within a few years these rivalries, too, were to have been resolved without war.

German *Weltpolitik*

The growth of tension between the two alliances which first became apparent during the first Moroccan crisis of 1905–6 was the result, not of the nature of the alliances themselves, but of the new course of German foreign policy, German *Weltpolitik*. *Weltpolitik* ('world policy') arose in part from Germany's consciousness of its own enormous strength. At the time of the Franco-Prussian War, Germany had been only marginally superior to France in the size of its population and economic production. For the remainder of the nineteenth century, however, Germany's birth rate was the highest in Europe while France's was the lowest, and the German economy expanded at almost twice the rate of the French.

At the end of the century Germany towered, both militarily and economically, over every other state in the continent of Europe. *Weltpolitik* was partly an expression of this strength. In part also, it was simply one expression of the imperialist mood common to other European powers.

Imperialism, in both France and Britain, became a popular movement only in the closing years of the nineteenth century, after the French and British Empires were virtually complete. World policy emerged in Germany at almost exactly the same moment. Its first acts were the seizure of the Chinese port of Kiaochow in 1897, and the decision by the German parliament, the *Reichstag*, a year later to build a new German battle fleet.

Weltpolitik reversed the assumptions on which Bismarck's foreign policy had been based. Germany was no longer 'a satiated power', content with its position in Europe. It aspired, instead, to become a world power, with world ambitions. 'The German Empire', declared the Kaiser optimistically, 'has become a world empire'. By the time that Germany began to demand a place in the sun, however, almost all the available places had been taken. Had the nineteenth-century scramble for Africa been followed, as many European statesmen expected, by a twentieth-century scramble for China, Germany might still have been able to satisfy its imperial ambitions. But it was not to be.

Largely because of the lack of outlets for its imperial ambitions, *Weltpolitik* assumed a peculiarly restless character, undecided on which area of the world to focus its ambitions. Even the purpose of the new German navy was never made quite clear. Bethmann-Hollweg, Germany's chancellor on the outbreak of war, said vaguely that Germany needed the new navy 'for the general purposes of German greatness'. The Kaiser was almost equally vague. He told the King of Italy: 'All the years of my reign my colleagues, the monarchs of Europe, have paid little attention to what I have to say. Soon, with my great navy to endorse my words, they will be more respectful.'

The fact that the ambitions of *Weltpolitik* were so ill-defined only increased the extent to which Britain, France and Russia all came to feel threatened by them. Each power interpreted these ambitions with a different emphasis. Britain came to look on *Weltpolitik* primarily as a threat to British naval supremacy, Russia as a challenge to Russian influence in the Near East, France as a threat to the French position in the Mediterranean.

It was partly because of the lack of overseas outlets for German imperialism that, during the early years of the twentieth century, the ambitions of *Weltpolitik* turned increasingly towards the European continent. Among some sections of German opinion there was growing interest in the idea of a German *Mitteleuropa*, a new order in central Europe embracing not merely Germany and Austria-Hungary but also large areas of the Balkans and eastern Europe and even parts of Belgium. Though this idea became the official policy of the German government only after the outbreak of war in 1914, *Mitteleuropa* was the logical outcome of these vaguer ambitions formulated before the war.

The most curious characteristic of Germany's foreign policy during the decade before the First World War was the degree to which it combined an often arrogant assertion of German strength with a chronic feeling of insecurity. To a considerable degree this insecurity was a product of its ambitions: a fear that Germany's neighbours were jealous of its growing strength and might conspire to deny it the world power status which was its by right. Germany's insecurity showed itself, for example, in a fear that England might attempt the destruction of the new German fleet before it had grown large enough to challenge the supremacy of the Royal Navy. This fear, though greatly exaggerated, was not entirely without foundation. Sir John Fisher, the volatile First Lord of the Admiralty, suggested just such a scheme to Edward VII in 1904. The king was horrified. 'Good God, Fisher,' he replied, 'you must be mad.'

Insecurity was a consequence also of Germany's geographic position in the heart of Europe which forced it, unlike its two main continental rivals, France and Russia, to face the possibility of war on two fronts. Bismarck himself confessed that he suffered throughout his career from 'a nightmare fear of coalitions'. Time and time again in the years before the First World War, German statesmen showed that they could feel secure only in a world in which Germany's neighbours were at odds with one another. Much of the confidence felt by the Kaiser and his ministers at the turn of the twentieth century derived from the deep hostility (which Germany was at pains to encourage) between both England and France and England and Russia. It was the violent German reaction to the relaxation of this hostility with the signing of the Entente Cordiale in 1904 which began the decade of tension in European affairs which was to culminate in the First World War.

Above, the ceremonial start to construction work on the Baghdad Railway, 1903: financed and built by Germany, the railway, which ran from Constantinople to Baghdad and was not completed until 1918, was viewed with anxiety in London and Paris as yet another attempt by Germany to extend her political and economic power.

The Entente Cordiale

The Entente Cordiale has come to seem a much more romantic agreement than it appeared to be to the statesmen who concluded it. President Auriol of France claimed, on its fiftieth anniversary, that 'the convention of 8 April 1904 embodied the agreement of our two peoples on the necessity of safeguarding the spiritual values of which we were the common trustees.' The interpretation given on the same occasion by the British foreign secretary, Sir Anthony Eden, was less romantic but more accurate. He told the House of Commons:

At the time when it was concluded the Entente Cordiale did not represent some great surge of public opinion on either side of the Channel. It was in fact an instrument of political policy at the time, calculated to attempt to remove the differences which had long complicated Anglo-French relations in Egypt and Morocco.

The solution to these differences was a somewhat unscrupulous arrangment, characteristic of the diplomacy of imperialism. England and France signed a public undertaking to respect the integrity of both Egypt and Morocco. Secretly, they simply agreed to take them over: Egypt was to go to Britain, Morocco to France.

In itself, the Entente Cordiale did nothing to make war between the two European alliances more likely than before. Nor did it give any indication that England was any readier than before to take part in a continental war. What made the Entente Cordiale a major turning-point in international relations was, quite simply, the German reaction to it. The sight of Germany's neighbours settling differences which the German Foreign Office had assumed to be permanent immediately revived in German statesmen their nightmare fear of hostile coalitions. Once the agreement was signed, Germany was determined to demonstrate publicly that it was worthless. Its attempt to do so provoked the first Moroccan crisis, the first in the series of European crises which characterized the decade before the outbreak of war in 1914.

The German government calculated that if it were to provoke a crisis with France over Morocco, Russia would be unable (because of its involvement in a war with Japan) and Britain unwilling to offer France effective support. At one stroke, therefore, Germany would demonstrate the ineffectiveness of both the Dual Alliance and the Entente Cordiale. Germany might then be able to draw France into dependence on it and transform the European balance of power dramatically in its favour.

The Moroccan crisis began with the Kaiser's visit to Tangier in the spring of 1905. At Tangier he declared that Germany regarded the sultan as the ruler of a free and independent state: a clear warning that

Germany would not be prepared to tolerate a French protectorate. The significance of his visit was summed up by the Moroccan grand vizier in a particularly picturesque metaphor. 'Whilst in the act of ravishing Morocco,' he declared, 'France has received a tremendous kick in the behind from the Emperor William.'

Supported by Germany, the sultan now demanded an international conference to discuss Moroccan affairs. Simultaneously, Germany began a war of nerves directed against France. Rouvier, the weak and inexperienced French prime minister, soon had visions of a second Franco-Prussian War, followed by a second Paris Commune. By the summer of 1905, his nerve had given way. As a peace-offering to Germany he forced the resignation of his foreign minister, Delcassé, the French architect of the Entente Cordiale. Germany's failure at this time to exploit the spectacular success of its war of nerves was one of the greatest missed opportunities in the entire history of German diplomacy.

For the first time since the Franco-Prussian War, a French prime minister appeared ready and even anxious to cooperate with Germany. Rouvier offered Germany compensation in the Congo for French supremacy in Morocco, as well as cooperation in a variety of other fields. Had Germany accepted these terms, France might well have been drawn into a policy of continuing cooperation with Germany, so shifting the balance of power decisively in Germany's favour.

The German government, however, found itself trapped by its own propaganda. Having publicly demanded an international conference and having posed as the defender

of Moroccan independence, it felt unable to back down and reach an agreement with France. By its inflexibility Germany alienated those Frenchmen most anxious for agreement with it. Even Rouvier gradually recovered his spirits. In November he told one of his advisers: 'If Berlin thinks it can intimidate me, it has made a mistake. Henceforth I shall make no further concessions, come what may.'

The German war of nerves against France strengthened the suspicions aroused in Britain by the building of the new German fleet. At the beginning of the crisis the British government denounced the attitude of Germany as 'most unreasonable' and offered France 'all the support in its power'. Sir John Fisher begged the Foreign Office to go further and 'send a telegram to Paris that the English and French fleets are one'. At the end of 1905 British and French service chiefs began secret talks about cooperation in a war with Germany. By its own policy, therefore, the German government had transformed the character of the Entente Cordiale. What had begun as a settlement of colonial differences had now become a defensive coalition against Germany, regarded by both Britain and France as essential to their own security.

The new significance of the Entente Cordiale was apparent as soon as the international conference on Morocco met at Algeciras in January 1906. Throughout the conference France depended on British support. Grey, the British foreign secretary, dared not refuse that support for fear of damaging the Entente Cordiale. Even when he thought the French unreasonable and believed they should make concessions towards Germany, he still maintained that

'we can't press our advice on them to the point of breaking up the Entente.'

The conference itself ended in a major defeat for German diplomacy. Germany had been convinced that France would find itself almost isolated at Algeciras and that neither Britain nor Russia would offer it effective support. In the event it was Germany which was almost isolated, supported only by Austria-Hungary and Morocco.

The first Moroccan crisis convinced Grey of the wisdom of turning the Entente with France into a Triple Entente with both France and Russia. He wrote during the Algeciras conference: 'An Entente between Russia, France, and ourselves would be absolutely secure. If it were necessary to check Germany it could then be done.' As soon as the conference was over, he began the negotiations, which led eventually to the Anglo-Russian agreement of August 1907 and the creation of the Triple Entente. Even now, Grey remained genuinely anxious to reduce the tension between Britain and Germany. Both he and his Foreign Office advisers, however, were constantly afraid of taking any initiative to improve relations with Germany which might endanger the Triple Entente with France and Russia on which, they believed, British security depended. 'If we sacrifice the other powers to Germany', Grey believed, 'we shall eventually be attacked.'

Tension in the Balkans

One of the unforeseen consequences of the first Moroccan crisis was its effect on Germany's relations with Austria-Hungary. Only a few years earlier, relations between the two countries had been rather distant.

At Algeciras, however, Austria-Hungary suddenly emerged as Germany's only reliable ally. In a Europe in which the other three great powers seemed to be uniting against it Germany now regarded the alliance with Austria as vital for its own security. Unhappily for the peace of Europe, the moment at which Germany found itself reduced to dependence on the Austrian alliance coincided almost exactly with the moment chosen by Austria to resume a forward policy in the Balkans.

The new course in Austrian foreign policy was partly the result of the rise of new men to power. In the autumn of 1906 Aehrenthal became Austrian foreign minister and Conrad chief of staff. Their predecessors had been cautious men, anxious not to disturb the understanding with Russia in the Balkans. Aehrenthal and Conrad were arrogant, aggressive and ambitious, eager to restore the prestige of the Austrian Empire by a dramatic success in the Balkans.

At a deeper level, however, Aehrenthal's foreign policy was a response to the internal tensions of the Austrian Empire. Like Turkey, Austria had to face the enormous problems involved in holding together a multinational empire beset by the growing nationalism of its subject peoples. Many European statesmen believed these problems to be insoluble and concluded that the Austrian, like the Turkish, Empire was doomed to disintegration.

The most restive nationality within the Austrian Empire were the South Slavs. Many were attracted by the prospect of joining with their fellow Slavs in the independent kingdom of Serbia and in the provinces of Bosnia-Herzegovina (still a part of the Turkish Empire though under

Austrian administration) to form a united South Slav state.

Serbia, which openly considered itself the nucleus of this future South Slav state, thus came to be considered by Austrian statesmen as a threat to the continued existence of Austria-Hungary. Austria-Hungary would be secure, Aehrenthal believed, 'only when we decide to grasp the nettle firmly and make a final end to the pan-Slav dream'. And for both Aehrenthal and Conrad the only 'final end to the pan-Slav dream' was the complete destruction of the kingdom of Serbia.

The signal for the revival of tension in the Balkans was the Young Turk revolution at Constantinople in the summer of 1908. The Turks, now fired, like their Balkan subjects, with a new spirit of nationalism, seemed likely to reclaim full sovereignty over the provinces of Bosnia-Herzegovina. Aehrenthal's reply was to announce the annexation of these provinces by the Austrian Empire. By bringing another million Slavs under Austrian rule, he believed that he had struck a first blow against South Slav dreams of a united South Slav state. So too did the Serbs. Serbia mobilized its forces and appealed for Russian support. Russia, as the largest of the Slav nations, considered itself the protector of the Balkan Slavs and demanded that the question of Bosnia-Herzegovina be submitted to an international conference.

Aehrenthal had planned the annexation without giving any warning to Berlin. He had acted, however, in the conviction that, once the crisis had begun, Germany dare not risk the defeat of its only reliable ally by denying it German support. In the event, Germany promised support, not merely over the annexation of Bosnia-Herzegovina but in whatever action Austria thought fit to deal with Serbia. The German chancellor wrote to Aehrenthal a fortnight after the annexation. 'I know you doubt whether the present nasty state of affairs in Serbia can be allowed to go on indefinitely. I trust your judgement and shall regard whatever decision you come to as appropriate to the circumstances.'

After six months of tension it was Germany which brought the crisis to an end. In March 1909 it presented Russia with what amounted to an ultimatum demanding that it recognize the annexation. With its army still unprepared for European war, Russia was forced to give way. Serbia, now deprived of Russian support, had no option but to follow suit. Germany, boasted the kaiser, had stood by its ally like a knight 'in shining armour'.

'Here', wrote the Austrian minister, in the Serbian capital soon after the crisis had ended, 'all think of revenge, which is only to be carried out with the help of the Russians.' Russia was unlikely to desert the Serbs a second time as it had done in 1909.

Having been humiliated once by Germany, it was unwilling to risk humiliation again. As soon as the crisis was over, Russia began a large-scale reconstruction of its armed forces. The settlement of the Bosnian crisis had only postponed a final showdown between Serbia and Austria-Hungary. When that showdown came, it was already clear what Germany's policy would be. It was Germany's willingness, and even eagerness, to underwrite Austrian action against Serbia – already clearly demonstrated in the crisis of 1908–9 – which, in August 1914, was to be the immediate cause of the First World War.

The naval arms-race

During the last five years before the outbreak of war two sources of European tension dominated all the rest: the Balkan rivalry between Austria and Serbia (and Serbia's protector, Russia) and the naval rivalry between Britain and Germany. Naval rivalry, unlike Balkan rivalry, did not cause a European war, but it did much to explain British participation in it.

Until the first Moroccan crisis the new German battle fleet had posed only a symbolic threat to British naval supremacy. The new fleet had succeeded in making Britain suspicious but not really apprehensive. The sheer size of the Royal Navy made it impossible, for the foreseeable future, to

envisage any real rival to it. Or so it seemed until the launching of the new British battleship *Dreadnought* in 1906. By its size and firepower the *Dreadnought* made all other battleships obsolete. With ten twelve-inch guns, each with a range of more than eight miles, it was more than a match for any two of its predecessors. Overnight the Royal Navy, like every other navy in the world, discovered that it was out of date.

The launching of the *Dreadnought* gave a new and more dangerous dimension to naval rivalry between Britain and Germany. The discovery by the British public that British naval supremacy was no longer secure was a traumatic experience. Almost inevitably, rumours spread that Germany was planning a secret acceleration of its naval programme which, within a few years, would give it more dreadnoughts than the Royal Navy. By the final stages of the Bosnian crisis in the spring of 1909 British public opinion had been roused to a state of almost frenzied agitation. Asquith's government, which had originally intended to build only four dreadnoughts during the next year, was assailed by the slogan 'We want eight and we won't wait' and capitulated to it.

Talks between Britain and Germany on methods of slowing down the naval arms race began in August 1909 and continued intermittently for two years. The stumbling block throughout the negotiations was

Germany's insistence that a naval agreement be accompanied by a political agreement. This was to bind each power to observe 'a benevolent neutrality' if the other went to war with other powers. To Britain it seemed increasingly clear that Germany's real aim in the negotiations was to destroy the Triple Entente. The slim prospect of a compromise agreement that still remained after nearly two years' negotiation was destroyed altogether by Germany's action in provoking the Agadir crisis in the summer of 1911.

Early in 1911 the Sultan of Morocco was forced to appeal for French troops in order to protect himself against a rebellion by his subjects. It soon became clear that a French protectorate would not be long delayed. Kiderlen, the German foreign minister, concluded that some dramatic gesture was necessary to make France offer Germany compensation for its absorption of Morocco. In his own words: 'It is necessary to thump the table, but the only object is to make the French negotiate.' Kiderlen's method of thumping the table was to send a gunboat to the Moroccan port of Agadir, allegedly for the protection of German citizens whose lives might be endangered by the Moroccan rising. Unfortunately, as A. J. P. Taylor has observed, the nearest German was at the more northerly port of Mogador. He was therefore ordered to proceed to Agadir at once, in order to put

Above, The Sure Shield of Britain and Her Empire, *painting dating from about 1914.*

Opposite, illustration from the Illustrated London News *of 21 September 1912 of 'the German Navy as it will be in the Near Future': the artist based his forecast on the provision recently made in a new German Navy Law for an increase in the size of the fleet. Command of the sea was essential for the survival of Britain and her empire and it was this German naval challenge above all other issues that alarmed both the government and public opinion in Britain.*

himself in danger and so justify the sending of a gunboat. The crisis was ended in November 1911 by a compromise. Germany agreed to recognize a French protectorate in Morocco and received a large slice of the French Congo in exchange.

Public reaction to this agreement was striking evidence of the serious worsening in Franco-German relations since the first Moroccan crisis of 1905. In 1905 most Germans had been indifferent to Morocco and most Frenchmen had been in favour of making concessions to Germany. In 1911, however, public opinion in both France and Germany was indignant at the conclusion of a compromise settlement. In Germany the minister of colonies resigned over the agreement, and attacks on it were ostentatiously applauded by the Crown Prince. To his fury the Kaiser found himself accused of loss of nerve for having let the settlement go through. In France public hostility to the treaty led to the overthrow of the government which had concluded it and to the rise to power, first as prime minister and then as president, of Raymond Poincaré, one of the leading advocates of a tough policy towards Germany.

The Agadir crisis was interpreted in Britain, like the first Moroccan crisis in 1905, as yet another German attempt to destroy the Entente Cordiale by a war of nerves against France. At the height of the crisis British and French chiefs of staff discussed, for the first time, the transfer of British troops to France to meet a German attack. At the same time Lloyd George, the chancellor of the exchequer, hitherto considered the most pro-German member of Asquith's cabinet, delivered the strongest public warning to Germany so far given by a British statesman. The British government, he said, would prefer war to a peace achieved 'by allowing Britain to be treated as if she were of no account in the cabinet of nations'. The British public believed that Germany had intended to make war on France and that Lloyd George's warning had stopped the German army in its tracks. The inevitable result of the passions aroused by the Agadir crisis was an intensification of Anglo-German naval rivalry. In Germany Tirpitz, the architect of the new German battle fleet, was able to use the crisis to push through a new German navy law. Britain replied with an enlarged naval programme of her own and a naval agreement with France.

The Balkan wars

The Agadir crisis led, by a roundabout route, to war in the Balkans. Italy took advantage of the crisis to begin an attack on Libya, now all that remained of the former Turkish empire on the north coast of Africa. In itself the Italian conquest of Libya was only a minor episode in the history of European imperialism. But, by making plain the unexpected extent of Turkey's military

vulnerability, it provided a powerful stimulus to the territorial ambitions of the Balkan states, anxious to divide between them what remained of Turkey's European empire. Bulgaria, Greece and Serbia temporarily set aside their differences, formed the Balkan League and declared war on Turkey in October 1912. The extent of their successes took the whole of Europe by surprise. After an illness lasting 150 years, European Turkey, the 'sick man of Europe', suddenly expired.

The First Balkan War, however, only strengthened the rivalries among the Balkan states themselves. It was followed in 1913 by a Second Balkan War in which the victors of the first fell out among themselves. In this war Serbia and Greece, the protégés of Russia, defeated Bulgaria, the protégé of Austria. Berchtold, who had succeeded Aehrenthal as Austrian foreign minister, declared at the beginning of the war: 'In view of the open hostility of Serbia towards us, a further material and moral strengthening of Serbia at the expense of Bulgaria would be absolutely contrary to our interests.' Yet this was precisely what the Second Balkan War achieved. It thus strengthened still further Austria's determination to put an end to the Serbian menace. Once again, the Kaiser reaffirmed Germany's readiness to support whatever action against Serbia Austria thought necessary. 'You can be certain', he told Berchtold, 'that I stand behind you, ready to draw sword whenever your action makes it necessary.'

The Sarajevo crisis

Bismarck had predicted, long ago, that the immediate cause of the next European war would be 'some damned foolish thing in the Balkans'. His prophecy was fulfilled by the murder of the Archduke Francis Ferdinand

at the Bosnian capital of Sarajevo on 28 June 1914. Francis Ferdinand had chosen as the date for his visit St Vitus' Day, the Serbian national festival. The effect on Serbian opinion has been compared to the likely effect in Ireland of a visit to Dublin on St Patrick's Day by a British monarch at the height of the Irish troubles. The Archduke and his wife only narrowly escaped a bomb attack soon after their arrival in Sarajevo. They were killed early in the afternoon while on their way to visit an officer wounded during the first assassination attempt a few hours earlier. The assassin, Gavrilo Princip, was a nineteen-year-old Bosnian, the first student revolutionary to change the course of European history.

Though Princip was an Austrian subject, the assassination had been planned in Serbia by a Serbian terrorist organization, the 'Union of Death' (better known as the 'Black Hand'), dedicated, as its name implies, to achieving the union of all South Slavs under the Serbian crown. Francis Ferdinand was selected as its victim, not merely because he was the heir to the throne of Austria-Hungary, but also, paradoxically, because he stood for a policy of conciliation towards the South Slavs of the Austrian Empire. He intended, once he became emperor, to offer the South Slavs an autonomy similar to that already enjoyed by the Magyars. Such a scheme was probably impracticable. The 'Black Hand', however, feared that it might succeed. If it did, it would end all hope of a united South Slav state. Francis Ferdinand was killed because, in his assassin's words, 'as future sovereign he would have prevented our union and carried out certain reforms which would have been clearly against our interests.'

Throughout the Sarajevo crisis the Austrian government possessed no proof whatever of Serbian complicity in the assassination. Even the existence of the 'Black Hand' was not discovered until much later. Conrad, nonetheless, insisted that the time had come for the Serbian nest of vipers' to be finally destroyed. Berchtold, after some hesitation, rallied to his view. The final decision of peace or war, however, rested not with the Austrian but with the German government. Even Conrad recognized that war with Serbia was out of the question unless Austria possessed a guarantee of German support.

Germany, however, not merely promised Austria support but urged it to lose no time in launching an attack. 'The Serbs', wrote the Kaiser, 'must be wiped out and quickly too.' Germany believed that Austria's survival as a great power was essential to its own security: and, in the opinion of both the Kaiser and his government, Austria could not remain a great power unless it dealt with Serbia. 'The maintenance of Austria, and in fact of the most powerful Austria possible', said Jagow, the foreign minister, 'is a necessity for us.'

But Germany's belligerence was not solely

dictated by concern for Austria-Hungary. Each succeeding crisis had strengthened the feeling in Berlin – as in other European capitals – that war between the two alliances was, sooner or later, inevitable. In the summer of 1914, German generals were agreed that now was the time to fight. 'Any delay', argued Moltke, 'means a worsening in our chances.' The alacrity with which the German government adopted the aim of a German *Mitteleuropa* once the war had started suggests, however, that Germany was not simply thinking in terms of a preventive war. Only through war could the frustrated ambitions of *Weltpolitik* hope to find fulfilment. The German writer, Plehn, wrote in 1913: 'It is an almost universal belief throughout the country that we shall only win our freedom to participate in world politics through a major European war.' Germany's ambitions did not cause the Sarajevo crisis, but once the crisis had arisen they inevitably conditioned its response to it.

Both Austria and Germany were careful to throw a smoke screen over their intentions. Early in July the Kaiser sent birthday greetings to the King of Serbia and left for his annual cruise off Scandinavia in his steam yacht. For almost a month after the assassination most European statesmen assumed that the crisis between Austria and Serbia would be settled without war. By mid-July the crisis was no longer headline news. English newspaper readers were more concerned with events in Ireland and French newspaper readers with the trial of a former prime minister's wife, accused of shooting a newspaper editor who had threatened to publish her husband's correspondence with his mistress. As late as 23 July, Lloyd George was confidently forecasting both 'substantial economies' in naval expenditure and a world-wide reaction against the growth of armaments. He told the House of Commons:

I cannot help thinking that civilization which is able to deal with disputes among individuals and small communities at home, and is able to regulate these by means of some sane and well-ordered arbitrament should be able to extend its operations to the larger sphere of disputes between states.

The approach to war

In the evening of 23 July, while Lloyd George was still speaking to the Commons, Austria delivered an ultimatum to Serbia, based on an assumption of Serbian responsibility for the assassination and making demands which were intended to be unacceptable. Serbia's refusal of these demands was intended to provide a pretext for war. To Austria's astonishment – and embarrassment – Serbia accepted, either outright or with reservations, all but one of Austria's demands. 'A great moral victory for Vienna!', wrote the Kaiser, when he learned of the reply, 'but with it every reason for war drops away.'

Though the Kaiser was beginning to have second thoughts, however, the German government continued to press Austria for an immediate declaration of war in order to make mediation impossible. In response to German pressure Austria formally declared war on Serbia on 28 July, a fortnight earlier than it had intended. The Kaiser's view that war was now unnecessary was passed on to Vienna by the German Foreign Office only when it was too late. Bethmann-Hollweg, the German chancellor, had no intention of trying to avert a war. He recognized that an Austrian war with Serbia would mean a European war with France and Russia but was confident of victory.

Bethmann-Hollweg, however, had counted on obtaining British neutrality. Only on 30 July, when he learned that it was not to be secured on the terms offered by Germany, did Bethmann-Hollweg at last make a serious attempt to restrain Austria. He urged Austria to halt its forces at Belgrade and agree to talks with Russia. By now, however, it was too late to hold Austria back. Nor was Germany speaking with a single voice. While Bethmann-Hollweg was counselling moderation, Moltke was telegraphing Conrad: 'Mobilize against Russia at once. Germany will follow suit.'

Even Bethmann-Hollweg's eleventh-hour attempt to hold Austria back was not wholly dictated by a desire to preserve the peace. He was also concerned – perhaps mainly concerned – to fix on Russia the responsibility for transforming a local war with Serbia into a continental war between the great powers of Europe. If Russia were the

first to mobilize its forces for a continental war, Bethmann-Hollweg believed it would be possible for Germany to brand Russia as the aggressor.

Russia went to war against Austria, as Austria went to war against Serbia, because it believed that its status as a great power left it no alternative. Just as Austria believed that it could not remain a great power without war with Serbia, so Russia believed that it could not remain a great power if it abandoned Serbia. On 30 July Russia became, as Bethmann-Hollweg had hoped, the first of the great powers to order general mobilization. This decision, however, reflected less a desire for war than a consciousness of its own military inferiority. Russia was well aware that its mobilization would be much slower, and less efficient, than that of Germany. Unlike Germany, therefore, Russia could not take the risk of allowing its opponents to be the first to mobilize.

Once Russia had decided to mobilize, control of German policy passed from the statesmen to the soldiers. The only plan of campaign which the German high command possessed was that devised by General Schlieffen ten years before. The Schlieffen Plan assumed (wrongly as it turned out) that Germany's only chance of victory in a war on two fronts was to win a quick victory over France by a sweep through Belgium before Russia was ready for war in the east. Once Russia had begun to mobilize, therefore, the Schlieffen Plan made it essential for war to begin without delay.

On 31 July Germany issued an ultimatum to Russia to demobilize within twelve hours. When this was refused, Germany declared

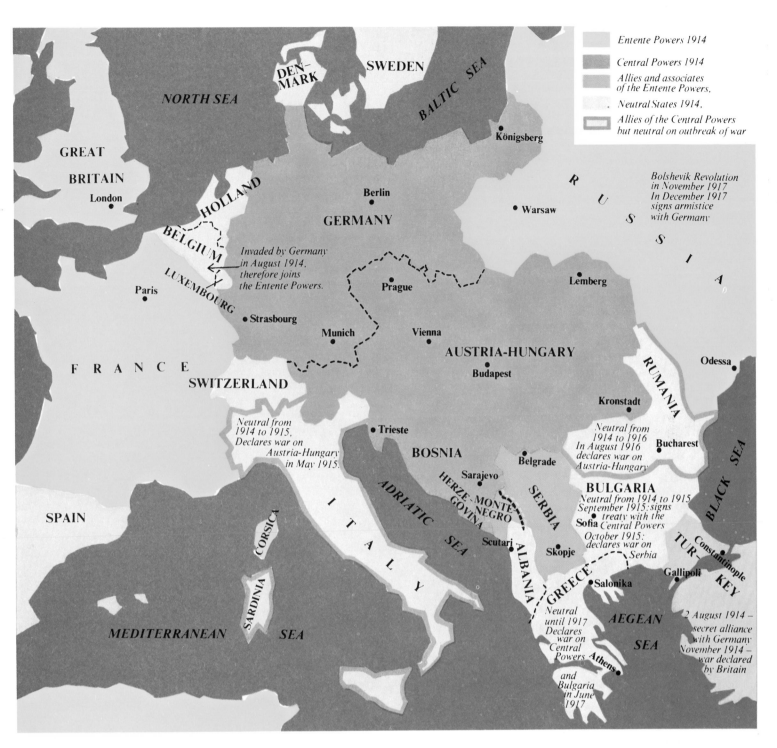

NORTH SEA

DEN-
MARK

SWEDEN

BALTIC SEA

GREAT
BRITAIN

London

HOLLAND

BELGIUM

LUXEMBOURG

Paris

Strasbourg

FRANCE

SWITZERLAND

Berlin

GERMANY

*Invaded by Germany
in August 1914,
therefore joins
the Entente Powers.*

Munich

Prague

Vienna

AUSTRIA-HUNGARY

Budapest

Warsaw

Lemberg

R
U
S
S
I
A

Königsberg

*Bolshevik Revolution
in November 1917
In December 1917
signs armistice
with Germany*

Odessa

RUMANIA

Kronstadt

Bucharest

*Neutral from
1914 to 1916
In August 1916
declares war on
Austria-Hungary*

*Neutral from
1914 to 1915.
Declares war on
Austria-Hungary
in May 1915.*

Trieste

BOSNIA

Sarajevo

HERZE-
GOVINA

MONTE-
NEGRO

Belgrade

SERBIA

Scutari

ALBANIA

Skopje

GREECE

*Neutral
until 1917
Declares
war on
Central
Powers*

Athens

*and
Bulgaria
in June
1917*

BULGARIA

*Neutral from 1914 to 1915
September 1915: signs
treaty with the
Central Powers*

Sofia

*October 1915:
declares war on
Serbia*

BLACK SEA

TUR-
KEY

Constantinople

Gallipoli

*2 August 1914 –
secret alliance
with Germany
November 1914 –
war declared
by Britain*

SPAIN

CORSICA

SARDINIA

ITALY

ADRIATIC
SEA

Salonika

AEGEAN
SEA

MEDITERRANEAN   SEA

war on 1 August. Two days later, on 3 August, Germany declared war on France, using the trumped-up pretext of French violations of the German frontier. Britain's last doubts about intervention were removed by the German ultimatum to Belgium, demanding free passage for an invasion of France. Britain replied with an ultimatum of her own, demanding German respect for Belgian neutrality. When Germany failed to reply, Britain entered the war at midnight on 4 August.

After forty-three years of peace the great powers of Europe went joyfully to war. Crowds in all the five main European capitals greeted the declaration of war with delirious enthusiasm. The social and political conflicts of the pre-war years seemed to be forgotten in the enthusiasm of the

moment. In Germany the Kaiser told cheering crowds, 'I see no more parties, I see only Germans.' In France all parties buried their differences in the *Union sacrée*. Even in Russia, the wave of strikes which had paralysed Russian industry in the spring and summer of 1914 ceased almost overnight. The Second International, which had sought to replace national rivalries by the international solidarity of the European working class, sank without a trace. Often, it was the young and idealistic who greeted war with the greatest enthusiasm. Peace had come to seem unheroic and they were bored by it, hoping to discover in war a sense of purpose lacking before. All over Europe a generation echoed the English poet, Rupert Brooke: 'Now God be thanked, Who has matched us with His hour.'

Above, Europe on the eve of the First World War.

Opposite top and centre, the last days of peace: citizens of Budapest read the mobilization order and Londoners demonstrate outside the War Office. How many of these, who confidently expected to be home from the front by Christmas, survived the four years' slaughter?

Opposite bottom, the first days of war: newly mobilized troops on their way to the front, a sight repeated in every town throughout Europe.

Chapter 49

The First World War

Almost no-one, in August 1914, had any idea of what war would be like. There had been moments in the decade before the war when at least some generals had had a premonition of what lay in store for them. Moltke had spoken in 1905 of 'a war that, even should we be victorious, will push our people to the limits of exhaustion'. Joffre, the French commander-in-chief, had spoken in 1912 of a war which might be 'of indefinite duration'. These fears seemed to be forgotten in August 1914. No country possessed plans for a war of more than a few months. Most generals on both sides thought such plans unnecessary. 'You will be home', the Kaiser told the German army, 'before the leaves have fallen from the trees.' Only Kitchener, recalled to become secretary of state for war on the day that Britain entered the conflict, foresaw a war which would involve millions of men and take years to decide.

And yet, on the Western Front at least, the war was almost won and lost within the space of one campaign. In both 1870 and 1940 the French were routed by the Germans in six weeks. The same thing very nearly happened in 1914. Though Joffre knew of the Schlieffen plan, he did not take it seriously. While the Germans were struggling through Belgium, the French would pour across the frontier into the heart of Germany. The whole French army in August 1914 shared Joffre's sublime confidence in attack. While the British and Germans tried to make themselves inconspicuous in khaki and field-grey, the French sought to make themselves as conspicuous as possible. Confident that their *élan* would shatter the enemy's nerve, their infantry went to battle in blue overcoats and red pantaloons. 'The French army', said its Field Regulations, 'knows no law but the offensive.' French *élan*, however, was no match for German firepower. The French assault on the German frontier ended in a series of disasters, collectively known as the Battles of the Frontiers. Unable to comprehend what had gone wrong, Joffre blamed the defeats on 'a lack of offensive spirit'.

The Germans, meanwhile, had swept through Belgium and were advancing into northern France. By early September they had reached the Marne, Paris was in a panic and the French government had left for Bordeaux. The very speed of its advance, however, had led the German army to over-reach itself. Corps commanders were often out of touch both with headquarters and with one another. Moltke hardly knew where his armies were for days on end. Instead of enveloping Paris, as Moltke had planned, the German army wheeled to the southeast, leaving its flank exposed to a brilliantly successful counterattack on the Marne by the Paris garrison.

Some historians have since concluded that the Schlieffen Plan was doomed from the beginning. The French, however, believed that they had been saved only by a miracle: 'the miracle of the Marne'. Perhaps the crucial factor in the German failure was that Moltke had been forced, at a critical stage of the French campaign, to transfer two army corps to the Eastern Front to meet an unexpected Russian attack in East Prussia. The miracle of the Marne was won as much in East Prussia as on the Marne itself.

The Western Front

The 'miracle of the Marne' was followed by a race to the sea, each side trying, unsuccessfully, to turn the other's flank before the sea was reached. Though Germany had failed to win a quick victory, it still retained the initiative in the war. When the race to the sea was over, Germany remained in control of one-tenth of France's territory, eighty percent of its coal and almost the whole of its iron ore. For the next three and a half years Germany was usually content to remain on the defensive behind an impregnable line of

trenches, against which the Allied armies battered in vain. At no time before the spring of 1918 did the front lines established during the race to the sea in 1914 vary in depth by as much as ten miles. 'The Western Front', wrote Robert Graves, 'was known among its embittered inhabitants as the Sausage Machine because it was fed with live men, churned out corpses, and remained firmly screwed in place.'

The reason for this stalemate was technological. The invention of barbed wire and the machine gun had given a temporary, but overwhelming, advantage to the defence. Only a further technological advance could turn the advantage once more in favour of attack. Some historians have argued that by the end of 1916 the invention of the tank already provided just such a technological advance and that only the blindness of both the French and British high commands

Above, a Cossack regiment on the march, September 1914: Russian casualties were enormous (3,800,000 in the first ten months of the war alone); so too were territorial losses, accompanied by mounting administrative and economic chaos.

Left, a German field telephone exchange in the trenches, where for four years men endured in unspeakable conditions, fighting for a few yards of devastated land.

Below left, wearing masks to shield themselves from possible gas attacks, British troops go 'over the top'.

Opposite top, British troops parade through Ypres, mid-October 1914, shortly before British and German forces, each hoping to outflank the other, met and fought an inconclusive battle; now the battleline was complete from Switzerland to the Belgian coast.

Opposite bottom, General Lord Kitchener (1850–1916), British secretary for war from August 1914: his face, familiar from countless recruiting posters, brought hundreds of thousands of eager volunteers to the colours.

prevented them from achieving a breakthrough. Until the closing months of the war, however, tanks were too deficient, both in quality and quantity, to end the stalemate on the Western Front. Even at their greatest victory, the Battle of Amiens, in August 1918, 270 of a total of 415 tanks were destroyed in one day's fighting. Deadlock in the west continued for so long not because generals were more incompetent than in the past but, quite simply, because they lacked the means to break it.

'The German lines in France', wrote Kitchener at the beginning of 1915, 'may be looked on as a fortress that cannot be carried by assault.' With the exception of Kitchener, however, most Allied generals were confident of an early breakthrough. The greatest criticism that can be levelled at the Allied commanders on the Western Front is not that they failed to make this

breakthrough but that they refused for so long, against all the evidence, to recognize the enormous strength of the enemy's position.

Joffre's plan to win the war in 1915 was for a gigantic pincer movement against the German lines, Anglo-French forces attacking in Artois and the French alone further south in Champagne. Offensives on these fronts continued intermittently throughout the year, none achieving an advance of more than three miles. At the end of the year Joffre comforted himself with the thought that, even if the Germans had yet to be defeated, they were being worn down by a war of attrition. Pinning his faith in inflated estimates of German losses, he refused, like most other Allied generals (and many later historians), to accept the simple truth that a war of attrition on the Western Front was bound to bear most heavily on the attacker. In fact, French and English losses in 1915 were almost double those of Germany: probably 1,600,000 killed and wounded as against 850,000 of the enemy.

Enormous though these losses were, they were surpassed by even greater losses in the east. In 1915 Falkenhayn, the new German commander-in-chief, had chosen to remain on the defensive in the west, while launching his main offensive in the east. In five months, between May and September 1915, Russia lost a million men in prisoners alone, at least a million more (perhaps far more) in killed and wounded and more territory than the whole area of France. Judging by size alone, Falkenhayn had won what has been called 'the greatest battle in history'. But it was not, and could not be, a decisive victory. Though the Russians had been forced to retreat three hundred miles,

they were left with a shorter line to defend and still possessed vast reserves of manpower. In the east, as in the west, 1915 ended in deadlock.

Verdun

The plan of campaign devised by the Allies for 1916 simply proposed to repeat the mistakes of 1915 on a larger scale. Joffre convinced himself and many others that, on the Western Front at least, the Allies had been on the verge of a breakthrough in 1915, robbed of a victory only by a lack of heavy guns and ammunition. Next year, with plenty of munitions and the first British conscript armies, things would be different. As soon as sufficient shells were available, Haig told *The Times* correspondent, 'we could walk through the German lines at several places'. To make sure of victory in 1916 it was agreed to launch all-out offensives simultaneously on both the Western and the Eastern Fronts. Italy, which had entered the war on the side of the Allies in 1915, would join in with an attack on Austria from the south.

Falkenhayn's plan for victory was much more subtle. He proposed to win the war not by defeating the enemy in battle but by bleeding him to death – a new and ingenious addition to the theory of warfare. The power on whom Falkenhayn proposed to perform this experiment was France:

Within our reach behind the French sector of the Western Front there are objectives for the retention of which the French General Staff would be compelled to throw in every man they have. If they do so, the forces of France will bleed to death – as there can be no question of voluntary withdrawal – whether we reach our goal or not.

Falkenhayn selected as his target the great French fortress of Verdun, already half encircled by German lines and one of the few places on the Western Front where the defenders seemed to be at a disadvantage. German communications to the Verdun salient were excellent, and their heavy guns had closed all French routes to the fortress, except for one light railway and one road, which became known as the *voie sacrée*. Throughout the Battle of Verdun supply remained as great a problem as the fighting itself. For months 3,000 lorries passed every day along the *voie sacrée* carrying 20,000 men and 4,000 tons of supplies.

The Battle of Verdun became, as Falkenhayn had intended, the supreme symbol of attrition even in a war of attrition. It lasted ten months, from February to November 1916, longer than any battle had ever lasted before. In no other battle in the history of warfare have so many died on so small an area of ground. As the battle progressed, however, it became increasingly clear that Falkenhayn had made one fatal miscalculation. 'Germany is perfectly free', he had written, 'to accelerate or draw out the offensive, to intensify it or to break it off from time to time as suits its purpose.'

Left, the western and Italian fronts during the
First World War.

Above and opposite top left and right, First
World War recruiting posters from Australia and
Great Britain.

Opposite bottom, French survivors from the
Battle of Verdun.

Map labels:

NORTH SEA

HOLLAND

Amiens

Ypres

Brussels
BELGIUM

Somme

Paris

Oise

Meuse

Liège

LUXEMBOURG

Rheims

Moselle

Seine

Marne

Verdun

Rhine

Strasbourg

Only Allied
occupation of
German territory
1914-1918

GERMANY

FRANCE

SWITZERLAND

Milan

MEDITERRANEAN
SEA

A U S T R I A

Po

Piave

Venice

Caporetto

I T A L Y

Trieste

ADRIATIC
SEA

Legend:

— Limit of German
advance 1914

--- Limit of German
advance 1918

▬▬▬ Limit of Austrian
advance

••• Armistice Line
November 1918

After the first week of the battle Falkenhayn's freedom of action had disappeared.
Just as French prestige was involved in the
defence of Verdun, so German prestige
increasingly demanded its capture. The
Battle of Verdun ended by bleeding the
German army almost as disastrously as it
bled the French.

Had Germany been able to press home
its attack after the capture of Fort Vaux
on 7 June however, it could, in the opinion
of the historian Alistair Horne, 'almost
certainly have broken through to Verdun'.
In June 1916, as in the other great crisis of the
war in September 1914, the French were
saved by a Russian offensive in the east.

Partly in response to desperate appeals from
France to relieve the pressure on Verdun,
Brusilov, the ablest of the Russian generals,
attacked the Austrians on the southeast front
with forty divisions. Many German officers
had long believed that, by its alliance with
Austria, 'Germany was fettered to a corpse'.
They were confirmed in this opinion by the
spectacular success of the Brusilov offensive.
What began as a diversionary attack rapidly
turned into a rout of the Austrian army
along a three hundred mile front. By the
time German troops arrived to try and
stem the Austrian retreat in September,
Brusilov had taken almost half a million
prisoners.

Despite its ultimate failure, the Brusilov offensive had far-reaching consequences on both the Eastern and Western Fronts. In the east it brought nearer the disintegration of the Austrian Empire. In the west it changed the course of the battle for Verdun. At a crucial moment, Falkenhayn was forced to divert to the Eastern Front divisions intended to push home the assault on Verdun. At a time when French reserves were almost exhausted, General Pétain, who had been summoned to the defence of Verdun, was given a vital ten days' breathing space in which to strengthen his defences and bring up fresh troops. When the Germans were able to resume their offensive, on 22 June, their chance of victory had gone.

The Somme offensive

Verdun was a turning point in the history of the Western Front. From now on, the main burden of the fighting passed from France to Britain. The French had been so weakened at Verdun that they were no longer capable of assuming the major role in the planned summer offensive on the Somme. When the battle began on 1 July the French contingent had been reduced by Verdun from forty to fourteen divisions alongside Haig's twenty-five. Yet what successes were achieved on the first day of the offensive were mainly because of the French. The latter moved swiftly in small groups supported by machine guns, using methods learnt from the Germans at Verdun, and overran most of the German front line. The British, weighed down by sixty-six pound packs, advanced at walking pace in even lines, presenting the German machine guns with their best target of the war. As one line was cut down, so others came on, regularly spaced at intervals of a hundred

yards. On 1 July the British lost almost 60,000 men killed and wounded in a single day, more than on any other day in the history of the British army and greater, too, than the losses suffered by any other army on any day of the First World War.

Neither Haig nor any of his staff officers had any idea of the extent of the catastrophe that had befallen them. Haig wrote in his diary on the following day: 'The enemy has undoubtedly been severely shaken. Our correct course, therefore, is to press him hard with the least possible delay.' The Battle of the Somme was to last five months. Only when the winter rains had reduced the battleground to a wilderness of mud was Haig, at last, forced to call a halt. When the battle ended, though the front line had here and there advanced about five miles, some of the objectives set for the first day's offensive had still not been achieved. Like Joffre after the Battle of Champagne a year before, Haig comforted himself with the

delusion, strengthened by inflated estimates of enemy casualties, that the Somme had been successful as a battle of attrition. 'The results of the Somme', he wrote, 'fully justify confidence in our ability to master the enemy's power of resistance.'

The wars that are won', it has been said, never are the wars that were begun.' Wars, once begun, invariably generate war aims for which the combatants would never at the outset have gone to battle. Thus it was after 1914, Russia would not have started a war to capture Constantinople and the Straits, nor Germany for the creation of a Belgian satellite, nor France for the recovery of Alsace-Lorraine. Yet once they had gone to war for other reasons, all these ambitions, and others like them, were swiftly adopted as war aims. And war aims multiplied still further as each side struggled to win over neutrals or retain existing allies by territorial bribes.

Italy's entry into the war in 1915 was preceded by a protracted auction in which each side competed for its favours and Italy played off one against the other. Much the same process preceded the entry of Bulgaria on the side of the Central Powers in 1915 and Romania on the side of the Allies a year later, though – like Italy – neither significantly influenced the outcome of the war.

Despite the stalemate in the war at the end of 1916, despite the growing exhaustion on each side, the extent of the war aims of each alliance condemned attempts to arrange a compromise peace to inevitable failure. Neither side was prepared to accept anything approaching a return to the status quo of July 1914, though both were understandably reluctant to reveal the full extent of their ambitions.

There was one further reason why a compromise peace was impossible. The French writer, de Tocqueville, had long ago predicted that though democracies might be reluctant to involve themselves in war, once embarked on war they would not readily make peace. In an age of mass education, the people of Europe were no longer content to accept the pretexts which for centuries had served as an excuse for war. They needed to believe, instead, that they were involved in a moral crusade to protect civilization itself. Only such a cause could justify the millions of lives whose sacrifice the war demanded. To bolster its belief in the rightness of its cause, each side convinced itself of the wickedness of its opponent. The people of Britain swiftly came to credit Germans with an enormous variety of mythical atrocities: priests hung as clappers in cathedral bells, crucified prisoners of war and children with their hands cut off. With so evil an enemy a compromise peace must be unthinkable. As Lloyd George put it shortly before he succeeded Asquith as prime minister in December 1916: 'The fight must be to a finish – to a knock-out.'

The war at sea

Britain possessed two decisive advantages over Germany at sea. The first was the size of her fleet: the British battle fleet – the 'Grand Fleet'– had thirty-one dreadnoughts against Germany's eighteen. Britain's strategic advantages were equally great. The fact that the British Isles lay between German ports and the seaways of the world meant that the German High Seas fleet could venture into the Atlantic only at the risk of having its retreat cut off – a risk it dare not take. For sixteen years the Germans had been building a fleet with which to challenge British supremacy at sea. When war came they dared not make the challenge. For almost two years the German battle fleet stayed cooped up in the Baltic, with only occasional sorties by detachments into the North Sea.

Yet the Grand Fleet did possess two serious weaknesses which the Germans failed either to detect or exploit. First, the fact that the fleet was based in the north at Scapa Flow and Rosyth made it impossible to offer real protection to the troop carriers taking British forces to the Western Front. Jellicoe, the commander of the Grand Fleet, later admitted that the German fleet 'could have stood a good chance of making the attack [on the troop carriers] and returning to his base before the [British] fleet could intervene'.

The second great weakness of the Grand Fleet was its lack, either at Rosyth or Scapa Flow, of a really secure naval base. Throughout the early stages of the war Jellicoe was constantly preoccupied by the danger of submarine attack. In November 1914 a false sighting of an enemy submarine off Scapa Flow actually succeeded in putting the Grand Fleet to flight. Once the war was over, Jellicoe himself expressed surprise that Germany had not attempted an attack on the Grand Fleet while it lay in harbour: 'It may have seemed impossible to the German mind that we should place our Fleet, on which the Empire depended for its very existence, in a position where it was open to submarine and destroyer attack.'

In past European wars Britain had traditionally used its command of the seas to land its forces at the most vulnerable point of the enemy's coastline. In accordance with this strategy the Admiralty had drawn up plans before 1914 for an amphibious assault on Germany's Baltic coast. Once the war began, however, the overwhelming demands of the Western Front forced Britain to follow a continental rather than a maritime strategy. The only large-scale amphibious operation launched by Britain during the war was the Gallipoli campaign of 1915. Its principal purpose was to force the Straits and re-establish a supply route to Russia, with whom communications had been broken by Turkey's entry into the war on the side of the Central Powers.

From first to last, however, the operation

was terribly bungled. An unsuccessful attempt by the Royal Navy, in February 1915, to force the Straits without the use of troops sacrificed the crucial advantage of surprise and allowed the Turks time in which to dig themselves in. Churchill himself later claimed, probably correctly, that: 'Three divisions in February could have occupied the Gallipoli peninsula with little fighting.'

By the time the first Allied landings were made in April, however, seven divisions were insufficient. Thereafter, reinforcements were either too few or failed to arrive in time. 'We have', said Churchill in June, 'always sent two-thirds of what was necessary a month too late.' Though fighting on the peninsula continued for the rest of the year, the operation had finally to be abandoned and Allied troops evacauted in December. The failure at Gallipoli had important consequences. By being interpreted as a failure of design, rather than a failure of execution, it discredited the whole policy of amphibious operations for the remainder of the war. And it seemed to clinch the argument of those who claimed that the only route to victory lay on the Western Front.

In Europe itself, the Royal Navy played a less direct part in the fighting than in previous European wars. Outside Europe, however, it won the war. The fact that Germany lost naval contact with its overseas empire meant that its colonies could be picked off one by one by Britain and its allies. Samoa and New Guinea fell to Australia and New Zealand within little more than a month of the outbreak of war. Early in November 1914 Japan, which entered the war as an ally of Britain, captured the German naval base at Kiaochow.

Above, troops and their horses on the beach at Suvla Bay, August 1915: the failure of the Gallipoli offensive, which might have removed Turkey from the war and would have opened a new supply route to Russia, meant that from now on the generals could pursue trench warfare on the western front undistracted by campaigns elsewhere.

Opposite top, the front line at Ovillers, July 1916, during the Battle of the Somme, in which the Allies gained ten miles and lost 600,000 men.

Opposite bottom, field hospital during the Battle of the Somme.

Togoland fell to the British, German South West Africa to the South Africans and the Cameroun, after an eighteen-month campaign, to English, French and Belgian forces advancing from three sides. Only in German East Africa, the largest and richest of the German colonies, did a commander of genius, General von Lettow-Vorbeck, succeed in continuing a guerrilla resistance until the end of the war.

The 'sideshows' in the German colonies, like other 'sideshows' nearer home, in Mesopotamia or at Salonika, had little influence on the outcome of the war in Europe. Even the fate of the German overseas empire was finally decided, not in the German colonies themselves, but on the Western Front. The true importance of the sideshows outside Europe – their impact on the growth of nationalism in India, China and Japan (and, to a far lesser extent, in Africa) became apparent only after the war was over.

In Europe itself the main function of the Royal Navy was to impose a naval blockade on Germany and its allies. Britain claimed the right to stop and search any ship suspected of making for German ports. Neutral countries bordering on Germany even had quotas imposed upon their imports, for fear that some of these might find their way to Germany. The United States protested that Britain was violating the freedom of the seas; but it protested more vigorously still against Germany's attempt to counter-

blockade Britain by the use of mines and submarines.

In April 1915 the British liner *Lusitania* was torpedoed by a German submarine and sank with the loss of 1,200 lives, of whom more than a hundred were American citizens. The reaction of American public opinion was so violent (and so well exploited by British propaganda) that Germany was deterred for the next two years from continuing unrestricted U-boat warfare.

The war at sea, like the war on land, defied most men's expectations. Instead of ending in the naval Armaggedon which both sides had expected, the war became instead a war of attrition aimed, not at destroying the enemy's fleet, but at destroying its economy and starving its civilian population into submission. The two great battle fleets, the source of so much pre-war rivalry, began to seem almost irrelevant.

In spring 1916, however, the growing success of the British blockade persuaded Admiral von Scheer, the new commander of the German High Seas Fleet, to make Germany's first direct challenge to British naval supremacy. Scheer's plan was to lure a part of the Grand Fleet into battle and then suddenly confront it with the whole of the German High Seas Fleet. On 31 May 1916 a decoy force under Admiral Hipper (followed at a distance by Scheer himself) succeeded in making contact with a British squadron commanded by Admiral Beatty. The battle which followed began very badly

for Britain. As Beatty himself laconically remarked, 'There seems to be something wrong with our bloody ships today.' In little more than half an hour two of his six battle-cruisers had been sunk and his flagship seriously damaged. At this point, however, Beatty himself became a decoy. Turning north, apparently in flight, he succeeded in luring Scheer towards the whole of the Grand Fleet. Suddenly, Scheer found himself heavily outnumbered. The Royal Navy seemed within sight of a decisive victory.

Jellicoe, however, was acutely conscious that he was, in Churchill's words, 'the only man on either side who could lose the war in an afternoon'. He was doubtful whether even a decisive victory would do much to improve Britain's existing naval supremacy. Starting from such premises, Jellicoe was unlikely to take risks. He was deeply concerned, too, by the possibility of serious damage to the Grand Fleet from enemy torpedoes. Ever since the beginning of the war he had been convinced that a pursuit of the German battle fleet would be a hazardous undertaking. In October 1914 he had written in a memorandum to the Admiralty: 'If . . . the enemy battle fleet were to turn away from our advancing fleet, I should assume that the intention was to lead us over mines and submarines and decline to be so drawn.' Twice during the Battle of Jutland the hail of fire from the Grand Fleet forced Scheer to break off the engagement and turn his fleet away. On both occasions a determined pursuit might have led to a decisive British victory. On both occasions Jellicoe refused a pursuit because of the danger of torpedo attack.

When night fell on 31 May, Jellicoe still lay between the German fleet and its home base and hoped for victory on the following day. Scheer, however, had two alternative routes back to base. Tragically, Jellicoe chose to cover the wrong one. Part of the blame for this critical decision lies with Jellicoe himself. Even with the information he possessed, he might have deduced that Scheer was heading for home, under cover of darkness, by the Horn Reef passage off the coast of Denmark.

An even greater share of the blame, however, belongs to the Admiralty. During the night of 31 May a series of signals from the German fleet was intercepted and deciphered in Whitehall. Some of the most important were, inexcusably, never passed on to Jellicoe. 'These errors', claimed Jellicoe later, 'were absolutely fatal, as the information if passed to me would have clearly shown that Scheer was making for the Horn Reef.' When morning came on, the German fleet was safe in Wilhelmshaven and the battle was over.

Both sides claimed the battle of Jutland as a victory: the British on the grounds that they had put the enemy to flight, the Germans on the more convincing grounds that, with a smaller fleet, they had inflicted the greater damage. The Grand Fleet had lost ships totalling 111,980 tons and 6,097 men killed, the Germans 62,233 tons and 2,551 men.

Jutland had shown serious deficiencies both in the construction of British warships and in the training of their crews. In the building of the Grand Fleet armour had been sacrificed to speed and firepower. All three British battlecruisers sunk at Jutland had been lost because their magazines were not protected against flash. Most serious of all was the inability of the Royal Navy to fight at night. German crews were already trained in the use of starshell and the co-ordination of guns and searchlights — techniques which were not adopted by the Royal Navy until ten years after the war had ended. It was the Grand Fleet's ignorance of these techniques which allowed Scheer to make his escape under cover of darkness.

Despite the failings of the Grand Fleet Scheer dared not risk another Jutland. He now concluded that Germany's only hope of surviving the British blockade was to step up her own blockade of Britain. This decision to intensify the German blockade was to lead in 1917 to the resumption of unrestricted U-boat warfare. Scheer was confident that German submarines could bring Britain to her knees before Britain had been able to ruin the German war economy. 'I guarantee', said the chief of the German naval staff, 'that the U-boat war will lead us to victory.' His prediction very nearly proved correct. In April 1917 alone, German U-boats sank 835,000 tons of Allied shipping. Britain's reserves of wheat rapidly diminished to a month and a half's supply. 'There is no good discussing plans for next spring', Jellicoe told the war cabinet in June, 'we cannot go on.' Only the convoy system, forced on the Admiralty by Lloyd George against its wishes, saved Britain from almost certain disaster.

Ultimately, however, the decision to resume unrestricted U-boat warfare was to have even more important consequences on land than on sea. By bringing about the intervention of the United States, it made the war, for the first time, truly a world war.

American intervention

At the beginning of 1917 the United States seemed to have done well out of its neutrality. Its overseas trading surplus had increased from $690 million in 1913 to $3,000 million in 1916. The first three years of the war saw the emergence of no less than 8,000 new American millionaires. The basis of this remarkable prosperity was the dependence of the Allied war economies on massive imports from the United States. While American exports to the Central Powers declined sharply as a result of the British blockade, her exports to France and Britain increased fourfold in two years. To finance their imports from the United States, the Allies were forced to rely on large

American loans. By the end of 1916 the Allied debt stood at almost $2,000 million. As the United States stake in Allies economies increased, so also did its stake in an Allied victory. If the Allies were to lose the war a vast American investment would stand at risk.

Though intervention on the Allied side may have been in the economic interests of the United States there is no convincing evidence that the decision to intervene was taken for economic reasons. There had been no sign, even at the end of 1916, that the United States proposed to abandon her neutrality. Indeed, Woodrow Wilson had been re-elected president in November on a

Above, American wartime recruiting poster.

Opposite, captured 'U' boats at Harwich on England's east coast: in 1917, German U-boat attacks on Allied and neutral shipping brought Britain to the brink of starvation (before the war she had imported 40 percent of her meat, 80 percent of her wheat), staved off only by the institution, in the face of Admiralty opposition, of the convoy system.

programme that proclaimed, 'He kept us out of war'.

Had the Russian revolution of March 1917 come only two months earlier the United States might never have entered the war at all. If Germany, at the beginning of 1917, had been able to foresee the possibility of a quick victory in the east which would allow it to concentrate all its forces on the Western Front, it might well have decided not to take the risks involved in trying to decide the war at sea. As Tirpitz was later to write: 'Had we been able to foresee in Germany the Russian revolution we should not have needed to regard the submarine campaign of 1917 as our last hope. But in January 1917 there was no visible sign of the revolution.'

Germany's decision to begin unrestricted submarine warfare was announced on 1 February 1917. It was followed in March by the sinking of American merchant vessels, without warning and with heavy loss of life. American intervention, as the German government itself realized, was now inevitable. The German Foreign Office, however, devised a comic opera scheme to cripple the American war effort in Europe by concluding a German alliance with Mexico, which, it was hoped, Japan might later be persuaded to join.

Unhappily for Zimmermann, the German foreign minister, a copy of his telegram outlining the terms of this alliance (and offering Texas, New Mexico and Arizona to Mexico as bait) was intercepted by British Intelligence, passed on to the United States government and published in the American press. Its publication caused a greater uproar even than the sinking of the *Lusitania*.

A second reason for America's decision to enter the war was, quite simply, American idealism. 'Sometimes', said Wilson, 'people call me an idealist. Well, that's the way I know I am an American. America, my fellow citizens, . . . is the only idealistic country in the world.' Time and again Wilson had tried as a neutral, without success, to bring the war in Europe to an end by American mediation. His failure had convinced him that the United States could bring its influence to bear, both on the course of the war and on the peace settlement which would follow it, only by being a belligerent. 'The world', Wilson told Congress, 'must be made safe for democracy.'

It was in this spirit that on 6 April 1917 the United States went to war. For many Americans, the news that Russia had overthrown the tsar and joined the ranks of the democracies for whom the world had to be made safe added a further reason for American intervention. 'The preservation and extension of the liberties so rapidly won in Russia', declared the New York *Nation*, 'are now inextricably bound up with the success of the Allies. A German victory would mean the collapse of free Russia.'

Revolution in Russia

Russian radicals had been predicting revolution in Russia ever since the middle of the nineteenth century. Nor was it only the radicals who made predictions. In 1884, the Russian minister of the interior confided to a foreign diplomat that, if tsarism were ever overthrown, its place would be taken by 'the communism of Mr Marx of London who has just died and whose theories I have

studied with much attention and interest'.

Even before 1914, it was already clear that war was the catalyst most likely to lead to revolution. Just as the Crimean War had been followed by the end of serfdom, and the war with Japan by the revolution of 1905, so Russia's involvement in the First World War led to the revolution of March 1917 (known in Russia as the February revolution because the tsarist calendar was thirteen days behind the West's).

By the beginning of 1917 it was clear that both the discontent and dislocation caused by the war were reaching a climax. Russia's casualties already numbered five million (perhaps far more – the government had lost count). On the home front, the cost of living had increased seven-fold since July 1914, and food supplies to the cities were breaking down. During the first two months of 1917 alone there were 1330 strikes, more than in the whole of the previous year. It was one of these strikes in Petrograd, the capital, which developed into the March revolution. The decisive factor in its success was the attitude of the Petrograd garrison. In 1905 the revolution had been broken by the army. In 1917 the army joined the revolution.

On 15 March, the tsar signed an act of abdication and handed over power to a provisional government of liberal politicians. The new government had, however, to contend with a rival authority. First in Petrograd, and then throughout the country, local soviets (councils) were formed, elected by factories and army units and claiming that the provisional government was responsible to them as the true representatives of the Russian people.

Soviet schoolchildren are still brought up on the myth that, in the words of one of their textbooks, 'the Romanovs collapsed under the shattering blows of the people inspired by the Bolshevik party'. In fact, the revolution took the Bolsheviks (the Russian communist party) by surprise. Their leader, Lenin, in exile in Switzerland, had said only a few weeks earlier: 'We, the old, will probably not live to see the decisive battles of the coming revolution.' Even after the March revolution, the Bolshevik following within the soviets lagged far behind that of their two socialist rivals – the Mensheviks and the Social Revolutionaries.

It was through the soviets, none the less – above all, through the Petrograd soviet – that Lenin planned to bring about a Bolshevik Russia. He depicted the rivalry between the soviets and the provisional government as an elemental struggle between the forces of light and darkness, a struggle between the bourgeois order and the revolutionary proletariat. The Bolsheviks must ensure the victory of the soviets in this struggle ('All power to the soviets!') while at the same time winning control of the soviets themselves.

Despite the small size of their following in March 1917, the Bolsheviks possessed one

overwhelming advantage over all their rivals. That advantage was the leadership of Lenin, the greatest political genius in Russian history. Without him, a Bolshevik victory would have been unthinkable.

When Lenin returned from exile in April, he found the Bolsheviks agreed on a policy of 'vigilant control' over the provisional government and contemplating cooperation with the Mensheviks. The first condition of the strategy which Lenin succeeded in imposing on his followers was that, on the contrary, they should adopt a policy of total opposition to the government and refuse all cooperation with other parties. The wisdom of this policy became clear in May when the Mensheviks and Social Revolutionaries joined the provisional government. While their rivals became increasingly compromised by the government's growing unpopularity, the Bolsheviks were able to claim that they alone put forward a truly independent programme.

The Bolshevik programme was based on the three simple slogans – peace, bread and land – which Lenin had formulated on his return from exile. No party could be against bread but, until Lenin's return, the Bolsheviks had been committed to neither peace nor land. Lenin himself had spoken many times in the past in favour of the nationalization of land as well as industry. The proposal that large estates be shared among the peasantry, which Lenin put forward in April 1917, was a policy borrowed by him from the Social Revolutionaries for the sole purpose of winning peasant support. After the March revolution the break-up of large estates was recognized as essential, even by most members of the provisional government. With the single exception of the Bolsheviks, however, all parties were agreed that an immediate redistribution of the land would risk paralysis of the war effort and was therefore impossible. Only the Bolsheviks demanded land for the peasant now.

As long as the war had been conducted by a tsarist government, the majority of Russian socialists had condemned it as an imperialist adventure. Once the tsar had been overthrown, however, the issues no longer seemed as simple. Both Mensheviks and Social Revolutionaries declared their support for 'peace without annexations and without indemnities'. Since there was no prospect of concluding a peace, this policy meant, in practice, reluctant support for a continuation of the war – an attitude shared at first by most Bolsheviks. The slogan 'Down with War!', wrote Joseph Stalin, the editor of *Pravda*, at the end of March, was irrelevant to the present situation. From the moment that Lenin returned to Petrograd, however, he demanded fraternization with the enemy and peace without a moment's delay.

For three months after Lenin's return Bolshevik support grew steadily both in the towns and in the army. Though they remained unable to reach the peasants in the villages, their policies won over large numbers of peasants at the front. Bolshevik party members in the army increased from 20,000 in February to 200,000 in July. During July the growth of support for Bolshevism persuaded a group of Lenin's followers, against Lenin's wishes, to attempt an unsuccessful coup d'état. The failure of the insurrection (which Lenin considered premature) and the publication of forged documents, alleging that Lenin was a German spy, produced a popular reaction against him and reduced the fortunes of the Bolshevik party to their lowest ebb since the March Revolution. Lenin himself had no option but to return to exile – this time in Finland.

The Bolsheviks seize power

It was not long before the Bolsheviks succeeded in re-establishing their position. While the provisional government was restoring order in Petrograd after the Bolshevik rising, General Brusilov was launching a massive new offensive on the Eastern Front in the hope of repeating his successes of the previous year. The collapse of this offensive meant the disintegration

Above, a women's meeting at Petrograd during the first weeks of the February Revolution: the banners call for women's rights. In the first weeks of the Revolution, unity was preserved between the provisional government and the Soviets established in the main towns; only after Lenin's return in April was the authority of the provisional government consistently challenged.

Above left, breadline in Petrograd, 1917: Russia had been prepared for revolution by years of military defeat and food and ammunition shortages and by the gradual collapse of the administration; it was the Bolshevik Party's good fortune to be able to take advantage of this situation.

Opposite, a US gun crew firing on German positions, 1918: though the effects of American entry into the war were not immediately noticeable, by the time of the armistice there were over a million American soldiers in France, a considerable boost to Allied morale as well as to fighting strength.

of most of the Russian army. By October there were no less than two million deserters. 'The soldiers', as Lenin said, 'voted for peace with their feet.' In the countryside the peasants were already dividing noble estates among themselves.

In September, alarmed at the collapse of the government's authority, General Kornilov, the Russian commander-in-chief, attempted to seize power. To defend Petrograd the provisional government was forced to appeal for Bolshevik support and to give arms to the Bolshevik Red Guards. In the event, Kornilov's troops refused even to march on Petrograd, and the insurrection collapsed without a shot being fired. Though unsuccessful, however, the rising destroyed most of the little authority which still remained in the hands of the provisional government. The Bolsheviks claimed to have saved Russia from counter-revolution and became the heroes of the hour. At the end of September they won majorities in the Petrograd and Moscow soviets for the first time.

Once these majorities had been won, Lenin demanded an immediate insurrection. The Bolshevik Central Committee, however, was more cautious and gave its consent only in the last week of October. The armed uprising itself was organized by a Military Revolutionary Committee, led by Leon Trotsky. Though Trotsky's name is now conspicuous by its absence from Russian accounts of the Revolution, it was Trotsky, nonetheless, who was mainly responsible for the immediate success of the Bolshevik seizure of power on 6–7 November 1917 (24–25 October according to the old Russian calendar). As Stalin was to write on the first anniversary of the November Revolution, in an article which must later have embarrassed him:

All the practical organization of the revolution was conducted under the direct leadership of the President of the Petrograd Soviet, Comrade Trotsky. It may be said, with certainty, that the swift passing of the [Petrograd] garrison to the side of the Soviet, and the bold execution of the work of the Military Revolutionary Committee, the party owes principally and above all to Comrade Trotsky.

Within little more than a decade, Stalin had turned himself into the chief architect of the revolution and Trotsky into its

principal opponent. Soviet historians have still to put the record straight.

On 8 November 1917, the day after their seizure of power, the Bolsheviks issued a decree calling for 'a just and democratic peace'. In December they signed an armistice with Germany and began peace negotiations at Brest-Litovsk. Germany demanded, as the price of a peace settlement, the dismemberment of western Russia: the cession to Germany of the Baltic provinces, White Russia, the Ukraine and the Caucasus. Lenin insisted that Russia had no option but to conclude a peace on Germany's terms. 'If you do not know how to adapt yourself', he said, 'if you are not inclined to crawl on your belly through the mud, then you are not a revolutionary but a chatterbox.'

A majority of the Bolshevik Central Committee, however, were unconvinced and wanted to continue the war rather than accept the German terms. Lenin's view prevailed only after he had twice threatened to resign. At last, on 3 March 1918, Russia signed the Peace of Brest-Litovsk. Russia, Lenin argued, had suffered only a temporary reverse which would soon be swept away by the tide of revolution advancing irresistibly across the continent of Europe. In the event, however, the Peace of Brest-Litovsk was to be swept away, not by the tide of revolution, but by the Allied victory on the Western Front.

Victory in the West

The new year in 1917 began with new men, all of them promising a knock-out blow that would bring final victory on the Western Front. In England Lloyd George had replaced Asquith as prime minister at the end of the previous year. In Germany civilian government gave way to a military dictatorship under the nominal leadership of the new supreme commander, Field Marshall Hindenburg, but with the real power resting in the hands of Hindenburg's deputy, General Ludendorff. In France General Nivelle, the youngest of the French army commanders, succeeded Joffre as commander-in-chief. Nivelle produced a plan for a lightning offensive to end the war in the spring of 1917 which seduced not only the French cabinet but, more surprisingly, Lloyd George, who was usually sceptical of the claims of generals.

Ignoring most of the lessons of the last two years, Nivelle pinned his faith on the 'violence' and 'brutality' of the French onslaught. 'Victory', he promised, would be 'certain, swift, and small in cost': 'One and a half million Frenchmen cannot fail.' The battle began in April and continued for three weeks. When it ended Nivelle had advanced up to four miles in depth along a sixteen-mile front, a result which compared well with the gains achieved in any previous Allied offensive. But it was not the decisive victory he had promised. In May Nivelle was replaced by Pétain, the hero of Verdun.

The failure of the Nivelle offensive to achieve a breakthrough brought to a climax the demoralization of the French army. It was followed by nothing less than a full-scale mutiny: 100,000 French soldiers were court-martialled and 23,000 found guilty. When French deserters revealed the scale of the mutiny to the Germans, their stories seemed so incredible that they were simply not believed. As a result Germany missed perhaps her best opportunity since the beginning of the war for a decisive breakthrough on the Western Front. As Painlevé,

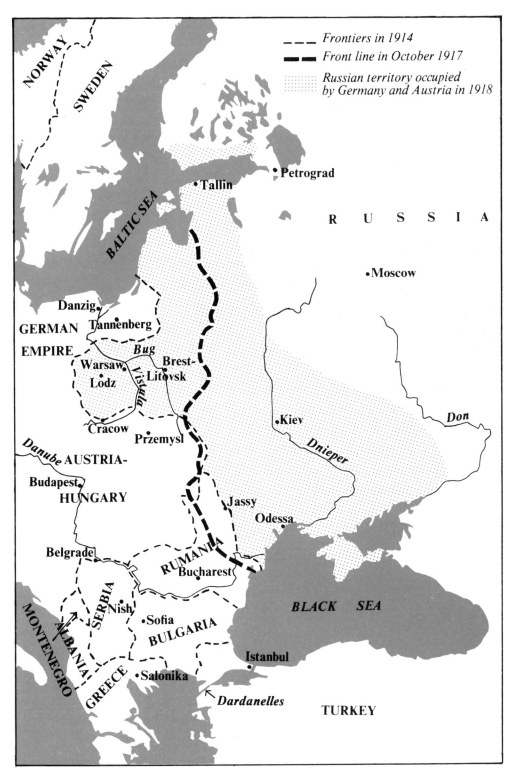

Left, the Eastern front during the First World War.

Opposite right, Lenin addresses a crowd in revolutionary Russia; Trotsky is standing on the right of the platform.

Opposite left, Bolsheviks pose by an armed car captured from forces loyal to the provisional government: in Petrograd the Bolsheviks took power in October without bloodshed, in Moscow after a week's uprising, though it needed years of fighting before the new regime's authority was established throughout the country.

the French minister of war, later admitted: 'There did not remain more than two divisions that could be absolutely relied upon if the Germans had launched a large-scale attack.'

Pétain was faced with an immensely difficult problem. If repression was too severe, the mutiny would become a rebellion. If he were not firm enough, the army might disintegrate. Pétain's success in quelling the mutiny was one of the most remarkable achievements by any Allied general during the war. A number of soldiers were shot *pour encourager les autres* (fifty-five officially, far more unofficially), but leave was doubled and conditions at the front improved. Most important of all, the French army gained the assurance that there would be no new French offensive for the remainder of the year. Pétain's strategy was summed up in the sentence, 'We must wait for the Americans', which meant, in effect, waiting for 1918.

Haig was undismayed by the French mutiny. 'For the last two years', he wrote in his diary at the end of May, 'most of us soldiers have realized that Great Britain must take the necessary steps to win the war by herself.' At the Battle of Passchendaele, fought from July to November 1917, Haig set out to do just that. The French high command condemned the whole offensive

in advance. Even Foch, though temperamentally inclined towards attack, described Haig's plan as a duck's march . . . 'futile, fantastic, and dangerous'.

The offensive coincided with the heaviest rains for thirty years. Even more than the Somme, Passchendaele became, as Lloyd George put it, 'the battle of the mud'. At times more than a dozen men were needed to wade across the battleground with one stretcher case. Haig and his staff officers, Lloyd George wrote bitterly,

never witnessed, not even through a telescope, the attacks [they] had ordained, except on carefully prepared charts where the advancing battalions were represented by the pencil which marched with ease across swamps and marked lines of triumphant progress without the loss of a single point. As for the mud, it never incommoded the movements of the irresistible pencil.

The few gains made in three and a half months' fighting were all to be abandoned without a fight early in 1918 in order to prepare for a new German offensive. Once again, as after the Somme, Haig pinned his faith in exaggerated estimates of German casualties and persuaded himself that he was wearing the Germans down. In fact, British casualties probably outnumbered those of Germany by more than three to two (over 300,000 as against less than 200,000) – and this at a time when Russia's withdrawal from the war made possible to transfer large numbers of German troops from the Eastern to the Western Front.

The last German offensive

As a result of her victory in the east, Germany had by March 1918 twenty divisions more in France than the combined total of the Allies. Ludendorff was well

aware, however, that this advantage was only a temporary one. As soon as American forces began to arrive in large numbers in France, the tables would be turned and the Allies could expect to win the war by sheer weight of numbers. Ludendorff drew the conclusion, therefore, that Germany must gamble on a last, all-out offensive, before her numerical advantage was lost.

After the first few days of the German offensive, Pétain was speaking as if the war was almost over. 'The Germans', he told Clemenceau, the French prime minister, 'will beat the English in the open field, after which they will beat us too.' To Haig Pétain 'had the appearance of a commander who was in a funk and had lost his nerve'.

It was Haig's alarm at Pétain's pessimism which led the British to take the initiative, early in April, in the appointment of Foch as the first 'Commander-in-chief of the Allied armies in France'. Even Foch, however, at first seemed less than optimistic. When congratulated by Clemenceau on his appointment, he replied, 'A fine gift! You give me a lost battle and tell me to win it.' By June 1918 the Germans were once more on the Marne and threatening Paris.

By now, though the Allies had little reason to suspect it, their greatest danger was past. Despite the fact that Germany's advance far exceeded anything achieved by the Allies since the opening of the Western Front, German troops had outstripped both their transport and artillery and were incapable of pressing home their attack. During July the tide of battle began to turn, at last, in favour of the Allies.

The real beginning of the German collapse was the British victory at Amiens, on 8 August. Ludendorff wrote later:

August 8th was the blackest day for the German army in the history of the war. This was the worst experience I had to

undergo. . . . Our losses had reached such proportions that the Supreme Command was faced with the necessity of having to disband a series of divisions.

The Battle of Amiens already foreshadowed the battles of the Second World War. It showed, too, how far methods of warfare had evolved since the war began. When Britain went to war in August 1914, officers' swords were still being sharpened by the regimental armourer and soldiers at the front were making home-made grenades out of empty tins of jam. At Amiens, in August 1918, British troops advanced behind a shield of tanks, protected by rudimentary air cover directed from the ground by radio.

During the final Allied offensive, Haig's invincible optimism, which had hitherto been something of a liability, became instead a valuable asset. While Foch, even after the Battle of Amiens, did not envisage a decisive breakthrough until April 1919, Haig was convinced that the war could, and must, be won by an all-out offensive in the autumn of 1918 before the enemy had an opportunity to recover. It was the British army, stiffened by strong divisions from Canada and Australia (the latter brilliantly commanded by General Monash), which bore the main brunt of the fighting during the final stages of the war. In the three months between the Battle of Amiens and the armistice of 11 November the British army, under Haig, captured 188,700 prisoners of war and 2,840 guns – almost as many as the other Allies put together. Foch himself was full of praise for Haig's achievement. 'Never at any time in its history', he said, 'has the British army achieved greater results in attack than in this unbroken offensive.'

Germany's defeat was hastened by the collapse of her partners. The Allied forces which had been cooped up in a Balkan bridgehead at Salonika for the past three years at last succeeded in launching a successful offensive and forced Bulgaria to make peace at the end of September. A month later Turkey followed suit, and Austria-Hungary, already in the throes of disintegration, appealed for an armistice.

Germany's collapse was only partly caused by the defeats inflicted on her and on her Allies in the closing months of the war. It was even more because of the conviction that the success of the British blockade and the prospect of large-scale American intervention made Germany's future prospects even bleaker than the present. The longer the war continued, the more the odds would turn against Germany.

In August, at a time when Germany's reserves were almost exhausted, the American army in Europe already numbered one and a half million men and was increasing at the rate of 300,000 a month. When the armistice was signed on 11 November 1918, Germany had still not been invaded, and her front line still lay on French and Belgian soil. Germany capitulated, not because she had been beaten in the field, but because her people and her leaders had lost hope for the future.

Victory, wrote Churchill, had been 'bought so dear as to be almost indistinguishable from defeat'. The war had killed not less than ten million people and maimed as many more. All the great powers of Europe felt, like Britain, that they had lost a generation. The mood of the British people now was very different from the enthusiastic jingoism of August 1914. Once the victory celebrations were over, the overwhelming feeling of the nation was that 'it must never happen again'. The young idealists who had flocked to the colours in 1914, hoping to find at the front a sense of purpose that had been lacking in peace, returned (if they returned at all) overwhelmed instead by the futility of war. The proud, patriotic poetry of Rupert Brooke had given way to the bitter, disillusioned verse of Wilfred Owen and Siegfried Sassoon.

Many men in the years between the wars sought to blame the enormous carnage that Europe had endured, not on the necessities of war, but on the stupidity of generals. And yet, despite the errors of the generals, victory could not have been achieved without the sacrifice of millions of lives. Without

the experience of the terrible battles of the past four years, the German army would not, in November 1918, have lost the will to resist. Despite the enormous technological advances of the next twenty years, no easier way to defeat Germany was discovered during the Second World War. Before Germany could be defeated for a second time in 1945, the massacres of Verdun and the Somme and Passchendaele were to be repeated at Leningrad and Stalingrad and Moscow.

Above, view of an armaments factory: though millions of civilians worked, often in extremely unpleasant conditions, in war-related industries, the very fact that the belligerent nations, except for Belgium, parts of Russia and a small part of France, were never invaded meant that behind the front line the real horror of the war was never fully comprehended and the gulf between soldier and civilian stayed unbridged.

Opposite top right, men of the Inniskillen Fusiliers advancing through the German second line at the Battle of Cambrai, 20 November 1917: tanks were used for the first time at Cambrai, where, instead of the usual yard by yard advance, they advanced five miles at very little cost; the infantry failed to keep up, however, and within ten days the Germans had recovered their position.

Opposite centre right, an early tank in action.

Opposite bottom right, Eddie Rickenbacker, the American ace pilot: considered useful only for front-line reconnaisance duties at the beginning of the war, four years later aircraft had become an important factor in military planning.

Opposite left, Anzacs (Australian and New Zealand Army Corps) at Passchendaele, 1917, described by AJP Taylor as 'the blindest slaughter of a blind war' and the last mass infantry assault of the war.

Chapter 50

Post-war Europe

President Wilson came to Europe in January 1919 expecting to build a new Europe on the ruins of the old, founded on the principles of national self-determination and the rule of law, with a League of Nations to uphold the peace. The rapturous reception given him by the peoples of Europe assured him of their confidence. When he visited London, rose petals were strewn before him. Wilson expected opposition from the Allied governments but was confident that he could overcome it. 'England and France', he had written in the summer of 1917, 'have not the same views with regard to peace that we have by any means. When the war is over, we can force them to our way of thinking.' England and France, however, were to prove less pliable than he supposed.

The basis of the post-war settlement was the Treaty of Versailles, negotiated at the peace conference of Paris, during the first six months of 1919. Unlike most such gatherings in the past, the Paris conference was not a conference between victor and vanquished. It was a conference instead where the victors decided, among themselves, the terms which were to be imposed upon the enemy. The details of the settlement were worked out by a series of more than fifty commissions, which held between them more than 1,600 sessions. Thirty-two states took part in these discussions, among them countries as remote from the fighting as Ecuador and Siam. All the major decisions, however, were taken by three men – Wilson, Lloyd George and Clemenceau, the 'Big Three'.

Two major difficulties stood in the way of the peace without annexations or indemnities which Wilson had come to build. The first was the problem of French security. There is almost no other example in the history of modern Europe of a nation so exhausted by its victory as France appeared to be in November 1918. Britain's security seemed to have been secured by the surrender of the German fleet at the armistice and the conquest of the German colonies during the war, most of which were soon to be shared out between Britain and the dominions.

France, however, seemed to have won something of a pyrrhic victory. Most of the destruction caused by the battles on the Western Front had been concentrated on French soil, and some of France's principal industries had been ruined. Worse still, with the lowest birth rate of any of the great powers, France had less chance than any other nation of making up its enormous losses in manpower. Even with the recovery of Alsace-Lorraine, France still remained far weaker, both in population and economic resources, than a defeated Germany. Moreover, the alliance with Russia, on which its security against Germany had formerly depended, had been swept away by the Bolshevik revolution.

Despite its victory in the First World War, therefore, the balance of power actually seemed more unfavourable to France at the end of war than at the beginning. Clemenceau at first insisted that the only way to make France secure was to separate the Rhineland from Germany and give France permanent bridgeheads on the right flank of the Rhine. Both Wilson and Lloyd George refused to consider such a scheme. Instead, they made two alternative proposals: first, an Allied occupation of the Rhineland for fifteen years, together with the permanent demilitarization both of the Rhineland itself and of a region fifty kilometres wide on the right bank of the Rhine; secondly, an occupation of the Saar, also for fifteen years (with its coal-mines ceded to France for that period), followed by a plebiscite to decide whether it should go to France or Germany.

France was persuaded to accept these terms only by an Anglo-American promise of immediate armed assistance against any German attack. This promise, however, was not to be honoured. The American Senate later refused to ratify the Versailles treaty, and Britain declared herself thereby released from her own undertaking to France.

The second great obstacle in the way of Wilson's hopes for a peace without victors was the demand for reparations. Public opinion in both France and Britain was in vengeful mood at the moment of victory. The election campaign which returned Lloyd George to power in December 1918 was conducted amid cries of 'Hang the Kaiser' and 'Make Germany Pay', orchestrated by conservative politicians and Lord Northcliffe's newspapers. Sir Eric Geddes, the First Lord of the Admiralty, assured his electors that the government would squeeze Germany 'until you can hear the pips squeak'. Even Lloyd George, though personally anxious to limit the extent of Germany's humiliation, felt compelled to promise that Britain would 'demand the whole cost of the war' in compensation.

Despite the cries for vengeance which surrounded it, the demand for reparations was perfectly justified. It was reasonable to expect that Germany, as the aggressor, should pay a proportion of the appalling losses inflicted by it on the rest of Europe – all the more so since its own economic losses had been lighter than those of most of its opponents.

Where the Allies were unwise was not in their demand for reparations but in the amount that they demanded and in the way that their demand was phrased. Since they were unable to agree among themselves on the size of reparations, they forced Germany to sign what amounted to a blank cheque. Then, in order to justify this blank cheque, they included in the Versailles treaty the famous war guilt clause, drafted by the young John Foster Dulles (later one of America's least successful secretaries of state):

The Allied and Associated Governments affirm and Germany accepts the responsibility of Germany and her allies for causing all the loss and damage to which the Allied and Associated Governments and their nationals have been subjected as a consequence of the war imposed upon them by the aggression of Germany and her allies.

That Germany should be forced to sign such a declaration was bound to be bitterly resented by the great majority of the German people as a gratuitous insult to the memory of the German dead. Outside Germany itself, the justification for reparations – 'the responsibility of Germany and her allies' for the outbreak of the First World War – is no longer seriously disputed. Most West German schoolchildren are still taught, however, that responsibility for the war was divided, more or less evenly, among all its main participants.

The peace with Germany was, in the words of one of its French critics, 'too mild for its severity' In certain respects the peace *was* severe. Germany lost its colonies, its air force, most of its fleet, all its army save 100,000 men and over thirteen percent of its territory (though most of its territorial losses, like the surrender of Polish territory or the return of Alsace-Lorraine to France, could be justified by the principle of self-determination). In addition, Germany was faced with a war indemnity, which it was expected to take half a century to pay. And yet the fundamental bases of German strength – the unity achieved by Bismarck in 1871, the great size of its population (even though diminished by ten percent) and the industrial strength which had given it in 1914 the most advanced economy in Europe – remained essentially unchanged. These were the factors which, before 1914, had made Germany incomparably the most powerful state on the continent of Europe. Sooner or later, it was inevitable that they should do so again.

France, Germany's main rival in western Europe, was destined to fall behind Germany economically and demographically even more rapidly after the First World War than it had done before. Already, in 1919, many French critics of Versailles advanced the thesis which was to become widely

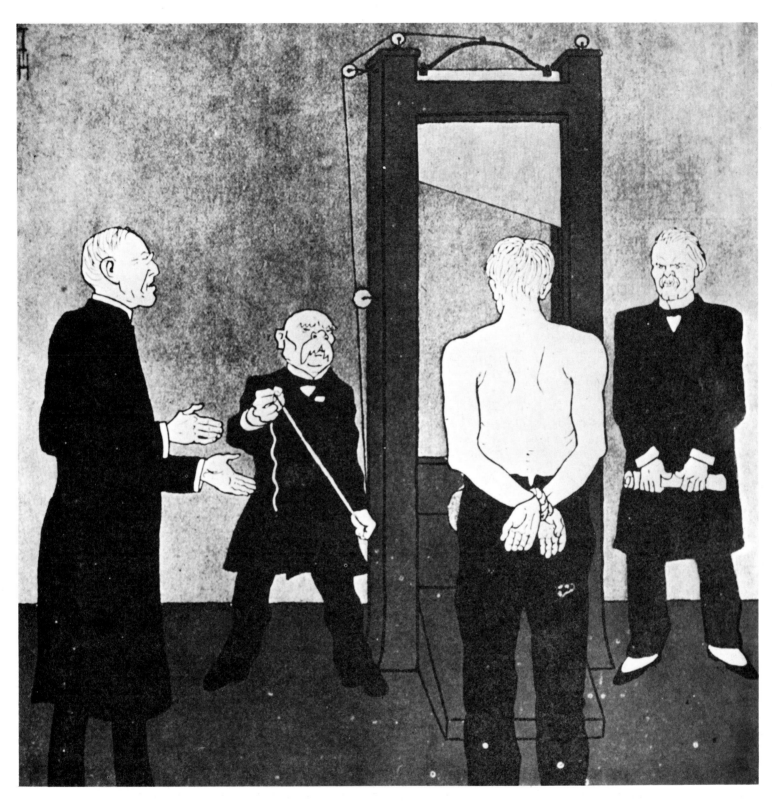

accepted after the Second World War: that European security demanded the sacrifice of the unity achieved in 1871 and the re-creation of a divided Germany.

Having failed to secure the peace without victors which he had come to build, Wilson pinned his faith instead on the League of Nations. Increasingly, as the Paris negotiations dragged on, he came to look on the League as a means whereby injustices in the peace with Germany, which he was powerless to prevent, could be put right as soon as the passions aroused by the war had died down. For that reason, he insisted that the Covenant of the League of Nations should be incorporated in the Versailles settlement itself. One of the articles of the Covenant contained express provision for 'the reconsideration of treaties which have become inapplicable' and the consideration of 'international conditions whose continuance might endanger the peace of the world. The Treaty of Versailles, even if imperfect, contained, in Wilson's view, the eventual remedy for its own imperfections.

Presenting the text of the Versailles treaty to the Senate after his return to the United States in July 1919, Wilson acknowledged that it contained many inadequacies. But he argued that these were redeemed by the

Above, cartoon from the German magazine Simplicissimus *attacking the Treaty of Versailles.*

Covenant which conferred on America the moral leadership of all mankind. He ended his speech with a remarkable peroration full of Wilsonian idealism:

The stage is set, the destiny disclosed. It has come about by no plan of our own conceiving, but by the hand of God who led us into this way. We cannot turn back. We can only go forward, with lifted eyes and freshened spirit, to follow the vision. It was this that we dreamed at our birth. America shall in truth show the way. The light streams upon the path ahead, and nowhere else.

The United States, however, refused Wilson's summons 'to follow the vision' Mainly because of objections to the Covenant of the League, the Senate refused to give the two-thirds majority required to ratify the Treaty of Versailles. That America failed to join the League of Nations was due not merely to Wilson's opponents but also to Wilson himself. The Senate was probably prepared to accept the Covenant with reservations which were no greater than those which most members of the League were in any case to exercise in practice. But Wilson was in no mood to repeat in Washington the kind of compromises which had been forced on him in Paris. All those who opposed him he denounced as 'contemptible quitters'. When officially informed by the French ambassador that the Allies were prepared to accept the reservations on American membership of the League demanded by an influential group of Republican senators, Wilson replied, 'Mr Ambassador, I shall consent to nothing. The Senate must take its medicine.' The Senate, however, refused to take its medicine; and the American people, by electing Warren Harding as their president in 1920, endorsed its decision.

The reshaping of eastern Europe

The second great task of the Paris peacemakers, after the peace with Germany, was the resettlement of eastern Europe. The almost simultaneous defeat of the Russian, German and Austrian empires meant, in effect, that the whole map of eastern Europe, from Finland in the north to the Black Sea in the south, had to be redrawn. The new map of eastern Europe took a year to make and was established by the Allies in three separate treaties: with Austria in September 1919, with Bulgaria in November 1919 and with Hungary in June 1920.

The Baltic states of Finland, Estonia, Latvia and Lithuania, formerly parts of the Russian Empire, all gained their independence. Poland, which in the seventeenth century had been a major European power and in the eighteenth had been divided by its neighbours, was reconstituted as an independent state. The Austrian Empire was divided among half a dozen 'succession

states', of which Austria and Hungary, formerly the two centres of power within the empire, were the smallest.

The guiding principle which underlay the resettlement of eastern Europe was the principle of nationality. Boundaries between states were to coincide as far as possible with boundaries between peoples. This principle was modified in practice by two other considerations. It was doubtless inevitable that Germany's allies in eastern Europe – Austria, Hungary and Bulgaria – should be less fairly treated than their neighbours, but it was difficult to justify either the annexation of German-speaking Austrian South Tyrol by Italy or the inclusion of large Magyar minorities in the territory of Hungary's neighbours. The second factor which limited the application of the principle of

nationality was fear of revolution. All the 'Big Three' were agreed on the need to make Russia's neighbours as large and strong as possible – even at the cost of including in them large alien minorities – in order to strengthen their ability to resist the westwards march of Bolshevism.

No Bolshevik had ever imagined that the revolution in Russia could be other than part of a world revolutionary movement. Early in 1919, Zinoviev, the head of the Communist International, forecast that 'within a year all Europe will be communist'. It is easy now to dismiss such predictions as hopelessly unrealistic. At the time they were taken very seriously indeed. 'Bolshevism', wrote Wilson, 'is moving steadily westward, has overwhelmed Poland, and is poisoning Germany.'

Many other statesmen at the Paris conference feared that the foundations of European society, as they knew it, were crumbling before their eyes. Lloyd George wrote in March: 'The whole of Europe is filled with the spirit of Revolution. The whole existing order in its political, social, and economic aspects is questioned by the masses of the population from one end of Europe to the other.'

Fear of the spread of Bolshevism was strengthened still further when a communist regime, led by Bela Kun, seized power in Hungary for a few months in the spring and summer of 1919. Even though an attempted communist rising in Berlin had been bloodily suppressed at the beginning of 1919, many European statesmen, like Lloyd George, saw a real danger that Germany might yet go the way of Hungary and bring the whole of central and eastern Europe within the Bolshevik orbit.

This fear continued to play upon the minds of the peacemakers throughout the negotiations of 1919. Secret offices were set up in New Scotland Yard and the American State Department to chart the course of Bolshevism as its poison spread through Europe. Ray Stannard Baker, one of Wilson's advisers at Paris, wrote later that the Bolsheviks 'without being represented at Paris at all, were important elements at every turn'. During 1919, western opinion was already coming round to the view expressed by Sir Henry Wilson, the British chief of staff, that 'our real danger is not the Boches but Bolshevism'.

The Civil War in Russia

While Allied statesmen were pondering the Bolshevik menace at the Paris conference, Russia itself was passing through a period of internal chaos usually, but inadequately, described as the 'Civil War'. The Bolsheviks were challenged by 'White' armies, attacking from three sides: from Siberia, the Gulf of Finland and the Caucasus.

That the Bolsheviks survived these attacks was in part because of Trotsky's brilliant leadership of the Red Army. Their survival owed even more, however, to the failures and divisions of their opponents, some of whom even fell to fighting among themselves. Increasingly, the White armies fell under the control of men of the old, discredited ruling class, hostile not merely to Bolshevism but to the March Revolution. Among the Russian peasant masses, on whom, in the last resort, the outcome of the war depended, the conviction grew that the Bolsheviks were fighting for the people of Russia against White generals whose only programme was reaction and the restoration of their former privileges.

The chaos of the Civil War offered western governments an opportunity which was never to return for reversing the decision of the November Revolution. Two or three Allied divisions landed in the Gulf of Finland in 1919 could probably have forced their way to Moscow (the new capital of Russia) and have overthrown the Bolshevik regime. But in the aftermath of the First World War not even two or three divisions could be found. In none of the Allied countries was public opinion prepared to tolerate intervention on more than a token scale. Those troops which were sent served mainly to discredit the White cause still further. They were too few to affect the outcome of the war but sufficient to allow the Bolsheviks to brand their opponents as the tools of western imperialism.

Above, weighing out an allocation of wood in Petrograd, 1919: the Russian economy had already virtually collapsed in 1917, but the Bolshevik policy of war communism, involving total control over all wealth, labour, commerce and agriculture, brought production of food and industrial goods to a standstill; only when Lenin introduced his New Economic Policy – vital if the Revolution were to be saved – did the situation improve.

Top, Admiral Kolchak (1874–1920), leader of the White Russian government based on Omsk, reviewing troops, September 1919: a few months later his advance collapsed (he himself was captured and executed), and by the end of 1920 foreign invervention had come to an end (with the exception of the Japanese occupation of Vladivostock, maintained until November 1922).

Opposite, cover of the October 1919 issue of The Communist International: *initially the Bolsheviks had hoped and expected that their revolution would be the harbinger of a Europe-wide movement towards communism, but by the early 1920s the opportunity for revolution had passed and the Bolshevik regime was forced to concentrate on the development of socialism in one country.*

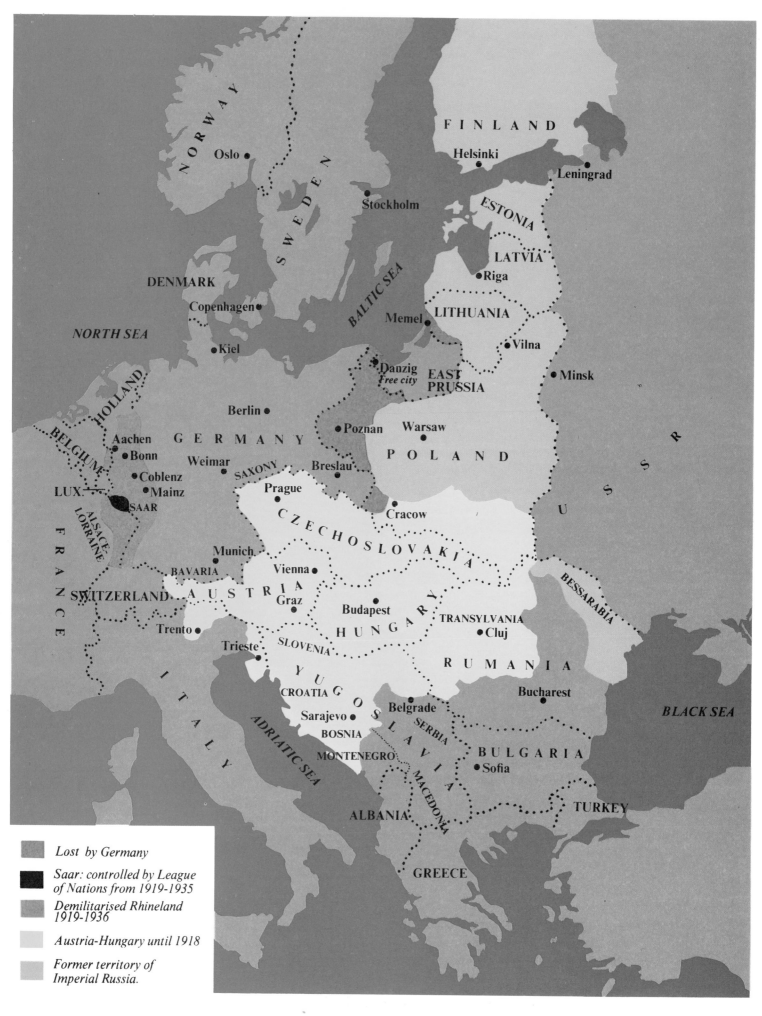

Lost by Germany

Saar: controlled by League
of Nations from 1919-1935

Demilitarised Rhineland
1919-1936

Austria-Hungary until 1918

Former territory of
Imperial Russia.

NORWAY

Oslo

SWEDEN

Stockholm

FINLAND

Helsinki

Leningrad

ESTONIA

LATVIA

Riga

DENMARK

Copenhagen

BALTIC SEA

LITHUANIA

Memel

Vilna

Minsk

NORTH SEA

Kiel

Danzig
Free city

EAST
PRUSSIA

HOLLAND

Berlin

GERMANY

Poznan

Warsaw

U S S R

Aachen
Bonn

POLAND

Weimar

SAXONY

Breslau

BELGIUM

Coblenz

Mainz

LUX.

SAAR

Prague

Cracow

ALSACE-
LORRAINE

CZECHOSLOVAKIA

FRANCE

Munich

BAVARIA

Vienna

BESSARABIA

SWITZERLAND

AUSTRIA

Graz

Budapest

TRANSYLVANIA

Cluj

Trento

HUNGARY

RUMANIA

Trieste

SLOVENIA

Bucharest

ITALY

YUGOSLAVIA

CROATIA

Belgrade

Sarajevo

SERBIA

BLACK SEA

BOSNIA

ADRIATIC SEA

MONTENEGRO

BULGARIA

Sofia

MACEDONIA

ALBANIA

TURKEY

GREECE

ЗА ЕДИНЯЮ РОССІЮ

Above, Tsarist poster from the time of the Russian Revolution: the dragon symbolizes the Bolsheviks devouring the heart of Russia, indicated by the outline of the buildings of Moscow.

Left, Russian revolutionary poster depicting the combatants in the First World War as capitalist, militaristic money-grabbers.

Opposite, Europe after the Treaty of Versailles, 1919.

By the beginning of 1920 the White forces, though not finally defeated, no longer seemed a serious threat to the Bolshevik regime. In April the Civil War within Russia itself became overshadowed by the beginning of war with Poland. The Poles invaded Russia, nominally in support of Ukrainian nationalists but with the real intention of acquiring the Ukraine for Poland. Within two months the Polish invasion of Russia had given way to a Russian invasion of Poland, followed by the creation of a provisional government of Polish communists.

For a few months in the summer of 1920 many Bolsheviks believed that they were engaged in building a Soviet Poland which would push the borders of Bolshevism to the frontiers of Germany and enable the German communists, with Russian help, to make a successful bid for power. Churchill, among others, was afraid they might succeed. In July 1920 he published an article in the *Evening News* luridly entitled 'The Poison Peril from the East', appealing to the Germans to build, before it was too late, 'a dyke of peaceful, lawful, patient strength and virtue against the flood of red barbarism flowing from the East'. By so doing, he assured them, they would find their way 'as the years pass by back to their own great place in the councils of Christendom'.

In August 1920 the victorious Russian advance was brought to a halt. The Poles, with French assistance, inflicted a decisive defeat on the Red Army at the battle of Warsaw and began a successful counter-offensive which carried them, once again, across the Russian border. In March 1921 the Russians were forced, by the Treaty of

Riga, to leave six million Ukrainians and White Russians in Polish hands. The failure of the Red Army in Poland ended all immediate hope of a European revolution and caused a sharp decline in the Bolsheviks' international prestige. In the year after the treaty of Riga the Italian and Czech communist parties lost more than half their members, the French almost half and the German about a third.

Only in the aftermath of the next European war was Bolshevism able to resume the conquest of eastern Europe. It succeeded after 1945 where it had failed after 1918 less because its ideological appeal had become more persuasive than because its military strength was now immeasurably greater. Between the wars, however, the most serious threat to liberal democracy in Europe came not from Russian communism but from the new menace of fascism, which emerged most rapidly in Italy and more slowly, though in a more vicious form, in Germany. Without the fears aroused by Bolshevism, however, fascism would have been much less serious a menace. Fascism owed its initial impetus in Italy to a panic fear of revolution. The Nazis sought to exploit the same fear in Germany. 'My ambition', said Adolf Hitler after his first, and unsuccessful, bid for power in 1923, 'was to become the destroyer of Marxism I am going to achieve this task.'

The birth of the Weimar Republic

On 14 August 1919 Germany became a democracy. The first article of the Weimar constitution (named after the city of its birth) proclaimed: 'The German Reich is a Republic. Political authority derives from the people.' Its drafters tried to combine in the new constitution all the best features of the British Bill of Rights, the French Declaration of the Rights of Man and the Citizen and the first Ten Amendments of the American Constitution. In all but one of its articles it was a model of democracy. The solitary exception was article 48, which allowed the president (who in normal circumstances reigned but did not rule) to confer absolute power on the chancellor 'if public order and security are seriously disturbed or endangered' Three chancellors during the final years of the Weimar Republic assumed absolute power. The last was Adolf Hitler.

The Weimar Republic was aptly described by its first chancellor as a candle burning at both ends. The right, which propagated the myth that the politicians, not the generals, were responsible for the capitulation of 1918, regarded the new republic as both the product and the instrument of Germany's shame. The communists, too, were dedicated to its destruction. From its supporters the Republic received only lukewarm loyalty. From its opponents it encountered passionate opposition. For thirteen years, none the less, the supporters of the Republic outnumbered its opponents. But in July and November 1932, at the last free elections held in a united Germany, the opponents of parliamentary democracy outnumbered its supporters.

During the first four years of its existence the Weimar Republic lived in a state of almost continuous economic and political crisis. The post-war inflation which affected every European state hit Germany worst of all. Reparations provided a convenient excuse for Germany's economic ills. The real cause, however, was the financial irresponsibility of her governments. In Britain during the war, income tax had reached the unheard-of rate of five shillings in the pound. In Germany, on the contrary, not a penny of the war effort was financed out of taxation. The government resorted instead to vast internal loans and the printing of paper money. It pursued the same policy after the war was over.

For the first four years of the Weimar Republic the government spent four times as much as it received in taxes. During these four years the German mark pursued a quickening decline. By 1923 it was worth less – literally – than the paper it was printed on. At its lowest point in November 1923 the mark stood at 4,200,000,000 to the dollar. The rapidity of Germany's financial recovery thereafter was further evidence of the financial irresponsibility of the past four years. That irresponsibility had put at risk not merely the future of the mark but the future of German democracy. By wiping out the savings of the German middle class it destroyed the security of the very class on which, in the long run, the security of the Weimar Republic itself depended.

Financial collapse in Weimar Germany was accompanied by the use of violence for political ends. The leading figures in this wave of violence were the *Freikorps*, groups of out-of-work officers who had earned a spurious respectability by their bloodthirsty suppression of the Bolshevik risings of 1919. In March 1920 5,000 men of the *Freikorps* led by Wolfgang Kapp, a former civil servant, occupied Berlin, declared the government deposed and the Weimar constitution null and void. The *Reichswehr* (the German army) refused to intervene. General von Seeckt refused a government request that he should do so with the curt rejoinder: 'Obviously there can be no question of letting *Reichswehr* fight against *Reichswehr*.' Instead, it was the people of Berlin themselves who paralysed the capital by a general strike and forced Kapp and his comrades to leave Berlin.

All those who had taken part in the Kapp putsch either escaped unpunished or were given an amnesty. Seeckt, who had refused to put the rising down, became head of the *Reichswehr* almost as soon as the rising was over. When workers in the Ruhr called for a purge of the *Reichswehr*, Seeckt branded them as Bolsheviks and sent against them the same *Freikorps* which had just tried to overthrow the government.

For three years after the Kapp putsch, the *Freikorps* took the lead in a well-organized campaign of political terrorism. In 1921 they arranged the assassination of the minister of finance, Mathias Erzberger, the man who had signed the armistice for Germany. 'Erzberger', said one right-wing paper, 'has suffered the fate which the vast majority of patriotic Germans desired for him.' A year later it was the turn of the foreign minister, Walter Rathenau, murdered partly because of his attitude to reparations but chiefly because of his Jewish origins. For several months before his death

STOSSTRUPP-HITLER
MÜNCHEN

Above, French troops occupy the Ruhr, January 1923, in an attempt to collect reparations in kind after the German government had defaulted on its payments. The reparations clauses of the Versailles Treaty, by which Germany was to pay substantial sums, chiefly to France, were ineptly enforced, and overall Germany paid out little.

Above left, members of the Freikorps, *early 1920s: large numbers of Germans felt no loyalty to the Weimar Republic, believing it to be the creation of disloyal politicians who had 'stabbed' the army 'in the back' by agreeing to the armistice and the Versailles treaty; they were fertile ground for Hitler's propaganda from the late 1920s onwards.*

Left, Hitler's stormtroops during the abortive Munich putsch, November 1923: arrested and tried, Hitler received a remarkably light sentence and spent much of his imprisonment writing Mein Kampf.

Opposite, members of the Berlin Soldiers' Council, November 1918: the Weimar Republic was founded to the accompaniment of uprisings of workers and soldiers throughout Germany, aimed at establishing revolutionary regimes, only put down by the Social Democratic government with the assistance of the army.

nationalists in beer-halls up and down Germany had sung a song which ended with the lines, 'Shoot down Walter Rathenau, The God-damned swine of a Jewish sow' The most disturbing aspect of these murders was their great popularity with large sections of the German people. Even the courts habitually assumed that right-wing violence (as opposed to left-wing violence) proceeded from praiseworthy motives and were lenient in their treatment of it.

The violence of the postwar years, like the spiral of inflation, reached its peak in 1923. The year began with the French occupation of the Ruhr, an action intended to enforce the payment of reparations which were overdue. For more than eight months, until the German government called a halt, the population of the Ruhr organized a massive campaign of passive, and occasionally violent, resistance. By the end of the summer the Kremlin concluded that Germany was ripe for revolution. On

orders from Moscow there were communist risings, during October, in Hamburg, Saxony and Thuringia. All were quickly suppressed by the *Reichswehr*.

Violence from the left was followed, as usual, by violence from the right. In November there was a nationalist putsch in Bavaria, in imitation of the earlier Kapp putsch in Berlin. As the nationalists marched into the centre of Munich the police opened fire and the putsch collapsed. At the head of the rising were Germany's two most prominent twentieth-century dictators: one, General Ludendorff, nearing the end of his career, the other, Adolf Hitler, at the beginning of his. Ludendorff bore himself splendidly in defeat. Ignoring the gunfire and the confusion around him, he continued to march forward, the police lines opening respectfully to allow him to pass through. Adolf Hitler emerged less creditably from his first bid for power. At the first shot he threw himself to the ground, then sprang up and fled

Was will
Spartakus?

Neuer Militarismus

Junkertum

Kapitalismus

·K·P·D·
(Spartakusbund)

for cover, leaving his followers to fend for themselves. Though many formidable problems still confronted the Weimar Republic at the end of 1923, Adolf Hitler did not seem to be one of them.

Fascism in Italy

Italy, as Bismarck had long ago observed, was gifted with a voracious territorial appetite but inadequate teeth. Its gains at Versailles – the South Tyrol, Trieste, islands in the Aegean and Adriatic – were an exaggerated reward for its minor contribution to the Allied victory. But Italy had wanted more – more, in particular, of the Dalmatian coast.

In September 1919 the nationalist poet, Gabriel D'Annunzio, marched into the

Dalmatian port of Fiume at the head of a thousand of his followers. To the embarrassment of the Italian government, which shared his ambitions but disavowed his methods, D'Annunzio announced the annexation of Fiume to Italy. For the next year, until the Italian government plucked up courage to dislodge him, he ruled a comic opera régime, which developed many of the theatrical absurdities later borrowed, without acknowledgement, by Mussolini. His followers wore black shirts, greeted one another with arms outstretched in the Roman salute and communed with their leader at open-air rallies through a rhythmic and platitudinous series of questions and answers.

But the mood of nationalist hysteria reflected in D'Annunzio's adventure was not,

as is often supposed, the mood of the Italian people as a whole. The general election of November 1919 (unlike the post-war elections in France and Britain) was remarkable for the poor showing not merely of the nationalists and conservatives but of all those groups which had favoured intervention in the war. The newly-founded fascist party, the most extreme of the nationalist groups, failed to win a single seat. Its leader, Benito Mussolini, standing in Milan, gained only two percent of the vote. The fascists were to come to power not by exploiting the nationalism of the Italian people but by playing on their fear of Bolshevism.

Until 1921 Italian socialists and communists were members of a single socialist party, united in its admiration for the Russian revolution. At the 1919 election the socialist party gained a third of the vote and trebled its pre-war representation in parliament. The socialist newspaper, *Avanti!*, declared in triumph, 'Revolutionary Italy is born!' The wave of social unrest which swept through Italy during 1919 and 1920 seemed to prove its point. Many thousands of peasants settled on large estates and seized holdings for themselves. The government seemed powerless to prevent them. Industrial unrest, too, was worse in Italy than anywhere else in Europe. It reached its peak in August 1920 when half a million workers occupied their factories and raised the red flag over them.

Ever since the end of the war the socialist party had been openly demanding 'the violent overthrow of bourgeois society'. In August 1920 its bluff was called. A Lenin would have used the occupation of the factories as the springboard for revolution. The Italian socialists, however, had not the slightest idea of how to put their revolutionary theories into practice. In September the factories were handed back to their owners, in return for a rise in wages and improved conditions.

The end result of all the talk of revolution in post-war Italy was not revolution itself but the rise of fascism. As the anarchist, Enrico Malatesta, prophetically remarked during the occupation of the factories: 'If we do not go on to the end we shall have to pay with blood and tears for the fear we are now causing the bourgeoisie.' With the return of the factories to their owners, all real danger of revolution had passed. 'Italian Bolshevism', wrote Mussolini privately, 'is mortally wounded.' The Italian middle classes, however, were more convinced than ever that Bolshevism was preparing for its final assault. It was by exploiting this fear, and by posing as the saviours of Italy from red revolution, that the fascists were able to raise themselves from obscurity to a position which enabled them to make a bid for power.

In July 1920, on the eve of the occupation of the factories, there were, at most, a hundred fascist groups (*fasci*) in the whole of Italy. Six months later, there were over a thousand. By now the fascists had the financial backing of many large industrialists and landowners who feared for their factories and estates. They had the support, too, of the same group of out-of-work army officers who made up the *Freikorps* in Germany. And, like the *Freikorps*, the paramilitary fascist *squadre d'azione* had the blessing of the government. Soon after the occupation of the factories, the ministry of war agreed to pay all ex-officers who led the *squadre* four-fifths of their former pay. In many parts of Italy, Mussolini and his followers were able to rely on the support of prefects, police and army commanders, anxious to pay off old scores against the socialists.

Confident of the collusion of the state authorities, the fascists began an intensive series of terrorist raids on left-wing organizations. They became quite open in boasting about their brutality. During one raid near Siena, for example, a fascist leader ordered one of his victims to balance a cup on his head so that he could demonstrate his markmanship. He missed and the man was killed. The incident was reported in the local newspaper under the humorous headline, 'An unfortunate William Tell'

The Italian middle classes found it impossible to conceive of a threat to the social order other than from the left. Impressed by years of socialist propaganda calling for the violent overthrow of bourgeois society, many were inclined to accept as legitimate the fascist argument that violence could be met only by violence. Even among liberals who deplored the fascists' methods, the illusion persisted that these excesses were no more than a passing phase. One of those who shared this illusion was the liberal minister Giolitti, who compared the fascists with the British irregulars in Ireland. 'The fascists', he told a British diplomat, 'are our Black and Tans.'

At the election of May 1921 Giolitti included the fascists on his own electoral list, thus helping them to gain a foothold in parliament for the first time. As yet few heeded Mussolini's warning that the fascists were destroying Bolshevism not as an end in itself but 'in preparation for the settling of accounts with the liberal state which survives'. When the liberal state finally recognized the nature of the fascist threat to its existence, it proved unequal to the challenge

There were two crucial turning points in the fascists' bid for power. The first was the government's failure to suppress the paramilitary *squadre d'azione* on which fascist power was based. Without the *squadre* the March on Rome would have been impossible. A government decree issued in December 1921 ordered the prefects throughout Italy to suppress all unofficial armed organizations. Mussolini immediately declared that all fascists were members of the *squadre*, confident that no government would dare dissolve the whole fascist party. His confidence proved to be well-founded, and the

decree remained a dead letter. 'The government', boasted Mussolini, 'can do nothing against us.' Its nerve had failed.

The fascist leader in Ferrara wrote in his diary on the first day of 1922: 'We have not only broken the resistance of our enemies but we also control the organs of the state. The prefect has to submit to orders given by me in the name of the fascists.' During the next nine months the fascists made themselves the masters of northern Italy, forcibly taking over most of its town councils. By October they were ready to make their bid for power. Mussolini told his followers on 24 October: 'Either the government will be given to us or we shall descend on Rome and take it.' Three days later the March on Rome began.

At the eleventh hour the Italian government seemed suddenly to recover its nerve. On the evening of 29 October the cabinet formally requested the king, Victor Emmanuel, to declare a state of martial law and use the army to put down the fascist march. Had the king granted this request, as constitutionally he was bound to do, the March on Rome would have ended in a fiasco from which the fascist movement would have had difficulty in recovering. Instead, Victor Emmanuel invited Mussolini

Above, Benito Mussolini (1883–1945), fascist dictator of Italy: authoritarian, militaristic, imperialist and pompous though his regime was, it never wholeheartedly espoused the racialist doctrines of Nazi Germany (though anti-Semitic campaigns were waged) and in 1943 simply crumbled away, leaving little or no mark on the nation.

Opposite, revolutionary poster issued in Germany 1918–19 depicting a spartacist slaying the forces of militarism, capitalism and the Junkers, *the great Prussian landowners.*

to become prime minister. Hitherto, Mussolini had taken no part in the March on Rome, preferring to remain out of harm's way in Milan. On receiving the king's invitation, however, he donned a bowler hat, boarded a sleeping car and arrived in Rome ahead of his followers. When the fascists entered Rome on 30 October, Mussolini was already prime minister.

Mussolini established his dictatorship only by degrees. For eighteen months he remained head of a coalition government. For more than two years opposition parties and an opposition press continued to exist. As late as the summer of 1924, after the murder by fascists of a socialist deputy, the opposition almost succeeded in bringing Mussolini down. In January 1925, as a result of this experience, Mussolini declared Italy a one-party state.

At the time of the March on Rome no-one, not even Mussolini, had had much idea what fascist government would be like. Like the rest of Italy, Mussolini discovered as he went along. He declared:

We do not believe in dogmatic programmes. . . . We permit ourselves the luxury of being aristocratic and democratic, conservative and progressive, reactionary and revolutionary, legalists and illegalists, according to the circumstances of the moment, the place and the environment.

Though he was vague about his policies Mussolini was clear about the poses which he wanted to adopt. He was, he informed the readers of his *Autobiography*, the man who had preserved Italy from the threat of Bolshevism, cleansed it from the corruption of parliamentary government and had given it a new sense of national pride. Many foreign statesmen were taken in. Winston Churchill called Mussolini 'the saviour of his country'; Sir Austen Chamberlain, the British foreign secretary, felt 'confident that he is a patriot and a sincere man'. Ramsay MacDonald, Britain's first Labour prime minister, wrote him friendly letters even while Mussolini was busy destroying the Italian socialist party. Mussolini made much of his friendship with British statesmen and their wives. In 1925 he ordered no less than one and a half million copies of a postcard showing himself in conversation with Lady Chamberlain and had them distributed all over Italy.

Whatever their attitude to Mussolini himself, almost all European observers during the 1920s utterly mistook the significance of the fascist movement. They regarded fascism not as the beginning of a European movement but as a peculiarly Italian response to a peculiarly Italian situation. Mussolini himself endorsed their judgement. 'Fascism', he declared as late as 1928, 'is not an article for export.' Only the Nazis seemed to understand the European significance of the fascist revolution. 'The March on Rome', wrote Goebbels later, 'was a warning, a storm-signal for liberal democracy. It was the first attempt to destroy the world of the liberal, democratic spirit.'

Chapter 51

Europe and the Outside World

یہ سپاہی ہندوستان کی حفاظت کر رہا ہے۔وہ اپنے گھر اور گھر والوں کی حفاظت کر رہا ہے۔

اپنے گھر والوں کی مدد کرنے کا سب سے اچھا طریقہ یہ ہے کہ فوج میں بھرتی ہو جاؤ

To acute political observers it had long been obvious that Europe's supremacy in world affairs would one day be replaced by global rivalry between the United States and Russia. These two nations, wrote de Tocqueville in 1835, were each of them 'marked out by the will of heaven to sway the destinies of half the globe'. The First World War seemed to have brought the prophecies of both Cobden and de Tocqueville to fulfilment. The United States, now beyond dispute the greatest economic power on earth, emerged from the war apparently intent on claiming what Wilson called 'the moral leadership of all mankind'. Russia shared the same ambition. The November Revolution had made it the centre of a new world faith which, within a single generation, was to rule the destiny of a third of mankind and of whose powers of attraction the statesmen gathered at Versailles seemed to have no doubt.

The age of European supremacy was not to end, however, with the First World War. It was reprieved for twenty years by the simultaneous retreat of the United States and Russia from world affairs. In his inaugural address, in January 1921, President Harding formally renounced the vision of the future which Wilson had laid before the American people. 'We seek no part', he said, 'in directing the destinies of the world.' Most Americans, during the 1920s, came to the conclusion that the United States ought never to have entered 'Wilson's war' at all. As late as 1937, an opinion poll showed that seventy percent of Americans were still of this opinion.

While the United States was unwilling to 'direct the destinies of the world', the Soviet Union (as Russia renamed itself in 1922) was anxious, but unable, to do so. By the time of Lenin's death, in January 1924, the prospect of European revolution, which had earlier seemed so real both to the Bolsheviks themselves and to the peacemakers in Paris, had become remote. In his last article before his death, Lenin consoled himself for the Bolsheviks' disappointments in Europe with the optimistic reflection that 'the East has already entered the revolutionary movement' and that 'Russia, India, China, etc., constitute a huge majority of the world's population.'

The torch of revolution had begun to pass from the peoples of industrial Europe, for whom it had been intended, to the backward peasant masses of Asia. But even in Asia there seemed no immediate prospect of a successful revolution. The communist risings in Chinese cities during the later 1920s were no more successful than the risings in German cities during the early 1920s. Revolution in Asia, like revolution in Europe, could come about only as a result of war.

Though the primacy of Europe continued after the First World War, its basis had been seriously undermined by the European powers themselves. The principle of self-determination proclaimed by the Allies in Europe was one which colonial peoples were bound to apply to the European empires: and which, a generation later, was to provide the ideological basis for decolonization. In both Asia and the Middle East (though not in Africa) it was the First World War which

Above, Indian recruiting poster issued during the First World War: the caption reads 'this soldier is guarding India. He is guarding his home and his household. Thus we are guarding your home and you must join the army.' Like other parts of the Empire, India contributed large numbers of troops to the Allied war effort.

Opposite, Mussolini's blackshirts at Milan railway station: it was from here that Mussolini embarked on his personal march on Rome in October 1922–by train.

621

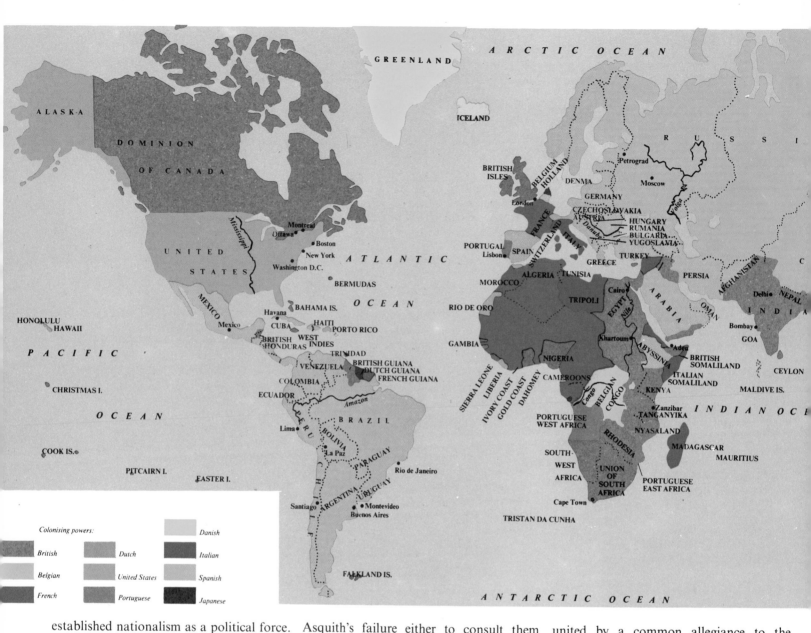

Map labels (selection):

ARCTIC OCEAN · GREENLAND · ICELAND · ALASKA · DOMINION OF CANADA · Montreal · Ottawa · Boston · New York · Washington D.C. · Mississippi · UNITED STATES · MEXICO · Mexico · Havana · CUBA · HAITI · PORTO RICO · BAHAMA IS. · BERMUDAS · ATLANTIC OCEAN · BRITISH HONDURAS · WEST INDIES · TRINIDAD · VENEZUELA · BRITISH GUIANA · DUTCH GUIANA · FRENCH GUIANA · COLOMBIA · ECUADOR · Amazon · BRAZIL · PERU · BOLIVIA · La Paz · Lima · PARAGUAY · CHILE · ARGENTINA · URUGUAY · Santiago · Montevideo · Buenos Aires · Rio de Janeiro · FALKLAND IS. · HONOLULU · HAWAII · PACIFIC OCEAN · CHRISTMAS I. · COOK IS. · PITCAIRN I. · EASTER I. · BRITISH ISLES · London · BELGIUM · HOLLAND · DENMA[RK] · GERMANY · CZECHOSLOVAKIA · AUSTRIA · HUNGARY · RUMANIA · BULGARIA · YUGOSLAVIA · FRANCE · SWITZERLAND · ITALY · PORTUGAL · Lisbon · SPAIN · GREECE · TURKEY · RUSSIA · Petrograd · Moscow · Volga · Danube · PERSIA · AFGHANISTAN · MOROCCO · ALGERIA · TUNISIA · TRIPOLI · EGYPT · Cairo · Nile · ARABIA · OMAN · Delhi · NEPAL · INDIA · Bombay · GOA · RIO DE ORO · GAMBIA · SIERRA LEONE · LIBERIA · IVORY COAST · GOLD COAST · DAHOMEY · NIGERIA · CAMEROONS · Khartoum · ABYSSINIA · Aden · BRITISH SOMALILAND · ITALIAN SOMALILAND · CEYLON · MALDIVE IS. · BELGIAN CONGO · Congo · KENYA · Zanzibar · TANGANYIKA · INDIAN OCEAN · PORTUGUESE WEST AFRICA · RHODESIA · NYASALAND · MADAGASCAR · MAURITIUS · SOUTH-WEST AFRICA · UNION OF SOUTH AFRICA · PORTUGUESE EAST AFRICA · Cape Town · TRISTAN DA CUNHA · ANTARCTIC OCEAN

Legend:

Colonising powers:

British · Belgian · French · Dutch · United States · Portuguese · Danish · Italian · Spanish · Japanese

---

established nationalism as a political force.

In the Middle East the Allies deliberately encouraged the growth of Arab nationalism against the Turkish Empire, only to find the same nationalism turning against themselves as soon as the war was over. In the two largest Asian colonies, India and Indonesia, the war witnessed the emergence of the National Congress and Sarekat Islam – hitherto middle class in membership and moderate in their demands – as mass movements demanding for the first time complete national independence.

The British Commonwealth of Nations

The First World War also transformed the relationship of the British dominions with the mother country. Responsibility for the foreign policy of the empire, Asquith had said in 1911, could never be shared with the dominions. In 1914 the dominions, like the rest of the empire, found themselves at war by a decision not of their own making but of the British government. Though the dominions accepted this decision without question, their governments came to resent

Asquith's failure either to consult them about the conduct of the war or even to keep them adequately informed about British policy. The very scale of the dominions' contribution to the war – 458,000 men from Canada, 332,000 from Australia, 112,000 from New Zealand, 76,000 from South Africa – made it inevitable that their voice should eventually be heard.

One of Lloyd George's earliest acts as prime minister was to announce the formation of an Imperial War Cabinet composed of the prime ministers and other representatives of Britain and the dominions. The new cabinet met in London for several weeks during both 1917 and 1918 to coordinate the imperial war effort and prepare for peace negotiations.

At the Imperial Conference of 1926 the dominions were formally conceded in theory the status which had been theirs in fact since 1917, couched in words which has passed into British constitutional history:

They are autonomous communities within the British Empire, equal in status, in no way subordinate one to another in any aspect of their domestic or external affairs, though

united by a common allegiance to the Crown, and freely associated as members of the British Commonwealth of Nations.

There was a deliberate and calculated ambiguity in the definition. Australian loyalists could pride themselves on remaining part of the British Empire; Afrikaaner nationalists, by contract, gained the satisfaction of being recognized as members of an autonomous community.

To many the whole idea of the Commonwealth of Nations was a piece of constitutional metaphysics which defied rational analysis. This was particularly true of the position of King George V, who, having begun his reign as ruler of a united empire, now found himself, rather to his annoyance, the owner of seven technically separate crowns: one for Britain and the colonies and one each for the six dominions (Australia, New Zealand, South Africa, Canada, Newfoundland, and, from 1922, Ireland). He was not amused by comments such as that of the sceptical Canadian historian, Professor Lower, who remarked: 'God in three persons is outnumbered by the British King in seven persons.'

Peking •

KOREA JAPANESE

Tokyo

EMPIRE

FORMOSA

Hong Kong

PACIFIC OCEAN

FRENCH
INDO
CHINA PHILIPPINE
ISLANDS

EAST INDIES

AYA

CELEBES

apore

BORNEO

NEW GUINEA

JAVA

GILBERT IS.

SOLOMON
ISLANDS

SAMOA

NEW
HEBRIDES FIJI IS.

TONGA

AUSTRALIA

Canberra • Sydney

Melbourne

NEW
ZEALAND

Wellington

Opposite, the colonial empires after the First World War.

For its supporters the Commonwealth had from the first a sentimental as much as a constitutional significance. Many probably shared the feelings of the future Australian prime minister, Sir Robert Menzies, who wrote later that the Commonwealth meant to him:

King George and Queen Mary coming to their Jubilee in Westminster Hall . . . at Canberra, at Wellington, at Ottawa, at Pretoria, the men of Parliament meeting as those who met at Westminster seven hundred years ago . . . Hammond at Sydney and Bradman at Lords and McCabe· at Trent Bridge, with the ghosts of Grace and Trumble looking on.

The First World War was followed by a steady drift of the dominions away from dependence on Britain. Between the wars most Canadian politicians accepted the dictum of Henri Bourassa, the leader of the French Canadians, that 'There is not a single problem of either internal or external policy which· we can settle without reference to the policy of the United States.' Sir Robert Borden, the Canadian prime minister, warned Lloyd George at the Paris

peace conference that 'if the future policy of the British Empire meant working in co-operation with some European nation as against the United States, that policy could not reckon on the approval or support of Canada.' In 1921 Borden's successor, Arthur Meighen, supported by South Africa, put pressure on Britain to abandon her alliance with Japan because of America's opposition to it.

Australasia followed, more slowly, the same path of growing dependence on the United States. For most of the interwar years Australia and New Zealand were overwhelmingly concerned with domestic problems, almost to the exclusion of foreign policy. Though their inhabitants were, by 1939, more prosperous than any other people in the world, neither as yet even possessed a diplomatic service in non-Commonwealth countries. As early as March 1914, however, Winston Churchill, as First Lord of the Admiralty, had warned Australasia that it could not depend on British naval support in the Pacific if Britain were involved in war in Europe. And without the Royal Navy to defend them, 'the only course of the five millions of white men in the Pacific would be to seek the protection of the United States'.

The rise of Japan during the 1930s and the realization that the Far East had now become, in the words of one New Zealand newspaper, 'Australasia's Near North', slowly convinced the governments of Australasia of the truth of Churchill's warning. At the beginning of 1942, even before the surrender of Singapore, the Australian prime minister, John Curtin, declared: 'Without any inhibitions of any kind, I make it quite clear that Australia looks to America, free of any pangs as to our traditional links of kinship with the United Kingdom.' Though the bluntness of Curtin's statement angered even Churchill (despite his earlier warning), it has remained ever since the underlying premise of Australia's defence policy.

The Irish Free State

The most restless of the dominions between the wars was also the newest and the nearest home. Until the First World War Ireland had been represented at Westminster by her own members of parliament, most of whom had demanded 'Home Rule', a formula which combined internal self-government with continued British sovereignty. The First World War made Irish nationalism, like the nationalism of other subject peoples, more extreme. At Easter 1916 a group of extremists seized the centre of Dublin and proclaimed an Irish republic 'in the name of God and of the dead generations'. After four days of street fighting the new republic surrendered and all but one of its leaders were executed. The single exception was the future president of

in the House of Commons, 'which would disgrace the blackest annals of the lowest despotism in Europe.' In the summer of 1921 Lloyd George abandoned hope of subduing Ireland by force, and the rebels agreed to a truce. In January 1922 the *Dáil* approved a treaty by which the Irish Free State was established with dominion status and Ulster was allowed to remain part of the United Kingdom.

In England the treaty helped to bring about the break-up of Lloyd George's coalition and the return to traditional party politics. In Ireland the bitterest phase of 'the troubles' now began. A republican minority, led by de Valéra, denounced the treaty as a surrender and began a civil war against their former colleagues. Some British ministers found it difficult to suppress a feeling of gratification at the sight of Irish nationalists tearing one another to pieces. Birkenhead, the lord chancellor, told the Lords in the summer of 1922: 'I, for one, rejoice, as I have said before in this House, that this task [the suppression of the rebellion], painful, costly, bloody as it must ultimately prove, is being undertaken by those to whom it properly falls.'

The atrocities committed by Irish against Irish after independence exceeded even those of the 'Black and Tans'. Government forces took to disposing of groups of their opponents by tying them to mines which were then exploded. Before the civil war ended in the spring of 1923, the Free State government had executed more than three times as many Irishmen as the British had done in the two years before independence. After independence de Valéra remained for a decade in the political wilderness. But in 1932 he returned to power at the head of a new party, the *Fianna Fáil* ('Soldiers of Destiny') and began gradually to dismantle Ireland's last links with Britain.

Imperial superiority

Few Europeans after the First World War realized that the decline of Europe had begun. The fact that Europe now controlled more of the outside world than ever before seemed more impressive than the faint stirrings of opposition to its rule. The British Empire had gained a million square miles at the expense of Turkey and Germany. It now contained a quarter of the earth's surface and a quarter of mankind. Few British people had any suspicion that the power of their empire was being weakened by the growth of a Commonwealth within it. The South African prime minister, Jan Smuts, the most persuasive advocate of the Commonwealth of Nations, emphatically denied that this was so. The British Empire, he told the Imperial Conference of 1921, 'emerged from the war quite the greatest power in the world, and it is only unwisdom or unsound policy that could rob her of that great position'.

Ireland, Eamon de Valéra, born in the United States of a Spanish father and Irish mother, whose American nationality earned him a reprieve.

In the short term the Easter Rising achieved only the destruction of much of central Dublin. In the longer term, it meant the abandonment of Home Rule. The 450 Irish lives lost during the rising, and the sixteen executions which followed it ('few but corroding', as Churchill described them), shocked most Irishmen outside Ulster into supporting the nationalist demand for complete independence.

By the end of the war most Irish MPs had already left Westminster. After the 1918 elections they established an independent Irish parliament, the *Dáil Eireann*, and an independent Irish government under Eamon de Valéra. The new government hoped at first, by levying its own taxes and administering its own justice, simply to take over peacefully from the discredited British administration. Over much of Ireland it might well have done so. The Irish Republican Army, however, thought otherwise. Against the wishes of the *Dáil*, it began its own guerrilla war against the British.

In 1920 the British brought in their own *Freikorps*, the so-called 'Black and Tans' and 'Auxis', whose atrocities rivalled, and perhaps exceeded, those of the IRA. 'Things are being done in Ireland', said Asquith

Patriotic pride in the British Empire was still a recent phenomenon. The idea that Britain possessed some kind of mission to the 'lesser breeds without the law' had captured a hold on the popular imagination only in the last decade of the nineteenth century. By 1918, however, most British people already regarded this mission as one of their oldest traditions. Their mood was reflected in the tune and words of 'Land of Hope and Glory', by now so popular that it had come to be regarded as a second national anthem. There were few who doubted the immense moral superiority of the British Empire over all other empires past and present. It was, said Lloyd George in 1921, 'the most hopeful experiment in human organization which the world has yet seen'. Hardly anyone was eccentric enough to suppose that within half a century the empire would have almost disappeared.

European rule in Africa

European rule over most of the African continent, though profound in its effects, was comparatively brief – less, in many cases, than a single lifetime. Between the wars, however, most British people thought of Africans as rather child-like people, probably incapable of ever running their own affairs, in general cheerful and easygoing but retaining beneath a thin layer of civilization an aura of primeval savagery.

This, at least, was the image of the peoples of Africa which most schoolchildren in Britain learned from their geography textbooks. One of the most popular of these textbooks was *Children Far Away*, by Ernest Young, a fellow of the Royal Geographical Society, which was first published in 1919 and reprinted twelve times in the next six years. Young's book devotes two of its seven chapters to the children of Africa: one to the negroes, the other to the pygmies. White negro children ('the little blackies') emerge from Young's description as mindless but moderately benevolent. Pygmy children are portrayed as both mindless and malevolent: 'The pygmy children do not love their father or mother, and their fathers and mothers do not love them. They care nothing for their own land or people. All they want is to hunt and to eat. They are cruel to one another.'

White rule in English-speaking Africa took two quite different forms. In West Africa and much of East Africa it was based on the system of 'indirect rule' made famous by the most celebrated of Britain's African proconsuls, Sir Frederick Lugard. Lugard believed in strengthening traditional government by tribal chiefs – if necessary even creating tribal goverments where there had been none before – and placing the chiefs themselves under the paternal care of British district officers. By these means he succeeded in governing the whole of Nigeria, the largest state in Africa (with one-fifth of Africa's population), with a civil service of

little more than a few hundred men.

Just as Lugard's Nigeria became the showcase of British imperial administration, so his book, *The Dual Mandate in Tropical Africa*, first published in 1922, became the bible of British imperialism between the wars. In it Lugard argued that Britain possessed a duty both to the peoples of Africa and to civilization itself: to the peoples of Africa, to watch over their political and economic advancement; and to civilized society as a whole, to make sure that Africa's natural resources were available to it. 'The merchant, the miner and the manufacturer', he wrote, 'do not enter the tropics on sufferance or employ their technical skill, their energy, and their capital as interlopers or as "greedy capitalists", but in fulfilment of the mandate of civilization.' The eventual goal of European rule should be to prepare the peoples of Africa to manage their own affairs. But Lugard warned against going at too fast a pace: 'The danger of going too fast with native races is more likely to lead to disappointment, if not to disaster, than the danger of not going fast enough.'

Neither South Africa nor Southern Rhodesia (which, though not independent, gained virtual self-government in 1923) had any thought of preparing their native populations for eventual independence, however remote that independence might be. Their aim, which was shared by many white settlers in other parts of East Africa, was to create new white nations in southern Africa and 'keep the kaffir in his place'. The case for white rule in southern Africa was bluntly put by a government official in Southern Rhodesia: 'We are in this country because we are better men. It is our only excuse for having taken the land. For us to turn round now and ask the natives to help in directing the government of ourselves is ridiculous.'

After the First World War many people in both Britain and South Africa (including both Churchill and Smuts) expected Southern Rhodesia to seek union with South Africa. To their surprise, a referendum in Southern Rhodesia in 1922 turned down a proposal for union. This decision was a momentous one for the whole of Africa. As a fifth province within the Union of South Africa, Southern Rhodesia might have tipped the balance in favour of the English-speaking population and made less likely both the dominance of the Afrikaner nationalists after World War Two and the era of apartheid which they inaugurated.

On the eve of World War Two there seemed no reason to anticipate either the racial tensions which were soon to show themselves in southern Africa or the pressures for independence which were soon to emerge within Africa as a whole. Though the phrase 'racial conflict' was in common use in southern Africa, it referred at that time not to tensions between black and white but to rivalry between the English and Afrikaner communities. Except in the Arab north, African opposition to European rule still seemed a negligible quantity. There was not a single nationalist movement of any importance struggling to achieve independence in any African colony south of the Sahara Desert.

The future of the African continent was decided far less by events in Africa itself between the wars than by India's struggle for independence. India, as the popular platitude put it, was 'the brightest jewel in the imperial crown'. Its population of 315,000,000 was three-quarters of that of the entire British Empire. It was in India that the decline of the British Empire began.

The Indian subcontinent

At the outbreak of the First World War British rule had seemed as secure in India as it appeared to be in Africa on the eve of the Second. The outburst of patriotism which greeted the declaration of war in Calcutta almost equalled that in London. In 1857 the use of Indian troops outside India had been one of the causes of the Indian Mutiny. Yet in 1914 Indian princes competed for the privilege of being the first to lead their forces to the front. While the princes offered troops, the middle classes offered money, and the Legislative Assembly volunteered to pay part of the cost of the war in Europe.

In retrospect, however, the war was to prove the beginning of the end of the British raj and the beginning of the end, also, of the British Empire. As the war continued the war-weariness which became common in Europe spread to India, but, while soldiers on the Western Front at least believed that they were fighting for national survival, Indians seemed to be giving their lives in Mesopotamia and the Middle East simply for the extension of the British Empire. At the beginning of the war there

had been no shortage of Indian recruits. During its later stages Britain was reduced to using press gangs.

Resentment against Britain was less serious for the future of the raj than the decline of British prestige. British rule in India rested, in the last resort, not on military coercion but on respect for the moral, as well as material, superiority of British civilization. As soon as belief in that superiority disappeared, as it began to do during the First World War, the days of the British raj were numbered.

The British government responded to the unrest caused by the war with a pledge – the Montagu Declaration of 1917 – which was interpreted in India as a promise of dominion status. But by raising hopes which Britain seemed reluctant to fulfil the Montagu Declaration only hastened the growth of opposition to British rule. The reforms introduced immediately after the war by the Government of India Act of 1919, though a substantial departure from the autocracy of the pre-war raj, seemed utterly inadequate as a preparation for self-government. As Adolf Hitler was later to observe, 'Britain has given to the Indians the opportunity of using as a weapon against her the non-fulfilment of her promises regarding a constitution.'

Before the First World War there had been no movement in India capable of organizing a mass demand for independence. The Indian National Congress was still a middle-class debating society which met briefly each December and then lapsed into inactivity for another year. There was nothing in 1914 to suggest that Congress would emerge from the war as a mass movement which would become the focus of resistance to the British raj. The man who brought about this transformation was Mohandas Gandhi, a barrister of the Inner Temple who, more than any other man, set in motion the process which was to lead to the downfall of the British Empire.

Until the war Gandhi had lived almost all his adult life outside India. He had made his name as the champion of the Indian community in South Africa, and it was there that he developed the technique of *satyagraha*, or passive resistance, which he was to use against the raj. Much of Gandhi's political success was a result of the aura of sanctity about his person which won him the devotion of the Hindu masses. After his return to India he abandoned western dress in favour of a loincloth, rigorously and ostentatiously adhered to the rules of poverty and chastity and identified himself with the cause of 'the untouchables', the lowest class in Indian society, whom he renamed the *Harijans*, or the sons of God. Gandhi sought not merely political freedom from British rule but spiritual emancipation from the materialism of western civilization. He claimed for India precisely that moral superiority which the British raj had hitherto assumed for himself.

The war was followed by an influenza epidemic which killed more Indians than the Western Front had killed Europeans. The epidemic added to the unrest caused by the war. The chief centre of unrest was the Punjab where most of the British press gangs had been concentrated. In April 1919 a prohibited meeting at the Punjabi town of Amritsar was dispersed without warning by troops using rifles and machine guns. The official casualty list was 379 dead and more than 1,000 wounded. General Dyer, the officer responsible for the order to open fire, was unrepentant. He followed the massacre by public floggings and forced all Indians using a street where a British woman missionary had been assaulted to crawl along it on all fours.

The Amritsar massacre has been called 'the worst atrocity in the history of the British Empire'. But it was less the massacre itself than the attempts to justify it in Britain which produced a revulsion against British rule. Though Dyer was dismissed by the Indian government, there were many in Britain who vigorously defended his conduct. The House of Lords passed, by a large majority, a motion in Dyer's favour, and the readers of the *Morning Post* subscribed £30,000 in appreciation of his action.

The result of Amritsar was to give Gandhi control of Congress and its endorsement for his view that 'cooperation in any shape or form with this satanic government is sinful.' In the summer of 1920 Gandhi began a campaign of non-cooperation which, he forecast optimistically, would bring the British raj to its knees within a year. But though thousands of students left their schools and colleges, and thousands of middle-class members of Congress began spinning cotton by hand (an activity to which Gandhi attributed spiritual as well as economic significance) instead of buying it from Lancashire, non-cooperation failed. It did so because thousands of Indian civil servants, even though sympathetic to Gandhi's aims, dared not take the enormous risk of resigning from their posts. By the end of 1921 many of Gandhi's followers were already losing heart.

Early in 1922, after twenty-two policemen had been burnt to death by a Hindu mob, Gandhi himself called off his campaign. The people of India, he concluded sadly, did not yet possess a sufficient understanding of the principle of non-violence for non-cooperation to achieve its aims. Soon afterwards, Gandhi was arrested and found guilty of incitement. 'It would be impossible', Gandhi was told by his judge, 'to ignore the fact that, in the eyes of millions of your countrymen, you are a great patriot and a great leader. Even those who differ from you in politics look upon you as a man of high ideals and of noble and even saintly life.' But Gandhi would 'not consider it unreasonable', the judge believed, that he should go to prison for six years: 'And I should like to say . . . that, if the course of events in India should make it possible for the government to reduce the period and release you, no one will be better pleased than I.'

On Gandhi's imprisonment, organized resistance to British rule seemed to have collapsed. By 1924 the Indian government felt, as Gandhi's judge had hoped, that it could safely release Gandhi from prison on the grounds of ill-health.

The British government still had no serious intention of preparing India for self-rule. Lord Birkenhead, the secretary of state for India, admitted in a letter to the viceroy in 1925: 'To me it is frankly inconceivable that India will ever be fit for Dominion self-government.' But Birkenhead thought it as well to anticipate further trouble by making some conciliatory gesture to Indian opinion. In 1927, therefore, the British government established the all-party Simon Commission (which included among its members the young Clement Attlee) to enquire into the Indian constitution.

By omitting to include on it any Indian member, however, Britain made the Simon Commission appear a calculated insult to the Indian people. Even those Indians best disposed towards Britain refused to have anything to do with it. Like the Amritsar massacre, the Simon Commission discredited the moderates and played into the hands of the militants. In December 1928 Congress issued an ultimatum to the British government demanding self-government within a year. When the year expired it declared India an independent state and authorized Gandhi to launch a new campaign of civil disobedience. The new campaign was to include, for the first time, sins of commission as well as omission: a programme of non-violent crime on so vast a scale that Gandhi believed the administration of justice would grind to a halt.

Gandhi began his campaign with a crime brilliantly calculated to show the raj at its most ridiculous and its most unjust. Probably the least defensible of all the methods of taxation used by the raj was its salt monopoly, reminiscent of the hated *gabelle* in pre-revolutionary France. It was an offence not merely to sell but even to possess salt not purchased from the British monopoly, and it was this monopoly which Gandhi decided to challenge. Amid the glare of world-wide publicity he began a three-week walk to the Indian Ocean. Having arrived at the seashore, he was photographed by newsreel cameras solemnly breaking the law by extracting salt from the sea. After a brief period of uncertainty while the raj made up its mind, Gandhi was sent to prison, soon to be joined by 60,000 of his followers. The British government hurriedly called a 'round-table conference' to discuss the future of India, but its discussions were made meaningless by the absence of any Congress representative.

Early in 1931 the British viceroy, Lord Irwin (later, as Lord Halifax, British foreign

secretary at the time of the Munich crisis), released Gandhi from prison and invited him to begin talks with him. Gandhi replied that he would like to meet 'not the viceroy but the man within the viceroy'. He displayed that the same flair for publicity in his meetings with Irwin that he had earlier shown on his walk to the sea. He went on foot each day to the viceroy's palace, surrounded by crowds of his supporters and large numbers of reporters and carrying an aluminium saucepan containing his food for the day. In Britain Winston Churchill fulminated against

the nauseating and humiliating spectacle of this one-time Inner Temple lawyer, now seditious fakir, striding half-naked up the steps of the viceroy's palace, there to negotiate and parley on equal terms with the representative of the King-Emperor.

Above, Mohandas (Mahatma) Gandhi (1869–1948) leading the Salt March, 1930: Gandhi's Congress Party played a central role in the campaign first for Indian self-government, then for complete independence.

Top, Indian demonstration against the Simon Commission: the Commission, headed by Sir John Simon (1873–1954), later to become foreign secretary, proposed indirect elections for the central legislature and increased local democracy, but the India Act passed in 1935 went considerably further in devolving power.

The result of the talks was the 'Gandhi-Irwin truce'. Irwin agreed to the release of all political prisoners, except those convicted of crimes of violence. Gandhi agreed to call off the civil disobedience campaign and attend a second round-table conference in London.

The truce, however, lasted less than a year. In London Gandhi demanded immediate dominion status, and the conference ended in deadlock. Within a few weeks of his return to India at the beginning of 1932, Gandhi was once again in prison. Congress fell, once more, into partial eclipse, as it had done ten years before when he was first imprisoned. Most Indians remained sympathetic towards its aims, but few were yet prepared to continue an indefinite struggle with the raj.

The British government and parliament continued nonetheless to be preoccupied with the future of the Indian subcontinent. A succession of 'fact-finding' commissions went back and forth to India, returning, as Churchill complained, laden with 'bulky and indigestible sheaves'. The final result of these deliberations was the Government of India Act of 1935, ridiculed by Churchill as 'a monstrous monument of sham built by the pygmies'. Under it central government remained safely in the hands of the viceroy but the provinces acquired a high degree of local autonomy and responsible government.

Congress was at first bitterly divided over its attitude to the new constitution, its left wing under Jawaharlal Nehru urging rejection of it. Eventually, however, Congress agreed to contest the first elections held under the new constitution in 1937 and won control of eight of the eleven provinces. The experience of government during the two years before the Second World War was a turning-point in the history of Congress. It marked its transformation from a movement seeking to gain its ends by unconstitutional means into a parliamentary party. Congress politicians and British officials, who had hitherto regarded each other with deep suspicion, now discovered that relations between them were often surprisingly good – a discovery which did much to smooth the course of independence negotiations after the war.

The great mistake made by Congress during the 1930s was in its treatment of the Muslims. During the 1920s Congress leaders had, on the whole, been conscious of the need for the Hindu majority to respect the rights of the Muslim minority. In ten years there had been five Muslim presidents of Congress. 'Hindu-Muslim unity', said Gandhi, 'is our breath of life.' The idea of Pakistan ('the land of the pure') originated, not on the Indian subcontinent itself, but among a group of Muslim undergraduates studying in England at Cambridge University in 1932.

Even in the middle of the 1930s, despite signs of tension between the Hindu and Muslim communities, a separate Muslim state after independence was still the ambition of only a small minority of Indian Muslims. Jinnah, the leader of the Muslim League, declared in 1937: 'There is really no difference between the League and Congress. . . . We shall always be glad to cooperate with Congress in their constructive programme.'

At the 1937 elections the League declared its willingness to form coalitions with Congress in the new provincial governments. Elated with their electoral success, however, Congress leaders refused to allow the Muslim League any share of power in the states which they controlled. No British government between the wars made any mistake of comparable magnitude in its Indian policy. Denied its rightful share in the government of India, the Muslim League was forced back on the idea of Pakistan: an ambition which was to be fulfilled only at the cost of a religious civil war on the Indian subcontinent and the loss of a million lives.

The Middle East

Britain's relations with the people of Egypt were worse than with any other of its subject peoples. The Egyptians became derisively known as 'wogs', a term later more broadly used to indicate the British image of the shifty foreigner. The British themselves, however, had shown a degree of shiftiness in establishing themselves in Egypt which had no parallel in the history of Victorian imperialism.

Britain had sent troops to Egypt in 1882 to put down an anti-European uprising, insisting that these troops would leave as soon as order had been restored. 'An indefinite occupation', declared Gladstone, the British prime minister, 'would be absolutely at variance with all the principles and views of Her Majesty's Government, and the pledges they have given Europe.' Though this pledge was many times repeated, the 'temporary occupation' was to last for seventy years.

Britain broke her word for strategic, rather than for economic, reasons. Even between the wars oil was still only a minor consideration in British policy in the Middle East. On the eve of the Second World War the whole of the Middle East produced no more than five percent of the world's oil. But the Suez canal, which ran through Egyptian territory, was regarded as the most vital link in Britain's imperial communications, the 'lifeline of the Empire'. In British eyes the safety of this lifeline demanded the permanent presence of British troops on Egyptian soil and British control of Egyptian foreign policy.

Despite the length of its military occupation, Britain's protectorate in Egypt lasted officially for only eight years. Its protectorate began soon after the outbreak of the First World War and came allegedly to an end in 1922 when Britain declared Egypt independent. Both British troops and the British high commissioner remained, however, and Britain claimed continued responsibility for Egypt's defence and foreign policy and for the protection of foreign interests in Egypt. The nationalist Wafd party reasonably declared that independence on these terms would be a farce. The sultan, Ahmed Fuad, was torn between his dislike of the British and his loathing for the politicians of the Wafd, most of whom combined nationalism and corruption in about equal proportions.

After a year's haggling, largely devoted to increasing his own powers, Fuad agreed to independence on terms which raised him from sultan to the status of a rather more than constitutional monarch. Though Britain slightly relaxed its grip on Egypt after the accession of King Farouk in 1936, British troops remained in Egypt for another twenty years.

The greater part of the Middle East in 1914 still belonged to the decaying Turkish Empire. Besides Egypt, only Cyprus and an assortment of sheikdoms under British protection in the Persian Gulf were under European control. The peace settlement which followed the First World War, however, established European rule over almost the whole of the Middle East. Britain's part in bringing about this transformation was more disreputable than any other episode in the history of its twentieth-century diplomacy. Ramsay MacDonald described it thus:

We encouraged a revolt in Turkey by a promise [in 1915] to create an Arab kingdom from the Arab provinces of the [Turkish] Empire including Palestine. At the same time we were encouraging the Jews to help us by promising them that Palestine would be placed at their disposal for settlement and government; and also at the same time, we were making with the French the Sykes-Picot Agreement partitioning the territories which we had instructed our governor-general in Egypt to promise to the Arabs. The story is one of crude duplicity, and we cannot expect to escape the reprobation which is bound to follow as a sequel.

As part of the post-war settlement Britain and France divided between them most of Turkey's former Arab empire. France took Syria and Lebanon, Britain acquired Iraq (formerly known as Mesopotamia), Transjordan and Palestine. Saudi Arabia, which neither country wanted, was given to the Arabs as an independent kingdom.

The horse-trading between Britain and France in the Middle East was made more respectable by the new principle of 'trusteeship'. Both countries acquired their shares of the Turkish Empire not as colonies but as mandates from the League of Nations and recognized a duty to watch over their

'progressive development . . . until such time as they can stand alone'. Most of the Middle East, however, gained its independence only after World War Two. Though the British mandate in Iraq ended formally in 1932, Britain continued, as in Egypt, a form of indirect rule by virtue of so-called 'treaty rights' which gave it military and financial control.

One unexpected by-product of British rule in Iraq was the birth of the Royal Air Force as an independent service. In 1922 Britain succeeded in quelling a tribal revolt in Iraq not, as in the past, by a military expedition but by bombing from the air. For the first time it seemed possible to envisage a European war decided as much in the air as on the ground. As a result, Britain became in 1923 the first country in the world to free its air force from dependence on the other services.

The most serious long-term problem bequeathed by Britain's devious wartime diplomacy in the Middle East arose from its promise to the Jews. The terms of Britain's mandate in Palestine made it responsible for putting this promise into effect by 'the establishment in Palestine of a national home for the Jewish people'. The Arabs, who made up more than ninety percent of the Palestinian population, were at once assured by Britain that the Jewish national home would not become a Jewish national state and that all their 'civil and religious rights' would be respected. A national state, however, was precisely what the Zionist movement (which was responsible for the idea of a 'national home' in Palestine) intended to achieve – a state which, in the words of Dr Weizmann, its leader, would be 'as Jewish as England is English'.

As a first step towards this goal, Zionists insisted on the strict separation of Arab and Jewish communities. Jewish parents refused to send their children to mixed government schools. Arab tenants and farm workers were evicted from all land bought by the Jewish National Fund. David Ben-Gurion, later the first prime minister of the state of Israel, organized a series of strikes against Jewish employers of Arab labour. The Jewish Agency, which coordinated Jewish settlement in Palestine, sought, with some success, to make itself a state within a state. Until the First World War the Arabs had been the only people living in contact with the Jews who had never persecuted them. The birth of Arab anti-semitism between the wars was the work not of Adolf Hitler but of the Zionists.

One of the first British ministers to deal with the Palestinian problem was Winston Churchill, colonial secretary during the final year of Lloyd George's coalition. In a White Paper published in 1922, Churchill correctly defined the crux of the problem (though in an uncharacteristically inelegant phrase) as one of relating Jewish immigration to Palestine's 'absorptive capacity'. During the 1920s Palestine's 'absorptive capacity' never seemed in danger. In most years, there were no more than 5,000 Jewish immigrants. At such a rate of immigration, Arab predominance in Palestine was not in danger, and British administrators could look forward to an eventual lessening of the tension between the two communities.

What no British government during the 1920s could be expected to foresee was the vast influx, in the next decade, of Jewish refugees from Nazi persecution. Though Britain tried in vain to stem the flow in 1939, the Second World War made it unstoppable. It was less the Zionists than Adolf Hitler who made possible the creation, in 1948, of the Jewish state of Israel out of most of pre-war Palestine.

The European empires

The British Empire was larger, both in size and population, than all other European empires put together. The empires of Italy, Belgium, Spain and Portugal were all virtually confined to Africa. That of the

Above, illegal Jewish immigrants to Palestine wading ashore, having dodged the Royal Navy's blockade, late 1930s: throughout that decade the British government restricted the number of Jews entering Palestine, so condemning many to remain in Europe to await eventual death in Hitler's concentration camps.

Above left, Chaim Weizmann (1874–1952), appointed head of the World Zionist Movement in 1920, with King Faisal I of Syria, later of Iraq (1885–1933), 1921: at this time, Jewish immigration into Palestine was small, and Jewish leaders tried to gain the cooperation of Arab leaders, though it was not long before open hostility broke out.

Netherlands consisted only of the Dutch East Indies and Dutch Guiana. Germany had no empire at all. Curiously, it was the oldest and most decrepit empires – those of Spain and Portugal – which were to last the longest. In Asia the last European colony to gain its independence was the tiny Portuguese enclave of Goa, on the Indian subcontinent. In Africa, by the end of the 1960s, Portugal's empire was larger than Great Britain's.

Apart from Britain, only France – with colonies in Africa, Asia, the Middle East, the West Indies and the Pacific – could claim to be a world power. But even France's empire, both in size and population, was less than half Britain's. It was also far more rebellious. In Africa, Asia and the Middle East, France was faced with armed rebellion on a scale not encountered by Britain until after the Second World War. During the 1920s there were serious revolts in both Syria and Morocco. The pacification of Morocco was not complete until the middle of the 1930s and Syria never really accepted French rule. In Indo-China the French administration seemed during 1930 to have caught a nationalist rebellion in its early stages and restored order by hundreds of executions. But by the beginning of the Second World War, there was already a powerful communist underground movement led by Ho Chi Minh which, once the war was over, was to launch a successful struggle for independence.

Though the French Empire was more autocratic than the British, Frenchmen were less troubled than Englishmen by racial differences between themselves and their colonial peoples. The long-term aim of the French colonial administration was to turn its subjects into Frenchmen. A British minister remarked in 1926:

In these matters we are apparently by nature the exact opposite of the French. The French have no doubt that the more French they can make French Africa in language, sentiment, custom, and outlook, the better. We cannot help doubting whether any persons not of our race can really become British in this way.

Increasingly French colonial enthusiasts regarded their colonies – especially in Africa – not as colonies at all but as extensions of France itself. For this reason many Frenchmen regarded their own empire, even though far smaller than the British, as superior to it. As one Gaullist minister was later to remark, referring to the supposed enthusiasm of Algerians for union with France: 'This is something unique! Whoever heard of any Pakistani shouting "*Pakistan anglais*"?'

The imperial mission was a transitory experience. Most people in France and Britain did not take it seriously until the very end of the nineteenth century. By the 1960s, most of them no longer believed in it. The young Disraeli had described most British colonies in the nineteenth century as 'wretched millstones'. Little more than a century later, such a description exactly fitted Britain's only remaining mainland colony, Rhodesia. But the imperial mission left a legacy behind. During the 1950s Dean Acheson described Britain as having 'lost an empire but not yet found a role'. Other peoples who were equally civilized and equally prosperous, like the Swiss and Scandinavians, did not feel that they needed to find a role precisely because they had never had an empire to lose. The imperial mission left in post-imperial Britain and in post-imperial France the conviction that the world still needed the light of their example.

Chapter 52

Prosperity and Depression

The later 1920s were the last period of real optimism in the history of Europe. The years of optimism began in 1925 with the treaty of Locarno, a non-aggression pact between France, Germany and Belgium, guaranteed by Britain and Italy. Locarno, said Sir Austen Chamberlain, would be remembered as 'the real dividing line between the years of war and the years of peace'. To many European statesmen it seemed a landmark in European history, the end of an era of deep hostility between France and Germany which had continued without a break from the Franco-Prussian war of 1870 to the occupation of the Ruhr in 1923. Geneviève Tabouis, the most famous French journalist of her generation, wrote of her reaction to Locarno:

I was literally drunk with joy. It seemed too good to be true that Germany, our enemy of yesterday, had actually signed the pact with its eight clauses of reconciliation! From now on, no more fears for the future! No more war!

The reconciliation between France and Germany was strengthened by the friendship of their foreign ministers, Aristide Briand and Gustav Stresemann. Briand was the greatest exponent of what A. P. Herbert called 'Locarno blarney', the emotional incantations to peace which flowed from the lips of most statesmen of the period. His oratory earned him the title of 'the archangel of peace', and he was regularly depicted by French cartoonists in the act of turning swords into ploughshares. Briand's most famous speech was his welcome to Stresemann on Germany's admission to the League of Nations in September 1926. In retrospect, his speech seems tinged with bathos: 'From this day forth women will be able to fix their eyes on little children without feeling their hearts torn by anxiety!' But it captured completely the mood of the Locarno honeymoon. No speech in European history has aroused so much enthusiasm over so much of Europe.

Soon after welcoming Stresemann to the League of Nations, Briand invited him to a private lunch at Thoiry in the French Alps. The two men announced after lunch that they had 'established the basis for a political understanding', though the nature of this understanding was never afterwards discovered. 'You can call it the mystery of Thoiry,' Briand told journalists, 'What a good title for a thriller!' But, he added whimsically, 'while we were sitting at luncheon we watched the clouds lift from the top of Mont Blanc, and we both agreed that its snows were no whiter than the bottom of our two hearts.'

The high point of the Locarno honeymoon was the Briand-Kellogg treaty of 1928. In April 1927 Briand proposed to the American government that France and the United States should celebrate the tenth anniversary of the American entry into the

Above, Gustav Stresemann (1878–1929), briefly chancellor of Germany in 1923 and then foreign minister until his death: he brought Germany out of her diplomatic isolation following the First World War.

Opposite, Moorish troops during the 1921 uprising in North Africa, when the Spanish garrisons in Morocco were overwhelmed: it was five years before Spanish control was firmly re-established.

First World War by a pact renouncing war as an instrument of national policy. Kellogg, the American secretary of state, replied six months later by suggesting (with one eye on the next presidential election) that such a pact should be extended to include the whole world. As a first step towards this end, the representatives of fifteen leading powers met in Paris in August 1928 to sign a treaty by which all agreed (though sometimes with reservations) to outlaw war.

The signature of the pact was surrounded by a slightly idiotic ceremonial, devised by Briand and satirized by one French newspaper as 'the celebration of Briand's spiritual wedding with peace'. Almost every state in the world hastened to add its signature to it, including even the Soviet Union which, like the United States, was not a member of the League. Only five states – Argentina, Bolivia, Brazil, Saudi Arabia and the Yemen – refused to sign. The pact was the supreme example of 'Locarno blarney', of the belief that words alone possessed the power to prevent aggression. Its only effect during the 1930s was possibly to make states more reluctant to declare war before they began to wage it.

The League of Nations

Looking back in 1930 on the achievements of the 1920s, most European statesmen still felt optimistic for the future. The League of Nations, though derided at its outset by those who considered themselves political realists, was now an accepted part of international diplomacy. It had, according to *The Times*, 'quietly made good'. The League had had so far to face only one major challenge to its authority: Mussolini's seizure of the Greek island of Corfu in 1923 after the murder in Greece of an Italian general. As a result of mediation through the League, Mussolini had undertaken to

withdraw from Corfu in return for fifty million lire from Greece. Though this settlement clearly favoured the stronger power, it was widely regarded as a victory for so new an organization. Without the League, it was argued, the seizure of Corfu might have developed into a European war. The fact that for the remainder of the 1920s the League had to face no further challenge to its authority from any major power seemed to demonstrate its growing authority.

Introducing a report on the League's first ten years in 1930, its secretary-general summed up the prospects for the future by quoting from a speech by General Smuts:

Looked at in its true light, in the light of the age and of the time-honoured ideas and practice of mankind, we are beholding an amazing thing – we are witnessing one of the great miracles of history. . . . The League may be a difficult scheme to work, but the significant thing is that the Powers have pledged themselves to work it . . . Mankind has, as it were, at one bound and in the short space of ten years, jumped from the old order to the new, across a gulf which may yet prove to be the greatest break or divide in human history.

The return of prosperity

The optimism of the Locarno honeymoon was in part a consequence of economic prosperity. In 1925, the year of the Locarno pact, European production for the first time reached its pre-war level. The return of prosperity was symbolized by Winston Churchill's decision as chancellor of the exchequer to put Britain back on the gold standard in the same year and make sterling once again freely convertible into gold. By 1928 all other European currencies had followed suit. Between 1925 and 1929, the volume of international trade rose by

almost twenty percent and by 1929 Europe's share of world production was once again as large as before the First World War.

The prosperous years of the later 1920s were characterized by conservative statesmen who contrived to make a virtue of their own inertia. Calvin Coolidge had won the 1924 election in the United States by telling the electorate to 'Keep Cool with Coolidge'. Stanley Baldwin, similarly, urged the British people to trust 'honest Stanley' and be content with a policy of 'safety first'. Though there were many gaps in the prosperity of the later 1920s, the Conservative governments of the time paid little attention to them. In Britain, for example, there were never less than a million unemployed. Yet, even after the General Strike of 1926, parliament contrived to spend more time discussing the revision of the Anglican Prayer Book than the problem of unemployment. Happily for the Conservative party, the inactivity of Baldwin's government enabled it to lose the 1929 election, just in time to leave a Labour government to face the depression.

The great flaw in the European prosperity of the Locarno era was that it depended for its continuance on the unstable prosperity of the American economy. This dependence was one of the most important consequences of the First World War. For a century before 1914 investment had flowed across the Atlantic from east to west. Ever since it has flowed emphatically in the opposite direction. The European economy in the 1920s depended for its prosperity on massive American investment. In the five years from 1925 to 1929 alone, this investment amounted to no less than $2,900 million. Germany, with a total debt of $1,000 million, depended on American investment not merely to remain prosperous but even to remain solvent. Yet the continued availability of American investment depended on the continuation of a speculative boom which ran increasingly out of control.

By the summer of 1929 share prices on Wall Street were nearly four times higher than four years before, and five million shares were changing hands every day. Most Americans seemed to imagine that the prosperity of the Locarno era would go on for ever. President Coolidge told Congress in his last message on the State of the Union, in December 1928:

No Congress of the United States ever assembled, on surveying the state of the Union, has met with a more pleasing prospect than that which appears at the present time. In the domestic field there is tranquillity and contentment and the highest record of years of prosperity. In the foreign field there is peace, the goodwill which comes from mutual understanding.

Herbert Hoover, Coolidge's successor as president of the United States, was equally optimistic. In his election campaign he promised Americans not merely 'a full

dinner pail but 'a full garage' too. Not even the economists seemed to have any premonition of what was coming. A fortnight before the biggest crash in the history of the American stock market, Professor Irving Fisher, the doyen of Yale economists confidently predicted, 'I expect to see the stock market a good deal higher than it is today within a few months.'

The Great Depression

On 'Black Thursday', 24 October 1929, the speculative bubble burst. In the next nine days $40,000 million were wiped off the value of American securities. With the collapse of the stock market, lending to Europe ceased and all existing loans were recalled as soon as their term expired. Since most American loans had been short-term, their withdrawal from Europe came with catastrophic suddenness. Yet, while calling in its loans, the United States continued until the summer of 1931 to demand punctilious payment of war debts owing to it. And by raising import duties to an average level of forty percent the United States made it impossible for its foreign debtors to pay their way by increased exports. As one country after another sought to balance its books by cutting imports, the inevitable result was the collapse of world trade.

The prosperity of the world economy depended not merely on American foreign investment but on a high rate of American consumption. In 1928 the United States consumed nearly forty percent of the world's nine chief primary products (food and raw materials). In the long run it was the primary producers who were hardest hit, both by the collapse of world trade and by the contraction of the American market. Even on the eve of the Second World War most primary producers were still unable to

afford much more than a third of what they had been able to buy from abroad before the Great Depression.

Contrary to popular belief, Britain was not one of the countries which suffered most from the depression. Despite its loss of foreign earnings, the slump in the price of its imports of food and raw materials meant that at the worst moments of the depression the net loss to its balance of payments was only £25,000,000 a year. While industrial production in Germany and the United States fell by almost fifty percent in three years, British production in 1932 was still eighty-four percent of the figure for 1929. Though there was heavy unemployment in Britain's export industries, there were also large sections of industry (especially in the southeast) which found themselves almost unaffected by the slump and in which real wages actually rose during the depression.

In the long run, the political consequences of the depression were more serious than

the economic. All over the world economic crisis was followed by political crisis. Even in Britain, famous for its political stability, the depression brought down the Labour government in August 1931 and replaced it by a National government, mainly composed of Conservative ministers under the nominal leadership of the former Labour leader, Ramsay MacDonald. In two continents, Latin America and Europe, the political consequences of the depression were particularly severe. In both, economic collapse produced a rapid growth of authoritarian regimes.

Latin America

For Latin America, as for Europe, the 1920s had been a period of relative stability. In most of the score of independent Latin American states revolution seemed, by 1930, to have become a thing of the past. Foreign investment had poured into Latin America at the rate of more than $5,000 million in a single decade, while Europe and North America provided steadily expanding markets for Latin American foodstuffs and raw materials. Then, in 1930, both the foreign capital and foreign markets,

on which the prosperity of the 1920s depended, were suddenly cut off.

For the first time in its history, Latin America had to face the problem of large-scale unemployment. In Brazil half the civil service was thrown out of work in a matter of months. In Chile 100,000 of the 140,000 miners lost their jobs within two years. The depression years were more violent than any others in Latin America's history since the early years of independence. In the first year of the depression the governments of the three major South American states, Argentina, Brazil and Chile (the 'ABC states') were all overthrown. In Argentina, none of whose governments had been forcibly overthrown for half a century, General José Uriburu, a professed admirer of Mussolini, established a military dictatorship. Two months later a military coup in Brazil handed power to another admirer of Mussolini, Getulio Vargas, who established what he called 'a disciplined democracy'. Chile, which suffered more severely from the depression than any other Latin American country, dissolved for eighteen months into a condition close to anarchy with, at one time, six governments being overthrown in the space of a hundred days. Of all the states of Latin America, only Colombia and Costa Rica managed to preserve relatively stable government throughout the 1930s.

Like Uriburu and Vargas, many of the men who came to power during the depression were attracted by the methods used by Mussolini in Italy. A few, like Calles, the Mexican dictator, claimed to model themselves on Hitler. It would be a mistake, however, to draw too close a parallel between the dictatorships of Europe and Latin America. Everywhere in Latin America dictatorship was tempered by incompetence. No government possessed the means to make itself totalitarian, even if it wished to do so. Political programmes, too, frequently contained a bewildering mixture of ideologies which would have been unthinkable in Europe. Calles, for example, though an admirer of Hitler, chose a moderate Marxist, Lázaro Cárdenas, to succeed him as President of Mexico in 1934. In 1938 a left-wing Popular Front government was established in Chile with the support of the Chilean Nazi party. The most striking characteristic of the regimes of the 1930s was their nationalism and xenophobia. Marxists, fascists and conservatives alike all blamed the outside world for Latin America's ills.

The depression in Europe

The first international consequence of the European depression was to strengthen France. France was not, like Germany, dependent on American investment, nor, like Britain, did she have to export to live. While the mark and the pound fell, the franc remained firm, supported by one third of the world's gold reserves. Dr Luther, the president of the German Reichsbank, was forced to fly cap in hand to Paris in search of credit, and France was able to make her financial goodwill dependent on German political concessions.

Until 1932 many Frenchmen thought they might escape the depression altogether. 'For our part', said *Le Figaro* in October 1931, 'let us rejoice in our timid yet prosperous economy in contrast to the presumptuous and decadent economy of the Anglo-Saxon races.' This euphoria was short-lived. Though the depression reached France last, it lingered longer there than anywhere else in western Europe. When Germany had recovered from the depression, and was planning its second bid for the mastery of Europe, France was still in the midst of an economic crisis. Even on the eve of the Second World War French industrial production was only three-quarters of the pre-depression level.

For more than half a century Marxists had been predicting the collapse of the European economy. Yet when the collapse came they were not the ones to profit from it. Not a single country became communist

as a result of the Great Depression. Instead, the depression changed fascism, communism's most virulent opponent, from an Italian to a European movement. The change in the nature of fascism is aptly reflected in the utterances of its founding father, Benito Mussolini. Having declared in 1928 that 'Fascism is not an article for export', he changed his mind soon after the depression had begun and declared in 1930, 'I never said that fascism is not an article for export.'

Over much of Europe democracy was still a new and fragile institution, unable to withstand the shock of an economic cataclysm. The greatest tragedy of the European depression was that it struck hardest in Germany, the great power where democracy was weakest. Once democracy had been destroyed in Germany, democracy in the rest of Europe stood at risk.

Above, Franklin D. Roosevelt (1882–1945, president from 1933), whose programme of New Deal legislation did much to alleviate the worst effects of the Depression.

Top, election poster issued by the French Communist Party, 1937, attacking bankers for working against the national interest.

Above left, combing a slag heap for coal during the 1930s.

Opposite top right, in Great Britain the effects of the Depression varied enormously from region to region and from class to class. The depressed areas of the north were especially badly hit, and in 1936 the Jarrow miners shown here marched to London to protest at continuing lack of work.

Opposite centre and bottom right, the upper and the lower classes face the camera: throughout the 1930s, and indeed well beyond that decade, Britain remained divided by class and wealth.

Opposite left, Dance Bar in Baden-Baden *by the German Expressionist painter Max Beckmann (1884–1950), a typical image of the inter-war period as it is now recalled. Galerie Günther Franke, Munich.*

Chapter 53

China and Japan

China is the oldest civilized state on earth. It is also the only large country in the world which has never at any time passed under European rule. For two thousand years after its unification in 221 BC the Chinese Empire came into contact with no civilization which could be considered the equal of its own.

China was not merely ignorant of the outside world. It was also uninterested in it. The Middle Kingdom found it inconceivable that the barbarians beyond its borders had anything of value to offer. Only the first Opium War of 1840–2 forced China to open its doors to the West. Its wars with the West led to the establishment of 'treaty ports', semi-colonial enclaves on Chinese territory which became the bases for the determined European exploitation of the Chinese economy. For a hundred years China itself became a semi-colonial nation. Its tax system, its ports and its largest industrial city fell into the hands of foreign powers. The Chinese government became, in the words of Mao Tse-tung, 'the counting house of our foreign masters'. The colonial privileges first established by the West in China in 1842 were finally abandoned only a hundred years later, in 1943, at a time when much of China was in Japanese hands.

For the first fifty years of its exploitation by western capital China still kept itself aloof from western ideas. Except for a half-hearted attempt to modernize its army, the Chinese government sought refuge in 'a return to old ways'. It was, paradoxically, not Europe but Japan which was responsible for bringing China's intellectual isolation from the West to an end. For centuries the Japanese had been contemptuously known in China as the 'dwarf pirates', inferior beings who had copied Chinese civilization. But in 1895 China was heavily defeated in a war with Japan and lost Formosa. Defeat by the 'dwarf pirates' was the greatest humiliation in the entire history of the Chinese Empire. Yet the reason for this humiliation seemed obvious. It lay in Japan's determination to learn from the West. The conclusion drawn by most educated Chinese was that China must end her traditional isolation and do the same.

The emergence of Japan

Japan's response to the challenge of the West was quite different from that of China. In the mid-eighteenth century Japan came swiftly to the conclusion that, if it were to avoid the fate of China, it must learn from the West the secrets of its strength.

The speed of Japan's modernization has no parallel in the history of the modern world. In the 1850s its islands had been defenceless even against a small detachment of American warships. Half a century later, in 1905, it inflicted a crushing defeat on Russia, which for most of the nineteenth century had been considered the greatest military power on earth. Japan's transformation into a modern state began with the accession of the Emperor Mitsuhito in 1867. For centuries the emperor had been a mere figurehead, dominated by a noble clan, the Tokugawa, who had been the real rulers of Japan. But in 1867 the Tokugawa were overthrown by reformers who restored the emperor and used his authority and prestige to gain acceptance for an ambitious programme of reforms.

Mitsuhito gave to his reign the name of Meiji, or 'enlightened rule'. When he died in 1912 Japan possessed a strong army, a modern navy and the basis of an industrialized economy. It had conquered Formosa and Korea and had gained the foothold in Manchuria from which in the 1930s it would begin the conquest of China. Though continuing to insist on his own divinity, Mitsuhito bestowed on Japan an autocratic system of government modelled on Bismarckian Germany, with the additional refinement that the army and navy ministers had always to be drawn from the armed services. This meant, in effect, that Japanese service chiefs had something approaching a power of veto over any cabinet of which they disapproved. The army thus acquired, with disastrous consequences for the future, an influence on government which it possessed in no other country in the world outside Latin America.

The First World War changed the balance of power in the Far East more than in any other part of the world. In Europe Germany's bid for European hegemony had only been interrupted. In the western hemisphere the war had merely confirmed the existing supremacy of the United States. But in the Far East the war established, for the first and only time in its history, the supremacy of Japan.

Before the First World War Japan had been only one of a number of powers competing among themselves for a priviledged position in China. On the outbreak of war, however, Japan's competitors were forced to abandon the struggle for influence in China and concentrate instead on the struggle in Europe. Japan took advantage of the war to capture the German base at Kiaochow on the Chinese mainland and

take possession of all the German islands in the north Pacific. Even the United States, hitherto deeply suspicious of Japan's ambitions, formally recognized after its entry into the war that 'Japan has special interests in China.' The Far Eastern problem', wrote the British minister in Peking at the end of the war, 'may now be defined as the problem of Japan's position in China.'

Japanese supremacy in the Far East was guaranteed by an international conference called at Washington in 1921 to discuss the limitation of naval armaments. Japan agreed to limit its navy to three-fifths the size of the navies of Britain and the United States and to give up Kiaochow, though it still retained the Pacific islands which it had won from Germany. In return for these concessions (which still left it with the third largest navy in the world and a strong foothold in China) Japan was able to insist that the West construct no naval bases within striking distance of its islands. Britain was to build no naval base north of Singapore, the United States no base west of Hawaii. Japan thus acquired the naval supremacy of the western Pacific.

This supremacy could have been challenged only by naval cooperation between the world's two greatest naval powers, Britain and the United States. Anthony Eden, as British foreign secretary in the years before the Munich crisis, tried several times to reach agreement on Far Eastern policy with the United States. He declared publicly that he was prepared to 'go from Melbourne to Alaska' to secure American cooperation. But the United States refused to commit itself to more than moral condemnation of Japanese aggression. Just as American isolation made possible Hitler's 'New Order' in Europe, so in the Far East it made possible Japan's 'New Order in East Asia'.

Besides transforming Japan's political position, the First World War also made it a fully industrial state for the first time. No country in the world – not even the United States – derived greater economic advantages from the war. All over Asia Japan was able to capture markets which Europe had once dominated but was now unable to supply because of the demands of the war effort. Part of Lancashire's economic troubles between the wars stemmed from Japan's conquest of much of the Asian cotton textile market during the First World War. Japan was transformed by the war from a debtor to a creditor nation. Until 1914 Japan had always been in deficit on its balance of payments. During the war years alone, it accumulated a trading surplus of 1,400 million yen – a greater sum than the total value of her industrial production in 1913. Its gold reserves in the same period increased almost a hundred times.

The causes of Japan's rise to Asian supremacy during the First World War, however, lie as much in China as in Japan. Throughout history the greatness of one power has invariably been built on the weakness of its neighbours. This principle was as true of twentieth-century Japan as of classical Rome, or the France of Louis XIV, or the Germany of Adolf Hitler. The real basis of Japanese power was less its own strength than the weakness of China. China was twelve times larger than Japan in area (even after the acquisitions of the Meiji era), eight times larger in the size of its population and richer by far in its natural resources. In the long term the modernization of China, begun at the turn of the twentieth century, was bound to make it, once again, the greatest power in Asia. In the short term, however, it destroyed China's internal cohesion. It was the interval of chaos in China which accompanied its emergence as a modern state which allowed Japan to make its bid for the mastery of Asia.

The Chinese warlords

Each of the dynasties which had ruled China for the past two thousand years had claimed to derive its throne from 'the Mandate of Heaven'. Each time a dynasty was overthrown its demise was interpreted by the Chinese people as a sign that heaven had withdrawn its mandate. Thus it was with the fall of the Manchus in 1911. But with their fall the traditional dynastic pattern of Chinese history was broken. They were succeeded not by a new dynasty but by a republic inspired by the alien ideals of western liberal democracy. 'History', said *The Times*, 'has witnessed few such surprising revolutions.' But *The Times* was less than optimistic for the future. It declared:

Some of those who know China best cannot but doubt whether a form of government so utterly alien to Oriental traditions as a Republic can be suddenly substituted for a monarchy in a nation of 400 millions of men whom Kings with semi-divine attributes have ruled since the first dim twilight of history.

The aim of the republican nationalists in the 1911 revolution was to replace the decentralized autocracy of the Manchu Empire with a strong and centralized Chinese state. In the short term, however, they achieved precisely the opposite. The new republic could not unite China because it could not control the army. Of the thirty-six divisions in the Manchu army in 1911, only five were paid and controlled directly by Peking. The other thirty-one were financed by the provinces in which they were stationed. The provincial commanders – 'warlords' as they were romantically called by the Western press – looked on the fall of the Manchus as an opportunity to entrench themselves as feudal rulers

of their respective provinces. Not until Mao Tse-tung proclaimed the Chinese People's Republic in 1949 was any government able to end the rule of the warlords.

The Chinese Republic was officially proclaimed on 1 January 1912. Six weeks later, in order to prevent civil war, its first president, Sun Yat-sen, was forced to hand over power to Yuan Shih-k'ai, the former commander of the Manchu army. Yuan was optimistically referred to by republican politicians as the 'Washington of the Chinese Republic'. His aim, however, was not to defend the Republic but to destroy it. On New Year's Day 1916 he proclaimed himself the founder of a new imperial dynasty. Yuan died six months later while trying, without success, to quell the rebellions which his proclamation had brought about.

The twelve years after Yuan's death were the most chaotic in Chinese history since the peasant rebellions which had brought down the Ming dynasty in the middle of the seventeenth century (at almost the same moment when the Stuart dynasty was being overthrown in England). In 1917 Sun Yat-sen and his republican followers left Peking and set up their own government in Canton. At the Paris peace conference two years later China was in the remarkable position of being jointly represented by separate delegations from the rival regimes in Peking and Canton, each claiming to be the only legitimate Chinese government and each conducting a civil war against the other. Neither government, however, controlled more than a fraction of the Chinese provinces, and both were at the mercy of the local warlords. Sun was forced on several occasions to flee for refuge to one of the foreign enclaves on Chinese soil.

Until the Japanese invasion of 1937 the real rulers of most of China were the warlords. Some made genuine, though sometimes misguided, attempts to modernize their provinces. One of the most famous,

Above, a warlord being received at American headquarters in Tientsin with full military honours: after the fall of the Manchu dynasty, numerous warlords – one estimate suggests that there were some 1300 between 1912 and 1928 – came forward to fill the political vacuum, but none succeeded in establishing a permanent, firmly based regime.

Feng Yu-hsiang, the 'Christian marshal', ordered the mass baptism of his troops with fire hoses and mounted his cavalry for a time on bicycles. Many warlords, however, were simply content to feather their own nests. Conscious that their reigns were likely to be brief, they were anxious to extract as much as possible from the population of their provinces before they could be deposed by a rival. No warlord after Yuan had any hope of founding even a local dynasty. Having amassed their fortunes, many then retired to the security of one of the 'treaty ports'. By 1926 Tientsin contained twenty-five major, and many minor, warlords living in retirement.

The consequences of the First World War in China were less dramatic than in Japan. In the long run, however, they were of even greater importance. The war produced a massive disillusionment among educated Chinese with the alien ideals which had inspired the foundation of the Chinese Republic. China's reaction against the West, like its earlier interest in western ideas, was once again the result of its humiliation by Japan. Japan took advantage of the war to deliver to Yuan Shih-k'ai in 1915 the notorious Twenty-one Demands, which were intended to turn China into a virtual Japanese protectorate. Japan tried to keep these demands secret for fear of their effect on the outside world. Precisely for that reason China made sure that knowledge of them reached Europe and the United States. Though the pressure of world opinion forced Japan to modify its more extreme demands, China was forced to concede to Japan both Kiaochow and the various privileges formerly enjoyed by Germany and to agree to an extension of Japan's existing foothold in Manchuria. The day on which Yuan agreed to these concessions became known in China as National Humiliation Day.

In August 1917 the Peking government yielded to American pressure to enter the war on the Allied side. By so doing, said the United States, China would win a place at the peace conference from which it could challenge Japan's encroachment on its soil. China's delegations set out for Paris at the end of the war confident that the principle of self-determination which the Allies had proclaimed in Europe would also be applied in China. What China did not know was that Britain and France were already committed by secret treaties to supporting Japan. The Treaty of Versailles brushed aside all China's claims and formally recognized the transfer to Japan of the former German base at Kiaochow. The American minister in Peking wrote:

Probably nowhere else in the world had expectations of America's leadership at Paris been raised so high as in China. The Chinese trusted America, they trusted the frequent declarations of principle uttered by President Wilson, whose words had

reached China in its remotest parts. The more intense was their disappointment and disillusionment due to the decisions of the old men controlling the Peace Conference. It sickened and disheartened me to think how the Chinese people would receive this blow which meant the blasting of their hopes and the destruction of their confidence in the equity of nations.

China's treatment by its allies made Chinese nationalism a mass movement for the first time. Its leaders were the Chinese students. On 4 May 1919 demonstrators taking part in a protest rally against the Paris peace conference organized by students from Peking University burned down the house of Ts'ao Ju-lin, who had negotiated the Chinese reply to the Twenty-one Demands and beat up Chang Tsung-hsiang, the former Chinese minister in Tokyo, whose life was saved only by the arrival of troops. The Fourth of May Movement, as it became known, spread to two hundred towns and cities throughout China, involving twenty million people in a series of strikes and demonstrations and a boycott of Japanese goods.

In response to pressure from the movement, the Chinese delegation at the Paris peace conference refused to sign the Versailles treaty (which thus did not receive the signature of any one of the world's three largest independent nations–China, Russia, and the United States). One of the leaders of the movement in Hunan was the young Mao Tse-tung, not yet a Marxist but already an ardent nationalist. His article, *The Great Union of the Popular Masses of the Whole Country*, written in July 1919, was widely read as far afield as Peking. In it Mao declared:

We students are already living in the twentieth century, and yet they [China's rulers] still compel us to observe the old ceremonies and the old methods. The country is about to perish, and yet they put up posters forbidding us to love our country.... The great union of the Chinese people must be achieved. Gentlemen! We must all exert ourselves, we must all advance with the utmost strength. Our golden age, our age of brilliance and splendour, lies ahead!

Western observers were taken aback by the student leadership of the Fourth of May Movement. The American philosopher, John Dewey, who came to lecture in Peking in 1919, wrote back to America: 'To think of kids in our country from fourteen on taking the lead in starting a big clean-up reform politics movement and shaming merchants and professional men into joining them! This is sure some country!'

In Europe student protest had begun to emerge as a political force only in the nineteenth century and even then on a small scale. But in China student protest was as old as the Empire itself. During the first century BC some 30,000 students from the

Imperial College had joined in an organized protest against the dismissal of an imperial official. At a number of times of crisis during the next two millenia, students at schools and colleges claimed the right to act as spokesmen for Chinese public opinion. The publications of the Fourth of May Movement make it clear that Chinese students in 1919 saw themselves in this traditional role.

Just as Soviet historians attribute the success of the March Revolution in Russia to the leadership of the Bolshevik party, so the few remaining historians on the Chinese mainland now claim to discern in the Fourth of May Movement the leadership of the Chinese Communist party – a remarkable achievement for a party which was not founded until two years later. The events of 4 May 1919 do, nonetheless, mark a turning-point in China's relations with the West, and the beginning of a new sympathy for Soviet Russia.

Until the First World War, Chinese intellectuals, though not entirely ignorant of Marxism, had been uninterested in it. Even Ch'en Tu-hsin, who in 1921 was to become the first leader of the Chinese communist party, had looked for the salvation of China not to ideas of Marx and Lenin but to 'Mr Democracy' and 'Mr Science', whom he considered the personifications of western civilization. China's betrayal at Versailles, however, left Ch'en, like most other Chinese intellectuals, disillusioned not merely with western governments but with western ideas as well. 'No sun', it was said, 'rises for China in the West.'

Less than a month after the Treaty of Versailles, Bolshevik Russia offered to renounce all the 'unequal treaties' imposed on China by the tsars and return all the territory taken from it. The contrast between Russia's behaviour towards China and that of the Western imperialists could hardly have seemed more striking. Sun Yat-sen, formerly an ardent admirer of the American system of government, now looked for inspiration not to Wilson but to Lenin. 'The only allies and brothers of the Chinese people in the struggle for national freedom', said Sun in a manifesto of July 1919, 'are the Russian workers and peasants of the Red Army.'

To most Chinese intellectuals the Russian revolution seemed to have changed Russia from a European to an Asian nation which had left the ranks of imperialist powers to side with the peoples of Asia in their struggle for freedom from foreign exploitation. 'Russia', said Sun, 'is attempting to separate from the white peoples of Europe. . . . She joins the East and leaves the West.'

Sun Yat-sen and the republicans at Canton (now renamed the Kuomintang or Nationalist party) were ignored by the Western powers, most of which hoped vaguely for the emergence of a warlord sufficiently strong to bring the whole country under his control. Only the Russian communists offered Sun and his followers their sympathy and support. In January 1922 Kuomintang delegates attended in Moscow a 'Congress of Toilers of the Far East'. In the following autumn one of the ablest Russian diplomats, Adolf Joffe, arrived in China to negotiate an alliance with Sun. By the terms of this alliance both men agreed that 'Communism was not suited to Chinese conditions' (Joffe doubtless adding 'not yet' under his breath).

The Kuomintang was promised Russian arms, money and political and military advisers. The political advisers, inspired by the principles of 'democratic centralism', made the Kuomintang an efficient political organization for the first time. The military advisers established the Whampoa military academy which, within a few years, had given the Canton government (previously at the mercy of the local warlords) the most powerful army in China. The first commandant of the new academy was the young and ambitious Nationalist general, Chiang Kai-shek.

The alliance with Russia brought with it the support of the still infant Chinese communist party. For several years, a number of communists held important posts in the Kuomintang administration. Mao Tse-tung ran the propaganda department of the Kuomintang Central Committee. Chou En-lai, later the first prime minister of the Chinese People's Republic, became chief political adviser at the Whampoa military academy. On his deathbed in 1925 Sun wrote a last letter to the Central Committee of the Russian communist party in which he looked forward to the alliance of 'a free and strong China' with the Soviet Union 'in the great fight for the emancipation of the oppressed peoples of the whole world'. In communist China today Sun's portraits are hung alongside those of Marx and Lenin. The places of his birth and burial have become centres of pilgrimage for the communist faithful.

Before his death Sun Yat-sen had dreamed of the day when the armies of the Kuomintang would sweep northwards from Canton and bring the whole of China under nationalist control. In July 1926 the Northern Expedition, commanded by General Chiang Kai-shek, set out from Canton to turn Sun's dreams into reality. Less than two years later, in June 1928, Chiang's forces entered the rival capital of Peking. In the following month he led his generals to the monastery of the Green Cloud, where for three years Sun's body had lain awaiting burial in a glass-topped coffin presented by the Russian government. In Sun's presence Chiang solemnly declared that the unity of China had been restored. That unity, however, was no more than nominal. Though Chiang had won the support of many of the warlords, he had not brought them under his control. The Nationalist government was never able to free itself from dependence on them.

Chiang was no friend of the West, but he had no faith either in the friendship of Soviet Russia. He returned from a visit to Moscow in 1923, privately convinced that 'what the Russians call "Internationalism" and "World Revolution" are nothing but old-fashioned imperialism.' Publicly Chiang proclaimed:

If Russia aids the Chinese revolution, does that mean she wants to oblige China to apply communism? No, she wants us to carry out the national revolution. If the communists join the Kuomintang, does this mean that they want to apply communism? No, they do not want to do that either.

Privately he believed the opposite. The Russians, though suspicious of Chiang's intentions, believed that Chinese communists should cooperate with him until they were strong enough to overthrow him. Chiang, said Stalin, 'should be squeezed like a lemon and then thrown away'.

Chiang, however, sought to use the Northern Expedition not merely to unify China but to destroy Chinese communism. In April 1927 a communist-led rising delivered Shanghai into his hands. Having gained control of Shanghai, Chiang then began the systematic massacre of the communists who had captured it for him. The 'purification movement', as the attempted extermination of the Chinese communist party was euphemistically described, spread quickly to other parts of China controlled by the Kuomintang and sympathetic warlords and continued for a year. The communists, on Stalin's instructions, replied with a series of armed risings – the Nanchang rising in August among units of the Nationalist army, the 'Autumn Harvest Rising' led by Mao Tse-tung in Hunan and the Canton Commune in December. All were disastrous failures.

In the late 1960s the leadership of Communist China consisted largely of

Above, Chiang Kai-shek (1887–1975): by the late 1920s Chiang had ordered the destruction of the communist wing of the Kuomintang, but he never succeeded in eradicating the party entirely. Commander-in-chief of Chinese forces fighting against Japan during the war, he failed to prevent the 1949 revolution and had to withdraw to Taiwan.

Left, Sun Yat-sen (centre) with Chiang Kai-shek (standing, centre): Sun Yat-sen, whose 'three principles' were national unification, democracy and social progress, accepted Soviet support, but the alliance with Russia was broken by Chiang after Sun Yat-sen's death.

men who by various means had survived the disasters of 1927. Mao himself was captured and almost executed but succeeded in escaping from his guards and hiding in a field of long grass. 'Once or twice', Mao said later, 'they came so close I could almost have touched them, but somehow I escaped discovery. At last when it was dusk they abandoned the search.' Chou En-lai had an even more fortunate escape. The officer in charge of his execution squad turned out to be one of Chou's former pupils at Whampoa and set him free.

Japan's bid for Asian mastery

Many Western observers in the 1920s thought of Japan as the 'Britain of the Far East'. Japan seemed rapidly to be establishing itself as Asia's only stable parliamentary democracy. In 1925, only seven years later than in Britain, all Japanese men gained the vote (though, as in France, women had to wait until after the Second World War). When Hirohito became emperor in the following year, he gave his reign the symbolic name of *showa* or 'enlightened peace'. At the time it seemed an appropriate title. The Japanese government, if not the Japanese army, appeared to have abandoned its wartime ambition of turning the Chinese Republic into a Japanese protectorate. 'Japan', said its foreign minister, Shidehara, 'has no intention of interfering in China's internal affairs.'

The most hopeful sign, both for the peace of Asia and the future of Japanese democracy, was the declining influence in the 1920s of the Japanese armed forces. The army suffered a severe blow to its prestige from its intervention in the Russian Civil War. In 1918, encouraged by its Western allies, Japan had sent an expedition to Siberia, which remained until 1922, long after all other foreign troops had .been withdrawn from Russia. The contrast between the long drawn-out failure of intervention against the Bolsheviks and the swift and crushing victory of 1905 could hardly fail to impress Japanese opinion.

In 1924 the army, despite the protests of its high command, was forced to cut its strength by four divisions. For the remainder of the 1920s it was refused the funds it needed to supply itself with up-to-date tanks and aircraft. The government was equally firm with the navy. It agreed at the London Naval Conference in 1930 to curtail its naval building programme, despite the resignation of the naval chief of staff. At the end of the 1920s there seemed less reason to suppose that the military would soon capture control of Japanese foreign policy than at any time since the dawn of the Meiji era.

The weaknesses of Japanese democracy derived mainly from its newness. The Japanese parliament still showed little of the decorum which Japanese people held so important to their way of life. Debates often ended in fist fights between the two main parties, the Seiyukai and the Kenseikai. On one occasion the Seiyukai even arranged for a poisonous snake to be thrown among its opponents from the public gallery, but the plan misfired and the snake landed on the Seiyukai's own benches.

Both parties, too, received regular bribes from rival groups within the *Zaibatsu*, the huge industrial and financial combines which dominated the Japanese economy. The inadequacies of Japanese democracy were tolerated as long as economic prosperity continued. But by destroying Japanese prosperity the Great Depression also destroyed the shallow roots of Japanese parliamentary government.

Within a year of the Wall Street crash the world price of silk, which accounted for two-fifths of Japanese exports, had fallen by half. Silk production provided a secondary source of income for almost half the farmers in Japan. Without it many were unable to make ends meet. Unrest in the countryside spread swiftly to the army. Until the Meiji era all Japanese army officers had been samurai, members of the old warrior aristocracy. By the 1920s, however, most officers, like the men they led, were the sons of peasants. The army's chief recruiting grounds in Japan were, significantly, also the areas worst hit by the depression. For most of the Japanese army the only answer to the problems created by the depression was strong government at home and expansion abroad. The depression created a climate of opinion in which the army was able to end its subjection to the politicians and win for its ambitions the support of the majority of the Japanese people.

The Manchurian incident

On 18 September 1931 Japanese troops stationed near the Japanese-owned South Manchurian railway blew up a section of the line. They then accused Chinese troops of responsibility for the explosion and used this as an excuse to begin the occupation of Manchuria. The Japanese government had been warned beforehand of the intentions of its army. On 15 September it had despatched an envoy to the Japanese commander in Manchuria with strict instructions to prevent any clash with Chinese troops. The envoy, however, was. waylaid by army officers and persuaded to break his journey in an officers' brothel. By the time he emerged to deliver his letter, the Manchurian incident had already taken place.

Control of Japanese foreign policy now. passed abruptly from the politicians to the soldiers. On 30 September 1931 the Japanese government accepted a resolution by the Council of the League of Nations calling for the withdrawal of Japanese troops to the South Manchuria railway zone. But in the face of the nationalist fervour which swept Japan, the government was powerless to carry out its promise. The army simply proceeded with the conquest of Manchuria. Early in 1932 it established in Manchuria the puppet state of Manchukuo, under the nominal rule of the last of the Manchu emperors.

For the next five years the Japanese army followed a policy of creeping imperialism by armed aggression and political intrigue in northern China. Western injunctions to Japan not to interfere in China were, said the minister of war, General Araki Sadao, in 1936, 'like telling a man not to get involved with a woman who was already pregnant by him'. When open war was declared between Japan and China in 1937, the Japanese army had already established indirect control over much of northeast China.

The Manchurian incident was to mark a turning-point in the history of the world between the wars. Eight days before it happened Lord Robert Cecil, the British delegate in Geneva, told the League of Nations: 'There has scarcely been a period in the world's history when war seemed less likely than it does at present.' For a year after war had started in Manchuria, most Western statesmen tried to persuade themselves that nothing had changed. Walter Lippmann, the most famous American journalist of his generation, insisted that 'the Japanese army is, in a word, carrying on not "a war" but "an intervention" ' which in no way contravened the Briand-Kellogg pact. The establishment of Manchukuo, *The Times* assured its readers, 'is undoubtedly intended to provide Manchuria with an efficient government and an honest financial administration.'

In October 1932 the illusion ended. The report of the League's commission of enquiry, though phrased in the most tactful language, condemned Japan. The Japanese delegate at Geneva compared his country to Jesus Christ; Japan, he claimed, was being 'crucified for her opinions'. Early in 1933 Japan left the League in protest. For the first time in its history, a great power had defied the authority of the League of Nations. Others were soon to follow Japan's example.

The Manchurian incident was a characteristic episode in the history of military imperialism. Throughout the period of the expansion of Europe, governments had tended to lose control of their colonial armies. At the dawn of European imperialism, in the sixteenth century, the government of Spain had lost control of its conquistadores in the New World. During the final phase of European imperialism, four centuries later, the government of France was overthrown by the rebellion of its armies in Algeria. Like many of the provincial armies in the later Roman Empire, the Japanese army in Manchuria possessed political as well as imperial ambitions. Not content with carving out an empire of its own, it

set out to destroy parliamentary democracy in Japan itself.

In May 1932, a group of young army and navy officers assassinated the prime minister, Inukai Tsuyoshi, after forcing their way into his official residence. The military high command, while disclaiming responsibility for the assassination, announced that it would no longer tolerate any government headed by a party leader. But the army did not in fact establish a military dictatorship until the Second World War. It failed to do so largely because for several years the army itself was torn between two rival factions: the Kodo-ha, which wanted war with Soviet Russia and something resembling a National-Socialist Japan, and the less radical and less adventurous Tosei-ha, whose ambitions were centred on China.

Their rivalry came to a head in February 1936 with an attempted coup d'état by the Kodo-ha and the victory of the Tosei-ha. Henceforth, the victorious Tosei-ha demanded the power to nominate, as well as to veto, ministerial appointments. From now on major policy decisions were made not by the Japanese cabinet but in meetings between the prime minister, the foreign minister and the service ministers and chiefs of staff.

Japan was never, in the European sense, a fascist state. It acquired neither a Führer nor a monolithic party system. But it shared with Nazi Germany (with whom Japan signed an alliance in 1936) both a violently aggressive nationalism and a conviction that parliamentary democracy was incompatible with national greatness. The argument used by Japan to justify its expansion on the Asia mainland was the same as that used by Germany in Europe: the need for *Lebensraum* or 'living space'. Without expansion, its rulers argued, the Japanese islands would soon find it impossible to support their teeming population. The extraordinary expansion of the Japanese (like the German) economy after the Second World War is a sufficient demonstration of the falsehood of their argument.

The rise of Mao Tse-tung

After the defeat of his Autumn Harvest Rising in 1927, Mao Tse-tung was forced to take to the hills with what remained of his followers. In 1928 he was joined by Chu Teh, who had led the army rising in Nanchang. Together the two men, soon collectively known as Chu-Mao, succeeded in establishing an independent communist soviet in the province of Kiangsi, protected by a Red Army commanded by Chu and with Mao as its political commissar.

In Kiangsi Mao began to evolve a new strategy of revolution. Hitherto, the object of all communist risings both in Europe and China (Mao's included) had been to capture the cities. This was the only strategy which Moscow understood. Once the cities had been taken, said Stalin, control of the countryside would automatically follow. Mao, however, reversed this strategy. He believed first in gaining control of the countryside by organizing the Chinese peasants into rural soviets and then in 'encircling the cities from the countryside'. The enemy, said Mao, would be defeated not by pitched battles or town risings but by guerrilla warfare waged in the countryside. He summed up his strategy of warfare in four famous sentences:

When the enemy advances, we retreat.
When he camps, we harass
When he tires, we attack
When he retreats, we pursue.

Mao spread revolution in the countryside by giving the peasants the land, often lynching landlords and moneylenders in the process. 'Whoever wins the peasants', he believed, 'will win China. Whoever solves the land question will win the peasants.' Mao's faith in the revolutionary potential of the Chinese countryside sprang partly from his experience in organizing peasant movements in his native Hunan. But it sprang also, like much of his thought, from his interpretation of the Chinese past.

Above, Pu Yi, the Japanese controlled puppet Emperor of Manchuria, arriving at his inauguration ceremony, March 1932: the Japanese seizure of Manchuria in 1931 was the first step towards the new Japanese order in Asia.

Above left, a Japanese armoured car in the streets of Shanghai, part of the forces that took over the city in 1932 in response to a Chinese boycott of Japanese goods in protest at the takeover of Manchuria. In 1933 they penetrated further inland, crossing the Great Wall.

Looking back on the two thousand years of the Chinese empire, Mao wrote in 1940:

The gigantic scale of the peasant uprisings and peasant wars in China's history is without parallel in the history of the world. These peasant uprisings and peasant wars alone have formed the real motive force of China's historical evolution.

To an orthodox Marxist, Mao's views could hardly fail to sound like heresy. Though Lenin had looked forward to the participation of the Asian peasant masses in an Asian revolutionary movement, he had never failed to insist that this movement must be led by the industrial working class. 'The city', he had said, 'inevitably leads the village. The village inevitably follows the city.' But Mao for many years paid little more than lip-service to the leadership of the working class, a class which, as he realized, as yet composed only a tiny fragment of China's population.

By the 1950s even Mao himself had concluded that his views of only twenty years before were insufficiently orthodox. Since then his earlier writings have been published in China only in bowdlerized editions which play down his earlier emphasis on the peasant base of the Chinese revolution and contain a number of insertions which stress, instead, the leading role of the proletariat.

By the end of 1930 there were eleven rural soviets in China, most of them modelled on the Chu-Mao soviet in Kiangsi. In 1931 delegates from these areas met in Mao's capital at Juchen and proclaimed the establishment of the Chinese Soviet Republic with Mao as its first chairman. Despite the failure of a second series of town risings in 1930, however, the official leadership of the Chinese communist party (all trained in Moscow and known in China as the 'Returned Students') remained deeply suspicious of Mao's preference for peasant guerrilla warfare. In 1931, the Central Committee, from which Mao had been dropped a few years earlier because of fears for his orthodoxy, moved to Juchen. It spent the next three years trying to reduce Mao's role as Chairman of the Soviet Republic to that of a figurehead.

The Long March

For three years after Mao's flight to the mountains Chiang Kai-shek had been unable, because of the intrigues of his warlord supporters, to send a large-scale expedition against him. At the end of 1930, however, he began the first of five 'annihilation campaigns' against the rural soviets. Even after the Manchurian incident Chiang still insisted that China's first priority, before resistance to the Japanese, must be the destruction of the communism within its borders. By 1934 he had come within an inch of success.

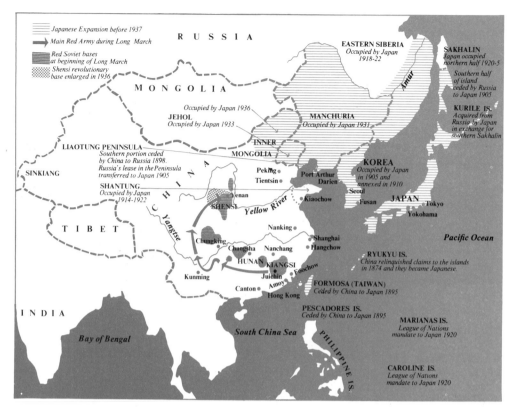

To avoid annihilation, the Kiangsi soviet, and what remained of the rest of the Chinese Soviet Republic were forced to begin a 6,000-mile march to the mountain stronghold of Shensi in northwest China. The Red Army later claimed to have crossed in its journey eighteen mountain ranges and twenty-four rivers, to have occupied at various times more than sixty cities and to have broken through the armies of ten warlords and dozens of Kuomintang regiments.

Of the 130,000 who set out (100,000 soldiers and 30,000 civilians), only 30,000 reached Shensi. But they arrived with their cohesion unbroken and their morale high. 'In the whole of history', wrote Mao, 'has there ever been a march like ours?' He was probably right to reply to his own question in the negative. Napoleon's retreat from Moscow had been a third as long and over less difficult ground, but the army of the greatest general in European history had been broken and demoralized by it.

Besides ensuring the survival of the Chinese communist party, the Long March also won it over to Mao's strategy of peasant revolution. In January 1935, while the March was still in its early stages, the Returned Students were forced to surrender power to Mao, who became the new chairman of the party's central committee. Mao's battle cry, from the moment the Red Army reached Shensi, was to call for a united front against Japan. Many of Chiang's own supporters were by now disillusioned with his policy of waging war on the communists while allowing Japan to strengthen her hold on northern China. In December 1936 he was kidnapped by some of his own troops and forced to agree to an alliance with Mao. This alliance was one of the factors which persuaded the Japanese army to end its previous policy of creeping imperialism and provoke an open war with China in the following year.

In 1937 few people, even in China, expected Mao and the Chinese communists to emerge from the war with Japan poised for the final conquest of power in China. Already, however, the Kuomintang possessed two crucial weaknesses which in the end were to prove decisive. Under the leadership of Chiang Kai-shek the Kuomintang, which had once considered itself a revolutionary party, had become an ideological vacuum. On the question of land reform, the most serious of all the internal problems facing China, it had no policy at all. In the areas which it recaptured from the communists, it took the land from the peasants and returned it to the landlords. In the long term it could not hope to compete with the communists for the loyalty of China's peasant masses.

The second great weakness of the Kuomintang was its inability to fight a guerrilla war. After 1939, with much of China in Japanese hands. Chiang went on the defensive for the remainder of the war. The communists, however, waged a continuous series of guerrilla campaigns within occupied China with the aim not merely of fighting the Japanese but of spreading the revolution in the countryside. The Red

Above, in 1937 war between China and Japan broke out again, and Japanese troops occupied the north of the country and almost all the coastline. Here, Japanese forces march through the streets of Hainan, 1939.

Top, the Long March, the epic journey to the Shensi stronghold, from where the communist revolution was planned, has inspired Mao's followers and provided propagandists with a central theme: this post-1949 painting shows Mao on the March.

Top left, Mao Tse-tung addressing a meeting in the Shensi stronghold.

Opposite top, the Far East in the 1920s and 1930s: the main features of these decades were the remorseless advance of Japanese power and the Chinese communists' abandonment of their bases in southern China, followed by the Long March and the establishment of their stronghold in Shensi.

Opposite bottom, Mao Tse-tung (1893–1976): his strategy of rural revolution, contrary to orthodox Marxist thinking, saved the communist party after it had been destroyed in the cities.

Army', wrote Mao, 'fights not merely for the sake of fighting, but to agitate the masses, to organize them, to arm them, and to help them establish revolutionary political power.' Just as Japanese aggression during the First World War had led China to turn her back on the West, so Japanese aggression on a far larger scale during the Second World War was to create the conditions for a communist victory.

The century from the Opium Wars to the birth of the Chinese People's Republic now seems, in retrospect, an abnormal interlude in the course of China's history. By the middle of the twentieth century China would once again find itself almost as isolated from the West as in the middle of the nineteenth century, as convinced as before that it had nothing of real importance to learn from the West. Once again China thought of itself as the Middle Kingdom, the centre of civilization in a world otherwise almost entirely composed of oppressed peoples, imperialists and revolutionists. But its experience of the outside world during the last century had left China convinced for the first time in its history of a world mission.

Mao's strategy of revolution, first devised during the days of the Kiangsi Soviet, though careful to emphasize the leading role of the proletariat, remained essentially unchanged. That strategy, however, was now applied on a world scale. 'Taking the entire globe', wrote Mao's 'close comrade in arms', Lin Piao, 'if North America and western Europe can be called "the cities of the world", Asia, Africa, and Latin America constitute "the countryside of the world". . . . In a sense, the contemporary world revolution presents a picture of the encirclement of the cities by the countryside.' The strategy of Chinese revolution had become the strategy of world revolution.

Chapter 54

The Decline of Democracy

The sheer frightfulness of Adolf Hitler has made historians reluctant to recognize his extraordinary genius. No other man in the history of modern Europe, perhaps not even Lenin, has seemed so able to bend history to his will. Yet Hitler began his political career in Germany with almost every conceivable disadvantage. He was, to begin with, not a German at all but an Austrian who acquired German citizenship only a year before he became German chancellor. Until the First World War when he became a lance-corporal in the German army, Hitler had lived in the slums of Vienna and Munich, struggling to earn a living as an unsuccessful artist selling poster designs and water colours painted on the back of postcards. After the war he was several times afraid that his new career as a political agitator in Germany would be cut short by deportation to Austria.

Unlike Lenin, Hitler did not have behind him an established political party bound together by a long revolutionary tradition. The Nazi party in Germany was Hitler's own creation. Yet Hitler's vision of the future, though far more malevolent than Lenin's, also came closer to fulfilment. The European revolution of which Lenin had been so confident in 1917 never came, and the party which he had believed would make Russia free became the instrument instead of the most absolute despotism in Russian history. But in 1924, at the lowest ebb of his political career after the failure of the Munich putsch, Hitler was already able in *Mein Kampf* to describe with horrifying accuracy the Europe which he later almost succeeded in creating.

The great Swiss historian, Jacob Burkhardt, writing at the end of the nineteenth century, had foreseen that the greatest danger to the future of the liberal state in twentieth-century Europe would come from 'terrible simplifiers' who would take control of it and 'rule with utter brutality'. This is what Hitler was. 'I have', he said privately in 1932, 'the gift of reducing all problems to their simplest proportions.' This gift, Hitler was convinced, was the key to his success. 'I shall tell you', he told a journalist,

what has carried me to the position I have reached. Our political problems appeared complicated. The German people could make nothing of them. . . . I, on the other hand, simplified these problems and reduced them to the simplest terms. The masses realized this and followed me.

Part of Hitler's political genius was his ability to provide a simple and persuasive explanation for Germany's complex misfortunes. He told his followers in 1925:

To make a struggle intelligible to the broad masses, it must always be carried on against two things, against a person and against a cause. Against whom did England fight? Against the German emperor as a person, and against militarism as a cause. . . . Against whom, therefore, must our movement fight? Against the Jew as a person and against Marxism as a cause.

Hitler portrayed Marxism itself as an essentially Jewish movement, the creation of 'that modern Mordecai, Karl Marx'. By a remarkable intellectual sleight of hand he convinced both himself and his followers that international capitalism, which was responsible for Germany's economic distress, and international communism, which sought to make Germany its captive, were both part of the same 'Judaeo-Bolshevik conspiracy' which was at the root of all Germany's misfortunes.

Despite the undoubted appeal to many of his followers of Hitler's simple diagnosis of Germany's misfortune, it was his even simpler solution to them which was the real secret of his success. This solution, Hitler insisted, was not a question of this or that policy but 'a matter of will-power'. 'No word', writes his biographer, Alan Bullock, 'was more frequently on Hitler's lips than "will".' Will-power alone, Hitler insisted – his own will-power – could make Germany prosperous and strong once more.

The fact that so many Germans believed Hitler was above all because of the extraordinary magnetism of his personality. Nor, as is sometimes implied, was his appeal confined to mass rallies of the simple-minded herded together in the Nuremberg stadium. Hitler excelled in varying his appeal according to his audience. Lloyd George, himself one of the most powerful personalities in the history of British politics, returned in 1936 from a visit to Germany convinced that Hitler was 'a born leader, a magnetic, dynamic personality' (with, incidentally, no desire 'to invade any other land'). A series of eminent visitors left Hitler's country retreat at Berchtesgaden with the same impression.

The collapse of German democracy

Until the Great Depression the mass resentments to which Hitler needed to appeal did not exist. After the fiasco of the Munich putsch in 1923 most people both inside

Opposite top, a village self-defence corps in Honan, 1938, where the communists had successfully organized the peasants as early as the late 1920s: the Japanese invasion united nationalists and communists in opposition to a common enemy.

Opposite bottom, guard duty on the Great Wall, 1938.

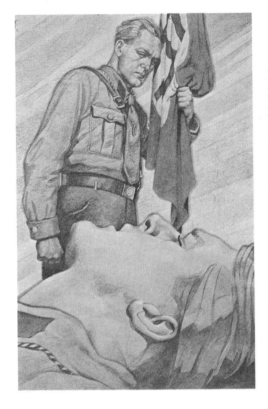

and outside Germany had written Hitler off. When Lord D'Abernon, the former British ambassador in Berlin, published two volumes of his memoirs in 1929, he mentioned Hitler only in a footnote. After referring briefly to Hitler's imprisonment after the putsch, he concluded: 'He was finally released after six months and bound over for the rest of his sentence, thereafter fading into oblivion.'

The early 1920s had already shown that the Nazis needed an economic crisis to come to power. In May 1924, during the aftermath of the postwar inflation, the Nazis gained thirty-two seats at their first general election, even though Hitler himself was still in prison. But at the next election in the following December, when the economic climate was beginning to improve, they held only fifteen of these seats. In 1928, when the Weimar Republic was at the height of its prosperity, the Nazis lost three more seats. As long as that prosperity continued the Nazis were doomed to remain on the fringe of German politics.

In the short term the depression did more damage to the German economy than to any other economy in Europe. By 1932 industrial production had fallen by almost a half, and six million men – one-third of the German labour force – were unemployed. Parliamentary government in Germany survived the Wall Street crash by only six months.

After the breakdown of the coalition government led by the social democrat, Hermann Müller, in March 1930, effective political power passed from the chancellor to President Hindenburg and the 'palace camarilla' which surrounded him, dominated by Hindenburg's son Oscar and Oscar's friend, General Schleicher. Ever since his

election in 1925 Hindenburg had been the model of a constitutional president, accepting the decisions of his ministers and the votes of the *Reichstag*. After Müller's resignation, however, no chancellor until Adolf Hitler was able to win a stable majority in the *Reichstag*. Hitler's three predecessors as chancellor (Bruning in March 1930, von Papen in April 1932, Schleicher in December 1932) were the nominees of the 'palace camarilla'. All relied not on the consent of the *Reichstag* but on emergency decrees signed by the president.

The depression made the Nazis a major political force for the first time. In 1930, at the first election after the Wall Street crash, Nazi seats in the *Reichstag* shot up from 12 to 107. In July 1932, at the worst moment of the Depression, the Nazis won thirty-seven percent of the vote and 230 seats, more than any other party in the history of the Weimar Republic (though still well short of an absolute majority in the *Reichstag*). By the autumn of 1932, however, it seemed that the party had passed its peak.

At the next election in November 1932 the Nazis lost two million votes. The party was on the verge of bankruptcy. By the end of the year it had run out of funds to finance the 400,000 men of the SA, its private army of stormtroopers. The SA were given collecting boxes and told to beg in the streets. 'This year', wrote Goebbels in his diary at the end of 1932, 'has brought us eternal ill luck.... The future looks dark and gloomy.' At the polls the Nazis seemed condemned to a gradual decline as prosperity returned. The only alternative appeared to be a Nazi coup d'état. But this was an alternative which Hitler himself had ruled out ever since the failure of the Munich putsch.

Above, Joseph Goebbels (1897–1945), Nazi propaganda chief from 1929: his enormous skills and unceasing work ensured the Party's success in the early 1930s and in the later part of the war did much to maintain morale.

Above left, Nazi election poster promising work, freedom and bread: the uncomplicated, direct appeal of Nazi propaganda won many converts in the early 1930s, at a time when the other parties seemed helpless and unimaginative, able only to react to events.

Above far left, honouring a fallen comrade: the simplicity and realism of this Nazi painting capture the essence of the movement's propaganda appeal.

Opposite, portrait of Hitler taken for his fiftieth birthday, 20 April 1939.

That the Nazis became the masters of Germany in 1933 was less because of their own strength than because of the failures of their opponents. At the elections of November 1932 the German left – the social democrats and communists – had won more votes than the Nazis. But the two parties of the left were hopelessly divided between themselves. The socialists had lost the will to govern. Like the Labour Party in England, they could not reconcile themselves to carrying out an economic policy of deflation which was bound to bear most heavily on their own supporters. The communists believed that a Nazi victory in Germany would signal the death throes of German capitalism. On instructions from Moscow they concentrated not on resisting Hitler but on establishing themselves as the only party of the left. 'Our principal struggle', said the party newspaper on the eve of Hitler's rise to power, 'is against social democracy.'

But the divisions of the left were less crucial than the miscalculations of the right. Baron von Papen, ousted as chancellor by General Schleicher, devised a scheme to use an alliance with Hitler to recover political power. As a preliminary he persuaded a group of Rhineland businessmen to save the Nazis from bankruptcy. Then he helped Hitler to arrange an alliance between the Nazis and the right-wing Nationalist party. At this critical moment the army high command came out in favour of a Hitler government. Hitler himself believed that its support was crucial. 'If the army had not stood on our side', he declared after he became chancellor, 'we should not have been standing here today.'

'You will not think it possible, gentlemen', Hindenburg told two of his generals on 26 January 1933, 'that I should appoint that Austrian lance-corporal chancellor.' He had the best constitutional reasons for changing his mind four days later. If, as then seemed possible, the Nazi-Nationalist alliance won the support of the Catholic Centre party, it would be the first coalition to win a majority in the *Reichstag* since the fall of Müller's government three years before. On 30 January 1933 Adolf Hitler became Chancellor of Germany.

Nazi Germany

The politicians, industrialists and generals who had brought Hitler to power had done so in the belief that they could use him for their own purposes. The coalition government which Hitler headed contained only two other Nazi ministers. Papen, as vice-chancellor, was confident that with nine non-Nazis in a cabinet of twelve real power would remain with him. But they failed to realize that with the two Nazi ministers, Frick and Goering, in control of internal affairs, and the pro-Nazi General Blomberg as minister of defence, Hitler effectively controlled the police and was assured of the army's benevolent neutrality.

Hitler's first act as chancellor was to ensure the failure of the negotiations with the Catholic Centre Party which might have given his government a majority in the *Reichstag*. His colleagues in the cabinet were then persuaded to agree to a new election, which Hitler intended to precede by a campaign of intimidation designed to

give him the absolute majority he could not win in a free election.

The mastermind of this campaign was Hermann Goering, whose gross exterior concealed surprising energy and ruthlessness. In only a few weeks Goering had laid the foundations of the Nazi police state: 40,000 men of the SA and the SS (Hitler's praetorian guard) were drafted into the police force and given unlimited opportunity to indulge the pent-up sadism accumulated during the years in opposition. Goering declared:

Police officers who make use of firearms in the execution of their duties will, without regard to the consequences of such use, benefit by my protection; those who, out of a misplaced regard for the consequences fail in their duty will be punished in accordance with the regulations.

In several parts of Germany local Nazi leaders founded concentration camps on their own initiative as centres of imprisonment and torture for anyone thought to oppose the regime. To assist them in tracking down their victims, Goering transformed the political police of the Weimar Republic into the infinitely more sinister Gestapo – the secret police.

Despite a brilliantly sustained campaign of intimidation, however, the Nazis won only forty-four percent of the vote at the March election. By outlawing all the communist deputies (most of whom were already in concentration camps) Hitler succeeded nonetheless in giving himself a clear overall majority. He then bullied the new *Reichstag*

into passing an 'Enabling Law' which made him the dictator of Germany.

Gleichschaltung

Hitler now began the subordination of every facet of German life to the control of the Nazi party, a process euphemistically described as *Gleichschaltung* or 'co-ordination'. All other political parties and the trade unions were abolished. The *Reichstag* was reduced to a cipher which met occasionally to be harangued by the Führer. Mass communications and German culture were handed over to Dr Goebbels whose preposterous title was 'minister of propaganda and public enlightenment'.

No legal redress was possible against Nazi tyranny. 'The law and the will of the Führer', said Goering, 'are one.' Hitler himself gave a striking practical demonstration of this principle on the 'Night of the Long Knives' in June 1934, when he ordered the simultaneous assassination of a number of past opponents and disaffected supporters (notably Röhm, the leader of the SA). In a speech to the *Reichstag* Hitler explained that he had acted as 'the supreme justiciar of the German people'.

After Hindenburg's death in August 1934 Hitler also became the head of state. The offices of chancellor and president, he announced, had now been combined in his person. As president (though he still preferred to call himself Führer) Hitler automatically became the new commander-in-chief of the German army, which was now required to pledge its loyalty not to the Fatherland but to Hitler himself.

Only one section of German society remained outside the process of *Gleichschaltung*. This was the Jewish community, which Hitler sought to isolate from the remainder of the German people in preparation for its eventual liquidation. Jews were excluded from the civil service, from the professions, from sport and from the arts. Boycotts were organized of Jewish shops, and blacklists were published of those housewives who dared to defy it.

In 1935 the Nuremberg Race Laws made illegal either marriage or sexual relations between Jews and other Germans. The so-called 'Crystal Night' in November 1938, when hundreds of Jews were murdered and synagogues throughout Germany were burnt to the ground, showed how far anti-semitism had been accepted by the German people as part of their way of life. A climate of opinion was emerging in which the majority of the German people, though not supporting the mass extermination of the Jews, would be prepared to turn a blind eye to it. And it was already clear what the fate of the Jewish people would be when Hitler went to war. He told the *Reichstag* at the beginning of 1939 that if the Jews brought about another world war (and, by definition, all world wars were brought about by Jews) its result would be 'the annihilation of the Jewish race in Europe'.

'I ask of you, German people', Hitler had said in January 1933, 'that after you have given the others fourteen years, you should give us four.' At the Nuremberg rally in November 1936 Hitler gave his own account of the achievements of those four years.

Below, left-wingers rounded up in the early days of the Nazi regime: the government acted quickly to silence all possible opposition.

Centre, Jews forced to scrub the pavements after the Nazi takeover of Austria, March 1938: the Jewish population of central Europe encountered vicious discrimination from the moment the Nazis came to power, though it was not until the early 1940s that the 'final solution', which Hitler had long had in mind, began to be put into operation.

Bottom, the Nuremberg rally, 1933: these massive, skilfully staged propaganda exercises served as a public reinforcement of the power of the Nazi movement.

No peacetime prime minister has ever been able to point to such a triumphant record of success. Unemployment had fallen in four years from six million to less than a million. Industrial production had recovered to the pre-depression level.

Hitler could claim, too, to have made Germany great as well as prosperous. In 1935 the Saar had voted to rejoin Germany and in March 1936 the German army had marched into the demilitarized Rhineland. The German government no longer recognized the restrictions of the Versailles treaty and had begun a massive programme of rearmament. For the first time since the First World War Germany was once again feared and respected as the greatest power on the continent of Europe.

Many Germans were so enthusiastic about Hitler's achievements that they were willing to overlook the methods which he used. But there were many too who were attracted by the violence of those methods. The *Freikorps* era had already shown the popularity of violence among large sections of the German public. After witnessing the organized brutality of Hitler's storm-troopers during the election campaign of 1933, Germans flocked to join them. In a single year membership of the SA rose from 400,000 to three million men. The smaller and even more sinister SS was also never short of recruits. Indeed it was somewhat embarrassed by the profusion of them. Its leader, Heinrich Himmler, declared in 1937:

'We still choose only fifteen out of every hundred candidates who present themselves to us.'

Hitler's supporters before he came to power had been concentrated among the members of the lower middle class: artisans, small shopkeepers, skilled craftsmen, minor civil servants. The depression threatened these men in a way in which it affected no other segment of German society. They felt menaced not merely with a lower standard of living (as did every class in German society) but with the loss of their middle-class status and reduction to the ranks of the working class which they despised.

Before he became chancellor Hitler did not succeed in making any serious inroads into the working-class vote. At both elections in 1932 the combined vote of the two working-class parties, the communists and social democrats, was higher than ever before. Once in power, however, Hitler rapidly established his claim to be the Führer of the whole German people.

During his first years as the ruler of Germany Hitler held a series of plebiscites to demonstrate the strength of his support. At the first of these, held only eighteen months after becoming chancellor, he gained ninety percent of the vote in a poll of ninety-six percent. In March 1936, after the re-occupation of the Rhineland, he won a majority of over ninety-eight percent. Whatever the reliability of these figures, there can be no doubt that the mood of the German

people as a whole was, in the words of Alan Bullock, one of 'overwhelming gratitude and approval'.

Nowhere was Hitler's support more secure than among the youth of Germany. The Nazis had captured control of the German student movement as early as 1931. Once the Nazis came to power, all German children aged six or over were compelled to join the Hitler Youth. At school their teachers brought them up in the Nazi faith. No wonder, then, that Hitler could declare in 1933: 'When an opponent says, "I will not come over to your side", I calmly reply, 'Your child belongs to us already.'

The opposition to Hitler was both weak and powerless. Even the concentration camps, to which the Nazis had no hesitation in despatching their opponents, had a population of only 25,000 at the outbreak of war out of a total German population which numbered eighty million. No government anywhere in the world between the wars commanded the enthusiasm which Adolf Hitler earned from the German people.

Stalin's Russia

'Having become General Secretary', wrote Lenin in his political testament, 'Comrade Stalin has acquired immense power in his hands, and I am not certain that he will always know how to use this power with

sufficient caution.' A few days later he added a final postscript suggesting that Stalin be replaced by someone 'more patient, more loyal, more polite and considerate to other comrades, less capricious and so on'. Lenin had intended that his testament should be read to delegates to the party congress after his death in January 1924. Instead Stalin ensured that it was not published in Russia during his lifetime. It is difficult to think of any other document in modern history whose suppression has had consequences of comparable magnitude.

Two things enabled Stalin to win the struggle for power which followed Lenin's death: his lack of any obvious talent and his control of the party machine. In 1924 Stalin was not even considered a serious candidate for the succession. Had it been otherwise his rivals would hardly have agreed to suppress Lenin's condemnation of him. As yet no one heeded Lenin's warning of the 'immense power' which Stalin had gathered in his hands. The most obvious candidate to succeed Lenin was Leon Trotsky, at once the party's leading intellectual, the organizer of the November Revolution and the hero of the Civil War. By comparison Stalin seemed what Trotsky called him: 'a dull mediocrity'.

To defeat Trotsky Stalin joined forces with his two main rivals, Kamenev and Zinoviev, the chairmen respectively of the Moscow and Leningrad (formerly Petro-

grad) Bolshevik parties. Trotsky lost the battle for power essentially because he was less unscrupulous than Stalin. His control of the Red Army gave him an even more powerful weapon than Stalin's command of the party machine, had he been prepared to use it. But Trotsky, unlike Stalin, had a horror of becoming the Bonaparte of the Russian Revolution. In January 1925 Stalin was able to force Trotsky's resignation from his key position as commissar for war. Having disposed of Trotsky, Stalin now turned on his former allies, Kamenev and Zinoviev, using his power as general secretary to undermine their control of the Moscow and Leningrad party machines. At the 1927 party congress Stalin emerged as the ruler of Russia.

The Bolsheviks in the 1920s found themselves out on a limb. In 1917 they had been sublimely confident that their own

Above, German troops occupying the demilitarized Rhineland, perhaps the biggest, and most successful, gamble of Hitler's career: all too well aware of their own military weakness, the western powers put up no resistance, though Germany would almost certainly have withdrawn had they done so.

Above left, Members of the Hitler Youth at one of the many ceremonial events designed to capture and retain their loyalty to the movement: the movement's appeal was especially attractive to the young, many of whom in the early 1930s felt that they had no future.

Opposite, Hitler amid some of his followers: as the head of the Nazi movement, Hitler acted as its entire focus and attracted devoted loyalty, the propaganda machine building him up as the one man who could save Germany.

revolution in Russia would quickly be followed by the rest of Europe. By the time of Lenin's death this confidence had gone. Europe by now showed little sign of following Russia's example. The most logical course of action, in Marxist terms, seemed either to concentrate all Russia's resources on an all-out attempt to spread the revolution to the rest of Europe (a view favoured by Trotsky) or else to postpone the establishment of socialism in Russia itself. In the autumn of 1924, however, Stalin instead formulated the slogan of 'socialism in one country'. Russia, he argued, must advance to socialism without waiting for the rest of Europe.

Stalin's excursion into the world of ideology took his colleagues by surprise. 'Don't make a fool of yourself', one old Marxist told him, 'Everyone knows that theory is not exactly your line.' But within a few years 'socialism in one country' had become the new test of orthodoxy: all those, like Trotsky, who disagreed were banished from the party. A few years more and Stalin was being hailed, with his evident approval, as the greatest philosopher the world had ever known – not merely the infallible head of the Marxist faith but the first man to solve certain problems in the interpretation of Aristotle and the only man who really understood both Kant and Hegel.

In the chaos left by the Civil War, Russia was at first in no position to build a fully socialist economy. 'We are paupers', Lenin had written in 1921, 'starving, destitute paupers. A comprehensive plan for us equals bureaucratic utopia.' By the New Economic Policy (NEP for short) begun in that year, though big business ('the commanding heights of the economy') was run by the state, almost all the land remained divided into individual peasant plots and a limited degree of private enterprise was allowed in the towns. Only in 1927 did production both on the land and in industry recover to the pre-war level.

The transformation of the Russian economy

The moderate wing of the Bolshevik party, led by Bukharin, was content to continue 'riding towards socialism at the pace of a peasant nag', continuing the gradual industrialization of the Russian economy while, at the same time, seeking slowly to persuade the peasants to merge their private holdings into collective farms. Stalin, however, decided that the doctrine of 'socialism in one country' made necessary a crash programme of rapid industrialization. A socialist Russia, Stalin argued, could survive encirclement by the imperialist powers only by ending her economic backwardness: 'We are fifty or a hundred years behind the advanced countries. We must make good this lag in ten years. Either we do it or they crush us.'

Rapid industrialization was necessary also for the security of the Bolshevik regime within Russia itself. A party which claimed to base itself on the dictatorship of the proletariat was bound to feel insecure so long as it ruled a predominantly peasant Russia. A crash programme of industrialization, however, could only be financed by larger agricultural surpluses from the Russian peasants, both to feed the increased labour force in the towns and to pay for imports of foreign machinery. The obvious way to obtain these surpluses was to encourage the *kulaks* or 'rich peasants' who were the most efficient producers. Since this solution was unacceptable for ideological reasons, the only alternative was compulsory collectivization.

In assessing the progress of the Russian economy after the end of NEP in 1928, the historian is faced with a massive falsification of evidence on a scale that has no parallel in the history of Europe. We know, for example, by the Soviet government's own subsequent admission, that even as late as 1952 grain production was deliberately exaggerated by no less than sixty percent. There is scarcely a single economic statistic published during the period of the first three five-year plans (begun respectively in 1928, 1933 and 1938) on whose accuracy it is possible to rely. Stalin himself lived during these years in a fantasy world largely of his own construction. In 1935, for example, he claimed that 'We have had no

poor now for two or three years' – and this at a time when, as Professor Nove has observed, the price of bread stood higher in relation to wages than at any other time in Soviet history.

And yet it is clear, despite the fantasy world of Soviet statistics, that by draconian methods and a massive rate of capital investment, Russia became a major industrial state in the space of a single decade – more rapidly than any other state in European history. By 1939 its total industrial production was probably exceeded only by that of Germany and the United States. Russia's industrial achievement compelled even Hitler's reluctant admiration. He admitted privately in 1942:

The arms and equipment of the Russian armies are the best proof of [Russia's] efficiency in handling industrial manpower . . . Stalin, in his own way, is a hell of a fellow. He knows his models, Genghis Khan and the others, very well.

The achievements of collectivized agriculture are far less impressive. In the short term they were nearly disastrous. The peasants' response to the collectivization of their livestock was simply to slaughter as much of it as possible. By 1934, even according to official statistics, the total number of horses, cattle and pigs had dropped by half and the total number of sheep by two thirds. Production on the collective farms did not recover to the 1928 level until the 1950s. A party congress, held soon after Stalin's death in 1953, was told that after twenty-five years of collectivized agriculture grain production per head of the population and numbers of livestock absolutely were still lower than in Tsarist Russia.

Both the failures of collectivized agriculture and the successes of Soviet industry were purchased at an appalling cost in human suffering. Stalin later told Churchill that of the ten million *kulaks* (a term rather loosely applied by Stalin) who had resisted collectivization, 'the great bulk' had been 'wiped out'. During the first five-year plan Stalin created the world's first man-made famine. To pay for imports of foreign machinery and feed the growing labour force in the towns, he insisted on a vast increase in food expropriations from the countryside at the very time when food production was in decline. In 1931, when the famine was beginning, five million tons of wheat were sold abroad. Though Stalin, characteristically, denied that a famine even existed, more than five million Russians died of starvation. 'We were', Bukharin was to say later, 'conducting a mass annihilation.'

The Great Terror

The barbarism which accompanied collectivization and the first five-year plan inevitably aroused opposition within the

653

Communist party itself. Those, like Bukharin, who opposed 'mass annihilation' seem to have pinned their hopes on the influence of Sergei Kirov, the party boss in Leningrad. Though a devoted admirer of Stalin, whom he described as 'the greatest man of all times and ages', Kirov was thought to be concerned by the brutality of Stalin's methods. In December 1934 he was murdered, probably on Stalin's orders. His death was the signal for the beginning of the Terror.

It seems increasingly clear that the immediate explanation for the Terror has to be sought less within the needs of Russian industrialization or the interests of the Russian communist party than in the personal paranoia of Joseph Stalin. For this paranoia we have the evidence of, amongst others, one of Stalin's successors, Nikita Krushchev:

Stalin was a very distrustful man, sickly suspicious; we knew this from our work with him. He could look at a man and say, 'Why are your eyes so shifty today?' or 'Why are you turning so much today and avoiding looking me directly in the eyes?' This sickly suspicion created in him a general distrust even toward eminent party workers whom he had known for years. Everywhere and in everything he saw 'enemies', 'double dealers', and 'spies'.

The most that can be said for Stalin is that, like many other despots, he probably convinced himself that his own enemies (real or imagined) were also the enemies of the state.

The Terror reached its peak in the years from 1936 to 1938. Everyone who had ever opposed Stalin on any issue was systematically sought out, accused of usually imaginary crimes and executed. This, however, was only the beginning. Many of the relatives of Stalin's victims were shot or sent to labour camps. Stalin had the penal code altered to permit the execution of children of twelve years and over. All those arrested had, in addition, to provide the names of their accomplices in their imaginary crimes. If they refused, they were tortured until they did so. By its very nature, therefore, the Terror provided itself with an increasing number of victims. 'Today', said the Russian writer, Isaac Babel, 'a man talks freely only with his wife – at night with the blankets drawn over his head.'

The purge began to slacken in the later months of 1938 largely because the administration of the Terror was beginning to collapse under the sheer weight of those it persecuted. By now perhaps one in twenty of the entire Russian population had been arrested. Even the vast network of Soviet labour camps had become hopelessly overstretched. At the height of the Terror probably some nine million people were in captivity, eight million of them in labour camps which could boast an annual death rate of twenty percent. 'We shall have no further need', Stalin told the 1939 party congress, 'of resorting to the method of mass purges.'

The section of Soviet society which suffered most from the Terror was, appropriately enough, the Russian communist party. Less than two percent of the ordinary delegates to the 1935 party congress reappeared at the next congress held four years later. Of those who failed to reappear, well over half had been shot. Of the 139 full members and candidate members of the Central Committee in 1934 only twenty-four were re-elected in 1939: ninety-eight of the remainder are known to have been shot. By a process of natural selection those members of the Soviet leadership who survived the jungle conditions of the Terror, or who rose to power during it, were likely to possess extremely unusual qualities of ruthlessness and servility. Both these qualities are aptly illustrated by the comments on a letter from General Yakir, before his execution on a trumped-up charge in 1937, pleading for the safety of his family. The letter was published by the Soviet government in 1961. It has on it four marginal comments:

Stalin: 'Yakir, trash and traitor.'
Voroshilov: 'An exact description.'
Molotov: 'Entire agreement with Stalin.'
Kaganovich: 'A traitor, a pig.'

By a curious coincidence Voroshilov, Molotov and Kaganovich were the only members of the Politburo at the time of Kirov's murder to escape the purges which followed. All three continued to hold high office after Stalin's death.

After the communist party, the Red Army was the principal target of Stalin's paranoia. Seventy-seven of its eighty-eight most senior commanders were purged. In all, about half the entire officer corps, totalling some 35,000 men, were shot or imprisoned, together with many of their wives and children. The Terror, as Krushchev later recognized, 'also undermined military discipline, because for several years officers of all ranks and even soldiers in the Party and Komsomol cells were taught to "unmask" their superiors as hidden enemies'.

The havoc wrought by the Terror was one of the factors which determined the timing of the German invasion in 1941. German intelligence reports concluded that it would be another three years before the Russian high command recovered from the consequences of the purges. Though a new and efficient command emerged under the pressure of the German invasion, the Terror had to be paid for during the war, as Robert Conquest observes, 'with the lives of hundreds of thousands of Russian soldiers, with hundreds of miles of Russian territory, and a great prolongation of the war itself'.

The cult of personality

While Stalin was busy decimating the Russian people he was also, in the words of his protégé, Krushchev, engaged in 'the glorification of his own person by all conceivable means'. Russian writers vied with one another in the extravagance of their praise. One of them, Avdeienko, told the Seventh Congress of Soviets in 1935:

I write books, I am an author; I dream of creating a lasting work. I love a girl in a new way; I am perpetuated in my children . . . All this is thanks to thee, O great teacher Stalin. Our love, our devotion, our strength, our heroism, our life – all are thine. Take them, great Stalin, all is thine, O leader of this great country . . . When the woman I love gives me a child the first word I shall teach it shall be 'Stalin'.

Almost every Soviet achievement in whatever field was invariably attributed at least in part to a personal initiative by Stalin himself. During April 1935, for example, *Pravda* reported that Stalin's ideas were 'invaluable directions for all the work done in the sphere of fruit-growing in this country'; that improvements in mechanized bakeries owed much to 'the genius of our leader and master, comrade Stalin'; and that 'the daily instructions of comrade Stalin were the decisive factors which ensured the victory of Soviet cinematography.'

The 'cult of personality' nowadays provides a convenient explanation in the Soviet Union for those enormities which are publicly admitted. But the abnormalities of Stalin's personality and the glorification of it provide only an immediate explanation. It still remains necessary to explain how a situation could develop in which it was possible for the personal paranoia of one man to hold to ransom a nation of two hundred million people. It is difficult to avoid the conclusion that the ultimate responsibility lies with Lenin.

Lenin had set out in November 1917 to establish the dictatorship of the proletariat, in order to prepare the way for the communist millenium. It had soon become clear, however, that the dictatorship of the proletariat meant in practice the dictatorship of the Bolshevik party. Before he came to power Lenin had insisted that 'what we do not want is the element of compulsion. We do not want to drive people into paradise with a bludgeon.' Once he became the ruler of Russia, however, he was prepared to argue that since the party knew the interests of the proletariat better than the proletariat itself it must, if necessary, use 'revolutionary violence' to defend the proletariat against itself. In 1921 he ordered the suppression of a mutiny of Kronstadt sailors, who had taken seriously his talk of the people's participation in the government of Russia and who felt themselves betrayed by him.

The Bolshevik party under Lenin's leadership was now, in Trotsky's words, persuaded that 'the party is always right'. From a state in which one party was always right it was to be only a short step to a state in which one man was always right.

The retreat from democracy

One of the most basic weaknesses of the Western democracies in the face of Hitler's Germany was their inability to grasp the extraordinary extent of Hitler's ambitions. Hitler had stated these ambitions quite clearly in *Mein Kampf*. Having first united all the German-speaking peoples, he proposed to revive the *Drang nach Osten*, the eastwards march of the Teutonic knights in the Middle Ages and then to recreate on a larger scale the slave empire they had founded in Eastern Europe: 'We start where they stopped six centuries before.' Germany, said Hitler, needed *Lebensraum* (living space) in the East. Once she had acquired it, the existing populations would either be removed or enslaved. Precisely because this malevolent vision of a new German empire seemed so fantastic, hardly anyone outside Germany took it seriously. And yet it was just such an empire that Hitler set out to build.

While communism claimed to have abandoned nationalism for internationalism, fascism prided itself instead on an exaggerated nationalism. And yet, during the 1930s at least, fascism was the more powerful international force. Fascist movements sprang up almost simultaneously all over Europe, looking for inspiration more to Hitler than to Mussolini. These movements took many different national forms, but everywhere they shared the same militarist nationalism (usually with racialist overtones) and the same militant hostility to both communism and democracy. Everywhere, too, they sought to establish a one-party state in which the party, as in Germany, would control every facet of national life.

Outside Germany and Italy fascism was strongest in the relatively backward countries of eastern Europe and the Iberian peninsula. Except in Spain, which experienced a brief interlude of democratic government from 1930 to 1936, democracy in these countries had already largely disappeared by the time of the Great Depression. The fascist parties of Portugal and eastern Europe (and in Spain after Franco became head of state) therefore aimed not, as Hitler and Mussolini had done, at the destruction of a democratic system of government but at the transformation of authoritarian regimes from within into fascist dictatorships.

Nowhere were they completely successful. Even in Spain, though the Falangists (the Spanish fascists) supported Franco's appointment by the army as head of state in 1936 in opposition to the legal government, they had, as they themselves privately admitted, little influence on his policies. Many European states during the 1930s – among them Spain, Portugal, Poland, Hungary, Romania, Yugoslavia and Greece – acquired fascist overtones or mouthed fascist slogans. None had the means, however, even had they wished to do so, to become fully-fledged fascist states. They lacked the highly developed machinery of oppression and control which enabled Hitler and Stalin to establish the world's first completely totalitarian societies. Even Mussolini, though he devised the celebrated fascist slogan, 'Everything for the state, nothing against the state, nothing outside the state', lacked the means to put that slogan fully into effect. *Gleichschaltung* in Italy was never complete.

Though the victory of fascism was still far from complete at the outbreak of the Second World War, it seemed clear that democracy was in decline. It survived (except in Switzerland) only on the north-western fringes of the European continent: in Britain, France, the Low Countries and Scandinavia. Even here democracy seemed to be losing faith in itself. The idea of progress which had been so popular only a generation earlier had now become desperately unfashionable. The inefficiency of democratic governments in finding effective solutions to the problems posed by the depression contrasted both with the rapid recovery of Nazi Germany and the apparent immunity of Stalin's Russia from the afflictions of capitalist economies.

The 1930s saw something like a *trahison des clercs* among liberal intellectuals. Instead of defending democracy when it was under siege they poured scorn on it. 'Contemporary society', said T. S. Eliot in 1935, 'is worm-eaten with liberalism.' Only Sir Arthur Quiller-Couch, the much mocked editor of the Oxford Book of English Verse, challenged Eliot's contempt for liberal democracy: 'What is the alternative? It is suppression; tyranny; in its final, brutal word-force. Look around Europe today.'

The resistance of the two great Western democracies, France and Britain, to the challenge of Hitler's Germany was far less determined than their opposition to the lesser menace of the kaiser's Germany only a quarter of a century before. But in the years before 1914 they had not been plagued by the economic crisis and intellectual doubts which beset them in the 1930s. There had been a profound change, too, in the mood of public opinion. During the decade before the First World War the peoples of France and Britain had grown steadily more convinced that war with Germany was sooner or later inevitable, and were ready for it. During the 1930s they tried instead to cling to the illusion that the Europe of the Locarno honeymoon had not really disappeared.

Appeasement

The classic example of the capitulation of Western democracy in the 30s is generally considered to be the Munich agreement of 1938, by which Britain and France jointly betrayed Czechoslovakia to Germany in the belief that they could thus appease Adolf Hitler. But the crucial capitulation had come two years earlier with Hitler's occupation of the Rhineland.

As long as the Rhineland remained demilitarized in accordance with the terms of the Versailles treaty, the heart of industrial Germany lay exposed to the menace of a French invasion. The French system of alliances with the smaller states of Eastern Europe (which since the First World War had replaced its earlier alliance with Tsarist Russia) made sense only if France was able to counter German aggression in the East with retaliation through the Rhineland. Hitler, equally, could embark on a policy

FRANÇAIS ALERTE !

E COMMUNISME A DEJA MIS LE FEU
AUX DEUX BOUTS DE L'EUROPE

Yo Mich

of expansion in eastern Europe only when he had protected his rear against French attack by the fortification of the Rhineland. The French journalist Alfred Fabre-Luce predicted in January 1936 the remilitarization of the Rhineland which took place two months later – and he accurately predicted its significance:

It would really be a way of asking France what her attitude would be in the event of war in eastern Europe. The lack of any military response on our part would be taken as a sufficient indication.... Germany would then prepare her war in the East, confident of being able to resist us on the Rhine which she had fortified.

Hitler's reoccupation of the Rhineland was, as he later admitted, one of the biggest gambles of his career:

If the French had then marched into the Rhineland we would have had to withdraw with our tails between our legs, for the military resources then at our disposal would have been wholly inadequate for even a moderate resistance.

Ten years, even five years before, there is no doubt that the French army would have

called Hitler's bluff. Even in 1936 France lacked not the ability to call Hitler's bluff but the will to do so. Britain, which grudgingly agreed to supply only two divisions if France invaded the Rhineland, heaved a sigh of relief when it failed to do so. Just as the achievements of Nazi Germany during the 1930s were not unfairly described by Hitler as 'the triumph of will', so the failures of Western democracy during the same period were, above all, a failure of will.

After Hitler's invasion of the Rhineland, Germany replaced France as the leading state on the continent of Europe. France herself was by now afflicted with a growing feeling of inferiority towards Germany. As late as 1931 France had seemed almost immune from the worst effects of the depression, while Germany had been forced to come cap in hand to Paris seeking financial help. By 1936 the tables had been turned with a vengeance. While the German economy forged rapidly ahead, France was still in the middle of an economic crisis. Worse still was the problem of France's declining manpower. During the 1930s deaths began to exceed births for the first time. France's population was actually

lower in 1940 than it had been fifty years before. The most striking fact about France's international position, observed Colonel Charles de Gaulle in 1934, was that two Germans were reaching military age for every one Frenchman.

During the middle of the 1930s European affairs seemed increasingly polarized into an international struggle between fascism and communism. In 1935 Stalin reversed his earlier instructions to European communists to concentrate on the destruction

LE PÉRIL JUIF

Above, bare-footed Abyssinian soldiers, 1935: they could do little against Italian airpower, poison gas and superior armaments.

Left, French anti-semitic poster issued during the 1930s: though at its most virulent there, anti-semitism was not confined to Germany, and Jews became a convenient scapegoat for Europe's political and economic ills.

Opposite top, right-wing French election poster of 1936 warning of the perils of communism: despite the fact that there had not been a single successful left-wing revolution anywhere in Europe, until the very late 1930s many people dreaded the Bolshevik menace, ignoring the far more real one posed by Germany.

Opposite bottom, Italian troops leaving Rome for Abyssinia, 1935: the League of Nations condemned Italy's aggression but failed to take any action.

of democratic socialism and advocated instead a new policy of 'Popular Front' alliances between socialists and communists against the menace of fascism. When the Civil War broke out in Spain in 1936 Hitler and Mussolini sent help to Franco, and an International Brigade of left-wing sympathizers partly supplied with Russian arms fought on the side of the republican government. Hitler, however, was in no hurry to ensure Franco's victory. The longer the war continued, he believed, the worse

would be the demoralization of liberal, democratic Europe.

The rest of Europe saw the Civil War in simplified terms as a struggle between fascism and communism. Many European conservatives were by now anxious that by opposing Hitler they might be playing into the hands of Stalin. This attitude was most prevalent in France. Ever since the beginning of the twentieth century the French right-wing parties had been the leading advocates in Europe of a tough,

uncompromising policy towards Germany. But in 1936 they suddenly changed their mind. Faced with the prospect of a Popular Front government in France led by the socialist, Léon Blum, they coined the slogan, 'Better Hitler than Blum!'

The policy of appeasement practised by the French and British governments during the 1930s reflected absolutely the wishes of their populations. The Munich agreement of 1938 was the most ignoble surrender in the history of modern British foreign policy. Yet as a direct result of that surrender Neville Chamberlain attained a peak of popularity which few, if any, other peacetime prime ministers have ever equalled. The British people as a whole greeted the betrayal of Czechoslovakia with an almost indecent relief of which they later felt ashamed.

The only British politician who might have rallied the British people from a policy of appeasement was Winston Churchill. But Churchill, after a brilliant early career

in which he had held almost every major cabinet office, had disappeared into the political wilderness. The eccentricity of his views on the Indian subcontinent only served to cast doubt on his constant warnings of Hitler's designs in Europe. His hour was yet to come.

The history of the 1930s suggests perhaps that the First World War, though a war caused by European rivalries and whose battles were overwhelmingly concentrated on the European continent, affected Europe less profoundly than it affected Asia. In Asia it set India on the path to independence, Japan on the road to Asian mastery and turned China's face against the West. In Europe, on the other hand, though the war acted as a catalyst to revolution in the East, in the West it only interrupted Germany's bid for the mastery of Europe. In 1919 Marshal Foch had described the peace settlement of Versailles as 'a twenty years' truce'. In Europe, at least, that was all it proved to be.

THE FIRST WORLD WAR AND THE WORLD BETWEEN THE WARS

Date	Western Europe	Central and Eastern Europe	The outside world
1914	Britain declares war on Germany (4 August) Battle of the Marne (5–12 September) Race for the sea (October–November)	Assassination of Francis Ferdinand (28 June) Austrian ultimatum to Serbia (23 July) Russia mobilizes (30 July) Germany declares war on Russia (1 August) Germany declares war on France and invades Belgium (3 August) Russian defeats in East Prussia (August-September)	New Zealand takes Samoa (August) Britain takes Togoland (August) Australia takes New Guinea (September) Turkey enters the war (October) Japan takes Kiaochow (November) British protectorate in Egypt (December)
1915	Allied offensives in Artois and Champagne (February–October) Italy enters the war (May) Haig British commander-in-chief (December)	Gallipoli campaign (February 1915–January 1916) Large German gains on the eastern front (May-October) Bulgaria enters the war (October)	Japan submits Twenty One Demands to China (January) South African troops take German Southwest Africa
1916	Conscription in Britain (January) Battle of Verdun (February–November) Easter Rising in Dublin Battle of Jutland (31 May) Battle of the Somme (July–November) Lloyd George prime minister (December)	Brusilov offensive (June-September) Romania enters the war (August)	Last German garrison in Cameroun surrenders (February) Sykes-Picot agreement on Middle-East Arab revolt against Turkey Wilson re-elected president of the United States (December)
1917	Imperial War Cabinet meets in London (March) Nivelle offensive (April–May) Mutinies in French army. Passchendaele (July–November)	Germany begins unrestricted submarine warfare (February) Tsar abdicates (15 March) Bolshevik revolution (7 November)	United States enters the war (April) China enters the war (June) Sun Yat-sen sets up rival government in Canton Montague declaration on India (August) Balfour declaration on Palestine (November)
1918	Final German offensive in the West (March–July) Foch 'commander-in-chief of the Allied armies in France' (April) Allied counter-offensive (July–November) Battle of Amiens (8–11 August) Armistice (11 November) Lloyd George coalition re-elected (December)	Treaty of Brest-Litovsk (March) Civil War begins in Russia (1918–20)	Wilson's Fourteen Points (January)
1919	Paris peace conference begins (January) Treaty of Versailles (28 June) Treaty of Saint-Germain with Austria (10 September) Treaty of Neuilly with Bulgaria (19 November)	Communist rising in Berlin (January) Bela Kun in power in Hungary (March–August) Weimar Republic in Germany (August) D'Annunzio occupies Fiume (September 1919–December 1920)	Amritsar massacre in India (April) Fourth of May Movement in China United States Senate rejects the Versailles treaty Government of India Act (December)
1920	Treaty of Trianon with Hungary (4 June) Treaty of Sèvres with Turkey (August) Italian workers occupy their factories (August)	Kapp putsch in Berlin (March) Battle of Warsaw (August)	Non-cooperation begins in India (August)
1921		Treaty of Riga (March) New Economic Policy in Russia	Harding President of the United States End of Anglo-Japanese alliance Foundation of Chinese communist party Washington Naval conference
1922	Irish *Dail* ratifies treaty establishing Irish Free State (January) Bonar Law British prime minister (October) Fascist March on Rome (October)	Stalin secretary-general of Russian communist party	End of British protectorate in Egypt Southern Rhodesia rejects union with South Africa Gandhi imprisoned (1922–24)
1923	Baldwin's first ministry (May)	Occupation of the Ruhr (January) German inflation at its height (November) Hitler leads unsuccessful Munich putsch (November)	Sun Yat-sen signs alliance with Russia (January) Coolidge President of the United States Southern Rhodesia gains virtual self-government
1924	Ramsay MacDonald Britain's first Labour prime minister (January) Matteoti assassinated in Italy (June) Baldwin's second ministry (November)	Death of Lenin (January)	
1925	Mussolini declares Italy a one-party state (January) Locarno treaties signed in London (December)	Hindenburg President of Germany	Death of Sun Yet-sen Abd-el Krim's rebellion in Morocco (1925–26) Druse rebellion in Syria (1925–27)
1926	General Strike in Britain (May)	Germany enters League of Nations	Chiang Kai-shek begins Northern Expedition Hirohito Emperor of Japan Imperial conference recognizes autonomy of dominions
1927		Stalin wins struggle for power in Russia	Chiang Kai-shek begins attack on Chinese communists Simon commission visits India
1928	Kellogg-Briand pact signed in Paris	First Five Year Plan begins in Russia	Chiang Kai-shek claims re-unification of China
1929	Ramsay MacDonald's second Labour government (June)	Trotsky leaves Russia	Hoover President of United States Chu-Mao soviet in Kiangsi Wall Street crash (October)
1930	London Naval Conference	Effective political power in Germany passes to Hindenburg and palace camarilla (March) Last Allied troops leave Rhineland (June)	Civil disobedience campaign in India Uriburu President of Argentina (September) Vargas President of Brazil (October) Rebellion in Indo-China
1931	National government in Britain led by Ramsay Macdonald (August) Statute of Westminster on British Commonwealth		Gandhi-Irwin truce Manchurian incident (18 September) Mao elected first chairman of Chinese Soviet Republic
1932	Worst year of the Great Depression	Worst year of the Great Depression Nazis emerge as largest party in Germany Russian famine at its height	Worst year of the Great Depression End of British protectorate in Iraq Japanese army establishes puppet state of Manchukuo
1933		Hitler becomes German Chancellor (30 January) Reichstag fire (27 February) Enabling law completes Hitler's dictatorship (23 March)	Franklin D. Roosevelt President of United States Japan leaves League of Nations
1934		Hitler's Night of the Long Knives (30 June) Death of Hindenburg. Hitler head of state (August) Kirov assassinated in Russia (December)	Long March in China (1934–35)
1935	Baldwin's third ministry (June)	Saar returns to Germany (January) Nuremberg race laws (March)	Government of India Act Italy invades Ethiopia
1936	Edward VIII King of England (January). Abdicates and succeeded by George VI (December) Popular Front government in France (1936–38) Spanish Civil War (1936–39)	Hitler reoccupies Rhineland (March) Stalin's Terror at its height (1936)	Italy annexes Ethiopia Anglo-Egyptian treaty Tosei-ha faction in Japanese army defeats Kodo-ha Alliance between Mao and Chiang (December)
1937	Neville Chamberlain prime minister (May)		Congress victory in Indian elections (February) War between China and Japan (1937–45)
1938		German annexation of Austria (March) Munich agreement (September)	
1939	Britain and France declare war on Germany (3 September)	German annexation of Czechoslovakia (March) Germany invades Poland (1 September)	

Part X

THE WORLD SINCE 1939

Introduction

Our age is one of rapid, far-reaching change. Change, by definition, means destruction as well as building up. As some fervently set out to sweep away outmoded institutions and hateful backwardness, others interpret their acts as wanton destruction of all that is good, true and beautiful. In such a situation, who is building and who destroying? Time, perhaps, will tell, but with a cruel partiality, praising whatever survives and portraying what goes under as deserving of its fate.

The confusion such a situation creates makes writing contemporary history in our age particularly difficult. The historian's effort must be to make sense of it all, but his appreciation of the tearing down and building up will not necessarily conform to others' viewpoints – or to the viewpoints of subsequent generations. Yet not to try to make sense of our world would amount to an abdication of the human effort to come to terms with life.

Human experience cannot be reduced to a simple formula. However it is true that a real thread runs through most of the human achievements since 1945. They are aspects of a remarkable growth in the range of human power, exerted usually through corporate organization of expertise rather than by individual men or by the unskilled masses of mankind. The most obvious examples are political and military: how enormously the destructive capacities of the world's armed forces have increased since 1945! How much the jurisdiction of governmental officials has enlarged during the same period, in backward and advanced countries alike. But the power and range of private corporations has also grown and often runs across national boundaries. Similarly, the less closely structured but nonetheless real communities of specialists in innumerable branches of science and technology have also become transnational and in some important respects continue to be self-regulating and capable of influencing even the greatest of the world's governments and corporations. Schools, sects, political parties, advertising agencies, news services and other corporate groupings that seek to affect men's minds have also attained greater scope and range. The globe-girdling television hook-up that reported the first human landing on the moon in 1969 is

only an unusually spectacular example of the interweaving of national information systems that has come to constitute a powerful political force in its own right, even in those lands where there is governmental control of information.

Cumulatively, the effect of such corporate activities is to make all society malleable – capable of being made over, this way or that, according to somebody's more or less rational plan. Zones of behaviour left to themselves – that is, to custom and to age-old traditional routine – have shrunk drastically. More than ever before, man has set out consciously to make and remake himself. The mushroom growth of corporate structures in the 'modernizing' sector of human society is matched by a no less remarkable disruption and breakdown of other types of corporate structures within which human life used to be led. Kindreds, tribes, village communities, as well as occupational, religious, ethnic and other groupings have become far less powerful, that is, far less able to guide men's actions through the vicissitudes of their lives. The great instrumentality breaking up these older structures is the enhanced range of modern communications. Since 1945 radio, television, and newspapers backed up by schools, political parties and ultimately by the whole array of 'modernizing' corporate structures have made most of the world's human beings dissatisfied with their traditional lot in life and hopeful of being able to enjoy other, usually urban, experiences of whose existence and possibility they had scarcely dreamed before.

Aptly named the 'revolution of rising expectations', this change in human attitudes

almost inescapably outruns the practical possibilities of realizing these new desires. To be sure, human life has always known pain and suffering. Traditional styles of life did not abolish suffering; perhaps they made it more tolerable by offering religious solace, but this in itself did not reduce the reality. What is new in our time is the potentiality – glimpsed and not yet attainable – of eliminating physical deprivation and many forms of disease that have haunted and deformed human lives for thousands of years. Yet, paradoxically, this bright vision is balanced by our increased awareness of the dark forces within human personalities that find expression in private, personal violence. On a public, political level, these same forces, allied with the social instincts that urge men to defend their own community – however defined – while fearing and often hating outsiders, open the possibility of mass destruction through war.

The irrational levels of human personality set limits to planning and check the growth of human capacity to control the world around them. Yet awareness of these levels may allow calculation of their effects in particular situations. Statistical regularities in criminal and other kinds of violent behaviour do exist. This may some day allow an ultimate triumph of rationality: planning for and deliberately making use of the irrational levels of the human psyche. Such a tour de force is still far away. In the meanwhile men must observe and take part in a fateful race between the party of construction and the party of destruction. The tricky part is to know which is which: and on this issue men may be expected to disagree in the future as they have in the past. Pending

an outcome, we cannot know for sure in any contested issue who in retrospect will appear right and who wrong. We remain too near, too closely engaged emotionally as well as intellectually in the struggles and debates of our age to see the overall patterns and master movements that will emerge for our descendants in a century or two. Yet each of us must do his best to understand his place in the world, to open new perspectives, batter down old prejudices and diminish narrow parochialisms.

Above, student riots at Kent State University, Ohio, in protest at US military action in Cambodia: the 1960s brought worldwide student protests against virtually every aspect of the established order, though by the late 1970s they could be seen to have had little long-term effect.

Left, Graham Sutherland's tapestry Christ of the Apocalypse *completed in 1962 for the rebuilt Coventry Cathedral.*

Opposite, Las Vegas, temple of American capitalism.

On page 662, at no time in the last four decades has the world been at peace; the Second World War has been followed by a succession of conflicts, more local in scale but no less bloody for those involved. The woman here is a Vietcong suspect being interrogated by a South Vietnamese policeman, but she could be almost anyone almost anywhere.

Chapter 55

The Second World War

Human experience cannot be reduced to a simple formula, but the historian has a duty to try and make sense of even its most recent past. For him not to do so would be to abdicate his professional responsibility. Therefore in offering an account of the last forty years of global history, the writer aims at eschewing bias while maintaining a viewpoint. That viewpoint consists of the belief that the historical process is an amalgam of political, economic and psychological forces, operating in varying conditions, subject to occasional deflection and modification at the touch of outstanding individual personalities and gradually raising the level of the sum total of mankind's consciousness of its own identity.

Unlike the outbreak of the First World War in 1914, which on the whole was unexpected, the hostilities beginning in September 1939 had been dreaded and anticipated for several years. The causes of both these major conflicts lie deep in the history of previous centuries; the causes of the second are rooted in the unfinished business of the first.

Politically they proceeded from the unchecked sovereignty of nation states, which the League of Nations had failed to curb. Economically they were the inevitable concomitant of competing economic systems, entrenched behind tariff barriers. The psychological causes of the war were the frustrations of peace time and were the result of human beings seeking compensatory outlets for their violent and aggressive instincts. All three of these were worldwide in their manifestations, but the occasion which finally triggered off war was entirely European.

That occasion was the German invasion of Poland on 1 September 1939. It, or something like it, had become unavoidable ever since the policies of Communism, Fascism, Nazism and the western democracies began during the 1930s to cut across each other. Directly or indirectly, these powers had all had a kind of dress-rehearsal interest in the Spanish Civil War. By the spring of 1939 this struggle was moving towards victory for General Franco's right-wing regime. The unopposed re-occupation of the demilitarized zone of the Rhineland by German troops in 1936 in defiance of the Treaty of Versailles, the proclamation of the agreement between Italy and Germany resulting in a Rome-Berlin Axis or collaboration pact in the same year, the anti-Comintern Pact (Germany–Italy–Japan) of 1937, which opposed international communism, the futile efforts of France, Britain and the Soviet Union to constitute a counter-alliance – these were stages towards catastrophe.

In March 1938 Hitler invaded Austria and incorporated her into the German Reich. In Czechoslovakia, Nazi Germany was giving more and more support to the Sudeten-Deutsch minority there and threatening military intervention to such a degree that in the late summer partial mobilization by the Great Powers in Europe began. However, on 29 September 1938, by a policy of appeasement towards Hitler, France and Britain bought off war for a few more months: this was the Munich agreement. Its hollowness, as expressed in Neville Chamberlain's fatuous claim that he had obtained 'peace with honour', was demonstrated by its terms. These involved the transfer of the Sudetenland to Germany in exchange for some vague guarantee about the inviolability of the remaining Czechoslovak frontiers – a fatal set-back to all attempts at anti-fascist and anti-Nazi solidarity.

In the ensuing months Czechoslovakia was virtually dismembered; in October 1938 its president, Benes, resigned; in March 1939 German troops occupied Bohemia and Moravia, and Germany annexed Memel from Lithuania. Hitler then proceeded to denounce the German non-aggression pact with Poland, and on 31 March France and Britain pledged their support to Poland in case she were attacked – a belated and ineffective gesture. On 16 April the Soviet Union proposed a defensive alliance with Britain, but it was not until 5 August that a British military mission left for Moscow. Then on 23 August there occurred a dramatic and complete reversal of alliances: suddenly a German-Soviet non-aggression pact was signed. What prompted this was Hitler's desire to guard against being involved in a possible war on two fronts and Stalin's eagerness to secure for the time being a screen behind which his own designs could be furthered.

Next, Germany demanded of Poland the right to build a military highway across the Polish Corridor, which since the First World War had separated west Germany from her eastern provinces, this was accompanied also by a demand for the ceding to Germany of the Free City of Danzig. Strengthened by the guarantee it had recently received from France and Britain, the Polish government refused that demand. This was the actual spark that set off the conflagration. The mixture of ruthless Nazi aggression, Soviet duplicity and Franco-British lethargy had shattered the frail defences of an uneasy armistice in Europe, which had lasted for exactly twenty years.

Before following the course of the Second World War and its extension beyond Europe across the planet, it is necessary to survey the rest of the world scene as it had been shaping during the 1930s and as it appeared in the summer of 1939.

Around the eastern end of the Mediterranean two forces were at work, one being the result of Egyptian national independence gained from Britain in 1936, which retained however certain strategic rights in the Suez canal area in case of war. The other was a legacy of the First World War, namely the problem of Arab-Jewish relations. It had been largely created by the incompatible promises of the British government of that day to the Arabs (Mac-Mahon Pledge 1916) and to the Jews (Balfour Declaration 1917), one guaranteeing rights of national self-determination to the Arab states, the other guaranteeing a national home for the Jews in their midst. This had resulted in the setting up under the League of Nations of a British Mandate for Palestine. By the middle of the 1930s terrorism in this area had become such a problem for the British administration that plans for the partition of Palestine between the two contestants, acceptable to neither Arab nor Jew, were being prepared. These became increasingly urgent under the stimulus of mounting immigration demands from Jewish refugees from Hitler's terror, but when the Second World War broke out no solution to the problem had been found. British arms controlled the strategic points of Cyprus, Malta and Gibraltar.

In North Africa there had been only two independent nations in 1933, Liberia and Ethiopia: the latter was invaded in 1935 and annexed in 1936 by Italy, its Emperor Haile Selassie going into exile. Elsewhere on that vast continent there was as yet, in striking contrast with many parts of Asia, an almost total absence of native nationalist leadership against the dominating European imperialist powers. Yet the policies of these same powers to their African dependencies varied: Belgium and Portugal were patriarchal, France had a policy of assimilation and Britain was paternalistically preparing both East and West Africa for eventual self-government. South Africa was a special case, where a small British and Afrikaans minority completely dominated a huge Bantu, Indian and 'Coloured' majority. This division is particularly notable because, although the then South African prime minister, Smuts, was to bring his country into the Second World War on the side of the Allies, there was a large measure of sympathy within the Afrikaans community for the Nazi cause.

Since 1937 India had been hovering on the verge of independence, but Anglo-Indian understanding was to receive a rude shock. All Congress office holders resigned in protest against the British government's inclusion of India, without consulting her, in the declaration of war on Germany in 1939.

Indian self-government was postponed for another eight years and even when it was achieved there were internal divisions. Meanwhile Indian troops fought on the Allied side, while a dissident anti-British group under Bose looked to the Japanese for support.

In China there had been two struggles going on since the early 1930s: one was between the Chinese and the Japanese invaders of their country (which had been formally in progress since 1937); the other was between Chiang Kai-shek's Chinese Nationalist party and the Communists under the leadership of Mao Tse-Tung. Between 1934 and 1937 the latter, in order to establish and consolidate a firm base for further revolutionary activities, had led his followers on the Long March of 6,000 miles to North East China, converting many of the peasantry to Communism on the way. Although for most of the Second World War the two Chinese leaders faced a common enemy in Japan, they neither trusted each other nor wished for reconciliation – in the end Mao's party was to prevail.

Undoubtedly the most striking phenomenon in the 1930s in the Far East had been the rise of Japanese power from the early days of Japan's violent aggression in Manchuria to the virtual declaration of a 'new order' in East Asia in October 1938. During the summer of 1939 there were Soviet-Japanese hostilities in Outer Mongolia, but with the signing of the Soviet-Nazi Pact Japan, because of her alliance with Germany, had to re-orientate her foreign policy. It was a year before she was ready for the next phase of her expansion. When it came, most of southeast Asia was ripe for shaking. Siam was traditionally pro-Japanese, Burma was restive under British control, Malaya was vulnerable in spite of the British stronghold at Singapore. The Dutch hold on the East Indies could be prised open, and French power in Indo-China was already being seriously challenged by the Vietnamese leader, Ho Chi Minh. The Philippines were on the point of obtaining their independence from the United States.

Of the remaining British Commonwealth countries in the eastern region Ceylon was still a crown colony and together with Australia and New Zealand supported Britain when she declared war in 1939.

Across the Atlantic the United States had been recovering under Roosevelt's New Deal from the post-1929 depression. Externally American policy was defined in terms of various Neutrality Acts and of her 'Good Neighbor' policy to the Latin American countries. Nevertheless, informed circles in the States had begun to sound the alarm against fascist, Nazi and communist movements in Europe and elsewhere, and in December 1938 there had been the joint United States-Latin American Declaration of Lima to the effect that any interference by an outside power in the affairs of the Latin

American continent would be regarded as an act of war.

As for the Latin American countries themselves, most of these had been striving to cope with the aftermath of the economic effects of the Great Depression, mainly by means of dictatorial forms of government. Although some of them displayed pro-Nazi sympathies, most were in due course to declare themselves supporters of the Allied cause. Canada, a young, highly industrialized country and part of the Commonwealth, ranged herself immediately with Britain on the outbreak of war.

Although on 23 September 1939 by the Panama Declaration of Neutrality the United States and the Latin American countries proclaimed their neutrality, this was not to endure. In Europe neutrality quickly became a casualty as Norway, Denmark, Greece, Belgium, the Netherlands, Luxembourg, Iceland and Yugoslavia were swallowed up by the belligerents' activities. Only nine countries retained their neutral status throughout the war years: Afghanistan, Saudi Arabia, Siam, Spain, Portugal, Sweden, Turkey, Switzerland and Eire. Fifty-seven nations went to war, forty-six on the Allied and eleven on the Axis side.

Blitzkrieg

Within the first three weeks of September 1939 German armies raced across Poland; on 17 September troops of the Soviet Union moved in from the East; on 27 September Warsaw itself capitulated to Hitler's might, and the Polish government went into exile. While these events were occurring the French and British military chiefs in the West acted indecisively, although logistically they enjoyed a marked superiority over the German forces opposed to them in that area. The mentality of the French High Command was symbolized by the Maginot

Above, inside the Maginot line, which ran the entire length of France's border with Germany: having constructed these enormous fortifications, the French General staff retired behind them, both mentally and physically, and utterly failed to appreciate the implications of German rearmament, being totally surprised by Hitler's rapid advance. Much of the Maginot line was surrendered without a fight.

Top, Polish cavalry during the September 1939 campaign: valiant though their resistance was, the Polish army could do nothing to withstand the onslaught of Hitler's forces.

line of fortification, behind which it sheltered. Although this was unfinished, it did not conceive of enemy infiltration. It seemed inhibited from advancing and assaulting the western front of Germany, while Nazi fanaticism and military expertise were triumphant in the East.

Yet the relationship between Germany and the Soviet Union was full of mistrust: Hitler had made up his mind to attack the Soviet Union at some stage, while Stalin was bent on securing his own defence by tightening his hold on the Eastern frontier lands of Poland and with German connivance wresting Lithuania, Latvia, Estonia and Finland to his own uses. On the other hand, these two powers could be of economic assistance to each other: food and materials could be brought from Siberia to Germany in return for manufactured goods and munitions from Germany to the Soviet Union.

Meanwhile throughout the autumn and winter months of 1939–40 all the Western Allies seemed capable of doing was to mount and increase the naval blockade of Germany and to await – in the case of Britain with some attempts at civilian defence precautions – the eventual switch of Hitler's *Blitzkrieg* from the Eastern to the Western front. A British expeditionary force had been sent across the channel to support the French armies. This came to be known as the 'phoney war'. At sea there had been a blow and counter-blow: the British battleship, *Royal Oak*, had been sunk when at anchor in Scapa Flow by a daring intrusive raid from a German submarine; the German pocket-battleship, *Admiral Graf Spee*, had been scuttled by her commander on 17 December in Montevideo harbour after being driven in there off the Atlantic by the British navy.

Military action in this first stage of the war was confined to Finland. On 30 November 1939 the Soviet Union attacked that country after failing to secure its unconditional cooperation by mere demand. The Finns, under Field-Marshal Mannerheim, put up an unexpectedly stiff resistance, but in March 1940 the Finnish army collapsed under renewed Soviet military pressure, and the Finnish government was forced to make peace, surrendering their naval base of Hango to the Russians.

Now although Hitler had already prepared for the seizure of power in Norway through the Norwegian Nazi leader, Quisling, he was still determined to finish off the French and British while the Soviet Union was preoccupied with Finland. He had in fact ordered an attack on the West for 17 January 1940, but on 10 January operational plans for this move had fallen into the hands of the Allies, who had also been secretly tipped off about Hitler's programme by the Italians. So, for a few weeks this 'Case Yellow', the code-name for Hitler's plan, was postponed. Instead, he went ahead with the invasion and occupation of Norway and

Denmark. He had strong reasons for doing so for he realized that the Allies were preparing to cut off Germany's imports of high-grade iron-ore via Norwegian territorial waters.

On 9 April 1940 German troops entered Denmark and Norway; the former yielded at once, the latter continued the struggle partly through internal resistance and partly through the Norwegian government which went into exile in London. In spite of a brief excursion of British troops in small numbers to Central Norway, the Germans obtained control of the whole country and Atlantic seaboard and safeguarded their supplies of iron-ore. The only compensation gained by the Allies was a successful British naval action against German warships near Narvik, whereby one-fifth of the

German navy's warship tonnage was destroyed.

In France Prime Minister Daladier was replaced by Paul Reynaud on 20 March 1940, a change which did not fundamentally alter the prevailing French attitude of defeatism. By contrast, in Britain Chamberlain was succeeded by Churchill on 10 May 1940 at the head of a coalition government, and under him the British will to resist stiffened.

Although still not in a position of numerical superiority in the West, the Germans at this stage possessed a clear advantage in morale and leadership. Their offensives in May through the Ardennes and their invasion of Belgium, Luxembourg and the Netherlands, the now fatal advance of British and French troops beyond their prepared positions and the demolition of the

myth of the Maginot line by the German flying columns – all these events meant that by the end of that one month the British forces were reeling back on Dunkirk, where they were to be joined by the defeated remnants of the French and Belgian armies: the Belgian government itself had surrendered on 28 May, and the Dutch government had escaped to England.

Two factors made possible the successful evacuation by 4 June of 222,500 British, 112,000 French and some 1,000 Belgian soldiers from Dunkirk to the shores of Britain. One was Hitler's decision to halt his tanks just south of Dunkirk in order to preserve them for further use elsewhere on the assurance of Goering that the Luftwaffe would suffice with its strafing from the air to prevent the evacuation of the Allied troops. The other was the extraordinary daring and skilful improvization of the British by means of which hundreds of small boats, mostly skippered by amateurs, ferried the soldiers back across the channel from the bombed and blazing beaches of Dunkirk.

Although Gamelin had been succeeded by Weygand as the French commander-in-chief, the latter had been unable to alter the course of France's collapse. On 10 June Mussolini declared war on France and Britain in order not to be left out of gaining some of the spoils of victory. On 22 June the French were forced to sign an armistice, and the old soldier, Marshal Pétain, took over the government of that part of defeated France which the Germans had decided not to occupy – roughly the southwest region with Vichy as the seat of government. General Charles de Gaulle had however escaped with a few followers and rallied what were to be known as the 'Free French' in

England, from where he continued to fight in the name of an undefeated France. A bitter dispute then ensued as regards the future of the French navy, the ships of which were impounded by the British navy either in home or in Mediterranean waters in so far as they were outside Vichy-controlled ports, although Vichy still claimed their allegiance.

Meanwhile the Soviet Union, uneasy at her partner's colourful successes in the West, attempted to make a bargain with Hitler for the partition of the Balkan countries. For the time being he had to concede Bessarabia to Stalin, but this was only because he was not yet ready to strike eastwards against the Soviet Union.

Across the Atlantic the dramatic successes of the Nazi *Blitzkrieg* had been forcing a reappraisal of American policy: neutrality was beginning to shade off into non-belligerence – a phrase which described an enormously increased production of munitions and in November 1940 the abandonment of the Neutrality Act. This meant rejecting the embargo on selling arms to belligerents to the extent of imposing 'cash and carry' terms which favoured the Allies.

This then was the position in the early summer of 1940 – a prostrate France, either occupied by Germany or controlled by Vichy, a victorious Germany in control of most of northern Europe, a watchful, predatory Soviet Union, a slowly awakening United States and a defiant Britain. In Churchill's words: 'the battle of France is over. I expect that the battle of Britain is about to begin . . . let us therefore brace ourselves to our duty, and so bear ourselves that, if the British Commonwealth and Empire last for a thousand years, men will still say, "This was their finest hour".'

669

With the repeated assurances of Goering that the Luftwaffe could gain dominance over the British navy and air force, Hitler decided that the invasion of Britain should take place during the month of August. In spite of this imminent peril, and relying on a huge increase in production of Hurricane and Spitfire fighter planes, the British government sent out reinforcements that summer to its commander in the Middle East, General Wavell, to help him to meet the onset of Italian forces in North Africa.

From 13 August to 17 September 1940 the Battle of Britain was fought, ending with the defeat of Goering's all-out effort to establish supremacy in the air and the calling off of the German invasion. If it is ever justifiable to pinpoint one event in history as being decisively important, then the victory of the Royal Air Force in the Battle of Britain was such an event. Churchill's phrase is the best comment: 'Never in the field of human conflict was so much owed by so many to so few'.

The eastern front

Hitler had been regarding the Soviet Union's propagandist activities in the Balkans with an alarm that only strengthened his determination to attack her early in the spring of 1941. Partly in preparation for this and partly to play on British, Dutch and French weaknesses in Asia, he listened attentively to the voice of Japan, which was about to state its claim to establish a so-called 'Greater Asia Co-prosperity Sphere'.

On 27 September 1940 a Tripartite Pact was signed between Germany, Italy and Japan by which the European partners agreed to underwrite a Japanese 'New Asia' and Japan agreed to underwrite a Nazi-Fascist 'New Europe'.

During the autumn events moved rapidly in southeast Europe: Hitler proclaimed his support for a newly established fascist regime in Romania under the 'Iron Front', anti-Communist General Antonescu, and at the end of October Italy invaded Greece. On 5 November 1940 Roosevelt was elected president of the United States for a third period of office. Thus he was able to lay plans for the granting of large-scale economic aid to Britain, which was to become effective by the Lend-Lease Act of 11 March 1941. Britain was enabled to procure ships and supplies in the form of a loan to be repaid only at some future date.

In April 1941 German troops began the invasion of Greece and Yugoslavia, compelling the Greek and Yugoslav governments to seek asylum in London together with the Free French, Polish, Belgian, Dutch, Norwegian and Czechoslovak governments already established there. Early in February Hitler had despatched one of his ablest generals, Rommel, to Africa with the famous 'Afrika Korps' which proceeded to conduct a massive onslaught against Wavell's forces.

It seemed that the whole world, with the exception of the Soviet Union, was convinced that Hitler was now about to turn eastwards, but Stalin spurned the British offer of a military alliance on 13 June. On 22 June at long last 'Operation Barbarossa', as the invasion of Russia was code-named at German headquarters, began. Hitler had a war on two fronts on his hands.

Turning-points in the struggle

Even at the time it was apparent to some that this action of Hitler must spell his eventual doom, although its manner could not be foretold – least of all the long-term ideological implications of it. With the Battle of the Atlantic causing heavy shipping losses to Britain, the German hold on western Europe from north to south firm, and the United States as yet only committed to economic aid through 'all measures short of war', Hitler's prospects looked bright.

The Nazi occupation of Europe therefore fell into four categories: first, those countries annexed outright and governed direct from Berlin: Austria, Sudetenland, northwest Poland including Danzig and the Polish Corridor, Alsace-Lorraine, Luxembourg and northwest Yugoslavia; second, the 'Eastern Lands': the 'Protectorate of Bohemia and Moravia, 'the Government-General of Poland' and eventually the Baltic states and the temporarily conquered areas of the Soviet Union; third, the 'occupied territories' granted a measure of self-government but under Nazi control: Norway, Denmark, Holland, Belgium, France, Serbia, Greece and (after September 1943) Northern Italy: fourth, Germany's satellite allies: Bulgaria, Hungary, Romania, Croatia, Slovenia and Finland.

Yet in spite of all this, three stubborn facts remained as pointers to the ultimate destruction of the Nazis, namely, an undefeated Britain, a mountingly hostile America and a Japan still neutral to the Soviet Union – a neutrality which, because it was maintained until very near the end of the war, meant that the Soviet Union had not to fear attack from her Asiatic rear while locked in desperate encounter with Hitler's invading armies.

Above, German news photo showing the citizens of Larissa, Greece, welcoming one of their invaders; the reality was rather different – the Greeks were among the dourest resisters, pinning down troops that could more usefully have been deployed elsewhere.

Above left, German reconnaissance group in Yugoslavia, April 1941: the German invasion took just one week, helped by the destruction of Belgrade from the air.

Opposite top, American B-17 Fortresses on a mission supported by a Mustang fighter escort.

Opposite bottom right, Reichsmarshal Herman Goering (1893–1946) visiting a Luftwaffe squadron, autumn 1940: the Luftwaffe's failure to win the Battle of Britain put paid to Hitler's hopes of invading England and helped to ensure his ultimate defeat.

Opposite bottom left, German Dornier 172 aircraft over the London docks in the first daylight bombing raid on London, 7 September 1940: with hindsight, this can be said to have been one of the most crucial days of the war, for the beginning of raids on London meant the end of the attacks on the airfields and radar stations of southern England, which, though still in action, had been severely damaged during the previous weeks, and so enabled the RAF to retain air superiority.

These were making spectacular advances into the Soviet Union on a 1,200-mile front, reaching the suburbs of Moscow and penetrating the Ukraine and the Crimea. But the reserves and resources of Siberia and the Urals remained beyond their reach, a knock-out blow was not achieved during the summer and soon the Russian winter closed in on the German armies.

In August 1941 Churchill and Roosevelt had their first meeting at sea and drew up the Atlantic Charter, a preliminary attempt to sketch the war aims of the Allies. The United States, though still neutral, had been edging nearer to participation by the way in which she was offering protection to convoys in large expanses of the Atlantic and by her steadily increasing deliveries of supplies to Britain.

In the Far East, Japan's governing regime became more and more militaristic as opportunities for further Japanese expansion

began to present themselves with the pre-occupation of the Western Powers in their own hostilities. The American government refused to countenance any accommodation of Japan as long as China remained un-liberated from Japanese pressure. On 17 October 1941, Tojo became head of the Japanese state, and although by then the Americans were expecting Japanese aggression somewhere in the East they were caught entirely by surprise when Japanese aircraft hurled themselves on the American naval base at Pearl Harbor on 7 December 1941. In less than one hour they inflicted greater naval losses than the United States had suffered throughout her First World War participation in 1917–18. This event brought the United States right into the Second World War as a full protagonist.

The war now began to take on its global but bi-partite character. On 1 January 1942, twenty-six of the Allied nations signed the Declaration of the United Nations, but al-ready there were signs both in Asia and Europe of those rifts which were, after 1945, to divide the victors. In China, Chiang Kai-shek, who had not been exerting himself much against the Japanese, was becoming more and more concerned with opposing the spread of Mao's influence and power; yet Roosevelt remained loyal to Chiang's nationalist regime.

In Europe the question was beginning to be raised as to whether the Russians and their Western Allies were prepared to recog-nize the same politicians as the legitimate government of Poland. For the time being they did, in the person of General Sikorski in London, but the problem of Poland's eventual eastern frontier was an unsolved and thorny one because the Russians naturally wished to see this ruled to their advantage and with a Polish regime favour-able to Soviet interests, and such a regime

Above, the Japanese attack on Pearl Harbor, 7 December 1941, which brought the Japanese strategic freedom for several months. The longer-term consequence – American entry into the war – was far graver for the Axis powers.

Opposite top right, Waffen SS troops in Yugoslavia. The Nazi belief in the inferiority of the peoples of eastern Europe deprived the Germans of much-needed support they might have gained from the population of the invaded territories.

Opposite top left, German officers watching the performance in a Paris nightclub.

Opposite centre right, German troops sweep into Russia, summer 1941. The German invaders became bogged down within six months, giving Russia time to recover herself and to draw on her enormous reserves of manpower.

Opposite bottom, Muscovites digging trenches during the German assault on the city.

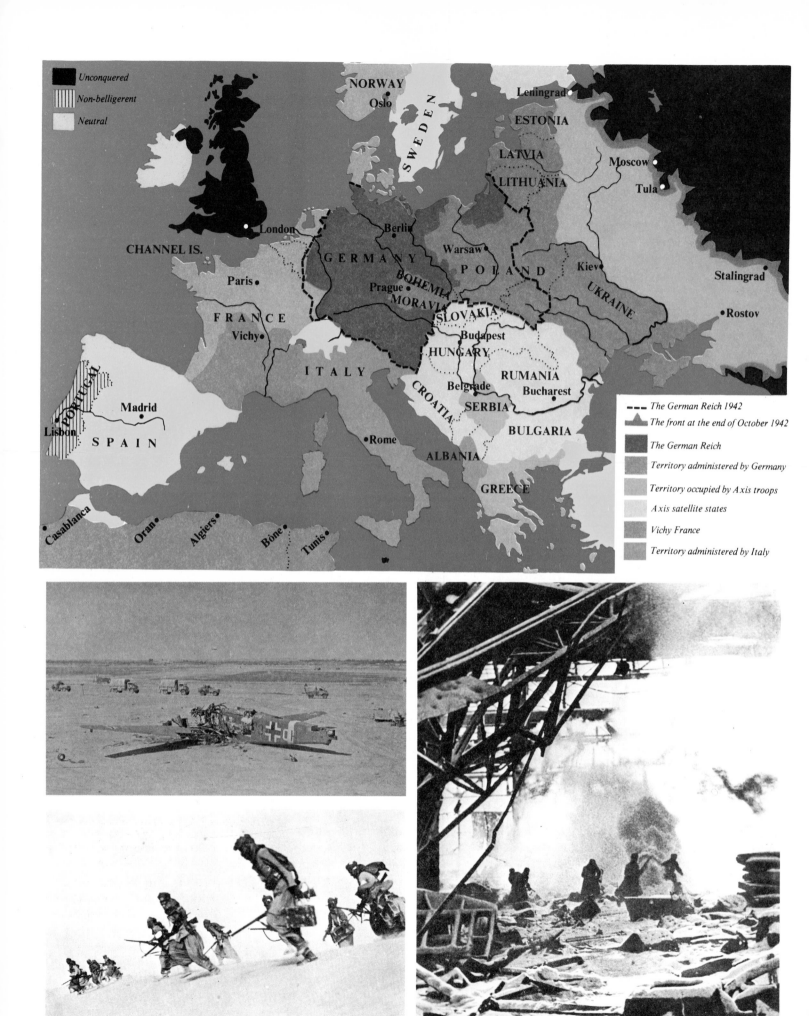

Legend (map):
- Unconquered
- Non-belligerent
- Neutral

NORWAY
Oslo
SWEDEN
Leningrad
ESTONIA
LATVIA
LITHUANIA
Moscow
Tula
CHANNEL IS.
London
Berlin
GERMANY
Warsaw
POLAND
Kiev
Stalingrad
Paris
BOHEMIA
Prague
MORAVIA
SLOVAKIA
UKRAINE
Rostov
FRANCE
Vichy
Budapest
HUNGARY
ITALY
RUMANIA
PORTUGAL
Madrid
Belgrade
Bucharest
Lisbon
SPAIN
CROATIA
SERBIA
BULGARIA
Rome
ALBANIA
Casablanca
Oran
Algiers
Bône
Tunis
GREECE

- - - The German Reich 1942
The front at the end of October 1942
The German Reich
Territory administered by Germany
Territory occupied by Axis troops
Axis satellite states
Vichy France
Territory administered by Italy

674

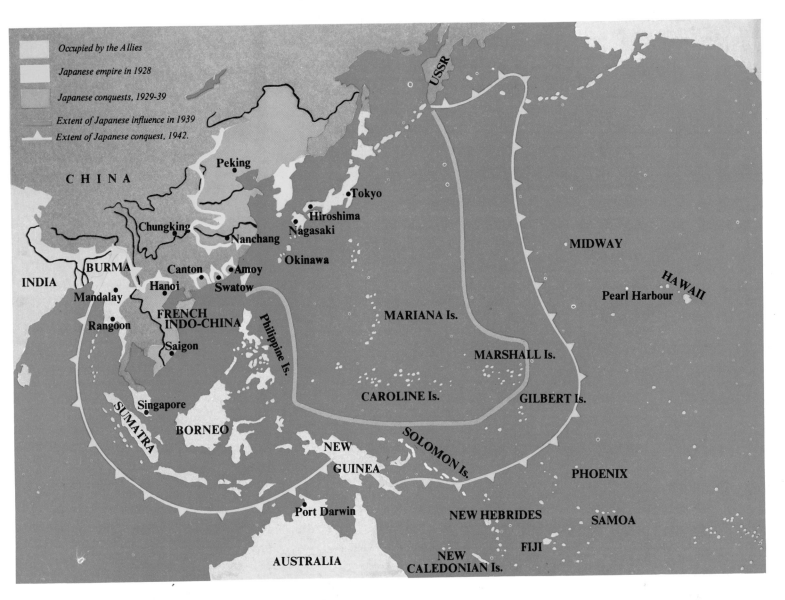

USSR

CHINA

Peking

Tokyo

Hiroshima
Nagasaki

Chungking

Nanchang

Okinawa

MIDWAY

BURMA

Canton   Amoy

HAWAII

INDIA

Hanoi   Swatow

Pearl Harbour

Mandalay

FRENCH
INDO-CHINA

MARIANA Is.

Rangoon

Saigon

Philippine Is.

MARSHALL Is.

CAROLINE Is.

GILBERT Is.

Singapore

SUMATRA

BORNEO

SOLOMON Is.

NEW
GUINEA

PHOENIX

Port Darwin

NEW HEBRIDES

SAMOA

FIJI

AUSTRALIA

NEW
CALEDONIAN Is.

was unlikely to emanate from the existing Polish government in exile in England.

The main features of the first six months of 1942 were the rapid expansion of Japanese control in southeast Asia, the start of the anti-British 'Quit India' campaign in India by the Congress leaders there, and the comparative lull in hostilities in the European section except for aerial bombing and the awakening of various anti-Axis resistance movements.

Two events dominated the autumn months. The first was the North African campaign with its climax in General Montgomery's victory at El Alamein on 22 October 1942. This was followed by the landing of an Anglo-American military force on the North African coast in November (Operation Torch). Shortly afterwards Admiral Darlan, who had been looked upon as Pétain's most probable successor as head of Vichy France, was persuaded to bring French Morocco and Algeria over to the Allied side. After his assassination on 24 December 1942, an uneasy co-presidency of the French side was established between General Giraud, commander of French troops in North Africa and the Middle East, and General de Gaulle of the French

Committee of National Liberation. On 11 November 1942, the Germans had already moved into and occupied the previously unoccupied France of the Vichy government.

The second event was Hitler's obsessive and ultimately fatal attempt to capture and hold the city of Stalingrad. His failure to do so, and the surrender on 31 January 1943 of Paulus, the general commanding there, meant that the Nazi initiative on the Eastern front was lost for ever.

Churchill and Roosevelt

When Churchill and Roosevelt met at Casablanca in North Africa in January 1943, their main topic of discussion was how Europe was to be invaded. The former urged the invasion of Italy, while the latter pressed for a direct invasion of northern France. As a compromise it was decided to attack Sicily.

In the early months of 1943 successful preparations were made for the opening up of the Burma road by means of which, as well as by flights over the mountains, supplies could reach Chiang Kai-shek from the

Above, the course of the Second World War in the Far East.

Opposite top, Europe during the Second World War.

Opposite bottom right, fighting during the battle for Stalingrad: 91,000 German soldiers surrendered (70,000 more had already been killed) in what was only one of a series of Russian victories that winter.

Opposite top left, a crashed German Ju-52 troop carrier in the North African desert.

Opposite bottom left, Italian troops in action in the North African desert: Italy became increasingly subordinate to Germany as the war progressed, counting for little in Hitler's calculations.

and Badoglio's government. This resulted in the overthrow of the latter and its replacement by Bonomi, chairman of the National Liberation Committee.

The Allies were now paying increasing attention to the question of how a defeated Germany should be treated, while Stalin pressed more and more vigorously for the opening of a Second Front in the west by Britain and the United States. From 28 November to 3 December 1943, Roosevelt, Churchill and Stalin met for consultation in Teheran. Here the main feature was the split between Churchill and Roosevelt. Roosevelt appeared ready to concede far more, both immediately and by implication for the future, to Stalin's demands for what was virtually the sovietization of the whole of eastern Europe. Moreover, in January 1944 Stalin set up a 'Polish National Council' made up of Polish Communists in Russia as a counterweight to the exiled Polish government in London – the very first seed of what came to be known as the Cold War.

Götterdammerung

General Eisenhower of the United States, Commander of 'Overlord' – the code-name for the invasion of France – settled on 6 June 1944, for D-Day. The landings on the French coast from across the English Channel were successful, but because of a number of factors, chiefly the unexpected and resilient stubbornness of the German resistance, the Allied follow-up into the interior of Europe was delayed for several months. During this time Hitler tried out V1s or flying-bomb weapons on London, but they were countered before they could do extensive damage to morale or material, as was the later V2 version.

On 20 July 1944, the German resistance movement finally failed, though by only the narrowest margin, to assassinate Hitler.

In August 1944 Paris was liberated from German occupation, while in the Balkans there had occurred an extraordinary division of the spoils between the Soviet Union and the Western Allies. This was the so-called 'percentage agreement' or deal between Churchill and Stalin by which ninety percent of Romania went to Russia and ten percent to others, ninety percent of Greece to Britain and ten percent to Russia, fifty percent of Yugoslavia and Hungary each to Russia and fifty percent to others, Bulgaria seventy-five percent to Russia and twenty-five per cent to others. Although things did not in fact work out like this, the arrangement provides a striking if unedifying example of diplomatic horse trading.

In August 1944 there occurred one of the most tragic and sinister events of the war, namely the uprising of the pro-Western Poles in Warsaw against their German oppressors in order to prevent, by anticipation, their being taken over by Stalin's

West. The activities of General Stilwell's American troops and Orde Wingate's 'Chindits' behind the Japanese lines ensured that in the event no Japanese reinforcement landing on the South China coast could succeed.

From January 1943 until July 1944 the Americans conducted an increasingly successful series of counter-offensives in the Pacific by means of which large numbers of Japanese troops, on their over-extended lines of communication, were cut off and left to wither. By spring 1943 the Battle of the Atlantic had at last been won by the Allies, and allied victory in North Africa was completed. In July the invasion of Sicily began, to the accompaniment of

anti-Mussolini movements in Italy. This resulted in the formation of a new Italian goverment under Marshal Badoglio, who immediately began secret talks with the Allies for taking his country out of the war.

Eventually Hitler decided to come to Mussolini's rescue: he despatched twenty-five divisions of German troops to north Italy, captured Rome in September 1943, kept the ignominiously rescued Mussolini under surveillance and delayed the slow and bloody advance of Allied troops up the long Italian peninsula until they eventually recaptured Rome in June 1944. Meanwhile a virtual civil war had developed between the leaders of the Italian resistance movement

Above, German officers in captivity after the liberation of Paris, 25 August 1944: its commander, General von Choltitz, had surrendered, disobeying Hitler's orders to destroy the city.

Above left, the Star-spangled Banner flutters over the citadel at Saint-Malo, surrendered, against his oath, by the German commander after a four-day American assault on 17 August 1944: such was the importance attached to the personal oath of loyalty sworn to Hitler by every officer and the strength of Nazi ideology that most – though not all – commanders resisted to the bitter end.

Left, a Russian soldier hoists the Red Flag over the ruined Reichstag in Berlin, symbolizing the defeat of Nazism and the start of Soviet hegemony over central and eastern Europe.

Opposite top, the monastery of Monte Cassino from the air: the Allied forces advancing up Italy towards Rome needed four months to take this heavily fortified stronghold.

Opposite bottom, Allied forces on the Normandy beaches shortly after D-Day: for Nazi Germany, this was the beginning of the end.

puppet 'Polish National Council' from Lublin. While this rising was ruthlessly and systematically crushed, Russian troops stood by without interfering – a cold piece of *Realpolitik* on Stalin's part and evidence of his determination to use any means to attain his national and ideological ends.

During the opening months of 1945 the Allied pincers closed on the crumbling German Reich, the Russians driving from the East, Americans and British from the West. On 30 April Hitler took his own life under the ruins of his Chancellery in Berlin. On 7 May the Germans surrendered unconditionally at General Eisenhower's headquarters in Reims, with a repeat of this act,

on Russian insistence, on the following day in Berlin. It was already evident that the understanding which Roosevelt and Churchill had thought they had reached with Stalin at the Yalta Conference in February 1944 was a hollow one, even though there did emerge from it the San Francisco Conference of April–June 1945 and eventually the United Nations Organization.

In the Far East Japan was reeling under the hammer blows of the victorious American offensive but was not yet invaded herself. The Allies shrank from the possible toll in casualties of such an invasion, especially as now there lay ready to hand the ultimate

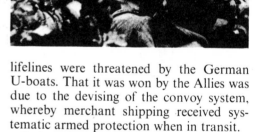

weapon – namely an atomic bomb, successfully tested on 16 July 1945. When Stalin, Churchill and the new American president, Truman, were meeting at Potsdam during that month, the latter two were informed of peace overtures which had been made and were being made through the Soviet Union, still in a state of neutrality with Japan. Nevertheless, on 26 July the Potsdam Declaration continued to demand Japan's unconditional surrender, under threat of 'prompt and utter destruction', which meant the use of an atomic bomb. When the Japanese government failed to respond to this ultimatum, the first atomic bomb was dropped by American aircraft on Hiroshima on 6 August, killing 78,000 people and destroying two-thirds of the city. On 8 August the Soviet Union shamelessly

declared war on Japan and invaded Manchuria, an act of unprovoked aggression. On 9 August a second atomic bomb was dropped, on Nagasaki. This led to complete Japanese surrender to the American General MacArthur on 2 September.

How the war was won

Once war begins, its outcome plainly depends on the skills of those waging it on the seas, on land and in the air, together with the immense resources in manpower, munitions, finance, transport and food essential to the support of both the armed forces and the civilian populations of the protagonists. There are two major considerations to be borne in mind in surveying the respective roles of navy, army and airforce: one is the concept and actuality of waging 'total' war, that is, war not confined to the military; the other is the occurrence of virtually two wars within one, the German and the Japanese, each only occasionally, though significantly, impinging on the other.

Naval affairs were chiefly significant in the long-fought Battle of the Atlantic, where, in the First World War, Britain's very

lifelines were threatened by the German U-boats. That it was won by the Allies was due to the devising of the convoy system, whereby merchant shipping received systematic armed protection when in transit.

It became clear that the day of large battle-fleets was over: carrier-borne aircraft and, as the Americans demonstrated in the Pacific naval operation against the Japanese, the use of a 'task force' supported by a 'fleet train' enabled lengthy operations to be conducted at long distance from the home base. The ever-increasing use made of radar was another distinctive feature of the war at sea, as was also the mounting of 'combined operations' for the invasion of an enemy-held coast line towards the end. Control of the seas still remained vital for whichever of the main contestants hoped to survive and win, but the manner in which that control was exercised was very different from that in previous wars and depended far more than previously on close and active cooperation with the air forces.

With regard to the conduct of armies, the Second World War was far more a war of manoeuvre than the First. This was dramatically demonstrated by the *Blitzkrieg* – the

Above, recruiting poster for the Waffen SS, Hitler's corps of elite troops who were responsible for many of the most atrocious excesses of the Nazi regime.

Left, Russian propaganda cartoon showing Hitler and Mussolini sheltering in vain beneath the Allied onslaught.

Opposite top right, photograph from Signal, *the German wartime propaganda magazine, of action at sea.*

Opposite top left, Allied poster produced in 1945 as a reminder that, despite victory in Europe, a foe still remained in the Far East.

Opposite bottom right, British paratroopers at Arnhem, September 1944: the airborne assault, an attempt to secure a bridgehead across the Rhine, failed.

Opposite bottom centre, a German tank crossing the Marne, June 1940: the success of the Blitzkrieg strategy throughout western Europe successfully disguised the fact that German reserves of armaments and vehicles were surprisingly low at the beginning of the war.

Opposite bottom left, the ruins of a Burman pagoda, January 1945: Japan lost the initiative in the Far East after the Battle of Midway, June 1942, but it took the Allied forces three years and two atomic bombs to achieve final victory.

lightning thrust of armed vehicles penetrating deep into enemy territory without waiting to advance on a uniform front: examples were the German invasion of Poland in 1939 and the German drive to the Channel ports in 1940. Another new feature was the use of airborne troops and the dropping of parachutists behind the enemy's lines, instances being the German drop on Crete (May 1941) and the British drop on Arnhem (September 1944). Further colourful expression of the war of manoeuvre was the North African Campaign with tanks taking the place of traditional cavalry in rapid encircling and outdistancing movements. It was only here that the old romantic elements of warfare still manifested themselves, in the admiration that each side accorded to the other's expertise.

Two other new types of soldiers emerged:

one was the commando unit on the Allied side, men specially selected, trained and toughened for short, violent bouts of intense aggressiveness, the other, also on the Allied side but in Britain alone, the mobilizing of a Home Guard. This consisted of civilians in full-time or part-time employment who drilled and prepared themselves in their free time to defend their homes in case of enemy landings from the sea or the air.

In the early months of the war three things became evident: one, the superb efficiency and high morale of the Germans on the offensive; two, the low morale and defeatism of the French armies hoodwinked by the myth of their own Maginot line and, three, the astonishingly contrived rescue of the bulk of the British expeditionary force from Dunkirk, albeit with the loss of most of its equipment. Later on, when the German

invasion of Russia took place, the Red Army, first in its 'scorched earth' retreat, then in its desperate beleaguering of Stalingrad and finally in its victorious counterattack right into the heart of Central Europe in 1945 vindicated to the full the years of ideological and military preparation. Two other developments may be noted: first, the degree to which women in most countries, but especially on the Allied side, were integrated into the war effort, and, second, the saving of life among the wounded as a result of improvements in medical treatment and the rapidity with which cases could be transported from the front to hospital.

Yet because control of the air proved to be the imperative condition for the successful waging of a naval or a land campaign, it was the contest between rival airforces which provided the truly decisive and dramatic issues. Three examples may be quoted. One was the Battle of Britain, when British fighter aircraft successfully denied the Luftwaffe that superiority over the English Channel and Southern England essential for effective German landings on the island coast. A second example was the Japanese air attack on the American fleet in Pearl Harbor, an event of shattering importance because of its effect on American public opinion and the way in which it dictated subsequent American strategy in the Pacific. A third example was the rather more controversial one of bombing: how much material and moral damage did sustained raids on cities and centres of industrial production actually do? The climax of this argument was expressed in the horrors of Dresden and Coventry, burning in nights of fire-storm, and in the ghastly effects of the atom bomb on Hiroshima and Nagasaki. Did events such as these finally tip the balance between acceptable war and genocide?

In conclusion it should be remembered that all the various naval, military and air encounters need to be surveyed in that confused context of strategic and political motivation which clouded the counsels of the great powers. As examples of 'miscalculations' there may be cited Hitler's underestimate of Russia's military strength and Roosevelt's underestimate of Russia's political ambitions. The tremendous dispute which went on so rancorously between Stalin and the Western Allies about the date for the opening of a Second Front can only be viewed as evidence of the underlying suspicions among the temporarily allied coalition against Hitler. It was because of this that the final German offensive in the west, although militarily a failure, was diplomatically a success in that it inserted still further the wedge of mistrust into the Allied ranks and meant that Berlin, Prague and Vienna were to be liberated not from the west but from the east.

In a very real sense Stalin obtained from Churchill and Roosevelt what he had failed to obtain from Hitler: a seat firmly astride the stricken countries of Central Europe.

Resistance

Any record of the Second World War would
be incomplete without reference to war-time
resistance movements in Europe and Asia,
leading on into full-scale national liberation
movements. In the case of the first, three
well-defined phases may be detected: one, a
period of stunned horror at the experience
of defeat and occupation; two, from 22 June
1941, the date when Germany's invasion of
the Soviet Union first really mobilized the
Communist elements in the resistance movements into active pro-Allied participation
and, three, the second half of the war when
most of the resistance movements went
over to the offensive with large-scale anti-
Nazi sabotage and regular liaison with the
invading Allied forces. Previously, they
had been mainly concerned with social
ostracism of the occupying forces, with
helping escaping prisoners on their way
and with labour strikes.

Of the European resistance movements
in the West, in Norway, Denmark, the
Netherlands, Belgium, Luxembourg and
France, the last was probably the most
important. A quite complex and intimate
relationship developed between the indigenous resistance fighters and General de
Gaulle and the Free French. For instance,
in January 1942 the Free French sent one
of their resistance heroes into France
by parachute to coordinate the various
groups into the National Liberation Movement. The organized groups of saboteurs
and guerrilla fighters were known collectively as the Maquis: this force liberated
Corsica on its own in 1943 and fought a
number of costly battles with the Germans

after the opening of the Second Front. It
would be fair to say that the leaders of the
various resistance movements represented
more or less honestly the interests of those
elements which were opposed to the Nazi
and fascist invaders of their countries – the
patriotic motive – and also, though not
nearly so cohesively, the interests of those
elements which wished to reform the pre-
war social system – the ideological motive.

It must also not be forgotten that resistance movements existed in the Axis countries themselves. In Italy this led eventually
to collaboration with the forces working
for the overthrow of Mussolini. In Germany
resistance was ill-organized and ineffective
– several attempts at Hitler's assassination
misfired: nevertheless, a number of liberal-
minded Germans from all sections of the
country strove persistently to undermine the
Nazi tyranny. They failed to interest the
Allies in their clandestine activities and
most of them suffered hideous execution at
the hands of the Gestapo after the last
abortive attempt of von Stauffenberg on
Hitler's life on 20 July 1944.

Grim though the story was in western
Europe, it was far grimmer and larger in
eastern Europe and also rather different.
For here, with almost daily massacres of his
neighbours going on around him, the
ordinary citizen and peasant was drawn
more rapidly into active opposition. In the
Soviet Union itself this took the form of
partisan activities directed by the Soviet
government as an ancillary to the campaigns
of the Red Army. In Yugoslavia there developed an extraordinarily complex and piti-
able situation. At first the Resistance was led
by the Serbian Colonal Mihailovitch and his

*Above, Soviet citizens executed by the Germans,
October 1941: the Soviet partisans could rely on
the wholehearted support of the population and
operated relatively freely behind the German
lines, though the consequences were brutal and
immediate if they were caught.*

*Above top left, a German firing-squad prepares
for its victims: Jews, left-wingers, resisters,
intellectuals, in fact all who failed to subscribe to
Nazi ideology, risked this treatment.*

*Above left, members of the Corsican Maquis:
throughout occupied Europe, resisters did much
to make life uncomfortable for the Germans, in
addition providing valuable intelligence and
assisting escapes; perhaps their most valuable
contribution for the future, though, was actually
to have resisted.*

*Opposite top, the City of London in flames
during the 1940 Blitz (miraculously, St Paul's
Cathedral was not destroyed): though the raids
on London and provincial centres did cause short-
term disruption, their main long-term effect
seems to have been to raise morale in the face of
adversity.*

*Opposite bottom, an oil refinery at Dortmund,
Germany, under bombardment by the US 8th Air
Force: as in Great Britain, enemy bombing
strengthened morale and had little effect on
industrial production, output in Germany
reaching a peak in 1944.*

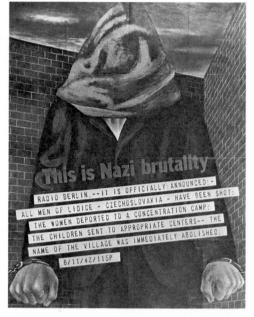

Cetniks, with the full support of the Allies and the Yugoslav government in exile. But although at first it launched actions against the Germans, Mihailovitch was more concerned with Serbian nationalism and anti-communism than with campaigning against the Nazis. So a second resistance movement developed, especially after the Soviet Union changed sides. This was led by Tito, eventually obtained full Allied support after this had been withdrawn from the Cetniks and was to prove victorious. The unfortunate Mihailovitch was tried and executed by Tito's government.

Whether or not Mihailovitch's policy can be justified, the extent of his resistance movement in the early days of the German invasion of Russia (and at the time there was virtually no other in Yugoslavia) delayed the German offensive by drawing off some of its troops for the Yugoslav front for as long as four to seven weeks, so that the German armies did not reach the gates of Moscow before winter had got them in its grip. This may well have contributed to one of the turning-points in the Second World War, for German success in Russia then could have prevented or completely altered the nature of the Western counter-measures slowly being prepared during this breathing-space.

With the Albanian resistance movement led by another Communist, the school teacher Enver Hoxha, it could be said that both Yugoslavia and Albania liberated themselves under Communist leadership.

In Poland, occupied by the Nazis for over five years, resistance took the form of sabotage and underground conspiracy. The fate of the Polish Home Army in the summer of 1944 has already been mentioned – a victim of Great Power politics. How could Polish resistance be communist-inspired when it feared Russian communism as much as German Nazi oppression? The very men and women who had heroically sustained the anti-Nazi underground movement were subsequently liquidated by the Russians as traitors and reactionaries because they were not communists.

In Asia, the great catalyst proved to be the Japanese seizure and occupation of vast areas previously under the imperial control of Britain, France, the Netherlands and the United States. In diverse ways this roused resistance movements against the Japanese in the Philippines, Vietnam, Indonesia, Malaya, Burma and, by indirect implication, in India. Much more than in Europe, these resistance movements not only aimed to eject the invader but to effect a social revolution internally, generally a socialist or communist one.

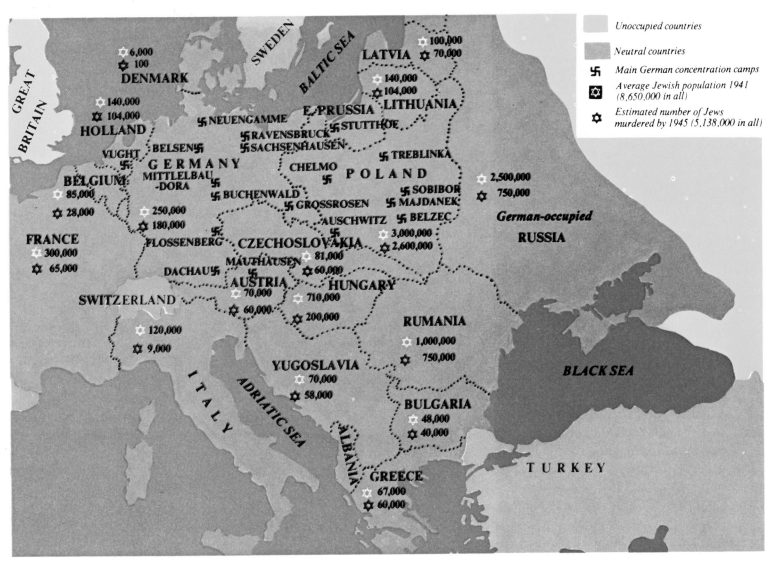

The map shows the following labels and figures:

GREAT BRITAIN

SWEDEN

BALTIC SEA

DENMARK
6,000
100

LATVIA
100,000
70,000

140,000
104,000

HOLLAND
140,000
104,000

E. PRUSSIA

LITHUANIA

NEUENGAMME
RAVENSBRUCK STUTTHOF
SACHSENHAUSEN

BELGIUM
85,000
28,000

VUGHT
BELSEN
GERMANY
MITTLELBAU
-DORA

TREBLINKA

CHELMO

POLAND

BUCHENWALD
GROSSROSEN

SOBIBOR
MAJDANEK

2,500,000
750,000

250,000
180,000

AUSCHWITZ
BELZEC

German-occupied
RUSSIA

FRANCE
300,000
65,000

FLOSSENBERG

CZECHOSLOVAKIA
81,000
60,000

3,000,000
2,600,000

DACHAU
MAUTHAUSEN

AUSTRIA
70,000
60,000

HUNGARY
710,000
200,000

RUMANIA
1,000,000
750,000

SWITZERLAND
120,000
9,000

YUGOSLAVIA
70,000
58,000

BLACK SEA

ITALY

ADRIATIC SEA

ALBANIA

BULGARIA
48,000
40,000

TURKEY

GREECE
67,000
60,000

Legend:
- Unoccupied countries
- Neutral countries
- Main German concentration camps
- Average Jewish population 1941 (8,650,000 in all)
- Estimated number of Jews murdered by 1945 (5,138,000 in all)

The concentration camps

Although the full horror and extent of the concentration camps did not become known until the end of hostilities, nevertheless the naked brutality and inhumanity which their existence symbolized were an essential issue around which the war was fought. The subject, however distressing, belongs to the history of the period and must not be evaded. It is necessary to distinguish clearly between concentration camps and the Warsaw ghetto, which was a particularly ghastly ante-chamber to them, on the one hand and prisoner-of-war camps, still largely governed by Red Cross conventions on the other. Questions which any student of our times is entitled to ask are: when and where were concentration camps set up, by whom and to what purpose and how could such bestiality exist within supposedly civilized societies?

Although concentration camps existed before, during and after the Second World War in the Soviet Union, our focus here will be on those established by the Nazis in Germany and the German-occupied or controlled territories. Their purpose was a double one: to detain all those who in any way could threaten the existence of the Nazi regime and, more ostensibly, to act as centres for forced labour vast numbers of men and women were often transported long distances in appalling conditions to constitute such a labour force. As well as all political deviationists, the inmates consisted of thousands of Jews and the majority of them perished either by deliberate extermination by gas ovens and shooting, or through starvation, overwork and neglect.

The most notorious of the concentration camps were Dachau, Buchenwald, Belsen, Sachsenhausen, Ravensbruck, Maüthausen, Auschwitz, Treblinka and Maidenek. The operations were conducted on a monstrous scale.

The walled ghetto

Although it was not strictly speaking a concentration camp, this is the place to record the story of a specific instance of the policy of genocide, the 'final solution' of the 'Jewish problem', decided on by Hitler in 1941. After the German conquest of Poland, 500,000 Jews were enclosed in one small area of the city of Warsaw. It was sealed off by a high brick wall and life within it was barely sustained at survival level. Then in June 1942 the Nazis decided to liquidate the ghetto, and by October of that year 310,000

Above, Hitler's progress towards the extermination of European Jewry.

Opposite top right, photomontage by John Heartfield (1891–1968), the German Communist propaganda artist, produced in response to the news of the massacre at Lidice: the village of Lidice was wiped from the ground – its men killed, women deported, houses burnt – as part of German reprisals for the assassination in 1942 of Reinhard Heydrich, SS leader in Bohemia.

Opposite centre right, Cetniks manning a mountainside position: Yugoslav resistance was determined and divided, Tito's forces eventually dominating.

Opposite bottom right, Japanese troops parading near Battery Road, Singapore: Singapore, thought by the British to be impregnable, fell on 15 February 1942, only ten weeks after Pearl Harbor.

Opposite left, Adolf Hitler (1889–1945), Chancellor of Germany from 1933: during the war his public appearances became less and less frequent, his health deteriorated, and his grip on reality vanished. Nevertheless he seems to have retained the loyalty of the vast majority of Germans until the very end.

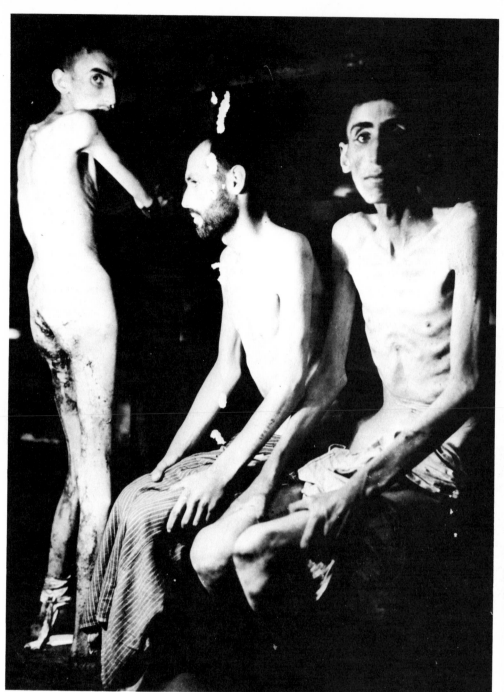

had been deported to extermination camps. News of this reached London via the Polish underground movement: for some weeks it was simply not believed. In April 1943 the 56,000 Jews who were all there were now left of the ghetto rose in heroic resistance against their Nazi tormentors: the SS major-general lost a thousand men in suppressing it and wiping out the ghetto.

This was one episode in the systematic slaughter of six million Jews by Hitler's orders. On 17 December 1942 the Allied governments officially condemned the extermination of the Jews and served notice that those concerned in organizing it would be held criminally responsible. One terrible assumption lay at the root of all these atrocities, namely that those outside the pale of the ruling regime or race were no longer human beings and could therefore be treated and used as mere objects.

Unconditional surrender

The formula of 'unconditional surrender' was hatched by Churchill and Roosevelt at the Casablanca Conference in January 1943. It was applied to Germany in April 1945 and to Japan in August 1945. It expressed a fierce determination to treat the defeated enemy with no other absolute consideration than to make future aggression impossible. Its pathos was twofold: first because its demand was unrealistic because, however unconditional the surrender, certain conditions, such as ensuring food and order, imposed themselves if the vanquished society was to exist at all, and to the establishment of these the victors would have to contribute; second because it veiled the irreconcilability of aims between the Soviet Union and the West, which when the formula was applied could no longer be concealed.

Of the original causes for which the war had been fought none had been realized: politically, in spite of the establishment of UNO, nationalism was as rampant as before, if not more so; economically, individual and collective competition was unrelenting; spiritually, human values had suffered abasement rather than elevation. The most that the historian can record on the credit side – and it is not negligible – is that the Allied victory left the human prospect less gloomy and more open to the chances of avoiding further declines into totalitarianism than if Hitler had triumphed.

The aftermath

As a consequence of hostilities, material damage and trade dislocation were great, but human displacement and penalties

were greater still. The major cities of Germany were heaps of rubble, and many urban centres in Europe and Britain bore the marks of heavy bombing. Railways, bridges, factories and private dwellings had been destroyed in the course of war; nor had the countryside escaped, for everywhere land had been 'scorched' by retreating armies. Yet material reconstruction proceeded surprisingly quickly. Far more long-term in their effects were the changed economic relationships between nations, the three chief examples of which were the virtual bankruptcy of the defeated powers in Europe, the impoverishment of Great Britain on such a scale as to transform her into a second-class power, deeply in debt, and the wrecking of much of the Soviet economy which in turn clamoured for disproportionate reparation from the countries she had helped to defeat.

Millions of people were homeless or in exile: refugees from war, enemy occupation and political persecution, prisoners of war in foreign captivity, conscripted workers forcibly driven into Germany to work for the Nazis and now in need of repatriation. Relief and rehabilitation were the crying needs of these postwar months even as the politicians, by the webs they were spinning, laid up further trouble for a peace-hungry, if not peace-loving, mankind. For although men might desire peace very few were prepared to pay its price, and this was the bitter knowledge on the basis of which governments had to shape their policies.

Already during the war much work had been done by the Western Allies in anticipation of postwar needs. This took two forms: one, plans for an emergency relief operation and, two, schemes for securing a social and economic world welfare society.

On 9 November 1943, forty-four Allied and associated nations established the United Nations Relief and Rehabilitation Administration (UNRRA):

Being determined that immediately upon the liberation of any area by the armed forces of the United Nations or as a consequence of retreat of the enemy, the population thereof shall receive aid and relief from their sufferings, food, clothing and shelter, aid in the prevention of pestilence and in the recovery of the health of the people, and that preparation and arrangements shall be made for the return of prisoners and exiles to their homes and for assistance in the resumption of urgently needed agricultural and industrial production and the restoration of essential services.

UNRRA headquarters were in Washington DC, and the organization consisted of a Council representing all the constituent members, a Central Committee and a Director-General and his internationally recruited staff. Relief and rehabilitation were to be distributed and dispersed fairly on the basis of the relative needs of the population in the areas and without discrimination because of race, creed or political belief. By the end of 1945 more than $3,500 million had been contributed to UNRRA funds.

Although UNRRA came in for various criticisms, some well justified on administrative grounds, its personnel laboured heroically and with a fair measure of success. Alongside the official UNRRA teams there worked teams from most of the great voluntary organizations of the world. As a result of this effort many of the war-devastated areas were redeemed and the mass outbreak of infectious epidemics avoided.

Of all UNRRA activities, those concerned with displaced persons were the most poignant and impressive. Many displaced persons were reluctant or unwilling to be repatriated, either because they had lost all ties with their countries of origin or because of changed political conditions there. At the beginning of 1946 some 1,675,000 persons were estimated to be refugees in need of new homes. The International Refugee Organization (IRO) took over this part of UNRRA's work in June 1947.

The need for long-term political and economic measures of reconstruction on a world scale had been realized quite early in the war: the political institutions, together with their social agencies which emerged, will be dealt with later; here may be conveniently summarized the early stages of the economic ones. Two concepts were dominant: one was the need to ensure conditions of full employment as widely as possible, the other was the desirability of establishing a stable international monetary system.

Normal trading relations having been disturbed during the war, and control by

Freedom of Speech   Freedom of Worship

Freedom from Want   Freedom from Fear

governments over the movements of goods having been greatly increased, the transition from wartime to peacetime economies was bound to prove difficult. For instance there was the wartime machinery employed to control the use of sterling in international transactions, which became the basis of a trading area in the post-war years encouraging freedom of payments and trade within the area. The fact that the United States had entered the war, with all that this implied for her subsequent involvement in world affairs, was another decisive factor. Beginning with the Atlantic Charter both the British and American governments had begun to take initiatives in designing a new economic as well as political order; the 1942 Mutual Aid Agreement between them was a further stage in this development.

By the summer of 1945 some $44 million worth of supplies had been provided to their allies by the Americans. Moreover Article 7 of the Agreement provided that the final settlement of Lend-Lease should include

provision for agreed action by the United States of America and the United Kingdom, open to participation by all other countries of like mind, directed to the expansion by

appropriate international and domestic measures, of production, employment, and the exchange and consumption of goods . . . to the elimination of all forms of discriminatory treatment in international commerce, and to the reduction of tariffs and trade barriers.

This declaration led to the establishment of an International Monetary Fund at a United Nations Monetary and Financial Conference at Bretton Woods in 1944; this became effective in 1947 and had some forty-eight members by 1949. Also discussed at Bretton Woods was a project for establishing another international fund for the provision of longer-term capital, which found realization in the setting up in 1946 of the International Bank for Reconstruction and Development, or World Bank. The third important institution to be founded was the General Agreement on Tariffs and Trade (GATT) in 1947, its constituents being twenty-three countries, which at that time controlled some seventy percent of world trade.

As the history of the international economy in the postwar years is so closely bound up with political developments, discussion of the Marshall Plan for European

Above, Churchill, Roosevelt and Stalin at the Yalta Conference, February 1945: here the three Allied leaders settled the post-war fate of eastern Europe and recognized Russia's de facto *control of the nations they liberated.*

Opposite top right, US wartime poster based on the Four Freedoms enunciated by President Roosevelt.

Opposite top left, Nazi posters proclaiming that 'Bolshevism brings war, unemployment and hunger': much of Nazi propaganda, before they came to power and again at the end of war, was directed at the national fear of communism and the even more traditional fear of the east.

Opposite bottom, Dutch anti-Nazi poster calling on a traditional theme of European iconography.

THE SECOND WORLD WAR

Date	The European sector	The war in Asia	Other events
1939			
March	Germany occupies Czechoslovakia		End of Spanish Civil War
April	Italian invasion of Albania		
August	German-Russian non-aggression pact		
	Britain signs pact with Poland		
Sept	Germany attacks Poland: Poland divided between Germany and Russia Britain and France declare war on Germany		
Sept–Oct	Soviet treaties with Estonia, Latvia, Lithuania		Accession of Pope Pius XII
Dec	Russia expelled from League of Nations		*Graf Spee* scuttled in Montevideo harbour
1940			
April	German fleet attacks Norway Germany occupies Denmark		
10 May	German troops invade Low Countries		Churchill leads coalition ministry
27 May–4 June	Evacuation of Dunkirk		
22 June	French sign armistice with Germany		
July	Start of the Battle of Britain German occupation of the Channel Islands		French government moves to Vichy
August	Italy and Britain clash in North Africa		Trotsky assassinated in Mexico
Sept		Japan joins Rome-Berlin axis. French Indo-China invaded	
Oct	Italy invades Greece		
1941			
March	Defeat of Italians at Cape Matapan		
April	Addis Ababa recaptured by British	Russo-Japanese neutrality pact	
May	Germany invades Greece and Yugoslavia Battle for Crete		
June	Free French and British enter Syria Turkey makes non-aggression pact with Germany		
22 June	Germany invades Russia		
14 Aug			Atlantic Charter signed by Churchill and Roosevelt
Oct	Attack on Moscow		
Dec		Attack on Pearl Harbor; USA declares war on axis powers Japanese capture Hong Kong	
1942			
Jan		Capture of Manila Dutch East Indies invasion	
Feb		Capture of Singapore, Rangoon	
March		Capture of Mandalay, Philippines Allied counter offensive in New Guinea	
May		Battle of the Coral Sea	
June	Rommel captures Tobruk		
July	Battle of el Alamein		
Sept	Battle of Stalingrad begins		
Nov	Germany enters unoccupied France		
1943			
Jan	British capture Tripoli Casablanca conference: 'unconditional surrender' terms agreed		
Feb	Germans surrender at Stalingrad		
May	Axis forces surrender in Tunisia		
July	Allied invasion of Sicily	Australians join American troops in the Pacific	
Sept	Italian government surrenders to Allies; joins Allies		
1944			
Jan	Allied landings at Anzio		
March	Bombardment of Monte Cassino		
June	Allied landings in Normandy	US forces bomb Japan	
July	Bunker bomb plot against Hitler fails		Iceland declares her independence
August	Liberation of Paris		
Sept	Battle of Arnhem		
Oct	Allied landings in Greece		
Nov			Roosevelt elected president for fourth term Butler Education Act
1945			
Jan	Hungary, Poland, Austria, overrun by Russia		
7 Feb	Yalta Conference		
April	Suicide of Hitler Mussolini shot	US forces invade Okinawa	Roosevelt dies; Truman President of America
May	Russians enter Berlin Unconditional surrender of Germany and Italy		
June			Formation of the United Nations
July	Start of Potsdam Conference		Labour wins British election
August		Russia declares war on Japan and invades Manchuria Surrender of Japan	

recovery and of the emergency of a number of regional economic groupings will be treated below in the account of ideological alignments and the waging of the Cold War.

Russia and America

At the end of the Second World War there were two great powers left in the world, the United States and the Soviet Union, for China was internally split between Nationalists and Communists and Great Britain was an impoverished victor. Her previous wealth had been stripped off her by vast war-time expenditures and her people were weary.

The Soviet Union had emerged from the conflict militarily victorious but at a terrible cost of human suffering and material damage: the loss both of manpower and resources was such as would require years of reinvestment and hard work for recuperation. Nevertheless the Red Army dominated eastern Europe, and Stalin's might threw long shadows right across Europe to the Channel ports and manifested itself as a no less challenging presence in northern Asia.

When hostilities ceased the United States was the greatest industrial power in the world. She had emerged from isolationism and could no longer seek alibis for her dominance of the global stage. Moreover, at this moment of history she alone possessed the secret of the atom bomb.

The two unsettled issues which straddled the postwar scene were the future of Germany and the fate of Poland. Both had begun to present themselves at the Yalta and Potsdam Conferences, although the former had not yet become as acute as the latter. The victorious Allies were agreed that conquered Germany should be administered by a Four Power Control Commission, American, British, French and Russian, the land being carved up regionally and the city of Berlin under special four-power control.

Reparations were to be exacted from Germany but not in the same totally unrealistic manner as in 1919, in spite of a first but unsuccessful attempt by the Soviet Union to assert a monstrous and disproportionate claim of her own. In general it was also agreed that a policy of denazification should be implemented by means of which all future controlling sectors of German society should be purged of those elements which had supported the Hitler regime. This project proved extremely difficult to execute both for administrative and ideological reasons and was to become one of the most bitter sources of quarrel between the Soviet Union and her Western partners. It was also further agreed that there should be a formal trial of war criminals. In due course this took place at an International War Crimes Court at Nuremberg at which a number of Nazi leaders were brought to trial as war criminals for the atrocities they had committed.

With regard to Poland, the Western Allies had virtually capitulated to the Russian demand for recognition of the former Lublin government as the legitimate government of Poland: the supposed counter-guarantee of 'free elections' to be held in the near future proving worthless in the light of Soviet prevarication and delay. The problem of frontiers was a menacing one, the very simplicity of its proposed solution being both brutal and sinister. The Soviet Union extended her frontiers westwards into former Polish territory, and for this Poland received territorial compensation by herself extending westwards into former German territory to the Oder Neisse line.

688

Chapter 56

The Headlines of History 1945–1965

In the distant perspective of history what lay behind the headlines often assumes greater significance than what was contained in them. Nevertheless the headlines are essential markers for our story.

The Anglo-American partnership had made an allied victory possible and Anglo-American relations coloured much of the next twenty years of world politics. That is why a glance at the domestic affairs of Britain and the United States during that period is necessary to start with. The first need to be viewed in the light of the decline in influence of a former Great Power; the second must be seen in the light of America's vast international responsibilities, as one of the two giant powers of the postwar world. Both countries are democracies, but each offers its own version of democratic principle and practice.

Great Britain

In July 1945 the Labour Party won a sweeping victory in the general election, which was conducted after the defeat of Germany (8 May 1945) but while the war against Japan was still being fought. In the words of the English historian A. J. P. Taylor: 'The electors cheered Churchill and voted against him.' Why? They believed, it seemed, that a war government was not the right government to tackle the problems of peace and that social reform, which had become a widely held expectation, would more probably be forthcoming from the Left than the Right. With Clement Attlee as prime minister, Herbert Morrison as deputy prime minister, Ernest Bevin at the Foreign Office and Sir Stafford Cripps as president of the Board of Trade until 1947 and then chancellor of the Exchequer, the new government commanded an impressive range of talents.

The team was successful in maintaining full employment and introducing a measure of nationalization in keeping with socialist principles: in 1946 the Bank of England, the coal industry and civil aviation were nationalized; in 1947 the British Transport Commission took over the railways, canals and road haulage, while the electricity and gas industries also came under state control.

In 1951 iron and steel began to be nationalized, but, unlike the others, this branch of the national life was almost entirely de-nationalized when the Conservatives came to power in 1951. Labour had only just retained its position after the general election of February 1950 with a majority of six; then illness and dissension disturbed its ranks, and, after the dissolution of parliament in September 1951, the Conservatives took office with a majority of seventeen.

Above, Princess Elizabeth (now Queen Elizabeth II), Queen Elizabeth (now Queen Elizabeth the Queen Mother), Sir Winston Churchill, King George VI and Princess Margaret greet the VE Day crowds from the balcony of Buckingham Palace, 8 May 1945. The royal family had worked continually throughout the war to maintain popular morale; in two months Churchill, despite his universal popularity, would be swept from power in a socialist landslide, reflection of the widespread belief that the nation was ready for radical reform.

Churchill resigns

Although Churchill headed the government, he had aged considerably. He suffered a heart attack in 1953 and finally resigned in 1955 from the premiership. He remained a member of parliament until a few months before his death in 1965, enjoying the veneration of his countrymen whose island he had saved from destruction. At the next general election in the early autumn of 1955 the Conservatives, with Anthony Eden as prime minister were returned to office with a majority of sixty. This was symptomatic of the country's general feeling of recovery and mild satisfaction with things as they were, of continuing friction between the right and left wings of the Labour Party and of the succession of Hugh Gaitskell as its leader.

After the fiasco of Suez and the retirement of Eden in 1957 the succession in the Conservative Party fell to Harold Macmillan, whose government continued from then until the end of 1963. It was a period when, for most of the British, it was true that they 'had never had it so good': there was better housing and more consumer

HELP THEM FINISH THEIR JOB!

Give them homes and work!

VOTE LABOUR

goods, increased car ownership and shorter working hours. In the election of October 1959 the Conservative majority was increased to a hundred. Yet beneath the calm, political surface there were serious economic problems, differences of opinion in both major political parties about expenditure on armaments and a growing coherence of viewpoint among the Labour opposition as Gaitskell asserted his leadership. In 1961 the Conservative government opened negotiations for British membership of the European Economic Community – a definite signal that the days of British supremacy as a first-class world power were at an end and that the reality of a united Commonwealth was rapidly disappearing. The rebuff which this initiative received from General de Gaulle, the personal scandal in connection with Mr Profumo, secretary of state for war, and his own ill-health accounted for Macmillan's resignation in October 1963. After an unedifying personal squabble over the leadership, he was succeeded by Sir Alec Douglas-Home, but in October 1964, at the next election, Labour returned to power under Harold Wilson with a tiny majority, Gaitskell having died unexpectedly in 1963.

Actually, the verdict of the polls revealed a three million Liberal vote and an almost equal division between the Conservative and Labour members returned to parliament. However, Labour succeeded in amassing an overwhelming majority at the next election eighteen months later, which implied a mission to do two things: re-align Britain's relations with the outside world in such a way that they corresponded to her actual status as a second-class power and tackle the balance of payments problem.

The end of this particular political sequence, 1945 to 1965, seemed to carry a tang of disillusionment about it. Were the real political decisions any longer being taken in parliament? Was not that august body now incapable of discharging its traditional functions of debate and questioning when the issues involved had become too complex and speculative for the legislative to pass judgment on them? Had the influence of the trade unions increased so enormously as to constitute a political menace? Was the office of prime minister itself assuming dangerously presidential-like powers? These are the kind of questions which an examination of the period brings into focus.

Embedded in wartime promises of social reform, of which Archbishop Temple and William Beveridge were the two most notable proponents, there was the implied assumption that Britain could and should spend more on her welfare services. How far this assumption was to prove well-founded must be judged in the context of her actual rate of economic growth in the postwar years and the relationship of that to her overseas balance of payments problem. Although the country was nothing like so rich relatively as she had been before 1939, the great majority of Britain's inhabitants enjoyed a higher standard of living than ever before at the very time that her share in world trade was steadily declining. Between 1953 and 1963, for example, the volume of British exports increased by less than forty percent while that of the Common Market countries increased by more than 140 percent. Two series of events illustrate this paradoxical tendency.

First, there was the achievement of the welfare state, the main landmarks of which were the Beveridge Report (1942), the creation of the National Health Service (1947) and the National Assistance Act (1948). It must be reckoned to the credit of

both government and governed that all this was achieved during a period when food rationing still continued and the price to be paid involved the public's putting up with the perpetuation in peacetime of many of the wartime austerities and controls. This whole enterprise in welfare democracy was however threatened by three factors. One was the dollar shortage (1949–50), shared with much of Europe and overcome by the imaginative and mass support of Marshall Aid. Another was the practice in business circles of living off expense accounts – particularly in the 1950s – an insidious method of evading taxation and damaging to public morale and efficiency. The third and easily the most important factor was Britain's balance of payments problem – the fact that she was not paying her way in terms of the world money market and was becoming increasingly dependent on foreign loans for the upkeep of her standard of living.

To offset these negative influences, particularly after 1953, attempts were made to invigorate the economy by the government's frequent exhortations to management and labour alike to modernize their methods and increase exports. In 1954 Britain attempted to re-establish her industrial and technological pre-eminence by setting-up the United Kingdom Atomic Energy Authority, which in subsequent years began to pay modest dividends. In 1963 came National Productivity Year, an attempt to infuse new life and energy into the national economic scene, but the notion smacked somewhat of 'whistling in the dark' and did not really catch on.

Another way of improving Britain's prospects was tried, namely, a belated formal move to join the European Community. Both political parties were divided on the issue when Macmillan's Conservative government applied for membership of the Treaty of Rome in July 1962. The chief economic argument was that the European Common Market could offer British manufacturers a larger and better market than the Commonwealth now did. General de Gaulle imposed his veto with a resounding

non in January 1963, on the grounds that the United Kingdom was not really genuine in her desire to join the community and was more likely to be a liability than an asset to it both economically and politically. In this he may not have been entirely incorrect, especially as one of the main arguments of those in Britain who were against 'going into Europe' was that Europe – the Europe of the Six – was not the real Europe, which stretched much further north, and south, but only a fragment of it. Hence Britain developed an alternative trade policy in collaboration with the European Free Trade Association (EFTA).

In the process of economic adjustment between 1945 and 1965 Britain could not help profiting from the general rise in material standards of living common to all the developed countries, but, it may be suggested, to the accompaniment of a degree of domestic demoralization and the derisive criticism of foreign controllers of capital: Britain had become the financial invalid of the international banking scene. In spite of all this Britain's welfare state had come to approximate rather more closely to the 'Great Society' than had the United States, where that slogan originated.

To come closer to an understanding of the political and economic phenomena so far discussed, it is necessary to pay attention to what might be called the spiritual and cultural groundswell of this population of fifty-two million – an average of six hundred of them to the square mile. A clue may be found in such phrases of the 1950s as 'I couldn't care less', 'I'm all right, Jack' and 'You've never had it so good' – themselves manifestations of the delayed shock induced by the huge and often heroic exertions of Britain during the Second World War.

The Festival of Britain in 1951 was an attempt on the part of the British to reassure themselves and their neighbours that they were the same and as good as if not better than their forefathers of 1851. Yet this was at any rate arguable, as was best demonstrated perhaps by the only truly popular movement of this period, the Campaign for Nuclear Disarmament

Above, **The Islanders,** *a sculpture produced for the 1951 Festival of Britain.*

Above left, a fight between two London dockers waiting for work: the system of competitive casual labour that prevailed in the London docks until the 1960s meant that only a bare minimum wage was guaranteed. It also reflected the widespread failure of British industry to reform its procedures and to attempt to overcome endemic class divisions.

Opposite, poster produced by the Labour Party during the 1945 election reflecting the current belief that the war had been fought not merely to defeat Germany but to create a fairer society at home: Conservative propaganda, by contrast, relied practically entirely on admiration for Churchill.

COMMITTEE of 100
ACTION FOR LIFE
DEFENCE MINISTRY
18 FEB. 1961

C. P. Snow, roamed the 'corridors of power' and helped to perpetuate the myth of two opposing cultures, science and the arts.

In the absence of broadly shared moral and political objectives, acceptable to the younger generation, there began the protest of youth. Symptomatic were the 'teddy-boys', the 'beats', the 'mods and rockers'. Also to be taken into account was the erosion of Christian belief, in spite of some attempts, such as the Bishop of Woolwich's book *Honest to God*, to bring fresh air into the stale theological atmosphere.

Yet the process of cultural adjustment to the postwar world was by no means entirely negative. Indeed, in the arts Britain experienced a veritable renaissance. Britten, Fonteyn, Piper, Moore, Murdoch these names suffice to indicate artistic variety and richness. Those in the younger age groups were seeking a new set of coherent values in the fields of politics and ethics – especially those to do with sexual conduct – which they could affirm as being relevant to the conditions of the mid-twentieth century. Perhaps the most hopeful sign of genuine progress was to be found in the sphere of education. The 1944 Education Act had been the climax of a 'silent social revolution' which had been occurring since 1870. Even though not all of its clauses were implemented, it led to a ferment of concern about the upbringing of the nation's children, not least in the desire to get away from selection for secondary education at the age of eleven. Education became news in a way which it had never been before: the Crowther Report on the education of the school child from fifteen to eighteen, the Newsom Report (*Half Our Future*) on the secondary school child of average or less than average ability, the Robbins Report on the expansion of the universities and their proliferation which followed from it, the Public Schools Report, the Plowden Report on primary education, the Albemarle Report on youth and many others all witnessed to a widely-spread feeling that Britain's future in reduced circumstances depended on the overhaul of her educational institutions at all levels to bring them into line with the demands of the atomic age.

By way of summary it may be suggested that after 1945 Britain steadily abandoned traditional forms of morality and religion, pursued material prosperity with inefficient eagerness, questioned her political institutions and placed a hopeful bet on the prospects of her schools and colleges.

The United States

In contrast with postwar Britain, there was in the United States no widespread demand for social reform, but rather for a return to things very much as they had been before the war. However, three mighty factors, which were to be operative throughout the four presidencies of the period

(CND). This effort to express outside official political circles the feeling among many sections of the population that Britain should no longer be a candidate for participation in, or preparation for, a Third World War of nuclear dimensions was a striking one. Although its influence was for a time considerable, it waned during the 1960s as the world seemed to be turning in the direction of several small-scale, contained wars rather than one total one. Another expression of discontent was to be found in literature and drama: J. B. Priestley's *Three Men in New Suits*, about men demobilized from the forces in 1946 and seeking a decent, commonsense way of

life who had turned into the 'angry young men' of the 1950s. What were they angry about? The false flush of health on Britain's body politic, as they saw it, the continuation of class differences and rivalries, the bogus nature of traditional figures of authority in the churches, the universities, the professions and business management.

It was then that much was heard of the 'establishment', a word used to describe the real as distinct from the apparent rulers of Britain – a mixture of the City, Oxford and Cambridge universities, top civil servants, the upper managerial class and a few high-ranking scientists. It was they who, in the words of the novelist and physicist

1945 to 1965, militated against that wish being fulfilled. One was the increasing size and vehemence of black protest, the consequence of black American participation in the armed forces and the experiences of wartime full employment and maximum productivity, with its resultant demand for full black civil rights. The second, to some extent provoked by the first, was a growing demand in the middle and late 1950s for measures to abolish such pockets of white poverty and misery as still existed in parts of the Union. The third was the realization by American citizens of some of the implications, not all of them welcome, of the unavoidable overseas responsibilities of the greatest power in the world.

Owing to the death of Franklin D. Roosevelt in office his vice-president, Harry Truman, automatically succeeded him in the early summer of 1945. Little was known or expected of the new president. He himself at first seemed aghast at the task which had fallen on his shoulders: he was indeed a 'president in the dark'. Yet in the course of his two periods of office, 1945 to 1948 and 1948 to 1952, his performance contradicted its lack of promise both in foreign affairs and in domestic policy. Two issues demonstrated Truman's capacity to interpret accurately the opinion of the mass of his fellow countrymen, who saw much of themselves reflected in his honest-to-goodness, practical common-sense, spiced with folksy humour and occasional outbursts of temper. The first of these was some appreciation of the plight of the negro: the fact that he boldly made the civil rights issue one of his main planks in his 1948 presidential election campaign, which he so unexpectedly won, showed the public that this was not a problem that could just be left; a plan, and when necessary direct federal guidance, were to be called for.

The second incident was his handling of the beginning of the 'Red Scare', which started in 1948 when Alger Hiss, a high-up state department official and president of the Carnegie Endowment for International Peace, was accused by Whittaker Chambers, himself an ex-communist, of having betrayed American secrets to the Russians

in the 1930s. This incident, which resulted in Hiss being convicted of perjury but not of treason by the Supreme Court in October 1950, triggered off long smouldering public alarm at what was felt to be the way in which American diplomacy was being outsmarted by Soviet guile in various parts of the world.

Although, a few days after the Hiss verdict, Truman announced that work was to proceed on the hydrogen bomb, this did not suffice to appease the Red-baiters, chief of whom was the Republican senator from Wisconsin, Joseph McCarthy. His main criticism of the Truman administration was that there were communists in high governmental positions. The Tydings Committee, which had been appointed to investigate these charges, reported in July 1950 that there was hardly any foundation in them and that they were a great deal to the discredit of McCarthy for the way in which he had brought them. Yet for a while the country as a whole fell for the attractions of a Red witch-hunt, and quite a number of liberals and moderates suffered from the operation of this scapegoat mechanism. McCarthyism was an ugly scar on the American body politic and undoubtedly exercised considerable influence in the 1951–52 presidential election by making the task of the Democratic candidate, Adlai Stevenson, a virtually impossible one.

The two periods of the Eisenhower presidency (1952–56 and 1956–60) were marked by substantial material progress, massive and often unthinking social conformism and the domination of the 'organization man'. Himself a national hero after his victorious command of the Allied Forces

Above, President Harry S. Truman (1884–1972, president 1945–53) holds aloft a copy of the Chicago Tribune *wrongly announcing his defeat in the 1948 presidential elections: his Republican opponent, Dewey, had widely been expected to win. The crucial decisions made by Truman – to drop atomic bombs on Japan, to commit the USA to the defence of western Europe, to send troops to Korea – set the course of international politics for the next decade and a half.*

Above left, Polish refugees arrive in New York, October 1948: the USA continued to welcome large numbers of immigrants after the Second World War, initially from Europe, later predominantly from the Caribbean, though restrictions ensured that numbers were never as great as they had been at the turn of the century.

Opposite top, CND demonstration against the construction of bases for Polaris submarines in Scotland, February 1961 (the philosopher Bertrand Russell is in the first line of the marchers): the disarmament campaign, the liveliest political movement of the late 1950s and early 1960s, petered out in the late 1960s, disillusion setting in as a result of the failure of the Labour Party, returned to power in 1964, to make any progress towards unilateral disarmament.

Opposite bottom, a scene from John Osborne's play Look Back in Anger, *first produced in 1956: its portrayal of personal relationships and the class society shocked the theatrical world, used to a more comfortable treatment, but the attitudes it embodied seem, twenty years on, as dated as those it attacked.*

at the end of the Second World War, 'Ike' was content to be a conscientious, golfing president, who presided over the counsels of his officials, listened to their advice, often took it and emerged ever more clearly as a beloved father-figure of the American people – the very personification at that time of their own desire to be left in peace to enjoy their affluence at home and not to be too much bothered by affairs abroad. As the following summary indicates, neither of these desires was to be realized.

McCarthyism, after a brief and sordid period of triumph in the summer of 1954, was most creditably exposed for the evil thing it was by the Senate resolution in December 1954 to the effect that McCarthy 'had acted contrary to Senatorial ethics and tended to bring the Senate into dishonour and disrepute, to obstruct the constitutional processes of the Senate, and

to impair its dignity – such conduct is hereby condemned'.

Eisenhower's cabinet, a conservative one by his own admission, concentrated on binding up the wounds of the Korean war, on reducing federal expenditure, eliminating corruption and tightening up the national defences. It was his second term of office that was to witness the outbreak of a series of troubles. Revolution in Cuba and the Lebanon, the Soviet launching of Sputnik I, the 'U2' incident and the bungling of the 1959 Paris summit conference need to be taken into review when surveying the American domestic scene. First, there was the school desegregation crisis of Little Rock, Arkansas: this was a definite alarm signal to the entire nation that black patience and white restraint, particularly in the southern states, were almost at an end. Black American citizens were prevented

from exercising their voting rights by such notorious devices as the 'literacy' tests: they were sent to inferior schools by means of the gerrymandering of school districts, and in most of the South they were excluded from jury service.

This therefore was the situation when there swung into more vigorous action the old-established National Association for the Advancement of Colored People and its Legal Defense and Education Fund: its first triumph was the Supreme Court's decision in May 1954 that 'in the field of education the doctrine of "equal but separate" has no place. Separate educational facilities are inherently unequal.' Eighteen months later segregated seating in buses in Montgomery, Alabama, was abolished as a result of a black bus boycott organized by the Reverend Martin Luther King.

Then at the beginning of the 1957 school year the Little Rock School Board decided to admit seventeen black students to the previously all-white Central High School. In defiance of federal law the governor of Alabama stationed the Arkansas National Guard outside the school, ostensibly 'to prevent racial violence' but actually to prevent blacks entering the school. This was a direct challenge to the federal constitution, and in spite of his own abhorrence of infringing state rights, President Eisenhower felt obliged to intervene to deal with the Little Rock situation, to suppress Governor Faubus' activities and to uphold the Supreme Court's decision. He did so by federalizing the Arkansas National Guard and despatching a thousand paratroopers to Little Rock to enforce law and order for the rest of the school year.

This was the beginning of a creeping malaise, which spread across the United States during the closing months of Eisenhower's presidency. It was compounded of white fears, black aspirations, a general shame at the shortcomings of many American schools, despondency and jealousy at

the achievements of Soviet science. Congress passed the National Defense Education Law for the appropriation of large funds for the financing of a great leap forward in the production of American scientists and political scientists.

Meanwhile the black revolt grew: cafe sit-ins were organized in 1960; the Congress of Racial Equality arranged a series of freedom rides. The Eisenhower era ended in a mood of deep national depression and self-questioning: obviously the political formula of the last eight years had proved inadequate, in spite of all the country's material affluence, to propound solutions to the persistent problems: the plight of blacks in such an affluent society and the international obligations of the United States.

The Kennedy presidency was as brief in duration as it was distinctive in style. At his inauguration in January 1961 John F. Kennedy, the youngest president ever elected and the first Roman Catholic to hold that office, declared his hope that the nations of the world would come together in joint harness, 'explore the stars, conquer the

deserts, eradicate disease, tap the ocean depths and encourage the arts and commerce'. Although thirty-four months later he was dead from an assassin's bullet, his 'new frontier' policy manifested itself vigorously both abroad, where the supreme test came with the Cuban crisis, and at home.

The black revolt continued: in September 1962 the University of Mississippi ('Ole Miss') admitted a black student. In August 1963 a quarter of a million people, black and white, representing all aspects of the civil rights movement, held a huge, peaceful rally in Washington DC. They were listened to sympathetically by Kennedy, who then recommended to Congress the strongest civil rights measure the country had ever seen. That measure became law at the hands of an otherwise reactionary Congress within a year, in spite of and partially because of Kennedy's assassination and by reason of the astute political management of his successor in office, former vice-president Lyndon Johnson.

Otherwise President Kennedy's domestic initiatives were hampered by nominally

Above, seconds after her husband has been shot, Mrs Kennedy drags a secret serviceman on to her car.

Opposite right, John F. Kennedy (1917–63, president 1961–63) addresses an Inaugural Gala on the eve of his inauguration as president, January 1961: Kennedy's administration brought new style and new hope to American politics, though much of the reforming legislation he promised was in fact enacted by his successor, Lyndon Johnson.

Opposite left, American advertisement dating from about 1950: the nation's enormous wealth has enabled it to set the lead in the development of a consumer society.

Democratic Congress with strong conservative prejudices. True, he did achieve the creation of the American Peace Corps for welfare services overseas, and he did see enacted the Trade Expansion Act. Yet, at the time of his assassination in November 1963, it was what he was promising rather than what he had actually achieved that was significant. His youth, intellectual brilliance, attractive family and general lifestyle had brought new energy and hope into American national life when it was badly needed.

Although Lyndon Johnson was personally the complete antithesis of Kennedy, he shared with him the same basic beliefs in progressive policies. As a result of the successful passing of the 1964 Civil Rights Act, integrated civil rights organizations operated in many parts of the United States, chiefly in the south. Their function was to test the degree to which the 'public accommodation' clauses were being implemented, to encourage voter registration and political education in the black communities and to foster urban renewal and slum clearance. Although their plight remained a desperate one in many areas, the blacks and their friends could begin to sing their song, 'We shall overcome', with a fair promise of success.

Yet the shadow of Vietnam spread ever more darkly over the Johnson administration, and there was a strange but understandable correspondence between the fears, doubts and honourable intentions of young Americans drafted to the Far East and the demands of black resistance at home and the small but increasing numbers of white Americans conscientious objectors to military service in Vietnam. It indicated a growing conviction among many Americans that the money being spent in Vietnam would be better spent at home. In the context of that correspondence President Johnson's hopes for the creation of the 'great society' grew paler.

If 'adjustment' is the correct verbal clue to an understanding of the British domestic scene since 1945, then, it may be suggested, 'complacency punctured by concern' is the appropriate phrase for the American one. Their respective accuracies may be tested by setting them in the wider context of the world's ideological alignments.

The beginnings of the Cold War

Ideology is a word used to describe two distinct but related notions, a science of ideas and a set of passionate beliefs. Together they combine to produce various forms of political life: those in which governmental authority is largely internalized may be deemed democratic; those where governmental authority is entirely externalized may be deemed dictatorial and, in the twentieth century, totalitarian. Both have been immensely affected in recent

history by the emergence on a world scale of working classes demanding their rights and by the gigantic leap forward in science and technology.

Where a society has been insufficiently sophisticated and mature to accommodate these forces by self-imposed, free-choice discipline, it has adopted a totalitarian government – fascism and Nazism on the Right, communism on the Left.

The origin of the Cold War is to be found in the Communist Manifesto of 1848, where an implicitly totalitarian challenge was issued to liberal and social democratic policies in the name of dialectical materialism, the dictatorship of the proletariat and a planned economy. That challenge received powerful reinforcement with the triumph of Leninism and Stalinism, the German-Soviet pact at the outbreak of the Second World War was only a tactical deviation from it, and by the time of the Potsdam Conference if not of the Yalta Conference in 1945, it had begun to emerge unmistakably once again. Because of the persistent strength of the power-politics of nation-states, the utopian ends of what is in theory an international communist policy became submerged in the conventional power-struggle of the Great Powers, which by 1945 had been reduced to two, the United States and the Soviet Union. No

wonder that the code name which Churchill used for Potsdam in 1945 was 'Terminal': no wonder that uneasy peace was to slither into cold war.

At the end of hostilities US policy rested on the assumption of harmonious cooperation with the Soviet Union and the strengthening of the United Nations: it continued so to rest for a year and a half, during which time the Soviet Union issued its own unmistakable challenge to the non-communist world. Soviet control was to extend between 1945 and 1948 across a vast area, from the 38th parallel in Korea to the Elbe; only in Yugoslavia did the Titoist regime presume to go its own way, while in Czechoslovakia there was but an interval of reprieve before the Soviet hand was outstretched over Prague in 1948. Soviet pressure was exerted on Turkey, Persia and Greece, and in the case of the last was to result in three years of civil war.

Recognition of the importance of these events was voiced by Churchill in the presence of President Truman at Fulton, Missouri, on 5 March 1946:

A shadow has fallen upon the scenes so lately lighted by the Allied victory. Nobody knows what Soviet Russia and its Communist international organization intends to do in the immediate future, or what are the

Above, the Potsdam Conference, July 1945, at which the Allied powers met to ratify the decisions made at Yalta about their spheres of influence in Europe and to discuss the future of Germany; initial attempts to govern Germany jointly failed, and by 1948 two separate states had already taken on an embryonic existence.

Opposite top, race riot in New York City, July 1964: in the mid- and late 1960s, the focus of racial tension moved from the south, where integration had at least in theory been enforced, to the urban areas of the north, where blacks formed a poorly housed, badly paid minority living in deprived city centres. Only in the 1970s did the tension seem to ease, though the inequalities that gave rise to it remained.

Opposite bottom, freedom marchers in Mississippi fleeing from their tents after highway patrolmen had attacked with tear gas, June 1966.

territory annexed by
the USSR in 1945

territory annexed by
Poland in 1945

territory occupied by US
and British forces 1945-55

the 'iron curtain' (the
curtain moved eastwards
in Austria in 1955 when
Russia, along with the
other Allies, withdrew its
forces of occupation)

····· post 1945 frontiers

········ 1937 frontiers

ALL OUR COLOURS TO THE MAST

began. 'I believe', said the President to Congress,

that it must be the policy of the United States to support free peoples who are resisting attempted subjugation by armed minorities or by outside pressures. . . . I believe that our help should be primarily through economic and financial aid, which is essential to economic stability and orderly political progress.

'Let us not be deceived', said the American financier, Bernard Baruch on 16 April 1947, 'today we are in the midst of a cold war.'

On 5 June 1947 the US secretary of state, General Marshall, made a speech offering substantial economic aid:

Our policy is directed not against any country or doctrine but against hunger, poverty, desperation and chaos. Its purpose shall be a revival of a working economy. . . . Any government that is willing to assist in the task of recovery will find full cooperation . . . on the part of the United States Government. . . . The initiative, I think, must come from Europe.

It did, chiefly from Britain and France, but the Soviet Union had such strong reservations, namely that the plan should be applied separately to each nation state and not to the continent as a whole, that in fact the Marshall Plan was confined to the West. Within a year the Organization of European Economic Cooperation (OEEC) had come into being, to implement the plan to the tune of some $17 billion from American resources.

At the same time as this economic buttressing of Western Europe, George Kennan, head of the State Department's

limits, if any, to their expansive and prose-lytising tendencies. . . . From Stettin, in the Baltic, to Trieste, in the Adriatic, an iron curtain has descended across the continent. Behind that line are all the capitals of the ancient states of central and eastern Europe – Warsaw, Berlin, Prague, Vienna, Buda-pest, Belgrade, Bucharest and Sofia. All these famous cities, and the populations around them, lie in the Soviet sphere, and all are subject in one form or another, not only to Soviet influence, but to a very high and increasing measure of control from Moscow. . . . Whatever the conclusions may be drawn from these facts – and facts they are – this is certainly not the liberated Europe we fought to build up. Nor is it one which contains the essentials of permament peace.

Germany was the focus of all this con-tention, for here the Soviet had sealed off

their zone from the British, French and American zones – not only politically but economically. This last fact meant that the Anglo-Americans were both supplying re-parations to the Soviet Union from their zones and at the same time pouring their own money into their own zones to enable the West German economy to function. This trend was reversed when in May 1946 reparations from the American zone were withheld; Bizonia was created in January 1947, and shortly after came an American declaration of intent to leave troops in Germany as long as there were occupation troops in Europe at all. When early in 1947 Britain informed the United States that she could no longer afford economic as-sistance to Turkey and Greece, America replied with the Truman doctrine of 12 March 1947. With this the phase of contain-ment of the Soviet Union by the West

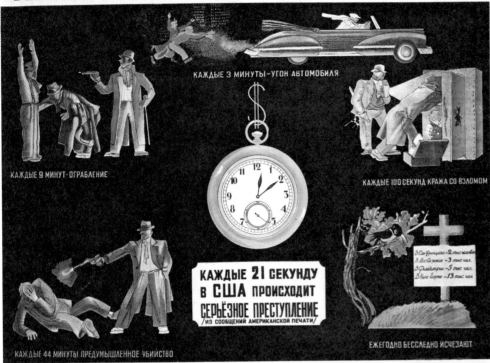

АМЕРИКАНСКИЙ ОБРАЗ ЖИЗНИ

КАЖДЫЕ 3 МИНУТЫ-УГОН АВТОМОБИЛЯ

КАЖДЫЕ 9 МИНУТ-ОГРАБЛЕНИЕ

КАЖДЫЕ 100 СЕКУНД-КРАЖА СО ВЗЛОМОМ

КАЖДЫЕ 21 СЕКУНДУ
в США ПРОИСХОДИТ
СЕРЬЁЗНОЕ ПРЕСТУПЛЕНИЕ
/ИЗ СООБЩЕНИЙ АМЕРИКАНСКОЙ ПЕЧАТИ/

КАЖДЫЕ 44 МИНУТЫ ПРЕДУМЫШЛЕННОЕ УБИЙСТВО

ЕЖЕГОДНО БЕССЛЕДНО ИСЧЕЗАЮТ

Above, bystanders weep as Russian tanks roll into Prague during the Communist takeover in 1948: hopes for the restoration of a democratic Czechoslovakia, faint enough at the end of the war, now vanished for twenty years.

Left, Russian poster produced in about 1950 for home consumption: its message, that the American way of life is corrupt, is supported by statistical evidence. Thus, 'every three minutes a car is stolen'; 'in San Francisco 2,000 people disappear every day,' etc.

Left, world communist leaders gathered in Moscow to celebrate Stalin's seventieth birthday, December 1949 (fourth from left at the front is Mao Tse-tung, at this time still closely supported by Russia): Stalin held power unchallenged until his death in 1953, but within three years his successor, Nikita Kruschev, had vehemently denounced his policies.

Opposite right, poster produced to commemorate the Marshall Plan of 1947, under which American aid was offered to Europe (and accepted by the nations of western Europe): the aid, vital to the rapid economic recovery of Europe, also helped to prevent a post-war slump in the USA.

Opposite left, Europe in the years immediately after the Second World War: though a Communist government came to power in Yugoslavia, in 1948 it broke with the USSR and has never been a member of the Soviet block.

Policy Planning Staff, developed a coherent policy of containment based on the conviction that Soviet Russia's plans were potentially aggressive and must be resisted not only by economic and defence measures on the part of the West but by a positive affirmation of Western civilization's political ideals.

Nine communist countries in eastern and central Europe responded to this by setting up a Communist Information Bureau (COMINFORM). This body described the Marshall Plan as 'a European brand of the general world plan of political expansion being realised by the US.' As a result of this counter-charge the Communist parties of western Europe immediately went into active opposition to their various national governments, and from the winter of 1948 onwards the cold war quickly became hotter.

During the spring and early summer of 1948 there were communist uprisings in Malaya against British colonial government and in the Philippines against the new independent Manila government: it was however in Indo-China that the communist offensive was most sustained and effective. Meanwhile, in Europe, a coup against Benes and Masaryk established a communist government in Czechoslovakia in February 1948; in June Yugoslavia was expelled from the Cominform, and between then and the autumn of 1949 Stalin's policy was responsible for the liquidation of communist leaders in eastern Europe suspected of deviation from the orthodox Moscow line.

The crux of the Cold War, however, was the city of Berlin, itself a symbol by reason of its municipal division, marking the rift between the Soviet Union and her former

States, the United Kingdom, France, Benelux, Italy, Iceland, Canada, Denmark, Norway and Portugal, it simply asserted: 'The Parties agree that an armed attack against one or more of them in Europe or North America should be considered an attack against them all.'

The policy of containment had been firmly and successfully initiated by the autumn of 1949, but its future was bound to be affected by two other events of that season: Soviet Russia's explosion of her own first atom bomb and the predominance of the Chinese People's Republic in Peking.

As we have already seen, conflict between Chiang Kai-shek and Mao Tse-tung had existed throughout the Second World War and in July 1946 it developed into a full-scale civil war in China. Chiang Kai-shek failed to make good his bid for victory in Manchuria, Mao's Communist armies triumphed, and by October 1949 the former had been compelled to retreat with the remnants of his troops to the island of Taiwan.

It is against this background that developments in the Far Eastern sector of the Cold War must be viewed. In 1945, to make the surrender of Japan easier, Korea had been divided at the 38th parallel, the northern half under Russian and the southern half under American supervision. By 1948 the now more or less independent Republic of Korea (in the south) and the Democratic People's Republic of Korea (in the north) each claimed sovereignty over both halves: the 38th parallel had become the Iron Curtain of the Far East.

In June 1949 American occupation troops were withdrawn from South Korea: this served as an opportunity for the Soviet Union, operating through its North Korean puppets, to instigate a North Korean invasion of the South, beginning on 25 June 1950. The Americans responded immediately to this challenge by dispatching troops and supplies to South Korea, and shortly afterwards the United Nations recommended military action by the UN 'to repel the armed attack'. In the end some fifteen member states contributed to the UN forces sent to Korea, although essentially they depended on the backing of American military power.

In September 1950 American troops landed at Inchon, and US policy was one of fighting a limited war, that is, one unlikely to provoke either the Soviet Union or China to participate in it. However, the American commander, General MacArthur, had more aggressive aims, and as in October 1950 the advance of his troops towards the Yalu river took place it seemed as if the traditional containment policy of the United States might be going to alter into a drive to 'liberate' a communist satellite country north of the 38th parallel.

However, the Soviet Union did not rise to this incitement: instead, Communist China under Mao came to the rescue of the reeling

allies. This was dramatically exposed by the fact that only a narrow corridor running through the Soviet zone connected Berlin's western half under British, American and French occupation by road and rail with the West.

In June 1948 the Western powers announced a currency reform in West Germany, including West Berlin, and at 6 a.m. on 24 June 1948 the Soviet forces closed all road and rail routes from Berlin to the West for reasons, as Moscow declared, of 'technical difficulties'. In fact, it was an attempt to drive out the Western

powers and starve West Berlin into submission. The Allies replied by organizing an air-lift of supplies into the beleaguered city and maintained this successfully until the blockade was lifted by the Russians in May 1949 – a resounding victory for the West.

This incident, combined with a worldwide series of Communist threats, led to closer ties between the United States and her West European allies. On 4 April 1949 the North Atlantic Treaty Organization (NATO) was initiated and came into force on 24 August 1949. Consisting of the United

North Korean armies and effectively halted the American forces – to such good purpose that in December 1950 America and Britain abandoned the aim of uniting North and South Korea and contented themselves with a declaration of their intention simply to stand firm on the 38th parallel.

In terms of world perspective the intervention of China was of the highest significance: it meant that the arena was changing from one dominated by two Great Powers to one dominated by three: America, the Soviet Union and China.

In April 1951 General MacArthur, who still advocated a forward, aggressive policy in Korea, was dismissed by his own president, who re-affirmed a US policy of containment and the conduct of a limited war only. Once again General Marshall defined the nature of the struggle:

There can be, I think, no quick and decisive solution to the global struggle short of resorting to another world war. The cost of such a conflict is beyond calculation. It is therefore our policy to contain Communist aggression in different fashions in different areas without resorting to total war.

Further Chinese and North Korean offensives in the peninsula in April and May 1951 were defeated by American and UN forces

Above, Korean war refugees: though the war ended as it had begun, with the country divided along the 38th parallel, it had brought a new power – the People's Republic of China – to the centre of international affairs and revealed the essentially defensive nature of the USA's role of guardian of the free world.

Left, General Douglas MacArthur (1880–1964) on his return to the USA after being dismissed as commander-in-chief of the UN forces in Korea: he had wanted to take the war into Chinese territory.

Opposite top, a British Dakota takes on passengers after delivering food supplies to blockaded Berlin, July 1948: the success of the airlift ensured the survival of West Berlin.

Opposite bottom, the ceremonial signing of the North Atlantic Treaty, 4 April 1949: the Treaty established NATO and formalized the USA's commitment to the defence of western Europe; it remains the backbone of the western defensive alliance today.

and negotiations for an armistice began. These extended for many more months while battles in the air and on the ground continued, accompanied by threats from the United States of unleashing atomic war on the Chinese mainland. Eventually an armistice was signed on 27 July 1953 at Panmunjom, confirming the partition of Korea.

Their experiences in the Far East, and the fact that although Stalin had died in March 1953 there was as yet no sign of change in the European sector of the Cold War, now led the Americans to embark on a huge rearmament programme and the establishment in Europe of the Supreme Headquarters Allied Powers Europe (SHAPE). This marked a new phase, namely the US policy of negotiation from strength, something sharper and, in the opinion of the American secretary of state, Dean Acheson, more likely to be effective as an international attitude. Aspects of this change were the signing of a peace treaty with Japan in September 1951 (to which the Soviet Union was *not* a party), the joining of NATO by Greece and Turkey, and the emergence of a virtually independent Western Germany – the German Federal Republic – soon to become a full and equal member of the Western alliance.

'Negotiation from strength' assumed extreme and flamboyant expression in the activities of Senator McCarthy, who whipped up an anti-communist witch hunt in the States. But on the election to the American presidency of the Republican candidate, General Eisenhower, in November 1952, and the death in March 1953 of Stalin, the position was once again greatly stabilized: neither communist expansion nor American counter-aggression were sustained for reasons which had to do with the

emergence of China as a third world power, the terror of nuclear weapons and the sensing of some degree of common interest between America and the Soviet Union. Power in the Soviet Union was passing via Malenkov to Kruschev: in June 1953 an uprising in East Germany was suppressed by Soviet troops; in March 1954 the Americans exploded a new nuclear device at Bikini – the hydrogen bomb.

The new American secretary of state, Foster Dulles, somewhat rhetorically practised the art of brinkmanship in international relations between East and West; there was talk of massive retaliation by the United States in case of attack; in September 1954 a further anti-communist bastion was established by the formation of the South East Asia Treaty Organization (SEATO), the United States, Britain, France, Thailand, Pakistan, Australia and New Zealand.

Yet in spite of, or because of, these events, the year 1954 marked a move towards mutual accommodation of a limited kind between Russia and America. There were signs that the Soviet Union might be ready to settle for a divided 'two Germany' agreement, and in April 1954 there had occurred the Geneva Conference, summoned to discuss the future of Korea and Indo-China. Nothing was achieved about the former, but as a result of the defeat of the French at Dien Bien Phu by the Vietminh yet another partition was agreed upon as a temporary modus vivendi, namely the partitioning of Vietnam into South and North. It seemed that a thaw in the cold war might be coming, not because of the end of the dispute but because of the deadlock of partition in Berlin and Germany, in Korea and in Vietnam.

The beginning of the year 1955 provided an epitome of the constant clash between the

major ideologies in the world. In January the offshore islands of Quemoy and Matsu, held by the Nationalist government in Formosa, were threatened with attack by Chinese communists from the mainland. Immediately the American president obtained authorization from Congress to resort to arms should they need to be defended. An apparent easing of tension followed soon after. In April 1955 there was an Afro-Asian conference in Bandung, Indonesia, where the Chinese foreign minister, Chou En-lai, carefully commended the 'peaceful' liberation of Formosa. This was the prelude to a lull of almost three years in the Far Eastern sector of the Cold War.

In Europe the German Federal Republic formally became a member of the Western Alliance on 6 May 1955. In the same month the Soviet Union organized a defence system for the Eastern countries, the Warsaw Pact; it came to terms with Tito's Yugoslavia and agreed to a treaty establishing the neutral state of Austria. At the same time the Soviet Union fired its first intermediate range ballistic missile. Both sides had been putting their respective houses in order before coming to the summit conference in Geneva in July 1955. Although this led nowhere, because of the basic intransigence of the United States and the Soviet Union, especially on the subject of Germany, a little progress towards some degree of coexistence was made in the shape of agreement to a measure of cultural exchange.

The Cold War drama was next played out in a Middle East setting. As part of US strategy there had come into existence in April 1955 the Baghdad Pact between Turkey, Iraq and Britain and a little later Pakistan and Persia – the so-called 'Northern Tier' of anti-communist defence in that region of the world. However, it was the cause of serious trouble, for Nasser of Egypt saw in it an increase in the power of Iraq to rival his own leadership of the Arab world. Unable to obtain arms to support his anti-Israel guerrilla warfare from the West, he acquired these in September 1956 from the Soviet Union via Czechoslovakia. At the same time he was planning the Aswan High Dam with the help of American capital. When in the spring of 1956 it was known that the Egyptian leader had recognized communist China, American and British promises of aid for the Aswan project were withdrawn.

This was the moment for Nasser to play his trump card: on 26 July 1956 he nationalized the Suez Canal. There then developed the Suez crisis, which revealed an Anglo-American split of the most serious kind, and that it coincided with the Hungarian uprising and its suppression by Russian tanks. A nationalistic and an ideological clash had become so confused that for a time Western anti-communist solidarity was ruptured, with the inevitable consequence that none but moral protests could be made against Soviet actions in Budapest.

Above, Egyptian ships blocking the entrance to the Suez Canal, November 1956: the abortive British and French attempt to wrest control of the Canal from Nasser failed to gain American support and caused an immediate financial crisis in London, demonstrating Britain's inability to sustain an imperial role.

Left, the citizens of Budapest wreck a statue of Stalin during the November 1956 uprising: resentment at low living standards and political repression turned into open revolt at the end of October, the revolutionary government promising to end the one-party state and withdraw from the Warsaw Pact and appealing in vain to the west for help. Russian tanks crushed the revolt in a few days.

Opposite, test hydrogen bomb explosion in the Pacific late 1940s.

Nevertheless it was sufficiently in the common interest of both the chief ideological protagonists, the United States and the Soviet Union, to prevent the spread of Middle Eastern hostilities into world war. However, the dispatch of a UN peace-keeping force to the Middle East was made possible largely by the prompt skill with which the then UN Secretary-General, Dag Hammarskjold acted.

In spite or because of these explosive situations, the era of coexistence was dawning. It was heralded in a sinister fashion by the bringing into production in 1957 of two neutralizing weapons of terror, the intermediate range ballistic missile and the intercontinental ballistic missile. Even more significantly, there had already occurred in February 1956 Khrushchev's 'secret speech'

to his Party, violently attacking Stalin and all his policies.

This speech had repercussions, first in Poland, where riots against the Stalinist regime broke out in June, to be succeeded in October by the establishment of a revisionist Polish government under Gomulka – the exact opposite of what occurred in Hungary, where Soviet intervention prevented such a liberalization of government.

With the launching of the Sputnik satellite in October 1957 the diplomatic phase of coexistence pursued its course, but to the accompaniment of a tremendously fierce race between America and the Soviet Union to obtain 'missile superiority'. Meanwhile the nations of western Europe had recovered economically from the ravages of war and six of them (France, Germany, Belgium,

failed to resolve the problem; Khrushchev's attempt to initiate a revisionist policy in European internal affairs to the advantage of the Soviet Union and the discomfiture of the West had not made much progress by the end of 1959. Its very stalemate served as a spur both to Khrushchev and to the new American president to attempt another Summit meeting in the hope of breaking deadlock without sacrificing what were conceived of as essential mutual interests.

Undoubtedly the single greatest factor to dominate these and succeeding years was the rift between the communist regimes of Moscow and Peking, the former failing to sustain its claim to be the sole and final arbitrator of Marxist-Leninism. The rift was caused by difference of opinion between Russia and China with regard to communist theory, tactics and strategy. The chief of these stemmed from the fact that Mao's revolution had been achieved by peasant-based guerrilla armies with little help from the Soviet Union. Moreover, in China the nationalist ingredient was as strong if not stronger than it had been in Russia. The Chinese Communist Party disapproved of Russia's coexistence policy; it regarded it as weak and deviating from true Marxist-Leninist principles. Furthermore, China was attempting her 'Great Leap Forward' during the late 1950s, an attempt to modernize and industrialize an age-old civilization and way of life overnight. In July 1960 at the Bucharest Conference of Communist Parties, Moscow was already abusing Peking as heretical and warmongering. The climax of the argument reached in November 1960 with a seeming compromise, which failed however to disguise underlying distrust and differences of policies with regard to world revolution and the pattern of national liberation movements.

Khrushchev had been continuing his version of coexistence with the West, not least by his attempt to wreck the November 1960 UN Congo peace-keeping effort. And by his insistence at the UN Assembly that 'there are no neutral men', when he tried unsuccessfully to have Hammarskjold replaced by a troika, or three-man committee.

The year 1961 could be reckoned as the decisive one in the long drawn-out Cold War, for with the assumption of the presidency by John Kennedy in January the stage was set for three great trials of strength, Cuba, Berlin and the Far East (Laos and Vietnam). In April 1961 there had been the ill-fated and misconceived attempt by the American Central Intelligence Agency to back a landing at the Bay of Pigs of Cubans opposed to the communistic regime of Fidel Castro. This was followed by the building of missile launching sites by the Soviet on Cuban soil and the ultimatum dispatched by Kennedy to Khrushchev on 22 October 1961 which virtually said that he

Italy, the Netherlands and Luxembourg) were entering into closer union, already economic and by intention political. This was signalized by the Treaty of Rome in March 1957, which brought the European Economic Community into formal existence on 1 January 1958. The diplomatic initiative still remained in the hands of Moscow, with the desire to establish a coexistence via a summit meeting on terms which would have meant the withdrawal of American military forces from Europe. However, in the summer of 1958 the Iraqi government was overthrown, and although British and American troops moved into Lebanon and Jordan to preclude any possible Soviet exploitation of the situation Iraq left the Baghdad Pact, which was later renamed the Central Eastern Treaty Organization

(CENTO). At about the same time threatening noises were heard in the Far East against the offshore islands, and these were met by strong pressure from the United States on Peking.

Once again the Berlin issue came alive to highlight the perpetual ideological quarrel. On 10 November 1958, Khrushchev proposed that the Potsdam signatories, the United States, the Soviet Union and Great Britain; should agree that Berlin should be turned into a demilitarized free city – on the territory, however, of the German Democratic Republic. This was in the nature of a Soviet notice to quit to the Western Allies, but its dangerous tone and the stiffening of Western resistance compelled Khrushchev eventually to withdraw it. Further consultations in Moscow, Paris and Washington

Left, the Berlin Wall, first erected on 13 August 1961 to prevent East Germans voting with their feet for the capitalist west: the flimsy structure shown in this picture has long since been replaced by a far more permanent collection of watchtowers, strips, fences and walls.

Opposite top, the formal signing of the Treaty of Rome, 25 March 1957, establishing the European Economic Community: its members were committed to a programme of measures designed to promote a customs union and to establish economic and commercial unity.

Opposite bottom, Vice-President Richard Nixon and Nikita Khruschev in the impromptu 'kitchen debate' held at a Moscow exhibition in 1959: the debate centred on the consumer society, Nixon vigorously defending the American way of life. Within little more than a decade Russian economists, in 1959 still trying to overcome wartime devastation, were placing far greater emphasis on the production of consumer goods.

must have the sites dismantled or be bombed out of existence. The Soviet Union capitulated: it did so in the knowledge that in case of non-compliance 144 Polaris, 103 Atlas, 105 Thor and Jupiter and 54 Titan missiles were ready to be used against them.

On 3 and 4 June 1961, Kennedy had met Khrushchev in Vienna, where he learned of the latter's determination to bring the Berlin issue to a head. Khrushchev repeated the Soviet demands of 1958, with a threat to sign a separate peace treaty with East Germany, and again suggested demilitarized status for West Berlin. Kennedy responded with a firm declaration of the American intention to protect the independence of West Berlin, and in the face of this and the alarming rate at which refugees were pouring through Berlin from East to West Germany Khrushchev decided to build the Berlin Wall. On 13 August 1961, that flow was brutally and effectively stopped.

In the Far East, events in Laos, which centred upon the emergence of pro-communist and anti-Western forces, resulted after mediation by the UN in a declaration of Laotian neutrality, but the situation in Vietnam developed into an open sore.

Apart from Vietnam, the next three years witnessed a continuing lull in East-West tensions. In August 1963 the nuclear test ban treaty was signed by the United States, Soviet Union and Britain, though not by China and France. Then on 1 June 1963, the so-called 'hot-line' was set up, a direct teleprinter circuit between Moscow and Washington, whereby the respective chiefs could make instantaneous contact in case of world crisis.

Yet armaments on each side remained huge and menacing, and such a balance as has been achieved between the previous two great contestants, America and the Soviet Union, must be regarded as one based on fear and not on trust, with the hope of survival as the only kind of cementing force.

A wave of nationalism

The nationalisms of Asia, Africa and elsewhere mostly developed in and after the Second World War as a consequence partly of the various resistance movements, partly of the disfigurement of the white man's image in the non-white world, partly of the increase in awareness among previously ignorant races of how other people in regions of the world hitherto unknown to them existed.

From a complete list of those which have either attained or reaffirmed in modern terms their independent national identities, a selection will be made to illustrate such points as underlying similarities or basic differences, types of government, relations with the ideological alignments of the Great Powers and the degree of domestic social alienation or solidarity. One touchstone of reality may usefully be John Stuart Mill's 1861 definition of the nation as

a portion of mankind . . . united among themselves by common sympathies which do not exist between them and any others – which make them cooperate with each other more willingly than with other people, desire to be under the same government, and desire that it should be government by

themselves or a portion of themselves exclusively.

The main nationalist movements of Asia were: Mongolian People's Republic (1945); Philippines (1946); India (1947); Pakistan (1947); Ceylon (1948); Burma (1948); Indonesia (1949); Laos (1949); Cambodia (1953–54); Vietnam (1954); Malaysia (1957–63); Singapore (1965); Maldive Islands (1965).

Because the entire Asian scene was deeply affected and continues to be strongly influenced by two events, it is appropriate that both should receive comment at the outset. One was the establishment of the Chinese People's Republic in 1949 under Mao Tse-tung and the emergence of a kind of renovated nationalism. In terms of ideology, domestic reform and potential power in foreign affairs Mao's China has taken its place as a third world power, whose word is listened to with admiration or revulsion not only throughout Asia but on the continents of Europe, Africa and Latin America and – most attentively of all – in the Kremlin. The other event was the manner of Japan's defeat at the end of the Second World War, and the reappearance of that country apparently shorn of its imperialistic and chauvinistic qualities as the small but immensely energetic and modernized industrial power of the Far East.

Asian nationalism was both cause and consequence of the retreat of the Western imperialism of America, Britain, France and the Netherlands. Three instances must suffice to illustrate a general phenomenon. The Dutch East Indies had, ever since the seventeenth century, formed a rich part of the Netherlands' overseas empire. Between 1929 and 1945 one man, the Indonesian Sukarno, had dreamed of and planned for the national independence of his country. When the Japanese occupation took place during the Second World War, the occupying power declared the country to be independent of the Netherlands. When at the end of the war the Dutch tried to re-establish their control, Sukarno led the

Indonesian National Party into action against them. For three and a half years a fierce, violent struggle took place, but when in 1949 Sukarno had to admit military defeat the United Nations, in response to world opinion, organized a conference at The Hague, as a result of which national independence was granted in 1950.

In spite of Sukarno's lofty speeches about the Indonesian Revolution occurring within the context of the revolution of mankind based on 'the awakened conscience of mankind', and in spite of the success with which Indonesia played host at the Bandung Conference of 1955, social reform did not go fast or far enough. As a result the local communist party gained rapidly in power. In a curious bid to stave it off Sukarno turned to Mao's China for help, but then the military stepped in, the generals demanding strong national government without foreign strings. These developments were viewed with alarm and suspicion by the United States, the Soviet Union and

China respectively, none of which could afford to see Indonesia fall exclusively into any one ideological lap. It has therefore remained so far a non-aligned dictatorship, still plagued with the problem of social alienation internally and with its original charismatic leader, Sukarno now having given place to Suharto.

India and Pakistan are two further examples of renovated nationalism. For two hundred years the two together had formed British India. After a long struggle for 'Swaraj' or Home Rule under the Hindu Gandhi and the Muslim Jinnah and, it must be stressed, a longer and more thorough administrative training for independence at the hands of its imperialist masters than any other part of the overseas empires of Europe, the Indian continent had to achieve liberation on the tragic basis of partition in 1947 into two independent nation states, Indian and Pakistan (West and East). That this occurred was a result of irreconcilable religious differences, and also

Left, road-building along the Chinese border with India, 1962: the ill-defined border between India and China was the subject of continual disputes, particularly serious in 1962, when the Chinese inflicted a serious defeat.

Opposite top right, Peking workers celebrating the first anniversary of the Republic: Mao Tse-tung (1893–1976) was the central figure in Chinese politics for nearly half a century, developing a specifically Chinese variety of Marxism.

Opposite top left, the residents of Peking welcoming the victorious Communist forces, 31 January 1949: in the long term the formal establishment of a communist regime in Peking was less significant than the continuing process of agricultural collectivization, started in the 1920s and completed in 1956, and the reassertion of Chinese power, unexercised since the fall of the Manchu dynasty in 1911.

Opposite bottom, Indonesians queuing for food in a refugee camp, July 1949: Dutch colonies in the east, like those of the other European empires, were a casualty of the war and the demands for independence it aroused.

because of the fact that independence which was almost achieved by 1939, was then deferred because of the war until the Allies had won – a period during which political and economic factions which might have come together went instead in opposite directions.

Enmity between the two countries thus partitioned continued long after 1947 and absorbed much of the energy which both the respective governments could more happily have applied to the solution of immense food and population problems. Prime Minister Nehru, the outstanding leader of independent India, steered his country on a course which sought to avoid communist extremes at home and to cultivate neutrality for India and create a Third World somewhere between the two Cold War power blocs.

What made any kind of rapprochement between India and Pakistan impossible was their dispute about Kashmir. It was claimed by India, but Pakistan objected on the grounds that seventy-five percent of Kashmir's population was Muslim. Military skirmishes took place, and in 1948–9 the United Nations attempted to impose truce and demarcation lines without obtaining any agreed settlement. Then the leadership changed: Ayub Khan took control in Pakistan in 1957, turning his country into a military state with pro-Chinese and anti-Russian tendencies; in 1964 Nehru died and was succeeded by Shastri. Shortly afterwards hostilities broke out again, chiefly as a result of Pakistan's offensives in Kashmir. These continued until a peace was patched up at Tashkent on Soviet initiative in January 1966.

The renovated emergent nationalisms of the Indian subcontinent have neither ministered to their domestic well-being nor to their external security, witness the ceaseless India-China frontier disputes after the Chinese occupation of Tibet.

The history of Vietnam was strangely interwoven with the total history of the

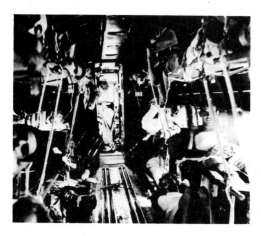

world: indeed, the story of the latter could be told in terms of the former, for here a renovated nationalism sought to emerge in a situation permeated with the ideological jealousies of the Great Powers beyond Vietnam herself.

Like Indonesia, Vietnam, or French Indo-China, of which it was then a part, was declared liberated from its former colonial status by the Japanese invaders. Even during the Japanese occupation guerrilla warfare had been started up against the Japanese troops by Ho Chi Minh. In 1945 he set up his own independent Democratic Republic of North Vietnam. As the French refused to recognize this, he organized further resistance (Viet Minh) against the French attempt to reassert their position. Under the brilliant leadership of General Giap the French were continually harassed, and 15,000 French soldiers were trapped by Giap in the fortress of Dien Bieu Phu and finally forced to surrender in May 1954.

Such an event bred alarm among all the leading powers for the future of Indo-China as a whole, and under their auspices the Geneva Conference convened. Here it was decided to make a fourfold division of the region: a communist North Vietnam under Ho Chi Minh, a non-communist South Vietnam and two neutral states to the west, Laos and Cambodia. The plan was that all foreign troops should then vacate Indo-China and that within two years free elections should be held in both parts of Vietnam to elect a government of the people's own choice for the whole area.

However, the very act of partition had serious consequences: essential rice supplies from the Mekong Delta were cut off from North Vietnam; moreover former Viet Minh now found themselves existing in the South, although many were communists and some were Buddhist-nationalists linked, if in nothing else, by their common hatred of the South Vietnam regime in Saigon, which was headed by the Roman Catholic Premier Diem.

In the years 1955–56 sporadic fighting against Diem's regime broke out, the rebels calling themselves Viet Cong (Vietnamese Communists). Diem appealed to the United States for help in suppressing them, and

16,000 American 'military advisers' soon arrived. In spite of this the Viet Cong had by 1961 gained control of more than half the South Vietnam countryside. A group of discontented army officers then turned on Diem and murdered him in 1963. One short-lived South Vietnamese government followed another, each supported more and more by the Americans, for the US government now began to see the Vietnam struggle as a great world issue and applied to it their theory that if what they regarded as the communist threat were not countered here, one after the other the other cards in the pack, Laos, Cambodia, Thailand, Burma, India, Pakistan, would collapse and go communist.

In August 1964 the war began to spread: communist torpedoes menaced US warships in the Bay of Tonking; US planes bombed North Vietnamese naval bases. Thousands more US troops were brought over the America, numbers of communist soldiers came down from the North by the 'Ho Chi Minh Trail' to help the Viet Cong. Soon a full-scale war was in progress around and among a piteously suffering native population. A military impasse seemed to have been reached, and largely

because of war-weariness in America and a fear shared by other powers that the Vietnam issue could at any moment spark off a world war, negotiations for a settlement at last began in Paris in January 1969 at a round table at which were seated representatives of North Vietnam, South Vietnam, the National Liberation front and the US Government.

Africa

African states which achieved independence were: (formerly under British control) South Africa, which became an independent Republic in 1961; Southern Rhodesia which issued its Unilateral Declaration of Independence (UDI) in 1965; South West Africa under UN and South African Trusteeship (special cases). Ghana (1957); Nigeria (1960); Sierra Leone (1960); Uganda (1962); Kenya (1963); Malawi (1964); Zambia (1964); Tanzania (1964); Gambia (1965); Botswana (1968); Lesotho (1966); Mauritius (1968); Swaziland (1968).

(Formerly under French control) Guinea (1958); Senegal (1958); Togo (1958); Cameroun Republic (1960); Central African Republic (1960); Chad (1960); Congo

(1960); Dahomey (1960); Gabon (1960); Ivory Coast (1960); Malagasy Republic (1960); Mali (1960); Mauritania (1960); Niger Republic (1960); Upper Volta (1960).

(Formerly under Belgian control) The Congolese Republic (1960); Rwanda (1961); Burundi (1962).

(Formerly under Italian rule) Libya (1949); Somali Republic (1960).

It is necessary to comment briefly on the special cases of the Independent Republic of South Africa (1961), South West Africa and Southern Rhodesia. In the first country a British-Afrikaans white minority of three and a half million rules over the remaining majority of fourteen millions (made up of Bantu, Coloured and Asiatics). The official policy of the government is one of apartheid or separate development. This has been implemented in two ways, by the creation under the Group Areas Act of segregated black African townships and job reservations, and by the state of Bantustan Transkei for the sole occupation of Bantus, which enjoys a measure of internal autonomy but in reality depends for its existence on the will of the white South African government. There were attempts on the part of the non-whites to organize resistance against this state of affairs, but in spite of the efforts of men like Luthuli and Mandela the African National Congress became a forbidden organization and almost all anti-white leaders are in gaol or exile. Because of the circumstances described above, South Africa was expelled from the United Nations on 6 November 1962 by resolution of the General Assembly.

To the northwest lies the former German colony, surrendered to South African mandate after the First World War. In spite of UN resolutions and a judgement of the International Court of Justice to the effect that the imposition of South African white

supremacy policy on this territory is illegal, it in fact continues. The black nationalist party was here led by Hosea Kutako, Paramount Chief of the Hereros.

After the break-up of the attempted Federation of Rhodesia in 1963, the northern part (Nyasaland) went its independent way as Malawi under Hastings Banda, and its eastern part (Northern Rhodesia) as Zambia under Kenneth Kaunda, leaving Southern Rhodesia still as a British colony with a white settler population of 224,000 ruling a black majority of four millions. Because of the mounting determination of successive white governments to perpetuate white supremacy and their refusal to make concessions to the British demand for eventual racial equality, under Ian Smith's premiership a Unilateral Declaration of Independence was made in 1965.

Those main features which characterized the emergence of Kenya as an independent nation-state can be clearly discerned. First, as a result of British colonization, the native population were able to gain some experience of administration and responsibility for a considerable period before independence. Together with this had gone the development by white settlers of the Kenya highlands which had served partly as a model and partly as a spur for the Africans. Secondly, there was the slow evolution from tribal conditions to the rudiments of party political life. Thirdly, there was the personality and leadership of an outstanding African leader in Jomo Kenyatta, who after a long spell in Britain (1934–46) returned to Kenya to head his country's national liberation movement. This was interrupted by imprisonment at the hands of the British between 1953 and 1959, while the movement had also from 1950 onwards acquired a terrorist wing in the shape of Mau Mau – an organization

Above, suspected Mau Mau guerrillas being led away for questioning, November 1952: Mau Mau violence was directed against both black and white (in fact it claimed some 8,000 African victims, 68 European) but failed in the end to prevent relatively peaceful progress towards independence.

Opposite right, a South Vietnamese poster warning of Communist brutalities: most peasants supported the Communists – or were in no position to do otherwise, since much of the south was under Viet Cong control by 1960 – rather than the government in Saigon, its existence only maintained by American aid, first financial, then military.

Opposite left, wounded French and Vietnamese troops being evacuated by air from Dien Bien Phu, May 1954: after their defeat and the division of Vietnam the French withdrew from Indo-China and were gradually replaced by the Americans.

709

which committed atrocities against white settlers. The combination of all these factors, especially the outstanding qualities of Kenyatta and the readiness, albeit gradual and reluctant, of the white rulers to acquiesce in their own dispossession meant that the transition from colonialism to independence in this East African country was managed with less friction than elsewhere on that continent.

On the opposite western flank of Africa the story is a sadder and more sombre one. The huge country of Nigeria, a former British colony with an almost entirely African population, had been evolving quite differently. With four hundred tribes, chief of which are the Hausa, Yoruba and Ibo, and many most able politicians, Nigeria failed to make her governmental institutions function effectively when white power was withdrawn. After a troubled period of six years a military takeover occurred in January 1966, federal and regional constitutions being suspended. In May 1967 the country was divided into twelve new states, but this action led to the break-away of the Ibo-controlled part of the country in a bid for complete independence as a nation with a name of its own, Biafra. After a bitter civil war waged with appalling sufferings for the civil population the break-away state finally succumbed to Nigeria's greater military strength.

After these two examples of post-British imperialism it is instructive to turn to the former French colony of Senegal. Here as elsewhere in their overseas empire the

French had attempted to turn the indigenous population into Frenchmen. Even under the pressure of wartime events and the growth of a strong *presence africaine* in the post-war years, when native leaders pressed with eventual success for independence, the French cultural influence lingered strongly. The President of Senegal, Leopold Senghor, contributed as poet and man of letters to the creation of that rich cultural concept known as 'negritude'. As a consequence of a prolonged period of governmental apprenticeship under the French, Senegalese political life developed with a strong, if violent, force, although it failed to maintain the attempted 1959 Federation of Mali, Senegal, French Sudan, Dahomey and Upper Volta.

The vast, sprawling, former Belgian Congo achieved its independence in 1960 with a shocking legacy from the past. This consisted of a period of extortionate exploitation by the imperialist power, especially in the days of its personal leadership by King Leopold II, and the deliberate policy of the Belgian government not to give higher education to more than a tiny fraction of the black African population. This meant that when the forces pressing for liberation from colonial rule became so menacing as to compel Belgian political withdrawal there was not an adequate supply of native leaders to carry on effective government.

Because of the commercial and industrial interests of two or three Western powers, especially in the mineral deposits of the

province of Katanga, and the accompanying Great Power rivalry for control of Congolese internal politics, that country very nearly became the occasion for a world conflict. That it did not do so was due to the skill and energy with which the then secretary-general of the United Nations, first in New York and subsequently with the aid of a UN peacekeeping force in the Congo, succeeded in balancing the rival power bids for a period of more than two years and avoiding Russian and American confrontation on African soil.

Even this short glance at only four of the emergent nationalisms of modern Africa will have sufficed to illustrate the immense importance of certain factors in determining the manner of post-colonial development. These are the presence or absence of white settlers, the pre-independence policies of the colonizing powers with regard to training the natives for independence, and the personalities of the African leaders. There are two further influences, neither of which has yet been explicitly mentioned. One is the economic resources of the particular African region in question, coffee in Kenya, cocoa in Nigeria for example, related to the natural climatic conditions prevailing; the other is education. On these the young independent country's future has depended.

In North Africa, nationalism centred upon three main issues: the Algerian struggle for independence, Nasser and Arab nationalism and the case of Israel.

The independent states of North Africa,

710

the Middle East and the Mediterranean are as follows: Tunisia (1956); Morocco (1956); Sudan (1956); Syria (1941); Egypt (1953); Algeria (1962); Yemen (1962); South Yemen People's Republic (1967); Israel (1948); Cyprus (1960); Malta (1964).

Acquired by the French in 1830, Algeria had in 1871 become three departments of metropolitan France, and many European immigrants had settled there. Between them and the government in Paris there had developed over the years a tension stemming from the resentment which the settlers felt at the amount of money being spent by the metropolitan government on the education of the native Muslim population of Algeria. After the First World War there were the first stirrings of native nationalism, and then in 1942 during the Second World War there appeared the Manifesto of the Algerian People, making a claim for independent Algerian sovereignty as soon as hostilities were over. The situation was a particularly delicate one, as during the closing months of the world struggle Algiers had become the seat of General de Gaulle's provisional French government. In an attempt to accommodate native demands, it allocated voting rights for the French Chamber in 1944 to all the population over twenty-one years of age, further evidence of the way in which national liberation movements could be influenced by their connection with events on a wider world stage. However, compromise on these lines proved impossible in the face of mounting terrorist activity on the part of the extremist national-

ists: these came to a head in the formation in March 1954 of a Revolutionary Council for Unity and Action. In spite of further attempts at settlement at the Evian Conference of 1962, what now constituted a full-scale civil war was in progress in Algeria.

This had three aspects: the French metropolitan government ineffectually seeking a compromise, the white settlers seeking to preserve their own position of privilege and power in Algeria, and the black African rebels seeking to overthrow both. By the end of 1962 General de Gaulle, with statesmanlike realism, conceded full independence to the *Front de la libération nationale* as the necessary price to be paid for the cessation of a ruinous and cruel war, which had had unsettling repercussions on political life in France herself. In August 1962 the now fully independent state of Algeria was admitted to the Arab League. The case of Algeria illustrated admirably the dual aspect of most national liberation movements, namely that independence of the former colonial power is a stage of development and that some degree of domestic social revolution is an inevitable accompaniment.

The Middle East

The seeds of Arab nationalism are in part religious, the common legacy of Islam, and in part political, resulting from growing,

Above, UN forces on the alert in Leopoldville, January 1963: some mistakes notwithstanding, the four-year UN presence in the Congo kept the Congolese economy going and prevented the secession of Katanga.

Opposite, Federal troops capture the airport at Enugu, the capital of the rebel Biafran state, October 1967: Biafra finally capitulated in January 1970 after three years' fighting, but reconciliation came about relatively quickly.

He proceeded energetically to galvanize his country, particularly concentrating on the building of the Aswan Dam as a vital contribution to Egypt's modernization. The international ramifications of this have already been traced and so all that needs to be noted here is the perpetuation of Arab-Israeli antagonism and the increased prestige of Nasser in other Arab countries. If the stories of the other Arab states over the last twenty years are studied, it will be found that two factors are constant. The first is a positive one, namely the attainment of their nationalist objectives in most cases, in the sense of abolishing foreign control. The second is a negative one, namely the failure of Arab nationalism to implement itself in the form of Pan-Arabism: this is a result of the deep mistrust persisting between Arab rulers.

The emergence of the modern state of Israel needs to be viewed against the background of Zionism, the 1917 Balfour Declaration guaranteeing the creation of a Jewish National Home, and Hitler's persecution of the Jews. When on 14 May 1948 the British Mandate of Palestine ended, partition took place. Immediate war brought victory for the Israelis, but the armistice of 1949 satisfied no one: Israel felt insecure and the Arab countries were still set on her destruction. This position was further exacerbated by Israeli policy during the Suez crisis and a long continuing series of border incidents culminating in the Arab-Israeli war of 1967, when the Arab armies were annihilated and considerable gains in territory were made by Israel.

The Caribbean and Latin America

Countries which achieved independence are: Jamaica (1962); Trinidad and Tobago (1962); Barbados (1966); Guyana (1966); Cuba (1959).

Nationalism in the Caribbean and Latin America has come under three dominant influences: former British imperialism in the West Indies, the economic pressures of US 'good neighbourliness' and the recent development of national liberation movements in Latin America, the origins of which lie in the nineteenth century.

The Caribbean group takes in the many islands with a population composed of white settlers, indigenous inhabitants, many of them of black slave origin, and half-castes and with an economy based mainly on the export of sugar, rum and bananas. With the cooperation of Britain, mother country of the British Commonwealth, its former members tried to establish their full independence in 1958 by forming the Federation of the West Indies. By 1962 this had collapsed, chiefly because of the unreadiness of Jamaica and Trinidad to give material assistance to the smaller islands. Unemployment remained a serious domestic

if ill-organized and sporadic, resistance to European imperialism, chiefly British, French and Italian. As a consequence of irreconcilable and opposed pledges given by the British to Jews and Arabs during the First World War (Balfour Declaration, 1917, and Mac-Mahon Pledge, 1916), the precursors of the contemporary Arab-Israeli conflict, interlaced with Great Power rivalry in the Middle East, particularly with regard to oil interests, helped to fan the flames of varying types of local Arab feeling. This took its most powerful shape in Egypt, where after the Second World War British power had to retreat in

the face of nationalist demands for complete independence, which was attained in 1953. Already in 1945 there had been formed an Arab League in the hope of building up concerted action for all the Middle Eastern Arab States to eliminate the Jews. However, in the 1948 Arab-Jewish war, which followed Britain's abandonment of her Palestine mandate and the failure of UN mediation, both Egypt and Jordan suffered humiliating military reverses. The truce of 1949 merely marked Arab ignominy and Jewish triumph. It was this defeat which paved the way for a military takeover in Egypt first under Neguib and then from 1954 under Nasser.

problem with the consequence that considerable numbers of West Indians emigrated to Britain.

The second and third influences are dramatically illustrated by the history of Cuba, which may be treated as a paradigm of many national liberation movements. From 1933 to 1958, with the exception of the years 1944 to 1952, Cuba existed under the dictatorial government of Fulgenicio Batista – a regime of brutality and terror. During this period US financial interests established a grip on the whole country, controlling its sugar industry, half the railways, most of the electronic and telegraph services and the tourist industry and mining. In spite of the rural poverty, illiteracy and disease which afflicted the population, the land itself was rich and had been industrialized with some success, but only to the benefit of a limited upper-middle class. This provided the opportunity for social revolution, which was seized by the young law student Fidel Castro. At his trial in 1953 after he had been arrested for attacking a barracks he made a long accusatory speech against Batista, outlining a programme of economic and political reform.

When, as a result of a general amnesty, Castro was released from prison two years after beginning to serve his fifteen years' sentence, he organized an expedition from Mexico in November 1956 but suffered complete defeat at the hands of Batista's troops. However, he retreated into the mountains with a faithful band of fellow-revolutionaries and then gradually built up a tiny but determined guerrilla band.

On 1 January 1959, as a result of successful harrying tactics, Castro came to power after the disintegration of the Batista regime; he established what at first seemed a just and not illiberal form of government. However, with the Agrarian Reform Law of May 1959, which provided for the expropriation of many properties, including foreign held ones, moderation vanished, and the Communist Party assumed a well-organized and tight control of affairs. This had international implications, for Castro not unnaturally sought support from the Soviet Union, an action which itself precipitated American counter-action in the shape of the suspension of the Cuban sugar quota. In July 1960 Castro expropriated all American interests, and this was followed by the series of events leading up to the missile site crisis in 1961. Once again an emergent nationalism had become entangled with ideology.

Above, Fidel Castro (b. 1927) (centre), whose Marxist revolution in Cuba survived American attempts to undermine it in the early 1960s but failed to extend to the rest of the Caribbean.

Opposite top, President Ben Bella of Algeria, Nikita Kruschev, President Nasser of Egypt and President Aref of Iraq at the temple of Karnak during a ceremony to divert the waters of the River Nile at Aswan, 1964: the Dam, begun in 1960, became a symbol of Egypt's membership of the modern world and a vital factor in international negotiations.

Opposite bottom, an immigrant ship arriving in Palestine, 1947: only in 1948, after the formation of the state of Israel, was unrestricted Jewish immigration permitted; before then, the British authorities had imposed a limited quota, turning away the survivors of the concentration camps and, before 1939, refugees from Nazi terror.

Chapter 57

The Headlines of History 1965–1978

While this period was dominated by the three giant powers, the United States, the Soviet Union and the People's Republic of China, the European continent began to assume an identity and to some degree an unity of its own. This tendency continued, however, to be sharply contradicted by the tensions between communist East and democratic, pluralist West, the two halves contriving an uneasy relationship of truce over which hovered the military preparedness of both sides to react offensively or defensively. A number of dominant features may be discerned.

The stabilization of the two Germanys: After Herr Willy Brandt became Chancellor of the German Federal Republic in October 1969, he and the Polish Premier signed a treaty in December 1970 which recognized the Oder/Neisse line as Poland's western frontier. After Walter Ulbricht, leader of the German Democratic Republic, retired in May 1971, to be succeeded by Herr Honecker, the way was clear for further accommodation between the two Germanys. In December 1971 agreement was reached regarding East-West German travel and traffic access, and in June 1973 the United Nations Organization admitted both the German Federal Republic and the German Democratic Republic as members. A final touch to stabilization was given by the signing of a Peace Treaty in May 1977 between Poland and East Germany. The cold war in Europe had given place after thirty years to a reluctant peace.

The European Economic Community and Great Britain's entry into it: In July 1966 the EEC became more closely knit through the adoption of a Common Agricultural Policy (CAP). In May 1967 Great Britain, Denmark and Eire registered applications for membership, but General de Gaulle firmly imposed his veto against the first. In July 1968 all EEC internal customs duties ended and a common external tariff was introduced. After the death of General de Gaulle in November 1970, and with the strong advocacy of the Conservative British Prime Minister, Edward Heath, the way was cleared for Great Britain, as well as Denmark and Eire, to enter the EEC in January 1973: British membership was sealed by a Referendum in its favour held in June 1975, with both Harold Wilson, then leader of a Labour government (until April 1976 when he was succeeded by James Callaghan) and Mrs Margaret Thatcher, newly elected leader of the opposition Conservative party, pledged to full British participation in Europe. Early in the 1970s Great Britain began to feel the economic benefits of her North Sea oil, while a fresh stage in the evolution of European unification began, in 1979 with direct elections to the European Parliament.

The USSR and the West: Growingly pre-occupied with the problem of its relations with the People's Republic of China, the Soviet Union made only one thrust on its Western side, namely the invasion of Czechoslovakia. Some clue as to Russia's internal condition may be obtained from the activities of a dissident minority within its borders, the expulsion of Alexander Solzhenitsyn in 1974 and the fact that, though the eminent Soviet scientist, Andrei Sakharov, received a message of

ICELAND

NORWEGIAN SEA

GREENLAND (DENMARK)

ICELAND

INSET

NORWAY

IRELAND

UNITED KINGDOM

NORTH SEA

DENMARK

NETHERLANDS

BELGIUM

LUXEMBOURG

FED. REP. GERMANY

ATLANTIC OCEAN

FRANCE

SWITZERLAND

AUSTR

also a member of EFTA

PORTUGAL

SPAIN

ITALY

MEDITERRANEAN SEA

714

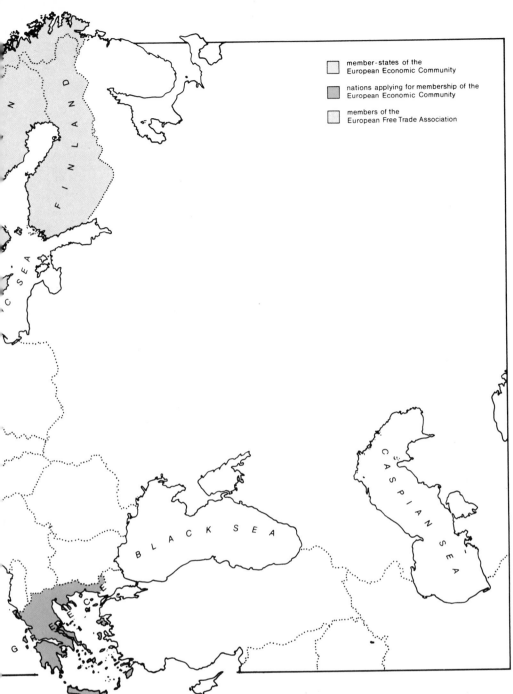

C

FINLAND

SEA

BLACK SEA

CASPIAN SEA

EEC

G

Left, the European Economic Community at the beginning of 1979: a large number of non-European nations, many from the developing world, have concluded trading agreements with the Community or have entered into associate status.

Opposite bottom, Alexander Solzhenitsyn (b. 1918), the Russian novelist expelled from his native land in 1974: his writings have done much to open western eyes to the true nature of the Soviet regime, though his quasi-religious, historical standpoint separates him from the majority of his fellow-dissidents, who are concerned to advocate a more democratic form of socialism.

encouragement from President Carter of the USA in February 1977, he still remains unapprehended. A visit to the German Federal Republic by Mr Brezhnev on behalf of the Soviet Union in May 1978 confirmed the success of German-Russian detente. A further aid to the improvement of relations between Communist and non-Communist countries was the election of Pope John Paul II – a Pole by nationality – in 1978.

Reform and reaction in Czechoslovakia: In January 1968 the Communist regime in Czechoslovakia began to be modified when Alexander Dubcek came to power as First Secretary of the Communist Party – 'socialism with a human face' was his slogan. However, removal of the censorship and other measures of relaxation, which were accompanied by clear indications that Czechoslovakia could no longer be regarded as politically reliable by its Russian neighbour, resulted in August 1968 in the invasion of the country by a Soviet military force. Ideologically, the clock was set back. In

January 1969 Jan Palach, a student of Prague University, burnt himself to death in protest against communist tyranny; in April 1969 Dubcek was forced to resign and a safely pro-Soviet Czechoslovak government installed. That the battle for liberalization had not been entirely lost was shown when in January 1977 Charter 77 was smuggled out of Czechoslovakia, a manifesto from those within proclaiming their anti-totalitarian convictions.

Northern Ireland: The relationships of Northern Ireland to the British parliament at Westminster and to the government of Eire in Dublin were darkened by the fierce and tragic internecine strife in Ulster. This was exacerbated in the autumn and winter of 1968–69 by clashes between Protestants and Catholics, Civil Rights marches and growing terrorist activities mainly, though not exclusively, perpetrated by the Irish Republican Army (IRA). By May 1972 conditions, in spite of the presence of British troops, had deteriorated so greatly

that the province became ungovernable locally, and direct rule from Westminster had to be substituted. Although terrorist activities subsided somewhat after a brief, but unsuccessful, attempt to export them to London, the underlying problems, political, economic and religious, remained no nearer resolution.

Post-Franco Spain: after nearly forty years of dictatorship, Spain became a constitutional monarchy after the death of General Franco in November 1975. Under King Juan Carlos I political life came more to resemble other pluralist democracies of

Western Europe, and Spain applied for
membership of the European Economic
Community.

Finally, no account of the European scene
during this period may omit the wave of
student unrest which swept across most
European universities in 1968 and after,
Paris and the London School of Economics
becoming notorious. It took the form of
protests, some of them violent, and 'sit ins'.
They were aimed against university curricula
and administration and were partly inspired
by left-wing agitation, partly by a sense of
genuine grievance at what appeared to many
students to be the irrelevance of their
prescribed studies to the burning issues of
the day, those of war and peace, capitalism
versus socialism, social equality and hierarchical privilege.

The Far East

There are two main features, the course of
the Vietnam war and the 'Cultural Revolution' and its aftermath in the People's
Republic of China. After some four years
of savage strife, in January 1969 North

Left, Red Guards assemble in Peking during the Cultural Revolution.

Opposite, survivors of the My Lai massacre, 1967, in which a US army unit killed 300 Vietnamese civilians.

Vietnam received her first diplomatic recognition from Sweden. In January 1973, after months of private and public diplomatic activity, a cease-fire between North and South was arranged. Fighting continued, however, and it was not until 30 April 1975, that President Minh of South Vietnam surrendered unconditionally to the Vietcong. In April 1976 the two halves of the country were re-united and Vietnam was recognized as one state. The most important aspect of the whole Vietnam war was that it demonstrated the inability, short of involvement in total war, of a great power (in this case the USA) to impose its will when met by determined opposition from a society (North Vietnamese) ideologically inspired and in some measure militarily supported from without.

After 1966 Chinese–Russian relations deteriorated, and the Chinese mainland scene was dominated by a mighty struggle within the governing Communist ranks. In August of that year the so-called Red Guards made their first appearance at one of Chairman Mao Tse-tung's huge rallies, and this marked the beginning of what came to be known as the 'Cultural Revolution'. This was an attempt by the ageing Marshall and his colleagues, 'the Rule of Four', to (in the words of its friends) preserve the purity of the original revolution, (in the words of its critics) to fasten a harsh, totalitarian regime on the whole country. In early 1967, after an incident between Russian diplomats at Peking airport and a period of closed schools and considerable social dislocation, Premier Chou en-lai called for discipline, and the Red Guards were ordered to desist from violence. In April 1975 General Chiang Kai-shek died in Taiwan, and on the mainland a Chinese National People's Congress, adopting a new constitution, headed the country in a new direction, towards some degree of domestic ideological relaxation, and of

719

international contacts, not least with the USA and Europe. On 9 September 1976, Chairman Mao died and was succeeded by Hua Kuo-feng, since when the reaction against the whole Maoist conception of communism as it had developed in Mao's latter years has continued to gain in force.

Other events in the Far East of note in this period are the secession of Singapore from Malaya in August 1965, the short-lived invasion of Laos in February 1971 by South Vietnamese troops supported by American aircraft, the fall of Cambodia in April 1975 to the Khmer Rouge communist forces and its subsequent invasion in 1979 by Vietnam, the establishment in Laos in December 1975 of a People's Democratic Republic. In concluding this summary it

may be noted that the cause of communism triumphed in the Far East, but that this did not lead to confrontation, in spite of armed stalemate within Korea, with the other great power of that hemisphere, namely Japan, which became a world industrial power during these years.

Africa

The dominant theme of events in this gigantic land-mass is the tremendous force of nationalism and its capacity to attract foreign aid, interest and intervention, e.g. the Chinese loan for the Tanzam (Tanzania/Zambia) railway.

Under the leadership of Verwoerd, Vorster and Botha successively, South

Africa continued its policy of white supremacy and apartheid, although its ultimate viability came more and more in question as various national liberation movements around its borders became successful, Angola and Mozambique to mention two.

In spite of sanctions, including an embargo on oil imports, the Smith regime in Rhodesia, in connivance with oil companies and with the tacit acquiescence of Britain, managed to survive for a number of years, declaring itself a Republic in March 1970. However, after an African National Council was set up in Rhodesia in December 1971 and in spite of lack of unity among the black opponents of the Smith regime, guerrilla warfare to destroy it and replace it by the independent state of Zimbabwe began and has not ceased. Under its pressure and that of the departure of many white settlers and constant admonition from the other Black African states, Britain and the USA, Ian Smith agreed in September 1976 to majority (i.e. black) rule within two years. To this end he proposed an internal settlement and took in to partnership two or three moderate Black Rhodesians, notably Bishop Muzarewa, but the Patriotic Front under Nkomo and Mugabe refused to go along with this policy and stepped up the fighting. As 1978 drew to an end, with majority rule now postponed by the Smith government until April 1979, the prospects of a peaceful settlement still eagerly canvassed by Britain and the USA seemed slim indeed.

Among numerous other African struggles, special mention may be made of the trials of Ghana first under President Nkrumah (deposed in 1966) and then an abortive civilian government of democratic style overthrown by the Army; after the deposition of Emperor Haille Selassie in September 1974, the conflict between Ethiopia and Somalia in 1977, and the independence struggle of Namibia (South-West Africa). Set against this pattern of tumultuous, bloody revolt and dislocation there may be posed the emergence of the Organization of African Unity, which held its sixteenth meeting in Khartoum in July 1978 and might possibly be regarded as an early harbinger of eventual black African solidarity.

The Indian Continent

In January 1966 Mrs Indira Gandhi became prime minister of India. In 1967, after a further series of minor border clashes India successfully resisted a sharp thrust by Chinese troops into Sikkim. In March 1971 Sheikh Mujib Rahman declared East Pakistan the free and independent state of Bangladesh, and in spite of bombing attacks from Pakistan, India recognized Bangladesh on 3 December 1971, and on 17 December the war between India and Pakistan ceased. By July 1972

Above, Mrs Indira Gandhi (b. 1917) prime minister of India 1966–77: despite the corruption of her administration and her authoritarian rule under the state of emergency between 1975 and 1977, in which thousands of people were imprisoned for alleged political offences, she retained a considerable personal and political following.

Left, a captured nationalist guerrilla amid the bodies of his dead comrades, slain by troops of the Rhodesian army: by 1979 divisions among black leaders within and outside Rhodesia and white reluctance to give up any real power had made a peaceful solution to the country's problems seem increasingly unlikely.

Opposite top, weeping members of Peking's Red Guard filing past Mao Tse-tung's coffin, September 1976: within a few years of Mao's death, the Chinese government had seemed to change ideological direction, developing far closer economical and cultural ties with the west.

Opposite bottom, window display in Luanda, Angola, featuring communist literature and portraits of Che Guevara and Fidel Castro: Angola independence, which followed immediately on the return to democracy in Portugal, was accompanied by Russian and Cuban military intervention.

Sheikh Mujib and Mrs Gandhi were co-operating, and she had also formed an accord with Mr Bhutto, who in August 1973 became prime minister of Pakistan.

However, in the course of her premiership the government for which she was responsible began to be attacked for corruption and intimidation of its opponents. In June 1975 Mrs Gandhi was found guilty of corrupt practices and disqualified from holding electoral office for six years. She was replaced in March 1977 by Mr Desai as prime minister but, determined to make a political comeback, she campaigned for election in a country district in Southern India and reentered Congress as the leading member of the Opposition in November 1978. Meanwhile in Bangladesh Sheikh Mujib and his family had been assassinated in August 1975, his place as President being taken by Mr Assad. In Pakistan General Muhammed Zia al-Hug overthrew Mr Bhutto in July 1977, since when the latter has been sentenced to death for treason to the state.

The Middle East

This ideologically volatile area continued to be plagued by Arab-Israeli conflict, anxieties all over the world on account of Middle Eastern oil supplies, and the constant fishing in troubled waters by the Great Powers, the United States with a leaning to Israel, the Soviet Union with a leaning to the Arab world.

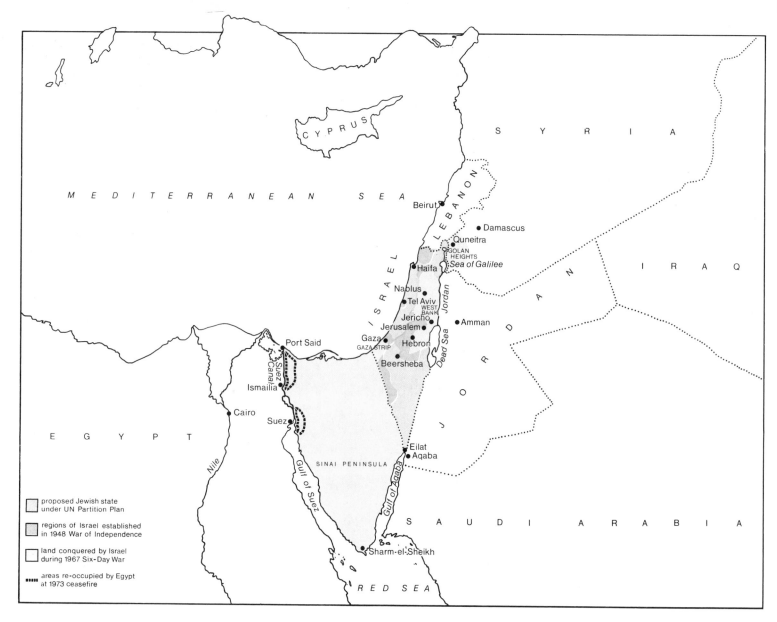

proposed Jewish state
under UN Partition Plan

regions of Israel established
in 1948 War of Independence

land conquered by Israel
during 1967 Six-Day War

••••• areas re-occupied by Egypt
at 1973 ceasefire

Of great significance was the coming into existence of the Palestine Liberation Organization (PLO), pledged to establish an independent Arab State of Palestine on the West bank of the river Jordan. This movement under the leadership of Yassir Arafat sought to promote its cause by methods of terrorism not confined to the Middle East: for example, it attacked an Israeli airplane on the ground at Zurich airport. In February 1969 Mrs Golda Meir became Israeli prime minister.

An additional complication in Middle Eastern affairs was caused by tensions between Syria and the Lebanon, which in the 1970s was to prove a disturbing factor in the internal politics of Lebanon. Meanwhile incidents of varying gravity continued to occur between Israel and Egypt, which were only slightly diminished by a 90-day ceasefire in the Arab-Israeli conflict in the summer of 1970. In September of 1970 Nasser was succeeded by Sadat as ruler of Egypt, and early in 1971 a United Nations mediator in the person of Mr Jarring strove ineffectively to discover a basis for serious peace talks. After King Hussein of Jordan's plan for an autonomous Palestine State

broke down and Israel occupied the whole of the West Bank, further full-scale war developed in October 1973 between Israel and Egypt. Peace talks, held in Geneva, in September 1975 led to the agreed withdrawal of Israeli troops in Sinai and the erection of a new UN buffer zone between them and the Egyptian forces.

Nothing further happened until in December 1977 the new Israeli Premier, Mena-

chem Begin, invited President Sadat to come to Jerusalem for talks, and the latter boldly accepted the invitation. Thus began a new era of life for Israeli-Egyptian rapprochement, eagerly encouraged by President Carter of the USA, who persuaded both men in 1978 to consult together under his aegis at Camp David, his country retreat. As a consequence there emerged the prospect of a real peace settlement

723

between Israel and Egypt, albeit somewhat dashed by the opposition of some of the other Arab states to any form of agreement which would seem to ratify the permanent status of the state of Israel.

Latin and North America

The main motif in the recent history of this continent of vast potential has been the continuing struggle between varying types of dictatorial government and movements of national liberation with a strong left-wing bias, both striving to be free of undue economic or ideological pressure from the USA. It is perhaps significant that in March

1977 the USA and Cuba resumed official contacts after a lapse of eighteen years. Comparable with the Organization of African Unity, there is an Organization of Latin American Solidarity which seeks to witness to some sense of continental solidarity, but essentially there are twenty-one nation-states (eighteen Spanish-speaking republics, plus Brazil, Haiti and Puerto Rico) with twenty-one histories. Three are mentioned here; Cuba has continued under the rule of General Fidel Castro; Argentina came for a while (1974–76) under the presidency of Senora Peron after the death of her husband and since March 1976 has been ruled by General Videla; and, thirdly, Chile, which between September

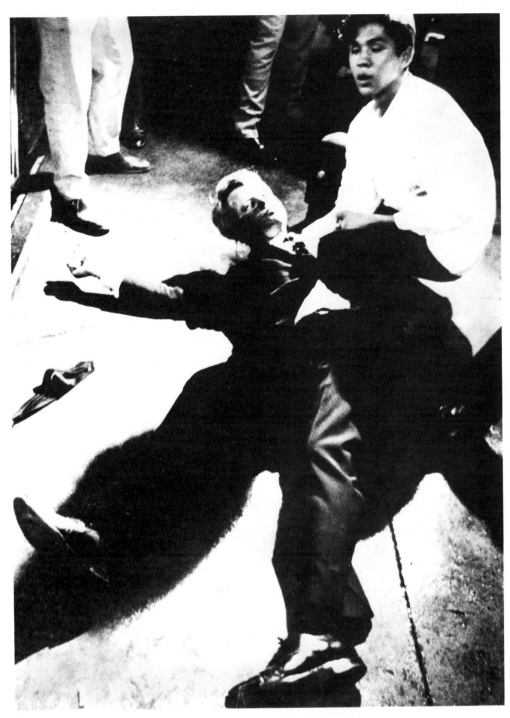

1970 and September 1973 experienced a brief period of Marxist revolutionary government under Dr Salvador Allende, but, after his reported suicide, reverted to the rule of a junta under General Pinochet.

In Canada the whiffs of French Separatism in Quebec grew stronger after 1967, though this has to some extent been checked by the premiership of Pierre Trudeau since April 1968.

The course of affairs in the USA can best be charted in the form of a chronological summary, keeping a watchful eye on four dominant features, her reversal in Vietnam, her Civil Rights problem with regard to race, the Watergate scandal, and her continuing international influence as still the most powerful of the world's three giants, the United States, the Soviet Union and the People's Republic of China.

In March 1968 it was announced that Robert Kennedy would challenge President Johnson as the Democratic presidential candidate; but in June of that year Kennedy was assassinated. In April 1968 the leader of the American blacks, Dr Martin Luther King, was assassinated, but in the same month a Civil Rights Bill passed through Congress. In August 1968 Mr Richard Nixon obtained the Republican and Mr Hubert Humphrey the Democratic party nominations respectively. During 1969 protests, especially from young Americans, against US involvement in Vietnam mounted steadily, and in December of that year Nixon, now president, announced the gradual withdrawal of American troops.

A beginning of rapprochement between the United States and the People's Republic of China was curiously enough signalled

WORLD EVENTS 1945–1979

Date	Europe	America	Asia and the Middle East	Africa
1945	War in Europe ends (May 1945) Potsdam talks between Allies (July 1945) Labour government elected in Britain (July 1945); nationalizes Bank of England, civil aviation, coal industry (1946), power and transport (1947) establishes National Health Service (1948) Communism established in: Bulgaria (1946) Poland (1947) Czechoslovakia (1948) Romania (1948) East Germany (1949) Hungary (1949) Marshall Aid instituted (1947) Organization of Europe; Community established (1948) Berlin air lift (1948) Federal Republic of West Germany founded (1949)	Death of F. D. Roosevelt, succeeded by Harry Truman (April 1945) Formation of Organization of American States (1948) Truman re-elected as president (1948)	Atomic bombs dropped on Hiroshima and Nagasaki, bringing war in Far East to an end (August 1945) Civil War in Indo-China (1946) Indian independence: Partition of India (1947) Assassination of Gandhi (1948) Arab-Israeli war: Zionist Jews declare new state of Israel (1948) Communists control North Korea and Northern China (1948) Ceasefire in Kashmir (1949) Laos, Indonesia, Cambodia, Vietnam declared independence (1949) Mao Tse-tung leader of Communist China (1949) Arab-Israeli armistice: Partition of Jerusalem (1949) Korean war starts (1949)	First African nominated for Kenya Legislative Council (1946) South Africa officially adopts apartheid policy (1948)
1950	North Atlantic Treaty Organization established (1950) Conservatives win British election (1951) Accession of Elizabeth II (1952) Death of Stalin (1953)	USA intervenes in Korean War (1950) Un-American Activities Committee set up (1950) Alger Hiss found guilty of perjury (1950) General MacArthur relieved of his command (1951) Dwight D. Eisenhower becomes president (1953)	India becomes an independent republic within the Commonwealth (1950) Iran nationalizes oil (1951) King Farouk of Egypt overthrown (1952) French defeated at Dien Bien Phu, withdraw from Indo-China (1954)	Fanatical anti-white sect, the Mau Mau, terrorizes Kenya (1952)
1955	Eden resigns over Suez (1956) Soviet troops quell revolt in Hungary (1956) British hydrogen bomb tested (1957) Launching of Sputnik I (1957) Charles de Gaulle president of France (1958) Nikita Krushchev (1958) prime minister of USSR (1958) Cyprus declared independent (1959)	Supreme Court rules against schools segregation (1955) Federal troops sent to Little Rock, Arkansas (1957)	Suez Crisis (1956) Syrian crisis (1957) New constitution for Singapore, CENTO established (1959)	Sir Roy Welensky prime minister of the Federation of Rhodesia (1956) Gold Coast becomes independent state of Ghana, Kwame Nkrumah as prime minister (1957) African National Congress banned in Rhodesia (1959)
1960	Uri Gagarin orbits the earth (1961) French veto British entry into Common Market (1963)	John F. Kennedy president (1961) Cuban crisis (1962) Kennedy assassinated: Lyndon Johnson becomes president (1963) Civil Rights Bill passed (1964)	Aswan dam begun (1960) Independence of Algeria (1962)	Nigeria becomes independent (1960) South Africa leaves Commonwealth (1961) Northern Rhodesia becomes Zambia (1964) Ian Smith prime minister of Southern Rhodesia (1964)
1965	Student riots (1968) Russia invades Czechoslovakia (1968) Willy Brandt becomes Chancellor of West Germany (1969) Solzhenitsyn expelled from Russia (1969)	Martin Luther King assassinated; Robert Kennedy assassinated; race riots (1968) Richard Nixon becomes president (1969) First man lands on moon (21 July 1969)	Cultural Revolution in China (1967) Six-day war between Israel and Arab states (1967)	Rhodesian UDI (Unilateral Declaration of Independence) (1965) Civil war in Nigeria (1967–70)
1970	Death of de Gaulle (1970) Death of Salazar and inauguration of democratic regime in Portugal (1970) Partition of Cyprus between pro-Greek and pro-Turkish governments (1973) Overthrow of right-wing colonels' regime in Greece (1973) Oil crisis (1973)	Nixon re-elected president (1972) Nixon visits China (1973) President Allende of Chile overthrown (1973) General Juan Peron returns to Argentina (1973) Mariner 10 probe reaches Venus (1974)	Bangladesh (formerly East Pakistan) becomes independent (1971) Yom Kippur war between Israel and Arab states followed by Arab restrictions on oil production (1973)	Emperor Haile Selassie of Ethiopia deposed (1974)
1975	Death of General Franco; succession of King Juan Carlos in Spain (1975) Election of a Pole, John-Paul II, as pope, the first non-Italian for four centuries (1978) Conservative election victory in Britain; Margaret Thatcher Europe's first woman prime minister (1979).	Jimmy Carter elected President (1976)	Civil war in Lebanon begins (1975) State of emergency in India (1975) US withdraws from South Vietnam, which falls to North Vietnam (1975) Death of Mao Tse-tung (1976) Mrs Gandhi defeated in elections (1977) Peace talks begin between Israel and Egypt (1977) Shah of Iran in exile (1979) Israel and Egypt sign peace treaty (1979)	Independence of Mozambique (1975) Death of Jomo Kenyatta (1978) First elected government to include non-whites takes office in Zimbabwe (Rhodesia) (1979)

by the visit in April 1971 of American table-tennis players to China.

In May 1972 President Nixon visited Moscow and in November was elected to a second term of office. However, in January 1973 the trial began of seven men accused of bugging Democratic headquarters in the Watergate building in Washington DC. Such damaging evidence then began to come to light concerning the malpractices of the Nixon administration that in October 1973 demands were heard from both the Republican and Democratic parties for the President's impeachment. In July 1974 the Supreme Court ruled that tapes carrying incriminating evidence against the president and his men must be handed over to the judicial enquiry, and on 8 August Nixon resigned his office, being immediately succeeded by the vice-president, Gerald Ford. In January 1975 the three chief defendants in the Watergate case were found guilty and received prison sentences, Nixon had received a pardon from President Ford and retired to his country estate. It would

be no exaggeration to state that Watergate gave a nasty smear to the image of American political life, which Ford and then his successor in November 1976 as Democratic president, Jimmy Carter, sought not unsuccessfully to remove.

Opposite top right, Vietnamese civilians vainly trying to scramble onto a departing transport as the Americans left Saigon, April 1975.

Opposite top left, President Nixon with Premier Chou En-Lai at a Peking banquet, 1972: since the early 1970s events in China have become more and more important to the West, and she must now be ranked with the USA and the USSR as a major world power.

Opposite bottom right, President Jimmy Carter (b. 1924, elected president 1977), walks down Pennsylvania Avenue from the Capitol with his wife and daughter after his inauguration as president. By 1979 Carter's popularity had declined considerably, as much because of changing views among Americans as to the president's role as because of his at times uninspiring performance.

Opposite centre left, cartoon by Herblock from the International Herald Tribune *published on 9 August 1974, the day President Nixon resigned.*

Opposite bottom left, Henry Kissinger (b. 1923), US Secretary of State 1973–77, famous for his 'shuttle diplomacy'.

727

Chapter 58

Headlines of History 1978-83

Europe

The oil crisis of 1973 marked the beginning of a world economic recession which, with ups and downs, lasted well into the 1980s. It affected all countries in varying degrees, though the most efficient manufacturing nations suffered least and the poorest producing nations suffered most. The recession was characterized by a problematic combination of falling production and rising prices: 'stagflation' ('stagnation' plus 'inflation') was the word coined for this unusual situation.

Opinions varied as to the means for curing these economic ills. In the West, harder times coincided with conservative governments, notably the Reagan administration in the USA and the Thatcher government in the UK. They regarded inflation as their worst enemy and attempted to combat it by control of the money supply and reduction of public-sector borrowing. The Federal Republic of Germany, the most prosperous European state, also gained a conservative (Christian Democratic) government in 1982 after the long and successful Social Democratic administrations of Brandt and Schmidt, but France opted for the socialists, led by François Mitterand, in 1981. Spain also elected a socialist government (1982).

In Britain the Thatcher government (elected in 1979) had considerable success in reducing inflation, though wages continued to rise at a faster rate and unemployment hovered around three million (over 12 per cent of the workforce) in 1982. Though Britain was fortunate in possessing the bonus of North Sea oil – an indirect effect of the 1973 oil crisis which encouraged exploitation of new reserves – the 1970s were a decade of economic failure. Inflation, unemployment, poor industrial relations (the so-called 'Winter of Discontent' in 1978-79 had brought down the Labour government), low productivity and falling output were problems common to industrial nations, but they were generally worse in Britain.

The poor economic performance lay behind some of Britain's social problems. In the summer of 1981 serious riots took place in impoverished metropolitan areas. High unemployment, especially among young blacks, was widely blamed. However, Celtic separatism, rising during the 1960s and '70s, petered out when less than the required forty per cent of Scottish and Welsh voters approved a bill for political devolution in a referendum (1979).

The Thatcher government gained in popularity after the successful expedition to expel Argentine forces from the Falklands in 1982, and it benefited from the weakness of the Labour Party, so badly divided that several Labour moderates resigned to form the new, centrist, Social Democratic Party in 1981. In the elections of 1983 the government increased its parliamentary majority.

No one could find a solution to the violence in Northern Ireland. Among numerous terrorist atrocities, Lord Mountbatten, Prince Philip's uncle, was assassinated in 1979. Ten internees committed suicide by hunger strike in the Maze prison in 1981, and the authorities adopted the doubtful expedient of granting favour to an informer, or 'supergrass', in an effort to convict republican terrorists.

Though fully committed to the Common Market, Britain remained an awkward member. It declined to join the European Monetary System, which was evolved in 1978 to stabilize exchange rates and was regarded by optimists as a step towards monetary union. Fisheries, the CAP and the budget also caused difficulties: by 1984 the Community's financial position was worrying. More positively, the first direct elections to the European assembly were held in 1979 and Greece joined the Community in 1981, with Spain, where democracy was reinforced by the failure of a right-wing coup in 1982, and Portugal to follow.

The policy of 'détente' which had improved relations between the USSR and the USA in the 1970s was destroyed by a series of developments of which the first and most important was the Soviet invasion of Afghanistan in December, 1979. Though generally allied to Moscow, Afghanistan was not a member of the Warsaw Pact, and the invasion provoked world-wide protest. The response from the West was ineffective: the USA (and some other countries) boycotted the 1980 Olympic Games in Moscow and briefly halted grain exports; the USSR promptly obtained their supplies from Argentina. However, in the excessively difficult terrain of Afghanistan, the Soviet forces became involved in a costly guerilla war with Afghan tribesmen.

Perhaps more worrying to the USSR were developments in Poland, where serious disturbances took place following food-price rises in 1980. The Polish Party chief, Edward Gierek, resigned, and a general programme of liberalization was forced on the government by the trade-

union movement known as Solidarity, with the vital support of the Roman Catholic Church (85 per cent of Poles were practising Roman Catholics and the current pope was a Pole). As the power of Solidarity, led by Lech Walesa, increased, Soviet intervention (as in Czechoslovakia in 1968) seemed probable: Warsaw Pact forces manoeuvred on the frontier. It was forestalled when the new prime minister, General Jaruzelski, declared martial law in December 1981; Walesa and other Solidarity leaders were interned. Martial law was suspended a year later, though Solidarity was still banned, and the economy showed little sign of improvement (Poland was effectively bankrupt by 1982 but kept afloat by Western banks). In 1983 Walesa was awarded the Nobel Peace Prize.

On the death of Leonid Brezhnev in November 1982, Yuri Andropov became First Secretary of the Communist Party of the USSR. Like his predecessor, he was in poor health and died in February 1984; the change in leadership had little effect on Soviet foreign policy. Relations with the USA were extremely unfriendly.

In Communist Europe generally, some tightening of security was evident. Dissatisfied East Germans found flight to the West more difficult (two families managed it in 1979 by hot-air balloon). In Rumania, despite some intense economic problems President Ceaucescu maintained his rela-

Above, anti-racialism rally in north London, late 1970s: the demonstrations held by the National Front, a tiny, fanatically racist party that never gained significant electoral support, provoked widespread counter-demonstrations in favour of racial equality and solidarity, though many people believed the consequent escalation of street violence harmed rather than helped the cause of racial integration.

Left, the body of German industrialist Hans Martin Schleyer, kidnapped and then shot by the Baader-Meinhof group, May 1977; by the late 1970s, kidnapping had become a favourite weapon of terrorist groups.

Above left, a British oil rig in the Brent oilfield off the Shetland Islands. Revenue from North Sea Oil provided a useful cushion for Britain's balance of payments difficulties but was not used to circumvent the general recession of the late 1970s.

tively independent foreign policy, including friendly relations with China and Israel. The death of that giant among political leaders, Marshal Tito, aroused fears for the stability and independence of Communist Yugoslavia in 1980, but the collective leadership which had already taken over held firm.

Many countries besides Britain experienced a rise in civil conflict which could be ascribed partly at least to the parlous times. In Turkey terrorism reached such a pitch (over 1,000 deaths in 1978) that the military coup of 1980, accompanied by suspension of the constitution, was widely welcomed. Under a new constitution, the military leader, General Evren, was elected president in 1982.

Since the Turkish invasion of 1974, Cyprus had been effectively partitioned into Turkish (the northern third) and Greek regions. Many Greek Cypriots lost their homes and livelihoods. Compromise between the Greek and Turkish Cypriot leaders (Kyprianou and Denktash) proved impossible, and the socialist government of Andreas Papandreou in Greece, which took a more militant attitude, helped to provoke Denktash into a unilateral declaration of independence in 1983.

The Far East

The difficulty of Westerners in understanding the affairs of China was exacerbated by a new Chinese phonetic system (1979), in which (for example) Mao Tse-tung becomes Mao Zedong. Internal liberalization and democracy proceeded at a modest pace: the 'Freedom Wall' in Peking (Beijing) where hitherto intolerable ideas could be posted up, came to an end in 1979 when criticism of the Communist system became too frank. New constitutional arrangements in 1982 reduced the powers of the high party officials and increased those of the prime minister and civil service. Contacts with the outside world, notably the West, also increased, but at a similarly cautious pace. A treaty of friendship with Japan (1978) was fiercely resented by the Soviet Union which, however, forfeited the possibility of Sino-Soviet reconciliation by its invasion of Afghanistan.

security threat in the Far East was responsible for its shooting-down of a South Korean airliner which had strayed over Soviet territory in 1983. South Korea suffered a series of shocks, notably assassinations (President Park in 1979, several cabinet ministers in 1983), riots and martial law (1980).

The Indian sub-continent

Following the collapse of the Janata coalition, Mrs Indira Gandhi staged one of the most remarkable political comebacks in history in the general election of 1979. Her party gained two-thirds of the seats. India's persistent social and economic problems, partly stemming from overpopulation, were no less, despite some improvements in agricultural productivity, and Mrs Gandhi suffered a personal blow when her son and close associate, Sanjay, was killed in an air accident (1980). The worst of India's many regional conflicts, which arose from Hindu resentment of the numerous Muslim immigrants from Bangladesh in Assam, resulted in over 4,000 deaths in 1983.

In Bangladesh itself, Ziaur Rahman

made himself a consitutional president and won popular elections in 1979, but he was assassinated in 1981. A year later the army again seized power. Similarly, General Zia of Pakistan delayed plans to return his country to democracy. His regime pursued a policy of 'Islamization' and Urdu nationalism and was characterized by shifts from relative liberality to harsh, authoritarian rule. The presence of Afghan refugees in the north-west caused a series of frontier 'incidents'.

Long-suppressed social hostilities also affected Sri Lanka, where the animosity of the Sinhalese towards the minority Tamils broke into violence little short of civil war in 1983. The government made insignificant attempts to defend the Tamils, many of whom sought refuge in southern India where Tamils form the majority of the population.

The Middle East

From 1978 to 1980 Western news media were dominated by the sensational events in Iran. Internal opposition to the pro-Western and repressive regime of the Shah reached such a pitch that in January 1979 his own appointed prime minister insisted on the Shah leaving the country as a condition of taking office. The government

Opposite, Lech Walesa leading a delegation of Solidarity workers in 1980. Walesa quickly assumed leadership of the trade union movement in Poland during the Gdansk shipyard strikes of 1980, and attempted to restrain it from posing an outright challenge to Communist Pary rule in Poland.

Left, Pope John Paul II (b. 1920), elected pope 1978), the first non-Italian pope for over 400 years: as a Pole, whose ministry had until his election as pope been entirely conducted under a Communist regime, he is thought by many to be particularly suitable to guide the Catholic church in its increasing dialogue with the non-Christian world.

even so failed to re-establish control of the country and in February the elderly religious leader, the Ayatollah (imam) Khomeini, returned from exile. The government collapsed and a revolutionary committee was set up consisting of religious leaders and dominated by the harsh grey eminence of Khomeini. According to the announced result of a referendum, 98 per cent voted for 'an Islamic republic' but the primitive type of 'Islamization' favoured by Khomeini was relentless to all opponents, including the Communists who had hitherto regarded themselves as allies of the Iranian revolution. An unknown number of citizens were judicially murdered after nonsense trials, besides the thousands killed in street fighting.

Animosity towards the USA, where the ailing Shah had gone for treatment, was expecially ferocious, and in November Iranian 'students' occupied the US embassy, holding fifty-two people as hostages for return of the Shah (the British embassy was also occupied, but for a few hours only). A US expedition to free the hostages was aborted in the Iranian Desert (April 1980) and they were finally released in January 1981 (six months after the Shah's death in Egypt). This episode clearly demonstrated the powerlessness of even the mightiest states in certain circumstances. Sporadic violence continued in Iran: the president and prime minister were killed by a bomb in August 1981.

Revolutionary energies were diverted into war when Iran was attacked by Iraq in September 1980. Iraq's expectation that the anarchic state of Iran would render it defensively feeble was disappointed, and neither side in the Gulf War could establish a decisive advantage.

The militant, extremist 'Islamization' of Khomeini and his associates signified a trend already evident in Gaddafi's Libya, which worried conservative Arab states like Saudi Arabia, where an obscure group succeeded in occupying the holy shrine of Mecca for three weeks in 1979, as well as the Soviet Union (with its large Muslim minority) and Western countries anxious about their oil supplies. The division between Shi'ite and Sunni Muslims was an increasingly likely source of conflict in countries like Iraq and Syria.

Syria, under the strong regime of President Assad and with heavy Soviet backing, appeared to have designs on the Lebanon, designs shared by its archenemy, Israel, supported by the USA. Both countries had differences with their sponsors; e.g. some US military supplies were witheld after an Israeli raid against an Iraqi nuclear plant in 1981.

The endemic fighting in the Lebanon took a new turn in June 1982 when Israel launched a full-scale invasion with the aim of driving out the Palestinian guerillas who

had mounted small but frequent raids over the border for some years. Beirut was surrounded and Yasser Arafat agreed to withdraw his men under Israeli pressure. Two weeks later Christian militiamen, incensed by the assassination of their leader (and Lebanese president) Bashir Gemayel, massacred hundreds of Palestinian civilians in the refugee camps. Israel, whose troops commanded the area at the time, was held responsible. Amin Gemayel replaced his more aggressive brother, and Israeli and Syrian troops withdrew from Beirut (though not from the Lebanon), being replaced by 'peace-keeping' forces from the USA, France, Italy and Britain. Violence continued, while the PLO defeat, following accusations of incompetence and

corruption, turned Syria against Arafat and in favour of a rebel PLO group. In 1983 Arafat was besieged in Tripoli, whose citizens suffered as had those of Beirut the year before, until Arafat's men were forced to leave. Early in 1984 Gemayel's government coalition collapsed and the peace-keeping forces left Beirut as the civil war resumed.

After the Israeli pull-back and the retirement of Prime Minister Begin in 1983, Israeli–US relations resumed their former warmth: President Reagan and Prime Minister Yitzhak Shamir reached new agreement on strategic co-operation in the region, signalling their intent to force the Syrians out of the Lebanon.

President Sadat of Egypt was assassi-

Left, the Ayatollah Khomeini as figurehead of the Islamic Republican Army in its overthrow of the Shah of Iran in 1979. Though virulently anti-American, fears that the Islamic nationalists were Moscow stooges seemed unjustified as Khomeini's regime won control of the country.

Opposite, an innocent victim of the Beirut civil war, which continued through the late 1970s and in the early 1980s drew in external powers such as Syria, Israel, the Palestinians and the United States.

nated in 1981 after civil disturbances and the imposition of authoritarian measures. His successor, Hosni Mubarak, pursued a more cautious foreign policy, softpedalling the Egyptian–Israeli rapprochment and seeking better relations with Arab neighbours.

Africa

For most Africans, as indeed other peoples, these years were dominated by economic considerations, with longestablished patterns of hardship aggravated by the results of the world recession.

Ethiopia's leaders failed to grapple with the huge economic difficulties but, thanks to Soviet support, drove back both the Somalis and the nationalist rebels of Eritrea. In Uganda, Amin's foolish attack on Tanzania in 1978 led to his downfall: Tanzanian troops invaded and he fled. In 1980 Milton Obote returned to rule Uganda after nine years.

The state of chronic civil war in Chad gained new significance with the intervention of Libya, which was suspected of coveting Chad's territory. In 1983 the Libyans halted their latest advance as French troops arrived in the south.

Economic problems lay behind a massive refugee problem in West Africa. Nigerian prosperity, based on oil, had attracted many immigrant workers but in the 1980s the recession caused high unemployment. Early in 1983 the Nigerian government expelled all 'foreigners' to leave at two weeks' notice. About two million people, the largest number from Ghana, were involved.

Nigeria had returned to civilian rule in 1980, but succumbed to a coup on the last day of 1983. Elsewhere the coup was a common occurrence: the unlikely-sounding Flight Lieutenant Jerry Rawlings took over in Ghana twice (1979 and 1981).

In the Republic of South Africa, the replacement of Vorster (later implicated in a political-corruption scandal nicknamed 'Muldergate') by Pieter Botha brought a breath of – by Afrikaner standards – liberalism. Botha's modest reforms caused a minor split in the Nationalist party, an ultra-Right group led by Andries Treurnicht breaking away. Botha's government introduced a measure of political representation for 'Coloureds' and Asians, but *apartheid* remained in force for blacks (the majority) and the government pursued the policy of creating black 'homelands' or Bantustans, regarded as autonomous states by the South African government but as glorified labour camps by the rest of the world. There were serious riots, notably in Soweto (the black suburb of

Johannesburg) in 1980, among other portents of larger conflict.

The future status of Namibia (South-West Africa), mandated to South Africa by the League of Nations in 1920, remained in doubt due to the insuperable difficulty of obtaining a government acceptable to both South Africa and the majority of the inhabitants, in particular the South West Africa People's Organization (SWAPO). South African operations against SWAPO guerillas included raids on their camps deep in Angola.

In Rhodesia the Smith regime finally surrendered to the pressure of the Patriotic Front. Agreement ending the seven-year civil war was reached at Lancaster House in London in 1979. The country, renamed Zimbabwe, held its first elections under majority rule in 1980, and Robert Mugabe, leader of ZANU, secured a sweeping victory. He headed a coalition government which included Nkomo, leader of ZAPU, and several white ministers. Although initial problems were largely overcome, a split between the two main African components, ZANU (essentially a Shona organization) and ZAPU (Ndebele) soon developed. Korean-trained government troops ravaged the Ndebele homeland and Nkomo, in fear of arrest, took temporary refuge in England in 1983.

The Americas

Jimmy Carter, the first Southern president of the USA since the Civil War, was elected in the year of the 200th anniversary of independence (1976), but his administration was beleaguered by the energy crisis, Congressional opposition, the falling value of the dollar and, above all, the problem of the diplomatic hostages in Iran. In 1980 the conservative Republican, Ronald Reagan, defeated him decisively.

Though wounded in an assassination attempt (March 1981), Reagan had considerable success in restoring the image of the USA as a mighty nation. He vastly increased military spending and reduced taxes at the expense of social welfare, though in practice his administration was generally less right-wing than its propaganda suggested. Excellent at public relations, Reagan announced at the age of seventy-two that he would seek re-election in 1984.

Reagan's tough foreign policy explicitly favoured pro-USA dictators in preference to hostile popular leaders, a doctrine which led to support of the much-hated governments in El Salvador, where civil war began in 1979, and Guatemala, as well as the rightist guerillas who attacked the leftist, Sandinista government in Nicara-

gua. In Latin America generally, economic problems (which brought potentially rich nations like Argentina and Brazil to the verge of bankruptcy) exacerbated the older political and social divisions. Democracy was in abeyance even in some countries which maintained the form of popular consent. Brazil returned to civil rule in 1982 but real power remained with the generals; Guyana's elections of 1980 were described by British observers as 'fraudulent'. The example of Bolivia was more typical: the military coup of 1979 was the 200th in its history.

In 1982 the military government in Argentina, led by General Galtieri, seized the Falkland Islands (Malvinas), occupied by the British for a century and a half. The act was condemned by the UN and, after negotiations had failed, the British sent a powerful 'task force' which, after a three-week campaign (with over 1,000 casualties) compelled an Argentine surrender. The discredited generals gave way to civilian rule in 1983, though the quarrel over possession of the Falklands ('two bald men fighting over a comb' – Jose Luis Borges) remained unsolved and Argentina's economic problems were worse than ever.

The leftist government which had held power in Grenada since the coup of 1979 was itself overthrown by a more extreme

Opposite, Soweto township, Johannesburg, the scene of severe riots during the summer of 1976: despite South Africa's increasing isolation from the international community and her occasional superficial attempts at integration in the mid 1980s the apartheid policy seemed as well entrenched as ever.

Left, British troops go ashore at San Carlos, on East Falkland, in May 1982. Despite their stretched lines of communication, and fierce opposition from the Argentinian air force, the professional and highly trained British forces were more than a match for their mainly conscripted opponents.

group, whose leaders were presumably backed by Cuba, in 1983. In co-operation with neighbouring Caribbean states and with the support of the Governor-General, the USA invaded Grenada and destroyed the new regime. This example of the Reagan government's determination to resist communism in 'its own backyard' contradicted international law and the UN charter, but was welcomed by the great majority of Grenadians.

Canada solved some constitutional problems in this period. The Canadian constitution itself was 'patriated', which necessitated a special act of the British parliament, in 1982. The separatist movement subsided when the Quebecois voted in a referendum to reject secession (1980). The veteran prime minister, Pierre Trudeau, having announced retirement after electoral defeat in 1979, was back in power a year later – a fact which probably influenced the Quebec referendum. He continued, tactfully, to distance Canada from its powerful neighbour, the USA, taking a less hostile stance against the USSR.

Chapter 59

The 1980s: Trends and Prospects

One world, many nations

There is one obvious, long-term trend in modern history, which has grown much more marked in the years since the Second World War and is often glibly summed up in the term 'One World'. This is fundamentally a matter of the dramatic improvement in forms of transport and communications. Five centuries ago Europeans did not know that North America existed; today, a European businessman can fly to New York in the morning, conduct a day's business and fly back at night. He can contact any city in the world by telephone in a matter of seconds, and he can transmit documents and photographs almost instantaneously. Moreover, none of this is expensive, relatively speaking; modern communications are not only much faster than the methods they replaced, they are also cheaper.

This has led to a certain superficial sameness. Our international businessman, attending conferences in London, New York, Hong Kong and Tel Aviv, will find his associates dressed in suits indistinguishable from his own. Whether he travels with Air India, Pan Am or Lufthansa, the actual aeroplane is likely to be identical. He may, if he likes, hire the same kind of car, stay in the same kind of hotel and eat much the same kind of food, although in this area, thank goodness, local variety is more easily obtainable. He will also find it much easier than—say—a Venetian merchant of the fifteenth century to conduct complicated business arrangements with foreigners. Though he may need an interpreter, in another sense international businessmen, like engineers and scientists, 'speak the same language'. Perhaps more significantly, the particular goods or services that the international businessman is engaged in producing probably have a world-wide market.

It is true that a large proportion of the world's population are still peasants living in rural areas where life has not changed greatly for centuries. But in the cities, which have always led the way in social change, the general similarity of everyday arrangements is striking. The significance of this is easily missed. The tourist in Britain may smile at the helmet of the policeman directing the London traffic. How quaint! But much more remarkable is the fact that there is a similar official, performing a similar task, back home in Texas or Tashkent.

In spite of the trend towards a similarity of experience throughout the world, largely the result of the successful export of the material forms of European civilization, there has been no significant reduction of human conflict in world terms. Since the World War ended in 1945 there has been scarcely a moment when there was no war of some kind going on somewhere in the world. However, most of the wars of the past forty years, even those that have involved the major powers in some capacity, have been local, and in many cases (e.g. the Vietnam War) they have been essentially civil wars. Notoriously, civil wars are the most vicious, but they are by definition conflicts between groups of people who have much in common.

To a great extent, human conflict arises from a failure to understand the point of view of one's opponent. If two motorists have a minor collision, no matter what the circumstances, even the driver who appears obviously at fault will have some reason to blame the other party. This universal human inability to adopt a neutral view in a personal disagreement is vastly magnified when larger groups, or nations, are involved. Just as no person who learns another language as an adult can hope to speak it without a trace of the accent that betrays his native tongue, no government, church or individual diplomat can ever negotiate, no matter how good their intentions, without an inbuilt and ineradicable cultural bias that colours their point of view. Thus, the terrorists and assassins of the Provisional IRA in Northern Ireland are subsidized by solid, conservative US citizens of Irish descent who would be utterly appalled by such a group as the Provisionals in any other context.

The similarity of experience which is so notable a feature of the modern world has so far made little impression on the fundamental difficulties of comprehension between peoples of a different cultural heritage. For the most part, people can agree to be different; indeed, most of us like it that way (the world would be a deadly boring place if we were really all the same). However, when a dispute

arises, such as the question of rightful sovereignty in the Falkland Islands, it is often impossible to settle it by objective reasoning. Debates in the UN General Assembly clearly reveal, not only that the delegates speak in many mutually incomprehensible languages, but that they have totally alien views of this or that subject, which cannot be reconciled by any interpreter.

The United Nations is the organization which most explicitly acknowledges the 'One World' doctrine. Its performance as a forum for peaceful resolution of international disputes since its foundation has disappointed many people, especially in the West, but the UN agencies have done immensely valuable work in combating numerous social and economic ills, and perhaps too much has been expected of the UN's political role. Western countries in particular have never been willing to make any sacrifice affecting their national sovereignty and have tended to underestimate the significance of the UN as a political organization to the Third World.

UN peace-keeping forces have been sent to many of the world's troublespots, including Zaire (during the civil war that followed independence), the Middle East and Cyprus. Though they provided an important service and in some places probably prevented many deaths, the UN did not and could not have much impact on the fundamental sources of those conflicts. Still less has the UN had a more than transitory effect on the conduct of the Cold War, the ideologically based hostility be-

tween the USSR and the USA with their satellites and allies. These two groups of nations, which included virtually all the industrialized, manufacturing countries, were numerically balanced by the countries of what has become known as the Third World, i.e. preponderantly the under-developed, producing countries (many of recent formation) of Asia and Africa. None of the three main groups, not even the Soviet bloc, were solid monoliths, and the world recession following the energy crisis of 1973 revealed very marked differences, economical as well as political, in the countries of the Third World, where some countries were desperately poor and some comparatively rich.

The long-delayed admission of China to the UN in 1971 apparently confirmed it as a third great power, alongside the USSR and the USA, with an obvious claim to leadership of the Third World. By weight of numbers if nothing else, China must be recognised as a great power, but its comparative backwardness in the economic sphere, its preoccupation with internal developments and its lack of imperialistic ambitions (despite the occupation of Tibet and border disputes with India), have so far combined to mask its international potential. There are several ironies in the Chinese situation. For example, though its system of government is Communist and totalitarian, it has become more hostile to the USSR than to the Western bloc. Should China's fears for its security be lulled, this situation may change.

Arms and man

One effect of war has often been a demand that in future it should be waged, if at all, in a less destructive way. In the Middle Ages, serious fears were expressed that the invention of the cross-bow would lead to the extermination of humanity; but disarmament was not taken very seriously at international level until after the carnage of the First World War. It was then believed that an international arms race not only imposed severe economic burdens but also made the eventual outbreak of war inevitable. After the Second World War, which had been concluded with the horrifying destruction of Hiroshima and Nagasaki by atom bombs, the question of disarmament assumed new importance. The atom bomb was soon superseded by more formidable nuclear weapons. The hydrogen bomb, first tested in 1952, employed nuclear fusion to a destructive effect hundreds of times greater than the atomic (fission) bomb, while the means of delivering the bombs to their targets also became far more effective. There were more sophisticated weapons, like the neutron bomb (approved by President Reagan in 1981), which was designed to minimise blast and maximise radiation, thus killing larger numbers of people but destroying less property. By 1980 some form of disarmament was universally recognized—with varying earnestness—as essential, since the existing stockpiles of nuclear weapons were more than enough to destroy all life on Earth.

Discussions and negotiations on disarmament have been held at the UN and at various levels between various parties since 1945. There have been some minor successes. The Nuclear Test-Ban Treaty of 1963 which outlawed all nuclear tests, was signed by the USSR, the USA and the UK, though France refused to sign since it made no attempt to restrict the build-up of nuclear weapons (it was cynically suggested that the signatories had no further need of tests whereas France's programme was incomplete). Many other countries have acceded to it since, but while it contributed to the preservation of the environment from the effects of radiation, it had no effect on the arms race. In 1967 agreement was reached on banning nuclear weapons in space, and 59 states signed a nuclear non-proliferation treaty. In 1969, the talks between the USSR and USA known as SALT (Strategic Arms Limitation Talks; there is another series ominously known as START) began; they resulted in rather limited agreements, SALT I (1974) and SALT II (1979), and the latter ran foul of the US Congress, which was particularly incensed by the Soviet invasion of Afghanistan.

The main strategic role of nuclear weapons has been deterrence. The USA and the USSR are each capable of inflicting devastating damage on each other even if attacked first (a situation known as Mutually Assured Destruction, or MAD!). Up to the early 1960s the USA held an undoubted advantage, creating a degree of

complacency in North America and some consternation in the USSR, which subsequently closed the gap and, by the end of the 1970s, had pulled ahead, at least in offensive striking power. Limited disarmament talks tended to founder on the inevitable disagreement as to what constituted parity. Thus in 1983 progress towards further disarmament came to a complete halt for a time when the USSR withdrew from talks in Geneva as a result of the deployment in Europe of Cruise and Pershing missiles, the latter in particular representing a new and direct threat to Soviet territory. However, these missiles had arrived to balance the extensive deployment of similar weapons in Europe by the USSR during previous years. The Soviet answer to that was that the USSR was already threatened by the largely sea-based nuclear arsenal (including Polaris submarines) of the Western powers—France and Britain as well as the USA.

In short, disarmament was a subject of much propaganda and little effective action. Both sides at Geneva tended to accuse the other of negotiating in bad faith; a series of proposals by President Reagan in Washington, including his 'zero option' of 1981, were regarded as mere public-relations exercises in Moscow.

Meanwhile, the fears of ordinary people in the West led to the growth of the so-called 'peace movement', which became more militant in the early 1980s as defence budgets soared and missiles proliferated. The earlier popular campaigns for nuclear disarmament had languished during the 1960s and Western governments were surprised by the intensity of this renewed protest. A substantial minority demanded unilateral disarmament, and US bases in Europe, such as Greenham Common in England, came under more-or-less permanent siege.

Governments took the view that unilateral disarmament would increase the chance of being attacked. It was true that deterrence had apparently worked—nuclear weapons had not been used since 1945—but nobody could be sure that it would work for ever or that the outbreak of nuclear war by accident, such as a computer fault, is impossible. Pessimists also pointed out that even if agreement should be reached on multilateral disarmament and all of the nuclear powers disposed of their weapons, what cannot be banned is the ability to make them. The knowledge that mankind is capable of destroying itself and every other species into the bargain is something the world had to learn to live with in the last quarter of the twentieth century.

The advances in weaponry were not confined to nuclear bombs and their delivery systems. The deadly little wars of recent times have been made possible by the effectiveness and availability of arms manufactured by a comparatively small group of

industrial nations. Terrorists in Northern Ireland carried Soviet rifles (allegedly supplied by Libya). It was significant that Iran, a commercial outcast after the Islamic revolution, was able to obtain highly sophisticated weapons, parts and ammunition sufficient to fight the Gulf War (although, like many terrorist organizations, it was apparently forced to employ unorthodox methods for at least some items).

Weapons, nuclear or 'conventional', are likely to become ever more commonplace. As with other current world problems, little can be expected from treatment of the symptoms (e.g. talks about limited disarmament) rather than the basic sources of conflict.

Population

It is now nearly two hundred years since Malthus wrote his *Essay on Population* in which he advanced the view that since population increases in a geometrical ratio while the means of subsistence increase only in an arithmetical ratio, population is bound to outrun resources unless checked by disaster such as war or famine. During the nineteenth century Malthus's theory seemed to have been conclusively disproved, mainly because of the vast increase in food production following from

colonization and transport improvements. Actually, Malthus got a lot of things wrong, for instance his assumption that population growth arose largely from a rising birth rate. The chief cause was—and is—a falling death rate. However, in the twentieth century, Malthus's fears, in a different form, have come to appear justified.

Since Malthus's time the world population has increased at a much faster rate than even he conceived. Moreover, Malthus was right about the geometrical ratio: the *rate* of population growth has constantly increased. The result is that the total population of the world today is roughly one-quarter of the total number of human beings who have ever lived. In 1976 the human population passed the four-billion mark, and if present trends continue that figure will double in forty-three years.

In modern industrial society, if each woman produces two children the population remains stable. Before about 1700, it was necessary for each woman to produce about seven children to keep the population level steady because of the high rate of infant mortality. Moreover, the average age of the world population is now very low: roughly one-third are children under the age of fourteen. This means that the proportion by which the birth rate

exceeds the death rate will increase.

As the Earth's resources are finite, it will be impossible to maintain the present rate of population growth indefinitely. Despite the millions who are hungry, there is in brutal fact no shortage of food in the world as a whole, nor has the Earth's food-producing potential reached anything like its limit. It may be that the dire prophecies of the present, like those of Malthus two centuries ago, will be contradicted by some unforeseen breakthrough in food production and distribution. And it was Malthus himself who said, 'no estimate of future population . . . can be depended upon.' Nevertheless, there must be a limit, and our current knowledge suggests that it is approaching rapidly.

The irony of the population explosion is that the means exist to control it. Recent historical research has shown that people in past ages did practise birth control to a greater extent than might have been expected, but it is only in the past generation that simple and effective devices to prevent unwanted pregnancy have become widely available. The first world conference on population was held in Rumania in 1974, and today, nearly every country in the world operates or subsidizes a family-planning programme. In some countries, like China, where 20 per cent of the present world population lives, there

are strong inducements to restrict family numbers. Family planning figures in the Chinese constitution and there are rewards for those couples who opt for sterilization after only one child. (There have been occasional reports, from India for example, of local officials enforcing sterilization in unjust and inhuman ways).

But apart from the problems involved in administering such programmes, there is a limit to the effectiveness of government policy in changing ancient social customs. For one reason or another, about 65 per cent of the world's families do not practise birth control and thus, although some countries have shown a decline in the rate of population growth as a result of family planning, the overall growth has not been greatly affected.

Action appropriate to one culture may be unworkable in another. The Indian government's intense propaganda efforts in support of birth control and sterilization have had very little effect in spite of some isolated cases (in the poverty-stricken state of Kerala, population growth in the 1970s and 1980s dipped sharply, for somewhat obscure reasons). It has become clear that the Indian government's approach to the population problem, based on Western practice, has been largely unsuccessful; publicity posters and family-planning clinics have not answered. More fundamental

forms of social change are required. For example, in the agrarian society which most of India still is, the status of women is low, their economic prospects are poor, and the result is that they get married at the first opportunity. Were the status of women to be raised to a level roughly equal with men, as in Western society by and large, woman would marry later in life and would have smaller families. There are numerous complications in the world population problem however; what appears superficially simple turns out, as in other world-wide social problems, to be involved with tradition and custom in ways that perhaps no one can fully understand. Until very recent times, in most societies it was regarded as desirable to have as many children (especially boys) as possible. This attitude is still very common—and not only in under-developed countries where a large family represents insurance for old age. Some of the highest rates of population growth at present are to be found in Latin America. In a country like Brazil or Argentina there is no compulsion towards smaller families, rather the contrary, since the nation's unexploited economic potential is thought to depend on a larger population.

These are also, of course, Roman Catholic countries, and the influence of the Roman Catholic Church is certainly a

Above, starvation in India: vital though the task of feeding the hungry is, it must be accompanied by efforts to release the developing world from its economic dependence on the richer nations.

Opposite, women from the Greenham Common peace-camp in Britain in January 1983, dancing on the silos built to receive the US 'cruise' missiles. This women-only camp withstood a barrage of official harassment from its foundation in 1981 and became the focus for the peace-movement's challenge to the basic assumptions of military planning.

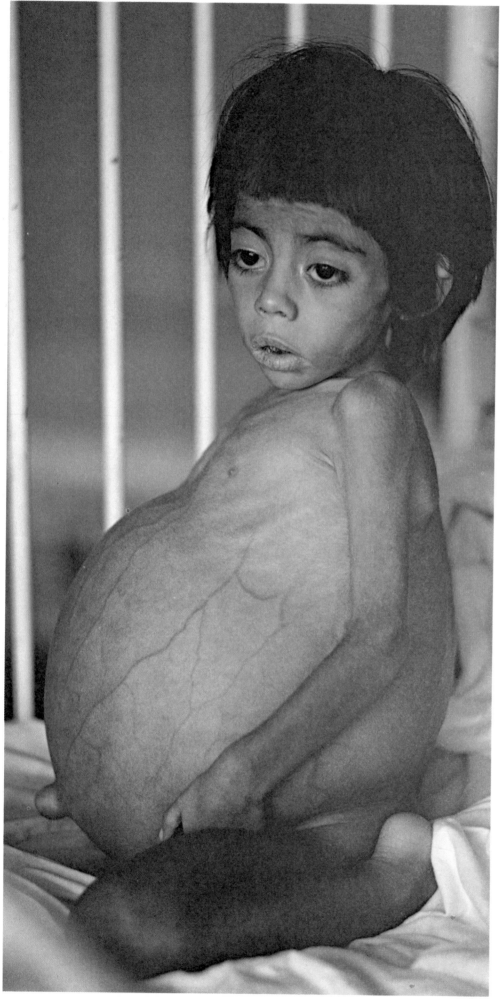

factor in encouraging large families. The Church condemns abortion utterly, and in most Roman Catholic countries it is illegal. The Church has also been traditionally hostile to artificial methods of birth control, though its attitude in this area is slightly more ambivalent.

Rich and poor

Despite the achievements of technologically advanced countries, the modern world remains divided into rich and poor; the gap, already immense, between the rich nations of the industrialized West and the impoverished lands of much of Africa and Asia has not been closed to any appreciable extent in the past generation; according to most estimates, it has actually widened. According to figures published by the World Bank (a UN agency which funds development in the Third World) in 1980, annual per capita income growth in the developing countries, 2.8 per cent, slightly exceeded the figure for developed countries (2.4 per cent). However, in 33 'least-developed' countries, the figure was under 2 per cent. The effects of the world recession of the 1970s were worst in the poor producing nations, which had to pay far more for vital fuel and imports while their own exports showed no comparable increase and, in terms of value, actually declined in some cases.

Since the world at large has embraced the Western idea that material improvement is a worthy, desirable and attainable aim for all people, the disparity between rich and poor, or 'industrialized' and 'under-developed', or between 'North' and 'South' (since the great majority of the rich countries are in the northern hemisphere and vice-versa), was widely recognized as posing serious political as well as economic problems. The report of a commission headed by former West German chancellor Willy Brandt (its distinguished membership included a former British prime minister, Edward Heath), published in 1980 under the title, 'North–South: a programme for survival', outlined the dangers and recommended solutions. It acknowledged many factors which have combined to thwart efforts to close the gap, including population growth that outpaces economic development, resistance to modernization in regions where non-Western cultural traditions are strong, and the unwillingness of the rich nations, especially during a recession, to make the kind of material sacrifice that is necessary.

The seventeen industrial countries of the Development Assistance Committee (DAC) provided £33 billion in aid in 1980, about half of which was private investment. The USA alone provided one-third of official development assistance. The aim of the DAC is that each member should

contribute at least 1 per cent of its GNP (gross national product) in aid, but not all members had achieved that modest ratio by 1983.

As long as the human race exists some people will no doubt be richer than others; that distinction still survives in relatively egalitarian, communist countries today, though it is less marked than in most capitalist countries. The contrast in the standard of life of people in rich and poor countries in the modern world is, however, as great as the contrast between European lord and peasant in the Middle Ages—indeed, probably greater in view of the effects of modern medicine in improving life in the developed countries.

The richest country in the world in the 1980s was the USA. Measured in terms of gross national product, the USA represented just over one-quarter of the world total. Four countries (the USA, USSR, Japan and West Germany) made up over half the total, leaving over 200 countries (including several relatively wealthy ones in Western Europe) to account for the remainder. In terms of GNP per head of the population, the league table was rather different. Among the leading states were Kuwait, the United Arab Emirates, Qatar and Libya, with Saudi Arabia one place higher than Japan and eight places higher than Britain. This of course reflected the value of oil exports.

GNP is not the only measure of national wealth, and is not necessarily a reliable indicator of the quality of life. In general, people in the modern world live longer than their ancestors, even in most poor countries, but there were extraordinary discrepancies in figures for the decade of the 1970s. There were 33 countries where life expectancy exceeded 70 (Norway was highest at 75). All but seven of these were in Europe or North America. By contrast, there were 25 countries where life expectancy was below 42 (the Upper Volta was lowest, at 32). All but three of these countries (Afghanistan, Indonesia and Laos) were in Africa. Of the 50 countries with life expectancy below 48, all were in Africa, Asia or South America.

Death rates gave a similar picture, though it was noticeable that the lowest death rates occurred in small countries, notably some of the islands of Oceania. (Andorra, Iceland and Lichtenstein were the lowest in Europe.)

The main causes of the low life expectancy in poor countries have been two:

Above, Pakistani women receiving family planning advice: controlling the rate of population growth is one of the greatest problems currently facing the world.

Opposite, a starving child, victim of the world's inability to organize its food supplies.

743

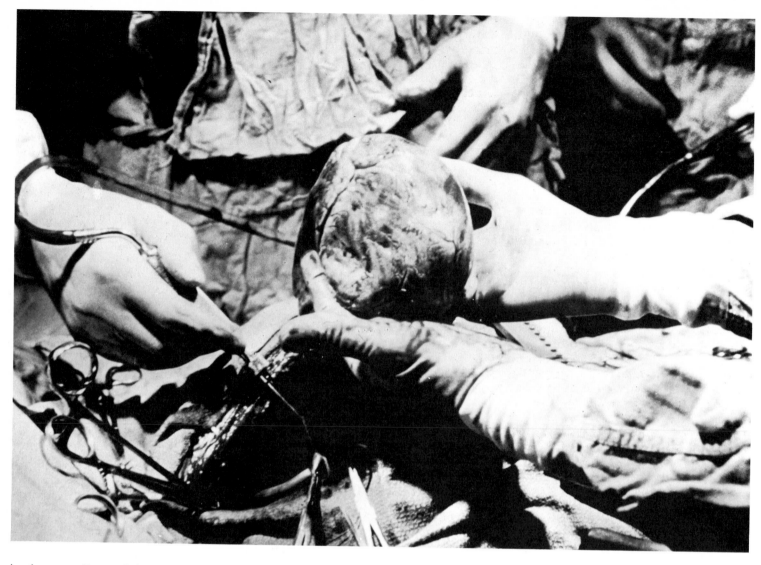

inadequate diet and inadequate medical care. According to UN estimates, the majority of people in the world in the early 1980s did not get enough to eat. In particular, prevailing diets in the poor countries of Africa and Asia were deficient in proteins and vitamins. This malnutrition alone gave rise, directly or indirectly, to disease on a massive scale. In large areas of the world, the child population lives continually on the brink of nutritional disaster. One slight mishap such as a poor harvest is enough to produce a clinical condition; while common diseases like measles, which pose no threat to healthy children, will kill the undernourished child.

The World Health Organization (WHO), a UN agency, is the body most intimately concerned with rectifying this situation on a world-wide basis. In 1982–83 it was active in 130 countries and had a budget of nearly $500 million. It has achieved some notable triumphs, such as the abolition of smallpox which (according to WHO) was eradicated throughout the world in 1980.

There are a great many diseases which are unknown in Europe (except for the odd outbreak like the rabies scare in the late 1970s) but afflict the tropical and semi-tropical countries of the Third World. Some are insect-borne, such as malaria (still one of the greatest killers though now absent from all Europe and most of North America), filariasis (elephantiasis), yellow fever (responsible for preventing possible economic development in South America), sleeping sickness (carried by the tse-tse fly which in the 1970s appeared to be spreading in parts of Africa) and plague (outbreaks still occur in India). Other diseases result from lack of sanitation, a prime concern of WHO which has the stated aim of bringing everyone within fifteen minutes walk of a safe water supply. They include typhoid, cholera (a new variety appeared in the Far East in the 1960s and within twelve years reached parts of south-west Europe) and various types of diarrhoeal disease which appeared to be increasing in the 1980s.

Other infections may not be fatal but have a dreadful effect on the quality of life. Bilharzia affected 200 million people in 1982, many being unable to walk. Leprosy, which is comparatively easy to control as prolonged contact (such as baby with mother) is required for infection, was decreasing, and can eventually be ex-

pected to disappear. The fight against vitamin-deficiency diseases like pellagra, beri-beri and scurvy produced encouraging results. More serious are the protein-deficiency diseases, which can only be overcome by a marked improvement in the diet of at least half the world's population.

Governments, charities and WHO have made great strides in improving health care, especially in establishing small, local clinics (found to be more effective than larger, less accessible hospitals). However, figures for infant mortality in the 1970s made grim reading. In Nigeria about 180 infants out of 1,000 died before they were a year old. The figure for Sweden was 13, for the USA 19, for India 139. The doctor-patient ratio in Nigeria was about 1:43,000, compared with 1:870 in Britain and 1:460 in the USSR.

Energy and resources

In the 1970s a fact previously asserted by a few became universally acknowledged: the consumption of non-renewable natural resources, especially fossil fuels, could not be continued on the current scale indefinitely. It was brought home to the ordinary individual by the energy crisis of 1973 when, following a boycott of several states by the Arab producing countries, OPEC (Organization of Petroleum Exporting Countries) raised the price of crude oil dramatically (it quadrupled within twelve months). This, the first effective example of concerted economic action by producer-countries against manufacturer-countries, had a salutory effect. Its immediate results, however, were severe economic recession and reduced oil consumption which led eventually to a glut of oil and falling prices—a sequence of events not foreseen by OPEC. Another effect of the 1973 crisis was the search for and exploitation of new oil (and gas) reserves, such as those in the North Seas and off Alaska. Production of North Sea oil, which would not have been worth the effort before 1973, was particularly valuable in Britain in its effect on the balance of payments. By the 1980s Britain was producing more oil than it consumed.

But North Sea supplies were expected to tail off in the 1990s; they were a useful stopgap, not a solution to the fundamental problem. It has been estimated that the human race consumed more energy in the twenty years between 1960 and 1980 than it had in all its previous existence; the sources of that energy were predominantly non-renewable.

A variety of alternatives were advocated and explored. Countries with appropriate terrain exploited hydro-electric power. The French pioneered experiments with tidal power; solar panels drawing energy from the Sun's rays appeared in some houses even in cloudy northern Europe; the Dutch took another look at windmills. But it is unlikely that these methods of harnessing power from renewable sources like the sun, tides and wind will be of more than marginal utility in supplying the enormous energy demands of the modern world, at least in the foreseeable future. The obvious alternative is, of course, nuclear energy.

Though nuclear energy also requires non-renewable resources (usually uranium), only a tiny amount is needed to produce a huge amount of energy. The grave drawback to nuclear-power development, however, was the safety factor. The prospect of an accident at a nuclear plant summoned up horrifying images—a nuclear reactor works in the same way as a nuclear bomb except that the explosion is controlled—and it was not surprising that any announcement of a planned reactor at a particular site immediately aroused the passionate opposition of local inhabitants. There have been many allegations of radio-active leakages in various places at various times; most were difficult to substantiate beyond doubt (the effects of radiation often being long-delayed), but there was a strong public suspicion in

industrialized countries where nuclear power was most common that the truth in these cases was being withheld by nervous governments. Moreover, the serious accident often forecast by opponents of nuclear energy almost occurred at Three-Mile Island, Pennsylvania, in 1979, when thousands of people were hastily evacuated to escape a radiation leak.

Additional problems arise when decisions have to be made as to the type of reactor to be built. The so-called fast-breeder reactor is particularly economical, both in terms of power output and because one of its by-products is new nuclear fuel. But it poses special technical problems and despite the success of the Dounreay prototype, which was in operation for seventeen years, proposals to build another reactor of that type in Britain were fiercely resisted. The opposition to nuclear power gained in strength in 1983 when beaches in north-west England were contaminated by radioactive waste from the advanced gas-cooled reactor at Windscale (Sellafield), which coincided with allegations of abnormal rates of cancer in neighbouring villages.

Nevertheless, it appeared in the 1980s that nuclear power was the only practical solution to the long-term world energy problem in sight.

Economic solutions to some of the problems posed by the Earth's diminishing resources have been and will continue to be prevented by political circumstances. The high-technology nations regarded requests for assistance to build nuclear reactors from Third-World countries with ambivalent feelings. Adequate safeguards against conversion of nuclear know-how to warlike purposes or against irresponsible disposal of radio-active waste were not easily achieved. Other ways of easing energy problems, like the planet-wide electrical grid advocated by the US technologist R. Buckminster Fuller (a practical and not outlandishly expensive idea) are likely to remain unrealizable dreams for the foreseeable future.

A truly revolutionary change in human behaviour, particularly as regards the industrial world, may be the only final answer, but there are other resources, more fundamental than fuels, which are also diminishing at a rate which cannot safely be maintained for many more generations. The two basic resources necessary for human life (and other forms of life) are land and water. There is still much uncultivated land which could be brought into future food production, but while the total area of cultivable land was increasing in 1980, in many areas it was declining because of the numerous other demands on land – for housing, roads, industry, etc. – and through natural processes such as soil erosion and drought. The Sahara Desert, for

Opposite, a surgeon examines his patient's heart during a heart transplant operation. Such glamorous and high-investment surgery became increasingly questioned in the 1980s as symbolizing the gap between the 'haves' and 'have-nots'.

Above, a worker in protective clothing at a nuclear power station in Britain. A drop in energy-consumption predictions, doubts about existing designs and the still-unresolved question of radio-active waste disposal made many countries less enthusiastic about nuclear power in the 1980s than a decade previously.

example, has been spreading south in recent years, rendering the northern Sahel unfit for the pastoral peoples of the region to maintain their flocks and herds. Water is also less abundant than our forefathers assumed. Only about two per cent of the total mass of water is available as fresh water, and over one family in five in the 1980s were without a safe water supply.

On this whole subject, there is much to engage those who view the world's future with foreboding. However, one of the lessons of history is that future developments can seldom be predicted from past trends. Things change quickly and unpredictably. Who in 1973, for instance, would have forecast that within five or six years the supply of crude oil would so far outdistance demand that oil prices would fall, or that the British government would be trying to influence OPEC to keep the price up?

Science and technology

Ever since explorers set out from Europe to new continents in the fifteenth century, the world has been shrinking. Conquerors and colonists made different peoples of the world at least aware of each other's existence; mutual understanding came less easily, although it is surely true that divisions of class race or religion can be overcome more easily in the modern world than they could five centuries ago. Science and technology have contributed to this development, not least in the ways in which they have eased communications and transport.

The most striking development in this area is recent years has been the exploration of space, which historians of the distant future may well see as the most important achievement of the twentieth century. Since the first successful launch of a man-made space satellite by the USSR in 1957, events have moved swiftly. The most spectacular single incident was the landing of men on the Moon by the USA in 1969, but that was to some extent a propaganda exercise and probably more important were the numerous unmanned spacecraft and satellites which penetrated deep into space, providing masses of information on the universe which could take years to process, or circled the Earth relaying TV signals, recording weather changes (a marked improvement in weather forecasting was just one beneficial by-product of the space age) or, indeed, spying. Nearly all this early activity came from the two nations able to afford it – the USA and the USSR – but there was increasing co-operation in the 1970s between the two superpowers themselves and with other countries. In the 1980s the first 'free-enterprise' space service was planned – rocket launchings on a commercial basis organized by a private company and not

subsidized directly by government.

The hectic pace of development in space exploration received a slight check in the 1970s, partly as a result of detente and a corresponding diminution of the fierce US–Soviet rivalry in space research, partly to divergent interests, and partly to financial restrictions in a recessionary period. The US Apollo programme run by NASA (National Aeronautics and Space Administration) which had achieved the Moon landing, ended in 1972 and NASA's next enterprise – the space 'shuttle' – was delayed by budget cuts and technical problems. Nevertheless, in 1981 *Columbia*, the first re-usable spaceship, made its successful maiden flight. Launched by disposable rockets and landing under its own power like an aeroplane, it represented a major advance in manned space vehicles.

Technology advanced rapidly in other fields also, notable automation and computers. In the more advanced vehicle-manufacturing plants, for example, the assembly-line method of production was gradually taken over by robots. As everyone agreed that working on an assembly line is an exceedingly unpleasant occupation, this was a great social advance. Unfortunately, automation destroys jobs, and in an economic recession even unattractive jobs are socially valuable. The high rates of unemployment which prevailed throughout the world in the 1980s were not caused by automation of industry alone – or even primarily. However, the rapid pace of technological development suggested that it would contribute to the continuation of high unemployment in future. Technology has been defined as 'doing more with less' but this has turned out to mean less labour as well as less machinery. In some strongly unionized

Above, Yuri Gagarin (1934–68), the first man to travel in space: his voyage inaugurated a space race between the USSR and the USA that lasted until well into the 1970s, when both governments found its cost increasingly prohibitive.

Opposite, a second New World, as men explore the moon's surface for the first time, July 1969.

industries, progress was effectively blocked by the resistance of workers fearful of losing jobs.

There has been a tendency in the modern world for social and economic advance to destroy jobs as well as to create them, in particular to destroy unskilled jobs while creating new ones for which the required skilled labour does not yet exist. In developing countries, the educated children of peasant farmers naturally expect a more rewarding role in life for themselves but, gravitating hopefully to the towns, discover that no opportunities exist.

There is no better illustration of technology achieving more with less than in computers. By the 1980s it was possible to carry out calculations on a pocket-sized instrument which, twenty years earlier, could not have been performed by a room-sized computer. Development seems to be accelerating. In 1983 'home' computers in Britain were little more expensive than television sets and were on the way to becoming almost as common. Yet less than three years earlier virtually no private citizen owned a computer. The whole computer industry has been growing faster than any other, with predictable effects on employment (the job losses through computers taking over from people being far more numerous than the jobs created in the industry itself).

The transistor and the silicon chip have made possible the miniaturization of computers and their increasing speed. New types appearing in the 1980s (and costing about £7 million each) could perform 100 million calculations per second, thanks partly to the technique known as pipelining which allows a large number of calculations to be performed simultaneously. But every advance brings new technical problems, and modern computers, with thousands of transistors to each tiny silicon chip, require an elaborate cooling system. It is possible that the next generation of 'supercomputers' will incorporate some alternative to transistors.

In technologically advanced countries there are now numerous computer networks, operated by private, academic or government bodies, in which, in the simplest form, the work is done by a central, host computer, to which other computers transmit data by telephonic links. Some consternation was caused in the 1980s by the demonstrated ability of skilful individuals to 'crash' a computer network to which they had no authorized connection. A few notable frauds were perpetrated in this way, while students in the USA succeeded in breaking into a computer network operated by the US Department of Defence.

The environment

Nuclear power has another vital advantage besides economy or resources. Providing the waste is properly disposed of – and barring 'accidents' – nuclear energy is 'clean'. During the past generation, concern has been rising for the future of the natural environment which the activities of modern, industrial man have been seriously damaging. This extends to every aspect of nature, but pollution of the air is possibly the most immediate menace.

Atmospheric pollution is chiefly caused by incomplete combustion of fossil fuels, especially coal. Disturbance of the carbon-dioxide balance could make the Earth hotter, with various undesirable results such as the melting of polar ice to raise the sea level and submerge such

places as New York or London; some scientists believe that this is beginning to happen already. Many city dwellers are familiar with 'smog', an atmospheric condition resulting from a mixture of smoke and fog. London was formerly a notorious victim of this condition, which in 1952 caused 2,000 deaths in the city, but London has been almost free of smog since passage of the Clean Air Act (1956), which outlawed smokey fuels and has increased winter sunshine in the British capital by 70 per cent. In a city like Los Angeles, however, a major culprit is exhaust fumes from motor vehicles. Among other undesirable substances, cars emit carbon monoxide, which is an invisible pollutant, like the sulphur dioxide produced primarily by power stations, factories and domestic heating.

In theory, most of the conditions that cause air pollution of this type can be cured fairly simply. Development of more efficient furnaces and the washing of flue gases have already made some contribution; car engines can be modified to reduce noxious exhaust, and this source is likely to be reduced by legislation in the countries most afflicted even if other developments (such as the cost of oil or the improvement of electrical vehicles) do not have the required effect.

Even more sinister is the phenomenon known as acid rain – precipitation contaminated with powerful acids such as nitric or sulphuric acid deriving from industrial effluents. Between 1940 and 1980 the amount of sulphur dioxide emitted in

Europe roughly doubled, and measurements in affected parts of North America have shown the rain to be over 100 times more acid than normal. The disappearance of fish from many lakes in Scandinavia, first noticed during the 1970s, was ascribed to acid rain, and in 1983 it was revealed that substantial parts of the Black Forest in southern Germany were dead or dying from the same cause. This is an international problem in a literal sense: the acids killing the Black Forest were believed to come mainly from factories in northern France.

The rise of acid can be reversed, though less swiftly than the reduction of smog-type pollution. What cannot be so easily rectified is the possible damage being done to the ozone layer in the upper atmosphere, which vitally protects the Earth from excessive, ultraviolent radiation, by fluoro-carbons (produced, among other sources, by aerosols). This potential threat was first publicized in 1974, but ten years later there was still considerable doubt as to whether or not the ozone layer is being significantly affected.

Pollution is a problem which has grown rapidly more prominent in recent years partly for the simple reason that it has become steadily much worse and partly because a concern for protection of the environment has become more widespread, assuming a political dimension in many industrialized countries. But pollution is an old problem. The last Atlantic salmon disappeared from the Thames about 150 years ago. The Thames having been successfully cleaned up in the 1970s, salmon have actually been introduced again, but hundreds of other rivers in Europe and North America, where once the silvery salmon ran, have long been little better than industrial sewers.

The growth in world population and the continuing progress of industrialization aroused fears that the human race, if it did not destroy the Earth by nuclear war, would destroy it piecemeal by pollution of the environment and depletion of natural resources which cannot be replaced. Every year naturalists reported more species of wild life extinct or in danger of extinction through destruction of their habitat in the name of material progress. One region of growing concern to conservationists was the huge forested region of Amazonia in South America. Besides the destruction wrought upon living creatures, plants, animals and human beings (the attractive but vulnerable forest-dwelling peoples in particular), it was said that the general destruction of forests throughout the world could have a dangerous effect on the level of oxygen in the atmosphere.

Modern society has produced other forms of 'pollution', the deleterious effects of which on the equality of life are said by those of reactionary cast to more than balance the benefits of progress. In a crowded industrialized country like England or Belgium, it has become difficult to find a spot where the ears are not afflicted by modern technological din. The Concorde supersonic airliner, a magnificent technical achievement by British and French engineers, was nevertheless rejected by most international airlines because of its excessive engine noise. The level of noise in the Place de l'Opéra in Paris in the 1970s was found to be greater than at Niagara Falls. The hearing of young people was said to be adversely affected by listening to amplified pop music.

Above, the Torrey Canyon, *broken in two off Land's End; her fate highlighted the environmental dangers brought by the development of vast supertankers.*

Above left, clearance of the Amazon rain forests, encouraged by the Brazilian government amid fears that the loss of so many trees would have drastic and irreversible effects on the world's climate.

Opposite left, the 1980s saw a huge proliferation in personal and micro-computers as integrated circuitry cut prices very quickly. Programming became a central element in the school curriculum in many countries.

Opposite right, the launch of Columbia, the US 'Space Shuttle', capable of landing like an aeroplane and being re-used. By cutting the cost of space travel, it brought a new commercial orientation to space development.

Index

752

Acknowledgements

The following illustrations were reproduced by gracious permission of Her Majesty the Queen 23 top, 28, 30, 99, 100, 194 right, 244.

Colour photographs
Archiv für Kunst und Geschichte, Berlin 657; Art Institute of Chicago, Illinois 530; Berliner Illustrierte Zeitung 646;Biblioteca Marucelliana, Florence 139; Bibliothèque Nationale, Paris 267 bottom, 345; Bildarchiv Preussischer Kulturbesitz, Berlin 155, 168, 181, 179 top, 482; Birmingham Museum and Art Gallery 398 top; Bisonte 698, 738 left; Bisonte – U.S. Atomic Energy Comm. 702;
Bo Bojesen, London 731, 742; British Museum, London 255 top right, 659 left; J. E. Bulloz, Paris 126 bottom; Camera Press, London 719; Chester Beatty Library, Dublin 35; Chicago Historical Society, Illinois 226, 455, 559 bottom left; Colorific, London 695, 718; Cooper-Bridgeman Library, London 134 top; Cooper-Bridgeman Library – Christie Manson and Woods 95; Henry Francis Du Pont Winterthur Museum, Delaware 282; Mary Evans Picture Library, London 299, 307 left, 310, 314, 318, 487, 502 top, 527; Galerie Günther Franke, München 633 left; Franshalsmuseum, Haarlem 115 top; Photographie Giraudon, Paris 162, 163 top, 206, 259, 303 right, 418, 430, 431 top left, 435 top, 439 bottom; Graphische Sammlung Albertina, Vienna 31 bottom left; Sonia Halliday, Weston Turville 34 top, 38, 43; Hamlyn Group Picture Library.63 top, 78 left, 79 right, 80, 86 top, 143 top left, 195 top right, 198, 242 top, 258, 270 top left, 302 left, 422, 454 top; Heeresgeschichtliches Museum, Vienna 415; Imperial War Museum, London 674 top left; Institute of Social History, Amsterdam 635 top, 658 top; Kongelige Bibliothek, Copenhagen 182; Library of Congress, Washington, D.C. 362, 372; MacClancy Press, London 287 top, 311 top, 327 bottom, 350 top, 350 bottom, 354, 355, 358–359, 462 top, 591, 598 left, 598 top right, 603, 615 left, 618, 643 left, 647 left, 670 top, 678 top left, 678 top right, 679 left, 679 right, 682 left, 682 top right, 686 top left, 686 bottom, 687, 690, 699 top; Mansell Collection, London 319, 390, 391, 502 bottom, 539 right; Marshall Cavendish, London 550, 694 left; Marshall Cavendish – National Maritime Museum 542; Mas, Barcelona 574 top; Metropolitan Museum of Art, New York 15 top; Photo Meyer, Vienna 570 bottom; NASA, Washington 746; National Army Museum 242 bottom, 503 left;National Library of Australia, Canberra 371; National Maritime Museum, London 130 top right; Nationalmuseum, Stockholm 295; National Portrait Gallery, London 98, 219, 400 top; National Scheepvaartmuseum, Antwerp 19 top; New York Historical Society 230 bottom; New York Public Library – Stokes Collection 451 left; Novosti Press Agency, London 131, 424 top; Orbis Publishing, London 291 left; Orbis – John Carter Brown Library 286; Orbis – Chicago Historical Society 450; Orbis – Giraudon 330; Orbis – New York Public Library 443; Pennsylvania Academy of Fine Arts, Philadelphia 230 top; Popperfoto, London 723 top; 742; Ann Ronan Picture Library, Loughton 138; Scala, Antella 310; Scala, Florence 55; Scala, Milan 414, 474 left, 475; Snark International, Paris 18 right; Taft Museum, Cincinatti, Ohio 559 top left; Time-Life – Ronald Haederle 718; Tokyo Gallery 534, 546, 551; Trades Union Congress, London 514; Western Americana Picture Library, Brentwood 243

Black and white photographs
Aberdeen Central Library 486 top; Alinari, Florence 66 centre, 207; Archives Photographiques, Paris 66 bottom, 68 bottom, 80, 203 top left; Ashmolean Museum, Oxford 106 bottom left; Associated Press, London 662, 724 bottom right; Barnaby's Picture Library, London 712 top, 724 top right, 749; Bibliothèque Albert I, Brussels 16 top right; Bibliothèque Nationale, Paris 14 bottom, 89 bottom, 321 bottom right, 345, 439 top left, 481 top; Bibliothèque Publique et Universitaire, Geneva 26; Bildarchiv der Österreichischen Nationalbibliothek, Vienna 411 top, 411 bottom left, 412, 413 right, 571 left, 571 right, 572 left; Bildarchiv Preussischer Kulturbesitz, Berlin 156, 157, 159 top left, 174 left, 178 left, 184 right, 186 top, 190, 289, 386, 389 left, 389 right, 406 top, 410, 464, 476, 477, 478, 479 top right, 479 centre, 479 bottom, 480, 481 centre, 483 top, 483 centre, 483 bottom, 485, 488 left, 489 bottom, 501, 564, 565, 566, 587, 589 right; Bernice P. Bishop Museum, Honolulu 272 left, 272 right; Bisonte 707; Bisonte – U.S. Army 697; Bill Brandt 635 left; Brighton Public Library 489 top right; British Library, London 271 top right, 273 top right; British Museum, London 23 bottom, 47 top, 105 top, 115 bottom, 118, 123 bottom, 137 top, 165 right, 179 bottom, 181 centre right, 199, 210–211, 215, 218 bottom, 221 top right, 222 bottom, 232 right, 268, 270 bottom, 273 top left, 273 bottom right, 274 bottom, 276, 302 bottom left, 311 centre left, 313 top left, 317 top, 321 bottom left, 324 bottom, 327 top, 334, 340–341, 343, 356 top; 423 bottom, 656; J. E. Bulloz, Paris 203 bottom, 434 bottom left; Camera Press, London 664, 708 right, 716–717 top, 716–717 bottom, 717 top right, 717 bottom right, 722, 726 top left, 729 top, 734, 736, 738–739 top; Central Press, London 624 bottom, 708 left; Chicago Historical Society 460 bottom right; P. & D. Colnaghi & Co., London 208 top; Colorific – Alon Reininger 723 bottom, 724 left; Colorific – Rick Smolan 726 bottom right; Comm. for European Communities 704 top; Computer Weekly Picture Library, Sutton 748 left; Country Life, London 148; Courtauld Institute of Art, London 152; Crown copyright reproduced with permission of the Controller of Her Majesty's Stationery Office 121; Deutsche Fotothek, Dresden 82, 90 bottom right, 146, 153, 159 right, 169, 173, 175 top, 183, 353 right, 427 bottom, 491, 563; East African Railways Confederation 501 right; European Picture Service 629 right; Mary Evans Picture Library, London 44 top, 107, 111 top right, 144 bottom, 185, 249 top left, 265 bottom, 275 left, 301 bottom, 303 top left, 303 bottom left, 304 top left, 304 top right, 304 bottom right, 305, 308 right, 309 left, 311 centre right, 311 bottom, 317 bottom, 322 top, 326 bottom, 328 top, 328 bottom, 329 top, 337 top, 356 bottom, 360, 375 left, 375 right, 376, 377 top left, 378, 379, 380, 381 left, 382, 578, 579; Fox Photos, London 689; Michael Freeman/World Wildlife Fund, Godalming 749 left; Frick Collection, New York 57 left; Gernsheim Collection, Humanities Research Center, University of Texas at Austin 577 right; Photographie Giraudon, Paris 14 bottom, 20 top, 22, 27 centre, 68 bottom right, 69 left, 69 right, 71, 73 right, 92, 123 bottom, 124 left, 125, 126 top, 128, 130 left, 147, 204, 205 top left, 205 top right, 250, 259 bottom, 301 top, 332, 333, 336, 337 bottom right, 352 left, 392 top, 392 bottom, 393 top, 431 top right, 432 bottom, 433 top, 433 bottom, 437, 496, 500; Guildhall Art Gallery, London 197 left; Hamlyn Group Picture Library 52, 65 bottom, 75 left, 81, 108, 114, 123, 137 bottom, 160, 175 bottom, 181 top, 232 right, 235 left, 251, 257, 263 top right, 267 top, 269 top, 269 bottom, 271 top left, 271 bottom, 297, 313 centre right, 320 top, 323, 329 bottom, 363, 368, 370, 375 bottom, 375 top right, 387, 388, 397 left, 398 bottom, 408, 409 right, 414, 415 bottom, 420 bottom, 436, 439 top right, 468, 490 top left, 497, 506 right, 517 bottom, 572 right, 701 top; Sonia Halliday, Weston Turville 17 bottom; Heeresgeschichtliches Museum, Vienna 479 top left, 570 top; Lewis W. Hine International Museum of Photography at George Eastman House, New York 459 right; Hispanic Society of America, New York 76 bottom left; Historisches Museum, Frankfurt am Main 348; George Howard 46 left; Imperial War Museum, London 419 top, 582, 596 top, 600 top, 601, 608 left, 608 top right, 609, 621; India Office, London, 259, 263 top left, 264, 403 top; International Herald Tribune 726 centre left; Kungl. Arméмuseum, Stockholm 86 bottom; Kungliga Biblioteket, Stockholm 132 bottom, 133, 184 left, 352 bottom right, 425 top right, 495 bottom; Kungl. Husgeradskammaren, Stockholm 85 bottom; Kungl. Livrustkammaren, Stockholm 89 top; Kunsthistorisches Museum, Vienna 19 bottom, 32 left; Kunstsammlungen, Coburg 36 right; Kupferstichkabinett, Berlin-Dahlem 17 top right; Larousse, Paris 129 top, 216 left, 233 top, 256, 307 bottom right, 308 left, 312 bottom, 321 top right; Library of Congress, Washington, D.C. 216–217, 217 right, 218 top, 220, 221 top left, 221 bottom, 222 top, 225 top, 227, 232 left, 234 left, 237 left, 237 right, 238, 266 bottom, 267 top, 361, 363 top, 369, 381 right, 383, 442, 447 bottom right, 448, 449, 451 top right, 452 left, 452 right, 453, 454 bottom, 456 top, 456 bottom, 459, 460 top right, 462 bottom left, 545, 554, 555 left, 555 right, 556 left, 560 top, 560 centre, 560 bottom, 561, 562, 633 bottom, 704 bottom; MacClancy Press, London 283 left, 283 top right, 283 bottom right, 287 bottom, 288 left, 289 top left, 291 right, 298, 306 right, 309 top right, 312 top left, 312 top right, 313 centre left, 313 bottom left, 313 bottom right, 321 top left, 322 bottom left, 322 bottom right, 325 bottom, 340 left, 341 right, 357, 460 left, 461 top, 461 bottom, 462 bottom right, 481 bottom, 484, 510, 544 top, 547 top, 547 bottom,548–549 bottom, 549 top left, 549 top right, 563 bottom, 584, 585, 588, 589 left, 592, 593 bottom, 594 top, 594 centre, 594 bottom, 596 bottom, 597 top left, 597 bottom left, 597 right, 598 bottom right, 600 bottom, 602, 608 centre right, 611, 612, 615 right, 616, 617 top left, 617 top right, 617 bottom, 619, 620, 633 top left, 633 top right, 635 right, 637, 639 right, 641 left, 641 right, 642, 643 bottom right, 644 top, 644 bottom, 647 centre, 647 right, 648–649, 649 top, 649 centre, 650 left, 650–651, 651 right, 658 bottom, 659 right, 660 top left, 660 top right, 660 bottom, 667 top, 667 bottom, 668 top, 668 bottom, 669 left, 670 bottom left, 670 bottom right, 671 left, 671 right, 672 left, 672 top right, 672 centre right, 674 bottom left, 677 top right, 678 bottom left, 678 bottom right, 680 top, 681 top left, 681 bottom left, 682 centre right, 682 bottom right, 684 left, 684 top right, 684 bottom right, 685 top, 685 bottom, 706 top left, 713; The Raymond Mander and Joe Mitchenson Theatre Collection, London 692 bottom; Mansell Collection, London 13 top, 17 top left, 18 top left, 18 bottom left, 20 bottom, 24, 31 bottom right, 33 bottom, 34 bottom, 37 top, 44 bottom, 45 right, 48 left, 48 right, 51 right, 57, 68 left, 68 top right, 69 right, 73 left, 75, 83, 84, 90 left, 90 top right, 142 right, 143 right, 145 top, 193 top, 211 bottom, 224, 246–247, 249 top right, 249 bottom, 306 left, 307 top right, 309 bottom right, 315, 325 top, 326 top, 393 bottom, 395 right, 396, 397 right, 401 left, 401 right, 402, 403 bottom, 404, 446, 447 top right, 469 left, 479 top left, 480 top right, 495 top, 503 top right, 503 bottom, 510 right, 532 bottom, 536 right, 536 left, 537, 538 left, 540 top, 540 bottom, 541, 543, 544 bottom, 552, 553, 580 top, 580 bottom, 590, 593 top, 606 right, 613 top, 632; Mansell-Alinari 64; Mansell-Bulloz 316; Mansell-Giraudon 302 right; Bildarchiv Foto Marburg 178 right, 252 top left, 252 top centre, 252 top right, 252 bottom right; Marshall Cavendish – Agence France-Presse 706 bottom; Marshall Cavendish – NATO 700 bottom; Marshall Cavendish – United Israel Appeal Photo Archives 712 bottom; Mas, Barcelona 54 top right, 65 top, 76 top, 210 bottom left, 211 top, 234 right, 366–367; 406 bottom, 573, 574 bottom, 576 top left, 576 bottom left; Musée de la Marine, Marseilles 337 bottom left; Musée de L'Armée, Paris 324 top, 346 bottom; Musée Guinet 253, 255; Musées Nationaux, Paris 70, 117 bottom, 119 right, 189; Musées Royaux des Beaux Arts de Belgique, Brussels 56; Museo del Prado, Madrid 76 bottom right; Museum of the City of New York – The Jacob A. Riis Collection 511; Muzeum Wojska Polskiego, Warsaw 93 top; NASA, Washington 748 right; National Archives, Washington 608 bottom right, 669 right, 676 bottom, 707; National Army Museum, London 150, 190, 193, 263 bottom, 351, 419 bottom; National Gallery, London 88; National Gallery of Art, Washington 47 right; National Library of Australia, Canberra 270 top right, 274 bottom; National Library of Ireland, Dublin 518, 519, 625; National Maritime Museum, London 14 top, 16 bottom, 41 right, 54 bottom, 49, 106 top left, 109 right, 111 bottom left, 112 top, 120, 129 bottom, 132 top, 265 top, 267, 333, 362–363; Nationalmuseum, Stockholm 134 bottom; National Portrait Gallery, London 45 left, 46 right, 51 left, 96, 97, 101, 103, 106 top right, 106 bottom right, 122 left, 122 right, 140 centre, 143 bottom, 144 top, 164 left, 195 top left, 195 bottom right, 196, 200, 202, 249 top centre, 395 left; Nederlandsch Historisch Scheepvaart Museum, Amsterdam 76–77, 251 bottom; Peter Newark's Western Americana, Brentwood 444 left, 444 right, 445 bottom, 447 top left; New York Historical Society 228 left, 228 right, 229, 240; New York Public Library 447 bottom left; Marquis of Northampton 49 bottom; Novosti Press Agency, London 130 left, 131, 159 bottom left, 181 centre left, 186 bottom, 425 top left, 425 bottom, 427 top, 486 bottom, 533 bottom left, 533 bottom right, 535, 538 top right, 539 top left, 605 left, 605 right, 606 left, 613 bottom, 652, 653, 654, 672 bottom, 674 right, 677 bottom, 681 right, 747; Orbis Publishing, London 279 right; Orbis – J. Banfield Art Galleries 280; Orbis – Bibliothèque Nationale 285 bottom right; Orbis – Bulloz 320 bottom; Orbis – Colonial Williamsburg 281 left; Orbis – Fogg Art Museum 293; Orbis – Library of Congress 281 right; Open Road Films, London 505 top; Österreichische Nationalbibliothek, Vienna 32 right, 172, 177 top, 177 bottom, 178 centre; Raissa Page/Format, London 740; Peabody Museum, Harvard University, Cambridge, Massachusetts 273 top right, 273 bottom left; The Photo Source/Fox, London 735; The Photo Source/Keystone, London 730, 732, 733, 745; Popperfoto, London 631, 634 top right, 634 centre right, 634 bottom right, 665 top, 692 top, 693 right, 694 right, 696 top, 696 bottom, 699 bottom, 700 top, 701 bottom, 703 top, 703 bottom, 705, 706 top right, 709, 710, 714, 716 left, 720 top, 720 bottom, 721 left, 721 right, 724 centre right, 725, 726 top right, 726 bottom left, 729 bottom, 744; Pracowinia Fotogratiezna, Prague 424; Prado Museum, Madrid 40; Enoch Pratt Free Library of Baltimore, Maryland 225 bottom; Public Library of Cincinati and Hamilton County 451 bottom right; Radio Times Hulton Picture Library, London 104, 109 left, 112 bottom, 124 top, 124 bottom, 135 left, 135 right, 140 right, 141 top, 141 bottom, 142 left, 167 top left, 167 top right, 194 left, 208 bottom, 235 top right, 235 bottom right, 248, 260, 266 left, 266 right, 292, 469 top, 469 bottom, 504 top left, 504 top right, 513, 515, 516, 517 top, 520 left, 538 bottom right, 576 right, 577 left, 628 top, 628 bottom, 632, 691 left; Rijksmuseum, Amsterdam 36 left, 111 top left; Ann Ronan Picture

Library, Loughton 145 bottom; H. Roger-Viollet, Paris 130 bottom, 163 bottom, 164 right, 165 left, 168, 174 right, 180, 201, 263 centre, 338, 344, 353 left, 409 left, 415 top, 429, 431 bottom, 432 top left, 432 top right, 434 top, 434 bottom right, 435 bottom left, 438 left, 438 right, 440, 441, 470, 488 right, 493, 505 bottom, 508, 521, 522, 523, 524, 525, 526 top, 526 bottom, 528, 529, 532 top, 532 centre, 533 top, 539 bottom left; Royal Geographical Society, London 247 bottom right, 506 left; Sammlung Handke, Berlin 289 top right; Scala, Milan 413 left, 496 top right, 469 bottom right, 471 left, 471 right, 472 top, 472 bottom, 473 left, 473 top right, 473 bottom right, 434 right; Shell, London 728–729; Smithsonian Institution, Washington 563 top; Staatliche Museen zu Berlin 25 bottom; Staatsgemaldesammlungen, Munich 33 top; The Star, Johannesburg – Barnett Collection 504 bottom; State Library of South Australia, Adelaide 490 bottom; Statens Museum for Kunst, Copenhagen 87; Tony Stone Associates, London 737; Svenska Porträt Arkivet, Nationalmuseum, Stockholm 85 top, 159 top right; Tate Gallery, London 167 bottom, 405; Thomas Gilcrease Institute, Tulsa, Oklahoma 212; Thompson, Coventry 665 bottom; Topix, London 624 top; UNICEF 743; Union Pacific Railroad Museum Collection 556 right; United Nations 711, 739; United Press International, Acme 693 left; U.S. Air Force, Washington 676 top, 680 bottom; U.S. National Archives, Washington 604; U.S. Naval Historical Center, Washington 445 top; U.S. Navy, Washington 673; U.S. Signal Corps, Washington 677 top left; U.S. War Department, General and Special Staff, Washington 460 centre right; University of Washington Library, Seattle 557; Victoria and Albert Museum, London 191, 197 top right, 339, 352 left, 399 bottom, 400, 420, 548 top, 691 right; Victoria Memorial Calcutta 261; Wallace Collection, London 27 bottom, 203 top right; Western Americana Picture Library, Brentwood 243; World Zionist Organization 629 left; Yale University Art Gallery, New Haven, Connecticut 287 centre, 288 right, 289 bottom.

U.S. research by Research Reports, New York